Feature	Description	Benefit
Chapter Objectives	Numbered list outlining the major topics and issues addressed in the chapter, and linked to specific content within the chapter	Alert students to the major topics they should recall after reading the chapter
Review Questions	Assessment questions to challenge students' understanding of the theories and topics covered within the chapter	Assist students in confirming whether they know what they need to know about the key topics presented in the chapter
Consumer Behavior Challenges	Questions designed to encourage discussion and application of the issues raised in the chapter	Drive students to delve deeper into both the theoretical and real-life implications of consumer behavior tactics and decisions
End-of-Chapter Case Studies	Cases that ask students to apply the material learned in the chapter	Help students learn how to use the chapter material in particular consumer behavior situations
CB as I See It	Leading consumer behavior professors and researchers discussing their areas of expertise	Give students further insight into the study of specific consumer behavior issues
CB as I Live It	Students discussing their own perspectives on key consumer behavior concepts	Connect key concepts from the book to students' everyday life and their consumer decisions
Mintel Memos and Data Exercises	Brief excerpts from Mintel market research data and application exercises	Provide students with an opportunity to manipulate and make sense of real, up-to-date market data on consumer trends
mymarketinglab	Interactive online component offering access to the e-book, online pretests and posttests, personalized study plans, and additional application exercises for enhanced understanding of consumer behavior concepts covered in the book	Simplifies the assessment experience for instructors and improves the remediation experience for students

PEARSON mymarketinglab™

mymarketinglab (www.mypearsonmarketinglab.com) gives students the opportunity to test themselves on key concepts and skills, track their progress through the course, and use the personalized study plan activities—all to help them achieve success in the classroom.

Features include:

- **Personalized study plans**—Pretests and posttests with remediation activities directed to help students understand and apply the concepts where they need the most help.

- **Self-assessments**—Prebuilt self-assessments give students the chance to test their understanding.

- **Interactive elements**—Students can discover consumer behavior through the online e-book where they can search for specific key words or page numbers, highlight specific sections, enter notes right on the e-book page, print reading assignments with notes for later review, complete critical-thinking exercises based on advertisements in the text, view videos with discussion questions, answer online end-of-chapter activities, and much more.

- **iQuizzes**—Students can study anytime, anywhere. iQuizzes contain questions specifically created for the iPod screen and work on any color-screen iPod.

Find out more at **www.mypearsonmarketinglab.com**

Critical Thinking in Consumer Behavior: Cases and Experiential Exercises, 2nd Edition

Instructors teaching Consumer Behavior and Customer Strategy can now:

- **Enhance student engagement and enthusiasm**
- **Create specific and measurable learning goals**
- **Assess student attainment of learning goals**

Give your students the skills and knowledge that are highly valued in this new customer-focused business world through the **concise, hands-on cases and exercises** in *Critical Thinking in Consumer Behavior: Cases and Experiential Exercises,* 2nd Edition.

With the adoption of this revised and expanded casebook, students will:

- **Use valuable new customer-centric business tools** such as Customer Experience Management and Net Promoter Score™.
- **Achieve mastery of classic customer behavior concepts** and gain proficiency in applying them in the current business world.
- Understand and **predict customer response** to new products and services.
- **Tap into vital customer insights** through the use of powerful qualitative customer research techniques, including laddering interviews, projective techniques, and mapping the customer experience.
- **Assess customers' attitudes and perceptions** through the use of straight-forward, efficient methodologies.
- Use creative skills to **develop attention-getting and memorable promotions,** anchored in a thorough understanding of how customers process information.
- **Examine customers' unconscious thought processes** and discover how these shape decision making.
- Uncover the power of word-of-mouth influence, and **strategize how businesses can harness W-O-M to enhance brand positioning**.
- **Craft compelling, persuasive communications** based on the principles of Social Judgment Theory, Balance Theory, the Elaboration Likelihood Model, and other key attitude-change theories.
- **Explore the diversity of customer behavior** across cultures, and zero in on the fascinating world of the Chinese consumer.

Instructors can learn more about *Critical Thinking in Consumer Behavior: Cases and Experiential Exercises,* **2nd Edition,** by visiting **www.pearsonhighered.com.** At this site, instructors may request an examination copy and explore the different ways to make this book available for their students, either as a stand-alone text using ISBN 0-13-602716-4, or in a valuepack with *Consumer Behavior: Buying, Having, and Being,* 9th Edition, at a reduced price using ISBN 0-13-215317-3.

OTHER MARKETING TITLES OF INTEREST

PRINCIPLES OF MARKETING

Marketing: An Introduction, 10/E
Armstrong & Kotler
ISBN-10: 0136102433 ■ ISBN-13: 9780136102434

Marketing Plan Handbook and Marketing Plan Pro Package, 4/E
Wood
ISBN-10: 0138020876 ■ ISBN-13: 9780138020873

Principles of Marketing, 13/E
Kotler & Armstrong
ISBN-10: 0136079415 ■ ISBN-13: 9780136079415

Marketing: Real People, Real Choices, 6/E
Solomon, Marshall & Stuart
ISBN-10: 0136054218 ■ ISBN-13: 9780136054214

Hasselback Marketing Faculty Guide, 13E
Hasselback
ISBN-10: 0136010024 ■ ISBN-13: 9780136010029

Marketing Ethics: Cases and Readings, 1/E
Murphy & Laczniak
ISBN-10: 0131330888 ■ ISBN-13: 9780131330887

Marketing in Virtual Worlds, 1/E
Wood
ISBN-10: 0136117171 ■ ISBN-13: 9780136117179

CONSUMER BEHAVIOR

Consumer Behavior, 9/E
Solomon
ISBN-10: 0136110924 ■ ISBN-13: 9780136110927

Consumer Behavior, 10/E
Schiffman & Kanuk
ISBN-10: 0135053013 ■ ISBN-13: 9780135053010

Critical Thinking in Consumer Behavior: Cases and Experiential Exercises, 2/E
Graham
ISBN-10: 0136027164 ■ ISBN-13: 9780136027164

Consumer Behavior and Managerial Decision Making, 2/E
Kardes
ISBN-10: 0130916021 ■ ISBN-13: 9780130916020

MARKETING RESEARCH

Basic Marketing Research Using Microsoft Excel Data Analysis, 2/E
Burns & Bush
ISBN-10: 0132059584 ■ ISBN-13: 9780132059589

Marketing Research: An Applied Orientation, 6/E
Malhotra
ISBN-10: 0136085431 ■ ISBN-13: 9780136085430

Basic Marketing Research: A Decision-Making Approach with Qualtrics Access Card, 3/E
Malhotra
ISBN-10: 013715593X ■ ISBN-13: 9780137155934

Marketing Research, 6/E
Burns & Bush
ISBN-10: 0136027040 ■ ISBN-13: 9780136027041

Multivariate Data Analysis, 7/E
Hair, Black, Babin & Anderson
ISBN-10: 0138132631 ■ ISBN-13: 9780138132637

INTERNATIONAL MARKETING

Global Marketing, 6/E
Keegan & Green
ISBN-10: 0137023863 ■ ISBN-13: 9780137023868

Global Marketing Management, 7/E
Keegan
ISBN-10: 0130332712 ■ ISBN-13: 9780130332714

International Marketing Research, 1/E
Kumar
ISBN-10: 0130453862 ■ ISBN-13: 9780130453860

MARKETING MANAGEMENT

Marketing Management, 13/E
Kotler & Keller
ISBN-10: 0136009980 ■ ISBN-13: 9780136009986

A Framework for Marketing Management, 4/E
Kotler & Keller
ISBN-10: 0136026605 ■ ISBN-13: 9780136026600

A Framework for Marketing Management Integrated with PharmaSim, 4/E
Kotler & Keller
ISBN-10: 0136083447 ■ ISBN-13: 9780136083443

Market-Based Management, 5/E
Best
ISBN-10: 0132336537 ■ ISBN-13: 9780132336536

Marketing Management, 3/E
Winer
ISBN-10: 0131963341 ■ ISBN-13: 9780131963344

Strategic Marketing Problems: Cases and Comments, 12/E
Kerin & Peterson
ISBN-10: 0136107060 ■ ISBN-13: 9780136107064

SELLING

Selling Today: Creating Customer Value, 11/E
Manning, Reece & Ahearne
ISBN-10: 013207995X ■ ISBN-13: 9780132079952

SALES MANAGEMENT

Sales Management: Shaping Future Sales Leaders, 1/E
Tanner, Honeycutt & Erffmeyer
ISBN-10: 0132324121 ■ ISBN-13: 9780132324120

RETAILING

Retail Management: A Strategic Approach, 11/E
Berman & Evans
ISBN-10: 0136087582 ■ ISBN-13: 9780136087588

ENTERTAINMENT AND SPORTS MARKETING

Sports Marketing: A Strategic Perspective, 4/E
Shank
ISBN-10: 0132285355 ■ ISBN-13: 9780132285353

Entertainment Marketing & Communication: Selling Branded Performance, People, and Places, 1/E
Sayre
ISBN-10: 0131986228 ■ ISBN-13: 9780131986220

SERVICES MARKETING

Services Marketing: People, Technology, Strategy, 7/E
Lovelock & Wirtz
ISBN-10: 0136107214 ■ ISBN-13: 9780136107217

Principles of Service Marketing and Management, 2/E
Lovelock & Wright
ISBN-10: 0130404675 ■ ISBN-13: 9780130404671

MARKETING CHANNELS

Marketing Channels, 7/E
Coughlan, Anderson, Stern & El-Ansary
ISBN-10: 0131913468 ■ ISBN-13: 9780131913462

LOGISTICS/SUPPLY CHAIN MANAGEMENT

Contemporary Logistics, 9/E
Murphy, Jr. & Wood
ISBN-10: 013156207X ■ ISBN-13: 9780131562073

Business Logistics/Supply Chain Management and Logware CD Package, 5/E
Ballou
ISBN-10: 0131076590 ■ ISBN-13: 9780131076594

BUSINESS TO BUSINESS MARKETING

Business Market Management: Understanding, Creating, and Delivering Value, 3/E
Anderson, Narus & Narayandas
ISBN-10: 0136000886 ■ ISBN-13: 9780136000884

NEW PRODUCT MANAGEMENT

Design and Marketing of New Products, 2/E
Urban & Hauser
ISBN-10: 0132015676 ■ ISBN-13: 9780132015677

HIGH TECH MARKETING

Marketing of High-Technology Products and Innovations, 3/E
Mohr, Sengupta & Slater
ISBN-10: 0136049966 ■ ISBN-13: 9780136049968

BRAND MANAGEMENT, BRAND STRATEGY

Best Practice Cases in Branding, 3/E
Keller
ISBN-10: 013188865X ■ ISBN-13: 9780131888654

Strategic Brand Management, 3/E
Keller
ISBN-10: 0131888595 ■ ISBN-13: 9780131888593

PRICING

The Strategy and Tactics of Pricing: A Guide to Growing More Profitably, 4/E
Nagle & Hogan
ISBN-10: 0131856774 ■ ISBN-13: 9780131856776

DIRECT MARKETING

Contemporary Direct & Interactive Marketing, 2/E
Spiller & Baier
ISBN-10: 0136086101 ■ ISBN-13: 9780136086109

MARKETING ON THE INTERNET

E-Marketing, 5/E
Strauss & Frost
ISBN-10: 0136154409 ■ ISBN-13: 9780136154402

Digital Business: Concepts and Strategy, 2/E
Coupey
ISBN-10: 0131400975 ■ ISBN-13: 9780131400979

NONPROFIT MARKETING

Strategic Marketing for Nonprofit Organizations, 7/E
Andreasen & Kotler
ISBN-10: 013175372X ■ ISBN-13: 9780131753723

INTRO TO ADVERTISING AND IMC

Advertising: Principles and Practices, 8/E
Moriarty, Mitchell & Wells
ISBN-10: 0132224151 ■ ISBN-13: 9780132224154

Kleppner's Advertising Procedure, 18/E
Lane, King & Reichert
ISBN-10: 0136110827 ■ ISBN-13: 9780136110828

Integrated Advertising, Promotion, and Marketing Communications, 4/E
Clow & Baack
ISBN-10: 0136079423 ■ ISBN-13: 9780136079422

PUBLIC RELATIONS

The Practice of Public Relations, 11/E
Seitel
ISBN-10: 0136088902 ■ ISBN-13: 9780136088905

Cutlip and Center's Effective Public Relations, 10/E
Broom
ISBN-10: 0136029698 ■ ISBN-13: 9780136029694

Public Relations Practices: Managerial Case Studies and Problems, 7/E
Center, Jackson, Smith & Stansberry
ISBN-10: 0132341360 ■ ISBN-13: 9780132341363

Consumers in the Marketplace

Consumers as Individuals

Consumers as Decision Makers

Consumers and Subcultures

Consumers and Culture

Section 3
Consumers as Decision Makers 303

Chapter 8: Decision Making 304

Chapter 9: Buying and Disposing 344

Section 4 Consumers and Subcultures 455

Section 5

Consumers and Culture 539

Chapter 15: Cultural Influences on Consumer Behavior 540

Chapter 16: Global Consumer Culture 572

Michael R. Solomon, Ph.D., is Professor of Marketing and Director of the Center for Consumer Research in the Haub School of Business at Saint Joseph's University in Philadelphia. He also is Professor of Consumer Behaviour at the Manchester School of Business, The University of Manchester, United Kingdom. Prior to joining the Saint Joseph's faculty in fall 2006, he was the Human Sciences Professor of Consumer Behavior at Auburn University. Before moving to Auburn in 1995, he was Chair of the Department of Marketing in the School of Business at Rutgers University, New Brunswick, New Jersey. Professor Solomon began his academic career in the Graduate School of Business Administration at New York University, where he also served as Associate Director of NYU's Institute of Retail Management. He earned B.A. degrees in psychology and sociology *magna cum laude* at Brandeis University and a Ph.D. in social psychology at The University of North Carolina at Chapel Hill. He was awarded the Fulbright/FLAD Chair in Market Globalization by the U.S. Fulbright Commission and the government of Portugal, and he served as Distinguished Lecturer in Marketing at The Technical University of Lisbon.

Professor Solomon's primary research interests include consumer behavior and lifestyle issues; branding strategy; the symbolic aspects of products; the psychology of fashion, decoration, and image; services marketing; marketing in virtual worlds, and the development of visually-oriented online research methodologies. He has published numerous articles on these and related topics in academic journals, and he has delivered invited lectures on these subjects in Europe, Australia, Asia, and Latin America. His research has been funded by the American Academy of Advertising, the American Marketing Association, the U.S. Department of Agriculture, the International Council of Shopping Centers, and the U.S. Department of Commerce. He currently sits on the editorial boards of the *Journal of Consumer Behaviour*, the *Journal of Retailing*, and *The European Business Review*, and he recently completed an elected 6-year term on the Board of Governors of the Academy of Marketing Science. Professor Solomon has been recognized as one of the 15 most widely cited scholars in the academic behavioral sciences/fashion literature, and as one of the 10 most productive scholars in the field of advertising and marketing communications.

Professor Solomon is a frequent contributor to mass media. His feature articles have appeared in such magazines as *Psychology Today, Gentleman's Quarterly,* and *Savvy*. He has been quoted in numerous national magazines and newspapers, including *Allure, Elle, Glamour, Mademoiselle, Mirabella, Newsweek,* the *New York Times, Self, USA Today,* and the *Wall Street Journal*. He frequently appears on television and speaks on radio to comment on consumer behavior issues, including *The Today Show, Good Morning America, Inside Edition, Newsweek on the Air,* the *Entrepreneur Sales and Marketing Show,* CNBC, Channel One, the Wall Street Journal Radio Network, the WOR Radio Network, and National Public Radio. He acts as consultant to numerous companies on consumer behavior and marketing strategy issues and often speaks to business groups throughout the United States and overseas. In addition to this text, Professor Solomon is coauthor of the widely used textbook *Marketing: Real People, Real Choices*. He has three children, Amanda, Zachary, and Alexandra, a son-in-law Orly, and a new granddaughter Rosi. He lives in Philadelphia with his wife Gail and their "other child"—a pug named Kelbie Rae.

● Eight new end-of-chapter cases covering topics such as consumer behavior during recessions (Chapter 1), the effect of avatars and virtual worlds on consumer behavior (Chapter 3), product endorsements (Chapter 7), online consumerism (Chapter 9), social media marketing (Chapter 8), and consumer "subcultures" (Chapters 13 and 14)

● Eight updated end-of-chapter cases (Chapters 2, 5, 6, 10, 11, 12, 15, and 16)

● Fourteen new *CB as I See It* boxes, feature consumer behavior professors and leading researchers who share their knowledge of and perspectives on their areas of expertise

● A brand new feature—*CB as I Live It*—highlights 18 individuals and student groups from schools across the country who contribute their own perspectives on key concepts

● Four brand-new end-of-section *Mintel Memos and Data Exercises* use data from recent consumer behavior market research to encourage "hands-on" applications of concepts

● New content added to every chapter, including the following topics and much more:

Transformative consumer research and the 80/20 rule (Chapter 1)

Anthropomorphism and schema processing (Chapter 2)

Online repetition and wearout (Chapter 3)

Consumer-generated content strategies and live advertising (Chapter 4)

Facial morphing, "sexting," and gender-bending products (Chapter 5)

Personality and media usage (Chapter 6)

Social media, widgets, "Japandering," and "spokescharacters" (Chapter 7)

Blissful ignorance effect, hyperopia, reputation economy, and brand advocates (Chapter 8)

Online gambling and gripe sites (Chapter 9)

Group influence, urban myths, and "Tweetups" (Chapter 10)

B2B promotional products and network effects (Chapter 11)

Tightwads, spendthrifts, and BRIC (Chapter 12)

Cosplay (Chapter 13)

Segmenting boomers, Gen Y, and media usage (Chapter 14)

Headbanging collective ritual, "Oprah devotion," and superstition (Chapter 15)

Gadget lovers, global obesity, and ideologies regarding technology (Chapter 16)

I love to people-watch, don't you? People shopping, people flirting, people consuming. Consumer behavior is the study of people and the products that help to shape their identities. Because I'm a consumer myself, I have a selfish interest in learning more about how this process works—and so do you.

In many courses, students are merely passive observers; they learn about topics that affect them indirectly, if at all. Not everyone is a plasma physicist, a medieval French scholar, or a marketing professional. But we are all consumers. Many of the topics in this book have both professional and personal relevance to the reader, regardless of whether he or she is a student, professor, or businessperson. Nearly everyone can relate to the trials and tribulations of last-minute shopping, primping for a big night out, agonizing over an expensive purchase, fantasizing about a week in the Caribbean, celebrating a holiday, or commemorating a landmark event, such as graduating, getting a driver's license, or (dreaming about) winning the lottery.

In this edition, I have tried to introduce you to the latest and best thinking by some very bright scientists who develop models and studies of consumer behavior. But that's not enough. Consumer behavior is an applied science, so we must never lose sight of the role of "horse sense" when we apply our findings to life in the real world. That's why you'll find a lot of practical examples to back up these fancy theories.

What Makes This Book Different: Buying, Having, and Being

As this book's subtitle suggests, my vision of consumer behavior goes well beyond studying the act of *buying*—*having* and *being* are just as important, if not more so. Consumer behavior is more than buying things; it also embraces the study of how having (or not having) things affects our lives and how our possessions influence the way we feel about ourselves and about each other—our state of being. I developed the *Wheel of Consumer Behavior* that appears at the beginning of text sections to underscore the complex—and often inseparable—interrelationships between the individual consumer and his or her social realities.

In addition to understanding why people buy things, we also try to appreciate how products, services, and consumption activities contribute to the broader social world we experience. Whether we shop, cook, clean, play basketball, hang out at the beach, or even look at ourselves in the mirror, the marketing system touches our lives. As if these experiences aren't complex enough, the task of understanding the consumer increases when we take a multicultural perspective.

Marketers like this Danish restaurant often rely on consumers' expectations based on country-of-origin cues.
Source: Courtesy of Reef 'N Beef/Saatchi

people spend roughly twice as much of their toilet paper budget on the top choice than on the second-ranked brand, about twice on the number two brand as on the third-ranked brand, and about twice on the number three brand as on the number four brand. One ramification is that a brand that moves from number two to number one in a category will see a much greater jump in sales than will, say, a brand that moves from number four to number three. Brands that dominate their markets are as much as 50 percent more profitable than their nearest competitors.[34]

Inertia: The Lazy Customer

Many people tend to buy the same brand just about every time they go to the store. Often this is because of **inertia**—we buy a brand out of habit merely because it requires less effort (see Chapter 4). If another product comes along that is cheaper (or if the original product is out of stock), we won't hesitate to change our minds. A competitor who tries to encourage this switch often can do so rather easily because the shopper won't hesitate to jump to the new brand if it offers the right incentive.

When we have little to no underlying commitment to a particular brand, marketers find it easy to "unfreeze" our habit with the help of promotional tools such as point-of-purchase displays, extensive couponing, or noticeable price reductions. Some analysts predict that we're going to observe this kind of fickle behavior more and more as consumers flit from one brand to the next. Indeed, one industry observer labels this variety-seeking consumer a *brand slut*; she points out that from

Net Profit

Our online behaviors also can satisfy needs at different levels of Maslow's hierarchy, especially when we participate in social networks like Facebook. Web-based companies can build loyalty if they keep these needs in mind when they design their offerings:

- We can satisfy physiological needs when we use the Web to research topics such as nutrition or medical questions.
- The Web enables users to pool information and satisfy safety needs when they call attention to bad practices, flawed products, or even dangerous predators.
- Profile pages on Facebook and MySpace let users define themselves as individuals.
- Online communities, blogs, and social networks provide recognition and achievement to those who cultivate a reputation for being especially helpful or expert in some subject.
- Users can seek help from others and connect with people who have similar tastes and interests.
- Access to invitation-only communities provides status.
- Spiritually-based online communities can provide guidance to troubled people.[20]

We'll explore these ideas with intriguing and current examples as we show how the consumer behavior discipline relates to your daily life. Throughout the ninth edition, you'll find up-to-the-minute discussions of topics such as social networking, tweetups, carbon footprints, sensory signatures, alternate-reality games, virtual identity and online avatars, frugalistas, sock puppeting, gripe sites, sexting, bromances, helicopter moms, cosplay, and headbanging rituals. If you can't identify all of these terms, I can suggest a textbook you should read immediately!

Going Global

The American experience is important, but it's far from the whole story. This book also considers the many other consumers around the world whose diverse experiences with buying, having, and being we must understand. That's why you'll find numerous examples of marketing and consumer practices relating to consumers and companies outside the United States throughout the book. If we didn't know it before the tragic events of September 11, 2001, we certainly know it now: Americans also are global citizens, and it's vital that we all appreciate others' perspectives.

Digital Consumer Behavior: A Virtual Community

As more of us go online every day, there's no doubt the world is changing—and consumer behavior evolves faster than you can say "the Web." This ninth edition continues to highlight and celebrate the brave new world of digital consumer behavior. Today, consumers and producers come together electronically in ways we have never known before. Rapid transmission of information alters the speed at which new trends develop and the direction in which they travel—especially because the virtual world lets consumers participate in the creation and dissemination of new products.

One of the most exciting aspects of the new digital world is that consumers can interact directly with other people who live around the block or around the world. As a result, we need to radically redefine the meaning of community. It's no longer enough to acknowledge that consumers like to talk to each other about products. Now we share opinions and get the buzz about new movies, CDs, cars, clothes—you name it—in electronic communities that may include a housewife in Alabama, a disabled senior citizen in Alaska, or a teen loaded with body piercings in Amsterdam. And many of us meet up in computer-mediated environments (CMEs) such as Facebook, Twitter, and *Second Life*. I'm totally fascinated by what goes on in virtual worlds, and you'll see a lot of material in this edition that relates to these emerging consumer playgrounds.

We have just begun to explore the ramifications for consumer behavior when a Web surfer can project her own picture onto a Web site to get a virtual makeover or a corporate purchasing agent can solicit bids for a new piece of equipment from vendors around the world in minutes. These new ways of interacting in the marketplace create bountiful opportunities for businesspeople and consumers alike. You will find illustrations of the changing digital world sprinkled liberally throughout this edition. In addition, each chapter features boxes I call *Net Profit,* which point to specific examples of the Net's potential to improve the way we conduct business.

But is the digital world always a rosy place? Unfortunately, just as in the "real world," the answer is no. The potential to exploit consumers, whether by invading their privacy, preying on the curiosity of children, or simply providing false product information, is always there. That's why you'll also find boxes I call *The Tangled Web* that point out some of the abuses of this fascinating new medium. Still, I can't imagine a world without the Web, and I hope you'll enjoy the ways it's changing our field. When it comes to the new virtual world of consumer behavior, you're either on the train or under it.

Consumer Research Is a Big Tent:
The Importance of a Balanced Perspective

Like most of you who will read this book, the field of consumer behavior is young, dynamic, and in flux. It is constantly cross-fertilized by perspectives from many different disciplines—the field is a big tent that invites many diverse views to enter. I try to express the field's staggering diversity in these pages. Consumer researchers represent virtually every social science discipline, plus a few from the physical sciences and the arts for good measure. From this blending of disciplines comes a dynamic and complex research perspective, including viewpoints regarding appropriate research methods, and even deeply held beliefs about what are and what are not appropriate issues for consumer researchers to study in the first place.

The book also emphasizes how strategically vital it is to understand consumers. Many (if not most) of the fundamental concepts in marketing emanate from a manager's ability to know people. After all, if we don't understand why people behave as they do, how can we identify their needs? If we can't identify their needs, how can we satisfy their needs? If we can't satisfy people's needs, we don't have a marketing concept, so we might as well fold our big tent and go home!

To illustrate the potential of consumer research to inform marketing strategy, the text contains numerous examples of specific applications of consumer behavior concepts by marketing practitioners as well as examples of windows of opportunity where we could use these concepts (perhaps by alert strategists after they take this course!). The *Marketing Opportunity* boxes you'll find in each chapter highlight the fascinating ways that marketing practitioners translate wisdom they glean from consumer research into actual business activities.

The Good, the Bad, and the Ugly

A strategic focus is great, but this book doesn't assume that everything marketers do is in the best interests of consumers or of their environment. Likewise, as consumers we do many things that are not so positive either. We suffer from addictions, status envy, ethnocentrism, racism, sexism, and many other isms. Regrettably, there are times when marketing activities—deliberately or not—encourage or exploit these human flaws. This book deals with the totality of consumer behavior, warts and all. We'll highlight marketing mistakes or ethically suspect activities in boxes I call *Marketing Pitfall.*

On a more cheerful note, marketers create wonderful (or at least unusual) things, such as holidays, comic books, Krispy Kreme donuts, nu-jazz music, Webkinz, and

---

The Tangled Web

In recent years we've witnessed a new attempt to manipulate attitudes that some call sock puppeting. This term describes a company executive or other biased source who poses as someone else as he touts his organization in social media. For example, in 2007 it came to light that the CEO of Whole Foods posted derogatory comments about rival Wild Oats without revealing his true identity. More recently a nonprofit research organization called GiveWell that rates the effectiveness of charities had to discipline two of its founders who pretended to be other people on blogs and then referred ... /eb site.[68]

... potentially dilute the ..., the open-source on-... beloved by many stu-... entries, so their relia-... Although other alert ... tually correct false or ... re is still room for or-... ontent in a way that ... example, a visitor ed-... try for the SeaWorld ... all mentions of "orcas" ... e or she also deleted a ... d SeaWorld's "lack of ... :as." It turns out the ... a computer located in ... ompany that happens ... employee of PepsiCo ... ... effects, ... n entry ... /ees. ... is so-... attempt ... brands ... e about ... s" can ... d to be ... rce rec-... warded ... rs who ... iences. ... nsumer ... re they ... c prod-... blogger ... nge for

Marketing Opportunity

The choice of a great brand name is so important that companies often hire *naming consultants* to come up with a winner. These experts try to find *semantic associations* that click because they evoke some desirable connection. That strategy brought us names such as Qualcomm ("quality" and "communications"), Verizon (*veritas* is Latin for "truth," and "horizon" suggests forward-looking), and Intel ("intelligent" and "electronics"). The name Viagra rhymes with the famous waterfall Niagara. People associate water with both sexuality and life, an... ... ... mecca. Phili... self Altria G... yond cigare... brewing. Thi... controversia... comments, '... company wi... in its brand

These se... to find, so ... more basic i... ages betwee... consonants ... sponses. Sti... that respon... guages asso... emotion-lad... alive and da... researchers ... sense name... phoneme, fo... and ask wh... nicer, and s... that come t... slowness, w... seem faster... sense of sp... When namin... to label a n... sistant (PDA... because the... seeds. They ... because the... letter *b* with... cated smallr... a linguist p... syllable and... fast connota... was born.[44]

Marketing Pitfall

Strongly held values can make life very difficult for marketers who sell personal-care products. This is the case with tampons; 70 percent of U.S. women use them, but only 100 million out of a potential market of 1.7 billion eligible women around the world do. Resistance to using this product posed a major problem for Tambrands. The company makes only one product, so it needs to sell tampons in as many countries as possible to continue growing. But Tambrands has trouble selling its feminine hygiene products in some cultures such as Brazil, where many young women fear they will lose their virginity if they use a tampon. A commercial it showed then featured an actress who says in a reassuring voice, "Of course, you're not going to lose your virginity."

Prior to launching a new global advertising campaign for Tampax in 26 countries, the firm's advertising agency divided the world into three clusters based on residents' resistance to using tampons. Resistance was so intense in Muslim countries that the agency didn't even try to sell there!

* In cluster 1 (including the United States, the United Kingdom, and Australia), women felt comfortable with the idea and offered little resistance. The agency developed a *teaser ad* to encourage more frequency of use: "Should I sleep with it, or not?"
* In cluster 2 (including France, Israel, and South Africa), about 50 percent of women use the product, but some concerns about the loss of virginity remain. To counteract these objections, the agency obtained endorsements from gynecologists within each country.
* In cluster 3 (including Brazil, China, and Russia), Tambrands encountered the greatest resistance. To try to make inroads in these countries, the researchers found that the first priority is simply to explain how to use the product without making women feel squeamish—a challenge they still try to figure out. If they do—and that's a big if—Tambrands will have changed the consumer behavior of millions of women and added huge new markets to its customer base in the process.[75]

the many stylistic options that beckon to us in the domains of clothing, home design, the arts, and cuisine. I also take pains to acknowledge the sizable impact of marketing on popular culture. Indeed, the final section of this book captures very recent work in the field that scrutinizes, criticizes, and sometimes celebrates consumers in their everyday worlds. I hope you will enjoy reading about such wonderful things as much as I enjoyed writing about them. Welcome to the fascinating world of consumer behavior!

Consumer Behavior in the Trenches

I'm a huge believer in the value of up-to-date information. Our field changes so rapidly that often yesterday's news is no news at all. True, there are "timeless" studies that demonstrate basic consumer behavior constructs as well today as they did 20 years ago or more (I may even have authored some of them!). Still, I feel a real obligation to present students and their professors with a current view of research, popular culture, and marketing activities whenever I can. For this reason, each time I start to contemplate my next edition, I write to colleagues to ask for copies of papers they have in press that they believe will be important in the future. Their cooperation with my request allows me to include a lot of fresh research examples; in some cases these articles will not yet have been published when this book comes out. I've listed those who help me in this endeavor in the Acknowledgments section, which follows.

I've taken this initiative to the next level with a feature I call *CB as I See It*. In every chapter you'll find a "flesh-and-blood" consumer behavior professor who shares his or her perspective as a leading researcher in a particular area of specialization about an appropriate topic. I've let these esteemed colleagues largely speak for themselves, so now you can benefit from other voices who chime in on relevant research issues. Again, I've listed these participants in the Acknowledgments section, and I'm grateful for their wonderful cooperation and for letting me share their words—and their photos!—with you.

But who says professors know everything (well, professors do . . .). As I've already noted, there's no doubt that consumer-generated content (in the form of buzz marketing strategies, commercials submitted by brand users, and so on) is fundamentally changing business—and consumer behavior. I believe we should "practice what we teach," and so this edition includes yet another new feature that lets real students have their way. For the new box, *CB as I Live It*, I invited individuals or student groups at schools across the United States to contribute their own views on key concepts. I gave these participants very explicit ground rules: Have fun. Tell or show us how an idea you read about in a chapter relates to your own life. In response I got essays, photos, poetry, even YouTube videos. You'll see them in the book and also posted on our *MyMarketingLab* site.

CB AS I SEE IT
Professor Jennifer Aaker, *Stanford University*

Imagine you are at Disneyland about to board the Space Mountain ride. As you climb into your rocket, you feel joy and apprehension—a mixed feeling that persists even after the ride is over. You grip the safety bar, at once thrilled and frightened. You leave the Space Mountain ride dizzy with mixed emotions. How will you recall your experience a week later? Will you remember the mixed emotions you experienced on the ride? Or will the memory of those mixed emotions fade?

Questions regarding the memory of mixed emotions are important. Many of life's most important events are defined by mixtures of emotions where people find themselves feeling both positive and negative emotions—e.g., graduating from college ("I'm making progress, but leaving my friends and family"), moving ("I'm starting a new life, but losing my old one"), or achieving major life goals ("I'm thrilled to have reached the destination, but I'm sad the journey is over").

To address these questions, we conducted a set of longitudinal experiments that show that the intensity of mixed emotions is underestimated at the time of recall—an effect that appears to increase over time and does not occur to the same degree with uniformly happy or sad emotions. Together, these results indicate that, as time passes, mixed emotions are increasingly difficult to recall, that memory for them fades, and that felt conflict underlies this recall bias.

The results of this work speak to several domains of research. For example, the results imply that individuals who are comfortable with inconsistency should recall mixed emotions more accurately. Similarly, if there is an increased desire to resolve the emotion of felt conflict, the effects documented here should be muted for individuals who are not disturbed by the ambiguity associated with mixed emotions. And, the effects should dissipate if the mixed emotions we experience consist of a dominant emotion (e.g., strong feelings of anger), thereby reducing the conflict we feel.

The results also speak to ongoing research in marketing, which suggests that emotional experiences can fundamentally impact purchase intent as well as foster brand loyalty. For example, the amount of warmth that emanates from a brand or the fun enjoyed by a brand (e.g., iPhone) can fundamentally influence our relationship with it. However, in reality, most consumer-brand relationships are defined, at some point or another, by a transgression that gives rise to negative feelings among consumers—such as when something you buy breaks. Our research suggests that the degree to which a negative event is categorized as part of a mixed experience (versus as a single negative event) impacts the probability that the consumer will remember that experience and be influenced by it. If the transgression is mentally clumped together with positive interactions with the brand, the memory of the mixed emotional experience may indeed fade—which would not be the case if the transgression stood alone as an isolated negative event.

CB AS I LIVE IT
Drew Rudebusch, *The University of Washington*

A quarter-life crisis. That is what some people called it. Others just said I was scared. Probably true, but who isn't scared when they are about to graduate. Call it whatever you want, but the one thing I know for certain is that my motivations have changed dramatically.

Coming out of a long-term relationship, with graduation quickly approaching, I found myself pondering every aspect of my life. Central to all of these musings were my motivations. I quickly realized that the motivation for many of my decisions was not sustaining me any longer. An altered living situation, coupled with a totally different perspective on the future, combined to make for a marketer's dream. I was truly on a mission to find myself, and provided an open door for marketers to inspire me with their "motivational" messaging. I grew less interested in the traditional material goods, such as cars, televisions, or a fancy house. Instead I was motivated by experiences that I want to strive for,

like traveling the world. I became more interested than ever before by travel discounts and advertisements about adventures abroad. Graduating and getting a job took on a totally different meaning than just months before. I looked forward to spending my paychecks in a drastically new way.

Does this mean my motivation for a nice car, a comfortable home, and tailored suits have gone away entirely? I doubt it. Those marketers will have their chance again one day, but for now because I have found a new motivation.

I'm actually sad to introduce a new chapter feature I call *ECONsumer Behavior*. You'd have to be living in a deep hole somewhere if you don't recognize the profound impact our current economic crisis has and will continue to have on consumer behavior. We can hope and trust that conditions will improve, but we can't ignore how high unemployment, bankruptcies of corporate icons like General Motors, and low consumer confidence influence what—and if—people want to buy. Some of these effects will reverse when the economy picks up steam, but others such as the value we place on "bling" may fundamentally change. This boxed feature that appears throughout the book focuses specifically on how marketer and consumer behavior is changing as a result. My only wish is that when I start to prepare the *next* edition of this book, I will no longer need to include this feature!

ECONsumer Behavior

Can our financial problems decrease our ability to remember even the coolest commercials? The research firm Gallup & Robinson says yes. In 2009 the company studied 12 years' worth of surveys about recall and likability of Super Bowl ads. It reports a direct relationship between the confidence people have in the economy and the amount of attention they pay to these spots. When consumer confidence is weak, recall is 11 percent lower than average and 36 percent lower than in good times.[87] Perhaps people are worrying too much about where they will get money to pay attention to ads that tell them how to spend it.

Mintel End-of-Section Feature

We've added a new feature to the end of each section of the ninth edition—*Mintel Memo and Dataset Exercises*. The folks at Mintel—a leading global provider of consumer and market research—have partnered with us to provide students with actual data the company obtained from recent consumer surveys. Each exercise contains Mintel data and some suggestions about how to use it to come up with answers to specific marketing questions. The challenge for students is to make sense of what the numbers tell us about how people actually consume.

Using data collected from both primary and secondary research sources, Mintel analyzes consumer trends across industries. As a global research leader, Mintel is eager to support research about consumer behavior trends and seeks to help students, businesses, and individuals better understand their markets.

Students can access Mintel Oxygen reports through their university libraries, as well as on- and off-campus. Using information from Mintel Oxygen reports, students can gain understanding of different markets, consumer behavior trends, and industry expectations. Professors can also access Mintel Oxygen reports through their university libraries. By using Mintel Oxygen reports in their curriculum, professors can stay on top of quickly changing consumer and market trends. You can learn more about Mintel at mintel.com. Full data sets to accompany these exercises can be downloaded from www.pearsonhighered.com/solomon.

MINTEL

SECTION 2

General Instructions for the *Mintel Memo and Dataset Exercises*

The dataset exercise in each Mintel section consists of a data-driven task. You should complete each task by analyzing the sample data tables provided in each Mintel section. (Each table includes data collected by Mintel International from actual respondents in the marketplace!)

In generating each data-driven "memo," you will provide your own interpretation of the data in the tables, paying close attention to significant differences among banner groups in the data tables (e.g., males versus females, 18- to 24-year-olds versus 55+ year-olds, single versus married, etc.). In the field of marketing research, marketing recommendations are typically generated from statistically significant differences among subgroups of respondents; therefore, your analyses and recommendations will be more useful and informed by focusing on statistically significant differences among the banner groups in the provided sets of data tables.

MINTEL MEMO

TO: Consumer Research Dept.
FROM: The Big Boss
RE: How are food and diet trends affecting consumer behavior today?

We need to provide consumer feedback to our new product development group ASAP. Based on what you know from reading Section 2 and from the data we have been given by Mintel, what would be a feasible idea for a new food product given today's market trends? Assume a reasonable but not an eye-popping budget.

Please provide us with actionable recommendations based on this information. As you analyze the data in the tables provided, remember to focus on general trends but also on specific subgroups (e.g., men versus women) that show a statistically significant difference in their responses—especially when there is some reason based on what you have learned in this section about consumer behavior to believe that this difference is important.

When you write your memo, please try to incorporate relevant concepts and information you learned when you read the designated chapters!

Critical Thinking in Consumer Behavior: Case Study

Learning by doing is an integral part of the classroom experience. In this edition, we've included a *Case Study* at the end of each chapter along with discussion questions to help students apply the case to the chapter's contents.

Also included in the ninth edition are the following items that will enhance the student learning experience.

- *Chapter Objectives* at the beginning of each chapter provide an overview of key issues to be covered in the chapter. Each *Chapter Summary* is then organized around the objectives to help students integrate the material they have read.
- *Review* at the end of each chapter helps students to study key issues.

Case Study

MICHAEL PHELPS: ENDORSEMENT DEALS GO UP IN SMOKE!

Michael Phelps made his Olympic debut at the age of 15. At 6'4" Phelps has a wingspan and a shoe size that eclipses most competitive swimmers. This physical advantage combined with years of extensive training positions him to become the greatest swimmer of all time. At the 2008 Beijing Olympics, Phelps won a record eight gold medals and broke four individual world records. He achieved what no athlete in the world had ever done in the history of the Olympics.

The United States had a new sports superstar! A hero for young kids to admire. An athlete who reflected the results of hard work and determination. During the Olympics,

Phelps' agents predicted the swimmer would earn over $100 million in endorsements over his lifetime.

Fast-forward to February 2009: A picture of Phelps smoking pot appears in the British tabloid *News of the World*. USA Swimming, the national governing body of competitive swimming in the United States, immediately suspended Phelps from competition for three months. Phelps' reputation began to unravel. Phelps quickly apologized to all his sponsors as the incriminating photo spread through the blogosphere. Kellogg and Subway dropped their sponsorship deals soon afterward.

However, other sponsors including Speedo, Omega, Visa, and Pure Sports continued to support Phelps. Speedo issued this statement: "Speedo would like to make it clear that it does not condone such behavior and we know that

● The *Consumer Behavior Challenge* at the end of each chapter is divided into two sections:
  ○ *Discuss* poses thoughtful issues that encourage students to consider pragmatic and ethical implications of the material they have read.
  ○ *Apply* allows students to "get their hands dirty" as they conduct miniexperiments and collect data in the real world to better grasp the application of consumer behavior principles.

CourseSmart

CourseSmart is an exciting new *choice* for students looking to save money. As an alternative to purchasing the print textbook, students can purchase an electronic version of the same content and save up to 50 percent off the suggested list price of the print text. With a CourseSmart eTextbook, students can search the text, make notes online, print out reading assignments that incorporate lecture notes, and bookmark important passages for later review. For more information or to purchase access to the CourseSmart eTextbook, visit coursesmart.com.

Supplements

Instructor's Resource Center (IRC)—The IRC online at pearsonhighered.com includes the Instructor's Manual with Video Guide, AACSB-accredited Test Item File, TestGen, PowerPoints, and the Image Library.

Videos—The ninth edition video package offers segments that take students on location, profiling well-known companies and their marketing strategies. In addition, we include in-depth examinations of the real world of global consumer behavior. These rich and thought-provoking films are drawn from the archives of the Association for Consumer Research Film Festivals. These festivals are held annually in North America and in the annual non–North America conference that rotates among Europe, Latin America, and the Asia Pacific region. The video library is available on DVD. Instructors can choose to have the DVD shrink-wrapped with the text.

Full Mintel Data Sets: Data sets to accompany the Mintel Exercises can be downloaded from www.pearsonhighered.com/solomon.

mymarketinglab

mymarketinglab is a series of text-specific, easily customizable online courses for Prentice Hall textbooks in consumer behavior. mymarketinglab gives you the tools you need to deliver all or a portion of your course online, whether your students are in a course setting or working from home.

Students can also use online tools, such as chapter objective study questions, chapter test assessments, and a multimedia textbook, to independently improve their understanding and performance.

Instructors can use mymarketinglab's homework and test managers to select and assign online exercises correlated directly to the textbook, and they can also create and assign their own online exercises and import TestGen tests for added flexibility. mymarketinglab's online grade book is designed to automatically track students' homework and test results and give the instructor control over the calculation of final grades. Instructors can also add off-line (paper-and-pencil) grades to the grade book.

Two bright doctoral students "kept me honest" as they helped me review recent literature. Thanks go to my "right brain" researcher Yesim Ozalp at York University and my "left brain" researcher Jesse Itzkowitz at The University of Florida. I'm also grateful for the many helpful comments on how to improve the ninth edition my peer reviewers provided. Special thanks go to the following individuals:

Elizabeth Blair, Ohio University–Athens
Mark Blake, York College
Sheri Bridges, Wake Forest University
Joshua Coplen, Santa Monica College
Julia Cronin-Gilmore, Bellevue University
Nitika Garg, University of Mississippi
Linda Goulet Crosby, Davenport University
Jan Hardesty, University of Arizona
Christopher D. Huseman, Culver Stockton College, John Wood Community
    College
Dale Kehr, University of Memphis
Ed Langlois, Palm Beach Atlantic University
Mike McCall, Ithaca College
Elaine Moore, Raritan Valley Community College
Hayden Noel, University of Illinois
Lois Patton, Shepherd University

These colleagues generously contributed their thoughts to my *CB as I See It* boxes:

Jennifer Aaker, Stanford University
Lauren Block, Baruch College of The City University of New York
Lisa Bolton, The Pennsylvania State University
Gordon Bruner, Southern Illinois University
Lan Chaplin, University of Arizona
Larry Compeau, Clarkson University
Susan Dobscha, Bentley University
Gavan Fitzsimmons, Duke University
Sonya Grier, American University
Aradhna Krishna, University of Michigan
George Loewenstein, Carnegie Mellon University
Edward McQuarrie, Santa Clara University
George Moschis, Georgia State University
Cele Otnes, University of Illinois at Urbana-Champaign
Julie Ozanne, Virginia Tech
Americus Reed, University of Pennsylvania
John Schouten, University of Portland
Alladi Venkatesh, University of California, Irvine

Many other colleagues and friends made significant contributions to this edition. I would like to thank, in particular, the following people who provided me with a sneak peek at their research materials and manuscripts now in press or under review:

Paul Albanese, Kent State University
Craig Andrews, Marquette University
Abe Biswas, Wayne State University
Lisa Bolton, The Pennsylvania State University
Lauren Block, Baruch College, The City University of New York
Amitava Chattopadhyay, INSEAD
June Cotte, University of Western Ontario
Aimee Drolet, UCLA
Sonya Grier, American University
Joel Huber, Duke University
Barbara Kahn, University of Miami
Aron Levin, Northern Kentucky University
Joan Meyers-Levy, University of Minnesota
Nicholas Lurie, Georgia Tech
David Mick, University of Virginia
Tom Novak, University of California, Riverside
Joseph Nunes, University of Southern California
Americus Reed, University of Pennsylvania
Martin Reimann, University of Southern California
Hope Schau, University of Arizona
Sharon Shavitt, University of Illinois
LJ Shrum, University of Texas at San Antonio
Kathleen Vohs, University of Minnesota
Tacli Yazicioglu, Bogazici University

A note of thanks to the colleagues who identified their best students to participate in my new *CB as I Live It* feature. You have good reason to be proud of your nominees!

JoAnn Atkin, University of Western Michigan
Paul Chao, Eastern Michigan University
Amber Epp, University of Wisconsin
Kivilcim Dogerlioglu-Demir, Washington State University
Karen Hood, University of Tennessee, Knoxville
Mark Lowenstein, College of St. Joseph's
Paula Peter, San Diego State University
Mary Beth Pinto, Penn State Behrend
Melanie Wallendorf, University of Arizona

Extra special thanks are due to the preparers of the ancillary materials: Tracy Tuten, East Carolina University; Bonnie Flaherty and Kathleen Zumpfe, Doane College. Deborah Utter, Boston University, for revising and creating new chapter cases; and Michael K. Coolsen, Shippensburg University, for preparation of the *Mintel Memo* feature.

I would also like to thank the good people at Prentice Hall who as always have done yeoman service on this edition. A special thanks to James Heine who wins "rookie of the year" honors and to Anne Fahlgren for her support. Karin Williams and Ana Jankowski did a great job keeping me on course, and Melissa Gill was her usual conscientious self.

Without the tolerance of my friends and colleagues, I would never have been able to sustain the illusion that I was still an active researcher while I worked on this edition. I am grateful to my department chair, John Lord, and to Dean Joe DiAngelo for supporting their high-maintenance faculty member. Also, I am grateful to my undergraduate students, who have been a prime source of inspiration, examples, and feedback. The satisfaction I have garnered from teaching them about consumer behavior motivated me to write a book I felt they would like to read.

Last but not least, I would like to thank my family and friends for sticking by me during this revision. They know who they are; their names pop up in chapter vignettes throughout the book. My apologies for "distorting" their characters in the name of poetic license! My gratitude and love go out to my parents, Jackie and Henry, and my in-laws, Marilyn and Phil. Ditto to my super children, Amanda, Zachary, and Alexandra—and my high-tech son-in-law Orly—who always made the sun shine on gray days (not to mention my favorite pug Kelbie Rae). My gorgeous new granddaughter Rosalia added a special thrill this past year. Finally, thanks above all to the love of my life—Gail, my wonderful wife, best friend, and the hottest grandmother on earth: I still do it all for you.

M.R.S.
Philadelphia, Pennsylvania
September 2009

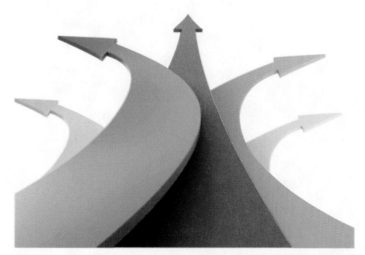

Consumer Behavior

HIS MOTHER'S EYES

HIS FATHER'S NOSE

HIS NEIGHBOUR'S LEG

LIVE AT AUCKLAND ZOO AND AT WWW.AUCKLANDZOOTIGERS.CO.NZ

Fed and watered by

Section 1 Consumers in the Marketplace

This introductory section provides an overview of the field of consumer behavior (CB). In Chapter 1, we look at how consumers influence the field of marketing and also at how marketers influence us. We describe the discipline of consumer behavior and some of the different approaches to understanding what makes consumers tick. We also highlight the importance of the study of consumer behavior to such public policy issues as addiction and environmentalism.

CHAPTER AHEAD

Chapter 1   Consumers Rule

1

Consumers Rule

When you finish this chapter you will understand:

1 How do consumers use products to help them define their identities in different settings?

2 Why is consumer behavior a process?

3 Why do marketers need to understand the wants and needs of different consumer segments?

4 How is the Web changing consumer behavior?

5 How does consumer behavior relate to other issues in our lives?

6 Why can consumer activities be harmful to individuals and to society?

7 How do different types of specialists study consumer behavior?

8 What are the two major perspectives that seek to understand and study consumer behavior?

*G*ail has some time to kill before her Accounting class, so she fires up her laptop and surfs the Web. Between studying for her Accounting and Marketing exams she hasn't checked out anything interesting in weeks—even her Facebook friends have been pretty quiet. Enough of the serious stuff, she decides. It's time for some *really* educational surfing.

So, where to go first? Gail figures she'll start at one of the popular women's portals and see what happens. She goes to iVillage.com, where she checks her horoscope (cool! a good day to start a new relationship), scans a few beauty tips, and takes a Great Date quiz (uh-oh, she may need to replace this new guy James she's been seeing). Similar stuff is going on at Oxygen.com; some community members chat about their obsession with *America's Next Top Model* while others tune in to *The Bad Girls Club* to learn more about what ". . . happens when you put seven bad girls under one roof."[1] Then she checks out the new Web site for her sorority at sigmadeltatau.com, which reminds her, "The mission of Sigma Delta Tau is to enrich the college experience of women of similar ideals, to build lasting friendships and to foster personal growth. . ."[2] Very nice, but she learned all that at Rush. Time to move on. . . .

After an hour of surfing some fascinating e-commerce sites—and vowing to return to some of them to reward herself with a present after exams—Gail decides to get the 411 on what "real people" are doing on the Web. First she checks in on the clubs she belongs to at teen.com—wow, more than 30 people from her campus are logged on right now! Looks like other students are studying as hard as she is! The site's *Campus Culture* link takes her to a story another female student posted, "I was a Hooter's Girl." She reads with a chuckle how she ". . . undergoes a babelicious transformation so she can serve wings to fat guys."[3] As Gail glances at the clock she realizes she'd better come back to the real world or she'll miss her class. In one final impulse, she logs on to RateMyProfessors.com and posts a nasty comment about her Accounting professor.[4] With a sly smile, Gail throws her laptop in her backpack and heads out to class. She can't wait to sit on the campus shuttle and Tweet her friends to check out the latest snide comments about Prof. Boring.

Consumer Behavior: People in the Marketplace

This book is about people like Gail—and YOU. It concerns the products and services we buy and use, and the ways these fit into our lives. This introductory chapter describes some important aspects of the field of consumer behavior and some reasons why it's essential to understand how people interact with the marketing system. For now, though, let's return to one "typical" consumer: Gail, the business major. The preceding vignette allows us to highlight some aspects of consumer behavior that we will cover in the rest of the book.

Gail is a consumer, so let's compare her to other consumers. For some purposes, marketers find it useful to categorize her in terms of her age, gender, income, or occupation. These are descriptive characteristics of a population, or **demographics**. In other cases, marketers would rather know something about Gail's interests in clothing or music, or the way she spends her leisure time. This sort of information comes under the category of **psychographics**, which refers to aspects of a person's lifestyle and personality. Knowledge of consumer characteristics plays an extremely important role in many marketing applications, such as defining the market for a product or deciding on the appropriate techniques to employ when a company targets a certain group of consumers.

Gail's sorority sisters strongly influence her purchase decisions. The conversations we have with others transmit a lot of product information, as well as recommendations to use or avoid particular brands; this content often is more influential than what we see on television commercials, magazines, billboards, or even MySpace. The growth of the Web has created thousands of online **consumption communities** where members share opinions and recommendations about anything from Barbie dolls to iPhone Apps. Gail forms bonds with fellow group members because they use the same products. There is also pressure on each group member to buy things that will meet with the group's approval. A consumer may pay a steep price in the form of group rejection or embarrassment when she doesn't conform to others' conceptions of what is good or bad, "in" or "out."

As members of a large society, such as the United States, people share certain cultural values, or strongly held beliefs about the way the world should be structured. Members of subcultures, or smaller groups within the culture, also share values; these groups include Hispanics, teens, Midwesterners, or even Lindsay Lohan fan clubs and *Hell's Angels*.

While examining Web sites, Gail was exposed to many competing *brands*. Numerous sites did not capture her attention at all, whereas she noticed and rejected others because they didn't relate to products, people, or ideas with which she identified or to which she aspired. The use of **market segmentation strategies** means targeting a brand only to specific groups of consumers rather than to everybody—even if it means that other consumers who don't belong to this target market aren't attracted to that product.

Brands often have clearly defined images, or "personalities," that advertising, packaging, branding, and other marketing strategies create. The choice of a favorite Web site is very much a *lifestyle* statement: It says a lot about a person's interests, as well as something about the type of person she would like to be. People often choose a product because they like its image or because they feel its "personality" somehow corresponds to their own. Moreover, a consumer may believe that if she buys and uses the product or service its desirable qualities will "magically" rub off onto her.

When a product, idea, or Web site succeeds in satisfying our specific needs or desires, we may reward it with many years of *brand loyalty*, a bond between product and consumer that is very difficult for competitors to break. Often a change in one's life situation or self-concept is required to weaken this bond.

The appearance, taste, texture, or smell of the item influences our evaluations of products. A good Web site helps people to feel, taste, and smell with their eyes. We may be swayed by the shape and color of a package, as well as by more subtle factors, such as the symbolism in a brand name, in an advertisement, or even in the choice of a cover model for a magazine. These judgments are affected by—and often reflect—how a society feels that people should define themselves at that point in time. If she were asked, Gail might not even be able to say exactly why she considered some Web sites and rejected others. Many product meanings are hidden below the surface of the packaging and advertising; we'll discuss some of the methods marketers and social scientists use to discover or apply these meanings.

Like Gail, our opinions and desires increasingly are shaped by input from around the world, which is becoming a much smaller place as a result of rapid advancements in communications and transportation systems. In today's global culture, consumers often prize products and services that "transport" them to different places and allow them to experience the diversity of other cultures—even if only to watch others brush their teeth on YouTube.

OBJECTIVE

How do consumers use products to help them define their identities in different settings?

What Is Consumer Behavior?

The field of **consumer behavior** covers a lot of ground: *It is the study of the processes involved when individuals or groups select, purchase, use, or dispose of products, services, ideas, or experiences to satisfy needs and desires.* Consumers take many forms, ranging from an 8-year-old child begging

The expanded view of consumer behavior embraces much more than the study of what and why we buy; it also focuses on how marketers influence consumers and how consumers use the products and services marketers sell. In this case, a hotel in Dubai promotes responsible behavior.
Source: Courtesy of Marco Polo Hotel/Dubai; Brandcom Agency.

Don't let alcohol alter your reality.
Drink responsibly. Don't drink and drive.

MARCO POLO
HOTELS
DUBAI

her mother for a Webkinz stuffed animal to an executive in a large corporation deciding on a multimillion-dollar computer system. The items we consume can include anything from canned peas to a massage, democracy, Reggaeton music, or a celebrity like Lady Gaga. Needs and desires we satisfy range from hunger and thirst to love, status, or even spiritual fulfillment. And, as we'll see throughout this book, people can get passionate about a broad range of products. For example, maybe you are a "sneakerhead" who covets rare models and measures time not by years but by Air Jordan editions. If so, get your kicks at Web sites such as <u>instyleshoes.com</u> and <u>kickz.com</u>.[5]

OBJECTIVE

Why is consumer behavior a process?

Consumer Behavior Is a Process

In its early stages of development, researchers referred to the field as *buyer behavior*; this reflected an emphasis on the interaction between consumers and producers at the time of purchase. Most marketers now recognize that consumer behavior is in fact an ongoing process, not merely what happens at the moment a consumer hands over money or a credit card and in turn receives some good or service.

The **exchange**, a transaction in which two or more organizations or people give and receive something of value, is an integral part of marketing.[6] Although *exchange theory* remains an important part of consumer behavior, the expanded view emphasizes the entire consumption process, which includes the issues that influence the consumer before, during, and after a purchase. Figure 1.1 illustrates some of the issues that we address during each stage of the consumption process.

Consumer Behavior Involves Many Different Actors

We generally think of a **consumer** as a person who identifies a need or desire, makes a purchase, and then disposes of the product during the three stages in the consumption process. In many cases, however, different people play a role in this

Figure 1.1 STAGES IN THE CONSUMPTION PROCESS

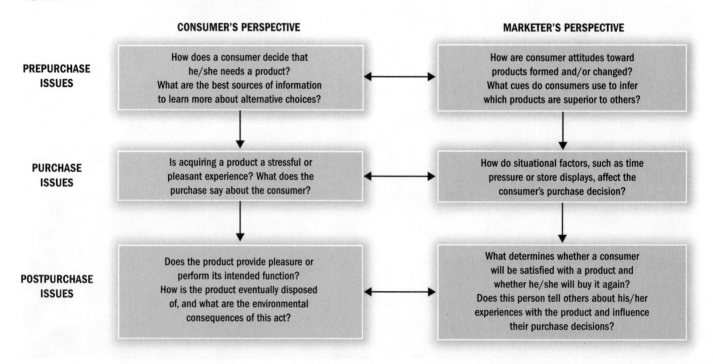

CONSUMER'S PERSPECTIVE | MARKETER'S PERSPECTIVE

PREPURCHASE ISSUES
How does a consumer decide that he/she needs a product? What are the best sources of information to learn more about alternative choices?
↔
How are consumer attitudes toward products formed and/or changed? What cues do consumers use to infer which products are superior to others?

PURCHASE ISSUES
Is acquiring a product a stressful or pleasant experience? What does the purchase say about the consumer?
↔
How do situational factors, such as time pressure or store displays, affect the consumer's purchase decision?

POSTPURCHASE ISSUES
Does the product provide pleasure or perform its intended function? How is the product eventually disposed of, and what are the environmental consequences of this act?
↔
What determines whether a consumer will be satisfied with a product and whether he/she will buy it again? Does this person tell others about his/her experiences with the product and influence their purchase decisions?

sequence of events. The purchaser and user of a product might not be the same person, as when a parent picks out clothes for a teenager (and makes selections that can result in "fashion suicide" in the view of the teen). In other cases, another person may act as an *influencer*, providing recommendations for or against certain products without actually buying or using them. A friend's grimace when you try on that new pair of pants may be more influential than anything your mother might say.

Finally, consumers may take the form of organizations or groups. One or several persons may make the decisions involved in purchasing products that many will use, as when a purchasing agent orders the company's office supplies. In other organizational situations, a large group of people may make purchase decisions—for example, company accountants, designers, engineers, sales personnel, and others—all of whom will have a say in the various stages of the consumption process. As we'll see in Chapter 11, one important type of organization is the family, where different family members play pivotal roles in making decisions regarding products and services all will use.

Consumers' Impact on Marketing Strategy

Surfing cool Web sites is a lot of fun. But, on the more serious side, why should managers, advertisers, and other marketing professionals bother to learn about consumer behavior? Very simply, *understanding consumer behavior is good business.* The basic marketing concept states that firms exist to satisfy needs. Marketers can only satisfy these needs to the extent that they understand the people or organizations who will use the products and services they are trying to sell.

Consumer response is the ultimate test of whether a marketing strategy will succeed. Thus, a marketer should incorporate knowledge about consumers into every facet of a successful marketing plan. Data about consumers help organizations to define the market and identify threats to and opportunities for a brand. And, in the wild and wacky world of marketing, nothing is forever: This knowledge also helps to ensure that the product continues to appeal to its core market.

The Sony Walkman is a good example of a successful product that needed to update its image—especially since the company faces fierce competition from the incredibly popular Apple iPod. Although Sony revolutionized the mobile music experience and sold almost 300 million Walkmans in the process, today's teens see portable cassette players as dinosaurs (assuming they've even heard of cassettes!). The company's advertising agency followed 125 teens to see how they use products in their day-to-day lives. Based on this consumer research, Sony relaunched the product with a removable "Memory Stick" instead of a cassette player so it works with MP3 files. The new S Series plays video and instantly creates channels based on a user's listening preferences.[7]

OBJECTIVE

Why do marketers need to understand the wants and needs of different consumer segments?

Consumers Are Different! How We Divide Them Up

As our society evolves from a mass culture where many consumers share the same preferences to a diverse one where we have almost an infinite number of choices, it's more important than ever to identify distinct market segments and develop specialized messages and products for those groups. McDonald's devotes a third of its U.S. marketing budget to television—compared with two-thirds a few years ago. The company uses that leftover money to sponsor closed-circuit sports programming

The woman in this Danish ad is fed up with bad financial news. Whether we like it or not, the global recession has affected all of us. Marketers are scrambling to adjust their strategies to this glum economic environment.

Source: Courtesy of Bianco Footwear & Co.

piped into Hispanic bars and for ads in *Upscale*, a custom-published magazine distributed to barber shops that cater to African American consumers. McDonald's advertises on Foot Locker's in-store video network to reach young men, and it zeroes in on mothers through ads in women's magazines such as *O: The Oprah Magazine* and Web sites such as iVillage.com.[8]

As we'll see later, building loyalty to a brand is a very smart marketing strategy, so sometimes companies define market segments when they identify their most faithful customers or **heavy users**. As a rule of thumb, marketers use the **80/20 rule**; 20 percent of users account for 80 percent of sales. This guideline often holds up well, and in some cases even this lopsided split isn't big enough: A recent study of 54 million shoppers reported that only 2.5 percent of consumers account for 80 percent of sales for the average package-goods brand. The 1 percent of pet owners who buy 80 percent of Iams pet food spend $93 a year on the brand, and the 1.2 percent of beer drinkers who account for 80 percent of Budweiser sales spend $170 on Bud each year. Of the 1,364 brands the researchers studied, only 25 had a consumer base of more than 10 percent that accounted for 80 percent of volume.[9] In the fast-food industry the heavy user (no pun intended) accounts for only one of five customers but for about 60 percent of all visits to fast-food restaurants. Taco Bell developed the Chalupa, a deep-fried and higher-calorie version of its Gordita stuffed taco, to appeal to its heavy users. The Checkers burger chain describes *its* core customer as a single male under age 30 who has a working-class job, loves loud music, doesn't read much, and hangs out with friends.[10] To attract the same customer, Hardee's unveiled its Monster Thickburger that weighs in at 1,418 calories—comedian Jay Leno joked that the burger comes in a cardboard box shaped like a coffin.[11] Finally, Burger King aims a lot of its promotions (including its weird but popular King character) to its "Super Fans"—mostly young men who pop into fast-food restaurants 16 times a month on average.[12]

Aside from heavy usage of a product, we use many other dimensions to divide up a larger market. As we've already seen, *demographics* are statistics that measure observable aspects of a population like birthrate, age distribution, and income. The U.S. Census Bureau is a major source of demographic data on U.S. families, but many private firms gather additional data on specific population groups as well. The changes and trends demographic studies reveal are of great interest to marketers because they can use the data to locate and predict the size of markets for many products, ranging from home mortgages to brooms and can openers. Imagine trying to sell baby food to a single male, or an around-the-world cruise to a couple making $15,000 a year!

In this book we explore many of the important demographic variables that make consumers the same or different from others. We also consider other important characteristics that are a bit more subtle, such as differences in consumers' personalities and tastes that we can't objectively measure yet may be tremendously important in influencing product choices. For now, let's summarize a few of the most important demographic dimensions, each of which we'll describe in more detail in later chapters.

Age

Consumers of different *age groups* obviously have very different needs and wants. Although people who belong to the same age group differ in many other ways, they do tend to share a set of values and common cultural experiences that they carry throughout life.[13] In some cases, marketers initially develop a product to attract one age group and then try to broaden its appeal later on. That's what the high-octane energy drink Red Bull does. The company aggressively introduced it in bars, nightclubs, and gyms to the product's core audience of young people. Over time, it became popular in other contexts, and the company began to sponsor the PGA European Tour to broaden its reach to older golfers (who probably aren't up partying all night). It also hands out free cans to commuters, cab drivers, and car rental agencies to promote the drink as a way to stay alert on the road.[14]

Gender

We start to make gender distinctions at a very early age—even diapers come in pink versions for girls and blue for boys. Many products, from fragrances to footwear, target either men or women. An all-female marketing team at Procter & Gamble (P&G), who jokingly call themselves "chicks in charge," introduced Crest Rejuvenating Effects, the first mass-market toothpaste positioned just for women. P&G communicates that this product is feminine when the company packages it in a teal tube nestled inside a glimmering "pearlescent" box. The toothpaste is sparkly, teal-toned, and tastes like vanilla and cinnamon.[15]

Family Structure

A person's family and marital status is yet another important demographic variable because this has such a big effect on consumers' spending priorities. Not surprisingly, young bachelors and newlyweds are the most likely to exercise; go to bars, concerts, and movies; and consume alcohol (enjoy it while you can!). Families with young children are big purchasers of health foods and fruit juices, whereas single-parent

A British anti-smoking ad appeals to a parent's guilt.
Source: Courtesy of Roy Castle Lung Cancer Foundation; CHI/London.

households and those with older children buy more junk food. Older couples and bachelors are most likely to use home maintenance services.[16]

Social Class and Income

People who belong to the same *social class* are approximately equal in terms of their incomes and social standing in the community. They work in roughly similar occupations, and they tend to have similar tastes in music, clothing, leisure activities, and art. They also tend to socialize with one another, and they share many ideas and values regarding the way one's life should be lived.[17] The distribution of wealth is of great interest to marketers because it determines which groups have the greatest buying power and market potential.

Race and Ethnicity

African Americans, Hispanic Americans, and Asian Americans are the three fastest-growing ethnic groups in the United States. As our society becomes increasingly

The Redneck Bank takes a unique approach to social class segmentation (yes, this is a real bank).
Source: Courtesy of www.redneckbank.com.

multicultural, new opportunities develop to deliver specialized products to racial and ethnic groups and to introduce other groups to these offerings. For example, Reebok introduced its RBK shoe line and signed popular urban artists like 50 Cent to promote it.

Geography
Many national marketers tailor their offerings to appeal to consumers who live in different parts of the country. Some southerners are fond of a "good ol' boy" image that leaves others scratching their heads. Although many northerners regard the name "Bubba" as a negative term, businesses in Dixie proudly flaunt the name. Bubba Co. is a Charleston-based firm that licenses products such as Bubba-Q-Sauce. In Florida, restaurants, sports bars, nightclubs, and a limousine firm all proudly bear the name Bubba.[18]

Lifestyles: Beyond Demographics
Consumers also have very different *lifestyles*, even if they share other demographic characteristics such as gender or age. The way we feel about ourselves, the things we value, the things we like to do in our spare time—all of these factors help to determine which products will push our buttons—or even those that make us feel

CAPTURE THE DREAM.

WWW.AZIMUTYACHTS.COM

AZIMUT YACHTS

This Italian ad for a yacht company appeals to people who have money—or who dream they will someday have enough to buy a yacht.

Source: Courtesy of Azimut Yachts.

better. Procter & Gamble developed its heartburn medicine Prilosec OTC with an ideal customer in mind based on a lifestyle analysis. Her name is Joanne, and she's a mother over 35 who's more likely to get heartburn from a cup of coffee than from an overdose of pizza and beer. A P&G executive observed, "We know Joanne. We know what she feels. We know what she eats. We know what else she likes to buy in the store."[19]

Marketers carefully define customer segments and listen to people in their markets as never before. Many of them now realize that a key to success is building relationships between brands and customers that will last a lifetime. Marketers who believe in this philosophy, called **relationship marketing**, interact with customers on a regular basis and give them reasons to maintain a bond with the company over time. A focus on relationships is even more vital during the tough economic conditions we've been experiencing—when times are tough, people tend to rely on their good friends for support!

Another revolution in relationship building is brought to us courtesy of the computer. **Database marketing** involves tracking specific consumers' buying habits very closely and crafting products and messages tailored precisely to people's wants and needs based on this information. Wal-Mart stores massive amounts of information on the 100 million people who visit its stores each week, and the company uses these data to fine-tune its offerings. When the company analyzed how shoppers' buying patterns react when forecasters predict a major hurricane, for example, it discovered that people do a lot more than simply stock up on flashlights. Sales of strawberry Pop-Tarts increase by about 700 percent, and the top-selling product of all is—beer. Based on these insights, Wal-Mart loads its trucks with toaster pastries and six-packs to stock local stores when a big storm approaches.[20]

**Many products help to define our identities.
Are you what you drive?**
Source: Courtesy of Automobile Magazine,
Source Interlink.

Marketing's Impact on Consumers

Does marketing imitate life, or vice versa? After the movie *The Wedding Crashers* became a big hit, hotels, wedding planners, and newlyweds reported an outbreak of uninvited guests who tried to gain access to parties across the United States.[21] For better or for worse, we all live in a world that the actions of marketers significantly influence.

Popular Culture

Marketing stimuli surround us as advertisements, stores, and products compete for our attention and our dollars. Marketers filter much of what we learn about the world, whether through the affluence they depict in glamorous magazines or the roles actors play in commercials. Ads show us how we should act with regard to recycling, alcohol consumption, the types of houses and cars we might wish to

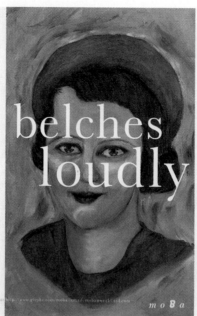

Some art speaks to you.
Some just **belches loudly** in your face.

Visit the permanent collection at 580 High Street, Dedham, Massachusetts – 617.325.8224 – Or on the Web at http://www.glyphic.com/moba email moba@world-std.com

moBa museum of bad art

We are surrounded by elements of popular culture—the good, the bad, and the ugly. This ad for the Museum of Bad Art reminds us of that.
Source: With permission of Museum of Bad Art.

own—and even how to evaluate others based on the products they buy or don't buy. In many ways we are also "at the mercy" of marketers because we rely on them to sell us products that are safe and that perform as promised, to tell us the truth about what they sell, and to price and distribute these products fairly.

Popular culture, consisting of the music, movies, sports, books, celebrities, and other forms of entertainment the mass market consumes, is both a product of and an inspiration for marketers. It also affects our lives in more far-reaching ways, ranging from how we acknowledge cultural events such as marriage, death, or holidays to how we view social issues such as global warming, gambling, and addictions. Whether it's the Super Bowl, Christmas shopping, national health care, newspaper recycling, body piercing, cigarette smoking, tweeting, or online video games, marketers play a significant role in our view of the world and how we live in it.

This cultural impact is hard to overlook, although many people do not seem to realize how much marketers influence their preferences for movie and musical heroes, the latest fashions in clothing, food, and decorating choices, and even the physical features that they find attractive or ugly in men and women. For example, consider the product icons that companies use to create an identity for their products. Many imaginary creatures and personalities, from the Pillsbury Doughboy to the Jolly Green Giant, at one time or another have been central figures in popular culture. In fact, it is likely that more consumers could recognize such characters than could identify past presidents, business leaders, or artists. Although these figures never really existed, many of us feel as if we "know" them, and they certainly are effective spokescharacters for the products they represent.

Consumer-Generated Content

Have you checked out one of those crazy Mentos/Diet Coke videos yet? At least 800 of them flooded the Internet after people discovered that when you drop the quarter-size candies into bottles of Diet Coke you get a geyser that shoots 20 feet into the air. Needless to say, Mentos got a gusher of free publicity out of the deal too.[22]

Consumer-generated content, where everyday people voice their opinions about products, brands, and companies on blogs, podcasts, and social networking sites such as Facebook and MySpace, and even film their own commercials that thousands view on sites such as YouTube, probably is the biggest marketing phenomenon of this decade. The ad a pair of brothers created for Doritos that ran during the 2009 Super Bowl scored top honors as the spot the most viewers remembered—it beat out other expensive entries by a lot of ad pros.[23]

This important trend helps to define the era of **Web 2.0**—the rebirth of the Internet as a social, interactive medium from its original roots as a form of one-way transmission from producers to consumers. We'll talk more about this phenomenon later, but for now it's worth noting because it's changing the way consumers relate to popular culture. Why? Because increasingly we see ourselves not just as consumers of culture but also as producers of culture. A recent survey reported that one-third of young people who use social media such as Facebook and YouTube consider themselves to be broadcasters in addition to audience members!

What Does It Mean to Consume?

What's the poop on Peeps? Every year, people buy about 1.5 billion of these mostly tasteless marshmallow chicks; about two-thirds of them sell around Easter. They have no nutritional value, but they do have a shelf life of 2 years. Maybe that's why not all Peeps get eaten. Devotees use them in decorations, dioramas, online slide shows, and sculptures. Some fans feel challenged to test their physical properties: On more than 200 Peeps Web sites, you can see fetishists skewering, microwaving, hammering, decapitating, and otherwise abusing the spongy confections.[24]

Peeps are objects of devotion—or of abuse—for many people.
Source: Courtesy of www.peepsresearch.org.

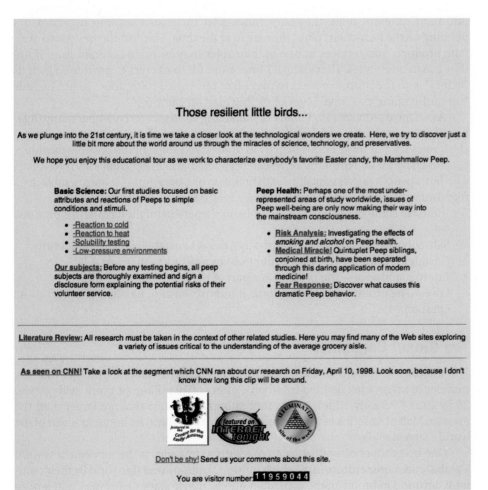

This fascination with a creepy little candy chick illustrates one of the fundamental premises of the modern field of consumer behavior: *People often buy products not for what they do but for what they mean.* This principle does not imply that a product's basic function is unimportant but rather that the roles products play in our lives extend well beyond the tasks they perform. The deeper meanings of a product may help it to stand out from other similar goods and services—all things being equal, we choose the brand that has an image (or even a personality!) consistent with our underlying needs.

For example, although most people probably couldn't run faster or jump higher if they were wearing Nikes instead of Reeboks, many die-hard loyalists swear by their favorite brand. These archrivals are largely marketed in terms of their images—meanings that have been carefully crafted with the help of legions of rock stars, athletes, slickly produced commercials, and many millions of dollars. So, when you buy a Nike "swoosh," you are doing more than choosing shoes to wear to the mall—you also make a lifestyle statement about the type of person you are or wish you were. For a relatively simple item made of leather and laces, that's quite a feat!

Our allegiances to sneakers, musicians, or even soft drinks help us define our place in modern society, and these choices also help each of us to form bonds with others who share similar preferences. This comment by a participant in a focus group captures the curious bonding that can be caused by consumption choices: "I was at a Super Bowl party, and I picked up an obscure drink. Somebody else across the room went 'yo!' because he had the same thing. People feel a connection when you're drinking the same thing."[25]

The sociological perspective of **role theory** takes the view that much of consumer behavior resembles actions in a play.[26] As in a play, each consumer has lines, props, and costumes necessary to put on a good performance. Because people act out many different roles, they sometimes alter their consumption decisions depending on the particular "play" they are in at the time. The criteria they use to evaluate products and services in one of their roles may be quite different from those they use in other roles. That's why it's important for marketers to provide each of us "actors" with the props we need to play all of our varied roles; these might include "up-and-coming executive," "geek," or "big man on campus."

As we have seen, one trademark of marketing strategies today is that many organizations try very hard to build relationships with customers. The nature of these relationships can vary, but these bonds help us to understand some of the possible meanings products have for us. Furthermore, researchers find that like friendships and love affairs with other people, our relationships with brands evolve over time—some resemble deep friendships, whereas others are more like exciting but short-lived flings.[27]

Here are some of the types of relationships a person might have with a product:

- **Self-concept attachment**—The product helps to establish the user's identity.
- **Nostalgic attachment**—The product serves as a link with a past self.
- **Interdependence**—The product is a part of the user's daily routine.
- **Love**—The product elicits emotional bonds of warmth, passion, or other strong emotion.[28]

The Global Consumer

The majority of people on Earth live in urban centers—analysts predict that the number of *megacities*, defined as urban centers of 10 million or more, will grow to 26 by 2015.[29] Already, China boasts four shopping centers that are larger than the massive Mall of America in Minnesota, and very soon it will be home to seven of the world's largest malls.[30]

One by-product of sophisticated marketing strategies is the movement toward a **global consumer culture**, one which unites people around the world by their common devotion to brand-name consumer goods, movie stars, celebrities, and leisure

activities.[31] Many multinational firms are "household names," widely recognized (though not necessarily liked) by literally billions of people. McDonald's Corp. and Microsoft Corp. are the most visible corporate brands on the planet.[32]

We owe much of this interconnectedness to exciting new developments in technology that allow us to link with companies—and with each other—regardless of our physical locations. Indeed, our old model that requires us to sit in front of a PC to surf the Web soon will disappear like the horse-and-buggy. **U-commerce** is the use of *ubiquitous networks* that will slowly but surely become a part of us, whether in the form of wearable computers or customized advertisements beamed to us on our cell phones ("Hey, you're walking by McDonald's. Come on in for today's burger special.").[33]

Many products already carry a plastic **RFID tag** that contains a computer chip and a tiny antenna that lets the chip communicate with a network. In the near future grocery items will tell the store what needs to be restocked and which items are past

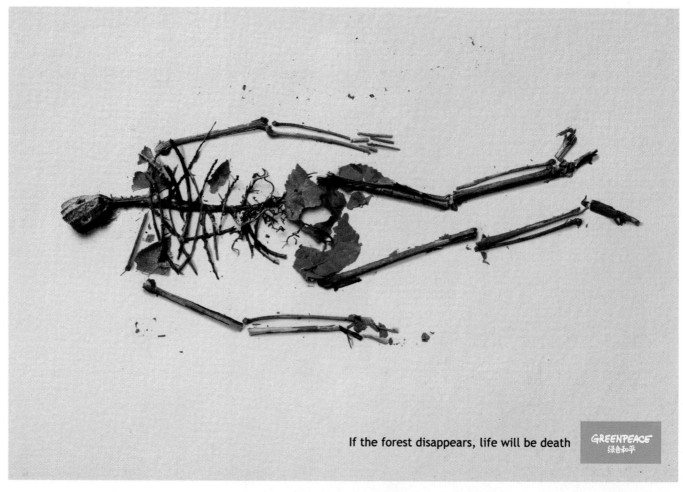

If the forest disappears, life will be death
绿色和平

The Greenpeace organization promotes environmental responsibility. This ad ran in Beijing.
Source: Courtesy of Dentsu, Japan.

their expiration dates, and your house will know when you're pulling in the driveway as it turns on the lights and starts your favorite tunes spinning before you walk in the door. Already, IBM introduced "smart" washers and dryers in some college dorms that let students keep tabs on their laundry from anywhere they can access the Internet—their dorm rooms, the library, or even a cell phone. Students can log onto a Web page to see if any machines are free and receive e-mail or a page when their load is finished.[34]

The rise of global marketing means that even small companies look to expand overseas—and this increases the pressure to understand how customers in other countries are the same or different from those in one's own country. In the restaurant industry, for example, Shakey's pizza restaurants are mushrooming in the Philippines, and food from the International House of Pancakes sells like hotcakes in Tokyo. But menu changes are sometimes called for to please local palates: Schlotzky's in Malaysia offers Smokey Mountain Chicken Crunch with "half-virgin" chicken, and diners at Bob's Big Boy in Thailand snap up Tropical Shrimp, deep fried with "exotic breading." This book will pay special attention to the good and bad aspects of this cultural homogenization.

④
OBJECTIVE

How is the Web changing consumer behavior?

Virtual Consumption and the Power of Crowds

There's little doubt that the digital revolution is one of the most significant influences on consumer behavior, and the impact of the Web will continue to expand as more and more people around the world log in. Many of us are avid Web surfers, and it's hard to imagine a time when texting, Twittering, or BlackBerrys and iPhones weren't an accepted part of daily life.

Electronic marketing has increased convenience because it breaks down many of the barriers time and location cause. You can shop 24/7 without leaving home, you can read today's newspaper without getting drenched picking up a hard copy in a rainstorm, and you don't have to wait for the 6:00 P.M. news to find out what the weather will be like tomorrow—at home or around the globe. And, with the increasing use of handheld devices and wireless communications, you can get that same information—from stock quotes to the weather—even when you're away from your computer.[35]

And, it's not all about businesses selling to consumers (**B2C e-commerce**). The cyberspace explosion has created a revolution in consumer-to-consumer activity (**C2C e-commerce**): Welcome to the new world of *virtual brand communities*. Just as e-consumers are not limited to local retail outlets in their shopping, they are not limited to their local communities when they look for friends or fellow fans of wine, hip-hop, or skateboarding.

Picture a small group of local collectors who meet once a month at a local diner to discuss their shared interests over coffee. Now multiply that group by thousands, and include people from all over the world who are united by a shared passion for sports memorabilia, Barbie dolls, Harley-Davidson motorcycles, refrigerator magnets, or massively multiplayer online games (MMOGs) such as *World of Warcraft*. The Web also provides an easy way for consumers around the world to exchange information about their experiences with products, services, music, restaurants, and movies. The Hollywood Stock Exchange (hsx.com) offers a simulated entertainment stock market where traders predict the 4-week box office take for each film. Amazon .com encourages shoppers to write reviews of books, and just like Gail did you can even rate your professors at RateMyProfessors.com (don't tell your prof about this one; it'll be our secret). The popularity of chat rooms where consumers can go to discuss various topics with like-minded "Netizens" around the world grows every day, as do immersive virtual worlds such as Second Life, Habbo Hotel, There.com, and Kaneva. News reports tell us of the sometimes wonderful and sometimes horrific romances that have begun on the Internet as people check out potential mates on sites such as Match.com or Lavalife.com (in a typical month, 26 million people visit online dating sites!).[36]

Will the Web bring people closer together or drive each of us into our own private virtual worlds? Wired Americans are spending less time with friends and family, less time shopping in stores, and more time working at home after hours. More than one-third of consumers who have access to the Internet report that they are online at least 5 hours a week. Also, 60 percent of Internet users say they have reduced their television viewing, and one-third say they spend less time reading newspapers—those that still remain as many fold due to a lack of readership and advertising revenue.

However, a study by the Pew Internet and American Life Project reported that more than half of users the group surveyed feel that e-mail actually strengthens family ties. Users reported far more off-line social contact than nonusers.[37] These results argue that people spend more time than ever with others. It's just that they form strong relationships over the Internet instead of in person. But the author of the first survey disagrees. As he observes, "If I go home at 6:30 in the evening and spend the whole night sending e-mail and wake up the next morning, I still haven't talked to my wife or kids or friends. When you spend your time on the Internet, you don't hear a human voice and you never get a hug."[38]

A follow-up study found that it works both ways—extroverts tend to make even more friends on the Web, whereas introverts feel even more cut off from the rest of the world. This has been termed the "rich get richer" model of Internet use.[39] So, it seems that just as in the offline world, our new digital reality is both good and bad. Throughout this book, we'll look at some examples of both the pros and cons of virtual consumer behavior in boxes called "Net Profit" and "The Tangled Web."

Blurred Boundaries: Marketing and Reality

There's no telling where advertising will turn up these days. Spirit Airlines' flight attendants protested when the company proposed new aprons that featured logos for alcoholic beverages including Budweiser beer.[40] A San Diego high school teacher sells ad space on exams to local businesses to defray the cost of printing the tests due to school budget cuts.[41]

Marketers and consumers coexist in a complicated, two-way relationship. It's often hard to tell where marketing efforts leave off and "the real world" begins. One result of these blurred boundaries is that we are no longer sure (and perhaps we don't care) where the line separating this fabricated world from reality begins and ends. Sometimes, we gleefully join in the illusion. A story line in a Wonder Woman comic book featured the usual out-of-this-world exploits of a vivacious superhero. But it also included the real-world marriage proposal of the owner of a chain of

Marketing messages often borrow imagery from other forms of popular culture to connect with an audience. This line of syrups adapts the "look" of a pulp detective novel.

Source: Courtesy of R. Torre and Company.

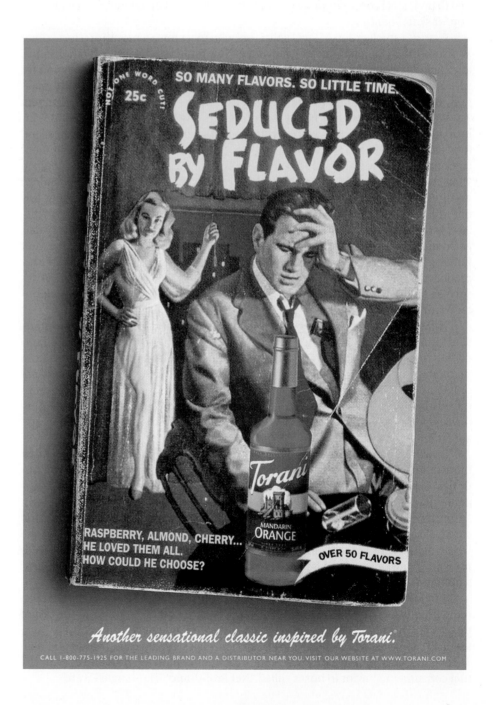

comic book stores, who persuaded DC Comics to let him woo his beloved in the issue.[42] One shudders to think what he has in mind for the honeymoon!

To what degree do marketers shape the world of popular culture—and even consumers' perceptions of reality? More than many of us believe, and this influence increases dramatically as companies experiment with new ways to command our attention. The changes Hasbro made to its hugely popular Monopoly board game illustrate the proliferation of brands in our daily lives. Seeking to offer "a representation of America in the twenty-first century," the game now includes tokens styled after name-brand products. Five of the eight tokens in the new *Monopoly Here and Now* edition are branded; players can choose from a Toyota Prius hybrid car, an order of McDonald's French fries, a New Balance running shoe, a cup of Starbucks coffee, or a Motorola Razr cell phone.[43]

OBJECTIVE

How does consumer behavior relate to other issues in our lives?

Marketing Ethics and Public Policy

In business, conflicts often arise between the goal to succeed in the marketplace and the desire to maximize the well-being of consumers by providing them with safe and effective products and services. However, consumers may expect too much from companies and try to exploit these obligations. A case involving the Wendy's fast-food chain made national headlines when a woman claimed she found a finger in her bowl of chili. The restaurants became the butt of jokes (some said they served nail clippers with their food instead of forks), and sales dropped dramatically at the company's franchises. This forced layoffs and reduced hours for many employees—until the woman was arrested for fraud.[45]

Business ethics are rules of conduct that guide actions in the marketplace—the standards against which most people in a culture judge what is right and what is wrong, good or bad. These universal values include honesty, trustworthiness, fairness, respect, justice, integrity, concern for others, accountability, and loyalty. Ethical business is good business. A Conference Board survey of U.S. consumers found the most important criterion when forming opinions about corporations is social responsibility in such areas as labor practices, business ethics, and environmental issues.[46] Consumers think better of products made by firms they feel behave ethically.[47]

Of course, notions of right and wrong differ among people, organizations, and cultures. Some businesses believe it is OK for salespeople to pull out all the stops to persuade customers to buy, even if it means giving them false information; other firms feel that anything less than total honesty with customers is terribly wrong. Because each culture has its own set of values, beliefs, and customs, companies around the world define ethical business behaviors quite differently. For example, one study found that because of differences in values (more on this in Chapter 4), Mexican firms are less likely to have formal codes of ethics and they are more likely to bribe public officials than are U.S. or Canadian companies. However, because of different attitudes about work and interpersonal relationships, these companies also are more likely to treat lower-level employees better than do their northern neighbors.[48]

These cultural differences certainly influence whether business practices such as bribery are acceptable. In Japan, it's called *kuroi kiri* (black mist); in Germany, it's *schmiergeld* (grease money), whereas Mexicans refer to *la mordida* (the bite), the French say *pot-de-vin* (jug of wine), and Italians speak of the *bustarella* (little envelope). They're all talking about *baksheesh*, the Middle Eastern term for a "tip" to grease the wheels of a transaction. Giving "gifts" in exchange for getting business from suppliers or customers is common and acceptable in many countries, even though this may be frowned on elsewhere.

Bribing foreigners to gain business has been against the law in the United States since 1977 under the Foreign Corrupt Practices Act. The Organization for Economic

A campaign for a clinic that serves low-income and uninsured families.
Source: Courtesy of Uptown Community Clinic Minneapolis/Olsen.

Cooperation and Development (OECD), to which most industrialized countries belong, also outlaws bribery. More than 800 business experts were asked to identify the countries where this practice is most flagrant. Russian and Chinese companies emerged at the top of the list, and Taiwan and South Korea were close behind. The "cleanest" countries were Australia, Sweden, Switzerland, Austria, and Canada.[49]

Regardless of whether they do it intentionally, some marketers do violate their bonds of trust with consumers. In some cases, these actions are actually illegal, as when a manufacturer deliberately mislabels the contents of a package. Or a retailer may adopt a "bait-and-switch" selling strategy that lures consumers into the store by offering inexpensive products with the sole intent of getting them to switch to higher-priced goods.

In other cases, marketing practices have detrimental effects on society even though they are not explicitly illegal. Some companies erect billboards for alcohol and tobacco products in low-income neighborhoods; others sponsor commercials depicting groups of people in an unfavorable light to get the attention of a target market. Civil rights groups, for example, charge that the marketing of menthol cigarettes by R.J. Reynolds to African Americans is illegal because menthol cigarettes are less safe than regular brands. A company spokeswoman responds, "This links to the bigger issue that minorities require some special protection. We find that offensive, paternalistic, and condescending."[50] Who is right? Throughout this book, we highlight ethical issues that relate to the practice of marketing. In boxes we call "Marketing Pitfall," we discuss questionable practices by marketers or the possible adverse effects of certain marketing strategies on consumers.

Needs and Wants:
Do Marketers Manipulate Consumers?

One of the most common and stinging criticisms of marketing is that companies convince consumers they "need" many material things and that they will be unhappy and inferior people if they do not have these "necessities." The issue is a complex one and is certainly worth considering: Do marketers give people what they want, or do they tell people what they *should* want?

Welcome to Consumerspace

Who controls the market—companies or consumers? This question is even more complicated as new ways of buying, having, and being are invented every day. It seems that the "good old days" of *marketerspace*—a time when companies called the shots and decided what they wanted their customers to know and do—are dead and gone. As we saw with Gail's surfing decisions, many people now feel empowered to choose how, when, or if they will interact with corporations as they construct their own **consumerspace**; an environment where individuals dictate to companies the types of products they want and how, when and where (or even if) they want to learn about them. In turn, companies need to develop and leverage brand equity in bold new ways to attract the loyalty of these consumer "nomads." People still "need" companies—but in new ways and on their own terms. As we'll see throughout this book, profound changes in consumer behavior are influencing how people search for product information and evaluate alternative brands. In the brave new world of consumerspace, we have the potential to shape our own marketing destinies.[54]

Do Marketers Create Artificial Needs?

The marketing system has come under fire from both ends of the political spectrum. On the one hand, some members of the Religious Right believe that marketers contribute to the moral breakdown of society by presenting images of hedonistic pleasure and encouraging the pursuit of secular humanism at the expense of spirituality and the environment. A coalition of religious groups called the National Religious Partnership for the Environment claims that gas-guzzling cars and other factors that cause climate change are contrary to Christian moral teachings about protecting people and the earth.[55]

On the other hand, some leftists argue that the same deceitful promises of material pleasure function to buy off people who would otherwise be revolutionaries working to change the system.[56] According to this argument, the marketing system creates demand—demand that only its products can satisfy.

A Response. *A **need** is a basic biological motive; a **want** represents one way that society has taught to satisfy the need.* For example, thirst is biologically based; we are taught to want Coca-Cola to satisfy that thirst rather than, say, goat's milk. Thus, the

The Tangled Web

To what extent should a consumer's personal information be available online? This is one of the most controversial ethical questions today. Scott McNealy, chief executive officer (CEO) of Sun Microsystems, once commented, "You already have zero privacy—get over it." Apparently, many consumers don't agree; they are not happy at the prospect of leaving an electronic trail behind. A poll conducted by the National Consumers League found that consumers are more worried about personal privacy than health care, education, crime, and taxes. People are particularly concerned that businesses or individuals will target their children.[51] Nearly 70 percent of consumers worry about keeping their information private, but according to a Jupiter Media Metrix survey, only 40 percent read privacy policies posted on business Web sites.[52]

How can these thorny ethical issues be solved? Some analysts predict that a market for privacy will emerge; we can ensure some degree of privacy, but it will cost us. Others believe that instead of paying to be left alone, we can actually make money by selling our personal data. As one online executive observed, "Slowly but surely consumers are going to realize that their profile is valuable. For loaning out their identity, they're going to expect something in return."[53]

This ad was created by the American Association of Advertising Agencies to counter charges that ads create artificial needs.

Source: Used with permission of American Association of Advertising Agencies.

DESPITE WHAT SOME PEOPLE THINK, ADVERTISING CAN'T MAKE YOU BUY SOMETHING YOU DON'T NEED.

Some people would have you believe that you are putty in the hands of every advertiser in the country.

They think that when advertising is put under your nose, your mind turns to oatmeal.

It's mass hypnosis. Subliminal seduction. Brain washing. Mind control. It's advertising.

And you are a pushover for it.

It explains why your kitchen cupboard is full of food you never eat.

Why your garage is full of cars you never drive.

Why your house is full of books you don't read, TV's you don't watch, beds you don't use, and clothes you don't wear.

You don't have a choice. You are forced to buy.

That's why this message is a cleverly disguised advertisement to get you to buy land in the tropics.

Got you again, didn't we? Send in your money.

ADVERTISING

ANOTHER WORD FOR FREEDOM OF CHOICE.

American Association of Advertising Agencies

need is already there; marketers simply recommend ways to satisfy it. A basic objective of marketing is to create awareness that needs exist, not to create needs.

Are Advertising and Marketing Necessary?

The social critic Vance Packard wrote more than 50 years ago, "Large-scale efforts are being made, often with impressive success, to channel our unthinking habits, our purchasing decisions, and our thought processes by the use of insights gleaned from psychiatry and the social sciences."[57] The economist John Kenneth Galbraith charged that radio and television are important tools to accomplish this manipulation of the masses. Because consumers don't need to be literate to use these media, repetitive and compelling communications can reach almost everyone. This criticism may even be more relevant to online communications, where a simple click delivers a world of information to us.

Many feel that marketers arbitrarily link products to desirable social attributes, fostering a materialistic society in which we are measured by what we own. One influential critic even argued that the problem is that we are not materialistic enough—that is, we do not sufficiently value goods for the utilitarian functions they deliver but instead focus on the irrational value of goods for what they symbolize. According to this view, for example, "Beer would be enough for us, without the additional promise that in drinking it we show ourselves to be manly, young at heart, or neighborly. A washing machine would be a useful machine to wash clothes, rather than an indication that we are forward-looking or an object of envy to our neighbors."[58]

A Response. *Products are designed to meet existing needs, and advertising only helps to communicate their availability.*[59] According to the **economics of information** perspective, advertising is an important source of consumer information.[60] This view emphasizes the economic cost of the time spent searching for products. Accordingly, advertising is a service for which consumers are willing to pay because the information it provides reduces search time.

Do Marketers Promise Miracles?

Through advertising, consumers are led to believe that products have magical properties; products will do special and mysterious things for consumers in a way that will transform their lives. Consumers will be beautiful, have power over others' feelings, be successful, and be relieved of all ills. In this respect, advertising functions as mythology does in primitive societies: It provides simple, anxiety-reducing answers to complex problems.

A Response. *Advertisers simply do not know enough about people to manipulate them.* Consider that the failure rate for new products ranges from 40 to 80 percent. Although people think that advertisers have an endless source of magical tricks and scientific techniques to manipulate them, in reality the industry is successful when it tries to sell good products and unsuccessful when it sells poor ones.[61]

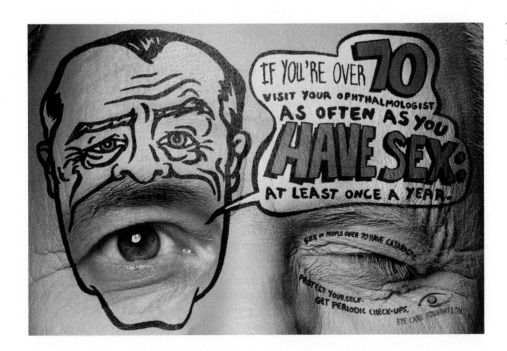

This Brazilian ad employs a novel message to encourage eye exams.
Source: Courtesy of Almap BBDO Communicacoes Ltda., photographer Alexandre Ermel.

Public Policy and Consumerism

Concern for the welfare of consumers has been an issue since at least the beginning of the twentieth century, and activists continue to voice concerns about a range of issues such as child labor, exploitative advertising, and genetically engineered food.[62] Recent deaths due to salmonella-infected peanut butter and contaminated toothpaste have added fuel to the fire.

Partly as a result of consumers' efforts in the United States, the U.S. government established many federal agencies to oversee consumer-related activities. These include the Department of Agriculture, the Federal Trade Commission, the Food and Drug Administration, the Securities and Exchange Commission, and the Environmental Protection Agency. After Upton Sinclair's 1906 book *The Jungle* exposed the awful conditions in the Chicago meatpacking industry, Congress was prompted to pass important pieces of legislation—the Pure Food and Drug Act in 1906 and the Federal Meat Inspection Act a year later—to protect consumers. A summary of some important consumer legislation enacted since that time appears in Table 1.1. You can find other information about consumer-related issues at consumerreports.org and cpsc.gov (The Consumer Product Safety Commission).

The Food and Drug Administration (FDA) polices advertising claims as well as the contents of edible products and pharmaceuticals, and its efforts have been more aggressive with the advent of the Obama administration. For example, as part of an FDA

TABLE 1.1	Sample of Federal Legislation Intended to Enhance Consumers' Welfare	
Year	**Act**	**Purpose**
1951	Fur Products Labeling Act	Regulates the branding, advertising, and shipment of fur products.
1953	Flammable Fabrics Act	Prohibits the transportation of flammable fabrics across state lines.
1958	National Traffic and Safety Act	Creates safety standards for cars and tires.
1958	Automobile Information Disclosure Act	Requires automobile manufacturers to post suggested retail prices on new cars.
1966	Fair Packaging and Labeling Act	Regulates packaging and labeling of consumer products. (Manufacturers must provide information about package contents and origin.)
1966	Child Protection Act	Prohibits sale of dangerous toys and other items.
1967	Federal Cigarette Labeling and Advertising Act	Requires cigarette packages to carry a warning label from the Surgeon General.
1968	Truth-in-Lending Act	Requires lenders to divulge the true costs of a credit transaction.
1969	National Environmental Policy Act	Established a national environmental policy and created the Council on Environmental Quality to monitor the effects of products on the environment.
1972	Consumer Products Safety Act	Established the Consumer Product Safety Commission to identify unsafe products, establish safety standards, recall defective products, and ban dangerous products.
1975	Consumer Goods Pricing Act	Bans the use of price maintenance agreements among manufacturers and resellers.
1975	Magnuson-Moss Warranty-Improvement Act	Creates disclosure standards for consumer product warranties and allows the Federal Trade Commission to set policy regarding unfair or deceptive practices.
1990	The Nutrition Labeling and Education Act	Reaffirms the legal basis for the Food and Drug Administration's new rules on food labeling and establishes a timetable for the implementation of those rules. Regulations covering health claims became effective May 8,1993. Those pertaining to nutrition labeling and nutrient content claims went into effect May 8,1994.
1998	Internet Tax Freedom Act	Established a moratorium on special taxation of the Internet, including taxation of access fees paid to America Online and other Internet Service Providers. An extension of the moratorium is being considered.

crackdown on consumer drug advertising, in 2009 Bayer HealthCare Pharmaceuticals launched a $20 million advertising campaign for Yaz, the most popular birth control pill in the United States. The twist is that the TV commercials, which ran during prime-time shows like *Grey's Anatomy* and on cable networks, warn that nobody should take Yaz hoping that it will also cure pimples or premenstrual syndrome. Bayer was required to run these ads to correct previous messages that regulators decided overstated the drug's ability to improve women's moods and clear up acne.[63]

In many cases, however, marketers modify their claims before the government forces them to. The National Advertising Division (NAD) unit of the Better Business Bureau often regulates industry members. In one recent decision, the self-governing body took issue with an online ad for Extra-Strength Excedrin. It shows a woman seated at an outdoor café who takes the medicine to relieve a headache. As a digital clock at the bottom of the screen nears 15 minutes, her grimace is replaced by a bright smile, indicating that the headache disappeared. The NAD (spurred to action by a complaint from rival drug maker Wyeth) decided that this claim wasn't supported and asked the brand to "modify or discontinue" it.[64]

Consumer Activism: America™?

"Absolut Impotence." So reads a parody vodka ad that Adbusters, a nonprofit organization that advocates for "the new social activist movement of the information age," created. The editor of the group's magazine argues that America is no longer a country, but rather a multitrillion-dollar brand subverted by corporate agendas. He claims that America™ is no different from McDonald's, Marlboro, or General Motors (well, let's at least hope our country's balance sheet starts to look a bit better than GM's).[65]

Social marketing encourages responsible behavior. This Belgian ad promotes the use of condoms.
Source: Used with the permission of Duval Guillaume Ad Agency.

This British social marketing campaign tries to change how people look at individuals with physical deformities.

Source: Courtesy of Changing Faces U.K. DDB, London; Photograph by Robert Wilson.

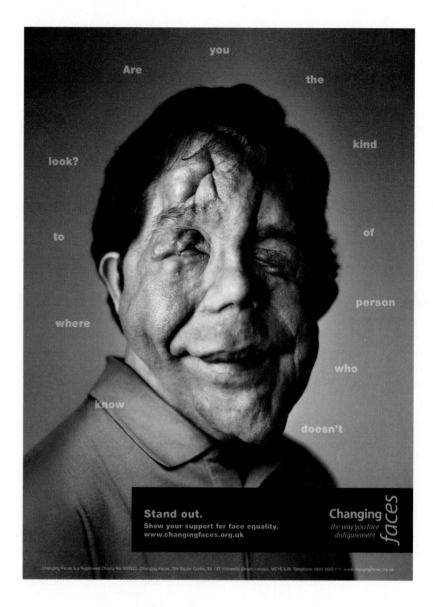

Adbusters sponsors numerous initiatives, including Buy Nothing Day and TV Turnoff Week, intended to discourage rampant commercialism. These efforts, along with biting ads and commercials that lampoon advertising messages, are examples of **culture jamming**; a strategy to disrupt efforts by the corporate world to dominate our cultural landscape. The movement believes "culture jamming" will change the way information flows; the way institutions wield power; the way TV stations are run; and the way the food, fashion, automobile, sports, music, and culture industries set their agendas.[66] The *Culture Jammers Manifesto* proclaims opposition to the "mind-polluters": "On the rubble of the old culture, we will build a new one with non-commercial heart and soul."[67] To protest against what the organization claims are Nike's unfair labor practices, Adbusters sells its own Blackspot sneakers. They are made from hemp in a Portuguese factory where workers receive pay higher than the country's minimum wage and where many employees belong to a union.[68]

Although some in corporate America may dismiss these extreme sentiments as the ravings of a lunatic fringe, they deserve to be taken seriously. The recent scandals involving such corporate icons as AIG, Enron, Martha Stewart, Arthur Andersen, and Merrill Lynch have fueled a growing bonfire of mistrust and skepticism among the consuming public. Time will tell if these backlashes against companies will die down or continue to grow as new scandals continue to come to light.

全球数亿人将和你一起关灯一小时，减缓气候变暖。
请登录 www.earthhour.org.cn 了解详情

地球一小时
3月28日20:30-21:30
关上灯，点亮希望

60
地球一小时

A Chinese ad for WWF—the planet's leading conservation organization—promotes a green message. The ad translates as: EARTH HOUR March 28 8:30–9:30 P.M. Turn off your lights for Earth Hour and protect our planet against climate change. Sign up at www.earthhour.org.cn.
Source: WWF China © text and graphics: 2009 WWF. All rights reserved.

Clearly, we need to take dramatic steps to restore public confidence as the business page of the newspaper starts to read like the crime blotter.

President John F. Kennedy ushered in the modern era of consumerism with his "Declaration of Consumer Rights" in 1962. These include the right to safety, the right to be informed, the right to redress, and the right to choice. The 1960s and 1970s were a time of consumer activism as consumers began to organize to demand better-quality products (and to boycott companies that did not provide them).

The publication of books such as Rachel Carson's *The Silent Spring* in 1962, which attacked the irresponsible use of pesticides, and Ralph Nader's *Unsafe at Any Speed* in 1965, which exposed safety defects in General Motors' Corvair automobile, prompted these movements. Many consumers have a vigorous interest in consumer-related issues ranging from environmental concerns such as global warming and climate change, toxic waste, and so on, to excessive violence and sex on television or in the lyrics of popular rock and rap songs. Recent controversies surrounding "shock jocks" such as Don Imus or Glenn Beck who use the public airwaves to hurl insults about racial or religious groups illustrate that people take these issues very seriously.

Indeed, some consumer researchers are themselves organizing to not only study but to rectify what they see as pressing social problems in the marketplace. This perspective is called *participatory action research (PAR)* or **Transformative Consumer Research (TCR)**. It promotes research projects that include the goal of

CB AS I SEE IT

Professor Julie Ozanne, *Virginia Tech*

$\mathcal{I}$f you want to work to make the world a better place, then it is essential to understand consumers' behavior. Consumption lies at the heart of the most important problems facing the global community. In economically developed countries, we are drowning in a sea of things that are depleting our limited global resources at an alarming rate. We are overconsuming food and raising a generation of overweight and unhealthy children. We are engaging in risky consumption behaviors such as smoking, drinking, and gambling. Yet most of the people in the world face limited consumption opportunities and struggle to meet even basic nutritional needs.

Transformative Consumer Research is a new movement of consumer researchers who want to improve consumer well-being. Transformative consumer researchers engage in rigorous research to understand the nature of these pressing social problems. But then they seek to move outside the university to forge alliances with external stakeholders who can build programs of social change to improve the quality of life. Consumer researchers stand in a unique position because they understand and respect the interests of both consumers and businesses. Thus, they have the potential to act as honest brokers working with consumer interest groups, public policy makers, and business leaders to foster positive social transformation.

This is an exciting time in which to create new models of business and new forms of consumption that are more sustainable and can strengthen our communities. Nobel Peace Prize winner Muhammad Yunis envisioned offering microcredit loans to poor consumers who wanted to start their own businesses, which is a new model of consumer financing that has literally pulled millions of people out of poverty. New models of consumption are also being created. Paris encourages bike-sharing by distributing bikes throughout the city and does not charge for the first half-hour of rental so that short trips are free. Similarly, carsharing, in which a fleet of cars is collectively owned and used, has grown to 600 cities worldwide.

My own research examines how the sharing of possessions can build and strengthen communities. For instance, toy-lending libraries operate similarly to book libraries by making toys available to children for a nominal fee. Networks of families form communities of sharing that become an important neighborhood resource for advice and support. Children get to enjoy a wide range of toys while learning important lessons, such as the pleasures of sharing and a respect for collective goods.

---

helping people or bringing about social change. Consumers are not objects of research, but collaborators who work with the researchers to realize this change. Adherents of TCR work with at-risk populations, such as children, the disadvantaged and the disabled or on such topics as materialism, consumption of dangerous products, and compulsive consumption.[69]

Social Marketing

As the emerging TCR perspective shows, the field of consumer behavior can play an important role in improving our lives as consumers.[70] **Social marketing** strategies use techniques marketers normally employ to sell beer or detergent to encourage positive behaviors such as increased literacy and to discourage negative activities such as drunk driving.[71] Many researchers help to evaluate or create public policies that ensure products are labeled accurately, that people can comprehend important information in advertising messages, or to prevent children from being exploited by program-length toy commercials that masquerade as television shows. For example, American Airlines and the American Association of People with Disabilities (AAPD) are joining forces to create television commercials that portray people with disabilities in a positive light.[72]

Green Marketing

In addition, **green marketing** is gaining in popularity. Firms that adopt this philosophy choose to protect or enhance the natural environment as they go about their business activities. Some have focused their efforts on reducing wasteful packaging, as when Procter & Gamble introduced refillable containers for Downy fabric softener.[73] We'll discuss this important trend in more detail in Chapter 4.

The Dark Side of Consumer Behavior

OBJECTIVE

Why can consumer activities be harmful to individuals and to society?

In late 2008, a crowd assembled for a big holiday sale at a Wal-Mart store in New York. When the doors opened, the crowd trampled a temporary worker to death as people rushed to grab discounted merchandise off of store shelves. A lawsuit filed on behalf of the man's survivors claimed that in addition to providing inadequate security, the retailer "engaged in specific marketing and advertising techniques to specifically attract a large crowd and create an environment of frenzy and mayhem."[74] Just how far will people go to secure a bargain?

Despite the best efforts of researchers, government regulators, and concerned industry people, sometimes consumers' worst enemies are themselves. We think of individuals as rational decision makers, calmly doing their best to obtain products and services that will maximize the health and well-being of themselves, their families, and their society. In reality, however, consumers' desires, choices, and

This ad from Singapore discourages young people from using ketamine, an animal tranquilizer.
Source: Used with permission of Saatchi & Saatchi of Singapore.

actions often result in negative consequences to individuals and the society in which they live.

Some of these actions are relatively harmless, but others have more onerous consequences. Some harmful consumer behaviors such as excessive drinking or cigarette smoking stem from social pressures, and the cultural value many of us place on money encourages activities such as shoplifting or insurance fraud. Exposure to unattainable ideals of beauty and success can create dissatisfaction with ourselves. We will touch on many of these issues later in this book, but for now let's review some dimensions of "the dark side" of consumer behavior.

Consumer Terrorism

The terrorist attacks of 2001 were a wake-up call to the free-enterprise system. They revealed the vulnerability of nonmilitary targets and reminded us that disruptions of our financial, electronic, and supply networks can potentially be more damaging to our way of life than the fallout from a conventional battlefield. These incursions may be deliberate or not—economic shockwaves of "mad cow" disease in Europe are still reverberating in the beef industry.[75] Assessments by the Rand Corporation and other analysts point to the susceptibility of the nation's food supply as a potential target of **bioterrorism**.[76]

Even prior to the anthrax scares of 2001, toxic substances placed in products threatened to hold the marketplace hostage. This tactic first drew public attention in the United States in 1982 when seven people died after they took Tylenol pills laced with cyanide. A decade later, Pepsi weathered its own crisis when more than 50 reports of syringes found in Diet Pepsi cans surfaced in 23 states. In that case, Pepsi pulled off a PR *coup de grace* by convincing the public that the syringes could not have been introduced during the manufacturing process. The company even showed an in-store surveillance video that caught a customer slipping a syringe into a Diet Pepsi can while the cashier's head was turned.[77] Pepsi's aggressive actions underscore the importance of responding to such a crisis head-on and quickly.

More recently, a publicity campaign for a late-night cartoon show backfired when it aroused fears of a terrorist attack and temporarily shut down the city of Boston. The "guerrilla marketing" effort consisted of 1-foot-tall blinking electronic signs with hanging wires and batteries that marketers used to promote the Cartoon Network TV show *Aqua Teen Hunger Force* (a surreal series about a talking milkshake, a box of fries, and a meatball). The signs were placed on bridges and in other high-profile spots in several U.S. cities. Most depicted a boxy, cartoon character giving passersby the finger. Bomb squads and other police personnel required to investigate the mysterious boxes cost the city of Boston more than $500,000—and a lot of frayed nerves.[78]

Addictive Consumption

Although most people equate addiction with drugs, consumers can use virtually any product or service to relieve (at least temporarily) some problem or satisfy some need to the point that reliance on it becomes extreme. It seems we can become dependent on almost anything—there is even a ChapStick Addicts support group with 250 active members! **Consumer addiction** is a physiological or psychological dependency on products or services. These problems of course include alcoholism, drug addiction, and nicotine addiction—and many companies profit from addictive products or by selling solutions for them.

CB AS I LIVE IT

Meghan McSkimming, *Fordham University*

Some use their "CrackBerrys" as adult security blankets. Instead, I have my iPod. I remember those middle school days of the Sony Walkman and Discman, the days when people bought CDs at the local music store instead of downloading the latest album from iTunes. I also remember receiving my first iPod as a high school graduation present and it revolutionized my music collection. All of its features—the little white headphones, sleek design, and interesting click wheel—were visually appealing and unlike anything I had ever seen or used before. Better yet, I could fit all of my music on one portable device. (Exactly how music, movies, and pictures fit on a small little machine is still a mystery to me.)

I've upgraded since that first gift, but the current model is still my constant companion. I am always listening to something—on the train into the city and riding the subway, walking the city streets while avoiding direct eye contact (as all good New Yorkers do), and on my way to class, even if my destination is only two minutes away. The convenience of having thousands of songs at my fingertips and on demand is one that I have become accustomed to. I always check to make sure my iPod is safely in my bag before leaving my room. If by chance I do temporarily misplace it, I feel like I'm missing a limb. What is typically a 22-minute Metro-North ride from the Bronx to Manhattan feels like a small eternity without music. Sitting in the library in complete silence, I am distracted by environmental noises— the flipping of pages, the "ping" of the elevator, and the footsteps and general rustling of other students. While a day without my iPod is definitely not disastrous, at certain times, it is a little less enjoyable.

Although I may not count myself among the ranks of the ChapStick addicts support group (ha ha), upon reading Chapter 1, I realized that I have a mild case of consumer addiction. Addiction is not limited to the stereotypical connotations of alcohol and drugs, as the book points out. The definition introduced is certainly very accurate—a reliance on something that fulfills a need, even if it is a material possession. Now that I am aware that I have a small dependency on this product, I have considered cutting down my usage. The concept of *consumer addiction* made me think about how this behavior impacts my life. It can even limit my interaction with the rest of the world, as evidenced by a casual stroll past my friends while blasting music, blissfully unaware of their screams to get my attention.

I am sure that my love for my iPod is a marketer's dream. Because I use it so much, I am interested in purchasing new models and downloading music, movies, and TV shows from the iTunes music store. Maybe my behavior is partially the consequence of their advertising campaigns. (Who could forget Apple's eye-catching black silhouettes contrasted with white iPods and vibrantly colored backgrounds?) Maybe they could even incorporate my experience into a new marketing strategy to show how their product really becomes a part of everyday life. Either way, I can honestly say, "Hello, my name is Meghan, and I'm an iPod-holic."

Even technology can be addicting—as anyone with a BlackBerry can attest: Some people call this little device by the nickname of "CrackBerry" because it's so hard to stop checking it constantly. Internet addiction already is a big problem in South Korea, where 90 percent of homes connect to cheap, high-speed broadband. Many young Koreans' social life revolves around the "PC bang," dim Internet parlors that sit on practically every street corner. A government study estimates that up to 30 percent of South Koreans under 18 are at risk of Internet addiction. Many already exhibit signs of actual addiction, like an inability to stop themselves from using computers, rising levels of tolerance that drive them to seek ever longer sessions online, and withdrawal symptoms like anger and craving when they can't log on. Some users have literally dropped dead from exhaustion after playing online games for days on end.[79]

A campaign to combat cigarette addiction.
Source: Courtesy of ADESF Association for Smoker Awareness; Neoqama/BBH.

IN 2066, BIN LADEN WILL BE CAUGHT.

LIVE TO SEE IT. QUIT SMOKING NOW.

ADESF

Marketing Pitfall

As the song says, "one is the loneliest number." A German print ad campaign for one-calorie PepsiMax depicts a lonely calorie trying to kill himself in a variety of grisly ways such as slitting his blue wrist with a razor blade. Suicide prevention groups reacted angrily. In the United States, General Motors encountered similar protests when it aired a Super Bowl commercial that showed a lonely robot considering suicide.[84]

Compulsive Consumption

Some consumers take the expression "born to shop" quite literally. They shop because they are compelled to do so rather than because shopping is a pleasurable or functional task. **Compulsive consumption** refers to repetitive shopping, often excessive, as an antidote to tension, anxiety, depression, or boredom.[80] "Shopaholics" turn to shopping much the way addicted people turn to drugs or alcohol.[81] One man diagnosed with *compulsive shopping disorder* (*CSD*) bought more than 2,000 wrenches and never used any of them. Therapists report that women clinically diagnosed with CSD outnumber men by four to one. They speculate that women are attracted to items such as clothes and cosmetics to enhance their interpersonal relationships, whereas men tend to focus on gadgetry, tools, and guns to achieve a sense of power.

One out of twenty U.S. adults is unable to control buying goods that he or she did not really want or need. Some researchers say compulsive shopping may be related to low self-esteem. It affects an estimated 2 to 16 percent of the adult U.S. population.[82] In some cases, like a drug addict the consumer has little or no control over his or her consumption. Whether it is alcohol, cigarettes, chocolate, diet colas, or even ChapStick, the products control the consumer. Even the act of shopping itself is an addicting experience for some people. Three common elements characterize many negative or destructive consumer behaviors:[83]

1 The behavior is not done by choice.
2 The gratification derived from the behavior is short-lived.
3 The person experiences strong feelings of regret or guilt afterward.

Gambling is an example of a consumption addiction that touches every segment of consumer society. Whether it takes the form of casino gambling, playing the "slots," betting on sports events with friends or through a bookie, or even buying lottery tickets, excessive gambling can be quite destructive. Taken to extremes, gambling can result in lowered self-esteem, debt, divorce, and neglected children. According to one psychologist, gamblers exhibit a classic addictive cycle: They experience a "high" while in action and depression when they stop gambling, which leads them back to the thrill of the action. Unlike drug addicts, however, money is the substance that hard-core gamblers abuse.

Consumed Consumers

Consumed consumers are people who are used or exploited, willingly or not, for commercial gain in the marketplace. The situations in which consumers themselves become commodities can range from traveling road shows that feature dwarfs and midgets to the selling of body parts and babies. Check out these consumed consumers:

- **Prostitutes**—Expenditures on prostitution in the United States alone are estimated at $20 billion annually. These revenues are equivalent to those in the domestic shoe industry.[85]
- **Organ, blood, and hair donors**—By one estimate, you could make about $46 million if you donated every reusable part of your body (do not try this at home).[86] In the United States, millions of people sell their blood. A lively market also exists for organs (e.g., kidneys), and some women sell their hair to be made into wigs. Bidding for a human kidney on eBay went to more than $5.7 million before the company ended the auction (it's illegal to sell human organs online—at least so far). The seller wrote, "You can choose either kidney . . . Of course only one for sale, as I need the other one to live. Serious bids only."[87]
- **Babies for sale**—Several thousand surrogate mothers have been paid to be medically impregnated and carry babies to term for infertile couples. A fertile woman between the ages of 18 and 25 can "donate" one egg every 3 months and rake in $7,000 each time. Over 8 years, that's 32 eggs for a total of $224,000.[88] In one recent case in Germany, police arrested a couple when they tried to auction their 8-month-old son on eBay. The parents claimed that the offer, which read "Baby—collection only. Offer my nearly new baby for sale because it cries too much. Male, 70 cm long" was just a joke.[89]

Illegal Activities

Many consumer behaviors are not only self-destructive or socially damaging but they are illegal as well. Analysts estimate the cost of crimes consumers commit against business at more than $40 billion per year. A survey the McCann-Erickson advertising agency conducted revealed the following tidbits:[90]

- Ninety-one percent of people say they lie regularly. One in three fibs about his or her weight, one in four about income, and 21 percent lie about their age. Nine percent even lie about their natural hair color.
- Four out of ten Americans have tried to pad an insurance bill to cover the deductible.
- Nineteen percent say they've snuck into a theater to avoid paying admission.
- More than three out of five people say they've taken credit for making something from scratch when they have done no such thing. According to Pillsbury's CEO, this ". . . behavior is so prevalent that we've named a category after it—speed scratch."

Consumer Theft and Fraud

Who among us has never received an e-mail offering us fabulous riches if we help to recover a lost fortune from a Nigerian bank account? Of course, the only money changing hands will be yours if you fall for the pitch from a so-called *advance fee fraud artist*. These con men have successfully fooled many victims out of hundreds

The Tangled Web

Crimes that *avatars* commit in virtual worlds can have real-life consequences. Dutch police arrested a teenager for stealing virtual furniture from rooms in Habbo Hotel (a large virtual world based in Finland). In South Korea, police commonly investigate online gaming-related crimes and warn that a cyber-Mafia is emerging where gangs demand protection money from new players. Japanese police arrested a Chinese exchange student after he organized a "mugging spree" in the fantasy game *Lineage II*. And, when a Chinese man who played *Legends of Mir 3* learned that the valuable virtual "dragon saber" he lent his friend was sold on eBay, he killed the friend in real life with a real sword and is now serving a real life sentence.[91]

of millions of dollars. However, a small but intrepid group of "counterscammers" sometimes give these crooks a taste of their own medicine by pretending to fall for a scam and humiliating the perpetrator. One common strategy is to trick the con artist into posing for pictures holding a self-mocking sign and then posting these photos on Internet sites. Both online and off-line, fraud is rampant.

Stealing from stores is the most common. Someone commits a retail theft every 5 seconds. **Shrinkage** is the industry term for inventory and cash losses from shoplifting and employee theft (not the condition George experienced in a famous episode of *Seinfeld*). This is a massive problem for businesses that gets passed on to consumers in the form of higher prices (about 40 percent of the losses can be attributed to employees rather than shoppers). Shopping malls spend $6 million annually on security, and a family of four spends about $300 extra per year because of markups to cover shrinkage.[92]

Indeed, shoplifting is America's fastest-growing crime. A comprehensive retail study found that shoplifting is a year-round problem that costs U.S. retailers $9 billion annually. The most frequently stolen products are tobacco products, athletic shoes, logo and brand-name apparel, designer jeans, and undergarments. The average theft amount per incident is $58.43, up from $20.36 in a 1995 survey.[93] The problem is equally worrisome in Europe; retailers there catch well over 1 million shoplifters every year. The United Kingdom has the highest rate of shrinkage (as a percent of annual sales), followed by Norway, Greece, and France. Switzerland and Austria have the lowest rates.[94]

The large majority of shoplifting is not done by professional thieves or by people who genuinely need the stolen items.[95] About 2 million Americans are charged with shoplifting each year, but analysts estimate that for every arrest, 18 unreported incidents occur.[96] About three-quarters of those caught are middle- or high-income people who shoplift for the thrill of it or as a substitute for affection. Shoplifting is also common among adolescents. Research evidence indicates that teen shoplifting is influenced by factors such as having friends who also shoplift. It is also more likely to occur if the adolescent does not believe that this behavior is morally wrong.[97]

And what about shoppers who commit fraud when they abuse stores' exchange and return policies? Some big companies such as Guess, Staples, and Sports Authority use new software that lets them track a shopper's track record of bringing items back. They are trying to crack down on "serial wardrobers" who buy an outfit, wear it once, and return it; customers who change price tags on items, then return one item for the higher amount; and shoppers who use fake or old receipts when they return a product. The retail industry loses approximately $16 billion a year to these and other forms of fraudulent behavior. Retail analysts estimate that about 9 percent of all returns are fraudulent.[98]

Anticonsumption

Some types of destructive consumer behavior are **anticonsumption**, events in which people deliberately deface or mutilate products and services. Some of these actions are relatively harmless, as when a person goes online at dogdoo.com to send a bag of dog manure to a lucky recipient. This site even lets customers calibrate the size of the "gift" by choosing among three "Poo Poo Packages": Econo-Poop (20-pound dog), Poo Poo Special (50-pound dog), and the ultimate in payback, the Poo Poo Grande (110-pound dog).[99] The moral: Smell your packages before opening.

Anticonsumption can range from relatively mild acts like spray-painting graffiti on buildings and subways to serious incidences of product tampering or even the release of computer viruses that can bring large corporations to their knees. It can also take the form of political protest in which activists alter or destroy billboards and other advertisements that promote what they feel to be unhealthy or unethical acts. For example, some members of the clergy in areas heavily populated by minorities have organized rallies to protest the proliferation of cigarette and alcohol advertising in their neighborhoods; these protests sometimes include the defacement of billboards promoting alcohol or cigarettes.

OBJECTIVE

How do different types of specialists study consumer behavior?

Consumer Behavior as a Field of Study

By now it should be clear that the field of consumer behavior encompasses many things, from the simple purchase of a carton of milk to the selection of a complex networked computer system; from the decision to donate money to a charity to devious plans to rip off a company.

There's an awful lot to understand, and many ways to go about it. Although people have certainly been consumers for a long time, it is only recently that consumption per se has been the object of formal study. In fact, although many business schools now require that marketing majors take a consumer behavior course, most colleges did not even offer such a course until the 1970s.

The study of consumer behavior applies to virtually every context. In this case a zoo in New Zealand tries to entice visitors.
Source: Courtesy of Ogilvy, Aukland Zoo.

Where Do We Find Consumer Researchers?

Just about anywhere we find consumers. Consumer researchers work for manufacturers, retailers, marketing research firms, governments and nonprofit organizations, and of course colleges and universities. You'll find them running sophisticated experiments in laboratories that involve advanced neural imaging machinery, or interviewing shoppers in malls. They may conduct focus groups or run large-scale polling operations. For example, when the advertising agency began to work on a new campaign for retailer JCPenney, it sent staffers to hang out with more than 50 women for several days. They wanted to really understand the respondents' lives, so they helped them to clean their houses, carpool, cook dinner, and shop. As one of the account executives observed, "If you want to understand how a lion hunts, you don't go to the zoo—you go to the jungle."[100]

And, researchers work on many types of topics, from everyday household products and high-tech installations to professional services, museum exhibits and public policy issues such as the effect of advertising on children. Indeed, no consumer issue is too sacred: Some intrepid investigators bravely explore "delicate" categories like incontinence products and birth control devices. The marketing director for Trojan condoms notes that, "Unlike laundry, where you can actually sit and watch people do their laundry, we can't sit and watch them use our product." For this reason Trojan relies on clinical psychologists, psychiatrists, and cultural anthropologists to understand how men relate to condoms.[101]

Interdisciplinary Influences on the Study of Consumer Behavior

Many different perspectives shape the young field of consumer behavior. Indeed, it is hard to think of a field that is more interdisciplinary. You can find people with training in a very wide range of disciplines—from psychophysiology to literature—doing consumer research. Universities, manufacturers, museums, advertising agencies, and governments employ consumer researchers. Several professional groups, such as the Association for Consumer Research and the Society for Consumer Psychology, have been formed since the mid-1970s.

To gain an idea of the diversity of interests of people who do consumer research, consider the list of professional associations that sponsor the field's major journal, the *Journal of Consumer Research*: the American Association of Family and Consumer Sciences, the American Statistical Association, the Association for Consumer Research, the Society for Consumer Psychology, the International Communication Association, the American Sociological Association, the Institute of Management Sciences, the American Anthropological Association, the American Marketing Association, the Society for Personality and Social Psychology, the American Association for Public Opinion Research, and the American Economic Association. That's a pretty mixed bag.

So, with all of these researchers from diverse backgrounds interested in consumer behavior, which is the "correct" discipline to look into these issues? You might remember a children's story about the blind men and the elephant. The gist of the story is that each man touched a different part of the animal and, as a result, the descriptions each gave of the elephant were quite different. This analogy applies to consumer research as well. Depending on the training and interests of the researchers studying it, they will approach the same consumer phenomenon in different ways and at different levels. Table 1.2 illustrates how a "simple" topic such as magazine usage can be understood in many different ways.

Figure 1.2 provides a glimpse of some of the disciplines working in the field and the level at which each tackles research issues. We can roughly characterize them in

TABLE 1.2	Interdisciplinary Research Issues in Consumer Behavior
Disciplinary Focus	**Magazine Usage Sample Research Issues**
Experimental Psychology: product role in perception, learning, and memory processes	How specific aspects of magazines, such as their design or layout, are recognized and interpreted; which parts of a magazine people are most likely to read.
Clinical Psychology: product role in psychological adjustment	How magazines affect readers' body images (e.g., do thin models make the average woman feel overweight?)
Microeconomics/Human Ecology: product role in allocation of individual or family resources	Factors influencing the amount of money a household spends on magazines.
Social Psychology: product role in the behavior of individuals as members of social groups	Ways that ads in a magazine affect readers' attitudes toward the products depicted; how peer pressure influences a person's readership decisions
Sociology: product role in social institutions and group relationships	Pattern by which magazine preferences spread through a social group (e.g., a sorority)
Macroeconomics: product role in consumers' relations with the marketplace	Effects of the price of fashion magazines and expense of items advertised during periods of high unemployment
Semiotics/Literary Criticism: product role in the verbal and visual communication of meaning	Ways in which underlying messages communicated by models and ads in a magazine are interpreted
Demography: product role in the measurable characteristics of a population	Effects of age, income, and marital status of a magazine's readers
History: product role in societal changes over time	Ways in which our culture's depictions of "femininity" in magazines have changed over time
Cultural Anthropology: product role in a society's beliefs and practices	Ways in which fashions and models in a magazine affect readers' definitions of masculine versus feminine behavior (e.g., the role of working women, sexual taboos)

terms of their focus on micro versus macro consumer behavior topics. The fields closer to the top of the pyramid concentrate on the individual consumer (micro issues), and those toward the base are more interested in the aggregate activities that occur among larger groups of people, such as consumption patterns members of a culture or subculture share (macro issues). As we make our way through this book, we'll focus on the issues at the top (micro) and then make our way to the bottom of the pyramid by the end of the course. Hang in there!

Should Consumer Research Have an Academic or an Applied Focus?

Many regard the field of consumer behavior as an applied social science. They argue that the value of the knowledge we generate should be judged in terms of its ability to improve the effectiveness of marketing practice. However, other researchers argue that consumer behavior should not have a strategic focus at all; the field should not be a "handmaiden to business." It should instead focus on the understanding of consumption for its own sake rather than marketers applying this knowledge to making a profit.[102] Most consumer researchers do not hold this rather extreme view, but it has encouraged many to expand the scope of their work beyond the field's

Figure 1.2 DISCIPLINES IN
CONSUMER RESEARCH

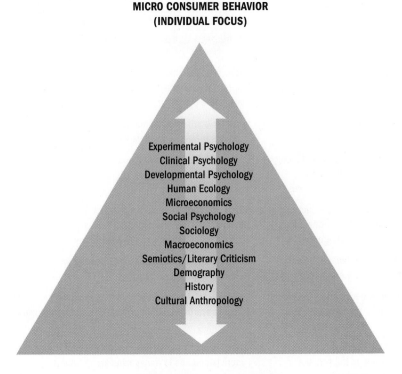

**MICRO CONSUMER BEHAVIOR
(INDIVIDUAL FOCUS)**

Experimental Psychology
Clinical Psychology
Developmental Psychology
Human Ecology
Microeconomics
Social Psychology
Sociology
Macroeconomics
Semiotics/Literary Criticism
Demography
History
Cultural Anthropology

**MACRO CONSUMER BEHAVIOR
(SOCIAL FOCUS)**

traditional focus on the purchase of consumer goods such as food, appliances, and cars to embrace social problems such as homelessness or preserving the environment. Certainly, it has led to some fiery debates among people working in the field!

OBJECTIVE

What are the two major perspectives that seek to understand and study consumer behavior?

Two Perspectives on Consumer Research

One general way we classify consumer research is in terms of the fundamental assumptions the researchers make about what they study and how to study it. We call a set of beliefs that guide our understanding of the world a **paradigm**. As in other fields of study, a paradigm dominates the discipline of consumer behavior, but some believe it is in the middle of a *paradigm shift*, which occurs when a competing paradigm challenges the dominant set of assumptions.

The basic set of assumptions underlying the dominant paradigm at this point in time is **positivism** (or sometimes *modernism*). This perspective has significantly influenced Western art and science since the late sixteenth century. It emphasizes that human reason is supreme and that there is a single, objective truth that science can discover. Positivism encourages us to stress the function of objects, to celebrate technology, and to regard the world as a rational, ordered place with a clearly defined past, present, and future.

The newer paradigm of **interpretivism** (or *postmodernism*) questions these assumptions.[103] Proponents of this perspective argue that our society emphasizes science and technology too much, and they feel that this ordered, rational view of behavior denies the complex social and cultural world in which we really live. Others feel that positivism puts too much emphasis on material well-being and that its logical outlook is directed by an ideology that stresses the homogenous views of a culture dominated by (dead) white males.

TABLE 1.3	Positivist Versus Interpretivist Approaches to Consumer Behavior	
Assumptions	**Positivist Approach**	**Interpretivist Approach**
Nature of reality	Objective, tangible Single	Socially constructed Multiple
Goal	Prediction	Understanding
Knowledge generated	Time-free, context independent	Time-bound Context dependent
View of causality	Existence of real causes	Multiple, simultaneous shaping events
Research relationship	Separation between researcher and subject	Interactive, cooperative with researcher being part of phenomenon under study

Source: Adapted from Laurel A. Hudson and Julie L. Ozanne, "Alternative Ways of Seeking Knowledge in Consumer Research," *Journal of Consumer Research* 14 (March 1988): 508–21. Reprinted with the permission of the University of Chicago Press. Copyright © 1988 JCR, Inc.

Interpretivists instead stress the importance of symbolic, subjective experience, and the idea that meaning is in the mind of the person—that is, we each construct our own meanings based on our unique and shared cultural experiences, so there are no right or wrong answers. In this view, the world in which we live is composed of a **pastiche**, or mixture of images.[104] This perspective rebukes the value we assign to products because they help us to create order; instead it focuses on regarding consumption as offering a set of diverse experiences. Table 1.3 summarizes the major differences between these two perspectives on consumer research.

We can illustrate an interpretative framework to understand marketing communications by referring to an analysis of one of the best-known and longest-running (1959–1978) advertising campaigns of all time: the work the advertising agency Doyle Dane Bernbach (DDB) did for the Volkswagen Beetle. This campaign, widely noted for its self-mocking wit, found many ways to turn the Beetle's homeliness, smallness, and lack of power into positive attributes at a time when most car ads were emphasizing just the opposite.

An interpretative analysis of these messages used concepts from literature, psychology, and anthropology to ground the appeal of this approach within a broader cultural context. Analysts linked the image DDB created for the humble car to other examples of what scholars of comedy call the "Little Man" pattern. This is a type of comedic character that is related to a clown or a trickster, a social outcast who is able to poke holes in the stuffiness and rigidity of bureaucracy and conformity. Other examples of the "Little Man" character include Hawkeye in the TV sitcom *M.A.S.H.*, the comedian Woody Allen, and Charlie Chaplin. When one looks at the cultural meaning of marketing messages this way, it is perhaps no coincidence that IBM chose the Charlie Chaplin character some years later to help it "soften" its stuffy, intimidating image as it tried to convince consumers that its new personal computer products were user-friendly.

Taking It from Here: The Plan of the Book

This book covers many facets of consumer behavior, and in the chapters to come we will highlight many of the research perspectives we briefly described in this one. The plan of the book is simple: It goes from micro to macro. Think of it as a sort of photograph album of consumer behavior: Each chapter provides a "snapshot" of consumers, but the lens used to take each picture gets successively wider. The book begins with issues related to the individual consumer and expands its focus until it eventually

Figure 1.3 THE WHEEL OF CONSUMER BEHAVIOR

- Cultural Influences on Consumer Behavior
- The Creation and Diffusion of Consumer Culture

- Perception
- Learning and Memory
- Values and Motivation
- The Self and Sex Roles
- Personality and Lifestyles
- Attitudes and Persuasion

Consumer Behavior

1 Consumers in the Marketplace
2 Consumers as Individuals
3 Consumers as Decision Makers
4 Consumers and Subcultures
5 Consumers and Culture

- Individual Decision Making
- Organizational and Housing Decision Making
- Buying and Disposing
- Groups

- Income and Social Class
- Ethnic, Racial, and Religious Subcultures
- Age Subcultures

considers the behaviors of large groups of people in their social settings. As Figure 1.3 shows, we can depict the topics we will cover as a "wheel of consumer behavior."

Section II, "Consumers as Individuals," considers the consumer at his or her most micro level. It examines how the individual receives information from his or her immediate environment and how this material is learned, stored in memory, and used to form and modify individual attitudes—both about products and about oneself. Section III, "Consumers as Decision Makers," explores the ways in which consumers use the information they have acquired to make decisions about consumption activities, both as individuals and as group members. Section IV, "Consumers and Subcultures," further expands the focus by considering how the consumer functions as part of a larger social structure. This structure includes the influence of different social groups with which the consumer belongs and identifies, including social class, ethnic groups, and age groups. Finally, Section V, "Consumers and Culture," completes the picture as it examines marketing's impact on mass culture. These effects include the relationship of marketing to the expression of cultural values and lifestyles; how products and services are related to rituals and cultural myths; and the interface between marketing efforts and the creation of art, music, and other forms of popular culture that are so much a part of our daily lives.

CHAPTER SUMMARY

Now that you have finished reading this chapter you should understand why:

 Consumers use products to help them define their identities in different settings.

A consumer may purchase, use, and dispose of a product, but different people may perform these functions. In addition, we can think of consumers as role players who need different products to help them play their various parts.

 Consumer behavior is a process.

Consumer behavior is the study of the processes involved when individuals or groups select, purchase, use, or dispose of products, services, ideas, or experiences to satisfy needs and desires.

Marketers need to understand the wants and needs of different consumer segments.

Market segmentation is an important aspect of consumer behavior. Consumers can be segmented according to many dimensions, including product usage, demographics (the objective aspects of a population, such as age and sex), and psychographics (psychological and lifestyle characteristics). Emerging developments, such as the new emphasis on relationship marketing and the practice of database marketing, mean that marketers are much more attuned to the wants and needs of different consumer groups. This is especially important as people are empowered to construct their own consumerspace—accessing product information where and when they want it and initiating contact with companies on the Internet instead of passively receiving marketing communications.

 The Web is changing consumer behavior.

The Web is transforming the way consumers interact with companies and with each other. Online commerce allows us to locate obscure products from around the world, and consumption communities provide forums for people to share opinions and product recommendations. Potential problems accompany these benefits, including the loss of privacy and the deterioration of traditional social interactions as people log more time online.

 Consumer behavior relates to other issues in our lives.

Marketing activities exert an enormous impact on individuals. Consumer behavior is relevant to our understanding of both public policy issues (e.g., ethical marketing practices) and the dynamics of popular culture.

 Consumer activities can be harmful to individuals and to society.

Although textbooks often paint a picture of the consumer as a rational, informed decision maker, in reality many consumer activities are harmful to individuals or to society. The "dark side" of consumer behavior includes terrorism, addiction, the use of people as products (consumed consumers), and theft or vandalism (anticonsumption).

 Different types of specialists study consumer behavior.

The field of consumer behavior is interdisciplinary; it is composed of researchers from many different fields who share an interest in how people interact with the marketplace. These disciplines can be categorized by the degree to which their focus is micro (the individual consumer) or macro (the consumer as a member of groups or of the larger society).

 There are two major perspectives that seek to understand and study consumer behavior.

There are many perspectives on consumer behavior, but we can roughly divide research orientations into two approaches: The positivist perspective emphasizes the objectivity of science and the consumer as a rational decision maker. The interpretivist perspective, in contrast, stresses the subjective meaning of the consumer's individual experience and the idea that any behavior is subject to multiple interpretations rather than to one single explanation.

KEY TERMS

80/20 rule, 10
Anticonsumption, 38
B2C e-commerce, 21
Bioterrorism, 34
Business ethics, 23
C2C e-commerce, 21
Compulsive consumption, 36
Consumed consumers, 37
Consumer, 8
Consumer addiction, 34
Consumer behavior, 7
Consumer-generated content, 16
Consumerspace, 25
Consumption communities, 6

Culture jamming, 30
Database marketing, 14
Demographics, 6
Economics of information, 27
Exchange, 8
Global consumer culture, 18
Green marketing, 32
Heavy users, 10
Interpretivism, 42
Market segmentation strategies, 6
Need, 25
Paradigm, 42
Pastiche, 43
Popular culture, 16

Positivism, 42
Psychographics, 6
Relationship marketing, 14
RFID tag, 19
Role theory, 18
Shrinkage, 38
Social marketing, 32
Transformative Consumer Research (TCR), 31
U-commerce, 19
Want, 25
Web 2.0, 17

REVIEW

1 Provide a definition of consumer behavior.

2 What are demographics? Give three examples of demographic characteristics.

3 What is the difference between a culture and a subculture?

4 Define market segmentation.

5 What is role theory, and how does it help us to understand consumer behavior?

6 What do we mean by an exchange?

7 Why is it important for businesses to learn about their heavy users?

8 What is database marketing? Give an example of a company that uses this technique.

9 What is popular culture, and how does this concept relate to marketing and consumer behavior?

10 What is the primary difference between transformative consumer research and "regular" consumer research?

11 This chapter states "people often buy products not for what they do but for what they mean." Explain the meaning of this statement and provide an example.

12 Describe two types of relationships a consumer can have with a product.

13 What do we mean by the term *global consumer culture*?

14 What is the difference between C2C and B2C e-commerce?

15 The economics of information perspective argues that advertising is important. Why?

16 Provide two examples of important legislation that relate to American consumers.

17 Define social marketing and give an example of this technique.

18 Define consumer addiction and give two examples.

19 What is an example of a consumed consumer?

20 What is shrinkage, and why is it a problem?

21 Define anticonsumption, and provide two examples of it.

22 Name two different disciplines that study consumer behavior. How would their approaches to the same issue differ?

23 What are the major differences between the positivist and interpretivist paradigms in consumer research?

CONSUMER BEHAVIOR CHALLENGE

■ DISCUSS

1 This chapter states that people play different roles and that their consumption behaviors may differ depending on the particular role they are playing. State whether you agree or disagree with this perspective, giving examples from your personal life. Try to construct a "stage set" for a role you play—specify the props, costumes, and script that you use to play a role (e.g., job interviewee, conscientious student, party animal).

2 A company introduced a teddy bear for Valentine's Day called "Crazy for You." This toy aroused the ire of mental health advocates because a straitjacket restrains the cuddly bear's paws and the stuffed animal comes with institutional commitment papers. Supporters of the company's decision to keep selling the bear say opponents are too "politically correct."[105] What do you think?

3 Nonprofit organizations routinely rely on generous corporate donations, and it's common to name facilities after benefactors. The Nationwide Children's Hospital in Ohio is no exception; its name recognizes the insurance company's $50 million donation. Now the hospital is adding the Abercrombie & Fitch Emergency Department and Trauma Center and there is also the Limited Too & Justice Main Lobby. Abercrombie & Fitch is notorious for its use of alluring young people. The Campaign for a Commercial-Free Childhood opposes this partnership. The group's director commented that "Abercrombie & Fitch is really among the worst of corporate predators. A company with such cynical disregard for children's well-being shouldn't be able to claim the mantle of healing. . . . And, personally, I find it very concerning that they named their hospital after an insurance company."[106] What do you think? Is this over the line, or does it matter where the money comes from so long as the end result is beneficial?

Some researchers believe that the field of consumer behavior should be a pure rather than an applied science. That is, research issues should be framed in terms of their scientific interest rather than their applicability to immediate marketing problems. Give your views on this issue.

4 From time to time advertisers use dark humor to get their messages across, as when a lonely calorie, repairman, or robot considers suicide. Or, an ad may imply that a shopper is "mentally ill" if they buy retail. Are these appeals a legitimate way to communicate a message, and if so under what circumstances?

5 Name some products or services that your social group uses a lot. State whether you agree or disagree with the notion that these products help to form group bonds. Support your argument with examples from your list of products your group uses.

6 Although marketers use demographic information on large numbers of consumers in many contexts, some people believe that the sale of data on customers' incomes, buying habits, and so on constitutes an invasion of privacy and should be stopped. Is Big Brother watching? Comment on this issue from both a consumer's and a marketer's point of view.

7 List the three stages in the consumption process. Describe the issues that you considered in each of these stages when you made a recent important purchase.

8 What aspects of consumer behavior would interest a financial planner? A university administrator? A graphic arts designer? A social worker in a government agency? A nursing instructor?

9 Critics of targeted marketing strategies argue that this practice is discriminatory and unfair, especially if such a strategy encourages a group of people to buy a product that may be injurious to them or that they cannot afford. For example, community leaders in largely minority neighborhoods have staged protests against billboards promoting beer or cigarettes in these areas. However, the Association of National Advertisers argues that banning targeted marketing constitutes censorship and thus is a violation of the First Amendment. What are your views regarding this issue?

10 Do marketers have the ability to control our desires or the power to create needs? Is this situation changing as the Internet creates new ways to interact with companies? If so, how?

11 An entrepreneur made international news when he set up a Web site to auction the egg cells of fashion models to the highest bidder (minimum bid: $15,000). The site was targeted to people who wanted to have very attractive babies because they believed this would maximize their chances of succeeding in our society. Is the buying and selling of humans just another example of consumer behavior at work? Do you agree that this service is simply a more efficient way to maximize the chance of having happy, successful children? Should this kind of marketing activity be allowed? Would you sell your eggs or sperm on a Web site?

12 A recent book bemoans the new wave of consumer-generated content, labeling it "the cult of the amateur." It compares the social networking phenomenon to the old story about the monkeys: If you put an infinite number of monkeys in a room with an infinite number of typewriters, eventually they will (by hitting keys randomly) reproduce all the major works of literature. In other words, the large majority of user-generated content is at about the same level, and the future of professionally produced, quality work is in doubt.[107] Do you agree or disagree with this assertion?

■ APPLY

1 To what degree will consumers trade lower prices for less privacy? Car owners now can let insurance companies monitor their driving using a new technology in exchange for lower rates. Customers who sign up for Progressive's TripSense program get a device the size of a Tic Tac box to plug into their cars. The device will track speed and how many miles are driven at what times of day. Every few months, customers unplug the device from the car, plug it into a computer, download the data, and send them to the company. Depending on results, discounts will range from 5 to 25 percent. In Great Britain, a major insurer is testing a program called Pay as You Drive. Volunteers will get a device the size of a Palm computer installed in their cars. The gadget will use global positioning satellite technology to track where the car goes, constantly sending information back to the insurance company. Cars that spend more time in safer areas will qualify for bigger discounts.[108] Of course, the potential downside to these efforts is that the insurance companies may be able to collect data on where you have driven, how long you stayed in one location, and so on. Conduct a poll of 10 drivers of various ages where you describe these programs and ask respondents if they would participate in order to receive a discount on their insurance premiums. What reasons do they give pro and con? Do you find any differences in attitudes based on demographic characteristics such as age or gender?

2 While you're talking to car owners, probe to see what (if any) relationships they have with their vehicles. Do these feelings correspond to the types of consumer/product attachments we discussed in this chapter? How are these relationships acted on (hint: see if any of the respondents have nicknames for their cars, or if they "decorate" them with personal items)?

3 Many college students "share" music by downloading clips from the Internet. Interview at least five people who have downloaded at least one song or movie without paying for it. Do they feel they are stealing? What explanations do they offer for this behavior? Try to identify any common themes as a result of these interviews. If you were devising an ad campaign to discourage free downloading, how might you use what you have learned to craft a convincing message?

Case Study

WILL CONSUMERS CONSUME?

Experts argue about when it started, what were really the first signs, who saw it coming, and who was surprised when it got here. The signs were undeniable by the early months of 2008: The U.S. economy was headed for big trouble. Bear Stearns, one of the largest and oldest investment firms, put itself up for sale. This Wall Street legend had survived the Great Depression, but it just couldn't cope with the Great Recession the mortgage crisis ignited. Six months later, Lehman Brothers, a company so old it was established before the Civil War, prepared to leave the marketplace. Grave economic news continued through the end of 2008 as the government bailed out banks and automakers. The year closed with the Dow Jones Industrial Average below 10,000 for the first time in four years.

As the country rolled into 2009, few things changed. The Dow continued to descend, reaching below 7,000 for the first time in a decade. Unemployment rose to 8.5 percent; nearly double the rate two years before, and the whole nation realized that the United States, and in fact the world, was in one of the deepest and most serious recessions most people had experienced in their lifetimes.

Consumers were confused and caught off guard; and they reacted quickly. They made swift changes in their consumer behavior and spending. People started staying home more—eating out less and cutting back on family vacations. Data from Nielsen research identified many product categories that were seeing a drop in sales and at the same time, categories with increases in their sales patterns.

Wait, increases? What do people buy more of in a recession? Baking staples and canning and freezing supplies began to pick up in sales. In addition to the expected baking goods—flour and sugar—there were increases in sales of jars and freezer bags. At the other extreme, Nielsen reports that cameras experienced the biggest sales drop among product categories. As people went out and traveled less, it's likely that photo opportunities would plummet as well. Pricey bottled water was another loser at retail as consumers reverted to good old (and inexpensive) tap water.

In addition to cutting back in certain categories, consumers started to save, many for the first time in their adult lives. The U.S. Department of Commerce tracks the personal savings rate, a measure of the fraction of personal income that people don't immediately spend. The rate jumped from .3 percent in early 2008 to 4.2 percent one year later in February 2009.

We expect a drop in consumer spending in a recession. But, customers' attitudes toward big business also declined. The Boston Consulting Group disclosed preliminary results from a survey showing that Americans and Europeans now have an intensified distrust of big business that might affect their future spending—even when the economic picture gets brighter. Large companies need to focus on rebuilding relationships with consumers to help reduce buyers' skepticism toward big brands.

Will Americans return to their old free-spending ways when the economy improves, or has their attitude toward spending versus saving changed forever? Will they trust big business again? What can brands do to gain back consumer trust?

DISCUSSION QUESTIONS

1 How have the changes in the economy led to changes in the consumption process? How might these influence the prepurchase, purchase, and postpurchase stages of consumer decision making?
2 Explain how the wheel of consumer behavior might help to explain the changes in consumer spending.
3 Will consumers continue to save? How can brands gain back consumer trust?
4 What effect might the recession have on priorities for consumer research—and perhaps opportunities for careers in this field?

Sources: Sean Gregory, "Inside the Cocoon." *Time* (2009): 59; "From Buy, Buy to Bye-Bye: Consumer Psychology," *The Economist* (2009): 67.

NOTES

1. Quoted in http://forums.oxygen.com, accessed June 27, 2009; www .ivillage.com, accessed June 27, 2009; http://oxygen.com, accessed June 27, 2009.
2. Quoted at www.sigmadeltatau.net, accessed June 27, 2009.
3. http://collegeclub.com, accessed June 27, 2009; Quoted at www.collegeclub.com/article/view/36;jsessionid=F04A1EFCB75138 6226EB3EC9C0C595CE, accessed August 12, 2007.
4. http://ratemyprofessors.com, accessed June 27, 2009.
5. Olivia Ma, "Sneaker Freaks," *Newsweek* (August 16, 2004): 69.
6. Michael R. Solomon and Elnora W. Stuart, *Marketing: Real People, Real Choices*, 2nd ed. (Upper Saddle River, NJ: Prentice Hall, 2000): 5–6.
7. "Sony Walkman Series S, E and B Music Players Features and Suppring [sic] Formats" (May 29, 2009), http://techwizardz.blogspot.com/ 2009/05/sony-walkman-series-s-e-and-b-music.html, accessed June 27, 2009; Evan Ramstad, "Walkman's Plan for Reeling in the Ears of Wired Youths," *Wall Street Journal Interactive Edition* (May 18, 2000).
8. Anthony Bianco, "The Vanishing Mass Market," *BusinessWeek* (July 12, 2004): 61–67.
9. Jack Neff, "Study: Package-Goods Brands' Consumer Bases Very Small, Yet Diverse," *Advertising Age* (December 8, 2008), www.adage .com, accessed December 8, 2008.
10. Jennifer Ordonez, "Cash Cows: Burger Joints Call Them 'Heavy Users'—But Not to Their Faces," *Wall Street Journal Interactive Edition* (January 12, 2000).
11. Steven Gray, "At Fast-Food Chains, Era of the Giant Burger (Plus Bacon) Is Here," *Wall Street Journal* (January 27, 2005), www.wsj.com, accessed January 27, 2005.
12. Allison Fass, "Kingdom Seeks Magic," *Forbes* (October 2006): 68–70.
13. Natalie Perkins, "Zeroing in on Consumer Values," *Advertising Age* (March 22, 1993): 23.
14. Hannah Karp, "Red Bull Aims at an Older Crowd," *Wall Street Journal* (June 7, 2004): B3.
15. Jack Neff, "Crest Spinoff Targets Women," *Advertising Age* (June 3, 2002): 1.
16. Charles M. Schaninger and William D. Danko, "A Conceptual and Empirical Comparison of Alternative Household Life Cycle Models," *Journal of Consumer Research* 19 (March 1993): 580–94; Robert E. Wilkes, "Household Life-Cycle Stages, Transitions, and Product Expenditures," *Journal of Consumer Research* 22 (June 1995): 27–42.
17. Richard P. Coleman, "The Continuing Significance of Social Class to Marketing," *Journal of Consumer Research* 10 (December 1983): 265–80.
18. Motoko Rich, "Region's Marketers Hop on the Bubba Bandwagon," *Wall Street Journal Interactive Edition* (May 19, 1999).
19. Sarah Ellison, "Prilosec OTC Blitz by P&G Represents New Drug Foray," *Wall Street Journal* (September 12, 2003), www.wsj.com, accessed September 12, 2003.
20. Constance L. Hayes, "What Wal-Mart Knows About Customers' Habits," *New York Times* (November 14, 2004), www.nytimes.com, accessed November 14, 2004.
21. Mylene Mangalindan, "Hollywood's 'Wedding Crashers' Inspires the Invitationless," *Wall Street Journal* (December 28, 2005): B1.
22. Suzanne Vranica and Chad Terhune, "Mixing Diet Coke and Mentos Makes a Gusher of Publicity," *Wall Street Journal* (June 12, 2006): B1.
23. Michael Learmonth, "Brands Team Up for User-Generated-Ad Contest:Ten Marketers to Launch Creative Competition That Will Culminate at Cannes," *Advertising Age* (March 23, 2009), www.adage .com, accessed March 23, 2009.
24. Thomas Vinciguerra, "Soft, Chewy and Taking Over the World," *New York Times* (July 5, 2006): Sec. 4, p. 2.
25. Quoted in "Bringing Meaning to Brands," *American Demographics* (June 1997): 34.
26. Erving Goffman, *The Presentation of Self in Everyday Life* (Garden City, NY: Doubleday, 1959); George H. Mead, *Mind, Self, and Society* (Chicago: University of Chicago Press, 1934); Michael R. Solomon, "The Role of Products as Social Stimuli: A Symbolic Interactionism Perspective," *Journal of Consumer Research* 10 (December 1983): 319–29.
27. Jennifer Aaker, Susan Fournier, and S. Adam Brasel, "When Good Brands Do Bad," *Journal of Consumer Research* 31 (2004): 1–16.
28. Susan Fournier, "Consumers and Their Brands. Developing Relationship Theory in Consumer Research," *Journal of Consumer Research* 24 (March 1998): 343–73.
29. Brad Edmondson, "The Dawn of the Megacity," *Marketing Tools* (March 1999): 64.
30. David Barbosa, "China, New Land of Shoppers, Builds Malls on Gigantic Scale," *New York Times* (May 25, 2005), www.nytimes.com, accessed May 25, 2005.
31. For a discussion of this trend, see Russell W. Belk, "Hyperreality and Globalization: Culture in the Age of Ronald McDonald," *Journal of International Consumer Marketing* 8 (1995): 23–38.
32. Ronald Alsop, "Best-Known Companies Aren't Always Best Liked," *Wall Street Journal* (November 15, 2004): B4.
33. Richard T. Watson, Leyland F. Pitt, Pierre Berthon, and George M. Zinkhan, "U-Commerce: Expanding the Universe of Marketing," *Journal of the Academy of Marketing Science* 30 (2002): 333–47.
34. "I.B.M. Unveils 'Smart' Laundry," *New York Times* (August 30, 2002), www.nytimes.com, accessed August 30, 2002.
35. Some material in this section was adapted from Michael R. Solomon and Elnora W. Stuart, *Welcome to Marketing.com: The Brave New World of E-Commerce* (Upper Saddle River, NJ: Prentice Hall, 2000).
36. Patricia Winters Lauro, "Marketing Battle for Online Dating," *New York Times* (January 27, 2003), www.nytimes.com, accessed January 27, 2003.
37. Rebecca Fairley Raney, "Study Finds Internet of Social Benefit to Users," *New York Times* (May 11, 2000), www.nytimes.com, accessed May 11, 2000.
38. John Markoff, "Portrait of a Newer, Lonelier Crowd Is Captured in an Internet Survey," *New York Times* (February 16, 2000), www.nytimes .com, accessed February 16, 2000.
39. Lisa Guernsey, "Professor Who Once Found Isolation Online Has a Change of Heart," *New York Times* (July 26, 2001), www.nytimes.com, accessed July 26, 2001.
40. Travis Reed, "Spirit Airlines Employees Upset Over Sexy Ads, Beer Uniforms," *Huffington Post* (January 28, 2009), www.huffingtonpost .com/2009/01/28/spirit-airlines-employees_n_162043.html, accessed June 28, 2009.
41. "Cash-Strapped Teacher Sells Ads on Tests," *CNN* (December 4, 2008), www.cnn.com/2008/LIVING/12/03/teacher.ads.on.tests/ index.html?eref=rss_us, accessed December 4, 2008.
42. Charles Sheehan, "Upcoming Comic Features Real-Life Marriage Proposal," *Montgomery Advertiser* (February 24, 2002).
43. Stuart Elliott, "Would You Like Fries with That Monopoly Game?" *New York Times* (September 12, 2006), www.nytimes.com, accessed September 12, 2006.
44. Edward Wyatt, "Times Are Tough on Wall Street and Wisteria Lane," *New York Times* (March 11, 2009), http://nytimes.com/2009/03/.../ 12plot.html?..., accessed March 11, 2009.
45. "Woman in Wendy's Finger Case Is Arrested," *New York Times* (April 22, 2005), www.nytimes.com, accessed April 22, 2005.
46. Reported in *American Demographics* (December 1999): 18.
47. Valerie S. Folkes and Michael A. Kamins, "Effects of Information About Firms' Ethical and Unethical Actions on Consumers' Attitudes," *Journal of Consumer Psychology* 8 (1999): 243–59.
48. Jacqueline N. Hood and Jeanne M. Logsdon, "Business Ethics in the NAFTA Countries: A Cross-Cultural Comparison," *Journal of Business Research* 55 (2002): 883–90.
49. Barbara Crossette, "Russia and China Called Top Business Bribers," *New York Times* (May 17, 2002), www.nytimes.com, accessed May 17, 2002. For more details about the survey see www.transparency.org.
50. Quoted in Ira Teinowitz, "Lawsuit: Menthol Smokes Illegally Targeted to Blacks," *Advertising Age* (November 2, 1998): 16.
51. Pamela Paul, "Mixed Signals," *American Demographics* (July 2001): 44.
52. R. Harris, "Most Customers Using Internet Fail to Read Retailers' Privacy Policies," *Ventura County Star* (June 6, 2002).
53. Quoted in Jennifer Lach, "The New Gatekeepers," *American Demographics* (June 1999): 41–42.
54. Michael R. Solomon, *Conquering Consumerspace: Marketing Strategies for a Branded World* (New York: AMACOM, 2003).

55. Jeffrey Ball, "Religious Leaders to Discuss SUVs with GM, Ford Officials," *Wall Street Journal Interactive Edition* (November 19, 2002); Danny Hakim, "The S.U.V. Is a Beast, and It's Hairy, Too," *New York Times* (February 2, 2005), www.nytimes.com, accessed February 2, 2005; www.nrpe.org/issues, accessed May 11, 2009.

56. William Leiss, Stephen Kline, and Sut Jhally, *Social Communication in Advertising: Persons, Products, and Images of Well-Being* (Toronto: Methuen, 1986); Jerry Mander, *Four Arguments for the Elimination of Television* (New York: William Morrow, 1977).

57. Packard (1957); quoted in Leiss et al., *Social Communication*, 11.

58. Raymond Williams, *Problems in Materialism and Culture: Selected Essays* (London: Verso, 1980).

59. Leiss et al., *Social Communication*.

60. George Stigler, "The Economics of Information," *Journal of Political Economy* (1961): 69.

61. Leiss et al., *Social Communication*, 11.

62. Robert V. Kozinets and Jay M. Handelman, "Adversaries of Consumption: Consumer Movements, Activism, and Ideology," *Journal of Consumer Research* 31 (December 2004): 691–704.

63. Natasha Singer, "A Birth Control Pill That Promised Too Much," *New York Times* (February 10, 2009), www.nytimes.com, accessed February 10, 2009.

64. Todd Wasserman, "Excedrin's Latest Headache," *Brandweek* (March 18, 2009), http://brandweek.com/.../e3ifaa96df164907....

65. "Adbusters," Adbusters Media Foundation, www.adbusters.org, accessed June 29, 2009.

66. Ibid.

67. www.nikesweatshop.net, accessed June 29, 2002.

68. Nat Ives, "Anti-Ad Group Tries Advertising," *New York Times* (September 21, 2004), www.nytimes.com, accessed September 21, 2004.

69. Julie L. Ozanne and Bige Saatcioglu. "Participatory Action Research." *Journal of Consumer Research*, 35 (October 2008): 423–39.

70. For consumer research and discussions related to public policy issues, see Paul N. Bloom and Stephen A. Greyser, "The Maturing of Consumerism," *Harvard Business Review* (November–December 1981): 130–39; George S. Day, "Assessing the Effect of Information Disclosure Requirements," *Journal of Marketing* (April 1976): 42–52; Dennis E. Garrett, "The Effectiveness of Marketing Policy Boycotts: Environmental Opposition to Marketing," *Journal of Marketing* 51 (January 1987): 44–53; Michael Houston and Michael Rothschild, "Policy-Related Experiments on Information Provision: A Normative Model and Explication," *Journal of Marketing Research* 17 (November 1980): 432–49; Jacob Jacoby, Wayne D. Hoyer, and David A. Sheluga, *Misperception of Televised Communications* (New York: American Association of Advertising Agencies, 1980); Gene R. Laczniak and Patrick E. Murphy, *Marketing Ethics: Guidelines for Managers* (Lexington, MA: Lexington Books, 1985): 117–23; Lynn Phillips and Bobby Calder, "Evaluating Consumer Protection Laws: Promising Methods," *Journal of Consumer Affairs* 14 (Summer 1980): 9–36; Donald P. Robin and Eric Reidenbach, "Social Responsibility, Ethics, and Marketing Strategy: Closing the Gap Between Concept and Application," *Journal of Marketing* 51 (January 1987): 44–58; Howard Schutz and Marianne Casey, "Consumer Perceptions of Advertising as Misleading," *Journal of Consumer Affairs* 15 (Winter 1981): 340–57; Darlene Brannigan Smith and Paul N. Bloom, "Is Consumerism Dead or Alive? Some New Evidence," in Thomas C. Kinnear, ed., *Advances in Consumer Research* 11 (1984): 369–73.

71. cf. Philip Kotler and Alan R. Andreasen, *Strategic Marketing for Nonprofit Organizations*, 4th ed. (Upper Saddle River, NJ: Prentice Hall, 1991); Jeff B. Murray and Julie L. Ozanne, "The Critical Imagination: Emancipatory Interests in Consumer Research," *Journal of Consumer Research* 18 (September 1991): 192–244; William D. Wells, "Discovery-Oriented Consumer Research," *Journal of Consumer Research* 19 (March 1993): 489–504.

72. Karl Greenberg, "American Airlines, AAPD To Create Positive Ads Featuring Disabled People," *Marketing Daily* (March 30, 2009), www.mediapost.com, accessed March 30, 2009.

73. "Concerned Consumers Push for Environmentally Friendly Packaging," *Boxboard Containers* (April 1993): 4.

74. Jack Neff, "Lawsuit: Marketing Blamed in Wal-Mart Trampling Death," *Advertising Age* (December 4, 2008), www.adage.com, accessed December 4, 2008; www.Freerepublic.Com/Focus/F-News/ 2142920/ Posts, accessed December 4, 2008.

75. "Japan Calls for Tighter Food Security Against Mad Cow Disease," *Xinhua News Agency* (May 20, 2002), cited June 29, 2002, www .xinhuanet.com/English, accessed June 29, 2002.

76. Kenneth E. Nusbaum, James C. Wright, and Michael R. Solomon, "Attitudes of Food Animal Veterinarians to Continuing Education in Agriterrorism," paper presented at the 53rd Annual Meeting of the Animal Disease Research Workers in Southern States, University of Florida (February 2001).

77. Betty Mohr, "The Pepsi Challenge: Managing a Crisis," *Prepared Foods* (March 1994): 13.

78. "Boston Officials Livid over Ad Stunt," *New York Times* (February 1, 2007), www.nytimes.com, accessed February 1, 2007.

79. Martin Fackler, "In Korea, A Boot Camp Cure for Web Obsession," *New York Times* (November 18, 2007), www.nytimes.com/2007/11/18/ Technology/18rehab.Html, accessed November 19, 2007.

80. Derek N. Hassay and Malcolm C. Smith, "Compulsive Buying: An Examination of the Consumption Motive," *Psychology & Marketing* 13 (December 1996): 741–52.

81. Thomas C. O'Guinn and Ronald J. Faber, "Compulsive Buying: A Phenomenological Explanation," *Journal of Consumer Research* 16 (September 1989): 154.

82. Curtis L. Taylor, "Guys Who Buy, Buy, Buy," *Newsday* (October 6, 2006); Jim Thornton, "Buy Now, Pay Later," *Men's Health* (December, 2004): 109–12.

83. Georgia Witkin, "The Shopping Fix," *Health* (May 1988): 73; see also Arch G. Woodside and Randolph J. Trappey III, "Compulsive Consumption of a Consumer Service: An Exploratory Study of Chronic Horse Race Track Gambling Behavior," working paper #90-MKTG-04, A. B. Freeman School of Business, Tulane University, 1990; Rajan Nataraajan and Brent G. Goff, "Manifestations of Compulsiveness in the Consumer-Marketplace Domain," *Psychology & Marketing* 9 (January 1992): 31–44; Joann Ellison Rodgers, "Addiction: A Whole New View," *Psychology Today* (September–October 1994): 32.

84. Matthew Creamer, "Pepsi Opens a Vein of Controversy with New Suicide-Themed Ads; Prints Ad Depict A Cartoonish Calorie Offing Itself," *Advertising Age* (December 2, 2008), http://Adage.Com/ Globalideanetwork/Post?Article_Id=132952; accessed December 3, 2008.

85. Helen Reynolds, *The Economics of Prostitution* (Springfield, IL: Thomas, 1986).

86. Patrick Di Justo, "How to Sell Your Body for $46 Million," *Wired* (August 2003): 47.

87. Amy Harmon, "Illegal Kidney Auction Pops Up on eBay's Site," *New York Times* (September 3, 1999), www.nytimes.com, accessed September 3, 1999.

88. Di Justo, "How to Sell Your Body for $46 Million," 47.

89. REUTERS, "German Parents Offer Baby on eBay," *New York Times* (May 25, 2008), www.nytimes.com/2008/05/25/world/europe/ 25ebayby.html?_r=1&scp=1&sq=baby..., accessed May 25, 2008.

90. "Advertisers Face Up to the New Morality: Making the Pitch," *Bloomberg* (July 8, 1997).

91. "Crimes of the Virtual Kind," *Times of London* (December 2, 2007), www.thetimes.co.za/PrintEdition/Lifestyle/Article.aspx?id=640972, accessed December 2, 2007.

92. "Shoplifting: Bess Myerson's Arrest Highlights a Multibillion-Dollar Problem That Many Stores Won't Talk About," *Life* (August 1988): 32.

93. "New Survey Shows Shoplifting Is a Year-Round Problem," *Business Wire* (April 12, 1994).

94. "Customer Not King, but Thief," *Marketing News* (December 9, 2002): 4.

95. Catherine A. Cole, "Deterrence and Consumer Fraud," *Journal of Retailing* 65 (Spring 1989): 107–20; Stephen J. Grove, Scott J. Vitell, and David Strutton, "Non-Normative Consumer Behavior and the Techniques of Neutralization," in Terry Childers et al., eds., *Marketing Theory and Practice*, 1989 AMA Winter Educators' Conference (Chicago: American Marketing Association, 1989): 131–35.

96. Mark Curnutte, "The Scope of the Shoplifting Problems," *Gannett News Service* (November 29, 1997).

97. Anthony D. Cox, Dena Cox, Ronald D. Anderson, and George P. Moschis, "Social Influences on Adolescent Shoplifting—Theory, Evidence, and Implications for the Retail Industry," *Journal of Retailing* 69 (Summer 1993): 234–46.

98. Stephanie Kang, "New Return Policy: Retailers Say 'No' to Serial Exchangers," *Wall Street Journal* (November 29, 2004): B1.

99. www.dogdoo.com, accessed June 12, 2007.

100. Suzanne Vranica, "Ad Houses Will Need to Be More Nimble, Clients Are Demanding More and Better Use of Consumer Data, Web," *Wall Street Journal* (January 2, 2008): B3.

101. Jack Neff, "Mucus to Maxi Pads: Marketing's Dirtiest Jobs, Frank Talk About Diapers and Condoms Lifts Taboos and Helps Make a

Difference in Consumers' Lives, Say Those in the Trenches, *Advertising Age* (February 17, 2009), www.adage.com, accessed February 17, 2009.

102. Morris B. Holbrook, "The Consumer Researcher Visits Radio City: Dancing in the Dark," in Elizabeth C. Hirschman and Morris B. Holbrook, eds., *Advances in Consumer Research* 12 (Provo, UT: Association for Consumer Research, 1985): 28–31.

103. For a recent overview, see Eric J. Arnould and Craig J. Thompson, "Consumer Culture Theory (CCT): Twenty Years of Research," *Journal of Consumer Research* 31 (March 2005): 868–82.

104. Alladi Venkatesh, "Postmodernism, Poststructuralism and Marketing," paper presented at the American Marketing Association Winter Theory Conference, San Antonio, February 1992; see also Stella Proctor, Ioanna Papasolomou-Doukakis, and Tony Proctor, "What Are Television Advertisements Really Trying to Tell Us? A Postmodern Perspective," *Journal of Consumer Behavior* 1 (February 2002): 246–55; A. Fuat Firat and Alladi Venkatesh, "The Making of Postmodern Consumption," in Russell W. Belk and Nikhilesh Dholakia, eds., *Consumption and Marketing: Macro Dimensions* (Boston: PWS-Kent, 1993).

105. Pam Belluck, "Toy's Message of Affection Draws Anger and Publicity," *New York Times* (January 22, 2005), www.nytimes.com, accessed January 22, 2005.

106. Natalie Zmuda, "Children's Hospital in Hot Water over Corporate Sponsorships, Critics Dismayed by Association with Racy Retailer Abercrombie & Fitch," *Advertising Age* (March 12, 2008), www.adage.com, accessed March 12, 2008.

107. Andrew Keen, *The Cult of the Amateur: How Today's Internet Is Killing Our Culture* (New York: Currency 2007).

108. Kevin Maney, "Drivers Let Big Brother in to Get a Break," *Ethics* (August 9, 2004): 1B.

Section 2 Consumers as Individuals

In this section, we focus on the internal dynamics of consumers. Although "no man is an island," each of us is to some degree a self-contained receptor of information about the outside world. Advertising messages, products, and other people constantly confront us—not to mention personal thoughts about ourselves that make us happy or sad. Each chapter in this section considers a different aspect of the individual that is "invisible" to others—but of vital importance to ourselves.

Chapter 2 describes the process of perception, where we absorb and interpret information about products and other people from the outside world. Chapter 3 focuses on the way we mentally store this information and how it adds to our existing knowledge about the world during the learning process. Chapter 4 discusses our reasons or motivations to absorb this information and how our cultural values influence what we do.

Chapter 5 explores how our views about ourselves—particularly our sexuality and our physical appearance—affect what we do, want, and buy. Chapter 6 goes on to consider how people's individual personalities influence these decisions and how the choices we make in terms of products, services, and leisure activities help to define our lifestyles.

Chapter 7 discusses how marketers form and change our attitudes—our evaluations of all these products and messages—and how we as individual consumers engage in an ongoing dialogue with the marketplace.

CHAPTERS AHEAD

2

Perception

When you finish this chapter you will understand:

Chapter
Objectives

*T*he European vacation has been wonderful, and this stop in Lisbon is no exception. Still, after 2 weeks of eating his way through some of the Continent's finest pastry shops and restaurants, Gary's getting a bit of a craving for his family's favorite snack—a good old American box of Oreos and an ice-cold carton of milk. Unbeknownst to his wife, Janeen, he had stashed away some cookies "just in case"—this was the time to break them out.

Now, all he needs is the milk. On an impulse, Gary decides to surprise Janeen with a midafternoon treat. He sneaks out of the hotel room while she's napping and finds the nearest *grosa.* When he heads to the small refrigerated section, though, he's puzzled—no milk here. Undaunted, Gary asks the clerk, *"Leite, por favor?"* The clerk quickly smiles and points to a rack in the middle of the store piled with little white square boxes. No, that can't be right—Gary resolves to work on his Portuguese. He repeats the question, and again he gets the same answer.

Finally, he investigates and sure enough he sees the boxes with labels saying they contain something called ultra heat treated (UHT) milk. Nasty! Who in the world would drink milk out of a little box that's been sitting on a warm shelf for who knows how long? Gary dejectedly returns to the hotel, his snack time fantasies crumbling like so many stale cookies.

1

OBJECTIVE

Why is perception a three-stage process that translates raw stimuli into meaning?

Sensory Systems

Gary would be surprised to learn that many people in the world drink milk out of a box every day. UHT is pasteurized milk that has been heated until the bacteria that cause it to spoil are destroyed, and it can last for 5 to 6 months without refrigeration if its aseptic container is unopened. The milk tastes slightly sweeter than fresh milk but otherwise it's basically the same stuff.

Shelf-stable milk is particularly popular in Europe, where refrigerator space in homes is smaller and stores tend to carry less inventory than in the United States. Seven out of ten Europeans drink it routinely. Manufacturers continue to try to crack the U.S. market as well, though analysts are dubious about their prospects. To begin with, milk consumption in the United States is declining steadily as teenagers choose soft drinks instead. Indeed, the Milk Industry Foundation pumped $44 million into an advertising campaign to promote milk drinking ("Got Milk?").

But it's even harder to entice Americans to drink milk out of a box. In focus groups, U.S. consumers say they have trouble believing the milk is not spoiled or unsafe. In addition, they consider the square, quart-sized boxes more suitable for dry food. Many schools and fast-food chains already buy UHT milk because of its' long shelf life.[1] Still, although Americans may not think twice about drinking a McFlurry from McDonald's made with shelf-stable milk, it's going to be a long, uphill battle to change their perceptions about the proper partner for a bagful of Oreos.

Whether it's the taste of Oreos, the sight of an Obsession perfume ad, or the sound of the music group OutKast, we live in a world overflowing with sensations. Wherever we turn, we are bombarded by a symphony of colors, sounds, and odors. Some of the "notes" in this symphony occur naturally, such as the loud barking of a dog, the shades of the evening sky, or the heady smell of a rose bush. Others come from people: The person who plops down next to you in class might sport tinted blonde hair, bright pink pants, and enough nasty perfume to make your eyes water.

Marketers certainly contribute to this commotion. Consumers are never far from advertisements, product packages, radio and television commercials, and billboards—all clamoring for our attention. Sometimes we go out of our way to experience "unusual" sensations, whether they are thrills from bungee jumping; playing virtual reality games; or going to theme parks such as Universal Studios, which offers "Fear Factor Live" attractions that ask vacationers to swallow gross things or perform stomach-churning stunts.[2]

Reality shows like *Survivor* attract people who want to test the limits of their sensations. On a popular Peruvian TV show called *Laura en America,* contestants show just what people are capable of experiencing (with the right incentive): For $20, two women stripped to their underwear and had buckets of slime and toads poured over their bodies. For the same amount, three men raced to gobble down bowls of large tree grubs from the Amazon jungle. For $30, a woman licked the armpits of a sweaty bodybuilder who had not bathed for 2 days.[3] And you thought college fraternity stunts were out there?

Game-show contestants or not, each of us copes with the bombardment of sensations by paying attention to some stimuli and tuning out others. The messages to which we *do* choose to pay attention often wind up differing from what the sponsors intended, as we each put our personal "spin" on things by adopting meanings consistent with our own unique experiences, biases, and desires. This chapter focuses on the process of perception, in which the consumer absorbs sensations and then uses these to interpret the surrounding world.

Sensation refers to the immediate response of our sensory receptors (eyes, ears, nose, mouth, fingers) to basic stimuli such as light, color, sound, odor, and texture. **Perception** is the process by which people select, organize, and interpret these sensations. The study of perception, then, focuses on what we *add* to these raw sensations in order to give them meaning.

Gary's encounter with milk in a box illustrates the perceptual process. He has learned to equate the cold temperature of refrigerated milk with freshness, so he experienced a negative physical reaction when confronted with a product that contradicted his expectations. Gary's evaluation was affected by factors such as the design of the package, the brand name, and even the section in the grocery store in which the milk was displayed. These expectations are largely affected by a consumer's cultural background. Europeans do not necessarily have the same perceptions of milk as Americans, and as a result their reactions to the product differ quite a bit from those of Americans.

Like computers, we undergo stages of *information processing* in which we input and store stimuli. Unlike computers, though, we do not passively process whatever information happens to be present. In the first place, we notice only a very small number of the stimuli in our environment. Of those we do notice we attend to an even smaller number. And we might not process the stimuli that do enter consciousness objectively. Each individual interprets the meaning of a stimulus to be consistent with his or her own unique biases, needs, and experiences. As Figure 2.1 shows, these three stages of exposure, attention, and interpretation make up the process of perception. Before considering each of these stages, let's step back and look at the sensory systems that provide sensations to us in the first place.

We receive external stimuli, or *sensory inputs*, on a number of channels. We may see a billboard, hear a jingle, feel the softness of a cashmere sweater, taste a new flavor of ice cream, or smell a leather jacket. The inputs our five senses detect are the raw data that begin the perceptual process. For example, sensory data emanating from the external environment (e.g., hearing a tune on the radio) can generate internal sensory experiences when the song triggers a young man's memory of his first dance and brings to mind the smell of his date's perfume or the feel of her hair on his cheek.

The unique sensory quality of a product helps it to stand out from the competition, especially if the brand creates a unique association with the sensation. The Owens-Corning Fiberglass Corporation was the first company to trademark a color when it used bright pink for its insulation material; it adopted the Pink Panther as its spokescharacter. Harley-Davidson actually tried to trademark the distinctive sound a "hog" makes when it revs up.[4] These responses are an important part of **hedonic consumption:** multisensory, fantasy, and emotional aspects of consumers' interactions with products.[5]

Figure 2.1 AN OVERVIEW OF THE PERCEPTUAL PROCESS

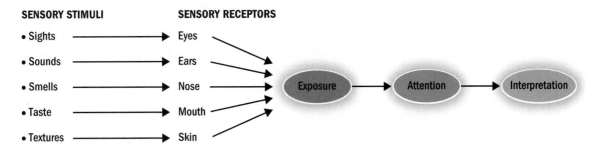

2
OBJECTIVE
Why is the design of a
product today a key
driver of its success or
failure?

Hedonic Consumption and the Design Economy

In recent years, the sensory experiences we receive from products and services play an even bigger role when we choose among competing options. As manufacturing costs go down and the amount of "stuff" that people accumulate goes up, consumers increasingly want to buy things that will give them hedonic value in addition to simply doing what they're designed to do. A Dilbert comic strip poked fun at this trend when it featured a product designer who declared: "Quality is yesterday's news. Today we focus on the emotional impact of the product." Fun aside, the new focus on emotional experience is consistent with psychological research that finds that people prefer additional experiences to additional possessions as their incomes rise.[6]

In this environment, form *is* function. Two young entrepreneurs named Adam Lowry and Eric Ryan discovered that basic truth when they quit their day jobs to develop a line of house-cleaning products they called Method. Cleaning products—what a yawn, right?

But, think again: For years companies such as Procter & Gamble have plodded along, peddling boring boxes of soap powder to generations of housewives who suffered in silence, scrubbing and buffing, yearning for the daily respite of martini time. Lowry and Ryan gambled that they could offer an alternative—cleaners in exotic scents such as cucumber, lavender, and ylang-ylang that come in aesthetically pleasing bottles. The bet paid off. Within 2 years, the partners were cleaning up, taking in more than $2 million in revenue. Shortly thereafter, they hit it big when Target contracted to sell Method products in its stores.[7]

There's a method to Target's madness. Design is no longer the province of upper-crust sophisticates who never got close enough to a cleaning product to be revolted by it. The red-hot store chain has helped to make designers such as Karim Rashid, Michael Graves, Philippe Starck, Todd Oldham, and Isaac Mizrahi household names. Mass-market consumers thirst for great design, and they reward those companies that give it to them with their enthusiastic patronage and loyalty. From razor blades such as the Gillette Sensor to the Apple iPhone and even to the lowly trash can, design *is* substance.

Sensory Marketing: Harnessing Perception for Competitive Advantage

When guests at Omni luxury hotels visit the hotel chain's Web site to reserve a room, they hear the sound of soft chimes playing. The signature scent of lemongrass and green tea hits them as they enter the lobby. In their rooms, they will find eucalyptus bath salts and Sensation Bars; minibars stocked with items such as mojito-flavored jelly beans and miniature Zen gardens. In a joint promotion with Starbucks, guests find small scented stickers on the front pages of their free copies of *USA Today*; a blackberry aroma suggests they start their day at the hotel with a cup of Starbucks coffee "paired with a fresh muffin."[8]

Welcome to the new era of **sensory marketing**, where companies pay extra attention to the impact of sensations on our product experiences. From hotels to carmakers to brewers, they recognize that our senses help us to decide which products appeal to us—and which ones stand out from a host of similar offerings in the marketplace. In this section, we'll take a closer look at how some smart marketers use our sensory systems to create a competitive advantage.

Vision

Philips makes its electronics products thinner and more colorful to impart a more youthful feel to the technology. Its audio products used to be all silver, but now each component comes in four vibrant colors such as electric green.[9] Marketers rely heavily on visual elements in advertising, store design, and packaging. They

CB AS I SEE IT

Professor Aradhna Krishna, *University of Michigan*

*W*hat is *sensory marketing*, what makes it important, and why is it so fascinating? I define it as "marketing that engages the consumers' senses and affects their behavior." The sensory characteristics of products such as the touch, smell, taste, sound, and look of products have a large impact on consumer behavior. These sensory inputs affect how we feel, how we think, what we remember, what we like, and even how we choose and use products. Specifically, by emphasizing the sensory characteristics of products and services, or even creating new sensations entirely, we can greatly enhance consumers' attitudes, perceptions, and satisfaction.

This concept of sensory marketing has received great attention from many top companies. Advertising within the food industry alone provides some illustrative examples as companies try to incorporate more senses than just taste into their product experiences. A new brand of chewing gum that produces a seemingly one-dimensional sensory experience (taste) is named "5" for all five senses, and the tagline again

incorporates this approach ("stimulate your senses"). Other examples include ads for Magnum 5 Senses Ice Cream and Denny's breakfast (". . .taste it with all five senses. . ."). Other products that provide a single sensory experience also try to stimulate the other senses. Axe Dark Temptation deodorant spray is advertised with an irresistible chocolate man that appeals to all the girls ("Become as irresistible as chocolate"). Even electronic products want to stimulate our senses with names like BlackBerry, Chocolate, and Touch.

With this increasing attention to sensory marketing, products and businesses need to act quickly to establish a **sensory signature**. Managers need to ask themselves— "Is there something about my brand that leaves a sensory impression in people's mind?" What sensory characteristic of their product sticks with consumers, helping them to remember the product in a positively unique way? Do they emphasize a sensory experience with the product, or have they constructed a new one entirely? Do they own a sensory experience and thus establish a sensory signature? A terrific example of a company with a definitive sensory signature, and consequently one of the most commonly cited by consultants in this area is Singapore Airlines. The

airline focuses on creating a distinct visual signature, but perhaps more interesting and memorable is its signature aroma, Floridian Waters. This fragrance was developed specifically for use by Singapore Airlines, and is infused into their hot towels, dispersed throughout the planes, and even worn by flight attendants. The smell is not only invigorating; it also remains in passengers' minds, leading to positive responses upon future exposure to the aroma.

Sensory signatures are just one aspect of sensory marketing. Managers need to look at their offerings and ask themselves whether they can emphasize any sensory aspect of the product to make the product more appealing or create a new sensation completely. Examples of the latter are Dippin' Dots, where the company's Web site claims that *"After overcoming the sight of their ice cream beads "pouring" into a cup there's the look of amazement that ice cream can be "tingly and almost crunchy" (their words!). When the smooth, creamy ice cream begins to melt in their mouth . . . a fan is born!"* or the new fish spas that are opening all over the world where tiny fish bite the dead skin off customers' feet and offer a different type of pedicure. There's more than one path to a distinctive sensory experience!

communicate meanings on the *visual channel* through a product's color, size, and styling.

Colors may even influence our emotions more directly. Evidence suggests that some colors (particularly red) create feelings of arousal and stimulate appetite, and others (such as blue) create more relaxing feelings—American Express launched its Blue card after its research found that people describe the color as "providing a sense of limitlessness and peace."[10] Advertisements of products presented against a backdrop of blue are better liked than when shown against a red background, and cross-cultural research indicates a consistent preference for blue whether people live in Canada or Hong Kong.[11]

People who complete tasks when the words or images appear on red backgrounds perform better when they have to remember details, while they excel at tasks that require an imaginative response when these are displayed on blue backgrounds. Olympic athletes who wear red uniforms are more likely to defeat competitors in blue uniforms, and men rate women who wear red as more attractive

This Finnish ad emphasizes the sensual reasons to visit the city of Helsinki.
Source: Used with permission of The City of Helsinki Information office.

Come to your senses.
Feel Helsinki.

than those who wear blue. In one study, interior designers created bars decorated primarily in red, yellow, or blue and people were invited to choose one to hang out in. More people chose the yellow and red rooms, and these guests were more social and active— and ate more. But, partygoers in the blue room stayed longer.[12] Maybe the moral is: Get your prof to give you multiple choice exams on red paper, essays on blue paper, celebrate afterward in a red room, and then recuperate from the party in a blue room.

Some reactions to color come from learned associations. In Western countries, black is the color of mourning, whereas in some Eastern countries, notably Japan, white plays this role. In addition, we associate the color black with power. Teams in both the National Football League and the National Hockey League who wear black uniforms are among the most aggressive; they consistently rank near the top of their leagues in penalties during the season.[13]

In Western culture the color black is often associated with sophistication while white connotes innocence.
Source: Used with permission of the San Francisco Ballet.

Other reactions are a result of biological and cultural differences. Women are drawn toward brighter tones and they are more sensitive to subtle shadings and patterns. Some scientists attribute this to biology because females see color better than males do and men are 16 times more likely to be color blind. Age also influences our responsiveness to color. As we get older, our eyes mature and our vision takes on a yellow cast. Colors look duller to older people, so they prefer white and other bright tones. This helps to explain why mature consumers are much more likely to choose a white car—Lexus, which sells heavily in this market, makes 60 percent of its vehicles in white. The trend toward brighter and more complex colors also reflects the increasingly multicultural makeup of the United States. For example, Hispanics tend to prefer brighter colors as a reflection of the intense lighting conditions in Latin America; strong colors keep their character in strong sunlight.[14] That's why Procter & Gamble uses brighter colors in makeup it sells in Latin countries.[15]

Scientists and philosophers talked about the meanings of colors since the time of Socrates in the fifth century B.C., but it took Sir Isaac Newton in the early seventeenth century to shine light through a prism and reveal the color spectrum. Even then, Newton's observations weren't totally scientific; he identified seven major colors to be consistent with the number of planets known at that time, as well as the seven notes of the diatonic scale.

We now know that perceptions of a color depend on both its physical wavelength and how the mind responds to that stimulus. Yellow is in the middle of wavelengths the human eye can detect so it is the brightest and attracts attention. The *Yellow Pages* originally were colored yellow to heighten the attention level of bored telephone operators.[16] However, our culture and even our language affect the colors we see. For example, the Welsh language has no words that correspond to green, blue, gray, or brown in English, but it uses other colors that English speakers don't (including one that covers part of green, part of gray, and the whole of our blue). Hungarian has two words for what we call red; Navajo has a single word for blue and green, but two words for black.[17]

Because colors elicit such strong emotional reactions, obviously the choice of a *color palette* is a key issue in package design. These choices used to be made casually. For example, Campbell's Soup made its familiar can in red and white because a company executive liked the football uniforms at Cornell University!

Today, however, color choices are a serious business. These decisions help to "color" our expectations of what's inside the package. When it launched a white cheese as a "sister product" to an existing blue "Castello" cheese, a Danish company introduced it in a red package under the name of Castello Bianco. They chose this color to provide maximum visibility on store shelves. Although taste tests were very positive, sales were disappointing. A subsequent analysis of consumer interpretations showed that the red packaging and the name gave the consumers wrong associations with the product type and its degree of sweetness. Danish consumers had trouble associating the color red with the white cheese. Also, the name "Bianco" connoted a sweetness that was incompatible with the actual taste of the product. The company relaunched it in a white package and named it "White Castello." Almost immediately, sales more than doubled.[18]

Some color combinations come to be so strongly associated with a corporation that they become known as the company's **trade dress**, and the company may even be granted exclusive use of these colors. For example, Eastman Kodak has successfully protected its trade dress of yellow, black, and red in court. As a rule, however, judges grant trade dress protection only when consumers might be confused about what they buy because of similar coloration of a competitor's packages.[19]

Of course, fashion trends strongly influence our color preferences so it's no surprise that we tend to encounter a "hot" color on clothing and in home designs in one season that something else replaces the next season (as when the *fashionistas* proclaim: "Brown is the new black!"). These styles do not happen by accident; most people don't know (but now *you* do) that a handful of firms produce *color forecasts* that manufacturers and retailers buy so they can be sure they stock up on the next hot hue. For example, Pantone, Inc. (one of these color arbiters), lists these colors as among its favorites for Spring 2010: Amparo Blue, Violet, Coral Fusion, and Pink Champagne.[20]

Dollars and Scents

We've all heard of "the Axe Effect" after we've been bombarded with commercials that show women chasing men who use Unilever's personal-care brand. Can it possibly be for real? A British researcher reported that women rated men as more attractive when they used Lynx deodorant (Axe's British counterpart) than when they reacted to men who used a "placebo" deodorant with no fragrance. Before you run out to the store, guys, keep in mind that the women didn't actually meet the men face-to-face; they watched 15-second videos the men made describing themselves. The men in the videos were instructed not to bathe for 48 hours, and those who used the unfra-

Tak akan terjadi dengan *Harpist*

granced deodorant to hide their "scent" rated themselves lower in self-confidence than did the Lynx users. A Unilever consumer scientist explained, "Deodorant is supposed to make you feel good about yourself and give you confidence in the mating game, which is what Axe says." Important note: The Axe effect only worked for women who watched the videos with no sound—those who actually heard the men talk didn't show a preference, which supports the idea that self-confidence translated into body language that in turn translated into attractiveness. As the researcher joked, "One way you could look at it is that the Axe Effect works as long as you're very quiet."[21]

Odors stir emotions or create a calming feeling. They invoke memories or relieve stress. One study found that consumers who viewed ads for either flowers or chocolate and who also were exposed to flowery or chocolaty odors spent more time processing the product information and were more likely to try different alternatives within each product category.[22] Many consumers control the odors in their environments and this growing interest has spawned a lot of new products since Glade marketed the first air freshener to suburban families in 1956. Today, younger people are at the forefront of scented air as they take advantage of plug-ins, fragrance fans, diffusers, and potpourri.

Some of our responses to scents result from early associations that call up good or bad feelings, and that explains why businesses explore connections among smell, memory, and mood.[24] Researchers for Folgers found that for many people the smell of coffee summons up childhood memories of their mothers cooking breakfast, so the aroma reminds them of home. The company turned this insight into a commercial in which a young man in an army uniform arrives home early one morning. He goes to the kitchen, opens a Folgers' package, and the aroma wafts upstairs. His mother opens her eyes, smiles, and exclaims, "He's home!"[25]

Speaking of coffee, Starbucks recently reverted to its old policy that requires *baristas* to grind a batch of coffee beans each time they brew a new pot instead of just once each morning. The idea is to reclaim lost customers by intensifying the smell of the beans when they enter the store. As the chain grew and adopted more efficient techniques that automated the process, the chain's founder reversed course. He declared that a switch to preground coffee had taken the "romance and theatre" out of a trip to Starbucks: "We achieved fresh-roasted bagged coffee, but at what cost? The loss of aroma—perhaps the most powerful nonverbal signal we had in our stores."[26]

ECONsumer Behavior

In a tight economy consumers want more bang for their buck—and this desire translates to "proof" that the products they buy actually do what they're supposed to do. In the scented products market, this means that fragrances get stronger. In 2008, twice as many new cleaning products had a fragrance (93 percent) compared to four years earlier.

Procter & Gamble reports that "fragrance megatrends" surface every decade or so. Past trends include cucumber melon (1980s), rain (1990s), and more recently linen. Now manufacturers focus on scents that aren't as delicate or even pleasant—Clorox bleach for example retains its original bleach scent even when it offers fragrances like fresh meadow. As the brand's director of research and development explained, "We tried covering it up, and it didn't work—consumers still want the bleach smell, just lighter."[23]

We process fragrance cues in the *limbic system,* the most primitive part of the brain and the place where we experience immediate emotions. One study even found that the scent of fresh cinnamon buns induced sexual arousal in a sample of male students![27] In another study, women sniffed T-shirts that men had worn for 2 days (wonder how much they paid them to do that?) and reported which they preferred. The women were most attracted to the odor of men who are genetically similar to themselves, though not *too* similar. The researchers claimed the findings were evidence that we are "wired" to select compatible mates, but not those so similar as to cause inbreeding problems.[28]

As scientists continue to discover the powerful effects of smell on behavior, marketers come up with ingenious ways to exploit these connections. Ad companies spend about $80 million per year on scent marketing; the Scent Marketing Institute estimates that number will reach more that $500 million by 2016.[29] This form of *sensory marketing* takes interesting turns as manufacturers find new ways to put scents into products, including men's suits, lingerie, detergents, and aircraft cabins. Here are a few recent smelly strategies:

- One hundred gas stations in California are testing technology that wafts a coffee aroma at the pump in a bid to tempt its pay-and-go customers into the store for a cup to go.
- Kraft Foods sponsored a special holiday issue of *People* magazine. Five of its ads in the issue allow readers to rub a spot to experience the smell of an advertised product, such as Chips Ahoy and Philadelphia Cream Cheese.
- Mars used scent technology to spread the aroma of chocolate around its M&M's World retail outlets, and it put Pedigree dog-food-scented stickers in front of supermarkets and pet stores.
- To launch its $2.99 Deals in several office buildings, Kentucky Fried Chicken (KFC) strategically placed a plate of chicken, a side item and a biscuit in mail carts that pass out interoffice mail. A spokesperson notes that "Mailroom staffers were all fed first so that they would have the strength to deal with the employees clamoring for the KFC." Perhaps the next time you get a letter that's still soggy with gravy you'll know why.[30]
- For a limited time, Burger King sold Flame, a body spray with "the scent of seduction" and a "hint of flame broiled meat."[31]

Sound

We're bombarded with the sound of voices and music (some good, some painful) all the time—but now advertisers can be more selective about just who hears what they have to say. As people age, many develop *aging ear*; they lose the ability to hear higher-frequency sounds. And some teens have figured out on their own that their parents don't have the same range of hearing that they do (probably as a result of years of listening to heavy metal music before the kids came along). Some teens download a special ring tone off the Internet to alert them to incoming text messages when they sit in class—their ancient teachers can't hear these sounds. Ironically, this tone is a spin-off of technology that was originally meant to *repel* teenagers. A Welsh security company developed what it called the "Mosquito" to help shopkeepers disperse young people loitering in front of their stores while it didn't affect adult customers.[33] In this case aging ear comes in handy; grownups couldn't hear the high, whining buzz that sent kids running.

Many aspects of sound (at least the ones we *can* hear) affect people's feelings and behaviors. Stores and restaurants often play certain kinds of music to create a certain mood. Now, even the airlines are looking to audible stimuli to help them board planes more efficiently. When Delta started to play contemporary, upbeat music during the boarding process, flight attendants reported that this seemed to encourage passengers to take their seats faster. Now, Delta deliberately chooses a different song line up each month to help "herd the cattle"—and then switches to lulling melodies to help passengers relax before takeoff.[35]

Touch

One recent study demonstrated the potential power of touch; the researchers found that participants who simply touched an item (an inexpensive coffee mug) for 30 seconds or less created a greater level of attachment to the product; this connection in turn boosted what they were willing to pay for it.[36] The classic, contoured Coca-Cola bottle also attests to the power of touch. The bottle was designed approximately 90 years ago to satisfy the request of a U.S. bottler for a soft-drink container that people could identify even in the dark.

Sensations that reach the skin, whether from a luxurious massage or the bite of a winter wind, stimulate or relax us. Researchers even have shown that touch can influence sales interactions. In one study, diners whom waitstaff touched gave bigger tips, and the same researchers reported that food demonstrators in a supermarket who lightly touched customers had better luck in getting shoppers to try a new snack product and to redeem coupons for the brand.[37] Britain's Asda grocery chain removed the wrapping from several brands of toilet tissue in its stores so that shoppers could feel and compare textures. The result, the retailer says, was soaring sales for its own in-store brand, resulting in a 50 percent increase in shelf space for the line.[38]

Some anthropologists view touch much like a primal language, one we learn well before writing and speech. Indeed, researchers are starting to identify the important role the *haptic* (touch) sense plays in consumer behavior. Haptic senses appear to moderate the relationship between product experience and judgment confidence—this confirms the commonsense notion that we're more sure about what we perceive when we can touch it (a major problem for those who sell products online).[40] Individuals who score high on a "Need for Touch" (NFT) scale are especially influenced by the haptic dimension. Those with a high need for touch respond positively to such statements as:

- When walking through stores, I can't help touching all kinds of products.
- Touching products can be fun.
- I feel more comfortable purchasing a product after physically examining it.[41]

Ironically, one recent study found that product judgments by individuals who do not normally possess a compulsion to touch products (low **autotelics**) are influenced by the "feel" of a package, while those who do have a compulsion to touch items (high autotelics) do not rely on this cue to infer a product's quality. Researchers gave subjects a glass of water in a flimsy cup that also holds a straw. Half of the subjects were told to hold the cup and drink from the straw, while the other half were told to leave the cup on the desk and drink from the straw. Participants who had been identified as high autotelics rated the water the same, regardless of whether or not they touched the cup. However, low autotelics downgraded the water if they had the opportunity to touch the cup as they drank from it.[42] How can we explain this finding? Presumably those who like to touch have learned over time that "you can't judge a book by its cover."

The Japanese take this idea a step farther with their practice of **Kinsei engineering**—a philosophy that translates customers' feelings into design elements. In one application, the designers of the Mazda Miata focused on young drivers who saw the car as an extension of their body, a sensation they call "horse and rider as one." After extensive research they discovered that making the stick shift exactly 9.5 centimeters long conveys the optimal feeling of sportiness and control.[43] Similar thinking went into the driver's seat of the Chrysler 300C, which is designed to make you feel a bit taller. In auto-industry speak, the car has a higher *H-point,* which refers to the location of the seated driver's hip. The change is prompted by the popularity of SUVs, pickups, and minivans that make drivers feel they are riding high on the highway. Ford calls its version "Command Seating" to reinforce the feeling of power it wants drivers to feel as they look down on all those little vehicles buzzing around below them.[44]

Marketing Opportunity

When players walk past a crack in a wall in the computer game *Broken Sword,* they feel a draft of air in the real world. When a virtual plane flies by, a set of fans next to the monitor generates a breeze to make them feel like they're on the runway. Philips' AMBX system includes a wrist pad that rumbles and lamps that flash to simulate thunder and lighting. As games get more realistic, manufacturers push the sensory envelope to let players experience them with all their senses. Some companies sell subwoofer devices that attach to the base of a chair to give gamers a sonic bump in the tailbone when they get blown up in a game. The ultimate game chair has 12 vibrating built-in motors—seven in the back, five in the seat—and a pair of speakers at the top. If a grenade goes off nearby in a video game, the chair gives the player a corresponding jolt to the back. Now if they can just simulate that day-old pizza taste.[39]

TABLE 2.1	Tactile-Quality Associations		
Perception	**Male**	**Female**	
High class	Wool	Silk	Fine
Low class	Denim	Cotton	↕
	Heavy ←——————→ Light		Coarse

Fragrance and cosmetics containers in particular tend to speak to consumers via their tactile appeal. Most modern perfume bottles still are made of glass because when women handle an elegantly sculpted glass container they experience a sense of luxury that more modern materials can't provide. For example, when Nina Ricci introduced L'Air du Temps perfume in 1948, the fragrance came in a Lalique crystal bottle with a stopper capped by a pair of crystal lovebirds. The bottle's elegance assured consumers who were not regular buyers of fragrances that this one was of high quality—why would anyone put anything less in such a nice container? In contrast, Calvin Klein's abstract bottle for its Euphoria fragrance is more futuristic, and the container looks like it's made of metal—but a touch still reassures that it is in fact still made of glass. The importance of the haptic dimension explains why people still buy most high-end fragrances in stores rather than online.[45]

We also link the perceived richness or quality of the material in clothing, bedding, or upholstery to its "feel," whether rough or smooth, flexible or inflexible. We equate a smooth fabric, such as silk, with luxury, whereas we consider denim to be considered practical and durable. Table 2.1 summarizes some of these tactile-quality associations. Fabrics composed of scarce materials or that require a high degree of processing to achieve their smoothness or fineness tend to be more expensive and thus we as-

This German ad reminds us that sometimes we bite off more than we can chew.
Source: Client: PowWow Bar & Restaurant. Agency: Jung von Matt/Spree, Germany.

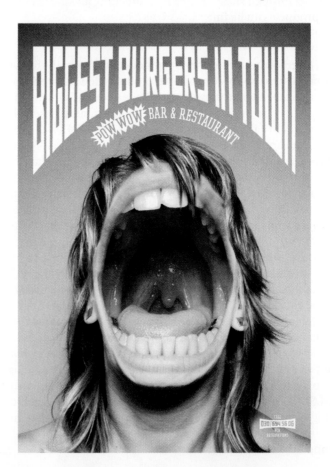

sume they are of a higher class. Similarly, we assume lighter, more delicate textures are feminine. Men often value a feeling of roughness, whereas women seek smoothness.

Taste

Our taste receptors obviously contribute to our experience of many products. So-called "flavor houses" develop new concoctions to please the changing palates of consumers. Scientists are right behind them as they build new devices to test these flavors. Alpha M.O.S. sells a sophisticated electronic tongue for tasting, and the company is working on what its executives call an electronic mouth, complete with artificial saliva, to chew food and to dissect its flavor. Coca-Cola and PepsiCo use the tongue to test the quality of corn syrups, whereas Bristol-Myers Squibb and Roche use the device to devise medicines that don't taste bitter.[46]

Cultural factors also determine the tastes we find desirable. A food item's image and the values we attach to it (such as how vegans regard beef menu items, which is not kindly) influence how we experience the actual taste.[47] For example, consumers' greater appreciation of different ethnic dishes contributes to increased desires for spicy foods, so the quest for the ultimate pepper sauce continues. More than 50 stores in the United States supply fiery concoctions with names such as Sting and Linger, Hell in a Jar, and Religious Experience (comes in Original, Hot, and Wrath).[48] Some of these sauces are so hot that stores ask customers to sign waivers of legal liability before they buy them. Purists measure the "heat" of peppers in units called Scovilles. In 1912, Wilbur Scoville asked a five-person panel to see how much sugar water it would take to eliminate the hotness of a pepper. How's this for a hot tip: It takes 1,981 gallons of sweetened water to neutralize a teaspoon of Da' Bomb, which claims to be the hottest sauce ever made.[49]

This Spanish ad for a hot chili-flavored chip uses a novel visual image to communicate the ferocity of the product's flavor.
Source: Tiempo BBDO Barcelona.

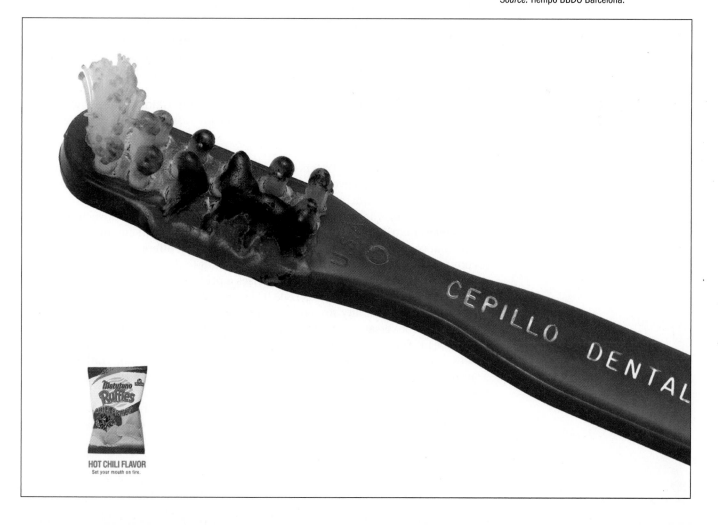

HOT CHILI FLAVOR
Set your mouth on fire.

Exposure

Exposure occurs when a stimulus comes within the range of someone's sensory receptors. Consumers concentrate on some stimuli, are unaware of others, and even go out of their way to ignore some messages. We notice stimuli that come within range for even a very short time—*if* we so choose. That's the reasoning behind Cadillac's ads for cars that can go from zero to 60 miles an hour in less than 5 seconds. Rather than using the traditional 30 seconds to get out this message, the company ran 5-second commercials to make its point.[50] However, getting a message noticed in such a short time (or even in a longer one) is no mean feat. Before we consider what else people may choose not to perceive, let's consider what they *are* capable of perceiving.

3

OBJECTIVE

Why is it that products and commercial messages often appeal to our senses, but we won't be influenced by most of them?

Sensory Thresholds

If you have ever blown a dog whistle and watched your pooch respond to a sound you cannot hear, you won't be surprised to learn that there are some stimuli that people simply can't perceive. Some of us pick up sensory information that others whose sensory channels have diminished due to disability or age cannot. **Psychophysics** is the science that focuses on how the physical environment is integrated into our personal, subjective world.

The Absolute Threshold

When we define the lowest intensity of a stimulus that can be registered on a sensory channel, we speak of its *threshold*. It sounds like a great name for a rock band, but the **absolute threshold** refers to the minimum amount of stimulation that can be detected on a given sensory channel. The sound a dog whistle emits is too high for human ears to detect, so this stimulus is beyond our auditory absolute threshold. The absolute threshold is an important consideration in designing marketing stimuli. A highway billboard might have the most entertaining copy ever written, but this genius is wasted if the print is too small for passing motorists to see it.

The Differential Threshold

The **differential threshold** refers to the ability of a sensory system to detect changes or differences between two stimuli. The minimum difference we can detect between two stimuli is the **j.n.d.** (just noticeable difference).

The issue of when and if consumers will notice a difference between two stimuli is relevant to many marketing situations. Sometimes a marketer may want to ensure that consumers notice a change, as when a retailer offers merchandise at a discount. In other situations, the marketer may want to downplay the fact that it has made a change, such as when a store raises a price or a manufacturer reduces the size of a package (see the "CB as I See It" box on reference prices).

A consumer's ability to detect a difference between two stimuli is relative. A whispered conversation that might be unintelligible on a noisy street can suddenly become public and embarrassingly loud in a quiet library. It is the *relative difference* between the decibel level of the conversation and its surroundings, rather than the absolute loudness of the conversation itself, that determines whether the stimulus will register.

In the nineteenth century, a psychophysicist named Ernst Weber found that the amount of change required for the perceiver to notice a change systematically

CB AS I SEE IT

Professor Larry Compeau, *Clarkson University*

*S*urveys consistently show that consumers consider price the most important factor when they buy, but marketers too often view price merely as an economic variable—that is, the amount of money the consumer must sacrifice to obtain the product. Years of recent research, however, show us that consumers regard price more than simply as the cost of a product.[52] To truly understand price, we need to think of it as an information stimulus, like color, aroma, and other more traditional stimuli we interpret. How consumers respond to and use price in their perceptual processes has been the focus of recent research. This research considers price as an information cue that is perceived and interpreted (attaching meaning to it). We call this area of research *behavioral pricing.*

One stream of behavioral pricing research looks at price as an information cue we use to judge a product.[53] You've certainly heard the old adage "You get what you pay for," which may or may not be true depending on the circumstances. Nonetheless, when consumers don't have other information on which they can rely, they often use price as an indicator of quality (more on this in Chapter 9). In this sense, price is an important information source consumers use to help them decide among product options.

In another stream of research, we expand the scope to consider the broader context and other information marketers often present along with the actual selling price.[54] We refer to the pieces of information that surround the actual selling price as *semantic*

cues because the consumer's interpretation or judgment of the selling price depends on how he or she interprets this information (semantics!).

When we conceptualize price as an information cue or stimulus, then we must also accept the fact that price is subject to the same types of perceptual processes that lead to different judgments depending on the context. A common strategy sellers use in providing contextual information for consumers is to present a *reference price* along with the selling price.

This refers to a price against which buyers compare the actual selling price. Marketers usually present it in price advertisements, on price tickets, or even on store displays. For example, how often have you seen an advertisement that states a selling price without some other "reference price" next to it showing the "regular price," "original price," "compare-at price," or "MSLP" (manufacturer's suggested list price)? It's pretty rare. When an item goes on sale and the old price and the new price are available to ascertain the savings, this price information is informative and helps the consumer.

A reference price communicates the value of the deal to the buyer. But if a seller knows that consumers rely on semantic cues to assess the deal, the seller can alter the cue information to enhance the deal's attractiveness:

Which is the better deal on an LCD television?

- Product A: 47 inch, 1080p, high definition—regular price: $2,499; sale price: $1,499
- Product B: 47 inch, 1080p, high definition—regular price: $1,799; sale price: $1,499

Like most consumers, you probably picked product A. Why? To make your decision, you used the reference prices. Getting a $2,500 television for $1,500 is a better deal than getting an $1,800 television for $1,500—you save more, and you get a better television, right? What if the televisions are identical? If the seller of product A deliberately exaggerates the regular price of $2,499, then the information may not be as informative as it is deceptive. Using higher reference prices, sellers can get consumers to increase their perceptions of the value of the deal, when in fact the deal is not better.[55] When this happens, consumers are more likely to purchase that item and less likely to shop around.[56] As a result, there is the potential for harm to consumers.

Important public policy implications (i.e., government rules and regulations) arise based on research on reference pricing.[57] We must consider how to protect consumers from deceptive practices, such as exaggerating reference prices, and this research plays a critical role in determining if deception occurs and what can be done about it. Many state and federal laws, along with guidelines from the Better Business Bureau, have specific regulations regarding the use of reference prices to avoid harming consumers, but a litany of court cases demonstrates that the research is critical to inform these laws and regulations and their interpretation by the courts.[58] Perception theory then is a critical base on which we can build a sophisticated understanding of how consumers use price. We then use this knowledge to protect consumers and enhance overall consumer welfare.

relates to the intensity of the original stimulus. The stronger the initial stimulus, the greater a change must be for us to notice it. This relationship is known as **Weber's Law**, which this equation summarizes:

$$K = \frac{\triangle i}{I}$$

where

K = a constant (this varies across the senses)
$\triangle i$ = the minimal change in intensity of the stimulus required to produce a j.n.d.
I = the intensity of the stimulus where the change occurs

Consider how Weber's Law works for a product when it goes on sale. A rule of thumb some retailers use is that a markdown should be at least 20 percent for the reduction to make an impact on shoppers. If this is the case, a pair of socks that retails for $10 should be put on sale for $8 (a $2 discount) for shoppers to realize a difference. However, a sports coat that sells for $100 would not benefit from a "mere" $2 discount—a retailer would have to mark it down to $80 to achieve the same impact.

Weber's Law, ironically, is a challenge to green marketers who try to reduce the sizes of packages when they produce concentrated (and more earth-friendly) versions of their products. Makers of laundry detergent brands have to convince their customers to pay the same price for about half the detergent. Also, because of pressure from powerful retailers such as Wal-Mart that want to fit more bottles on their shelves, the size of detergent bottles is shrinking significantly. Procter & Gamble, Unilever, and Henkel all maintain that their new concentrated versions will allow people to wash the same number of loads with half the detergent. One perceptual trick they're using to try to convince consumers of this is the redesign of the bottle cap: Both P&G and Church & Dwight use a cap with a broader base and shorter sides to persuade consumers that they need a smaller amount.[59]

Perceptual thresholds pose a challenge to brands that need to update their images without sacrificing the brand image they've worked years to cultivate. The trick is to make a product, logo, trademark, or package different enough so that people will notice the change, yet not *so* different that consumers will think it's no longer the same product. If a marketer tries to change too much, it courts disaster. Mattel found this out in 1993 when it gave Barbie's boyfriend Ken a purple mesh T-shirt, a pierced ear, and the name "Earring Magic Ken." Not a pretty picture.[60]

Here's how a few venerable marketers deal with this problem:

- Pepsi took five months to revamp its famous logo after top executives decided the company needed to define the drink as a "cultural leader."[61]
- As figure 2.2 shows, The lonely Maytag repairman first appeared in national commercials in 1967. Now he's getting a makeover to become more active and outgoing for a new generation of shoppers. Formerly known as "Ol' Lonely," the new spokescharacter takes the initiative to repair other things that Maytag implies ought to be as dependable as its appliances, such as office copiers and cable TV.[62]
- Strawberry Shortcake, a popular doll and cartoon character in the 1980s, doesn't connect with modern girls—maybe it's the bloomers she wears. Her owner American Greetings Properties launched what the company calls a "fruit-forward" makeover. The doll now prefers fresh fruit to gumdrops, wears a dab of lipstick (but no rouge), and has abandoned her calico cat in favor of a cell phone.

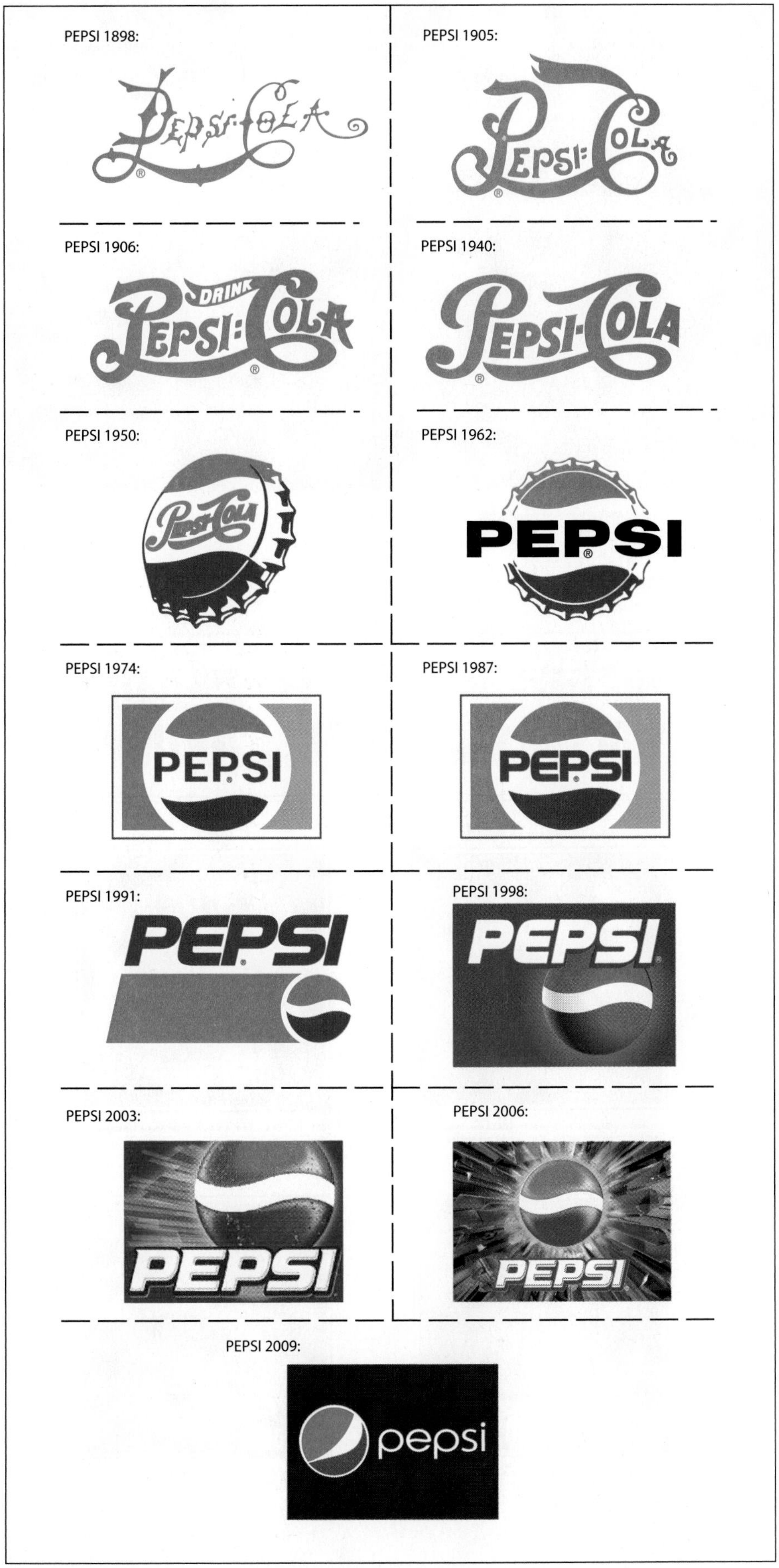

Figure 2.2 THE PEPSI LOGO OVER TIME

PEPSI 1898:

PEPSI 1905:

PEPSI 1906:

PEPSI 1940:

PEPSI 1950:

PEPSI 1962:

PEPSI 1974:

PEPSI 1987:

PEPSI 1991:

PEPSI 1998:

PEPSI 2003:

PEPSI 2006:

PEPSI 2009:

Maytag Corp. puts its lonely repairman to work fixing other companies' brands of home appliances.
Source: Erik S. Lesser/AP Wide World Photos.

This Canadian beer ad pokes fun at subliminal advertising.
Source: © 2005. Molson USA, LLC.

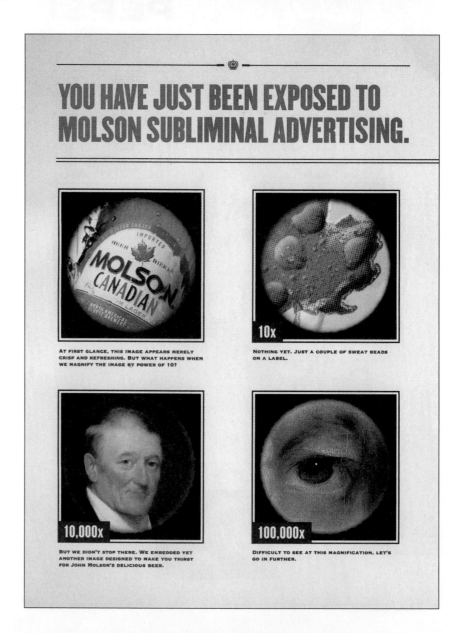

4
OBJECTIVE

Why is subliminal advertising a controversial—but largely ineffective—way to talk to consumers?

Subliminal Perception

Most marketers want to create messages *above* consumers' thresholds so people will notice them. Ironically, a good number of consumers instead believe marketers design many advertising messages so they will perceive them unconsciously, or *below* the threshold of recognition. Another word for threshold is *limen* (just remember "the secret of Sprite"), and we term stimuli that fall below the limen *subliminal*. **Subliminal perception** occurs when the stimulus is below the level of the consumer's awareness.

Subliminal perception is a topic that has captivated the public for more than 50 years, despite the fact that there is virtually no proof that this process has *any* effect on consumer behavior. A survey of American consumers found that almost two-thirds believe in the existence of subliminal advertising, and more than one-half are convinced that this technique can get them to buy things they do not really want.[63] ABC rejected a Kentucky Fried Chicken (KFC) commercial that invited viewers to slowly replay the ad to find a secret message, citing the network's long-standing policy against subliminal advertising. KFC argued that the ad wasn't subliminal at all because the company told viewers about the message and how to find it. The network wasn't convinced.[64]

YOU MAY NOT BE AWARE OF IT, BUT RIGHT NOW YOUR SUBCONSCIOUS IS JONESING FOR A COLD, CRISP MOLSON. WHY? BECAUSE WE SLIPPED THROUGH THE BACK DOOR OF YOUR BRAIN AND PLANTED A FEW VISUAL CUES DEEP IN YOUR MIND. ANY OF THE IMAGES BELOW SEEM STRANGELY FAMILIAR?

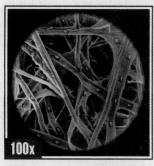

100x

MAGNIFIED AT 100X HOWEVER, WE BEGIN TO SEE SOMETHING.

1,000x

AN IMAGE OF JOHN MOLSON PRINTED ON THE PAPER FIBER OF THE BEER LABEL. THOUGH MINUTE, YOUR BRAIN PICKED UP ON THIS SUBLIMINAL CUE TO A 219-YEAR HERITAGE OF BREWING GREAT-TASTING BEER.

1,000,000x

AH, THERE IT IS: AN IMAGE OF PEOPLE SOCIALIZING WITH AN ICE-COLD MOLSON.

10,000,000x

A MICROSCOPIC REMINDER THAT MOLSON HAS BEEN BRINGING FRIENDS TOGETHER SINCE 1786. SHOULD YOU SUDDENLY AWAKEN IN A CROWDED BAR ORDERING A ROUND OF MOLSON FOR EVERYONE, WE DID THAT. AND YOU'RE WELCOME.

Like this KFC ad, most examples of subliminal advertising that people "discover" are not subliminal at all—on the contrary, the images are quite apparent. Remember, if you can see it or hear it, it's not subliminal; the stimulus is above the level of conscious awareness. Nonetheless, the continuing controversy about subliminal persuasion has been important in shaping the public's beliefs about advertisers' and marketers' abilities to manipulate consumers against their will.

Subliminal Techniques

Marketers supposedly send *subliminal messages* on both visual and aural channels. **Embeds** are tiny figures they insert into magazine advertising via high-speed photography or airbrushing. These hidden figures, usually of a sexual nature, supposedly exert strong but unconscious influences on innocent readers. Some limited evidence hints at the possibility that embeds can alter the moods of men when they're exposed to sexually suggestive subliminal images, but the effect (if any) is very subtle—and may even work in the opposite direction if this creates negative feelings among viewers.[65] To date, the only real impact of this interest in hidden messages is to sell more copies of "exposés" written by a few authors and to make some consumers (and students taking a consumer behavior class) look a bit more closely at print ads—perhaps seeing whatever their imaginations lead them to see.

The possible effects of messages hidden on sound recordings also fascinate many consumers. We can see one attempt to capitalize on subliminal auditory perception techniques in the growing market for self-help audios. CDs and tapes, which typically feature the sounds of crashing waves or other natural sounds, supposedly contain subliminal messages to help listeners stop smoking, lose weight, gain confidence, and so on. Despite the rapid growth of this market, there is little evidence that subliminal stimuli transmitted on the auditory channel can bring about desired changes in behavior.[66]

Does Subliminal Perception Work? Let's Evaluate the Evidence

Some research by clinical psychologists suggests that subliminal messages can influence people under very specific conditions, though it is doubtful that these techniques would be of much use in most marketing contexts. For this kind of message to have a prayer of working, an advertiser has to tailor it specifically to an individual rather than the mass messages suitable for the general public.[67] The stimulus should also be as close to the liminal threshold as possible. Here are other discouraging factors:

● There are wide individual differences in threshold levels. In order for a message to avoid conscious detection by consumers who have low thresholds, it would have to be so weak that it would not reach those who have high thresholds.
● Advertisers lack control over consumers' distance and position from a screen. In a movie theater, for example, only a small portion of the audience would be in exactly the right seats to be exposed to a subliminal message.
● The viewer must pay absolute attention to the stimulus. People who watch a television program or a movie typically shift their attention periodically, and they might not even notice when the stimulus appears.
● Even if the advertiser induces the desired effect, it works only at a very general level. For example, a message might increase a person's thirst—but not necessarily for a specific drink. Because the stimulus just affects a basic drive, a marketer could find that after all the bother and expense of creating a subliminal message, demand for competitors' products increases as well!

Clearly, there are better ways to get our attention—let's see how.

Attention

As you sit in a lecture, you might find your mind wandering (yes, even you!). One minute you are concentrating on the professor's words, and the next you catch yourself daydreaming about the upcoming weekend. Suddenly, you tune back in as you hear your name being spoken. Fortunately, it's a false alarm—the professor has called on another "victim" who has the same first name. But, she's got your attention now.

Attention refers to the extent to which processing activity is devoted to a particular stimulus. As you know from sitting through both interesting and "less interesting" lectures, this allocation can vary depending on both the characteristics of the stimulus (i.e., the lecture itself) and the recipient (i.e., your mental state at the time).

Although we live in an "information society," we can have too much of a good thing. Consumers often are in a state of **sensory overload**, where they are exposed to far more information than they can process. In our society, much of this bombardment comes from commercial sources, and the competition for our attention is steadily increasing. The average adult is exposed to about 3,500 pieces of advertising information every single day—up from about 560 per day 30 years ago.

Getting the attention of young people in particular is a challenge—as your professor probably knows! By one estimate, 80 percent of teens today engage in **multitasking**, where they process information from more than one medium at a time as they attend to their cell phones, TVs, instant messages, and so on.[68] One study observed 400 people for a day and found that 96 percent of them were multitasking about a third of the time they used media.[69] Marketing researchers struggle to understand this new condition as they figure out how to reach people who do many things at once.

As we'll also see in later chapters, marketers constantly search for ways to break through the clutter and grab people's attention—at times with mixed results:

● Networks try to engage viewers during commercial breaks when they wedge original content into the blocks of advertising time so that viewers will anticipate seeing something fun if they sit through a few ads. Fox Broadcasting televised a series of clips about an animated character named Oleg, a New York cab driver, who popped up in 8-second vignettes during commercial breaks in series such as *24*. In a Greek accent, Oleg urged viewers to visit Fox's Web site. In one clip, Oleg sang about himself to the Barry Manilow tune "Copacabana." In others, he drove celebrities such as Tom Cruise and Rosie O'Donnell. Although Oleg generated more than 100,000 Web site hits on some nights, some viewers complained that he was an ethnic stereotype and others couldn't understand what he was saying—so Oleg is history. But, it was a good idea in principle.[70]

This camera ad from Singapore reminds us that consumers tune out many stimuli that compete for their attention.
Source: Courtesy of Nikon/Euro RSCG/Singapore.

- The CW television network runs *content wraps,* which mix sponsors' products into program snippets. Sometimes these wraps involve the cast of the shows in which the commercials appear. This is hardly a new strategy, however; so-called "cast commercials" were common in the days of *I Love Lucy, The Beverly Hillbillies,* and even *The Flintstones.*

- In the online world, advertisers are trying more tricks to get visitors to watch their messages. One of the most popular today is **rich media**—this technique uses movement to get viewers' attention. <u>LowerMyBills.com</u> is notorious for its endless loops of silhouetted dancers and surprised office workers, whereas other ads spring into action when you move the cursor over them. Other rich media are online versions of familiar TV commercials that sit frozen on the Web site until you click them. *Teaser ads,* much like those you see on TV that give you a taste of the story but make you return later for the rest, also turn up on Web sites.[71]

- Of course, a sure-fire way to grab our attention is to do something outrageous, or at least unusual, in a public place. To promote a new class at the New York Health and Racquet Club, six men and women stood outside the city's Grand Central Terminal flashing their underwear at strangers. The garments featured the club's logo and "Booty Call," the name of the class.

Because the brain's capacity to process information is limited, consumers are very selective about what they pay attention to. The process of **perceptual selection** means that people attend to only a small portion of the stimuli to which they are exposed. Consumers practice a form of "psychic economy," picking and choosing among stimuli to avoid being overwhelmed. How do they choose? Both personal and stimulus factors help to decide.

Personal Selection Factors

The actions of a Colorado judge illustrate how powerful our own tastes can be in determining what we want to see and hear. He requires young people convicted of violating the city's noise ordinance to listen to music they don't like—including a heavy dose of such "favorites" as Wayne Newton, Dean Martin, and bagpipe recordings.[72] What, no Jonas Brothers? **Experience**, which is the result of acquiring and processing stimulation over time, is one factor that determines how much exposure to a particular stimulus a person accepts. **Perceptual filters** based on our past experiences influence what we decide to process.

Perceptual vigilance is one such factor. Consumers are more likely to be aware of stimuli that relate to their current needs. A consumer who rarely notices car ads will become very much aware of them when she or he is in the market for a new car. A newspaper ad for a fast-food restaurant that would otherwise go unnoticed becomes significant when one sneaks a glance at the paper in the middle of a five o'clock class.

The flip side of perceptual vigilance is **perceptual defense**. This means that people see what they want to see—and don't see what they don't want to see. If a stimulus is threatening to us in some way, we may not process it—or we may distort its meaning so that it's more acceptable. For example, a heavy smoker may block out images of cancer-scarred lungs because these vivid reminders hit a bit too close to home.

Still another factor is **adaptation**, the degree to which consumers continue to notice a stimulus over time. The process of adaptation occurs when consumers no longer pay attention to a stimulus because it is so familiar. A consumer can "habituate" and require increasingly stronger "doses" of a stimulus to notice it. A commuter *en route* to work might read a billboard message when it is first installed, but after a few days, it simply becomes part of the passing scenery. Several factors can lead to adaptation:

- **Intensity**—Less-intense stimuli (e.g., soft sounds or dim colors) habituate because they have less sensory impact.
- **Duration**—Stimuli that require relatively lengthy exposure in order to be processed habituate because they require a long attention span.
- **Discrimination**—Simple stimuli habituate because they do not require attention to detail.
- **Exposure**—Frequently encountered stimuli habituate as the rate of exposure increases.
- **Relevance**—Stimuli that are irrelevant or unimportant habituate because they fail to attract attention.

Stimulus Selection Factors

In addition to the receiver's mind-set, characteristics of the stimulus itself play an important role in determining what we notice and what we ignore. Marketers need to understand these factors so they can create messages and packages that will have a better chance to cut through the clutter. This idea even applies to getting animals' attention: A British ad agency created a TV commercial aimed at felines that used fish and mouse images and sounds to attract catty consumers. In trials, 60 percent of cats showed some form of response to the ad, from twitching their ears to tapping the television screen.[73] That's a better track record than some "people commercials" have shown!

In general, we are more likely to notice stimuli that differ from others around them (remember Weber's Law). A message creates **contrast** in several ways:

- **Size**—The size of the stimulus itself in contrast to the competition helps to determine if it will command attention. Readership of a magazine ad increases in proportion to the size of the ad.[75]
- **Color**—As we've seen, color is a powerful way to draw attention to a product or to give it a distinct identity. For example, Black & Decker developed a line of tools it called DeWalt to target the residential construction industry. B&D colored the new line yellow instead of black, which made it stand out against other "dull" tools.[76]
- **Position**—Not surprisingly, we stand a better chance of noticing stimuli that are in places we're more likely to look. That's why the competition is so heated among suppliers to have their products displayed in stores at eye level. In magazines, ads that are placed toward the front of the issue, preferably on the right-hand side, also win out in the race for readers' attention. (Hint: The next time you read a magazine, notice which pages you're more likely to spend time looking at.)[77] A study that tracked consumers' eye movements as they scanned telephone directories also illustrates the importance of a message's position. Consumers scanned listings in alphabetical order, and they noticed 93 percent of quarter-page display ads but only 26 percent of plain listings. Their eyes were drawn to color ads first, and these were viewed longer than black-and-white ones. In addition, subjects spent 54 percent more time viewing ads for businesses they ended up choosing, which illustrates the influence of attention on subsequent product choice.[78]
- **Novelty**—Stimuli that appear in unexpected ways or places tend to grab our attention. One solution is to put ads in unconventional places, where there will be less competition for attention. These places include the backs of shopping carts, walls of tunnels, floors of sports stadiums, and yes, even public restrooms.[79] An outdoor advertising agency in London constructs huge ads in deserts and farm fields adjacent to airports so that passengers who look out the window can't help but pay attention. It prints the digital ads on pieces of PVC mesh that sit on

ECONsumer Behavior

While consumers are more reluctant to pull out their wallets in tough times, marketers redouble efforts to introduce a steady stream of new products. The reason? Marketers need new reasons to reach out to their customers whose impulse is to decrease their connection to the marketplace. Cold Stone Creamy is launching numerous new ice cream products as well as coffee drinks and a line of cheesecakes. A company executive explained that while consumers are changing their buying habits, hopefully ". . . they're still looking for that 10-minute vacation at Cold Stone."[74]

An oversized ad for Air Dubai cuts through the clutter.

Source: Haakson Dewing/Haakon Photographic Services.

frames a few inches above the ground.[80] Other entrepreneurs equip billboards with tiny cameras that use software to determine that a person is standing in front of an outdoor ad. Then the program analyzes the viewer's facial features (like cheekbone height and the distance between the nose and the chin) to judge the person's gender and age. Once the software categorizes the passerby, it selects an advertisement tailored to this profile—an Hispanic teenager for example sees a different message than the middle-aged Asian woman who walks behind him.[81]

Indeed, one recent study indicates that novelty in the form of interruptions actually *intensifies* our experiences; distraction increases our enjoyment of pleasant stimuli as it amplifies our dislike of unpleasant stimuli. In fact, the study reported that people actually enjoy TV shows *more* when commercials interrupt them. A group of undergraduates watched an episode of an old sitcom (*Taxi*) with which they were unfamiliar. Half viewed the original broadcast that included ads for a jeweler, a lawyer, and other businesses while the other half saw the show with all commercials deleted. Students who saw the original actually gave higher evaluations to it. The researchers found a similar pattern when they interrupted people who got a massage. On the other hand, subjects reported that the irritating sound of a vacuum cleaner was even worse when they got a break from listening to it and then had to hear it resume! The researchers interpret these results as the outcome of adaptation—we experience events more intensely at first but then get used to them. When we experience an interruption and then start over, we revert back to the original intensity level.[82]

lus, the degree to which students saw infractions and the blame they assigned for those they did see depended on which college they attended.[89]

As this experiment demonstrates, we tend to project our own desires or assumptions onto products and advertisements. This interpretation process can backfire for marketers. Planters LifeSavers Company found this out when it introduced Planters Fresh Roast, a vacuum-packed peanuts package. The idea was to capitalize on consumers' growing love affair with fresh-roast coffee by emphasizing the freshness of the nuts in the same way. A great idea—until irate supermarket managers began calling to ask who was going to pay to clean the peanut gook out of their stores' coffee-grinding machines.[90]

Another experiment demonstrated how our assumptions influence our experiences; in this case, the study altered beer drinkers' taste preferences simply by telling them different stories about a specific brew's ingredients. The researcher offered bar patrons free beer if they would participate in a taste test (guess what: very few refused the offer). Participants tasted two beers each, one a regular draft of Budweiser or Samuel Adams and the other the same beer with a few drops of balsamic vinegar added. Although most beer *aficionados* would guess that vinegar makes the drink taste bad, in fact 60 percent of the respondents who did not know which beer contained the vinegar actually preferred the doctored version to the regular one! But when tasters knew in advance which beer had vinegar in it before they took a swig, only one-third preferred that version.[91]

Semiotics: The Symbols Around Us

OBJECTIVE

Why does the field of semiotics help us to understand how marketers use symbols to create meaning?

As we've just seen, when we try to "make sense" of a marketing stimulus we interpret it in light of our prior associations. For this reason, much of the meaning we take away influences what we make of the symbolism we perceive. After all, on the surface many marketing images have virtually no literal connection to actual products. What does a cowboy have to do with a bit of tobacco rolled into a paper tube? How can a celebrity such as the basketball player Shaquille O'Neal or the singer Rihanna enhance the image of a soft drink or a fast-food restaurant?

To help them understand how consumers interpret the meanings of symbols, some marketers turn to **semiotics**—the field of study that studies the correspondence between signs and symbols and their roles in how we assign meanings.[92] Semiotics is a key link to consumer behavior because consumers use products to express their social identities. Products carry learned meanings, and we rely on marketers to help us figure out what those meanings are. As one set of researchers put it, "Advertising serves as a kind of culture/consumption dictionary; its entries are products, and their definitions are cultural meanings."[93]

From a semiotic perspective, every marketing message has three basic components: an *object,* a *sign* (or symbol), and an *interpretant.* The **object** is the product that is the focus of the message (e.g., Marlboro cigarettes). The **sign** is the sensory image that represents the intended meanings of the object (e.g., the Marlboro cowboy). The **interpretant** is the meaning we derive from the sign (e.g., rugged, individualistic, American). Figure 2.3 diagrams this relationship.

According to semiotician Charles Sanders Peirce, signs relate to objects in one of three ways: They can resemble objects, connect to them, or tie to them conventionally. An **icon** is a sign that resembles the product in some way (e.g., the Ford Mustang has a galloping horse on the hood). An **index** is a sign that connects to a product because they share some property (e.g., the pine tree on some of Procter & Gamble's Spic and Span cleanser products conveys the shared property of fresh

Figure 2.3 SEMIOTIC RELATIONSHIPS

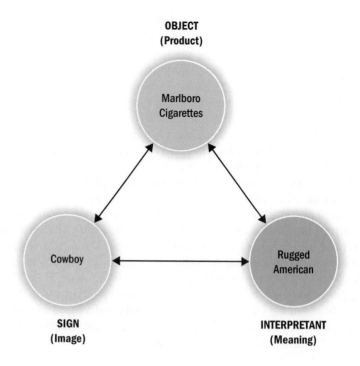

scent). A **symbol** is a sign that relates to a product by either conventional or agreed-on associations (e.g., the lion in Dreyfus Fund ads provides the conventional association with fearlessness and strength that it carries [or hopes to carry] over to the company's approach to investments).[94]

A lot of time, thought, and money go into creating brand names and logos that clearly communicate a product's image (even when a name like Exxon is generated by a computer!). The Nissan Xterra combines the word *terrain* with the letter *X*, which many young people associate with extreme sports, to give the brand name a cutting-edge, off-road feel.

The choice of a logo is even more difficult when the brand has to travel across cultures. For example, as Chinese business becomes more global, companies re-fashion ancient Chinese pictograms into new corporate logos that resonate with both the East and the West. Chinese pictograms really are icons because the ancient symbols were once graphic depictions of the words they signify. For example, China Telecom's logo features two interlocking letter *C*'s that together form the Chinese character for China but also represent the concept of "customer" and "competition," the firm's new focus. In addition, though, the symbol also resembles the horns of an ox, a hard-working animal. The software company Oracle redesigned its logo for the Chinese market; it added three Chinese characters that signify the literal translation of the word *oracle*: "writing on a tortoise shell." The expression dates back to ancient China when mystics scrawled prophecies on bones. The California firm was enthu-siastic about the translation because it conveyed Oracle's core competency—data storage.[95]

Hyperreality

One of the hallmarks of modern advertising is that it creates a condition of **hyperreality**. This refers to the process of making real what is initially simulation or "hype." Advertisers create new relationships between objects and interpretants when they invent new connections between products and benefits, such as when an ad equates Marlboro cigarettes with the American frontier spirit. In a hyperreal en-vironment, over time it's no longer possible to discern the true relationship between the symbol and reality. The "artificial" associations between product symbols and the real world take on lives of their own. Here are some recent hyperreal sightings:

- A furniture designer launched a dining room set inspired by the TV series *Dexter*—the main character is a police blood splatter analyst who moonlights as a serial killer. The all-white table and chairs are festooned with big splotches of red.[96]
- "It's so easy even a caveman can do it." The "yuppie" cavemen from the insurance company GEICO's ad campaign became so popular they actually spawned a (short-lived) TV sitcom. Now, ESPN signed the characters to star in a series of vignettes to promote its *SportsCenter* program and fantasy football offering.[97]
- We'll learn later on in the book about the popular strategy of product placement, where TV shows and movies incorporate real products on sets and in plotlines. **Reverse product placement** is a great example of hyperreality; in these cases fictional products that appear in shows become popular in the real world. The e-commerce site LastExitToNowhere.com sells T-shirts that bear the logos of companies featured in works of fiction. These include such made-up companies as Tyrell (the manufacturer of genetic replicants in the movie classic *Blade Runner*), Polymer Records (a music label in the cult movie *This Is Spinal Tap)*, and the Weyland-Yutani Corporation (it made the spaceship freighter Nostromo in the *Alien* movies). Another online store—80sTees.com—proclaimed Duff beer, from *The Simpsons* TV show the number one fake brand. Coming in second was Dunder Mifflin, the paper company on *The Office* series.[98]
- Bertie Bott's Every Flavor Beans originated in the *Harry Potter* book series before the product moved to actual retail shelves; the movie *Forrest Gump* inspired the Bubba Gump Shrimp Company restaurant chain; and Nestlé sells Wonka candy (from the *Willy Wonka* movie).[99]

Perceptual Positioning

So, we know that we often interpret a product stimulus in light of what we've learned about a product category and the characteristics of existing brands. Our perception of a brand comprises both its functional attributes (e.g., its features, its price, and so on) and its symbolic attributes (its image and what we think it says about us when we use it). We'll look more closely at issues such as brand image in later chapters, but for now it's important to keep in mind that (as we stated in Chapter 1) our evaluation of a product typically is the result of what it means rather than what it does. This meaning—as consumers perceive it—constitutes the product's market position, and it may have more to do with our expectations of product performance as communicated by its color, packaging, or styling than with the product itself.

How does a marketer determine where a product actually stands in the minds of consumers? One technique is to ask them what attributes are important to them and how they feel competitors rate on these attributes. We use this information to construct a **perceptual map**—a vivid way to paint a picture of where consumers locate products or brands in their minds. GRW Advertising created a perceptual map for HMV music stores, a British company. The agency wanted to know more about how its target market, frequent buyers of CDs, perceived different music stores. GRW plotted perceptions of such attributes of competitors as selection, price, service, and hipness on an imaginary street map. Based on this research, the firm determined that HMV's strengths were service, selection, and the stores' abilities to cater to local tastes because store managers order their own stock. It used this map as part of its strategic decision to specialize in music products as opposed to trying to compete against other stores that sell video games, fragrances, and computer CD-ROMs.[101]

This decision became part of HMG's **positioning strategy**, which is a fundamental component of a company's marketing efforts as it uses elements of the marketing mix (i.e., product design, price, distribution, and marketing communications) to influence the consumer's interpretation of its meaning in the marketplace relative to its competitors. For example, although consumers' preferences for the

Marketing Pitfall

There's no doubt that traditional newspapers are in trouble. Many are searching for new ways to attract advertisers and boost circulation in an era where a lot of people get their news from Web sites or blogs instead. The *Los Angeles Times* took a controversial step when the paper ran a front-page ad for an NBC television show that was deliberately designed to look like a news article. Although the top of the column was labeled "Advertisement" and it included NBC's peacock logo, many critics complained that this form of hyperreality crossed an inappropriate line between marketing and reality.[100]

taste of one product over another are important, this functional attribute is only one component of product evaluation.

Coca-Cola found this out the hard way when it committed its famous New Coke marketing blunder in the 1980s. Consumers preferred New Coke to Pepsi in *blind taste tests* (in which researchers did not identify the products) by an average of 55 to 45 percent in 17 markets, yet New Coke hit a wall when it replaced the older version. Consumers' impassioned protests and letter-writing campaigns eventually forced the company to bring back "Classic Coke." Why the reversal? People do not buy a cola for taste alone; they buy intangibles such as brand image as well.[102] Coca-Cola's unique position as part of an American, fun-loving lifestyle is based on years of marketing efforts that involve a lot more than its literal taste.

Marketers can use many dimensions to carve out a brand's position in the marketplace. These include the following:[103]

- **Lifestyle**—Grey Poupon mustard is a "higher-class" condiment.
- **Price leadership**—L'Oréal sells its Noisôme brand face cream in upscale beauty shops, whereas its Plenitude brand is available for one-sixth the price in discount stores—even though both are based on the same chemical formula.[104]
- **Attributes**—Bounty paper towels are "the quicker picker upper."
- **Product class**—The Spyder Eclipse is a sporty convertible.
- **Competitors**—Northwestern Insurance is "the quiet company."
- **Occasions**—Wrigley's gum is an alternative at times when smoking is not permitted.
- **Users**—Levi's Dockers target men in their 20s to 40s.
- **Quality**—At Ford, "Quality is job 1."

CHAPTER SUMMARY

Now that you have finished reading this chapter you should understand why:

Perception is a three-stage process that translates raw stimuli into meaning.

Perception is the process by which physical sensations, such as sights, sounds, and smells, are selected, organized, and interpreted. The eventual interpretation of a stimulus allows it to be assigned meaning. A perceptual map is a widely used marketing tool that evaluates the relative standing of competing brands along relevant dimensions.

The design of a product today is a key driver of its success or failure.

In recent years the sensory experiences we receive from products and services have become a high priority when we choose among competing options. Consumers increasingly want to buy things that will give them hedonic value in addition to functional value. They often believe that most brands perform similarly, so they weigh a product's aesthetic qualities heavily when they select a brand.

Products and commercial messages often appeal to our senses, but we won't be influenced by most of them.

Marketing stimuli have important sensory qualities. We rely on colors, odors, sounds, tastes, and even the "feel" of products when we evaluate them. Not all sensations successfully make their way through the perceptual process. Many stimuli compete for our attention, and we don't notice or accurately interpret the majority of them. People have different thresholds of perception. A stimulus must be presented at a certain level of intensity before our sensory detectors can detect it. In addition, a consumer's ability to detect whether two stimuli are different (the differential threshold) is an important issue in many marketing contexts, such as package design, the size of a product, or its price.

Subliminal advertising is a controversial—but largely ineffective—way to talk to consumers.

So-called subliminal persuasion and related techniques that expose people to visual and aural messages below the sensory threshold are controversial. Although evidence that subliminal persuasion is effective is virtually nonexistent, many consumers continue to believe that advertisers use this technique.

Some of the factors that determine which stimuli (above the threshold level) do get perceived include the amount of exposure to the stimulus, how much attention it generates, and how it is interpreted. In an increasingly crowded stimulus environment, advertising clutter occurs when too many marketing-related messages compete for attention.

We interpret the stimuli to which we do pay attention according to learned patterns and expectations.

We don't attend to a stimulus in isolation. We classify and organize it according to principles of perceptual organization. A *Gestalt,* or overall pattern, guides these principles. Specific grouping principles include closure, similarity, and figure-ground relationships. The final step in the process of perception is interpretation. Symbols help us make sense of the world by providing us with an interpretation of a stimulus that others often share. The degree to which the symbolism is consistent with our previous experience affects the meaning we assign to related objects.

 The field of semiotics helps us to understand how marketers use symbols to create meaning.

Marketers try to communicate with consumers by creating relationships between their products or services and desired attributes. A semiotic analysis involves the correspondence between stimuli and the meaning of signs. The intended meaning may be literal (e.g., an icon such as a street sign with a picture of children playing). Or it may be indexical if it relies on shared characteristics (e.g., the red in a stop sign means danger). Meaning also can be conveyed by a symbol in which an image is given meaning by convention or by agreement of members of a society (e.g., stop signs are octagonal, whereas yield signs are triangular). Marketer-created associations often take on lives of their own as consumers begin to believe that hype is, in fact, real. We call this condition hyperreality.

KEY TERMS

Absolute threshold, 68
Adaptation, 76
Attention, 75
Autotelics, 65
Closure principle, 81
Contrast, 77
Differential threshold, 68
Embeds, 74
Experience, 76
Exposure, 68
Figure-ground principle, 82
Gestalt, 81
Hedonic consumption, 57
Hyperreality, 84
Icon, 83

Index, 83
Interpretant, 83
Interpretation, 79
j.n.d., 68
Kinsei engineering, 65
Multitasking, 75
Object, 83
Perception, 57
Perceptual defense, 76
Perceptual filters, 76
Perceptual map, 85
Perceptual selection, 76
Perceptual vigilance, 76
Positioning strategy, 85
Priming, 79

Principle of similarity, 82
Psychophysics, 68
Reverse product placement, 85
Rich media, 76
Schema, 79
Semiotics, 83
Sensation, 57
Sensory marketing, 58
Sensory overload, 75
Sensory signature, 59
Sign, 83
Subliminal perception, 73
Symbol, 84
Trade dress, 62
Weber's Law, 70

REVIEW

1 Define hedonic consumption and provide an example.
2 Does the size of a package influence how much of the contents we eat? Provide an example.
3 How does the sense of touch influence consumers' reactions to products?
4 Identify and describe the three stages of perception.
5 What is the difference between an absolute threshold and a differential threshold?
6 Does subliminal perception work? Why or why not?
7 "Consumers practice a form of 'psychic economy.'" What does this mean?
8 Describe two factors that can lead to stimulus adaptation.

9 Define a "schema" and provide an example of how this concept is relevant to marketing.
10 "The whole is greater than the sum of its parts." Explain this statement.
11 List the three semiotic components of a marketing message, giving an example of each.
12 What do we mean by the concept of hyperreality? Give an example that is not discussed in the chapter.
13 What is a positioning strategy? What are some ways marketers can position their products?

CONSUMER BEHAVIOR CHALLENGE

■ DISCUSS

1 Many studies have shown that our sensory detection abilities decline as we grow older. Discuss the implications of the absolute threshold for marketers who want to appeal to the elderly.

2 Assuming that some forms of subliminal persuasion may have the desired effect of influencing consumers, do you think the use of these techniques is ethical? Explain your answer.

3 Do you believe that marketers have the right to use any or all public spaces to deliver product messages? Where would you draw the line in terms of places and products that should be off limits?

4 The slogan for the movie *Godzilla* was "Size does matter." Should this be the slogan for America as well? Many marketers seem to believe so. The average serving size for a fountain drink has gone from 12 ounces to 20 ounces. An industry consultant explains that the 32-ounce Big Gulp is so popular because "people like something large in their hands. The larger the better." Hardee's Monster Burger, complete with two beef patties and five pieces of bacon, weighs in at 63 grams of fat and more than 1,000 calories. The standard for TV sets used to be 19 inches; now it's 32 inches and growing.

Hulking sport utility vehicles (SUVs) have replaced tiny sports cars as the status vehicle of the new millennium. What's up with our fascination with bigness? Is this a uniquely American preference? Do you believe that "bigger is better"? Is this a sound marketing strategy?

5 Playmobil toys recreate real-life settings such as a police station or hospital. A new offering the company calls Security Check Point features armed airport security officers, a metal detector, and an X-ray screening machine. Some parents protested; one wrote this comment on Amazon.com: "I applaud Playmobil for attempting to provide us with the tools we need to teach our children to unquestioningly obey the commands of the State Security Apparatus. But unfortunately, this product falls short of doing that. There's no brown figure for little Josh to profile, taser, and detain." A Playmobil executive comments, "The whole premise behind Playmobil toys is to familiarize the child with the realities of life through play. If you're taking a child for a first flight to Florida from New Jersey to visit grandparents, you say, 'This is what the terminal looks like, and when we get here we have to take our shoes off and walk though security.'"[105] Where should toymakers draw the line between reality and play?

■ APPLY

1 Interview three to five male and three to five female friends about their perceptions of both men's and women's fragrances. Construct a perceptual map for each set of products. Based on your map of perfumes, do you see any areas that are not adequately served by current offerings? What (if any) gender differences did you notice regarding both the relevant dimensions raters use and how they place specific brands along these dimensions?

2 Assume that you are a consultant for a marketer who wants to design a package for a new premium chocolate bar targeted to an affluent market. What recommendations would you provide in terms of such package elements as color, symbolism, and graphic design? Give the reasons for your suggestions.

3 Using magazines archived in the library, track the packaging of a specific brand over time. Find an example of gradual changes in package design that may have been below the j.n.d.

4 Visit a set of Web sites for one type of product (e.g., personal computers, perfumes, laundry detergents, or athletic shoes) and analyze the colors and other design principles they employ. Which sites "work" and which don't? Why? Look through a current magazine and select one ad that captures your attention over the others. Explain why this ad attracts you.

5 Find ads that use the techniques of contrast and novelty. Give your opinion of the effectiveness of each ad and whether the technique is likely to be appropriate for the consumers the ad targets.

Case Study

THE BRAVE NEW WORLD OF SUBWAY ADVERTISING

What do American Express, Target Stores, Coca-Cola, the Discovery Channel, Cadillac, Minute Maid, the Cartoon Network, Royal Caribbean, and Calvin Klein have in common? They all break through the clutter of traditional ad spaces to grab the attention of potential customers. And in the process, they dazzle them right out of the boredom of riding the subway.

Subway advertising has been around nearly as long as the subway itself. But advertising media pioneers Submedia, Sidetrack Technologies, and MotionPoster give the old venue a new twist. By employing an innovative technology similar to that of a childhood flip book, they illuminate dark subway tunnels and turn them into valuable showcases for major advertisers.

At the core of this new method is a series of lit panels that contain static images. The panels occupy 500 to 1,000 feet of space that normally hold only graffiti, grime, and the occasional rat. When you view one from a standstill, they appear as simple still images. But when a subway passes by, they come to life for riders as a 15- to 30-second full-motion commercial.

Having just another place to air a commercial might not seem so appealing to advertisers. But in a media environment where consumers increasingly bypass ads (think TiVo), the placement of these ads in subway tunnels presents exceptional possibilities. Advertisers clamor for opportunities to break through the typical clutter. And these ads are so unique, most consumers have never seen anything like them. "We think this will catch people so totally by surprise that when they see them, they can't help but watch them," said Dan Hanrahan, Royal Caribbean's senior vice president of marketing and sales.

But the uniqueness of this medium is only part of the formula that makes these ad agencies believe they're on to something. The rest is based on the nature of the subway audience: captive and bored. "Everybody overwhelmingly says it takes away from the boredom of the ride," said Joshua Spodek, founder of New York City–based Submedia. "It's not like it's taking away from a beautiful view, like a billboard as you're driving around a beautiful area in Vermont. A subway tunnel is a semi-industrial environment."

Whether it's because the ads give a bored audience something to do or because this new wave of out-of-home advertisements is truly cutting-edge, industry officials claim that the public reaction has been overwhelmingly positive. Submedia reports that 87 percent of riders look forward to seeing the next Submedia advertisement and 60 percent said the ad made their ride more enjoyable.

Comments like this make it easy to believe the claims of underground advertising agencies. One estimate asserts that more than 92 percent of consumers remember the advertised product while only 13 percent have that same level of recall for televisions ads. This means big ad revenues, and not just for the agencies. Mass transit organizations potentially can realize a big source of secondary income when they lease out this unused real estate.

Currently brightening the tunnels of numerous mass transit systems in North and South America, Asia, and Europe, these advertisements represent something every advertiser dreams of: an ad that people go out of their way to look at. In a world that is increasingly skeptical about too much advertising, this new platform is an express ride to success.

DISCUSSION QUESTIONS

1 Based on the principles of attention the chapter presents, explain why riders receive these new ads so positively.
2 Using the same principles, what should the ads' creators consider to avoid the potential burnout of this medium?

Sources: Media kit, www.submediaworld.com, accessed May 23, 2009; Katy Bachman, "Underground Film," *Mediaweek* 18, no. 15 (April 14, 2008): 24. Louis M. Brill, "Subway In-tunnel Advertising Gives Outdoor a New Direction," www.sub-media.com/press, accessed May 23, 2009.

NOTES

1. Craig Baumrucker, "Why Does Organic Milk Last So Much Longer Than Regular Milk?" *Scientific American* (June 6, 2008), www.scientificamerican.com/article.cfm?id=experts-organic-milk-lasts-longer, accessed June 30, 2009; "Going Organic," *Prepared Foods* (August 2002): 18; Cathy Sivak, "Purposeful Parmalat: Part 1 of 2," *Dairy Field* 182, no. 9 (September 1999): 1; "North Brunswick, NJ-Based Food Company Signs Deal with OnlineGrocer," *Home News Tribune* (March 21, 2000).

2. Nat Ives, "Putting Some Terror in Family Outings," *New York Times* (January 17, 2005), www.nytimes.com, accessed January 17, 2005.

3. Rick Vecchio, "'Reality TV' Peru Style: Trashy Shows Entertain, Distract During Election Year," *Opelika-Auburn News* (March 15, 2000): 15A.

4. Glenn Collins, "Owens-Corning's Blurred Identity," *New York Times* (August 19, 1994): D4.

5. Elizabeth C. Hirschman and Morris B. Holbrook, "Hedonic Consumption: Emerging Concepts, Methods, and Propositions," *Journal of Marketing* 46 (Summer 1982): 92–101.

6. Virginia Postrel, "The New Trend in Spending," *New York Times* (September 9, 2004), www.nytimes.com, accessed September 9, 2004.

7. Emily Cadei, "Cleaning Up: S.F. Duo Putting a Shine on Its Product Line," *San Francisco Business Times Online Edition* 17, no. 16 (December 6, 2002).

8. Stuart Elliott, "Joint Promotion Adds Stickers to Sweet Smell of Marketing" *New York Times* (April 2, 2007), www.nytimes.com, accessed April 2, 2007.

9. Gabriel Kahn, "Philips Blitzes Asian Market as It Strives to Become Hip," *Wall Street Journal Interactive Edition* (August 1, 2002).

10. Adam Bryant, "Plastic Surgery at AmEx," *Newsweek* (October 4, 1999): 55.

11. Amitava Chattopadhyay, Gerald J. Gorn, and Peter R. Darke, "Roses Are Red and Violets Are Blue—Everywhere? Cultural Universals and Differences in Color Preference Among Consumers and Marketing Managers" (unpublished manuscript, University of British Columbia, Fall 1999); Joseph Bellizzi and Robert E. Hite, "Environmental Color, Consumer Feelings, and Purchase Likelihood," *Psychology & Marketing* 9 (1992): 347–63; Ayn E. Crowley, "The Two-Dimensional Impact of Color on Shopping," *Marketing Letters* 4 (January 1993); Gerald J. Gorn, Amitava Chattopadhyay, and Tracey Yi, "Effects of Color as an Executional Cue in an Ad: It's in the Shade," (unpublished manuscript, University of British Columbia, 1994).

12. Pam Belluck, "Reinvent Wheel? Blue Room. Defusing a Bomb? Red Room," *New York Times* (February 5, 2009), www.nytimes.com, accessed February 5, 2009.

13. Mark G. Frank and Thomas Gilovich, "The Dark Side of Self and Social Perception: Black Uniforms and Aggression in Professional Sports," *Journal of Personality and Social Psychology* 54 (1988): 74–85.

14. Pamela Paul, "Color by Numbers," *American Demographics* (February 2002): 31–36.

15. Paulette Thomas, "Cosmetics Makers Offer World's Women an All-American Look with Local Twists," *Wall Street Journal* (May 8, 1995): B1.

16. Marc Gobé, *Emotional Branding: The New Paradigm for Connecting Brands to People* (New York: Allworth Press, 2001).

17. Dirk Olin, "Color Cognition," *New York Times* (November 30, 2003), www.nytimes.com, accessed November 30, 2003.

18. "Ny Emballage og Nyt Navn Fordoblede Salget," *Markedsføring* 12 (1992): 24. Adapted from Michael R. Solomon, Gary Bamossy, and Soren Askegaard, *Consumer Behavior: A European Perspective*, 2nd ed. (London: Pearson Education, 2001).

19. Meg Rosen and Frank Alpert, "Protecting Your Business Image: The Supreme Court Rules on Trade Dress," *Journal of Consumer Marketing* 11 (1994): 50–55.

20. http://www.fashiontrendsetter.com/content/color_trends/2009/Pantone-Fashion-Color-Report-Summer-2010.html, accessed November 6, 2009.

21. Jack Neff, "Scientists Prove the 'Axe Effect' Is Real," *Advertising Age* (January 7, 2009), www.adage.com, accessed January 7, 2009.

22. Deborah J. Mitchell, Barbara E. Kahn, and Susan C. Knasko, "There's Something in the Air: Effects of Congruent or Incongruent Ambient Odor on Consumer Decision-Making," *Journal of Consumer Research* 22 (September 1995): 229–38; for a review of olfactory cues in store environments, see also Eric R. Spangenberg, Ayn E. Crowley, and Pamela W. Henderson, "Improving the Store Environment: Do Olfactory Cues Affect Evaluations and Behaviors?" *Journal of Marketing* 60 (April 1996): 67–80.

23. Quoted in Ellen Byron, "Is the Smell of Moroccan Bazaar Too Edgy for American Homes? New Products Aimed at 'Scent Seekers' Are Fast Changing the Fragrance of Clean," *Wall Street Journal* (February 3, 2009), http://online.wsj.com/article/SB123362286186141795.html, accessed February 3, 2009.

24. Pam Scholder Ellen and Paula Fitzgerald Bone, "Does It Matter If It Smells? Olfactory Stimuli as Advertising Executional Cues," *Journal of Advertising* 27 (Winter 1998): 29–40.

25. Jack Hitt, "Does the Smell of Coffee Brewing Remind You of Your Mother?" *New York Times Magazine* (May 7, 2000): 73–77.

26. Quoted in Julie Jargon, "At Starbucks, It's Back to the Grind," *Wall Street Journal* (June 17, 2009), online.wsj.com/article/SB124517480498919731.html, accessed June 17, 2009.

27. Maxine Wilkie, "Scent of a Market," *American Demographics* (August 1995): 40–49.

28. Nicholas Wade, "Scent of a Man Is Linked to a Woman's Selection," *New York Times* (January 22, 2002), www.nytimes.com, accessed January 22, 2002.

29. Newman, Kara, "How to Sell with Smell," *Business 2.0* (April 2007): 36.

30. Nina M. Lentini, "KFC Targets the Nostrils of Hungry Office Workers" *Marketing Daily* (August 29, 2007), www.mediapost.com, accessed August 29, 2007.

31. Emily Bryson York, "Make Your Man a Flamer, Mmmmmmm. Fresh Meat," *Advertising Age* (December 15, 2008), http://adage.com/adages/post?article_id=133264, accessed December 15, 2008.

32. Jesse McKinley, "City Sours on Cookie-Scented Ads" *New York Times* (December 6, 2006), www.nytimes.com, accessed December 6, 2006.

33. Maria Aspan, "Horror Movie at High Pitch in TV Ad Aimed at Teenagers" *New York Times* (February 19, 2007), www.nytimes.com, accessed February 19, 2007; "Students Find Ring Tone Adults Can't Hear," *New York Times* (June 12, 2006), www.nytimes.com, accessed June 12, 2006.

34. Andrew Hampp, "Hear Voices? It May Be an Ad, An A&E Billboard 'Whispers' a Spooky Message Audible Only in Your Head in Push to Promote Its New 'Paranormal' Program," December 10, 2007; Advertising Age, http://adage.com/article?article_id=122491; accessed December 10, 2007.

35. Nathan Hurst, "Delta: Right Tunes Make Boarding Faster, Carrier Uses a Mix of Popular Songs to Get Travelers Moving," *Detroit News* (August 18, 2008), www.detnews.com/apps/pbcs.dll/article?AID=/20080818/BIZ/808180349/1001/BIZ, accessed August 18, 2008.

36. "You Can Look—But Don't Touch," *Science Daily* (January 20, 2009), www.sciencedaily,com, accessed January 30, 2009.

37. Jacob Hornik, "Tactile Stimulation and Consumer Response," *Journal of Consumer Research* 19 (December 1992): 449–58.

38. Sarah Ellison and Erin White, "'Sensory' Marketers Say the Way to Reach Shoppers Is the Nose," *Advertising Age* (November 24, 2000): 1–3.

39. Mike Musgrove, "Bringing Senses into Play: Gaming Gadgets Create Whoooshes and Rumbles," *Washington Post* (June 19, 2007): D1.

40. Douglas Heingartner, "Now Hear This, Quickly," *New York Times* (October 2, 2003), www.nytimes.com, accessed October 2, 2003.

41. J. Peck and T. L. Childers, "Individual Differences in Haptic Information Processing: The 'Need for Touch' Scale," *Journal of Consumer Research* 30, no. 3 (2003): 430–42.

42. Aradhna Krishna and Maureen Morrin, "Does Touch Affect Taste? The Perceptual Transfer of Product Container Haptic Cues," *Journal of Consumer Research* 34 (April 2008): 807–18.

43. Material adapted from a presentation by Glenn H. Mazur, QFD Institute, 2002.

44. Joseph B. White, "Taller in the Saddle: Higher Driver's Seats in Sedans Are Effort to Appeal to Fans of SUVs and Minivans," *Wall Street Journal* (August 23, 2004), www.wsj.com, accessed August 23, 2004.

45. Randall Frost, "Feeling Your Way in a Global Market," Brand Channel (October 18, 2006), www.brandchannel.com, accessed October 18, 2006.

46. John Tagliabue, "Sniffing and Tasting with Metal and Wire," *New York Times* (February 17, 2002), www.nytimes.com, accessed February 17, 2002.

47. Michael W. Allen, Richa Gupta, and Arnaud Monnier. "The Interactive Effect of Cultural Symbols and Human Values on Taste Evaluation," *Journal of Consumer Research*, 35 (August 2008): 294–308.

48. Becky Gaylord, "Bland Food Isn't So Bad—It Hurts Just to Think about This Stuff," *Wall Street Journal* (April 21, 1995): B1.

49. Dan Morse, "From Tabasco to Insane: When You're Hot, It May Not Be Enough," *Wall Street Journal Interactive Edition* (May 15, 2000).

50. Stuart Elliott, "TV Commercials Adjust to a Shorter Attention Span," *New York Times* (April 8, 2005), www.nytimes.com, accessed April 8, 2005.

51. Brian Steinberg, "How to Keep Ad Skippers from Fast-Forwarding Your Ad," *Advertising Age* (March 31, 2009), www.adage.com, accessed March 31, 2009.

52. Dhruv Grewal and Larry D. Compeau, "Consumer Responses to Price and Its Contextual Information Cues: A Synthesis of Past Research, a Conceptual Framework, and Avenues for Further Research," *Review of Marketing Research* 3 (2007): 109–31; Kent B. Monroe, *Pricing: Making Profitable Decisions*, 3rd ed. (New York: McGraw-Hill, 2003); Dhruv Grewal, Kent B. Monroe, and R. Krishnan, "The Effects of Price Comparison Advertising on Buyers' Perceptions of Acquisition Value and Transaction Value," *Journal of Marketing* 62 (April 1998): 46–60.

53. William B. Dodds, Kent B. Monroe, and Dhruv Grewal, "Effects of Price, Brand, and Store Information on Buyers' Product Evaluations," *Journal of Marketing Research* 28 (August 1991): 307–19; Merrie Brucks, Valerie Zeithaml, and Gillian Naylor, "Price and Brand Name as Indicators of Quality Dimensions of Consumer Durables," *Journal of the Academy of Marketing Science* 28, no. 3 (2000): 359–74.

54. Dhruv Grewal and Larry D. Compeau, "Comparative Price Advertising: Informative or Deceptive?" *Journal of Public Policy and Marketing* 11 (Spring 1991): 52–62; Larry D. Compeau and Dhruv Grewal, "Comparative Price Advertising: An Integrative Review," *Journal of Public Policy and Marketing* 17 (Fall 1998): 257–73; Larry D. Compeau, Dhruv Grewal, and Joan Lindsey-Mullikin, "An Analysis of Consumers' Interpretations of Semantic Phrases Found in Reference Price Advertisements," *Journal of Consumer Affairs* 38 (Summer 2004): 178–87.

55. Larry D. Compeau and Dhruv Grewal, "Adding Value by Communicating Price Deals Effectively: Does It Matter How You Phrase It?" *Pricing Strategy and Practice: An International Journal* 2, no. 2 (1994): 28–36.

56. Joel E. Urbany, William O. Bearden, and Don C. Weilbaker, "The Effect of Plausible and Exaggerated Reference Prices on Consumer Perceptions and Price Search," *Journal of Consumer Research* 15 (1998): 95–110.

57. Larry D. Compeau and Dhruv Grewal, "Comparative Price Advertising: An Integrative Review," *Journal of Public Policy and Marketing* 17 (Fall 1998): 257–73; Dhruv Grewal and Larry D. Compeau, "Pricing and Public Policy: A Research Agenda and an Overview," *Journal of Public Policy and Marketing* 18 (Spring 1999): 3–10.

58. Larry D. Compeau, Dhruv Grewal, and Diana S. Grewal, "Adjudicating Claims of Deceptive Advertised Reference Prices: The Use of Empirical Evidence," *Journal of Public Policy and Marketing* 13 (Fall 1994): 312–18; Dhruv Grewal and Larry D. Compeau, *Journal of Public Policy and Marketing: Special Issue on Pricing and Public Policy* 18 (Spring 1999), Chicago, IL: American Marketing Association. Also see www.bbb.org/membership/codeofad.asp#Comparative%20Price, www.ftc.gov/bcp/guides/decptprc.htm for guidelines on use of reference prices.

59. Ellen Byron, "Selling Detergent Bottles' Big Shrink Suds Makers' Challenge: Convince Consumers Less Isn't Really Less," *Wall Street Journal* (May 21, 2007), www.wsj.com, accessed May 21, 2007.

60. Brooks Barnes, "Beloved Characters as Reimagined for the 21st Century," *New York Times* (June 11, 2008), www.Nytimes.Com/2008/06/11/Business/Media/11cartoons.Html?_R=1&Ref=Business, accessed June 11, 2008.

61. Natalie Zmuda, "What Went into the Updated Pepsi Logo? Experts Estimate Cost to Roll Out New Look in the Hundreds of Millions," *Advertising Age* (October 27, 2008), http://Adage.Com/Article?Article_Id=132016; accessed October 27, 2008.

62. Stuart Elliott, "The Names Are Vintage, The Touches Modern," *New York Times* (May 1, 2007), www.nytimes.com/2007/05/01/Business/Media/01adco.html, accessed May 1, 2007.

63. Michael Lev, "No Hidden Meaning Here: Survey Sees Subliminal Ads," *New York Times* (May 3, 1991): D7.

64. "ABC Rejects KFC Commercial, Citing Subliminal Advertising," *Wall Street Journal* (March 2, 2006), www.wsj.com, accessed March 2, 2006.

65. Andrew B. Aylesworth, Ronald C. Goodstein, and Ajay Kalra, "Effect of Archetypal Embeds on Feelings: An Indirect Route to Affecting Attitudes?" *Journal of Advertising* 28, no. 3 (Fall 1999): 73–81.

66. Philip M. Merikle, "Subliminal Auditory Messages: An Evaluation," *Psychology & Marketing* 5, no. 4 (1988): 355–72.

67. Joel Saegert, "Why Marketing Should Quit Giving Subliminal Advertising the Benefit of the Doubt," *Psychology & Marketing* 4 (Summer 1987): 107–20; see also Dennis L. Rosen and Surendra N. Singh, "An Investigation of Subliminal Embed Effect on Multiple Measures of Advertising Effectiveness," *Psychology & Marketing* 9 (March–April 1992): 157–73; for a more recent review, see Kathryn T. Theus, "Subliminal Advertising and the Psychology of Processing Unconscious Stimuli: A Review of Research," *Psychology & Marketing* (May–June 1994): 271–90.

68. Jennifer Pendleton, "Multi-Taskers," *Advertising Age* (March 29, 2004): S8.

69. Sharon Waxman, "At an Industry Media Lab, Close Views of Multitasking," *New York Times* (May 15, 2006).

70. Stuart Elliott, "Trying to Keep the Viewers When the Ads Come On," *New York Times* (May 14, 2007), www.nytimes.com, accessed May 14, 2007.

71. Lee Gomes, "As Web Ads Grow, Sites Get Trickier About Targeting You," *Wall Street Journal* (May 9, 2007): B1.

72. "Court Orders Bagpipes for Noise Violations," *Montgomery Advertiser* (March 6, 1999): 1A.

73. Lucy Howard, "Trying to Fool a Feline," *Newsweek* (February 8, 1999): 8.

74. Stuart Elliott, "A Strategy When Times Are Tough: 'It's New!' One," *New York Times* (March 24, 2009), http://topics.nytimes.com/top/reference/timestopics/people/e/stuart_elliott/index.html?offset=60&&, accessed March 24, 2009.

75. Roger Barton, *Advertising Media* (New York: McGraw-Hill, 1964).

76. Suzanne Oliver, "New Personality," *Forbes* (August 15, 1994): 114.

77. Adam Finn, "Print Ad Recognition Readership Scores: An Information Processing Perspective," *Journal of Marketing Research* 25 (May 1988): 168–77.

78. Gerald L. Lohse, "Consumer Eye Movement Patterns on Yellow Pages Advertising," *Journal of Advertising* 26 (Spring 1997): 61–73.

79. Michael R. Solomon and Basil G. Englis, "Reality Engineering: Blurring the Boundaries Between Marketing and Popular Culture," *Journal of Current Issues and Research in Advertising* 16, no. 2 (Fall 1994): 1–18; Michael McCarthy, "Ads Are Here, There, Everywhere: Agencies Seek Creative Ways to Expand Product Placement," *USA Today* (June 19, 2001): 1B.

80. Linda Stern, "Bigger Than at Times Square," March 24, 2008, www.newsweek.com.

81. Stephanie Clifford, "Billboards That Look Back," *New York Times* (May 31, 2008), www.nytimes.com, accessed May 31, 2008.

82. Benedict Carey, "Liked the Show? Maybe It Was the Commercials," *New York Times* (March 2, 2009), http://topics.nytimes.com/topics/reference/timestopics/people/c/benedict_carey/index.html, accessed March 3, 2009.

83. Nicholas Bakalar, "If It Says McDonald's, Then It Must Be Good," *New York Times* (August 14, 2007), www.nytimes.com, accessed August 14, 2007.

84. Robert M. McMath, "Image Counts," *American Demographics* (May 1998): 64.

85. Brian Wansink, James Painter, and Koert van Ittersum, "Descriptive Menu Labels' Effect on Sales," *Cornell Hotel and Restaurant Administration Quarterly* (December 2001): 68–72.

86. Xiaoyan Deng and Barbara E. Kahn, "Is Your Product on the Right Side? The 'Location Effect' on Perceived Product Heaviness and Package Evaluation," *Journal of Marketing Research* (December 2009).

87. Pankaj Aggarwal and Ann L. McGill, "Is That Car Smiling at Me? Schema Congruity as a Basis for Evaluating Antropomorphized Products," *Journal of Consumer Behavior* 34 (December 2007): 468–79.

88. Anthony Ramirez, "Lessons in the Cracker Market: Nabisco Saved New Graham Snack," *New York Times* (July 5, 1990): D1.

89. Albert H. Hastorf and Hadley Cantril, "They Saw a Game: A Case Study," *Journal of Abnormal and Social Psychology* 49 (1954): 129–34; see also Roberto Friedmann and Mary R. Zimmer, "The Role of Psychological Meaning in Advertising," *Journal of Advertising* (1988): 31–40.

90. Robert M. McMath, "Chock Full of (Pea)nuts," *American Demographics* (April 1997): 60.

91. Benedict Carey, "Knowing the Ingredients Can Change the Taste," *New York Times* (December 12, 2006), www.nytimes.com, accessed December 12, 2006.

92. See David Mick, "Consumer Research and Semiotics: Exploring the Morphology of Signs, Symbols, and Significance," *Journal of Consumer Research* 13 (September 1986): 196–213.

93. Teresa J. Domzal and Jerome B. Kernan, "Reading Advertising: The What and How of Product Meaning," *Journal of Consumer Marketing* 9 (Summer 1992): 48–64.

94. Arthur Asa Berger, *Signs in Contemporary Culture: An Introduction to Semiotics* (New York: Longman, 1984); David Mick, "Consumer Research and Semiotics: Exploring the Morphology of Signs, Symbols, and Significance," 196–213; Charles Sanders Peirce, in Charles Hartshorne, Paul Weiss, and Arthur W. Burks, eds., *Collected Papers* (Cambridge, MA: Harvard University Press, 1931–1958); cf. also V. Larsen, D. Luna, and L. A. Peracchio, "Points of View and Pieces of Time: A Taxonomy of Image Attributes," *Journal of Consumer Research* 31, no. 1 (2004): 102–11.

95. Gabriel Kahn, "Chinese Characters Are Gaining New Meaning as Corporate Logos," *Wall Street Journal Interactive Edition* (July 18, 2002).

96. Dexter Dining Room and Kitchen, *Metropolitan Home* (March 2009), www.metropolitanhome.com, accessed January 27, 2009.

97. Jeremy Mullman, "GEICO Cavemen Get a New Gig with ESPN, Will Act as Fantasy-Football Salesmen and Star in 'SportsCenter' Ads," *Advertising Age* (August 14, 2008), accessed August 14, 2008.

98. Rob Walker, "False Endorsement," *New York Times Magazine* (November 18, 2007), www.nytimes.com/2007/11/18/magazine/18wwln-consumed-t.html?_r=1&..., accessed November 24, 2007; David Edery, "Reverse Product Placement in Virtual Worlds," *Harvard Business Review* (December 2006).

99. Walker, "False Endorsement."

100. Stephanie Clifford, "Front of *Los Angeles Times* Has an NBC 'Article,'" *New York Times* April 9, 2009, http://topics.nytimes.com/top/news/business/small_business/marketing_and_advertising/index.html?s=closest&&query=NEWSPAPERS&field=des&match=exact, accessed April 9, 2009.

101. Stuart Elliott, "Advertising: A Music Retailer Whistles a New Marketing Tune to Get Heard Above the Cacophony of Competitors," *New York Times* (July 2, 1996): D7; personal communication, GRW Advertising (April 1997).

102. See Tim Davis, "Taste Tests: Are the Blind Leading the Blind?" 43–44; Betsy McKay, "Pepsi to Revive a Cola-War Barb: The Decades-Old Blind Taste Test," *Wall Street Journal Interactive Edition* (March 21, 2000).

103. Adapted from Michael R. Solomon and Elnora W. Stuart, *Marketing: Real People, Real Choices*, 2nd ed. (Upper Saddle River, NJ: Prentice Hall, 2000).

104. William Echikson, "Aiming at High and Low Markets," *Fortune* (March 22, 1993): 89.

105. Adam Newman, "Playmobil Finds Fun in the Police State," *New York Times* (February 15, 2009), www.nytimes.com, accessed February 15, 2009.

3 Learning and Memory

Chapter Objectives

When you finish this chapter you will understand:

1. Why is it important for marketers to appreciate how consumers learn about products and services?

2. Why does conditioning result in learning?

3. Why do learned associations with brands generalize to other products, and why is this important to marketers?

4. What is the difference between classical and instrumental conditioning?

5. How do we learn by observing others' behavior?

6. How do memory systems work?

7. Why do the other products we associate with an individual product influence how we will remember it?

8. How do products help us to retrieve memories from our past?

9. How do marketers measure our memories about products and ads?

*A*h, Sunday morning! The sun is shining, the birds are singing, and Joe is feeling groovy! He puts on his vintage Levi's 501 jeans (circa 1968) and his Woodstock T-shirt (the "real" Woodstock, not that fake abomination they put on in 2009, thank you) and saunters down to the kitchen. Joe smiles in anticipation of his morning plans. He's just returned from his college reunion and now it's time to "process" all the people he's seen and the stories he heard about their old antics. Joe cranks up the Lava Lamp, throws a Jefferson Airplane record on the turntable (ah, the sublime joys of vinyl), and sits back on his Barcalounger as he clutches a huge bowl filled to the brim with his all-time favorite cereal, Cap'n Crunch. Let the memories begin!

OBJECTIVE
Why is it important for marketers to appreciate how consumers learn about products and services?

Learning

Joe journeys through time with the aid of many products that make him feel good because they remind him of earlier parts of his life. These days it's easy to do, as marketers recycle memories of the hippie era in ads. First, Ameriprise Financial unveiled a campaign that featured Dennis Hopper, who starred in the quintessential '60s film *Easy Rider*. *The Bachelorette* TV show refers to "the summer of love" in its promotions. A print ad for Luvs diapers includes a cartoon version of a VW Microbus festooned with psychedelic designs. The election of Barack Obama added fuel to the fire as the idealism from an earlier time started to reassert itself. Volkswagen's ads feature vintage Bugs to promote its new models. A VW marketing executive explains, "[The 1960s] . . . evokes a time when young people were seeking to change society and trying to break free from a stale, tired way of life. I see a lot of similarities with what's going on with today's youth."[1]

Many marketers realize that long-standing, learned connections between products and memories are a potent way to build and keep brand loyalty. Some companies are bringing their old trademark characters out of retirement, including the Campbell's Soup Kids, the Pillsbury Doughboy, Betty Crocker, the Jolly Green Giant, Charlie the Tuna, and Planters' Mr. Peanut.[2] In this chapter, we'll learn why learned associations among feelings, events, and products—and the memories they evoke—are an important aspect of consumer behavior.

Learning is a relatively permanent change in behavior that experience causes. The learner need not have the experience directly; we can also learn when we observe events that affect others.[3] We learn even when we don't try: We recognize many brand names and hum many product jingles, for example, even for products we don't personally use. We call this casual, unintentional acquisition of knowledge **incidental learning**.

Learning is an ongoing process. Our knowledge about the world constantly updates as we are exposed to new stimuli and as we receive ongoing feedback that allows us to modify our behavior when we find ourselves in similar situations at a later time. The concept of learning covers a lot of ground, ranging from a consumer's simple association between a stimulus such as a product logo (e.g., Coca-Cola) and a response (e.g., "refreshing soft drink") to a complex series of cognitive activities (e.g., writing an essay on learning for a consumer behavior exam).

Psychologists who study learning advance several theories to explain the learning process. These theories range from those that focus on simple stimulus–response connections (*behavioral theories*) to perspectives that regard consumers as complex-problem solvers who learn abstract rules and concepts when they observe what others say and do (*cognitive theories*). It's important for marketers to understand these theories as well, because basic learning principles are at the heart of many consumer purchase decisions.

OBJECTIVE
Why does conditioning result in learning?

Behavioral Learning Theories

Behavioral learning theories assume that learning takes place as the result of responses to external events. Psychologists who subscribe to this viewpoint do not focus on internal thought processes. Instead, they approach the mind as a "black box" and emphasize the observable aspects of behavior, as Figure 3.1 depicts. The observable aspects consist of things that go into the box (the stimuli or events perceived from the outside world) and things that come out of the box (the responses, or reactions to these stimuli).

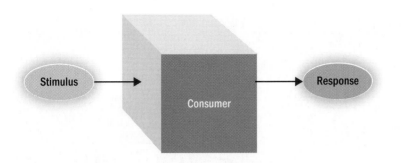

Figure 3.1 THE CONSUMER AS A "BLACK BOX": A BEHAVIORIST PERSPECTIVE ON LEARNING

Two major approaches to learning represent this view: *classical conditioning* and *instrumental conditioning*. According to the behavioral learning perspective, the feedback we receive as we go through life shapes our experiences. Similarly, we respond to brand names, scents, jingles, and other marketing stimuli because of the learned connections we form over time. People also learn that actions they take result in rewards and punishments; this feedback influences the way they will respond in similar situations in the future. Consumers who receive compliments on a product choice will be more likely to buy that brand again, while those who get food poisoning at a new restaurant are not likely to patronize it in the future.

Classical conditioning occurs when a stimulus that elicits a response is paired with another stimulus that initially does not elicit a response on its own. Over time, this second stimulus causes a similar response because we associate it with the first stimulus. Ivan Pavlov, a Russian physiologist who conducted research on digestion in animals, first demonstrated this phenomenon in dogs. Pavlov induced classically conditioned learning when he paired a neutral stimulus (a bell) with a stimulus known to cause a salivation response in dogs (he squirted dried meat powder into their mouths). The powder was an **unconditioned stimulus (UCS)** because it was naturally capable of causing the response. Over time, the bell became a **conditioned stimulus (CS)**—it did not initially cause salivation, but the dogs learned to associate the bell with the meat powder and began to salivate at the sound of the bell only. The drooling of these canine consumers because of a sound, now linked to feeding time, was a **conditioned response (CR)**.

This basic form of classical conditioning that Pavlov demonstrated primarily applies to responses the autonomic (e.g., salivation) and nervous (e.g., eye blink) systems control. That is, it focuses on visual and olfactory cues that induce hunger, thirst, sexual arousal, and other basic drives. When marketers consistently pair these cues with conditioned stimuli, such as brand names, consumers may learn to feel hungry, thirsty, or aroused when they encounter these brand cues at a later point.

Classical conditioning can have similar effects for more complex reactions, too. Even a credit card becomes a conditioned cue that triggers greater spending, especially because as a stimulus it's present only in situations where we spend money. People learn they can make larger purchases with credit cards, and they also leave larger tips than when they pay by cash.[4] Small wonder that American Express reminds us, "Don't leave home without it."

Repetition

Conditioning effects are more likely to occur after the conditioned (CS) and unconditioned (UCS) stimuli have been paired a number of times.[5] Repeated exposures increase the strength of stimulus–response associations and prevent the decay of these associations in memory. Some research indicates that the intervals between exposures may influence the effectiveness of this strategy as well as the type of medium the marketer uses; the most effective repetition strategy is a combination of spaced exposures that alternate in terms of media that are more and less involving, such as television advertising complemented by print media.[6]

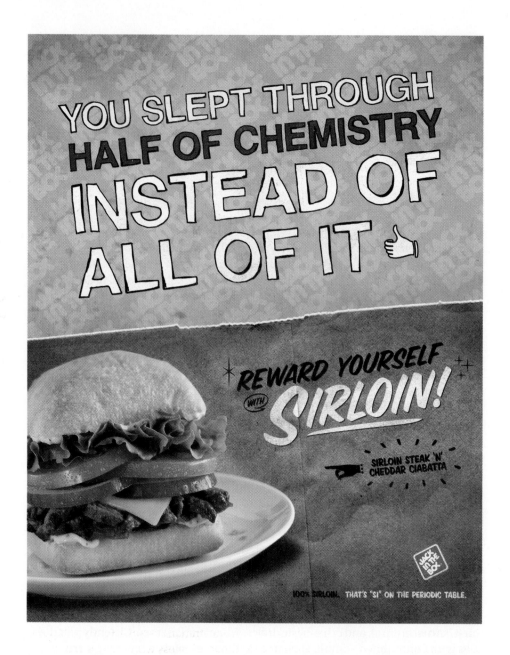

Many classic advertising campaigns consist of product slogans that companies repeat so often they are etched in consumers' minds. Conditioning will not occur or will take longer if the CS is only occasionally paired with the UCS. One result of this lack of association is **extinction**, which occurs when the effects of prior conditioning diminish and finally disappear. This can occur, for example, when a product is over-exposed in the marketplace so that its original allure is lost. The Izod Lacoste polo shirt, with its distinctive crocodile crest, is a good example of this effect. When the once-exclusive crocodile started to appear on baby clothes and many other items, it lost its cachet. Other contenders, such as the Ralph Lauren polo player, successfully challenged it as a symbol of casual elegance. Now that Izod is being more careful about where its logo appears, the brand is starting to regain its "cool" in some circles.

Stimulus Generalization
Stimulus generalization refers to the tendency of stimuli similar to a CS to evoke similar, conditioned responses. For example, Pavlov noticed in subsequent studies that his dogs would sometimes salivate when they heard noises that only resembled a bell, such as keys jangling.

People also react to other, similar stimuli in much the same way they responded to the original stimulus; we call this generalization a **halo effect**. A drugstore's bottle of private brand mouthwash it deliberately packages to resemble Listerine mouthwash may evoke a similar response among consumers, who assume that this "me-too" product shares other characteristics of the original. Indeed, consumers in one study on shampoo brands tended to rate those with similar packages as similar in quality and performance as well.[8] This "piggybacking" strategy can cut both ways: When the quality of the me-too product turns out to be lower than that of the original brand, consumers may exhibit even more positive feelings toward the original. However, if they perceive the quality of the two competitors to be about equal, consumers may conclude the price premium they pay for the original is not worth it.[9]

In a twist on this principle, some companies now use a strategy they call **masked branding**, where they deliberately *hide* a product's true origin. For example Levi Strauss markets its Red Tab line to appeal to young consumers who don't want to be associated with an "old" brand. Miller Brewing Co. actually created a dummy company called Plank Road Brewery when it launched its Icehouse and Red Dog beers.[10]

Stimulus Discrimination

Stimulus discrimination occurs when a UCS does not follow a stimulus similar to a CS. When this happens, reactions weaken and will soon disappear. Part of the learning process involves making a response to some stimuli but not to other, similar stimuli. Manufacturers of well-established brands commonly urge consumers not to buy "cheap imitations" because the results will not be what they expect.

OBJECTIVE

Why do learned associations with brands generalize to other products, and why is this important to marketers?

Marketing Applications of Classical Conditioning Principles

Behavioral learning principles apply to many consumer phenomena, such as creating a distinctive brand image or linking a product to an underlying need. The transfer of meaning from an unconditioned stimulus to a conditioned stimulus explains why "made-up" brand names, such as Marlboro, Coca-Cola, or Reebok, exert such powerful effects on consumers. The association between the Marlboro man and the cigarette is so strong that in some cases the company no longer even bothers to include the brand name in its ads.

When researchers pair *nonsense syllables* (meaningless sets of letters) with such evaluative words as *beauty* or *success*, the meaning transfers to the fake words. This change in the symbolic significance of initially meaningless words shows that fairly simple associations can condition even complex meanings and the learning that results can last a long time.[11] These associations are crucial to many marketing strategies that rely on the creation and perpetuation of **brand equity**, in which a brand has strong positive associations in a consumer's memory and commands a lot of loyalty as a result.[12]

Marketing Applications of Repetition

One advertising researcher argued that any more than three exposures to a marketing communication are wasted. The first exposure creates awareness of the product, the second demonstrates its relevance to the consumer, and the third reminds him or her of the product's benefits.[13] However, even this bare-bones approach implies that we need repetition to ensure that the consumer is actually exposed to (and processes) the message at least three times. As we saw in Chapter 2, this exposure is by no means guaranteed because people tend to tune out or distort many marketing communications. Marketers that attempt to condition an association must ensure that the consumers they target will be exposed to the stimulus a sufficient number of times to make it "stick."

Net Profit

How often should an advertiser repeat ads it places on Web sites? Recent research indicates the answer depends on whether the ad relates to the Web site's content as well as to whether or not there are also competing ads present on the site. The study found support for the general idea that repetitive ad messages resulted in higher recall and interest in learning more about the advertised product (in this case, a laptop). However, repeating the same ad was primarily effective when competitors also showed ads on the site. Otherwise it was better to vary the ad messages for the laptop (presumably because people tuned out the ad if it appeared repeatedly). And, these ads were more effective when they appeared on a site where the content related to the advertised product.[7]

Marketing Pitfall

At least on the surface, it's easier to accept some brand extensions than others. Consider the new line of wines that now sell under the Ed Hardy brand—better known for tattoo-themed streetwear. As one reviewer wrote, "Wine is a cultivated taste of a delicately cultivated product, a source of savored satisfaction and nuance, a living liquid that rewards reflection and restraint. The haute-trash Ed Hardy brand—as near as I can parse it—represents getting wasted in Las Vegas and leaving your $50 trucker hat in the cab on the way to the airport."[20] Cheers!

However, it is possible to have too much of a good thing. Consumers can become so used to hearing or seeing a marketing stimulus that they no longer pay attention to it. Varying the way in which the marketer presents the basic message can alleviate this problem of **advertising wear-out**. Toyota ran a commercial featuring a reworked version of The Fixx's 1983 hit "Saved by Zero" to promote its no-interest payment options so many times that close to 10,000 fed-up viewers organized a Facebook group to petition the company for mercy. As one worn-out group member posted, "There have been worse commercials, and there have been commercials that were played this often; but never before has a commercial this bad been aired so much."[14]

Marketing Applications of Conditioned Product Associations

Advertisements often pair a product with a positive stimulus to create a desirable association. Various aspects of a marketing message, such as music, humor, or imagery, can affect conditioning. In one study, for example, subjects who viewed a slide of pens paired with either pleasant or unpleasant music were more likely later to select the pen that appeared with the pleasant music.[15]

The order in which the conditioned stimulus and the unconditioned stimulus occur also can affect the likelihood that learning will occur. Generally speaking, a marketer should present the conditioned stimulus prior to the unconditioned stimulus. The opposite sequence of *backward conditioning*, such as when the company plays a jingle (the UCS) and then shows a soft drink (the CS), generally is not effective.[16] Because sequential presentation is desirable for conditioning to occur, classical conditioning is not as effective in static situations, for example, in magazine ads where (in contrast to TV or radio) the marketer cannot control the order in which the reader perceives the CS and the UCS.

Because of the danger of extinction, a classical conditioning strategy may not be as effective for products that consumers frequently encounter because there is no guarantee the CS will accompany them. A bottle of Pepsi paired with the refreshing sound of a carbonated beverage poured over ice may seem like a good application of conditioning. Unfortunately, people would also see the product in many other contexts in which this sound was absent, so this reduces the effectiveness of a conditioning strategy.

By the same reasoning, a marketer is better off if she chooses to pair a novel tune rather than a popular one with a product because people will also hear the popular song in many situations where the product is absent.[17] Music videos in particular may serve as effective UCSs because they often have an emotional impact on viewers, and this effect may transfer to ads that accompany the video.[18]

Marketing Applications of Stimulus Generalization

The process of stimulus generalization often is central to branding and packaging decisions that try to capitalize on consumers' positive associations with an existing brand or company name. We can clearly appreciate the value of this kind of linkage when we look at universities with winning sports teams where loyal fans snap up merchandise, from clothing to bathroom accessories, emblazoned with the school's name. This business did not even exist 20 years ago when schools were reluctant to commercialize their images. Texas A&M was one of the first schools that even bothered to file for trademark protection, and that was only after someone put the Aggie logo on a line of handguns. Today, it's a different story. Many college administrators crave the revenue they receive from sweatshirts, drink coasters, and even toilet seats emblazoned with school logos. Strategies marketers base on stimulus generalization include the following:

- **Family branding**—Many products capitalize on the reputation of a company name. Companies such as Campbell's, Heinz, and General Electric rely on their positive corporate images to sell different product lines.
- **Product line extension**—Marketers add related products to an established brand. Dole, which we associate with fruit, introduced refrigerated juices and juice bars, whereas Sun Maid went from raisins to raisin bread. The gun manufacturer

Smith & Wesson launched its own line of furniture and other home items, whereas makers of the two top diaper brands, Huggies and Pampers, both introduced lines of toiletries for babies and small children. Starbucks Corp. and Jim Beam Brands recently brought out Starbucks Coffee Liqueur. Meanwhile, Procter & Gamble cleans up with its Mr. Clean brand of liquid cleanser; it aggressively puts the name on new products such as Mr. Clean Magic Eraser, for removing crayon marks from walls and scuff marks from chair rails, and Mr. Clean Autodry, for leaving a freshly washed car spot-free without hand drying.[19]

- **Licensing**—Companies often "rent" well-known names. This strategy is increasingly popular as marketers try to link their products and services with popular brands or designers. *Prevention* magazine introduced vitamins, and *Runner's World* magazine puts its name on jogging suits. Even New York City firefighters and police got into the act following 9/11 when they licensed such products as Billy Blazes Firefighter dolls by Fisher-Price, bottled water, and fire department computer software games by Activision.[21]
- **Look-alike packaging**—Distinctive packaging designs create strong associations with a particular brand. Companies that make generic or private-label brands and want to communicate a quality image often exploit this linkage when they put their products in similar packages to those of popular brands.[22] How does this strategy affect consumers' perceptions of the original brand? One study found that a negative experience with an imitator brand actually *increased* consumers' evaluations of the original brand, whereas a positive experience with the imitator had the opposite effect of decreasing evaluations of the original brand.[23] Another study found that consumers tend to react positively to "copycat brands" as long as the imitator doesn't make grandiose claims that it can't fulfill.[24]

Of course, this strategy can make a lot of work for lawyers if the copycat brand gets *too* close to the original. Marketers of distinctive brands work hard to protect their designs and logos, and each year companies file numerous lawsuits in so-called *Lanham Act* cases that hinge on the issue of "consumer confusion"; how likely is it that one company's logo, product design, or package is so similar to another that the typical shopper would mistake one for the other? For example, Levi Strauss has sued almost 100 other apparel manufacturers that it claims have borrowed its trademark pocket design of a pentagon surrounding a drawing of a seagull in flight or its distinctive tab that it sews into its garments' vertical seams.[25]

Companies with a well-established brand image try to encourage stimulus discrimination when they promote the unique attributes of their brand—hence the constant reminders for American Express Travelers Cheques: "Ask for them by name." However, a brand name that a firm uses so widely that it is no longer distinctive becomes part of the public domain and competitors are free to borrow it—think of well-worn names such as aspirin, cellophane, yo-yo, escalator, and even google (which started as a noun and is now also a verb). This high degree of acceptance can be a mixed blessing. Now, Microsoft hopes we will choose to "bing" rather than "google" when we want information.

Instrumental Conditioning

OBJECTIVE

What is the difference between classical and instrumental conditioning?

Instrumental conditioning (or *operant conditioning*) occurs when we learn to perform behaviors that produce positive outcomes and avoid those that yield negative outcomes. We most closely associate this learning process with the psychologist B. F. Skinner, who demonstrated the effects of instrumental conditioning by teaching pigeons and other animals to dance, play Ping-Pong, and perform other activities when he systematically rewarded them for desired behaviors.[27]

Whereas responses in classical conditioning are involuntary and fairly simple, we make those in instrumental conditioning deliberately to obtain a goal, and these may be more complex. We may learn the desired behavior over a period of time as a **shaping** process rewards our intermediate actions. For example, the owner of a new store may award prizes to shoppers who simply drop in; she hopes that over time they will continue to drop in and eventually even buy something.

Also, whereas classical conditioning involves the close pairing of two stimuli, instrumental learning occurs when a learner receives a reward *after* she performs the desired behavior. In these cases learning takes place over time, while the learner attempts and abandons other behaviors that don't get reinforced. A good way to remember the difference is to keep in mind that in instrumental learning the person makes a response because it is *instrumental* to gain a reward or avoid a punishment. Over time, consumers come to associate with people who reward them and to choose products that make them feel good or satisfy some need.

Instrumental conditioning occurs in one of three ways:

1 When the environment provides **positive reinforcement** in the form of a reward, this strengthens the response and we learn the appropriate behavior. For example, a woman who gets compliments after wearing Obsession perfume learns that using this product has the desired effect, and she will be more likely to keep buying the product.

2 **Negative reinforcement** also strengthens responses so that we learn the appropriate behavior. A perfume company might run an ad showing a woman sitting home alone on a Saturday night because she did not wear its fragrance. The message this conveys is that she could have avoided this negative outcome if only she had used the perfume.

3 In contrast to situations where we learn to do certain things in order to avoid unpleasantness, **punishment** occurs when unpleasant events follow a response (such as when our friends ridicule us if we wear a nasty-smelling perfume)—we learn the hard way not to repeat these behaviors.

To help you understand the differences among these mechanisms, keep in mind that reactions from a person's environment to his behavior can be either positive or negative and that marketers can either apply or remove these outcomes (or anticipated outcomes). That is, under conditions of both positive reinforcement and punishment, the person receives a reaction when he does something. In contrast, negative reinforcement occurs when the person avoids a negative outcome—the removal of something negative is pleasurable and hence is rewarding.

Finally, when a person no longer receives a positive outcome, *extinction* is likely to occur, and the learned stimulus–response connection will not be maintained (as when a woman no longer receives compliments on her perfume). Thus, positive and negative reinforcement strengthen the future linkage between a response and an outcome because of the pleasant experience. This tie is weakened under conditions of both punishment and extinction because of the unpleasant experience. Figure 3.2 will help you to "reinforce" the relationships among these four conditions.

It's important for marketers to determine the most effective reinforcement schedule to use because this decision relates to the amount of effort and resources they must devote when they reward consumers who respond as they hope to their requests. Several schedules are possible:

● **Fixed-interval reinforcement**—After a specified time period has passed, the first response you make brings the reward. Under such conditions, people tend to respond slowly right after they get reinforced, but their responses get faster as the time for the next reinforcement approaches. For example, consumers may crowd into a store for the last day of its seasonal sale and not reappear until the next one.

● **Variable-interval reinforcement**—The time that must pass before you get reinforced varies based on some average. Because you don't know exactly when to expect the reinforcement, you have to respond at a consistent rate. This is the

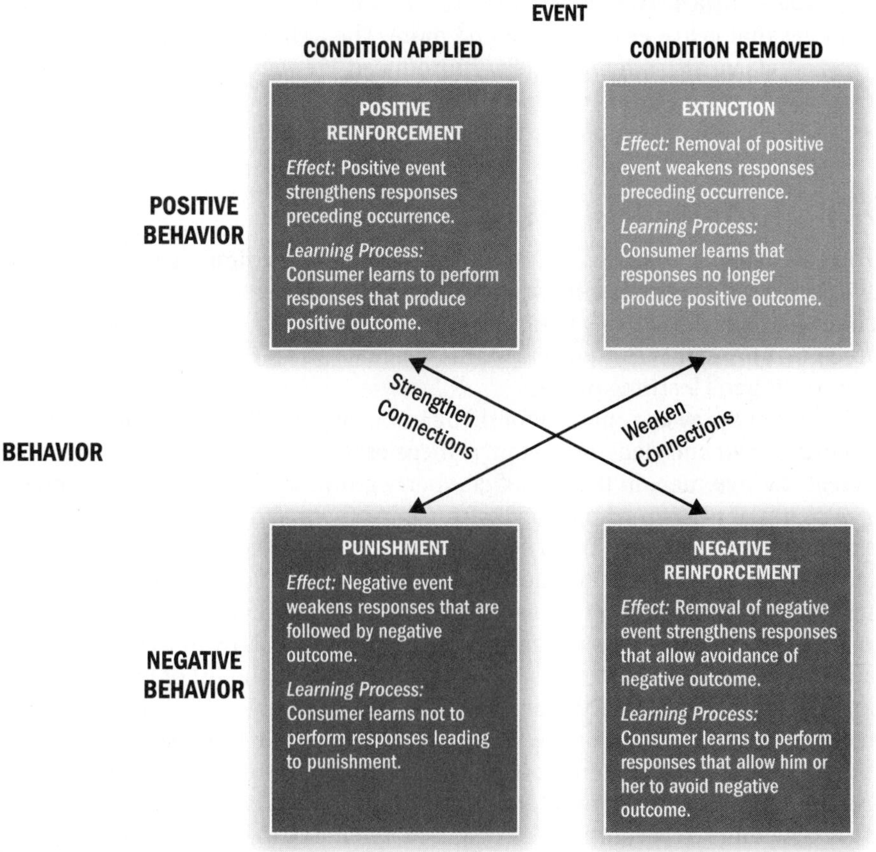

Figure 3.2 TYPES OF REINFORCEMENT

EVENT

| | **CONDITION APPLIED** | **CONDITION REMOVED** |

POSITIVE BEHAVIOR

POSITIVE REINFORCEMENT

Effect: Positive event strengthens responses preceding occurrence.

Learning Process: Consumer learns to perform responses that produce positive outcome.

EXTINCTION

Effect: Removal of positive event weakens responses preceding occurrence.

Learning Process: Consumer learns that responses no longer produce positive outcome.

BEHAVIOR

Strengthen Connections

Weaken Connections

NEGATIVE BEHAVIOR

PUNISHMENT

Effect: Negative event weakens responses that are followed by negative outcome.

Learning Process: Consumer learns not to perform responses leading to punishment.

NEGATIVE REINFORCEMENT

Effect: Removal of negative event strengthens responses that allow avoidance of negative outcome.

Learning Process: Consumer learns to perform responses that allow him or her to avoid negative outcome.

logic behind retailers' use of so-called *secret shoppers;* people who periodically test for service quality when they pose as customers at unannounced times. Because store employees never know exactly when to expect a visit, they must maintain high quality constantly "just in case."

● **Fixed-ratio reinforcement**—Reinforcement occurs only after a fixed number of responses. This schedule motivates you to continue performing the same behavior over and over. For example, you might keep buying groceries at the same store in order to earn a prize when you collect 50 register receipts.

● **Variable-ratio reinforcement** —You get reinforced after a certain number of responses, but you don't know how many responses are required. People in such situations tend to respond at very high and steady rates, and this type of behavior is very difficult to extinguish. This reinforcement schedule is responsible for consumers' attractions to slot machines. They learn that if they keep throwing money into the machine, they will eventually win something (if they don't go broke first).

Marketing Applications of Instrumental Conditioning Principles

Principles of instrumental conditioning are at work when a marketer rewards or punishes a consumer for a purchase decision. Businesspeople shape behavior when they gradually reinforce the appropriate actions consumers take. For example, a car dealer might encourage a reluctant buyer to simply sit in a floor model, then suggest a test drive, and then try to close the deal.

Marketers have many ways to reinforce consumers' behaviors, ranging from a simple thank you after a purchase to substantial rebates and follow-up phone calls. For example, a life insurance company obtained a much higher rate of policy renewal among a group of new customers who received a thank you letter after each payment, compared to a control group that did not receive any reinforcement.[28]

Frequency marketing is a popular technique that rewards regular purchasers with prizes that get better as they spend more. The airline industry pioneered this instrumental learning strategy when it introduced "frequent flyer" programs in the early 1980s to reward loyal customers. The practice has spread to many other businesses as well, ranging from video stores to fast-food places.

Cognitive Learning Theory

In contrast to behavioral theories of learning, **cognitive learning theory** approaches stress the importance of internal mental processes. This perspective views people as problem solvers who actively use information from the world around them to master their environments. Supporters of this view also stress the role of creativity and insight during the learning process.

An Ocean Spray commercial for diet cranberry juice illustrates how marketers can harness their knowledge of cognitive theories to tweak marketing messages. The spot features two men, in the role of cranberry growers, who stand knee-deep in a bog. A group of women who are exercising joins them. Originally, the ad depicted the women having a party, but a cognitive scientist who worked on the campaign nixed that idea; she argued that the exercise class would send the diet message more quickly, whereas the party scene would confuse viewers who would spend too much time trying to figure out why the group was celebrating. This extra cognitive activity would distract from the ad's message. And, contrary to standard practice in advertising that the actors name the product as early as possible, she decided that the main characters should wait a few seconds before they mention the new diet product. She reasoned that viewers would need a second or so more time to process the images because of the additional action in the ad (the exercising). In a test of which ads get remembered best, this new version scored in the top 10 percent.[29]

Is Learning Conscious or Not?

A lot of controversy surrounds the issue of whether or when people are aware of their learning processes.[30] Whereas behavioral learning theorists emphasize the routine, automatic nature of conditioning, proponents of cognitive learning argue that even these simple effects are based on cognitive factors: They create expectations that a response will follow a stimulus (the formation of expectations requires mental activity). According to this school of thought, conditioning occurs because subjects develop conscious hypotheses and then act on them.

There is some evidence to support the existence of *nonconscious procedural knowledge*. People apparently do process at least some information in an automatic, passive way, a condition researchers call "mindlessness" (we've all experienced that!).[31] When we meet someone new or encounter a new product, for example, we have a tendency to respond to the stimulus in terms of existing categories we have learned, rather than taking the trouble to formulate new ones. In these cases a *trigger feature*, some stimulus that cues us toward a particular pattern, activates a reaction. For example, men in one study rated a car in an ad as superior on a variety of characteristics if a seductive woman (the trigger feature) was present, despite the fact that the men did not believe the woman's presence actually had an influence on their evaluations.[32]

Another recent study also illustrates this process. Undergraduates who were on their way to participate in a psychology experiment "accidentally" encountered a laboratory assistant who was laden with textbooks, a clipboard, papers, and a cup of hot or iced coffee—and asked for a hand with the cup. Guess what? The students who held a cup of iced coffee rated a hypothetical person they later read about as much colder, less social, and more selfish than did their fellow students who had helped out by holding a cup of hot coffee. Other researchers report similar findings; people tidy up more thoroughly when there's a faint tang of cleaning liquid in the air and they act more competitively if there's a briefcase in the room. In each case they change their behavior without being aware of doing so.[33] Indeed, a controversial

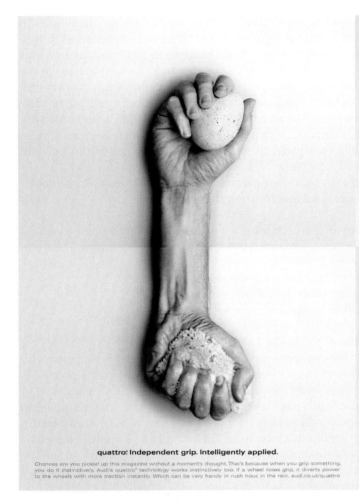
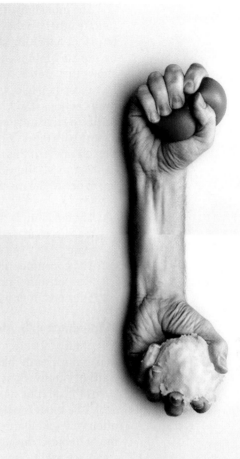

quattro: Independent grip. Intelligently applied.

Chances are you picked up this magazine without a moment's thought. That's because when you grip something, you do it instinctively. Audi's quattro® technology works instinctively too. If a wheel loses grip, it diverts power to the wheels with more traction instantly. Which can be very handy in rush hour, in the rain. audi.co.uk/quattro

Vorsprung durch Technik **Audi**

This British car ad captures the idea of mindlessness when it says, "Chances are you picked up this magazine without a moment's thought. That's because when you grip something, you do it instinctively. Audi's quattro technology works instinctively too."

Source: Used with permission of Volkswagen Group of America, Inc.

best-selling book, *Blink: The Power of Thinking Without Thinking,* argues that we often make snap judgments that result in superior decisions compared to those we think about a lot because we rely on our "adaptive unconscious" to guide us.[34]

Nonetheless, many modern theorists regard some instances of automatic conditioning as cognitive processes, especially where people form expectations about the linkages between stimuli and responses. Indeed, studies using *masking effects,* which make it difficult for subjects to learn CS/UCS associations, show substantial reductions in conditioning.[35] An adolescent girl may observe that women on television and in real life seem to be rewarded with compliments and attention when they smell nice and wear alluring clothing. She figures out that the probability of these rewards occurring is greater when she wears perfume, so she deliberately wears a popular scent to obtain the reward of social acceptance.

5

OBJECTIVE

How do we learn by observing others' behavior?

Observational Learning

Observational learning occurs when people watch the actions of others and note the reinforcements they receive for their behaviors. In these situations learning occurs as a result of *vicarious* rather than direct experience. This type of learning is a complex process; people store these observations in memory as they accumulate knowledge and then they use this information at a later point to guide their own behavior. **Modeling** (not the runway kind) is the process of imitating the behavior of others. For example, a woman who shops for a new kind of perfume may remember the reactions her friend received when she wore a certain brand several months earlier, and she will mimic her friend's behavior with the hope of getting the same feedback.

The modeling process is a powerful form of learning, and people's tendencies to imitate others' behaviors can have negative effects. Of particular concern is the potential of television shows and movies to teach violence to children. Children may be exposed to new methods of aggression by models (e.g., cartoon heroes) in the shows they watch. At some later point, when the child becomes angry, he may imitate these behaviors. A classic study demonstrates the effect of modeling on children's actions. Kids, who watched an adult stomp on, knock down, and otherwise torture a large inflated "Bobo doll" repeated these behaviors when later left alone in a room with the doll; children who did not witness these acts did not.[36] Unfortunately, the relevance of this study to violent TV shows seems quite clear.

Figure 3.3 shows that in order for observational learning in the form of modeling to occur, the marketer must meet four conditions:[37]

1 The consumer's attention must be directed to the appropriate model, whom, for reasons of attractiveness, competence, status, or similarity, he must want to emulate.
2 The consumer must remember what the model says or does.
3 The consumer must convert this information into actions.
4 The consumer must be motivated to perform these actions.

Marketing Applications of Cognitive Learning Principles

Our ability to learn vicariously when we observe the outcomes of what others do makes the lives of marketers much easier. They don't necessarily have to directly reward or punish consumers when they make a purchase (think how expensive or even ethically questionable that might be!). Instead, they can show what happens to desirable models who use or do not use their products; they know that consumers often will imitate these actions at a later time. For example, a perfume commercial might depict a throng of admirers who compliment a glamorous woman when she wears a certain fragrance. Needless to say, this learning process is more practical than providing the same attention to each woman who actually buys the perfume (unless your brand's market share is really, really small!).

Consumers' evaluations of the people they model go beyond simple stimulus–response connections. For example, a celebrity's image elicits more than a simple reflexive response of good or bad.[38] It is a complex combination of many attributes. In general, the degree to which a person emulates someone else depends on that model's level of *social attractiveness*. Attractiveness comes from several components, including physical appearance, expertise, or similarity to the evaluator (more on this in Chapter 7).

Figure 3.3 THE OBSERVATIONAL LEARNING PROCESS

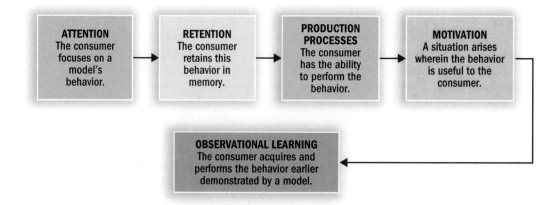

A French clothing ad relies on the models'
social attractiveness to get across its
message.
Source: Courtesy of Callegari-Berville Grey, Paris;
Executive Creative Director: Andrea Stillacci.
Creative Director: Giovanni Settesoldi / Luissandro
del Sobbo. Art Director: Giovanni Settesoldi.
Copywriter: Luissandro del Sobbo.

Memory

Memory is a process of acquiring information and storing it over time so that it will
be available when we need it. Contemporary approaches to the study of memory
employ an *information-processing approach.* They assume that the mind is in some
ways like a computer: Data are input, processed, and output for later use in revised
form. In the **encoding** stage, information enters in a way the system will recognize.
In the **storage** stage, we integrate this knowledge with what is already in memory
and "warehouse" it until it is needed. During **retrieval**, we access the desired information.[39] Figure 3.4 summarizes the memory process.

Figure 3.4 THE MEMORY PROCESS

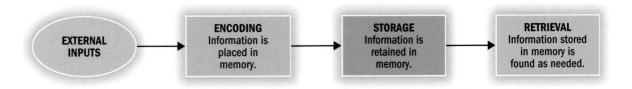

The choice of a great brand name is so important that companies often hire *naming consultants* to come up with a winner. These experts try to find *semantic associations* that click because they evoke some desirable connection. That strategy brought us names such as Qualcomm ("quality" and "communications"), Verizon (*veritas* is Latin for "truth," and "horizon" suggests forward-looking), and Intel ("intelligent" and "electronics"). The name Viagra rhymes with the famous waterfall Niagara. People associate water with both sexuality and life, and Niagara Falls is a honeymoon mecca. Philip Morris Companies renamed itself Altria Group to convey its expansion beyond cigarettes into packaged foods and brewing. This word means "high," which is a controversial choice; one brand consultant comments, "I'm not sure 'high' is right for a company with many mood-altering products in its brand portfolio."[43]

These semantic combinations get harder to find, so some consultants appeal to our more basic instincts when they focus on linkages between the raw sounds of vowels and consonants (*phonemes*) and emotional responses. Studies on sound symbolism show that respondents who speak different languages associate the same sounds with such emotion-laden qualities as sad and insecure, alive and daring. To get at these associations, researchers usually give subjects pairs of nonsense names that differ in only a single phoneme, for example, *paressa* and *taressa*, and ask which sounds faster, more daring, nicer, and so on. They've found that sounds that come to a full stop (*p, b, t, d*) connote slowness, whereas the *f, v, s,* and *z* sounds seem faster. Prozac and Amazon convey a sense of speed (of recovery or of delivery). When naming consultants got the assignment to label a new handheld personal digital assistant (PDA), they first thought of Strawberry because the little keyboard buttons resembled seeds. They liked the "berry" part of the name because they knew that people associated the letter *b* with reliability and a berry communicated smallness compared to other PDAs. But a linguist pointed out that "straw" is a slow syllable and the product needed to have a fast connotation. Voila! The BlackBerry PDA was born.[44]

Many of our experiences are locked inside our heads, and they may surface years later if the right cues prompt them. Marketers rely on consumers to retain information they collect about products and services so they will apply it to future purchase decisions. During the *consumer decision-making process* (which we will learn about in detail in Chapter 8), we combine this *internal memory* with *external memory*. This includes all the product details on packages and other marketing stimuli that permit us to identify and evaluate brand alternatives in the marketplace.[40]

The grocery shopping list is a good example of a powerful external memory aid. When consumers use shopping lists, they buy approximately 80 percent of the items on the list. And the likelihood that a shopper will purchase a particular list item is higher if the person who wrote the list also participates in the shopping trip. This means that, if marketers can induce a consumer to plan to purchase an item before she goes shopping, there is a high probability she will buy it. One way to encourage this kind of advance planning is to provide peel-off stickers on packages so that, when the consumer notices the supply is low, she can simply peel off the label and place it directly on a shopping list.[41]

How Our Brains Encode Information

The way we *encode*, or mentally program, information helps to determine how we will represent it in memory. In general, it's more likely we'll retain incoming data when we associate it with other information already in memory. For example, we tend to remember brand names we link to physical characteristics of a product category (e.g., Coffee-Mate creamer or Sani-Flush toilet bowl cleaner) or that we can easily visualize (e.g., Tide detergent or Ford Mustang cars) compared to more abstract brand names.[42]

Types of Meaning

Sometimes we process a stimulus simply in terms of its *sensory meaning*, such as the literal color or shape of a package. We may experience a feeling of familiarity when, for example, we see an ad for a new snack food we have recently tasted. In many cases, though, we encode meanings at a more abstract level. *Semantic meaning* refers to symbolic associations, such as the idea that rich people drink champagne or that fashionable women have navel piercings. Let's take a closer look at how we encode these deeper meanings.

Episodic memories relate to events that are personally relevant.[45] As a result, a person's motivation to retain these memories will likely be strong. Couples often have "their song," which reminds them of their first date or wedding. We call some especially vivid associations *flashbulb memories* (for example, where were you when you first heard about the attack on The World Trade Center?). And recall of the past may affect future behavior. A college fund-raising campaign can raise more money when it evokes pleasant college memories than when it reminds alumni of unpleasant ones.

A **narrative**, or story is often an effective way to convey product information. Our memories store a lot of the social information we acquire in story form; it's a good idea to construct ads in the form of a narrative so they resonate with the audience. Narratives persuade people to construct mental representations of the information they see or hear. Pictures aid in this construction and allow us to develop more detailed mental representations.[46] Research supports the idea that we are more likely to positively evaluate and purchase brands when they connect with us like this.[47]

Memory Systems

OBJECTIVE 6
How do memory systems work?

According to the information-processing perspective, there are three distinct memory systems: *sensory memory*, *short-term memory (STM)*, and *long-term memory (LTM)*. Each plays a role in processing brand-related information. Figure 3.5 summarizes the interrelationships among these memory systems.

Sensory Memory

Sensory memory stores the information we receive from our senses. This storage is very temporary; it lasts a couple of seconds at most. For example, a man who walks past a donut shop gets a quick, enticing whiff of something baking inside. Although this sensation lasts only a few seconds, it is sufficient to allow him to consider whether

Marketing Opportunity

It's common for marketers to give a brand a vivid name that conjures up an image or story in our minds. Research suggests this strategy results in higher consumer evaluations versus brand names composed of meaningless letters or numbers. One study reported that consumers rated cell phones from Samsung and LG more positively after they were the first in the industry to break the practice of naming the phones with combinations of letters and numbers—LG's phones instead sport names like Chocolate, Shine, Vu, Voyager, Dare, and Decoy while Samsung started things off with the BlackJack, UpStage, FlipShot, and Juke and later added the Access, Instinct, and Glyde. During the same period these companies increased market share in this category. Compared to other phone brands, consumers rated these models as modern, creative, engaging, original, cool, and easy to remember.[48]

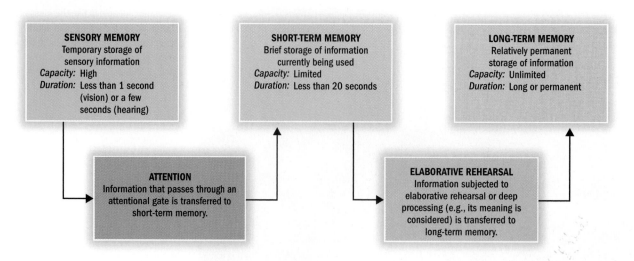

Figure 3.5 THE MEMORY PROCESS

he should investigate further. If he retains this information for further processing, it passes through an **attentional gate** and transfers to short-term memory.

Short-Term Memory

Short-term memory (STM) also stores information for a limited period of time, and it has limited capacity. Similar to a computer, this system is *working memory*; it holds the information we are currently processing. Our memories can store verbal input *acoustically* (in terms of how it sounds) or *semantically* (in terms of what it means).

We store this information by combining small pieces into larger ones in a process we call **chunking**. A chunk is a configuration that is familiar to the person and that he or she can think about as a unit. For example, a brand name such as Seven For All Mankind is a chunk that summarizes a great deal of detailed information about the product.

Initially, researchers believed that our STM was capable of processing between five and nine chunks of information at a time—they described this basic property as "the magical number 7 + / − 2." This is the reason our phone numbers today (at least in the United States) have seven digits.[49] It now appears that three to four chunks is the optimal size for efficient retrieval (we remember seven-digit phone numbers because we chunk the individual digits, so we may remember a three-digit exchange as one piece of information).[50] Phone calls aside, chunking is important to marketers because it helps determine how consumers keep prices in short-term memory when they comparison shop.[51]

Long-Term Memory

Long-term memory (LTM) is the system that allows us to retain information for a long period of time. A cognitive process we call **elaborative rehearsal** allows information to move from short-term memory into long-term memory. This involves thinking about the meaning of a stimulus and relating it to other information already in memory. Marketers sometimes assist in the process when they devise catchy slogans or jingles that consumers repeat on their own.

How Our Memories Store Information

The relationship between short-term memory and long-term memory is a source of some controversy. The traditional *multiple-store* perspective assumes that STM and LTM are separate systems. More recent research has moved away from the distinction between the two types of memory; it emphasizes the interdependence of the systems. According to this work, depending on the nature of the processing task, different levels of processing occur that activate some aspects of memory rather than others. We call these approaches **activation models of memory**.[52] The more effort it takes to process information (so-called "deep processing"), the more likely it is that information will transfer into LTM.

OBJECTIVE

Why do the other products we associate with an individual product influence how we will remember it?

Associative Networks

According to activation models of memory, an incoming piece of information gets stored in an **associative network** that contains many bits of related information. We each have organized systems of concepts that relate to brands, manufacturers, and stores stored in our memories; the contents, of course, depend on our own unique experiences.

Think of these storage units, or *knowledge structures,* as complex spider webs filled with pieces of data. Incoming information gets put into nodes that connect to one another (if you haven't guessed, this is also why we call cyberspace the World Wide Web). When we view separate pieces of information as similar for some reason, we chunk them together under some more abstract category. Then, we interpret new, incoming information to be consistent with the structure we have created (recall the discussion in Chapter 2 about how prior expectations influence current experiences).[53] This helps explain why we are better able to remember brands or stores that we believe "go together," for example, when Spalding rather than Chanel sponsors a golf tournament. Recent research indicates that people can recall brands that are not as obviously linked (for example, when an unlikely product sponsors an event), but in these cases marketers have to work harder to justify why the two things go together.[54]

In the associative network, links form between nodes. For example, a consumer might have a network for "perfumes." Each node represents a concept related to the category. This node can be an attribute, a specific brand, a celebrity the consumer identifies with a specific perfume brand, or even a related product. A network for perfumes might include concepts such as the names Brit for Women, Light Blue, and CKOne, as well as attributes such as sexy and elegant.

When we ask the consumer to list perfumes, this consumer recalls only those brands that show up in the appropriate category. This group constitutes her **evoked set**. The task of a new entrant that wants to position itself as a category member (e.g., a new luxury perfume) is to provide cues that facilitate its placement in the appropriate category. Figure 3.6 shows a sample network for perfumes.

Spreading Activation

A marketing message may activate our memory of a brand directly (for example, when it shows us a picture of the package) or it may do so indirectly when it links to something else that's related to the brand in our knowledge structure. If it activates a node, it will also activate other linked nodes much as tapping a spider's web in one spot sends movement reverberating across the web. Meaning thus spreads across the network, and we recall concepts, such as competing brands and relevant attributes, that we use to form attitudes toward the brand.

This process of **spreading activation** allows us to shift back and forth among levels of meaning. The way we store a piece of information in memory depends on the type of meaning we initially assign to it. This meaning type, in turn, will determine how and when something activates the meaning. For example, we could store the memory trace for an Axe men's fragrance ad in one or more of the following ways:

- **Brand-specific**—Memory is stored in terms of claims the brand makes ("it's macho").

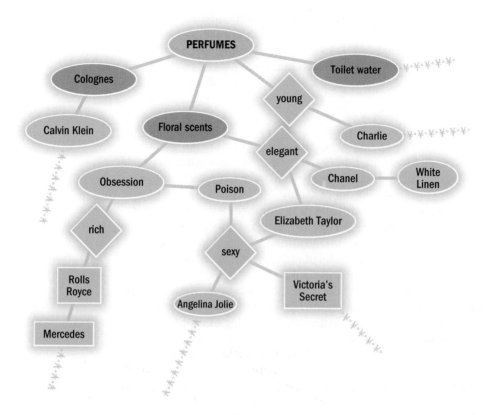

Figure 3.6 AN ASSOCIATIVE NETWORK FOR PERFUMES

- **Ad-specific**—Memory is stored in terms of the medium or content of the ad itself (a macho-looking guy uses the product).
- **Brand identification**—Memory is stored in terms of the brand name (e.g., "Axe").
- **Product category**—Memory is stored in terms of how the product works or where it should be used (a bottle of Axe sits in a guy's medicine cabinet).
- **Evaluative reactions**—Memory is stored as positive or negative emotions ("that looks cool").[55]

Levels of Knowledge

Within a knowledge structure we code elements at different levels of abstraction and complexity. *Meaning* concepts (such as "macho") get stored as individual nodes. We may combine these concepts into a larger unit we call a *proposition* (or a *belief*). A proposition links two nodes together to form a more complex meaning, which can serve as a single chunk of information. For example, "Axe is cologne for macho men" is a proposition (not necessarily a correct one!).

In turn, we integrate propositions to produce an even more complex unit called a *schema*, which we saw in Chapter 2. A schema is a cognitive framework we develop through experience. We encode information more readily that is consistent with an existing schema.[56] The ability to move up and down among levels of abstraction greatly increases processing flexibility and efficiency. For this reason, young children who do not have well-developed schemas yet are not able to make as efficient use of purchase information as are older children.[57]

One type of schema especially relevant to consumer behavior is a **script**, a sequence of events an individual expects to occur. As consumers we learn *service scripts* that guide our behavior in commercial settings. We expect a certain sequence of events, and we may become uncomfortable if the service departs from our script. A service script for a visit to the dentist might include such events as (1) drive to the dentist, (2) read old magazines in the waiting room, (3) hear name called and sit in dentist's chair, (4) dentist injects something into gums, (5) dentist turns on high-pitched drill, and so on. This desire to follow a script helps to explain why such service innovations as automatic bank machines, self-service gas stations, or "scan-your-own" grocery checkouts have met with resistance by some consumers who have trouble adapting to new sequences of events.[58]

How We Retrieve Memories When We Decide What to Buy

In a study conducted by Information Resources Inc., *New Products* magazine, comScore, and Schneider Associates, only 23 percent of the respondents could recall a new product introduced in the past year.[59] Not a pretty picture for marketers.

Retrieval is the process whereby we recover information from long-term memory. As evidenced by the popularity of the board game *Trivial Pursuit*, people have a vast quantity of information stored in their heads—a lot of which is not very useful unless you're playing the game! Although most of the information that enters our long-term memory does not go away, it may be difficult or impossible to retrieve unless the appropriate cues are present. What factors influence the likelihood we will remember the marketing messages that organizations work so hard to create?

Individual cognitive or physiological factors are responsible for some of the differences in retrieval ability among people.[60] Older adults consistently display inferior recall ability for current items, such as prescription drug instructions, although they may recall events that happened to them when they were younger with great clarity.[61] The recent popularity of puzzles, such as Sudoku, and centers that offer "mental gymnastics" attests to emerging evidence that we can keep our retrieval abilities sharp by exercising our minds just as we keep our other muscles toned when we work out on a regular basis.

Situational factors also influence retrieval; these relate to the environment in which we encounter the message. Not surprisingly, recall is enhanced when we pay more attention to the message in the first place. Some evidence indicates that we can retrieve information about a *pioneering brand* (the first brand to enter a market) more easily from memory than we can for *follower brands* because the first product's introduction is likely to be distinctive and, for the time being, no competitors divert

HBO wants to be sure fans of the series *Big Love* don't forget about the show.
Source: Courtesy of HBO.

our attention.[62] In addition, we are more likely to recall descriptive brand names than those that do not provide adequate cues as to what the product is.[63]

Not surprisingly, the way a marketer presents her message influences the likelihood we'll be able to recall it later. The **spacing effect** describes the tendency for us to recall printed material more effectively when the advertiser repeats the target item periodically rather than presenting it repeatedly in a short time period.[64] The viewing environment of a marketing message also affects recall. For example, commercials we see during baseball games yield the lowest recall scores among sports programs because the activity is stop-and-go rather than continuous. Unlike football or basketball, the pacing of baseball gives many opportunities for attention to wander even during play. Similarly, General Electric found that its commercials fared better in television shows with continuous activity, such as stories or dramas, compared to variety shows or talk shows that are punctuated by a series of acts.[65] Finally, a large-scale analysis of TV commercials found that viewers recall commercials shown first in a series of ads better than those they see last.[66]

Finally, it goes without saying that the nature of the ad itself plays a big role in determining whether it's memorable. One study on print advertising reported that we are far more likely to remember spectacular magazine ads, including multipage spreads, three-dimensional pop-ups, scented ads, and ads with audio components. For example, a Pepsi Jazz two-page spread with a three-dimensional pop-up of the opened bottle and a small audio chip that played jazz music from the bottle's opening as well as a scratch-and-sniff tab that let readers smell its black cherry vanilla flavor scored an amazing 100 percent in reader recall.[67] Unfortunately, that kind of multimedia treatment is very expensive; not every ad can mimic a Broadway production!

What Makes Us Forget?

Marketers obviously hope that consumers will not forget about their products. However, in a poll of more than 13,000 adults, more than half were unable to remember any specific ad they had seen, heard, or read in the past 30 days. How many can you remember right now? Clearly, forgetting by consumers is a big headache for marketers (not to mention a problem for students when they study for exams!).

Early memory theorists assumed that memories simply fade with the passage of time. In a process of **decay**, the structural changes learning produces in the brain simply go away. Forgetting also occurs as a result of **interference**; as we learn additional information, it displaces the earlier information. Consumers may forget stimulus–response associations if they subsequently learn new responses to the same or similar stimuli; we call this process *retroactive interference*. Or prior learning can interfere with new learning, a process we term *proactive interference*. Because we store pieces of information in memory as nodes that link to one another, we are more likely to retrieve a meaning concept that is connected by a larger number of links. But as we learn new responses, a stimulus loses its effectiveness in retrieving the old response.[68]

These interference effects help to explain problems in remembering brand information. Consumers tend to organize attribute information by brand.[69] Additional attribute information regarding a brand or similar brands may limit the person's ability to recall old brand information. Recall may also be inhibited if the brand name is composed of frequently used words. These words cue competing associations and, as a result, we retain less brand information.[70]

In one study, brand evaluations deteriorated more rapidly when ads for the brand appeared with messages for 12 other brands in the same category than when researchers showed the ad along with ads for 12 dissimilar products.[71] Thus, when we increase the uniqueness of one brand it impairs the recall of other brands.[72] However, when we call a competitor by name this can result in poorer recall for our own brand.[73]

Finally, the **part-list cueing effect** allows marketers to strategically use the interference process. When they present only a portion of the items in a category to consumers, they don't recall the omitted items as easily. For example, comparative advertising that mentions only a subset of competitors (preferably those that the marketer is not very worried about) may inhibit recall of the *unmentioned* brands with which the product does not favorably compare.[74]

State-Dependent Retrieval

Is it true that you'll do better on an exam if you study for it in the classroom in which you'll take the test? Perhaps. The process we call **state-dependent retrieval** illustrates that we are better able to access information if our internal state is the same at the time of recall as when we learned the information. So, we are more likely to recall an ad if our mood or level of arousal at the time of exposure is similar to that in the purchase environment. When marketers re-create the cues that were present when they first presented the information they can enhance recall. For example, Life cereal uses a picture of "Mikey" from its commercial on the cereal box, which facilitates recall of brand claims and favorable brand evaluations.[75]

Familiarity and Recall

As a general rule, when we are already familiar with an item we're more likely to recall messages about it. Indeed, this is one of the basic goals of marketers who try to create and maintain awareness of their products. The more experience a consumer has with a product, the better use he or she makes of product information.[76] However, there is a possible fly in the ointment: As we noted earlier in this chapter, some evidence indicates that extreme familiarity can result in inferior learning and recall. When consumers are highly familiar with a brand or an advertisement, they may attend to fewer attributes because they do not believe that any additional effort will increase their knowledge.[77] For example, when researchers expose consumers to a radio ad that repeats the audio track from a television ad they've already seen, they do very little critical, evaluative processing and instead mentally replay the video portion of the ad.[78]

Salience and Recall

The **salience** of a brand refers to its prominence or level of activation in memory. As we noted in Chapter 2, stimuli that stand out in contrast to their environments are more likely to command attention, which, in turn, increases the likelihood that we will recall them. Almost any technique that increases the novelty of a stimulus also improves recall (a result we call the **von Restorff Effect**).[79] This explains why unusual advertising or distinctive packaging tends to facilitate brand recall.[80]

Introducing a surprise element in an ad can be particularly effective in aiding recall, even if it is not relevant to the factual information the ad presents.[81] In addition, *mystery ads*, in which the ad doesn't identify the brand until the end, are more effective if we want to build associations in memory between the product category and that brand—especially in the case of relatively unknown brands.[82]

And, the intensity and type of emotions we experience at the time also affect the way we recall the event later. We recall mixed emotions (e.g., those with positive and negative components) differently than **unipolar emotions** (e.g., those that are either wholly positive or wholly negative). The latter become even more polarized over time, so that we recall good things as even better than they really were and bad things as even worse (maybe the "good old days" weren't really so good after all!).[83]

The Viewing Context

Regardless of how awesome a commercial is, the show in which it appears influences its impact. Nielsen (the company that measures who watches which media) reports that viewers who enjoy a program are more likely to respond positively to a commercial and to say they want to buy the advertised product. Nielsen studied the responses of 10,000 people across 50 shows and 200 brands. Viewers are almost one-third more likely to remember brands whose products were placed in shows they

CB AS I SEE IT

Professor Jennifer Aaker, *Stanford University*

*I*magine you are at Disneyland about to board the Space Mountain ride. As you climb into your rocket, you feel joy and apprehension—a mixed feeling that persists even after the ride is over. You grip the safety bar, at once thrilled and frightened. You leave the Space Mountain ride dizzy with mixed emotions. How will you recall your experience a week later? Will you remember the mixed emotions you experienced on the ride? Or will the memory of those mixed emotions fade?

Questions regarding the memory of mixed emotions are important. Many of life's most important events are defined by mixtures of emotions where people find themselves feeling both positive and negative emotions—e.g., graduating from college ("I'm making progress, but leaving my friends and family"), moving ("I'm starting a new life, but losing my old one"), or achieving major life goals ("I'm thrilled to have reached the destination, but I'm sad the journey is over").

To address these questions, we conducted a set of longitudinal experiments that show that the intensity of mixed emotions is underestimated at the time of recall—an effect that appears to increase over time and does not occur to the same degree with uniformly happy or sad emotions. Together, these results indicate that, as time passes, mixed emotions are increasingly difficult to recall, that memory for them fades, and that felt conflict underlies this recall bias.

The results of this work speak to several domains of research. For example, the results imply that individuals who are comfortable with inconsistency should recall mixed emotions more accurately. Similarly, if there is an increased desire to resolve the emotion of felt conflict, the effects documented here should be muted for individuals who are not disturbed by the ambiguity associated with mixed emotions. And, the effects should dissipate if the mixed emotions we experience consist of a dominant emotion (e.g., strong feelings of anger), thereby reducing the conflict we feel.

The results also speak to ongoing research in marketing, which suggests that emotional experiences can fundamentally impact purchase intent as well as foster brand loyalty. For example, the amount of warmth that emanates from a brand or the fun enjoyed by a brand (e.g., iPhone) can fundamentally influence our relationship with it. However, in reality, most consumer-brand relationships are defined, at some point or another, by a transgression that gives rise to negative feelings among consumers—such as when something you buy breaks. Our research suggests that the degree to which a negative event is categorized as part of a mixed experience (versus as a single negative event) impacts the probability that the consumer will remember that experience and be influenced by it. If the transgression is mentally clumped together with positive interactions with the brand, the memory of the mixed emotional experience may indeed fade—which would not be the case if the transgression stood alone as an isolated negative event.

---

enjoy. The impact of this factor varies across show format; it's weaker in sitcoms but much stronger in "lifestyle programs" like *Extreme Makeover Home Edition*.[84]

It also helps when the marketer's message is consistent with the theme or events in the program—and it's even better when the advertised product actually makes a reference to the show. The Discovery Channel documented this effect during a broadcast of its program *Mythbusters*, which uses science to test the validity of urban legends. The network ran a brief ad for Guinness beer where a character asked another whether it was a ". . . myth that Guinness only has 125 calories." Viewers who saw this ad remembered the name of the Guinness brand 41 percent more often than they did when they saw a traditional ad for the beer. Other similar **hybrid ads** that include a program tie-in deliver similar results.[85] In fact, Turner Entertainment Network launched a new initiative it calls *TV in Context* for the 2009–2010 television season that explicitly tailors commercials to the shows in which they appear. For example after viewers watch a car crash scene in the movie *The Bourne Supremacy*, they see a spot for General Motors' OnStar service that asks, "Are you counting on your cell phone to be your lifeline in a crash?"[86]

Pictorial Versus Verbal Cues: Is a Picture Worth a Thousand Words?

There is some evidence for the superiority of visual memory over verbal memory, but this advantage is unclear because it is more difficult to measure recall of pictures.[88] However, the available data indicate that we are more likely to recognize information we see in picture form at a later time.[89] Certainly, visual aspects of an ad are more likely to grab a consumer's attention. In fact, eye-movement studies indicate that about 90 percent of viewers look at the dominant picture in an ad before they bother to view the copy.[90]

Although pictorial ads may enhance recall, they do not necessarily improve comprehension. One study found that television news items presented with illustrations (still pictures) as a backdrop result in improved recall for details of the news story, even though understanding of the story's content does not improve.[91] Another study confirmed that typically consumers recall ads with visual figures more often and they like them better.[92]

8

OBJECTIVE

How do products help us to retrieve memories from our past?

Products as Memory Markers

Products and ads can themselves serve as powerful retrieval cues. Indeed, the three types of possessions consumers most value are furniture, visual art, and photos. These objects are most likely to jog memories of the past.[93] Researchers find that valued possessions can evoke thoughts about prior events on several dimensions, including sensory experiences, friends and loved ones, and breaking away from parents or former partners.[94]

An Australian ad for hair products evokes memories of an earlier time—that some of us might prefer to forget.
Source: Courtesy of Fudge Australia.

Fossil's product designs evoke memories of earlier, classic styles.

Source: Used with permission of Fossil Inc. Photography by Thom Jackson and Jon Kirk.

Food can do the same thing: One study looked at how favorite recipes stimulate memories of the past. When the researchers asked informants to list three of their favorite recipes and to talk about these choices, they found that people tended to link them with memories of past events such as childhood memories, family holidays, milestone events (such as dishes they only make on special holidays like corned beef and cabbage on St. Patrick's Day), heirlooms (recipes handed down across generations), and the passing of time (e.g., only eating blueberry cobbler in the summer).[95]

Products are particularly important as markers when our sense of the past is threatened, as for example, when an event, such as divorce, relocation, or graduation challenges a consumer's current identity.[96] Our cherished possessions often have *mnemonic* qualities that serve as a form of external memory when they prompt us to retrieve episodic memories. For example, family photography allows consumers to create their own retrieval cues; the 11 billion amateur photos we take annually form a kind of external memory bank for our culture. A stimulus is, at times, able to evoke a weakened response even years after we first perceived it. We call this effect **spontaneous recovery**, and this reestablished connection may explain consumers' powerful emotional reactions to songs or pictures they have not been exposed to in quite a long time.

OBJECTIVE

How do marketers measure our memories about products and ads?

How We Measure Consumers' Recall of Marketing Messages

Because marketers pay so much money to place their messages in front of consumers, they hope that people will actually remember these ads at a later point. It seems that they have good reason to be concerned. In one study, fewer than

40 percent of television viewers made positive links between commercial messages and the corresponding products, only 65 percent noticed the brand name in a commercial, and only 38 percent recognized a connection to an important point.[97]

Ironically, we may be more likely to remember companies that we don't like—perhaps because of the strong negative emotions they evoke. In a 2007 survey, for example, that assessed both recall of companies and their reputations, 4 of the 10 best-remembered companies also ranked in the bottom 10 of reputation rankings: Halliburton Co., Ford Motor Co., General Motors Corp., and Exxon Mobil Corp. In fact, Halliburton, with the lowest reputation score, scored the highest media recall of all 60 companies in the survey.[98]

Even more sadly, only 7 percent of television viewers can recall the product or company featured in the most recent television commercial they watched. This figure represents less than half the recall rate recorded in 1965. We can explain this drop-off in terms of such factors as the increase of 30- and 15-second commercials and the practice of airing television commercials in clusters rather than in single-sponsor programs.[99]

Recognition Versus Recall

One indicator of good advertising is, of course, the impression it makes on us. But how can we define and measure this impact? Two basic measures of impact are **recognition** and **recall**. In the typical *recognition test*, researchers show ads to subjects one at a time and ask if they have seen them before. In contrast, *free recall tests* ask consumers to independently think of what they have seen without being prompted for this information first—obviously, this task requires greater effort on their part.

Intermedia Advertising Group is a research firm that measures advertising effectiveness by monitoring the TV-viewing population's ability to remember an ad within 24 hours. The firm assigns a *recall index* to each ad to indicate the strength of the impact it had. In one recent year, whereas ads with well-known celebrities such as Britney Spears, Austin Powers, and Michael Jordan had very high recall rates, three of the top five most-remembered ads starred another (and taller) celebrity: Toys "R" Us spokesanimal Geoffrey the Giraffe![100]

Under some conditions, these two memory measures tend to yield the same results, especially when the researchers try to keep the viewers' interest in the ads constant (though as we've already seen, that may be an overly artificial way to study true memory for ads).[101] Generally, though, recognition scores tend to be more reliable and do not decay over time the way recall scores do.[102] Recognition scores are almost always better than recall scores because recognition is a simpler process and the consumer has more retrieval cues available.

Both types of retrieval play important roles in purchase decisions, however. Recall tends to be more important in situations in which consumers do not have product data at their disposal, so they must rely on memory to generate this information.[103] However, recognition is more likely to be an important factor in a store, where retailers confront consumers with thousands of product options (i.e., external memory is abundantly available) and the task simply may be to recognize a familiar package. Unfortunately, package recognition and familiarity can have negative consequences—consumers may ignore warning labels because they take their messages for granted and don't really notice them.[104]

Problems with Memory Measures

Although measuring an ad's memorability is important, analysts have questioned whether existing measures accurately assess these dimensions for several reasons. First, the results we obtain from a measuring instrument are not necessarily based on what we measure but rather on something else about the instrument or the respondent. This form of contamination is a **response bias**. For example, people tend to give "yes" responses to questions, regardless of what the item asks. In addition, experimental subjects often are eager to be "good subjects;" they try to figure out what the experimenter is looking for and give the response they think they are supposed to give. This tendency is so strong that in some studies the rate at which subjects claim they recognize *bogus ads* (ads they have not seen before) is almost as high as their recognition rate for those they have seen![105]

Memory Lapses

People are also prone to forgetting information or retaining inaccurate memories (yes, even younger people). Typical problems include *omitting* (leaving facts out), *averaging* (the tendency to "normalize" memories by not reporting extreme cases), and *telescoping* (inaccurate recall of time).[106] These distortions are not just a problem in court cases that rely on eyewitness testimony; they also call into question the accuracy of product usage databases that rely on consumers to recall their purchase and consumption of food and household items. For example, one study asked people to describe what portion of various foods—small, medium, or large—they ate in a typical meal. However, the researchers used different definitions of "medium." Regardless of the definition they gave, about the same number of people claimed they typically ate "medium" portions.[107]

Another study documented the **illusion of truth effect**, where telling people (especially elderly subjects) that a consumer claim is false can make them misremember it as true. Respondents were repeatedly told that a claim was false; after a 3-day delay they were likely to remember it as true. This is because the repetition of the claim increases familiarity with it but respondents don't retain their memories

This ad from Chile uses a retro appeal.
Source: Courtesy of Volkswagen.

of the context (where the claim was debunked). This effect has potentially important implications, especially for social marketing campaigns that try to educate people about false claims.[108]

Finally, although researchers continue to work on techniques that increase the accuracy of memory scores, these improvements do not address the more fundamental issue of whether recall is even necessary for advertising to have an effect. In particular, some critics argue that these measures do not adequately tap the impact of "feeling" ads whose objective is to arouse strong emotions rather than to convey concrete product benefits. Many ad campaigns, including those for Hallmark cards, Chevrolet, and Pepsi, use this approach.[109] In these cases, the marketers hope to create a long-term buildup of positive feelings rather than relying on a one-shot attempt to convince consumers to buy their products.

Also, it is not clear that recall translates into preference. We may recall the benefits touted in an ad but not believe them. Or the ad may be memorable because it is so obnoxious and the product becomes one we "love to hate." The bottom line: Although recall is important, especially to create brand awareness, it is not necessarily sufficient to alter consumer preferences. To accomplish this, we need more sophisticated attitude-changing strategies. We'll discuss these issues in Chapter 7.

Bittersweet Memories:
The Marketing Power of Nostalgia

Marketers often resurrect popular characters and stories from days gone by; they hope that consumers' fond memories will motivate them to revisit the past. We had a 1950s revival in the 1970s, and consumers in the 1980s got a heavy dose of memories from the 1960s. Today, it seems that popular characters only need to be gone for a few years before someone tries to bring them back.

Nostalgia describes a bittersweet emotion where we view the past with both sadness and longing.[110] References to "the good old days" are increasingly common, as advertisers call up memories of youth—and hope these feelings will translate to what they're selling today.

A **retro brand** is an updated version of a brand from a prior historical period (such as the PT Cruiser we'll talk about in Chapter 16). These products trigger nostalgia, and researchers find that they often inspire consumers to think back to an era where (at least in our memories) life was more stable, simple, or even utopian—they let us "look backward through rose-colored glasses."[111]

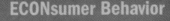

ECONsumer Behavior

There's nothing like tough economic times to trigger longing for the past. Many companies have responded as they dig deep into their vaults to bring back old favorites such as these:

- Mattel is reviving Barbie's little sister Skipper, as well as a Barbie camper based on an earlier 1971 version.
- Hasbro is bringing back the 60-year-old popular board game Candy Land (this time as a 3-D version) as well as its Super Soaker water gun and Care Bears characters.[112]
- General Mills uses retro box designs for cereals—Cheerios, Honey Nut Cheerios, Lucky Charms, Cocoa Puffs, and Trix cereals.
- Sales of well-loved candies like Mary Janes, Tootsie Rolls, and Gummy Bears are booming. The first candy boom occurred during the Great Depression in the 1930s when Snickers, Tootsie Pops, Mars bars, and Three Musketeers debuted to provide cheap treats to cash-poor consumers.
- Target periodically features "retro toys" in its catalogs like sock monkeys and gumball machines.
- Commercials for I Can't Believe It's Not Butter feature a make-believe 1950s family named the Buttertons.
- Cotton Inc. reintroduced its jingle "The Fabric of Our Lives," that it used in commercials in the 1990s after its research found that its target audience of women in their 20s and 30s had positive memories of it.

Strawberry Shortcake returns.
Source: Reproduced by Permission. Those Characters From Cleveland, Inc. © TCFC, Inc.

Our prior experiences also help to determine what we like today. Consumer researchers created a *nostalgia index* that measures the critical ages during which our preferences are likely to form and endure over time. It turns out that a good predictor of whether a person will like a specific song is how old she was when that song was popular. On average, we are most likely to favor songs that were popular when we were 23.5 years old (so pay attention to the hot songs if you haven't turned 23 yet). Our preferences for fashion models peak at age 33, and we tend to like movie stars that were popular when we were 26 or 27 years old.[113]

CHAPTER SUMMARY

Now that you have finished reading this chapter you should understand why:

 It's important for marketers to understand how consumers learn about products and services.

Learning is a change in behavior that experience causes. Learning can occur through simple associations between a stimulus and a response or via a complex series of cognitive activities.

 Conditioning results in learning.

Behavioral learning theories assume that learning occurs as a result of responses to external events. Classical conditioning occurs when a stimulus that naturally elicits a response (an unconditioned stimulus) is paired with another stimulus that does not initially elicit this response. Over time, the second stimulus (the conditioned stimulus) elicits the response even in the absence of the first.

 Learned associations can generalize to other things and why this is important to marketers.

This response can also extend to other, similar stimuli in a process we call stimulus generalization. This process is the basis for such marketing strategies as licensing and family branding, where a consumer's positive associations with a product transfer to other contexts.

 There is a difference between classical and instrumental conditioning.

Operant, or instrumental, conditioning occurs as the person learns to perform behaviors that produce positive outcomes and avoid those that result in negative outcomes. Whereas classical conditioning involves the pairing of two stimuli, instrumental learning occurs when reinforcement occurs following a response to a stimulus. Reinforcement is positive if a reward follows a response. It is negative if the person avoids a negative outcome by not performing a response. Punishment occurs when an unpleasant event follows a response. Extinction of the behavior will occur if reinforcement no longer occurs.

 We learn by observing others' behavior.

Cognitive learning occurs as the result of mental processes. For example, observational learning occurs when the consumer performs a behavior as a result of seeing someone else performing it and being rewarded for it.

 Memory systems work.

Memory is the storage of learned information. The way we encode information when we perceive it determines how we will store it in memory. The memory systems we call sensory memory, short-term memory, and long-term memory each play a role in retaining and processing information from the outside world.

 The other products we associate with an individual product influence how we will remember it.

We don't store information in isolation; we incorporate it into knowledge structure where our brains associate it with other related data. The location of product information in associative networks, and the level of abstraction at which it is coded, help to determine when and how we will activate this information at a later time. Some factors that influence the likelihood of retrieval include the level of familiarity with an item, its salience (or prominence) in memory, and whether the information was presented in pictorial or written form.

 Products help us to retrieve memories from our past.

Products also play a role as memory markers; consumers use them to retrieve memories about past experiences (autobiographical memories), and we often value them because they are able to do this. This function also encourages the use of nostalgia in marketing strategies.

 Marketers measure our memories about products and ads.

We can use either recognition or recall techniques to measure memory for product information. Consumers are more likely to recognize an advertisement if it is presented to them than they are to recall one without being given any cues. However, neither recognition nor recall automatically or reliably translates into product preferences or purchases.

KEY TERMS

REVIEW

1   What is the difference between an unconditioned stimulus and a conditioned stimulus?

2   Give an example of a halo effect in marketing.

3   How can marketers use repetition to increase the likelihood that consumers will learn about their brand?

4   Why is it not necessarily a good idea to advertise a product in a commercial where a really popular song plays in the background?

5   What is the difference between classical conditioning and instrumental conditioning?

6   How do different types of reinforcement enhance learning? How does the strategy of frequency marketing relate to conditioning?

7   What is the major difference between behavioral and cognitive theories of learning?

8   Name the three stages of information processing.

9   What is external memory and why is it important to marketers?

10   Give an example of an episodic memory.

11   Why do phone numbers have seven digits?

12   List the three types of memory, and tell how they work together.

13   How is associative memory like a spider web?

14   How does the likelihood that a person wants to use an ATM machine relate to a schema?

15   Why does a pioneering brand have a memory advantage over follower brands?

16   If a consumer is familiar with a product, advertising for it can work by either enhancing or diminishing recall. Why?

17   How does learning new information make it more likely that we'll forget things we've already learned?

18   Define *nostalgia*, and tell why it's such a widely used advertising strategy.

19   Name the two basic measures of memory and describe how they differ from one another.

20   List three problems with measures of memory for advertising.

CONSUMER BEHAVIOR CHALLENGE

▪ DISCUSS

1   In his book, *Blink: The Power of Thinking Without Thinking,* author Malcolm Gladwell argues that hallowed marketing research techniques such as focus groups aren't effective because we usually react to products quickly and without much conscious thought, so it's better simply to solicit consumers' first

impressions rather than getting them to think at length about why they buy. What's your position on this issue?

2 Some die-hard fans were not pleased when The Rolling Stones sold the tune "Start Me Up" for about $4 million to Microsoft, which wanted the classic song to promote its Windows 95 launch. The Beach Boys sold "Good Vibrations" to Cadbury Schweppes for its Sunkist soft drink, Steppenwolf offered his "Born to Be Wild" to plug the Mercury Cougar, and even Bob Dylan sold "The Times They Are A-Changin'" to Coopers & Lybrand (now called PriceWaterhouseCoopers).[114] Other rock legends have refused to play the commercial game, including

Bruce Springsteen, The Grateful Dead, Led Zeppelin, Fleetwood Mac, R.E.M., and U2. According to U2's manager, "Rock 'n roll is the last vestige of independence. It is undignified to put that creative effort and hard work to the disposal of a soft drink or beer or car."[115] Singer Neil Young is especially adamant about not selling out; in his song "This Note's for You," he croons, "Ain't singing for Pepsi, ain't singing for Coke, I don't sing for nobody, makes me look like a joke." What's your take on this issue? How do you react when one of your favorite songs turns up in a commercial? Is this use of nostalgia an effective way to market a product? Why or why not?

■ APPLY

1 Devise a "product jingle memory test." Compile a list of brands that are or have been associated with memorable jingles, such as Chiquita Banana or Alka-Seltzer. Read this list to friends, and see how many jingles they remember. You may be surprised at their level of recall.

2 A physician borrowed a page from product marketers when she asked for their advice to help persuade people in the developing world to wash their hands habitually with soap. Diseases and disorders caused by dirty hands—like diarrhea—kill a child somewhere in the world about every 15 seconds, and about half those deaths could be prevented with the regular use of soap. The project adapted techniques that major marketers use to encourage habitual product usage of items such as skin moisturizers, disinfecting wipes, air fresheners, water purifiers, toothpaste, and vitamins. For example beer commercials often depict a group of guys together, because research shows that being with a group of friends tend to trigger habitual drinking! The researchers found that when people in Ghana experienced a feeling of disgust, this was a cue to wash their hands. However, as in many developing countries, toilets are actually a symbol of cleanliness because they

have replaced pit latrines. So, an advertising campaign included messages that reminded people of the germs they could still pick up even in modern bathrooms—mothers and children walked out of restrooms with a glowing purple pigment on their hands that contaminated everything they touched. These images in turn triggered the habit of hand-washing and the project resulted in a significant increase in the number of consumers who washed their hands with soap.[116] How can other organizations that work to improve public health, the environment, or other social issues harness our knowledge about consumer learning and habitual behavior to create or reenergize positive habits?

3 Identify some important characteristics of a product with a well-known brand name. Based on these attributes, generate a list of possible brand extension or licensing opportunities, as well as some others that consumers would not be likely to accept.

4 Collect some pictures of "classic" products that have high nostalgia value. Show these pictures to others, and allow them to free associate. Analyze the types of memories that they evoke, and think about how a marketer might employ these associations in a product's promotional strategy.

Case Study

DO OUR AVATARS LEARN?

When he ventures online, he's a muscular, bronzed 23-year-old surfer. But, after a few hours chilling in the virtual world of Second Life, it's time for this 110-pound shy student to get back to work. Sound weird? It's not. He is one of the 38,000 "residents" who is logged into Second Life at any given time. Welcome to the world of avatars! Marketers are just beginning to understand how the time people spend in virtual worlds influences the way they learn about brands.

Second Life, which Linden Labs first launched in 2002, is one of the largest virtual worlds. It's free to use the site al-

though there is a premium membership of $9.95 a month that is required for some online activities. In Second Life, and other sites, users create an avatar to represent themselves online. Some people create avatars that look a lot like them in the real world, but many residents choose avatars that represent the person they would like to be, fantasy creatures, or even individuals of the opposite gender. With these alternate personalities they go out and explore virtual worlds. So what does this mean to marketers? Many things. Avatars interact with real brands in these virtual worlds. They can purchase products such as jeans for their avatars, and they can attend events such as concerts or lectures.

But it's not just virtual worlds like Second Life that want to understand how to make money from the legions of avatars out there. Web site designers and developers also realize the importance of avatars that interact with visitors on corporate Web sites. Several companies offer software applications that design avatars to greet and guide visitors (for one example, check out Sitepal.com). Some of these avatars take the form of famous people including rock stars, actors, and historical figures. Research indicates that these avatars might increase users' satisfaction with the Web sites and affect purchases.

Organizations and educators are just beginning to realize the impact of avatars and virtual worlds. Many companies now host their business meetings online; they encourage employees to develop their own avatars when they attend the meetings. Several university presidents hold online forums with students and create avatars to discuss current issues of concern with their students. The world of avatars and virtual worlds will continue to challenge marketers in the years to come.

DISCUSSION QUESTIONS

1 How might classical conditioning operate for a consumer who visits a new tutoring Web site and is greeted by the Web site's avatar who resembles Albert Einstein?

2 How might a consumer who purchases a new outfit for his avatar on a virtual world be influenced by instrumental conditioning?

3 Do consumers build associative networks from their avatar's experience? Do you think this network is part of the consumer's overall associative network for that brand or is it a separate network?

Source: Natalie Wood, Michael R. Solomon, Basil G. Englis, "Personalization of the Web Interface: The Impact of Web Avatars on Users' Responses to E-commerce Sites," *Journal of Website Promotion* 2, no. 1/2 (2006): 53–69; Natalie T. Wood and Michael R. Solomon, "Virtual Worlds, Real Impact: Advertising in Immersive Digital Environments" in Matthew S. Eastin, Terry Daugherty, and Neal M. Burns, eds., *Handbook of Research on Digital Media and Advertising: User Generated Content Consumption*, IGI Global, in press.

NOTES

1. Quoted in Stuart Elliott, "Kickin' Down Madison Ave., Feelin' Groovy," *New York Times* (June 16, 2009), www.nytimes.com, accessed June 16, 2009.
2. Stuart Elliott, "At 75, Mr. Peanut Is Getting Expanded Role at Planters," *New York Times* (September 23, 1991): D15.
3. Robert A. Baron, *Psychology: The Essential Science* (Boston: Allyn & Bacon, 1989).
4. Richard A. Feinberg, "Credit Cards as Spending Facilitating Stimuli: A Conditioning Interpretation," *Journal of Consumer Research* 13 (December 1986): 348–56.
5. R. A. Rescorla, "Pavlovian Conditioning: It's Not What You Think It Is," *American Psychologist* 43 (1988): 151–60; Elnora W. Stuart, Terence A. Shimp, and Randall W. Engle, "Classical Conditioning of Consumer Attitudes: Four Experiments in an Advertising Context," *Journal of Consumer Research* 14 (December 1987): 334–39.
6. C. Janiszewski, H. Noel, and A. G. Sawyer, "A Meta-analysis of the Spacing Effect in Verbal Learning: Implications for Research on Advertising Repetition and Consumer Memory," *Journal of Consumer Research* 30, no. 1 (2003): 138–49.
7. Yaveroglu and Naveen Donthu, "Advertising Repetition and Placement Issues in On-Line Environments," *Journal of Advertising* 37 (Summer 2008): 31–43.
8. James Ward, Barbara Loken, Ivan Ross, and Tedi Hasapopoulous, "The Influence of Physical Similarity of Affect and Attribute Perceptions from National Brands to Private Label Brands," in Terence A. Shimp et al., eds., *American Marketing Educators' Conference* (Chicago: American Marketing Association, 1986): 51–56.
9. Judith Lynne Zaichkowsky and Richard Neil Simpson, "The Effect of Experience with a Brand Imitator on the Original Brand," *Marketing Letters* 7, no. 1 (1996): 31–39.
10. Janice S. Griffiths and Mary Zimmer, "Masked Brands and Consumers' Need for Uniqueness," *American Marketing Association* (Summer 1998): 145–53.
11. Randi Priluck Grossman and Brian D. Till, "The Persistence of Classically Conditioned Brand Attitudes," *Journal of Advertising* 21, no. 1 (1998): 23–31; Chris T. Allen and Thomas J. Madden, "A Closer Look at Classical Conditioning," *Journal of Consumer Research* 12 (December 1985): 301–15; Chester A. Insko and William F. Oakes, "Awareness and the Conditioning of Attitudes," *Journal of Personality and Social Psychology* 4 (November 1966): 487–96; Carolyn K. Staats and Arthur W. Staats, "Meaning Established by Classical Conditioning," *Journal of Experimental Psychology* 54 (July 1957): 74–80.
12. Kevin Lane Keller, "Conceptualizing, Measuring, and Managing Customer-Based Brand Equity," *Journal of Marketing* 57 (January 1993): 1–22.
13. Herbert Krugman, "Low Recall and High Recognition of Advertising," *Journal of Advertising Research* (February–March 1986): 79–80.
14. Brian Steinberg, "Ad Nauseam: Repetition of TV Spots Risks Driving Consumers Away, Fragmenting Media, Smaller Budgets Make for More of the Same Ads," *Crain's Detroit Business* (December 1, 2008), www.Crainsdetroit.Com/Article/20081201/Email01/812010278/1092, accessed December 1, 2008.
15. Gerald J. Gorn, "The Effects of Music in Advertising on Choice Behavior: A Classical Conditioning Approach," *Journal of Marketing* 46 (Winter 1982): 94–101.
16. Noreen Klein, Virginia Tech, personal communication (April 2000); Calvin Bierley, Frances K. McSweeney, and Renee Vannieuwkerk, "Classical Conditioning of Preferences for Stimuli," *Journal of Consumer Research* 12 (December 1985): 316–23; James J. Kellaris and Anthony D. Cox, "The Effects of Background Music in Advertising: A Reassessment," *Journal of Consumer Research* 16 (June 1989): 113–18.
17. Frances K. McSweeney and Calvin Bierley, "Recent Developments in Classical Conditioning," *Journal of Consumer Research* 11 (September 1984): 619–31.
18. Basil G. Englis, "The Reinforcement Properties of Music Videos: 'I Want My . . . I Want My . . . I Want My . . . MTV,'" paper presented at the meetings of the Association for Consumer Research, New Orleans, 1989.
19. Anand Natarajan, "Branding: Interiors by Smith & Wesson," *BusinessWeek* (November 10, 2003): 16; James B. Arndorfer, "Starbucks Wakes Up to Liquor Possibilities," *Advertising Age* (November 22, 2004): 4; Claudia Deutsch, "Will Real Men Buy Mr. Clean?" *New York Times* (September 24, 2003), www.nytimes.com, accessed September 24, 2003; Jane L. Levere, "Huggies and Pampers Seek to Extend Brands into Toiletries," *New York Times* (January 18, 2005), www.nytimes.com, accessed January 18, 2005.
20. Quoted in Dan Neil, "Ed Hardy Wines? Christian Audigier's Branding Machine Grinds On," *Los Angeles Times* (April 28, 2009), www.latimes.com/business, accessed April 28, 2009.
21. Tracie Rozhon, "Read Our Article, and Purchase Our Hair Color While You're at It," *New York Times* (June 17, 2004), www.nytimes.com, accessed June 17, 2004; Patricia Winters Lauro, "Fire and Police Try to Market Goods," *New York Times* (June 10, 2002), www.nytimes.com, accessed June 10, 2002.
22. "Look-Alikes Mimic Familiar Packages," *New York Times* (August 9, 1986): D1.
23. Zaichkowsky and Simpson, "The Effect of Experience with a Brand Imitator on the Original Brand," 31–39.
24. Luk Warlop and Joseph W. Alba, "Sincere Flattery: Trade-Dress Imitation and Consumer Choice," *Journal of Consumer Psychology* 14, nos. 1 & 2 (2004): 21–27.

25. Michael Barbaro and Julie Creswell, "Levi's Turns to Suing Its Rivals," *New York Times* (January 29, 2007), www.nytimes.com/2007/01/29/business/29jeans.html, accessed June 30, 2009.

26. Gordon Fairclough, "From Hongda to Wumart, Brand Names in China Have Familiar, if Off-Key, Ring," *Wall Street Journal* (October 19, 2006): B1.

27. For a comprehensive approach to consumer behavior–based operant conditioning principles, see Gordon R. Foxall, "Behavior Analysis and Consumer Psychology," *Journal of Economic Psychology* 15 (March 1994): 5–91.

28. J. Blaise Bergiel and Christine Trosclair, "Instrumental Learning: Its Application to Customer Satisfaction," *Journal of Consumer Marketing* 2 (Fall 1985): 23–28.

29. Suzanne Vranica, "Agencies Don Lab Coats to Reach Consumers, Firms Deploy Scientists Within Creative Groups to Make Messages Stick," *Wall Street Journal* (June 4, 2007): B8.

30. Cf. for example E. M. Eisenstein and J. W. Hutchinson, "Action-Based Learning: Goals and Attention in the Acquisition of Market Knowledge," *Journal of Marketing Research* 43, no. 2 (2006): 244–58.

31. Ellen J. Langer, *The Psychology of Control* (Beverly Hills, CA: Sage, 1983).

32. Robert B. Cialdini, *Influence: Science and Practice*, 2nd ed. (New York: William Morrow, 1984); Y. Rottenstreich, S. Sood, and L. Brenner, "Feeling and Thinking in Memory-Based Versus Stimulus-Based Choices," *Journal of Consumer Research* 33, no. 4 (2007): 461–69.

33. Benedict Carey, "Who's Minding the Mind?" *New York Times Online* (July 31, 2007).

34. Malcolm Gladwell, *Blink: The Power of Thinking Without Thinking* (New York: Little, Brown, 2005).

35. Chris T. Allen and Thomas J. Madden, "A Closer Look at Classical Conditioning," *Journal of Consumer Research* 12 (December 1985): 301–15; see also Terence A. Shimp, Elnora W. Stuart, and Randall W. Engle, "A Program of Classical Conditioning Experiments Testing Variations in the Conditioned Stimulus and Context," *Journal of Consumer Research* 18 (June 1991): 1–12.

36. Terence A. Shimp, "Neo-Pavlovian Conditioning and Its Implications for Consumer Theory and Research," in Thomas S. Robertson and Harold H. Kassarjian, eds., *Handbook of Consumer Behavior* (Upper Saddle River, NJ: Prentice Hall, 1991).

37. Albert Bandura, *Social Foundations of Thought and Action: A Social Cognitive View* (Upper Saddle River, NJ: Prentice Hall, 1986).

38. Ibid.

39. R. C. Atkinson and I. M. Shiffrin, "Human Memory: A Proposed System and Its Control Processes," in K. W. Spence and J. T. Spence, eds., *The Psychology of Learning and Motivation: Advances in Research and Theory*, vol. 2 (New York: Academic Press, 1968): 89–195.

40. James R. Bettman, "Memory Factors in Consumer Choice: A Review," *Journal of Marketing* (Spring 1979): 37–53. For a study that explores the relative impact of internal versus external memory on brand choice, see Joseph W. Alba, Howard Marmorstein, and Amitava Chattopadhyay, "Transitions in Preference over Time: The Effects of Memory on Message Persuasiveness," *Journal of Marketing Research* 29 (1992): 406–16.

41. Lauren G. Block and Vicki G. Morwitz, "Shopping Lists as an External Memory Aid for Grocery Shopping: Influences on List Writing and List Fulfillment," *Journal of Consumer Psychology* 8, no. 4 (1999): 343–75.

42. Kim Robertson, "Recall and Recognition Effects of Brand Name Imagery," *Psychology & Marketing* 4 (Spring 1987): 3–15.

43. Stuart Elliott, "A Name Change at Philip Morris," *New York Times* (November 19, 2001).

44. Sharon Begley, "StrawBerry Is No BlackBerry: Building Brands Using Sound," *Wall Street Journal* (August 26, 2002), www.wsj.com, accessed August 26, 2002.

45. Endel Tulving, "Remembering and Knowing the Past," *American Scientist* 77 (July–August 1989): 361.

46. Rashmi Adaval and Robert S. Wyer, Jr., "The Role of Narratives in Consumer Information Processing," *Journal of Consumer Psychology* 7, no. 3 (1998): 207–46; cf. also R. F. Baumeister and L. S. Newman, "How Stories Make Sense of Personal Experiences: Motives that Shape Autobiographical Narratives," *Personality and Social Psychology Bulletin* 20, no. 6 (1994): 676–90; J. Bruner, *Actual Minds, Possible Worlds* (Cambridge, MA: Harvard University Press, 1986).

47. Jennifer Edson Escalas, "Narrative Processing: Building Consumer Connections to Brands," *Journal of Consumer Psychology* 14, nos. 1 & 2 (2004): 168–80.

48. Beth Snyder Bulik, "What's in a (Good) Product Name? Sales Cellphone Study Finds 'Cognitive' Monikers Work; Numerics Flop," February 2, 2009, www.namedevelopment.com/Articles/Good-Cellphone-Names.html, accessed February 27, 2009.

49. George A. Miller, "The Magical Number Seven, Plus or Minus Two: Some Limits on Our Capacity for Processing Information," *Psychological Review* 63 (1956): 81–97.

50. James N. MacGregor, "Short-Term Memory Capacity: Limitation or Optimization?" *Psychological Review* 94 (1987): 107–8.

51. M. Vanhuele, G. Laurent, and X. Dréze, "Consumers' Immediate Memory for Prices," *Journal of Consumer Research* 33, no. 2 (2006): 163–72.

52. See Catherine A. Cole and Michael J. Houston, "Encoding and Media Effects on Consumer Learning Deficiencies in the Elderly," *Journal of Marketing Research* 24 (February 1987): 55–64; A. M. Collins and E. F. Loftus, "A Spreading Activation Theory of Semantic Processing," *Psychological Review* 82 (1975): 407–28; Fergus I. M. Craik and Robert S. Lockhart, "Levels of Processing: A Framework for Memory Research," *Journal of Verbal Learning and Verbal Behavior* 11 (1972): 671–84.

53. Walter A. Henry, "The Effect of Information-Processing Ability on Processing Accuracy," *Journal of Consumer Research* 7 (June 1980): 42–48.

54. T. B. Cornwell, M. S. Humphreys, A. M. Maguire, C. S. Weeks, and C. L. Tellegen, "Sponsorship-Linked Marketing: The Role of Articulation in Memory," *Journal of Consumer Research* 33, no. 3 (2006): 312–21.

55. Kevin Lane Keller, "Memory Factors in Advertising: The Effect of Advertising Retrieval Cues on Brand Evaluations," *Journal of Consumer Research* 14 (December 1987): 316–33. For a discussion of processing operations that occur during brand choice, see Gabriel Biehal and Dipankar Chakravarti, "Consumers' Use of Memory and External Information in Choice: Macro and Micro Perspectives," *Journal of Consumer Research* 12 (March 1986): 382–405.

56. Susan T. Fiske and Shelley E. Taylor, *Social Cognition* (Reading, MA: Addison-Wesley, 1984).

57. Deborah Roedder John and John C. Whitney Jr., "The Development of Consumer Knowledge in Children: A Cognitive Structure Approach," *Journal of Consumer Research* 12 (March 1986): 406–17.

58. Michael R. Solomon, Carol Surprenant, John A. Czepiel, and Evelyn G. Gutman, "A Role Theory Perspective on Dyadic Interactions: The Service Encounter," *Journal of Marketing* 49 (Winter 1985): 99–111.

59. Aaron Baar, "New Product Messages Aren't Making Intended Impressions," *Marketing Daily* (March 6, 2008), http://publications.mediapost.com/Index.Cfm?Fuseaction=Articles.Showarticle&Art_Aid=779, accessed March 6, 2008.

60. S. Danziger, S. Moran, and V. Rafaely, "The Influence of Ease of Retrieval on Judgment as a Function of Attention to Subjective Experience," *Journal of Consumer Psychology* 16, no. 2 (2006): 191–95.

61. Roger W. Morrell, Denise C. Park, and Leonard W. Poon, "Quality of Instructions on Prescription Drug Labels: Effects on Memory and Comprehension in Young and Old Adults," *The Gerontologist* 29 (1989): 345–54.

62. Frank R. Kardes, Gurumurthy Kalyanaram, Murali Chandrashekaran, and Ronald J. Dornoff, "Brand Retrieval, Consideration Set Composition, Consumer Choice, and the Pioneering Advantage" (unpublished manuscript, the University of Cincinnati, Ohio, 1992).

63. Judith Lynne Zaichkowsky and Padma Vipat, "Inferences from Brand Names," paper presented at the European meeting of the Association for Consumer Research, Amsterdam, June 1992.

64. H. Noel, "The Spacing Effect: Enhancing Memory for Repeated Marketing Stimuli," *Journal of Consumer Psychology* 16 no. 3 (2006): 306–20; for an alternative explanation, see S. L. Appleton-Knapp, R. A. Bjork, and T. D. Wickens, "Examining the Spacing Effect in Advertising: Encoding Variability, Retrieval Processes, and Their Interaction," *Journal of Consumer Research* 32, no. 2 (2005): 266–76.

65. Herbert E. Krugman, "Low Recall and High Recognition of Advertising," *Journal of Advertising Research* (February–March 1986): 79–86.

66. Rik G. M. Pieters and Tammo H. A. Bijmolt, "Consumer Memory for Television Advertising: A Field Study of Duration, Serial Position, and Competition Effects," *Journal of Consumer Research* 23 (March 1997): 362–72.

67. Erik Sass, "Study Finds Spectacular Print Ads Get Spectacular Recall," *Marketing Daily* (February 23, 2007), www.mediapost.com, accessed February 23, 2007.

68. Raymond R. Burke and Thomas K. Srull, "Competitive Interference and Consumer Memory for Advertising," *Journal of Consumer Research* 15 (June 1988): 55–68.

69. Eric J. Johnson and J. Edward Russo, "Product Familiarity and Learning New Information," *Journal of Consumer Research* 11 (June 1984): 542–50.

70. Joan Meyers-Levy, "The Influence of Brand Name's Association Set Size and Word Frequency on Brand Memory," *Journal of Consumer Research* 16 (September 1989): 197–208.

71. Michael H. Baumgardner, Michael R. Leippe, David L. Ronis, and Anthony G. Greenwald, "In Search of Reliable Persuasion Effects: II. Associative Interference and Persistence of Persuasion in a Message-Dense Environment," *Journal of Personality and Social Psychology* 45 (September 1983): 524–37.

72. Joseph W. Alba and Amitava Chattopadhyay, "Salience Effects in Brand Recall," *Journal of Marketing Research* 23 (November 1986): 363–70.

73. Margaret Henderson Blair, Allan R. Kuse, David H. Furse, and David W. Stewart, "Advertising in a New and Competitive Environment: Persuading Consumers to Buy," *Business Horizons* 30 (November–December 1987): 20.

74. John G. Lynch and Thomas K. Srull, "Memory and Attentional Factors in Consumer Choice: Concepts and Research Methods," *Journal of Consumer Research* 9 (June 1982): 18–37.

75. Kevin Lane Keller, "Memory Factors in Advertising: The Effect of Advertising Retrieval Cues on Brand Evaluations," *Journal of Consumer Research* 14 (December 1987): 316–33.

76. Eric J. Johnson and J. Edward Russo, "Product Familiarity and Learning New Information," *Journal of Consumer Research* 11 (June 1984): 542–50.

77. Eric J. Johnson and J. Edward Russo, "Product Familiarity and Learning New Information," in Kent Monroe, ed., *Advances in Consumer Research* 8 (Ann Arbor, MI: Association for Consumer Research, 1981): 151–55; John G. Lynch and Thomas K. Srull, "Memory and Attentional Factors in Consumer Choice: Concepts and Research Methods," *Journal of Consumer Research* 9 (June 1982): 18–37.

78. Julie A. Edell and Kevin Lane Keller, "The Information Processing of Coordinated Media Campaigns," *Journal of Marketing Research* 26 (May 1989): 149–64.

79. John G. Lynch and Thomas K. Srull, "Memory and Attentional Factors in Consumer Choice: Concepts and Research Methods," *Journal of Consumer Research* 9 (June 1982): 18–37.

80. Joseph W. Alba and Amitava Chattopadhyay, "Salience Effects in Brand Recall," *Journal of Marketing Research* 23 (November 1986): 363–70; Elizabeth C. Hirschman and Michael R. Solomon, "Utilitarian, Aesthetic, and Familiarity Responses to Verbal Versus Visual Advertisements," in Thomas C. Kinnear, ed., *Advances in Consumer Research* 11 (Provo, UT: Association for Consumer Research, 1984): 426–31.

81. Susan E. Heckler and Terry L. Childers, "The Role of Expectancy and Relevancy in Memory for Verbal and Visual Information: What Is Incongruency?" *Journal of Consumer Research* 18 (March 1992): 475–92.

82. Russell H. Fazio, Paul M. Herr, and Martha C. Powell, "On the Development and Strength of Category-Brand Associations in Memory: The Case of Mystery Ads," *Journal of Consumer Psychology* 1, no. 1 (1992): 1–13.

83. Jennifer Aaker, Aimee Drolet, Dale Griffin, "Recalling Mixed Emotions," *Journal of Consumer Research* 35 (August 2008): 268–78.

84. Alex Mindlin, "Commercials Bask in a Show's Glow," *New York Times Online* (December 17, 2007), www.nytimes.com, accessed December 17, 2008.

85. Suzanne Vranica, "New Ads Take On Tivo, Tie-Ins to TV Shows Aim to Prevent Fast-Forwarding," *Wall Street Journal* (October 5, 2007): B4.

86. Stuart Elliott, "We Interrupt This Show for an Ad (Very Similar)," *New York Times* (May 20, 2009): B6.

87. Brian Steinberg, "Bad Times Affect Ad Recall for Bowl Spots, Gallup: Weak Consumer Confidence Can Mean Less Attention," *Advertising Age* (January 20, 2009), www.adage.com, accessed January 20, 2009.

88. Hirschman and Solomon, "Utilitarian, Aesthetic, and Familiarity Responses to Verbal Versus Visual Advertisements."

89. Terry Childers and Michael Houston, "Conditions for a Picture-Superiority Effect on Consumer Memory," *Journal of Consumer Research* 11 (September 1984): 643–54; Terry Childers, Susan Heckler, and Michael Houston, "Memory for the Visual and Verbal Components of Print Advertisements," *Psychology & Marketing* 3 (Fall 1986): 147–50.

90. Werner Krober-Riel, "Effects of Emotional Pictorial Elements in Ads Analyzed by Means of Eye Movement Monitoring," in Thomas C. Kinnear, ed., *Advances in Consumer Research* 11 (Provo, UT: Association for Consumer Research, 1984): 591–96.

91. Hans-Bernd Brosius, "Influence of Presentation Features and News Context on Learning from Television News," *Journal of Broadcasting & Electronic Media* 33 (Winter 1989): 1–14.

92. Edward F. McQuarrie and David Glen Mick, "Visual and Verbal Rhetorical Figures Under Directed Processing Versus Incidental Exposure to Advertising," *Journal of Consumer Research* (March 2003): 29, 579–87; cf. also Ann E. Schlosser, "Learning through Virtual Product Experience: The Role of Imagery on True Versus False Memories," *Journal of Consumer Research* 33, no. 3 (2006): 377–83.

93. Russell W. Belk, "Possessions and the Extended Self," *Journal of Consumer Research* 15 (September 1988): 139–68.

94. Morris B. Holbrook and Robert M. Schindler, "Nostalgic Bonding: Exploring the Role of Nostalgia in the Consumption Experience," *Journal of Consumer Behavior* 3, no. 2 (December 2003): 107–27.

95. Stacy Menzel Baker, Holli C. Karrer, and Ann Veeck, "My Favorite Recipes: Recreating Emotions and Memories Through Cooking," *Advances in Consumer Research* 32, no. 1 (2005): 304–305.

96. Russell W. Belk, "The Role of Possessions in Constructing and Maintaining a Sense of Past," in Marvin E. Goldberg, Gerald Gorn, and Richard W. Pollay, eds., *Advances in Consumer Research* 16 (Provo, UT: Association for Consumer Research, 1989): 669–78.

97. "Only 38% of T.V. Audience Links Brands with Ads," *Marketing News* (January 6, 1984): 10.

98. Ronald Alsop, "How Boss's Deeds Buff A Firm's Reputation," *Wall Street Journal* (January 31, 2007), www.wsj.com, accessed January 31, 2007.

99. "Terminal Television," *American Demographics* (January 1987): 15.

100. Vanessa O'Connell, "Toys 'R' Us Spokesanimal Makes Lasting Impression: Giraffe Tops List of Television Ads Viewers Found the Most Memorable," *Wall Street Journal* (January 2, 2003), www.wsj.com, accessed January 2, 2003.

101. Richard P. Bagozzi and Alvin J. Silk, "Recall, Recognition, and the Measurement of Memory for Print Advertisements," *Marketing Science* 2 (1983): 95–134.

102. Adam Finn, "Print Ad Recognition Readership Scores: An Information Processing Perspective," *Journal of Marketing Research* 25 (May 1988): 168–77.

103. James R. Bettman, "Memory Factors in Consumer Choice: A Review," *Journal of Marketing* (Spring 1979): 37–53.

104. Mark A. Deturck and Gerald M. Goldhaber, "Effectiveness of Product Warning Labels: Effects of Consumers' Information Processing Objectives," *Journal of Consumer Affairs* 23, no. 1 (1989): 111–25.

105. Surendra N. Singh and Gilbert A. Churchill, Jr., "Response-Bias-Free Recognition Tests to Measure Advertising Effects," *Journal of Advertising Research* (June–July 1987): 23–36.

106. William A. Cook, "Telescoping and Memory's Other Tricks," *Journal of Advertising Research* 27 (February–March 1987): 5–8.

107. "On a Diet? Don't Trust Your Memory," *Psychology Today* (October 1989): 12.

108. I. Skurnik, C. Yoon, D. C. Park, and N. Schwarz, "How Warnings About False Claims Become Recommendations," *Journal of Consumer Research* 31, no. 4 (2005): 713–24.

109. Hubert A. Zielske and Walter A. Henry, "Remembering and Forgetting Television Ads," *Journal of Advertising Research* 20 (April 1980): 7–13; Cara Greenberg, "Future Worth: Before It's Hot, Grab It," *New York Times* (1992): C1; S. K. List, "More Than Fun and Games," *American Demographics* (August 1992): 44.

110. Susan L. Holak and William J. Havlena, "Feelings, Fantasies, and Memories: An Examination of the Emotional Components of Nostalgia," *Journal of Business Research* 42 (1998): 217–26.

111. Stephen Brown, Robert V. Kozinets, and John F. Sherry, "Teaching Old Brands New Tricks: Retro Branding and the Revival of Brand Meaning," *Journal of Marketing* 67 (July 2003): 19–33.

112. Nicholas Casey, "Toy Makers Reach into Product Attic," *Wall Street Journal* (March 2, 2009), www.wsj.com, accessed March 3, 2009; Emily Bryson York, "Retro Designs of Their Youth Appeal to Stressed Shoppers' Desire for Comfort," *Advertising Age* (March 3, 2009), www.adage.com, accessed March 3, 2009; Christine Haughney, "When Economy Sours, Tootsie Rolls Soothe Souls," *New York Times* (March 23, 2009), http://community.nytimes.com/article/comments/2009/.../nyregion/24candy.html, accessed March 23, 2009; Stuart Elliott, "Warm and Fuzzy Makes a Comeback," *New York Times* (April 6, 2009), http://topics.nytimes.com/top/reference/timestopics/people/e/stuart_elliott/index.html?offset=50&, accessed April 6, 2009.

113. Robert M. Schindler and Morris B. Holbrook, "Nostalgia for Early Experience as a Determinant of Consumer Preferences," *Psychology & Marketing* 20, no. 4 (April 2003): 275–302; Morris B. Holbrook and Robert M. Schindler, "Some Exploratory Findings on the Development of Musical Tastes," *Journal of Consumer Research* 16 (June 1989): 119–24; Morris B. Holbrook and Robert M. Schindler, "Market Segmentation Based on Age and Attitude Toward the Past: Concepts, Methods, and Findings Concerning Nostalgic Influences on Consumer Tastes," *Journal of Business Research* 37 (September 1996): 27–40.

114. Thomas F. Jones, "Our Musical Heritage Is Being Raided," *San Francisco Examiner* (May 23, 1997).

115. Kevin Goldman, "A Few Rockers Refuse to Turn Tunes into Ads," *New York Times* (August 25, 1995): B1.

116. Charles Duhigg, "Warning: Habits May Be Good for You," *New York Times Magazine* (July 17, 2008), www.newyorktimesimes.com/2008/07/13/Business/13habit.html, accessed July 17, 2008.

4

Motivation and Values

Chapter Objectives

When you finish this chapter you will understand:

1. Why is it important for marketers to recognize that products can satisfy a range of consumer needs?

2. Why does the way we evaluate and choose a product depend on our degree of involvement with the product, the marketing message, and/or the purchase situation?

3. Why do our deeply held cultural values dictate the types of products and services we seek out or avoid?

4. Why do consumers vary in the importance they attach to worldly possessions, and why does this orientation in turn impact on their priorities and behaviors?

*A*s Basil scans the menu at the trendy health-food restaurant Paula has dragged him to, he reflects on what a man will give up for love. Now that Paula has become a die-hard vegetarian, she's slowly but surely working on him to forsake those juicy steaks and burgers for healthier fare. He can't even hide from tofu and other delights at school; the dining facility in his dorm just started to offer "veggie" alternatives to its usual assortment of greasy "mystery meats" and other delicacies he loves.

Paula is totally into it; she claims that eating this way not only cuts out unwanted fat but also is good for the environment. Just his luck to fall head-over-heels for a "tree-hugger." As Basil gamely tries to decide between the stuffed artichokes with red pepper vinaigrette and the grilled marinated zucchini, fantasies of a sizzling 14-ounce T-bone dance before his eyes.

OBJECTIVE

Why is it important for
marketers to recognize
that products can satisfy
a range of consumer
needs?

The Motivation Process: Why Ask Why?

Paula certainly is not alone in her belief that eating green is good for the body, the soul, and the planet. About 7 percent of the general population is vegetarian, and women and younger people are even more likely to adopt a meatless diet. An additional 10 to 20 percent of consumers explore vegetarian options in addition to their normal dead animal fare. And, more and more people take the next step as they adopt a vegan lifestyle. *Veganism* links to a set of ethical beliefs about cruelty to animals. In addition to objecting to hunting or fishing, adherents protest cruel animal training, the degrading use of animals in circuses, zoos, rodeos, and races (Eagles quarterback and part-time dogfight entrepreneur Michael Vick probably would not qualify) and they also oppose the testing of drugs and cosmetics on animals.[1] Although the proportion of vegetarian or vegan consumers is quite small compared to those of us who still like to pound down a Quarter Pounder, big companies are taking notice of this growing interest in vegetarian and cruelty-free products. Colgate purchased a controlling interest in Tom's of Maine, and Dean Foods (America's largest processor of dairy foods) bought Silk and its parent company White Wave. PETA (People for the Ethical Treatment of Animals) offers resources to promote an animal-friendly lifestyle, including an Online Vegetarian Starter Kit for kids.[2] The beef industry fights back with its high-profile advertising campaign—"Beef. It's What's for Dinner" and a Web site to promote meat consumption (beefitswhatsfordinner.com).[3] It's obvious our menu choices have deep-seated consequences.

The forces that drive people to buy and use products are generally straightforward, for example, when a person chooses what to have for lunch. As hard-core vegetarians demonstrate, however, even the basic food products we consume also relate to wide-ranging beliefs regarding what we think is appropriate or desirable. In some cases, these emotional responses create a deep commitment to the product. Sometimes people are not even fully aware of the forces that drive them toward some products and away from others.

To understand motivation is to understand why consumers do what they do. Why do some people choose to bungee jump off a bridge or compete on reality shows, whereas others spend their leisure time playing chess or gardening? Whether it is to quench a thirst, kill boredom, or attain some deep spiritual experience, we do everything for a reason, even if we can't articulate what that reason is. We teach marketing students from Day 1 that the goal of marketing is to satisfy consumers' needs. However, this insight is useless unless we can discover what those needs are and why they exist. A beer commercial once asked, "Why ask why?" In this chapter, we'll find out.

Motivation refers to the processes that lead people to behave as they do. It occurs when a need is aroused that the consumer wishes to satisfy. The need creates a state of tension that drives the consumer to attempt to reduce or eliminate it. This need may be *utilitarian* (i.e., a desire to achieve some functional or practical benefit, as when a person loads up on green vegetables for nutritional reasons) or it may be *hedonic* (i.e., an experiential need, involving emotional responses or fantasies, as when Basil longs for a juicy steak). The desired end state is the consumer's **goal**. Marketers try to create products and services to provide the desired benefits and help the consumer to reduce this tension.

Whether the need is utilitarian or hedonic, the magnitude of the tension it creates determines the urgency the consumer feels to reduce it. We call this degree of arousal a **drive**. We can satisfy a basic need in any number of ways, and the specific path a person chooses is influenced both by her unique set of experiences and by the values her culture instills.

These personal and cultural factors combine to create a **want**, which is one manifestation of a need. For example, hunger is a basic need that all of us must satisfy;

the lack of food creates a tension state that we reduce when we eat cheeseburgers, double-fudge Oreo cookies, raw fish, or bean sprouts. The specific route to drive re-duction is culturally and individually determined. When a person attains the goal, this reduces the tension and the motivation recedes (for the time being). We describe motivation in terms of its *strength*, or the pull it exerts on the consumer, and its *direction*, or the particular way the consumer attempts to reduce it.

Motivational Strength

The degree to which a person will expend energy to reach one goal as opposed to an-other reflects his or her motivation to attain that goal. Psychologists have advanced

This ad for exercise equipment shows an ideal body (as dictated by contemporary Western culture), and suggests a solution (purchase of the equipment) to attain it.
Source: Used with permission of Soloflex.

This ad from the United Arab Emirates appeals to our basic drive to reduce hunger.
Source: Designed & released by Publinet Advertising & Publicity LLC, Dubai, UAE.

Give in.

many theories to explain why people behave the way they do. Most share the basic idea that people have some finite amount of energy that we direct toward our goals.

Early work on motivation ascribed behavior to *instinct*, the innate patterns of behavior that are universal in a species. This view is now largely discredited. For one thing, the existence of an instinct is difficult to prove or disprove because we infer the instinct from the behavior it is supposed to explain (we call this type of circular explanation a *tautology*).[4] It is like saying that a consumer buys products that are status symbols because he is motivated to attain status—hardly a satisfying explanation.

Biological Versus Learned Needs

Drive theory focuses on biological needs that produce unpleasant states of arousal (e.g., your stomach grumbles during a morning class). The arousal this tension causes motivates us to reduce it. Some researchers feel this need to reduce arousal is a basic mechanism that governs much of our behavior.

In a marketing context, tension refers to the unpleasant state that exists if a person's consumption needs are not fulfilled. A person may be grumpy if he hasn't eaten, or he may be dejected or angry if he cannot afford that new car he wants. This state activates goal-oriented behavior, which attempts to reduce or eliminate this unpleasant state and return to a balanced one we call **homeostasis**.

If a behavior reduces the drive, we'll naturally tend to repeat it. (We discussed this process of *reinforcement* in Chapter 3.) Your motivation to leave class early to grab a snack would be greater if you hadn't eaten in 24 hours than if you had eaten only 2 hours earlier. If you did sneak out and got indigestion afterward, say, from wolfing down a package of Twinkies, you would be less likely to repeat this behavior the next time you want a snack. One's degree of motivation, then, depends on the distance between one's present state and the goal.

Drive theory runs into difficulties when it tries to explain some facets of human behavior that run counter to its predictions. People often do things that increase a drive state rather than decrease it. For example, people may *delay gratification*. If you know you are going out for a lavish dinner, you might decide to forego a snack earlier in the day even though you are hungry at that time.

Most current explanations of motivation focus on cognitive factors rather than biological ones to understand what motivates behavior. **Expectancy theory** suggests that expectations we will achieve desirable outcomes—positive incentives—rather than being pushed from within motivate our behavior. We choose one product over another because we expect this choice to have more positive consequences for us. Thus, we use the term drive here loosely to refer to both physical and cognitive processes.

Motives have direction as well as strength. They are goal-oriented in that they drive us to satisfy a specific need. We can reach most goals by a number of routes, and the objective of a company is to convince consumers that the alternative it offers provides the best chance to attain the goal. For example, a consumer who decides that she needs a pair of jeans to help her reach her goal of being admired by others can choose among Levi's, Wranglers, True Religion, Diesel, Seven for All Mankind, and many other alternatives, each of which promises to deliver certain benefits.

Needs Versus Wants

The specific way we choose to satisfy a need depends on our unique history, learning experiences, and cultural environment. Two classmates may feel their stomachs rumble during a lunchtime lecture. If neither person has eaten since the night before, the strength of their respective needs (hunger) would be about the same. However, the ways each person goes about satisfying this need might be quite different. The first person may be a vegetarian like Paula who fantasizes about gulping down a big handful of trail mix, whereas the second person may be a meat hound like Basil who gets turned on by the prospect of a greasy cheeseburger and fries.

What Do We Need?

We are born with a need for certain elements necessary to maintain life such as food, water, air, and shelter. These are *biogenic needs*. We have many other needs, however, that are not innate. We acquire *psychogenic needs* as we become members of a specific culture. These include the needs for status, power, and affiliation. Psychogenic needs reflect the priorities of a culture, and their effect on behavior will vary from environment to environment. For example, a U.S. consumer devotes a good chunk of his income to products that permit him to display his individuality, whereas his Japanese counterpart may work equally hard to ensure that he does not stand out from his group.

We also can be motivated to satisfy either utilitarian or hedonic needs. When we focus on a *utilitarian need,* we emphasize the objective, tangible attributes of products, such as miles per gallon in a car; the amount of fat, calories, and protein in a cheeseburger; or the durability of a pair of blue jeans. *Hedonic needs* are subjective and experiential; here we might look to a product to meet our needs for excitement, self-confidence, or fantasy—perhaps to escape the mundane or routine aspects of life.[5] Of course, we can also be motivated to purchase a product because it provides *both* types of benefits. For example, a woman (perhaps a politically incorrect one) might buy a mink coat because of the luxurious image it portrays and because it also happens to keep her warm through the long, cold winter.

Motivational Conflicts

A goal has *valence*, which means that it can be positive or negative. We direct our behavior toward goals we value positively; we are motivated to *approach* the goal and to seek out products that will help us to reach it. However as we saw in the previous chapter's discussion of negative reinforcement, sometimes we're also motivated to *avoid* a negative outcome rather than achieve a positive outcome. We structure purchases or consumption activities to reduce the chances we will experience a nasty result. For example, many consumers work hard to avoid rejection by their peers, a negative goal. They will stay away from products that they associate with social disapproval. Products such as deodorants and mouthwash frequently rely on consumers' negative motivation when ads depict the onerous social consequences of underarm odor or bad breath.

Because a purchase decision can involve more than one source of motivation, consumers often find themselves in situations in which different motives, both positive and negative, conflict with one another.[6] Marketers attempt to satisfy consumers' needs by providing possible solutions to these dilemmas. As Figure 4.1 shows, there are three general types of conflicts we should understand. Let's review each kind.

Approach–Approach Conflict

A person has an **approach–approach conflict** when she must choose between two desirable alternatives. A student might be torn between going home for the holidays and going on a skiing trip with friends. Or she might have to choose between two CDs to download (assuming she's going to pay for one of them!). The **theory of cognitive dissonance** is based on the premise that people have a need for order and consistency in their lives and that a state of *dissonance* (tension) exists when beliefs

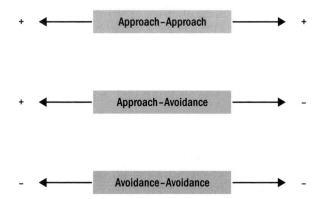

Figure 4.1 TYPES OF MOTIVATIONAL
CONFLICTS

or behaviors conflict with one another. We resolve the conflict that arises when we choose between two alternatives through a process of *cognitive dissonance reduction*, where we look for a way to reduce this inconsistency (or dissonance) and thus we eliminate unpleasant tension.

Dissonance occurs when a consumer must choose between two products, both of which possess good and bad qualities. When he chooses one product and not the other, the person gets the bad qualities of the product he buys and loses out on the good qualities of the one he didn't buy. This loss creates an unpleasant, dissonant state he wants to reduce. We tend to convince ourselves, after the fact, that the choice we made was the smart one as we find additional reasons to support the alternative we did choose—perhaps when we discover flaws with the option we did not choose (sometimes we call this "rationalization"). A marketer can bundle several benefits together to resolve an approach–approach conflict. For example, Miller Lite's claim that it is "less filling" *and* "tastes great" allows the drinker to "have his beer and drink it too."

Many of the products and services we desire have negative consequences attached to them as well. We may feel guilty or ostentatious when we buy a luxury product like a fur coat (especially when others around us lose their jobs) or we might feel like a glutton when we crave a tempting package of Twinkies. An **approach– avoidance conflict** occurs when we desire a goal but wish to avoid it at the same time.

Some solutions to these conflicts include the proliferation of fake furs, which eliminate guilt about harming animals to make a fashion statement, and the success of diet programs like Weight Watchers that promise good food without the calories.[7] Many marketers try to help consumers overcome guilt when they convince them they deserve these luxuries. As the model for L'Oréal cosmetics exclaims, "Because I'm worth it!"

Sometimes we find ourselves "caught between a rock and a hard place." We may face a choice with two undesirable alternatives; for instance the option of either spending more money on an old car or buying a new one. Don't you hate when that happens? Marketers frequently address an **avoidance–avoidance conflict** with messages that stress the unforeseen benefits of choosing one option (e.g., when they emphasize special credit plans to ease the pain of car payments).

How We Classify Consumer Needs

Some analysts set out to define a universal inventory of needs they could trace systematically to explain virtually all behavior. One such inventory that the psychologist Henry Murray developed delineates a set of 20 *psychogenic needs* that (sometimes in combination) result in specific behaviors. These needs include such dimensions as *autonomy* (being independent), *defendance* (defending the self against criticism), and even *play* (engaging in pleasurable activities).[8]

Murray's framework is the basis for a number of personality tests modern-day psychologists use, such as the Thematic Apperception Test (TAT). In the TAT, the analyst shows test subjects four to six ambiguous pictures and asks them to write answers to four direct questions about the pictures:

1 What is happening?
2 What led up to this situation?
3 What is being thought?
4 What will happen?

The researcher then analyzes each answer for references to certain needs. The theory behind the test is that people will freely project their own subconscious needs onto the neutral stimulus. By getting responses to the pictures, the analyst really gets at the person's true needs for achievement or affiliation or whatever other need may be dominant. Murray believed that everyone has the same basic set of needs but that individuals differ in their priority rankings of these needs.[9]

How Do Our Needs Influence What We Buy?

Other motivational approaches focus on specific needs and their ramifications for behavior. For example, individuals with a high *need for achievement* strongly value personal accomplishment.[10] They place a premium on products and services that signify success because these consumption items provide feedback about the realization of their goals. These consumers are good prospects for products that provide evidence of their achievement. One study of working women found that those who were high in achievement motivation were more likely to choose clothing they considered businesslike and less likely to be interested in apparel that accentuated their femininity.[11] Some other important needs that are relevant to consumer behavior include these:

● **Need for affiliation**—(to be in the company of other people):[12] The need for affiliation is relevant to products and services for people in groups, such as participating in team sports, frequenting bars, and hanging out at shopping malls.
● **Need for power**—(to control one's environment):[13] Many products and services allow us to feel that we have mastery over their surroundings (to quote the

A need like safety that may be largely irrelevant in one culture may be quite prominent in another. This Chilean ad for Renault touts the protective value of shield window film.
Source: Courtesy of Renault.

famous line from *Seinfeld*, we are "... masters of our domain")! These products range from "hopped-up" muscle cars and loud boom boxes (large portable radios that impose one's musical tastes on others) to luxury resorts that promise to respond to every whim of their pampered guests.

● **Need for uniqueness**—(to assert one's individual identity):[14] Products satisfy the need for uniqueness when they pledge to bring out our distinctive qualities. For example, Cachet perfume claims to be "as individual as you are."

Maslow's Hierarchy of Needs

Psychologist Abraham Maslow originally developed his influential approach to motivation when he sought to understand personal growth and how people attain spiritual "peak experiences." Marketers later adapted his work to understand consumer motivations.[15] Maslow proposed a hierarchy of biogenic and psychogenic needs that specifies certain levels of motives. This *hierarchical* structure implies that the order of development is fixed—that is, we must attain a certain level before we activate a need for the next, higher one. Marketers embraced this perspective because it (indirectly) specifies certain types of product benefits people might look for, depending on their stage of mental or spiritual development or on their economic situation.[16]

Figure 4.2 summarizes this model. At each level, the person seeks different kinds of product benefits. Ideally, an individual progresses up the hierarchy until his or her dominant motivation is a focus on "ultimate" goals, such as justice and beauty. Unfortunately, this state is difficult to achieve (at least on a regular basis); most of us have to be satisfied with occasional glimpses, or *peak experiences*. One study of men aged 49 to 60 found these respondents engaged in three types of activities to attain self-fulfillment: (1) *sport and physical activity*, (2) *community and charity*, and (3) *building and renovating*. Regardless of whether these activities were related to their professional work, these so-called *magnetic points* gradually took the place of those that were not as fulfilling.[17]

The basic lesson of Maslow's hierarchy is that we must first satisfy basic needs before we progress up the ladder (a starving man is not interested in status symbols,

Figure 4.2 MASLOW'S HIERARCHY

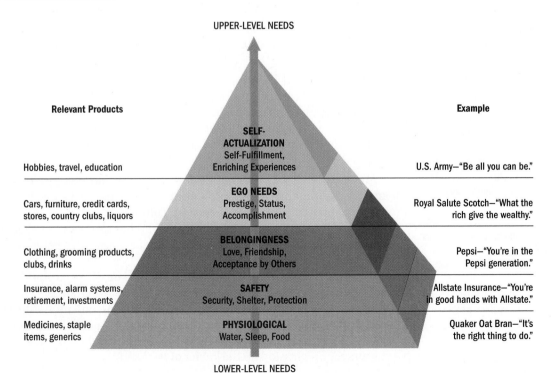

A study that compared Dutch and American students' conceptions of paradise asked respondents to construct collages that expressed their vision of an ideal life. This Dutch collage emphasizes higher-order needs relating to interpersonal harmony and environmental awareness.

Source: Courtesy of Dr. Gary Bamossy, Georgetown University.

Net Profit

Our online behaviors also can satisfy needs at different levels of Maslow's hierarchy, especially when we participate in social networks like Facebook. Web-based companies can build loyalty if they keep these needs in mind when they design their offerings:

- We can satisfy physiological needs when we use the Web to research topics such as nutrition or medical questions.
- The Web enables users to pool information and satisfy safety needs when they call attention to bad practices, flawed products, or even dangerous predators.
- Profile pages on Facebook and MySpace let users define themselves as individuals.
- Online communities, blogs, and social networks provide recognition and achievement to those who cultivate a reputation for being especially helpful or expert in some subject.
- Users can seek help from others and connect with people who have similar tastes and interests.
- Access to invitation-only communities provides status.
- Spiritually-based online communities can provide guidance to troubled people.[20]

friendship, or self-fulfillment). That implies that consumers value different product attributes depending on what is currently available to them. For example, consumers in the former Eastern bloc are now bombarded with images of luxury goods, yet may still have trouble obtaining basic necessities. In one study, Romanian students named the products they hoped to acquire. Their wish lists included not only the expected items such as sports cars and the latest model televisions but also staples such as water, soap, furniture, and food.[18] In today's economic environment, the hierarchy helps to explain why many consumers take a closer look at the price and reliability of a product rather than whether it will impress their friends.

Marketers' application of this hierarchy has been somewhat simplistic, especially as the same product or activity can gratify different needs. For example, one study found that gardening could satisfy needs at every level of the hierarchy:[19]

- **Physiological**—"I like to work in the soil."
- **Safety**—"I feel safe in the garden."
- **Social**—"I can share my produce with others."
- **Esteem**—"I can create something of beauty."
- **Self-actualization**—"My garden gives me a sense of peace."

Another problem with taking Maslow's hierarchy too literally is that it is culture-bound; its assumptions may apply only to Western culture. People in other cultures (or, for that matter, even some in Western cultures as well) may question the order of the levels it specifies. A religious person who has taken a vow of celibacy would not necessarily agree that physiological needs must be satisfied before self-fulfillment can occur.

Similarly, many Asian cultures value the welfare of the group (belongingness needs) more highly than needs of the individual (esteem needs). The point is that this hierarchy, although marketers widely apply it, is helpful primarily because it reminds us that consumers may have different need priorities in different consumption situations and at different stages in their lives—not because it *exactly* specifies a consumer's progression up the ladder of needs.

Consumer Involvement

OBJECTIVE

Why does the way we evaluate and choose a product depend on our degree of involvement with the product, the marketing message, and/or the purchase situation?

Do consumers form strong relationships with products and services? If you don't believe so, consider these events:

● A consumer in Brighton, England, loves a local restaurant called the All in One so much that he had its name and phone number tattooed on his forehead. The owner remarked, "Whenever he comes in, he'll go straight to the front of the queue."[21]

● *Lucky* is a magazine devoted to shopping for shoes and other fashion accessories. The centerfold of the first issue featured rows of makeup sponges. The editor observed, "It's the same way that you might look at a golf magazine and see a spread of nine irons. *Lucky* is addressing one interest in women's lives, in a really obsessive, specific way."[22]

● After his girlfriend jilted him, a Tennessee man tried to marry his car. His plan was thwarted, however, when he listed his fiancée's birthplace as Detroit, her father as Henry Ford, and her blood type as 10W40. Under Tennessee law, only a man and a woman can legally wed.[23] So much for that exciting honeymoon at the carwash.

Clearly, we can get pretty attached to products. Our motivation to attain a goal increases our desire to acquire the products or services we believe will satisfy it. However, not everyone is motivated to the same extent—one person might be convinced he can't live without the latest Apple iPhone, whereas another is perfectly happy with his 3-year-old LG.

Involvement is "a person's perceived relevance of the object based on their inherent needs, values, and interests."[24] We use the word *object* in the generic sense to refer to a product (or a brand), an advertisement, or a purchase situation. Consumers can find involvement in all these *objects*. Figure 4.3 shows that different factors may create it. These factors can be something about the person, something about the object, or something about the situation.

Product involvement often depends on the situation we're in. The Charmin toilet tissue brand sponsors a Web site, appropriately named SitOrSquat.com. The site helps travelers find the cleanest public restrooms wherever they happen to be on Earth. The brand manager explains, "Our goal is to connect Charmin with innovative conversations and solutions as a brand that understands the importance of bringing the best bathroom experience to consumers, even when they're away from home." According to Charmin, SitOrSquat lists over 52,000 toilets in 10 countries.
Source: Courtesy of P&G/Charmin.

Figure 4.3 CONCEPTUALIZING INVOLVEMENT

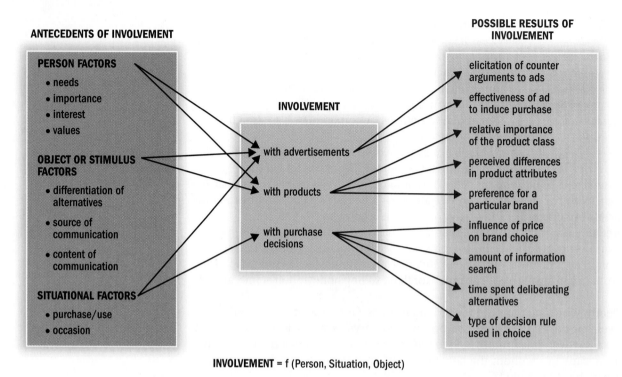

INVOLVEMENT = f (Person, Situation, Object)

The level of involvement may be influenced by one or more of these three factors. Interactions among persons, situation, and object factors are likely to occur.

Involvement reflects our level of motivation to process information.[25] To the degree that you feel knowing more about a product will help you to achieve some goal, you'll be motivated to pay attention to information about it. And as our involvement with a product increases, we devote more attention to ads related to the product, we exert more cognitive effort to understand these ads, and we focus more attention on the product-related information in the ads.[26]

Levels of Involvement: From Inertia to Passion

The type of information processing that occurs depends on the consumer's level of involvement. It can range from *simple processing*, where she considers only the basic features of a message all the way to *elaboration*, where she links this information to her preexisting knowledge system.[27]

Inertia

Think of a person's degree of involvement as a continuum that ranges from absolute lack of interest in a marketing stimulus at one end to obsession at the other. **Inertia** describes consumption at the low end of involvement, where we make decisions out of habit because we lack the motivation to consider alternatives. At the high end of involvement, we find the devotion we reserve for people and objects that carry great meaning for us. For example, the passion of some consumers for famous people (those living, such as Oprah Winfrey, or—supposedly—dead, such as Elvis Presley) demonstrates the high end of the involvement continuum.

When consumers are truly involved with a product, an ad, or a Web site, they enter a **flow state**. This experience is the Holy Grail of Web designers who want to create sites that are so entrancing the surfer loses all track of time as he becomes en-

This German ad hopes to ramp up involvement with potatoes, a low involvement product. The ad for ready-to-serve potato dishes declares, "Good stuff from potatoes."
Source: Courtesy of Unilever/Germany.

grossed in the site's contents (and hopefully buys stuff in the process!). Flow is an optimal experience with these qualities:

- A sense of playfulness
- A feeling of being in control
- Concentration and highly focused attention
- Mental enjoyment of the activity for its own sake
- A distorted sense of time
- A match between the challenge at hand and one's skills.[28]

Cult Products

In 2007, a momentous event shook the modern world: Apple puts its first iPhone on sale. Thousands of adoring iCultists around the country (including the mayor of Philadelphia) waited in front of Apple stores for days to be one of the first to buy the

Loyal users can log in and hang out at the Jones Soda Web site.

Source: Courtesy of Jones Soda Co.

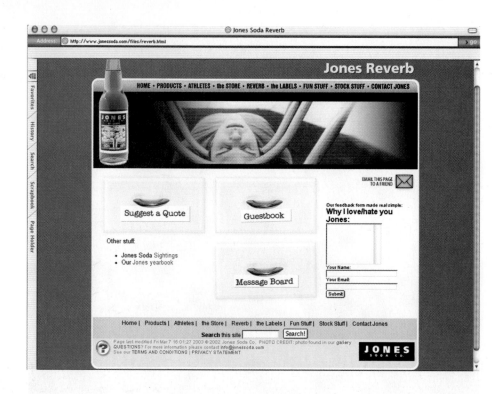

Apple boosts involvement with its popular iPhone as it provides numerous apps for users to download. The company ran into a storm of protest however after it unveiled a "Baby Shaker" app—it features a crying baby that stops howling only when the user shakes the phone vigorously. Although Apple didn't create the app, it does approve all offerings before it posts them at its online store. A spokeswoman for a consumer group that protested the product (her 2-year-old son suffered irreversible brain damage when he was shaken by his biological father as an infant) said in a press release, "This horrible iPhone app will undoubtedly be downloaded thousands of times by others in that same young-male demographic—the population group that is already statistically the most likely to shake babies." Apple pulled the application two days after it launched.[30]

device—even though they could order the phone online and have it delivered in 3 days. Somehow that was too long to wait for a cell phone with a touch screen. As one loyal consumer admitted, "If Apple made sliced bread, yeah, I'd buy it."[29]

OK, a useful product like a Smartphone is one thing—but a cookie? When Kellogg surrendered to the all-powerful Oreo and took its Hydrox cookies off the market, hard-core fans were bereft. As one wrote on a Web site devoted to the product, "This is a dark time in cookie history. And for those of you who say, 'Get over it, it's only a cookie,' you have not lived until you have tasted a Hydrox."[31] **Cult products** like Hydrox, Apple, Harley-Davidson, Jones Soda, Manolo Blahnik designer shoes (think Carrie on *Sex and the City*), and the Boston Red Sox command fierce consumer loyalty, devotion, and maybe even worship by consumers.[32]

The Many Faces of Involvement

A freelance software programmer who calls himself Winter is on a mission to visit every Starbucks in the world. To date he's been to more than 9,000 outlets in numerous countries. When he learned that a Starbucks store in British Columbia was scheduled to close the next day, he spent $1,400 to fly there immediately just to order a cup of coffee in the nick of time. He chronicles his odyssey on his Web site, starbuckseverywhere.net.[33]

Involvement takes many forms. It can be cognitive, as when a "gearhead" is motivated to learn all he can about the latest specs of a new multimedia personal computer (PC), or emotional, as when the thought of a new Armani suit gives a clotheshorse goose bumps.[34] The very act of buying the Armani may be very involving for people who are passionately devoted to shopping.

To further complicate matters, advertisements such as those Nike or Adidas produce may themselves be involving for some reason (e.g., because they make us laugh or cry, or inspire us to exercise harder). So, it seems that involvement is a fuzzy concept because it overlaps with other things and means different things to different people. Indeed, the consensus is that there are actually several broad types of involvement we can relate to the product, the message, or the perceiver.[35]

Dairy Queen helped to create the DQ Tycoon videogame, which boosts involvement as it lets players run their own fast-food franchise. They have to race against the clock to complete mundane tasks such as preparing Peanut Buster Parfaits, taking orders, restocking the refrigerator, and dipping cones.

Source: Courtesy of American Dairy Queen Corporation.

Product Involvement

Product involvement refers to a consumer's level of interest in a particular product. Many sales promotions aim to increase this type of involvement—consider the woman who won Roto-Rooter's "Pimped-Out John" contest (winning out over 318,000 other entries). Her prizes to maximize her bathroom experience included these goodies:[36]

- An Avanti 4.3-cubic-foot compact refrigerator with a beer tap
- A Gateway eMachines Notebook
- A dual-sided magnification mirror
- A Microsoft Xbox 360 core system
- A Philips Progressive-Scan DVD player
- A TiVo Series2 Digital Video Recorder
- A Philips 20-inch LCD Flat-Panel TV
- A personal cooling fan
- An Apple 30 GB iPod
- An iCarta Stereo Dock for iPod with bath tissue holder
- A Baseline Resistive Pedal Exerciser
- A Roto-Rooter Service button
- A megaphone so anyone in the house can hear you from up to 300 feet away

Talk about satisfying utilitarian and hedonic needs at the same time!

Message–Response Involvement

Media platforms possess different qualities that influence how motivated we are to pay attention to what they tell us. Television is a *low-involvement medium* because it requires a passive viewer who exerts relatively little control (remote-control "zipping" notwithstanding) over content. In contrast, print is a *high-involvement medium.* The reader actively processes the information and is able to pause and reflect on what he or she has read before moving on.[39] We'll discuss the role of message characteristics in changing attitudes in Chapter 7.

Marketing Opportunity

Mass customization is the personalization of products and services for individual customers at a mass-production price.[37] This strategy applies to a wide range of products and services, from newspaper Web sites that allow readers to choose which sections of the paper they want to see to Dell computers you can configure to Levi's blue jeans you can buy that have a right leg that's one inch shorter than a left leg to fit an asymmetrical body (this is more common than you think). Mars Snackfood USA introduced M&M's Faces to encourage consumers to bond with its chocolates: At mymms.com you can upload a photo and order a batch of M&M's with a face and personal message printed on the candy shell. Amazon.com offers a version of a book called *The Obama Time Capsule* that a buyer can personalize with his or her name on the cover as an author, a dedication, or even a picture on a page next to pictures of "other" celebrities like Oprah Winfrey. Lexus sponsors a project with Time Inc. and American Express Publishing (AEP) to produce a customized magazine it calls *Mine.* Consumers choose content from a set of magazines that includes *Time, Sports Illustrated,* and *Food & Wine.* They get their personalized magazine either in print or online as well as via RSS feeds on their cell phones.[38]

The winner of Roto-Rooter's "Pimped-Out John" Contest satisfies both utilitarian and hedonic needs at the same sitting.
Source: © Copyright 2007, Roto-Rooter, Inc.

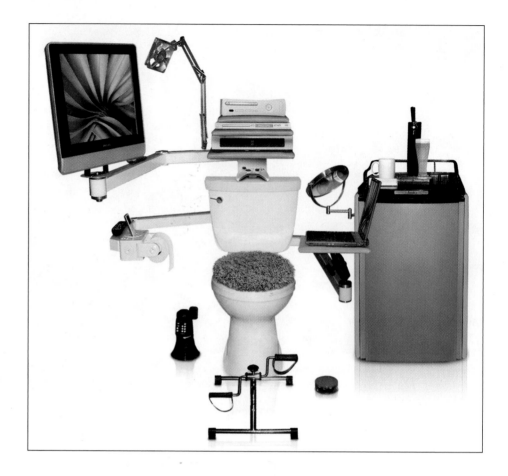

Although consumers differ in their levels of involvement with respect to a product message, marketers do not have to simply sit back and hope for the best. By being aware of some basic factors that increase or decrease attention, they can take steps to increase the likelihood that product information will get through. A marketer can boost a person's motivation to process relevant information via one or more of the following techniques:[40]

● **Appeal to the consumers' hedonic needs**—Ads that use sensory appeals like those we discussed in Chapter 2 generate higher levels of attention.[41]
● **Use novel stimuli, such as unusual cinematography, sudden silences, or unexpected movements, in commercials**—When a British firm called Egg Banking introduced a credit card to the French market, its ad agency created unusual commercials to make people question their assumptions. One ad stated, "Cats always land on their paws," and then two researchers in white lab coats dropped a kitten off a rooftop—never to see it again (animal rights activists were not amused).[42]
● **Use prominent stimuli, such as loud music and fast action, to capture attention in commercials**—In print formats, larger ads increase attention. Also, viewers look longer at colored pictures than at black-and-white ones.
● **Include celebrity endorsers to generate higher interest in commercials**—As we'll see in Chapter 7, people process more information when it comes from someone they admire.
● **Provide value customers appreciate**—Charmin bathroom tissue set up public toilets in Times Square that hordes of grateful visitors used. Thousands more people (evidently with time on their hands) visited the brand's Web site to view the display.[43]
● **Let customers make the messages**—*Consumer-generated content* where freelancers and fans film their own commercials for favorite products is one of the

hottest trends in marketing right now. This practice creates a high degree of *message–response involvement* (also called *advertising involvement*), which refers to the consumer's interest in processing marketing communications.[44]

What are some other options to increase message involvement? One is to invent new media platforms to grab our attention. Procter & Gamble printed trivia questions and answers on its Pringles snack chips with ink made of blue or red food coloring, and a company called Speaking Roses International patented a technology to laser-print words, images, or logos on flower petals.[46] An Australian firm creates hand stamps nightclubs use to identify paying customers; the stamps include logos or ad messages so partiers' hands become an advertising platform.[47]

Another tactic is to create **spectacles** or *performances*, where the message is itself a form of entertainment. In the early days of radio and television, ads literally were performances—show hosts integrated marketing messages into the episodes. Today live advertising is making a comeback as marketers try harder and harder to captivate jaded consumers:

- Jimmy Kimmel did a skit on his night-show program about Quiznos Subs.
- In the summer of 2009 Axe body products sponsored a posh Hamptons (New York) nightclub for the whole season where it became The Axe Lounge with branding on the DJ booth and menu and Axe products in the restrooms.[48]
- A British show broadcast a group of skydivers who performed a dangerous jump to create a human formation in the air that spelled out the letters *H, O, N, D,* and *A.*
- Honda built a musical road in Lancaster, PA; grooves in the cement create a series of pitches that play the William Tell Overture when a car drives over them.
- A public health campaign to promote awareness of colorectal cancer erected a 20-foot long inflatable colon in the middle of Times Square.[49]
- A New York campaign for Jameson Irish Whiskey projects an ad onto a wall—an operator scans the street for pedestrians that fit the brand's profile and inserts live text messages directed at them into the display.[50]
- To promote the 25th anniversary of the Michael Jackson album *Thriller,* which featured zombies dancing in a music video, Sony BMG staged such a performance on the London Underground. A group of "passengers" suddenly burst into a zombie-like dance before they disappeared into the crowd—and this

Marketing Pitfall

Chevrolet learned the hard way about the potential downside when a marketer gives up control over its brand to consumers. The carmaker introduced a Web site that allowed visitors to take existing video clips and music, insert their own words, and create customized 30-second commercials for the Chevrolet Tahoe. The idea was to generate interest in the Tahoe by encouraging satisfied drivers to circulate videos on the Web of themselves. Sure enough, plenty of videos circulated—but many of the messages for the gas-hungry SUV weren't exactly flattering. One ad used a sweeping view of the Tahoe driving through a desert. "Our planet's oil is almost gone," it said. "You don't need G.P.S. to see where this road leads." Another commercial asked, "Like this snowy wilderness? Better get your fill of it now. Then say hello to global warming."

A spokeswoman for Chevrolet said, "We anticipated that there would be critical submissions. You do turn over your brand to the public, and we knew that we were going to get some bad with the good. But it's part of playing in this space."[45]

Parachuters form an "H" for Honda in the sky during Honda's FreeFly TV ad shown in the U.K.
Source: Courtesy of Honda (UK).

An inflatable colon in Manhattan promotes awareness of colorectal cancer.
Source: Courtesy of Prevent Cancer Foundation.

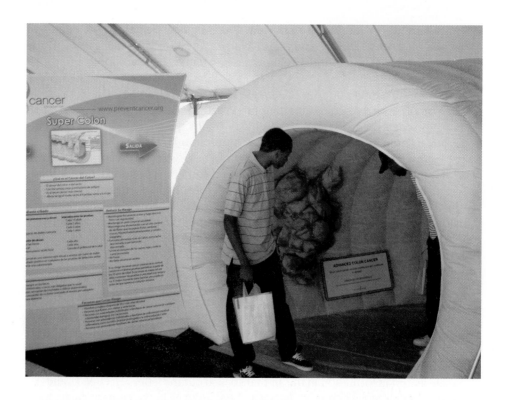

videotaped scene was posted online. The video inspired similar performances in other countries, and within a week more than a million people had downloaded these films.[51] In a similar stunt for T-Mobile, several hundred commuters at the Liverpool rail station broke into a dance—more than 15 million people watched the performance on YouTube in the following weeks.[52]

● In Hollywood 500 guests showed up for what they thought was the debut of a new TV series called *Scarlet*. The event was in reality part of a new campaign for LG Electronics' new line of Scarlet TVs.[53]

The quest to heighten message involvement also fuels the rapid growth of **interactive mobile marketing**, where consumers participate in real-time promotional campaigns via their trusty cell phones, usually by text-messaging entries to on-air TV contests. These strategies are very popular in the United Kingdom, for example, where revenue from phone and text-messaging services for TV programs brings in almost a half billion dollars a year.

In the United States, people now send more text messages than they do e-mails. Although a handful of U.S. TV shows, such as *American Idol*, invite viewers to use their cell phones to vote on contestants, this wasn't a popular strategy until recently. There was little money to be made because consumers generally paid only about 10 cents per message and the cell phone companies typically kept most of the revenue. The United States also has been slow to adopt text voting because programmers have to deal with several time zones and several different wireless network technologies, whereas in many other countries there is only one time zone and one dominant wireless network technology. Also a few major cell phone operators wouldn't let marketers use their networks because of concerns about network overload. However, this all changed in 2006 when the leading wireless operators agreed on "consumer best practices guidelines" for text-message voting on TV shows. The guidelines now allow programmers to charge as much as 99 cents a message as long as viewers are aware of the cost. And programmers no longer run the risk they will frustrate audience members who have the wrong cell phone service now that all major operators participate.[54]

To build involvement with a message, a movie theater audience controls a screen game with their body movements as part of a campaign for MSNBC.com.
Source: Scott Gries/Getty Images.

The latest version of mobile marketing that intends to involve consumers at a higher level is the **alternate-reality game** that blends online and off-line clues and encourages players to collaborate to solve a puzzle. McDonald's got into the act with The Lost Ring promotion the chain ran during the 2008 Olympics. First, 50 bloggers received packages with an Olympic-themed poster and a clue pointing them to TheLostRing.com that described the game in a video. It was only when players started to discover additional clues that they learned McDonald's was behind the game.[55]

Purchase Situation Involvement

If you happen to be walking through the Shibuya Station in Tokyo, you might come across a giant vending machine that dispenses—a car. Well, not exactly—but it does give you a canister with a brochure for the Smart car as well as a **QR code** that you can photograph with your cell phone. This advanced version of a barcode activates your phone's browser, which takes you to the Smart digital portal that lets you create your own car with a funky paint job and graphics and then race around a 3-D track. You can even print a color version of your pimped-out ride to help you create a real-life model of your design.[56]

Purchase situation involvement refers to differences in motivation when people buy the same product but in different contexts. For example, when you want to impress someone, you may try to buy a brand with a certain image that you think reflects good taste. When you have to buy a gift for someone in an obligatory situation, such as a wedding gift for a cousin you do not really like, you may not care what image the gift portrays. Again, some smart retailers are waking up to the value of increasing purchase situation involvement when they appeal to hedonic shoppers who look to be entertained or otherwise engaged in addition to simply "buying stuff."[57] We'll learn more about how they're doing this via the creation of themed retailing venues and other strategies in Chapter 10.

Measuring involvement is important for many marketing applications. For example, research evidence indicates that a viewer who is more involved with a television show will respond more positively to commercials he sees during that show and that these spots will have a greater chance to influence his purchase intentions.[59] Table 4.1 shows one of the most widely used scales researchers use to assess level of involvement.

Marketing Opportunity

As a next step in the steady march toward personalized messaging, a few marketers tailor the recommendations they give shoppers in a store based on what they picked up on a shelf—and in the near future based on their appearance. At a few Dunkin' Donuts locations, a person who orders a morning coffee sees an ad at the cash register that pushes hash browns or breakfast sandwiches. At a German store, Procter & Gamble places RFID (radio-frequency identification) tags on products; when a shopper lifts a package off a shelf, this action changes the message on a digital screen in front of him or her. For example, if you pull out shampoo for thick hair, the screen recommends the best conditioner or other hair products. One company is almost ready to deploy similar technology that includes facial-recognition technology; this will actually classify shoppers into groups based on their approximate age and their likely gender (some hairstyles and facial piercings will make this challenge "interesting"). The technology analyzes features like the size and shape of the nose, eyes, cheekbones, and jaw line and compares these to databases to make a guess as to which category the person should belong.[58]

Chinese people look at a Smart Fortwo exhibited in a vending machine at a shopping mall in Beijing. Consumers can get a magic cube with more information about the Smart model after they insert a one-yuan coin into a vending slot. Potential buyers can also file applications for test drives and even reserve Smart cars through the machine.

Source: AP Wide World Photos.

TABLE 4.1	Measuring Involvement	
To Me [Object to Be Judged] Is		
1. important	_:_:_:_:_:_:_	unimportant*
2. boring	_:_:_:_:_:_:_	interesting
3. relevant	_:_:_:_:_:_:_	irrelevant*
4. exciting	_:_:_:_:_:_:_	unexciting*
5. means nothing	_:_:_:_:_:_:_	means a lot to me
6. appealing	_:_:_:_:_:_:_	unappealing*
7. fascinating	_:_:_:_:_:_:_	mundane*
8. worthless	_:_:_:_:_:_:_	valuable
9. involving	_:_:_:_:_:_:_	uninvolving*
10. not needed	_:_:_:_:_:_:_	needed

Values

A religious official in Saudi Arabia recently decreed that children there should not be allowed to watch Mickey Mouse because the cartoon character is a "soldier of Satan."[60] This may surprise most of us, but then again we don't live in this deeply conservative Islamic culture. A **value** is a belief that some condition is preferable to its opposite. For example, it's safe to assume that most people prefer freedom to slavery. Others avidly pursue products and services that will make them look younger rather than older. A person's set of values plays a very important role in consumption activities. Consumers purchase many products and services because they believe these products will help to attain a value-related goal.

Two people can believe in the same behaviors (e.g., vegetarianism), but their underlying *belief systems* may be quite different (e.g., animal activism versus health concerns). The extent to which people share a belief system is a function of individual, social, and cultural forces. Advocates of a belief system often seek out others with similar beliefs so that social networks overlap, and as a result, believers tend to be exposed to information that supports their beliefs (e.g., "tree-huggers" rarely hang out with loggers).[61]

Core Values

OBJECTIVE

Why do our deeply held cultural values dictate the types of products and services we seek out or avoid?

More than 8.2 million women in 50 countries read versions of *Cosmopolitan* in 28 different languages—even though due to local norms about modesty some of them have to hide the magazine from their husbands! It's a bit tricky to adapt the *Cosmo* credo of "Fun, Fearless Female" in all these places. Different cultures emphasize varying belief systems that define what it means to be female, feminine, or appealing—and what people consider appropriate to see in print on these matters. Publishers of the Chinese version aren't even permitted to mention sex at all, so they replace articles about uplifting cleavage with uplifting stories about youthful dedication. Ironically, there isn't much down-and-dirty material in the Swedish edition either—but for the opposite reason: The culture is so open about this topic that it doesn't grab readers' attention the way it would in the United States.[62]

In India, you won't come across any *Cosmo* articles about sexual positions. And *Playboy* recently announced plans to publish a magazine in India—but without nudes. The magazine views the country as a promising, new market with values similar to those of people in the United States in the 1950s when *Playboy* was first published: India is on the verge of a sexual revolution, but it's not quite there yet. In a sharp departure even from fairly recent times, today pollsters report that in India one-quarter of urban, unmarried women have sex; one-third read erotic literature; and half go on dates. And there is a small but growing class of young, urban Indian men with disposable incomes who are eager to learn about the good life. However, as one Indian analyst observed, "In urban India, the concept of single men living alone is quite new. Here, most men, until they're married, live at home. Once you're married, your wife wonders what you're reading."[63]

CB AS I LIVE IT
Drew Rudebusch, *The University of Washington*

A quarter-life crisis. That is what some people called it. Others just said I was scared. Probably true, but who isn't scared when they are about to graduate. Call it whatever you want, but the one thing I know for certain is that my motivations have changed dramatically.

Coming out of a long-term relationship, with graduation quickly approaching, I found myself pondering every aspect of my life. Central to all of these musings were my motivations. I quickly realized that the motivation for many of my decisions was not sustaining me any longer. An altered living situation, coupled with a totally different perspective on the future, combined to make for a marketer's dream. I was truly on a mission to find myself, and provided an open door for marketers to inspire me with their "motivational" messaging. I grew less interested in the traditional material goods, such as cars, televisions, or a fancy house. Instead I was motivated by experiences that I want to strive for, like traveling the world. I became more interested than ever before by travel discounts and advertisements about adventures abroad. Graduating and getting a job took on a totally different meaning than just months before. I looked forward to spending my paychecks in a drastically new way.

Does this mean my motivation for a nice car, a comfortable home, and tailored suits have gone away entirely? I doubt it. Those marketers will have their chance again one day, but they can focus on someone else for now because I have found a new motivation.

ECONsumer Behavior

The Italian preference for deep-down cleaning crops up more in the U.S.A., especially as our wallets shrink. Companies that make household cleaning products are tuning in to current values in the United States the economic situation influences: Frugality, environmentalism, and disclosure about how and where products are manufactured. SC Johnson announced that it will reveal ingredient information over and above federal guidelines for brands like Windex and Glade. Several major firms including Clorox and Church & Dwight have come out with green versions of their cleaners. As one industry analyst observed, "Consumers want to do-it-yourself, make-it-yourself, grow-it-yourself and clean-it-yourself these days. People are saying, 'I don't have control of what's out there—but I do have control over my home.' The banking system has failed us, the stock market has failed us, even the electrical grid is starting to fail us. It's a way people have of saying, 'I don't trust the system.'" A survey from the Soap and Detergent Association (SDA) reported that 60 percent of Americans say they're doing more cleaning themselves instead of hiring a cleaning service.

What's more, 22 percent make their own cleaning products at home.[67] The trend toward making things yourself that you used to buy from others shows up in other product categories as well. It's so widespread that some marketers even invented a new term for it: **insourcing**. We see a spike in sales of sewing kits and garden seeds, while Procter & Gamble reports that more consumers call with questions about how to dye their hair at home.

These differences in values often explain why marketing efforts that are a big hit in one country flop in another. For example, a hugely successful advertisement in Japan promoted breast cancer awareness when it showed an attractive woman in a sundress who drew stares from men on the street as a voice-over says, "If only women paid as much attention to their breasts as men do." The same ad flopped in France because the use of humor to talk about a serious disease offended the French.[64]

Values regarding issues such as sexuality are important in the United States also. A recent flap over a condom commercial illustrates how these beliefs can touch a nerve (in fact, it was only recently that we started to see prophylactic advertising on TV at all!). In the Trojan spot, women in a bar sit next to pigs. One magically turns into a handsome suitor after it buys a condom from a vending machine. The tag line reads, "Evolve. Use a condom every time." The CBS and FOX networks rejected the ad, and some local NBC affiliates refused to run it. A blogger noted the ambiguity of our values about this sensitive issue: "I'm offended by the reality that television is so hypersexualized and glorifies sexual excess and promiscuity, and then runs screaming into the megachurch and drops to its knees when someone wants to run an advertisement that urges people to be responsible about their sexual expression."[65]

Or take the core value of cleanliness—everyone wants to be clean, but some societies are more fastidious than others and won't accept products and services that they think cut corners. Italian women on average spend 21 hours a week on household chores other than cooking—compared with only 4 hours for Americans according to Procter & Gamble's research. The Italian women wash kitchen and bathroom floors at least four times a week, Americans only once. Italian women typically iron nearly all their wash, even socks and sheets, and they buy more cleaning supplies than women elsewhere do.

So they should be ideal customers for cleaning products, right? That's what Unilever thought when it launched its all-purpose Cif spray cleaner there, but it flopped. Similarly, P&G's best-selling Swiffer wet mop bombed big time. Both companies underestimated this market's desire for products that are tough cleaners, not timesavers. Only about 30 percent of Italian households have dishwashers because many women don't trust machines to get dishes as clean as they can get them by hand, manufacturers say. Many of those who do use machines tend to thoroughly rinse the dishes before they load them in the dishwasher The explanation for this value: After World War II, Italy remained a poor country until well into the 1960s, so labor-saving devices, such as washing machines, which had become popular in wealthy countries, arrived late. Italian women joined the workforce later than many other European women and in smaller numbers. Young Italian women increasingly work outside the home, but they still spend nearly as much time as their mothers did on housework.

When Unilever did research to determine why Italians didn't take to Cif, they found that these women weren't convinced that a mere spray would do the job on tough kitchen grease or that one product would adequately clean different surfaces (it turns out that 72 percent of Italians own more than eight different cleaning products). The company reformulated the product and reintroduced it with different varieties instead of as an all-in-one. It also made the bottles 50 percent bigger because Italians clean so frequently and changed its advertising to emphasize the products' cleaning strength rather than convenience. P&G also reintroduced its Swiffer, this time adding beeswax and a Swiffer duster that is now a bestseller. It sold 5 million boxes in the first 8 months, twice the company's forecasts.[66]

In many cases, of course, values are universal. Who does not desire health, wisdom, or world peace? What sets cultures apart is the *relative importance*, or ranking, of these universal values. This set of rankings constitutes a culture's **value system**.[68] For example, one study found that North Americans have more favorable attitudes toward advertising messages that focus on self-reliance, self-improvement, and the achievement of personal goals as opposed to themes stressing family integrity, collective goals, and the feeling of harmony with others. Korean consumers exhibited the reverse pattern.[69]

We characterize every culture in terms of its members' endorsement of a value system. Every individual may not endorse these values equally, and in some cases, values may even seem to contradict one another (e.g., Americans appear to value both conformity and individuality, and try to find some accommodation between the two). Nonetheless, it is usually possible to identify a general set of **core values** that uniquely define a culture. Core values such as freedom, youthfulness, achievement, materialism, and activity characterize American culture.

In contrast, most Japanese are happy to trade off a bit of independence for security and a feeling of safety—especially when it comes to their children. It's common for communities to post guards along school routes and for parents to place global positioning system (GPS) devices and safety buzzers in their kids' backpacks. Numerous indoor parks in Japan are highly secure environments designed to ease parents' minds. At a typical one called the Fantasy Kids Resort, there are uniformed monitors, security cameras, and antibacterial sand. Visitors spray their stroller wheels with antiseptic soap, and guards require identification from visitors before they admit them.[70]

How do we determine what a culture values? We term the process of learning the beliefs and behaviors endorsed by one's own culture **enculturation**. In contrast, we call the process of learning the value system and behaviors of another culture (often a priority for those who wish to understand consumers and markets in foreign countries) **acculturation** (more on this in Chapter 13). *Socialization agents*, including parents, friends, and teachers, impart these beliefs to us.

Another important type of agent is the media; we learn a lot about a culture's priorities when we look at the values advertising communicates. For example, sales strategies differ significantly between the United States and China. U.S. commercials are more likely to present facts about products and suggestions from credible authorities, whereas Chinese advertisers tend to focus more on emotional appeals

CB AS I LIVE IT

Rachel Miller, *University of Virginia*

*N*avigating a foreign culture can be a headache. And in Spain, the search for relief might make you feel even worse. When I spent a semester in Madrid during my third year of college, one of the more aggravating differences for me, a blue-blooded American girl, was the business model of Spanish pharmacies. Rather than discretely slipping into CVS for tampons/hemorrhoid cream/miscellaneous embarrassing first aid item, customers must personally ask a pharmacist for the cure to whatever ails them, even for products that don't require a prescription. When I felt sick,

I found myself weighing my physical suffering against the emotional trauma of describing my symptoms to a stranger in the middle of a store.

I think the concept at work was a difference in cultural values. Whereas Spaniards value expert advice for even the least severe of medical woes, as an American I prioritize privacy. My experience reflects Chapter 4's lesson that cultural values strongly influence consumer behavior. As the chapter illustrates, shoppers tend to reject products and services that conflict with their core values. In my case, I searched for substitutes, avoided pharmacies unless a visit was absolutely necessary, and asked my mom to bring a supply from home when she came to visit.

I felt an aversion to Spanish pharmacies even before I could explain why. However, I will be sure to consider differences in values when I undertake my own business ventures in the future. Although marketers in Spain may not cater to American consumers, my experience reemphasizes the point that it is important to design products and services that are in line with a market's regional values. For instance, the full-service drugstore may thrive in Spain, but executives should think twice before they try to bring the same model to America. Or perhaps an entrepreneur may see an opportunity to design hassle-free first aid shopping for ex-pats in Europe.

without bothering too much to substantiate their claims. U.S. ads tend to be youth-oriented, whereas Chinese ads are more likely to stress the wisdom of older people.[71]

How Do Values Link to Consumer Behavior?

Despite their importance, values haven't helped us to understand consumer behavior as much as we might expect. One reason is that broad-based concepts such as freedom, security, or inner harmony are more likely to affect general purchasing patterns than to differentiate between brands within a product category. This is why some researchers distinguish among broad-based *cultural values* such as security or happiness, *consumption-specific values* such as convenient shopping or prompt service, and *product-specific values* such as ease of use or durability, which affect the relative importance people in different cultures place on possessions.[72]

A recent study of product-specific values looked in depth at Australians who engage in extreme sports such as surfing, snowboarding, and skateboarding. The researchers identified four dominant values that drove brand choice: freedom, belongingness, excellence, and connection. For example, one female surfer they studied embraced the value of belongingness. She expressed this value when she wore popular brands of surfing apparel even when these major brands had lost their local roots by going mainstream. In contrast, another surfer in the study valued connection—he expressed this as he selected only locally made brands and supported local surfing events.[73]

Some aspects of brand image such as sophistication tend to be common across cultures, but others are more likely to be relevant in specific places. The Japanese tend to value peacefulness, whereas Spaniards emphasize passion, and the value of ruggedness appeals to Americans.[74] Because values drive much of consumer behavior (at least in a very general sense), we might say that virtually *all* consumer research ultimately relates to identifying and measuring values. In this section we'll describe some specific attempts by researchers to measure cultural values and apply this knowledge to marketing strategy.

The positive value we place on the activities of large corporations is changing among some consumers who prefer to go "anti-corporate." This ad for a coffee shop in Boulder, Colorado, reflects that sentiment.
Source: Used with permission of Ink! Coffee and Cultivator Advertising & Design.

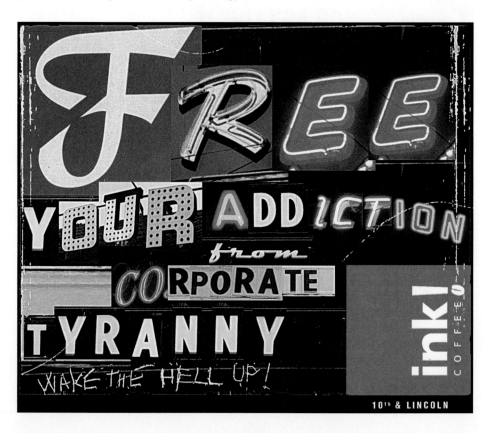

Hofstede's Cultural Dimensions

One of the most widely used measures of cross-cultural values is an instrument developed by Geert Hofstede, a Dutch researcher.[76] This measure scores a country in terms of its standing on five dimensions so that users can compare and contrast values:[77]

- **Power Distance**—The extent to which the less powerful members of organizations and institutions (like the family) accept and expect that power is distributed unequally.
- **Individualism**—The degree to which individuals are integrated into groups.
- **Masculinity**—The distribution of roles between the genders.
- **Uncertainty Avoidance**—A society's tolerance for uncertainty and ambiguity.
- **Long-Term Orientation**—Values associated with Long-Term Orientation are thrift and perseverance; values associated with Short-Term Orientation are respect for tradition, fulfilling social obligations, and protecting one's "face."

The Rokeach Value Survey

The psychologist Milton Rokeach identified a set of **terminal values**, or desired end states, that apply to many different cultures. The *Rokeach Value Survey* also includes a set of **instrumental values**, or actions we need to take to achieve these terminal values.[78] Table 4.2 lists these two sets of values.

Some evidence indicates that differences in these global values do translate into product-specific preferences and differences in media usage. Nonetheless, marketing researchers have not widely used the Rokeach Value Survey.[79] One reason is that

TABLE 4.2	Terminal and Instrumental Values
Instrumental Values	**Terminal Values**
Ambitious	A comfortable life
Broad-minded	An exciting life
Capable	A sense of accomplishment
Cheerful	A world of peace
Clean	A world of beauty
Courageous	Equality
Forgiving	Family security
Helpful	Freedom
Honest	Happiness
Imaginative	Inner harmony
Independent	Mature love
Intellectual	National security
Logical	Pleasure
Loving	Salvation
Obedient	Self-respect
Polite	Social recognition
Responsible	True friendship
Self-controlled	Wisdom

Source: Richard W. Pollay, "Measuring the Cultural Values Manifest in Advertising," *Current Issues and Research in Advertising* (1983): 71–92. Reprinted by permission, CtC Press. All rights reserved.

Marketing Pitfall

Strongly held values can make life very difficult for marketers who sell personal-care products. This is the case with tampons; 70 percent of U.S. women use them, but only 100 million out of a potential market of 1.7 billion eligible women around the world do. Resistance to using this product posed a major problem for Tambrands. The company makes only one product, so it needs to sell tampons in as many countries as possible to continue growing. But Tambrands has trouble selling its feminine hygiene products in some cultures such as Brazil, where many young women fear they will lose their virginity if they use a tampon. A commercial it showed there featured an actress who says in a reassuring voice, "Of course, you're not going to lose your virginity."

Prior to launching a new global advertising campaign for Tampax in 26 countries, the firm's advertising agency divided the world into three clusters based on residents' resistance to using tampons. Resistance was so intense in Muslim countries that the agency didn't even try to sell there!

- In cluster 1 (including the United States, the United Kingdom, and Australia), women felt comfortable with the idea and offered little resistance. The agency developed a *teaser ad* to encourage more frequency of use: "Should I sleep with it, or not?"
- In cluster 2 (including France, Israel, and South Africa), about 50 percent of women use the product, but some concerns about the loss of virginity remain. To counteract these objections, the agency obtained endorsements from gynecologists within each country.
- In cluster 3 (including Brazil, China, and Russia), Tambrands encountered the greatest resistance. To try to make inroads in these countries, the researchers found that the first priority is simply to explain how to use the product without making women feel squeamish—a challenge they still try to figure out. If they do—and that's a big if—Tambrands will have changed the consumer behavior of millions of women and added huge new markets to its customer base in the process.[75]

our society is evolving into smaller and smaller sets of *consumption microcultures* within a larger culture, each with its own set of core values (more on this in Chapter 12). For example, in the United States, a sizable number of people are strong believers in natural health practices and alternative medicine. This focus on wellness instead of mainstream medical approaches to sickness influences many of their behaviors, from food choices to the use of alternative medical practitioners, as well as their opinions on political and social issues.[80]

The List of Values (LOV)

The **List of Values (LOV) Scale** isolates values with more direct marketing applications. This instrument identifies nine consumer segments based on the values members endorse and relates each value to differences in consumption behaviors. These segments include consumers who place priorities on such values as a sense of belonging, excitement, warm relationships with others, and security. For example, people who endorse the sense-of-belonging value are older, are more likely to read *Reader's Digest* and *TV Guide*, drink and entertain more, and prefer group activities more than people who do not endorse this value as highly. In contrast, those who endorse the value of excitement are younger and prefer *Rolling Stone* magazine.[81]

The Means–End Chain Model

Another research approach that incorporates values is the *means–end chain model*. This approach assumes that people link very specific product attributes (indirectly) to terminal values: We choose among alternative means to attain some end state we value (such as freedom or safety). Thus, we value products to the extent that they provide the means to some end we desire. A technique researchers call **laddering** uncovers consumers' associations between specific attributes and these general consequences. Using this approach, they help consumers climb up the "ladder" of abstraction that connects functional product attributes with desired end states.[82] Based on consumer feedback, they then create *hierarchical value maps* that show how specific product attributes get linked to end states.

Figure 4.4 shows three different hierarchical value maps from a study of consumers' perceptions of cooking oils in three European countries.[83] The laddering technique illustrates stark differences among product/values links across cultures. For Danish people, health is the most important end state. The British also focus on health, but saving money and avoiding waste are more important for them than for people elsewhere. And unlike the other two countries, French people link olive oil to their cultural identity.

Syndicated Surveys

A number of companies track changes in values through large-scale surveys. They sell the results of these studies to marketers, who receive regular updates on changes and trends. This approach originated in the mid-1960s, when Playtex was concerned about sagging girdle sales (pun intended). The company commissioned the market research firm of Yankelovich, Skelly & White to see why sales dropped. Their research linked the decline to a shift in values regarding appearance and naturalness. Playtex went on to design lighter, less restrictive garments, whereas Yankelovich went on to track the impact of these types of changes in a range of industries.

Gradually, the firm developed the idea of one big study to track U.S. attitudes. In 1970, it introduced the Yankelovich *Monitor*™, which is based on 2-hour interviews with 4,000 respondents.[84] This survey attempts to pick up changes in values; for example, it reported a movement among American consumers toward simplification and away from hype as people try to streamline their hectic lives and reduce their concerns about gaining the approval of others through their purchases. **Voluntary simplifiers** believe that once we satisfy our basic material needs, additional income does not add to happiness. Instead of adding yet another SUV to the

Figure 4.4 HIERARCHICAL VALUE MAPS FOR VEGETABLE OIL IN THREE COUNTRIES
Source: N. A. Nielsen, T. Bech-Larsen, and K. G. Grunert, "Consumer Purchase Motives and Product Perceptions: A Laddering Study on Vegetable Oil in Three Countries," *Food Quality and Preference* 9(6) (1998): 455–66. © 1998 Elsevier. Used with permission.

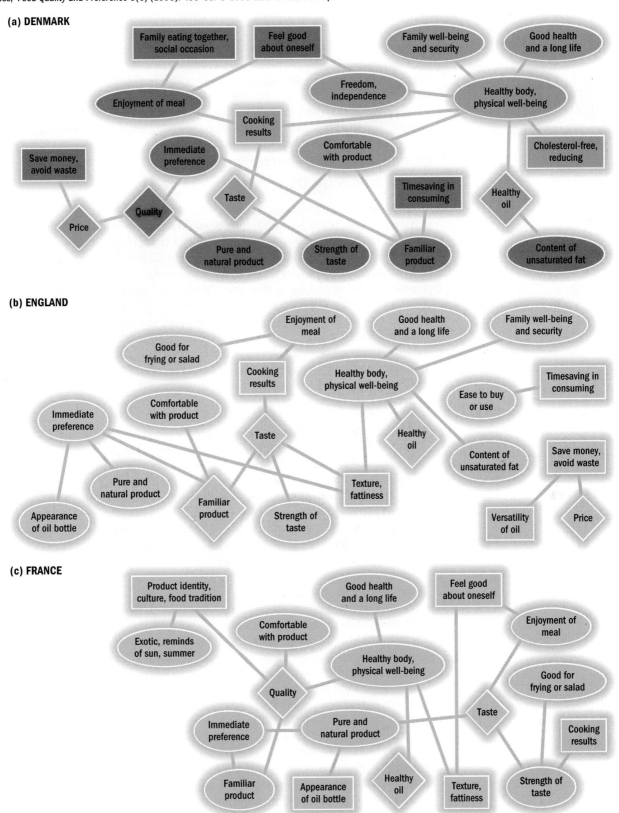

(a) DENMARK

(b) ENGLAND

(c) FRANCE

collection in the garage, simplifiers are into community building, public service, and spiritual pursuits (think about the self-actualization level we saw in Maslow's hierarchy earlier in the chapter).[85] Members range from senior citizens who downsize their homes to young, mobile professionals who don't want to be tied down to their possessions.

Today, many other syndicated surveys also track changes in values. Advertising agencies operate some of these so that they can stay on top of important cultural trends and help shape the messages they craft for clients. These services include VALS2™ (more on this in Chapter 6), GlobalScan (operated by the advertising agency Backer Spielvogel Bates), New Wave (the Ogilvy & Mather advertising agency), and the Lifestyles Study the DDB World Communications Group conducts.

Conscientious Consumerism: A New American Core Value?

Are U.S. consumers finally going green—for real? In one survey, 8 in 10 consumers said they believe it's important to buy green brands and products from green companies, and that they'll pay more to do so. The U.S. consumer's focus on personal health is merging with a growing interest in global health. Some analysts call this new value **conscientious consumerism**.[86] In another survey conducted in 2009, 71 percent of consumers agree that they "avoid purchasing from companies whose practices they disagree with and about 1/2 claim they tell others to either patronize or avoid products based on manufacturers' social and environmental practices."[87]

However, it's important to note that (as we'll see in Chapter 7) attitudes don't always predict behavior—especially for pocketbook issues. When people have less money to spend, they may not purchase environmentally friendly or healthy products if they have to pay a premium for them. As the old saying goes, "The road to hell is paved with good intentions."

Still, it's clear that at least a sizable number of Americans' values are shifting. In particular, marketers point to a segment of consumers they call *LOHAS*—an acronym for "lifestyles of health and sustainability." This label refers to people who worry about the environment, want products to be produced in a sustainable way, and spend money to advance what they see as their personal development and potential. These so-called "Lohasians" (others refer to this segment as *cultural creatives*) represent a great market for products such as organic foods, energy-efficient appliances, and hybrid cars, as well as alternative medicine, yoga tapes, and ecotourism. One organization that tracks this group estimates they make up about 16 percent of the adults in the United States or 35 million people; it values the market for socially conscious products at more than $200 billion.[88]

Whereas in the past it was sufficient for companies to offer recyclable products, this new movement creates a whole new vocabulary as consumers "vote with their forks" when they demand food, fragrances, and other items made without genetically modified ingredients (GMOs); hormone-free, which don't involve animal clones or animal testing; locally grown; and cage-free, just to name a few of consumers' concerns and requirements.

Although Lohasians have fueled demand for ecofriendly products for several years, the big news today is that conscientious consumerism now is spreading to the mass market as well. In fact, even the retailing behemoth Wal-Mart is making significant strides in this area. The world's largest retailer developed a survey called the "Live Better Index" that allows it to monitor customers' feelings about ecofriendly products. The first wave of research polled more than 2,500 Americans on five products: compact fluorescent light bulbs (CFLs), organic milk, concentrated/reduced-packaging liquid laundry detergents, extended-life paper products, and organic baby food. In this survey, 62 percent of respondents said they would buy more ecofriendly products *if* there was no price difference. Nearly half (47 percent) said they completely agree that buying environmentally friendly products makes them feel like smart consumers, and 68 percent agree that "even the small act of recycling at home has an impact on the environment."[89] Numerous companies respond to these desires as they develop new "green" formulations or partner with other organizations to promote environmentally friendly behavior. Clorox teamed up with the Sierra Club to promote a new line of ecofriendly Clorox products in exchange for a share of the profit. The cleaners are made from natural ingredients such as coconuts and lemon oil, contain no phosphorus or bleach, are biodegradable, and are not animal-tested. Their packaging bottles are recyclable and bear the Sierra Club's name and logo—a giant sequoia tree framed by mountain peaks.[90]

Ethical behavior aside for a moment, is there a financial reward waiting for those companies that pay closer attention to what goes into their products and who makes them? One study that examined this question suggests the answer is yes. The researchers gave subjects a description of a coffee company that either used or did not use Fair Trade principles to buy its beans. They found that participants were willing to pay an additional $1.40 for a pound of the coffee if it was ethically sourced and they were very negative about the company if it did not adhere to these principles. The study obtained similar results for shirts that were made with organic cotton.[91]

The Carbon Footprint and Offsets

The **carbon footprint** measures, in units of carbon dioxide, the impact human activities have on the environment in terms of the amount of greenhouse gases they produce. The average American is responsible for 9.44 tons of CO_2 per year![93] As Figure 4.5 shows, a carbon footprint comes from the sum of two parts, the direct, or primary, footprint and the indirect, or secondary, footprint:

1 The *primary footprint* is a measure of our direct emissions of CO_2 from the burning of fossil fuels, including domestic energy consumption and transportation (e.g., cars and planes).
2 The *secondary footprint* is a measure of the indirect CO_2 emissions from the whole life cycle of products we use, from their manufacture to their eventual breakdown.[94]

Thousands of consumers use services such as Climate Clean and TerraPass that sell them *greenhouse gas (GHG) offsets*. These businesses enable individuals and busi-

Marketing Pitfall

How much green is too much? As companies jump on the environmental bandwagon, some make inflated claims about just how green they are. Some marketers fear a backlash they've called **greenwashing** where consumers push back and refuse to believe all the hype. According to one report, almost one-fourth of American consumers say they have "no way of knowing" if a product is green or actually does what it claims. And, big corporations still have their work cut out for them—41 percent of survey respondents could not name a single company they consider socially and environmentally responsible.[92]

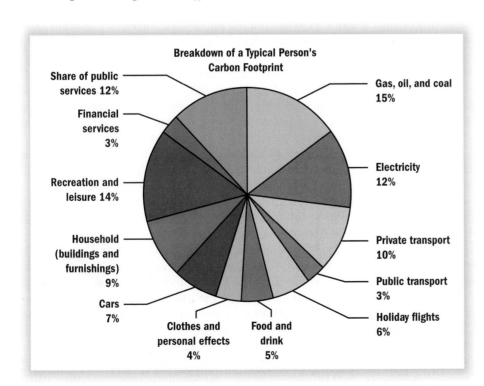

Figure 4.5 CARBON FOOTPRINT BREAKDOWN

nesses to reduce their GHG emissions as they offset, reduce or displace the GHG to another place, typically where it is more economical to do so. GHG offsets typically include using renewable energy, energy efficiency, and methane capture that reduce the emission of gases scientists tell us contribute to global warming. For example, if your company flies you to another city for a business trip, it might purchase an "offset" equal to the amount of emissions the airplane created to get you there.[95]

Even the television industry is starting to think about its carbon footprint. The hit show *24* became the first "carbon neutral" TV series. The show brought in consultants to measure how much carbon dioxide it produces during production, installed motion monitors in bathrooms and kitchens to make the lighting more efficient, bought carbon offsets, and sharply reduced the number of car crashes included in the scripts. NBC Universal committed to "greening" several shows, including the *Nightly News with Brian Williams* and *Saturday Night Live*—the network uses alternative fuels and increased its recycling and composting.[96]

Materialism: "He Who Dies with the Most Toys, Wins"

OBJECTIVE

Why do consumers vary in the importance they attach to worldly possessions, and why does this orientation in turn impact on their priorities and behaviors?

Our possessions play a central role in our lives, and our desire to accumulate them shapes our value systems. **Materialism** refers to the importance people attach to worldly possessions.[97] We sometimes take the bounty of products and services for granted, until we remember how recent this abundance is. For example, in 1950, two of five American homes did not have a telephone, and in 1940, half of all households still did not possess complete indoor plumbing.

During World War II, members of "cargo cults" in the South Pacific literally worshiped cargo salvaged from crashed aircraft or washed ashore from ships. They believed that their ancestors piloted the ships and planes passing near their islands so they tried to attract them to their villages. They went so far as to construct fake planes from straw to lure the real ones![98]

We may not worship products to that extent, but many of us certainly work hard to attain our vision of the good life, which abounds in material comforts. Most young people can't imagine a life without cell phones, MP3 players, and other creature comforts. In fact, we can think of marketing as a system that provides certain standards of living to consumers. To some extent, then, the standards of living we expect and desire influence our lifestyles—either by personal experience or as a result of the affluent characters we see on TV and in movies.[99] These expectations of course vary across cultures—for example today about 70 percent of Korean households have refrigerators specially designed to hold *kimchi*, the fermented vegetables that Koreans eat with just about every meal.[100]

Materialistic values tend to emphasize the well-being of the individual versus the group, which may conflict with family or religious values. That conflict may help to explain why people with highly material values tend to be less happy.[101] And, materialism is highest among early adolescents (12 to 13 years old) in comparison to children or late adolescents—perhaps it's no coincidence that this is the age group that also has the lowest level of self-esteem.[102]

Materialists are more likely to value possessions for their status and appearance-related meanings, whereas those who do not emphasize this value tend to prize products that connect them to other people or that provide them with pleasure when they use them.[103] As a result, high materialists prefer expensive products they publicly consume. A study that compared specific items that low versus high materialists value found that people low on the materialism value cherished items such as a mother's wedding gown, picture albums, a rocking chair from childhood, or a garden, whereas those who scored high preferred things such as jewelry, china, or a vacation home.[104] Materialistic people appear to link more of their self-identity to products (more on this

CB AS I SEE IT

Professor Lon Chaplin, *The University of Arizona*

*T*oday's children are arguably the most materialistic generation ever. At age 2, toddlers are already showing clear signs of developing into savvy consumers with strong preferences for products and brands across a variety of product categories. When we look at adults, we know that although they believe that material possessions will make them happy, those who are more materialistic tend to be less happy. Is this true for children as well? What individual traits are associated with materialistic tendencies in children? What causes children to be materialistic? What socialization factors influence children's materialism (e.g., parents, peers, media, and marketing)?

My research examines how materialism develops throughout childhood and adolescence. *Materialism* is the importance a person places on the acquisition of material possessions at the expense of self-transcendent and/or prosocial pursuits, such as helping others in the

community, volunteering, and donating, to achieve happiness. Although some research on youth materialism exists, most of the studies focus on adolescents. Only a handful of studies including younger children are beginning to emerge. Studies with a wide age range (e.g., 6- to 18-year-olds) would be ideal, as they would help parents and educators to understand how developmental changes in children's cognitive abilities and social awareness affect the degree to which they focus on acquiring material goods to achieve happiness.

To have confidence in the results, materialism researchers must use reliable and valid measures that are appropriate for younger populations who have less sophisticated verbal and reading skills. As such, one of my research interests involves developing creative measurement tools that are more amenable to measuring materialism in a children's population. My collaborator, Professor Deborah Roedder John, and I have found that projective techniques such as collages work well to study children's materialism. We essentially ask children to create a "Happiness" collage made of people, pets, material

things, achievements, sports, and achievements that make them happy. When they describe what makes them happy, kids who place more importance on material things as opposed to less materialistic sentiments are considered to be more materialistic. Not only is the collage a familiar and engaging task that allows for more thoughtful responses, but it also masks the fact that we are studying a value that society deems to be negative.

Understanding children's materialism will continue to be an important topic for many reasons. No other consumer segment has grown as much in purchasing power and influence in the last decade than the children and adolescent segment. Additionally, materialism is a topic in consumer research that holds considerable interest from a public policy perspective, especially given recent concerns over children's well-being and the role that marketers play in convincing children that they *need* certain products or brands to be "cool." I look forward to the challenges that lie ahead, as the benefits to having happier, less materialistic children are substantial.

---

in the next chapter). One study found that when people who score high on this value fear the prospect of dying, they form even stronger connections to brands.[105]

The disenchantment among some people with big corporations shows up in events that promote uniqueness and anticorporate statements. Probably the most prominent movement is the annual Burning Man project. This is a week-long annual anti-market event, where thousands of people gather at Black Rock Desert in Nevada to proclaim their emancipation from corporate America. The highlight of the festival involves the burning of a huge wooden figure of a man, which symbolizes freedom from market domination. Ironically, some critics point out that even this high-profile, antimarket event is being commercialized as it becomes more popular each year![106] Although the event is supposed to run on what participants call a "gift economy" where no U.S. currency changes hands, the 2007 event broke with tradition by allowing green energy companies to exhibit products. Ironically, it turns out that this huge countercultural event uses huge amounts of fossil fuel (lots of gas to burn that man)—the group wants to offset the 28,000 tons of carbon it generates.[107]

A value that's related to materialism is **cosmopolitanism**. Researchers define a *cosmopolitan* as someone who tries to be open to the world and who strives for diverse experiences. This is a quality that used to be linked to the wealthy, but now with

Participants at the anti-corporate Burning Man Festival find novel ways to express their individuality.

Source: Courtesy of Professor Robert Kozinets, York University.

improved access to media and of course the Internet it's no longer necessary to be rich to express an interest in a range of culturally diverse products. Cosmopolitans respond well to brands that have a "worldly" (i.e., international) image. They think it's important to own consumer electronics products and are more likely to engage in electronic media activities such as e-mail, Web surfing, and buying DVDs.[108] A scale to identify these consumers includes measures like these:

- I enjoy exchanging ideas with people from other cultures or countries.
- I am interested in learning more about people who live in other countries.
- I find people from other cultures stimulating.

CHAPTER SUMMARY

Now that you have finished reading this chapter you should understand why:

1 **It's important for marketers to recognize that products can satisfy a range of consumer needs.**

Marketers try to satisfy consumer needs, but the reasons people purchase any product can vary widely. The identification of consumer motives is an important step to ensure that a product will satisfy appropriate needs. Traditional approaches to consumer behavior focus on the abilities of products to satisfy rational needs (utilitarian motives), but hedonic motives (e.g., the need for exploration or for fun) also play a key role in many purchase decisions.

As Maslow's hierarchy of needs demonstrates, the same product can satisfy different needs, depending on the consumer's state at the time. In addition to this objective situation (e.g., have basic physiological needs already been satisfied?), we must also consider the consumer's degree of involvement with the product.

2 **The way we evaluate and choose a product depends on our degree of involvement with the product, the marketing message, and/or the purchase situation.**

Product involvement can range from very low, where purchase decisions are made via inertia, to very high, where consumers form very strong bonds with what they buy. In addition to considering the degree to which consumers are involved with a product, marketing strategists also need to assess their extent of involvement with marketing messages and with the purchase situation.

3 **Our deeply held cultural values dictate the types of products and services we seek out or avoid.**

Underlying values often drive consumer motivations. Products thus take on meaning because a person thinks they will help him or her to achieve some goal that is linked to a value, such as individuality or freedom. A set of core values characterizes each culture, to which many of its members adhere.

Consumers vary in the importance they attach to worldly possessions, and this orientation in turn has an impact on their priorities and behaviors.

Materialism refers to the importance people attach to worldly possessions. Although we describe many Americans as materialists, there are indications of a value shift within a sizable portion of the population—and this accompanies much greater interest in environmentally sustainable products and services.

KEY TERMS

Acculturation, 149
Alternate-reality game, 145
Approach–approach conflict, 132
Approach–avoidance conflict, 133
Avoidance–avoidance conflict, 133
Carbon footprint, 155
Conscientious consumerism, 154
Core values, 149
Cosmopolitanism, 157
Cult products, 140
Drive, 128
Drive theory, 130
Enculturation, 149
Esteem need, 136
Expectancy theory, 131

Flow state, 138
Goal, 128
Greenwashing, 155
Homeostasis, 130
Inertia, 138
Insourcing, 148
Instrumental values, 151
Interactive mobile marketing, 144
Involvement, 137
Laddering, 152
List of Values (LOV) Scale, 152
LOHAS, 154
Mass customization, 141
Materialism, 156
Motivation, 128

Need for affiliation, 134
Need for power, 134
Need for uniqueness, 135
Physiological need, 136
QR code, 145
Safety need, 136
Self-actualization, 136
Social, 136
Spectacles, 143
Terminal values, 151
Theory of cognitive dissonance, 132
Value, 146
Value system, 148
Voluntary simplifiers, 152
Want, 128

REVIEW

1 What is motivation, and how is this idea relevant to consumer behavior?
2 Describe three types of motivational conflicts, citing an example of each from current marketing campaigns.
3 Explain the difference between a need and a want.
4 What is cognitive dissonance?
5 Name the levels in Maslow's hierarchy of needs, and give an example of a marketing appeal that is focused at each level.
6 What is consumer involvement? How does this concept relate to motivation?
7 Why would marketers want their customers to enter into a flow state when shopping for their products?

8 List three types of consumer involvement, giving an example of each type.
9 What are some strategies marketers can use to increase consumers' involvement with their products?
10 What are values, and why should marketers care?
11 What is the difference between enculturation and acculturation?
12 What is LOHAS, and why are people who follow this lifestyle important?
13 Describe at least two alternative techniques marketing researchers have used to measure values.
14 What is materialism and why is it relevant to marketing?

CONSUMER BEHAVIOR CHALLENGE

■ DISCUSS

1 "College students' concerns about the environment and vegetarianism are simply a passing fad; a way to look 'cool.'" Do you agree?
2 Some market analysts see a shift in values among young people. They claim that this generation has not had a lot of stability in their lives. They are fed up with superficial relationships and yearn for a return to tradition. This change is reflected in attitudes toward marriage and family. One survey of 22- to 24-year-old women found that 82 percent thought motherhood was the most important job in the world. *Bride's* magazine reports a swing toward traditional weddings—80 percent of brides today

toss their garters, and Daddy walks 78 percent of them down the aisle.[109] So, what's your take on this? Are young people indeed returning to the values of their parents (or even their grandparents)? How have these changes influenced your perspective on marriage and family?

3 How (if at all) do you think consumers have changed as a result of 9/11? Are these changes long-term or will we start to revert back to our pre-2001 mind-set?

4 Core values evolve over time. What do you think are the three to five core values that best describe Americans today?

5 Which of the needs in Maslow's hierarchy do you satisfy when you participate in social networks like Facebook and MySpace? How could these sites add new features to help you satisfy these needs?

6 The chapter mentions new facial recognition technology that marketers will soon use to classify shoppers in terms of their appearance so they can serve up ads that appeal to people in certain demographic categories. This makes advertising more useful because it reduces the amount of irrelevant information we will see. However, is there a down side to this technique? Do you see any potential for negative applications that use (for example) racial profiling to decide what information consumers should receive? Do the potential benefits outweigh these negative applications?

■ APPLY

1 Devise separate promotional strategies for an article of clothing, each of which stresses one of the levels of Maslow's hierarchy of needs.

2 Collect a sample of ads that appeals to consumers' values. What value is being communicated in each ad, and how is this done? Is this an effective approach to designing a marketing communication?

3 When you pay to enter a club, you may find your hand stamped with an advertising message. Do companies have the right to use your body as a billboard? Is this an effective media platform?

4 Describe how a man's level of involvement with his car would affect how different marketing stimuli influence him. How might you design a strategy for a line of car batteries for a segment of low-involvement consumers, and how would this strategy differ from your attempts to reach a segment of men who are very involved in working on their cars?

5 Interview members of a celebrity fan club. Describe their level of involvement with the "product," and devise some marketing strategies to reach this group.

6 Survey your class: Do your classmates "worship" a specific brand? What do these cult products have in common? How can other marketers try to turn their brands into cult products?

Case Study

CAMPAIGNING FOR MORE THAN BEAUTY

They are thin, possess flawless skin, and have beautiful hair. They are the models and celebrities we see in television, print, and billboards that tout the latest shampoos, antiaging creams, and skin cleansers. The message is clear—buy our product and you will attain this goal—you will look like these models.

Beginning in 2004, Dove, a division of Unilever, started on a bold advertising trail it called the "Campaign for Real Beauty." The first step in Dove's campaign, a tactic to support its skin firming cream, introduced the nation to billboards that showed untouched photographs of "normal" women of various sizes in just their underwear.

Dove sent the message that women do not need to conform to the standards of beauty the fashion industry determines. Everybody, of any age or size, is beautiful and should feel strong and proud. The campaign continued to build strongly over the next couple of years, and gained more steam with the viral release of the video "Evolution." The ad featured an average-looking woman who enters a film studio. The video then speeds through a series of hair, makeup, and shocking computer-enhancement techniques. At the end we see what is now a gorgeous woman on a billboard ad. Immediately after the final shot of the billboard, the video blacks out to the statement, "No wonder our perception of beauty is distorted." This viral video was followed with "Onslaught," an equally powerful ad, which shows the intensity of personal care, diet, and exercise advertising when viewed through the eyes of a young girl. The ad ends with another powerful message, "Talk to your daughter before the beauty industry does."

An important part of the Campaign for Real Beauty is the Dove Self-Esteem Fund. With young girls reporting alarmingly low levels of self-esteem, this arm of the campaign works to provide confidence-building tools and workshops for young girls. As of 2009, Dove connected with over 2 million girls and hopes to continue with the program.

Dove has enjoyed strong PR results with this campaign. It received mentions on various talk shows including the strongly influential *Oprah Winfrey Show*. In addition, the Evolution ad won the Cannes Lion Grand Prix Award in the film category at the 2007 award ceremony.

But the campaign is not without its critics. Some charge that Unilever, which owns Dove, is as guilty as the rest of the industry in promoting false ideals of beauty. Ads for the company's Axe brand often are cited as flagrant examples of messages that objectify women. In addition, the antiaging and firming creams Unilever sells thrive on women's insecurities about their looks. If she is supposed to be satisfied with her natural beauty, then why does a woman need these products? And finally, there was controversy concerning the airbrush techniques Dove used to photograph these "normal" women. An article in the *New Yorker* cited a prominent photo editor who claimed that he had done a large amount of retouching and mentioned what a challenge it was to make the women look attractive. Unilever's response was that it did not digitally alter the photos but retouched them only to correct color and remove dust. Still, this was a damaging accusation against Dove and its ad agency Ogilvy & Mather since the "Evolution" campaign criticizes retouching tricks.

Finally, there is the question of whether such an emotionally charged campaign actually boosts sales. It certainly helps to break through the clutter and bring recognition to the brand, but does it resonate with the consumer over the long-term? Dove reported a doubling of its sales from 2002–2007, but we are yet to see what the next five years will bring. Will this theme continue to strike a chord—while it sells beauty products at the same time?

DISCUSSION QUESTIONS

1 Describe the level of consumer involvement with personal care products in general. How might the Dove brand be different?

2 What terminal values relate to the Campaign for Real Beauty? Do they tie into the consumer's needs for this product?

Sources: Neol Bussey, "Dove Abandons Its Soapbox to Focus on the Soap," *Campaign* (August 28, 2008); Molly Prior, "Reality Check: Would You Buy Beauty Products from These Women?" *WWD* (April 20, 2007); Jack Neff, "Retouching Ruckus Leaves Dove Flailing," *Advertising Age* (May 12, 2008).

NOTES

1. www.afa-online.org/vegan.html, accessed August 12, 2007.
2. www.petakids.com, accessed June 30,2009.
3. http://beefitswhatsfordinner.com, accessed June 30, 2009.
4. Robert A. Baron, *Psychology: The Essential Science* (Boston: Allyn & Bacon, 1989).
5. Russell W. Belk, Guliz Ger, and Søren Askegaard, "The Fire of Desire: A Multisited Inquiry into Consumer Passion," *Journal of Consumer Research* 30 (2003): 326–51.
6. Thomas Kramer and Song-Oh Yoon, "Approach-Avoidance Motivation and the Use of Affect as Information," *Journal of Consumer Psychology* 17, no. 2 (2007): 128–38.
7. www.weightwatchers.com/index.aspx, accessed June 30, 2009.
8. See Paul T. Costa and Robert R. McCrae, "From Catalog to Classification: Murray's Needs and the Five-Factor Model," *Journal of Personality and Social Psychology* 55 (1988): 258–65; Calvin S. Hall and Gardner Lindzey, *Theories of Personality*, 2nd ed. (New York: Wiley, 1970); James U. McNeal and Stephen W. McDaniel, "An Analysis of Need-Appeals in Television Advertising," *Journal of the Academy of Marketing Science* 12 (Spring 1984): 176–90.
9. Michael R. Solomon, Judith L. Zaichkowsky, and Rosemary Polegato, *Consumer Behaviour: Buying, Having, and Being—Canadian Edition* (Scarborough, Ontario: Prentice Hall Canada, 1999).
10. See David C. McClelland, *Studies in Motivation* (New York: Appleton-Century-Crofts, 1955).
11. Mary Kay Ericksen and M. Joseph Sirgy, "Achievement Motivation and Clothing Preferences of White-Collar Working Women," in Michael R. Solomon, ed., *The Psychology of Fashion* (Lexington, MA: Lexington Books, 1985): 357–69.
12. See Stanley Schachter, *The Psychology of Affiliation* (Stanford, CA: Stanford University Press, 1959).
13. Eugene M. Fodor and Terry Smith, "The Power Motive as an Influence on Group Decision Making," *Journal of Personality and Social Psychology* 42 (1982): 178–85.
14. C. R. Snyder and Howard L. Fromkin, *Uniqueness: The Human Pursuit of Difference* (New York: Plenum, 1980).
15. Abraham H. Maslow, *Motivation and Personality*, 2nd ed. (New York: Harper & Row, 1970).
16. An integrative view of consumer goal structures and goal-determination processes proposes six discrete levels of goals wherein higher-level (versus lower-level) goals are more abstract, more inclusive, and less mutable. In descending order of abstraction, these goal levels are life themes and values, life projects, current concerns, consumption intentions, benefits sought, and feature preferences. See Cynthia Huffman, S. Ratneshwar, and David Glen Mick, "Consumer Goal Structures and Goal-Determination Processes: An Integrative Framework," in S. Ratneshwar, David Glen Mick, and Cynthia Huffman, eds., *The Why of Consumption* (London: Routledge, 2000): 9–35.
17. Paul Henry, "Magnetic Points for Lifestyle Shaping: The Contribution of Self-Fulfillment, Aspirations and Capabilities," *Qualitative Market Research* 9 no. 2 (2006): 170.
18. Russell W. Belk, "Romanian Consumer Desires and Feelings of Deservingness," in Lavinia Stan, ed., *Romania in Transition* (Hanover, NH: Dartmouth Press, 1997): 191–208, quoted on p. 193.
19. Study conducted in the Horticulture Department at Kansas State University, cited in "Survey Tells Why Gardening's Good," *Vancouver Sun* (April 12, 1997): B12; see also Paul Hewer and Douglas Brownlie, "Constructing 'Hortiporn': On the Aesthetics of Stylized Exteriors," *Advances in Consumer Research* 33, no. 1 (2006).
20. Adapted in part from Jack Loechner, "Emotional Business Bonding on Social Networks," *Research Brief*, Center for Media Research (December 27, 2007), http://blogs.mediapost.com/research_brief/?p=1603, accessed December 27, 2007.
21. "Forehead Advertisement Pays Off," *Montgomery Advertiser* (May 4, 2000): 7A.
22. Alex Kuczynski, "A New Magazine Celebrates the Rites of Shopping," *New York Times Online* (May 8, 2000).
23. "Man Wants to Marry His Car," *Montgomery Advertiser* (March 7, 1999): 11A.
24. Judith Lynne Zaichkowsky, "Measuring the Involvement Construct in Marketing," *Journal of Consumer Research* 12 (December 1985): 341–52.
25. Andrew Mitchell, "Involvement: A Potentially Important Mediator of Consumer Behavior," in William L. Wilkie, ed., *Advances in Consumer Research* 6 (Provo, UT: Association for Consumer Research, 1979): 191–96.
26. Richard L. Celsi and Jerry C. Olson, "The Role of Involvement in Attention and Comprehension Processes," *Journal of Consumer Research* 15 (September 1988): 210–24.
27. Anthony G. Greenwald and Clark Leavitt, "Audience Involvement in Advertising: Four Levels," *Journal of Consumer Research* 11 (June 1984): 581–92.
28. Mihaly Csikszentmihalyi, *Flow: The Psychology of Optimal Experience* (New York: HarperCollins, 1991); Donna L. Hoffman and Thomas P. Novak, "Marketing in Hypermedia Computer-Mediated Environments: Conceptual Foundations," *Journal of Marketing* (July 1996): 50–68.
29. Jeremy W. Peters, "Gave Up Sleep and Maybe a First-Born, but at Least I Have an iPhone," *New York Times Online* (June 30, 2007).

30. Quoted in Beth Snyder Bulik, "Apple Pulls 'Baby Shaker' iPhone App," *Advertising Age* (April 26, 2009), www.adagae.com, accessed April 26, 2009.

31. Christopher Rhoads, "The Hydrox Cookie Is Dead, and Fans Won't Get Over It," *Wall Street Journal* (January 19, 2008): A1.

32. Robert W. Pimentel and Kristy E. Reynolds, "A Model for Consumer Devotion: Affective Commitment with Proactive Sustaining Behaviors," *Academy of Marketing Science Review*, no. 5 (2004), www.amsreview.org/articles/pimentel05-2004.pdf.

33. starbuckseverywhere.net, accessed June 26, 2009; Julie Jargon, "A Fan Hits a Roadblock on Drive to See Every Starbucks," *Wall Street Journal* (May 23, 2009), http://online.wsj.com/article/SB124301100481847767.html, accessed May 25, 2009.

34. Judith Lynne Zaichkowsky, "The Emotional Side of Product Involvement," in Paul Anderson and Melanie Wallendorf, eds., *Advances in Consumer Research* 14 (Provo, UT: Association for Consumer Research): 32–35.

35. For a discussion of interrelationships between situational and enduring involvement, see Marsha L. Richins, Peter H. Bloch, and Edward F. McQuarrie, "How Enduring and Situational Involvement Combine to Create Involvement Responses," *Journal of Consumer Psychology* 1, no. 2 (1992): 143–53. For more information on the involvement construct, see "Special Issue on Involvement," *Psychology & Marketing* 10, no. 4 (July–August 1993).

36. "A Woman Wins Roto-Rooter's Tricked Out Toilet," *PROMO* (April 3, 2007), www.promomagazine.com/news/woman_wins_roto_rooters_toilet_043007/index.html; www.designnews.com/blog/1080000108/post/650006865.html, accessed June 27, 2007.

37. Joseph B. Pine, II, and James H. Gilmore, *Markets of One—Creating Customer-Unique Value Through Mass Customization* (Boston: Harvard Business School Press, 2000); www.managingchange.com/masscust/overview.htm, accessed May 30, 2005.

38. Neeraj Arora, Xavier Dréze, Anindya Ghose, James D. Hess, Reghuram Iyengar, Bing Jing, Yogesh Joshi, V. Kumar, Nicholas Lurie, Scott Neslin, S. Sajeesh, Meng Su, Niladri Syam, Jacquelyn Thomas, and Z. John Zhang, "Putting One-to-One Marketing to Work: Personalization, Customization, and Choice," *Marketing Letters* (2008): 305–21; Mike Beirne, "Mars Gives M&M's A Face," *Brandweek* (May 22, 2008), www.Brandweek.Com/Bw/News/Recent_Display.Jsp?Vnu_Content_Id=1003807134; accessed May 22, 2008; Edward C. Baig, "Technology Allows You to Be a Part of History in Obama Book," *USA Today* (May 21, 2009), www.usatoday.com/tech/news/2009-05-20-obama-time-capsule-amazon_N.htm?csp=34, accessed May 21, 2009; Karl Greenberg, "Lexus Backs First Consumer-Customized Magazine," *Marketing Daily* (March 19, 2009), www.mediapost.com, accessed March 19, 2009.

39. Herbert E. Krugman, "The Impact of Television Advertising: Learning Without Involvement," *Public Opinion Quarterly* 29 (Fall 1965): 349–56.

40. David W. Stewart and David H. Furse, "Analysis of the Impact of Executional Factors in Advertising Performance," *Journal of Advertising Research* 24 (1984): 23–26; Deborah J. MacInnis, Christine Moorman, and Bernard J. Jaworski, "Enhancing and Measuring Consumers' Motivation, Opportunity, and Ability to Process Brand Information from Ads," *Journal of Marketing* 55 (October 1991): 332–53.

41. Morris B. Holbrook and Elizabeth C. Hirschman, "The Experiential Aspects of Consumption: Consumer Fantasies, Feelings, and Fun," *Journal of Consumer Research* 9 (September 1982): 132–40.

42. Elaine Sciolino, "Disproving Notions, Raising a Fury," *New York Times* (January 21, 2003), www.nytimes.com, accessed January 21, 2003.

43. Louise Story, "Times Sq. Ads Spread via Tourists' Cameras," *New York Times* (December 11, 2006), www.nytimes.com, accessed December 11, 2006.

44. Rajeev Batra and Michael L. Ray, "Operationalizing Involvement as Depth and Quality of Cognitive Responses," in Alice Tybout and Richard Bagozzi, eds., *Advances in Consumer Research* 10 (Ann Arbor, MI: Association for Consumer Research, 1983): 309–13.

45. Julie Bosman, "Chevy Tries a Write-Your-Own-Ad Approach, and the Potshots Fly," *New York Times* (April 4, 2006), www.nytimes.com, accessed April 4, 2006.

46. "Read My Chips? Pringles Has Plans to Print Jokes, Trivia on Its Potatoes," *Wall Street Journal* (May 20, 2004): C13; David Serchuk, "A Rose with Another Name," *Forbes* (December 27, 2004): 52.

47. "Ads That Stay with You," November 19, 2007; *Newsweek*, www.Newsweek.Com/Id/68904, accessed November 19, 2007.

48. Stephanie Clifford, "Axe Body Products Puts Its Brand on the Hamptons Club Scene," *New York Times* (May 22, 2009): B6.

49. Alana Semuels, "Honda Finds a Groovy New Way to Pitch Products: The Musical Road," *Los Angeles Times* (October 13, 2008), www.latimes.com/Business/La-Fi-Roads13-2008oct13,0,4147014.Story; accessed October 13, 2008; Eric Pfanner, "A Live Promotion, At 14,000 Feet," *New York Times* (June 6, 2008), accessed June 6, 2008; Giant

50. Les Luchter, "Jameson Whiskey Texts Targets on N.Y. Streets," *Marketing Daily* (August 8, 2008), www.mediapost.com, accessed August 8, 2008.

51. Doreen Carvajal, "Dancers in the Crowd Bring Back 'Thriller,'" *New York Times* (March 10, 2008), www.nytimes.com, accessed March 10, 2008.

52. Eric Pfanner, "When Consumers Help, Ads Are Free," *New York Times* (June 21, 2009), www.nytimes.com, accessed June 22, 2009.

53. Suzanne Vranica, "New to the TV Lineup: A Flat-Panel Teaser," *Wall Street Journal* (April 29, 2008): B6.

54. Li Yuan, "Television's New Joy of Text Shows with Vote by Messaging Are on the Rise as Programmers Try to Make Live TV Matter," *Wall Street Journal* (July 20, 2006): B1.

55. Stephanie Clifford, "An Online Game so Mysterious Its Famous Sponsor Is Hidden," *New York Times* (April 1, 2008), www.nytimes.com/2008/04/01/Business/Media/01adco.Html?_R=1&Ref=Business&Oref..., accessed April 1, 2008.

56. "Play Smart," *Contagious* (June 24, 2008), www.contagiousmagazine.com, accessed June 25, 2008.

57. Mark J. Arnold and Kristy E. Reynolds, "Hedonic Shopping Motivations," *Journal of Retailing* 79 (2003): 77–95.

58. Emily Steel, "The Ad Changes with the Shopper in Front of It," *Wall Street Journal* (August 21, 2008): B7.

59. Kevin J. Clancy, "CPMs Must Bow to 'Involvement' Measurement," *Advertising Age* (January 20, 1992): 26.

60. Robert F. Worth, "Arab TV Tests Societies' Limits with Depictions of Sex and Equality," *New York Times* (September 26, 2008), www.nytimes.com/2008/09/27/World/Middleeast/27beirut.Html?_R=1&Scp=1&Sq=N..., accessed September 26, 2008.

61. Ajay K. Sirsi, James C. Ward, and Peter H. Reingen, "Microcultural Analysis of Variation in Sharing of Causal Reasoning About Behavior," *Journal of Consumer Research* 22 (March 1996): 345–72.

62. David Carr, "Romance in *Cosmo*'s World Is Translated in Many Ways," *New York Times* (May 26, 2002), www.nytimes.com, accessed May 26, 2002.

63. Anand Giridharadas, "*Playboy* Makes Move in India, but Without the Centerfold," *New York Times* (January 2, 2006), www.nytimes.com, accessed January 2, 2006.

64. Sarah Ellison, "Sexy-Ad Reel Shows What Tickles in Tokyo Can Fade Fast in France," *Wall Street Journal Interactive Edition* (March 31, 2000), www.wsj.com, accessed March 31, 2000.

65. Quoted in Andrew Adam Newman, "With Condoms in Particular, Local Stations Can Say No," *New York Times* (July 16, 2007), www.nytimes.com, accessed July 16, 2007.

66. Deborah Ball, "Women in Italy Like to Clean but Shun the Quick and Easy: Convenience Doesn't Sell When Bathrooms Average Four Scrubbings a Week," *Wall Street Journal* (April 25, 2006): A1.

67. Sarah Mahoney, "Consumers Seek Self-Reliance in the Home" *Marketing Daily* (March 25, 2009), www.mediapost.com, accessed March 25, 2009; Peter St. Onge, "Have You Become an 'Insourcer'?" *The Charlotte Observer* (April 14, 2009), www.thecharlotteobserver.com, accessed April 14, 2009.

68. Milton Rokeach, *The Nature of Human Values* (New York: Free Press, 1973).

69. Sang-Pil Han and Sharon Shavitt, "Persuasion and Culture: Advertising Appeals in Individualistic and Collectivistic Societies," *Journal of Experimental Social Psychology* 30 (1994): 326–50.

70. Chisaki Watanabe, "Japanese Parents Embrace Ultra-secure Children's Park," *Philadelphia Inquirer* (September 4, 2006): A2.

71. Carolyn A. Lin, "Cultural Values Reflected in Chinese and American Television Advertising," *Journal of Advertising* 30 (Winter 2001): 83–94.

72. Donald E. Vinson, Jerome E. Scott, and Lawrence R. Lamont, "The Role of Personal Values in Marketing and Consumer Behavior," *Journal of Marketing* 41 (April 1977): 44–50; John Watson, Steven Lysonski, Tamara Gillan, and Leslie Raymore, "Cultural Values and Important Possessions: A Cross-Cultural Analysis," *Journal of Business Research* 55 (2002): 923–31.

73. Pascale Quester, Michael Beverland, and Francis Farrelly, "Brand-Personal Values Fit and Brand Meanings: Exploring the Role Individual Values Play in Ongoing Brand Loyalty in Extreme Sports Subcultures," *Advances in Consumer Research* 33, no. 1 (2006): 21–28.

74. Jennifer Aaker, Veronica Benet-Martinez, and Jordi Garolera, "Consumption Symbols as Carriers of Culture: A Study of Japanese and Spanish Brand Personality Constructs," *Journal of Personality and Social Psychology* (2001).

75. Yumiko Ono, "Tambrands Ads Try to Scale Cultural, Religious Obstacles," *Wall Street Journal Interactive Edition* (March 17, 1997).

76. Geert Hofstede, *Culture's Consequences: Comparing Values, Behaviors, Institutions, and Organizations Across Nations* (Thousand Oaks CA: Sage Publications, 2001). For a recent critique of this instrument

Human Colon Makes Times Square PR Debut," *Advertising Age* (March 3, 2009), www.adage.com, accessed March 3, 2009.

cf. Aron M. Levin, Irwin P. Levin, and Michael P. Cook, "Measuring and Accounting for Cross-Country Response Biases in Marketing Food and Drink Products," *International Journal of Consumer Marketing*, in press.

77. Adapted from "What Are Hofstede's Five Cultural Dimensions?" www .geert-hofstede.com, accessed May 22, 2009.

78. Milton Rokeach, *Understanding Human Values* (New York: Free Press, 1979); see also J. Michael Munson and Edward McQuarrie, "Shortening the Rokeach Value Survey for Use in Consumer Research," in Michael J. Houston, ed., *Advances in Consumer Research* 15 (Provo, UT: Association for Consumer Research, 1988): 381–86.

79. B. W. Becker and P. E. Conner, "Personal Values of the Heavy User of Mass Media," *Journal of Advertising Research* 21 (1981): 37–43; Scott Vinson and Lamont Vinson, "The Role of Personal Values in Marketing and Consumer Behavior," 44–50.

80. Craig J. Thompson and Maura Troester, "Consumer Value Systems in the Age of Postmodern Fragmentation: The Case of the Natural Health Microculture," *Journal of Consumer Research* 28 (March 2002): 550–71.

81. Sharon E. Beatty, Lynn R. Kahle, Pamela Homer, and Shekhar Misra, "Alternative Measurement Approaches to Consumer Values: The List of Values and the Rokeach Value Survey," *Psychology & Marketing* 2 (1985): 181–200; Lynn R. Kahle and Patricia Kennedy, "Using the List of Values (LOV) to Understand Consumers," *Journal of Consumer Marketing* 2 (Fall 1988): 49–56; Lynn Kahle, Basil Poulos, and Ajay Sukhdial, "Changes in Social Values in the United States During the Past Decade," *Journal of Advertising Research* 28 (February–March 1988): 35–41; see also Wagner A. Kamakura and Jose Alfonso Mazzon, "Value Segmentation: A Model for the Measurement of Values and Value Systems," *Journal of Consumer Research* 18 (September 1991): 28; Jagdish N. Sheth, Bruce I. Newman, and Barbara L. Gross, *Consumption Values and Market Choices: Theory and Applications* (Cincinnati: South-Western Publishing Co., 1991).

82. Thomas J. Reynolds and Jonathan Gutman, "Laddering Theory, Method, Analysis, and Interpretation," *Journal of Advertising Research* (February–March 1988): 11–34; Beth Walker, Richard Celsi, and Jerry Olson, "Exploring the Structural Characteristics of Consumers' Knowledge," in Melanie Wallendorf and Paul Anderson, eds., *Advances in Consumer Research* vol. 14 (Provo, UT: Association for Consumer Research, 1986): 17–21; Veludo-de-Oliveira, Tania Modesto, Ana Akemi Ikeda, and Marcos Cortez Campomar, "Laddering in the Practice of Marketing Research: Barriers and Solutions," *Qualitative Market Research: An International Journal* 9, no. 3 (2006): 297–306. For a recent critique of this technique, cf. Elin Brandi Sørenson and Søren Askegaard, "Laddering: How (Not) to Do Things with Words," *Qualitative Market Research: An International Journal* 10, no. 1 (2007): 63–77.

83. This example was adapted from Michael R. Solomon, Gary Bamossy, and Søren Askegaard, *Consumer Behaviour: A European Perspective*, 2nd ed. (London: Pearson Education Limited, 2002).

84. "25 Years of Attitude," *Marketing Tools* (November–December 1995): 38–39.

85. Amitai Etzioni, "The Good Society: Goals Beyond Money," *The Futurist* 35, no. 4 (2001) 68–69; D. Elgin, *Voluntary Simplicity: Toward a Way of Life That Is Outwardly Simple, Inwardly Rich* (New York: Quill, 1993); *Ascribe Higher Education News Service*, "PNA Trend in Consumer Behavior Called 'Voluntary Simplicity' Poses Challenges for Marketers" (December 6, 2001); Caroline Bekin, Marylyn Carrigan, and Isabelle Szmigin, "Defying Market Sovereignty: Voluntary Simplicity at New Consumption Communities," *Qualitative Market Research* 8, no. 4 (2005): 413.

86. Emily Burg, "Whole Foods Is Consumers' Favorite Green Brand," *Marketing Daily*, www.mediapost.com, accessed May 10, 2007.

87. "Consumers Want Proof It's Green," *Research Brief*, Center for Media Research (April 9, 2009), www.mediapost.com, accessed April 9, 2009.

88. www.lohas.com/about.htm, accessed June 30, 2007.

89. Sarah Mahoney, "Wal-Mart: The Average Joe Is Greener Than You Think," *Marketing Daily* (April 19, 2007), www.mediapost.com, accessed April 19, 2007.

90. "Deal with Clorox Spurs Sierra Club Feud," *Los Angeles Times* (July 17, 2008), www.latimes.com/Business/La-Fi-Clorox17-2008jul17,0,1163469 .Story?Track=Rss, accessed July 17, 2008.

91. Remi Trudel and June Cotte, "Does It Pay to Be Good?" *MIT Sloan Management Review* 61 (Winter 2009): 61–68.

92. Suzanne Vranica, "Ad Houses Will Need to Be More Nimble, Clients Are Demanding More and Better Use of Consumer Data, Web," *Wall Street Journal* (January 2, 2008): B3; "Consumers Want Proof It's Green."

93. http://green.yahoo.com/index.php?q=action, accessed June 30, 2007.

94. www.carbonfootprint.com/carbon_footprint.html, accessed June 30, 2007.

95. www.climateclean.net, accessed June 30, 2007; www.terrapass.com, accessed June 30, 2007.

96. Leslie Kaufman, "Car Crashes to Please Mother Nature," *New York Times* (March 1, 2009), http://www.nytimes.com/2009/03/02/ arts/television/02twen.html?_r=1, accessed March 1, 2009.

97. Susan Schultz Kleine and Stacy Menzel Baker, "An Integrative Review of Material Possession Attachment," *Academy of Marketing Science Review*, no. 1 (2004).

98. Russell W. Belk, "Possessions and the Extended Self," *Journal of Consumer Research* 15 (September 1988): 139–68; Melanie Wallendorf and Eric J. Arnould, "'My Favorite Things': A Cross-Cultural Inquiry into Object Attachment, Possessiveness, and Social Linkage," *Journal of Consumer Research* 14 (March 1988): 531–47.

99. L. J. Shrum, James E. Burroughs, and Aric Rindfleisch, "Television's Cultivation of Material Values," *Journal of Consumer Research* 32, no. 3 (2005): 473–79.

100. Matthew Creamer, "On the Rise in South Korea: Kimchi Refrigerators Soju Consumption Rises Too, at the Expense of Beer, According to Cheil Study," *Advertising Age* (February 26, 2009), www.adage.com, accessed February 26, 2009.

101. James E. Burroughs and Aric Rindfleisch, "Materialism and Well-Being: A Conflicting Values Perspective," *Journal of Consumer Research* 29 (December 2002): 348–70.

102. Lan Nguyen Chaplin and Deborah Roedder John. "Growing Up in a Material World: Age Differences in Materialism in Children and Adolescents," *Journal of Consumer Research* 34 (December 2007): 480–93.

103. Marsha L. Richins, "Special Possessions and the Expression of Material Values," *Journal of Consumer Research* 21 (December 1994): 522–33.

104. Ibid.

105. Aric Rindfleisch, James E. Burroughs, and Nancy Wong. "The Safety of Objects: Materialism, Existential Insecurity, and Brand Connection" *Journal of Consumer Research* 36 (June 2009): 1–16.

106. Robert V. Kozinets, "Can Consumers Escape the Market? Emancipatory Illuminations from Burning Man," *Journal of Consumer Research* 29 (June 2002): 20–38; see also Douglas B. Holt, "Why Do Brands Cause Trouble? A Dialectical Theory of Consumer Culture and Branding," *Journal of Consumer Research* 29 (June 2002): 70–90.

107. Chris Taylor, "Burning Man Grows Up" *Business 2.0* (June 28, 2007), http://money.cnn.com/magazines/business2/business2_archive/2007/ 07/01/100117064/, accessed June 30, 2007.

108. Mark Cleveland, Michel Laroche, and Nicolas Papadopoulos, "Cosmopolitanism, Consumer Ethnocentrism, and Materialism: An Eight-Country Study of Antecedents and Outcomes," *Journal of International Marketing* 17, no. 1 (2009): 116–46.

109. Helene Stapinski, "Y Not Love?" *American Demographics* (February 1999): 62–68.

5

The Self

When you finish this chapter you will understand:

1. Why does the self-concept strongly influence consumer behavior?

2. Why do products often play a pivotal role in defining the self-concept?

3. Why is sex-role identity different from gender, and how do society's expectations of masculinity and femininity help to determine the products we buy to be consistent with these expectations?

4. Why is the way we think about our bodies (and the way our culture tells us we should think) a key component of self-esteem?

5. Why can our desire to live up to cultural expectations of appearance be harmful?

6. Why does every culture dictate certain types of body decoration or mutilation that help to identify its members?

*L*isa is trying to concentrate on the report her client expects by 5:00 P.M. She has worked hard to maintain this important account for the firm, but today she is distracted thinking about her date with Eric last night. Although things seemed to go OK, she couldn't shake the feeling that Eric regards her more as a friend than as a potential romantic partner.

As she leafs through *Glamour* and *Cosmopolitan* during her lunch hour, Lisa is struck by all the articles about ways to become more attractive by dieting, exercising, and wearing sexy clothes. She begins to feel depressed as she looks at the svelte models in the many advertisements for perfumes, apparel, and makeup. Each woman is more glamorous and beautiful than the last. Surely they've had "adjustments"—women simply don't look that way in real life. Then again, it's unlikely that Eric could ever be mistaken for Brad Pitt on the street.

In her down mood, Lisa actually thinks that maybe she should look into cosmetic surgery. Even though she's never considered herself unattractive, maybe if she got a new nose or removed that mole on her cheek she'd feel better about herself. Who knows, she might look so good she'll get up the nerve to submit a photo to that Web site <u>hotornot.com</u> that everyone's talking about. But wait—on second thought is Eric even worth it?

OBJECTIVE

Why does the self-concept strongly influence consumer behavior?

What Is the Self?

Lisa isn't the only person who feels that her physical appearance and possessions affect her "value" as a person. Consumers' insecurities about their appearance are rampant. We buy many products, from cars to cologne, because we want to highlight or hide some aspect of the self. In this chapter, we'll focus on how consumers' feelings about themselves shape their consumption practices, particularly as they strive to fulfill their society's expectations about how a male or female should look and act.

Does the Self Exist?

New Line Cinema hired street teams to go to 80 bars or events such as the Super Bowl across the country with a confession booth and a video camera so that people could confess their obsessions and post them on a Web site to promote the movie *The Number 23*. One woman owned up to being infatuated with the singer Justin Timberlake and another revealed that she used to put Visine eye drops in the beers of customers when she was a bartender![1] Don't have video access but still feel a need to let your peeps know exactly what you're doing 24/7? Just *Tweet* them on the increasingly popular text-messaging service at <u>twitter.com</u>.[2] The growth of social networking services such as these enables everyone to focus on him- or herself and share mundane or scintillating details about their lives with anyone who's interested (why they are is another story!).

Today it seems natural to think of ourselves as a potential celeb waiting for our 15 minutes of fame (as the pop icon Andy Warhol once predicted). However, the idea that each single human life is unique rather than a part of a group only developed in late medieval times (between the eleventh and fifteenth centuries). Furthermore, the emphasis on the unique nature of the self is much greater in Western societies.[3] Many Eastern cultures stress the importance of a *collective self*, where a person derives his or her identity in large measure from a social group. Both Eastern and Western cultures believe the self divides into an inner, private self and an outer, public self. But where they differ is in terms of which part they see as the "real you"—the West tends to subscribe to an independent understanding of the self, which emphasizes the inherent separateness of each individual.

Non-Western cultures, in contrast, tend to focus on an interdependent self where we define our identities largely by our relationships with others.[4] For example, a Confucian perspective stresses the importance of "face"—others' perceptions of the self and maintaining one's desired status in their eyes. One dimension of face is *mien-tzu*—the reputation one achieves through success and ostentation. Some Asian cultures developed explicit rules about the specific garments and even colors that certain social classes and occupations were allowed to display. These traditions live on today in Japanese style manuals that provide very detailed instructions for dressing and how to address people of differing status.[5]

That orientation is a bit at odds with such Western conventions as "casual Friday," which encourages employees to express their unique selves (at least short of muscle shirts and flip-flops). To further illustrate these cross-cultural differences, a Roper Starch Worldwide survey compared consumers in 30 countries to see which were the most and least vain. Women who live in Venezuela were the chart toppers— 65 percent said they thought about their appearance all the time.[6] Other high-scoring countries included Russia and Mexico. The lowest scorers lived in the Philippines and in Saudi Arabia, where only 28 percent of consumers surveyed agreed with this statement.

Subject   Hillary Clinton   Morph
                                                      (35% Subject, 65% Clinton)

Study participants tend to prefer photos of political candidates whose features have been combined with their own.

Source: Photos courtesy of Prof. Jeremy Bailenson, Stanford University.

Self-Concept

The **self-concept** summarizes the beliefs a person holds about his own attributes and how he evaluates the self on these qualities. Although your overall self-concept may be positive, there certainly are parts of it you evaluate more positively than others. For example, Lisa feels better about her professional identity than she does about her feminine identity.

The self-concept is a very complex structure. We describe attributes of self-concept along such dimensions as *content* (e.g., facial attractiveness versus mental aptitude), *positivity* (i.e., self-esteem), *intensity and stability* over time, and *accuracy* (i.e., the degree to which one's self-assessment corresponds to reality).[7] As we'll see later in this chapter, consumers' self-assessments can be quite distorted, especially with regard to their physical appearance.

However, most people feel reasonably positive about themselves, and we are drawn to others who we feel are similar in personality or appearance. One study demonstrated just how powerful this attraction can be: Researchers used "morphing" software to manipulate photos of political candidates from the 2008 presidential primaries and other elections. This technique combines the facial features of the study participant with the candidate so that the resulting photo actually is a mixture of the two. Subjects who saw the morphed photos of the candidates liked them better than those who saw the undoctored photos—even though they were unaware that the images included their own features![8]

Self-Esteem

Self-esteem refers to the positivity of a person's self-concept. People with low self-esteem expect that they will not perform very well, and they will try to avoid embarrassment, failure, or rejection. When it developed a new line of snack cakes, for example, Sara Lee found that consumers low in self-esteem preferred portion-controlled snack items because they felt they lacked self-control.[9]

Alberto Culver uses a self-esteem appeal to promote a product that reflects our changing society: Soft & Beautiful Just for Me Texture Softener, an alternative to hair pressing or relaxing. It's targeted to white mothers who don't know how to care for the hair of their multiracial children who have "hair texture" issues. The self-esteem portion of the campaign, dubbed "Love Yourself. Love Your Hair," includes a Web site, texturesoftener.com that offers "conversation starters" to help parents find ways to talk to their daughters about self-image.[10]

How do marketers influence self-esteem? Exposure to ads such as the ones Lisa checked out can trigger a process of *social comparison*, where the person tries to evaluate her appearance by comparing it to the people these artificial images depict.[11] This is a basic human tendency, and many marketers tap into our need for benchmarks when they supply idealized images of happy, attractive people who just happen to use their products. An ad campaign for Clearasil is a good example. In one typical ad, two teenage boys enter a kitchen where a 40-ish mother is mixing something in a bowl. When her son leaves the room, his friend hits on Mom. The ad's tagline: "Clearasil may cause confidence."

In a study that illustrates the social comparison process, female college students who were exposed to beautiful women in advertisements afterward expressed lowered satisfaction with their own appearance, as compared to other participants who did not view ads with attractive models.[13] Another study reported that young women alter their perceptions of their own body shapes and sizes after they watch as little as 30 minutes of TV programming.[14] Researchers report similar findings for men.[15]

Real and Ideal Selves

When a consumer compares some aspect of himself to an ideal, this judgment influences his self-esteem. He might ask, "Am I as good-looking as I would like to be?" or "Do I make as much money as I should?" The **ideal self** is a person's conception of how he would like to be, whereas the **actual self** refers to our more realistic appraisal of the qualities we have and don't have. We choose some products because we think they are consistent with our actual self, while we buy others to help us reach an ideal standard. And we often engage in a process of **impression management** where we work hard to "manage" what others think of us; we strategically choose clothing and other products that will show us off to others in a good light.[16]

This process applies to all sorts of behaviors, from professional contexts and dating to markers of religious observance. For example, an increasing number of Islamic men in Egypt have a *zebibah* (Arabic for "raisin"); a dark circle of callused skin or a bump, between the hairline and the eyebrows. It marks the spot where the worshipper repeatedly presses his forehead into the ground during his daily prayers (observant Muslims pray five times a day). Some add prayers so that the bump will become even more pronounced; the owner of the mark thus broadcasts his degree of piousness on his head. As an Egyptian newspaper editor explains, ". . . there is a kind of statement in it. Sometimes as a personal statement to announce that he is a conservative Muslim and sometimes as a way of outbidding others by showing them that he is more religious or to say that they should be like him."[17]

This impression management process is very apparent when people exaggerate their positive qualities on their MySpace or Facebook pages. And those who post photos of their actual selves in unflattering situations (that must have been a pretty wild party . . .) may come to regret their actions as potential employers start to check out their pages before they look at their résumés. Some even turn to services such as Reputation Defender that scour the Internet to remove embarrassing postings before the boss (or Mom) sees them.[18] What can visitors learn about you when they visit your profile?

Fantasy: Bridging the Gap Between the Selves

Most people experience a discrepancy between their real and ideal selves, but for some consumers this gap is especially large. These people are especially good targets for marketing communications that employ *fantasy appeals*.[19] A **fantasy** or daydream is a self-induced shift in consciousness, which is sometimes a way to compensate for a lack of external stimulation or to escape from problems in the real world.[20] Many products and services succeed because they appeal to our fantasies. An ad may transport us to an unfamiliar, exciting situation; things we purchase may permit us to "try on" interesting or provocative roles. And with today's technology,

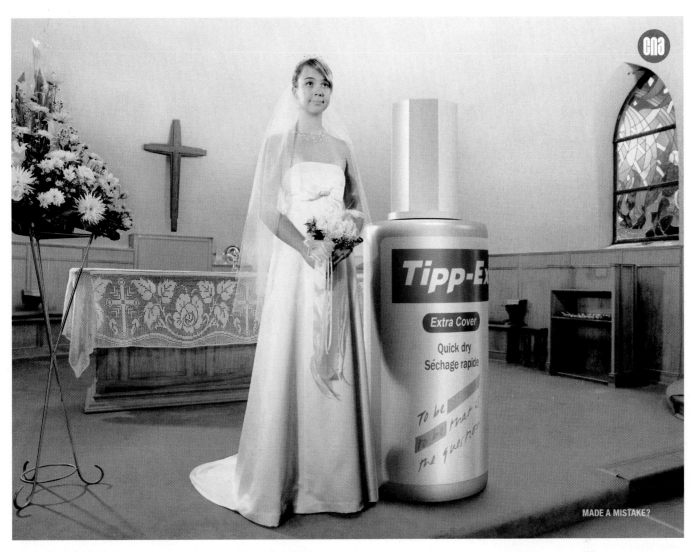

A South African ad conveys a feeling of insecurity.
Source: Courtesy of Tipp-Ex/Jupiter Drawing Room, South Africa.

such as *virtual makeovers* that several Web sites offer, consumers can experiment with different looks before they actually take the plunge in the real world.[21]

Multiple Selves

In a way, each of us really is a number of different people—your mother probably would not recognize the "you" that emerges at a party at 2:00 in the morning! We have as many selves as we do different social roles. Depending on the situation, we act differently, use different products and services, and even vary in terms of how much we *like* the aspect of ourselves we put on display. A person may require a different set of products to play each of her roles: She may choose a sedate, understated perfume when she plays her professional self but splash on something more provocative on Saturday night as she transitions to her *femme fatale* self. A word to the wise: Corporate recruiters often complain about students who show up for job interviews in sloppy or revealing clothing—these applicants failed to "read the program" about which role they're expected to play in professional settings!

As we saw in Chapter 1, the dramaturgical perspective on consumer behavior views people as actors who play different roles. We each play many roles, and each has its own script, props, and costumes.[22] The self has different components, or *role identities,* and only some of these are active at any given time. Some identities (e.g., husband, boss, student) are more central to the self than others, but other identities (e.g., dancer, gearhead, or advocate for the homeless) may dominate in specific situations.[23]

A German shampoo helps users to fantasize.

Source: Courtesy of JWT/Frankfurt.

Strategically, this means a marketer may want to ensure the appropriate role identity is active before she pitches products customers need to play a particular role. One obvious way to do that is to place advertising messages in contexts where people are likely to be well aware of that role identity—for example, when fortified drink and energy bar product companies hand out free product samples to runners at a marathon.

Virtual Identity

In the influential cyberpunk novel *Snow Crash,* author Neal Stephenson envisioned a virtual world he called the *Metaverse* as a successor to the Internet. In the *Metaverse,* everyday people take on glamorous identities in a 3-D immersive digital world. The book's main character delivers pizza in real life (RL), but in the Metaverse, he's a warrior prince and champion sword fighter.[24] The hugely popular *Matrix* movie trilogy paints a similar (though more sinister) picture of a world that blurs the lines between physical and digital reality.

Today these fictional depictions come to life as we witness the tremendous growth of real-time, interactive virtual worlds that allow people to assume **virtual identities** in cyberspace. More than 11 million people worldwide belong to the virtual world of *Second Life,* more than 8 million play the online game *World of Warcraft,* and the majority of Korean adults belong to *CyWorld.* Add to that the millions more who play *The Sims Online* or who visit other **computer-mediated environments (CMEs)** such as *Webkinz, There, Habbo Hotel,* MTV's *Virtual Laguna Beach,* and more than 150 other virtual worlds and you're looking at a lot of serious role-playing.

The barriers between real life and virtual identities get more difficult to distinguish. People who participate in the growing movement called **cosplay** dress as their online avatars or as other favorite characters from comic books and movies.
Source: Courtesy of Elena Dorfman.

On these sites people assume visual identities, or **avatars**, that range from realistic versions of themselves to tricked-out versions with exaggerated physical characteristics or winged dragons or superheroes. Researchers are just starting to investigate how these online selves will influence consumer behavior and how the identities we choose in CMEs relate to our RL (or "meat-world") identities. Already we know that when people take on avatar forms, they tend to interact with other avatars much as their meat-world selves interact with other RL people. For example, just as in the RL, males in *Second Life* leave more space between them when they talk to other males versus females and they are less likely to maintain eye contact than females are. And when avatars get very close to one another, they tend to look away from each other—the norms of the RL steadily creep into the virtual world.[25]

Symbolic Interactionism

If each person potentially has many social selves, how does each develop? How do we decide which self to "activate" at any point in time? The sociological tradition of **symbolic interactionism** stresses that relationships with other people play a large part in forming the self.[26] According to this perspective, we exist in a symbolic environment. As we saw in Chapter 2, we assign meaning to any situation or object when we interpret the symbols in this environment. As members of society, individuals learn to agree on shared meanings. Thus, we "know" that a red light means stop, the "golden arches" means fast food, and "blondes have more fun." That's important to understand consumer behavior because it implies that our possessions play a key role as we evaluate ourselves and decide "who we are."[27]

Each of us, then, interprets our identity, and this assessment continually evolves as we encounter new situations and people. In symbolic interactionist terms, we *negotiate* these meanings over time. Essentially, each of us poses the question, "Who am I in this situation?" Those around us greatly influence how we answer this query, and we ask, "Who do *other people* think I am?" We tend to pattern our behavior on the perceived expectations of others as a form of *self-fulfilling prophecy.* When we act the way we assume others expect us to act, we often confirm these perceptions.

The Looking-Glass Self

Some clothing stores are testing an interactive mirror that doubles as a high-resolution digital screen. When you choose a garment, the mirror superimposes it on your reflection so that you can see how it would look on your body. A camera relays live images of you modeling your virtual outfit to an Internet site where your friends can log in to instant message (IM) you to tell you what they think; their comments pop up on the side of the mirror for you to read. They can also select virtual items for you to try on that the "magic" mirror will reflect.[28]

A customer tries on a "virtual dress."
Source: Courtesy of Redux. Photos/Photographer Andrea Mohin.

Sociologists call the process of imagining others' reactions "taking the role of the other," or the **looking-glass self**.[29] According to this view, our desire to define ourselves operates as a sort of psychological sonar: We take readings of our own identity when we "bounce" signals off others and try to project their impression of us. Like the distorted mirrors in a funhouse, our appraisal of who we are varies depending on whose perspective we consider and how accurately we predict their evaluations of us. A confident career woman like Lisa may sit morosely at a nightclub—she imagines that others see her as a dowdy, unattractive woman with little sex appeal (regardless of whether these perceptions are true). A *self-fulfilling prophecy* like the one we described comes into play here because these "signals" influence Lisa's actual behavior. If she doesn't believe she's attractive, she may choose frumpy, unflattering clothing that actually does make her less attractive. The next morning at work, however, her self-confidence at the office may cause her to assume that others hold her "executive self" in even higher regard than they actually do (we all know people like that)!

Self-Consciousness

If you have ever walked into a class in the middle of a lecture and you were convinced that all eyes were on you as you awkwardly searched for a seat, you can understand the feeling of *self-consciousness*. In contrast, sometimes we behave with shockingly little self-consciousness. For example, we may do things in a stadium, a riot, or at a fraternity party we would never do if we were highly conscious of our behavior (and add insult to injury when we post these escapades to our Facebook page!).[30]

Some people seem to be more sensitive in general to the image they communicate to others. However, we all know people who act as if they're oblivious to the impression they are making. A heightened concern about the nature of one's public "image" also results in more concern about the social appropriateness of products and consumption activities.

Consumers who score high on a scale of *public self-consciousness* express more interest in clothing and use more cosmetics than others who score lower.[31] In one recent study, highly self-conscious subjects expressed greater willingness to buy personal products like a douche or a gas-prevention remedy that are somewhat embarrassing to buy but may avoid awkward public incidents later.[32]

BMW 3 SERIES CONVERTIBLE. THE WORLD IS LOOKING AT YOU.

This Italian ad reminds us of the power of self-consciousness: "The world is looking at you."

Source: Used with permission of D'Adda Lorenzini, Vigorelli BBDO.

Similarly, high *self-monitors* are more attuned to how they present themselves in their social environments, and their estimates of how others will perceive their product choices influence what they choose to buy.[33] A scale to measure self-monitoring asks consumers how much they agree with statements such as "I guess I put on a show to impress or entertain others" or "I would probably make a good actor." Perhaps not surprisingly, publicly visible types such as college football players and fashion models tend to score higher on these dimensions.[34]

Consumption and Self-Concept

Identity marketing is a promotional strategy where consumers alter some aspects of their selves to advertise for a branded product:[35]

- A British marketing firm paid five people to legally change their names for one year to "Turok," the hero of a video game series about a time-traveling Native American who slays bionically enhanced dinosaurs.
- The Internet Underground Music Archive (IUMA) paid a Kansas couple $5,000 to name their baby boy Iuma.
- Air New Zealand created "cranial billboards" in exchange for a round-trip ticket to New Zealand—30 Los Angeles participants shaved their heads and walked around with an ad for the airline on their skulls.
- The Casa Sanchez restaurant in San Francisco gives free lunches for life to anyone who gets its logo tattooed on their body. The Daytona Cubs baseball team awards free season tickets for life to anyone who will tattoo the Cubs logo on

their body. According to the International Trademark Association, the Harley tattoo is still the most widespread corporate logo tattoo in North America, but other contenders include Nike, Adidas, Budweiser, Corona, Apple computers, Ford, Chevy, and Volkswagen.

Are You What You Consume?

OBJECTIVE

Why do products often play a pivotal role in defining the self-concept?

Remember that the reflected self helps shape self-concept, which implies that people see themselves as they imagine others see them. Because what others see includes a person's clothing, jewelry, furniture, car, and so on, it stands to reason that these products also help to create the perceived self. A consumer's possessions place her into a social role, which helps to answer the question, "Who am I now?"

People use an individual's consumption behaviors to identify that person's social identity. In addition to checking out a person's clothes and grooming habits, we make inferences about personality based on her choice of leisure activities (e.g., squash versus bowling), food preferences (e.g., tofu and beans versus steak and potatoes), cars, and home decorating choices. When researchers show people pictures of someone's living room, for example, they make surprisingly accurate guesses about the occupant's personality.[36] In the same way that a consumer's use of products influences others' perceptions, the same products can help to determine his own self-concept and social identity.[37]

We are *attached* to an object to the extent we rely on it to maintain our self-concept.[38] Objects act as a security blanket when they reinforce our identities, especially in unfamiliar situations. For example, students who decorate their dorm rooms with personal items are less likely to drop out of college. This coping process may protect the self from being diluted in a strange environment.[39] When a pair of researchers asked children of various ages to create "who am I?" collages where they chose pictures that represented their selves, older kids between middle childhood and early adolescence inserted more photos of branded merchandise. And, as they aged, their feelings about these objects evolved from concrete relationships (e.g., "I own it") to more sophisticated, abstract relationships (e.g., "It is like me").[40]

Our use of consumption information to define the self is especially important when we have yet to totally form a social identity, such as when we have to play a new role in life. Think, for example, of the insecurity many of us felt when we first started college or reentered the dating market after we left a long-term relationship. **Symbolic self-completion theory** suggests that people who have an incomplete self-definition tend to complete this identity when they acquire and display symbols they associate with that role.[41]

Adolescent boys, for example, may use "macho" products such as cars and cigarettes to bolster their developing masculinity; these items act as a "social crutch" during a period of uncertainty about their new identity as adult males. As we mature into a role, we actually rely less on the products people associate with it: For example, when kids start to skateboard they often invest in pro skateboard "decks" with graphics and branding that cost between $40 and $70 even without the "trucks" (wheels and axles). But—to the chagrin of the skateboard industry—as they get more serious about boarding, many think it's just fine to buy "blank decks," the plain wood boards that cost only $15 to $30.[42]

The contribution of possessions to self-identity is perhaps most apparent when we lose these treasured objects. One of the first acts of institutions such as prisons or the military that want to repress individuality and encourage group identity is to confiscate personal possessions.[43] Victims of burglaries and natural disasters commonly report feelings of alienation, depression, or of being "violated." One consumer's comment after she was robbed is typical: "It's the next worse thing to being bereaved; it's like being raped."[44] Burglary victims exhibit a diminished sense of community, lowered feelings of privacy, and less pride in their houses' appearance than do their neighbors.[45]

A study of postdisaster conditions, where consumers may have lost literally everything but the clothes on their backs following a fire, hurricane, flood, or earthquake, highlights the dramatic impact of product loss. Some people are reluctant to undergo the process of re-creating their identities by acquiring new possessions. Interviews with disaster victims reveal that some hesitate to invest the self in new possessions and so become more detached about what they buy. This comment from a woman in her 50's is representative of this attitude: "I had so much love tied up in my things. I can't go through that kind of loss again. What I'm buying now won't be as important to me."[46]

Self/Product Congruence

Because many consumption activities relate to self-definition, it is not surprising to learn that consumers demonstrate consistency between their values (see Chapter 4) and the things they buy.[47] **Self-image congruence models** suggest that we choose products when their attributes match some aspect of the self.[48] These models assume a process of *cognitive matching* between product attributes and the consumer's self-image.[49]

An exploration of the conflicts Muslim women who choose to wear headscarves experience illustrates how even a simple piece of cloth reflects a person's aesthetic, political, and moral dimensions.[50] The Turkish women in the study expressed the tension they felt in their ongoing struggle to reconcile ambiguous religious principles that simultaneously call for modesty and beauty. Society sends Muslim women contradictory messages in modern-day Turkey. Although the Koran denounces waste, many of the companies that produce religious headscarves introduce new designs each season and, as styles and tastes change, women are encouraged to purchase more scarves than necessary. Moreover, the authors point out that a wearer communicates her fashion sense by the fabrics she selects and by the way she drapes and ties her scarf. In addition, veiling sends contradictory images about the proper sex roles of men and women. On the one hand, women who cover their heads by choice feel a sense of empowerment. On the other, the notion that Islamic law exhorts women to cover themselves lest they threaten men's self-restraint and honor is a persistent sign that men exert control over women's bodies and restrict their freedom. As a compromise solution Nike designed a uniform for observant women in Somalia who want to play sports without abandoning the traditional *hijab* (a robe that wraps around the head and loosely drapes over the entire body). The company streamlined the garment so that volleyball players could move but still keep their bodies covered.[51]

Although research results are somewhat mixed, the ideal self appears to be more relevant than the actual self as a comparison standard for highly expressive social products such as perfume. In contrast, the actual self is more relevant for everyday, functional products. These standards are also likely to vary by usage situation.[52] For example, a consumer might want a functional, reliable car to commute to work every day and a flashier model when he goes out on a date in the evening.

Research tends to support the idea of congruence between product usage and self-image. One of the earliest studies to examine this process found that car owners' ratings of themselves tended to match their perceptions of their cars: Pontiac drivers saw themselves as more active and flashy than did Volkswagen drivers.[53] Indeed, a German study found that observers were able to match photos of male and female drivers to pictures of the cars they drove almost 70 percent of the time.[54] Researchers also report congruity between consumers and their most preferred brands of beer, soap, toothpaste, and cigarettes relative to their least preferred brands, as well as between consumers' self-images and their favorite stores.[55] Some specific attributes useful to describe matches between consumers and products include rugged/delicate, excitable/calm, rational/emotional, and formal/informal.[56]

Although these findings make some intuitive sense, we cannot blithely assume that consumers will always buy products whose characteristics match their own. It is not clear that consumers really see aspects of themselves in down-to-earth, functional products that don't have very complex or humanlike images. It is one thing to consider a brand personality for an expressive, image-oriented product, such as perfume, and quite another to impute human characteristics to a toaster.

Another problem is the old "chicken-and-egg" question: Do people buy products because the they see these as similar to the themselves, or do people assume that these products must be similar to themselves because they bought them? The similarity between a person's self-image and the images of products he purchases does tend to increase over the time he owns the product, so we can't rule out this explanation.

The Extended Self

As we noted earlier, many of the props and settings consumers use to define their social roles become parts of their selves. Those external objects that we consider a

This Italian ad demonstrates that our favorite products are part of the extended self.
Source: Used with permission of Francesco Biasia and D'Adda, Lorenzini, Vigorelli BBDO.

FRANCESCO**BIASIA**
HANDBAGS

CB AS I LIVE IT

Eric Fleury, Will Hincks, Eric Ruiz, Jeffrey Creps, Stephen Hattersley,
San Diego State University

ouTube video link:
http://www.youtube.com/
watch?v=oaCgXwOMXmc&fmt=
18&fmt=5

Matt DeCelles grew up in the country. Growing up in the suburbs, many people take concrete and asphalt for granted. But when Matt was 10 years old, he purchased a skateboard to use on a small sidewalk-like slab of concrete that made a small path around his backyard; this was all he had to practice on. The skateboard at first was only something to keep him from boredom, since he lived out in the country, a good distance from the city and his friends. However as time went by, he became more and more attached to his skateboard and the image it was transforming him into. His clothes soon reflected the brand of skateboards he liked, the music he listened to could be heard off skating videos he would see on television, and a pile of destroyed shoes torn and worn down from the grip tape on his board, lay in the corner of his room. His skateboard had become his "extended self."

We agree with the chapter's description of the "extended self," that we sometimes cherish items enough to consider them a part of ourselves. Ever since Matt got his skateboard, it opened him up to a completely new lifestyle and set of products. From the different brands of skateboards themselves and their parts, to different kinds of shoes designed specifically to endure the abuse of skating, and other clothing and apparel that showed off the brands he associated with.

To Matt, his skateboard is a hobby, a mode of transportation, and a lifestyle. A marketer can learn from Matt's experience by trying to focus on the image of the lifestyle for the person, and by providing products for consumers to choose, to complete that lifestyle. Provide the pieces, and the person will complete the puzzle themselves.

part of us comprise the **extended self.** In some cultures, people literally incorporate objects into the self—they lick new possessions, take the names of conquered enemies (or in some cases eat them), or bury the dead with their possessions.[57]

We don't usually go that far, but some people do cherish possessions as if they were a part of them. In fact, some of us willingly (and perhaps eagerly) label ourselves as *fanatics* about a cherished product.[58] Consider shoes, for example: You don't have to be Carrie of *Sex and the City* fame to acknowledge that many people feel a strong bond to their footwear. One study found that people commonly view their shoes as magical emblems of self, Cinderella-like vehicles for self-transformation. Based on data collected from consumers, the researcher concluded that (like their sister Carrie) women tend to be more attuned to the symbolic implications of shoes than men. A common theme that emerged was that a pair of shoes obtained when younger—whether a first pair of leather shoes, a first pair of high heels, or a first pair of cowboy boots—had a big impact even later in life. These experiences were similar to those that occur in such well-known fairy tales and stories as Dorothy's red shoes in *The Wizard of Oz* (1939), Karen's magical red shoes in Hans Christian Anderson's *The Red Shoes* (1845), and Cinderella's glass slippers.[59]

In addition to shoes, of course, many material objects ranging from personal possessions and pets to national monuments or landmarks help to form a consumer's identity. Just about everyone can name a valued possession that has a lot of the self "wrapped up" in it, whether it is a beloved photograph, a trophy, an old shirt, a car, or a cat. Indeed, usually we can construct a pretty accurate "biography" of someone when we simply catalog the items he displays in his bedroom or office.

The extended self helps to explain why to the Japanese it's a deal killer if you mishandle a business card. Japanese businesspeople view a card as an extension of their self and they expect the recipient to treat it respectfully. If you bend the card or make it do double duty as a toothpick, you are insulting the card's owner big time. Arriving in Japan without an ample stock of business cards is akin to arriving barefoot. There is an elaborate etiquette connected to giving and receiving cards. This should be done solemnly and you need to study the card intently rather than shoving it into your coat pocket to file later.[60]

We describe four levels of the extended self, ranging from very personal objects to places and things that allow people to feel as though they are rooted in their larger social environments:[61]

1 **Individual level**—Consumers include many of their personal possessions in self-definition. These products can include jewelry, cars, clothing, and so on. The saying "You are what you wear" reflects the belief that one's things are a part of one's identity.

2 **Family level**—This part of the extended self includes a consumer's residence and the furnishings in it. We can think of the house as a symbolic body for the family, and the place where we live often is a central aspect of who we are.

3 **Community level**—It is common for consumers to describe themselves in terms of the neighborhood or town from which they come. For farm families or other residents with close ties to a community, this sense of belonging is particularly important.

4 **Group level**—We regard our attachments to certain social groups as a part of the self—we'll consider some of these consumer *subcultures* in later chapters. A consumer also may feel that landmarks, monuments, or sports teams are a part of the extended self.

CB AS I LIVE IT

Alyssa Williams, Kimberly Guzman, Mackenzie Haggerty, Max Malanga, Kelsey Wells, *San Diego State University*

*Y*ouTube video link: http://www.youtube.com/watch?v=4i9BrjQWuk8

This is the story of Max Malanga. Throughout his high school life, Max had a very strong connection to a particular pair of footwear. The white leather Reebok Classics was his shoe of choice for almost four years. The first pair he bought was simply due to the fact that he saw his best friend wearing a pair of these Reebok Classics, and they were the exact look he was going for. Whether it was the signature red and white Reebok logo that appeared on the tongue, or the way the pearly white shoes sparkled as you took them out of the box for the first time, these shoes would become his everyday shoe for a significant period in his life. Over time,

people began to know him as the kid who wore the grandpa-like Reeboks every day. He was fine with that because he felt as if these shoes had given people in his school something to affiliate Max with, something to remember Max by. These perfect white shoes had become a symbol of Max Malanga. The white leather Reebok Classics had become a part of his *extended self*. The book defines the extended self as "external objects that we consider a part of ourselves." We believe the Reebok Classics to be a perfect example of his extended self as he wore these shoes literally every day of his high school career, receiving comments daily about how he did wear these shoes that no one else dared to wear on the basis that the shoes were notoriously worn by the elderly.

We strongly agree with the chapter's description of the concept of the extended self. The main reason Max kept on buying new pairs of the

Reebok Classics is because people expected him to keep wearing the "geezer shoes." If he had come to school one day wearing a pair of Vans or Nikes, he would be overwhelmed with an array of accusatory questions, wondering what happened to his beloved Reeboks. At first he had worn the shoes to display a new sense of style, and over time the shoes became a part of his identity, a part of his character, a part of Max Malanga.

Max's knowledge of this concept will have very little effect on his consumer behavior in the future. Max was consciously aware of the concept of the extended self back in high school, and he knew that this was what was making him a repeat buyer of the Reebok Classics. If in the future Max comes across a product that he feels will be an extension of his identity and personal characteristics, he will not hesitate to purchase the product.

OBJECTIVE

Why is sex role identity different from gender, and how do society's expectations of masculinity and femininity help to determine the products we buy to be consistent with these expectations?

Sex Roles

The Indian government recently banned a TV spot for Axe men's deodorant. The spot shows a man who turns into a walking chocolate figurine after he sprays himself with the brand's Dark Temptation deodorant. As he walks through the city, women throw themselves at him as they lick him and bite off various parts of his body. Although the same ad played in Argentina and Europe without any problem, traditional Indian culture doesn't approve of such blatant imagery. The government yanked another ad for Amul Macho underwear—when a young woman comes to a river to do her husband's laundry, she pulls out a pair of boxer shorts and begins to wash them by hand as she gives sultry looks to the camera and throws her head back in a suggestive manner as a voice-over says, "Amul Macho. Crafted for fantasies." And, a court issued an arrest warrant for actor Richard Gere after he kissed an Indian actress at an AIDS awareness event in New Delhi because he broke a public-obscenity law. Members of a Hindu organization called The Army of Ram (a Hindu god) attacked a group of female college students in a bar because they were drinking and dancing with men.[63] Clearly, sex roles are not set in stone around the world.

Sexual identity is a very important component of a consumer's self-concept. People often conform to their culture's expectations about how those of their gender should act, dress, or speak. Of course, these guidelines change over time, and

This Israeli poster that appeared in men's restrooms illustrates cultural assumptions about sex role differences.
Source: Courtesy of Goldstar.

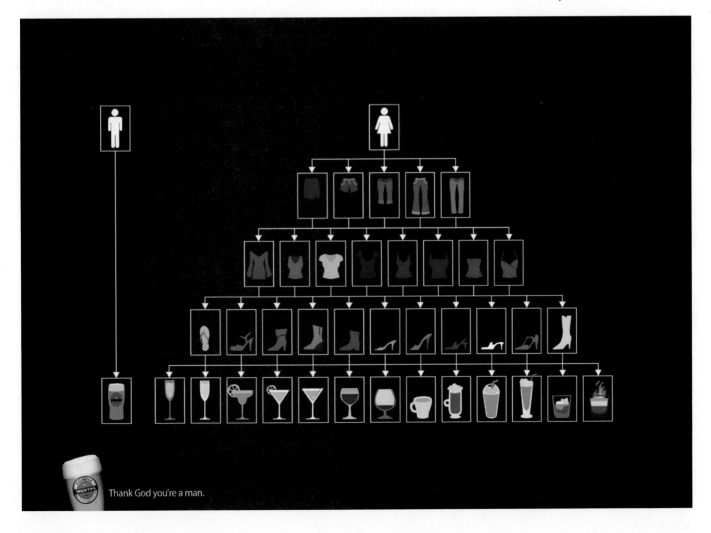

Thank God you're a man.

they differ radically across societies. In India and elsewhere, a society communicates its assumptions about the proper roles of men and women as it defines ideal behaviors for each gender.

It's not clear to what extent gender differences are innate versus culturally shaped—but they're certainly evident in many consumption situations. Consider the gender differences market researchers observe when they compare the food preferences of men to those of women. Women eat more fruit; men are more likely to eat meat. As one food writer put it, "Boy food doesn't grow. It is hunted or killed."[64] The sexes also differ sharply in the quantities of food they eat: When researchers at Hershey discovered that women eat smaller amounts of candy, they created a white chocolate confection called Hugs, one of the most successful food introductions of all time. However, a man in a Burger King Whopper ad ditches his date at a fancy restaurant, complaining that he is "too hungry to settle for chick food." Pumped up on Whoppers, a swelling mob of men shake their fists, punch one another, toss a van off a bridge, and sing, "I will eat this meat until my innie turns into an outie," and "I am hungry. I am incorrigible. I am man."[65]

Gender Differences in Socialization

Can the smell of burning rubber and gasoline light the fires of love? Harlequin, a major publisher of romance novels with a predominantly female readership, partnered with male-dominated NASCAR to turn out racing-themed stories. In one, the heroine is an ex-kindergarten teacher who falls in love with a real NASCAR driver named Lance Cooper after he hits her with his car (subtle, right?); she winds up driving his racing team's motor coach from race to race. In a typical passage, the novel describes a kiss: "It wasn't gentle, it wasn't passive, it was a kiss that instantly proved the two of them were like high-octane fuel, their flesh sparking off each other...."[66] Yet another case of boy meets girl, boy runs over girl.

Many commercial sources, in addition to parents and friends, provide lessons in *gender socialization* for both girls and boys:

- Mattel partnered with Bonne Bell to market a line of cosmetics to young girls aged 6 to 9. The popular Bratz doll line already licenses its name to a cosmetics line that also targets this age group.
- ESPN Zone in Chicago is a male preserve that lets boys be boys and men be . . . boys. Customers perceive the venue as a safe haven where buddies can watch men's sports and establish camaraderie with other men.[67]
- Sony created a TV ad for its Bravia line of liquid-crystal-display (LCD) televisions that offers different endings to each gender. The spot shows a man and a woman gazing through a storefront window at a Bravia LCD. Unaware of each other, the two simultaneously whisper: "Nice picture." Suddenly, two buttons appear on the screen that read: "Ending for Men" and "Ending for Women." The male ending is either a funny clip from a sports show or a cartoon spoof of a martial-arts movie. Women see either a 1950s-era musical centered on shoes or a tear-jerker about a female doctor who saves the life of an orphan.[68]

As these examples illustrate, manufacturers and retailers tend to reinforce a society's expectations regarding the "correct" way for boys and girls, men and women, to look and act. Even countries that are physically close to each other may send very different messages. In comparing Malaysian and Singaporean commercials, for example, researchers found that Malaysian males tend to dominate ads for technical products, whereas females dominate the Singaporean ones, which suggests that in Singapore people accept women to a greater degree when they assume professional roles. To support this argument, they also found that ads in Malaysia portray men more often in high-level business or professional roles, whereas those in Singapore portray both genders equally.[69]

Many societies expect males to pursue **agentic goals,** which stress self-assertion and mastery. However, they teach females to value **communal goals,** such as affiliation and the fostering of harmonious relations.[71] One study even found that people perceived a male voice emanating from a computer to be more accurate and authoritative than a female voice that reads the very same words. And participants valued computer-generated words of praise to a greater extent when the voice was male![72] Similarly, an analysis of TV commercials aimed at children in the United States and Australia found that they depict boys as more knowledgeable, active, aggressive, and instrumental.[73]

These differences in orientation show up early in our development. When Mattel decided to develop Ello, a building toy for girls, its designers carefully observed the play patterns of 5- to 10-year-olds. The toy features interconnecting plastic squares, balls, triangles, squiggles, flowers, and sticks, in pastel colors and with rounded corners that let users snap pieces together to create houses, people, jewelry, and picture frames. As one of the developers observed, "boys enjoy stacking blocks and working towards a goal, such as finishing a building. Their play is more physically active, and they like to create conflict between characters. Girls don't like repetitive stacking. They prefer to create relationships between characters, building communities and decorative spaces."[74]

New research indicates that our brains are "wired" to react differently to males and females—and it may help to explain why men tend to objectify women. A study that used brain-scanning technology showed photos of women wearing bikinis to a group of heterosexual male college students and tracked which areas of their brains lit up. The activated areas were the same as those that get aroused when males handle tools. In a follow-up study, men tended to associate bikini-clad women with first-person action verbs such as I "push," "handle" and "grab" instead of the third-person forms such as she "pushes," "handles" and "grabs." On the other hand, when they saw photos of fully clothed women, they reverted to the third-person forms, which implied they perceived these women as being in control of their own actions. Female subjects who responded to both sets of pictures did not display this difference.[75]

Gender Versus Sexual Identity

Gender-role identity is a state of mind as well as body. A person's biological gender (i.e., male or female) does not totally determine whether he or she will exhibit **sex-typed traits**, characteristics we stereotypically associate with one gender or the other. A consumer's subjective feelings about his or her sexuality are crucial as well.[76]

Unlike maleness and femaleness, masculinity and femininity are *not* biological characteristics. A behavior one culture considers to be masculine might get a different response in another. For example, the norm in the United States is that male friends avoid touching each other (except in "safe" situations such as on the football field). In some Latin and European cultures, however, it is common for men to hug and kiss one another as a form of greeting. Note that even this norm continues to evolve, as American teenagers of both sexes adopt the new fad of hugging as a standard form of greeting (sometimes accompanied by the high-five or the fist-bump) and male friends (encouraged by the MTV show of the same name) feel free to talk about having a **bromance** (affection between straight male friends).[77]

Sex-Typed Products

A popular book once proclaimed, *Real Men Don't Eat Quiche*. Many products (in addition to quiche) also are "sex-typed." They take on masculine or feminine attributes, and consumers associate them with one gender or another.[78] Marketers often encourage the sex typing of products such as Princess telephones, boys' and girls' bicycles, or Luvs color-coded diapers. A vodka brand called Thor's Hammer illustrates this stereotyping. The booze comes in a short, squat bottle, and the company's vice president of marketing describes it as "bold and broad and solid. This is a man's kind of vodka . . . it's not your frosted . . . girly-man vodka." Thor was the Norse god of

This ad for Bijan illustrates how sex role identities are culturally bound by contrasting the expectations of how women should appear in two different countries.
Source: Courtesy of Bijan Fragrances c/o Fashion World.

thunder, and the company claims the name has no connection to the slang phrase "getting hammered," which can happen if you drink too much of the stuff.[79] On the other hand, Dell recently launched *Della*, a female-targeted microsite to attract women who want to buy Netbooks. The home page featured three women whose clothes matched their laptops, along with "Tech Tips" that includes advice on how to count calories and share recipes online. Many people didn't appreciate this treatment: A Twitter comment sums up the reaction: "Della, new website 4 women who r 2 stupid 2 go 2 dell.com."[80]

Androgyny

Androgyny refers to the possession of both masculine and feminine traits.[82] Researchers make a distinction between *sex-typed people*, who are stereotypically masculine or feminine, and *androgynous people*, whose orientation isn't as clearly defined. People who don't neatly fit into one gender category or another may create uncertainty among others who aren't sure how to relate to them. A study demonstrated that sex-role assumptions travel into cyberspace as well. The researchers asked each volunteer to interact with another respondent via a chat room. They showed subjects an avatar to represent the other person, with images ranging from "an obviously female" blonde to one with no clear gender to a strong-jawed male. The subjects rated their partners as less "credible" when they saw an androgynous avatar than when they saw one with sex-typed facial characteristics.[83]

Of course, the "normality" of sex-typed behaviors varies across cultures. For example, although acceptance of homosexuality varies in Asian cultures, it doesn't occur to most Asians to assume that a man with some feminine qualities is gay. A recent survey of Korean consumers found that more than 66 percent of men and 57 percent of women younger than age 40 were living self-described "androgynous" lifestyles—with men having more traditionally female traits and women having more traditionally male ones than they might have years ago. But the respondents didn't link that with sexual orientation. Although Koreans nickname males with feminine interests "flower men," they don't consider this to be a derogatory term.[84] In Japan, men that people call *gyaru-o* ("male gals") are common on city streets. Tanned and meticulously dressed (and usually heterosexual), these fops cruise Tokyo's stylish boutiques.[85]

Differences in sex-role orientation can influence how we respond to marketing stimuli, at least under some circumstances.[86] For example, females are more likely to undergo more elaborate processing of message content, so they tend to be more sensitive to specific pieces of information when they form a judgment, whereas males are more influenced by overall themes.[87] In addition, women with relatively strong masculine components in their sex-role identity prefer ad portrayals that include nontraditional women.[88] Some research indicates that sex-typed people are more sensitive to the sex-role depictions of characters in advertising, although women appear to be more sensitive generally to gender-role relationships than are men.

In one study, subjects read two versions of a beer advertisement couched in either masculine or feminine terms. The masculine version contained phrases such as "X beer has the strong aggressive flavor that really asserts itself with good food and good company," and the feminine version made claims such as "Brewed with tender care, X beer is a full-bodied beer that goes down smooth and gentle." People who rated themselves as highly masculine or highly feminine preferred the version that was described in (respectively) very masculine or feminine terms.[89] Sex-typed people in general are more concerned with ensuring that their behavior is consistent with their culture's definition of gender appropriateness.

Researchers developed a scale to identify "nontraditional males" (NTMs) who exhibit stereotypically female tendencies. The scale included statements such as these:

- I enjoy looking through fashion magazines.
- In our family, I take care of the checkbook and pay the bills.
- I am concerned about getting enough calcium in my diet.
- I am good at fixing mechanical things.
- I would do better than average in a fistfight.

Not too surprisingly, strong differences emerged between men who rated the statements along traditional sex-role lines versus those who had nontraditional orientations. When asked how they would like others to see them, NTMs were more likely than traditional males (TMs) to say that they would like to be considered stylish, sophisticated, up to date, and trendsetting. They were also more likely to say that they would like to be seen as sensitive, spiritual, affectionate, organized, and thrifty but less likely to say they would like to be seen as "outdoorsy."[90]

Gender-Bending Products

Smart marketers try to think about new markets for their products. Some companies that sell exclusively to one gender therefore may decide to test the waters with the other sex when they promote **gender-bending products**—a traditionally sex-typed item adapted to the opposite gender. Here are some recent gender benders:[91]

- Taking a page from a classic *Seinfeld* TV episode, Japanese lingerie retailer Wish Room discovered that some men secretly would like to wear a bra. It sold hundreds of "mansierres."
- Rubbermaid introduced a line of grooming tools specifically for men, including tweezers and clippers. As a manager explained, "Most men don't want to go to what we call the 'pink aisle' of the store to get tweezers and clippers that are made

The Tangled Web

At a Web site called Zack16, a series of blogs, Tweets, and videos tells the story of a 16-year-old boy who wakes up one morning to find his "guy parts" gone and replaced with "girl parts." One entry says, "So something weird happened to me last night and I'm just trying to deal. Went to the bathroom this morning to find that I suddenly possessed the aiming ability of a defective garden sprinkler. Soon thereafter I discovered that a super important body part of mine had gone missing. . . . Decided to seek medical attention. Had an awkward discussion with the school nurse. . . . " It turns out that Procter & Gamble's Tampax brand created the site. The only clue to the site's origin is when the boy (Zack Johnson) experiences his first period during French class and sneaks into the girls' restroom to use a Tampax vending machine.[81]

for women. They want products that look masculine and are made for their specific grooming needs." The tools fit better in men's hands and are stronger as well as address issues such as thicker toenails and hair that grows in different places. In addition to drug stores, men can buy the products at Home Depot. The company that designed the line now is trying to launch a women's product it calls "Siren"—a condom designed to fit in a lipstick-like tube.

- Frito-Lay's salty snacks traditionally appeal to men, but the company is working hard to change that with baked versions of chips and 100-calorie packages of snacks. After conducting extensive research (including asking several hundred women to keep detailed journals of their daily activities), the company's marketers concluded that the typical woman looks for a reminder that she's eating something healthy. As one result of this work, the bag for Baked Lay's will change from shiny yellow to a matte beige that displays pictures of the ingredients like spices or ranch dressing.

- Harley-Davidson backed a Guinness World Record attempt for the number of women motorcycle riders trained in one weekend. Its dealerships host women-only Garage Parties.

- Best Buy opened an electronics store designed for women in Aurora, Colorado, that displays flat-screen TVs and appliances in home-like settings. The company enlisted local women to provide ideas; the design includes a private room for new moms complete with free diapers and a rocking chair.

- As fewer men take up the sport of hunting, the industry is going after women—and former Alaska Governor Sarah Palin (who apparently knows how to shoot and field-dress a moose) probably helped to publicize the sport during the 2008 presidential election. As one female hunter observed, companies first tried simply to "Pink it and shrink it," but now they're taking more sophisticated steps. They manufacture lighter crossbows and produce TV shows that star women shooters such as *American Huntress* and *Family Traditions with Haley Heath.* Apparel makers including SHE Safari and Foxy Huntress sell women's camouflage clothing.

Female Sex Roles

In the 1949 movie *Adam's Rib,* Katherine Hepburn played a stylish and competent lawyer. This film was one of the first to show that a woman can have a successful career and still be happily married. Today, the evolution of a new managerial class of women has forced marketers to change their traditional assumptions about women as they target this growing market. For example, Suzuki appeals to the growing number of women in India who achieve financial independence and buy their own cars. Its Zen Estilo (*estilo* means "style" in Spanish) model comes in eight colors, including "purple fusion," "virgin blue," and "sparkling olive."[92]

Still, it's premature to proclaim the death of traditional sex-role stereotypes. This is certainly true in traditional Islamic countries, such as Saudi Arabia, that require women to be completely covered in public and that prohibit them to work as salespeople in stores open to the public (even if the store sells female intimate apparel).[93] Back home, Spirit Airlines has received complaints about recent fare promotions such as the "Threesome Sale," which invited customers to "come join in the fun," and the boast, "We're Proud of our DDs" (which in this case stands for deep discounts).[94]

To further complicate matters, sex roles constantly evolve—in a complex society like ours we often encounter contradictory messages about "appropriate" behavior and we may find ourselves putting on a very different face as we jump from situation to situation. A recent exploration of what the authors labeled **Contemporary Young Mainstream Female Achievers (CYMFA)** identified different roles these women play in different contexts. For example as a mother or partner they enact a highly feminine role, as a tough pitiless businesswoman they play a masculine role, and with a friend they might evoke both roles at once.[95]

Women consume many products intended to alter their appearance to be in line with cultural expectations.

Source: Agency: Downtown Partners Chicago. Writer: Sean Austin. Art Directors: Joe Stuart and Tom Kim.

And, like other fashion phenomena that we'll talk about in Chapter 16, a wave in one direction may set off a ripple in another. We can clearly see this in the messages girls have been getting from the media for the last several years: It's cool to be slutty. Role models like Paris Hilton, Lindsay Lohan, Britney Spears, and even Bratz dolls convey standards about how far preteens and teens should go when they broadcast their sexuality. Now, as these messages seem to go over the top (at least in the eyes of some concerned parents), we start to see early signs of a backlash. At the Pure Fashion Web site, girls get style tips including skirts and dresses that fall no more than four fingers above the knee and no tank tops without a sweater or jacket over them. Several other sites such as ModestApparelUSA.com, ModestByDesign.com, and DressModestly.com advocate a return to styles that leave almost everything to the imagination.[96] Is our culture moving from a celebration of "girls gone wild" to "girls gone mild?" Stay tuned.

As we'll see in the next chapter, it's not realistic to paint a huge group of consumers with the same brush, so we often need to subdivide them into segments that share important characteristics. This logic certainly applies to women, and smart marketers understand that they can't assume all female consumers have been socialized the same way. For example, a research company called Cohorts identifies nine segments of single women alone. Cohorts describes the three most promising segments:[97]

1 **Megan**—A stylish, tech-savvy student with a median income of $16,000. She reads *Self, Rolling Stone, InStyle,* and *Us Weekly.* She is likely to channel surf when ads come on TV and she wouldn't watch TV at all without cable. Her favorite channels are Oxygen, Nick at Nite, Disney Channel, MTV, VH1, E!, and

TBS. She's turned on by what's cool or the latest thing, she's liberal, seizes opportunities, and she spends on a whim.

2 **Allison**—An educated working woman with a median income of $52,000. She reads *Elle, Shape, Cosmopolitan,* and *Entertainment Weekly.* Her favorite channels are Lifetime, Bravo, Cartoon Network, E!, FX, TBS, and TLC. She's into travel and her career, and she prides herself on her sophisticated tastes.

3 **Elizabeth**—An affluent career woman with a median income of $174,000. She reads *Vogue, Harper's Bazaar, People,* and *Martha Stewart Living.* When she takes time to watch TV, she tunes in to networks such as Lifetime, WE, Comedy Central, MTV, CNBC, E!, HBO, A&E, Bravo, and AMC. She values foreign travel, fitness, and her career, and she's savvy and spontaneous.

Male Sex Roles

Our culture's stereotype of the ideal male is a tough, aggressive, muscular man who enjoys "manly" sports (and MavTV—"TV created by men for men").[98] Just as for women, however, the true story is more complicated than that. Indeed, scholars of **masculinism** study the male image and the complex cultural meanings of masculinity.[99] Like women, men receive mixed messages about how they are supposed to behave and feel.

Some analysts argue that men are threatened because they don't necessarily recognize themselves in the powerful male stereotypes against which feminists protest.[100] One study examined how American men pursue masculine identities through their everyday consumption. The researchers suggest that men are trying to make sense out of three different models of masculinity that they call *breadwinner, rebel,* and *man-of-action hero,* as they figure out just who they are supposed to be. On the one hand, the breadwinner model draws from the American myth of success

This German car ad refers to a male stereotype.
Source: Courtesy of Lamborghini.

SHIFTING. STEERING. BRAKING.
WHO SAID MEN CAN'T MULTITASK?

LAMBORGHINI GALLARDO SUPERLEGGERA

This Dutch beer ad communicates
expectations about the male sex role.
Source: KesselsKramer, Amsterdam.
KesselsKramer, Sabine Gilhuijs, Lauriergracht 39,
1016 RG Amsterdam. The Netherlands.

and celebrates respectability, civic virtues, pursuit of material success, and organized achievement. The rebel model, on the other hand, emphasizes rebellion, independence, adventure, and potency. The man-of-action hero is a synthesis that
draws from the better of the other two models.[101]

One consequence of the continual evolution of sex roles is that men are concerned as never before with their appearance. Men spend $7.7 billion on grooming
products globally each year. A wave of male cleansers, moisturizers, sunscreens, de-
pilatories, and body sprays washes up on U.S. shores, largely from European marketers. L'Oréal Paris reports that men's skincare products is now its fastest-growing
sector. In Europe, 24 percent of men younger than age 30 use skincare products—
and 80 percent of young Korean men do. In the United States Norelco reported a 24
percent rise in facial hair grooming products in 2008. Mintel reports big growth, especially in products with antiaging and exfoliating ingredients. And, even some cosmetics products like foundation and eyeliner are catching on in some segments,
though men aren't comfortable owning up to using them. In fact, a British makeup
product looks like a ballpoint pen so men can apply it secretly at the office.[103]

No doubt one of the biggest marketing buzzwords over the past few years is the
metrosexual, a straight, urban male who is keenly interested in fashion, home design, gourmet cooking, and personal care. A gay writer named Mark Simpson actually coined the term way back in a 1994 article when he "outed" British (and now
American) soccer star and pop icon David Beckham as a metrosexual. Simpson
noted that Beckham is "almost as famous for wearing sarongs and pink nail polish
and panties belonging to his wife, Victoria (aka Posh from the Spice Girls), as he is
for his impressive ball skills."[104]

Hype aside, how widespread is the metrosexual phenomenon? Although there's
no doubt that "everyday guys" are expanding their horizons, many actively resist this

ECONsumer Behavior

Post Foods developed an
ad campaign it targets to
males that touts its Grape
Nuts cereal while it also
tries to help men cope with a loss of income
or a job. It includes a big collection of two-
minute online Webisodes that offer advice on
topics including how to ask for a raise during
a recession. The voice-over proclaims, "When
you tackle something tough at work or at
home, that doesn't just take know-how—that
takes Grape Nuts."[102]

The Axe line of male personal care products puts a twist on an old stereotype by depicting men as sex objects.

Source: Courtesy of Bartle Bogle Hegarty New York aka BBH.

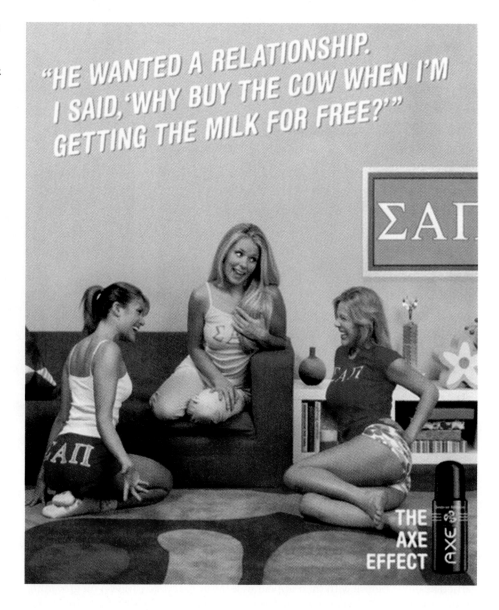

label because they don't want others to question their sexual preferences (as we'll see in Chapter 10, this is a great example of a *negative reference group*). Clearly, our cultural definition of masculinity is evolving as men try to redefine sex roles while they stay in a "safety zone" of acceptable behaviors bounded by danger zones of sloppiness at one extreme and effeminate behavior at the other. For example, a man may decide that it's OK to use a moisturizer but draw the line at an eye cream that he considers too feminine.[105] And, much like the "girls gone milder" trend we discussed earlier in the chapter, some cultural observers report the emergence of "retrosexuals;" men who want to emphasize their old-school masculinity via plastic surgery to create a more rugged look that includes hairier chests and beards, squarer chins, and more angular jaw lines.[106]

Indeed, in many circles the "M word" has become taboo and other (perhaps less threatening) labels pop up instead. One such label is the **übersexual**, which *The Urban Dictionary* defines as

metro-sexuality for the noughties (2000–2009). . . . In German it means the best, the greatest, super, or above. Übersexuals are the most attractive (not just physically), most dynamic, and most compelling men of their generations. They are confident, mascu-

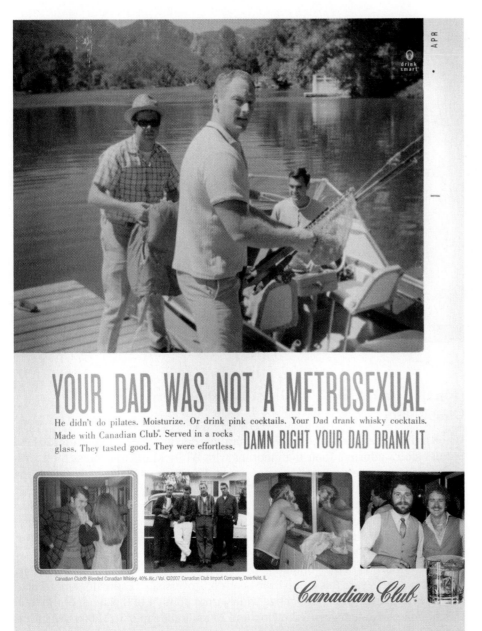

YOUR DAD WAS NOT A METROSEXUAL

He didn't do pilates. Moisturize. Or drink pink cocktails. Your Dad drank whisky cocktails. Made with Canadian Club. Served in a rocks glass. They tasted good. They were effortless. **DAMN RIGHT YOUR DAD DRANK IT**

Canadian Club® Blended Canadian Whisky, 40% Alc./Vol. ©2007 Canadian Club Import Company, Deerfield, IL.

Canadian Club

How valid is the metrosexual stereotype today?
Source: Canadian Club ® Blended Canadian Whisky, 40%-50% alc./vol. © 2009 Canadian Club Import Company, Deerfield, IL.

line, stylish, and committed to uncompromising quality in all areas of life. Übersexuals also have depth, subtlety and individuality . . . a male who is similar to a metro-sexual but has the traditional manly qualities such as confidence, strength, and class . . . without giving into the negative stereotypes such as chauvinism, emotional unavailability and a brain only filled with sports stats, beer and burgers. Compared with the metro-sexual, the übersexual is more into relationships than self. It is a masculinity that combines the best of traditional manliness (strength, honor, character) with positive traits traditionally associated with females such as nurturance, communicativeness, and co-operation. . . .

The current icon of übersexuals is Bono. He's global and socially aware, confident, and compassionate, and he commands a huge base of followers who are fans of his music and his humanitarianism. Other notable übersexuals are Bill Clinton, George Clooney, Jon Stewart, Pierce Brosnan, Donald Trump, and Ewan McGregor.[107]

The label "metrosexual" is a turnoff to many men.

Source: Courtesy of Zippo.

Gay, Lesbian, Bisexual, and Transgender (GLBT) Consumers

When California voters upheld the gay marriage ban in a 2009 referendum, 20 Levi Strauss stores adorned their mannequins with White Knots to express their solidarity with the same-sex marriage movement. The company's 501 button-fly jeans line partners with the Logo unit of MTV Networks (a network aimed at gay and lesbian viewers) in a campaign it calls "Logo Unbuttoned." The network has also signed sponsorship deals with other mainstream marketers like Orbitz, Stolichnaya, and Subaru.[108] Clearly these companies see value in coming out of the marketing closet.

The proportion of the population that is gay or lesbian is difficult to determine, and efforts to measure this group have been controversial.[109] Estimates among academics and marketing experts range widely from about 4 to 8 percent of the total U.S. population, or between 11 million and 23 million people. The 2000 Census reported 1.2 million same-sex "unmarried" partners in the United States, and this number excludes single gays and lesbians.[110] The respected research company Yankelovich Partners Inc., which, as we saw in Chapter 4, has tracked consumer values and attitudes since 1971 in its annual *Monitor*™ survey, now includes a question about sexual identity in its instrument and reports that about 6 percent of respondents identify themselves as gay/homosexual/lesbian. This study was virtually the first to use a sample that reflects the population as a whole instead of polling only smaller or biased groups (such as readers of gay publications) whose responses may not be as representative of all consumers.

To put things in perspective, the GLBT market is at least as large, if not larger, than the Asian American population (currently at about 12 million people). These consumers spend in the range of $250 billion to $350 billion a year. A Simmons study of readers of gay publications found that readers are almost 12 times more likely to hold professional jobs, twice as likely to own a vacation home, and eight times more likely to own a notebook computer compared to heterosexuals.[111]

CB AS I SEE IT

Professor Susan Dobscha, *Bentley University*

Imagine the excitement a young couple feels when they find out they are pregnant with their first child. They may learn this from a doctor's visit or from a pregnancy test they purchased at the drugstore. Once the pregnancy is confirmed and friends and relatives receive the good news, the couple must now begin the extensive planning process that gets them ready for this new addition to their family. Not surprisingly, a large portion of this process requires the planning and purchasing of goods and services. There are thousands of books on how to be a new parent, most of them geared toward the mother. While there are several books that give advice on how to be a new father, the book market reflects the still widely-accepted cultural norms that mothers are the primary caretakers of children, while fathers largely play a secondary role. A recent study found that while both new mothers and new fathers believed that responsibilities of parenting should be shared equally, the majority of those same mothers and fathers did not feel like responsibility was shared in their household. Sex roles remain fairly stable over time, even if expectations about them change dramatically.

The VOICE Group, an international research team currently undertaking a global study of motherhood, asked new mothers about their husbands' role in the planning process as a run up to the new baby arriving. While most of our participants claimed that their husbands were "excited" and "involved," the reality for most women was that their partner's level of involvement was lower than their own. Our study focused on mothers' perceptions of fathers' attitudes toward consumption decisions related to the introduction of the first child in the family. The data revealed that men, according to their wives' perceptions, used consumption as a virtual umbilical cord, although levels of consumption involvement varied from co-involvement for most purchases, to limited involvement, and/or involvement for big-ticket items, particularly travel systems and technical products. This research also revealed that men partook in highly masculinized forms of "nesting," and in general shunned pregnancy book reading; although some did engage in "research" activities such as searching the Internet for product safety information. We concluded from this study that the transition into parenthood can be difficult for men due to their lack of a physical connection to the pregnancy, a perception that the baby industry is not designed for them, the continuance of male stereotypes in the media, and also the time available to men to become involved in consumption activities immediately prior to a baby's birth.

An interesting question for consumer researchers is, how do sex roles change over time and to what extent does the marketplace reflect or in some cases hinder that change? In this study, we found that the books geared toward new dads typically displayed a tongue-in-cheek tone; they implied that new dads are incapable of taking a serious look at their new role as caretaker of a young child. The baby stores are also somewhat intimidating to men (although the women felt just as intimidated by the large box baby stores) because of men's general lack of experience with caring for infants and lack of information or awareness on what that infant's needs were once he or she arrived.

If men have an expectation about themselves that they will be co-parents, equally responsible in the caretaking of their child, does the lack of marketplace offerings directed at new dads hinder those dads from enacting those new roles? And, are there opportunities here for enterprising marketers who can develop products to better meet these needs?

American Express, Stolichnaya vodka, Atlantic Records, and Naya bottled water are among those corporations that run ads in lesbian publications (an ad for American Express Travelers Cheques for Two shows two women's signatures on a check). Acting on research that showed lesbians are four times as likely as the average consumer to own one of their cars, Subaru of America decided to target this market in a big way. And in one of the first mainstream pitches to directly address the controversy over gay marriage, Grand Marnier, a French cognac, launched print ads that read, "Your sister is finally getting remarried. Her fiancée's name is Jill."[113]

Marketing Opportunity

The Asterix Group conducted a large-scale segmentation study of the gay market. This survey reminds us of the perils of assuming that everyone in a large market is the same. It identified five distinct segments:

1 "Super Gays" (26 percent of respondents) are highly educated, earn high incomes, and describe themselves as sophisticated, activist, complex, intellectual, mature, risk-taking and extroverted. Nearly 90 percent report that they are "completely out," and about the same percentage report that they consider being gay to be a big part of who they are. About three-quarters of them live in big cities. They are the segment most likely to connect to a company that "actively speaks on behalf of LGBT causes."

2 "Habitaters" (25 percent) are older and most likely to be in a stable, living-together relationship. They describe themselves as serious, down-to-earth, emotional, simple, traditional, responsible, and mature. They are the most likely to live in suburban areas and watch the most TV of any segment. Habitaters are most likely to connect with a company that offers domestic partner benefits to employees.

3 "Gay Mainstream" (23 percent) tend to be conservative. Fewer than half are "completely out," but over half are in stable relationships. They are most likely to say that they prefer to watch TV programs in which being gay is part of the story.

4 "Party People" (14 percent) are young and the least-educated; most live in big cities. They describe themselves as youthful, down-to-earth, simple, cutting-edge, extroverted, rebellious, and risk-taking. They are far more likely than other segments to agree that "being gay is a choice." Three-quarters say they visit LGBT bars/clubs frequently, and they spend more time and money in restaurants.

5 The "Closeted" segment (12 percent) is older, and just 4 percent are "completely out." They describe themselves as serious, sideliners, traditional, introverted, mature, and cautious. Nearly half live in rural areas, and they're the most likely to connect to a company that "reaches out to gays and lesbians in traditional media."[112]

OBJECTIVE

Why is the way we think about our bodies (and the way our culture tells us we should think) a key component of self-esteem?

Body Image

A person's physical appearance is a large part of his self-concept. **Body image** refers to a consumer's subjective evaluation of his physical self. As with a person's overall self-concept, this image is not necessarily accurate. A man may think of himself as being more muscular than he really is, or a woman may feel she appears fatter than is the case. Some marketers exploit consumers' tendencies to distort their body images when they prey on our insecurities about appearance. They try to create a gap between the real and ideal physical self and consequently motivate a person to purchase products and services he thinks will narrow that gap.

As part of a campaign to promote the Broadway show *Reasons to be Pretty*, a casting call went out to the general public to show up and expose the part of their body they disliked the most—eight winners had these parts photographed for use in ads.[114] **Body cathexis** refers to a person's feelings about his body. The word *cathexis* refers to the emotional significance of some object or idea; we know that some parts of the body are more central to self-concept than are others. One study of young adults' feelings about their bodies found that the respondents were the most satisfied with their hair and eyes and they had the least positive feelings about their waists. These feelings also linked to grooming products the respondents said they used. Consumers who were more satisfied with their bodies were more frequent users of such "preening" products as hair conditioner, blow dryers, cologne, facial bronzer, tooth polish, and pumice soap.[115]

Ideals of Beauty

Our satisfaction with the physical image we present to others depends on how closely we think the image corresponds to the ideal our culture values.[116] An **ideal of beauty** is a particular model, or *exemplar*, of appearance. Ideals of beauty for both men and women may include physical features (e.g., big breasts or small, bulging muscles or not) as well as clothing styles, cosmetics, hairstyles, skin tone (pale versus tan), and body type (petite, athletic, voluptuous, etc.).

Is Beauty Universal?

It's no secret that despite the popular saying "You can't judge a book by its cover," people can and do. Fairly or not, we assume that more attractive people are smarter, more interesting, and more competent—researchers call this the *"what is beautiful is good"* stereotype.[117] By the way, this bias affects both men and women—men with above-average looks earn about 5 percent more than those of average appearance, and those who are below average in appearance make an average of 9 percent less than the norm. Hitting close to home, in one study researchers collected teaching evaluations for 463 courses taught by 94 faculty members at the University of Texas at Austin, along with some characteristics of the instructors, such as sex and race and whether they were on tenure track. They asked a panel of undergrads to rate photos of the professors in terms of their physical attractiveness. Guess what? Good-looking professors got significantly higher scores—and this effect was even more pronounced for male professors than for females. Fortunately, your consumer behavior professor is no doubt near the top of the scale.[118]

And virtually every culture displays this beauty bias, even though the standards by which people judge what is hot and what is not may differ. Communist China once banned beauty contests as "spiritual pollution," but then again China recently hosted the "Miss World" pageant. The Chinese consider appearance so important that they view plastic surgery as a commercial investment, and it's common for people to take out loans to fund procedures.[119]

Recent research indicates that preferences for some physical features rather than others are "wired in" genetically, and that these preferences tend to be the same among people around the world. When researchers show babies as young as 5 hours old pictures of faces adults rate as beautiful and not so beautiful, they report that the infants spend more time looking at the attractive faces.[121] Specifically, people appear to favor features we associate with good health and youth, attributes we link to reproductive ability and strength. These characteristics include large eyes, high cheekbones, and a narrow jaw. Another cue that people across ethnic and racial groups use to signal sexual desirability is whether the person's features are balanced. People with symmetrical features on average start having sex 3 to 4 years earlier than those with unbalanced features.[122]

Men also are more likely to use a woman's body shape as a sexual cue; an evolutionary explanation is that feminine curves provide evidence of reproductive potential. During puberty, a typical female gains almost 35 pounds of "reproductive fat" around the hips and thighs that supply the approximately 80,000 extra calories she will need to support a pregnancy. Most fertile women have waist–hip ratios of 0.6 to 0.8, an hourglass shape that also happens to be the one men rank highest. Even though preferences for overall weight change over time, waist–hip ratios tend to stay in this range. Even the superthin model Twiggy (who pioneered the "waif look" decades before Kate Moss) had a ratio of 0.73.[123]

Women, however, favor men with heavy lower faces (an indication of a high concentration of androgens that impart strength), those who are slightly above average in height, and those with prominent brows. A recent study provided evidence that women judge potential mates by how masculine their features are. Respondents viewed a series of male headshots that had been digitally altered to exaggerate or minimize masculine traits. They saw men with square jaws and well-defined brow ridges as good short-term partners, whereas they preferred those with feminine traits, such as rounder faces and fuller lips, for long-term mates.

The Tangled Web

Millions of people have posted photos at Hot or Not (www.hotornot.com), a hot Web site two engineers founded where visitors rate each picture on a scale from 1 to 10. One of the site's creators remembers, "Basically, we were sitting around drinking beers in the middle of the afternoon when a comment Jim made about a woman he had seen at a party made us think, wouldn't it be cool if there was a Web site where you could tell if a girl was a perfect 10?"

The phenomenal success of the site spawned hundreds of copycats, many of them not exactly the PG-rated environment this site offers. Some of the photos people send in aren't what you would call flattering (especially the ones submitted as jokes on unsuspecting friends); one possible explanation is the psychological concept of *self-handicapping* where we set ourselves up for failure so that in case ratings are low we can blame the picture rather than ourselves. Another is that the world is crowded with people so hungry for attention that they will submit to any number of indignities to have others look at them. What do you think?[120]

The "beautification engine" of a new computer program uses a mathematical formula to alter the original form into a theoretically more attractive version, while maintaining what programmers call an "unmistakable similarity" to the original. The software program, developed by computer scientists in Israel, is based on the responses of study participants who viewed photographs of white male and female faces and picked the most attractive ones. The researchers used these data to develop an algorithm that uses several hundred measurements between facial features to identify what makes a face attractive; important factors include symmetry between features, smoothness of skin, and vivid color in the eyes and hair. A woman's real photo (left) and the computer-enhanced version (right).

Source: Lars Klove/Redux Pictures.

Overwhelmingly, participants said those with more masculine features were likely to be risky and competitive and also more apt to fight, challenge bosses, cheat on spouses, and put less effort into parenting. They assume men with more feminine faces would be good parents and husbands, hard workers, and emotionally supportive mates.[124]

One study found these preferences actually fluctuate during the course of a woman's menstrual cycle: Researchers showed women in Japan and Scotland a series of computer-generated photos of male faces that were systematically altered in terms of such dimensions as the size of the jaw and the prominence of the eyebrow ridge.[125] Women in the study preferred the heavier masculine features when they were ovulating, but these choices shifted during other parts of their monthly cycles. If these results are valid, they indicate a "wired-in" preference for strong men who can pass on this trait to offspring.

Another study supplied tantalizing evidence that these preferences, indeed, are triggered physiologically: The researchers tested female university students who came to their lab when they were ovulating and when they were not. They photographed each woman twice—once in her fertile phase and once in her least-fertile phase. Then the researchers asked a separate panel of men and women to look at these pairs of photos (with the faces blacked out) and choose the one in which the person tries to look more attractive. These judges were more likely to select the photo of each woman when she was ovulating, and in these pictures the women tended to wear flashier clothing and jewelry; the researchers compared this behavior to animals that commonly signal when they are fertile via scents or changes in skin color.[126]

Of course, the way we "package" these faces still varies enormously, and that's where marketers come in: Advertising and other forms of mass media play a significant role in determining which forms of beauty we consider desirable at any point in time. An ideal of beauty functions as a sort of cultural yardstick. Consumers compare themselves to some standard (often one the fashion media advocates at that time), and they are dissatisfied with their appearance to the extent that they don't match up to it. This may lower their own self-esteem or, in some cases, possibly diminish the effectiveness of an ad because of negative feelings a highly attractive model arouses.[127]

Our language provides phrases to sum up these cultural ideals. We may talk about a "bimbo," a "girl-next-door," or an "ice queen," or we may refer to specific women who have come to embody an ideal, such as J-Lo, Gwyneth Paltrow, or the late Princess Diana.[128] Similar descriptions for men include "jock," "pretty boy," and "bookworm," or a "Brad Pitt type," a "Wesley Snipes type," and so on.

The Western Ideal of Beauty

Beauty is about more than aesthetics—we use cues such as skin color and eye shape to make inferences about a person's status, sophistication, and social desirability. People in less powerful cultures tend to adopt the standards of beauty prevalent in dominant cultures. For example, an ad on Malaysian television showed an attractive college student who can't get a second glance from a boy at the next desk. "She's pretty," he says to himself, "but. . . ." Then, she applies Pond's Skin Lightening Moisturizer by Unilever PLC and she reappears looking several shades paler. Now the boy wonders, "Why didn't I notice her before?" In many Asian cultures, people historically equate light skin with wealth and status, and they associate dark skin with the laboring class that toils in the fields. This stereotype persists today: In a survey, 74 percent of men in Malaysia, 68 percent in Hong Kong, and 55 percent in Taiwan said they are more attracted to women with fair complexions. And about a third of the female respondents in each country said they use skin-whitening products. Olay has a product it calls White Radiance, and L'Oréal sells a White Perfect line.[129]

As media images of glamorous American (Caucasian) celebrities proliferate around the globe, women who buy into the Western ideal of beauty—big round eyes, tiny waists, large breasts, blond hair, and blue eyes—literally go under the knife to achieve these attributes:

- A few years ago, a model named Cindy Burbridge, who was the local spokeswoman for Lux soap and Omega watches, became the first blue-eyed Miss Thailand. She's one of a generation of racially mixed Thais who now dominate the local fashion and entertainment industries as the public abandons the round face, arched eyebrows, and small mouth of the classical Thai look in favor of a Western ideal. Many buy blue contact lenses to enhance their looks. In a poll to name the sexiest men and the sexiest women in Thailand, seven out of the nine top scorers were of mixed blood.[130] The Thai language reflects the stigma of darker skin. One common insult is *tua dam,* or "black body," and another is *dam tap pet,* or "black like a duck's liver."[131]

- Year after year, winners of the Most Beautiful Girl in Nigeria performed very poorly in the Miss World competition. Local organizers had about given up on the idea that an African woman could win a contest Western beauties dominated. Then a Nigerian woman went on to win the Miss World title. She was the first African winner in the contest's 51-year history. However, pride mixed with puzzlement: The new Miss World didn't possess the voluptuous figure African culture prized. In West and Central Africa, people revere big women; many beauty contestants weigh more than 200 pounds. In Niger, women even eat livestock feed or special vitamins to bulk up. The Calabari in southeastern Nigeria send prospective brides to fattening farms, where they are fed huge amounts of food and massaged into rounder shapes. After weeks of this regimen, the bigger brides proudly parade in the village square.[132] As one African explained, "Plumpness means prosperity. Thin represents everything you don't want: poverty, AIDS, and other diseases, misery and hunger." In contrast, the contest winner is 6 feet tall and skinny. Older Nigerians did not find the winner especially attractive at all, and some bitingly described her as a white girl in black skin. But younger people feel different. For them, thin is in. In Lagos, fashionable thin girls are called *lepa* and there is even a popular song with this title. A movie called *Lepa Shandi* celebrates the more svelte look—the title means a girl as slim as a 20-naira bill.[133]

- Japanese retailers are scrambling to stock larger dress sizes to keep up with a new look the fashion industry calls *bonkyu-bon.* This means "big-small-big" and it stands for a change in that culture's body ideal: Japanese women are getting curvier. Today, the average Japanese woman's hips, at 35 inches, are about an inch wider than those of women a generation older. Women in their 20s wear bras at least two sizes larger than those of their mothers, whereas waist sizes have gotten smaller. The government reports that the average 20-year-old is also nearly 3 inches taller than she was in 1950. These changes are the result of a diet that is becoming more Westernized; the traditional meal of fish, vegetables, and tofu is now more likely to consist of red meat, dairy, and decadent desserts such as Krispy Kreme doughnuts and Cold Stone Creamery ice cream. Juicy Couture, known for its figure-hugging terrycloth tracksuits, opened one of its biggest stores in Tokyo, and other department stores feature larger sizes from other American designers. Wacoal Corp., Japan's largest lingerie company, was once known for its super-padded brassieres. Now the company has a new bestseller: the "Love Bra," a cleavage-boosting creation with less padding, aimed at curvier women in their 20s.[134]

Ideals of Beauty over Time

Although beauty may be only skin deep, throughout history women have worked very hard to attain it. They have starved themselves; painfully bound their feet; inserted plates into their lips; spent countless hours under hair dryers, in front of mirrors, and beneath tanning lights; and opted for breast reduction or enlargement operations to alter their appearance and meet their society's expectations of what a beautiful woman should look like.

We often characterize periods of history by a specific "look," or ideal of beauty. Often these relate to broader cultural happenings, such as today's emphasis on fitness and toned bodies. A look at U.S. history reveals a succession of dominant ideals. For example, in sharp contrast to today's emphasis on health and vigor, in the early 1800s it was fashionable to appear delicate to the point of looking ill. The poet John Keats described the ideal woman of that time as "a milk white lamb that bleats for man's protection." Other past looks include the voluptuous, lusty woman that Lillian Russell made popular; the athletic Gibson Girl of the 1890s; and the small, boyish flapper of the 1920s that the silent movie actress Clara Bow exemplified.[135]

In much of the nineteenth century, the desirable waistline for U.S. women was 18 inches, a circumference that required the use of corsets pulled so tight that they routinely caused headaches, fainting spells, and possibly even the uterine and spinal disorders common among women of the time. Although modern women are not quite as "straight-laced," many still endure such indignities as high heels, body waxing, eye-lifts, and liposuction. In addition to the millions women spend on cosmetics, clothing, health clubs, and fashion magazines, these practices remind us that—rightly or wrongly—the desire to conform to current standards of beauty is alive and well.

Our culture communicates these standards—subtly and not so subtly—virtually everywhere we turn: on magazine covers, in department store windows, on TV shows. Feminists argue that fashion dolls, such as the ubiquitous Barbie, reinforce an unnatural ideal of thinness. When we extrapolate the dimensions of these dolls to average female body sizes, indeed they are unnaturally long and thin.[136] If the traditional Barbie doll were a real woman, her dimensions would be 38–18–34! Mattel conducted "plastic surgery" on Barbie to give her a less pronounced bust and slimmer hips, but she is still not exactly dumpy.[137] The company now sells an even more realistic Barbie featuring wider hips and a smaller bust (and for the first time Barbie has a belly button).[138]

As we've seen, the ideal body type of Western women changes over time—check out portraits of models from several hundred years ago by Botticelli and others to appreciate by just how much. These changes periodically cause us to redefine *sexual dimorphic markers*—those aspects of the body that distinguish between the sexes. The first part of the 1990s saw the emergence of the controversial "waif" look in which successful models (most notably Kate Moss) were likely to have bodies that resembled those of young boys. Using heights and weights from winners of the Miss America pageant, nutrition experts concluded that many beauty queens were in the undernourished range. In the 1920s, contestants had a body mass index in the range now considered normal—20 to 25. Since then, an increasing number of winners have had indexes under 18.5, which is the World Health Organization's standard for undernutrition.[139]

Similarly, a study of almost 50 years of *Playboy* centerfolds shows that the women have become less shapely and more androgynous since Marilyn Monroe graced the first edition with a voluptuous hourglass figure of 37–23–36. However, a magazine spokesman comments, "As time has gone on and women have become more athletic, more in the business world and more inclined to put themselves through fitness regimes, their bodies have changed, and we reflect that as well. But I would think that no one with eyes to see would consider playmates to be androgynous."[140] Fair enough. Indeed, a recent reexamination of centerfold data for the years 1979 to 1999 shows that the trend toward increasing thinness seems to have stabilized and actually may have begun to reverse. Still, although the women shown in the magazine became somewhat heavier over the 21-year period the researchers reviewed, the Playmates remain markedly below weights medical experts consider normal for their age group.[141]

Is the Ideal Getting Real?

Fed up because you don't get mistaken for a svelte supermodel on the street? Dove's well-known Campaign for Real Beauty that features women with imperfect bodies in their underwear may help. One ad reads, "Let's face it, firming the thighs of a size

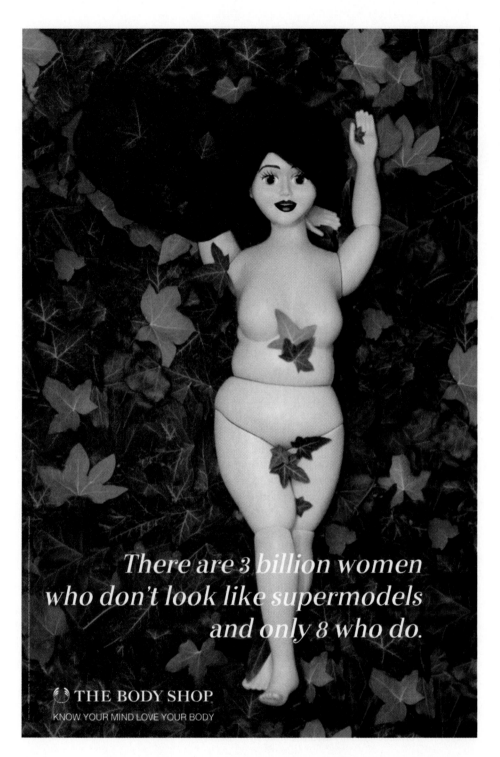

8 supermodel wouldn't have been much of a challenge." Unilever initiated the campaign after its research showed that many women didn't believe its products worked because the women shown using them were so unrealistic.[142] When the company asked 3,200 women around the world to describe their looks, most summed themselves up as "average" or "natural." Only 2 percent called themselves "beautiful."

Marketers of its Dove brand sensed an opportunity, and they set out to reassure women about their insecurities by showing them as they are—wrinkles, freckles, pregnant bellies, and all. Taglines ask "Oversized or Outstanding?" or "Wrinkled or Wonderful?" Dove even has a Web site (campaignforrealbeauty.com) where visitors can view the ads and cast their votes. The brand also sponsored a survey of 1,800 American

Dove's use of real women in its advertising has contributed to changes in how we think about ideals of beauty.
Source: Courtesy of Unilever Home and Personal Care NA.

women to assess how they felt about their looks. Overall, they found that women were satisfied with who they are, and these positive feelings were even stronger in subgroups such as African American and Hispanic women, younger women, and wealthier women. Fifty-two percent of women between the ages of 18 and 39 said that "looking beautiful" describes them very well, whereas 37 percent of women aged 40 and older feel the same. And 75 percent of the women agree that beauty does not come from a woman's looks but from her spirit and love of life. Only 26 percent feel that our society uses reasonable standards to evaluate women's beauty.[143]

However, Unilever's experience with Chinese women reminds us again that appearance norms are strongly rooted in culture. Dove's Campaign for Real Beauty flopped in China—after the fact Unilever's research showed that many Chinese women *do* believe they can attain the kind of airbrushed beauty they see in advertising. As a result the company scrapped the campaign there and instead launched a Chinese version of *Ugly Betty*—a successful American sitcom, which was in turn adapted from a Colombian telenovela. The show, *Ugly Wudi*, focuses on fictional ad agency employee Lin Wudi, who strives to unveil her own beauty—aided by the numerous Dove products that appear in the show. As you might expect, it helps that the actress who plays Wudi has perfect skin and actually is quite attractive once you strip away the oversized glasses and the fake braces.[144]

Male Ideals of Beauty

We also distinguish among ideals of beauty for men in terms of facial features, musculature, and facial hair—who could confuse Nick Jonas with Johnny Depp? In fact, one national survey that asked both men and women to comment on male aspects of appearance found that the dominant standard of beauty for men is a strongly masculine, muscled body—though women tend to prefer men with less muscle mass than men themselves strive to attain.[145] Advertisers appear to have the males' ideal in mind—a study of men who appear in advertisements found that most sport the strong and muscular physique of the male stereotype.[146]

And menswear designers and fashion magazines are starting to choose male models who look more like "regular" guys as they try to broaden the industry's appeal to the mass market. Until recently, most male models have been either super-thin and boyish looking or overly muscular. Now, with more men than ever before doing their own clothes shopping, some designers see an opportunity to cater to men who want to dress fashionably but who are turned off by the edgy looks they see in magazines. One industry insider credits celebrities such as actor Ashton Kutcher—a former model himself—and TV shows such as *Entourage* and *Grey's Anatomy* with showing men that guys can be stylish without being too muscular, too thin, or too manicured. He describes this look as "Chiseled without being too pretty."[147]

OBJECTIVE

Why can our desire to live up to cultural expectations of appearance be harmful?

Working on the Body

The Japanese company Wacoal recently launched a men's girdle to flatten big stomachs. Levi Strauss introduced Levi's Ultimate Lift 544, a new figure-enhancing jean for women. The new style creates a cup shape in each seat panel to mold the wearer's derriere.[148] No doubt, there's a lot of shaping going on out there.

Because many consumers experience a gap between their real and ideal physical selves, they often go to great lengths to change aspects of their appearance. From girdles to bras, cosmetics to plastic surgery, tanning salons to diet drinks, a multitude of products and services promise to alter aspects of the physical self. It is difficult to overstate the importance of the physical self-concept (and consumers' desires to improve their appearances) to many marketing activities.

Fattism

As the expression "You can never be too thin or too rich" reminds us, it's no secret our society has an obsession with weight. The media continually bombard us with images of thin, happy people. In one survey, more than twice as many female respondents said they were concerned about their weight than about cancer, heart disease, or diabetes. Only 40 percent said they were satisfied with their physical appearance.[149] Fattism is deeply ingrained in our culture: As early as nursery school age, children prefer drawings of peers in wheelchairs, on crutches, or with facial disfigurements to those of fat children. One survey of girls aged 12 to 19 reported that 55 percent said they see ads "all the time" that make them want to go on a diet.[150]

Although Americans' obsession with weight is legendary worldwide, a cultural priority on thinness is spreading—even as obesity rates around the globe skyrocket:

- In traditional Fijian culture the body ideal for females is, to put it delicately, robust. When a woman started to lose weight in Fiji, this was cause for concern and a sign of probable illness. Then, a few years ago the island finally got satellite TV feeds that exposed Fijians for the first time to American TV shows such as *Melrose Place* and *Beverly Hills 90210* that feature casts of skinny stars. Now, the tables have turned as teenage girls in Fiji exhibit eating disorders. A study found that teens who watched TV three or more nights per week were 50 percent more likely to feel too fat than were other girls. Participants cited actresses such as Heather Locklear as inspiration to change their bodies.[151]
- As in Fiji, Egyptians traditionally preferred somewhat plumper women—and the belly dancing tradition encouraged this. Now, though, weight loss diets are fashionable. The head of Egyptian television announced that overweight female newscasters had 3 months to shed those extra pounds (10 to 20 pounds in most cases) or he would fire them. A popular television exercise show encourages weight loss—but in deference to Islamic sensibilities, the female exercisers wear only loose-fitting clothes even though they do aerobic exercises, and the women aren't allowed to breathe too heavily.[152]
- Japan now requires companies and local governments to measure the waistlines of citizens between the ages of 40 and 74 as part of their annual checkups. If a

A poster at a public health clinic in Japan reads, "Goodbye, Metabo," a word associated with being overweight. The Japanese government is mounting an ambitious weight-loss campaign.

Source: Ko Sasaki/Redux Pictures.

Marketing Opportunity

The size and shape of the "average" U.S. consumer today is dramatically different from what it was 60 years ago. The U.S. government estimates that two-thirds of American adults are overweight or obese. Nevertheless, apparel companies still develop clothing lines based on a 1941 military study that set sizing standards based on a small sample of mostly white, young (and presumably physically fit) female soldiers.

Those standards are finally starting to change because the typical woman's body is no longer as "petite" as it used to be. The most commonly purchased dress today is a size 14; it was a size 8 in 1985! Slowly but surely, standards change as many women reject the unrealistic body ideal of the waif and subscribe to the battle cry: "Big is beautiful!" The popularity of "full-figured" women, such as Oprah, Queen Latifah, and Rosie O'Donnell, and plus-size spokesmodels, such as Emme, also has helped to improve the self-esteem of larger women.

In addition, standards based on this outdated snapshot of U.S. women need to recognize the diversity of today's ethnic population: According to current criteria, 78 percent of African American women and 72 percent of Hispanic women are overweight, compared with 58 percent of white women. And non-Caucasian body shapes differ as well—for example, Hispanic Americans and Asian Americans

person exceeds government limits—33.5 inches for men and 35.4 inches for women—he is provided with medical education. Eventually the government plans to impose financial penalties on organizations that fail to meet weight targets.[153]

- Jump over to Europe, where the diet brand Slim-Fast tackled a common stereotype: British women are the plump ones on the beaches of Europe. The United Kingdom has the highest obesity rate in Europe—nearly one in five of all 15-year-olds are overweight. The company ran ads that rally British women to lose weight or lose face to their sexier Continental counterparts in France, Spain, and Sweden. In one Slim-Fast ad, a French model says, "I love British women. They make me look great." In another spot, a shapely Spanish woman scolds, "Face it, British women, it's not last year's bikini getting smaller."[154]

Cosmetic Surgery

Consumers increasingly choose to have cosmetic surgery to change a poor body image or simply to enhance appearance.[156] According to the American Academy of Cosmetic Surgery, doctors perform nearly 860,000 cosmetic-surgery procedures each year—and men make up more than 150,000 of the patients. As cosmetic surgery becomes increasingly acceptable (even expected in some circles), consumers and the medical profession expand the scope of body parts they want to alter. Perhaps spurred by fashions such as low-rise jeans and spandex workout gear that call attention to the derrière, for example, buttock augmentation surgery is gaining in popularity. The operation typically costs about $20,000, so clearly it's not intended for the bottom of the market.[157]

Virtually any body part is fair game for surgical alteration. Bellybutton reconstruction is a popular form of cosmetic surgery in Japan. The navel is an important part of Japanese culture, and mothers often save a baby's umbilical cord in a wooden box. In Japanese, a "bent navel" is a grouch, and a phrase meaning "give me a break" translates as "yeah, and I brew tea in my bellybutton." A popular insult among children is "Your mother has an outie."[158] Interest in the United States tends to center elsewhere. Popular operations for men include the implantation of silicon pectoral muscles (for the chest) and even calf implants to fill out "chicken legs."[159]

Traveling upward, our culture tends to equate breast size with sex appeal. Consumer research an underwear company performed demonstrates the impact of breast size on self-concept. While she conducted focus groups on bras, an analyst noted that small-chested women typically reacted with hostility when they discussed the subject. The participants would unconsciously cover their chests with their arms as they spoke and complained that the fashion industry ignored them. To meet this overlooked need, the company introduced a line of A-cup bras it called "A-OK" and gave birth to a new market segment.

Some women elect to have breast augmentation procedures because they feel that larger breasts will increase their allure.[160] Although some of these procedures have generated controversy as a result of negative side effects, it is unclear whether potential medical problems will deter large numbers of women from choosing surgical options to enhance their (perceived) femininity. And as Lisa discovered, many companies promote nonsurgical alterations by pushing push-up bras that merely create the illusion of larger cleavage. These products offer "cleavage enhancement" that uses a combination of wires and internal pads (the industry calls them "cookies") to create the desired effect.

6

OBJECTIVE

Why does every culture dictate certain types of body decoration or mutilation that help to identify its members?

Body Decoration and Mutilation

People in every culture adorn or alter their bodies in some way. Decorating the self serves a number of purposes:[161]

- **To separate group members from nonmembers**—The Chinook, Native Americans of North America, pressed the head of a newborn between two boards for a year, which permanently altered its shape. In our society, teens go out of their way to adopt distinctive hair and clothing styles that will separate them from adults.

- **To place the individual in the social organization**—Many cultures engage in puberty rites during which a boy symbolically becomes a man. Some young men in part of Ghana paint their bodies with white stripes to resemble skeletons to symbolize the death of their child status. In Western cultures, this rite may involve some form of mild self-mutilation or engaging in dangerous activities.

- **To place the person in a gender category**—The Tchikrin, Native Americans of South America, insert a string of beads in a boy's lip to enlarge it. Western women wear lipstick to enhance femininity. At the turn of the twentieth century, small lips were fashionable because they represented women's submissive role at that time.[162] Today, big, red lips are provocative and indicate an aggressive sexuality. Some women, including a number of famous actresses and models, receive collagen injections or lip inserts to create large, pouting lips (insiders in the modeling industry call them "liver lips").[163]

- **To enhance sex-role identification**—We can compare the modern use of high heels, which podiatrists agree are a prime cause of knee and hip problems, backaches, and fatigue, with the traditional Asian practice of foot binding to enhance femininity. As one doctor observed, "When [women] get home, they can't get their high-heeled shoes off fast enough. But every doctor in the world could yell from now until Doomsday, and women would still wear them."[164]

- **To indicate desired social conduct**—The Suya of South America wear ear ornaments to emphasize the importance placed on listening and obedience in their culture. In Western society, some gay men may wear an earring in the left or right ear to signal what role (submissive or dominant) they prefer in a relationship.

- **To indicate high status or rank**—The Hidates, Native Americans of North America, wear feather ornaments that indicate how many people they have killed. In our society, some people wear glasses with clear lenses, even though they do not have eye problems, to enhance their perceived status.

- **To provide a sense of security**—Consumers often wear lucky charms, amulets, and rabbits' feet to protect them from the "evil eye." Some modern women wear a "mugger whistle" around their necks for a similar reason.

tend to be shorter than their Caucasian counterparts.

The clothing industry can't take the market potential of this segment lightly—women spend about $47 billion on plus-size garments each year, which accounts for 20 percent of the total apparel market. Now, the apparel industry sponsors Size USA, an ambitious project to revamp the way we think about body size and shape. This survey uses sophisticated 3-D body scanners to measure the complete physical dimensions of 10,000 people who represent the entire U.S. population. If and when these new standards make their way into designers' lines, today's size 14 might become tomorrow's size 8.

And, while many companies such as NutriSystem, Jenny Craig, and Weight Watchers address the need to lose weight, other companies see a chance to earn their weight in gold. One of these is the Casual Male Retail Group, which owns Casual Male XL, the nation's largest chain of men's plus-size clothing and apparel stores. The company targets the largely untapped market for specialty products that make life easier for the growing population of obese men and women. In its LivingXL catalog, you can buy a lawn chair that supports up to 800 pounds, or a "Big John" toilet seat with a 1,200-pound capacity.[155]

Body piercing has become a form of
expression for young people the world over.
Source: Used with permission of Tattoo Arts
Magazine and Art and Ink Enterprise.

Tattoos

Mattel Inc. recently released Totally Stylin' Tattoos Barbie, which comes with tiny tattoos girls can put on her body. The doll also comes with wash-off tats kids can use to ink themselves.[165] Tattoos—both temporary and permanent—today are a popular form of body adornment.[166] While consumers young and old (okay, mostly young) sport body art to make statements about the self, these skin designs actually serve some of the same functions that other kinds of body painting do in primitive cultures. Tattoos (from the Tahitian *ta-tu*) have deep roots in folk art. Until recently, the images were crude and were primarily death symbols (e.g., a skull), animals (especially panthers, eagles, and snakes), pinup women, or military designs. More current influences include science fiction themes, Japanese symbolism, and tribal designs.

Historically, people associated tattoos with social outcasts. For example, authorities in sixth-century Japan tattooed the faces and arms of criminals to identify them, and these markings served the same purpose in nineteenth-century prisons and twentieth-century concentration camps. Marginal groups, such as bikers or Japanese *yakuze* (gang members), often use these emblems to express group identity and solidarity.

Today, a tattoo is a fairly risk-free way to express an adventurous side of the self. A Harris Poll reported that one-third of Americans aged 25 to 29 and one-fourth of those between 30 and 39 have tattoos. And, consistent with our previous discussion, when we compare respondents who sport a tattoo to those who don't, the latter are more likely to think that people who have one are deviant and rebellious. On the other hand, one-third of those who do have a tattoo say it makes them feel sexier.[167]

Body Piercing

Decorating the body with various kinds of metallic inserts also has evolved from a practice we associate with fringe groups to become a popular fashion statement. Historians credit the initial impetus for the mainstreaming of what had been an underground West Coast fad to Aerosmith's 1993 video "Cryin'," in which Alicia Silverstone gets both a navel ring and a tattoo.[169] Piercings can range from a hoop protruding from a navel to scalp implants, where metal posts are inserted in the skull (do not try this at home!). Publications such as *Piercing Fans International Quarterly* see their circulations soar, and Web sites attract numerous followers.

Body Image Distortions

In less than 2 months, 4 young Brazilian women died in widely publicized cases of anorexia, which sparked an international debate about body image and eating disorders. The first to die was a 21-year-old model who stood 5 feet, 8 inches tall but weighed slightly more than 80 pounds when she collapsed at a fashion shoot in Japan. In Spain, the government imposed a controversial ban on extremely thin models as measured by their body mass index, or BMI (a formula that takes into account both height and weight). It requires a BMI greater than 17.4 for female models younger than 18 years old, or 18.5 for models older than 18 years old. For a 5-foot, 9-inch model older than 18, that translates to a weight requirement of 126 pounds. Unilever, in turn, banned the use of so-called "size 0" models in its ads for products ranging from Lux shower gel and Sunsilk shampoo to Slim-Fast diet drinks.[170]

Some people exaggerate the connection between self-esteem and appearance to such an extent that they sacrifice their health to attain what they consider to be a desirable body image. Women in particular tend to pick up messages from the media that the quality of their bodies reflects their self-worth, so it is not surprising that most (though certainly not all) major distortions of body image occur among females.

Men do not tend to differ in ratings of their current figure, their ideal figure, and the figure they think is most attractive to women. In contrast, women rate both the figure they think is most attractive to men and their ideal figure as much thinner than their actual figure.[171] In one survey, two-thirds of college women admitted they resort to unhealthy behavior to control weight. Advertising messages that convey an image of slimness help to reinforce these activities when they arouse insecurities about weight.[172]

Researchers link a distorted body image to eating disorders, which are particularly prevalent among young women. People with *anorexia* perceive themselves as too fat, and they virtually starve themselves in the quest for thinness. This condition often results in *bulimia,* which involves two stages. First, binge eating occurs (usually in private), in which a person may consume more than 5,000 calories at one time. The binge is followed by induced vomiting, abuse of laxatives, fasting, or overly strenuous exercise—a "purging" process that reasserts the woman's sense of control.

Most eating disorders occur among white, upper-middle-class teens and college-age women. Victims often have brothers or fathers who are hypercritical of their weight, and these disorders are also associated with a history of sexual abuse.[173] In addition, one's peers can encourage binge eating; groups such as athletic teams, cheerleading squads, and sororities may reinforce this practice. In one study of a college sorority, members' popularity within the group increased the more they binged.[174]

Marketing Opportunity

As more people jump on the tattoo bandwagon (the FDA estimates that 17 million Americans have gotten inked), it's inevitable that some of them will regret this decision later (perhaps when they wake up in the morning?). Tattoo removal centers with names such as Dr. Tattoff, Tat2BeGone, and Tattoo MD meet the need to deal with so-called "tattoo regret." One industry member estimates that as many as 100,000 Americans undergo tattoo removal each year. Unfortunately, at least for now, it's a lot more complicated to remove a tattoo than to put one on you. A design that cost several hundred dollars could require several thousand dollars and many laser sessions to remove. A special laser device shatters tattoo pigment into particles that the body's lymphatic system clears. Full removal takes an average of eight treatments, spaced at least a month apart, using different lasers for different colored inks.[168] The moral: Before you get a significant other's name etched onto your body, be pretty sure you plan to stay together.

The Tangled Web

At least 400 Web sites attract young people with "ana" and "mia," nicknames for anorexia and bulimia. These "communities" offer tips on crash dieting, bingeing, vomiting, and hiding weight loss from concerned parents. **Group dieting** is a growing problem as consumers patronize blog rings devoted to excessive weight loss—especially when they challenge female college students to lose as much weight as possible before events such as spring break. In one typical post, a woman confessed to eating ". . . one cracker, one strawberry and a little bit of soup" in a 24-hour period, whereas another recounted a lunch of a slice of mango and a stick of gum. These sites, often adorned with photos of ultrathin celebrities and slogans such as "Diet Coke Is Life" appeal to followers of an underground movement called *pro-ana* (pro-anorexia) who sometimes identify themselves in public when they wear red bracelets.[175]

Although about 90 percent of teens doctors treat for eating disorders are female, body image disturbances in men may be more widespread than most of us believe. Psychiatrists report increasing cases of *body dysmorphic disorder* (an obsession with perceived flaws in appearance) among young males (the average age of onset is 15). Symptoms of this disorder include excessive checking of mirrors and attempts to camouflage imagined deformities. Eating disorders in males are especially common among jockeys, boxers, and other athletes who must conform to weight requirements.[176]

As with women, media images and products encourage men to attain an unrealistic physique; as we've seen recently in the steroid scandals plaguing major league sports, professional athletes certainly are not immune to this pressure. Consider, for example, that if the dimensions of the original GI Joe action figure were projected onto a real 5-foot 10-inch man, he would have a 32-inch waist, a 44-inch chest, and 12-inch biceps. Or how about the same exercise for the Batman action figure: If this superhero came to life, he would boast a 30-inch waist, 57-inch chest, and 27-inch biceps.[177] Holy steroids, Robin!

CHAPTER SUMMARY

Now that you have finished reading this chapter you should understand why:

 1 **The self-concept strongly influences consumer behavior.**

Consumers' self-concepts are reflections of their attitudes toward themselves. Whether these attitudes are positive or negative, they will help to guide many purchase decisions; we can use products to bolster self-esteem or to "reward" the self.

 2 **Products often play a pivotal role in defining the self-concept.**

We choose many products because we think that they are similar to our personalities. The symbolic interactionist perspective of the self implies that each of us actually has many selves, and we require a different set of products as props to play each role. We view many things other than the body as part of who we are. People use valued objects, cars, homes, and even attachments to sports teams or national monuments to define the self, when they incorporate these into the extended self.

 3 **Sex-role identity is different from gender, and society's expectations of masculinity and femininity help to determine the products we buy to be consistent with these expectations.**

A person's sex-role identity is a major component of self-definition. Conceptions about masculinity and femininity, largely shaped by society, guide the acquisition of "sex-typed" products and services.

The media play a key role in teaching us how to behave as "proper" males and females. Advertising and other media play an important role because they socialize consumers to be male and female. Although traditional women's roles have often been perpetuated in advertising depictions, this situation is changing somewhat. The media do not always portray men accurately either.

 4 **The way we think about our bodies (and the way our culture tells us we should think) is a key component of self-esteem.**

A person's conception of his or her body also provides feedback to self-image. A culture communicates specific ideals of beauty, and consumers go to great lengths to attain these. Many consumer activities involve manipulating the body, whether through dieting, cosmetic surgery, piercing, or tattooing.

 5 **Our desire to live up to cultural expectations of appearance can be harmful.**

Sometimes these activities are carried to an extreme, as people try too hard to live up to cultural ideals. One common manifestation is eating disorders, diseases in which women in particular become obsessed with thinness.

 6 **Every culture dictates certain types of body decoration or mutilation that help to identify its members.**

Body decoration or mutilation may serve such functions as separating group members from nonmembers, marking the individual's status or rank within a social organization or within a gender category (e.g., homosexual), or even providing a sense of security or good luck.

KEY TERMS

Actual self, 168
Agentic goals, 181
Androgyny, 182
Avatars, 171
Body cathexis, 192
Body image, 192
Bromance, 181
Communal goals, 181
Computer-mediated environments, 170
Contemporary Young Mainstream
    Female Achievers (CYMFA), 184

Cosplay, 171
Extended self, 176
Fantasy, 168
Gender-bending products, 183
Group dieting, 203
Ideal of beauty, 192
Ideal self, 168
Identity marketing, 173
Impression management, 168
Looking-glass self, 172

Masculinism, 186
Metrosexual, 187
Self-concept, 167
Self-image congruence models, 175
Sexting, 178
Sex-typed traits, 181
Symbolic interactionism, 171
Symbolic self-completion theory, 174
Übersexual, 188
Virtual identities, 170

REVIEW

1 How do Eastern and Western cultures differ in terms of how people think about the self?

2 List three dimensions that describe the self-concept.

3 Compare and contrast the real versus the ideal self. List three products for which a person is likely to use each type of self as a reference point when he or she considers a purchase.

4 What does "the looking-glass self" mean?

5 How do feelings about the self influence the specific brands people buy?

6 Define the extended self and provide three examples.

7 What is the difference between agentic and communal goals?

8 Is masculinity/femininity a biological distinction? Why or why not?

9 Give two examples of sex-typed products.

10 What is body cathexis?

11 Have ideals of beauty in the United States changed during the past 50 years? If so, how?

12 What is fattism?

13 How did tattoos originate?

CONSUMER BEHAVIOR CHALLENGE

■ DISCUSS

1 The term *metrosexual* is a big buzzword in marketing, but is it real or simply media hype? Do you see men in your age group changing their ideas about acceptable interests for males (e.g., home design, cooking, etc.)?

2 How prevalent is the Western ideal of beauty among your peers? How do you see this ideal evolving now (if at all)?

3 Some historians and social critics say our obsession with thinness is based less on science than on morality. They equate our society's stigmatizing obese people (treating them as "sick," disabled, or weak) with the Salem witch trials or McCarthyism (the paranoid anti-communism movement of the 1950s). These critics argue that the definition of obesity has often arbitrarily shifted throughout history. Indeed, being slightly overweight was once associated with good health (as we've seen, in some parts of the world, it still is) in a time when many of the most troubling illnesses were wasting diseases such as tuberculosis. Plumpness used to be associated with affluence and the aristocracy (King Louis XIV of France padded his body to look more imposing),

whereas today it is associated with the poor and their supposedly bad eating habits.[178] What do you think?

4 Some authorities are so concerned about the practice of *sexting* that they are trying to prosecute young people who do this for distributing child pornography. How does sexting reflect on a consumer's self-concept? Should it be a matter for concern?

5 Should fast-food restaurants be liable if customers sue them for contributing to their obesity?

6 How might the creation of a self-conscious state be related to consumers who are trying on clothing in dressing rooms? Does the act of preening in front of a mirror change the dynamics by which people evaluate their product choices? Why?

7 Is it ethical for marketers to encourage infatuation with the self?

8 To date, the bulk of advertising targeted to gay consumers has been placed in exclusively gay media. If it were your decision to make, would you consider using mainstream media as well to reach gays, who constitute a significant

proportion of the general population? Or, remembering that members of some targeted segments have serious objections to this practice, especially when the product (e.g., liquor, cigarettes) may be viewed as harmful in some way, should marketers single out gays at all?

9 Some consumer advocates have protested the use of super-thin models in advertising, claiming that these women encourage others to starve themselves in order to attain the waif look. Other critics respond that the media's power to shape behavior has been overestimated, and that it is insulting to people to assume that they are unable to separate fantasy from reality. What do you think?

10 Does sex sell? There's certainly enough of it around, whether in print ads, television commercials, or on Web sites. When Victoria's Secret broadcast a provocative fashion show of skimpy lingerie live on the Web (after advertising the show on the Super Bowl), 1.5 million visitors checked out the site before it crashed as a result of an excessive number of hits. Of course, the retailer was taking a risk because, by its own estimate, 90 percent of

its sales are to women. Some of them did not like this display of skin. One customer said she did not feel comfortable watching the Super Bowl ad with her boyfriend: "It's not that I'm offended by it; it just makes me feel inferior." Perhaps the appropriate question is not does sex sell, but *should* sex sell? What are your feelings about the blatant use of sex to sell products? Do you think this tactic works better when selling to men than to women? Does exposure to unbelievably attractive men and women models only make the rest of us "normal" folks unhappy and insecure? Under what conditions (if any) should sex be used as a marketing strategy?

11 Some activists object to Axe's male-focused marketing; they claim that its commercials demean women. On the other hand, Dove's campaign has been applauded because it promotes a healthy body image for girls. Guess what? Both Axe and Dove are owned by Unilever. Is it hypocritical for a big company to sponsor positive messages about women in one of its divisions while it sends a different message in another?[179]

■ APPLY

1 Watch a set of ads on TV that feature men and women. Try to imagine the characters with reversed roles (i.e., the male parts played by women and vice versa). Can you see any differences in assumptions about sex-typed behavior?

2 Construct a "consumption biography" of a friend or family member. Make a list of or photograph his or her favorite possessions, and see if you or others can describe this person's personality just from the information provided by this catalog.

3 Interview victims of burglaries, or people who have lost personal property in floods, hurricanes, or other natural disasters. How do they go about reconstructing their possessions, and what effect did the loss appear to have on them? Similarly, poll your class: If their house or apartment was on fire and they could only take one possession with them as they evacuate, what would it be?

4 Locate additional examples of self-esteem advertising. Evaluate the probable effectiveness of these appeals—is it true that "Flattery gets you everywhere?"

Case Study

RIDING THE PLUS-SIZE WAVE

For years, Hollywood and the advertising media perpetuated a stereotypical image of women. As a result, many consumers have the unrealistic expectation that many women are (or should be) poreless, hipless, silken-haired, high-cheekboned, size 0, 20-year-old goddesses. But is this beauty myth finally changing? Companies like Charming Shoppes, Inc., parent to plus-size retailer Lane Bryant, are doing their darnedest to see that it does.

Lane Bryant was founded in 1900 in New York as the first women's apparel retailer devoted exclusively to plus sizes. Acquired by Charming Shoppes, Inc., in 2001 from Limited Brands Inc., Lane Bryant is part of the retail holding company's strategic plan to pull itself back from the brink of bankruptcy. Now, 74 percent of Charming Shoppes' revenue comes from sales of plus-size apparel.

The future looks even brighter. The apparel industry defines plus-size as 14 and up—today that includes 62 percent of American women. According to Mintel, the plus-size-clothing sector rang up $34 billion in sales in 2008. While this shift in demographics bodes well for Lane Bryant, the increase in the plus-size market does not directly translate into heftier sales. Plus-size customers tend to spend less as a percentage of their disposable income on apparel compared with women who are junior and misses sizes. Most analysts attribute this gap to the fact that retailers have not done a good job of making fashionable clothing available to larger women. According to one executive, "People are more accepting of their bodies today, and I think there has been a positive influence with role models. Years ago, manufacturers were only interested in making low-end plus-size merchandise because they thought customers were always in transition. Now no longer."

Lane Bryant is fighting this tide. With new product lines and promotional campaigns, the company sends the message that it's not only OK to be a plus-size, but that women in this category can be as stylish as anyone. Lane Bryant focuses on *en vogue* styles previously available only to more modestly sized shoppers. Its strategy includes offering larger sizes in the upscale Seven Jean Collection. It also includes an expansion into the lingerie category with its new Cacique brand. In addition to selling lingerie in Lane Bryant stores, Charming Shoppes is positioning itself as a Victoria's Secret competitor by opening dozens of stand-alone Cacique stores.

Other retailers are noticing this market and beginning to make a move. Will Lane Bryant's efforts change how society perceives the "typical" woman? Charming Shoppes' recent financial performance seems to indicate that this may be the case. Revenue for 2008 was at just over $3 billion. In addition, the company claims to rank number two in women's plus-size sales overall behind Wal-Mart.

Other retailers are also getting in the game. Hot Topic, Gap/Old Navy, Target, Lands' End, Saks Fifth Avenue, and Macy's are among national retailers offering or expanding their assortments of plus apparel sizes and increasing promotional efforts for this category. With these industry changes, who knows what images of women the media of the future will celebrate?

DISCUSSION QUESTIONS

1 Explain the success that Lane Bryant is currently experiencing in relation to self-concept, self-esteem, and self-consciousness. How can the plus-size industry leverage what we know about consumer behavior to address self-esteem issues?

2 Discuss the real-world changes that appear to be occurring with respect to media images of women. What are the reasons for this?

3 How do you reconcile the greater degree of acceptance of plus-size women with the parallel emphasis our society continues to place on thinness (as evidenced by the billions we spend on diet products, exercise, and so on)? Given the health problems associated with obesity (heart disease, diabetes, etc.) should the industry continue to encourage this acceptance?

Sources: www.spoke.com, accessed May 23, 2009; "Plus Size Teens and Women—US—November 2008," *Mintel Oxygen*, accessed May 23, 2009; Leigh Gragan, "Looking Good: Plus-Size Styles Are All About the Fashion," *McClatchy Tribune Business News* (March 26, 2008); Keiko Morris, "Finding Both Fashion and Fit: Plus-Size Retailing Is Becoming Hot as Demand Grows for Trendy Clothing in Size 14 and Up," *Knight Ridder Tribune Business News* (May 28, 2007): 1.

NOTES

1. Louise Story, "Forgive Me, Viewer, for I Have Confessed in a Banner Ad," *New York Times* (February 10, 2007), www.nytimes.com, accessed February 10, 2007.
2. http://twitter.com, accessed June 30, 2009.
3. Harry C. Triandis, "The Self and Social Behavior in Differing Cultural Contexts," *Psychological Review* 96, no. 3 (1989): 506–20; H. Markus and S. Kitayama, "Culture and the Self: Implications for Cognition, Emotion, and Motivation," *Psychological Review* 98 (1991): 224–53.
4. Markus and Kitayama, "Culture and the Self."
5. Nancy Wong and Aaron Ahuvia, "A Cross-Cultural Approach to Materialism and the Self," in Dominique Bouchet, ed., *Cultural Dimensions of International Marketing* (Denmark: Odense University, 1995): 68–89.
6. Lisa M. Keefe, "You're So Vain," *Marketing News* (February 28, 2000): 8.
7. Morris Rosenberg, *Conceiving the Self* (New York: Basic Books, 1979); M. Joseph Sirgy, "Self-Concept in Consumer Behavior: A Critical Review," *Journal of Consumer Research* 9 (December 1982): 287–300; www.mediapost.com, accessed February 15, 2007; Roy F. Baumeister, Dianne M. Tice, and Debra G. Hutton, "Self-Presentational Motivations and Personality Differences in Self-Esteem," *Journal of Personality* 57 (September 1989): 547–75; Ronald J. Faber, "Are Self-Esteem Appeals Appealing?" in Leonard N. Reid, ed., Proceedings of the 1992 Conference of the American Academy of Advertising (1992): 230–35.
8. Jeremy N. Bailenson, Shanto Iyengar, Nick Yee, and Nathan A. Collins, *Public Opinion Quarterly* 72, no. 5 (2008): 935–61.
9. Emily Yoffe, "You Are What You Buy," *Newsweek* (June 4, 1990): 59.
10. Christine Bittar, "Alberto-Culver Ties Hair Relaxer to Self-Esteem," www.mediapost.com, accessed February 15, 2007; www.texturesoftener.com, accessed May 29, 2009.
11. Michael Hafner, "How Dissimilar Others May Still Resemble the Self: Assimilation and Contrast After Social Comparison," *Journal of Consumer Psychology* 14, nos. 1 & 2 (2004): 187–96.
12. Andrew Adam Newman, Quoted in "If You're Nervous, Deodorant Makers Have a Product for You," *New York Times* (February 16, 2009), www.nytimes.com, accessed February 16, 2009.
13. Marsha L. Richins, "Social Comparison and the Idealized Images of Advertising," *Journal of Consumer Research* 18 (June 1991): 71–83; Mary C. Martin and Patricia F. Kennedy, "Advertising and Social Comparison: Consequences for Female Preadolescents and Adolescents," *Psychology & Marketing* 10 (November–December 1993): 513–30.
14. Philip N. Myers, Jr., and Frank A. Biocca, "The Elastic Body Image: The Effect of Television Advertising and Programming on Body Image Distortions in Young Women," *Journal of Communication* 42 (Summer 1992): 108–33.
15. Charles S. Gulas and Kim McKeage, "Extending Social Comparison: An Examination of the Unintended Consequences of Idealized Advertising Imagery," *Journal of Advertising* 29 (Summer 2000): 17–28.
16. For the seminal treatment of this process, cf. Erving Goffman, *The Presentation of Self in Everyday Life* (New York: Doubleday, 1959).
17. Quoted in Michael Slackman, "Fashion and Faith Meet, on Foreheads of the Pious," *New York Times* (December 18, 2007), www.nytimes.com, accessed December 18, 2007.
18. www.reputationdefender.com, accessed May 29, 2009.
19. Harrison G. Gough, Mario Fioravanti, and Renato Lazzari, "Some Implications of Self Versus Ideal-Self Congruence on the Revised Adjective Check List," *Journal of Personality and Social Psychology* 44, no. 6 (1983): 1214–20.
20. Steven Jay Lynn and Judith W. Rhue, "Daydream Believers," *Psychology Today* (September 1985): 14.
21. www.taaz.com, accessed May 29, 2009; www.dailymakeover.com, accessed May 29, 2009.
22. Erving Goffman, *The Presentation of Self in Everyday Life* (Garden City, NY: Doubleday, 1959); Michael R. Solomon, "The Role of Products as Social Stimuli: A Symbolic Interactionism Perspective," *Journal of Consumer Research* 10 (December 1983): 319–29.
23. A. Reed, "Activating the Self-Importance of Consumer Selves: Exploring Identity Salience Effects on Judgments," *Journal of Consumer Research* 31, no. 2 (2004): 286–95.
24. Neal Stephenson, *Snow Crash* (New York: Bantam Books, 1992).
25. Natalie Wood and Michael R. Solomon (2010), eds., *Virtual Social Identity* (Newport Beach, CA: Sage); Peter Svensson, "Study: Virtual

Men Are Standoffish Too" *MyFox 21* (February 2007), http://matei
.org/ithink/2007/02/22/study-virtual-men-are-standoffish-too-
yahoo-news/, accessed February 22, 2007.

26. George H. Mead, *Mind, Self and Society* (Chicago: University of Chicago Press, 1934).

27. Debra A. Laverie, Robert E. Kleine, and Susan Schultz Kleine, "Reexamination and Extension of Kleine, Kleine, and Kernan's Social Identity Model of Mundane Consumption: The Mediating Role of the Appraisal Process," *Journal of Consumer Research* 28 (March 2002): 659–69.

28. Natasha Singer, "If the Mirror Could Talk (It Can)," *New York Times* (March 18, 2007), accessed March 18, 2007.

29. Charles H. Cooley, *Human Nature and the Social Order* (New York: Scribner's, 1902).

30. J. G. Hull and A. S. Levy, "The Organizational Functions of the Self: An Alternative to the Duval and Wicklund Model of Self-Awareness," *Journal of Personality and Social Psychology* 37 (1979): 756–68; Jay G. Hull, Ronald R. Van Treuren, Susan J. Ashford, Pamela Propsom, and Bruce W. Andrus, "Self-Consciousness and the Processing of Self-Relevant Information," *Journal of Personality and Social Psychology* 54, no. 3 (1988): 452–65.

31. Arnold W. Buss, *Self-Consciousness and Social Anxiety* (San Francisco: Freeman, 1980); Lynn Carol Miller and Cathryn Leigh Cox, "Public Self-Consciousness and Makeup Use," *Personality and Social Psychology Bulletin* 8, no. 4 (1982): 748–51; Michael R. Solomon and John Schopler, "Self-Consciousness and Clothing," *Personality and Social Psychology Bulletin* 8, no. 3 (1982): 508–14.

32. Loraine Lau-Gesk and Aimee Drolet, "The Publicly Self-Conscious Consumer: Prepare to Be Embarrassed," *Journal of Consumer Psychology* 18 (April 2008): 127–36.

33. Morris B. Holbrook, Michael R. Solomon, and Stephen Bell, "A Re-Examination of Self-Monitoring and Judgments of Furniture Designs," *Home Economics Research Journal* 19 (September 1990): 6–16; Mark Snyder, "Self-Monitoring Processes," in Leonard Berkowitz, ed., *Advances in Experimental Social Psychology* (New York: Academic Press, 1979): 85–128.

34. Mark Snyder and Steve Gangestad, "On the Nature of Self-Monitoring: Matters of Assessment, Matters of Validity," *Journal of Personality and Social Psychology* 51 (1986): 125–39; Timothy R. Graeff, "Image Congruence Effects on Product Evaluations: The Role of Self-Monitoring and Public/Private Consumption," *Psychology & Marketing* 13 (August 1996): 481–99; Timothy R. Graeff, "Image Congruence Effects on Product Evaluations: The Role of Self-Monitoring and Public/Private Consumption," *Psychology & Marketing* 13 (August 1996): 481–99; Richard G. Netemeyer, Scot Burton, and Donald R. Lichtenstein, "Trait Aspects of Vanity: Measurement and Relevance to Consumer Behavior," *Journal of Consumer Research* 21 (March 1995): 612–26.

35. "Video Game Company Tries Human Branding," *New York Times* (August 12, 2002), www.nytimes.com, accessed August 12, 2002; Angela Orend-Cunningham, "Corporate Logo Tattoos: Literal Corporate Branding?" *Consumers, Commodities & Consumption*, American Sociological Association 5, no. 1 (December 2003); www .airnewzealand.com/aboutus/mediacentre/cranial-billboards-campaign .htm, accessed May 29, 2009.

36. Jack L. Nasar, "Symbolic Meanings of House Styles," *Environment and Behavior* 21 (May 1989): 235–57; E. K. Sadalla, B. Verschure, and J. Burroughs, "Identity Symbolism in Housing," *Environment and Behavior* 19 (1987): 579–87.

37. Solomon, "The Role of Products as Social Stimuli," 319–28; Robert E. Kleine III, Susan Schultz-Kleine, and Jerome B. Kernan, "Mundane Consumption and the Self: A Social-Identity Perspective," *Journal of Consumer Psychology* 2, no. 3 (1993): 209–35; Newell D. Wright, C. B. Claiborne, and M. Joseph Sirgy, "The Effects of Product Symbolism on Consumer Self-Concept," in John F. Sherry Jr. and Brian Sternthal, eds., *Advances in Consumer Research* 19 (Provo, UT: Association for Consumer Research, 1992): 311–18; Susan Fournier, "A Person-Based Relationship Framework for Strategic Brand Management" (doctoral dissertation, University of Florida, 1994).

38. A. Dwayne Ball and Lori H. Tasaki, "The Role and Measurement of Attachment in Consumer Behavior," *Journal of Consumer Psychology* 1, no. 2 (1992): 155–72.

39. William B. Hansen and Irwin Altman, "Decorating Personal Places: A Descriptive Analysis," *Environment and Behavior* 8 (December 1976): 491–504.

40. Lan Nguyen Chaplin and Deborah Roedder John, "The Development of Self-Brand Connections in Children and Adolescents," *Journal of Consumer Research* 32 (June 2005): 119–29.

41. R. A. Wicklund and P. M. Gollwitzer, *Symbolic Self-Completion* (Hillsdale, NJ: Erlbaum, 1982).

42. Paul Glader, "Avid Boarders Bypass Branded Gear;" *Wall Street Journal* (July 27, 2007): B1.

43. Erving Goffman, *Asylums* (New York: Doubleday, 1961).

44. Floyd Rudmin, "Property Crime Victimization Impact on Self, on Attachment, and on Territorial Dominance," *CPA Highlights, Victims of Crime Supplement* 9, no. 2 (1987): 4–7.

45. Barbara B. Brown, "House and Block as Territory," paper presented at the Conference of the Association for Consumer Research, San Francisco, 1982.

46. Shay Sayre and David Horne, "I Shop, Therefore I Am: The Role of Possessions for Self-Definition," in Shay Sayre and David Horne, eds., *Earth, Wind, and Fire and Water: Perspectives on Natural Disaster* (Pasadena, CA: Open Door Publishers, 1996), 353–70; cf. also Jill G. Klein and Laura Huang, "After All Is Lost: Meeting the Material Needs of Adolescent Disaster Survivors," *Journal of Public Policy and Marketing* 26, no. 1 (Spring 2007): 1–12.

47. Deborah A. Prentice, "Psychological Correspondence of Possessions, Attitudes, and Values," *Journal of Personality and Social Psychology* 53, no. 6 (1987): 993–1002.

48. Jennifer L. Aaker, "The Malleable Self: The Role of Self-Expression in Persuasion," *Journal of Marketing Research* 36 (February 1999): 45–57; Sak Onkvisit and John Shaw, "Self-Concept and Image Congruence: Some Research and Managerial Implications," *Journal of Consumer Marketing* 4 (Winter 1987): 13–24. For a related treatment of congruence between advertising appeals and self-concept, see George M. Zinkhan and Jae W. Hong, "Self-Concept and Advertising Effectiveness: A Conceptual Model of Congruency, Conspicuousness, and Response Mode," in Rebecca H. Holman and Michael R. Solomon, eds., *Advances in Consumer Research* 18 (Provo, UT: Association for Consumer Research, 1991): 348–54.

49. C. B. Claiborne and M. Joseph Sirgy, "Self-Image Congruence as a Model of Consumer Attitude Formation and Behavior: A Conceptual Review and Guide for Further Research," paper presented at the Academy of Marketing Science Conference, New Orleans, 1990.

50. Özlem Sandikci and Güliz Ger, "Aesthetics, Ethics and Politics of the Turkish Headscarf,", in Susanne Küchler and Daniel Miller, eds., *Clothing as Material Culture* (Oxford: Berg, 2005): Chapter 4.

51. Marc Lacey, "Where Showing Skin Doesn't Sell, a New Style Is a Hit," *New York Times* (March 20, 2006).

52. Jennifer L. Aaker, "The Malleable Self: The Role of Self-Expression in Persuasion," *Journal of Marketing Research* 36 (February 1999): 45–57.

53. A. L. E. Birdwell, "A Study of Influence of Image Congruence on Consumer Choice," *Journal of Business* 41 (January 1964): 76–88; Edward L. Grubb and Gregg Hupp, "Perception of Self, Generalized Stereotypes, and Brand Selection," *Journal of Marketing Research* 5 (February 1986): 58–63.

54. Benedict Carey, "With That Saucy Swagger, She Must Drive a Porsche," *New York Times* (June 13, 2006), www.nytimes.com, accessed June 13, 2006.

55. Ira J. Dolich, "Congruence Relationship Between Self-Image and Product Brands," *Journal of Marketing Research* 6 (February 1969): 80–84; Danny N. Bellenger, Earle Steinberg, and Wilbur W. Stanton, "The Congruence of Store Image and Self Image as It Relates to Store Loyalty," *Journal of Retailing* 52, no. 1 (1976): 17–32; Ronald J. Dornoff and Ronald L. Tatham, "Congruence Between Personal Image and Store Image," *Journal of the Market Research Society* 14, no. 1 (1972): 45–52.

56. Naresh K. Malhotra, "A Scale to Measure Self-Concepts, Person Concepts, and Product Concepts," *Journal of Marketing Research* 18 (November 1981): 456–64.

57. Ernest Beaglehole, *Property: A Study in Social Psychology* (New York: Macmillan, 1932).

58. Scott Smith, Dan Fisher, and S. Jason Cole. "The Lived Meanings of Fanaticism: Understanding the Complex Role of Labels and Categories in Defining the Self in Consumer Culture," *Consumption, Markets and Culture* 10 (June 2007): 77–94.

59. Russell W. Belk, "Shoes and Self," *Advances in Consumer Research* (2003): 27–33.

60. James Brooke, "Learning to Avoid a Deal-Killing *Faux Pas* in Japan," *New York Times* (September 17, 2002), www.nytimes.com, accessed September 17, 2002.

61. Russell W. Belk, "Possessions and the Extended Self," *Journal of Consumer Research* 15 (September 1988): 139–68.

62. Sean D. Hamill, "Students Sue Prosecutor in Cellphone Photos Case," *New York Times* (March 25, 2009), www.nytimes.com/2009/03/26/us/26sextext.html, accessed March 26, 2009.

63. Somini Sengupta, "Attack on Women at an Indian Bar Intensifies a Clash of Cultures," *New York Times* (February 8, 2009), www.nytimes.com, accessed February 8, 2009; Niraj Sheth and Tariq Engineer, "As The Selling Gets Hot, India Tries to Keep Cool, New-Age Dilemma: Too Sexy? Just Fun? The Chocolate Man," *Wall Street Journal* (September 9, 2008), www.wsj.com, accessed September 9, 2008.

64. Diane Goldner, "What Men and Women Really Want . . . to Eat," *New York Times* (March 2, 1994): C1 (2).

65. Nina M. Lentini, "McDonald's Tests 'Angus Third Pounder' in California," *Marketing Daily* (March 27, 2007), www.mediapost.com, accessed March 27, 2007.

66. Charles McGrath, "In Harlequin-NASCAR Romance, Hearts Race," *New York Times* (February 19, 2007), www.nytimes.com, accessed February 19, 2007.

67. John F. Sherry, Jr., Robert V. Kozinets, Adam Duhachek, Benet DeBerry-Spence, Krittinee Nuttavuthisit, and Diana Storm, "Gendered Behavior in a Male Preserve: Role Playing at ESPN Zone Chicago," *Journal of Consumer Psychology* 14, nos. 1 & 2 (2004): 151–58.

68. Suzanne Vranica, "Sony Tries to Lure DVR Ad-Skippers," *Wall Street Journal* (September 20, 2006): A20.

69. Thomas Tsu Wee Tan, Lee Boon Ling, and Eleanor Phua Cheay Theng, "Gender-Role Portrayals in Malaysian and Singaporean Television Commercials: An International Advertising Perspective," *Journal of Business Research* 55 (2002): 853–61.

70. Doreen Carvajal, "Europe Takes Aim at Sexual Stereotyping in Ads," *New York Times* (September 9, 2008), www.nytimes.com/2008/09/10/Business/Media/10adco.Html?_R=1&Ei=5070&Emc=Et..., accessed September 10, 2008.

71. Joan Meyers-Levy, "The Influence of Sex Roles on Judgment," *Journal of Consumer Research* 14 (March 1988): 522–30.

72. Anne Eisenberg, "Mars and Venus, on the Net: Gender Stereotypes Prevail," *New York Times* (October 12, 2000), www.nytimes.com, accessed October 12, 2000.

73. Beverly A. Browne, "Gender Stereotypes in Advertising on Children's Television in the 1990s: A Cross-National Analysis," *Journal of Advertising* 27 (Spring 1998): 83–97.

74. Lisa Bannon, "Mattel Sees Untapped Market for Blocks: Little Girls," *Wall Street Journal* (June 6, 2002): B1.

75. Elizabeth Landau, "Men See Bikini-Clad Women as Objects, Psychologists Say," *CNN* (February 19, 2009), www.cnnhealth.com, accessed February 19, 2009.

76. Eileen Fischer and Stephen J. Arnold, "Sex, Gender Identity, Gender Role Attitudes, and Consumer Behavior," *Psychology & Marketing* 11 (March–April 1994): 163–82.

77. Sarah Kershaw, "For Teenagers, Hello Means 'How About a Hug?'" *New York Times* (May 27, 2009), www.nytimes.com, accessed May 28, 2009.

78. Clifford Nass, Youngme Moon, and Nancy Green, "Are Machines Gender Neutral? Gender-Stereotypic Responses to Computers with Voices," *Journal of Applied Social Psychology* 27, no. 10 (1997): 864–76; Kathleen Debevec and Easwar Iyer, "Sex Roles and Consumer Perceptions of Promotions, Products, and Self: What Do We Know and Where Should We Be Headed," in Richard J. Lutz, ed., *Advances in Consumer Research* 13 (Provo, UT: Association for Consumer Research, 1986): 210–14; Joseph A. Bellizzi and Laura Milner, "Gender Positioning of a Traditionally Male-Dominant Product," *Journal of Advertising Research* (June–July 1991): 72–79.

79. Hillary Chura, "Barton's New High-End Vodka Exudes a 'Macho Personality,'" *Advertising Age* (May 1, 2000): 8; www.thorshammervodka.com, accessed May 29, 2009.

80. Teressa Iezzi, " Dell's Della Debacle an Example of Wrong Way to Target Women," *Advertising Age* (May 25, 2009), www.adage.com, accessed May 25, 2009.

81. Quoted in http://zack16.com, accessed June 26, 2009; Jack Neff, "You Won't Believe Who's Behind These Viral Videos," *Advertising Age* (June 16, 2009), www.adage.com, accessed June 16, 2009.

82. Sandra L. Bem, "The Measurement of Psychological Androgyny," *Journal of Consulting and Clinical Psychology* 42 (1974): 155–62; Deborah E. S. Frable, "Sex Typing and Gender Ideology: Two Facets of the Individual's Gender Psychology That Go Together," *Journal of Personality and Social Psychology* 56, no. 1 (1989): 95–108.

83. "Gender-Bending Avatars Suffer Lack of Trust," *SAWF News* (July 11, 2007), http://news.sawf.org/Lifestyle/39848.aspx, accessed July 11, 2007.

84. Geoffrey A. Fowler, "Asia's Lipstick Lads," *Wall Street Journal* (May 27, 2005), www.wsj.com, accessed May 27, 2005.

85. Matt Alt and Hiroko Yoda, "Big Primpin' in Toyko," *Wired* (May 2007): 46.

86. See D. Bruce Carter and Gary D. Levy, "Cognitive Aspects of Early Sex-Role Development: The Influence of Gender Schemas on Preschoolers' Memories and Preferences for Sex-Typed Toys and Activities," *Child Development* 59 (1988): 782–92; Bernd H. Schmitt, France Le Clerc, and Laurette Dube-Rioux, "Sex Typing and Consumer Behavior: A Test of Gender Schema Theory," *Journal of Consumer Research* 15 (June 1988): 122–27.

87. Carol Gilligan, *In a Different Voice: Psychological Theory and Women's Development* (Cambridge, MA: Harvard University Press, 1982); Joan Meyers-Levy and Durairaj Maheswaran, "Exploring Differences in Males' and Females' Processing Strategies," *Journal of Consumer Research* 18 (June 1991): 63–70.

88. Lynn J. Jaffe and Paul D. Berger, "Impact on Purchase Intent of Sex-Role Identity and Product Positioning," *Psychology & Marketing* (Fall 1988): 259–71; Lynn J. Jaffe, "The Unique Predictive Ability of Sex-Role Identity in Explaining Women's Response to Advertising," *Psychology & Marketing* 11 (September–October 1994): 467–82.

89. Leila T. Worth, Jeanne Smith, and Diane M. Mackie, "Gender Schematicity and Preference for Gender-Typed Products," *Psychology & Marketing* 9 (January 1992): 17–30.

90. Qimei Chen, Shelly Rodgers, and William D. Wells, "Better Than Sex: Identifying Within-Gender Differences Creates More Targeted Segmentation," *Marketing Research* (Winter 2004): 17–22.

91. Rupal Parekh, "Gender-Bending Brands an Easy Way to Increase Product Reach," *Advertising Age* (March 2, 2009), www.adage.com, accessed March 2, 2009; Sarah Mahoney, "Best Buy Opens Store Designed For Women," *Marketing Daily* (October 6, 2008), www.mediapost.com, accessed October 6, 2008; Kevin Helliker, "The Solution to Hunting's Woes? Setting Sights on Women," *Wall Street Journal* (October 1, 2008), http://online.wsj.com/Article/Sb122281550760292225.Html?Mod=Dist_Smartbrief, accessed October 2, 2008; Stephanie Clifford, "Frito-Lay Tries to Enter the Minds (and Lunch Bags) of Women," *New York Times* (February 24, 2009), www.nytimes.com, accessed February 24, 2009; Karl Greenberg, "Harley Says Guys Ride Back Seat in May," *Marketing Daily* (February 3, 2009), www.mediapost.com, accessed February 3, 2009.

92. Eric Bellman, "Suzuki's Stylish Compacts Captivate India's Women," *Wall Street Journal* (May 11, 2007): B1.

93. Craig S. Smith, "Underneath, Saudi Women Keep Their Secrets," *New York Times* (December 3, 2002), www.nytimes.com, accessed December 3, 2002.

94. Nathan Hurst, "Spirit Flight Attendants Not Happy with Airline's Proposed Uniforms," *The Detroit News* (January 28, 2009).

95. Marylouise Caldwell, Ingeborg Astrid Kelppe, and Paul Henry. "Prosuming Multiple Gender Role Identities: A Multi-Country Written and Audio-Visual Exploration of Contemporary Young Mainstream Female Achievers," *Consumption, Markets and Culture* 10 (June 2007): 95–115.

96. Jennie Yabroff, "Girls Going Mild(er): A New 'Modesty Movement' Aims to Teach Young Women They Don't Have to Be Bad, or Semiclad," *Newsweek* (July 23, 2007), http://boards.youthnoise.com/eve/forums/a/tpc/f/573295355/m/38310644, accessed July 18, 2007; www.purefashion.com, accessed May 29, 2009; www.modestapparelusa.com, accessed May 29, 2009; www.lightplanet.com/mormons/modesty/dress.html, accessed May 29, 2009; www.modestbydesign.com/Home, accessed May 29, 2009.

97. Adapted from www.cohorts.com/meet_the_cohorts.html, accessed June 1, 2007.

98. www.mavtv.com.

99. Barbara B. Stern, "Masculinism(s) and the Male Image: What Does It Mean to Be a Man?" in Tom Reichert and Jacqueline Lambiase, eds., *Sex in Advertising: Multi-Disciplinary Perspectives on the Erotic Appeal* (Mahwah, NJ: Erlbaum, 2003).

100. Ibid., 215–28.

101. Douglas B. Holt and Craig J. Thompson, "Man-of-Action Heroes: The Pursuit of Heroic Masculinity in Everyday Consumption," *Journal of Consumer Research* 31 (September): 425–40.

102. Suzanne Vranica, "Grape Nuts Takes Aim at Men: New Post Strategy Marks Departure for Cereal Campaigns," *Wall Street Journal* (March 26, 2009), http://online.wsj.com/article/SB123801803460241457.html?mod=wsjcrmain, accessed March 26, 2009.

103. Vivian Manning-Schaffel, "Metrosexuals: A Well-Groomed Market?" *Brand Channel* (May 22, 2006), www.brandchannel.com, accessed May 22, 2006; Jack Neff, "A Lipstick Index for Men? Philips' Norelco Posits That Guys Are Growing Beards to Protest Recession," *Advertising Age* (April 2, 2009), www.adage.com, accessed April 2, 2009; Aaron Baar, "Move Over, Ladies; Men Are Walking Down Beauty Aisles," *Marketing Daily* (December 22, 2008), www.mediapost.com, accessed December 22, 2008.

104. "Defining Metro Sexuality" *Metrosource* (September/October/November 2003).

105. Diego Rinallo, "Metro/Fashion/Tribes of Men: Negotiating the Boundaries of Men's Legitimate Consumption," in B. Cova, R. Kozinets, and A. Shankar, eds., *Consumer Tribes: Theory, Practice and Prospects* (Oxford: Elsevier/Butterworth-Heinemann, 2007); Susan Kaiser, Michael R. Solomon, Janet Hethorn, Basil Englis, Van Dyk Lewis, and Wi-Suk Kwon, "Menswear, Fashion, and Subjectivity," paper presented in Special Session: Susan Kaiser, Michael Solomon, Janet Hethorn, and Basil Englis (Chairs), "What Do Men Want? Media Representations, Subjectivity, and Consumption," at the ACR Gender Conference, Edinburgh, Scotland, June 2006.

106. Catharine Skipp and Arian Campo-Flores, "Looks: A Manly Comeback," *Newsweek* (August 20, 2007), www.msnbc.msn.com/id/20218432/site/newsweek, accessed August 17, 2007.

107. www.urbandictionary.com/define.php?term=ubersexual, accessed July 2, 2007.

108. Ari Karpel, "Levi's Adopts a Tie-In with a Gay Marriage Symbol," *New York Times* (May 26, 2009), www.nytimes.com, accessed May 26, 2009; Stuart Elliott, "Levi's, Unbuttoned and Out of the Closet," *New York Times* (September 14, 2008), www.nytimes.com/2008/09/15/Business/Media/15adcol.Html?_R=1&Scp=1&Sq=Levi..., accessed September 16, 2008.

109. Projections of the incidence of homosexuality in the general population often are influenced by assumptions of the researchers, as well as the methodology they employ (e.g., self-report, behavioral measures, fantasy measures). For a discussion of these factors, see Edward O. Laumann, John H. Gagnon, Robert T. Michael, and Stuart Michaels, *The Social Organization of Homosexuality* (Chicago: University of Chicago Press, 1994).

110. Lee Condon, "By the Numbers (Census 2000)," *The Advocate: The National Gay and Lesbian Newsmagazine* (September 25, 2001): 37.

111. For a recent academic study of this subculture, cf. Steven M. Kates, "The Dynamics of Brand Legitimacy: An Interpretive Study in the Gay Men's Community," *Journal of Consumer Research* 31 (September 2004): 455–64.

112. Karlene Lukovitz, "Consumer Preferences Vary Among Gay/Lesbian Segments," *Marketing Daily* (October 24, 2007), www.mediapost.com/publications/?fa=Articles.showArticle&art_aid=69729; accessed October 24, 2007.

113. Ellen Byron, "Cognac and a Splash of Controversy," *Wall Street Journal* (April 29, 2004): B5.

114. "New Broadway Show to Use Body-Part Confessional Ads," *Advertising Age* (January 19, 2009), www.adage.com, accessed January 19, 2009.

115. Dennis W. Rook, "Body Cathexis and Market Segmentation," in Michael R. Solomon, ed., *The Psychology of Fashion* (Lexington, MA: Lexington Books, 1985), 233–41; for research that examines how body image influences the likelihood of using virtual models, cf. Ellen C. Garbarino and José Antonio Rosa, "Body Esteem, Body Image Discrepancy and Body Boundary Aberration as Influencers of the Perceived Accuracy of Virtual Models," working paper, Weatherhead School of Management, Case Western Reserve University (2006).

116. Carrie Goerne, "Marketing to the Disabled: New Workplace Law Stirs Interest in Largely Untapped Market," *Marketing News* 3 (September 14, 1992): 1; "Retailers Find a Market, and Models, in Disabled," *New York Times* (August 6, 1992): D4.

117. Karen K. Dion, "What Is Beautiful Is Good," *Journal of Personality and Social Psychology* 24 (December 1972): 285–90.

118. Hal R. Varian, "The Hunk Differential," *New York Times* (August 28, 2003), www.nytimes.com, accessed August 28, 2003.

119. "Saving Face," *The Economist* (July 10, 2004): 55.

120. Gary Rivlin, "Facing the World with Egos Exposed," *New York Times* (June 3, 2004), www.nytimes.com, accessed June 3, 2004.

121. Emily Flynn, "Beauty: Babes Spot Babes," *Newsweek* (September 20, 2004): 10.

122. Ibid.

123. For some recent results that provide exceptions to this overall phenomenon, cf. Elizabeth Cashdan, "Waist-to-Hip Ratio Across Cultures: Trade-Offs between Androgen- and Estrogen-Dependent Traits," *Current Anthropology* 49, no. 6 (2008): 1099–1107.

124. Abigail W. Leonard, "How Women Pick Mates vs. Flings," *LiveScience* (January 2, 2007), www.livescience.com/health/070102_facial_features.html, accessed January 3, 2007.

125. Corky Siemaszko, "Depends on the Day: Women's Sex Drive a Very Cyclical Thing," *New York Daily News* (June 24, 1999): 3.

126. http://science.netscape.com/story/2006/10/10/fertile-women-dress-to-impress, accessed February 1, 2007.

127. Amanda B. Bower, "Highly Attractive Models in Advertising and the Women Who Loathe Them: The Implications of Negative Affect for Spokesperson Effectiveness," *Journal of Advertising* 30 (Fall 2001): 51–63.

128. Basil G. Englis, Michael R. Solomon, and Richard D. Ashmore, "Beauty Before the Eyes of Beholders: The Cultural Encoding of Beauty Types in Magazine Advertising and Music Television," *Journal of Advertising* 23 (June 1994): 49–64; Michael R. Solomon, Richard Ashmore, and Laura Longo, "The Beauty Match-Up Hypothesis: Congruence Between Types of Beauty and Product Images in Advertising," *Journal of Advertising* 21 (December 1992): 23–34.

129. Thomas Fuller, "A Vision of Pale Beauty Carries Risks for Asia's Women," *International Herald Tribune Online* (May 14, 2006), accessed May 16, 2006.

130. Seth Mydans, "Oh Blue-Eyed Thais, Flaunt Your Western Genes!" *New York Times* (August 29, 2002), www.nytimes.com, accessed August 29, 2002.

131. Thomas Fuller, "A Vision of Pale Beauty Carries Risks for Asia's Women," *International Herald Tribune Online* (May 14, 2006), accessed May 16, 2006.

132. Norimitsu Onishi, "Globalization of Beauty Makes Slimness Trendy," *New York Times* (October 3, 2002), www.nytimes.com, accessed October 3, 2002.

133. Ellen Knickermeyer, "Full-Figured Females Favored," *Opelika-Auburn News* (August 7, 2001).

134. Amy Chozick, "Developing Nation: Japanese Clothiers Update Their Lines Changes in Diet Produce Curvier Bodies in Women; "The 'Love Bra' Catches Fire," *Wall Street Journal* (May 7, 2007): A1.

135. Lois W. Banner, *American Beauty* (Chicago: University of Chicago Press, 1980); for a philosophical perspective, see Barry Vacker and Wayne R. Key, "Beauty and the Beholder: The Pursuit of Beauty Through Commodities," *Psychology & Marketing* 10 (November–December 1993): 471–94.

136. Elaine L. Pedersen and Nancy L. Markee, "Fashion Dolls: Communicators of Ideals of Beauty and Fashion," paper presented at the International Conference on Marketing Meaning, Indianapolis, IN, 1989; Dalma Heyn, "Body Hate," *Ms.* (August 1989): 34; Mary C. Martin and James W. Gentry, "Assessing the Internalization of Physical Attractiveness Norms," *Proceedings of the American Marketing Association Summer Educators' Conference* (Summer 1994): 59–65.

137. Lisa Bannon, "Barbie Is Getting Body Work, and Mattel Says She'll Be 'Rad,'" *Wall Street Journal Interactive Edition* (November 17, 1997).

138. Lisa Bannon, "Will New Clothes, Bellybutton Create 'Turn Around' Barbie," *Wall Street Journal Interactive Edition* (February 17, 2000).

139. "Report Delivers Skinny on Miss America," *Montgomery Advertiser* (March 22, 2000): 5A.

140. "Study: Playboy Models Losing Hourglass Figures" CNN.com (December 20, 2002).

141. Anthony H. Ahrensa, Sarah F. Etua, James J. Graya, James E. Mosimanna, Mia Foley Sypecka, and Claire V. Wisemanb, "Cultural Representations of Thinness in Women, Redux: *Playboy* Magazine's Depiction of Beauty from 1979 to 1999," *Body Image* (September 2006): 229–35.

142. Erin White, "Dove 'Firms' with Zaftig Models: Unilever Brand Launches European Ads Employing Non-Supermodel Bodies," *Wall Street Journal* (April 21, 2004): B3.

143. "The Dove Report: Challenging Beauty," *Unilever* 2004, www.dove.com/real_beauty/article.asp?id=430, accessed June 15, 2005.

144. Geoffrey A. Fowler, "Unilever Gives 'Ugly Betty' A Product-Plug Makeover in China," *Wall Street Journal* (December 29, 2008), www.wsj.com, accessed December 29, 2008.

145. Jill Neimark, "The Beefcaking of America," *Psychology Today* (November–December 1994): 32.

146. Richard H. Kolbe and Paul J. Albanese, "Man to Man: A Content Analysis of Sole-Male Images in Male-Audience Magazines," *Journal of Advertising* 25 (Winter 1996): 1–20.

147. Ray A. Smith, "Male Models Get a New Look as Fashion Targets Regular Guys," *Wall Street Journal* (February 2, 2007): B1.

148. Nina Lentini, "Levi's Launches 'Ultimate Lift' for Female Derriere," (November 17, 2008), *Marketing Daily*, www.mediapost.com/Publications/?Fa=Articles.Showarticle&Art_Aid=94943, accessed November 23, 2008; Miho Inada, "Is a Girdle Just for Men a Stretch? Japanese Company Calls Product 'Exercise Wear,' Says It Tones Muscles," *Wall Street Journal* (December 28, 2007): B3.

149. Jack Loechner, "Appearance and Weight Trumps Disease in Women's Concerns," Center for Media Research (May 26, 2008), http://blogs.mediapost.com/Research_Brief/?P=1714, accessed May 26, 2008.

150. David Goetzl, "Teen Girls Pan Ad Images of Women," *Advertising Age* (September 13, 1999): 32; Carey Goldberg, "Citing Intolerance, Obese People Take Steps to Press Cause," *New York Times* (November 5, 2000).

151. "Fat-Phobia in the Fijis: TV-Thin Is In," *Newsweek* (May 31, 1999): 70.

152. Amy Dockser Marcus, "With an Etiquette of Overeating, It's Not Easy Being Lean in Egypt," *Wall Street Journal Interactive Edition* (March 4, 1998).

153. Norimitsu Onishi, "Japan, Seeking Trim Waists, Measures Millions," *New York Times* (June 13, 2008), www.nytimes.com, accessed June 13, 2008.

154. Erin White and Deborah Ball, "Slim-Fast Pounds Home Tough Talk Ads Aimed at U.K. Women," *Wall Street Journal* (May 28, 2004): B3.

155. www.livingxl.com/store/en_US/index.jsp, accessed May 29, 2009; "Retailer Has Big Plans for Big Customers: LivingXL Sells Lifestyle Products for an Increasingly Obese America," www.MSNBC.com, accessed May 30, 2007; Rebecca Gardyn, "The Shape of Things to Come," *American Demographics* (July/August 2003): 25–49.

156. John W. Schouten, "Selves in Transition: Symbolic Consumption in Personal Rites of Passage and Identity Reconstruction," *Journal of Consumer Research* 17 (March 1991): 412–25; Janet Whitman, "Extreme Makeovers Blur Line Between Medicine and Cosmetics," *Wall Street Journal* (January 7, 2004), www.wsj.com, accessed January 7, 2004.

157. Natasha Singer, "How to Stuff a Wild Bikini Bottom," *New York Times* (March 2, 2006), www.nytimes.com, accessed March 2, 2006.

158. Jane E. Brody, "Notions of Beauty Transcend Culture, New Study Suggests," *New York Times* (March 21, 1994): A14; Norihiko Shirouzu, "Reconstruction Boom in Tokyo: Perfecting Imperfect Belly-Buttons," *Wall Street Journal* (October 4, 1995): B1.

159. Emily Yoffe, "Valley of the Silicon Dolls," *Newsweek* (November 26, 1990): 72.

160. Jerry Adler, "New Bodies for Sale," *Newsweek* (May 27, 1985): 64.

161. Ruth P. Rubinstein, "Color, Circumcision, Tattoos, and Scars," in Michael R. Solomon, ed., *The Psychology of Fashion* (Lexington, MA: Lexington Books, 1985), 243–54; Peter H. Bloch and Marsha L. Richins, "You Look 'Mahvelous': The Pursuit of Beauty and Marketing Concept," *Psychology & Marketing* 9 (January 1992): 3–16.

162. Sondra Farganis, "Lip Service: The Evolution of Pouting, Pursing, and Painting Lips Red," *Health* (November 1988): 48–51.

163. Michael Gross, "Those Lips, Those Eyebrows; New Face of 1989 (New Look of Fashion Models)," *New York Times Magazine* (February 13, 1989): 24.

164. "High Heels: Ecstasy's Worth the Agony," *New York Post* (December 31, 1981).

165. Tiffany Hsu and Don Lee, "At 50 Years Old, Barbie Gets Tattoos—And a Megastore in China," *Los Angeles Times* (March 6, 2009), http://articles.latimes.com/2009/mar/06/business/fi-tattoobarbie6, accessed March 6, 2009.

166. Dannie Kjeldgaard and Anders Bengtsson, "Consuming the Fashion Tattoo," in Geeta Menon and Akshay R. Rao, eds., *Advances in Consumer Research*, vol. 32 (Duluth, MN: Association for Consumer Research, 2005): 172–77.

167. "Three in Ten Americans with a Tattoo Say Having One Makes Them Feel Sexier," (February 12, 2008), www.harrisinteractive.com/harris_poll/index.asp?PID=868, accessed May 29, 2009.

168. Natasha Singer, "Erasing Tattoos, Out of Regret or for a New Canvas," *New York Times* (June 17, 2007), www.nytimes.com, accessed June 17, 2007.

169. www.pathfinder.com:80/altculture/aentries/p/piercing.html, accessed August 22, 1997.

170. Caroline Muspratt, "Unilever Bans 'Size Zero' Models in Ads," *London Telegraph* (May 9, 2007), www.telegraph.co.uk, accessed May 9, 2007; Larry Rohter, "Burst of High-Profile Anorexia Deaths Unsettles Brazil," *New York Times* (December 30, 2006), www.nytimes.com, accessed December 30, 2006; Eric Wilson, "Doctors Fault Designers' Stance over Thin Models," *New York Times* (January 9, 2007), www.nytimes.com, accessed January 9, 2007.

171. Debra A. Zellner, Debra F. Harner, and Robbie I. Adler, "Effects of Eating Abnormalities and Gender on Perceptions of Desirable Body Shape," *Journal of Abnormal Psychology* 98 (February 1989): 93–96.

172. Robin T. Peterson, "Bulimia and Anorexia in an Advertising Context," *Journal of Business Ethics* 6 (1987): 495–504.

173. Jane E. Brody, "Personal Health," *New York Times* (February 22, 1990): B9.

174. Christian S. Crandall, "Social Contagion of Binge Eating," *Journal of Personality and Social Psychology* 55 (1988): 588–98.

175. Doreen Carvajal, "French Bill Takes Chic out of Being too Thin," *New York Times* (April 16, 2008), www.nytimes.com, accessed April 16, 2008; Alex Williams, "Before Spring Break, the Anorexic Challenge," *New York Times* (April 2, 2006), www.nytimes.com, accessed April 2, 2006.

176. Judy Folkenberg, "Bulimia: Not for Women Only," *Psychology Today* (March 1984): 10.

177. Stephen S. Hall, "The Bully in the Mirror," *New York Times Magazine*, (August 22, 1999), www.nytimes.com, accessed August 22, 1999; Natalie Angier, "Drugs, Sports, Body Image and G.I. Joe," *New York Times* (December 22, 1998): D1.

178. Dinitia Smith, "Demonizing Fat in the War on Weight," *New York Times* (May 1, 2004), www.nytimes.com, accessed May 1, 2004.

179. Stephanie Clifford, "Axe Body Products Puts Its Brand on the Hamptons Club Scene," *New York Times* (May 22, 2009): B6.

6

Personality and Lifestyles

When you finish this chapter you will understand:

𝒥ackie and Hank, executives in a high-powered Los Angeles advertising agency, are exchanging ideas about how they are going to spend the big bonus everyone in the firm is getting for landing a new account—quite a feat when most agencies are laying off people instead of adding new business! They can't help but snicker at their friend Anne in accounting, who avidly surfs the Internet for information about a state-of-the-art home theater system she plans to install in her condo. What a couch potato! Hank, who fancies himself a bit of a thrill seeker, plans to blow his bonus on a wild trip to Colorado, where a week of outrageous bungee jumping awaits him (assuming he lives to tell about it, but that uncertainty is half the fun). Jackie replies, "Been there, done that . . . Believe it or not, I'm staying put right here—heading over to Santa Monica to catch some waves." Seems that the surfing bug has bitten her since she stumbled on Jetty Girl, an online resource for women who surf.[1]

Jackie and Hank marvel at how different they are from Anne, who's content to spend her down-time watching sappy old movies or actually reading books. All three make about the same salary, and Jackie and Susan were sorority sisters at USC. How can their tastes be so different? Oh well, they figure, that's why they make chocolate and vanilla.

OBJECTIVE

Why does a consumer's
personality influence the
way he responds to
marketing stimuli, but
efforts to use this
information in marketing
contexts meet with mixed
results?

Personality

Jackie and Hank are typical of many people who search for new (and even risky) ways to spend their leisure time. This desire translates into big business for the "adventure travel" industry, which provides white-knuckle experiences.[2] In the old days, the California beach culture relegated women to the status of landlocked "Gidgets" who sat on shore while their boyfriends rode the surf. Now (spurred by the female surfers in the movie *Blue Crush*), women fuel the sport's resurgence in popularity. Roxy rides the wave with its collections of women's surf apparel; it even includes a feature on its Web site that lets users design their own bikinis.[3]

Just what does make Jackie and Hank so different from their more sedate friend Anne? One answer may lie in the concept of **personality**, which refers to a person's unique psychological makeup and how it consistently influences the way a person responds to her environment. Do all people *have* personalities? Certainly we can wonder about some we meet! Actually, even though the answer seems like a no-brainer, some psychologists argue that the concept of personality may not be valid. Many studies find that people do not seem to exhibit stable personalities. Because people don't necessarily behave the same way in all situations, they argue that this is merely a convenient way to categorize people.

Intuitively, this argument is a bit hard to accept because we tend to see others in a limited range of situations, and so they *do* appear to act consistently. However, we each know that *we* are not all *that* consistent; we may be wild and crazy at times and serious and responsible at others. Although certainly not all psychologists have abandoned the idea of personality, many now recognize that a person's underlying characteristics are but one part of the puzzle, and situational factors often play a very large role in determining behavior.[4] Still, marketing strategies often include some aspects of personality. We usually employ these dimensions in conjunction with a person's choices of leisure activities, political outlooks, aesthetic tastes, and other individual factors to segment consumers in terms of *lifestyles*, a process we'll focus on more fully later in this chapter.

Consumer Behavior on the Couch: Freudian Theory

Sigmund Freud proposed the idea that much of one's adult personality stems from a fundamental conflict between a person's desire to gratify her physical needs and the necessity to function as a responsible member of society. This struggle is carried out in the mind among three systems. (Note: These systems do *not* refer to physical parts of the brain.) Let's quickly review each.

Freudian Systems

The **id** is about immediate gratification—it is the "party animal" of the mind. It operates according to the **pleasure principle**; our basic desire to maximize pleasure and avoid pain guides our behavior. The id is selfish and illogical. It directs a person's psychic energy toward pleasurable acts without regard for any consequences.

The **superego** is the counterweight to the id. This system is essentially the person's conscience. It internalizes society's rules (especially as parents teach them to us) and tries to prevent the id from seeking selfish gratification. Finally, the **ego** is the system that mediates between the id and the superego. It's basically a referee in the fight between temptation and virtue. The ego tries to balance these opposing forces according to the **reality principle**, which means it finds ways to gratify the id that the outside world will find acceptable. (Hint: This is where Freudian theory applies to

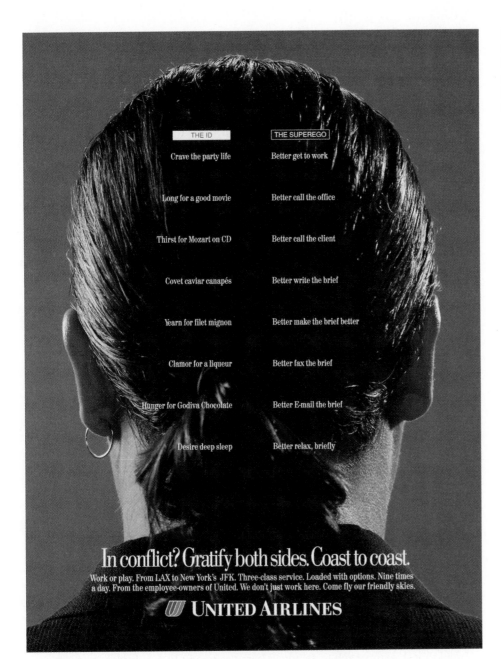

The ad caption:

This ad focuses on the conflict between the desire for hedonic gratification (represented by the id) versus the need to engage in rational, task-oriented activities (represented by the superego).
Source: Used with permission of United Airlines.

marketing). These conflicts occur on an unconscious level, so the person is not necessarily aware of the underlying reasons for his or her behavior.

Consumer researchers have adapted some of Freud's ideas. In particular, his work highlights the potential importance of unconscious motives that guide our purchases. The implication is that consumers cannot necessarily tell us their true motivation when they choose products, even if we can devise a sensitive way to ask them directly. The Freudian perspective also raises the possibility that the ego relies on the symbolism in products to compromise between the demands of the id and the prohibitions of the superego. The person channels her unacceptable desire into acceptable outlets when she uses products that signify these underlying desires. This is the connection between product symbolism and motivation: The product stands for, or represents, a consumer's true goal, which is socially unacceptable or unattainable. By acquiring the product, the person vicariously experiences the forbidden fruit.

Sometimes a Cigar Is Just a Cigar

Most Freudian applications in marketing relate to a product's supposed sexual symbolism. For example, some analysts speculate that owning a sports car is a substitute for sexual gratification (especially for men going through a "midlife crisis"). Indeed, some people do seem inordinately attached to their cars and may spend many hours lovingly washing and polishing them. An Infiniti ad reinforces the belief that cars symbolically satisfy consumers' sexual needs in addition to their functional ones when it describes one model as "what happens when you cross sheet metal and desire." Other approaches focus on male-oriented symbolism—so-called *phallic symbols*—that appeals to women. Although Freud joked "sometimes a cigar is just a cigar," many popular applications of Freud's ideas revolve around the use of objects that resemble sex organs (e.g., cigars, trees, or swords for male sex organs; tunnels for female sex organs). This focus stems from Freud's analysis of dreams, which he believed communicate repressed desires in the form of symbolically rich stories.

Motivational Research

In the 1950s, **motivational research** borrowed Freudian ideas to understand the deeper meanings of products and advertisements. This approach adapted psychoanalytical (Freudian) interpretations with a heavy emphasis on unconscious motives. It basically assumed that we channel socially unacceptable needs into acceptable outlets—including product substitutes.

This perspective relies on *depth interviews* with individual consumers. Instead of asking many consumers a few general questions about product usage and combining these responses with those of many other consumers in a representative statistical sample, a motivational researcher talks to only a few people, but she probes deeply into each respondent's purchase motivations. A depth interview might take several hours, and it's based on the assumption that the respondent cannot immediately articulate his *latent* or underlying motives. A carefully trained interviewer can derive these only after extensive questioning and interpretation.

Ernest Dichter, a psychoanalyst who trained with Freud's disciples in Vienna in the early part of the twentieth century, pioneered this work. Dichter conducted in-depth interview studies on more than 230 different products, and actual marketing campaigns incorporated many of his findings.[5] For example, Esso (now Exxon in the United States) for many years reminded consumers to "Put a Tiger in Your Tank" after Dichter found that people responded well to this powerful animal symbolism containing vaguely sexual undertones. Table 6.1 provides a summary of major consumption motivations he identified.

Some critics reacted to the motivational studies ad agencies conducted much the same way that they had to subliminal perception studies (see Chapter 2). They charged that this approach gave advertisers the power to manipulate consumers.[6] On the other hand, many consumer researchers felt the research lacked sufficient rigor and validity because the interpretations are so subjective.[7] Since the analyst bases his conclusions on his own judgment after he interviews a small number of people, they were dubious about whether the findings would generalize to a larger market. In addition, because the original motivational researchers were heavily influenced by orthodox Freudian theory, their interpretations usually involved sexual themes. This emphasis tends to overlook other plausible causes for behavior. Still, motivational research had great appeal to at least some marketers for several reasons, including these:

- Motivational research is less expensive to conduct than large-scale, quantitative survey data collection because interviewing and data-processing costs are relatively minimal.
- The knowledge a company derives from motivational research may help it develop marketing communications that appeal to deep-seated needs and thus

TABLE 6.1	A Motivational Researcher Identifies Consumption Motives
Motive	**Associated Products**
Power-masculinity-virility	Power: Sugary products and large breakfasts (to charge oneself up), bowling, electric trains, hot rods, power tools Masculinity-virility: Coffee, red meat, heavy shoes, toy guns, buying fur coats for women, shaving with a razor
Security	Ice cream (to feel like a loved child again), full drawer of neatly ironed shirts, real plaster walls (to feel sheltered), home baking, hospital care
Eroticism	Sweets (to lick), gloves (to be removed by woman as a form of undressing), a man lighting a woman's cigarette (to create a tension-filled moment culminating in pressure, then relaxation)
Moral purity-cleanliness	White bread, cotton fabrics (to connote chastity), harsh household cleaning chemicals (to make housewives feel moral after using), bathing (to be equated with Pontius Pilate, who washed blood from his hands), oatmeal (sacrifice, virtue)
Social acceptance	Companionship: Ice cream (to share fun), coffee Love and affection: Toys (to express love for children), sugar and honey (to express terms of affection) Acceptance: Soap, beauty products
Individuality	Gourmet foods, foreign cars, cigarette holders, vodka, perfume, fountain pens
Status	Scotch: ulcers, heart attacks, indigestion (to show one has a high-stress, important job!), carpets (to show one does not live on bare earth like peasants)
Femininity	Cakes and cookies, dolls, silk, tea, household curios
Reward	Cigarettes, candy, alcohol, ice cream, cookies
Mastery over environment	Kitchen appliances, boats, sporting goods, cigarette lighters
Disalienation (a desire to feel connectedness to things)	Home decorating, skiing, morning radio broadcasts (to feel "in touch" with the world)
Magic-mystery	Soups (having healing powers), paints (change the mood of a room), carbonated drinks (magical effervescent property), vodka (romantic history), unwrapping of gifts

Source: Adapted from Jeffrey F. Durgee, "Interpreting Dichter's Interpretations: An Analysis of Consumption Symbolism," in *The Handbook of Consumer Motivation, Marketing and Semiotics: Selected Papers from the Copenhagen Symposium*, eds. Hanne Hartvig-Larsen, David Glen Mick, and Christian Alstead (Copenhagen, 1991).

provide a more powerful hook to reel in consumers. Even if they are not necessarily valid for all consumers in a target market, these insights still can be valuable to an advertiser who wants to create copy that will resonate with customers.
● Some of the findings seem intuitively plausible after the fact. For example, motivational studies concluded that we associate coffee with companionship, that we avoid prunes because they remind us of old age, and that men fondly equate the first car they owned as an adolescent with the onset of their sexual freedom.

Other interpretations were hard for some researchers to swallow; such as the observation that women equate the act of baking a cake with birth, or that men are reluctant to give blood because they feel it drains their vital fluids. However, we do sometimes say a pregnant woman has "a bun in the oven," and Pillsbury claims, "nothing says lovin' like something from the oven." When the Red Cross hired motivational researcher Dichter to boost blood donation rates, he did report that men (but not women) tend to drastically overestimate the amount of blood they give. As a result the Red Cross counteracted men's fear of losing their virility when the organization symbolically equated the act of giving blood with fertilizing a female egg: "Give the gift of life." Despite its drawbacks, some ad agencies today still use some forms of motivational research. The approach is most useful, however, when we use it as an exploratory technique to provide insights that inform more rigorous research approaches.

Neo-Freudian Theories

Freud's work had a huge influence on subsequent theories of personality. Although he opened the door to the realization that explanations for behavior may lurk beneath the surface, many of his colleagues and students felt that an individual's personality is more influenced by how he handles relationships with others than by how he resolves sexual conflicts. We call these theorists *neo-Freudian* (meaning following from or being influenced by Freud).

Karen Horney

One of the most prominent neo-Freudians was Karen Horney. This pioneering psychotherapist described people as moving toward others *(compliant)*, away from others *(detached)*, or against others *(aggressive)*.[8] Indeed, one early study found that compliant people are more likely to gravitate toward name brand products, detached types are more likely to be tea drinkers, and males the researchers classified as aggressive preferred brands with a strong masculine orientation (e.g., Old Spice deodorant).[9] Other well-known neo-Freudians include Alfred Adler, who proposed that a prime motivation is to overcome feelings of inferiority relative to others, and Harry Stack Sullivan, who focused on how personality evolves to reduce anxiety in social relationships.[10]

Carl Jung

Carl Jung was also a disciple of Freud (and Freud was grooming him to be his successor). However, Jung was unable to accept Freud's emphasis on sexual aspects of personality, and this was a contributing factor in the eventual dissolution of their relationship. Jung went on to develop his own method of psychotherapy, which he called *analytical psychology*.

Jung believed that the cumulative experiences of past generations shape who we are today. He proposed that we each share a *collective unconscious;* a storehouse of memories we inherit from our ancestors. For example, Jung would argue that many people are afraid of the dark because their distant ancestors had good reason to fear it. These shared memories create **archetypes**, or universally recognized ideas and behavior patterns. Archetypes involve themes, such as birth, death, or the devil, that appear frequently in myths, stories, and dreams.

Jung's ideas may seem a bit far-fetched, but advertising messages in fact do often include archetypes. For example, some of the archetypes Jung and his followers identified include the "old wise man" and the "earth mother."[11] These images appear frequently in marketing messages that use characters such as wizards, revered teachers, or even Mother Nature. Our culture's current infatuation with stories such as *Harry Potter* and *The Lord of the Rings* speaks to the power of these images—to say nothing of the "wizard" that helps you to repair your laptop.

Young & Rubicam (Y&R), a major advertising agency, uses the archetype approach in its BrandAsset® Archetypes model that Figure 6.1 depicts. The model proposes healthy relationships among Archetypes as well as unhealthy ones. A healthy personality is one in which the Archetypes overwhelm their corresponding Shadows; a sick personality results when one or more Shadows prevail. When a brand's Shadows dominate, this cues the agency to take action to guide the brand to a healthier personality, much like one would try to counsel a psychologically ill person. The agency feels that this approach has numerous advantages:

- Because Archetypes are grounded in the human psyche across all cultures and points in time it is easy to understand a brand's personality—oftentimes multinationally—using such a structure.
- Archetypes telegraph instantly to those responsible for brand communication; indeed, the best of this group already incorporates these notions into how they think of the brand: The model helps the rest of them "catch up."

Figure 6.1 BRANDASSET VALUATOR® ARCHETYPES
Source: BrandAsset® Consulting: A Young & Rubicam Brands Company.

Characteristics

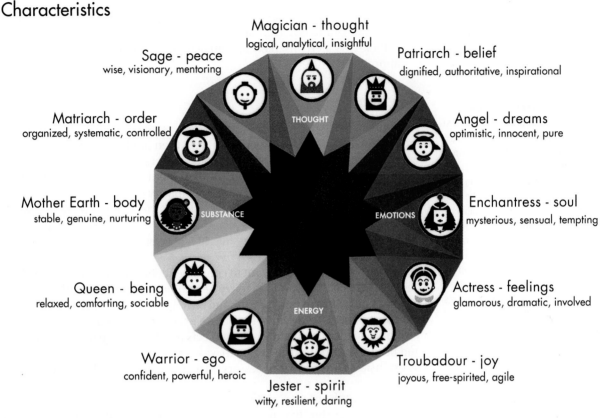

Shadow Characteristics

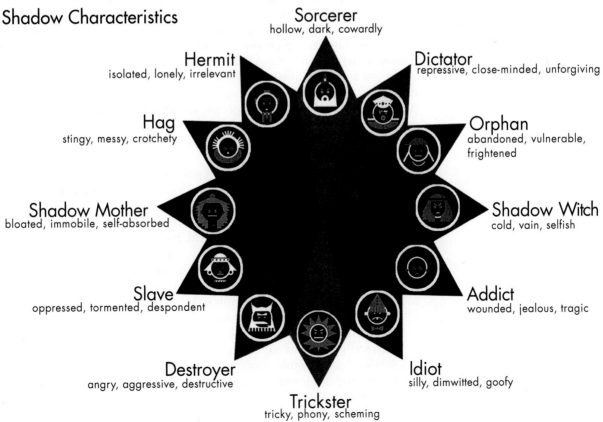

ECONsumer Behavior

Another trait relevant to consumer behavior is *frugality*. Frugal people deny short-term purchasing whims; they choose instead to resourcefully use what they already own. For example, this personality type tends to favor cost-saving measures such as timing showers and bringing leftovers from home to have for lunch at work.[16] Obviously during tough economic times many people reveal their "inner frugalista" as they search for ways to save money. Indeed, in 2008 Google searches for the term *frugality* increased by roughly 2500 percent. As of April 2009 the savings rate—or percentage of income consumers sock away rather than spend—climbed to almost 6 percent, which is a 14-year high. While many of us splurged on expensive cars or Jimmy Choo shoes (or both) in the past, many analysts predict that more of us will be frugal down the road, even if/when the economy improves. They expect to see us buy smaller houses and (gasp!) live within our means as we forsake heavy credit card debt. How accurate is this prediction? Maybe the answer depends on how many of us truly have frugal personality traits versus those who are merely "taking a break" until the economy improves.

● Linking measures of BrandAsset® Archetypes to more objective brand perception measures provides strong evidence to assure marketing decision makers that the changes Y&R recommends will achieve concrete business objectives.
● Measuring the health of a brand's personality can act as an "early warning" signal that a brand is in trouble, sometimes years in advance of marketplace indicators. This alerts marketing managers in enough time to tweak the brand as appropriate.[12]

Trait Theory

Popular online matchmaking services such as <u>match.com</u> and <u>eharmony.com</u> offer to create your "personality profile" and then hook you up with other members whose profiles are similar. This approach to personality focuses on the quantitative measurement of **personality traits**; the identifiable characteristics that define a person. For example, we distinguish people by the degree to which they are socially outgoing (the trait of *extroversion*)—Anne is an *introvert* (quiet and reserved), whereas her coworker Jackie is an *extrovert*.[13] Some research evidence suggests that ad messages that match how a person thinks about himself are more persuasive.[14]

Some specific traits relevant to consumer behavior include: *innovativeness* (the degree to which a person likes to try new things), *materialism* (the amount of emphasis a person places on acquiring and owning products, we discussed in Chapter 4), *self-consciousness* (the degree to which a person deliberately monitors and controls the image of the self that he or she projects to others, as we discussed in Chapter 5), and *need for cognition* (the degree to which a person likes to think about things and, by extension, expends the necessary effort to process brand information).[15]

Are You an Innie or an Outie?

One trait dimension that interests many consumer researchers distinguishes between those of us who consume to please others versus those who aren't very concerned about what others think. Sociologist David Reisman first introduced the terms *inner-directed* and *outer-directed* to our culture more than 30 years ago, and these ideas remain important today.[17] We think about individuals in terms of this distinction as well as larger social groups: As we'll see in Chapter 15, some cultures in general tend to stress individualism, whereas others reward those who try to fit in.

When researchers classified people as either **idiocentric** (an individualist orientation) or as **allocentric** (a group orientation), they identified numerous differences between these two personality types:[18]

● **Contentment**—Idiocentrics score higher than allocentrics on the statement "I am very satisfied with the way things are going in my life these days." They also are more satisfied with their financial situations.
● **Health consciousness**—Allocentrics are more likely to avoid foods that are high in cholesterol, have a high salt content, have additives in them, or have a high amount of fat.
● **Food preparation**—The kitchen is an allocentric's favorite room, and these types spend more time in meal preparation than do idiocentrics.
● **Workaholics**—Idiocentrics are more likely to say they work very hard most of the time, and they stay late at work more than do allocentrics.
● **Travel and entertainment**—Idiocentrics are more interested in other cultures and traveling than are allocentrics. They also are more likely to go to movies, art galleries, and museums. Compared to idiocentrics, allocentrics visit the public library more often and read more books. Allocentrics report working on crafts projects such as needlework and model building. However, idiocentric individuals are more likely to collect stamps and rocks, work on do-it-yourself projects, and take photos.[19]

Problems with Trait Theory in Consumer Research

Because consumer researchers categorize large numbers of consumers according to whether they exhibit various traits, we can apply this approach to segment markets. If a car manufacturer for example determines that drivers who fit a given trait profile prefer a car with certain features, it can use this information to great advantage. The notion that consumers buy products that are extensions of their personalities makes intuitive sense. As we'll see shortly, many marketing managers endorse this idea as they try to create *brand personalities* to appeal to different types of consumers.

Unfortunately, the use of standard personality trait measurements to predict product choices has met with mixed success at best. In general, marketing researchers simply have not been able to predict consumers' behaviors on the basis of measured personality traits. These are some logical explanations for these less-than-stellar results:[21]

- Many of the scales are not sufficiently valid or reliable; they do not adequately measure what they are supposed to measure, and their results may not be stable over time.
- Psychologists typically develop personality tests for specific populations (e.g., people who are mentally ill); marketers then "borrow" them to apply to a more general population where they have questionable relevance.
- Often marketers don't administer the tests under the appropriate conditions; people who are not properly trained may give them in a classroom or at a kitchen table.
- The researchers often make changes in the instruments to adapt them to their own situations, in the process they add or delete items and rename variables. These *ad hoc* changes dilute the validity of the measures and also reduce researchers' ability to compare results across consumer samples.
- Many trait scales measure gross, overall tendencies (e.g., emotional stability or introversion); marketers then use these results to make predictions about purchases of specific brands.
- In many cases, marketers ask consumers to respond to a large number of scales with no advance thought about how they will relate these measures to consumer behavior. The researchers then use a "shotgun approach," as they follow up on anything that happens to look interesting. As any statistician will tell you, this approach capitalizes on chance and can produce distorted results that may not surface in other studies.

Although marketing researchers largely abandoned the use of personality measures after many studies failed to yield meaningful results, some researchers have not given up on the early promise of this line of work. More recent efforts (mainly in Europe) try to benefit from past mistakes. Researchers use more specific measures of personality traits that they have reason to believe are relevant to economic behavior. They try to increase the validity of these measures, primarily when they include multiple measures of behavior rather than just a single personality scale. In addition, these researchers toned down their expectations of what personality traits can tell them about consumers. They now recognize that traits are only part of the solution; they have to incorporate personality data with information about people's social and economic conditions for it to be useful.[22] As a result, some more recent research has had better success at relating personality traits to such consumer behaviors as alcohol consumption among young men or shoppers' willingness to try new, healthier food products.[23]

Brand Personality

In 1886, a momentous event occurred in marketing history—the Quaker Oats man first appeared on boxes of hot cereal. Quakers had a reputation in nineteenth-century America for being shrewd but fair, and peddlers sometimes dressed as

Marketing Opportunity

According to research firm Mindset Media, personality traits are better predictors of the type of media consumers choose than demographic variables such as age, gender, and income. The agency developed a set of 21 personality traits such as leadership, openness, perfectionism, and dynamism. Based on a large-scale survey of over 5,000 consumers, here are some of its findings:[20]

- Heavy Web users rank high in *openness*. Light Web users rank high in *dogmatism*; they are socially conservative people who tend to look to a religious or moral authority for guidance.
- *Optimists* spend more time with newspapers than with any other medium. *Dynamic* people and *leaders* also are heavy users. *Bravados* (who are impulsive and prefer to leap before they look) are least likely to read the paper.
- People low in *dynamism* are likely to be heavy TV watchers, as are those who rank on the low end for openness and leadership. People who score high in *bravado* also watch a lot of tube. *Dynamic* people or those who rank high in *openness* and *leadership* are only half as likely to watch TV as the average person.
- *Dynamic* people are very heavy radio users; this medium allows them to multitask. On the other hand *introverts* are extremely light listeners.

Yes, colleges have brand personalities too—though as with other products these images aren't always an accurate (or desirable) reflection of the place. ESPN had to pull the plug on an advertising campaign for its collegiate basketball coverage after managers learned that Anomaly, the advertising agency it retained for the campaign, intended to recruit actors who would play the part of stereotypical students at numerous schools. The idea was to have the students stationed at a call center; they would phone consumers to convince them to watch their school play on TV. Here are just a few of the "brand personalities" a leaked memo described:

- U. Tennessee: " . . . a slutty girl who would hang out at the cowgirl hall of fame."
- Duke: " . . . a smart, with it, young white male. He's handsome. He's from money. He is, in short, the kind of guy everyone can't stand. He is the kind of guy everyone wants to be."
- Oklahoma: " . . . is awesome and he thinks everything is awesome. He's very enthusiastic about all things call center and all things life and he wants to share this contagious enthusiasm with everyone he meets. Wide-eyed, as naive as they come."
- Purdue: " . . . child prodigy. 14-year-old. Or open to an 18-year-old who looks 14. Aeronautical engineering. Wiz kid. Think McLovin from *Superbad*."
- Kansas: " . . . straight off the farm. However, he takes great pains to point out that Kansas is very cosmopolitan, as witnessed by their record, their burgeoning tech industry, and their hybrid corns (bonus: modified by fish genes!)."
- Villanova: " . . . the poor man's Duke—he's not quite as handsome, he's not quite as rich, he's not quite as dapper. After 2 or 3 beers though, who cares? . . . he's friendly enough."
- Pittsburgh: " . . . a tomboy. She obviously grew up in the neighborhood and isn't going to take any guff from anyone and she'll wallop you in the eye with a crowbar if you suggest different. So don't. Think Tina Fey type."
- Georgetown: " . . . a 4.36 GPA who's lived in 9 world-class cities, but all the time in her sister's shadow (her GPA is 4.37). She's sort of the female Duke, except most people like her. Think Reese Witherspoon."[32]

members of this religious group to cash in on their credibility. When the cereal company decided to "borrow" this imagery for its packaging, it recognized that its customers might make the same association.[24]

Today thousands of brands also borrow personality traits of individuals or groups to convey an image they want customers to form of them. A **brand personality** is the set of traits people attribute to a product as if it were a person. An advertising agency wrote the following memo to help it figure out how to portray one of its clients. Based on this description of the "client," can you guess who he is? "He is creative . . . unpredictable . . . an imp. . . . He not only walks and talks, but has the ability to sing, blush, wink, and work with little devices like pointers. . . . He can also play musical instruments. . . . His walking motion is characterized as a 'swagger.' . . . He is made of dough and has mass."[25] Of course, we all know today that packaging and other physical cues create a "personality" for a product (in this case, the Pillsbury Doughboy).

Many of the most recognizable figures in popular culture are spokescharacters for long-standing brands, such as the Jolly Green Giant, the Keebler Elves, Mr. Peanut, or Charlie the Tuna.[26] These personalities periodically get a makeover to keep their meanings current. For example, Bayer recently recast Speedy Alka-Seltzer: In the 1950s and later he was an all-around good guy who was ready to help with any sort of indigestion. Today he appears as a "wing man" for men in their 20s and 30s who tend to "overindulge" on food and drink. Do you know anyone who fits this description? The creative director on the campaign explained that the goal is to introduce Speedy as " . . . the good-times enabler who shows up whenever guys are being guys."[27]

Like people, brand personalities do change over time—whether marketers like Alka-Seltzer want them to or not. To give you an idea of how much things change, Americans ranked these brands as the most stylish in 1993:

1 Levi's
2 Nike
3 Bugle Boy
4 Guess
5 L.A. Gear

By 2008, these were the top five:

1 Victoria's Secret
2 Ralph Lauren
3 Nine West
4 Calvin Klein
5 Coach[28]

Forging a successful brand personality often is key to build brand loyalty, but it's not as easy to accomplish as it looks. One reason is that many consumers (particularly younger ones) have a very sensitive "BS detector" that alerts them when a brand doesn't live up to its claims or is somehow inauthentic. When this happens, the strategy may backfire as consumers rebel. They may create Web sites to attack the brand or post parodies that make fun of it on YouTube. One set of researchers terms this phenomenon a **Doppelgänger brand image** (one that looks like the original but is in fact a critique of it). For example, many consumers were immensely loyal to the Snapple brand until Quaker purchased it. These loyalists felt that Quaker had stripped the brand of its offbeat, grassroots sensibility; one shock jock renamed it "Crapple" on his radio show.[29]

Our feelings about a brand's personality are part of *brand equity*, which refers to the extent to which a consumer holds strong, favorable, and unique associations with a brand in memory—and the extent to which she or he is willing to pay more for the branded version of a product than for a nonbranded (generic) version.[30] Building strong brands is good business—if you don't believe it consider that, in a study of 760 *Fortune* 1,000 companies after the stock market took a nosedive in October 1997, the 20 strongest corporate brands (e.g., Microsoft, GE) actually gained in market value whereas the 20 weakest lost an average of $1 billion each.[31]

So, how do people think about brands? Advertisers are keenly interested in this question, and ad agencies often conduct extensive consumer research to help them understand how consumers will relate to a brand before they roll out campaigns. DDB Worldwide does a global study called "Brand Capital" of 14,000 consumers; Leo Burnett's "Brand Stock" project involves 28,000 interviews. WPP Group has "BrandZ" and Young & Rubicam uses its BrandAsset Valuator®. DDB's worldwide brand planning director observes, "We're not marketing just to isolated individuals. We're marketing to society. How I feel about a brand is directly related to and affected by how others feel about that brand."[33] Table 6.2 shows some of the things a marketer can do to influence consumers' perceptions of a brand's personality.

We use some personality dimensions to compare and contrast the perceived characteristics of brands in various product categories including these:[34]

- Old-fashioned, wholesome, traditional
- Surprising, lively, "with it"
- Serious, intelligent, efficient
- Glamorous, romantic, sexy
- Rugged, outdoorsy, tough, athletic

Indeed, consumers appear to have little trouble assigning personality qualities to all sorts of inanimate products, from personal care products to more mundane, functional ones—even kitchen appliances. Whirlpool's research showed that people saw its products as more feminine than they saw competing brands. When respondents were asked to imagine the appliance as a person, many of them pictured a modern, family-oriented woman living in the suburbs—attractive but not flashy. In contrast, they envisioned the company's Kitchen Aid brand as a modern professional woman who was glamorous, wealthy, and enjoyed classical music and the theater.[36]

A product that creates and communicates a distinctive brand personality stands out from its competition and inspires years of loyalty. However, personality analysis helps marketers identify a brand's weaknesses that have little to do with its functional qualities: Adidas asked kids in focus groups to imagine that the brand came to life and was at a party, and to tell what they would expect the brand to be doing there. The kids responded that Adidas would be hanging around the keg with its pals, talking about girls. Unfortunately, they also said Nike would *be with* the girls![37] The results reminded Adidas' brand managers they had some work to do. We

Marketing Pitfall

It looks like the marketers who came up with the logo for the 2012 Olympic Games in London won't be winning any gold medals. The British tabloids have been less than kind; one paper described the design as a "toileting monkey." An antilogo group got 50,000 people to sign a petition demanding that organizers change the design. Some marketing experts feel that this outcry is a good thing because most young Britons are very blasé about the prospect of the Olympics taking place in their backyard so this will get their blood pumping.[35]

TABLE 6.2	Brand Behaviors and Possible Personality Trait Inferences	
Brand Action		**Trait Inference**
Brand is repositioned several times or changes its slogan repeatedly		Flighty, schizophrenic
Brand uses continuing character in its advertising		Familiar, comfortable
Brand charges a high price and uses exclusive distribution		Snobbish, sophisticated
Brand frequently available on deal		Cheap, uncultured
Brand offers many line extensions		Versatile, adaptable
Brand sponsors show on PBS or uses recycled materials		Helpful, supportive
Brand features easy-to-use packaging or speaks at consumer's level in advertising		Warm, approachable
Brand offers seasonal clearance sale		Planful, practical
Brand offers five-year warranty or free customer hotline		Reliable, dependable

Source: Adapted from Susan Fournier, "A Consumer-Brand Relationship Framework for Strategic Brand Management," unpublished doctoral dissertation, University of Florida, 1994, Table 2.2, p. 24.

The logo for the 2012 Olympics in London has received a mixed response from the British public.
Source: Daniel Berehulak/Getty Images.

compare this process to **animism**, the common cultural practice whereby people give inanimate objects qualities that make them somehow alive.[38]

We tend to *anthropomorphize* objects, which happens when we give them human characteristics. We may think about a cartoon character or mythical creation as if it were a person and even assume it has human feelings. Again, think about familiar spokescharacters such as Charlie the Tuna, the Keebler Elves, or the Michelin Man, or consider the frustration some people feel when they come to believe their computer is smarter than they are or even that it's "conspiring" to make them crazy! In research for its client Sprint Business Services, Grey Advertising found that when customers imagined long-distance carriers as animals, they envisioned AT&T as a lion, MCI as a snake, and Sprint as a puma. Grey used these results to position Sprint as a company that could "help you do more business" rather than taking the more aggressive approach of its competitors.[39]

In a sense a brand personality is a statement about the brand's market position. Understanding this is crucial to marketing strategy, especially if consumers don't see the brand the way its makers intend them to and they must attempt to *reposition* the product (i.e., give it a personality makeover). That's the problem Volvo now faces; its cars are renowned for safety but drivers don't exactly see them as exciting or sexy. A safe and solid brand personality makes it hard to sell a racy convertible like the C70 model, so a British ad tries to change that perception with the tagline, "Lust, envy,

Personality Traits		Low	High
Sincerity	Down-to-earth Honest Wholesome Cheerful		
Excitement	Daring Spirited Imaginative Up-to-date		
Competence	Reliable Intelligent Successful		
Sophistication	Upper class Charming		
Ruggedness	Outdoorsy Tough		

A recent study found that consumers infer strong differences in a wine's "personality" based on the bottle's label design.

Source: Reprinted with permission from *Journal of Marketing*, published by the American Marketing Association, Ulrich R. Orth & Keven Malkewitz, May 2008, Vol. 72, p. 73.

jealousy. The dangers of a Volvo." Just as with people, however, you can only go so far to convince others that your personality has changed. Volvo has been trying to jazz up its image for years, but for the most part consumers aren't buying it. In an earlier attempt in the United Kingdom, the company paired action images like a Volvo pulling a helicopter off a cliff with the headline "Safe Sex"—but market research

The Zaltman Metaphor Elicitation Technique (ZMET) is one tool used to assess the strategic aspects of brand personality and is based on the premise that brands are expressed in terms of metaphors; that is, a representation of one thing in terms of another. These associations often are nonverbal, so the ZMET approach is based on a nonverbal representation of brands. Participants collect a minimum of twelve images representing their thoughts and feelings about a topic, and are interviewed in depth about the images and their feelings. Eventually, digital imaging techniques are used to create a collage summarizing these thoughts and feelings, and the person tells a story about the image created. This collage was created by a young woman to express her feelings about Tide detergent. It includes such images as a sunrise to represent freshness and a teddy bear that stands for the soft and comfortable way her laundry feels when she's done. However, the facial expressions also give a clue about her "fondness" for doing laundry!

Source: Harvard Graduate School of Business Administration.

showed people didn't believe the new image. As one brand consultant observed, "You get the sort of feeling you get when you see your grandparents trying to dance the latest dance. Slightly amused and embarrassed."[40]

OBJECTIVE

Why are consumers' lifestyles key to many marketing strategies?

Lifestyles and Psychographics

Jackie, Hank, and Anne strongly resemble one another demographically. They all were raised in middle-class households, have similar educational backgrounds, are about the same age, and work for the same company. However, as their leisure choices show it would be a big mistake to assume that their consumption choices are similar as well. Each person chooses products, services, and activities that help define a unique *lifestyle*. This section first explores how marketers approach the issue of lifestyle and then how they use information about these consumption choices to tailor products and communications to individual lifestyle segments.

Lifestyle: Who We Are, What We Do

In traditional societies, class, caste, village, or family largely dictate a person's consumption options. In a modern consumer society, however, each of us is free (at least within our budgets) to select the set of products, services, and activities that define our self and, in turn, create a social identity we communicate to others. One's choice of goods and services indeed makes a statement about who one is and about the types of people with whom one desires to identify—and even those whom we wish to avoid.

Lifestyle defines a pattern of consumption that reflects a person's choices of how to spend her time and money. In an economic sense, your lifestyle represents the way you elect to allocate income, both in terms of relative allocations to different products and services, and to specific alternatives within these categories.[41] Other somewhat similar distinctions describe consumers in terms of their broad patterns of consumption, such as those that differentiate people in terms of those who devote a high proportion of their total expenditures to food, or advanced technology, or to such information-intensive goods as entertainment and education.[42]

A *lifestyle marketing perspective* recognizes that people sort themselves into groups on the basis of the things they like to do, how they like to spend their leisure time, and how they choose to spend their disposable income.[44] The growing number of niche magazines and Web sites that cater to specialized interests reflects the spectrum of choices available to us in today's society. The downside of this is obvious to the newspaper industry; several major papers have already had to shut down their print editions because people consume most of their information online.

Colorado appeals to tourists who prefer to spend their leisure time in outdoor pursuits.
Source: Courtesy of MMG Worldwide.

An energy drink links itself to a lifestyle statement.
Source: Courtesy of Blue Media, Bliss Beverage.

These finely tuned choices do however create opportunities for market segmentation strategies that recognize the potency of a consumer's chosen lifestyle to determine both the types of products he or she purchases as well as the specific brands most likely to appeal to a certain lifestyle segment. For example, the popularity of wrestling (or at least watching it) creates other lifestyle marketing opportunities: The WWE (World Wrestling Entertainment) lends its name to the Socko Energy line of beverages that Wal-Mart sells. The drinks include "WWE Slammin' Citrus Powered by Socko" and "WWE Raw Attitude Powered by Socko," and, in turn, Bliss Beverages, which makes the beverages, will sponsor WWE pay-per-view matches. Now that's opening a can of lifestyle marketing Whoop-ass.[45]

OBJECTIVE

Why do psychographics go beyond simple demographics to help marketers understand and reach different consumer segments?

Lifestyles as Group Identities

Economic approaches are useful when we want to track changes in broad societal priorities, but they do not begin to embrace the symbolic nuances that separate lifestyle groups. Lifestyle is more than how we allocate our discretionary income. It is a statement about who one is in society and who one is not. Group identities, whether of hobbyists, athletes, or drug users, gel around forms of expressive symbolism. Social scientists use a number of terms to describe such self-definitions including *lifestyle, taste public, consumer group, symbolic community,* and *status culture.*[46]

Many people in similar social and economic circumstances may follow the same general consumption pattern. Still, each person also provides a unique "twist" to the pattern that allows him to inject some individuality into a lifestyle. For example, a "typical" college student (if there is such a thing) may dress much like his friends, hang out in the same places, and like the same foods yet still

The White Aryan Resistance is one of many hate groups with an active presence on the World Wide Web.
Source: Courtesy of White Aryan Resistance.

indulge a passion for marathon running, stamp collecting, or acid jazz that makes him unique.

Lifestyles are not set in stone. Unlike the deep-seated values we discussed in Chapter 4, people's tastes and preferences evolve over time. In fact, down the road we may laugh at consumption patterns we follow now. If you don't believe that,

The recreational-vehicle ad shown here demonstrates how a market segment is defined by a particular allocation of time and money to leisure activity. The ad's claim that the RV dealer has the product that "says you're you!" implies that dedicated RVers derive a significant portion of their self-identities from the activities associated with this lifestyle.
Source: Courtesy of Jayco Inc.

CB AS I SEE IT

Professor Lisa Bolton, *Penn State University*
Professor Americus Reed II, *The University of Pennsylvania*

The concept of "branding" is fundamental to marketing. It communicates benefits and establishes differentiation between product offerings in a category. However, sometimes the category label itself can have unforeseen consequences for consumers. Take the situation of consumers who seek to pursue a "healthy lifestyle"—especially those who are at high risk for consumer health complications (such as cholesterol and obesity).

We have been investigating how the labeling of health remedies affect healthy lifestyles. Imagine how consumers react to the same health remedy, labeled as either a "drug" or a "supplement." Do you think it will affect their plans to exercise and what they eat? If so, how?

When they consider a health remedy labeled as a "DRUG," consumers tend to discount the health risks associated with the remedy (such as health risks of high-fat foods). As a result, consumers are more likely to engage in risky behavior (such as high-fat eating). Ironically, this "boomerang" effect of drug marketing is more pronounced for consumers who are at greater risk (such as consumers with high cholesterol or obesity problems). In other words, the drug remedy hurts most the consumers it is designed to help!

At-risk consumers perceive the drug as a "get out of jail free card" that takes the risk out of risky behavior—in other words, bring on the cheesecake![47] Indeed, the boomerang effect has also been observed on actual behavior—for example, in one study consumers ate more M&M candy after a single exposure to a drug remedy advertisement.[48]

In contrast, the label "SUPPLEMENT" does not boomerang.[49] Consumers seem to realize that the label "means" that the remedy must be taken in conjunction with some kind of change in lifestyle (healthier eating, more exercise). Although supplements do not appear to undermine a healthy lifestyle, the researchers acknowledge other issues with supplement marketing (the category is somewhat notorious!) that merit future research.

Aside from the negative consequences for consumer health and welfare, the boomerang effect has important implications for marketers. Will a more responsible approach help to "undo" the boomerang effect on healthy behavior?

Marketing Opportunity

Companies have always exerted a big influence on the music industry as they sponsor tours and sign artists as endorsers. Their role as patrons of music continues to grow and in some cases it's getting hard to tell a hit song from a commercial jingle. The singer Estelle performed her hit song "American Boy" at the 2009 Grammy Awards with Kanye West—but she also appeared before the ceremony to introduce a new song called "Star." This wasn't part of the show—it was in a commercial for Crystal Light drink mix. Similarly, the Wm. Wrigley Jr. division of Mars signed Chris Brown to record a song, "Forever," that is actually a new version of the company's Doublemint gum jingle. In this case the company subsequently dropped Brown due to his legal problems; we'll talk more about the potential pitfalls of celebrity endorsers in Chapter 7.[51]

simply think back to what you and your friends wore 5 or 10 years ago—where *did* you find those clothes? Because people's attitudes regarding physical fitness, social activism, sex roles for men and women, the importance of home life and family, and so on do change, it is vital for marketers to continually monitor the social landscape to try to anticipate where these changes will lead.

OBJECTIVE
Why is identifying patterns of consumption superior to knowledge of individual purchases when a marketer crafts a lifestyle marketing strategy?

Products Are the Building Blocks of Lifestyles

Nike makes a lot of shoes and athletic apparel, but now the company wants to play an even bigger role in defining your lifestyle. It commissioned original workout music for its "Nike + Original Run" series you can buy at Apple's iTunes Music Store. It teamed up with Apple to offer the Nike + shoes that feature a built-in pocket under the insole for the Nike + iPod sensor that lets you track your run and set goals while listening to your favorite tunes. It's releasing other CDs featuring music and voice-over coaching in activities such as yoga, dance, and weight training.[50] At the running clubs its retail stores sponsor, Nike's staff keeps track of members' performances and hails members who log more than 100 miles.

At the Whole Foods supermarket in Seattle, shoppers take part in a "singles" night the first Friday of every month. The store's marketing staff organizes a wine tasting or sets out snacks in a room they use for cooking classes. Customers wear a red or blue ribbon to indicate whether they are looking for a male or a female

A unique lifestyle appeal for bathroom fixtures.
Source: Photograph courtesy of Kohler Co.

partner. REI offers training in kayaking and mountain biking at its stores; PetSmart and PETCO provide training classes for pet owners; and Cabela's, a hunting store, offers classes on "trout tactics" and gun cleaning.[52]

These are smart moves, especially when marketers encourage a sense of *community* among product users (think of the reasons you faithfully check your Facebook account). We often choose a product precisely because we associate it with a certain lifestyle. For this reason, lifestyle marketing strategies attempt to position a product by fitting it into an existing pattern of consumption and thus create a brand personality that is relevant to a variety of products and situations.

A goal of lifestyle marketing is to allow consumers to pursue their chosen ways to enjoy their lives and express their social identities. For this reason a key aspect of this strategy is to focus on people who use products in desirable social settings. The desire to associate a product with a social situation is a long-standing one for advertisers, whether they include the product in a round of golf, a family barbecue,

Figure 6.2 CONSUMPTION STYLE

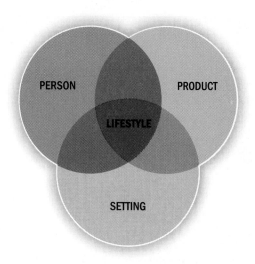

or a night at a glamorous club surrounded by the hip-hop elite.[53] Thus, people, products, and settings combine to express a *consumption style,* as Figure 6.2 diagrams.

We get a clearer picture of how people use products to define lifestyles when we see how they make choices in a variety of product categories. A lifestyle marketing perspective implies that we must look at *patterns of behavior* to understand consumers. As one study noted, "All goods carry meaning, but none by itself. . . . The meaning is in the relations between all the goods, just as music is in the relations marked out by the sounds and not in any one note."[54]

Indeed, many products and services do seem to "go together," usually because the same types of people tend to select them. In many cases, products do not seem

Interior designers rely on consumption constellations when they choose items to furnish a room. A decorating style involves integrating products from many different categories—such as appliances, furnishings, knick-knacks, and even artwork—into a unified whole that conveys a certain "look."
Source: Courtesy of General Electric.

Monogram, by GE. It solves the riddle of how to integrate the appliances into custom kitchen design.

No matter what design theme you choose, the one thing you don't have to worry about nowadays is how the appliances will look.

The Monogram line of built-in appliances now offers such an array of models that you have virtually infinite choice and options.

This year we add the first 36" built-in refrigerator that is trimless and completely cabinet friendly. The decorative door panels accept custom handles, so they co-ordinate with the pulls on your cabinets. Because there is no bottom air vent, the base of the cabinet can now extend across the bottom of the refrigerator. No other built-in refrigerator integrates so beautifully.

Monogram™ now offers a built-in convection wall oven that provides new technology for faster cooking and sleek flush design.

Our Component Cooktops continue to be the only ones that can be installed perpendicular or horizontal to the counter edge to form clusters in gas, electric, updraft and downdraft. And there's also a 5-burner gas cooktop.

The remarkable idea of getting everything from your dishwasher to your microwave from *one* manufacturer also simplifies the complex process of shopping and delivery. And when you buy Monogram, you buy the assurance of the appliance industry's most extensive network of factory service professionals.

Going one step further is the extraordinary GE Answer Center™ service on duty 24 hours a day *every* day of the year at 800.626.2000. We're there to help in any way. If you would like a brochure that tells you more about Monogram, and if you would like to know where you can see the line, please call.

Monogram, from GE. A synonym for the best in built-in appliances.

Monogram.™

to "make sense" if companion products don't accompany them (e.g., fast food and paper plates, or a suit and tie) or are incongruous in the presence of other products that have a very different personality (e.g., a Chippendale chair in a high-tech office or Lucky Strike cigarettes with a solid gold lighter).

Therefore, an important part of lifestyle marketing is to identify the set of products and services that consumers associate with a specific lifestyle. In fact, research evidence suggests that even a relatively unattractive product becomes more appealing when consumers link it with other products they do like.[55] The meshing of objects from many different categories to express a single lifestyle idea is at the heart of many consumption decisions—these include coordinating an outfit for a big date (shoes, garments, fragrance, etc.), decorating a room (tables, carpet, wallpaper, etc.), or designing a restaurant (menu, ambiance, waitperson uniforms, etc.). Many people today evaluate products not just in terms of function but also how well their design coordinates with other objects and furnishings. For example, Procter & Gamble's new line of Febreze fabric freshener, called Décor Collection, features a clear bottle with a simple botanical or raindrop design on the back panel. It has a removable wrapper that promises "a bottle so nicely designed" that it is "perfect to leave out in the bedroom or living room."[56]

Marketers who understand these cross-category relationships often pursue **co-branding strategies** where they team up with other companies to promote two or more items. For example, Wendy's and Procter & Gamble joined forces to offer Wendy's Custom Bean, a Folgers Gourmet Selection coffee that the restaurant chain says will become a centerpiece of its new breakfast menu.[57] Some marketers even match up their spokescharacters in ads; the Pillsbury Doughboy appeared in a commercial with the Sprint Guy to pitch cell phones, the lonely Maytag repairman was in an ad for the Chevrolet Impala, and the Taco Bell Chihuahua (now retired) showed up in a commercial for GEICO insurance.[58]

Product complementarity occurs when the symbolic meanings of different products relate to one another.[59] Consumers use these sets of products we call a **consumption constellation** to define, communicate, and perform social roles.[60] For example, we identified the American "yuppie" of the 1980s by such products as a Rolex watch, a BMW automobile, a Gucci briefcase, a squash racket, fresh pesto, white wine, and brie cheese. We find somewhat similar constellations for "Sloane Rangers" in the United Kingdom and "Bon Chic Bon Genres" in France. Although people today take pains to avoid being classified as yuppies, this social role had a major influence on defining cultural values and consumption priorities in the 1980s.[61] What consumption constellation might characterize you and your friends today?

Psychographics

When Cadillac introduced its Escalade sport utility vehicle, critics scoffed at the bizarre pairing of this old-line luxury brand with a truck. However, consumers quickly associated the vehicle with the hip-hop lifestyle. Artists such as Jennifer Lopez, Outkast, and Jay-Z referred to it in songs, and Jermaine Dupri proclaimed, "Gotta have me an Escalade." Three years later, Cadillac went even further when it rolled out its 18-foot Escalade EXT pickup with a sticker price of $50,000.

The Escalade brand manager describes the target customer for luxury pickups as a slightly earthier version of the SUV buyer. She says that although the two drivers may own $2 million homes next door to each other, the typical luxury SUV driver is about 50, has an MBA from Harvard, belongs to a golf club, maintains connections with his college friends, and works hard at keeping up with the Joneses. In contrast, the luxury pickup driver is roughly 5 years younger. He might have inherited his father's construction business, and he's been working since he was 18 years old. He may or may not have attended college, and unlike the SUV driver, he is absolutely still connected to his high school friends.[63]

NASCAR is a long-time proponent of cross-promotion as its drivers sport a sea of corporate logos on their uniforms.
Source: Jason Smith/Getty Images.

As this example shows, marketers often find it useful to develop products that appeal to different lifestyle groups—simply knowing a person's income doesn't predict whether he or she will drive a Cadillac Escalade SUV, pickup, or a Cadillac El Dorado sedan. As Jackie's, Hank's, and Anne's choices demonstrated, consumers can share the same demographic characteristics and still be very different people. For this reason, marketers need a way to "breathe life" into demographic data to really identify, understand, and target consumer segments that will share a set of preferences for their products and services.

Earlier in this chapter we discussed some of the differences in consumers' personalities that may influence their product choices. When marketers combine personality variables with knowledge of lifestyle preferences, they have a powerful lens they can focus on consumer segments. Adidas, for example, describes different types of shoe buyers in terms of lifestyles so that it can address the needs of segments such as *Gearheads* (hard-core, older runners who want high-performance shoes), *Popgirls* (teeny-boppers who hang out at the mall and wear Skechers), and *Fastidious Eclectus* (Bohemian, cutting-edge types who want hip, distinctive products).[64] It's fairly common for companies to divide up their customers along lifestyle dimensions and

NORESUND
estructura de cama
€119,00

DORMITORIOS COMO TÚ.

Redecora tu vida

label them to quickly communicate to their creative and strategy people just how to talk to different groups. For example, the makers of the popular Sigg water bottle that is available in many different designs actually choose from about 3,000 different concepts each year with specific customers in mind. These include the *Whole Foods Woman* who lives in a city, practices yoga, and buys organic produce; and the *Geek Chic Guy* who listens to Radiohead and wears vintage Converse sneakers.[65]

We call this approach **psychographics**, which involves the "use of psychological, sociological, and anthropological factors . . . to determine how the market is segmented by the propensity of groups within the market—and their reasons—to make a particular decision about a product, person, ideology, or otherwise hold an attitude or use a medium."[66]

Sigg water bottles are designed with specific types of users in mind.
Source: Bill Hogan/Chicago Tribune/Newscom.

Psychographics can help a marketer fine-tune its offerings to meet the needs of different segments. For example, the Best Buy consumer electronics chain decided to revamp its stores according to the types of customers they serve. The company identified five prototypical customers:

1 "Jill," a busy suburban mom who wants to talk about how electronics can help her family.
2 "Buzz," a focused, active younger male who likes to buy (and show off) the latest gadgets.
3 "Ray," a family man who likes practical technology.
4 "BB4B" (short for Best Buy for Business), a small employer.
5 "Barry," an affluent professional male who's likely to drop tens of thousands of dollars on a home theater system and who is an action-movie enthusiast.

The chain identifies the two most dominant customer types who patronize each of its outlets and plans accordingly. Store clerks receive hours of training to help them pick out the most likely category to which a customer belongs. They are told to label a shopper who says his family has a regular "movie night," as a "Ray" or "Jill" and to steer him or her toward home-theater equipment. Stores that cater to the "Jill" segment will feature play areas for kids. Instead of a booming bass beat, the soundtrack that plays in the background will be instrumental and children's music.[67]

The Roots of Psychographics

Marketers first developed psychographic research in the 1960s and 1970s to address the shortcomings of two other types of consumer research: motivational research and quantitative survey research. Recall that motivational research, which involves intensive, one-to-one interviews and projective tests, yields a lot of information about a few people. As we've seen, though, this information is often idiosyncratic and therefore it may not be very reliable. At the other extreme, quantitative survey research, or large-scale demographic surveys, yields only a little information about a lot of people. As some researchers observed, "The marketing manager who wanted to know why people ate the competitor's cornflakes was told '32 percent of the respondents said taste, 21 percent said flavor, 15 percent said texture, 10 percent said price, and 22 percent said don't know or no answer.'"[68]

Marketers use many psychographic variables to segment consumers, but all of these dimensions go beyond surface characteristics to understand consumers' motivations for purchasing and using products. Demographics allow us to describe *who* buys, but psychographics tells us *why* they do. A classic example involves a very popular Canadian advertising campaign for Molson Export beer that included insights from psychographic findings. The company's research showed that Molson's target customers tend to be like boys who never grew up, who were uncertain about the future, and who were intimidated by women's newfound freedoms. Accordingly, the ads featured a group of men, "Fred and the boys," whose get-togethers emphasize male companionship, protection against change, and the reassuring message that the beer "keeps on tasting great."[69]

How Do We Do a Psychographic Analysis?

Some early attempts at lifestyle segmentation "borrowed" standard psychological scales (that psychologists use to measure pathology or personality disturbances) and related test scores to product usage. As we saw earlier in the chapter, such efforts were largely disappointing. These tests were never intended to be related to everyday consumption activities, so they didn't do much to explain people's purchases. The technique is more effective when the marketers include variables that are more closely related to actual consumer behaviors. If you want to understand purchases of household cleaning products, you are better off asking people about their attitudes toward household cleanliness than to test for personality disorders!

Psychographic studies take several different forms:

- A **lifestyle profile** looks for items that differentiate between users and nonusers of a product.
- A **product-specific profile** identifies a target group and then profiles these consumers on product-relevant dimensions.
- A **general lifestyle segmentation** places a large sample of respondents into homogenous groups based on similarities of their overall preferences.
- A **product-specific segmentation study** tailors questions to a product category. For example, if a researcher wants to conduct research for a stomach medicine, she might rephrase the item, "I worry too much" as, "I get stomach problems if I worry too much." This allows her to more finely discriminate among users of competing brands.[70]

AIOs

Most contemporary psychographic research attempts to group consumers according to some combination of three categories of variables—activities, interests, and opinions—that we call **AIOs**. Using data from large samples, marketers create profiles of customers who resemble each other in terms of their activities and patterns of product usage.[72] Table 6.3 lists commonly used AIO dimensions.

To group consumers into AIO categories, researchers give respondents a long list of statements and ask them to indicate how much they agree with each one. Thus, we can "boil down" a person's lifestyle by discovering how he spends his time, what he finds interesting and important, and how he views himself and the world around him.

Typically, the first step in conducting a psychographic analysis is to determine which lifestyle segments yield the bulk of customers for a particular product. According to a very general rule of thumb that marketers call the **80/20 rule**—only

Marketing Pitfall

Target Corp. decided to cancel a survey that would have let the retailer compare the psyches of its customers to those of rival Wal-Mart shoppers. Some people complained to the company that items were too personal and inappropriate, including statements such as "My partner is likely to reject me at some point unless I am better (smarter, better looking, etc.) than any other potential mate" and "I could disappear from the face of the earth and no one would notice."[71]

TABLE 6.3	Lifestyle Dimensions		
Activities	**Interests**	**Opinions**	**Demographics**
Work	Family	Themselves	Age
Hobbies	Home	Social issues	Education
Social events	Job	Politics	Income
Vacation	Community	Business	Occupation
Entertainment	Recreation	Economics	Family size
Club membership	Fashion	Education	Dwelling
Community	Food	Products	Geography
Shopping	Media	Future	City size
Sports	Achievements	Culture	Stage in life cycle

Source: William D. Wells and Douglas J. Tigert, "Activities, Interests, and Opinions," *Journal of Advertising Research* 11 (August 1971): 27–35. © 1971 by The Advertising Research Foundation. Used with permission.

20 percent of a product's users account for 80 percent of the volume of product a company sells. Researchers attempt to determine who uses the brand and try to isolate heavy, moderate, and light users. They also look for patterns of usage and attitudes toward the product. In many cases, only a few lifestyle segments account for the majority of brand users.[73] Marketers primarily target these heavy users, even though they may constitute a relatively small number of total users.

After marketers identify and understand their heavy users, they consider more specifically how these customers relate to the brand. Heavy users may have quite different reasons for using the product; often we can further subdivide them in terms of the *benefits* they derive from using the product or service. For instance, marketers at the beginning of the walking-shoe craze assumed that all purchasers were basically burned-out joggers. Subsequent psychographic research showed that there were actually several different groups of "walkers," ranging from those who walk to get to work to those who walk for fun. This realization resulted in shoes that manufacturers aimed at different segments, from Footjoy Joy-Walkers to Nike Healthwalkers.

How Do We Use Psychographic Data?
Marketers use the results of these studies in several ways:

- **To define the target market**—This information allows the marketer to go beyond simple demographic or product usage descriptions (e.g., middle-aged men or frequent users).
- **To create a new view of the market**—Sometimes marketers create their strategies with a "typical" customer in mind. This stereotype may not be correct because the actual customer may not match these assumptions. For example, marketers of a face cream for women were surprised to find that older, widowed women were their heavy users rather than the younger, sociable women to whom they were pitching their appeals.
- **To position the product**—Psychographic information can allow the marketer to emphasize features of the product that fit in with a person's lifestyle. A company that wants to target people whose lifestyle profiles show a high need to be around other people might focus on its product's ability to help meet this social need.
- **To better communicate product attributes**—Psychographic information can offer very useful input to advertising creatives who must communicate something about the product. The artist or copywriter obtains a much richer mental image

Model shown is Honda Civic Hybrid 1.4 IMA in mpg (L/100km): Urban 54.3 (5.2), Extra Urban 65.7 (4.3), Combined 61.4 (4.6). CO2 Emissions 109 g/km.

In this British ad, Honda targets eco-conscious consumers.
Source: Courtesy of Honda/Wieden & Kennedy, London.

of the target consumer than she can simply by looking at dry statistics. For example, research Schlitz beer conducted found that heavy beer drinkers tended to feel that life's pleasures were few and far between. In response the brewer developed commercials with the tagline, "You only go around once, so reach for all the gusto you can."[74]

- **To develop product strategy**—Understanding how a product fits, or does not fit, into consumers' lifestyles allows the marketer to identify new product opportunities, chart media strategies, and create environments most consistent and harmonious with these consumption patterns.

- **To market social and political issues**—Psychographic segmentation can be an important tool in political campaigns and policy makers also can employ the technique to find commonalities among consumers who engage in destructive behaviors, such as drug use or excessive gambling. A psychographic study of men aged 18 to 24 who drink and drive highlights the potential for this perspective to help in the eradication of harmful behaviors. Researchers divided this segment into four groups: "good timers," "well adjusted," "nerds," and "problem kids." They found that one group in particular—"good timers"—is more likely to believe that it is fun to be drunk, that the chances of having an accident while driving drunk are low, and that drinking increases one's appeal to the opposite sex. Because the study showed that this group is also the most likely to drink at rock concerts and parties, is most likely to watch MTV, and tends to listen to album-oriented rock radio stations, reaching "good timers" with a prevention campaign became easier.[75]

Psychographic Segmentation Typologies

Marketers constantly search for new insights so they can identify and reach groups of consumers united by common lifestyles. To meet this need, many research companies and advertising agencies develop their own *segmentation typologies*. Respondents answer a battery of questions that allow the researchers to cluster them into a set of distinct lifestyle groups. The questions usually include a mixture of AIOs plus other items relating to feelings about specific brands, favorite celebrities, and media preferences. Companies that want to learn more about their customers and potential customers then buy one or more of these systems for their own use.

At least at a superficial level, many of these typologies are fairly similar to one another; they usually divide the population into roughly five to eight segments. Researchers give each cluster a descriptive name, and clients receive a profile of "typical" members. Unfortunately, it is often difficult to compare or evaluate different typologies because the methods and data that analysts use to devise these systems frequently are *proprietary;* that is, the company owns the information and does not share its findings with outsiders. Let's review a few typical approaches to classifying consumers in terms of lifestyles.

VALS2™

One well-known segmentation system is *The Values and Lifestyles System* (**VALS2™**) that SRI International developed. SRI built the original VALS™ system on consumers' extent of agreement with various social issues such as abortion rights. After about 10 years, SRI discovered that the social issues it used to categorize consumers were not as predictive of consumer behavior as they once had been. SRI searched for a more powerful way to segment consumers, and the company discovered that certain lifestyle indicators such as "I like a lot of excitement in my life" were better predictors of purchase behavior than the degree to which a person agreed or disagreed with a social value.

The current VALS2™ system uses a battery of 39 items (35 psychological and 4 demographic) to divide U.S. adults into groups, each with distinctive characteristics. As Figure 6.3 shows, the typology arranges groups vertically by their resources (including such factors as income, education, energy levels, and eagerness to buy) and horizontally by self-orientation.

Three self-orientations comprise the horizontal dimension. Consumers with an *Ideals* orientation rely on a belief system to make purchase decisions, and they are not concerned with the views of others. People with an *Achievement* orientation are more competitive; they take into account what their peers will think about their decisions and how these choices will reflect on them. Finally, those with a *Self-Expression* orientation are more concerned with the emotional aspects of purchases and the satisfaction they will personally receive from products and services.

- **Innovators**—the top VALS2™ group, are successful consumers with many resources. This group is concerned with social issues and is open to change.

The next three groups also have sufficient resources but differ in their outlooks on life:[76]

- **Thinkers**—are satisfied, reflective, and comfortable.
- **Achievers**—are career oriented and prefer predictability to risk or self-discovery.
- **Experiencers**—are impulsive, young, and enjoy offbeat or risky experiences.

The next four groups have fewer resources:

- **Believers**—have strong principles and favor proven brands.
- **Strivers**—are similar to Achievers but have fewer resources. They are very concerned about the approval of others.
- **Makers**—are action oriented and tend to focus their energies on self-sufficiency. They will often be found working on their cars, canning their own vegetables, or building their own houses.
- **Strugglers**—are at the bottom of the economic ladder. They are most concerned with meeting the needs of the moment and have limited ability to acquire anything beyond the basic goods needed for survival.

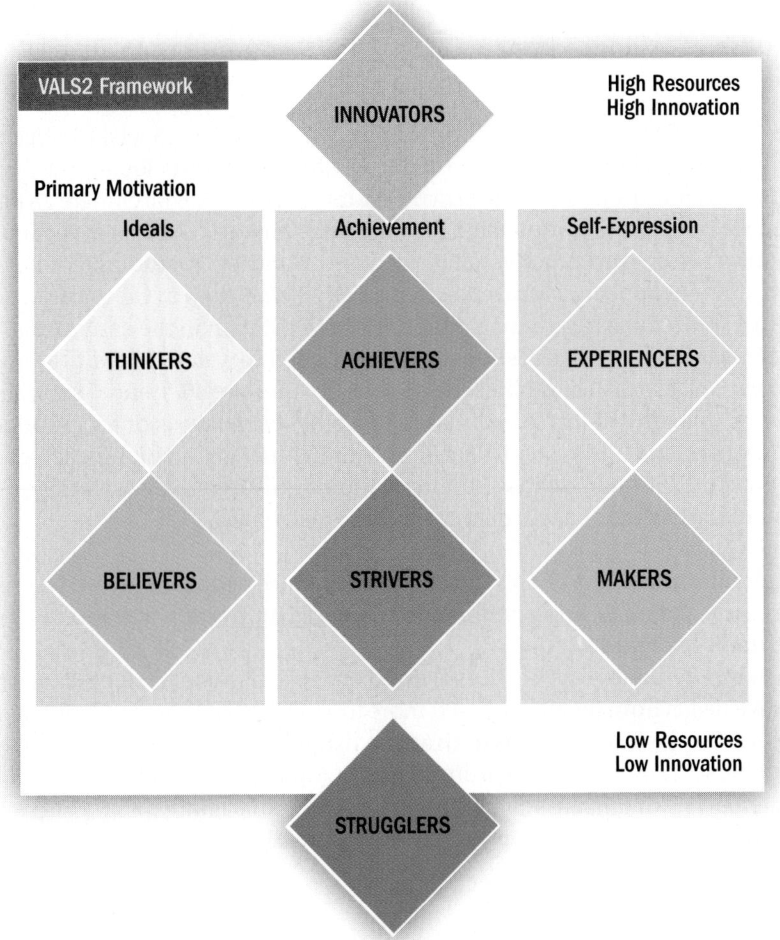

Figure 6.3 VALS2™.
Source: SRI International.

The VALS2™ system is a useful way to understand people like Jackie and Hank. SRI estimates that 12 percent of American adults are thrill seekers, who tend to fall into the system's Experiencer category and who are likely to agree with statements such as, "I like a lot of excitement in my life" and "I like to try new things." Experiencers like to break the rules, and extreme sports such as sky surfing or bungee jumping attract them. Not too surprisingly, one-third of consumers aged 18 to 34 belong in this category, so it has attracted the interest of many marketers who are trying to appeal to younger people. For example, VALS2™ helped Isuzu market its Rodeo sport utility vehicle by focusing on Experiencers, many of whom believe it is fun to break rules in ways that do not endanger others. Isuzu positioned the Rodeo as a vehicle that lets a driver do just that. It created advertising to support this idea by showing kids jumping in mud puddles, running with scissors, and coloring outside the lines.[77] Isuzu sales increased significantly after this campaign. If you want to see what VALS type you are, go to sric-bi.com/VALS/presurvey.shtml.

Global MOSAIC

The British firm Experian developed Global MOSAIC. This system analyzes consumers in 19 countries including Australia, South Africa, and Peru. Experian boiled down 631 different MOSAIC types to come up with 14 common lifestyles, classifying 800 million people who produce roughly 80 percent of the world's GDP. This allows marketers to identify consumers who share similar tastes around the world.

An Experian executive explained, "The yuppie on the Upper East Side of New York has more in common with a yuppie in Stockholm than a downscale person in Brooklyn."

RISC

Since 1978, the Paris-based organization Research Institute on Social Change (RISC) has conducted international measurements of lifestyles and sociocultural change in more than 40 countries.[78] Its long-term measurement of the social climate around the world makes it possible to anticipate future change and to identify signs of change in one country before it eventually spreads to other countries. For example, concern for the environment appeared in Sweden in the early 1970s, then in Germany in the late 1970s, in France in the beginning of the 1980s, and in Spain in the early 1990s.

RISC asks a battery of questions to identify people's values and attitudes about a wide range of issues. It combines the answers to measure 40 "trends" such as "spirituality" or "blurring of the sexes." Based on statistical analysis of the respondent's score on each trend, the system locates each individual in a virtual space described by three axes. RISC then divides the population into 10 segments referring to their position in this virtual space. The three axes are as follows:

1 **Exploration/stability**— The vertical axis separates people motivated by change, creativity, volatility, and openness from people motivated by stability, familiarity, tradition, and structure.
2 **Social/individual**—The horizontal axis distinguishes people oriented toward collective needs from people oriented more toward satisfaction of individual needs.
3 **Global/local**—The third axis indicates a distance between people who are comfortable with unfamiliar environments, multiple loose connections, and large-scale networking from people preferring close-knit relationships and a desire for the elements of life to be connected in a predictable manner.

Geodemography

Geodemography refers to analytical techniques that combine data on consumer expenditures and other socioeconomic factors with geographic information about the areas in which people live, in order to identify consumers who share common con-

Geodemography is based on the assumption that "birds of a feather flock together." A frat house next to an all-girls' school means one of them needs to relocate, according to the moving company that created this ad.
Source: Courtesy of 86 The Onion Ad Agency.

sumption patterns. Researchers base this approach on the common assumption that "birds of a feather flock together"—people who have similar needs and tastes also tend to live near one another, so it should be possible to locate "pockets" of like-minded people who marketers can reach more economically by direct mail and other methods. For example, a marketer who wants to reach white, single consumers who are college educated and tend to be fiscally conservative may find that it is more efficient to mail catalogs to zip codes 20770 (Greenbelt, MD) and 90277 (Redondo Beach, CA) than to adjoining areas in either Maryland or California, where there are fewer consumers who exhibit these characteristics.

Food Cultures

Are you what you eat? One of the most obvious lifestyle domains that our place of residence influences is food. Many marketers regionalize their offerings to appeal to different tastes, as for example, when Campbell's Soup puts a stronger dose of jalapeño pepper in its nacho cheese soup in the Southwest. In Philadelphia, a serving of Philadelphia cream cheese contains 14 percent more calories than the same size serving in Milan. A jar of Hellmann's mayonnaise you purchase in London will have half the saturated fat of the one you buy in Chicago. And a Kellogg's All-Bran bar you buy in the United States has nearly three times the sodium as one the company sells across the border in Mexico.

Our food preferences say a lot about us, and many of our likes and dislikes are learned responses to dishes that people who matter to us value—or don't value. Saudis consider sheep eyeballs a delicacy, whereas the Chinese prize a good snake dish. People in Spain and Portugal consume 10 times the amount of fresh fish as those in Austria or the United Kingdom, and the consumption of pork in Denmark is about 10 times that of France. Not surprisingly, the Irish eat a lot of potatoes—but not as many as the Greeks. In contrast, Italians avoid the tuber; instead they consume approximately four times more pasta per person than the Swiss, who are the second most avid spaghetti eaters.[79]

A **food culture** is a pattern of food and beverage consumption that reflects the values of a social group. Because these patterns vary so dramatically, food companies often find it rough going when they try to standardize their recipes. Sometimes these preferences are based on tastes and traditions, but in other cases people in other countries differ in terms of their focus on health. In China, Cadbury Schweppes PLC makes its Cadbury milk chocolate less milky and less sweet compared with that in the United Kingdom to suit the low-dairy diet of most Chinese consumers, whereas Kraft adds calcium to the Ritz crackers it sells in China to underscore the Chinese government's efforts to get its citizens to eat more calcium. Unilever actually had to reduce the size of its Magnum chocolate-covered ice cream bars sold in China because consumers there were more health-conscious than Europeans and resisted the bigger bar.

Our food preferences say a lot about our lifestyles and values.
Source: Courtesy of Saskatoon Restaurant, Greenville, SC.

CB AS I LIVE IT

Rochelle Affias, *University of Wisconsin–Madison*

*I*f what they say is true, that you are what you eat, then I am a bull's you-know-what. I am an entire shrimp (eyes, tail, shell, and all). I am pancakes, pancakes, and more pancakes. And I am four hot dogs, a heaping cup of orzo rice smothered in tomato sauce, a Mediterranean salad, a loaf of fresh bread, a whole rotisserie chicken, and a yogurt. Since moments define our memories and memories become our stories, I'd like to share a bit of one with you. My experience living abroad for a semester in Granada, Spain, helped me understand how a *food culture* truly reflects the values and perceptions of social groups and societies.

"I'll try anything once." It's a personal motto. So, off I went to Spain, ready to try everything. The first day living with my host family I realized I was in for a whole ton, both literally and figuratively. Wanting to make me feel welcome, my family put together the largest lunch I'd ever seen in my life (see journal entry that follows). After I'd made a substantial dent in my lunch, between the unbuttoning of my pants and the gasping for air, I embarked on the five-month learning lesson that led me to my understanding of how a food culture influences both the decisions of consumers and marketers alike. A food culture, as defined in the text, embodies the values of a society. In Spain, as I began to learn, the values reflected by this culture include a relaxed and carefree lifestyle, the importance of family and relationships, and the desire to *put on a show* at all times.

It wasn't just the obvious differences in food timing, preparation, and consuming that surprised me, but rather a number of subtle differences embedded within the cultures of my upbringing in the United States and my journey abroad that aided in my understanding of the Spanish food culture. I learned that almost any type of meat can be cured (and hung on the wall in kitchens and bars alike), I learned that Spaniards keep pots and pans in their ovens because baking never happens (the same reason it is almost impossible to find chocolate chips in a grocery store or market), I learned the difference between a *sandwich* (Spanish-American version of a snack on white, sliced bread) and a *bocadillo* (a REAL Spanish sandwich on a full loaf of bread), I learned that you don't eat the eyes, shell, nor tails of shrimp—rather using your fingers to peel these off is acceptable. I learned that yogurt and fruit are considered desserts, while donuts and muffins are considered breakfast. I learned that if I taught my señora how to make something (pancakes, for example) she would assume that I loved them, making them for every subsequent meal. And finally I learned that, unlike many Spaniards, I do not find that a bull's you-know-what nor blood sausage can make my mouth water in the same way the thought of ice cream on a hot, summer day ever could.

A food culture needs to be understood and embraced by marketers in order to successfully modify a product to appeal to consumers across cultural borders. I realize that being immersed in a culture different from my own helped me understand why it is vital for marketers to recognize cultural differences and use this understanding to adapt products to the lifestyles and values of their international and regional customers. In an age of globalization, understanding and adapting a product to a certain food culture is absolutely necessary for success. Whether it is a McDonald's in Saudi Arabia or one in Germany, being able to understand the food culture of these countries makes the golden arches popular across the world. Since Saudi Arabia is a country with a strong Islamic influence, you won't find pork on their menu, however you will find beer on every McDonald's menu in Germany. It is only through experience and understanding that marketers are able to modify and effectively mold products to appeal to a host of different cultures. Without the firsthand knowledge and experience that came out of my five months of living abroad, I would still not understand the food culture of Spain. My "I'll try anything once" philosophy is exactly what marketers need to embrace when delving into other cultures. Throw anything at me, and I'll gladly try it. Either I'll like it, or I'll learn from it.

This is my **food culture** experience...
A semester abroad in Granada, Spain

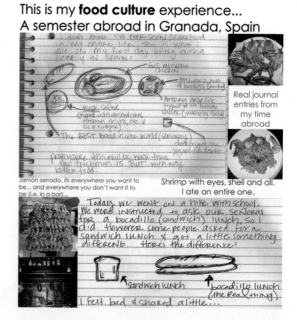

Real journal entries from my time abroad

Jamón serrado, its everywhere you want to be... and everywhere you don't want it to be (i.e. in a bar)...

Shrimp with eyes, shell and all. I ate an entire one.

Figure 6.4 EUROPEAN FOOD CULTURES

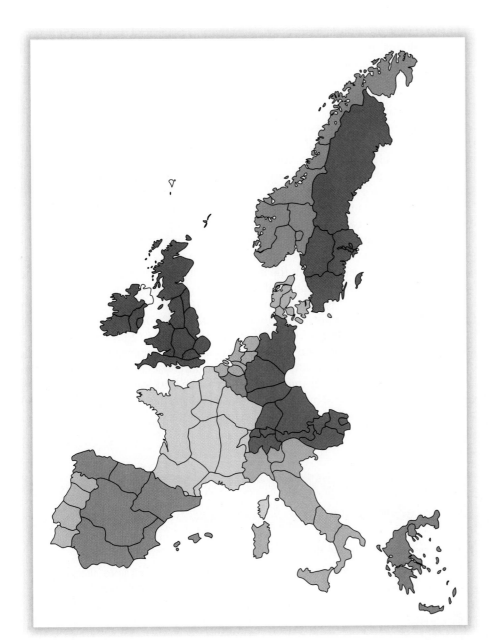

As Figure 6.4 shows, a large-scale analysis of food cultures in 15 European countries revealed 12 distinct food cultures, many of which parallel national or linguistic borders. For example, the study characterized the French/French-Swiss, Wallonian, and Italian cultures by the importance of the sensory pleasure and high consumption of red wine; the Germanic cluster of countries exhibit a high degree of health consciousness; the Portuguese and Greek food cultures show relatively traditional eating patterns with a fascination for new "global" food; the Norwegian and Danish food cultures are unique in their openness to convenience products (and, for the Danes, also for the love of beer); and it distinguishes the British and Irish by their extraordinary desire for sweets and tea.[80]

PRIZM

One popular clustering technique is the **PRIZM NE** (PRIZM stands for Potential Rating Index by Zip Market) system by Claritas, Inc. This system classifies every U.S. zip code into 1 of 66 categories, ranging from the most affluent "Blue-Blood Estates"

More than 27 million people have taken a test on <u>RealAge.com</u> that promises to take years off your age. The test includes about 150 questions about lifestyle and family history and then it tells you your "biological age," which is how much older or younger your lifestyle makes you (e.g., stress, exercise, eating habits). Then the site delivers recommendations to take years off your age. Here's the hitch: The site makes money because it sells responses to pharmaceutical firms that contact members to suggest drug solutions to their problems. Companies including Pfizer, Novartis, and GlaxoSmithKline can learn whether a respondent takes antidepressants, how sexually active they are, or if they have a happy marriage. They can even notify a person that his responses indicate the symptoms of a disease before he gets a diagnosis from his doctor. The company does state that " . . . we will share your personal data with third parties to fulfill the services that you have asked us to provide to you," and you must agree to become a member before you get added to their database. Still, critics claim that consumers join without understanding this process. According to an analyst at one public interest group, "[The company] can create a group of people, and hit them up and create anxiety even though the person does not have a diagnosis."[85]

to the least well-off "Public Assistance."[81] It terms a resident of Southern California "Money & Brains" if she lives in Encino (zip code 91316), whereas someone living in Sherman Oaks (zip code 91423) is a "Young Influential."[82] Claritas updated the system from its original set of 40 clusters to reflect the growing ethnic and economic diversity of the United States; some new clusters include "American Dreams," "Kids & Cul-de-Sacs," and "Young Literati."[83]

Residents of different clusters display marked differences in their consumption of products, from annuities to Ziploc bags. The system also ranks these groupings by income, home value, and occupation (i.e., a rough index of social class) on a ZQ (Zip Quality) scale. Table 6.4 provides an idea of how dramatically different the consumption patterns of two clusters can be. This table compares consumption data for "Furs & Station Wagons," the third-highest-ranking cluster, with "Tobacco Roads," the third-lowest. You can check out your own zip code at <u>MyBestSegments.com</u>.[84]

Although consumers in two very different clusters may purchase a product at an equivalent rate, these similarities end when we take their other purchases into account. These differences highlight the importance of going beyond simple product-category purchase data and demographics to really understand a market (remember the earlier discussion of product complementarity). For example, people in "Urban Gold Coast," "Money & Brains," and "Blue-Blood Estates" communities buy a lot of high-quality binoculars, but so do those in the "Grain Belt," "New Homesteaders," and "Agri-Business" clusters. The difference is that the former groups use the binoculars to watch birds and other wildlife, whereas the latter use them to help line up the animals in their gun sights. Furthermore, whereas the bird watchers do a lot of foreign travel, listen to classical music, and host cocktail parties, the bird hunters travel by bus, like country music, and belong to veterans' clubs.

TABLE 6.4 A Comparison of Two PRIZM Clusters

Furs & Station Wagons (ZQ3)		Tobacco Roads (ZQ38)	
New money, parents in 40s and 50s		Racially mixed farm towns in the South	
Newly built subdivisions with tennis courts, swimming pools, gardens		Small downtowns with thrift shops, diners, and laundromats; shanty-type homes without indoor plumbing	
Sample neighborhoods:		Sample neighborhoods:	
Plano, TX (75075)		Belzoni, MI (39038)	
Dunwoody, GA (30338)		Warrenton, NC (27589)	
Needham, MA (02192)		Gates, VA (27937)	
High Usage	**Low Usage**	**High Usage**	**Low Usage**
Country clubs	Motorcycles	Travel by bus	Knitting
Wine by the case	Laxatives	Asthma relief remedies	Live theater
Lawn furniture	Nonfilter cigarettes	Malt liquors	Smoke detectors
Gourmet magazine	Chewing tobacco	*Grit* magazine	*Ms.* magazine
BMW 5 Series	*Hunting* magazine	Pregnancy tests	Ferraris
Rye bread	Chevrolet Chevettes	Pontiac Bonnevilles	Whole-wheat bread
Natural cold cereal	Canned stews	Shortening	Mexican foods

Note: Usage rates as indexed to average consumption across all 40 clusters.
Source: "A Comparison of Two Prizm Clusters" from *The Clustering of America* by Michael J. Weiss. Copyright © 1988 by Michael J. Weiss. Reprinted by permission of the Sagalyn Literacy Agency.

Behavioral Targeting

The latest and hottest extension of lifestyle marketing is **behavioral targeting**, where e-commerce marketers serve up customized ads on Web sites or cable TV stations based on a customer's prior activity.[86] A long-term study Comcast conducted reported that people who lived in households that received targeted ads were about one-third less likely to change the channel than those who were shown traditional ads.[87] Customized messaging continues to entice advertisers; CBS Mobile recently announced a partnership with the social networking service Loopt to track participating families on their cell phones—the idea is to tailor promotions to consumers so specifically that they can receive special offers as they walk by specific stores and restaurants.[88]

Some critics feel behavioral targeting is a mixed blessing, because it implies that big companies track where we go so this threatens our privacy. In a few cases protests by privacy advocates have been strong enough to cause media companies to reverse course. For example, Denver-based Wide Open West stopped its plans to use NebuAd's software that tracks where customers surf on the Web and subdivides them by their browsing habits. If you've searched for "male enhancement products" within the last 30 days the software might group you with others who have done the same so that online advertisers can reach you. Proponents of these technologies argue that the data they collect is anonymous and can't be traced back to individuals. They also intend to notify customers that they track their surfing and to give them the choice to opt out of the service.[89]

Indeed, there are important privacy issues still to be resolved, but interestingly many consumers seem more than happy to trade off some of their personal

This digital billboard is equipped with a camera that gathers details on passersby; it displays customized messages depending on the characteristics it observes.
Source: Hiroko Masuike/Redux Pictures.

information in exchange for information they consider more useful to them. A 2006 survey on this issue reported that 57 percent of the consumers it polled say they are willing to provide demographic information in exchange for a personalized online experience. And three-quarters of those involved in an online social network felt that this process would improve their experience because it would introduce them to others who share their tastes and interests. However, a majority still express concern about the security of their personal data online.[90]

CHAPTER SUMMARY

Now that you have finished reading this chapter you should understand why:

 A consumer's personality influences the way he responds to marketing stimuli, but efforts to use this information in marketing contexts meet with mixed results.

The concept of *personality* refers to a person's unique psychological makeup and how it consistently influences the way a person responds to her environment. Marketing strategies based on personality differences have met with mixed success, partly because of the way researchers have measured and applied these differences in *personality traits* to consumption contexts. Some analysts try to understand underlying differences in small samples of consumers by employing techniques based on Freudian psychology and variations of this perspective, whereas others have tried to assess these dimensions more objectively in large samples using sophisticated, quantitative techniques.

 Consumers' lifestyles are key to many marketing strategies.

A consumer's *lifestyle* refers to the ways she chooses to spend time and money and how her consumption choices reflect these values and tastes. Lifestyle research is useful to track societal consumption preferences and also to position specific products and services to different segments. Marketers segment based on lifestyle differences; they often group consumers in terms of their AIOs (activities, interests, and opinions).

 Psychographics go beyond simple demographics in helping marketers understand and reach different consumer segments.

Psychographic techniques classify consumers in terms of psychological, subjective variables in addition to observable characteristics (demographics). Marketers have developed a variety of systems, such as VALS, to identify consumer "types" and to differentiate them in terms of their brand or product preferences, media usage, leisure time activities, and attitudes toward broad issues such as politics and religion.

 Identifying patterns of consumption can be superior to knowledge of individual purchases when organizations craft a lifestyle marketing strategy.

We associate interrelated sets of products and activities with social roles to form *consumption constellations*. People often purchase a product or service because they associate it with a *constellation* that, in turn, they link to a lifestyle they find desirable. *Geodemography* involves a set of techniques that use geographical and demographic data to identify clusters of consumers with similar psychographic characteristics.

KEY TERMS

80/20 rule, 237
AIOs, 237
Allocentric, 220
Animism, 224
Archetypes, 218
Behavioral targeting, 247
Brand personality, 222
Co-branding strategies, 233
Consumption constellation, 233

Doppelgänger brand image, 222
Ego, 214
Food culture, 243
Geodemography, 242
Id, 214
Idiocentric, 220
Lifestyle, 227
Motivational research, 216
Personality, 214

Personality traits, 220
Pleasure principle, 214
PRIZM NE, 245
Product complementarity, 233
Psychographics, 235
Reality principle, 214
Superego, 214
VALS2™, 240

REVIEW

1 Describe the id, ego, and superego and tell how they work together according to Freudian theory.
2 What is motivational research? Give an example of a marketing study that used this approach.
3 Describe three personality traits relevant to marketers.
4 Contrast idiocentrics and allocentrics.
5 List three problems when we apply trait theory to marketing contexts.
6 Define a brand personality and give two examples.
7 How does lifestyle differ from income?

8 What is the basic philosophy behind a lifestyle marketing strategy?
9 Define psychographics, and describe three ways marketers can use it.
10 What are three specific kinds of AIOs?
11 What is VALS2™, and how do marketers use it?
12 Alcohol drinkers vary sharply in terms of the number of drinks they may consume, from those who occasionally have one at a cocktail party to regular imbibers. Explain how the 80/20 rule applies to this product category.

CONSUMER BEHAVIOR CHALLENGE

■ DISCUSS

1 What consumption constellation might characterize you and your friends today?
2 Geodemographic techniques assume that people who live in the same neighborhood have other things in common as well. Why do they make this assumption, and how accurate is it?
3 Wireless devices have quickly become an indispensable part of many consumers' lifestyles. How do you view this rapid transition to a situation where many of us are lost without our "CrackBerrys" or iPhones? What impact on other lifestyle activities do you predict as a result?
4 We live in a time where many people live frugally; they cut back on visits to restaurants, buy fewer high-end clothes and other luxury goods and hold on to their cars much longer. Are we witnessing a long-term shift in consumer behavior, or do you believe this is just a temporary situation?
5 The chapter lists the most stylish brands in 2008; all denote luxurious consumption. As concern about the economy and the environment continues to mount, do

you predict that our definition of "style" will shift? Can we expect to see eco-conscious brands like Patagonia on future lists of "stylish" brands?
6 Behavioral targeting techniques give marketers access to a wide range of information about a consumer when they tell them what Web sites he visits. Do you believe this "knowledge power" presents any ethical problems with regard to consumers' privacy? Should the government regulate access to such information? Should consumers have the right to limit access to these data?
7 Should organizations or individuals be allowed to create Web sites that advocate potentially harmful practices? Should hate groups such as al-Qaeda be allowed to recruit members online? Why or why not?
8 The chapter notes the growing trend of marketers that commission recording artists to create original songs for their commercials. Do you see this as just another way to encourage new music when other funding dries up, or is there something ominous about companies that influence the creativity of artists?

■ APPLY

1 Construct a brand personality inventory for three different brands within a product category. Ask a small number of consumers to rate each brand on about 10 different personality dimensions. What differences can you identify? Do these "personalities" relate to the advertising and packaging strategies used to differentiate these products?
2 Compile a set of recent ads that attempt to link consumption of a product with a specific lifestyle. How does a marketer usually accomplish this goal?
3 Political campaigns may use psychographic analyses. Conduct research on the marketing strategies a candidate used in a recent, major election. How did the cam-

paign segment voters in terms of values? Can you find evidence that the campaign's communications strategies used this information?
4 Construct separate advertising executions for a cosmetics product that targets the Believer, Achiever, Experiencer, and Maker VALS2™ types. How would the basic appeal differ for each group?
5 New "types" (or more often, updated versions of old types) emerge from popular culture on a regular basis, whether they are shredders, tuners, or geeks. In recent years, for example, some analysts identify the resurrection of the *hipster*. One source describes a person who follows this lifestyle as someone with a "complicated"

hairstyle (dyed black or white-blonde) who reads *Nylon* magazine; listens to indie rock; majored in art or writing; drinks Pabst Blue Ribbon beer; wears tight black pants, scarves, and ironic T-shirts; and is addicted to coffee and cigarettes—and denies being a hipster![91] How valid is this lifestyle type in your area? Can you identify people who belong to it or to a similar group?

6 Using media that targets college students, construct a consumption constellation for this social role. What set of products, activities, and interests tend to appear in advertisements depicting "typical" college students? How realistic is this constellation?

7 Extreme sports. You Tube. Blogging. Veganism. Can you predict what will be "hot" in the near future? Identify a lifestyle trend that is just surfacing in your universe. Describe this trend in detail, and justify your prediction. What specific styles or products are part of this trend?

Case Study

THE MAGIC OF IPOD

MP3 players are all the rage. It's no surprise then that the list of manufacturers that sell these pint-sized musical powerhouses continues to grow: Microsoft, Creative Zen, Creative, Sony, iRiver . . . all have their own versions. And yet Apple, with its line of iPods, continues to dominate this segment with 50 percent market share.

Why does Apple still run over the competition? One could say that it is because the iPods are technologically superior. And yet new players from other companies offer more features at lower prices. Perhaps iPod's commanding lead is due to greater flexibility and compatibility with online music services? That's not likely either, since devices from other companies are compatible with several online music stores, while the iPod only works with Apple's iTunes Store.

The hysteria surrounding the iPod hints that the answer to this question perhaps isn't so rational. Whether they intended to or not, the folks at Apple created a product that has achieved cult status. The Apple version of the MP3 player is instantly recognizable. It sports a svelte design with rounded edges, circles as control buttons, and distinctive white earbud headphones. No one will mistake an iPod for some other brand. Danika Cleary, a senior marketing manager for Apple, guesses that this artsy look and feel has propelled the iPod's success. She explains, "Users kind of covet it, in a way. We've seen people caress them."

Caress them? As though they are alive? Maybe that explains why some people even dress their iPods. Devoted users fit their tiny round music boxes with everything from socks and mohair slipcovers to "hoodie" sweatshirts and stick-on tattoos. It's not just enough to have the product anymore. Accessorizing the iPod has become a major trend fueled by a cottage industry of companies that make over 400 supporting products. You can even buy iPod cases from Louis Vuitton for $265—more than several iPod models cost.

From dressing an iPod in Louis Vuitton apparel, it may not be so big a step to believing that the device has its own tiny little mind. Maybe that's why some of us actually name our iPods. That's right, somewhere out there are iPods answering to "Steve," "Jaime," and "Gerald." One household with two units has named them "Bert" and "Ernie." "People attribute all sorts of personalities to their iPods," says Cleary. "I've heard many stories of people who think their iPods have certain preferences in music."

If iPods have assumed these brand personalities, then we shouldn't be surprised when they become part of social networks. *Pod-poaching* (swapping iPods with friends, coworkers, and other acquaintances) has become quite popular. This practice even occurs between total strangers (people call this "podjacking").

Apple has indeed achieved something almost all brands can only aspire to. It has a product with a brand image so strong that competitors find it almost impossible to gain ground. But beyond that, Apple has achieved something it may have never anticipated. The company created a product that has culture-shifting effects, which has changed the way we consume music. And with Apple's addition of the iPhone and iTouch to the iPod line, it may just end up changing the way that we do a lot of other things as well.

DISCUSSION QUESTIONS

1 Describe the brand personality of the iPod. Compare this personality to other high-tech brands, such as Nokia cell phones.

2 According to the information in this case, do iPod users seem to have a unique lifestyle? Describe it. Discuss the changes that iPod has had on the music-listening lifestyle in general.

Sources: Nick Wingfield, "Apple Price Cut on New iPhone Shakes Investors," *Wall Street Journal* (September 6, 2007): A1; Mike Musgrove, "Apple's iPod Still Calls the Tune," *Washington Post* (May 30, 2007): D8; Dan Moren, "Is the iPod Slipping," *Macworld* (April 2008): 24; "MP3 Players and Accessories–US–June 2008," *Mintel Oxygen*, accessed May 23, 2009.

NOTES

1. www.jettygirl.com, accessed June 30, 2009.
2. For an interesting ethnographic account of skydiving as a voluntary high-risk consumption activity, see Richard L. Celsi, Randall L. Rose, and Thomas W. Leigh, "An Exploration of High-Risk Leisure Consumption Through Skydiving," *Journal of Consumer Research* 20 (June 1993): 1–23.
3. www.roxy.com/home/index.jsp, accessed June 30, 2009.
4. See J. Aronoff and J. P. Wilson, *Personality in the Social Process* (Hillsdale, NJ: Erlbaum, 1985); Walter Mischel, *Personality and Assessment* (New York: Wiley, 1968).
5. Ernest Dichter, *A Strategy of Desire* (Garden City, NY: Doubleday, 1960); Ernest Dichter, *The Handbook of Consumer Motivations* (New York: McGraw-Hill, 1964); Jeffrey J. Durgee, "Interpreting Dichter's Interpretations: An Analysis of Consumption Symbolism," in *The Handbook of Consumer Motivations* (unpublished manuscript, Rensselaer Polytechnic Institute, Troy, New York, 1989); Pierre Martineau, *Motivation in Advertising* (New York: McGraw-Hill, 1957).
6. Vance Packard, *The Hidden Persuaders* (New York: D. McKay, 1957).
7. Harold Kassarjian, "Personality and Consumer Behavior: A Review," *Journal of Marketing Research* 8 (November 1971): 409–18.
8. Karen Horney, *Neurosis and Human Growth* (New York: Norton, 1950).
9. Joel B. Cohen, "An Interpersonal Orientation to the Study of Consumer Behavior," *Journal of Marketing Research* 6 (August 1967): 270–78; Pradeep K. Tyagi, "Validation of the CAD Instrument: A Replication," in Richard P. Bagozzi and Alice M. Tybout, eds., *Advances in Consumer Research* 10 (Ann Arbor, MI: Association for Consumer Research, 1983): 112–14.
10. For a comprehensive review of classic perspectives on personality theory, see Calvin S. Hall and Gardner Lindzey, *Theories of Personality*, 2nd ed. (New York: Wiley, 1970).
11. See Carl G. Jung, "The Archetypes and the Collective Unconscious," in H. Read, M. Fordham, and G. Adler, eds., *Collected Works*, vol. 9, part 1 (Princeton, NJ: Princeton University Press, 1959).
12. This material was contributed by Rebecca H. Holman, senior vice president and director, Consumer Knowledge Structures, The Knowledge Group, Young & Rubicam Brands, July 2005.
13. For an application of trait theory, cf. Adam Duhachek and Dawn Iacobucci, "Consumer Personality and Coping: Testing Rival Theories of Process," *Journal of Consumer Psychology* 15, no. 1 (2005): 52–63.
14. S. Christian Wheeler, Richard E. Petty, and George Y. Bizer, "Self-Schema Matching and Attitude Change: Situational and Dispositional Determinants of Message Elaboration," *Journal of Consumer Research* 31 (March, 2005): 787–97.
15. Linda L. Price and Nancy Ridgway, "Development of a Scale to Measure Innovativeness," in Richard P. Bagozzi and Alice M. Tybout, eds., *Advances in Consumer Research* 10 (Ann Arbor, MI: Association for Consumer Research, 1983): 679–84; Russell W. Belk, "Three Scales to Measure Constructs Related to Materialism: Reliability, Validity, and Relationships to Measures of Happiness," in Thomas C. Kinnear, ed., *Advances in Consumer Research* 11 (Ann Arbor, MI: Association for Consumer Research, 1984): 291; Mark Snyder, "Self-Monitoring Processes," in Leonard Berkowitz, ed., *Advances in Experimental Social Psychology* (New York: Academic Press, 1979), 85–128; Gordon R. Foxall and Ronald E. Goldsmith, "Personality and Consumer Research: Another Look," *Journal of the Market Research Society* 30, no. 2 (1988): 111–25; Ronald E. Goldsmith and Charles F. Hofacker, "Measuring Consumer Innovativeness," *Journal of the Academy of Marketing Science* 19, no. 3 (1991): 209–21; Curtis P. Haugtvedt, Richard E. Petty, and John T. Cacioppo, "Need for Cognition and Advertising: Understanding the Role of Personality Variables in Consumer Behavior," *Journal of Consumer Psychology* 1, no. 3 (1992): 239–60.
16. John L. Lastovicka, Lance A. Bettencourt, Renee Shaw Hughner, and Ronald J. Kuntze, "Lifestyle of the Tight and Frugal: Theory and Measurement," *Journal of Consumer Research* 26 (June 1999): 85–98; "The Continuing Economic Maelstrom & the US Consumer: Implications for CPG, Restaurant and Retail January 2009," The Hartman Group: 9; Joseph Lazzaro, "US Savings Rate Soars to 14-Year High," *Daily Finance* (June 1, 2009), www.dailyfinance.com/2009/06/01/us-savings-rate-soars-to-14-year-high, accessed June 1, 2009; Andrea K. Walker, "Economy Breeds a Frugal Consumer," *Baltimore Sun* (April 20, 2009), www.baltimoresun.com/business/bal-te.bz.shoppinghabits19apr20,0,1577826.story, accessed June 1, 2009.
17. David Reisman, *The Lonely Crowd: A Study of the Changing American Character* (New Haven, CT: Yale University Press, 1969).
18. Kelly Tepper Tian, William O. Bearden, and Gary L. Hunter, "Consumers' Need for Uniqueness: Scale Development and Validation," *Journal of Consumer Research* 28 (June 2001): 50–66; Bennett Courtney, "Robotic Voices Designed to Manipulate," *Psychology Today* (January–February 2002): 20.
19. Mohan J. Dutta-Bergman and William D. Wells, "The Values and Lifestyles of Idiocentrics and Allocentrics in an Individualist Culture: A Descriptive Approach," *Journal of Consumer Psychology* 12 (March 2002): 231–42.
20. Beth Snyder Bulik, "How Personality Can Predict Media Usage," *Advertising Age* (May 4, 2009), http://adage.com/article?article_id=136408, accessed May 4, 2009.
21. Jacob Jacoby, "Personality and Consumer Behavior: How Not to Find Relationships," in *Purdue Papers in Consumer Psychology*, no. 102 (Lafayette, IN: Purdue University, 1969); Harold H. Kassarjian and Mary Jane Sheffet, "Personality and Consumer Behavior: An Update," in Harold H. Kassarjian and Thomas S. Robertson, eds., *Perspectives in Consumer Behavior*, 4th ed. (Glenview, IL: Scott Foresman, 1991): 291–353; John Lastovicka and Erich Joachimsthaler, "Improving the Detection of Personality Behavior Relationships in Consumer Research," *Journal of Consumer Research* 14 (March 1988): 583–87. For an approach that ties the notion of personality more directly to marketing issues, see Jennifer L. Aaker, "Dimensions of Brand Personality," *Journal of Marketing Research* 34 (August 1997): 347–57.
22. See Girish N. Punj and David W. Stewart, "An Interaction Framework of Consumer Decision-Making," *Journal of Consumer Research* 10 (September 1983): 181–96.
23. J. F. Allsopp, "The Distribution of On-Licence Beer and Cider Consumption and Its Personality Determinants Among Young Men," *European Journal of Marketing* 20, no. 3 (1986): 44–62; Gordon R. Foxall and Ronald E. Goldsmith, "Personality and Consumer Research: Another Look," *Journal of the Market Research Society* 30, no. 2 (April 1988): 111–25.
24. Thomas Hine, "Why We Buy: The Silent Persuasion of Boxes, Bottles, Cans, and Tubes," *Worth* (May 1995): 78–83.
25. Bradley Johnson, "They All Have Half-Baked Ideas," *Advertising Age* (May 12, 1997): 8.
26. Yongjun Sung and Spencer F. Tinkham, "Brand Personality Structures in the United States and Korea: Common and Culture-Specific Factors," *Journal of Consumer Psychology* 15, no. 4 (2005): 334–50; Beverly T. Venable, Gregory M. Rose, Victoria D. Bush, and Faye W. Gilbert, "The Role of Brand Personality in Charitable Giving: An Assessment and Validation," *Journal of the Academy of Marketing Science* 33 (July 2005): 295–312.
27. Quoted in Stuart Elliott, "A 1950s Brand Mascot Fights 21st-Century Indigestion," *New York Times* (March 5, 2008), www.nytimes.com, accessed March 5, 2008.
28. Susan Nelson, "Our Changing View of Style," *Marketing Daily* (February 17, 2009), www.mediapost.com, accessed February 17, 2009.
29. Craig J. Thompson, Aric Rindfleisch, and Zeynep Arsel, "Emotional Branding and the Strategic Value of the Doppelganger Brand Image," *Journal of Marketing* 70, no. 1 (2006): 50.
30. Kevin L. Keller, "Conceptualization, Measuring, and Managing Customer-Based Brand Equity," *Journal of Marketing* 57 (January 1993): 1–22.
31. Linda Keslar, "What's in a Name?" *Individual Investor* (April 1999): 101–2.
32. Michael Hiestand, "ESPN Drops Ad Campaign That Was to Portray College Stereotypes," *USA Today* (November 14, 2008), www.usatoday.com/money/advertising/2008-11-13-espn-ad-campaign-killed_N.html, accessed November 14, 2008.
33. Kathryn Kranhold, "Agencies Beef Up Brand Research to Identify Consumer Preferences," *Wall Street Journal Interactive Edition* (March 9, 2000), accessed March 9, 2000.
34. Aaker, "Dimensions of Brand Personality."
35. Eric Pfanner, "Mocking an Olympics Logo, but Loving the Attention," *New York Times* (June 12, 2007), www.nytimes.com, accessed June 12, 2007.
36. Tim Triplett, "Brand Personality Must Be Managed or It Will Assume a Life of Its Own," *Marketing News* (May 9, 1994): 9.
37. Seth Stevenson, "How to Beat Nike," *New York Times* (January 5, 2003), www.nytimes.com, accessed January 5, 2003.
38. Susan Fournier, "Consumers and Their Brands: Developing Relationship Theory in Consumer Research," *Journal of Consumer Research* 24, no. 4 (March 1998): 343–73.

39. Rebecca Piirto Heath, "The Frontiers of Psychographics," *American Demographics* (July 1996): 38–43.

40. Quoted in Erin White, "Volvo Sheds Safe Image for New, Dangerous Ads," *Wall Street Journal* (June 14, 2002), www.wsj.com, accessed June 14, 2002; Viknesh Vijayenthiran, "Volvo's Upmarket Plans Hindered by Brand Image, Poor CO2 Emissions," *Motor Authority* (November 24, 2008), www.motorauthority.com/volvo-continuing-with-plans-to-move-upmarket.html, accessed June 1, 2009.

41. Benjamin D. Zablocki and Rosabeth Moss Kanter, "The Differentiation of Life-Styles," *Annual Review of Sociology* (1976): 269–97.

42. Mary Twe Douglas and Baron C. Isherwood, *The World of Goods* (New York: Basic Books, 1979).

43. "Precious Little Time," Center for Media Research (December 24, 2008), www.mediapost.com, accessed December 24, 2008.

44. Zablocki and Kanter, "The Differentiation of Life-Styles."

45. Karl Greenberg, "World Wrestling Brands Bliss Beverages, Launching Integrated Marketing Effort," *Marketing Daily* (May 16, 2007), www.mediapost.com, accessed May 16, 2007.

46. Richard A. Peterson, "Revitalizing the Culture Concept," *Annual Review of Sociology* 5 (1979): 137–66.

47. Lisa E. Bolton, Joel B. Cohen, and Paul N. Bloom (2006), "Does Marketing Products as Remedies Create 'Get Out of Jail Free Cards'?" *Journal of Consumer Research* 33 (June): 71–81.

48. Amit Bhattacharjee, Lisa E. Bolton, and Americus Reed, II, "License to Lapse: The Effects of Weight Management Product Marketing on a Healthy Lifestyle," working paper, *Wharton*, 2009.

49. Lisa E. Bolton, Americus Reed II, Kevin Volpp, and Katrina Armstrong, "How Does Drug and Supplement Marketing Affect a Healthy Lifestyle?" *Journal of Consumer Research* 34, no. 5 (2008): 713–26.

50. Stephanie Kang and Ethan Smith, "Music for Runners, Volume 2: Nike Releases Second Recording," *Wall Street Journal* (October 23, 2006): B6; http://nikeplus.nike.com/nikeplus/#tutorials, accessed July 6, 2007.

51. Stuart Elliott, "Commercials and Musicians Share the Need to Be Heard," *New York Times* (February 5, 2009), www.nytimes.com, accessed February 5, 2009.

52. Jonathan Birchall, "Just Do It, Marketers Say: Nike, Petsmart and Other Companies Are Trying to Sell Their Brands by Inviting Consumers to Take Part in Activities Linked to the Product or Service," *Los Angeles Times* (April 30, 2007), www.latimes.com/business/la-ft-brands30apr30, accessed April 30, 2007.

53. William Leiss, Stephen Kline, and Sut Jhally, *Social Communication in Advertising* (Toronto: Methuen, 1986).

54. Douglas and Isherwood, *The World of Goods*, quoted on pp. 72–73.

55. Christopher K. Hsee and France Leclerc, "Will Products Look More Attractive When Presented Separately or Together?" *Journal of Consumer Research* 25 (September 1998): 175–86.

56. Ellen Byron, "Consumer Products Getting a Makeover, Packaging Gets Stylish as P&G, Rivals Plan to Get out of the Closet," *Wall Street Journal* (June 2, 2008): B9; www.febreze.com/en_US/home.do, accessed June 3, 2009.

57. Nina M. Lentini, "Wendy's, P&G Couple to Offer Folgers Coffee for Breakfast," *Marketing Daily* (May 21, 2007), www.mediapost.com, accessed May 21, 2007.

58. Brian Steinberg, "Whose Ad Is This Anyway? Agencies Use Brand Icons to Promote Other Products; Cheaper Than Zeta-Jones," *Wall Street Journal* (December 4, 2003), www.wsj.com, accessed December 4, 2003.

59. Michael R. Solomon, "The Role of Products as Social Stimuli: A Symbolic Interactionism Perspective," *Journal of Consumer Research* 10 (December 1983): 319–29.

60. Michael R. Solomon and Henry Assael, "The Forest or the Trees? A *Gestalt* Approach to Symbolic Consumption," in Jean Umiker-Sebeok, ed., *Marketing and Semiotics: New Directions in the Study of Signs for Sale* (Berlin: Mouton de Gruyter, 1988), 189–218; Michael R. Solomon, "Mapping Product Constellations: A Social Categorization Approach to Symbolic Consumption," *Psychology & Marketing* 5, no. 3 (1988): 233–58; see also Stephen C. Cosmas, "Life Styles and Consumption Patterns," *Journal of Consumer Research* 8, no. 4 (March 1982): 453–55.

61. Russell W. Belk, "Yuppies as Arbiters of the Emerging Consumption Style," in Richard J. Lutz, ed., *Advances in Consumer Research* 13 (Provo, UT: Association for Consumer Research, 1986): 514–19.

62. Sarah Mahoney, "Milk Next to Cereal? Piggly Wiggly Rethinks Design," *Marketing Daily* (April 8, 2008), http://publications.mediapost.com/index.cfm?fuseaction=Articles.san&s=80124&Nid=412..., accessed April 8, 2008.

63. Danny Hakim, "Cadillac, Too, Shifting Focus to Trucks," *New York Times Online* (December 21, 2001).

64. Seth Stevenson, "How to Beat Nike," *New York Times* (January 5, 2003), www.nytimes.com, accessed January 5, 2003.

65. Helen Coster, "The $25 Water Bottle," *Forbes* (March 19, 2009), www.forbes.com, accessed March 19, 2009; www.mysigg.com, accessed June 3, 2009.

66. See Lewis Alpert and Ronald Gatty, "Product Positioning by Behavioral Life Styles," *Journal of Marketing* 33 (April 1969): 65–69; Emanuel H. Demby, "Psychographics Revisited: The Birth of a Technique," *Marketing News* (January 2, 1989): 21; William D. Wells, "Backward Segmentation," in Johan Arndt, ed., *Insights into Consumer Behavior* (Boston: Allyn & Bacon, 1968): 85–100.

67. Gary McWilliams, "Analyzing Customers, Best Buy Decides Not All Are Welcome; Retailer Aims to Outsmart Dogged Bargain-Hunters, and Coddle Big Spenders Looking for 'Barrys' and 'Jills,'" *Wall Street Journal* (November 8, 2004): A1; Joshua Freed, "Best Buy Stores Adapting to Help Customers They Serve," *Montgomery Advertiser* (May 23, 2004): 31.

68. William D. Wells and Douglas J. Tigert, "Activities, Interests, and Opinions," *Journal of Advertising Research* 11 (August 1971): 27.

69. Ian Pearson, "Social Studies: Psychographics in Advertising," *Canadian Business* (December 1985): 67.

70. Piirto Heath, "Psychographics: Qu'est-Ce Que C'est ?," *Marketing Tools* (Nov.-Dec. 1995): pages n.a.

71. Doris Hajewski, "Halted Poll Hits Close to Home: Target Ends Survey That Asks Shoppers Personal Questions," *Milwaukee Journal Sentinel* (June 11, 2007), www.jsonline.com/story/index.aspx?id=617780, accessed June 11, 2007.

72. Alfred S. Boote, "Psychographics: Mind over Matter," *American Demographics* (April 1980): 26–29; William D. Wells, "Psychographics: A Critical Review," *Journal of Marketing Research* 12 (May 1975): 196–213.

73. Joseph T. Plummer, "The Concept and Application of Life Style Segmentation," *Journal of Marketing* 38 (January 1974): 33–37.

74. Berkeley Rice, "The Selling of Lifestyles," *Psychology Today* (March 1988): 46.

75. John L. Lastovicka, John P. Murry, Erich A. Joachimsthaler, Gurav Bhalla, and Jim Scheurich, "A Lifestyle Typology to Model Young Male Drinking and Driving," *Journal of Consumer Research* 14 (September 1987): 257–63.

76. Martha Farnsworth Riche, "VALS 2," *American Demographics* (July 1989): 25. Additional information provided by William D. Guns, Director, Business Intelligence Center, SRI Consulting, Inc., personal communication, May 1997.

77. Rebecca Piirto Heath, "You Can Buy a Thrill: Chasing the Ultimate Rush," *American Demographics* (June 1997): 47–51.

78. Some of this section is adapted from material presented in Michael R. Solomon, Gary Bamossy, and Søren Askegaard, *Consumer Behaviour: A European Perspective*, 2nd ed. (London: Prentice Hall Europe, 2002).

79. "Euromonitor," *European Marketing Data and Statistics* (1997): 328–31.

80. Deborah Ball, Sarah Ellison, Janet Adamy, and Geoffrey A. Fowler, "Recipes Without Borders? Big Food Marketers Adjust Levels of Fat and Sodium to Fit Regulations, Tastes," *Wall Street Journal* (August 18, 2004): B1; Søren Askegaard and Tage Koed Madsen, "The Local and the Global: Patterns of Homogeneity and Heterogeneity in European Food Cultures," *International Business Review* 7, no. 6 (1999): 549–68; Michael R. Solomon, Suzanne C. Beckmann, and Basil G. Englis, "Exploring and Understanding of Cultural Meaning Systems: Visualizing the Underlying Meaning Structure of Brands," presented at Branding: Activating & Engaging Cultural Meaning Systems Conference, Innsbruck, Austria, May 2003.

81. Michael J. Weiss, *The Clustering of America* (New York: Harper & Row, 1988).

82. Bob Minzesheimer, "You Are What You Zip," *Los Angeles Times* (November 1984): 175.

83. Christina Del Valle, "They Know Where You Live and How You Buy," *BusinessWeek* (February 7, 1994): 89; www.claritas.com, accessed June 3, 2005.

84. www.claritas.com/MyBestSegments/Default.jsp, accessed June 3, 2009.

85. Stephanie Clifford, "Cable Companies Target Commercials to Audience," *New York Times* (March 3, 2009), www.nytimes.com/2009/03/04/business/04cable.html?_r=1, accessed March 4, 2009.

86. Stephanie Kang and Vishesh Kumar, "TV Learning Importance of Targeting," *Wall Street Journal* (April 4, 2008): B7.

87. Laura M. Holson, "In CBS Test, Mobile Ads Find Users," *New York Times* (February 6, 2008), www.nytimes.com, accessed February 6, 2008.

88. Emily Steel and Vishesh Kumar, "Targeted Ads Raise Privacy Concerns, Pressure Could Imperil Online Strategy Shared by Phone and Cable-TV Firms," *Wall Street Journal* (July 8, 2008): B1.

89. "Consumers Willing to Trade Off Privacy for Electronic Personalization," Center for Media Research (January 23, 2007), www.mediapost.com, accessed January 23, 2007.

90. Stephanie Clifford, "Online Age Quiz Is a Window for Drug Makers," *New York Times* (March 25, 2009), www.nytimes.com/2009/03/26/technology/internet/26privacy.html?hp, accessed March 26, 2009; www.realage.com/ralong/entry4.aspx?cbr=GGLE806&gclid=CIfH6Muj7poCFQVfFQodvWQvBw, accessed June 3, 2009.

91. Robert Lanham, *The Hipster Handbook* (New York: Anchor, 2003); www.urbandictionary.com/define.php?term=hipster, accessed July 5, 2007.

7

Attitudes and Persuasion

Chapter Objectives

When you finish this chapter you will understand:

1 Why is it so important for consumer researchers to understand the nature and power of attitudes?

2 Why are attitudes more complex than they first appear?

3 Why do we form attitudes in several ways?

4 Why does a need to maintain consistency among all of our attitudinal components motivate us to alter one or more of them?

5 Why do we use attitude models to identify specific components and combine them to predict a consumer's overall attitude toward a product or brand?

6 Why does the communications model identify several important components for marketers when they try to change consumers' attitudes toward products and services?

7 Why is the consumer who processes a message not necessarily the passive receiver of information marketers once believed him to be?

8 Why do several factors influence a message source's effectiveness?

9 How does the way a marketer structures his message determine how persuasive it will be?

10 How do audience characteristics help to determine whether the nature of the source or the message itself will be relatively more effective?

*N*atalie is sorting through today's mail: bill, ad, bill, fund-raising letter from political candidate, offer for another credit card.

Aha! Here it is—the envelope she's been waiting for: an invitation to a posh cocktail party at her friend Tracy's ad agency. This will be her chance to see and be seen, to mingle, network, and maybe even land a job offer. But, what to wear? Somehow her industrial grunge clothes don't seem appropriate for the new life she imagines as an account executive. Natalie needs help, so she does what comes naturally. First, she Tweets her friends to let them know about the event; then she fires up her computer to check out what the *fashionistas* who roam the blogosphere recommend this season.[1] As she browses shoppingblog.com, she quickly learns there's a return to bright colors, bold patterns, and feminine flourishes.[2] On the other hand, she might make a real entrance if she shows up in an all-white Calvin Klein one-sleeve outfit inspired by the *Star Trek* movie that *Shopping the Trend* raves about.[3] Natalie quickly copies some snapshots from a bunch of Web sites and e-mails them to her buddies to get their votes. It's fun to get input from "real people" in addition to fashion industry snobs.

The Power of Attitudes

1

OBJECTIVE

Why is it so important for consumer researchers to understand the nature and power of attitudes?

People use the term *attitude* in many contexts. A friend might ask you, "What is your attitude toward abortion?" A parent might scold, "Young man, I don't like your attitude." Some bars even euphemistically refer to happy hour as "an attitude adjustment period." For our purposes, though, an **attitude** is a lasting, general evaluation of people (including oneself), objects, advertisements, or issues.[4] We call any-thing toward which one has an attitude an **attitude object (***A*o**).**

An attitude is lasting because it tends to endure over time. It is general because it applies to more than a momentary event, such as hearing a loud noise, though you might, over time, develop a negative attitude toward all loud noises. Consumers have attitudes toward a wide range of attitude objects, from very product-specific behaviors (e.g., you use Crest toothpaste rather than Colgate) to more general, consumption-related behaviors (e.g., how often you should brush your teeth). Attitudes help to determine whom you choose to date, what music you listen to, whether you will recycle aluminum cans, or whether you choose to become a consumer researcher for a living.

In this chapter we'll consider the contents of an attitude, how we form attitudes, and how we measure them. We will also review some of the surprisingly complex relationships between attitudes and behavior and then take a closer look at how marketers can change these attitudes.

Psychologist Daniel Katz developed the **functional theory of attitudes** to explain how attitudes facilitate social behavior.[5] According to this pragmatic approach, attitudes exist *because* they serve some function for the person. Consumers who expect that they will need to deal with similar situations at a future time will be more likely to start to form an attitude in anticipation.[6] Two people can each have an attitude toward some object for very different reasons. As a result, it's helpful for a marketer to know *why* an attitude is held before she tries to change it. These are different attitude functions:

- **Utilitarian function**—The **utilitarian function** relates to the basic principles of reward and punishment we learned about in Chapter 3. We develop some attitudes toward products simply because they provide pleasure or pain. If a person likes the taste of a cheeseburger, that person will develop a positive attitude toward cheeseburgers. Ads that stress straightforward product benefits (e.g., you should drink Diet Coke "just for the taste of it") appeal to the utilitarian function.
- **Value-expressive function**—Attitudes that perform a **value-expressive function** relate to the consumer's central values (Chapter 4) or self-concept (Chapter 5). A person forms a product attitude in this case because of what the product says about him as a person (e.g., "What sort of man reads *Playboy*?"). Value-expressive attitudes also are highly relevant to the lifestyle analyses we discussed in Chapter 6, which consider how consumers cultivate a cluster of activities, interests, and opinions to express a particular social identity.
- **Ego-defensive function**—Attitudes we form to protect ourselves either from external threats or internal feelings perform an **ego-defensive function**. An early marketing study showed that housewives in the 1950s resisted the use of instant coffee because it threatened their conception of themselves as capable home-makers (this doesn't seem to be a very big issue for most anymore!).[7] Products that promise to help a man project a "macho" image (e.g., Marlboro cigarettes) appeal to his insecurities about his masculinity. Another example is deodorant campaigns that stress the dire, embarrassing consequences when you're caught with underarm odor in public.
- **Knowledge function**—We form some attitudes because we need order, structure, or meaning. A **knowledge function** applies when a person is in an ambigu-ous situation ("it's OK to wear casual pants to work, but only on Friday") or she confronts a new product (e.g., "Bayer wants you to know about pain relievers").

2

OBJECTIVE

Why are attitudes more complex than they first appear?

The ABC Model of Attitudes

When Subaru of America began work on a new marketing strategy, the automaker discovered that even though most auto buyers had heard of the brand very few had strong emotional connections to it. However, Subaru owners expressed strong passion and even love for the brand. To ramp up this emotional connection, the new campaign targets people who are in three different stages of buying a car—what Subaru calls the heart, the head, and the wallet. The heart stage focuses on the love owners show for their cars as commercials share personal stories of their attachment. The "head" stage ads, in contrast, present a rational side of specific models as they emphasize how the cars benefit their owners in terms of reliability, economy, etc. The "wallet" ads deal with the financial side of actually buying a Subaru such as local dealer offers.[8]

Like the Subaru campaign, an attitude has three components: affect, behavior, and cognition. **Affect** describes how a consumer *feels* about an attitude object. **Behavior** refers to his intentions to *take action* about it (but, as we will discuss at a later point, an intention does not always result in an actual behavior). **Cognition** is what he *believes* to be true about the attitude object. You can remember these three components of an attitude as the **ABC model of attitudes.**

The ABC model emphasizes the interrelationships among knowing, feeling, and doing. We can't determine consumers' attitudes toward a product if we just identify their cognitions (beliefs) about it. For example, a researcher may find that shoppers "know" a particular camcorder has an 8:1 power zoom lens, auto focus, and a flying erase head, but simply knowing this doesn't indicate whether they feel these attributes are good, bad, or irrelevant, or whether they would actually buy the camcorder.

Hierarchies of Effects

Which comes first: knowing, feeling, or doing? It turns out that each element may lead things off depending on the situation. Attitude researchers developed the concept of a **hierarchy of effects** to explain the relative impact of the three components. Each hierarchy specifies that a fixed sequence of steps occurs en route to an attitude. Figure 7.1 summarizes these three different hierarchies.

Figure 7.1 HIERARCHIES OF EFFECTS

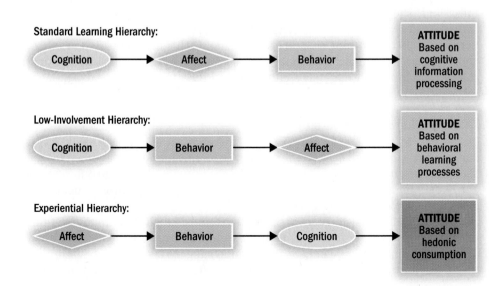

This ad for New York's famous Smith & Wollensky restaurant emphasizes that marketers and others associated with a product or service are often more involved with it than are their customers.

Source: Courtesy of Smith & Wollensky Steak House.

Steak is our life. All we ask is that you make it your lunch.

Smith & Wollensky.
The quintessential New York City steakhouse.
49th St. & 3rd Ave. (212) 753-1530.

Winner of The *Wine Spectator's* 1987 Grand Award.

The Standard Learning Hierarchy

Think → Feel → Do: The **standard learning hierarchy** assumes that a person approaches a product decision as a problem-solving process. First, she forms beliefs about a product as she accumulates knowledge (*beliefs*) regarding relevant attributes. Next, she evaluates these beliefs and forms a feeling about the product (*affect*).[10] Then she engages in a relevant behavior, such as when she buys the product that offers the attributes she feels good about. This hierarchy assumes that a consumer is highly involved when she makes a purchase decision.[11] She's motivated to seek out a lot of information, carefully weigh alternatives, and come to a thoughtful decision.

The Low-Involvement Hierarchy

Do → Feel → Think: The **low-involvement hierarchy of effects** assumes the consumer initially doesn't have a strong preference for one brand over another; instead she acts on the basis of limited knowledge and she forms an evaluation only *after* she has bought the product.[12] The attitude is likely to come about through behavioral learning—good or bad experiences reinforce her initial choice.

The possibility that consumers simply don't care enough about many decisions to carefully assemble a set of product beliefs and then evaluate them is important. This implies that all of our concern about influencing beliefs and carefully communicating information about product attributes often may be wasted. Consumers aren't necessarily going to pay attention anyway; they are more likely to respond to simple stimulus–response connections when they make purchase decisions. For example, a consumer choosing among paper towels might remember that "Bounty is the quicker picker-upper" rather than bothering to systematically compare all the brands on the shelf.

The notion of consumers' low involvement is a bitter pill for some marketers to swallow. Who wants to admit that what they market is not very important or involving? A brand manager for, say, a brand of bubble gum or cat food may find it hard to believe that consumers don't put that much thought into purchasing her product because she herself spends many of her waking (and perhaps sleeping) hours thinking about it.

For marketers, the ironic silver lining to this low-involvement cloud is that under these conditions, consumers are not motivated to process a lot of complex, brand-related information. Instead, they will be swayed by principles of behavioral learning, such as the simple responses that conditioned brand names or point-of-purchase displays elicit, which we discussed in Chapter 3.

The Experiential Hierarchy

Feel → Think → Do: According to the **experiential hierarchy of effects**, we act on the basis of our emotional reactions. The experiential perspective highlights the idea that intangible product attributes, such as package design, advertising, brand names, and the nature of the setting in which the experience occurs, can help shape our attitudes toward a brand. We may base these reactions on hedonic motivations, such as whether using the product is exciting (like the Nintendo Wii).

Even the emotions the communicator expresses have an impact. A smile is infectious; in a process we term *emotional contagion*, messages happy people deliver enhance our attitude toward the product.[13] Numerous studies indicate that the mood a person is in when she sees or hears a marketing message influences how she will process the ad, the likelihood that she will remember the information she sees, and how she will feel about the advertised item and related products in the future.[14]

OBJECTIVE

Why do we form attitudes in several ways?

How Do We Form Attitudes?

We all have lots of attitudes, and we don't usually question how we got them. Certainly, you're not born with the conviction that, say, Pepsi is better than Coke, or that alternative music liberates the soul. From where do these attitudes come?

We form an attitude in several different ways, depending on the particular hierarchy of effects that operates. As we saw in Chapter 3, we may form an attitude toward a brand due to classical conditioning—a marketer repeatedly pairs an attitude object such as the Pepsi name with a catchy jingle ("You're in the Pepsi Generation"). Or we can form an attitude due to instrumental conditioning—the marketer reinforces us when we consume the attitude object (e.g., you take a swig of Pepsi and it quenches your thirst). Or this learning can result from a very complex cognitive process. For example, a teenager may model the behavior of friends and media endorsers, such as Beyoncé, who drink Pepsi because they believe that this will allow them to fit in with the desirable lifestyle Pepsi commercials portray.

All Attitudes Are Not Created Equal

It's important to distinguish among types of attitudes because not all are formed in the same way.[15] One consumer may be highly brand-loyal; she has an enduring, deeply held positive attitude toward an attitude object, and it would be difficult to weaken this involvement. However, another woman may be a more fickle consumer: She may have a mildly positive attitude toward a product but be quite willing to abandon it when something better comes along. In this section, we'll consider the differences between strongly and weakly held attitudes and briefly review some of the major theoretical perspectives researchers use to explain how attitudes form and relate to our other attitudes.

Consumers vary in their *commitment* to an attitude; the degree of commitment relates to their level of involvement with the attitude object (see Chapter 4).[16] Let's look at three (increasing) levels of commitment:

1. **Compliance**—At the lowest level of involvement, **compliance**, we form an attitude because it helps us to gain rewards or avoid punishment. This attitude is very superficial; it is likely to change when others no longer monitor our behavior or when another option becomes available. You may drink Pepsi because the cafeteria sells it, and it is too much trouble to go elsewhere for a Coca-Cola.

2. **Identification**—**Identification** occurs when we form an attitude to conform to another person's or group's expectations. Advertising that depicts the dire social consequences when we choose some products over others relies on the tendency of consumers to imitate the behavior of desirable models (more on this in Chapter 10).

3. **Internalization**—At a high level of involvement we label **internalization**, deep-seated attitudes become part of our value system. These attitudes are very difficult to change because they are so important to us. The infamous Coke debacle of the 1980s (still a standard in marketing textbooks today) illustrates what can happen when a marketer messes with strongly held attitudes. In this case Coca-Cola decided to change its flavor formula to meet the needs of younger consumers who often preferred a sweeter taste (more characteristic of Pepsi). The company conducted rigorous blind *taste tests* that showed people who didn't know what brands they were drinking preferred the flavor of the new formula. Much to its surprise, when New Coke hit the shelves the company faced a consumer revolt as die-hard Coke fans protested. This allegiance to Coke was obviously more than a minor taste preference for these people—the brand had become intertwined with their social identities and took on intense patriotic and nostalgic properties.

OBJECTIVE

Why does a need to maintain consistency among all of our attitudinal components motivate us to alter one or more of them?

The Consistency Principle

Have you ever heard someone say, "Pepsi is my favorite soft drink. It tastes terrible," or "I love my boyfriend. He's the biggest idiot I've ever met?" Probably not (at least until the couple gets married!) because these beliefs or evaluations don't go together. According to the **principle of cognitive consistency**, we value harmony among our thoughts, feelings, and behaviors, and a need to maintain uniformity among these elements motivates us. This desire means that, if necessary, we change our thoughts, feelings, or behaviors to make them consistent with other experiences. That boyfriend may slip up and act like an idiot occasionally, but usually his girlfriend (eventually) will find a way to forgive him—or dump him. The consistency principle is an important reminder that we don't form our attitudes in a vacuum. Instead, a big factor is how well they fit with other, related attitudes we already hold.

The **theory of cognitive dissonance** states that when a person is confronted with inconsistencies among attitudes or behaviors, he will take some action to resolve this "dissonance"—perhaps he will change his attitude or modify his behavior to restore consistency. The theory has important ramifications for consumer behavior because situations often confront us where there is some conflict between our attitudes toward a product or service and what we actually do or buy.[17]

According to the theory, our motivation to reduce the negative feelings of dissonance makes us find a way for our beliefs and feelings to fit together. The theory focuses on situations in which two cognitive elements clash. A *cognitive element* can be something a person believes about himself, a behavior he performs, or an observation about his surroundings. For example, the two cognitive elements "I know smoking cigarettes causes cancer" and "I smoke cigarettes" are *dissonant* with one another. This psychological inconsistency creates a feeling of discomfort that the smoker tries to reduce. The magnitude of dissonance depends on both the importance and number of dissonant elements.[18] In other words, we're more likely to observe dissonance in high-involvement situations where there is more pressure to reduce inconsistencies.

We reduce dissonance when we eliminate, add, or change elements. For example, a person can stop smoking (*eliminating*), or remember Great-Aunt Sophie who smoked until the day she died at age 90 (*adding*). Alternatively, he might question the research that links cancer and smoking (*changing*), perhaps by believing industry-sponsored studies that try to refute this connection.

Dissonance theory can help to explain why evaluations of a product tend to increase *after* we buy the product. The cognitive element, "I made a stupid decision," is dissonant with the element, "I am not a stupid person," so we tend to find even more reasons to like something after it becomes ours. A classic study at a horse race demonstrated this *postpurchase dissonance*. Bettors evaluated their chosen horse more highly and were more confident of its success *after* they placed a bet than before. Because the bettor financially commits to the choice, she reduces dissonance as she increases the attractiveness of the chosen alternative relative to the unchosen ones.[19] One implication of this phenomenon is that consumers actively seek support for their decisions so they can justify them; therefore, marketers should supply their customers with additional reinforcement after they purchase to bolster these decisions.

Self-Perception Theory

Do we always change our attitudes to be in line with our behavior because we're motivated to reduce cognitive dissonance? **Self-perception theory** provides an alternative explanation of dissonance effects.[20] It assumes that we observe our own behavior to determine just what our attitudes are, much as we assume that we know what another person's attitude is when we watch what he does. The theory states that we maintain consistency as we infer that we must have a positive attitude toward an object if we have bought or consumed it (assuming that we freely made this choice). Thus, you might say to yourself, "I guess I must be into Facebook pretty big time. I seem to spend half my life on it."

Self-perception theory helps to explain the effectiveness of a strategy salespeople call the **foot-in-the-door technique**—they know that a consumer is more likely to comply with a big request if he agrees to a smaller one.[21] The name for this technique comes from the practice of door-to-door selling—salespeople learn to plant their foot in a door so the prospect (hopefully) doesn't slam it on them. A good salesperson knows that she is more likely to get an order if she can persuade the customer to open the door and talk. By agreeing to do so, the customer signals that he's willing to listen to the salesperson's pitch. Placing an order is consistent with the self-perception that "I'm the kind of person who is willing to buy something from a salesperson who knocks on my door." Recent research also points to the possibility that when salespeople ask consumers to make a series of choices these decisions are cognitively demanding and they deplete the resources the person has available to monitor his behavior. As a result the target will opt for easier decisions down the road; in some cases it may be easier just to comply with the request than to search for reasons why you shouldn't.[22]

Social Judgment Theory

Social judgment theory also assumes that people assimilate new information about attitude objects in light of what they already know or feel.[23] The initial attitude acts as a frame of reference, and we categorize new information in terms of this existing standard. Just as our decision that a box is heavy depends in part on the weight of other boxes we lift, we develop a subjective standard when we judge attitude objects.

One important aspect of the theory is that people differ in terms of the information they will find acceptable or unacceptable. They form **latitudes of acceptance and rejection** around an attitude standard. They will evaluate ideas falling within a latitude favorably, but they are more likely to reject those that fall outside of this zone. People tend to perceive messages within their latitude of acceptance as more consistent with their position than they actually are. We call this exaggeration an *assimilation effect*.

However, we tend to see messages that fall in our latitude of rejection as even more unacceptable than they actually are—this results in an exaggeration we call a *contrast effect*.[24] As a person becomes more involved with an attitude object, her latitude of acceptance gets smaller. In other words, the consumer accepts fewer ideas farther from her own position and she tends to oppose even mildly divergent positions. Discriminating buyers have a smaller latitude of acceptance (e.g., "choosy mothers choose Jif peanut butter"). However, relatively uninvolved consumers consider a wider range of alternatives. They are less likely to be brand loyal and are more likely to switch brands.[25]

Have you ever heard the expression, "Any friend of Joe's is a friend of mine?" How about "My enemy's enemy is my friend?" **Balance theory** considers how a person perceives relations among different attitude objects, and how he alters his attitudes so that these remain consistent (or "balanced").[26] This perspective involves relations (always from the perceiver's subjective point of view) among three elements, so we call the resulting attitude structures *triads*. Each triad contains (1) a person and his perceptions of (2) an attitude object and (3) some other person or object. The theory specifies that we want relations among elements in a triad to be harmonious. If they are unbalanced, this creates tension that we are motivated to reduce by changing our perceptions in order to restore balance.

We link elements together in one of two ways: They can have either a *unit relation* where we think that a person is somehow connected to an attitude object (something like a belief), or they can have a *sentiment relation*, where a person expresses liking or disliking for an attitude object. You might perceive that a dating couple has a positive sentiment relation. On getting married, they will have a positive unit relation. If they get divorced, they sever the unit relation.

To see how balance theory might work, consider the following scenario:

- Alex would like to date Larry, who is in her consumer behavior class. In balance theory terms, Alex has a positive sentiment relation with Larry.
- One day, Larry shows up in class wearing an earring. Larry has a positive unit relation with the earring.
- Alex is turned off by men who wear earrings. She has a negative sentiment relation with men's earrings.

According to balance theory, Alex faces an unbalanced triad. As Figure 7.2 shows, she will experience pressure to restore balance by altering some aspect of the triad. How can she do this? She could decide that she does not like Larry after all. Or her liking for Larry could prompt her to decide that earrings on men are really pretty cool. She might even try to negate the unit relation between Larry and the earring by deciding that he must wear it as part of a fraternity initiation (this reduces the free-choice element). Finally, she could choose to "leave the field" by accepting a date with Larry's roommate Brad who doesn't wear an earring (but who has an awesome tattoo). Note that although the theory does not specify which of these routes Alex will choose, it does predict that she will change one or more of her perceptions to achieve balance. Although this example is an oversimplified representation of most attitude processes, it helps to explain a number of consumer behavior phenomena.

Balance theory reminds us that when we have balanced perceptions our attitudes also are likely to be stable. However, when we experience inconsistencies we also are more likely to change our attitudes. Balance theory also helps explain why consumers like to be linked to positively valued objects. Forming a unit relation with a popular product (e.g., buying and wearing fashionable clothing, driving a flashy car, or even being part of a rap singer's posse) may improve the chances that other people will include you as a positive sentiment relation in their triads.

This "balancing act" is at the heart of celebrity endorsements, in which marketers hope that the star's popularity will transfer to the product or when a nonprofit organization recruits a celebrity to discourage harmful behaviors.[27] We will consider this strategy at length later in the chapter. For now, it pays to remember that creating a unit relation between a product and a star can backfire if the public's opinion of the celebrity endorser shifts from positive to negative. This happened when Pepsi pulled an ad that featured Madonna after she released a controversial music video involving religion and sex and when celebrity bad girl Paris Hilton got busted. The

Marketing Opportunity

Consumers often like to publicize their connections with successful people or organizations (no matter how shaky the connection) to enhance their own standing. Researchers call this tactic **basking in reflected glory**. A series of studies at Arizona State University (ASU) showed how students' desires to identify with a winning image—in this case, ASU's football team—influenced their consumption behaviors. After the team played a game each weekend, observers recorded the incidence of school-related items, such as ASU T-shirts and caps, students walking around campus wore. The researchers correlated the frequency of these behaviors to the team's performance. If the team won on Saturday, students were more likely to show off their school affiliation (basking in reflected glory) the following Monday than if the team had lost. And the bigger the point spread, the more likely they were to observe students who wore clothes with the ASU logo.

At the college level, many schools in addition to ASU reap huge revenues when they license their school's name and logo. Schools with strong athletic programs, such as Michigan, Penn State, and Auburn, clean up when they sell millions of dollars worth of merchandise (everything from T-shirts to toilet seats). Yale was a relative latecomer to this game, but the director of licensing explained the decision to profit from the use of the school's name and the likeness of bulldog mascot Handsome Dan: "We recognize that our name means a lot—even to people who didn't go here. Plus, this way we can crack down on the Naked Coed Lacrosse shirts out there with Yale on them."[28]

Figure 7.2 BALANCE THEORY

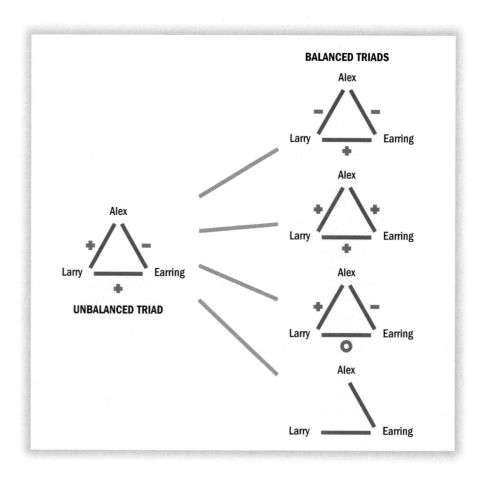

OBJECTIVE

Why do we use attitude models to identify specific components and combine them to predict a consumer's overall attitude toward a product or brand?

strategy can also cause trouble if people question the star–product unit relation: This happened when the late singer Michael Jackson, who also did promotions for Pepsi, subsequently confessed that he didn't even drink soda.

Attitude Models

When market researchers want to assess consumers' attitudes toward beer brands, they might simply go to a bar and ask a bunch of guys, "How do you feel about Budweiser?" However, as we saw earlier, attitudes can be a lot more complex than that. One problem is that many attributes or qualities may link to a product or service and, depending on the individual, some of these will be more or less important ("Less filling!" "Tastes great!"). Another problem is that when a person decides to take action toward an attitude object, other factors influence his behavior such as whether he feels that his family or friends would approve. *Attitude models* specify the different elements that might work together to influence people's evaluations of attitude objects.

Multiattribute Attitude Models

A simple response does not always tell us everything we need to know, either about *why* the consumer feels a certain way toward a product or about what marketers can do to change his attitude. Our beliefs (accurate or not) about a product often are key to how we evaluate it. Warner-Lambert discovered this while doing research for its Fresh Burst Listerine mouthwash. A research firm paid 37 families to allow it to set up cameras in their bathrooms and watch their daily routines (maybe they should have just checked out YouTube). Participants who bought both Fresh Burst and rival Scope said they used mouthwash to make their breath smell good. But Scope users swished around the liquid and then spit it out, while Listerine users kept the product in their mouths for a long time (one respondent held the stuff in until he got in the car and finally spit it out in a sewer a block away!). These findings told Listerine the brand still hadn't shaken its medicine-like image.[29]

Because attitudes are so complex, marketing researchers may use **multiattribute attitude models** to understand them. This type of model assumes that a consumer's attitude toward an attitude object (A_o) depends on the beliefs she has about several of its attributes. When we use a multiattribute model, we assume that we can identify these specific beliefs and combine them to derive a measure of the consumer's overall attitude. We'll describe how these models work with the example of a consumer who evaluates a complex attitude object that should be very familiar to you: a college.

Basic multiattribute models contain three specific elements:[30]

- *Attributes* are characteristics of the A_o. A researcher tries to identify the attributes that most consumers use when they evaluate the A_o. For example, one of a college's attributes is its scholarly reputation.
- *Beliefs* are cognitions about the specific A_o (usually relative to others like it). A belief measure assesses the extent to which the consumer perceives that a brand possesses a particular attribute. For example, a student might believe that the University of North Carolina is strong academically.
- *Importance weights* reflect the relative priority of an attribute to the consumer. Although people might consider an A_o on a number of attributes, some are likely to be more important than others (i.e., they will give them greater weight). Furthermore, these weights are likely to differ across consumers. In the case of colleges and universities, for example, one student might stress research opportunities, whereas another might assign greater weight to athletic programs.

The Fishbein Model. The most influential multiattribute model is called the *Fishbein model*, named after its primary developer.[31] The model measures three components of attitude:

1 *Salient beliefs* people have about an A_o (i.e., those beliefs about the object a person considers during evaluation).
2 *Object-attribute linkages*, or the probability that a particular object has an important attribute.
3 *Evaluation* of each of the important attributes.

When we combine these three elements, we compute a consumer's overall attitude toward an object (we'll see later how researchers modify this equation to increase its accuracy). The basic formula is:

$$A_{jk} = \Sigma \beta_{ijk} I_{ik}$$

where

i = attribute
j = brand
k = consumer
I = the importance weight given attribute i by consumer k
β = consumer k's belief regarding the extent to which brand j possesses attribute i
A = a particular consumer's (k's) attitude score for brand j

We obtain the overall attitude score (*A*) when we multiply a consumer's rating of each attribute for all the brands she considered by the importance rating for that attribute.

To see how this basic multiattribute model works, let's suppose we want to predict which college a high school senior is likely to attend. After months of waiting anxiously, Saundra gets accepted to four schools. Because she must now decide among these, we would first like to know which attributes Saundra will consider when she forms an attitude toward each school. We can then ask Saundra to assign a rating regarding how well each school performs on each attribute and also determine the relative importance of the attributes to her.

By summing scores on each attribute (after we weight each by its relative importance), we compute an overall attitude score for each school. Table 7.1 shows these hypothetical ratings. Based on this analysis, it seems that Saundra has the most favorable attitude toward Smith. She is clearly someone who would like to attend a college for women with a solid academic reputation rather than a school that offers a strong athletic program or a party atmosphere.

Marketing Applications of the Multiattribute Model

Suppose you were the director of marketing for Northland College, another school Saundra considered. How might you use the data from this analysis to improve your image?

Capitalize on Relative Advantage. If prospective students view one brand as superior on a particular attribute, a marketer needs to convince consumers like Saundra that this particular attribute is important. For example, although Saundra rates Northland's social atmosphere highly, she does not believe this attribute is a valued aspect for a college. As Northland's marketing director, you might emphasize the importance of an active social life, varied experiences, or even the development of future business contacts that a student forges when she makes strong college friendships.

Strengthen Perceived Product/Attribute Linkages. A marketer may discover that consumers do not equate his brand with a certain attribute. Advertising campaigns often address this problem when they stress a specific quality to consumers (e.g., "new and improved"). Saundra apparently does not think much of Northland's academic quality, athletic programs, or library facilities. You might develop an informational campaign to improve these perceptions (e.g., "little known facts about Northland").

TABLE 7.1	The Basic Multiattribute Model: Saundra's College Decision				
		Beliefs (*B*)			
Attribute (*i*)	**Importance (*I*)**	**Smith**	**Princeton**	**Rutgers**	**Northland**
Academic reputation	6	8	9	6	3
All women	7	9	3	3	3
Cost	4	2	2	6	9
Proximity to home	3	2	2	6	9
Athletics	1	1	2	5	1
Party atmosphere	2	1	3	7	9
Library facilities	5	7	9	7	2
Attitude score		163	142	153	131

Note: These hypothetical ratings are scored from 1 to 10, and higher numbers indicate "better" standing on an attribute. For a negative attribute (e.g., cost) higher scores indicate that the school is believed to have "less" of that attribute (i.e., to be cheaper).

Add a New Attribute. Product marketers frequently try to distinguish themselves from their competitors when they add a product feature. Northland College might try to emphasize some unique aspect, such as a hands-on internship program for business majors that takes advantage of ties to the local community.

Influence Competitors' Ratings.   Finally, you can decrease your competitors' higher ratings with a *comparative advertising* strategy. In this case, you might publish an ad that lists the tuition rates of a number of area schools with which Northland compares favorably and emphasize the value for the money its students get.

Do Attitudes Predict Behavior?

Consumer researchers have used multiattribute models for many years, but a major problem plagues them: In many cases, a person's attitude doesn't predict her behavior. In a classic demonstration of "do as I say, not as I do," many studies report a very low correlation between a person's reported attitude toward something and her actual behavior toward it. Some researchers are so discouraged that they question whether attitudes are of any use at all in understanding behavior.[32]

This questionable linkage between attitudes and behavior is a big headache for advertisers: Consumers can love a commercial yet still not buy the product. For example, one of the most popular TV commercials in recent years featured basketball player Shaquille O'Neal for Pepsi. Although the company spent $67 million on this spot and other similar ones in a single year, sales of Pepsi-Cola fell by close to 2 percent, even as sales of archrival Coca-Cola increased by 8 percent during the same period.[33]

The Extended Fishbein Model

In response, researchers tinkered with the Fishbein model to improve its predictive ability. They call the newer version the **theory of reasoned action**.[34] This model contains several important additions to the original, and although the model is still not perfect, it does a better job of prediction.[35] Let's look at some of the modifications to this model.

Intentions Versus Behavior

Like the motivations we discussed in Chapter 4, attitudes have both direction and strength. A person may like or dislike an attitude object with varying degrees of confidence or conviction. It is helpful to distinguish between firmly held attitudes and those that are more superficial, especially because a person who holds an attitude with greater conviction is more likely to act on it.[36] One study on environmental issues and marketing activities found, for example, that people who express greater conviction in their feelings regarding environmentally responsible behaviors such as recycling show greater consistency between attitudes and behavioral intentions.[37]

However, as the old expression goes, "the road to hell is paved with good intentions." Many factors might interfere with performing the intended behavior. Say you save up to buy a new Apple iPhone. Although you have every intention to get it, stuff happens: You might lose your job, get mugged on the way to the Apple store, or arrive at the store only to find they've run out of the item. It is not surprising, then, that in some instances researchers find that instead of knowing our intentions, our past purchase behavior does a better job of predicting our future behavior (this is one of the foundations of direct marketing techniques that identify likely customers based on their purchase histories).[38] The theory of reasoned action aims to measure *behavioral intentions*—it recognizes that certain uncontrollable factors (such as that mugger) limit our ability to predict the future with 100 percent accuracy.

Social Pressure

Perhaps most importantly, the theory acknowledges the power of other people to influence what we do. Much as we may hate to admit it, what we think others would *like* us to do may override our own preferences. Some research approaches assess the extent to which people's "public" attitudes and purchase decisions might differ from what they do in private. For example, one firm uses a technique it calls "engineered theatre." Researchers go to the actual site where people use a product, such as a bar. They arrange for the bartender to "mistakenly" serve the wrong drink and then observe the consumer's "naked response" to the new brand and her reaction to consuming the brand in a social context.[39]

Returning to Saundra's college choice, you can see in Table 7.1 that she was very positive about going to a predominantly female school. However, if she felt that this choice would be unpopular (perhaps her friends would think she was crazy), she might ignore or downgrade this preference when she made her decision. Researchers added a new element, the **subjective norm (SN)**, to account for the effects of what we believe other people think we should do. They use two factors to measure SN: (1) the intensity of a *normative belief (NB)* that others believe we should take or not take some action and (2) the *motivation to comply (MC)* with that belief (i.e., the degree to which the consumer takes others' anticipated reactions into account when she evaluates a purchase).

Attitude Toward Buying

The newer model also measures **attitude toward the act of buying (A_{act})**, rather than only the attitude toward the product itself. In other words, it focuses on the perceived consequences of a purchase. Knowing how someone feels about buying or using an object turns out to be more valid than merely knowing the consumer's evaluation of the object itself.[41]

This Vietnamese ad employs social pressure (the subjective norm) to address people's attitudes toward wearing helmets.
Source: Courtesy of Ogilvy & Mather/Asia Injury Prevention Foundation; Photo by Pro-I Studio.

"I WON'T WEAR A **HELMET**
(PHAN DINH - MENTAL AGE 2YRS)
IT **MAKES** ME LOOK **STUPID**"

EVERY YEAR OVER 12,000 PEOPLE DIE ON OUR ROADS AND 30,000 ARE SERIOUSLY INJURED. THAT MEANS THOUSANDS OF FAMILIES LEFT PICKING UP THE PIECES. FAMILIES TORTURED BY THE LOSS OF A LOVED ONE, CRIPPLED BY REDUCED INCOME OR THE SUDDEN NEED TO CARE FOR A RELATIVE WITH PERMANENT BRAIN DAMAGE. THE SAD TRUTH IS THAT MOST OF THESE CASES COULD HAVE BEEN PREVENTED BY SIMPLY WEARING A HELMET. WHEN YOU THINK ABOUT IT, THERE ARE NO EXCUSES.

WEAR A **HELMET**. THERE ARE NO EXCUSES.

To understand this distinction, consider a marketing researcher who wants to measure college students' attitudes toward safe sex and wearing condoms. Although many college students she interviews would probably report a positive attitude toward condom use, can she conclude from these responses that these respondents will actually buy and use them? She might get more accurate results if she simply asks the same students how likely they are to *buy* condoms. A person might have a positive A_o toward condoms, but A_{act} (attitude toward the act of obtaining the attitude object) might be negative because of the embarrassment or the hassle involved.

Obstacles to Predicting Behavior in the Theory of Reasoned Action

Despite improvements to the Fishbein model, problems arise when researchers misapply it. Like our discussion about measuring personality traits in Chapter 6, sometimes researchers use the model in ways it was not intended or where certain assumptions about human behavior may not be warranted.[42] Here are some other obstacles to predicting behavior:

- The model tries to predict actual behavior (e.g., taking a diet pill), not the *outcomes* of behavior that some studies assess (e.g., losing weight).
- Some outcomes are beyond our control, such as when the purchase requires the cooperation of other people. For instance, a woman might *want* to get a mortgage, but this intention will be worthless if she cannot find a banker to give her one.
- The basic assumption that behavior is intentional may be invalid in a variety of cases, including impulsive acts, sudden changes in one's situation, novelty seeking, or even simple repeat buying. One study found that such unexpected events as having guests, changes in the weather, or reading articles about the healthfulness of certain foods significantly affected actual behaviors.[43]
- Measures of attitude often do not really correspond to the behavior they are supposed to predict, either in terms of the A_o or when the act will occur. One common problem is a difference in the level of abstraction researchers employ. For example, knowing a person's attitude toward sports cars may not predict whether she will purchase a BMW Z4. It is very important to match the level of specificity between the attitude and the behavioral intention.
- A similar problem relates to the *time frame* of the attitude measure. In general, the longer the time between the attitude measurement and the behavior it is supposed to assess, the weaker the relationship will be. For example, predictability improves greatly if we ask a consumer the likelihood that she would buy a house in the next week as opposed to within the next 5 years.
- We form stronger and more predictive attitudes through direct, personal experience with an A_o than those we form indirectly through advertising.[44] According to the *attitude accessibility perspective*, behavior is a function of the person's immediate perceptions of the A_o, in the context of the situation in which we encounter it. An attitude will guide the evaluation of the object but *only* if a person's memory activates it when she encounters the object. These findings underscore the importance of strategies that induce trials (e.g., by widespread product sampling to encourage the consumer to try the product at home, by taste tests, test drives, etc.) as well as those that maximize exposure to marketing communications.[45]

In addition, most researchers apply the theory of reasoned action in Western settings. Certain assumptions inherent in the model may not necessarily apply to consumers from other cultures. Several cultural roadblocks diminish the universality of the theory of reasoned action:

- The model predicts the performance of a voluntary act. Across cultures, however, many activities, ranging from taking exams and entering military service to receiving an inoculation or even choosing a marriage partner, are not necessarily voluntary.

Marketing Opportunity

Social pressure can play a useful role in motivating consumers to engage in socially responsible behaviors. One study assessed this possibility when it compared the effectiveness of different ways a hotel might encourage guests to reuse their towels. When researchers used a social appeal ("the majority of guests reuse their towels") this worked better than a functional appeal ("help save the environment"). They also found that they boosted compliance when they phrased the requests in terms of directly relevant others ("the majority of guests in this room reuse their towels") compared to more general group appeals (such as the "majority of men and women reuse their towels").[40]

- The relative impact of subjective norms may vary across cultures. For example, Asian cultures tend to value conformity and "face saving," so it is possible that subjective norms that involve the anticipated reactions of others to the choice will have an even greater impact on behavior for many Asian consumers. Indeed, a recent study conducted among voters in Singapore was able to predict voting for political candidates from their voting intentions, which in turn were influenced by such factors as voters' attitudes toward the candidate, attitudes toward the political party, and subjective norms—which in Singapore includes an emphasis on harmonious and close ties among members of the society.
- The model measures behavioral intentions and thus presupposes that consumers are actively thinking ahead and planning future behaviors. The intention concept assumes that consumers have a linear time sense; they think in terms of past, present, and future. As we'll discuss in Chapter 9, not all cultures subscribe to this perspective on time.
- A consumer who forms an intention (implicitly) claims that he is in control of his actions. Some cultures (e.g., Muslim peoples) tend to be fatalistic and do not necessarily believe in the concept of free will. Indeed, one study that compared students from the United States, Jordan, and Thailand found evidence for cultural differences in assumptions about fatalism and control over the future.[46]

Trying to Consume

Other theorists propose different perspectives on the attitude–behavior connection. For example, a recent model its authors call the **multiple pathway anchoring and adjustment (MPAA) model** emphasizes multiple pathways to attitude formation, including outside-in (object-centered) and inside-out (person-centered) pathways.[47]

Another perspective tries to address some of these problems as it focuses instead on consumers' goals and what they believe they have to do to attain them. The **theory of trying** states that we should replace the criterion of behavior in the reasoned action model with *trying* to reach a goal.[48] As Figure 7.3 shows, this per-

Figure 7.3 THEORY OF TRYING

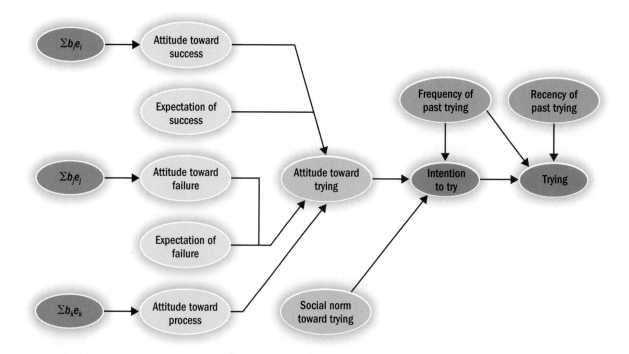

spective recognizes that additional factors might intervene between intent and performance—both personal and environmental barriers might prevent the individual from attaining the goal. For example, a person who intends to lose weight may have to deal with numerous issues: He may not believe he is capable of slimming down, he may have a roommate who loves to cook and who leaves tempting goodies lying around the apartment, his friends may be jealous of his attempts to diet and encourage him to pig out, or he may be genetically predisposed to obesity and cutting down on calories simply will not produce the desired results.

How Do Marketers Change Attitudes?

BUY NOW! Advertisers constantly bombard us with messages imploring us to change our attitudes—and of course buy their products. These persuasion attempts can range from logical arguments to graphic pictures, from peers who try to intimidate us to celebrities who try to charm us. Now we'll review some of the factors that help to determine the effectiveness of marketing communications. Our focus will be on some basic aspects of communication that specifically help to determine how and if consumers will form new attitudes or modify existing ones.

Persuasion involves an active attempt to change attitudes. This is of course job number one for many marketing communications. We'll learn more about how marketers try to accomplish this later, but for now we'll set the stage when we list some basic psychological principles that influence people to change their minds or comply with a request:[49]

- **Reciprocity**—We are more likely to give if first we receive. That's why including money in a mail survey questionnaire increases the response rate by an average of 65 percent over surveys that come without financial incentives in the envelope.
- **Scarcity**—Like people, items are more attractive when they aren't available. In one study, researchers asked people to rate the quality of chocolate chip cookies. Participants who only got one cookie liked them better than did those who evaluated more of the same kind of cookie. That helps explain why we tend to value "limited edition" items.
- **Authority**—We believe an authoritative source much more readily than one that is less authoritative. That explains why the American public's opinion on an issue can shift by as much as 2 percent when the *New York Times* (but not the *National Enquirer*) runs an article about it.
- **Consistency**—As we saw earlier in this chapter, people try not to contradict themselves in terms of what they say and do about an issue. In one study, students at an Israeli university who solicited donations to help disabled people doubled the amount they normally collected in a neighborhood if they first asked the residents to sign a petition supporting this cause 2 weeks before they actually asked for the donations.
- **Liking**—We agree with those we like or admire. In one study, good-looking fundraisers raised almost twice as much as other volunteers who were not as attractive.
- **Consensus**—We consider what others do before we decide what to do. People are more likely to donate to a charity if they first see a list of the names of their neighbors who have already done so.

Decisions, Decisions:
Tactical Communications Options

Suppose a car company wants to create an advertising campaign for a new ragtop it targets to young drivers. As it plans this campaign, the automaker must develop a message that will arouse desire for the car. To craft persuasive messages that might persuade someone to buy this car instead of the many others available, we must answer several questions:

● Who will drive the car in the ad? A NASCAR driver? A career woman? A hip-hop star? The source of a message helps determine whether consumers will accept it.
● How should we construct the message? Should it emphasize the negative consequences of being left out when others drive cool cars and you still tool around in your old clunker? Should it directly compare the car with others already on the market, or maybe present a fantasy in which a tough-minded female executive meets a dashing stranger while she cruises down the highway?
● What media should we use? Should the ad run in a magazine? Should we air it on TV? Sell the product door-to-door? Post the material on a Web site or create a Facebook group? Convince bloggers to write about it? If we do produce a print ad, should we run it in the pages of *Vogue*? *Good Housekeeping*? *Car and Driver*? Sometimes *where* you say something is as important as *what* you say. Ideally, we should match the medium's attributes with those of what we sell. For example, advertising in magazines with high prestige is more effective when we want to communicate messages about overall product image and quality, whereas specialized expert magazines do a better job when we want to convey factual information.[50]
● What characteristics of the target market might lead them to accept the ad? If targeted users are frustrated in their daily lives, they might be more receptive to a fantasy appeal. If they're status-oriented, maybe a commercial should show bystanders who swoon with admiration as the car cruises by.

OBJECTIVE

Why does the communications model identify several important components for marketers when they try to change consumers' attitudes toward products and services?

The Elements of Communication

Marketers traditionally rely on the **communications model** that you see in Figure 7.4. This model specifies the elements they need to control in order to communicate with their customers. One of these is a source, where the communication originates. Another is the message itself. There are many ways to say something, and the structure of the message has a significant effect on how we perceive it. We must transmit the message via a medium, which could be TV, radio, magazines, billboards, personal contact, or even a matchbook cover. One or more *receivers* (such as Natalie) interpret the message in light of their own experiences. Finally, the source receives *feedback* so that the marketer can use receivers' reactions to modify aspects of the message as necessary.

An Updated View: Interactive Communications

Although Natalie managed to ignore most of the "junk mail" that arrived at her door, she didn't avoid every marketing message—instead she chose which ones she wanted to see. The traditional communications model is not entirely wrong. But, it also doesn't tell the whole story—especially in today's dynamic world of interactivity where consumers have many more choices available to them and greater control over which messages they *choose* to process.[51]

In fact, the popular strategy we call **permission marketing** acknowledges that a marketer will be much more successful when he communicates with consumers who have already agreed to listen to him—consumers who "opt out" of listening to the message probably weren't good prospects in the first place.[52] In contrast, those who say they want to learn more are likely to be receptive to marketing communications they have chosen to see or hear. As the permission marketing concept reminds us, we don't have to simply sit there and take it. We have a voice in deciding what messages we choose to see and when—and we exercise that option more and more.

Figure 7.4 THE TRADITIONAL
COMMUNICATIONS MODEL

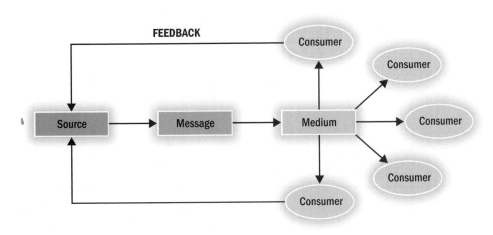

Social scientists developed the traditional model to understand mass communications in which a source transmits information to many receivers at one time—typically via a *broadcast* medium such as television. This perspective essentially views advertising as the process of transferring information to the buyer before a sale. It regards a message as *perishable*—the marketer repeats the same message to a large audience and then the message "vanishes" when a new campaign takes its place. As we'll see, that model doesn't work as well now that we can *narrowcast*, or finely tune our messages to very small groups of receivers (sometimes even one person at a time).

OBJECTIVE

Why is the consumer who processes a message not necessarily the passive receiver of information marketers once believed him to be?

How long has it been since you posted to your Facebook page? Exciting technological and social developments make us rethink the picture of passive consumers as people increasingly play more proactive roles in communications. In other words, we are to a greater extent *partners*—rather than couch potatoes—in the communications process. Our input helps to shape the messages we and others like us receive, and furthermore we may seek out these messages rather than sit home and wait to see them on TV or in the paper. Figure 7.5 illustrates this updated approach to interactive communications.

Viral marketing techniques rely on consumers to spread an ad message to others in their social network because they find it cool, interesting, or just plain funny. The "subservient chicken" viral campaign for Burger King was a very successful application to promote BK's chicken sandwiches. You can type a command into the box and the "chicken" will execute it in real-time.
Source: The BURGER KING® trademarks and image are used with permission from Burger King Corporation.

Figure 7.5 AN UPDATED COMMUNICATIONS MODEL

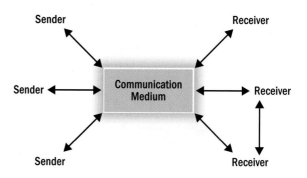

One of the early instigators of this communications revolution was the humble handheld remote control device. As VCRs (remember them?) began to be commonplace in homes, suddenly consumers had more input into what they wanted to watch—and when. No longer did the TV networks decide when we could watch our favorite shows, and we didn't have to miss the new episode of *Mork and Mindy* because it was on at the same time as the Bears game.

Since that time, of course, our ability to control our media environment has mushroomed. Just ask some of the millions of us who use digital video recorders (DVRs) such as TiVo to watch TV shows whenever we wish—and who blithely skip over the commercials.[53] Many others have access to video-on-demand or pay-per-view TV. Home-shopping networks encourage us to call in and discuss our passion for cubic zirconium jewelry live on the air. Caller ID devices and answering machines allow us to decide if we will accept a phone call during dinner and to know if a telemarketer lurks on the other end before we pick up the phone. A bit of Web surfing allows us to identify kindred spirits around the globe, to request information about products, and even to provide suggestions to product designers and market researchers.

New Message Formats

An array of new ways to transmit information in both text and picture form offers marketers exciting alternatives to traditional advertising on TV, billboards, magazines, and so on.[54] **M-commerce** (mobile commerce), where marketers promote their goods and services via wireless devices, including cell phones, PDAs, and iPods, is red-hot. European and Asian consumers already rely on their cell phones to connect them to the world in ways we are only starting to realize in the United States. In Asia, tiny cell phone screens have become electronic wallets that buy Cokes from vending machines and devices that dole out McDonald's coupons on the phone screen. Among the Chinese, cell phones have become such important status symbols that relatives at funeral rites burn paper cell phone effigies so the dead will have their mobiles in the afterlife.

If you're on Facebook or MySpace (and the odds are good you are), you're one of the one billion people that analysts project will use **social media** applications globally within five years.[55] This label refers to the set of technologies that enable users to create content and share it with a large number of others. Social media is so widespread that in the United States and other developed countries more people use these platforms than use e-mail—and the time people spend on these networks is growing three times faster than the rate of overall participation online.[56] Social media platforms include:

- **Blogs**—Users post messages to the Web in diary form. Blogging started as a grassroots movement where individuals shared their thoughts on a range of topics from the mundane to the profound. Analysts estimate that two-thirds of all American Internet users will post and read blogs on a regular basis by 2012.[57]

Video blogging (vlogging)—You can post video diaries on sites such as YouTube or photos on Flickr.

Podcasting—You can create your own radio show that people can listen to either on their computers or iPods.

Virtual worlds—Immersive 3-D digital environments (e.g., Second Life). The research firm Gartner predicts that by the year 2011, over 250 million people will participate in one or more virtual worlds.

Twitter—Postings limited to 140 characters. By the end of 2008, Twitter had close to 2 million users and the site continues to grow exponentially as more celebrities (like Shaquille O'Neal and Oprah) post "tweets" to their followers.

Widgets—Small programs that users can download onto their desktops, or embed in their blogs or profile pages, that import some form of live content. For example, a football blogger can place an <u>ESPN.com</u> widget on his blog that displays up-to-the-minute NFL rankings.

8
OBJECTIVE
Why do several factors influence a message source's effectiveness?

⊕ The Source

Regardless of whether we receive a message by "snail mail" (netheads' slang for the postal service) or e-mail, common sense tells us that if different people say or write the very same words, the message can affect us differently. Researchers have discussed the power of *source effects* for more than 50 years. When we attribute the same message to different sources and measure the degree of attitude change that occurs after listeners hear it, we can isolate which characteristics of a communicator cause attitude change.[58]

Under most conditions, the source of a message can have a big impact on the likelihood that receivers will accept it. Marketers can choose a spokesperson because she is an expert, attractive, famous, or even a "typical" consumer who is both likable and trustworthy. *Credibility* and *attractiveness* are two particularly important source characteristics (i.e., how much we either believe or like the communicator).[59]

How do marketing specialists decide whether to stress credibility or attractiveness when they select a message source? There should be a match between the needs of the recipient and the potential rewards the source offers. When this match occurs, the recipient is more motivated to process the message. An attractive source, for example, is more effective for receivers who tend to be sensitive about social acceptance and others' opinions, whereas a credible, expert source is more powerful when she speaks to internally oriented people.[60] However, even a credible source's trustworthiness evaporates if she endorses too many products.[61]

The choice may also depend on the type of product. A positive source can reduce risk and increase message acceptance overall, but particular types of sources are more effective to reduce different kinds of risk. Experts excel when we want to change attitudes toward utilitarian products that have high performance risk, such as vacuums, because they are complex and may not work as we expect. Celebrities work better when they focus on products such as jewelry and furniture that have high social risk, where the user is more concerned about the impression others have of him. Finally, "typical" consumers, who are appealing sources because of their similarity to the recipient, tend to be most effective when they provide real-life endorsements for everyday products that are low risk, such as cookies.[62]

⊕ Source Credibility

Source credibility refers to a communicator's expertise, objectivity, or trustworthiness. This dimension relates to consumers' beliefs that this person is competent and

ECONsumer Behavior

When Chrysler was struggling in the 1980s, CEO Lee Iacocca took to the airwaves to urge consumers to buy his cars. Since the current economic crisis hit, we've seen a lot more CEOs on TV to promote their companies. The chief executives from companies as diverse as Sprint, Charles Schwab, and S.C. Johnson try to project an image of dependability and value during uncertain times. These authoritative sources may be effective, though not every CEO is telegenic enough to pull this off. When (the former) DaimlerChrysler used its CEO Dieter Zetsche in a series of ads starring "Dr. Z," the campaign produced more cringes than sales.[65]

that she will provide the necessary information we need when we evaluate competing products. Sincerity is particularly important when a company tries to publicize its *corporate social responsibility (CSR)* activities that benefit the community in some way. When consumers believe it's genuinely doing good things, a company's image can skyrocket. But this effort can backfire if people question the organization's motivations (e.g., if they think the firm spends more to talk about its good deeds than to actually do them).[63] Not too surprisingly, people who see deceptive advertising experience a feeling of distrust that carries over to other messages from that source and even to other sources because they are more likely to assume that advertising in general is not very credible—a true case of poisoning the well for other marketers![64]

A credible source is particularly persuasive when the consumer has yet to learn much about a product or form an opinion of it.[66] The decision to pay an expert or a

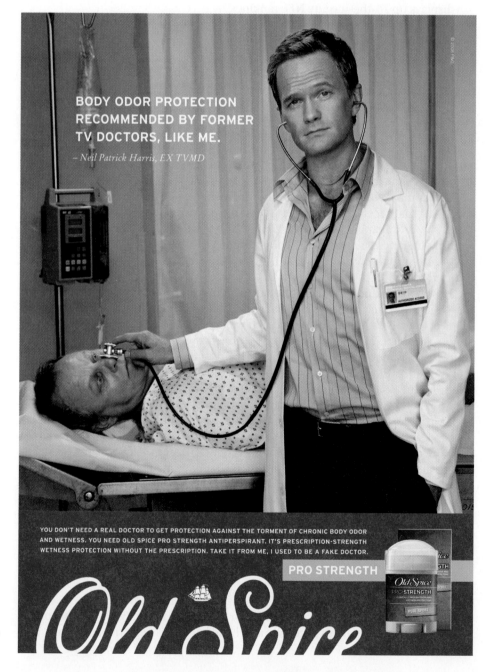

Even actors who play doctors on TV may be credible communicators.
Source: Courtesy of Old Spice/The Procter & Gamble Company.

celebrity to tout a product can be a very costly one. However, typically the investment is worth it simply because market analysts use the announcement of an endorsement contract to evaluate a firm's potential profitability, which affects its expected return. On average, then, the impact of endorsements on stock returns appears to be so positive that it offsets the cost of hiring the spokesperson.[67]

Although in general more positive sources tend to increase attitude change, there are exceptions to this rule. Sometimes we can think a source is obnoxious, yet still it is effective. A case in point is Mr. Whipple, the irritating but well-known TV character who scolds toilet paper shoppers, "Please don't squeeze the Charmin!" In some instances the differences in attitude change between positive sources and less positive sources become erased over time. After a while, people appear to "forget" about the negative source and change their attitudes anyway. We call this process the **sleeper effect**.[69]

What Factors Affect Credibility?

A message's credibility increases if receivers think the source's qualifications are relevant to the product he or she endorses. This linkage can overcome other objections people may have to the endorser or the product. Ronald Biggs, whose claim to fame was his 1963 role in the Great Train Robbery in the United Kingdom, successfully served as a spokesman in Brazil for a company that makes door locks—a topic about which he is presumably knowledgeable![70]

It's important to note that what is credible to one consumer segment may be a turnoff to another. Indeed, rebellious or even deviant celebrities may be attractive to some simply for that reason. Tommy Hilfiger cultivated a rebellious, street-smart image when he used rapper Snoop Doggy Dogg (who was acquitted of murder charges) to help launch his clothing line and Coolio, a former crack addict and thief, as a runway model.[71] Parents may not be thrilled by these message sources—but isn't that the point?

A consumer's beliefs about a product's attributes will weaken if he or she perceives that the source is biased.[72] *Knowledge bias* implies that a source's knowledge about a topic is not accurate. *Reporting bias* occurs when a source has the required knowledge but we question his willingness to convey it accurately—as when a racket manufacturer pays a star tennis player to use its products exclusively. The source's credentials might be appropriate, but the fact that consumers see the expert as a "hired gun" compromises believability. The Federal Trade Commission is considering steps to toughen the rules for testimonials by requiring advertisers to produce evidence that the results of a spokesperson are likely to be typical for others. One other possible measure will require celebrities who mention products in TV interviews to disclose any connections they have to the manufacturers of those products. And, bloggers who receive free products and recommend them in their blogs will have to document that they got the items at no charge.[73]

Source Attractiveness: "What Is Beautiful Is Good"

Recently a British dairy company enlisted Johnny Rotten, the lead singer of the Sex Pistols, to appear in a commercial (or *advert*, as they say in the United Kingdom) to promote its butter. Sales went up 85 percent when the punk legend plugged the product.[74] **Source attractiveness** refers to the social *value* recipients attribute to a communicator. This value relates to the person's physical appearance, personality, social status, or similarity to the receiver (we like to listen to people who are like us).

Some sources like Johnny Rotten appeal to us because they are cool, brainy, or just plain famous. However, many simply are nice to look at. Almost everywhere we turn, beautiful people try to persuade us to buy or do something. As Chapter 5 showed us, our society places a very high premium on physical attractiveness. We assume that good-looking people are smarter, hipper, and happier than the rest of us. This is an example of a *halo effect*, which occurs when we assume that persons who rank high on one dimension excel on others as well. We can explain this effect in

The Tangled Web

In recent years we've witnessed a new attempt to manipulate attitudes that some call **sock puppeting**. This term describes a company executive or other biased source who poses as someone else as he touts his organization in social media. For example, in 2007 it came to light that the CEO of Whole Foods posted derogatory comments about rival Wild Oats without revealing his true identity. More recently a non-profit research organization called GiveWell that rates the effectiveness of charities had to discipline two of its founders who pretended to be other people on blogs and then referred people to the group's Web site.[68]

Similar problems potentially dilute the credibility of *Wikipedia*, the open-source online encyclopedia that is beloved by many students. Anyone can edit entries, so their reliability is not assured. Although other alert contributors may eventually correct false or self-serving entries, there is still room for organizations to color content in a way that serves their goals. For example, a visitor edited the *Wikipedia* entry for the SeaWorld theme parks to change all mentions of "orcas" to "killer whales" and he or she also deleted a paragraph that criticized SeaWorld's "lack of respect toward its orcas." It turns out the changes originated at a computer located in Anheuser-Busch—the company that happens to own SeaWorld. An employee of PepsiCo deleted several paragraphs of the Pepsi entry that focused on its detrimental health effects, and a person at Wal-Mart altered an entry about how the retailer pays its employees.

Another form of sock puppeting is so-called **paid influencer programs** that attempt to start online conversations about brands when they encourage bloggers to write about them. These "sponsored conversations" can be effective, but again marketers need to be careful about the potential to distort source recommendations. For example, Kmart awarded a shopping spree to a group of bloggers who agreed to post about their experiences. Panasonic flew bloggers to the Consumer Electronics Show in Las Vegas, where they posted about the show and Panasonic products unveiled there. Mercedes gave a blogger use of an SUV for a week in exchange for posts about it.

terms of the consistency principle we discussed earlier in this chapter; we are more comfortable when all of our judgments about a person correspond.

Clearly, beauty sells—so how does this happen?[75] One explanation is that physical attractiveness is a cue that facilitates or modifies information processing because it directs our attention to the message. Some evidence indicates that consumers pay more attention to ads that contain attractive models, though not necessarily to the ad copy.[76] In other words, we're more likely to notice an ad with a beautiful person in it, but we won't necessarily read it. We may enjoy looking at a handsome person, but these positive feelings do not necessarily affect product attitudes or purchase intentions.[77]

Under the right circumstances, however, beauty can indeed be a source of information—especially when the advertised product actually (or so the marketer claims) enhances attractiveness or sexuality.[78] The *social adaptation perspective* assumes that the perceiver weights information more heavily if he feels it will help him to evaluate the subject of a message. As we saw in Chapter 2, we filter out irrelevant information to minimize cognitive effort. So in these situations, a hot endorser provides appropriate information and this becomes a central, task-relevant cue. For example, attractiveness affects attitudes toward ads about perfume or cologne (where attractiveness is relevant) but not toward coffee ads (where attractiveness is not relevant).[79]

Star Power: Celebrities as Communications Sources

Celebrities hawk everything from grills (George Foreman) to perfumes (J. Lo). As our discussion about the consistency principle illustrates, these messages are more effective when there's a logical connection between the star and the product. When Bob Dylan—who wrote lyrics such as "Advertising signs that con you/Into thinking you're the one/That can do what's never been done/That can win what's never been won. . . ."—pitches Victoria's Secret lingerie (yes he really did), marketers may need to reread their consumer behavior textbook.[80]

Believe it or not, stars don't endorse products for free—they may not even use the brands they ask you to buy (sorry to burst your bubble). Celebs typically make a lot of money to appear in advertising—is this a smart marketing investment? Actually the evidence says yes (assuming they're not caught in the act of taking a bong hit at a party). One study found that compared to "ordinary" faces, our brains pay more attention to famous faces and more efficiently process information about these images.[81] Celebrities increase awareness of a firm's advertising and enhance both company image and brand attitudes.[82] A celebrity endorsement strategy can be an effective way to differentiate among similar products. This is especially important when consumers do not perceive many actual differences among competitors, as often occurs when brands are in the mature stage of the product life cycle.

Star power works because celebrities embody *cultural meanings*—they symbolize important categories like status and social class (a "working-class hero," such as Kevin James of *King of Queens*), gender (a "ladies man," such as Brad Pitt), age (the boyish Michael J. Fox), and even personality types (the nerdy but earnest Hiro on *Heroes*). Ideally, the advertiser decides what meanings the product should convey (that is, how it should position the item in the marketplace) and then chooses a celebrity who embodies a similar meaning. The product's meaning thus moves from the manufacturer to the consumer, using the star as a vehicle.[84]

Nonhuman Endorsers

Celebrities can be effective endorsers, but there are drawbacks to using them. As we previously noted, their motives may be suspect if they plug products that don't fit their images or if consumers begin to believe the celebrities never met a product they didn't like (for a fee). They may be involved in a scandal or deviate from a brand's desired image—the Milk Processor Education Program suspended "Got Milk?" ads featuring Mary-Kate and Ashley Olsen after Mary-Kate entered a treatment facility for an undisclosed health issue.

For these reasons, some marketers seek alternative sources, including cartoon characters and mascots (in 2009 Milk-Bone named its first-ever "spokesdog," a Great Dane named Winston).[85] As the marketing director for a company that manufactures costumed characters for sports teams and businesses points out, "You don't have to worry about your mascot checking into rehab."[86] And researchers report that **spokescharacters**, such as the Pillsbury Doughboy, Chester the Cheetah, and the Snuggle Bear, do, in fact, boost viewers' recall of claims that ads make and also yield higher brand attitude.[87] The most popular spokescharacters today are M&M's, the GEICO Gecko, the AFLAC duck, Poppin' Fresh (aka The Pillsbury Doughboy) and that old standby Tony the Tiger.[88]

As we saw in Chapter 5, an *avatar* is an alternative to a flesh-and-blood endorser. *Avatar* is a Hindu term for a deity that appears in superhuman or animal form. In the computing world, it means a character you can move around inside a visual, graphical world. Consumers who inhabit virtual worlds such as Second Life, There, and Entropia Universe design their avatars to reflect their own unique personalities, desires, and fantasies.

The advantages of using virtual avatars compared to flesh-and-blood models include the ability to change the avatar in real time to suit the needs of the target audience. From an advertising perspective, they are likely to be more cost effective than hiring a real person. From a personal selling and customer service perspective, they handle multiple customers at one time, they are not geographically limited, and they are operational 24/7 so they free up company employees and sales personnel to perform other activities.[89]

OBJECTIVE

How does the way a marketer structures his message determine how persuasive it will be?

' The Message

A major study of more than 1,000 commercials identified factors that determine whether a commercial message will be persuasive. The single most important feature: Does the communication stress a unique attribute or benefit of the product?[90] Table 7.2 lists some other good and bad elements.

Characteristics of the message itself help determine its impact on attitudes. These variables include *how* we say the message as well as *what* we say. These are some issues a marketer faces when she creates a message:

- Should she convey the message in words or pictures?
- How often should she repeat the message?
- Should it draw a conclusion or should this be left up to the listener?
- Should it present both sides of an argument?
- Should it explicitly compare the product to competitors?
- Should it include a blatant sexual appeal?
- Should it arouse negative emotions such as fear?
- How concrete or vivid should the arguments and imagery be?
- Should it be funny?

How Do We Send the Message?

Pictures or words? The saying, "One picture is worth a thousand words" captures the idea that visuals are very effective, especially when the communicator wants to influence receivers' emotional responses. For this reason, advertisers often rely on vivid illustrations or photography.[91]

TABLE 7.2	Characteristics of Good and Bad Messages
Positive Effects	**Negative Effects**
Showing convenience of use	Extensive information on components, ingredients, or nutrition
Showing new product or improved features	Outdoor setting (message gets lost)
Casting background (i.e., people are incidental to message)	Large number of on-screen characters
Indirect comparison to other products	Graphic displays
Demonstration of the product in use	
Demonstration of tangible results (e.g., bouncy hair)	
An actor playing the role of an ordinary person	
No principal character (i.e., more time is devoted to the product)	

Source: Adapted from David W. Stewart and David H. Furse, "The Effects of Television Advertising Execution on Recall, Comprehension, and Persuasion," *Psychology & Marketing* 2 (Fall 1985): 135–60. Copyright © 1985 by John Wiley & Sons, Inc. Reprinted by permission.

This British clothing ad uses vivid (and perhaps a bit scary?) imagery to communicate.
Source: Courtesy of DDB, London.

However, a picture is not always as effective when it communicates factual information. Ads that contain the same information elicit different reactions when the marketer presents them in visual versus verbal form. The verbal version affects ratings on the utilitarian aspects of a product, whereas the visual version affects aesthetic evaluations. Verbal elements are more effective when an accompanying picture reinforces them, especially if they *frame* the illustration (the message in the picture strongly relates to the copy).[92]

Because it requires more effort to process, a verbal message is most appropriate for high-involvement situations, such as print contexts where the reader really pays attention to the advertising. Verbal material decays more rapidly in memory, so these messages require more frequent exposures to obtain the desired effect. Visual images, in contrast, allow the receiver to *chunk* information at the time of encoding (see Chapter 3). Chunking results in a stronger memory trace that aids retrieval over time.[93]

Powerful descriptions or graphics command attention and are more strongly embedded in memory. This may be because *vivid* images tend to activate mental imagery, whereas abstract stimuli inhibit this process.[94] Of course, this effect can cut both ways: Negative information a marketer presents in a vivid manner may result in more negative evaluations at a later time.[95]

The concrete discussion of a product attribute in ad copy also influences the importance of that attribute because it draws more attention. For example, in a study where participants read two versions of ad copy for a watch, the version that claimed "According to industry sources, three out of every four watch breakdowns are due to water getting into the case," was more effective than the version that simply said, "According to industry sources, many watch breakdowns are due to water getting into the case."[96]

Repeat the message? Repetition can be a double-edged sword for marketers. As we noted in Chapter 3, we usually need multiple exposures to a stimulus before learning occurs. Contrary to the saying "familiarity breeds contempt," people tend to like things that are more familiar to them, even if they were not that keen on them initially.[97] Psychologists call this the *mere exposure* phenomenon.

Advertisers find positive effects for repetition even in mature product categories—repeating product information boosts consumers' awareness of the brand, even though the marketer says nothing new.[98] However, as we saw in Chapter 2, too much repetition creates *habituation*, whereby the consumer no longer pays attention to the stimulus because of fatigue or boredom. Excessive exposure can cause advertising wear-out, which can result in negative reactions to an ad after we see it too much.[99]

The **two-factor theory** explains the fine line between familiarity and boredom; it proposes that two separate psychological processes operate when we repeatedly

Figure 7.6 TWO-FACTOR THEORY

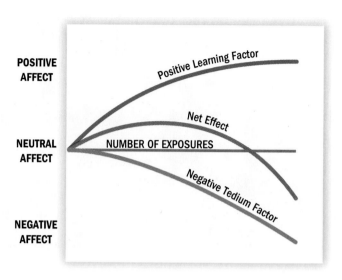

show an ad to a viewer. The positive side of repetition is that it increases familiarity and thus reduces uncertainty about the product. The negative side is that over time boredom increases with each exposure. At some point the amount of boredom exceeds the amount of uncertainty the message reduces, and this results in wear-out. Figure 7.6 depicts this pattern. Its effect is especially pronounced when each exposure is of a fairly long duration (such as a 60-second commercial).[100]

The theory implies that advertisers can overcome this problem if they limit the amount of exposure per repetition (e.g., use 15-second spots instead of longer commercials). They can also maintain familiarity but alleviate boredom if they slightly vary the content of ads over time—although each spot differs, the campaign still revolves around a common theme. Recipients who see varied ads about the product absorb more information about product attributes and experience more positive thoughts about the brand than do those who see the same information repeatedly. This additional information also allows the person to resist attempts to change his or her attitude in the face of a counterattack by a competing brand.[101]

How Do We Structure the Argument?

Many marketing messages are like debates or trials—a source presents an argument and tries to convince the receiver to shift his or her opinion. As you've no doubt guessed, the *way* we present the argument may be as important as *what* we say.

Most messages merely present one or more positive attributes about the product or reasons to buy it. These are *supportive arguments.* An alternative is to use a *two-sided message,* in which the message presents both positive and negative information. Research indicates that two-sided ads can be quite effective, yet marketers rarely use them.[102]

Why would a marketer want to devote advertising space to publicize a product's negative attributes? Under the right circumstances, **refutational arguments** that first raise a negative issue and then dismiss it can be quite effective. This approach increases source credibility because it reduces *reporting bias.* Also, people who are skeptical about the product may be more receptive to a balanced argument instead of a "whitewash."[104] For example, after General Motors declared bankruptcy, an ad declared: "Let's be completely honest: No company wants to go through this."[105]

This is not to say that the marketer should go overboard and confess to major problems with the product (though hopefully there aren't any major ones to admit to). The typical refutational strategy discusses relatively minor attributes that may present a problem or fall short when the customer compares a product to competitors. Positive, important attributes then refute these drawbacks. For example, Avis got a lot of mileage when it claimed to be only the "No. 2" car rental company, whereas an ad for Volkswagen woefully described one of its cars as a "lemon" because there was a scratch on the glove compartment chrome strip.[106] A two-sided strategy appears to be the most effective when the audience is well-educated (and presumably more impressed by a balanced argument).[107] It is also best to use when receivers are not already loyal to the product—"preaching to the choir" about possible drawbacks may raise doubts unnecessarily.

Should the argument draw conclusions, or should the marketer merely present the facts and let the consumer arrive at his own decision? On the one hand, consumers who make their own inferences instead of having them spoon-fed to them will form stronger, more accessible attitudes. On the other hand, leaving the conclusion ambiguous increases the chance that the consumer will not form the desired attitude.

The response to this issue depends on the consumer's motivation to process the ad and the complexity of the arguments. If the message is personally relevant, people will pay attention to it and spontaneously form inferences. However, if the arguments are hard to follow or consumers lack the motivation to follow them, it's safer for the ad to draw conclusions.[108]

Should we compare our product to our competitors? In 1971, the FTC issued guidelines that encouraged advertisers to name competing brands in their ads. The government did this to improve the information available to consumers in ads, and indeed recent evidence indicates that, at least under some conditions, this type of presentation does result in more informed decision making.[109] **Comparative advertising** refers to a strategy in which a message compares two or more recognizable brands and weighs them in terms of one or more specific attributes.[110] A recent Arby's campaign to promote its chicken sandwiches uses this approach: One commercial, set in a fictitious McDonald's boardroom, features a young man trying to convince McDonald's executives to serve a healthier type of chicken as he proclaims, "I propose that McDonald's stops putting phosphates, salt and water into its chicken. Consider replacing your chicken that is only about 70 percent chicken, with 100 percent all-natural chicken." The room erupts with laughter. At the end of the spot, a voice-over chimes in: "Unlike McDonald's, all of Arby's chicken sandwiches are made with 100 percent all-natural chicken. . . ."[111] Research indicates that this strategy is more effective for products that already have a positive brand image.[112]

This strategy can cut both ways, especially if the sponsor depicts the competition in a nasty or negative way. Although some comparative ads result in desired attitude changes, they may also be lower in believability and stir up *source derogation* (i.e., the consumer may doubt the credibility of a biased presentation).[114] Indeed, in some cultures (such as Asia) comparative advertising is rare because people find such a confrontational approach offensive.

Types of Message Appeals

A persuasive message can tug at the heartstrings or scare you, make you laugh, make you cry, or leave you yearning to learn more. In this section, we'll review the major alternatives available to communicators.

Emotional Versus Rational Appeals

Colgate-Palmolive's Total brand was the first toothpaste to claim that it fights gingivitis, a benefit that let Colgate inch ahead of Procter & Gamble's Crest for the first time in decades. Colgate initially made a scientific pitch for its new entry as it emphasized Total's germ-fighting abilities. In newer ads, however, former model Brooke Shields cavorts with two children (not hers) as soft music plays in the background. She states, "Having a healthy smile is important to me. Not just as an actress but as a mom."[115]

ECONsumer Behavior

When money is tight many companies try to steal market share from their competitors instead of trying to attract new users—and so they're more likely to take off the gloves and run attack ads that directly name their rivals. Domino's Pizza claimed its sandwiches were preferred two to one over Subway's; its competitor's lawyer sent the company a letter to challenge this assertion. In a follow-up ad, Domino's president burned the letter onscreen. To add insult to injury, Domino's gave away free sandwiches to the first 1,000 customers named Jared—a reference to Subway's well-known spokesman Jared Fogle. Dunkin' Donuts announced that consumers preferred its coffee to Starbucks on a Web site called dunkinbeatstarbucks.com. Visitors can send friends e-cards that say "Friends don't let friends drink Starbucks." Apple has shredded PC operating systems with its successful "I'm a PC" campaign. In the words of one well-known brand strategist, "When hard times hit, the singing, dancing and emotional ads go out the window, and clients say, 'How do I nail my competitor?'"[113]

The Crest Pro-Health campaign emphasizes information over emotion as it focuses on the toothpaste's health benefits.

Source: © Procter & Gamble Company, 2007. Used with permission.

ECONsumer Behavior

In a departure for mainstream advertising, several ad campaigns deal with the recession as they evoke strong negative emotions that acknowledge the fear and uncertainty many consumers experience. Eastman Kodak's ads for a line of printers and inkjet cartridges rant about a "$5 billion stain" on the economy when companies overpay for other ink brands. Post Shredded Wheat cereal proclaims that "Progress is overrated" and "Innovation is not your friend." JetBlue Airways pokes fun at senior executives who no longer fly on corporate jets as it greets them with a sarcastic "Welcome aboard." A blue-collar character in Miller High Life ads gleefully removes the brand from fancy bars and restaurants that he thinks take advantage of customers. An agency executive commented, "You need to walk in the shoes of the average consumers today. They're a little beat up and their wallets are lighter, and the people they trusted stole from them."[117] At least for now, it's not all hearts and flowers in the ad biz.

So, which is better: to appeal to the head or to the heart? The answer often depends on the nature of the product and the type of relationship consumers have with it. It's hard to gauge the precise effects of rational versus emotional appeals. Although recall of ad content tends to be better for "thinking" ads than for "feeling" ads, conventional measures of advertising effectiveness (e.g., day-after recall) may not be adequate to assess cumulative effects of emotional ads. These open-ended measures assess cognitive responses, and they may penalize feeling ads because the reactions are not as easy to articulate.[116]

Sex Appeals

Mars recently introduced Fling, a low-calorie chocolate bar targeted to women it describes as "Naughty, but not that naughty." In the candy's first commercial spot, a woman enters a dressing room that already has a man inside and the two get undressed and do uncandy-like things. But as the camera pans over the top it turns out they're actually in two separate rooms and in reality she's nibbling on a Fling. The campaign uses taglines like "Your boyfriend doesn't need to know," and "Pleasure yourself."[118]

Echoing the widely held belief that "sex sells," many marketing communications for products from perfumes to autos feature heavy doses of erotic suggestions that range from subtle hints to blatant displays of skin. Of course, the prevalence of sexual appeals varies from country to country. Even American firms run ads elsewhere that would not go over at home. For example, a "cheeky" ad campaign designed to boost the appeal of American-made Lee jeans among Europeans features a series of bare buttocks. The messages are based on the concept that if bottoms could choose jeans, they would opt for Lee: "Bottoms feel better in Lee Jeans."[119]

Perhaps not surprisingly, female nudity in print ads generates negative feelings and tension among female consumers, whereas men's reactions are more positive—although women with more liberal attitudes toward sex are more likely to be receptive.[120] In a case of turnabout being fair play, another study found that males dislike nude males in ads, whereas females responded well to undressed males—but not totally nude ones.[121] Women also respond more positively to sexual themes when they occur in the context of a committed relationship rather than just gratuitous lust.[122]

So, does sex work? Although erotic content does appear to draw attention to an ad, its use may actually be counterproductive. In one survey, an overwhelming 61 percent of the respondents said that sexual imagery in a product's ad makes them less likely to buy it.[123] Ironically, a provocative picture can be *too* effective; it can attract so much attention as to hinder processing and recall of the ad's contents. Sexual appeals appear to be ineffective when marketers use them merely as a "trick" to grab attention. They do, however, appear to work when the product is *itself* related to sex (e.g., lingerie or Viagra).[124]

A research firm recently explored how men and women look at sexually themed ads and what effect, if any, what they choose to look at might have on the ads' effectiveness. One part of the study used special software to follow the visual behavior of respondents as they looked at 10 print ads. The ad sample consisted of two U.S. print ads, one sexual and one nonsexual, from each of five product categories. When the participants looked at a sexual ad, men tended to ignore the text as they focused instead on the woman in it, whereas the women participants tended first to explore the ad's text elements. Men said they liked the sexual ads more, liked the products advertised in them more, and would be more likely to buy those products. Women scored the sexual ads lower than the nonsexual ones on all three of those criteria.[125]

Humorous Appeals

A TV commercial for Metamucil showed a National Park Service ranger who pours a glass of the laxative down Old Faithful and announces that the product keeps the famous geyser "regular." Yellowstone National Park started getting letters from offended viewers such as this one who wrote, "I suppose that in an era when people sell naming rights to sports arenas . . . that some in the National Park Service would see nothing wrong with selling the image of a National Park ranger for the marketing of a product promoting bowel regularity." Park officials also had their own concerns—they didn't want people to think that the geyser needed "help" or that it's OK to throw things down into it![127]

Does humor work? Overall, humorous advertisements do get attention. One study found that recognition scores for humorous liquor ads were better than average. However, the verdict is mixed as to whether humor affects recall or product attitudes in a significant way.[128] One reason silly ads may shift opinions is that they provide a source of *distraction*. A funny ad inhibits *counterarguing* (in which a consumer thinks of reasons why he doesn't agree with the message), so this increases the likelihood of message acceptance because he doesn't come up with arguments against the product.[129]

Humor is more likely to be effective when the ad clearly identifies the brand and the funny material does not "swamp" the message. This danger is similar to one we've already discussed about beautiful models who divert attention from copy points. Subtle humor is usually better, as is humor that does not make fun of the potential consumer. Finally, humor should be appropriate to the product's image. Hint: An undertaker or a bank might want to avoid humor, as well as a company that accepted U.S. government bailout money.

Fear Appeals

Volkswagen's advertising campaign to promote the safety of its Jetta model really got people's attention. The spots depict graphic car crashes from the perspective of the passengers who chatter away as they drive down the street. Without warning, other

Marketing Pitfall

The Campaign for a Commercial-Free Childhood (CCFC) protested when Nickelodeon and Burger King showed what it called a "highly sexualized" commercial for Burger King's SpongeBob Kids Meal. In the spot BK's weird spokescharacter The King sings a remix of Sir Mix-A-Lot's 1990s hit song "Baby Got Back," with the new lyrics: "I like square butts and I cannot lie." The CCFC objected to the inclusion of women who shake their rear ends as SpongeBob dances and to Sir Mix-A-Lot's statement (in reference to the offer): "Booty is booty." Burger King responded that the commercial's intent is to speak to adults who take their kids to BK, and it requires the purchase of an adult Value Meal.[126]

Marketing Pitfall

A series of funny ads a German agency created didn't make everyone laugh. Grey Germany did three condom ads for a pharmacy chain. They implied that if more people used condoms the world would have been spared such figures as Mao Tse-Tung, Adolf Hitler, and Osama bin Laden. Each execution depicted a swimming sperm with a likeness of one of the despised characters. Critics complained the ads were racist, offensive, and inappropriate; the campaign apparently didn't exactly enhance the retailer's image.[130]

Humorous appeals can be effective when marketers use them properly.
Source: © 2009 The Clorox Pet Products Company. Reprinted with permission.

vehicles come out of nowhere and brutally smash into their cars. In one spot, viewers see a passenger's head striking an airbag. The spots end with shots of stunned passengers, the damaged Jetta, and the slogan: "Safe happens." The ads look so realistic that consumers called the company to ask if any of the actors were hurt.[131]

Fear appeals emphasize the negative consequences that can occur unless the consumer changes a behavior or an attitude. Fear appeals are fairly common in advertising, although they are more common in social marketing contexts in which organizations encourage people to convert to healthier lifestyles by quitting smoking, using contraception, relying on a designated driver, or perhaps driving a Jetta. In a typical recent campaign for Brink's Home Security, sales jumped 10 percent after ads depicted families' peaceful lives that get disrupted by a home invasion. In one spot, a Brink's siren saves a woman who is home alone after a creepy-looking guy tries to kick in her door.[132]

This tactic worked for Brink's—but does a fear appeal work more generally for marketers that don't happen to be in the security business? Most research on this topic indicates that these negative messages are most effective when the advertiser uses only a moderate threat and when the ad presents a solution to the problem. Otherwise, consumers will tune out the ad because they can do nothing to solve the threat.[133]

When a weak threat is ineffective, there may be insufficient elaboration of the harmful consequences of engaging in the behavior. When a strong threat doesn't work, there may be too much elaboration that interferes with the processing of the recommended change in behavior—the receiver is too busy thinking of reasons the message doesn't apply to her to pay attention to the offered solution.[134] A study that manipulated subjects' degree of anxiety about AIDS, for example, found that they evaluated condom ads most positively when they used a moderate threat. Copy that promoted the use of the condom because "Sex is a risky business" (moderate threat) resulted in more attitude change than either a weaker threat that emphasized the product's sensitivity or a strong threat that discussed the certainty of death from AIDS.[135]

Similarly, scare tactics have not generally been an effective way to convince teenagers to curb their use of alcohol or drugs. Teens simply tune out the message or deny its relevance to them.[136] However, a study of adolescent responses to social versus physical threat appeals in drug prevention messages found that social threat (such as being ostracized by one's peer) is a more effective strategy.[137]

The Message as Art Form: Metaphors Be with You

Just like novelists, poets, and artists, marketers are storytellers. Their communications take the form of stories because they describe intangible product benefits. The storyteller, therefore, must express these in some concrete form so that consumers will get the message.

Advertising creatives rely (consciously or not) on well-known literary devices to communicate these meanings. For example, characters such as Mr. Goodwrench, the Jolly Green Giant, and Charlie the Tuna may personify a product or service.

This Chinese detergent ad uses a handcuff metaphor as it urges the viewer, "Free yourself from the burden of handwash."
Source: Courtesy of Saatchi & Saatchi.

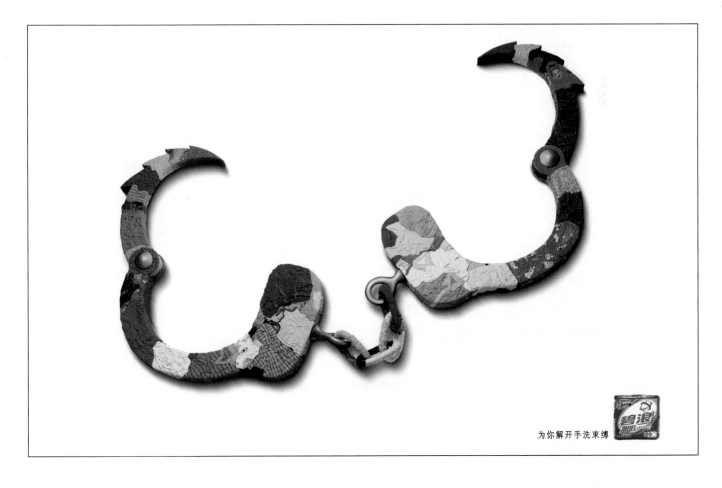

为你解开手洗束缚

Many ads take the form of an **allegory**—a story about an abstract trait or concept that advertisers tell in the context of a person, animal, vegetable, or object.

A **metaphor** places two dissimilar objects into a close relationship such that "A is B," whereas a **simile** compares two objects, "A is like B." A and B, however dissimilar, share some quality that the metaphor highlights. Metaphors allow the marketer to apply meaningful images to everyday events. In the stock market "white knights" battle "hostile raiders" with the help of "poison pills" while Tony the Tiger equates cereal with strength and "you're in good hands with Allstate" insurance.[138]

Resonance is another type of literary device advertisers frequently use. It is a form of presentation that combines a play on words with a relevant picture. Table 7.3 gives some examples of ads that rely on resonance. Whereas metaphor substitutes one meaning for another by connecting two things that are in some way similar, resonance employs an element that has a double meaning—such as a *pun* where two words sound similar but have different meanings. For example, an ad for a diet strawberry shortcake dessert might bear the copy "berried treasure" so that the brand conveys qualities we associate with buried treasure such as valuable and hidden. Because the text departs from expectations, it creates a state of tension or uncertainty on the part of the viewer until he figures out the wordplay. Once the consumer "gets it," he may prefer the ad to a more straightforward message.[139]

Just as a novelist or artist can tell a story in words or pictures, we can choose several ways to address our consumer audiences. Advertisers structure commercials like other art forms; as we've seen they borrow conventions from literature and art to communicate.[142] One important distinction is between a *drama* and a *lecture*.[143] A lecture is like a speech: The source speaks directly to the audience to inform them about a product or to persuade them to buy it. Because a lecture clearly implies an attempt at persuasion, the audience will regard it as such. Assuming it motivates listeners, they weigh the merits of the message along with the source's credibility. Cognitive responses occur (e.g., "How much did Coke pay him to say that?"). Consumers accept the appeal if it overcomes objections and is consistent with their beliefs.

In contrast, a drama is similar to a play or movie. Whereas a lecture holds the viewer at arm's length, a drama draws the viewer into the action. The characters indirectly address the audience—they interact with each other about a product or service in an imaginary setting. Dramas are experiential—they involve the audience emotionally. The *transformational advertising* method encourages the recipient to

TABLE 7.3	Some Examples of Advertising Resonance
Product/Headline	**Visual**
Embassy Suites: "This Year, We're Unwrapping Suites by the Dozen"	Chocolate kisses with hotel names underneath each
Toyota auto parts: "Our Lifetime Guarantee May Come as a Shock"	Man holding a shock absorber
Bucks filter cigarettes: "Herd of These?"	Cigarette pack with a picture of a stag
Bounce fabric softener: "Is There Something Creeping Up Behind You?"	Woman's dress bunched up on her back due to static
Pepsi: "This Year, Hit the Beach Topless"	Pepsi bottle cap lying on the sand
ASICS athletic shoes: "We Believe Women Should Be Running the Country"	Woman jogging in a rural setting

Source: Adapted from Edward F. McQuarrie and David Glen Mick, "On Resonance: A Critical Pluralistic Inquiry into Advertising Rhetoric," *Journal of Consumer Research* 19 (September 1992): 182. Table 1. Reprinted with permission of the University of Chicago Press.

CB AS I SEE IT
Professor Edward McQuarrie, *Santa Clara University*

*E*arly in my career, I became fascinated by *wordplay* in magazine advertisements. Puns, rhymes, and much more complex figures of speech abound in advertising headlines. In fact, virtually any figure of speech catalogued by the ancient Greeks can be found in the headlines of American advertisements today. But why is that? After all, advertisers are under a lot of pressure. They have to spend tons of money in the often forlorn hope of getting a consumer to spend a second or two glancing at an ad. Why mess around with complicated wordplay and risk confusing or alienating consumers?

The answer, my colleague Professor David Mick and I discovered, goes to the heart of what makes mass-media advertising a distinctive kind of human communication.[140] The thing to

remember is that no one has to look at a magazine ad, or spend much time on it. It's the exact opposite of being in school, where you have to pay attention—or flunk. And that's why advertisers put puns, rhymes, and every other rhetorical device in ad headlines: Such wordplay functions as a lure and a snare for attention. It's fun to get the joke. Result: Consumers linger a second longer, and absorb at least one point from the ad, even if they never read the rest. And a small jot of pleasure gets associated with the brand.

Traditional consumer research is tied to an experimental paradigm where the subjects are forced to read the whole ad; within that paradigm, there is no way to discover the importance of rhetorical figures. A related problem that I believe continues to handicap consumer research is an excessive focus on persuasion by means of words. Open a contemporary magazine and look at the full-page color ads: How many

words do you see? Not very many anymore. What you will see is carefully crafted photographic imagery, heavily altered by computer graphics software. In fact you will see visual puns, and visual metaphors—figures of speech in pictorial form. My colleague Professor Barbara Phillips and I have shown why it might be smart for advertisers to make their pitch in pictures rather than words; briefly, the very ambiguity of pictorial persuasion makes it more effective, because the reader has to generate more inferences to comprehend the ad.[141]

What I like about being a consumer researcher is that I get to study reality. Every ad represents an attempt by someone working very hard, under the gun to keep his or her job, to get an invisible mass of consumers to spend a second or two more with his or her creation. In my view, it's the study of these real efforts at persuasion that hold the most promise for advancing scientific understanding.

associate the experience of product usage with some subjective sensation—like the feeling you get when you watch a silhouetted actor on TV as he dances energetically to his iPod.

OBJECTIVE

How do audience characteristics help to determine whether the nature of the source or the message itself will be relatively more effective?

The Source Versus the Message: Do We Sell the Steak or the Sizzle?

We've discussed two major components of the communications model: the source and the message. At the end of the day, which component persuades consumers to change their attitudes? Should we worry more about *what* we say or *how* we say it and *who* says it?

Surprise! The answer is it depends. As we saw in Chapter 4, a consumer's level of involvement determines which cognitive processes will activate when she receives a message. This in turn influences which aspects of a communication she processes. Like a traveler who comes to a fork in the road, she chooses one path or the other. The direction she takes determines which aspects of the marketing communication will work and which will fall on deaf ears.

The **elaboration likelihood model (ELM)** assumes that under conditions of high involvement we take the *central route* to persuasion. Under conditions of low involvement, we take a *peripheral route* instead. Figure 7.7 diagrams this model.[144]

Figure 7.7 THE ELABORATION LIKELIHOOD MODEL (ELM) OF PERSUASION

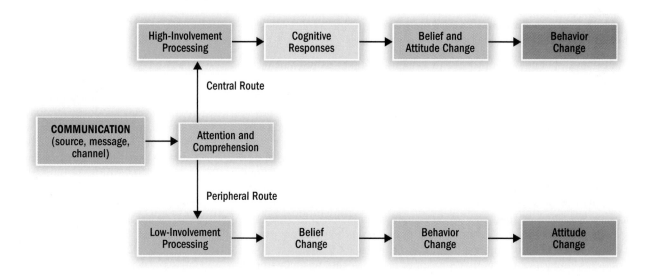

The Central Route to Persuasion

According to the ELM, when we find the information in a persuasive message relevant or interesting, we pay careful attention to it. In this event we focus on the arguments the marketer presents and generate *cognitive responses* to this content. An expectant mother who hears a radio message that warns about drinking while pregnant might say to herself, "She's right. I really should stop drinking alcohol now that I'm pregnant." Or she might offer counterarguments, such as "That's a bunch of baloney. My mother had a cocktail every night when she was pregnant with me, and I turned out fine." If a person generates counterarguments in response to a message, it's less likely that she will yield to the message, whereas if she generates further supporting arguments, it's more likely she'll comply.[145]

The central route to persuasion involves the standard hierarchy of effects we discussed earlier in the chapter. Recall this assumes that we carefully form and evaluate beliefs and the strong attitudes that result guide our behavior. The implication is that message factors, such as the quality of arguments an ad presents, will determine attitude change. Prior knowledge about a topic results in more thoughts about the message and also increases the number of counterarguments.[146]

The Peripheral Route to Persuasion

In contrast, we take the peripheral route when we're not really motivated to think about the marketer's arguments. Instead, we're likely to use other cues to decide how to react to the message. These cues include the product's package, the attractiveness of the source, or the context in which the message appears. We call sources of information extraneous to the actual message *peripheral cues* because they surround the actual message.

The peripheral route to persuasion highlights the paradox of low involvement we discussed in Chapter 4: When we *don't* care about a product, the style in which it's presented (e.g., who endorses it or the visuals that go with it) increase in importance. The implication here is that we may buy low-involvement products chiefly because the marketer designs a "sexy" package, chooses a popular spokesperson, or creates a stimulating shopping environment (more on that in Chapter 9).

To recap, the basic idea of the ELM is that highly involved consumers look for the "steak" (e.g., strong, rational arguments). Those who are less involved go for the "sizzle" (e.g., the colors and images in packaging or famous people's endorsements).

It is important to remember, however, that the *same* communications variable can be both a central and a peripheral cue, depending on its relation to the attitude object. The physical attractiveness of a model might serve as a peripheral cue in a car commercial, but her beauty might be a central cue for a product such as shampoo where a major product benefit is to enhance attractiveness.[147]

CHAPTER SUMMARY

Now that you have finished reading this chapter you should understand why:

 It's important for consumer researchers to understand the nature and power of attitudes.

An *attitude* is a predisposition to evaluate an object or product positively or negatively. We form attitudes toward products and services that often determine whether we will purchase them or not.

 Attitudes are more complex than they first appear.

Three components make up an attitude: beliefs, affect, and behavioral intentions.

 We form attitudes several ways.

Attitude researchers traditionally assumed that we learn attitudes in a fixed sequence: First we form beliefs (*cognitions*) about an attitude object, then we evaluate that object (*affect*), and then we take some action (*behavior*). Depending on the consumer's level of involvement and the circumstances, though, his attitudes can result from other hierarchies of effects as well. A key to attitude formation is the function the attitude holds for the consumer (e.g., is it utilitarian or ego defensive?).

 A need to maintain consistency among all of our attitudinal components motivates us to alter one or more of them.

One organizing principle of attitude formation is the importance of consistency among attitudinal components—that is, we alter some parts of an attitude to be in line with others. Such theoretical approaches to attitudes as *cognitive dissonance theory, self-perception theory,* and *balance theory* stress the vital role of our need for consistency.

 We use attitude models to identify specific components and combine them to predict a consumer's overall attitude toward a product or brand.

Multiattribute attitude models underscore the complexity of attitudes—they specify that we identify and combine a set of beliefs and evaluations to predict an overall attitude. Researchers integrate factors such as subjective norms and the specificity of attitude scales into attitude measures to improve predictability.

 The communications model identifies several important components for marketers when they try to change consumers' attitudes toward products and services.

Persuasion refers to an attempt to change consumers' attitudes. The communications model specifies the elements marketers need to transmit meaning. These include a source, a message, a medium, a receiver, and feedback.

 The consumer who processes a message is not necessarily the passive receiver of information marketers once believed him to be.

The traditional view of communications regards the perceiver as a passive element in the process. New developments in interactive communications highlight the need to consider the active roles a consumer plays when he or she obtains product information and builds a relationship with a company. Advocates of permission marketing argue that it's more effective to send messages to consumers who have already indicated an interest in learning about a product than trying to hit people "cold" with these solicitations.

 Several factors influence a message source's effectiveness.

Two important characteristics that determine the effectiveness of a source are its attractiveness and credibility. Although celebrities often serve this purpose, their credibility is not always as strong as marketers hope. Marketing messages that consumers perceive as buzz (those that are authentic and consumer generated) tend to be more effective than those they categorize as hype (those that are inauthentic, biased, and company generated).

 The way a marketer structures his message determines how persuasive it will be.

Some elements of a message that help to determine its effectiveness include the following: The marketer conveys the message in words or pictures; the message employs an emotional or a rational appeal; how often it's repeated; whether it draws a conclusion; whether it presents both sides of the argument; and whether the message includes fear, humor, or sexual references. Advertising messages often incorporate elements from art or literature, such as dramas, lectures, metaphors, allegories, and resonance.

Audience characteristics help to determine whether the nature of the source or the message itself will be relatively more effective.

The relative influence of the source versus the message depends on the receiver's level of involvement with the communication. The elaboration likelihood model (ELM) specifies that source effects are more likely to sway a less-involved consumer, whereas a more-involved consumer will be more likely to attend to and process components of the actual message.

KEY TERMS

ABC model of attitudes, 257
Affect, 257
Allegory, 288
Attitude, 256
Attitude object, 256
Attitude toward the act of buying (A_{act}), 268
Balance theory, 263
Basking in reflected glory, 263
Behavior, 257
Blogging, 274
Cognition, 257
Communications model, 272
Comparative advertising, 283
Compliance, 260
Ego-defensive function, 256
Elaboration likelihood model (ELM), 289
Experiential hierarchy of effects, 259
Fear appeals, 286
Foot-in-the-door technique, 262
Functional theory of attitudes, 256

Hierarchy of effects, 257
Identification, 260
Internalization, 260
Knowledge function, 256
Latitudes of acceptance and rejection, 262
Low-involvement hierarchy of effects, 258
M-commerce, 274
Metaphor, 288
Multiattribute attitude models, 265
Multiple pathway anchoring and adjustment (MPAA) model, 270
Paid Influencer programs, 277
Permission marketing, 272
Persuasion, 271
Podcasting, 275
Principle of cognitive consistency, 260
Refutational arguments, 282
Resonance, 288
Self-perception theory, 262

Simile, 288
Sleeper effect, 277
Social judgment theory, 262
Social media, 274
Social pressure, 269
Sock puppeting, 277
Source attractiveness, 277
Source credibility, 275
Spokescharacters, 279
Standard learning hierarchy, 258
Subjective norm (SN), 268
Theory of cognitive dissonance, 260
Theory of reasoned action, 267
Theory of trying, 270
Twitter, 275
Two-factor theory, 281
Utilitarian function, 256
Value-expressive function, 256
Video blogging (vlogging), 275
Virtual worlds, 275
Widgets, 275

REVIEW

1 How can an attitude play an ego-defensive function?
2 Describe the ABC model of attitudes.
3 List the three hierarchies of attitudes, and describe the major differences among them.
4 How do levels of commitment to an attitude influence the likelihood that it will become part of the way we think about a product in the long term?
5 We sometimes enhance our attitude toward a product after we buy it. How does the theory of cognitive dissonance explain this change?
6 What is the foot-in-the-door technique? How does self-perception theory relate to this effect?
7 What are latitudes of acceptance and rejection? How does a consumer's level of involvement with a product affect his latitude of acceptance?
8 According to balance theory, how can we tell if a triad is balanced or unbalanced? How can consumers restore balance to an unbalanced triad?

9 Describe a multiattribute attitude model and list its key components.
10 "Do as I say, not as I do." How does this statement relate to attitude models?
11 What is a subjective norm, and how does it influence our attitudes?
12 What are three obstacles to predicting behavior even if we know a person's attitudes?
13 Describe the theory of reasoned action. Why might it not be equally valuable when we apply it to non-Western cultures?
14 List three psychological principles related to persuasion.
15 Describe the elements of the traditional communications model, and tell how the updated model differs.
16 What are blogs and how can marketers use them?
17 What is source credibility, and what are two factors that influence whether we decide a source is credible?

18 What is the difference between buzz and hype? How does this difference relate to the *corporate paradox*?

19 What is a halo effect, and why does it happen?

20 What is an avatar, and why might an advertiser choose to use one instead of hiring a celebrity endorser?

21 When should a marketer present a message visually versus verbally?

22 How does the two-factor theory explain the effects of message repetition on attitude change?

23 When is it best to present a two-sided message versus a one-sided message?

24 Do humorous ads work, and if so, under what conditions?

25 Should marketers ever try to arouse fear in order to persuade consumers?

26 Why do marketers use metaphors to craft persuasive messages? Give two examples of this technique.

27 What is the difference between a lecture and a drama?

28 Describe the elaboration likelihood model, and summarize how it relates to the relative importance of *what* is said versus *how* it's said.

CONSUMER BEHAVIOR CHALLENGE

■ DISCUSS

1 Contrast the hierarchies of effects the chapter outlines. How should marketers take these different situations into account when they choose their marketing mix?

2 Many universities contact with commercial companies to run campus Web sites and e-mail services. These agreements provide Web services to colleges at little or no cost. But these actions arouse controversy because major companies pay to place advertising on the sites. That gives marketers the opportunity to influence the attitudes of thousands of students who are involuntarily exposed to product messages. University administrators argue that they could not provide the services by themselves—students expect to be able to fill out financial aid forms and register for classes online. Colleges that do not offer such services may lose their ability to attract students. How do you feel about this situation? Should companies be able to buy access to your eyeballs from the school you pay to attend if it means you get access to enhanced online services in return?

3 A recent antismoking ad sponsored by The New York City Department of Health crossed the line for many viewers. The spot showed a young boy who cries hysterically as a crowd of adults walk by him. The voiceover says, "This is how your child feels after losing you for a minute. Just imagine if they lost you for life."

   The ad aroused a lot of controversy because it wasn't clear if the child was merely acting or if the spot's producers provoked his tears for the camera. Is this genre of "scared straight" advertising an effective way to convince people to curb unhealthy behaviors like smoking?

4 A *flog* is a fake blog a company posts to build buzz around its brand. Is this ethical?

5 The sleeper effect implies that perhaps we shouldn't worry too much about how positively people evaluate a source. Similarly, there's a saying in public relations that "any publicity is good publicity." Do you agree?

6 Discuss some conditions where you would advise a marketer to use a comparative advertising strategy.

7 The American Medical Association encountered a firestorm of controversy when it agreed to sponsor a line of health-care products Sunbeam manufactured (a decision it later reversed). Should trade or professional organizations, journalists, professors, and others endorse specific products at the expense of other offerings?

8 A marketer must decide whether to incorporate rational or emotional appeals in its communications strategy. Describe conditions that are more favorable to one or the other.

9 Many, many companies rely on celebrity endorsers as communications sources to persuade. Especially when they target younger people, these spokespeople often are "cool" musicians, athletes, or movie stars. In your opinion, who would be the most effective celebrity endorser today, and why? Who would be the least effective? Why?

10 Swiss Legend, a watch brand, gets famous people to wear its colorful timepieces. One way it does this is to give away its products at awards shows. Publicists call this common practice "gifting the talent"—companies provide stars with "goody bags" full of complimentary products.[148] What do you think about the practice of "gifting the talent" in order to accumulate endorsements? Is this a sound strategy? Is it ethical for celebrities to accept these gifts?

■ APPLY

1 Think of a behavior someone does that is inconsistent with his or her attitudes (e.g., attitudes toward cholesterol, drug use, or even buying things to make him or her stand out or attain status). Ask the person to elaborate on why he or she does the behavior, and try to identify the way the person resolves dissonant elements.

2 Devise an attitude survey for a set of competing automobiles. Identify areas of competitive advantage or disadvantage for each model you include.

3 Construct a multiattribute model for a set of local restaurants. Based on your findings, suggest how restaurant managers can improve an establishment's image via the strategies the chapter describes.

4 Locate foreign ads at sites like japander.com in which celebrities endorse products they don't pitch on their home turf. Ask friends or classmates to rate the attractiveness of each celebrity, then show them these ads and ask them to rate the celebrities again. Does the star's "brand image" change after it's paired with cheesy ads? What advice would you give to a manager who has to choose among endorsement offers for a famous client based on these results?

5 A government agency wants to encourage people who have been drinking to use designated drivers. What advice could you give the organization about constructing persuasive communications? Discuss some factors that might be important, including the structure of the communications, where they should appear, and who should deliver them. Should it use fear appeals, and if so, how?

6 Why would a marketer consider saying negative things about her product? When is this strategy feasible? Can you find examples of it?

7 Collect ads that rely on sex appeal to sell products. How often do they communicate benefits of the actual product?

8 Observe the process of counterargumentation by asking a friend to talk out loud while he watches a commercial. Ask him to respond to each point in the ad or to write down reactions to the claims the message makes. How much skepticism regarding the claims can you detect?

9 Make a log of all the commercials a network television channel shows during a 2-hour period. Assign each to a product category and decide whether each is a drama or an argument. Describe the types of messages the ads use (e.g., two-sided arguments), and keep track of the types of spokespeople who appear (e.g., TV actors, famous people, animated characters). What can you conclude about the dominant forms of persuasive tactics marketers currently employ?

10 Collect examples of ads that rely on the use of metaphors or resonance. Do you feel these ads are effective? If you were marketing the products, would you feel more comfortable with ads that use a more straightforward, "hard-sell" approach? Why or why not?

11 Create a list of current celebrities whom you feel typify cultural categories (e.g., clown, mother figure, etc.). What specific brands do you feel each could effectively endorse?

12 Conduct an "avatar hunt" on e-commerce Web sites, online video game sites, and online communities such as *The Sims* that let people select what they want to look like in cyberspace. What seem to be the dominant figures people choose? Are they realistic or fantasy characters? Male or female? What types of avatars do you believe would be most effective for each of these different kinds of Web sites and why?

Case Study

MICHAEL PHELPS: ENDORSEMENT DEALS GO UP IN SMOKE!

Michael Phelps made his Olympic debut at the age of 15. At 6'4" Phelps has a wingspan and a shoe size that eclipses most competitive swimmers. This physical advantage combined with years of extensive training positions him to become the greatest swimmer of all time. At the 2008 Beijing Olympics, Phelps won a record eight gold medals and broke four individual world records. He achieved what no athlete in the world had ever done in the history of the Olympics.

The United States had a new sports superstar! A hero for young kids to admire. An athlete who reflected the results of hard work and determination. During the Olympics,

Phelps' agents predicted the swimmer would earn over $100 million in endorsements over his lifetime.

Fast-forward to February 2009: A picture of Phelps smoking pot appears in the British tabloid *News of the World*. USA Swimming, the national governing body of competitive swimming in the United States, immediately suspended Phelps from competition for three months. Phelps' reputation began to unravel. Phelps quickly apologized to all his sponsors as the incriminating photo spread through the blogosphere. Kellogg and Subway dropped their sponsorship deals soon afterward.

However, other sponsors including Speedo, Omega, Visa, and Pure Sports continued to support Phelps. Speedo issued this statement: "Speedo would like to make it clear that it does not condone such behavior and we know that

Michael truly regrets his actions. Michael Phelps is a valued member of the Speedo team and a great champion. We will do all that we can to support him and his family."

The marketing community's response was mixed. Many agreed with Kellogg's decision to terminate its endorsement deal. Phelps was, after all, a spokesman for products the company markets to impressionable kids. Phelps' brand personality was of a hard-working, clean-cut athlete—not a bong-wielding party animal. However, others felt that he made a youthful mistake and deserved a second chance.

What about public opinion? The David Brown Index (DBI) is one measure of a celebrity's image. It's based on feedback from a panel of 1.5 million consumers who evaluate more than 1,500 celebrities each year. Although Phelps' overall DBI rating did not change significantly after the photograph broke, he did lose points on measures of "aspiration" and "trust." Ironically, panelists' awareness of his name increased after the incident.

DISCUSSION QUESTIONS

1 In the context of source effects, discuss why companies scrambled to sign endorsement deals with Michael Phelps immediately after the Olympics. How did these source effects change after the picture was published?

2 Using a multiattribute model for Kellogg's cereal, describe how consumers might develop a positive or negative attitude toward the Corn Flakes brand. How would Michael Phelps' picture in the British paper influence the multiattribute model?

Sources: Emily Bryson York, "Phelps Brand Takes a Hit," *Advertising Age* (2009): 1; Suzanne Vranica and Emily Steel, "Phelps Image as Hero Hurt by Photos," *Wall Street Journal*, (February 3, 2009):4; Karl Greenberg, "Phelps' Celeb Index Unchanged; 'Trust' Down," *MediaPost News* (February 10, 2009), www.mediapost.com, accessed February 10, 2009.

NOTES

1. http://shoppingblog.com, accessed June 30, 2009.
2. http://ezinearticles.com/?Current-Trends-In-Womens-Fashion&id= 1196799, accessed June 30, 2009.
3. www.shoppingthetrend.com/celebrity/Actresses/Zoe-Saldana/Fab-White-Dresses-Zoe-Saldana-at-BET-Awards-Cameron-Diaz-in-J.-Mendel.html, accessed June 30, 2009.
4. Robert A. Baron and Donn Byrne, *Social Psychology: Understanding Human Interaction*, 5th ed. (Boston: Allyn & Bacon, 1987).
5. Daniel Katz, "The Functional Approach to the Study of Attitudes," *Public Opinion Quarterly* 24 (Summer 1960): 163–204, Richard J. Lutz, "Changing Brand Attitudes Through Modification of Cognitive Structure," *Journal of Consumer Research* 1 (March 1975): 49–59.
6. Russell H. Fazio, T. N. Lenn, and E. A. Effrein, "Spontaneous Attitude Formation," *Social Cognition* 2 (1984): 214–34.
7. Sharon Shavitt, "The Role of Attitude Objects in Attitude Functions," *Journal of Experimental Social Psychology* 26 (1990): 124–48; see also J. S. Johar and M. Joseph Sirgy, "Value Expressive Versus Utilitarian Advertising Appeals: When and Why to Use Which Appeal," *Journal of Advertising* 20 (September 1991): 23–34.
8. Aaron Baar, "New Subaru Campaign Takes Aim with Cupid's Arrow," *Marketing Daily* (April 28, 2008), http://publications.mediapost.com/Index.Cfm?Fuseaction=Articles.San&S=81435&Nid=420..., accessed April 28, 2008.
9. Quoted in Stuart Elliott, "Down Economic Times Elicit Upbeat Campaigns," *New York Times* (March 9, 2009), http://www.nytimes.com/2009/03/10/business/media/10adco.html?_r=1, accessed March 9, 2009; Betsy McKay and Suzanne Vranica, "Coca-Cola to Uncap 'Open Happiness' Campaign New Ad Push," *Wall Street Journal* (January 14, 2009), www.wsj.com, accessed January 14, 2009.
10. Michael Ray, "Marketing Communications and the Hierarchy-of-Effects," in P. Clarke, ed., *New Models for Mass Communications* (Beverly Hills, CA: Sage, 1973), 147–76.
11. Herbert Krugman, "The Impact of Television Advertising: Learning Without Involvement," *Public Opinion Quarterly* 29 (Fall 1965): 349–56; Robert Lavidge and Gary Steiner, "A Model for Predictive Measurements of Advertising Effectiveness," *Journal of Marketing* 25 (October 1961): 59–62.
12. Stephanie Thompson, "Bad Breakup? There, There, B&J Know Just How You Feel," *Advertising Age* (January 24, 2005): 8.
13. For some recent studies, see Andrew B. Aylesworth and Scott B. MacKenzie, "Context Is Key: The Effect of Program-Induced Mood on Thoughts About the Ad," *Journal of Advertising* 27 (Summer 1998): 17; Angela Y. Lee and Brian Sternthal, "The Effects of Positive Mood on Memory," *Journal of Consumer Research* 26 (September 1999): 115–28; Michael J. Barone, Paul W. Miniard, and Jean B. Romeo, "The Influence of Positive Mood on Brand Extension Evaluations," *Journal of*

Consumer Research 26 (March 2000): 386–401. For a study that compared the effectiveness of emotional appeals across cultures, see Jennifer L. Aaker and Patti Williams, "Empathy Versus Pride: The Influence of Emotional Appeals Across Cultures," *Journal of Consumer Research* 25 (December 1998): 241–61. For research that relates mood (depression) to acceptance of health-related messages, see Punam Anand Keller, Isaac M. Lipkus, and Barbara K. Rimer, "Depressive Realism and Health Risk Accuracy: The Negative Consequences of Positive Mood," *Journal of Consumer Research* 29 (2002): 57–69.
14. Punam Anand, Morris B. Holbrook, and Debra Stephens, "The Formation of Affective Judgments: The Cognitive–Affective Model Versus the Independence Hypothesis," *Journal of Consumer Research* 15 (December 1988): 386–91; Richard S. Lazarus, "Thoughts on the Relations Between Emotion and Cognition," *American Psychologist* 37, no. 9 (1982): 1019–24; Robert B. Zajonc, "Feeling and Thinking: Preferences Need No Inferences," *American Psychologist* 35, no. 2 (1980): 151–75.
15. See Sharon E. Beatty and Lynn R. Kahle, "Alternative Hierarchies of the Attitude–Behavior Relationship: The Impact of Brand Commitment and Habit," *Journal of the Academy of Marketing Science* 16 (Summer 1988): 1–10.
16. J. R. Priester, D. Nayakankuppan, M. A. Fleming, and J. Godek, "The A(2)SC(2) Model: The Influence of Attitudes and Attitude Strength on Consideration Set Choice," *Journal of Consumer Research* 30, no. 4 (2004): 574–87.
17. Chester A. Insko and John Schopler, *Experimental Social Psychology* (New York: Academic Press, 1972).
18. Robert E. Knox and James A. Inkster, "Postdecision Dissonance at Post Time," *Journal of Personality and Social Psychology* 8, no. 4 (1968): 319–23.
19. Daryl J. Bem, "Self-Perception Theory," in Leonard Berkowitz, ed., *Advances in Experimental Social Psychology* (New York: Academic Press, 1972), 1–62.
20. Jonathan L. Freedman and Scott C. Fraser, "Compliance Without Pressure: The Foot-in-the-Door Technique," *Journal of Personality and Social Psychology* 4 (August 1966): 195–202. For further consideration of possible explanations for this effect, see William DeJong, "An Examination of Self-Perception Mediation of the Foot-in-the-Door Effect," *Journal of Personality and Social Psychology* 37 (December 1979): 221–31; Alice M. Tybout, Brian Sternthal, and Bobby J. Calder, "Information Availability as a Determinant of Multiple-Request Effectiveness," *Journal of Marketing Research* 20 (August 1988): 280–90.
21. David H. Furse, David W. Stewart, and David L. Rados, "Effects of Foot-in-the-Door, Cash Incentives and Follow-ups on Survey Response," *Journal of Marketing Research* 18 (November 1981): 473–78; Carol A. Scott, "The Effects of Trial and Incentives on Repeat Purchase Behavior," *Journal of Marketing Research* 13 (August 1976): 263–69.

22. Bob Fennis, Loes Janssen, and Kathleen D. Vohs, "Acts of Benevolence: A Limited-Resource Account of Compliance with Charitable Requests," *Journal of Consumer Research* (2009): 906–25.

23. See Joan Meyers-Levy and Brian Sternthal, "A Two-Factor Explanation of Assimilation and Contrast Effects," *Journal of Marketing Research* 30 (August 1993): 359–68.

24. Mark B. Traylor, "Product Involvement and Brand Commitment," *Journal of Advertising Research* (December 1981): 51–56.

25. Fritz Heider, *The Psychology of Interpersonal Relations* (New York: Wiley, 1958).

26. Quoted in Jon Weinbach, "Ad Score! Major League Soccer Teams Will Sell Ad Space on Players' Jerseys," *Wall Street Journal* (September 28, 2006): B1.

27. Leslie Kaufman, "Enough Talk," *Newsweek* (August 18, 1997): 48–49.

28. Debra Z. Basil and Paul M. Herr, "Attitudinal Balance and Cause-Related Marketing: An Empirical Application of Balance Theory," *Journal of Consumer Psychology* 16, no. 4, (2006): 391–403.

29. William L. Wilkie, *Consumer Behavior* (New York: Wiley, 1986).

30. M. Fishbein, "An Investigation of the Relationships Between Beliefs About an Object and the Attitude Toward That Object," *Human Relations* 16 (1983): 233–40.

31. Allan Wicker, "Attitudes Versus Actions: The Relationship of Verbal and Overt Behavioral Responses to Attitude Objects," *Journal of Social Issues* 25 (Autumn 1969): 65.

32. Laura Bird, "Loved the Ad. May (or May Not) Buy the Product," *Wall Street Journal* (April 7, 1994): B1.

33. Icek Ajzen and Martin Fishbein, "Attitude–Behavior Relations: A Theoretical Analysis and Review of Empirical Research," *Psychological Bulletin* 84 (September 1977): 888–918.

34. Morris B. Holbrook and William J. Havlena, "Assessing the Real-to-Artificial Generalizability of Multi-Attribute Attitude Models in Tests of New Product Designs," *Journal of Marketing Research* 25 (February 1988): 25–35; Terence A. Shimp and Alican Kavas, "The Theory of Reasoned Action Applied to Coupon Usage," *Journal of Consumer Research* 11 (December 1984): 795–809.

35. R. P. Abelson, "Conviction," *American Psychologist* 43 (1988): 267–75; R. E. Petty and J. A. Krosnick, *Attitude Strength: Antecedents and Consequences* (Mahwah, NJ: Erlbaum, 1995); Ida E. Berger and Linda F. Alwitt, "Attitude Conviction: A Self-Reflective Measure of Attitude Strength," *Journal of Social Behavior and Personality* 11, no. 3 (1996): 557–72.

36. Ida E. Berger and Linda F. Alwitt, "Attitude Conviction: A Self-Reflective Measure of Attitude Strength," *Journal of Social Behavior and Personality* 11, no. 3 (1996): 557–72.

37. Richard P. Bagozzi, Hans Baumgartner, and Youjae Yi, "Coupon Usage and the Theory of Reasoned Action," in Rebecca H. Holman and Michael R. Solomon, eds., *Advances in Consumer Research* 18 (Provo, UT: Association for Consumer Research, 1991): 24–27; Edward F. McQuarrie, "An Alternative to Purchase Intentions: The Role of Prior Behavior in Consumer Expenditure on Computers," *Journal of the Market Research Society* 30 (October 1988): 407–37; Arch G. Woodside and William O. Bearden, "Longitudinal Analysis of Consumer Attitude, Intention, and Behavior Toward Beer Brand Choice," in William D. Perrault, Jr., ed., *Advances in Consumer Research* 4 (Ann Arbor, MI: Association for Consumer Research, 1977): 349–56.

38. Andy Greenfield, "The Naked Truth (Studying Consumer Behavior)," *Brandweek* (October 13, 1997): 22.

39. Michael J. Ryan and Edward H. Bonfield, "The Fishbein Extended Model and Consumer Behavior," *Journal of Consumer Research* 2 (1975): 118–36.

40. Noah J. Goldstein, Robert B. Cialdini, Vladas Griskevicius, "A Room with a Viewpoint: Using Social Norms to Motivate Environmental Conservation in Hotels," *Journal of Consumer Research* 35 (October 2008): 472–482.

41. Blair H. Sheppard, Jon Hartwick, and Paul R. Warshaw, "The Theory of Reasoned Action: A Meta-Analysis of Past Research with Recommendations for Modifications and Future Research," *Journal of Consumer Research* 15 (December 1988): 325–43.

42. Joseph A. Cote, James McCullough, and Michael Reilly, "Effects of Unexpected Situations on Behavior–Intention Differences: A Garbology Analysis," *Journal of Consumer Research* 12 (September 1985): 188–94.

43. Russell H. Fazio, Martha C. Powell, and Carol J. Williams, "The Role of Attitude Accessibility in the Attitude-to-Behavior Process," *Journal of Consumer Research* 16 (December 1989): 280–88; Robert E. Smith and William R. Swinyard, "Attitude–Behavior Consistency: The Impact of Product Trial Versus Advertising," *Journal of Marketing Research* 20 (August 1983): 257–67.

44. For a recent similar application, cf. N. T. Tavassoli and G. J. Fitzsimons, "Spoken and Typed Expressions of Repeated Attitudes: Matching

Response Modes Leads to Attitude Retrieval Versus Construction," *Journal of Consumer Research* 33, no. 2 (2006): 179–87.

45. Kulwant Singh, Siew Meng Leong, Chin Tiong Tan, and Kwei Cheong Wong, "A Theory of Reasoned Action Perspective of Voting Behavior: Model and Empirical Test," *Psychology & Marketing* 12, no. 1 (January 1995): 37–51; Joseph A. Cote and Patriya S. Tansuhaj, "Culture Bound Assumptions in Behavior Intention Models," in Thom Srull, ed., *Advances in Consumer Research* 16 (Provo, UT: Association for Consumer Research, 1989): 105–9.

46. Joel B. Cohen and Americus Reed, "A Multiple Pathway Anchoring and Adjustment (MPAA) Model of Attitude Generation and Recruitment," *Journal of Consumer Research* 33 (June 2006): 1–15.

47. Richard P. Bagozzi and Paul R. Warshaw, "Trying to Consume," *Journal of Consumer Research* 17 (September 1990): 127–40.

48. Barbara Presley Noble, "After Years of Deregulation, a New Push to Inform the Public," *New York Times* (October 27, 1991): F5.

49. Robert B. Cialdini and Kelton V. L. Rhoads, "Human Behavior and the Marketplace," *Marketing Research* (Fall 2001): 13.

50. Gert Assmus, "An Empirical Investigation into the Perception of Vehicle Source Effects," *Journal of Advertising* 7 (Winter 1978): 4–10. For a more thorough discussion of the pros and cons of different media, see Stephen Baker, *Systematic Approach to Advertising Creativity* (New York: McGraw-Hill, 1979).

51. Alladi Venkatesh, Ruby Roy Dholakia, and Nikhilesh Dholakia, "New Visions of Information Technology and Postmodernism: Implications for Advertising and Marketing Communications," in Walter Brenner and Lutz Kolbe, eds., *The Information Superhighway and Private Households: Case Studies of Business Impacts* (Heidelberg: Physica-Verlag, 1996), 319–37; Donna L. Hoffman and Thomas P. Novak, "Marketing in Hypermedia Computer-Mediated Environments: Conceptual Foundations," *Journal of Marketing* 60, no. 3 (July 1996): 50–68. For an early theoretical discussion of interactivity in communications paradigms, see R. Aubrey Fisher, *Perspectives on Human Communication* (New York: Macmillan, 1978).

52. Seth Godin, *Permission Marketing: Turning Strangers into Friends, and Friends into Customers* (New York: Simon & Schuster, 1999).

53. Brad Stone, "The War for Your TV," *Newsweek* (July 29, 2002): 46–47.

54. Geoffrey A. Fowler, "Asia's Mobile Ads," *Wall Street Journal* (April 25, 2005), www.wsj.com, accessed April 25, 2005; Brooks Barnes, "Coming to Your Cell: Paris Hilton," *Wall Street Journal* (March 17, 2005), www.wsj.com, accessed March 17, 2005; Alice Z. Cuneo, "Marketers Dial in to Messaging," *Advertising Age* (November 1, 2004): 18; Stephen Baker and Heather Green, "Blogs Will Change Your Business," *BusinessWeek* (May 2, 2005): 56.

55. "The People's Revolution: Implications of Web 2.0 and Social Media Applications," Strategy Analytics, 2008.

56. "Social Nets and Blogs More Popular Than E-Mail," March 17, 2009; e.marketer.com, accessed March 17, 2009.

57. "U.S. Blog Readers 2007–2012," *Emarketer* (April 15, 2009), www.emarketer.com, accessed April 15, 2009.

58. Carl I. Hovland and W. Weiss, "The Influence of Source Credibility on Communication Effectiveness," *Public Opinion Quarterly* 15 (1952): 635–50; for a recent treatment, cf. Yong-Soon Kang and Paul M. Herr, "Beauty and the Beholder: Toward an Integrative Model of Communication Source Effects," *Journal of Consumer Research* 33 (June 2006): 123–30.

59. Herbert Kelman, "Processes of Opinion Change," *Public Opinion Quarterly* 25 (Spring 1961): 57–78; Susan M. Petroshius and Kenneth E. Crocker, "An Empirical Analysis of Spokesperson Characteristics on Advertisement and Product Evaluations," *Journal of the Academy of Marketing Science* 17 (Summer 1989): 217–26.

60. Kenneth G. DeBono and Richard J. Harnish, "Source Expertise, Source Attractiveness, and the Processing of Persuasive Information: A Functional Approach," *Journal of Personality and Social Psychology* 55, no. 4 (1988): 541–46.

61. Joseph R. Priester and Richard E. Petty, "The Influence of Spokesperson Trustworthiness on Message Elaboration, Attitude Strength, and Advertising Effectiveness," *Journal of Consumer Psychology* 13, no. 4 (2003): 408–21.

62. Hershey H. Friedman and Linda Friedman, "Endorser Effectiveness by Product Type," *Journal of Advertising Research* 19, no. 5 (1979): 63–71. For a study that looked at nontarget market effects—the effects of advertising intended for other market segments—see Jennifer L. Aaker, Anne M. Brumbaugh, and Sonya A. Grier, "Non-Target Markets and Viewer Distinctiveness: The Impact of Target Marketing on Advertising Attitudes," *Journal of Consumer Psychology* 9, no. 3 (2000): 127–40.

63. Yeosun Yoon, Zeynep Gurhan-Canli, and Norbert Schwarz, "The Effect of Corporate Social Responsibility (CSR) Activities on Companies with Bad Reputations," *Journal of Consumer Psychology* 16, no. 4 (2006): 377–90.

64. Peter R. Darke and Robin J. B. Ritchie, "The Defensive Consumer: Advertising Deception, Defensive Processing, and Distrust," *Journal of Marketing Research* 44 (February 2007): 114–27.

65. Suzanne Kapner, "Pitchmen-In-Chief: Are CEOs Enticing or Alienating to Consumers? Sprint and S.C. Johnson Will Soon Find Out," *Fortune* (January 26, 2009), www.fortune.com, accessed January 26, 2009.

66. S. Ratneshwar and Shelly Chaiken, "Comprehension's Role in Persuasion: The Case of Its Moderating Effect on the Persuasive Impact of Source Cues," *Journal of Consumer Research* 18 (June 1991): 52–62.

67. Jagdish Agrawal and Wagner A. Kamakura, "The Economic Worth of Celebrity Endorsers: An Event Study Analysis," *Journal of Marketing* 59 (July 1995): 56–62.

68. Stephanie Strom, "Nonprofit Punishes a 2nd Founder for Ruse," *New York Times*, January 15, 2008, www.nytimes.com/2008/01/15/us/15givewell.html?ex=1201064400&en=97effb249..., accessed January 15, 2008; Ross D. Petty and J. Craig Andrews, "Covert Marketing Unmasked: A Legal and Regulatory Guide for Practices that Mask Marketing Messages," *Journal of Public Policy and Marketing* (Spring 2008): 7–18; James B. Stewart, "Whole Foods CEO Threatens Merger, Fuels Arbitrage," *Smart Money* (July 18, 2007), www.smartmoney.com/investing/stocks/whole-foods-ceo-threatens-merger-fuels-arbitrage-21550/?hpadref=1, accessed June 4, 2009; Brian Morrissey, "'Influencer Programs' Likely to Spread," *Adweek* (March 2, 2009), adweek.com/.../e3i9b282d63be07572..., accessed March 2, 2009; Katie Hafner, "Seeing Corporate Fingerprints in Wikipedia Edits," *New York Times* (August 19, 2007), www.nytimes.com/2007/08/19/technology/19wikipedia.html?_r=1&oref=slogin, accessed August 19, 2007; Brian Bergstein, "New Tool Mines: Wikipedia Trustworthiness Software Analyzes Reputations of the Contributors Responsible for Entries," *MSNBC* (September 5, 2007), www.msnbc.msn.com/id/20604175, accessed September 5, 2007; http://wikiscanner.virgil.gr, accessed June 4, 2009.

69. Anthony R. Pratkanis, Anthony G. Greenwald, Michael R. Leippe, and Michael H. Baumgardner, "In Search of Reliable Persuasion Effects: III. The Sleeper Effect Is Dead, Long Live the Sleeper Effect," *Journal of Personality and Social Psychology* 54 (1988): 203–18.

70. "Robber Makes It Biggs in Ad," *Advertising Age* (May 29, 1989): 26.

71. Robert LaFranco, "MTV Conquers Madison Avenue," *Forbes* (June 3, 1996): 138.

72. Alice H. Eagly, Andy Wood, and Shelly Chaiken, "Causal Inferences About Communicators and Their Effect in Opinion Change," *Journal of Personality and Social Psychology* 36, no. 4 (1978): 424–35.

73. Ira Teinowitz, "'Results May Vary' Won't Be Enough Under New FTC Rules, Proposed Changes Could Put Squeeze on Ads for Diet Plans and Fitness Equipment," *Advertising Age* (March 12, 2009), www.adage.com, accessed March 12, 2009.

74. Patrick Loughran, "Sex Pistol Sends Dairy Crest Butter Sales Soaring," *Times of London* (February 3, 2009), www.timesonline.co.uk, accessed February 4, 2009.

75. Michael J. Baker and Gilbert A. Churchill, Jr., "The Impact of Physically Attractive Models on Advertising Evaluations," *Journal of Marketing Research* 14 (November 1977): 538–55; Marjorie J. Caballero and William M. Pride, "Selected Effects of Salesperson Sex and Attractiveness in Direct Mail Advertisements," *Journal of Marketing* 48 (January 1984): 94–100; W. Benoy Joseph, "The Credibility of Physically Attractive Communicators: A Review," *Journal of Advertising* 11, no. 3 (1982): 15–24; Lynn R. Kahle and Pamela M. Homer, "Physical Attractiveness of the Celebrity Endorser: A Social Adaptation Perspective," *Journal of Consumer Research* 11 (March 1985): 954–61; Judson Mills and Eliot Aronson, "Opinion Change as a Function of Communicator's Attractiveness and Desire to Influence," *Journal of Personality and Social Psychology* 1 (1965): 173–77.

76. Leonard N. Reid and Lawrence C. Soley, "Decorative Models and the Readership of Magazine Ads," *Journal of Advertising Research* 23, no. 2 (1983): 27–32.

77. Marjorie J. Caballero, James R. Lumpkin, and Charles S. Madden, "Using Physical Attractiveness as an Advertising Tool: An Empirical Test of the Attraction Phenomenon," *Journal of Advertising Research* (August–September 1989): 16–22.

78. Baker and Churchill, Jr., "The Impact of Physically Attractive Models on Advertising Evaluations"; George E. Belch, Michael A. Belch, and Angelina Villareal, "Effects of Advertising Communications: Review of Research," in *Research in Marketing*, no. 9 (Greenwich, CT: JAI Press, 1987): 59–117; A. E. Courtney and T. W. Whipple, *Sex Stereotyping in Advertising* (Lexington, MA: Lexington Books, 1983).

79. Lynn R. Kahle and Pamela M. Homer, "Physical Attractiveness of the Celebrity Endorser: A Social Adaptation Perspective," *Journal of Consumer Research* 11 (March 1985): 954–61.

80. Brian Steinberg, "Bob Dylan Gets Tangled Up in Pink: Victoria's Secret Campaign Drafts Counterculture Hero; Just Like the Rolling Stones," *Wall Street Journal* (April 2, 2004): B3.

81. Heather Buttle, Jane E. Raymond, and Shai Danziger, "Do Famous Faces Capture Attention?" Paper presented at Association for Consumer Research Conference, Columbus, Ohio (October 1999).

82. Michael A. Kamins, "Celebrity and Noncelebrity Advertising in a Two-Sided Context," *Journal of Advertising Research* 29 (June–July 1989): 34; Joseph M. Kamen, A. C. Azhari, and J. R. Kragh, "What a Spokesman Does for a Sponsor," *Journal of Advertising Research* 15, no. 2 (1975): 17–24; Lynn Langmeyer and Mary Walker, "A First Step to Identify the Meaning in Celebrity Endorsers," in Rebecca H. Holman and Michael R. Solomon, eds., *Advances in Consumer Research* 18 (Provo, UT: Association for Consumer Research, 1991): 364–71.

83. Quoted in www.japander.com, accessed June 6, 2009.

84. Grant McCracken, "Who Is the Celebrity Endorser? Cultural Foundations of the Endorsement Process," *Journal of Consumer Research* 16, no. 3 (December 1989): 310–21.

85. Karlene Lukovitz, "Milk-Bone Picks First-Ever 'Spokesdog,'" February 25, 2009, *Marketing Daily*, www.mediapost.com, accessed February 25, 2009.

86. Nat Ives, "Marketers Run to Pull the Plug When Celebrity Endorsers Say the Darnedest Things," *New York Times* (July 16, 2004), www.nytimes.com, accessed July 16, 2004.

87. Judith A. Garretson and Scot Burton, "The Role of Spokescharacters as Advertisement and Package Cues in Integrated Marketing Communications," *Journal of Marketing* 69 (October, 2005): 118–32.

88. Lacey Rose, "America's Most-Loved Spokescreatures," *Forbes* (July 9, 2008), www.forbes.com/home/2008/07/08/Advertising-Mars-Geico-Biz-Media-Cx_Lr_0708spokescreatures.html, accessed July 17, 2008.

89. Natalie T. Wood and Michael R. Solomon, eds., *Virtual Social Identity* (Newport, CA: Sage, 2010).

90. David W. Stewart and David H. Furse, "The Effects of Television Advertising Execution on Recall, Comprehension, and Persuasion," *Psychology & Marketing* 2 (Fall 1985): 135–60.

91. R. C. Grass and W. H. Wallace, "Advertising Communication: Print vs. TV," *Journal of Advertising Research* 14 (1974): 19–23.

92. Elizabeth C. Hirschman and Michael R. Solomon, "Utilitarian, Aesthetic, and Familiarity Responses to Verbal Versus Visual Advertisements," in Thomas C. Kinnear, ed., *Advances in Consumer Research* 11 (Provo, UT: Association for Consumer Research, 1984): 426–31.

93. Terry L. Childers and Michael J. Houston, "Conditions for a Picture-Superiority Effect on Consumer Memory," *Journal of Consumer Research* 11 (September 1984): 643–54.

94. John R. Rossiter and Larry Percy, "Attitude Change Through Visual Imagery in Advertising," *Journal of Advertising Research* 9, no. 2 (1980): 10–16.

95. Jolita Kiselius and Brian Sternthal, "Examining the Vividness Controversy: An Availability–Valence Interpretation," *Journal of Consumer Research* 12 (March 1986): 418–31.

96. Scott B. MacKenzie, "The Role of Attention in Mediating the Effect of Advertising on Attribute Importance," *Journal of Consumer Research* 13 (September 1986): 174–95.

97. Robert B. Zajonc, "Attitudinal Effects of Mere Exposure," *Journal of Personality and Social Psychology* 8 (1968): 1–29.

98. Giles D'Souza and Ram C. Rao, "Can Repeating an Advertisement More Frequently Than the Competition Affect Brand Preference in a Mature Market?" *Journal of Marketing* 59 (April 1995): 32–42.

99. George E. Belch, "The Effects of Television Commercial Repetition on Cognitive Response and Message Acceptance," *Journal of Consumer Research* 9 (June 1982): 56–65; Marian Burke and Julie Edell, "Ad Reactions over Time: Capturing Changes in the Real World," *Journal of Consumer Research* 13 (June 1986): 114–18; Herbert Krugman, "Why Three Exposures May Be Enough," *Journal of Advertising Research* 12 (December 1972): 11–14.

100. Robert F. Bornstein, "Exposure and Affect: Overview and Meta-Analysis of Research, 1968–1987," *Psychological Bulletin* 106, no. 2 (1989): 265–89; Arno Rethans, John Swasy, and Lawrence Marks, "Effects of Television Commercial Repetition, Receiver Knowledge, and Commercial Length: A Test of the Two-Factor Model," *Journal of Marketing Research* 23 (February 1986): 50–61.

101. Curtis P. Haugtvedt, David W. Schumann, Wendy L. Schneier, and Wendy L. Warren, "Advertising Repetition and Variation Strategies: Implications for Understanding Attitude Strength," *Journal of Consumer Research* 21 (June 1994): 176–89.

102. Linda L. Golden and Mark I. Alpert, "Comparative Analysis of the Relative Effectiveness of One- and Two-Sided Communication for Contrasting Products," *Journal of Advertising* 16 (1987): 18–25; Michael A.

Kamins, "Celebrity and Noncelebrity Advertising in a Two-Sided Context," *Journal of Advertising Research* 29 (June–July 1989): 34; Robert B. Settle and Linda L. Golden, "Attribution Theory and Advertiser Credibility," *Journal of Marketing Research* 11 (May 1974): 181–85.

103. Leon Festinger, *A Theory of Cognitive Dissonance* (Stanford, CA: Stanford University Press, 1957).

104. Cf. Alan G. Sawyer, "The Effects of Repetition of Refutational and Supportive Advertising Appeals," *Journal of Marketing Research* 10 (February 1973): 23–33; George J. Szybillo and Richard Heslin, "Resistance to Persuasion: Inoculation Theory in a Marketing Context," *Journal of Marketing Research* 10 (November 1973): 396–403.

105. Rupal Parekh and Jean Halliday, "New Ad Introduces Consumers to 'New GM,'" *Advertising Age* (June 1, 2009), http://adage.com/article?article_id=137010, accessed June 6, 2009.

106. Golden and Alpert, "Comparative Analysis of the Relative Effectiveness of One- and Two-Sided Communication for Contrasting Products"; Gita Venkataramani Johar and Anne L. Roggeveen, "Changing False Beliefs from Repeated Advertising: The Role of Claim-Refutation Alignment," *Journal of Consumer Psychology* 17, no. 2 (2007): 118–27.

107. George E. Belch, Michael A. Belch, and Angelina Villareal, "Effects of Advertising Communications: Review of Research," in *Research in Marketing*, no. 9 (Greenwich, CT: JAI Press, 1987): 59–117.

108. Frank R. Kardes, "Spontaneous Inference Processes in Advertising: The Effects of Conclusion Omission and Involvement on Persuasion," *Journal of Consumer Research* 15 (September 1988): 225–33.

109. George E. Belch, Michael A. Belch, and Angelina Villareal, "Effects of Advertising Communications: Review of Research," in *Research in Marketing*, no. 9 (Greenwich, CT: JAI Press, 1987): 59–117; Cornelia Pechmann and Gabriel Esteban, "Persuasion Processes Associated with Direct Comparative and Noncomparative Advertising and Implications for Advertising Effectiveness," *Journal of Consumer Psychology* 2, no. 4 (1994): 403–32.

110. Cornelia Dröge and Rene Y. Darmon, "Associative Positioning Strategies Through Comparative Advertising: Attribute vs. Overall Similarity Approaches," *Journal of Marketing Research* 24 (1987): 377–89; D. Muehling and N. Kangun, "The Multidimensionality of Comparative Advertising: Implications for the FTC," *Journal of Public Policy and Marketing* (1985): 112–28; Beth A. Walker and Helen H. Anderson, "Reconceptualizing Comparative Advertising: A Framework and Theory of Effects," in Rebecca H. Holman and Michael R. Solomon, eds., *Advances in Consumer Research* 18 (Provo, UT: Association for Consumer Research, 1991): 342–47; William L. Wilkie and Paul W. Farris, "Comparison Advertising: Problems and Potential," *Journal of Marketing* 39 (October 1975): 7–15; R. G. Wyckham, "Implied Superiority Claims," *Journal of Advertising Research* (February–March 1987): 54–63.

111. Suzanne Vranica, "Arby's TV Spots Play Game of Fast-Food Chicken," *Wall Street Journal* (July 5, 2006): A16.

112. Mehmet I. Yagci, Abhijit Biswas, and Sujay Dutta, "Effects of Comparative Advertising Format on Consumer Responses: The Moderating Effects of Brand Image and Attribute Relevance," *Journal of Business Research*, forthcoming.

113. Quoted in Suzanne Vranica, "And in This Corner. . . . Marketers Take Some Jabs," *Wall Street Journal* (October 2, 2008), http://online.wsj.com/article/Sb122289868915095901.html accessed October 2, 2008; Stuart Elliott, "Dueling Brands Pick Up Where Politicians Leave Off," *New York Times* (November 3, 2008), www.newyorktimes.com/2008/11/04/Business/Media/04adco.Html?_R=1&Oref=Slogin11/4/2008, accessed November 4, 2008.

114. Stephen A. Goodwin and Michael Etgar, "An Experimental Investigation of Comparative Advertising: Impact of Message Appeal, Information Load, and Utility of Product Class," *Journal of Marketing Research* 17 (May 1980): 187–202; Gerald J. Gorn and Charles B. Weinberg, "The Impact of Comparative Advertising on Perception and Attitude: Some Positive Findings," *Journal of Consumer Research* 11 (September 1984): 719–27; Terence A. Shimp and David C. Dyer, "The Effects of Comparative Advertising Mediated by Market Position of Sponsoring Brand," *Journal of Advertising* 3 (Summer 1978): 13–19; R. Dale Wilson, "An Empirical Evaluation of Comparative Advertising Messages: Subjects' Responses to Perceptual Dimensions," in B. B. Anderson, ed., *Advances in Consumer Research* 3 (Ann Arbor, MI: Association for Consumer Research, 1976): 53–57.

115. Louise Kramer, "In a Battle of Toothpastes, It's Information vs. Emotion," *New York Times* (January 17, 2007): C6.

116. H. Zielske, "Does Day-After Recall Penalize 'Feeling' Ads?" *Journal of Advertising Research* 22 (1982): 19–22.

117. Quoted in Stuart Elliott, "Angry Ads Seek to Channel Consumer Outrage," *New York Times* (May 14, 2009), www.nytimes.com, accessed May 14, 2009.

118. Rupal Parekh and Emily Bryson York, "Mars Encourages Women to Have a Fling," *Advertising Age* (March 27, 2009), www.adage.com, accessed March 27, 2009.

119. Allessandra Galloni, "Lee's Cheeky Ads Are Central to New European Campaign," *Wall Street Journal* (March 15, 2002), www.wsj.com, accessed March 15, 2002.

120. George E. Belch, Michael A. Belch, and Angelina Villareal, "Effects of Advertising Communications: Review of Research," in *Research in Marketing*, no. 9 (Greenwich, CT: JAI Press, 1987): 59–117; Courtney and Whipple, *Sex Stereotyping in Advertising*; Michael S. LaTour, "Female Nudity in Print Advertising: An Analysis of Gender Differences in Arousal and Response," *Psychology & Marketing* 7, no. 1 (1990): 65–81; B. G. Yovovich, "Sex in Advertising—The Power and the Perils," *Advertising Age* (May 2, 1983): M4–M5. For an interesting interpretive analysis, see Richard Elliott and Mark Ritson, "Practicing Existential Consumption: The Lived Meaning of Sexuality in Advertising," in Frank R. Kardes and Mita Sujan, eds., *Advances in Consumer Behavior* 22 (1995): 740–45; Jaideep Sengupta and Darren W. Dahl, "Gender-Related Reactions to Gratuitous Sex Appeals," *Journal of Consumer Psychology* 18 (2008): 62–78.

121. Penny M. Simpson, Steve Horton, and Gene Brown, "Male Nudity in Advertisements: A Modified Replication and Extension of Gender and Product Effects," *Journal of the Academy of Marketing Science* 24, no. 3 (1996): 257–62.

122. Jaideep Sengupta and Darren W. Dahl, "Gender-Related Reactions to Gratuitous Sex Appeals," *Journal of Consumer Psychology* 18 (2008): 62–78; Darren W. Dahl, Jaideep Sengupta, and Kathleen Vohs, "Sex in Advertising: Gender Differences and the Role of Relationship Commitment," *Journal of Consumer Research* 36 (August 2009): in press.

123. Rebecca Gardyn, "Where's the Lovin'?" *American Demographic* (February 2001): 10.

124. Michael S. LaTour and Tony L. Henthorne, "Ethical Judgments of Sexual Appeals in Print Advertising," *Journal of Advertising* 23, no. 3 (September 1994): 81–90.

125. "Does Sex Really Sell?" *Adweek* (October 17, 2005): 17.

126. Karlene Lukovitz, "Burger King SpongeBob Ad Too Sexual?" *Marketing Daily* (April 10, 2009), www.mediapost.com, accessed April 10, 2009.

127. Katharine Q. Seelye, "Metamucil Ad Featuring Old Faithful Causes a Stir," *New York Times* (January 19, 2003), www.nytimes.com, accessed January 19, 2003.

128. Thomas J. Madden, "Humor in Advertising: An Experimental Analysis," working paper, no. 83-27, University of Massachusetts, 1984; Thomas J. Madden and Marc G. Weinberger, "The Effects of Humor on Attention in Magazine Advertising," *Journal of Advertising* 11, no. 3 (1982): 8–14; Weinberger and Spotts, "Humor in U.S. versus U.K. TV Commercials"; see also Ashesh Mukherjee and Laurette Dubé, "The Use of Humor in Threat-Related Advertising" (unpublished manuscript, McGill University, June 2002).

129. David Gardner, "The Distraction Hypothesis in Marketing," *Journal of Advertising Research* 10 (1970): 25–30.

130. Chris Abraham, "Global Web Means Your 'Fart Jokes' Can Be Heard out of Context," *Advertising Age* (June 15, 2009), http://adage.com/digitalnext/article?article_id=137273, accessed June 16, 2009.

131. Brian Steinberg, "VW Uses Shock Treatment to Sell Jetta's Safety," *Wall Street Journal* (April 19, 2006): B4.

132. Rich Thomaselli, "Fear Factor Gets Brink's Buzz—and a Sales Boost," *Advertising Age* (April 13, 2009), www.adage.com, accessed April 13, 2009.

133. Michael L. Ray and William L. Wilkie, "Fear: The Potential of an Appeal Neglected by Marketing," *Journal of Marketing* 34, no. 1 (1970): 54–62.

134. Punam Anand Keller and Lauren Goldberg Block, "Increasing the Effectiveness of Fear Appeals: The Effect of Arousal and Elaboration," *Journal of Consumer Research* 22 (March 1996): 448–59.

135. Ronald Paul Hill, "An Exploration of the Relationship Between AIDS-Related Anxiety and the Evaluation of Condom Advertisements," *Journal of Advertising* 17, no. 4 (1988): 35–42.

136. Randall Rothenberg, "Talking Too Tough on Life's Risks?" *New York Times* (February 16, 1990): D1.

137. Denise D. Schoenbachler and Tommy E. Whittler, "Adolescent Processing of Social and Physical Threat Communications," *Journal of Advertising* 25, no. 4 (Winter 1996): 37–54.

138. Barbara B. Stern, "Medieval Allegory: Roots of Advertising Strategy for the Mass Market," *Journal of Marketing* 52 (July 1988): 84–94.

139. Edward F. McQuarrie and David Glen Mick, "On Resonance: A Critical Pluralistic Inquiry into Advertising Rhetoric," *Journal of Consumer Research* 19 (September 1992): 180–97.

140. Edward F. McQuarrie and David G. Mick, "Figures of Rhetoric in Advertising Language," *Journal of Consumer Research* 22, 4 (1996): 420–34.

141. Barbara J. Phillips and Edward F. McQuarrie, "Beyond Visual Metaphor: A New Typology of Visual Rhetoric in Advertising," *Marketing Theory*, 4 (March/June 2004): 113–36.

142. Cf. Linda M. Scott, "The Troupe: Celebrities as Dramatis Personae in Advertisements," in Rebecca H. Holman and Michael R. Solomon, eds., *Advances in Consumer Research* 18 (Provo, UT: Association for Consumer Research, 1991): 355–63; Barbara Stern, "Literary Criticism and Consumer Research: Overview and Illustrative Analysis," *Journal of Consumer Research* 16 (1989): 322–34; Judith Williamson, *Decoding Advertisements* (Boston: Marion Boyars, 1978).

143. John Deighton, Daniel Romer, and Josh McQueen, "Using Drama to Persuade," *Journal of Consumer Research* 16 (December 1989): 335–43.

144. Richard E. Petty, John T. Cacioppo, and David Schumann, "Central and Peripheral Routes to Advertising Effectiveness: The Moderating Role of Involvement," *Journal of Consumer Research* 10, no. 2 (1983): 135–46.

145. Jerry C. Olson, Daniel R. Toy, and Philip A. Dover, "Do Cognitive Responses Mediate the Effects of Advertising Content on Cognitive Structure?" *Journal of Consumer Research* 9, no. 3 (1982): 245–62.

146. Julie A. Edell and Andrew A. Mitchell, "An Information Processing Approach to Cognitive Responses," in S. C. Jain, ed., *Research Frontiers in Marketing: Dialogues and Directions* (Chicago: American Marketing Association, 1978).

147. Richard E. Petty, John T. Cacioppo, Constantine Sedikides, and Alan J. Strathman, "Affect and Persuasion: A Contemporary Perspective," *American Behavioral Scientist* 31, no. 3 (1988): 355–71.

148. Rob Walker, "The Gifted Ones," *New York Times Magazine* (November 14, 2004), www.nytimes.com, accessed September 29, 2007.

MINTEL

SECTION 2

General Instructions for the *Mintel Memo and Dataset Exercises*

*T*he dataset exercise in each Mintel section consists of a data-driven task. You should complete each task by analyzing the sample data tables provided in each Mintel section. (Each table includes data collected by Mintel International from actual respondents in the marketplace!)

In generating each data-driven "memo," you will provide your own interpretation of the data in the tables, paying close attention to significant differences among banner groups in the data tables (e.g., males versus females, 18- to 24-year-olds versus 55+ year-olds, single versus married, etc.). In the field of marketing research, marketing recommendations are typically generated from statistically significant differences among subgroups of respondents; therefore, your analyses and recommendations will be more useful and informed by focusing on statistically significant differences among the banner groups in the provided sets of data tables.

MINTEL MEMO

TO: Consumer Research Dept.
FROM: The Big Boss
RE: How are food and diet trends affecting consumer behavior today?

We need to provide consumer feedback to our new product development group ASAP. Based on what you know from reading Section 2 and from the data we have been given by Mintel, what would be a feasible idea for a new food product given today's market trends? Assume a reasonable but not an eye-popping budget.

Please provide us with actionable recommendations based on this information. As you analyze the data in the tables provided, remember to focus on general trends but also on specific subgroups (e.g., men versus women) that show a statistically significant difference in their responses—especially when there is some reason based on what you have learned in this section about consumer behavior to believe that this difference is important.

When you write your memo, please try to incorporate relevant concepts and information you learned when you read the designated chapters!

What can we learn from the following data to help our company create and market a new food product?

Section 3 Consumers as Decision Makers

This section explores how we make consumption decisions and discusses the many influences others exert during this process. Chapter 8 focuses on the basic sequence of steps we undergo when we make decisions. Chapter 9 considers how the particular situation in which we find ourselves affects these decisions and how we go about evaluating the results of our choices. Chapter 10 provides an overview of group processes and discusses the reasons we are motivated to conform to the expectations of others when we choose and display our purchases. Chapter 11 goes on to consider the many instances where we make our purchase decisions in conjunction with others, especially coworkers or family members.

CHAPTERS AHEAD

8

Decision Making

When you finish this chapter you will understand:

Chapter
Objectives

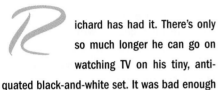 ichard has had it. There's only so much longer he can go on watching TV on his tiny, antiquated black-and-white set. It was bad enough trying to listen to the scratchy music in MTV videos and squinting through *It's On with Alexa Chung*. The final straw was when he couldn't tell the Titans from the Jaguars during an NFL football game. When he went next door to watch the second half on Mark's home theater setup, he finally realized what he was missing. Budget or not, it was time to act: A man has his priorities.

Where to start looking? The Web, naturally. Richard checks out a few comparison-shopping Web sites, including pricegrabber.com and bizrate.com. After he narrows down his options, he ventures out to scope out a few sets in person. He figures he'll probably get a decent selection (and an affordable price) at one of those huge new warehouse stores. Arriving at Zany Zack's Appliance Emporium, Richard heads straight for the Video Zone in the back—he barely notices the rows of toasters, microwave ovens, and stereos on his way. Within minutes, a smiling salesperson in a cheap suit accosts him. Even though he could use some help, Richard tells the salesperson he's only browsing—he figures these guys don't know what they're talking about, and they're simply out to make a sale no matter what.

Richard examines some of the features on the 60-inch color sets. He knew his friend Carol had a set by Prime Wave that she really liked, and his sister Diane warned him to stay away from the Kamashita. Although Richard finds a Prime Wave model loaded to the max with features such as a sleep timer, on-screen programming menu, cable-compatible tuner, and picture-in-picture, he chooses the less expensive Precision 2000X because it has one feature that really catches his fancy: stereo broadcast reception.

Later that day, Richard is a happy man as he sits in his easy chair and watches Lauren, Audrina, Spencer, and the others doing their thing on MTV's *The Hills*. If he's going to be a couch potato, he's going in style.

Why is consumer decision making a central part of consumer behavior, but the way we evaluate and choose products (and the amount of thought we put into these choices) varies widely, depending on such dimensions as the degree of novelty or risk in the decision?

We Are Problem Solvers

A consumer purchase is a response to a problem, which in Richard's case is the need for a new TV. His situation is similar to those that we encounter virtually every day of our lives (even if you decide to make no decisions on your day off, that's still a decision!). He realizes that he wants to make a purchase, and he undergoes a series of steps in order to make it. We describe these steps as (1) problem recognition, (2) information search, (3) evaluation of alternatives, and (4) product choice. Of course, after we make a decision, its outcome affects the final step in the process, in which learning occurs based on how well the choice worked out. This learning process, of course, influences the likelihood that we'll make the same choice the next time the need for a similar decision occurs. And so on and so on . . .

Figure 8.1 provides an overview of this decision-making process. As we begin this chapter we'll review different approaches we might use when we need to make a purchase decision. We then focus on three of the steps in the decision process:

1 How we recognize the problem, or need for a product;
2 How we search for information about product choices; and
3 How we evaluate alternatives to arrive at a decision.

Because some purchase decisions are more important than others, the amount of effort we put into each one differs. Sometimes the decision-making process is almost automatic—we seem to make snap judgments based on very little information. At other times, when we decide what to buy the process resembles a full-time job. A person may literally spend days or weeks agonizing over an important purchase such as a new home, a car, or even Mac versus PC. This intensive decision-making process gets even more complicated in today's environment where we have so many options from which to choose. Ironically, for many modern consumers one of the biggest problems they face is not having *too few* choices but having *too many*. We describe this profusion of options as **consumer hyperchoice**—a condition where the large number of available options forces us to make repeated choices that may drain psychological energy while it saps our abilities to make smart decisions.[1]

A purchase is a response to a problem.
Source: Darko Novakovic/Shutterstock.

Figure 8.1 STAGES IN CONSUMER
DECISION MAKING

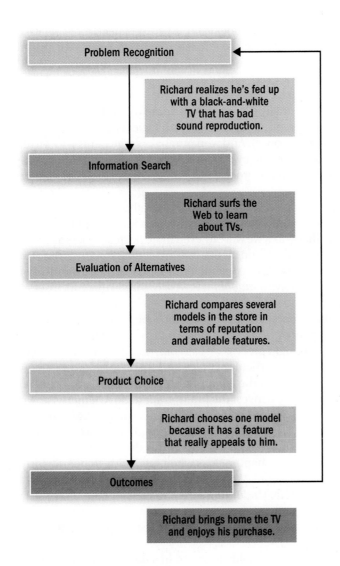

Perspectives on Decision Making

Consumer researchers typically apply a **rational perspective** to understand decision making. In this view, we calmly and carefully integrate as much information as possible with what we already know about a product, painstakingly weigh the pluses and minuses of each alternative, and make a satisfactory decision. This traditional perspective relates the *economics of information* approach to the search process—it assumes that we collect just as much data as we need to make an informed decision. We form expectations of the value of additional information and continue to search to the extent that the rewards of doing so (what economists call the *utility*) exceed the costs. This utilitarian assumption also implies that we collect the most valuable units of information first. We absorb additional pieces only to the extent that we think they will add to what we already know.[2] In other words, we'll put ourselves out to collect as much information as we can, so long as the process isn't too onerous or time-consuming.[3]

This rational outlook implies that marketing managers should carefully study steps in decision making to understand how consumers obtain information, how they form beliefs, and what criteria they use to make product choices. Then, companies can develop products that emphasize the appropriate attributes, and marketers can tailor promotional strategies to deliver the types of information customers are most likely to desire and in the most effective formats.[4]

It all sounds good, but how valid is this perspective? Sure, we do follow these decision-making steps when we make some purchases, but this rational process doesn't accurately portray many of our purchase decisions.[5] We simply don't go through this elaborate sequence every time we buy something. If we did, we'd spend our entire lives making these decisions. This would leave us very little time to enjoy the things we eventually decide to buy. Some of our buying behaviors simply don't seem "rational" because they don't serve a logical purpose (you don't use that belly ring to hold a beach towel). And, you purchase some items with virtually no advance planning at all—have you ever impulsively thrown a fattening candy bar into your cart while you wait at the grocery checkout? (Hint: That's why candy bars and celeb magazines are there.)

Still other actions actually contradict what those rational models predict. For example, **purchase momentum** occurs when our initial impulse purchases actually increase the likelihood that we will buy even more (instead of less as we satisfy our needs); it's like we get "revved up" and plunge into a spending spree (we've all been there!).[6] And, recent research hints that people differ in terms of their **cognitive processing style**. Some of us tend to have a *rational system of cognition* that processes information analytically and sequentially using roles of logic, while others rely on an *experiential system of cognition* that processes information more holistically and in parallel.[7]

Researchers now realize that decision makers actually possess a *repertoire* of strategies—in a thought process we call *constructive processing,* we evaluate the effort we'll need to make a particular choice and then we tailor the amount of cognitive "effort" we expend to get the job done.[8] When the task requires a well-thought-out, rational approach, we'll invest the brainpower to do it. Otherwise, we look for shortcuts or fall back on learned responses that "automate" these choices.

We make some decisions under conditions of low involvement, as we discussed in Chapter 4. In many of these situations, our decision is a learned response to environmental cues (see Chapter 3), as when we decide to buy something on impulse because it just looks cool. We explain these types of decisions as the **behavioral influence perspective**. Under these circumstances, managers should focus on the peripheral cues Chapter 7 describes such as an attention-grabbing package rather than on factual details (i.e., as we said in the last chapter, sell the "sizzle" rather than the "steak").[9]

In other cases, we're highly involved in a decision, but still we can't explain our selections rationally. For example, the traditional approach is hard-pressed to account for our choice of art, music, or even a spouse ("OMG, how did she ever wind up with *him*?"). In these cases, no single quality determines the decision. Instead, the **experiential perspective** stresses the *Gestalt*, or totality (see Chapter 2), of the product or service.[10] In these contexts marketers need to assess consumers' affective responses to products or services and then develop offerings that create a positive emotional response.

Types of Consumer Decisions

It helps to understand the decision-making process when we think about the amount of effort that goes into a decision each time we must make it. Consumer researchers think in terms of a continuum, anchored on one end by *habitual decision making* and at the other extreme by *extended problem solving*. Many decisions fall somewhere in the middle so we describe these as *limited problem solving*. Figure 8.2 presents this continuum.

Extended Problem Solving

Decisions involving **extended problem solving** correspond most closely to the traditional decision-making perspective. As Table 8.1 indicates, we usually initiate this careful process when the decision we have to make relates to our self-concept (see Chapter 5), and we feel that the outcome may be risky in some way. In that case we

Figure 8.2 A CONTINUUM OF BUYING DECISION BEHAVIOR

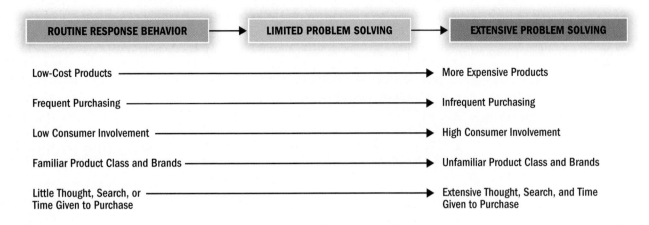

try to collect as much information as possible, both from our memory (internal search) and from outside sources such as Google (external search). Then we carefully evaluate each product alternative—often we consider the attributes of one brand at a time and see how each brand's attributes relate to the results we hope to get from our choice.

Limited Problem Solving

Limited problem solving is usually more straightforward and simple. In this case we're not nearly as motivated to search for information or to evaluate each alternative rigorously. Instead, we're likely to use simple *decision rules* as we choose among alternatives. These cognitive shortcuts (more about these later) enable us to fall back on general guidelines, instead of having to start from scratch every time we need to decide.

Habitual Decision Making

Both extended and limited problem-solving modes involve some degree of information search and deliberation. At the other end of the choice continuum, however, lies **habitual decision making**—choices we make with little to no conscious effort. Many purchase decisions are so routinized that we may not realize we've made them until we look in our shopping carts! We make these choices without conscious control—researchers call this process *automaticity*.[11]

TABLE 8.1	Characteristics of Limited Versus Extended Problem Solving	
	Limited Problem Solving	**Extended Problem Solving**
Motivation	Low risk and involvement	High risk and Involvement
Information Search	Little search Information processed passively In-store decision likely	Extensive search Information processed actively Multiple sources consulted prior to visits
Alternative Evaluation	Weakly held beliefs Only most prominent criteria used Alternatives perceived as basically similar Noncompensatory strategy used	Strongly held beliefs Many criteria used Significant differences perceived among alternatives Compensatory strategy used
Purchase	Limited shopping time; may prefer self-service Choice often Influenced by store displays	Many outlets shopped if needed Communication with store personnel often desirable

Although this kind of thoughtless activity may seem dangerous or at best stupid in many cases, it actually makes sense! When we develop these habitual, repetitive behaviors, we minimize the time and energy we spend on mundane purchase decisions. However, habitual decision making poses a problem when a marketer tries to introduce a new way to do an old task. In this case she must convince us to "unfreeze" our former habit and replace it with a new one—perhaps to use an ATM instead of a live bank teller, or switch to a self-service gas pump instead of having an attendant wait on us.

Steps in the Decision-Making Process

Richard didn't suddenly wake up and crave a new TV. He went through several steps between the time he felt the need for a new boob tube and when he actually brought one home. Let's review the basic steps in this process.

Problem Recognition

Ford's plan to promote its 2010 Fusion hybrid model focuses on people who aren't thinking about buying a new car—at least not right now. Its TV commercials target what the auto industry terms the "upper funnel," or potential buyers down the road. Ford's research found that 40 percent of U.S. drivers still are unaware of the Fusion. The company is confident that it can close sales if and when customers decide to buy a new car. But, its weak spot is to get people into the frame of mind where they want to do that. To create desire where there is none now, visitors to <u>weraceyouwin.com</u> can enter to win a trip and a new Fusion. Ford publicized the sweepstakes on Twitter and Facebook; during the first two weeks of the promotion, almost 70,000 people requested more information about the car.[13]

Problem recognition occurs at what Ford terms "the upper funnel" when we experience a significant difference between our current state of affairs and some state

This Dutch ad encourages consumers to recognize a problem: They need to get out and go to the movies asap!
Source: © KesselsKramer, Amsterdam.

we desire. We realize that to get from here to there we need to solve a problem, which may be small or large, simple or complex. A person who unexpectedly runs out of gas on the highway has a problem, as does the person who becomes dissatisfied with the image of his car, even though there is nothing mechanically wrong with it. Although the quality of Richard's TV had not changed, he altered his *standard of comparison,* and as a result he had a new problem to solve—how to improve his TV experience?

Figure 8.3 shows that a problem arises in one of two ways. The person who runs out of gas experiences a decline in the quality of his *actual state* (*need recognition*). In contrast the person who craves a newer, flashier car moves his *ideal state* upward (*opportunity recognition*). Either way, there is a gulf between the actual state and the ideal state.[14] Richard perceived a problem due to opportunity recognition—he moved his ideal state upward in terms of the quality of TV reception he craved.

Need recognition occurs in several ways. A person's actual state can decrease if she runs out of a product, or if she buys a product that doesn't adequately satisfy her needs, or if she realizes she has a new need or desire. For example, when you buy a house, this sets off an avalanche of other choices because now you need to buy many new things to fill it—assuming there's any money left over! In contrast, opportunity recognition often occurs when we're exposed to different or better-quality products. This happens because our circumstances change, as when we start college or land a new job. As our frame of reference shifts, we make purchases to adapt to the new environment. That awesome pair of True Religion jeans you just scored somehow won't make it on a job interview.

Information Search

Once a consumer recognizes a problem, she needs the 411 to solve it. **Information search** is the process by which we survey the environment for appropriate data to make a reasonable decision. In this section we'll review some of the factors this search involves.[15]

Types of Information Search

You might recognize a need and then search the marketplace for specific information (a process we call *prepurchase search*). However, many of us, especially veteran shoppers, enjoy browsing just for the fun of it or because we like to stay up-to-date on what's happening in the marketplace. Those shopaholics engage in *ongoing search*.[17] Table 8.2 describes some differences between these two search modes.

Marketing Pitfall

Some consumers really have trouble searching for information—because they have difficulty reading. When we do consumer research, we typically assume that our respondents are fully literate so they are able to find information, identify products, and conduct transactions with few problems. However, it's worth noting that, in fact, more than half of the U.S. population reads at or below a sixth-grade level—and that roughly half are unable to master specific aspects of shopping. This fact reminds us to think more about the **low-literate consumer** who is at a big disadvantage in the marketplace. Some of these people (whom researchers term *social isolates*) cope with the stigma of illiteracy by avoiding situations where they will have to reveal this problem. They may choose not to eat at a restaurant with an unfamiliar menu, for example. Low-literate consumers rely heavily on visual cues, including brand logos and store layouts, to navigate in retail settings, but they often make mistakes when they select similarly packaged products (for example, brand line extensions). They also encounter problems with *innumeracy* (understanding numbers)—many low-literate people have difficulty knowing, for example, whether they have enough money to purchase the items in their cart and unethical merchants may cheat them out of the correct amount of change. Not surprisingly, these challenges create an emotional burden for low-literate consumers, who experience stress, anxiety, fear, shame, and other negative emotions before, during, and after they shop.[16]

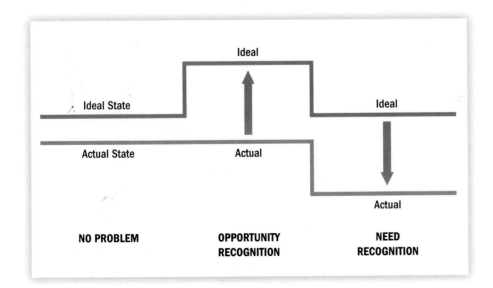

Figure 8.3 PROBLEM RECOGNITION: SHIFTS IN ACTUAL OR IDEAL STATES

When it comes to efficient information search, don't look to American men who do the grocery shopping. According to an industry analyst who conducted a study on store behavior, men are " . . . often overwhelmed by the experience." She says they " . . . roam the aisles like lost sheep, and are afraid to make their wives mad by bringing home the wrong brand of cereal bar or toothpaste. . . . They do not want to catch any flak for coming home with the wrong thing. They'd say, 'I'll just tell my wife the store is out of this brand,' rather than admit that they couldn't find it." She notes that grocery stores aren't organized to make life easier for male shoppers. They tend to circle back through aisles multiple times in their searches, become overwhelmed in center-store aisles, and focus their attention within a fairly narrow visual range. But, they're more likely to call their spouses on a cell phone than to ask store employees for help. Kind of like stopping on the road to ask for directions—not happening.[18]

The proliferation of powerful online search engines creates a new breed of consumers—one research company labels them the **new info shoppers**. This term refers to people who almost automatically search for information online before they buy just about anything. They tend to work in information-based jobs, are well-educated, and fairly affluent. In one survey of these new info shoppers, over three-quarters agreed that TV conventional media advertising no longer provides enough information, and over 90 percent said they have more confidence in what they learn online than from any other source (including salesclerks). More generally, 70 percent of Americans now say they consult product reviews or consumer ratings before they decide what to buy, and three-quarters of those under the age of 45 spend at least half an hour online every week to research purchases. So, we can expect to see a new wave of online applications that cater to our desires to search. Many of the new wave of iPhone apps provide a search function—as one example Kraft Foods offers the iFood

It helps to distinguish between internal and external search. As a result of our prior experience and the fact that we live in a consumer culture, each of us has some degree of knowledge already in memory about many products. When a purchase decision confronts us, we may engage in *internal search* as we scan our own memory banks to assemble information about different product alternatives (see Chapter 3). Usually, though, even those of us who are the most market-savvy need to supplement this knowledge with external search so we also obtain information from advertisements, friends, or just plain people watching. A Finnish study demonstrated how what our neighbors buy impacts our own decision making. The researchers discovered that when one of a person's 10 nearest neighbors bought a car, the odds that he would buy a car of the same make during the next week and a half jumped 86 percent.[19]

Deliberate Versus "Accidental" Search. We may know about a product due to directed learning: On a previous occasion we've already searched for relevant information. A parent who bought a birthday cake for one child last month, for example, probably has a good idea of the best kind to buy for another child this month.

Other times, however we acquire information in a more passive manner. Even though a product may not be of direct interest to us today, we still encounter advertising, packaging, and sales promotion activities that result in *incidental learning*. Mere exposure over time to conditioned stimuli and observations of others makes us learn a lot of information that we may not need for some time, if ever (think of all those advertising jingles you can't get out of your head). For marketers, this is one of the benefits of steady, "low-dose" advertising; they establish and maintain product associations until the time we need them.

In some cases, we may be so expert about a product category (or at least believe we are) that we don't conduct any additional search. Frequently, however, our own

TABLE 8.2	A Framework for Consumer Information Search
Prepurchase Search	**Ongoing Search**
Determinants	
Involvement in the purchase	Involvement with the product
Market environment	Market environment
Situational factors	Situational factors
Motives	
Making better purchase decisions	Building a bank of information for future use
	Experiencing fun and pleasure
Outcomes	
Increased product and market knowledge	Increased product and market knowledge leading to
Better purchase decisions	• future buying efficiencies
	• personal influence
Increased satisfaction with the purchase outcome	Increased impulse buying
	Increased satisfaction from search and other outcomes

Source: Peter H. Bloch, Daniel L Sherrell, and Nancy M. Ridgway. "Consumer Search: An Extended Framework," *Journal of Consumer Research* 13 (June 1986): 120. Copyright © 1986 JCR. Inc. Reprinted with permission of the University of Chicago Press.

existing state of knowledge is not sufficient to make an adequate decision, and we must look elsewhere for more information. The sources we consult for advice vary: They may be impersonal and marketer-dominated sources, such as retailers and catalogs; they may be friends and family members; or they may be unbiased third parties, such as *Consumer Reports.*[20]

Online Search

When we search online for product information, we're a perfect target for advertisers because we declare our desire to make a purchase. Recognizing this, many companies pay **search engines** like <u>Google</u> as well as <u>Bing</u>, <u>Yahoo!</u>, and <u>Ask.com</u> to show ads to users who search for their brand names. However, when DoubleClick (an online marketing company) looked closely at what people search for, its analysts found we rarely specify brand names in our queries. Instead, most prepurchase searches use only generic terms, such as *hard drive*. Consumers tend to make these searches early on and then conduct a small flurry of brand-name queries right before they buy.[21]

OBJECTIVE

Why is decision making not always rational?

Do We Always Search Rationally?

As we've seen, we don't necessarily engage in a rational search process where we carefully identify every alternative before we choose the one we want. In fact, the amount of external search we do for most products is surprisingly small, even when we would benefit if we had more information. And lower-income shoppers, who have more to lose when they make a bad purchase, actually search less before they buy than do more affluent people.[22]

Like our friend Richard, some consumers typically visit only one or two stores and rarely seek out unbiased information sources before they make a purchase decision, especially when they have little time available to do so.[23] This pattern is especially prevalent for decisions about durable goods, such as appliances or autos, even when these products represent significant investments. One study of Australian car buyers found that more than a third had made two or fewer trips to inspect cars prior to buying one.[24]

This tendency to avoid external search is less prevalent when consumers consider the purchase of symbolic items, such as clothing. In those cases, not surprisingly, people tend to do a fair amount of external search, although most of it involves asking peers' opinions.[25] Although the stakes may be lower financially, people may see these self-expressive decisions as having dire social consequences if they make the wrong choice. The level of risk, a concept we'll discuss shortly, is high.

In addition, we often engage in *brand switching*, even if our current brand satisfies our needs. When researchers for British brewer Bass Export studied the American beer market, they discovered that many drinkers have a repertoire of two to six favorite brands rather than one clear favorite.[26]

Sometimes, it seems we simply like to try new things—we crave variety as a form of stimulation or to reduce boredom. **Variety seeking**, the desire to choose new alternatives over more familiar ones, even influences us to switch from our favorite products to ones we like less! This can occur even before we become *satiated,* or tired, of our favorite. Research supports the idea that we are willing to trade enjoyment for variety because the unpredictability *itself* is rewarding.[27]

We're especially likely to look for variety when we are in a good mood, or when there isn't a lot of other stuff going on.[28] In the case of foods and beverages, we may decide to try new things due to *sensory-specific satiety*. Put simply, this means the

Assistant to make it easier to search recipes, plan meals, and locate the nearest store that sells the ingredients you need.

Obviously our thirst for information is what drives the growth of search-engine advertising, where marketers bid on key words (like *pizza delivery*) in a continuous auction. When a consumer searches for any of the words, a marketer's ad will appear with the results if the company has bid enough and the engine's software determines the ad is relevant. That process in turn has spawned the industry of **search engine optimization (SEO)**—the small army of consultants who help companies to "game" the search engines to insure that their links turn up near the top of the list when we hop online to find a pizza or even a Picasso.

Our quest for information takes us beyond traditional Web sites as social media continue to grow; for example, in addition to buying advertising space on Google, Pizza Hut now places messages that people access through their mobile phones and on Facebook. One-third of Americans who use cell phones recalled seeing mobile advertising (most as SMS text messages) during the fourth quarter of 2008—and 40 percent of iPhone users did. Women were almost twice as likely as men to say they responded in some way to a mobile ad they'd received and not surprisingly 18- to 24-year-olds were the most responsive. Overall, one in seven people said they'd bought a product or visited a store after they saw an ad on their mobile. Our reliance on our cells to find anything and perhaps anyone will increase as technology advances. Using its mobile maps service, Google's new Latitude service enables you to share your location with your friends, and see where your friends are (or at least where they want you to "think" they are). For marketers, this is another step toward integrating social networking into our daily lives—not just reaching us when we've stopped what we're doing to check in on Facebook.

CB AS I LIVE IT

Jason Calcano, *Rutgers University, New Brunswick*

I have been working out ever since my freshman year in high school. I began exercising consistently because of my participation in football, basketball, and baseball. Throughout high school, my exercising consisted of weightlifting and conditioning programs set by my coaches. Once I enrolled in college, I continued weightlifting but my cardio workouts had pretty much ended. Recently, my gym membership was coming to an end, and I decided that I would try and change up my workout routine. I went to four different gyms and they all felt the same. Finally, a friend of mine told me about mixed martial arts classes she was taking at Tiger Schulmann's Mixed Martial Arts. I decided to look into it and was able to take a trial class. The workout was a lot different than what I was used to, but I really enjoyed it. The classes at Tiger Schulmann's gave me a full workout in an hour and taught me self-defense techniques as well. The workout improved my strength, cardio,

flexibility, and the self-defense techniques made me a lot more confident. I felt that this workout was very refreshing, and I decided to join Tiger Schulmann's program instead of joining a new gym.

My situation best illustrates the concept of *variety seeking*. I wanted to switch up the same workout routine that I had been using for the past 8 years. Also, I wanted to get more cardio in my workouts and try something different because my normal routine was starting to bore me, especially since I could not get any of my friends to join the gym with me. I was working out by myself for the past 2 years, and it was hard to stay motivated. When I found Tiger Schulmann's, I immediately knew it was something that I have never tried before and the challenge motivated me. Another great factor was that I would be in classes working out with other people and not going by myself.

I agree with the chapter's description of variety seeking. I definitely chose Tiger Schulmann's as a form of stimulation and to reduce my monotonous workouts. Even though I loved going to the gym, I felt that I

needed a change. This decision was just what I needed. I went from lifting heavy weights and normally just working out my upper body to getting a great cardio workout and training my whole body. Knowing about the variety seeking concept will probably affect some of my decisions in the future. Knowing that there are many alternatives out there will force me to try out different brands or activities that I normally would not.

I believe a marketer could learn a lot from my experience. Marketers can present their products as alternatives to the normal, repetitive routines that get boring. I would never have tried to work out at Tiger Schulmann's if it was not for my friend's advice. I feel that if marketers can show that their products or brands are different and can offer variety in your life, they can greatly increase the amount of sales they make. Marketers should try to explain that their product can reinvigorate or stimulate someone's life and that would make their product more successful. I believe people are always looking for something different and if you can market your product as a refreshing alternative, you will be a lot better off.

pleasantness of a food item we have just eaten drops, whereas the pleasantness of uneaten foods remains unchanged.[29] So even though we have favorites, we still like to sample other possibilities. However, when the decision situation is ambiguous, or when there is little information about competing brands, we tend to opt for the safe choice. Figure 8.4 shows the brand attributes consumers consider most important when they choose among alternatives, according to a survey *Advertising Age* conducted.

Mental Accounting:
Biases in the Decision-Making Process

Consider the following scenario: You've scored a free ticket to a major football game. At the last minute, though, a sudden snowstorm makes it somewhat dangerous to get to the stadium. Would you still go? Now, assume the same game and snowstorm— except this time you paid a small fortune for the ticket. Would you head out in the storm in this case?

Figure 8.4 *ADVERTISING AGE* POLL: IMPORTANCE OF BRAND ATTRIBUTES

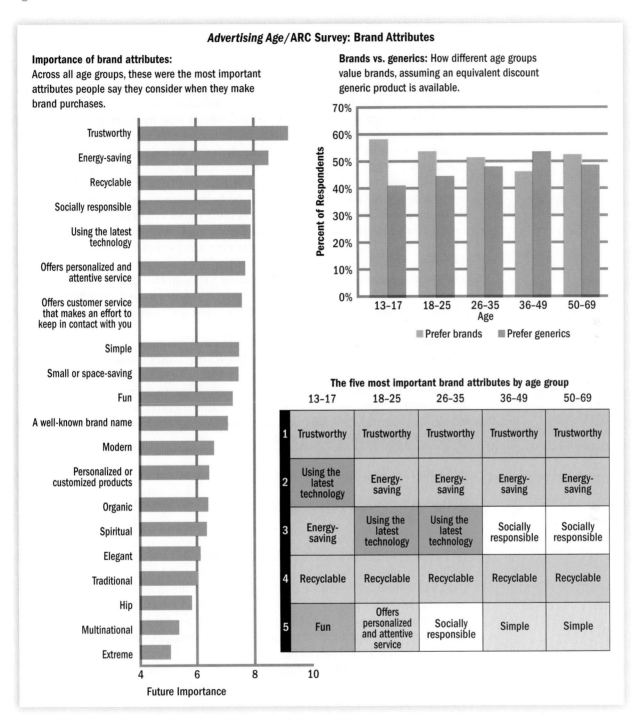

Analyses of people's responses to this situation and to other similar puzzles illustrate principles of **mental accounting**. This process demonstrates that the way we pose a problem (we call this *framing*) and whether it's phrased in terms of gains or losses influences our decisions.[30] In this case, researchers find that people are more likely to risk their personal safety in the storm if they paid for the football ticket than if it's a freebie. Only the most die-hard fan would fail to recognize that this is an irrational choice because the risk is the same regardless of whether you got a great deal on the ticket. Researchers call this decision-making bias the *sunk-cost fallacy*—if we've paid for something we're more reluctant to waste it.

Whether we focus on the present or the future is another example of how the way we frame an issue influences the options we choose and how we feel about them. The condition of **hyperopia** (the medical term for people who have far-sighted vision) describes people who are so obsessed with preparing for the future that they can't enjoy the present. College students who participated in a study on this phenomenon reported that they regretted not working, studying, or saving money during their winter breaks. But, when researchers asked them to imagine how they will feel about this break a year from now, their biggest regrets were that they didn't have enough fun or travel enough. In another study, female subjects received a ticket for a lottery that would be held three months later. They had to choose in advance from one of two prizes if they won: either $85 in cash or an $80 voucher for a massage or facial at a spa. Even though they were reminded that they could use the $85 in cash to get a spa treatment and pocket the $5 difference, more than a third of the women chose the voucher. Researchers found similar results in other situations; when people had to choose between cash and prizes like bottles of wine or dinners out, many of them chose the luxuries even though the cash was a better deal. One participant observed, "If I took the cash it would end up going into the rent."[31]

Loss aversion is another bias. This means that we emphasize our losses more than our gains. For example, for most people losing money is more *unpleasant* than gaining money is *pleasant*. **Prospect theory** describes how people make choices—it defines utility in terms of gains and losses. We evaluate the riskiness of a decision differently if it's put to us in terms of what we stand to gain rather than what we stand to lose.[32] To illustrate this bias, consider the following choices. For each, would you take the safe bet or choose to gamble?

- **Option 1**—You're given $30 and a chance to flip a coin: Heads you win $9, tails you lose $9.
- **Option 2**—You get $30 outright or you accept a coin flip that will win you either $39 or $21.

In one study, 70 percent of those who got option 1 chose to gamble, compared to only 43 percent of those who got option 2. Yet the odds are the same for both options! The difference is that we prefer to "play with the house money"—we're more willing to take risks when we think we're using someone else's resources. So, contrary to a rational decision-making perspective, we value money differently depending on its source. This explains, for example, why the same person who chooses to blow a big bonus on a $2,000 pair of Manolo Blahnik heels would never consider taking that same amount out of her savings account to buy shoes.

Finally, research in mental accounting demonstrates that extraneous characteristics of the choice situation can influence our selections, even though they wouldn't *if* we were totally rational decision makers. Researchers gave survey participants one of the two versions of this scenario:

You are lying on the beach on a hot day. All you have to drink is ice water. For the past hour you have been thinking about how much you would enjoy a nice cold bottle of your favorite brand of beer. A companion gets up to go make a phone call and offers to bring back a beer from the only nearby place where beer is sold (either a fancy resort hotel or a small, run-down grocery store, depending on the version you're given). He says that the beer might be expensive and so asks how much you are willing to pay for it. What price do you tell him?

CB AS I SEE IT

Professor Gavan Fitzsimons, *Duke University*

*F*or many years consumer researchers have thought of the consumer largely as a conscious, thinking machine. Consumers consider what is important to them, evaluate choice options on those alternatives on those dimensions, and make a decision. Recently, however, a growing group of consumer researchers has started to revisit an old idea that had been largely considered debunked—namely that much of what goes on in the life of a consumer occurs outside of his or her conscious awareness.

The idea that consumers are influenced outside of their conscious awareness is frightening to many consumers, and has thus received considerable resistance. And yet, the data become more and more clear that consumers are influenced by stimuli they don't realize they have been exposed to, processes occur in the consumers' minds they are unaware of, and consumers even engage in behavior that they are not conscious of (e.g., consider many habitual behaviors). These nonconscious processes are often adaptive and helpful for the consumer, but can also at times be detrimental.

One interesting recent example from our own lab involved subliminally exposing consumers to brand logos—in several studies either an Apple or an IBM logo. Incidental brand exposures occur every day—recent estimates range between 3,000 and 10,000 times in a single day for the typical American consumer—and thus we were curious if they could influence consumer behavior in meaningful ways. Apple or IBM logos were flashed on a screen for very brief intervals—from 10 to 50 milliseconds—to mimic this real-world incidental brand exposure. Participants had no conscious experience of seeing a brand, and believed they were only seeing a box on the left or right of the screen. Our results showed that nonconscious exposure to the Apple logo led consumers to be significantly more creative than consumers similarly exposed to an IBM logo. This **incidental brand exposure** activated a goal in consumers that they actively pursued until they could satisfy it. Similar studies have shown dramatic increases in choices of one brand versus another as a result of incidental brand exposure.

The future of research on unconscious consumer behavior is likely to continue to document domains in which the consumer is influenced outside of his or her awareness. Contexts in which consumers find themselves taxed, exhausted, or overwhelmed are all ripe for unconscious influence, which sadly have become the default rather than the exception for most consumers. Some of the most interesting questions remaining deal with exactly how nonconscious processes work, and when they may be adaptive versus harmful. If helpful, how can consumers, firms, and public policy makers embrace and encourage them. For example, many consumers might like to be more creative, or faster, for example, and thus might strategically surround themselves with Apple or Speedo logos. Over time exposure to these logos will become incidental and they may find themselves increasingly creative or faster. If such exposures are harmful, what can these groups do to minimize their effects? Preliminary evidence suggests that pre-warnings can, at least in part, dampen these nonconscious effects.

In the survey, the median price participants who read the fancy resort version gave was $2.65, but those who got the grocery store version were only willing to pay $1.50. In both versions the consumption act is the same, the beer is the same, and they don't consume any "atmosphere" because they drink the beer on the beach.[33] So much for rational decision making!

How Much Do We Search?

As a general rule, we search more when the purchase is important, when we have more of a need to learn more about the purchase, or when it's easy to obtain the relevant information.[34] Consumers differ in the amount of search they tend to undertake, regardless of the product category in question. All things being equal, younger, better-educated people who enjoy the shopping/fact-finding process

Figure 8.5 THE RELATIONSHIP
BETWEEN AMOUNT OF INFORMATION
SEARCH AND PRODUCT KNOWLEDGE

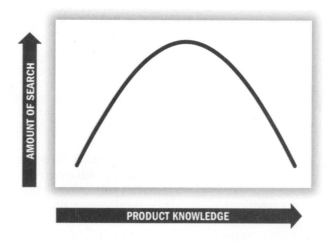

tend to conduct more information search. Women are more inclined to search than men are, as are those who place greater value on style and the image they present.[35]

Does knowing something about the product make it more or less likely that we will engage in search? The answer to this question isn't as obvious as first appears: Product experts and novices use very different procedures during decision making. Novices who know little about a product should be the most motivated to find out more about it. However, experts are more familiar with the product category—they should be better able to understand the meaning of any new product information they might acquire.

So who searches more? The answer is neither: Search tends to be greatest among those consumers who are *moderately knowledgeable* about the product. We find an inverted-U relationship between knowledge and external search effort, as Figure 8.5 shows. People with very limited expertise may not feel they are competent to search extensively. In fact, they may not even know where to start. Richard, who did not spend a lot of time researching his purchase, is typical. He visited one store, and he looked only at brands with which he was already familiar. In addition, he focused on only a small number of product features.[36]

Because experts have a better sense of what information is relevant to the decision, they engage in *selective search*, which means their efforts are more focused and efficient. In contrast, novices are more likely to rely on the opinions of others and on "nonfunctional" attributes, such as brand name and price, to distinguish among alternatives. Finally, novice consumers may process information in a "top-down" rather than a "bottom-up" manner—they focus less on details than on the big picture. For instance, they may be more impressed by the sheer amount of technical information an ad presents than by the actual significance of the claims it makes.[37]

Ironically, people who have details about a product before they buy it do *not* expect to be as happy with it as do those who got only ambiguous information. The so-called **blissful ignorance effect** apparently occurs because we want to feel like we've bought the right thing—and if we know precisely how the product performs it's not as easy to rationalize away any shortcomings. In one experiment some subjects were told of a manufacturer's claims about a hand lotion and informed that separate research had shown that 50 percent of people in fact obtained these benefits. Another set of subjects also heard about the manufacturers' claims, but they were told the results from independent research were not yet available. Those who were provided with less information (the latter group) actually expected the product to perform better. In other words, the less we know about something the easier it is to persuade ourselves that we like it.[38]

Perceived Risk

As a rule, purchase decisions that involve extensive search also entail **perceived risk**, or the belief that there may be negative consequences if you use or don't use a product or service. This may occur when the product is expensive or is complex and hard to understand. Alternatively, perceived risk can be a factor when others can see what we choose, and we may be embarrassed if we make the wrong choice.[39]

Figure 8.6 lists five kinds of risk—including objective (e.g., physical danger) and subjective (e.g., social embarrassment) factors—as well as the products each type tends to affect. Perceived risk is less of a problem for consumers who have greater "risk capital" because they have less to lose from a poor choice. For example, a highly self-confident person might worry less than a vulnerable, insecure person who chooses a brand that peers think isn't cool.

Minolta features a no-risk guarantee as a way to reduce the perceived risk in buying an office copier.
Source: Courtesy of Minolta Corporation.

MAYBE THE BEST WAY TO HANDLE RISK IS TO AVOID IT ALTOGETHER.

That's why Minolta created the No-Risk Guarantee. It takes you out of harm's way by letting you decide whether you're happy with the copier's performance.

Even better, it covers our EP 9760 Pro Series Copier, which was recently voted first overall in productivity in the high-volume class.

Here's how it works: If you're not completely satisfied with our copier within the first three years of normal operation, we will replace it with an identical or comparably equipped model, free of charge. In other words, it works or it walks. An award-winning copier combined with an iron-clad guarantee? The only risk involved is passing this opportunity up.

For more information, call 1-800-9-MINOLTA.

NO-RISK COPIERS
ONLY FROM THE MIND OF MINOLTA

MINOLTA

Figure 8.6 FIVE TYPES
OF PERCEIVED RISK

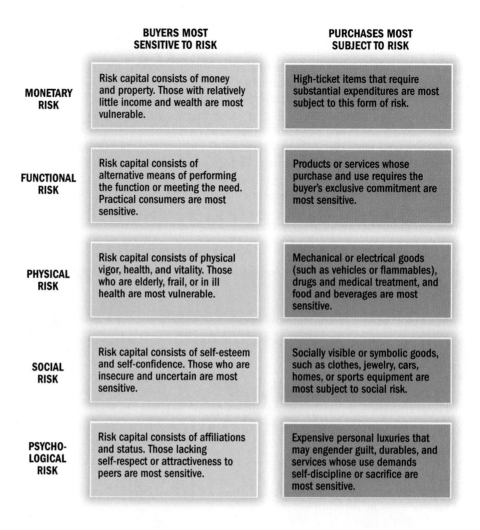

	BUYERS MOST SENSITIVE TO RISK	PURCHASES MOST SUBJECT TO RISK
MONETARY RISK	Risk capital consists of money and property. Those with relatively little income and wealth are most vulnerable.	High-ticket items that require substantial expenditures are most subject to this form of risk.
FUNCTIONAL RISK	Risk capital consists of alternative means of performing the function or meeting the need. Practical consumers are most sensitive.	Products or services whose purchase and use requires the buyer's exclusive commitment are most sensitive.
PHYSICAL RISK	Risk capital consists of physical vigor, health, and vitality. Those who are elderly, frail, or in ill health are most vulnerable.	Mechanical or electrical goods (such as vehicles or flammables), drugs and medical treatment, and food and beverages are most sensitive.
SOCIAL RISK	Risk capital consists of self-esteem and self-confidence. Those who are insecure and uncertain are most sensitive.	Socially visible or symbolic goods, such as clothes, jewelry, cars, homes, or sports equipment are most subject to social risk.
PSYCHO-LOGICAL RISK	Risk capital consists of affiliations and status. Those lacking self-respect or attractiveness to peers are most sensitive.	Expensive personal luxuries that may engender guilt, durables, and services whose use demands self-discipline or sacrifice are most sensitive.

How Do We Decide Among Alternatives?

Much of the effort we put into a purchase decision occurs at the stage where we have to put the pedal to the metal and actually choose a product from several alternatives. This may not be easy—modern consumer society abounds with choices. In some cases, there may be literally hundreds of different brands (as in cigarettes) or different variations of the same brand (as in shades of lipstick).

Ask a friend to name all the brands of perfume she can think of. The odds are she will reel off three to five names rather quickly, then stop and think awhile before she comes up with a few more. She's probably very familiar with the first set of brands, and in fact she probably wears one or more of these. Her list may also contain one or two brands that she doesn't like—to the contrary they come to mind because she thinks they smell nasty or are unsophisticated. Note also that there are many, many more brands on the market that she did not name at all.

If your friend goes to the store to buy perfume, it is likely that she will consider buying some or most of the brands she listed initially. She might also entertain a few more possibilities if these come to her attention while she's at the fragrance counter—for example, if an employee "ambushes" her with a scent sample as she walks down the aisle.

How do we decide which criteria are important, and how do we narrow down product alternatives to an acceptable number and eventually choose one instead of others? The answer varies depending on the decision-making process we use. A person who engages in extended problem solving may carefully evaluate several brands, whereas someone who makes a habitual decision may not consider any

This British ad appeals to social risk.
Source: © Abbott Mead Vickers BBDO, London. Ad created and produced by Simon Langley, Richard Morgan, and John Offenbach.

alternatives to his normal brand. Furthermore, some evidence indicates that we do more extended processing in situations that arouse negative emotions because of conflicts we feel among the available choices. This is most likely to occur when there are difficult trade-offs; for example when a person has to choose between the risks involved in having a bypass operation versus the potential improvement in his life if the operation succeeds.[40]

We call the alternatives a consumer knows about his **evoked set** and the ones that he actually considers his **consideration set** (often we don't seriously consider every single brand we know about because it's out of our price range or we've had a bad experience with it).[41] Recall that Richard did not know much about the technical aspects of television sets, and he had only a few major brands in memory. Of these, two were acceptable possibilities and one was not.

Consumers often consider a surprisingly small number of alternatives—especially with all the choices available to us. A cross-national study found that people generally include just a few products in their consideration, although this amount varies by product category and across countries. For example, on average American beer consumers considered only three brands whereas Canadian consumers typically considered seven brands. In contrast, while auto buyers in Norway studied two alternatives, American consumers on average looked at more than eight models before they decided.[42] We seem to be a lot more picky about our wheels than our brews.

This ad for Sunkist lemon juice attempts to establish a new category for the product by repositioning it as a salt substitute.
Source: Courtesy of Sunkist Growers.

For obvious reasons, a marketer who finds that his brand is not in his target market's evoked set has cause to worry. You often don't get a second chance to make a good first impression; a consumer isn't likely to place a product in his evoked set after he already considered it and rejected it. Indeed, we're more likely to add a new brand to the evoked set than one that we previously considered but passed over, even after a marketer has provided additional positive information about it.[43] For marketers, a consumer's reluctance to give a rejected product a second chance underscores the importance of ensuring that it performs well from the time the company introduces it.

An advertising campaign for Hyundai illustrates how hard a company sometimes has to work to get its brand into consumers' consideration sets. Many people think of Hyundai strictly as a low-cost vehicle, even though it has received high marks for quality in recent years. The carmaker's "Think About It" campaign encouraged consumers to reconsider their long-held beliefs through frank statements like "The logo is there to tell you what the car is, not who you are" and "When a car company charges for roadside assistance, aren't they just helping themselves?" As Hyundai's vice president for marketing in America explained, "Unless we give people a compelling reason to shuffle the brand deck, they'll stand with the brands they know rather than make that switch."[44]

How Do We Put Products into Categories?

Remember that when consumers process product information, they don't do it in a vacuum. They evaluate its attributes in terms of what they already know about the item or other similar products. A person who thinks about a particular 35mm camera will most likely compare it to other 35mm cameras rather than to a disposable camera. Because the *category* in which a consumer places a product determines the other products she will compare it to, the way we classify a brand in our minds plays a big role in how we evaluate it.

The products in a consumer's evoked set are likely to share some similar features. This process can either help or hurt a product, depending on what people compare it to. For example, in one survey about 25 percent of consumers said they would be less likely to buy a product made of hemp if they know it's derived from the same plant from which marijuana comes (but without any of the latter's effects). When we come across a new product, we tend to place it into an existing category rather than create a new category.[46] Of course, that's one of the big hurdles a new form of technology has to clear—before a person will buy a microwave oven, MP3 player, or GPS, they need to make sense out of the category to which it belongs.

It is important to understand how we cognitively represent this information in a **knowledge structure**—this term refers to a set of beliefs and the way we organize these beliefs in our minds.[47] We discussed these knowledge structures in Chapter 4. Their makeup matters to marketers because they want to ensure that customers correctly group their products. For example, General Foods brought out a new line of Jell-O flavors, such as Cranberry Orange, that it called Jell-O Gelatin Flavors for Salads. Unfortunately the company discovered that people used the product only for salad because the name encouraged them to put the product in their "salad" structure rather than in their "dessert" structure. General Foods dropped the product line.[48]

Typically we represent a product in a cognitive structure at one of three levels. To understand this idea, consider how someone might respond to these questions about an ice cream cone: What other products share similar characteristics, and which would you consider as alternatives to eating a cone?

These questions may be more complex than they first appear. At one level, a cone is similar to an apple because you could eat both as a dessert. At another level, a cone is similar to a piece of pie because you could eat either for dessert and both are fattening. At still another level, a cone is similar to an ice cream sundae—you could eat either for dessert, both are made of ice cream, and both are fattening. Figure 8.7 depicts these three levels.

It's easy to see that the foods a person associates with, the category "fattening dessert," influence his or her decision about what to eat after dinner. The middle level, or *basic level category*, is typically the most useful to classify products. At this level the items we group together tend to have a lot in common with each other but still permit us to consider a broad enough range of alternatives. The broader *superordinate category* is more abstract, whereas the more specific *subordinate category* often includes individual brands.[50] Of course, not all items fit equally well into a category. Apple pie is a better example of the subordinate category "pie" than is rhubarb pie, even though both are types of pies. This is because it's more *prototypical*, and most people would think of apple as a pie flavor before they thought of rhubarb. In contrast, true pie experts probably know a lot about both typical and atypical category examples.[51]

Marketing Pitfall

Kimberly-Clark Corp., which makes well-known paper products including Kleenex and Scott tissues, learned the hard way about the perils of product categorization and consumers' resistance to products they find hard to assign to a well-known category. The company announced "the most significant category innovation since toilet paper first appeared in roll form in 1890." Even Jay Leno covered the news of the new product: Cottonelle Fresh Rollwipes, a roll of moist wipes in a plastic dispenser that clips onto a regular toilet-paper holder. To quiet skeptics who questioned whether Americans would change their bathroom habits so dramatically, Kimberly-Clark unveiled its research showing that 63 percent of adults were already in the habit of wetting toilet paper or using a wipe.

Although the company spent more than $100 million to develop the roll and dispenser and guards it with more than 30 patents, high hopes for the product have gone down the toilet. Part of the problem is that the company is dealing with a product most people don't even want to discuss in the first place, and its advertising failed to show consumers what the wipes even do. Its ad agency tried to create a fun image with TV ads showing shots of people splashing in the water from behind with the slogan, "sometimes wetter is better." A print ad with an extreme close-up of a sumo wrestler's *derriere* was a flop. To make matters worse, the company didn't design a version in small product sizes, so it couldn't pass out free samples. And, the wipes come in a container that is immediately visible in a bathroom—another strike for people already bashful about buying the product.[49]

Figure 8.7 LEVELS OF ABSTRACTION IN DESSERT CATEGORIES

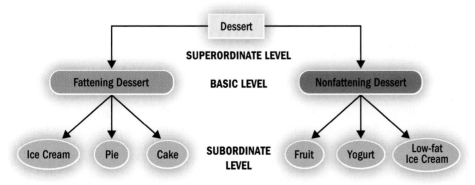

Strategic Implications of Product Categorization

The way we categorize products has a lot of strategic implications. That's because this process affects which products consumers will compare to our product and also the criteria they'll use to decide if they like us or the other guys.

Position a Product. The success of a *positioning strategy* hinges on the marketer's ability to convince the consumer to consider its product within a given category. For example, the orange juice industry tried to reposition orange juice as a drink people can enjoy all day long ("It's not just for breakfast anymore"). However, soft-drink companies attempt the opposite when they portray sodas as suitable for breakfast consumption. They are trying to make their way into consumers' "breakfast drink" category, along with orange juice, grapefruit juice, and coffee. Of course, this strategy can backfire, as Pepsi-Cola discovered when it introduced Pepsi A.M. and positioned it as a coffee substitute. The company did such a good job of categorizing the drink as a morning beverage that customers wouldn't drink it at any other time, and the product failed.[52]

Identify Competitors. At the abstract, superordinate level, many different product forms compete for membership. The category "entertainment" might comprise both bowling and the ballet, but not many people would substitute one of these activities for the other. Products and services that on the surface are quite different, however, actually compete with each other at a broad level for consumers' discretionary dollars. Although bowling or ballet may not be a likely trade-off for many people, a symphony might try to lure away season ticket holders to the ballet by positioning itself as an equivalent member of the superordinate category "cultural event."[53]

We're often faced with choices between noncomparable categories, where we can't directly relate the attributes in one to those in another (the old problem of comparing apples and oranges). When we can create an overlapping category that encompasses both items (e.g., entertainment, value, usefulness) and then rate each alternative in terms of that superordinate category comparison, the process is easier.[54]

Create an Exemplar Product. As we saw with the case of apple pie versus rhubarb pie, if a product is a really good example of a category it is more familiar to consumers and they more easily recognize and recall it.[55] The characteristics of **category exemplars** tend to exert a disproportionate influence on how people think of the category in general.[56] In a sense, brands we strongly associate with a category get to "call the shots"—they define the criteria we use to evaluate all category members.

Being a bit less than prototypical is not necessarily a bad thing, however. Products that are moderately unusual within their product category may stimulate more information processing and positive evaluations because they are neither so familiar that we will take them for granted nor so different that we won't consider them at all.[57] A brand that is strongly discrepant (such as Zima, a clear malt beverage) may occupy a unique niche position, whereas those that are somewhat different (e.g., local microbrews) remain in a distinct position within the general category.[58]

Locate Products in a Store. Product categorization also can affect consumers' expectations regarding the places they can locate a desired product. If products do not clearly fit into categories (e.g., is a rug furniture?), this may diminish our ability to find them or figure out what they're supposed to be once we do. For instance, a frozen dog food that pet owners had to thaw and cook before they served it to Fido failed in the market, partly because people could not adapt to the idea of buying dog food in the "frozen foods for people" section of their grocery stores.

Product Choice:
How Do We Select from the Alternatives?

Once we assemble and evaluate the relevant options in a category, eventually we have to choose one.[59] Recall that the decision rules that guide our choices range from very simple and quick strategies to complicated processes that require a lot of attention and cognitive processing.[60] Our job isn't getting any easier as companies overwhelm us with more and more features. We deal with 50-button remote controls, digital cameras with hundreds of mysterious features and book-length manuals, and cars with dashboard systems worthy of the space shuttle. Experts call this spiral of complexity **feature creep**. As evidence that the proliferation of gizmos is counterproductive, Philips Electronics found that at least half of the products buyers return have nothing wrong with them—consumers simply couldn't figure out how to use them! What's worse, on average the buyer spent only 20 minutes trying to figure out how to use the product and then gave up.

Why don't companies avoid this problem? One reason is that we often assume the more features the better. It's only when we get the product home that we realize the virtue of simplicity. In one study consumers chose among three models of a digital device that varied in terms of how complex each was. More than 60 percent chose the one with the most features. Then, the participants got the chance to choose from up to 25 features to customize their product—the average person chose 20 of these add-ons. But when they actually used the devices, it turns out that the large number of options only frustrated them—they ended up being much happier with the simpler product. As the saying goes, "Be careful what you wish for. . . . "[61]

Evaluative Criteria

When Richard looked at different television sets, he focused on one or two product features and completely ignored several others. He narrowed down his choices as he only considered two specific brand names, and from the Prime Wave and Precision models, he chose one that featured stereo capability.

Evaluative criteria are the dimensions we use to judge the merits of competing options. When he compared alternative products, Richard could have chosen from among many criteria that ranged from very functional attributes ("Does this TV come with remote control?") to experiential ones ("Does this TV's sound reproduction make me imagine I'm in a concert hall?").

Another important point is that criteria on which products *differ* from one another carry more weight in the decision process than do those where the alternatives are *similar*. If all brands a person considers rate equally well on one attribute (e.g., if all TVs come with remote control), Richard needs to find other reasons to choose one over another. **Determinant attributes** are the features we actually use to differentiate among our choices.

Marketers often educate consumers about which criteria they should use as determinant attributes. For example, consumer research from Church & Dwight indicated that many consumers view the use of natural ingredients as a determinant attribute. As a result, the company promoted its toothpaste made from baking soda, which the company already manufactured for Church & Dwight's Arm & Hammer brand.[62]

And sometimes, the company actually invents a determinant attribute: Pepsi-Cola accomplished this when it stamped freshness dates on soda cans. It spent about $25 million on an advertising and promotional campaign to convince consumers that there's nothing quite as horrible as a stale can of soda—even though people in the industry estimate that drinkers consume 98 percent of all cans well before this could be a problem. Six months after it introduced the campaign, lo and behold an independent survey found that 61 percent of respondents felt that freshness dating is an important attribute for a soft drink![63] In order for a marketer

This Indonesian ad shows us one of bubblegum's determinant attributes.
Source: Courtesy of draft FCB Jakarta Indonesia.

to effectively recommend a new decision criterion, it should convey three pieces of information:[64]

1. It should point out that there are significant differences among brands on the attribute.
2. It should supply the consumer with a decision-making rule, such as *if* . . . (deciding among competing brands), *then* . . . (use the attribute as a criterion).
3. It should convey a rule that is consistent with how the person made the decision on prior occasions. Otherwise, she is likely to ignore the recommendation because it requires too much mental work.

Neuromarketing: How Your Brain Reacts to Alternatives

Is there a "buy button" in your brain? Some corporations have teamed up with neuroscientists to find out.[66] **Neuromarketing** uses *functional magnetic resonance imaging* (or *fMRI*), a brain-scanning device that tracks blood flow as we perform mental tasks. In recent years, researchers discovered that regions in the brain, such as the amygdala, the hippocampus, and the hypothalamus, are dynamic switchboards that blend memory, emotions, and biochemical triggers. These interconnected neurons shape the ways that fear, panic, exhilaration, and social pressure influence our choices.

Scientists know that specific regions of the brain light up in these scans to show increased blood flow when a person recognizes a face, hears a song, makes a decision, or senses deception. Now they hope to harness this technology to measure consumers' reactions to movie trailers, automobiles, the appeal of a pretty face, and even their loyalty to specific brands. British researchers recorded brain activity as shoppers toured a virtual store. They claim they identified the neural region that becomes active when a shopper decides which product to pluck from a supermarket shelf. DaimlerChrysler took brain scans of men as they looked at photos of cars and confirmed that sports cars activated their reward centers. The company's scientists found that the most popular vehicles—the Porsche- and Ferrari-style sports cars—triggered activity in a section of the brain they call the *fusiform face area*, which governs facial recognition. A psychiatrist who ran the study commented, "They were reminded of faces when they looked at the cars. The lights of the cars look a little like eyes."

A study that took brain scans of people as they drank competing soft-drink brands illustrates how loyalty to a brand affects our reactions, even at a very basic, physiological level. When the researchers monitored brain scans of 67 people who took a blind taste test of Coca-Cola and Pepsi, each soft drink lit up the brain's reward system, and the participants were evenly split as to which drink they preferred—even though three out of four participants *said* they preferred Coke. When told they were drinking Coke, the regions of the brain that control memory lit up, and this activation drowned out the area that simply reacts to taste cues. In this case, Coke's strong brand identity trumped the sensations coming from respondents' taste receptors.

In another study, researchers reported that pictures of celebrities triggered many of the same brain circuits as did images of shoes, cars, chairs, wristwatches, sunglasses, handbags, and water bottles. All of these objects set off a rush of activity in a part of the cortex that neuroscientists know links to our sense of identity and social image. The scientists also identified types of consumers based on their responses. At one extreme were people whose brains responded intensely to "cool" products and celebrities with bursts of activity but who didn't respond at all to "uncool" images. They dubbed these participants "cool fools" who are likely to be impulsive or compulsive shoppers. At the other extreme were people whose brains reacted only to the unstylish items—this pattern fits well with people who tend to be anxious, apprehensive, or neurotic. Many researchers remain skeptical about how helpful this technology will be for consumer research. If indeed researchers can reliably track consumers' brand preferences by seeing how their brains react, there may be many interesting potential opportunities for new research techniques that rely on what we (or at least our brains) do rather than what we say.

OBJECTIVE

Why is our access to online sources changing the way we decide what to buy?

Cybermediaries

As anyone who's ever typed a phrase such as "home theaters" into Google or another search engine, the Web delivers enormous amounts of product and retailer information in seconds. In fact (recall our earlier discussion of the problem of *hyperchoice*), the biggest problem Web surfers face these days is to narrow down their choices, not to beef them up. In cyberspace, simplification is key.

With the tremendous number of Web sites available and the huge number of people surfing the Web each day, how can people organize information and decide where to click? A **cybermediary** often is the answer. This is an intermediary that helps to filter and organize online market information so that customers can identify and evaluate alternatives more efficiently.[67] Many consumers regularly link to comparison-shopping sites, such as Bizrate.com or Pricegrabbers.com, for example, that list many online retailers that sell a given item along with the price each charges.[68]

Cybermediaries take different forms:[69]

● *Directories* and *portals* such as Yahoo! or The Knot are general services that tie together a large variety of different sites.
● *Forums, fan clubs*, and *user groups* offer product-related discussions to help customers sift through options (more on these in Chapter 10). It's clear that customer product reviews are a key driver of satisfaction and loyalty. In one large survey, about half of the respondents who bought an item from a major Web site remembered seeing customer product reviews. This group's satisfaction with the online shopping experience was 5 percent higher than for shoppers who didn't recall customer reviews.[70] Another advantage is that consumers get to experience a much wider array of options—and at the same time products such as

movies, books, and CDs that aren't "blockbusters" are more likely to sell. At Netflix, the online DVD rental company, for example, fellow subscribers recommend about two-thirds of the films that people order. In fact, between 70 and 80 percent of Netflix rentals come from the company's back catalog of 38,000 films rather than recent releases.[71]

And, this aspect of online customer review is one important factor that's fueling a new way of thinking one writer calls the **long tail**.[72] The basic idea is that we need no longer rely solely on big hits (such as blockbuster movies or best-selling books) to find profits. Companies can also make money if they sell small amounts of items that only a few people want—if they sell enough different items. For example, Amazon.com maintains an inventory of 3.7 million books compared to the 100,000 or so you'll find in a Barnes & Noble retail store. Most of these will sell only a few thousand copies (if that), but the 3.6 million books that Barnes & Noble <u>doesn't</u> carry make up a quarter of Amazon's revenues! Other examples of the long tail include successful microbreweries and TV networks that make money on reruns of old shows on channels such as the Game Show Network.

Intelligent agents are sophisticated software programs that use *collaborative filtering* technologies to learn from past user behavior in order to recommend new purchases.[73] When you let Amazon.com suggest a new book, the site uses an intelligent agent to propose novels based on what you and others like you have bought in the past. Collaborative filtering is still in its infancy. In the next few years, expect to see many new Web-based methods to simplify the consumer decision-making process. Now if only someone could come up with an easier way to pay for all the great stuff you find courtesy of shopping bots!

Researchers work hard to understand how consumers find information online, and in particular how they react to and integrate recommendations they receive from different kinds of online agents into their own product choices. An **electronic recommendation agent** is a software tool that tries to understand a human decision maker's multiattribute preferences for a product category as it asks the user to communicate his preferences. Based on that data, the software then recommends a list of alternatives sorted by the degree that they fit these criteria. These agents do appear to influence consumers' decision making though some evidence indicates they're more effective when they recommend a product based on utilitarian attributes (functionality like nutritional value) than hedonic attributes (like design or taste).[74]

Although engineers continually improve the ability of electronic recommendations agents to suggest new things we might like, we still rely on other people to guide our search. About 80 percent of online shoppers rely on customer reviews before they buy. We call the people who supply these reviews **brand advocates**. Yahoo! estimates that 40 percent of people who spend time online are advocates and that they influence purchases two to one over nonadvocates. Marketers who adjust their strategies to acknowledge this impact find it's worth their while. For example, PETCO saw a 500 percent increase in its click-through rate when it included consumers' reviews in its online ads.[75]

The huge growth in demand for user reviews in turn fuels new opinion-based sites including Yelp for local businesses, TripAdvisor for travel, and Urbanspoon for restaurants. Yelp for example offers over 4 million reviews of everything from corner cafés to dog groomers. People who take the time to post to these sites don't do it for money, but they do generate an income in the form of props for good recommendations. Analysts refer to this reward system as the **reputation economy**—many thousands of consumers devote significant time to editing Wikipedia entries, serving as brand advocates, or uploading clips to YouTube simply because they enjoy the process and want to boost their reputation as knowledgeable advisors.[76]

Heuristics: Mental Shortcuts

Do we actually perform complex mental calculations every time we make a purchase decision? Get a life! When we don't rely on a Web site to steer us to the right place, we often use other decision rules to simplify our choices. For example, Richard made certain assumptions instead of engaging in prolonged information search. In particular, he assumed the selection at Zany Zack's was more than sufficient, so he did not bother to shop at any of Zack's competitors.[78]

Especially when limited problem solving occurs prior to making a choice, we often fall back on **heuristics**, or mental rules-of-thumb to make a speedy decision. These rules range from the very general ("higher-priced products are higher-quality products" or "buy the same brand I bought last time") to the very specific ("buy Domino, the brand of sugar my mother always bought").[79] Sometimes these shortcuts may not be in our best interests. A car shopper who personally knows one or

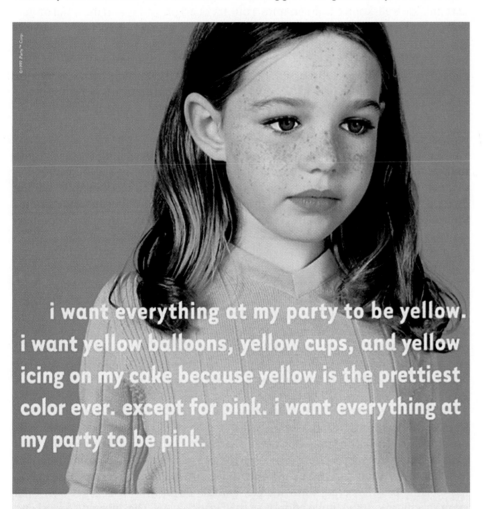

Consumers often simplify choices when they use heuristics such as automatically choosing a favorite color or brand.
Source: Courtesy of iParty Retail Store Corp.

Marketing Pitfall

Companies fall all over one another in their quest to be "green." Unfortunately, many consumers who want to buy earth-friendly products aren't sure how to tell if an item really is as green as it says. They would like to rely on a convenient heuristic like the environmental equivalent of a *Good Housekeeping* Seal of Approval. Unfortunately, so many organizations offer their own version of this seal it's hard to know which are legitimate. The Web site ecolabelling.org reports that more than 300 of these labels currently certify items from seafood to coffee. While some of these programs such as Green Seal and EcoLogo obtain independent verification of product manufacturers' green claims, many others don't expend the time and money to do that. A few major retailers try to reduce confusion as they perform their own ratings—these include Home Depot's "Eco Options" designation for items such as energy-efficient lightbulbs and Office Depot's "Green Book" catalog it distributes to business buyers. Still, the potential for confusion and misleading claims is huge—one study of almost 4,000 consumer products found evidence of rampant **greenwashing**, where manufacturers make untrue or misleading green claims.[84]

two people who have had problems with a particular vehicle, for example, might assume he would have similar trouble with it rather than taking the time to find out it has an excellent repair record.[80]

How Do We Rely on Product Signals?

One shortcut we often use is to *infer* hidden dimensions of products from attributes we observe. In these cases the visible element is a **product signal** that communicates some underlying quality. This explains why someone who tries to sell a used car makes sure the car's exterior is clean and shiny: Potential buyers often judge the vehicle's mechanical condition by its appearance, even though this means they may drive away in a clean, shiny clunker.[81]

When we only have incomplete product information, we often base our judgments on our beliefs about *covariation*—the associations we have among events that may or may not actually influence one another.[82] For example, a shopper may judge product quality by the length of time a manufacturer has been in business. Other signals or attributes consumers tend to believe coexist with good or bad products include well-known brand names, country of origin, price, and the retail outlets that carry the product.

Unfortunately, many of us estimate covariation quite poorly. And, our erroneous beliefs persist despite evidence to the contrary. In a process similar to the consistency principle we discussed in Chapter 7, we tend to see what we're looking for. In other words, we'll look for product information that confirms our guesses and ignore or explain away information that contradicts what we already think.[83]

Market Beliefs: Is It Better if I Pay More for It?

We constantly form assumptions about companies, products, and stores. These **market beliefs** then become shortcuts that guide our decisions—as our discussion of green-washing indicates, these beliefs are not necessarily accurate.[85] Recall that Richard chose to shop at a large "electronics warehouse store" because he *assumed* the selection would be better there than at a specialty store. Table 8.3 lists some market beliefs researchers have identified—how many do you share?

Do higher prices mean higher quality? The link we assume between price and quality is one of the most pervasive market beliefs.[86] Novice consumers, in fact, may consider price as the only relevant product attribute. Experts also consider this information although they tend to use price for its informational value when they evaluate products (e.g., virgin wool) that they know vary widely in quality. When this quality level is more standard or strictly regulated (e.g., Harris Tweed sport coats), experts do not weigh price in their decisions. For the most part, this belief is justified—you do tend to get what you pay for. However, let the buyer beware: The price–quality relationship is not always justified.[87]

Country of Origin as a Product Signal

Does a shrimp have a personality? As cheap foreign imports flood the market, U.S. shrimpers hope they do. They know that consumers prefer coffee from exotic places such as Kenya and salmon from Alaska, so they hope to persuade consumers to prefer American shrimp. At the Lark restaurant in Seattle, diners can read on the menu whether the prawns come from Georgia, Florida, or Alaska. Other places get even more specific about the home address of their crustaceans. The Silverado Resort and Spa in Napa, California, serves "local West Texas white shrimp."[88]

A product's "address" matters. We Americans like to buy Italian shoes, Japanese cars, clothing imported from Taiwan, and microwave ovens built in South Korea. **Country of origin** often is a determinant attribute in the decision-making process. Consumers strongly associate certain items with specific countries, and products from those countries often attempt to benefit from these linkages. The consumer's own expertise with the product category moderates the effects of this attribute. When other information is available, experts tend to ignore country-of-origin infor-

TABLE 8.3	Common Market Beliefs
Brand	All brands are basically the same.
	Generic products are just name brands sold under a different label at a lower price.
	The best brands are the ones that are purchased the most.
	When in doubt, a national brand is always a safe bet.
Store	Specialty stores are great places to familiarize yourself with the best brands; but once you figure out what you want, it's cheaper to buy it at a discount outlet.
	A store's character is reflected in its window displays.
	Salespeople in specialty stores are more knowledgeable than other sales personnel.
	Larger stores offer better prices than small stores.
	Locally owned stores give the best service.
	A store that offers a good value on one of its products probably offers good values on all of its items.
	Credit and return policies are most lenient at large department stores.
	Stores that have just opened usually charge attractive prices.
Prices/Discounts/Sales	Sales are typically run to get rid of slow-moving merchandise.
	Stores that are constantly having sales don't really save you money.
	Within a given store, higher prices generally indicate higher quality.
Advertising and Sales Promotion	"Hard-sell" advertising is associated with low-quality products.
	Items tied to "giveaways" are not a good value (even with the freebie).
	Coupons represent real savings for customers because they are not offered by the store.
	When you buy heavily advertised products, you are paying for the label, not for higher quality.
Product/Packaging	Largest-sized containers are almost always cheaper per unit than smaller sizes.
	New products are more expensive when they're first introduced; prices tend to settle down as time goes by.
	When you are not sure what you need in a product, it's a good idea to invest in the extra features, because you'll probably wish you had them later.
	In general, synthetic goods are lower in quality than goods made of naturals materials.
	It's advisable to stay away from products when they are new to the market; it usually takes the manufacturer a little time to work the bugs out.

Source: Adapted from Calvin P. Duncan, "Consumer Market Beliefs: A Review of the Literature and an Agenda for Future Research," in Marvin E. Goldberg. Gerald Gorn, and Richard W. Pollay eds., *Advances in Consumer Research* 17 (Provo, UT: Association for Consumer Research, 1990):729–35.

mation, whereas novices continue to rely on it. However, when other information is unavailable or ambiguous, both experts and novices will rely on a product's birthplace to make a decision.

Swadeshi describes an Indian nationalist movement that started in the Nineteenth century in reaction to the British decision to divide the country into separate provinces. Adherents boycott multinational brands like Coca-Cola and express their ideology as they buy products made in India. Men buy Godrej or Emani shaving creams instead of Old Spice or Gillette; women make a point of shampooing with Lakme, Nirma, or Velvet instead of Western brands that sell in India such as Halo, All Clear, Sunsilk, Head & Shoulders, or Pantene.[89] **Ethnocentrism** is the tendency to prefer products or people of one's own culture to those of other countries. Ethnocentric consumers are likely to feel it is wrong to buy products made elsewhere, particularly because this may have a negative effect on the domestic economy.

Marketing campaigns that stress the desirability of "buying American" obviously appeal to ethnocentric consumers. The Consumer Ethnocentric Scale (CETSCALE) measures this trait: Ethnocentric consumers agree with statements such as the following:[90]

- Purchasing foreign-made products is un-American.
- Curbs should be put on all imports.
- American consumers who purchase products made in other countries are responsible for putting their fellow Americans out of work.[91]

A Dutch shoe ad reminds us that a product's address matters.

Source: Coutesy of Grey/Copenhagen.

Made from fine
Italian canvas

www.kappa.dk

Do We Choose Familiar Brand Names Because of Loyalty or Habit?

When you fall in love with a brand, it may be your favorite for a lifetime. In a study the Boston Consulting Group conducted of the market leaders in 30 product categories, 27 of the brands that were number one in 1930 (such as Ivory Soap and Campbell's Soup) still were at the top more than 50 years later.[93] Clearly "choose a well-known brand name" is a powerful heuristic. As this study demonstrates, some brands in a sense are well-known *because* they are well-known—we assume that if so many people choose a product it must be good.

Indeed, our tendency to prefer a number one brand to the competition is so strong that it seems to mimic a pattern scientists find in other domains from earthquakes to linguistics. **Zipf's Law** describes this pattern. In the 1930s, a linguist named George Kingsley Zipf found that *the*—the most-used English word—occurs about twice as often as *of* (second place), about three times as often as *and* (third), and so on. Since then, scientists have found similar relationships between the size and frequency of earthquakes and a variety of other natural and artificial phenomena.

A marketing researcher decided to apply Zipf's Law to consumer behavior. His firm asked Australian consumers to identify the brands of toilet paper and instant coffee they use and to rank them in order of preference. As the model predicted,

Marketers like this Danish restaurant often rely on consumers' expectations based on country-of-origin cues.
Source: Courtesy of Reef 'N Beef/Saatchi

people spend roughly twice as much of their toilet paper budget on the top choice than on the second-ranked brand, about twice on the number two brand as on the third-ranked brand, and about twice on the number three brand as on the number four brand. One ramification is that a brand that moves from number two to number one in a category will see a much greater jump in sales than will, say, a brand that moves from number four to number three. Brands that dominate their markets are as much as 50 percent more profitable than their nearest competitors.[94]

Inertia: The Lazy Customer

Many people tend to buy the same brand just about every time they go to the store. Often this is because of **inertia**—we buy a brand out of habit merely because it requires less effort (see Chapter 4). If another product comes along that is cheaper (or if the original product is out of stock), we won't hesitate to change our minds. A competitor who tries to encourage this switch often can do so rather easily because the shopper won't hesitate to jump to the new brand if it offers the right incentive.

When we have little to no underlying commitment to a particular brand, marketers find it easy to "unfreeze" our habit with the help of promotional tools such as point-of-purchase displays, extensive couponing, or noticeable price reductions. Some analysts predict that we're going to observe this kind of fickle behavior more and more as consumers flit from one brand to the next. Indeed, one industry observer labels this variety-seeking consumer a *brand slut*; she points out that from

2004 to 2007 the number of women who say a manufacturer's brand name is very influential in their decision to buy a beauty product decreased by 21 percentage points to stand at 19 percent.[95]

Brand Loyalty: A "Friend," Tried-and-True

This kind of "promiscuity" will not occur if true brand loyalty exists. In contrast to inertia, **brand loyalty** describes repeat purchasing behavior that reflects a conscious decision to continue buying the same brand.[96] This definition implies that the consumer not only buys the brand on a regular basis but she also has a strong positive attitude toward it rather than that she simply buys it out of habit. In fact we often find that a brand-loyal consumer has more than simply a positive attitude—she is passionate about the product. Because of these emotional bonds, "true-blue" users react more vehemently when a company alters, redesigns, or (God forbid) eliminates a favorite brand.[97]

OBJECTIVE

Why do consumers rely on different decision rules when they evaluate competing options?

Decision Rules We Use When We Care

We've seen that we use different rules when we choose among competing products that depend on the decision's complexity and how important the choice is to us. Sometimes we use a simple heuristic, but at other times we carefully weigh alternatives. We describe the processes we use when we give more thought to these decisions as we divide the rules we

To reinforce brand loyalty, MiniUSA delivered custom messages to Mini Cooper owners on digital signs the company calls "talking" billboards. The boards are programmed to identify approaching Mini drivers through a coded signal from a radio chip embedded in their key fob. The messages are personal, based on questionnaires that owners filled out. For example, if a lawyer completed the survey the message might say, "Mary, moving at the speed of justice."
Source: Photo Courtesy of Newscast and MINI, a Divison of **BMW of North America, LLC.**

TABLE 8.4	Hypothetical Alternatives for a TV Set			
		Brand Ratings		
Attribute	**Importance Ranking**	**Prime Wave**	**Precision**	**Kamashita**
Size of screen	1	Excellent	Excellent	Excellent
Stereo broadcast capability	2	Poor	Excellent	Good
Brand reputation	3	Excellent	Excellent	Poor
Onscreen programming	4	Excellent	Poor	Poor
Cable-ready capability	5	Good	Good	Good
Sleep timer	6	Excellent	Poor	Good

use into two categories: *compensatory* and *noncompensatory*. To aid in the discussion of some of these rules, Table 8.4 summarizes the attributes of the TV sets that Richard considered. Now, let's see how some of these rules result in different brand choices.

We use **noncompensatory decision rules** when we feel that a product with a low standing on one attribute can't compensate for this flaw even if it performs better on another attribute. In other words, we simply eliminate all options that do not meet some basic standards. A consumer like Richard who uses the decision rule, "Only buy well-known brand names," would not consider a new brand, even if it were equal or superior to existing ones. When people are less familiar with a product category or are not very motivated to process complex information, they tend to use simple, noncompensatory rules such as the ones we summarize next.[98]

The Lexicographic Rule. When a person uses the *lexicographic rule*, he selects the brand that is the best on the most important attribute. If he feels two or more brands are equally good on that attribute, he then compares them on the second most important attribute. This selection process goes on until the tie is broken. In Richard's case, because both the Prime Wave and Precision models were tied on his most important attribute (a 60-inch screen), he chose the Precision because of its rating on this second most important attribute—its stereo capability.

The Elimination-by-Aspects Rule. Using the *elimination-by-aspects rule*, the buyer also evaluates brands on the most important attribute. In this case, though, he imposes specific cutoffs. For example, if Richard had been more interested in having a sleep timer on his TV (i.e., if it had a higher importance ranking), he might have stipulated that his choice "must have a sleep timer." Because the Prime Wave model had one and the Precision did not, he would have chosen the Prime Wave.

The Conjunctive Rule. Whereas the two former rules involve processing by attribute, the *conjunctive rule* entails processing by brand. As with the elimination-by-aspects procedure, the decision maker establishes cutoffs for each attribute. He chooses a brand if it meets all the cutoffs, but failure to meet any one cutoff means he will reject it. If none of the brands meet all the cutoffs, he may delay the choice, change the decision rule, or modify the cutoffs he chooses to apply.

If Richard stipulated that all attributes had to be rated "good" or better, he would not have been able to choose any of the options. He might then have modified his decision rule, conceding that it was not possible to attain these high standards in his price range. In this case, perhaps Richard could decide that he could live without on-screen programming, so he would reconsider the Precision model.

Compensatory Decision Rules

Unlike noncompensatory rules, **compensatory decision rules** give a product a chance to make up for its shortcomings. Consumers who employ these rules tend to be more involved in the purchase, so they're willing to exert the effort to consider the entire picture in a more exacting way.[99]

If we're willing to allow good and bad product qualities to cancel each other out, we arrive at a very different choice. For example, if Richard were not concerned about having stereo reception, he might have chosen the PrimeWave model. But because this brand doesn't feature this highly ranked attribute, it doesn't stand a chance when he uses a noncompensatory rule.

Researchers identify two basic types of compensatory rules. A person uses a *simple additive rule* if he merely chooses the alternative that has the largest number of positive attributes. This is most likely to occur when his ability or motivation to process information is limited. One drawback to this approach for the consumer is that some of these attributes may not be very meaningful or important. An ad that presents a long list of product benefits may be persuasive, despite the fact that many of the benefits it names are actually standard within the product class.

The *weighted additive rule* is a more complex version.[100] When he uses this rule, the consumer also takes into account the relative importance of positively rated attributes, essentially multiplying brand ratings by importance weights. If this process sounds familiar, it should. The calculation process strongly resembles the multiattribute attitude model we described in Chapter 7.

CHAPTER SUMMARY

Now that you have finished reading this chapter you should understand why:

Consumer decision making is a central part of consumer behavior, but the way we evaluate and choose products (and the amount of thought they put into these choices) varies widely, depending on such dimensions as the degree of novelty or risk related to the decision.

We almost constantly need to make decisions about products. Some of these decisions are very important and entail great effort, whereas we make others on a virtually automatic basis. The decision-making task is further complicated because of the sheer number of decisions we need to make in a marketplace environment characterized by consumer hyperchoice.

Perspectives on decision making range from a focus on habits that people develop over time to novel situations involving a great deal of risk in which consumers must carefully collect and analyze information prior to making a choice. Many of our decisions are highly automated and we make them largely by habit. This trend is

accelerating as marketers begin to introduce smart products that enable silent commerce, where the products literally make their own purchase decisions (e.g., a malfunctioning appliance that contacts the repairperson directly).

A decision is actually composed of a series of stages that results in the selection of one product over competing options.

A typical decision process involves several steps. The first is problem recognition, where we realize we must take some action. This recognition may occur because a current possession malfunctions or perhaps because we have a desire for something new.

Once the consumer recognizes a problem and sees it as sufficiently important to warrant some action, he begins the process of information search. This search may range from scanning simple scan of his memory to determine what he's done before to resolve the same problem to extensive fieldwork where he consults a variety of sources to amass as much information as possible. In many cases, people engage in surprisingly little search. Instead, they rely on various mental shortcuts, such as brand names or price, or they may simply imitate others' choices.

In the evaluation of alternatives stage, the product alternatives a person considers comprise his evoked set. Members of the evoked set usually share some characteristics; we categorize them similarly. The way the person mentally groups products influences which alternatives she will consider, and usually we associate some brands more strongly with these categories (i.e., they are more prototypical).

 Decision making is not always rational.

Research in the field of behavioral economics illustrates that decision making is not always strictly rational. Principles of mental accounting demonstrate that the way a problem is posed (called framing) and whether it is put in terms of gains or losses influences what we decide.

 Our access to online sources is changing the way we decide what to buy.

The World Wide Web has changed the way many of us search for information. Today, our problem is more likely to weed out excess detail than to search for more information. Comparative search sites and intelligent agents help to filter and guide the search process. We may rely on cybermediaries, such as Web portals, to sort through massive amounts of information as a way to simplify the decision-making process.

 We often fall back on well-learned "rules-of-thumb" to make decisions.

Very often, we use heuristics, or mental rules-of-thumb, to simplify decision making. In particular, we develop many market beliefs over time. One of the most common beliefs is that we can determine quality by looking at the price. Other heuristics rely on well-known brand names or a product's country of origin as signals of product quality. When we consistently purchase a brand over time, this pattern may be the result of true brand loyalty or simply to inertia because it's the easiest thing to do.

 Consumers rely on different decision rules when evaluating competing options.

When the consumer eventually must make a product choice from among alternatives, he uses one of several decision rules. Noncompensatory rules eliminate alternatives that are deficient on any of the criteria we've chosen. Compensatory rules, which we are more likely to apply in high-involvement situations, allow us to consider each alternative's good and bad points more carefully to arrive at the overall best choice.

KEY TERMS

Behavioral influence perspective, 308
Blissful ignorance effect, 318
Brand advocates, 328
Brand loyalty, 334
Category exemplars, 324
Cognitive processing style, 308
Compensatory decision rules, 336
Consideration set, 321
Consumer hyperchoice, 306
Country of origin, 330
Cybermediary, 327
Determinant attributes, 325
Electronic recommendation agent, 328
Ethnocentrism, 331
Evaluative criteria, 325
Evoked set, 321

Experiential perspective, 308
Extended problem solving, 308
Feature creep, 325
Green-washing, 330
Habitual decision making, 309
Heuristics, 329
Hyperopia, 316
Incidental brand explosive, 317
Inertia, 333
Information search, 311
Intelligent agents, 328
Knowledge structure, 323
Limited problem solving, 309
Low-literate consumer, 311
Market beliefs, 330
Mental accounting, 315

Neuromarketing, 326
New info shopper, 312
Noncompensatory decision rules, 335
Perceived risk, 319
Problem recognition, 310
Product signal, 330
Prospect theory, 316
Purchase momentum, 308
Rational perspective, 307
Reputation economy, 328
Search engine optimization (SEO), 313
Search engines, 313
Long tail, 328
Variety seeking, 313
Zipf's Law 332

REVIEW

1 Why do we say that "mindless" decision making can actually be more efficient than when we devote a lot of thought to what we buy?

2 List the steps in the model of rational decision making.

3 What is purchase momentum, and how does it relate (or not) to the model of rational decision making?

4 What is the difference between the behavioral influence and experiential perspectives on decision making? Give an example of the type of purchase that each perspective would most likely explain.

5 Name two ways a consumer problem arises.

6 Give an example of the sunk-cost fallacy.

7 What is prospect theory? Does it support the argument that we are rational decision makers?

8 Describe the relationship between a consumer's level of expertise and how much he is likely to search for information about a product.

9 List three types of perceived risk, and give an example of each.

10 "Marketers need to be extra sure their product works as promised when they first introduce it." How does this statement relate to what we know about consumers' evoked sets?

11 Describe the difference between a superordinate category, a basic level category, and a subordinate category.

12 What is an example of an exemplar product?

13 List three product attributes that consumers use as product quality signals and provide an example of each.

14 How does a brand name work as a heuristic?

15 Describe the difference between inertia and brand loyalty.

16 What is the difference between a noncompensatory and a compensatory decision rule? Give one example of each.

CONSUMER BEHAVIOR CHALLENGE

■ DISCUSS

1 This chapter argues that for many of today's consumers it's a bigger problem to have too many choices than to not have enough choices. Do you agree? Is it possible to have too much of a good thing?

2 How big a problem is greenwashing? What is the potential impact of this practice on consumer decision making?

3 Commercial Alert, a consumer group, is highly critical of neuromarketing. The group's executive director wrote, "What would happen in this country if corporate marketers and political consultants could literally peer inside our brains and chart the neural activity that leads to our selections in the supermarket and voting booth? What if they then could trigger this neural activity by various means, so as to modify our behavior to serve their own ends?"[101] What do you think? Is neuromarketing dangerous?

4 If people are not always rational decision makers, is it worth the effort to study how they make purchasing decisions? What techniques might marketers employ to understand experiential consumption and to translate this knowledge into marketing strategy?

5 Why is it difficult to place a product in a consumer's evoked set after the person has already rejected it? What strategies might a marketer use to accomplish this goal?

6 Discuss two different noncompensatory decision rules and highlight the difference(s) between them. How might the use of one rule versus another result in a different product choice?

7 Technology has the potential to make our lives easier as it reduces the amount of clutter we need to work through in order to access the information on the Internet that really interests us. However, perhaps intelligent agents that make recommendations based only on what we and others like us have chosen in the past limit us—they reduce the chance that we will stumble on something (e.g., a book on a topic we've never heard of or a music group that's different from the style we usually listen to). Will the proliferation of "shopping bots" make our lives too predictable by only giving us more of the same? If so, is this a problem?

8 It's increasingly clear that many postings on blogs and product reviews on Web sites are fake or are posted there to manipulate consumers' opinions. How big a problem is this if consumers increasingly look to consumer-generated product reviews to guide their purchase decisions? What steps if any can marketers take to nip this problem in the bud?

■ APPLY

1 Find examples of electronic recommendation agents on the Web. Evaluate these—are they helpful? What characteristics of the sites you locate are likely to make you buy products you wouldn't have bought on your own?

2 In the last few years several products made in China including toothpaste and toys have been recalled because they are dangerous to use or even fatal. In one survey, about 30 percent of American respondents indicated that they have stopped purchasing some Chinese goods as a result of the recalls or that they usually don't buy products from China.[102] If the Chinese government hired you as a consultant to help it repair some of the damage to the reputation of products made there, what actions would you recommend?

3 Conduct a poll based on the list of market beliefs you'll find in Table 8.3. Do people agree with these beliefs, and how much do they influence their decisions?

4 Pepsi invented freshness dating and managed to persuade consumers that this was an important product attribute. Devise a similar strategy for another product category by coming up with a brand new product attribute. How would you communicate this attribute to your customers?

5 Define the three levels of product categorization the chapter describes. Diagram these levels for a health club.

6 Choose a friend or parent who grocery shops on a regular basis and keep a log of his or her purchases of common consumer products during the term. Can you detect any evidence of brand loyalty in any categories based on consistency of purchases? If so, talk to the person about these purchases. Try to determine if his or her choices are based on true brand loyalty or on inertia. What techniques might you use to differentiate between the two?

7 Form a group of three. Pick a product and develop a marketing plan based on each of the three approaches to consumer decision making: rational, experiential, and behavioral influence. What are the major differences in emphasis among the three perspectives? Which is the most likely type of problem-solving activity for the product you have selected? What characteristics of the product make this so?

8 Locate a person who is about to make a major purchase. Ask that person to make a chronological list of all the information sources they consult prior to deciding what to buy. How would you characterize the types of sources he or she uses (i.e., internal versus external, media versus personal, etc.)? Which sources appeared to have the most impact on the person's decision?

9 Perform a survey of country-of-origin stereotypes. Compile a list of five countries and ask people what products they associate with each. What are their evaluations of the products and likely attributes of these different products? The power of a country stereotype can also be demonstrated in another way. Prepare a brief description of a product, including a list of features, and ask people to rate it in terms of quality, likelihood of purchase, and so on. Make several versions of the description, varying only the country from which it comes. Do ratings change as a function of the country of origin?

10 Ask a friend to "talk through" the process he or she used to choose one brand rather than others during a recent purchase. Based on this description, can you identify the decision rule that he most likely employed?

11 Give one of the scenarios described in the section on biases in decision making to 10 to 20 people. How do the results you obtain compare with those the chapter reported?

12 Think of a product you recently shopped for online. Describe your search process. How did you become aware that you wanted or needed the product? How did you evaluate alternatives? Did you wind up buying online? Why or why not? What factors would make it more or less likely that you would buy something online versus in a traditional store?

Case Study

DOMINO'S DILEMMA

Social media sites are so much part of mainstream culture that the Internet Advertising Bureau (IAB) recently reported they have exceeded the reach of television. *Social media marketing* describes the use of social media to engage with customers to meet marketing goals. It's about reaching customers via online dialogue. According to Lloyd Salmons, chairman of the IAB, it's really about brands having conversations.

But sometimes social media backfires for companies. Domino's, the national pizza delivery company, found itself in a crisis in April 2009. Two employees of a North Carolina Domino's store posted a YouTube video of themselves in the kitchen as they performed disgusting practices with pizza ingredients:

In about five minutes it'll be sent out on delivery where somebody will be eating these, yes, eating them, and little did they know that cheese was in his

nose and that there was some lethal gas that ended up on their salami . . . that's how we roll at Domino's.

What steps should a company take when it faces a social media marketing disaster like this? Should Domino's just ignore the videos and assume that the buzz will die down, or should it take quick action? Domino's did nothing for the first 48 hours but eventually—after more than one million people viewed the spot—got the video removed from YouTube. Domino's also posted a YouTube clip of its CEO who stated:

We sincerely apologize for this incident. We thank members of the online community who quickly alerted us and allowed us to take immediate action. Although the individuals in question claim it's a hoax, we are taking this incredibly seriously.

Domino's also announced the store where the videos were taken was shut down and sanitized. In addition, the company opened a Twitter account to deal with consumer questions. The two employees involved were charged with the felony of delivering prohibited foods and Domino's is preparing a civil lawsuit against them.

Was this a strong enough response by Domino's? Most social media marketing experts grade Domino's actions as excellent but a bit delayed. In fact, an *Advertising Age* survey revealed that 64 percent of readers believed that the company did the best it could to deal with the crisis. Still, there's no doubt this incident was a pie in the eye for the company.

DISCUSSION QUESTIONS

1 Is the decision about what to eat for dinner and more specifically what type of pizza to order an example of extended, limited, or habitual problem solving?

2 Describe how the video would influence a consumer during the information search stage of this purchase decision.

3 How might this incident affect brand loyalty for Domino's in the short-term? In the long-term?

4 Would you have done anything differently if your employees posted a disparaging or obscene video?

Sources: Stephanie Clifford, "Video Prank at Domino's Taints Brand," *New York Times* (April 15, 2009), www.nytimes.com, accessed May 23, 2009; Ben Levisohm and Ellen Gibson, "An Unwelcomed Delivery," *BusinessWeek* (May 4, 2009):15; Emily Bryson York, "What Domino's Did Right—and Wrong—in Squelching Hubbub over YouTube Video," *Advertising Age* (April 20, 2009), http://adage.com/article?article_id= 136086, accessed June 8, 2009.

NOTES

1. David Glen Mick, Susan M. Broniarczyk, and Jonathan Haidt, "Choose, Choose, Choose, Choose, Choose, Choose, Choose: Emerging and Prospective Research on the Deleterious Effects of Living in Consumer Hyperchoice," *Journal of Business Ethics* 52 (2004): 207–11; see also Barry Schwartz, *The Paradox of Choice: Why More Is Less* (New York: Ecco, 2005).
2. Itamar Simonson, Joel Huber, and John Payne, "The Relationship Between Prior Brand Knowledge and Information Acquisition Order," *Journal of Consumer Research* 14 (March 1988): 566–78.
3. John R. Hauser, Glenn L. Urban, and Bruce D. Weinberg, "How Consumers Allocate Their Time When Searching for Information," *Journal of Marketing Research* 30 (November 1993): 452–66; George J. Stigler, "The Economics of Information," *Journal of Political Economy* 69 (June 1961): 213–25. For a set of studies focusing on online search costs, see John G. Lynch, Jr., and Dan Ariely, "Wine Online: Search Costs and Competition on Price, Quality, and Distribution," *Marketing Science* 19, no. 1 (2000): 83–103.
4. John C. Mowen, "Beyond Consumer Decision-Making," *Journal of Consumer Marketing* 5, no. 1 (1988): 15–25.
5. Richard W. Olshavsky and Donald H. Granbois, "Consumer Decision-Making—Fact or Fiction," *Journal of Consumer Research* 6 (September 1989): 93–100.
6. Ravi Dhar, Joel Huber, and Uzma Khan, "The Shopping Momentum Effect," paper presented at the Association for Consumer Research, Atlanta, Georgia, October 2002.
7. Thomas P. Novak and Donna L. Hoffman, "The Fit of Thinking Style and Situation: New Measures of Situation-Specific Experiential and Rational Cognition," *Journal of Consumer Research* 36 (December 2009): 56–72.
8. James R. Bettman, "The Decision Maker Who Came in from the Cold" (presidential address), in Leigh McAllister and Michael Rothschild, eds., *Advances in Consumer Research* 20 (Provo, UT: Association for Consumer Research, 1993): 7–11; John W. Payne, James R. Bettman, and Eric J. Johnson, "Behavioral Decision Research: A Constructive Processing Perspective," *Annual Review of Psychology* 4 (1992): 87–131. For an overview of recent developments in individual choice models, see Robert J. Meyers and Barbara E. Kahn, "Probabilistic Models of Consumer Choice Behavior," in Thomas S. Robertson and Harold H. Kassarjian, eds., *Handbook of Consumer Behavior* (Upper Saddle River, NJ: Prentice Hall, 1991): 85–123.
9. Mowen, "Beyond Consumer Decision-Making."
10. The Fits-Like-a-Glove (FLAG) framework is a decision-making perspective that views consumer decisions as a holistic process shaped by the person's unique context; cf. Douglas E. Allen, "Toward a Theory of Consumer Choice as Sociohistorically Shaped Practical Exper-

ience: The Fits-Like-a-Glove (FLAG) Framework," *Journal of Consumer Research* 28 (March 2002): 515–32.
11. Joseph W. Alba and J. Wesley Hutchinson, "Dimensions of Consumer Expertise," *Journal of Consumer Research* 13 (March 1988): 411–54.
12. Examples provided by Dr. William Cohen, personal communication, October 1999.
13. Jean Halliday, "With Fusion Campaign, Ford Targets 'Upper Funnel' Car Buyers: $60M to $80M Ad Blitz Aimed at Consumers Not Yet Ready to Buy New Vehicle," *Advertising Age* (March 2, 2009), www.advertisingage.com, accessed March 2, 2009.
14. Gordon C. Bruner, II, and Richard J. Pomazal, "Problem Recognition: The Crucial First Stage of the Consumer Decision Process," *Journal of Consumer Marketing* 5, no. 1 (1988): 53–63.
15. For a study that examined trade-offs in search behavior among different channels, cf. Judi Strebel, Tulin Erdem, and Joffre Swait, "Consumer Search in High Technology Markets: Exploring the Use of Traditional Information Channels," *Journal of Consumer Psychology* 14, nos. 1 & 2 (2004): 96–104.
16. Natalie Ross Adkins and Julie L. Ozanne, "The Low Literate Consumer," *Journal of Consumer Research* 32, no. 1 (2005): 93; Madhubalan Viswanathan, José Antonio Rosa, and James Edwin Harris "Decision-Making and Coping of Functionally Illiterate Consumers and Some Implications for Marketing Management," *Journal of Marketing* 69, no. 1 (2005): 15.
17. Peter H. Bloch, Daniel L. Sherrell, and Nancy M. Ridgway, "Consumer Search: An Extended Framework," *Journal of Consumer Research* 13 (June 1986): 119–26.
18. Sarah Mahoney, "Study Finds Men Bamboozled by Choices in Supermarkets," *Marketing Daily* (May 31, 2007), www.mediapost.com, accessed May 31, 2007.
19. David Leonhardt, "The Neighbors as Marketing Powerhouses," *New York Times* (June 13, 2005), www.nytimes.com, accessed June 13, 2005.
20. Girish Punj, "Presearch Decision-Making in Consumer Durable Purchases," *Journal of Consumer Marketing* 4 (Winter 1987): 71–82.
21. Laurie Peterson, "Study Places Value on Marketing at Consumer Research Stage," *Marketing Daily* (June 27, 2007), www.mediapost.com, accessed June 27, 2007.
22. Alex Mindlin, "Buyers Search Online, but Not by Brand," *New York Times* (March 13, 2006), www.nytimes.com, accessed March 13, 2006.
23. Cathy J. Cobb and Wayne D. Hoyer, "Direct Observation of Search Behavior," *Psychology & Marketing* 2 (Fall 1985): 161–79.
24. Sharon E. Beatty and Scott M. Smith, "External Search Effort: An Investigation Across Several Product Categories," *Journal of Consumer Research* 14 (June 1987): 83–95; William L. Moore and Donald R.

Lehmann, "Individual Differences in Search Behavior for a Nondurable," *Journal of Consumer Research* 7 (December 1980): 296–307.

25. Geoffrey C. Kiel and Roger A. Layton, "Dimensions of Consumer Information Seeking Behavior," *Journal of Marketing Research* 28 (May 1981): 233–39; see also Narasimhan Srinivasan and Brian T. Ratchford, "An Empirical Test of a Model of External Search for Automobiles," *Journal of Consumer Research* 18 (September 1991): 233–42.

26. David F. Midgley, "Patterns of Interpersonal Information Seeking for the Purchase of a Symbolic Product," *Journal of Marketing Research* 20 (February 1983): 74–83.

27. Cyndee Miller, "Scotland to U.S.: 'This Tennent's for You,'" *Marketing News* (August 29, 1994): 26.

28. Rebecca K. Ratner, Barbara E. Kahn, and Daniel Kahneman, "Choosing Less-Preferred Experiences for the Sake of Variety," *Journal of Consumer Research* 26 (June 1999): 1–15.

29. Harper A. Roehm and Michelle L. Roehm, "Revisiting the Effect of Positive Mood on Variety Seeking," *Journal of Consumer Research* 32 (September 2005): 330–336; Satya Menon and Barbara E. Kahn, "The Impact of Context on Variety Seeking in Product Choices," *Journal of Consumer Research* 22 (December 1995): 285–95; Barbara E. Kahn and Alice M. Isen, "The Influence of Positive Affect on Variety Seeking Among Safe, Enjoyable Products," *Journal of Consumer Research* 20 (September 1993): 257–70.

30. J. Jeffrey Inman, "The Role of Sensory-Specific Satiety in Consumer Variety Seeking Among Flavors" (unpublished manuscript, A. C. Nielsen Center for Marketing Research, University of Wisconsin–Madison, July 1999).

31. Quoted in John Tierney, "Oversaving, a Burden for Our Times," *New York Times* (March 23, 2009), www.nytimes.com/2009/03/24/science/24tier.html?_r=1, accessed March 23, 2009.

32. Gary Belsky, "Why Smart People Make Major Money Mistakes," *Money* (July 1995): 76; Richard Thaler and Eric J. Johnson, "Gambling with the House Money or Trying to Break Even: The Effects of Prior Outcomes on Risky Choice," *Management Science* 36 (June 1990): 643–60; Richard Thaler, "Mental Accounting and Consumer Choice," *Marketing Science* 4 (Summer 1985): 199–214.

33. Daniel Kahneman and Amos Tversky, "Prospect Theory: An Analysis of Decision Under Risk," *Econometrica* 47 (March 1979): 263–91; Timothy B. Heath, Subimal Chatterjee, and Karen Russo France, "Mental Accounting and Changes in Price: The Frame Dependence of Reference Dependence," *Journal of Consumer Research* 22, no. 1 (June 1995): 90–97.

34. Richard Thaler, "Mental Accounting and Consumer Choice," *Marketing Science* 4 (Summer 1985): 199–214, quoted on p. 206.

35. Girish N. Punj and Richard Staelin, "A Model of Consumer Search Behavior for New Automobiles," *Journal of Consumer Research* 9 (March 1983): 366–80. For recent work on online search that decomposes search strategies in terms of type of good, cf. Peng Huang, Nicholas H. Lurie, and Sabyasachi Mitra, "Searching for Experience on the Web: An Empirical Examination of Consumer Behavior for Search and Experience Goods," *Journal of Marketing*, in press.

36. Cobb and Hoyer, "Direct Observation of Search Behavior"; Moore and Lehmann, "Individual Differences in Search Behavior for a Nondurable"; Punj and Staelin, "A Model of Consumer Search Behavior for New Automobiles"; Brian T. Ratchford, M. S. Lee, and D. Toluca, "The Impact of the Internet on Information Search for Automobiles," *Journal of Marketing Research* 40, no. 2 (2003): 193–209.

37. James R. Bettman and C. Whan Park, "Effects of Prior Knowledge and Experience and Phase of the Choice Process on Consumer Decision Processes: A Protocol Analysis," *Journal of Consumer Research* 7 (December 1980): 234–48.

38. Alina Tugend, "Some Blissful Ignorance Can Cure Chronic Buyer's Remorse," *New York Times* (March 15, 2008), www.nytimes.com/2008/03/15/Business/15shortcuts.Html?Scp=1&Sq=Tugend&St=Nyt, accessed March 15, 2008.

39. Alba and Hutchinson, "Dimensions of Consumer Expertise"; Bettman and Park, "Effects of Prior Knowledge and Experience and Phase of the Choice Process on Consumer Decision Processes"; Merrie Brucks, "The Effects of Product Class Knowledge on Information Search Behavior," *Journal of Consumer Research* 12 (June 1985): 1–16; Joel E. Urbany, Peter R. Dickson, and William L. Wilkie, "Buyer Uncertainty and Information Search," *Journal of Consumer Research* 16 (September 1989): 208–15.

40. For an interpretive treatment of risk, cf. Craig J. Thompson, "Consumer Risk Perceptions in a Community of Reflexive Doubt," *Journal of Consumer Research* 32, no. 2 (2005): 235.

41. Mary Frances Luce, James R. Bettman, and John W. Payne, "Choice Processing in Emotionally Difficult Decisions," *Journal of Experimental Psychology: Learning, Memory, and Cognition* 23 (March 1997): 384–405; example provided by Professor James Bettman, personal communication (December 17, 1997).

42. Some research suggests that structural elements of the information available, such as the number and distribution of attribute levels, will influence how items in a consideration set are processed; cf. Nicholas H. Lurie, "Decision-Making in Information-Rich Environments: The Role of Information Structure," *Journal of Consumer Research* 30 (March 2004): 473–86.

43. John R. Hauser and Birger Wernerfelt, "An Evaluation Cost Model of Consideration Sets," *Journal of Consumer Research* 16 (March 1990): 393–408.

44. Robert J. Sutton, "Using Empirical Data to Investigate the Likelihood of Brands Being Admitted or Readmitted into an Established Evoked Set," *Journal of the Academy of Marketing Science* 15 (Fall 1987): 82.

45. Quoted in Sarah Mahoney, "Small-Brand Solution: The Non-Branded Site," *Marketing Daily* (March 13, 2009), www.mediapost.com, accessed March 13, 2009; www.musthaveshoes.com, accessed June 6, 2009.

46. Quoted in Stuart Elliott, "A Brand Tries to Invite Thought," *New York Times* (September 7, 2007), www.nytimes.com, accessed September 7, 2007.

47. Cyndee Miller, "Hemp Is Latest Buzzword," *Marketing News* (March 17, 1997): 1.

48. Alba and Hutchison, "Dimensions of Consumer Expertise"; Joel B. Cohen and Kunal Basu, "Alternative Models of Categorization: Toward a Contingent Processing Framework," *Journal of Consumer Research* 13 (March 1987): 455–72.

49. Emily Nelson, "Moistened Toilet Paper Wipes Out After Launch for Kimberly-Clark," *Wall Street Journal* (April 15, 2002), www.wsj.com, accessed April 15, 2002.

50. Robert M. McMath, "The Perils of Typecasting," *American Demographics* (February 1997): 60.

51. Eleanor Rosch, "Principles of Categorization," in E. Rosch and B. B. Lloyd, eds., *Recognition and Categorization* (Hillsdale, NJ: Erlbaum, 1978); cf. also Joseph Lajos, Zsolt Katona, Amitava Chattopadhyay, and Miklos Savary, "Category Activation Model: A Spreading Activation Network Model of Subcategory Positioning When Categorization Uncertainty Is High," *Journal of Consumer Research* (June 2009), Vol. 36, No. 1: pp. 122-136.

52. Michael R. Solomon, "Mapping Product Constellations: A Social Categorization Approach to Symbolic Consumption," *Psychology & Marketing* 5, no. 3 (1988): 233–58.

53. McMath, "The Perils of Typecasting."

54. Elizabeth C. Hirschman and Michael R. Solomon, "Competition and Cooperation Among Culture Production Systems," in Ronald F. Bush and Shelby D. Hunt, eds., *Marketing Theory: Philosophy of Science Perspectives* (Chicago: American Marketing Association, 1982): 269–72.

55. Michael D. Johnson, "The Differential Processing of Product Category and Noncomparable Choice Alternatives," *Journal of Consumer Research* 16 (December 1989): 300–39.

56. Mita Sujan, "Consumer Knowledge: Effects on Evaluation Strategies Mediating Consumer Judgments," *Journal of Consumer Research* 12 (June 1985): 31–46.

57. Rosch, "Principles of Categorization."

58. Joan Meyers-Levy and Alice M. Tybout, "Schema Congruity as a Basis for Product Evaluation," *Journal of Consumer Research* 16 (June 1989): 39–55.

59. Mita Sujan and James R. Bettman, "The Effects of Brand Positioning Strategies on Consumers' Brand and Category Perceptions: Some Insights from Schema Research," *Journal of Marketing Research* 26 (November 1989): 454–67.

60. See William P. Putsis, Jr., and Narasimhan Srinivasan, "Buying or Just Browsing? The Duration of Purchase Deliberation," *Journal of Marketing Research* 31 (August 1994): 393–402.

61. Robert E. Smith, "Integrating Information from Advertising and Trial: Processes and Effects on Consumer Response to Product Information," *Journal of Marketing Research* 30 (May 1993): 204–19.

62. Ronald Alsop, "How Boss's Deeds Buff a Firm's Reputation," *Wall Street Journal* (January 31, 2007): B1.

63. Jack Trout, "Marketing in Tough Times," *Boardroom Reports* 2 (October 1992): 8.

64. Stuart Elliott, "Pepsi-Cola to Stamp Dates for Freshness on Soda Cans," *New York Times* (March 31, 1994): D1; Emily DeNitto, "Pepsi's Gamble Hits Freshness Dating Jackpot," *Advertising Age* (September 19, 1994): 50.

65. Quoted in Sarah Mahoney, "JoS. A. Bank Guarantees Suit if Job Is Lost," (March 17, 2009), *Marketing Daily*, mediapost.com, accessed March 17, 2009; Sheryl Jean, "Companies Marketing Peace of Mind for Layoff-Fearing Customers," *Dallas Morning News*, (March 13, 2009), www.dallasnews.com/sharedcontent/dws/bus/personalfinance/stories/031309dnbuslayoffmarketing.3985f89.html, accessed June 7, 2009; Rob Walker, "S.U.V. and Sympathy: Hyundai Assurance," *New York Times Magazine* (March 16, 2009), www.nytimes.com/2009/03/22/magazine/22wwln-consumed-t.html, accessed March 16, 2009.

66. Martin Reimann, Andreas Aholt, Carolin Neuhaus, Thorsten Teichert, and Bernd Weber, "On the Use of Functional Magnetic Resonance Imaging in Consumer Research: Review, Procedures and Own Empirical Results," unpublished manuscript, 2009; Robert Lee Hotz, "Searching for the Why of Buy," *Los Angeles Times Online* (February 27, 2005), www.latimes.com/news/science/la-sci-brain27feb27,0,3899978.story?coll=la-home-headlines; Sandra Blakeslee, "If You Have a 'Buy Button' in Your Brain, What Pushes It?" *New York Times* (October 19, 2004) www.nytimes.com, accessed October 19, 2004; Clive Thompson, "There's a Sucker Born in Every Medial Prefrontal Cortex," *New York Times* (October 26, 2003), www.nytimes.com, accessed September 29, 2007.

67. www.neurosciencemarketing.com/blog, accessed June 7, 2009; Robert Lee Hotz, "Searching for the Why of Buy," *Los Angeles Times Online* (February 27, 2005), www.latimes.com/news/science/la-sci-brain27feb27,0,3899978.story?coll=la-home-headlines; Sandra Blakeslee, "If You Have a 'Buy Button' in Your Brain, What Pushes It?"; Clive Thompson, "There's a Sucker Born in Every Medial Prefrontal Cortex."

68. Michael Porter, *Competitive Advantage* (New York: Free Press, 1985).

69. Linda Stern, "Wanna Deal? Click Here," *Newsweek* (March 22, 2004): 65.

70. Material in this section was adapted from Michael R. Solomon and Elnora W. Stuart, *Welcome to Marketing.com: The Brave New World of E-Commerce* (Upper Saddle River, NJ: Prentice Hall, 2001).

71. "Customer Product Reviews Drive Online Satisfaction and Conversion," *Marketing Daily* (January 24, 2007), www.mediapost.com, accessed January 24, 2007.

72. Chris Anderson, *The Long Tail: Why the Future of Business Is Selling Less of More* (New York: Hyperion, 2006).

73. Jeffrey M. O'Brien, "You're Sooooooo Predictable," *Fortune* (November 27, 2006): 230.

74. Joseph Lajos, Amitava Chattopadhyay, and Kishore Sengupta, "When Electronic Recommendation Agents Backfire: Negative Effects on Choice Satisfaction, Attitudes, and Purchase Intentions," 2009, *INSEAD Working Paper Series*.

75. Emily Burg, "Leverage User-Generated Content to Boost Brands," *Marketing Daily* (March 13, 2007), www.mediapost.com, accessed March 13, 2007.

76. www.yelp.com/Philadelphia, accessed June 7, 2009; Anya Kamenetz, "The Perils and Promise of the Reputation Economy," *Fast Company* (December 3, 2008), www.fastcompany.com/magazine/131/on-the-internet-everyone-knows-youre-a-dog.html, accessed December 3, 2008.

77. www.goodguide.com, accessed June 25, 2009; Claire Cain Miller, "On Web and iPhone, a Tool to Aid Careful Shopping," *New York Times* (June 14, 2009), www.nytimes.com, accessed June 14, 2009.

78. Laurie J. Flynn, "Like This? You'll Hate That (Not All Web Recommendations Are Welcome)" *New York Times* (January 23, 2006), www.nytimes.com, accessed January 23, 2006. For recent work that uses consumers' self-reported need for cognition as a moderator of heuristic usage, cf. Aimee Drolet, Mary Frances Luce, and Itamar Simonson, "When Does Choice Reveal Preference? Moderators of Heuristic vs. Goal Based Choice," *Journal of Consumer Research* (June 2009): 137–147.

79. Robert A. Baron, *Psychology: The Essential Science* (Boston: Allyn & Bacon, 1989); Valerie S. Folkes, "The Availability Heuristic and Perceived Risk," *Journal of Consumer Research* 15 (June 1989): 13–23; Kahneman and Tversky, "Prospect Theory: An Analysis of Decision Under Risk."

80. Wayne D. Hoyer, "An Examination of Consumer Decision-Making for a Common Repeat Purchase Product," *Journal of Consumer Research* 11 (December 1984): 822–29; Calvin P. Duncan, "Consumer Market Beliefs: A Review of the Literature and an Agenda for Future Research," in Marvin E. Goldberg, Gerald Gorn, and Richard W. Pollay, eds., *Advances in Consumer Research* 17 (Provo, UT: Association for Consumer Research, 1990): 729–35; Frank Alpert, "Consumer Market Beliefs and Their Managerial Implications: An Empirical Examination," *Journal of Consumer Marketing* 10, no. 2 (1993): 56–70.

81. Michael R. Solomon, Sarah Drenan, and Chester A. Insko, "Popular Induction: When Is Consensus Information Informative?" *Journal of Personality* 49, no. 2 (1981): 212–24.

82. Beales et al., "Consumer Search and Public Policy."

83. Gary T. Ford and Ruth Ann Smith, "Inferential Beliefs in Consumer Evaluations: An Assessment of Alternative Processing Strategies," *Journal of Consumer Research* 14 (December 1987): 363–71; Deborah Roedder John, Carol A. Scott, and James R. Bettman, "Sampling Data for Covariation Assessment: The Effects of Prior Beliefs on Search Patterns," *Journal of Consumer Research* 13 (June 1986): 38–47; Gary L. Sullivan and Kenneth J. Berger, "An Investigation of the Determinants of Cue Utilization," *Psychology & Marketing* 4 (Spring 1987): 63–74.

84. Gwendolyn Bounds, "As Eco-Seals Proliferate, So Do Doubts," *Wall Street Journal* (April 2, 2009), http://online.wsj.com/article/SB123862823846680371.html, accessed April 2, 2009; www.ecolabelling.org, accessed June 7, 2009.

85. John et al., "Sampling Data for Covariation Assessment."

86. Duncan, "Consumer Market Beliefs."

87. Chr. Hjorth-Andersen, "Price as a Risk Indicator," *Journal of Consumer Policy* 10 (1987): 267–81; David M. Gardner, "Is There a Generalized Price–Quality Relationship?" *Journal of Marketing Research* 8 (May 1971): 241–43; Kent B. Monroe, "Buyers' Subjective Perceptions of Price," *Journal of Marketing Research* 10 (1973): 70–80.

88. Katy McLaughlin, "Shrimp Gets a Makeover, As Foreign Imports Rise U.S. Fishermen Try Giving Prawns Regional Identities," *Wall Street Journal* (August 19, 2004): D1.

89. Rohit Varman and Russell W. Belk. "Nationalism and Ideology in an Anti-consumption Movement," *Journal of Consumer Research* (December 2009), in press.

90. Items excerpted from Terence A. Shimp and Subhash Sharma, "Consumer Ethnocentrism: Construction and Validation of the CETSCALE," *Journal of Marketing Research* 24 (August 1987): 282.

91. See Sung-Tai Hong and Dong Kyoon Kang, "Country-of-Origin Influences on Product Evaluations: The Impact of Animosity and Perceptions of Industriousness Brutality on Judgments of Typical and Atypical Products," *Journal of Consumer Psychology* 16, no. 3, (2006): 232–39; Richard Jackson Harris, Bettina Garner-Earl, Sara J. Sprick, and Collette Carroll, "Effects of Foreign Product Names and Country-of-Origin Attributions on Advertisement Evaluations," *Psychology & Marketing* 11 (March–April 1994): 129–45; Terence A. Shimp, Saeed Samiee, and Thomas J. Madden, "Countries and Their Products: A Cognitive Structure Perspective," *Journal of the Academy of Marketing Science* 21 (Fall 1993): 323–30; Durairaj Maheswaran, "Country of Origin as a Stereotype: Effects of Consumer Expertise and Attribute Strength on Product Evaluations," *Journal of Consumer Research* 21 (September 1994): 354–65; Ingrid M. Martin and Sevgin Eroglu, "Measuring a Multi-Dimensional Construct: Country Image," *Journal of Business Research* 28 (1993): 191–210; Richard Ettenson, Janet Wagner, and Gary Gaeth, "Evaluating the Effect of Country of Origin and the 'Made in the U.S.A.' Campaign: A Conjoint Approach," *Journal of Retailing* 64 (Spring 1988): 85–100; C. Min Han and Vern Terpstra, "Country-of-Origin Effects for Uni-National and Bi-National Products," *Journal of International Business* 19 (Summer 1988): 235–55; Michelle A. Morganosky and Michelle M. Lazarde, "Foreign-Made Apparel: Influences on Consumers' Perceptions of Brand and Store Quality," *International Journal of Advertising* 6 (Fall 1987): 339–48.

92. Natalie Zmuda, "New Balance Plays Patriotism Card in New Marketing Push," *Advertising Age* (June 15, 2009), www.adage.com, accessed June 16, 2009.

93. Adam Bryant, "Message in a Beer Bottle," *Newsweek* (May 29, 2000): 43.

94. Richard W. Stevenson, "The Brands with Billion-Dollar Names," *New York Times* (October 28, 1988): A1; Eric Pfanner, "Zipf's Law, or the Considerable Value of Being Top Dog, as Applied to Branding," *New York Times* (May 21, 2007); Ronald Alsop, "Enduring Brands Hold Their Allure by Sticking Close to Their Roots," *Wall Street Journal*, centennial ed. (1989): B4.

95. Greg Morago, "Envy: The Brand Sluts—Many Who Covet Their Retailers' Garb No Longer Look at the Logo," *Hartford Courant on the Web* (January 1, 2007).

96. Jacob Jacoby and Robert Chestnut, *Brand Loyalty: Measurement and Management* (New York: Wiley, 1978).

97. Ibid.

98. C. Whan Park, "The Effect of Individual and Situation-Related Factors on Consumer Selection of Judgmental Models," *Journal of Marketing Research* 13 (May 1976): 144–51.

99. For an examination of cultural differences in analytical versus holistic attribute evaluation, cf. Alokparna Basu Monga and Deborah Roedder John. "Cultural Differences in Brand Extension Evaluation: The Influence of Analytic Versus Holistic Thinking." *Journal of Consumer Research*, 33(March 2007): 529–36.

100. Joseph W. Alba and Howard Marmorstein, "The Effects of Frequency Knowledge on Consumer Decision-Making," *Journal of Consumer Research* 14 (June 1987): 14–25.

101. Sandra Blakeslee, "If You Have a 'Buy Button' in Your Brain, What Pushes It?"

102. "Americans Are Open to Chinese Goods, Poll Finds," *New York Times* (October 22, 2007), www.nytimes.com/2007/10/22/business/22bizpoll .html?ex=1350705600&en=1615df5334b6437f&ei=5088&partner= rssnyt&emc=rss, accessed October 22, 2007.

9

Buying and Disposing

When you finish this chapter you will understand:

*K*yle is really psyched. The big day has actually arrived: He's going to buy a car! He's had his eye on that silver 2005 Malibu parked in the lot of Jon's Auto-Rama for weeks now. Although the sticker says $2,999, Kyle figures he can probably get this baby for a cool $2,000—with GM going bankrupt, these Chevy dealers are desperate to move their inventory. Besides, Jon's dilapidated showroom and seedy lot makes it look like just the kind of place that's hungry to move some cars.

Kyle did his homework on the Web. First he found out the wholesale value of similar used Malibus from the Kelley Blue Book (kbb.com), and then he scouted out some cars for sale in his area at autobytel.com. So, Kyle figures he's coming in loaded for bear—he's going to show these guys they're not dealing with some rube.

Unlike some of the newer, flashy car showrooms he's been in lately, this place is a real nuts-and-bolts operation—it's so dingy and depressing he can't wait to get out of there and take a shower. Kyle dreads the prospect of haggling over the price, but he hopes to convince the salesperson to take his offer because he knows the real market value of the car he wants. At the Auto-Rama lot, big signs on all the cars proclaim that today is Jon's Auto-Rama Rip Us Off Day! Things look better than Kyle expected—maybe he can get the Malibu for even less than he hoped. He's a bit surprised when a salesperson comes over to him and introduces herself as Rhoda. He expected to deal with a middle-aged man in a loud sport coat (a stereotype he has about used-car salespeople), but this is more good luck: He figures he won't have to be so tough if he negotiates with a woman his age.

Rhoda laughs when he offers her $1,800 for the Malibu; she points out that she can't take such a low bid for such a sweet car to her boss or she'll lose her job. Rhoda's enthusiasm for the car convinces him all the more that he has to have it. When he finally writes a check for $2,700, he's exhausted from all the haggling. What an ordeal! In any case, Kyle reminds himself that he at least convinced Rhoda to sell him the car for less than the sticker price—and maybe he can fix it up and sell it for even more in a year or two. That Web surfing really paid off—he's a tougher negotiator than he thought.

Why do many factors over and above the qualities of the product or service influence the outcome of a transaction? Why do factors at the time of purchase dramatically influence the consumer decision-making process?

Situational Effects on Consumer Behavior

Even in today's buyer's market, many consumers dread the act of buying a car. In fact, a survey by Yankelovich Partners found that this transaction is the most anxiety-provoking and least satisfying of any retail experience.[1] But change is in the wind as dealers transform the car showroom. Car shoppers like Kyle log onto Internet buying services, call auto brokers who negotiate for them, buy cars at warehouse clubs, and visit giant auto malls where they can easily comparison shop.

Kyle's experience when he bought a car illustrates some of the concepts we'll discuss in this chapter. Making a purchase is often not a simple, routine matter where you just pop into a store and make a quick choice. As Figure 9.1 illustrates, many contextual factors affect our choice, such as our mood, whether we feel time pressure to make the purchase, and the particular reason we need the product. In some situations, such as when we buy a car or a home, the salesperson or realtor plays a pivotal role in our final selection. And today people often use the Web to arm themselves with product and price information before they even enter a dealership or a store; this puts more pressure on retailers to deliver the value their customers expect.

But the sale doesn't end at the time of purchase. A lot of important consumer activity occurs after we bring a product home. Once we use a product, we have to decide whether we're satisfied with it. The satisfaction process is especially important to savvy marketers who realize that the key to success is not to sell a product *one* time, but rather to forge a relationship with the consumer so that he will come back for more. Finally, just as Kyle thought about the resale value of his car, we must also consider how consumers dispose of products and how we often rely on secondary markets (e.g., used-car dealers) to obtain what we want. We'll consider these issues in this chapter.

The Denny's chain hopes to motivate college students to drop in for a munch between 10 P.M. and 5 A.M. It introduced a "Pick 3" appetizer promotion for $9.99 on weekdays and gives a 20 percent discount with a college ID on Saturday nights. A company executive explains, ". . . [We] treat each day-part as a specific business. Late-night is one. We wanted to create a marketing and promotions program that targets what we know are our predominate [sic] late-night visitors—college kids."[2] Even some online advertisers tailor content to time of day. McDonald's advertises

Figure 9.1 ISSUES RELATED TO PURCHASE AND POSTPURCHASE ACTIVITIES

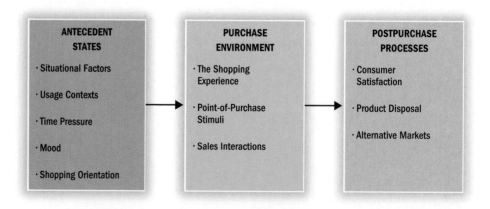

breakfast meals in the morning hours on Yahoo! whereas Sanofi-Aventis runs ads for its sleep-aid drug Ambien CR in the middle of the night on CBSNews.com.[3]

These companies understand that a *consumption situation* includes a buyer, a seller, a product or service—but also many other factors, such as the reason we want to make a purchase and how the physical environment makes us feel.[4] Common sense tells us that we tailor our purchases to specific occasions and that the way we feel at a specific point in time affects what we want to do—or buy. Smart marketers understand these patterns and plan their efforts to coincide with situations in which we are most prone to purchase. For example, book clubs invest heavily in promotional campaigns in June because many people want to stock up on "beach books" to read during the summer.[5] Our moods even change radically during the day, so at different times we might be more or less interested in what a marketer offers.

A study used a technique researchers call the *day reconstruction method* to track these changes. More than 900 working women kept diaries of everything they did during the day, from reading the paper in the morning to falling asleep in front of the TV at night. The next day they relived each diary entry and rated how they felt at the time (annoyed, happy, etc.). Overall, researchers found the study participants woke up a little grumpy but soon entered a state of mild pleasure. This mood increased by degrees through the day though it was punctuated by occasional bouts of anxiety, frustration, and anger. Not surprisingly the subjects were least happy when they engaged in mundane activities like commuting to work and doing housework, whereas they rated sex, socializing with friends, and relaxing as most enjoyable. Contrary to prior findings, however, the women were happier when they watched television than when they shopped or talked on the phone. They ranked taking care of children low, below cooking and not far above housework. The good news: Overall, people seem to be pretty happy, and these ratings aren't influenced very much by factors such as household income or job security. By far, the two factors that most upset daily moods were a poor night's sleep and tight work deadlines.[6]

In addition to the functional relationships between products and usage situation, another reason to take environmental circumstances seriously is that a person's *situational self-image*—the role she plays at any one time—helps to determine what she wants to buy or consume (see Chapter 5).[7] A guy who tries to impress his date as he plays the role of "man-about-town" may spend more lavishly, order champagne instead of beer, and buy flowers—purchases he would never consider when he hangs out with his friends, slurps beer, and plays the role of "one of the boys." Let's see how these dynamics affect the way people think about what they buy.

If we systematically identify important usage situations, we can tailor market segmentation strategies to insure that our offerings meet the specific needs these situations create. For example, we often tailor our furniture choices to specific settings. We prefer different styles for a city apartment, a beach house, or an executive suite. Similarly, we distinguish motorcycles in terms of how riders use them, including commuting, riding them as dirt bikes, or on a farm versus highway travel.[8]

Coach, the maker of luxury leather goods, decided to overhaul its marketing strategy to convince women that they need more than simply a bag for everyday use and one for dressy occasions. Now, the company helps women (at least those who can still afford Coach!) to update their wardrobes when it offers them weekend bags, evening bags, backpacks, satchels, clutches, totes, briefcases, diaper bags, coin purses, duffels, and even a "wristlet"—a mini-handbag that doubles as a bag-within-a-bag. Coach also makes new bags to fill what it calls "usage voids"—activities that range from weekend getaways to trips to the grocery store. Coach introduced its Hamptons Weekend collection with a display of bags it stuffed with beach towels and colorful flip-flops. Have bag, will travel.[9]

Clothing choices are often heavily influenced by the situation in which we need to wear them.
Source: Courtesy of Hart Schaffner Marx/Hartmarx.

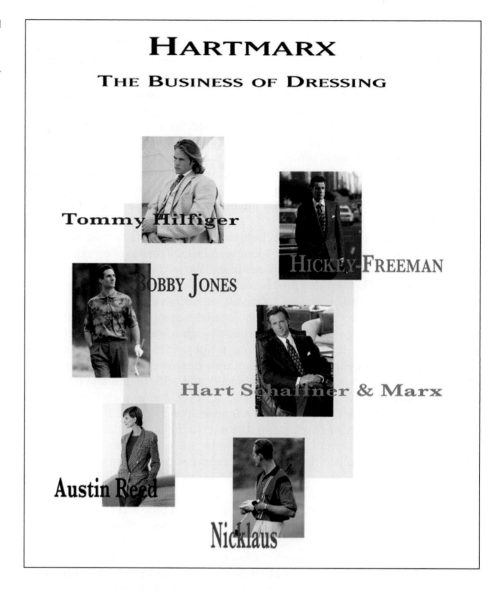

Table 9.1 gives one example of how a marketer fine-tunes its segmentation strategy to the usage situation. When we list the major contexts in which people use a product (e.g., snow skiing and sunbathing for a suntan lotion) and the different types of people who use the product, we can construct a matrix that identifies specific product features we should emphasize for each situation. During the summer a lotion manufacturer might promote the fact that the bottle floats and is hard to lose, but during the winter season it could tout its nonfreezing formula.

Our Social and Physical Surroundings

A consumer's physical and social environment affects her motives to use a product as well as how she will evaluate the item. Important cues include her immediate environment as well as the amount and type of other consumers who are there as well. Dimensions of the physical environment, such as decor, odors, and even temperature can significantly influence consumption. One study even found that if a Las Vegas casino pumped certain odors into the room, patrons fed more money into the slot machines![10] We'll take a closer look at some of these factors a bit later in this chapter when we consider how important store design is to consumer behavior.

In addition to physical cues, though, groups or social settings significantly affect many of our purchase decisions. In some cases, the sheer presence or absence of

TABLE 9.1   A Person-Situation Segmentation Matrix for Suntan Lotion

Situation	Young Children		Teenagers		Adult Women		Adult Men		Benefits/Features
	Fair Skin	Dark Skin	Fair Skin	Dark Skin	Fair Skin	Dark Skin	Fair Skin	Dark Skin	
Beach/boat sunbathing	Combined insect repellent				Summer perfume				a. Product serves as windburn protection b. Formula and container can stand heat c. Container floats and is distinctive (not easily lost)
Home-poolside sunbathing					Combined moisturizer				a. Product has large pump dispenser b. Product won't stain wood, concrete, furnishings
Sunlamp bathing					Combined moisturizer and massage oil				a. Product is designed specifically for type of lamp b. Product has an artificial tanning ingredient
Snow skiing					Winter perfume				a. Product provides special protection from special light rays and weather b. Product has antifreeze formula
Person benefit/features	Special protection a. Protection is critical b. Formula is non-poisonous		Special protection a. Product fits in jean pocket b. Product used by opinion leaders		Special protection Female perfume		Special protection Male perfume		

Source: Adapted from Peter R. Dickson, "Person-Situation: Segmentation's Missing Link," *Journal of Marketing* 46 (Fall 1982): 62. Copyright © 1982 American Marketing Association. By permission of American Marketing Association.

co-consumers, the other patrons in a setting, actually is a product attribute—think about an exclusive resort or boutique that promises to provide privacy to privileged customers. At other times, the presence of others can have positive value. A sparsely attended ball game or an empty bar can be a depressing sight.

Have you ever experienced a panicky feeling if you're trapped in the middle of a big crowd? The presence of large numbers of people in a consumer environment increases *physiological arousal levels*, so our experiences are more intense. This boost, however, can be positive or negative—the experience depends on how we *interpret* this arousal. It is important to distinguish between *density* and *crowding* for this reason. The former term refers to the actual number of people who occupy a space; whereas the unpleasant psychological state of crowding exists only if a negative affective state occurs as a result of this density.[11] For example, 100 students packed into a classroom designed for 75 may result in an unpleasant situation for all, but the same number of people jammed together at a party—and who occupy a room of the same size—might just make for a great time.

In addition, the *type* of consumers who patronize a store or service or who use a product affects our evaluations. We often infer something about a store when we examine its customers. For this reason, some restaurants require men to wear jackets for dinner (and supply rather tacky ones if they don't), and bouncers at some "hot" nightspots handpick people who wait in line based on whether they have the right "look" for the club. To paraphrase the comedian Groucho Marx, "I would never join a club that would have me as a member!"

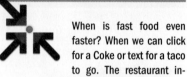

Marketing Opportunity

When is fast food even faster? When we can click for a Coke or text for a taco to go. The restaurant industry is investing in technology to attract on-the-go consumers who live or die by their BlackBerrys or mobile phones. The average American 18 years old and older buys a snack or a meal from a restaurant five times a week on average, and the industry finds that most people won't wait more than 5 minutes in a drive-through line. According to the National Restaurant Association, about 13 percent of Americans placed online food orders in 2006, and industry experts expect this number to mushroom as more eateries offer this service. As one busy salesperson who orders both breakfast and lunch online observed, "I'm saving time. I'm so adept at it now that I can actually do business on the phone while I'm placing my food order."[16]

Temporal Factors

Time is one of consumers' most precious resources. We talk about "making time" or "spending time" and we frequently remind others that "time is money." Common sense tells us that we think more about what we want to buy when we have the luxury to take our time. Even a normally meticulous shopper who never buys before she compares prices might sprint through the mall at 9:00 P.M. on Christmas Eve to scoop up anything left on the shelves if she needs a last-minute gift.

Economic Time

Time is an economic variable; it is a resource that we must divide among our activities.[12] We try to maximize satisfaction when we allocate our time to different tasks. Of course, people's allocation decisions differ; we all know people who seem to play all of the time, and others who are workaholics. An individual's priorities determine his *timestyle*.[13] People in different countries also "spend" this resource at different rates. A social scientist compared the pace of life in 31 cities around the world as part of a study on timestyles.[14] He and his assistants timed how long it takes pedestrians to walk 60 feet and the time postal clerks take to sell a stamp. Based on these responses, he claims that the fastest and slowest countries are:

> **Fastest countries**—(1) Switzerland, (2) Ireland, (3) Germany, (4) Japan, (5) Italy
>
> **Slowest countries**—(31) Mexico, (30) Indonesia, (29) Brazil, (28) El Salvador, (27) Syria

Many consumers believe they are more pressed for time than ever before; marketers label the feeling **time poverty**. This problem appears to be more perception than fact. The reality is we simply have more options to spend our time, so we feel pressured by the weight of all of these choices. The average working day at the turn of the nineteenth century was 10 hours (6 days per week), and women did 27 hours of housework per week, compared to less than 5 hours weekly now. Of course, there are plenty of husbands who share these burdens more, and in some families it's not as important as it used to be to maintain an absolutely spotless home as our values change (see Chapter 4). Ironically, though husbands do help out a lot more than they used to, married women spend a lot more time on housework than do single women (having kids to take care of figures in there). Married men and single women do roughly the same amount each week and (surprise!) single men average the least time of anyone (about 7 to 8 hours per week). Still, about a third of Americans report always feeling rushed—up from 25 percent of the population in 1964.[15]

Psychological Time

"Time flies when you're having fun," but other situations (like some classes?) seem to last forever. Our experience of time is very subjective; our immediate priorities and needs determine how quickly time flies. The fluidity of time is important for marketers to understand because we're more likely to be in a consuming mood at some times than at others.

A study examined how the timestyles of a group of American women influence their consumption choices.[17] The researchers identified four dimensions of time: (1) the *social dimension* refers to individuals' categorization of time as either "time for me" or "time with/for others"; (2) the *temporal orientation dimension* depicts the relative significance individuals attach to past, present, or future; (3) the *planning orientation dimension* alludes to different time management styles varying on a continuum from analytic to spontaneous; and (4) the *polychronic orientation dimension* distinguishes between people who prefer to do one thing at a time from those who have multitasking timestyles. After they interviewed and observed these women, the researchers identified a set of five metaphors that they say capture the participants' perspectives on time:

Too busy to eat? Help is at hand.

Introducing Campbell's® Soup at Hand.™
A whole new way to eat right when you're on the run.

Now you can enjoy sippable soup, anytime, anywhere, with new Campbell's Soup at Hand. Four deliciously satisfying soups in sippable, heat-and-go microwavable cups. Sure your hands are full, but it's amazing what you can do with new Soup at Hand from Campbell's.

M'm! M'm! Good!®

© 2002 Campbell Soup Company

Time poverty is creating opportunities for many new products (like portable soups) that let people multitask.
Source: Courtesy of Campbell Soup Company.

Time is a pressure cooker—These women are usually analytical in their planning, other-oriented, and monochronic in their timestyles. They treat shopping in a methodical manner and they often feel under pressure and in conflict.

Time is a map—These women are usually analytical planners; they exhibit a future temporal orientation and a polychronic timestyle. They often engage in extensive information search and comparison shop.

Time is a mirror—Women in this group are also analytic planners and have a polychronic orientation. However, they have a past temporal orientation. Because of their risk averseness in time use, these women are usually loyal to products and services they know and trust. They prefer convenience-oriented products.

Time is a river—These women are usually spontaneous in their planning orientation and have a present focus. They go on unplanned, short, and frequent shopping trips.

Time is a feast—These women are analytical planners with a present temporal orientation. They view time as something they consume to pursue sensory pleasure and gratification, and for this reason they value hedonic consumption and variety-seeking.

Our experience of time is largely a result of our culture because people around the world think about the passage of time very differently. To most Western consumers, time is a neatly compartmentalized thing: We wake up in the morning, go to school or work, come home, eat dinner, go out, go to sleep, wake up, and do it all over again. We call this perspective *linear separable time*—events proceed in an orderly sequence and "There's a time and a place for everything." There is a clear sense of past, present, and future. We perform many activities as the means to some end that will occur later, as when we "save for a rainy day."

This perspective seems "natural" to us, but not all others share it. Some cultures run on *procedural time* and ignore the clock completely—people simply decide to do something "when the time is right." For example, in Burundi people might arrange to meet when the cows return from the watering hole. If you ask someone in Madagascar how long it takes to get to the market, you will get an answer such as, "in the time it takes to cook rice."

Alternatively, in *circular* or *cyclic* time, natural cycles such as the regular occurrence of the seasons govern people's sense of time (a perspective many Hispanic cultures share). To these consumers, the notion of the future does not make sense—that time will be much like the present. Because the concept of future value does not exist, these consumers often prefer to buy an inferior product that is available now rather than wait for a better one that may be available later. Also, it is hard to convince people who function on circular time to buy insurance or save for a rainy day when they don't think in terms of a linear future.

To appreciate all the different ways people think about time, consider those who speak Aymara, an Indian language of the high Andes. They actually see the future as behind them and the past ahead of them! Aymara call the future *qhipa pacha/timpu*, meaning back or behind time, and the past *nayra pacha/timpu*, meaning front time. And they gesture ahead of them when remembering things past and backward when talking about the future. Anthropologists explain that people in this culture distinguish primarily between what they know and what they don't—and they know what they see in front of them with their own eyes. So, because they know the past, it lies ahead of them. The future is unknown, so it lies behind them where they can't see it.[18] Just imagine trying to sell them life insurance!

The sketches in Figure 9.2 illustrate what happened when a researcher asked college students to draw pictures of time. The drawing at the top left represents procedural time; there is lack of direction from left to right and little sense of past, present, and future. The three drawings in the middle denote cyclical time, with markers that designate regular cycles. The bottom drawing represents linear time, with a segmented time line moving from left to right in a well-defined sequence.[19]

The psychological dimension of time—how we actually experience it—is an important factor in **queuing theory**, the mathematical study of waiting lines. As we all know, our experience when we wait has a big effect on our evaluations of what we get at the end of the wait. Although we assume that something must be pretty good if we have to wait for it, the negative feelings that long waits arouse can quickly turn people off.[20] In a survey, NCR Corp. found that standing around the local Department or Division of Motor Vehicles is the most dreaded wait of all. Waiting on line at retail outlets came in a close second, followed by registering at clinics or hospitals, checking in at airports, and ordering at fast-food restaurants or deli counters. On average, consumers estimate that they spend more than 2 days per year waiting in line for service, and half believe they waste between 30 minutes and 2 hours each week on lines.[21]

Marketers use "tricks" to minimize psychological waiting time. These techniques range from altering customers' perceptions of a line's length to providing distractions that divert attention away from waiting:[22]

Net Profit

The Walt Disney Co. is counting on our cell phones to enhance our theme park experiences. Guests who wait in line for a comedy show at Walt Disney World can text message jokes that may be included in the show they go to see. As one executive explained, "It works as our warm-up act essentially for the show, but it also . . . keeps them entertained while they're waiting." In a deal with Verizon Wireless, park visitors will use their mobiles to save a spot in a line at a popular ride or even to determine where they can find Mickey Mouse at the moment to get an autograph. Visitors will be able to download an app to plan their trips, make hotel reservations, and create a checklist of must-see attractions. They'll be able to check wait times at rides or locate the closest pizza vendor. Disney will be able to recommend alternative activities with faster wait times and even suggest places to see based on the user's current location in the park. They can follow up with personalized mementoes of the trip, such as a digital photo of Sleeping Beauty who thanks a child for coming.[25]

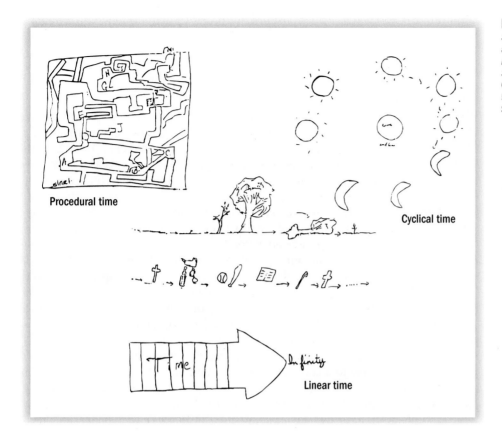

Figure 9.2 DRAWINGS OF TIME
Source: Esther S. Page-Wood, Carol J. Kaufman, and Paul M. Lane, (1990) "The Art of Time." *Proceedings of the 1990 Academy of Marketing Science* conference, ed B. J. Dunlap, Vol. xiii, Cullowhee, NC: Academy of Marketing Science, 56–61. Copyright © 1990 Academy of Marketing Science. Used with permission.

- One hotel chain received excessive complaints about the wait for elevators so it installed mirrors near the elevator banks. People's natural tendency to check their appearance reduced complaints, even though the actual waiting time was unchanged.
- Airline passengers often complain about the wait to claim their baggage. In one airport, they would walk 1 minute from the plane to the baggage carousel and then wait 7 minutes for their luggage. When the airport changed the layout so that the walk to the carousel took 6 minutes and bags arrived 2 minutes after that, complaints disappeared.[23]
- Restaurant chains are scrambling to put the fast back into fast food, especially for drive-through lanes, which now account for 65 percent of revenues. In a study that ranked the speed of 25 fast-food chains, cars spent an average of 203.6 seconds from the menu board to departure. Wendy's was clocked the fastest at 150.3 seconds. To speed things up and eliminate spills, McDonald's created a salad that comes in a container to fit into car cup holders. Arby's is working on a "high viscosity" version of its special sauce that's less likely to spill. Burger King is testing see-through bags so customers can quickly check their orders before speeding off.[24]

Queuing theory needs to take cultural differences into account because these affect how we behave while in line. One Hong Kong researcher maintains, for example, that Asians and others in more collective cultures compare their situation with those around them. This means they're more likely to patiently stand in a long line— they are likely to compare their situation to the number of people *behind* them rather than to the number ahead of them. By contrast, Americans and others in more individualistic societies don't make these "social comparisons." They don't necessarily feel better that more people are behind them, but they feel bad if too many people are in front of them. A Disney executive claims that Europeans also exhibit different behaviors depending on their nationality. He notes that at the

Disneyland Resort Paris, British visitors are orderly but the French and Italians "never saw a line they couldn't be in front of."[26]

OBJECTIVE

Why does the information a store or Web site provides strongly influence a purchase decision in addition to what a shopper already knows or believes about a product?

The Shopping Experience

Whole Foods wants you to feel really, really mellow before you cruise its grocery aisles. The natural supermarket chain is testing a spa-within-a-food-store concept. You'll find its Refresh—The Everyday Spa at Whole Foods Market prototype in Dallas enclosed with a soundproof lounge complete with fountains, several treatment rooms, and a private balcony where clients can order lunch.[27] After a Shiatsu massage, it's unlikely you'll care too much if those exotic guavas are on sale before you throw them in your cart.

Our mood at the time of purchase can really impact what we feel like buying.[28] Recall that in Chapter 4 we talked about how we direct our behavior to satisfy certain goal states. If you don't believe it, try grocery shopping on an empty stomach! Or make a decision when you're stressed and you'll understand how a physiological state impairs information-processing and problem-solving abilities.[29]

Two basic dimensions, *pleasure* and *arousal*, determine whether we will react positively or negatively to a consumption environment.[30] What it boils down to is that you can either enjoy or not enjoy a situation, and you can feel stimulated or not. As Figure 9.3 indicates, different combinations of pleasure and arousal levels result in a variety of emotional states. An arousing situation can be either distressing or exciting, depending on whether the context is positive or negative (e.g., a street riot versus a street festival). So, a specific mood is some combination of pleasure and arousal. The state of happiness is high in pleasantness and moderate in arousal, whereas elation is high on both dimensions.[31] A mood state (either positive or negative) biases our judgments of products and services in that direction.[32] Put simply, we give more positive evaluations when we're in a good mood (this explains the popularity of the business lunch!).

Many factors including store design, the weather, or whether you just had a fight with your significant other affect your mood. Music and television programming do as well.[33] When we hear happy music or watch happy programs, we experience more positive reactions to commercials and products.[34] And when we're in a good mood,

Figure 9.3 DIMENSIONS OF EMOTIONAL STATES

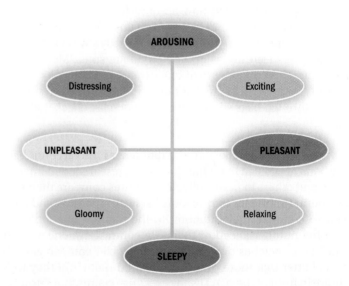

we process ads with less elaboration. We pay less attention to specifics of the message and we rely more on heuristics (see Chapter 8).[35]

Our emotional reactions to marketing cues are so powerful that some high-tech companies study mood in very small doses (in 1/30 of a second increments) as they analyze people's facial reactions when they see ads or new products. They measure happiness as they look for differences between, for example, a *true smile* (which includes a relaxation of the upper eyelid) and a *social smile* (which occurs only around the mouth). Whirlpool used this technique to test consumers' emotional reactions to a yet-to-be-launched generation of its Duet washers and dryers. The company's goal: To design an appliance that will actually make people happy. Researchers discovered that even though test subjects said they weren't thrilled with some out-of-the-box design options, such as unusual color combinations, their facial expressions said otherwise.[36]

When the Going Gets Tough, the Tough Go Shopping

We all know some people who shop simply for the sport of it, and others whom we have to drag to a mall. Shopping is how we acquire needed products and services, but social motives for shopping also are important. Thus, shopping is an activity that we can perform for either utilitarian (functional or tangible) or hedonic (pleasurable or intangible) reasons.[37]

So, do people hate to shop or love it? We segment consumers in terms of their **shopping orientation**, or general attitudes about shopping. These orientations vary depending on the particular product categories and store types we consider. Rob hates to shop for a car, but he may love to browse in music stores. A shopper's motivation influences the type of shopping environment that will be attractive or annoying; for example a person who wants to locate and buy something quickly may find loud music, bright colors, or complex layouts distracting; while someone who is there to browse may enjoy the sensory stimulation.[38]

Some scale items researchers use to assess our shopping motivations illustrate the diverse reasons we may shop. One item that measures hedonic value is "During the trip, I felt the excitement of the hunt." When we compare that type of sentiment to a functional statement, "I accomplished just what I wanted to on this shopping trip," there's a clear contrast between these two dimensions.[39] Hedonic shopping motives include the following:[40]

- **Social experiences**—The shopping center or department store replaces the traditional town square or county fair as a community gathering place. Many people (especially in suburban or rural areas) have almost no other places to spend their leisure time. That probably explains the popularity of late-night games college students in some rural areas play at their local Wal-Mart. In addition to sports such as scavenger hunts, aisle football, and a relay race limbo under the shopping-cart stand, "10 in 10" is a big attraction. To play this game, students form into teams; each team has 10 minutes to put 10 items from anywhere in the store in a shopping cart. Then they turn their cart over to the opposing team, which has to figure out where the items came from and return them to the shelves where they belong (not so easy in a store stocked with more than 100,000 different items). The first team back to the checkout counters with an empty cart wins.[41] Note: If you get busted for playing this game, you did NOT learn about it here.
- **Sharing of common interests**—Stores frequently offer specialized goods that allow people with shared interests to communicate.
- **Interpersonal attraction**—Shopping centers are a natural place to congregate. The shopping mall is a favorite "hangout" for teenagers. It also represents a controlled, secure environment for the elderly, and many malls now feature "mall walkers' clubs" for early morning workouts.

● **Instant status**—As every salesperson knows, some people savor the experience of being waited on, even though they may not necessarily buy anything. One men's clothing salesman offered this advice: "Remember their size, remember what you sold them last time. Make them feel important! If you can make people feel important, they are going to come back. Everybody likes to feel important!"[42] When a team of researchers conducted in-depth interviews with women to understand what makes shopping a pleasurable experience, they found one motivation was role-playing. For example, one respondent dressed up for shopping excursions to upscale boutiques because she likes to pretend she is wealthy and have salespeople fall all over her.[43]

● **The thrill of the hunt**—Some people pride themselves on their knowledge of the marketplace. Unlike our car-buying friend Rob, they may love to haggle and bargain.

E-Commerce: Clicks Versus Bricks

As more and more Web sites pop up to sell everything from refrigerator magnets to Mack trucks, marketers continue to debate how the online world affects their business.[44] In particular, many lose sleep as they wonder whether e-commerce will replace traditional retailing, work in concert with it, or perhaps even fade away to become another fad your kids will laugh about someday (OK, that's not real likely).

One thing to keep in mind is that the experience of acquiring the good may be quite different off line versus online. This aspect of the transaction can provide value added over and above the good or service you buy. We clearly see this difference between the two worlds when we compare how people gamble in casinos versus online. When researchers interviewed 30 gamblers to explore these experiences, they found sharp contrasts. Those who enjoy casino gambling have a strong sense of connection to fellow gamblers so it's very much a social experience. Online gamblers enjoy the anonymity of the Internet. Casino gamblers get turned on by the sensual experiences and excitement of the casino, while online gamblers gravitate more to the feeling of safety and control they get because they stay at home. Casino gamblers talked about the friendly atmosphere, while those who stayed online reported behaviors that a real casino wouldn't tolerate such as taunts and bullying.[45] Although both groups aim to have fun and hopefully make money, it's a safe bet their experiences are quite different.

For marketers, the growth of online commerce is a sword that cuts both ways: On the one hand, they reach customers around the world even if they're physically located 100 miles from nowhere. On the other hand, they now compete not only with the store across the street but also thousands of Web sites that span the globe. Also, when consumers obtain products directly from the manufacturer or wholesaler, this eliminates the intermediary—the loyal, store-based retailers that carry the firm's products and that sell them at a marked-up price.[46]

So what makes e-commerce sites successful? Some e-tailers take advantage of technology to provide extra value to their customers that their land-locked rivals can't. For example, Lands' End (LandsEnd.com) offers men and women a Virtual Model that lets them design a model to match their own body type so they can then "try on" the clothing they see on the Web site. Soon MTV viewers will be able to use their remote controls to purchase the CDs that go with the music videos they watch.

More generally, these online shoppers value these aspects of a Web site:

● The ability to click on an item to create a pop-up window with more details about the product including price, size, colors, and inventory availability.

● The ability to click on an item and add it to your cart without leaving the page you're on.

● The ability to "feel" merchandise through better imagery, more product descriptions, and details.

tuesday, 11:15 p.m.
buying a new dress.

bluefly℠

www.bluefly.com℠
the outlet store in your home℠

Women's, men's and kid's designer fashions.
Save up to 75%.   90-day money back guarantee.

E-commerce sites like Bluefly give shoppers the option of shopping without leaving home.
Source: Courtesy of Bluefly.com.

- The ability to enter all data related to your purchase on one page, rather than going through several checkout pages.
- The ability to mix and match product images on one page to determine whether they look good together.[47]

Table 9.2 summarizes some of the pros and cons of e-commerce. It's clear that traditional shopping isn't quite dead yet—but brick-and-mortar retailers do need to work harder to give shoppers something they can't get (yet anyway) in the virtual world—a stimulating or pleasant environment. Now let's check out how they're doing that.

Retailing as Theater

At several U.S. malls shoppers show up in shorts and flip-flops. They're turning out to ride a Flowrider—a huge wave-making machine.[48] Shopping center developers turn to attractions like this to lure reluctant customers back to malls. The

TABLE 9.2 Pros and Cons of E-Commerce	
Benefits of E-Commerce	**Limitations of E-Commerce**
For the Consumer	**For the Consumer**
Shop 24 hours a day	Lack of security
Less traveling	Fraud
Can receive relevant information in seconds from any location	Can't touch items
More choices of products	Exact colors may not reproduce on computer monitors
More products available to less-developed countries	Expensive to order and then return
Greater price information	Potential breakdown of human relationships
Lower prices so that less affluent can purchase	
Participate in virtual auctions	
Fast delivery	
Electronic communities	
For the Marketer	**For the Marketer**
The world is the marketplace	Lack of security
Decreases costs of doing business	Must maintain site to reap benefits
Very specialized business can be successful	Fierce price competition
Real-time pricing	Conflicts with conventional retailers
	Legal issues not resolved

Source: Adapted from Michael R. Solomon and Elnora W. Stuart, *Welcome to Marketing.com: The Brave New World of E-Commerce* (Upper Saddle River, NJ: Prentice Hall, 2001).

competition for customers becomes even more intense as nonstore alternatives, from Web sites and print catalogs to TV shopping networks and home shopping parties, continue to multiply.

With all of these shopping alternatives available, how can a traditional store compete? Many malls are giant entertainment centers, almost to the point that their traditional retail occupants seem like an afterthought. Today, it's commonplace to find carousels, miniature golf, skating rinks, or batting cages in a suburban mall. Hershey opened a make-believe factory smack in the middle of Times Square. It features four steam machines, 380 feet of neon lighting, plus a moving message board that let consumers program messages to surprise their loved ones.[49]

The quest to entertain means that many stores go all out to create imaginative environments that transport shoppers to fantasy worlds or provide other kinds of stimulation. We call this strategy **retail theming**. Innovative merchants today use four basic kinds of theming techniques:

1 *Landscape themes* rely on associations with images of nature, Earth, animals, and the physical body. Bass Pro Shops, for example, creates a simulated outdoor environment including pools stocked with fish.
2 *Marketscape themes* build on associations with man-made places. An example is The Venetian hotel in Las Vegas that lavishly recreates parts of the Italian city.
3 *Cyberspace themes* build on images of information and communications technology. eBay's retail interface instills a sense of community among its vendors and traders.
4 *Mindscape themes* draw on abstract ideas and concepts, introspection and fantasy, and often possess spiritual overtones. The Kiva day spa in downtown Chicago offers health treatments based on a theme of Native American healing ceremonies and religious practices.[50]

One popular theming strategy is to convert a store into a **being space**. This environment resembles a commercial living room where we can go to relax, be entertained, hang out with friends, escape the everyday, or even learn. When you think of

A Flowrider machine attracts mall shoppers.
Source: Courtesy of Barbara P. Fernandez/Redux Pictures.

being spaces, Starbucks probably comes to mind. The coffee chain's stated goal is to become our "third place" where we spend the bulk of our time in addition to home and work. Starbucks led the way when it outfitted its stores with comfy chairs and Wi-Fi. But there are many other marketers who meet our needs for exciting commercial spaces—no matter what those needs are. In Asia, venues such as Manboo and Fujiyama Land provide havens where gamers can do their thing 24/7—and even take a shower on-site during a break. Other spaces cater to the needs of **minipreneurs** (one-person businesses) as they offer work-centered being spaces. At New York's Paragraph, writers who need a quiet place to ruminate can hang out in a loft that's divided into a writing room and a lounge area. TwoRooms ("You Work, They Play") provides office space and child care for home-based workers.

Temporary stores, like this Kiehl's pop-up store at the University of Colorado, are fashion brands' latest attempt to develop brand loyalty among college students.
Source: Photo by Zachary Tolber, Kiehl's Since 1851.

CB AS I SEE IT

Professor Cele Otnes, *University of Illinois at Urbana-Champaign*

*H*ow can retailers make consumers' in-store experiences more meaningful in order to positively influence key attitudinal and behavioral measures, such as brand loyalty and likelihood of repeat purchasing? One research topic that relates to this question is how retailers use in-store rituals to shape consumers' experiences. *Rituals* are expressive, dramatic events we repeat over time (for more on rituals, see Chapter 15).

Our research explores whether and how these types of rituals actually impact customers' experience with a brand. We have interviewed more than 20 retailers and service providers who identify themselves as using rituals designed for their employees or customers in order to enhance their relationships with these stakeholders, to improve efficiency, and to differentiate themselves from their competitors. We're exploring such issues as how consumers resist rituals, how consumers help co-create rituals with other shoppers and with retailers (as is the case at Build-A-Bear, when consumers engage in grooming rituals with the toys they've just created), and whether and how these rituals actually enhance consumers' retail experiences. From a strategic perspective, we will also explore whether ritualizing the shopping experience allows retailers to charge premium prices, to be forgiven more easily if they make mistakes with consumers, and to allocate less of their money to marketing communications. So next time you stand in line at Marble Slab Creamery or wear a "birthday sombrero" on your head at your favorite Mexican restaurant, remember—you've been ritualized!

Reflecting the ever-quickening pace of our culture, many of these *being spaces* come and go very rapidly—on purpose. **Pop-up stores** appear in many forms around the world. Typically, these are temporary installations that do business only for a few days or weeks and then disappear before they get old. The Swatch Instant Store sells limited edition watches in a major city until the masses discover it; then it closes and moves on to another "cool" locale. The Dutch beer brand Dommelsch organized pop-up concerts—fans entered barcodes they found on cans, beer bottles, and coasters on the brewer's Web site to discover dates and locations. You may even run into a pop-up store on your campus; several brands including the Brazilian flip-flop maker Havaianas, Victoria's Secret's Pink, and sustainable-clothing brand RVL7 run pop-up projects around the United States.[51]

Store Image

As so many stores compete for customers, how do we ever pick one over others? Just like products (see Chapter 6), stores have "personalities." Some shops have very clearly defined images (either good or bad). Others tend to blend into the crowd. What factors shape this personality, or **store image**? Some of the important dimensions of a store's image are location, merchandise suitability, and the knowledge and congeniality of the sales staff.[52]

These design features typically work together to create an overall impression. When we think about stores, we don't usually say, "Well, that place is fairly good in terms of convenience, the salespeople are acceptable, and services are good." We're more likely to proclaim, "That place gives me the creeps," or "It's so much fun to shop there." We quickly get an overall impression of a store, and the feeling we get may have more to do with intangibles, such as interior design and the types of people we find in the aisles, than with the store's return policies or credit availability. As a result, some stores routinely pop up in our consideration sets (see Chapter 9), whereas we never consider others ("Only geeks shop there!").[53]

A recent makeover of FedEx retail outlets illustrates the crucial role design can play in communicating a desirable store image. As shown in the before-and-after shots, consumer research conducted by Ziba Design for FedEx indicated that compared to its main competitors, the firm's brand personality was more innovative, leading-edge, and outgoing—but this impression was certainly not reinforced by its cluttered storefront locations where customers go to drop off packages for delivery. The designers used colors and shapes associated with these attributes to makeover the stores.
Source: Ziba Design.

Atmospherics

Retailers want you to come in—and stay. Careful store design increases the amount of space the shopper covers, and stimulating displays keep them in the aisles longer. This "curb appeal" translates directly to the bottom line: Researchers tracked grocery shopper's movements by plotting the position of their cell phones as they moved about a store. They found that when people lingered just 1 percent longer sales rose by 1.3 percent. Of course, grocers know a lot of tricks after years of observing shoppers. For example, they call the area just inside a supermarket's entrance the "decompression zone"—people tend to slow down and take stock of their surroundings when they enter the store so store designers use this space to promote bargains rather than to sell. Similarly, Wal-Mart's "greeters" help customers to settle in to their shopping experience. Once they get a serious start, the first thing shoppers encounter is the produce section. Since fruits and vegetables can easily be damaged, it would be more logical to buy these items at the end of a shopping trip. But fresh, wholesome food makes people feel good (and righteous) so they're less guilty when they throw the chips and cookies in the cart later.[55]

Because marketers recognize that a store's image is a very important part of the retailing mix, store designers pay a lot of attention to **atmospherics**, the "conscious designing of space and its various dimensions to evoke certain effects in buyers."[56] These dimensions include colors, scents, and sounds. For example, stores with red interiors tend to make people tense, whereas a blue decor imparts a calmer feeling.[57] As we noted in Chapter 2, some preliminary evidence also indicates that odors (olfactory cues) influence our evaluations of a store's environment.[58]

A store's atmosphere in turn affects what we buy. In one study, researchers asked shoppers how much pleasure they felt 5 minutes after they entered a store. Those who enjoyed their experience spent more time and money.[59] To boost the entertainment value of shopping (and to lure online shoppers back to brick-and-mortar stores), some retailers offer **activity stores** that let consumers participate in the production of the products or services they buy there. One familiar example is the Build-A-Bear Workshop chain where customers dress bear bodies in costumes.[60]

Retailers cleverly engineer their store designs to attract customers. Light colors impart a feeling of spaciousness and serenity; signs in bright colors create excitement. When the fashion designer Norma Kamali replaced fluorescent lights with pink ones in department store dressing rooms to flatter shoppers' faces and banish wrinkles, women were more willing to try on (and buy) the company's bathing suits.[61] Wal-Mart found that sales were higher in areas of a prototype store

Expo-Xplore, part of a new shopping complex near Durban, South Africa, is the next wave in retail and entertainment design. The courtyard, lined with retailers selling clothes and gear for a variety of outdoor adventure sports, leads to Planet Blue, the ocean-themed heart of the project, with stores oriented around scuba diving, boating, surfing, and other water sports.
Source: Design Group.

ECONsumer Behavior

The Washington Mutual bank was one of the first victims of the recession. Before it went under, the company spent about $1 billion to build new branches with modern, free-flowing designs that replaced bank-teller windows with free-standing counters and signs that promised "free checking, free smiles." When JPMorgan Chase took over the bank, it reversed course. The industry (or what's left of it) is abandoning recent experiments with a "warm and fuzzy" store image as customers search for stability in uncertain times. As a JPMorgan executive observed, "[traditional branches] are superior in every way. They might be boring, but they're practical."[54]

lit in natural daylight compared to the artificial light in its regular stores.[62] One study found that shoppers in stores with brighter in-store lighting examined and handled more merchandise.[63]

In addition to visual stimuli, all sorts of sensory cues influence us in retail settings.[64] For example, patrons of country-and-western bars drink more when the jukebox music is slower. According to a researcher, "Hard drinkers prefer listening to slower-paced, wailing, lonesome, self-pitying music."[65] Music also can affect eating habits. Another study found that diners who listened to loud, fast music ate more food. In contrast, those who listened to Mozart or Brahms ate less and more slowly. The researchers concluded that diners who choose soothing music at mealtimes can increase weight loss by at least 5 pounds a month![66]

In-Store Decision Making

Despite all their efforts to "pre-sell" consumers through advertising, marketers increasingly recognize that the store environment exerts a strong influence on many purchases. Women tell researchers, for example, that store displays are one of the major information sources they use to decide what clothing to buy.[67] This influence is even stronger when we shop for food—analysts estimate that shoppers decide on about two out of every three supermarket purchases while they walk through the aisles.[68]

Marketers work hard to engineer purchasing environments that allow them to connect with consumers at the exact time they make a decision. This strategy even applies to drinking behavior: Diageo, the world's largest liquor company, discovered that 60 percent of bar customers don't know what they will drink until seconds before they place their orders. To make it more likely that the customer's order will include Smirnoff vodka, Johnnie Walker Scotch, or one of its other brands, Diageo launched its Drinks Invigoration Team to increase what it calls its "share of throat." The Dublin-based team experiments with bar "environments" and bottle-display techniques, and comes up with drinks to match customers' moods. For example, the company researchers discovered that bubbles stimulate the desire for spirits, so it developed bubble machines it places in back of bars. Diageo even categorizes bars into types and identifies types of drinkers—and the drinks they prefer—who frequent each. These include "style bars," where cutting-edge patrons like to sip fancy

CB AS I LIVE IT

Heather O'Brien, *Eastern Michigan University*

*S*ince my sixth birthday party at a "paint your own" pottery store, I have not been able to escape my attraction to *activity stores*. Visiting retailers such as Creative Design, a "paint your own pottery" store, Build-A-Bear that allows consumers to choose the features they want on their teddy bear, and Dream Dinners, which is a store of kitchens that consumers pay to use

while they follow the directions of a cooking instructor has become a hobby of mine. Another kind of activity store that I have recently discovered is one including dining and the preparation of food. Restaurants such as Mongolian Barbecue, where you create your own stir fry, and Melting Pot, which allows diners to cook their own meal fondue style creates a new reason to dine out.

The idea behind these activity stores and restaurants is to lure customers in because they will not only be satisfied with the final product

but they will enjoy the experience leading up to it. The entertainment value of this kind of shopping and dining allows consumers to use these stores as a way to socialize with others. This concept of an activity store does not come without a price however; these companies are able to charge a premium because they also provide an enjoyable experience. While it may seem ridiculous to some people that activity restaurants charge more when consumers have to cook their own food, I find it engaging and well worth the money!

---

fresh-fruit martinis, and "buzz bars," where the clientele likes to drink Smirnoff mixed with energy brew Red Bull.[69]

Spontaneous Shopping
When a shopper suddenly decides to buy something in the store, one of two different processes explains this:

1 She engages in **unplanned buying** when she's unfamiliar with a store's layout or perhaps she's under some time pressure. Or, if she sees an item on a store shelf this might remind her she needs it. About one-third of all unplanned buying occurs because a shopper recognizes a new need while she's in the store.[70]
2 She engages in **impulse buying** when she experiences a sudden urge she simply can't resist.[71] A consumer who researchers asked to sketch a typical impulse purchaser drew Figure 9.4.

Retailers typically place so-called *impulse items*, such as candy and gum, near the checkout to cater to these urges. Similarly, many supermarkets install wider aisles to encourage browsing, and the widest tend to feature products with the highest profit margins. They stack low markup items that shoppers purchase regularly in narrower aisles to allow shopping carts to speed through. Starbucks encourages impulse purchasing when it charges customers who want to download songs they hear over the store's speakers directly onto their iPhones.[72]

Point-of-Purchase Stimuli
A well-designed in-store display boosts impulse purchases by as much as 10 percent. That explains why U.S. companies spend more than $13 billion each year on **point-of-purchase (POP) stimuli**. A POP can be an elaborate product display or demonstration, a coupon-dispensing machine, or an employee who gives out free samples of a new cookie in the grocery aisle. Now the pace of POP spending will probably pick up even more—an alliance of major marketers including Procter & Gamble, Coca-Cola, 3M, Kellogg, Miller Brewing, and Wal-Mart is using infrared sensors to measure the reach of in-store marketing efforts. Retailers have long counted the number of shoppers who enter and exit their stores, and they use product barcode data to track what shoppers buy. But big consumer-products

Net Profit

The ShopText company introduced a system that's an impulse buyer's dream (or nightmare). It lets you buy a product instantly when you send a text message—you don't even have to visit a store or a Web site. A woman who spies an ad for a pocketbook in a magazine can order it on the spot as she uses her cell phone to send the code she finds printed next to the item. This type of system is already in limited use. Ads for a CD by singer Tim McGraw carry a texting code, as did magazine write-ups for the final Harry Potter novel. Some charities now accept donations via text messages. To use the system, a consumer must first call ShopText to set up an account and specify a shipping address and credit card number. After that, she can buy everything by thumb.[73]

Figure 9.4 ONE CONSUMER'S IMAGE OF AN IMPULSE BUYER
Source: Dennis Rook, "Is Impulse Buying (Yet) a Useful Marketing Concept?" (unpublished manuscript, University of Southern California, Los Angeles, 1990): Fig. 7-A.

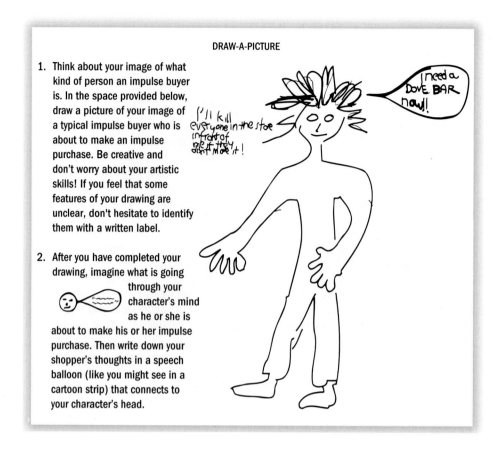

companies also need to know how many people actually walk by their promotional displays so they can evaluate how effective these are. Although it's possible to fool these sensors (they still can't tell if someone simply cuts through to reach the other end of the store), this sophisticated measurement system is a valuable first step that many advertisers eagerly await.[74]

The importance of POP in shopper decision making explains why product packages increasingly play a key role in the marketing mix as they evolve from the functional to the fantastic:

- In the last 100 years, Pepsi changed the look of its can, and before that its bottles, only 10 times. Now the company switches designs every few weeks. And, it's testing cans that spray an aroma when you open one to match the flavor of the drink—such as a wild cherry scent misting from a Wild Cherry Pepsi can.
- Coors Light bottles sport labels that turn blue when the beer is chilled to the right temperature.
- Huggies' Henry the Hippo hand soap bottles have a light that flashes for 20 seconds to show children how long they should wash their hands.
- Evian's "palace bottle" turns up in restaurants and luxury hotels. The bottle has an elegant swanlike neck and sits on a small silver tray.
- Unilever North America sells Axe shower gel bottles shaped like video game joysticks.
- Some companies are considering the insertion of a computer chip and tiny speaker inside a package. This gimmick might be useful for cross-promotion. For example, a package of cheese could say "I go well with Triscuit crackers" when a shopper takes it off the shelf. Of course, this attention-getting trick could backfire if everyone starts to do it. As one ad executive commented, "If you're walking down a row in a supermarket and every package is screaming at you, it sounds like a terrifying, disgusting experience."[75]

The growing practice of mobile couponing encourages in-store decision making.
Source: Courtesy of Hardees.

An in-store kiosk dispenses drug-related information and products.
Source: Courtesy Evincii, Inc.

The Décor bottle by Febreze illustrates how marketers focus on package design to provide a value-added experience. The company boasts that the bottle has a removable wrapper and is ". . . perfect to leave out in the bedroom or living room."

Source: Courtesy of Proctor & Gamble.

Marketing Pitfall

Consumers aren't the only ones who get angry about frustrating service interactions. Many employees have an axe to grind as well. At a Web site a disgruntled former employee of a certain fast-food franchise put up, we share the pain of this ex-burger flipper: "I have seen the creatures that live at the bottom of the dumpster. I have seen the rat by the soda machine. I have seen dead frogs in the fresh salad lettuce." Fries with that?

At the customerssuck.com Web site, restaurant and store workers who have to grin and bear it all day go to vent. Once off the clock, they share their frustrations about the idiocy, slovenliness, and insensitivity of their customers. Some contributors to the Web site share stupid questions their customers ask, such as "How much is a 99-cent cheeseburger?" whereas others complain about working conditions and having to be nice to not-so-nice people. The slogan of the site is "the customer is never right."[78]

3

OBJECTIVE

Why is a salesperson often the crucial link between interest in a product and its actual purchase?

The Salesperson: A Lead Role in the Play

The salesperson is one of the most important players in the retailing drama—as Rob learned in his interaction with Rhoda.[76] As we saw way back in Chapter 1, exchange theory stresses that every interaction involves a trade of value. Each participant gives something to the other and hopes to receive something in return.[77] A (competent) salesperson offers a lot of value because his expert advice makes the shopper's choice easier.

A buyer–seller situation is like many other *dyadic encounters* (two-person groups); it's a relationship where both parties must reach some agreement about the roles of each participant during a process of *identity negotiation*.[79] For example, if Rhoda immediately establishes herself as an expert (and Rob accepts this designation), she is likely to have more influence over him through the course of the relationship. Some of the factors that help to define a salesperson's role (and effectiveness) are her age, appearance, educational level, and motivation to sell.[80]

In addition, more effective salespersons usually know their customers' traits and preferences better than do ineffective salespersons, and they adapt their approach to meet the needs of each specific customer.[81] The ability to be adaptable is especially vital when customers and salespeople have different *interaction styles*.[82] We each vary

NXT body wash/moisturizer cans light up on the store shelf.
Source: Courtesy of NXT/Clio Designs Incorporated.

in the degree of assertiveness we bring to interactions. At one extreme, *nonassertive* people believe it's not socially acceptable to complain, and sales situations may intimidate them. *Assertive* people are more likely to stand up for themselves in a firm but nonthreatening way. *Aggressives* may resort to rudeness and threats if they don't get their way (we've all run into these folks).[83]

4
OBJECTIVE

Why do marketers need to be concerned about a consumer's evaluations of a product after he buys it as well as before?

Postpurchase Satisfaction

Our overall feelings about a product after we've bought it—what researchers call **consumer satisfaction/dissatisfaction (CS/D)**—obviously play a big role in our future behavior. It's a lot easier to sell something once than to sell it again if it bombed the first time. We evaluate the things we buy as we use them and integrate them into our daily consumption activities.[86] In a sense, each of us is a product reviewer whether or not we bother to talk or blog about our experiences.

Companies that score high in customer satisfaction often have a big competitive advantage—especially when so many firms skimp on the attention they pay to customers. A 5-year study of customer satisfaction in the Canadian banking industry provides typical results—banks that provided better service commanded a larger "share of wallet" than did others (i.e., their customers entrusted them with a larger proportion of their money).[87]

Good marketers constantly look for reasons why their customers might be dissatisfied so they can try to improve.[88] For example, United Airlines' advertising agency wanted to identify specific aspects of air travel that ticked people off. Researchers gave frequent flyers crayons and a map that showed different stages in a long-distance trip. Respondents colored in these stages—they used hot hues to symbolize areas that cause stress and anger and cool colors for parts of the trip they associate with satisfaction and calm feelings. Although many of them painted jet cabins in a serene aqua, they colored the ticket counters orange and terminal waiting areas fire-red. As a result, United focused more on improving its overall operations instead of only the in-flight experience.[89]

Just What *Is* Quality?

What do consumers look for in products? That's easy: They want quality and value.[90] However, these terms have slippery meanings that are hard for us to pin down. We

Marketing Pitfall

Not all sales interactions are positive, but some *really* stand out. Here are a few incidents that make the rest of them easier to swallow:

- A woman sued a car dealer in Iowa, claiming that a salesperson persuaded her to climb into the trunk of a Chrysler Concorde to check out its spaciousness. He then slammed the trunk shut and bounced the car several times, apparently to the delight of his coworkers. The manager offered a prize of $100 to the salesperson who could get a customer to climb in.[84]

- A Detroit couple filed a $100 million lawsuit against McDonald's, alleging three McDonald's employees beat them after they tried to return a watery milkshake.

- In Alabama, a McDonald's employee was arrested on second-degree assault charges after she stabbed a customer in the forehead with a ballpoint pen.[85]

infer quality when we rely on cues as diverse as brand name, price, product warranties, and even our estimate of how much money a company invests in its advertising.[91]

In the book *Zen and the Art of Motorcycle Maintenance*, a cult hero of college students in an earlier generation literally went crazy as he tried to figure out the meaning of quality.[93] Marketers appear to use the word *quality* as a catchall term for *good*. Because of its wide and imprecise usage, the attribute of *quality* threatens to become a meaningless claim. If everyone has it, what good is it?

To muddy the waters a bit more, satisfaction or dissatisfaction is more than a reaction to how well a product or service performs. According to the **expectancy disconfirmation model**, we form beliefs about product performance based on prior experience with the product or communications about the product that imply a certain level of quality.[94] When something performs the way we thought it would, we may not think much about it. If it fails to live up to expectations, this may create negative feelings. However, if performance happens to exceed our expectations, we're happy campers.

To understand this perspective, think about how you decide if a restaurant is good or bad depending on the type of place it is. You expect sparkling clear glassware at a fancy eating establishment, and you're not happy if you discover a grimy glass. However, you may not be surprised if you see fingerprints on your beer mug at a lo-

This ad for Ford relies on a common claim about quality.
Source: Courtesy of Ford Motor Co.

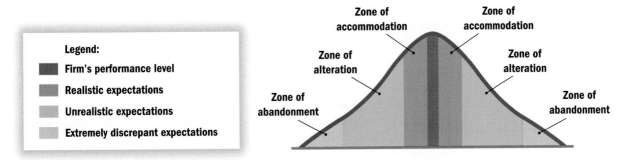

Figure 9.5 CUSTOMER EXPECTATION ZONES
Source: Jagdish N. Sheth and Banwari Mittal, "A Framework for Managing Customer Expectations," *Journal of Market Focused Management* 1 (1996): 137–58.

cal greasy spoon; you may even shrug off this indiscretion because it's part of the place's "charm."

This perspective underscores how important it is to *manage expectations*—we often trace a customer's dissatisfaction to his erroneous expectations of the company's ability to deliver a product or service. NO company is perfect. It's just not realistic to think that everything will always turn out perfectly (although some firms don't even come close!).

Figure 9.5 illustrates the alternative strategies a firm can choose when customers expect too much. The organization can either accommodate these demands as it improves the range or quality of products it offers, alter these expectations, or perhaps choose to "fire the customer" if it is not feasible to meet his needs (banks and credit card companies often do this when they identify customers who don't make them enough money to justify keeping their accounts).[95] How can a marketer alter expectations? For example, a waiter can tell a diner in advance that the portion size she ordered isn't very big, or a car salesperson can warn a buyer that he may smell some strange odors during the break-in period. A firm also can *underpromise*, as Xerox routinely does when it inflates the time it will take for a service rep to visit. When the rep arrives a day earlier, this impresses the customer.

When a product doesn't work as we expect or turns out to be unsafe (like the recent spate of hazardous products from China, ranging from toothpaste to dog food), it's the understatement of the year to say we're not satisfied. In these situations, marketers must immediately take steps to reassure us or risk losing a customer for life. If the company confronts the problem truthfully, we are often willing to forgive and forget; we've seen this happen in incidents over the years when a firm suffers from a negative incident. Examples include Tylenol (product tampering), Chrysler (the company disconnected the odometers on executives' cars and resold them as new— well before the carmaker declared bankruptcy!), or Perrier (traces of the chemical benzene turned up in the drink). But if the firm seems to be dragging its heels or covering up, our resentment grows. This is what happened during Union Carbide's chemical disaster in India, the massive Alaskan oil spill the tanker *Exxon Valdez* caused, and recent corporate scandals such as the collapse of Enron and AIG.

What Can We Do When We're Dissatisfied?

Fifty-four million dollars for a pair of missing pants? A judge in Washington, D.C., made headlines when he filed a $54 million lawsuit against his neighborhood dry cleaner because it lost a pair of his pinstriped suit paints. He claimed that a local consumer protection law entitled him to thousands of dollars for each day over nearly 4 years in which signs at the shop promised "same day service" and "satisfaction guaranteed." The suit dragged on for several months, but at the end of the day the plaintiff went home with empty pockets.[96] And some people charge we have too many lawsuits in this country!

If you're not happy with a product or service, what can you do about it? You have three possible courses of action (though sometimes you can take more than one):[97]

1 **Voice response**—You can appeal directly to the retailer for redress (e.g., a refund).
2 **Private response**—You can express your dissatisfaction to friends and boycott the product or the store where you bought it.
3 **Third-party response**—Like the pantless judge, you can take legal action against the merchant, register a complaint with the Better Business Bureau, or write a letter to the newspaper.

In one study, business majors wrote complaint letters to companies. When the firm sent a free sample in response, this action significantly improved how they felt about it. This didn't happen, however, when they *only* received a letter of apology—but no swag. Even worse, students who got no response reported an even more negative image than before—this shows that *any* kind of response is better than none.[98]

A number of factors influence which route we choose. People are more likely to take action if they're dissatisfied with expensive products such as household durables, cars, and clothing than for inexpensive products.[99] Ironically, consumers who are satisfied with a store in general are more likely to complain if they experience something bad; they take the time to complain because they feel connected to the store. Older people are more likely to complain, and they are much more likely to believe the store will actually resolve the problem. And, if a company resolves the problem, a customer feels even better about it than if she hadn't complained in the first place![100]

However, if the consumer does not believe that the store will respond to her complaint, she will be more likely to simply switch than fight as she just takes her business elsewhere.[101] The moral: Marketers should actually *encourage* consumers to complain to them: People are more likely to spread the word about unresolved negative experiences to their friends than they are to boast about positive occurrences.[102]

TQM: Going to the Gemba

Many analysts who study consumer satisfaction, or those who design new products or services to increase it, recognize that it is crucial to understand how people actually interact with their environment to identify potential problems. To do so they typically conduct *focus groups*—a small set of consumers comes into a facility to try a new item while company personnel observe them from behind a mirror. However, some researchers advocate a more up-close-and-personal approach that allows them to watch people in the actual environment where they consume the product. This perspective originated in the Japanese approach to **total quality management (TQM)**—a complex set of management and engineering procedures that aims to reduce errors and increase quality.

To help them achieve more insight, researchers go to the **gemba**, which to the Japanese means "the one true source of information." According to this philosophy, it's essential to send marketers and designers to the precise place where consumers use the product or service rather than to ask laboratory subjects to use it in a simulated environment.

Figure 9.6 illustrates this idea in practice. Host Foods, which operates food concessions in major airports, sent a team to the *gemba*—in this case, an airport cafeteria—to identify problem areas. Employees watched as customers entered the facility, and then followed them as they inspected the menu, procured silverware, paid, and found a table. The findings were crucial to Host's redesign of the facility. For example, the team identified a common problem many people traveling solo experience: the need to put down one's luggage to enter the food line and the feeling of panic you get because you're not able to keep an eye on your valuables when you get your meal. This simple insight allowed Host to modify the design of its facilities to improve a patron's line-of-sight between the food area and the tables.[104]

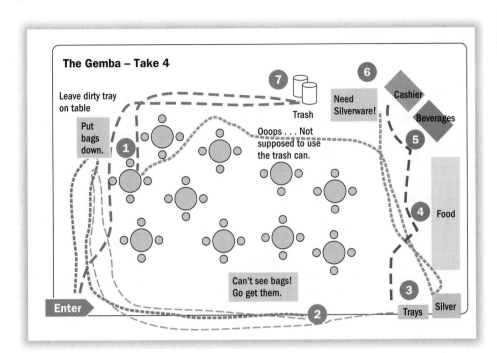

Figure 9.6 GOING TO THE GEMBA
Source: © Quality Function Deployment Institute.
Used with permission.

5

OBJECTIVE

Why is getting rid of products when consumers no longer need or want them a major concern both to marketers and to public policy makers?

Product Disposal

Because we do form strong attachments to some products, it can be painful to dispose of some of our things. Our possessions anchor our identities; our past lives on in our things.[105] Some Japanese ritually "retire" worn-out sewing needles, chopsticks, and even computer chips when they burn them in a ceremony to thank them for years of good service.[106]

Still, we all have to get rid of our "stuff" at some point, either because it's served its purpose or perhaps because it no longer fits with our view of ourselves (like when newlyweds "upgrade" to a real place). Concern about the environment coupled with a need for convenience makes ease of product disposal a key attribute in categories from razors to diapers. And our demand for sustainable products that don't harm the environment when we're done with them creates new markets (such as the carbon offsets we discussed in Chapter 4) and new opportunities for entrepreneurs who find a better alternative.

For example, Terra Cycle is a start-up brand that sells an "exotic" product: A key ingredient on its label is "liquefied worm poop." A 25-year-old college dropout founded the company—company literature confesses that he was trying to grow "certain plants" in a worm bin inside his college apartment in order to "harvest the buds" when he stumbled on the idea. Inspiration comes from many sources! Terra Cycle makes fertilizer products it packages in used plastic bottles, many of which the company itself collects through a nationwide recycling program it organized. Terra Cycle claims that waste packaged in waste makes it the "ultimate eco-friendly" product. The fertilizer comes from containers filled with shredded newspaper, food scraps—and worms who eat this waste and digest it. The resulting "poop" happens to make great plant food.[107]

Disposal Options

In many cases, we acquire a new product even though the old one still functions—perhaps that's one of the hallmarks of our materialistic society. Some reasons to replace an item include a desire for new features, a change in the individual's environment (e.g., a refrigerator is the wrong color for a freshly painted kitchen), or a change in the person's role or self-image.[108]

The issue of product disposition is vital because of its enormous public policy implications. We live in a throwaway society, which creates problems for the environment and also results in a great deal of unfortunate waste. One study reported that we never use as much as 12 percent of the grocery products we buy; consumers buy nearly two-thirds of these *abandoned products* for a specific purpose such as a recipe and then change their plans. Because we don't use these items immediately, they slowly get pushed to the back of the cupboard and forgotten.[109] Some of those "science projects" that grow in the back of your refrigerator might qualify. In another survey, 15 percent of adults admitted they are *pack rats,* and another 64 percent said they are selective savers. In contrast, 20 percent say they throw out as much garbage as they can. The consumers most likely to save things are older people and those who live alone.[110]

Training consumers to recycle has become a priority in many countries. In Japan, residents sort their garbage into as many as 44 different categories; for example, if they discard one sock it goes into a bin for burnables, but if they throw out a pair it goes into used cloth, though only if the socks "are not torn, and the left and right sock match."[111]

A study examined the relevant goals consumers have when they recycle. It used a means–end chain analysis of the type we described in Chapter 4 to identify how consumers link specific instrumental goals to more abstract terminal values. Researchers identified the most important lower-order goals to be "avoid filling up landfills," "reduce waste," "reuse materials," and "save the environment." They linked these to the terminal values of "promote health/avoid sickness," "achieve life-sustaining ends," and "provide for future generations."

Another study reported that the perceived effort involved in recycling was the best predictor of whether people would go to the trouble—this pragmatic dimension outweighed general attitudes toward recycling and the environment in predicting intention to recycle.[112] When researchers apply these techniques to study recycling and other product disposal behaviors, it will be easier for social marketers to design advertising copy and other messages that tap into the underlying values that will motivate people to increase environmentally responsible behavior.[113]

Lateral Cycling: Junk Versus "Junque"

During **lateral cycling**, one consumer exchanges something she owns with someone else for something she owns. Reusing other people's things is especially important in our throwaway society because, as one researcher put it, "there is no longer an 'away' to throw things to."[114] Although traditional marketers don't pay much attention to used-product sellers, factors such as concern about the environment, demands for quality, and cost and fashion consciousness make these "secondary" markets more important.[115] In fact, economic estimates of this **underground economy** range from 3 to 30 percent of the gross national product of the United States and up to 70 percent of the gross domestic product of other countries. Trade publications such as *Yesteryear, Swap Meet Merchandising, Collectors Journal, The Vendor Newsletter,* and *The Antique Trader* offer reams of practical advice to consumers who want to bypass formal retailers and swap merchandise.

In the United States alone, there are more than 3,500 flea markets—including at least a dozen huge operations such as the 60-acre Orange County Marketplace in California—that operate nationwide to produce upward of $10 billion in gross sales.[116] Other growth areas include student markets for used computers and textbooks, as well as ski swaps, at which consumers exchange millions of dollars worth of used ski equipment. A new generation of secondhand store owners is developing markets for everything from used office equipment to cast-off kitchen sinks. Many are nonprofit ventures started with government funding. A trade association called the Reuse Development Organization (redo.org) encourages them.[117]

The Internet revolutionizes the lateral cycling process, as millions of people flock to eBay to buy and sell their "treasures." And entrepreneurs keep coming up with new ways to facilitate online bartering. At Peerflix 250,000 members post titles of DVDs they want to trade; the company helps out by providing printable forms that include postage and the recipient's address. PaperBackSwap's members trade 30,000 books weekly for $1.59 apiece.[118]

Lateral cycling is literally a lifestyle for some people with an anticonsumerist bent who call themselves **freegans** (this label is a takeoff on *vegans,* who shun all animal products). Freegans are modern-day scavengers who live off discards as a political statement against corporations and consumerism. They forage through supermarket trash and eat the slightly bruised produce or just-expired canned goods that we routinely throw out, and negotiate gifts of surplus food from sympathetic stores and restaurants. Freegans dress in castoff clothes and furnish their homes with items they find on the street. They get the word on locations where people throw out a lot of stuff (end-of-semester dorm cleanouts are a prime target) as they check out postings at <u>freecycle.org</u> where users post unwanted items and at so-called *freemeets* (flea markets where no one exchanges money).[119]

If our possessions do indeed come to be a part of us, how do we bring ourselves to part with these precious items? The way we divest ourselves of our things may make a statement (think about throwing out things an ex-partner gave you). One study found that people who are very attached to their "stuff" may engage a *professional organizer* to help them declutter and simplify their lives; in essence the organizer is an intermediary who helps the person to detach from reminders of his former life so that he can move on.[120]

Some researchers examined how consumers practice **divestment rituals**, where they take steps to gradually distance themselves from things they treasure so that they can sell them or give them away (more on rituals in Chapter 15). As they observed people getting items ready to be sold at garage sales, the researchers identified these rituals:

- **Iconic transfer ritual**—Taking pictures and videos of objects before we sell them.
- **Transition-place ritual**—Putting items in an out-of-the way location such as a garage or attic before we dipose of them.
- **Ritual cleansing**—Washing, ironing, and/or meticulously wrapping the item.[121]

CHAPTER SUMMARY

Now that you have finished reading this chapter you should understand why:

 Many factors over and above the qualities of the product or service influence the outcome of a transaction. Factors at the time of purchase dramatically influence the consumer decision-making process.

Many factors affect a purchase. These include the consumer's antecedent state (e.g., his or her mood, time pressure, or disposition toward shopping). Time is an important resource that often determines how much effort and search will go into a decision. Our moods are influenced by the degree of pleasure and arousal a store environment creates.

The usage context of a product is a segmentation variable; consumers look for different product attributes depending on the use to which they intend to put their purchase. The presence or absence of other people (co-consumers)—and the types of people they are—can also affect a consumer's decisions.

The shopping experience is a pivotal part of the purchase decision. In many cases, retailing is like theater—the con-sumer's evaluation of stores and products may depend on the type of "performance" he witnesses. The actors (e.g., sales-people), the setting (the store environment), and props (e.g., store displays) influence this evaluation. Like a brand personality, a number of factors, such as perceived convenience, sophistication, and expertise of salespeople, determine store image. With increasing competition from nonstore alternatives, creating a positive shopping experience has never been more important. Online shopping is growing in importance, and this new way to acquire products has both good (e.g., convenience) and bad (e.g., security) aspects.

 In addition to what a shopper already knows or believes about a product, information a store or Web site provides can strongly influence a purchase decision.

Because we don't make many purchase decisions until we're actually in the store, point-of-purchase (POP) stimuli are very important sales tools. These include product samples, elaborate package displays, place-based media, and in-store promotional materials such as "shelf talkers." POP stimuli are particularly useful in promoting impulse buying, which happens when a consumer yields to a sudden urge for a product.

A salesperson can be the crucial link between interest in a product and its actual purchase.

The consumer's encounter with a salesperson is a complex and important process. The outcome can be affected by such factors as the salesperson's similarity to the customer and his or her perceived credibility.

 Marketers need to be concerned about a consumer's evaluations of a product after he buys it as well as before.

A person's overall feelings about the product after he buys determine consumer satisfaction/dissatisfaction. Many fac-

tors influence our perceptions of product quality, including price, brand name, and product performance. Our degree of satisfaction often depends on the extent to which a product's performance is consistent with our prior expectations of how well it will function.

 Getting rid of products when consumers no longer need or want them is a major concern both to marketers and to public policy makers.

Product disposal is an increasingly important problem. Recycling is one option that will become more crucial as consumers' environmental awareness grows. Lateral cycling occurs when we buy, sell, or barter secondhand objects.

KEY TERMS

Activity stores, 361
Atmospherics, 361
Being space, 358
Co-consumers, 349
Consumer satisfaction/
    dissatisfaction (CS/D), 367
Divestment rituals, 373
Expectancy disconfirmation model, 368

Freegans, 373
Gemba, 370
Gripe sites, 370
Impulse buying, 363
Lateral cycling, 372
Minipreneurs, 359
Point-of-purchase (POP) stimuli, 363
Pop-up stores, 360

Queuing theory, 352
Retail theming, 358
Shopping orientation, 355
Store image, 360
Time poverty, 350
Total quality management (TQM), 370
Underground economy, 372
Unplanned buying, 363

REVIEW

1 What do we mean by situational self-image? Give an example of this phenomenon.
2 Describe the difference between density and crowding. Why is this difference relevant in purchase environments?
3 What is time poverty, and how can it influence our purchase decisions?
4 What are the two dimensions that determine whether we will react positively or negatively to a purchase environment?
5 List three separate motivations for shopping, and give an example of each.

6 What are some important pros and cons of e-commerce?
7 List three factors that help to determine store image.
8 What is the difference between unplanned buying and impulse buying?
9 How do a consumer's prior expectations about product quality influence his satisfaction with the product after he buys it?
10 List three actions a consumer can take if he is dissatisfied with a purchase.
11 What is the underground economy and why is it important to marketers?

CONSUMER BEHAVIOR CHALLENGE

■ DISCUSS

1 Is the customer always right? Why or why not?
2 Are pop-up stores simply a fad or a retailing concept that's here to stay?
3 Discuss some of the shopping motivations the chapter describes. How might a retailer adjust its strategy to accommodate these motivations?
4 What are some positive and negative aspects of a policy that requires employees who interact with customers to wear a uniform?

5 Think about exceptionally good and bad salespeople you have encountered as a shopper. What qualities seem to differentiate them from others?
6 Discuss the concept of "timestyle." Based on your own experiences, how might we segment consumers in terms of their timestyles?
7 Several men's clothing retailers nationwide now provide free booze to their male clientele to encourage

them to hang out in their stores.[122] Is it ethical to encourage customers to get wasted before they shop?

8   Compare and contrast different cultures' conceptions of time. What are some implications for marketing strategy within each of these frameworks?

9   The movement away from a "disposable consumer society" toward one that emphasizes creative recycling creates many opportunities for marketers. Can you identify some?

10   Some retailers work hard to cultivate a certain look or image, and they may even choose employees who fit this look. Abercrombie & Fitch, for example, seems to link itself to a clean-cut, all-American image. At one point a lawsuit claimed that Abercrombie & Fitch systematically "refuses to hire qualified minority applicants as brand representatives to work on the sales floor and discourages applications from minority applicants" (Abercrombie replied that it has "zero tolerance for discrimination")[123] And, we know the Hooters restaurant chain is notorious for its attractive female waitresses. Should a retailer have the right to recruit employees who are consistent with its image even if this means excluding certain types of people (e.g., non-Caucasians, men) from the sales floor?

11   The mall of the future will most likely be less about purchasing products than about exploring them in a physical setting. This means that retail environments will have to become places to build brand images, rather than simply places to sell products. What are some strategies stores can use to enhance the emotional/sensory experiences they give to shoppers?

12   The store environment is heating up as more and more companies put their promotional dollars into point-of-purchase efforts. Some stores confront shoppers with videos at the checkout counter, computer monitors attached to their shopping carts, and ads stenciled on the floors. And we're increasingly exposed to ads in nonshopping environments. A health club in New York was forced to remove TV monitors that showed advertising on the Health Club Media Networks—exercisers claimed they interfered with their workouts. Do you feel that these innovations are overly intrusive? At what point might shoppers rebel and demand some peace and quiet when they shop? Do you see any market potential in the future for stores that "countermarket" by promising a "hands-off" shopping environment?

13   Courts often prohibit special interest groups from distributing literature in shopping malls. Mall managements claim that these centers are private property. However, these groups argue that the mall is the modern-day version of the town square and as such is a public forum. Find some recent court cases involving this free-speech issue, and examine the arguments pro and con. What is the current status of the mall as a public forum? Do you agree with this concept?

■ APPLY

1   Conduct naturalistic observation at a local mall. Sit in a central location and observe the activities of mall employees and patrons. Keep a log of the nonretailing activity you observe (e.g., special performances, exhibits, socializing, etc.). Does this activity enhance or detract from business the mall conducts? As malls become more like high-tech game rooms, how valid is the criticism that shopping areas only encourage more loitering by teenage boys, who don't spend a lot in stores and simply scare away other customers?

2   Select three competing clothing stores in your area and conduct a store image study for them. Ask a group of consumers to rate each store on a set of attributes and plot these ratings on the same graph. Based on your findings, are there any areas of competitive advantage or disadvantage you could bring to the attention of store management?

3   Using Table 9.1 as a model, construct a person–situation segmentation matrix for a brand of perfume.

4   What applications of queuing theory can you find that local services use? Interview consumers as they wait in line to determine how their experience affects their satisfaction with the service.

5   Interactive tools allow surfers on sites such as LandsEnd.com to view apparel product selections on virtual models in full, 360-degree rotational view. In some cases, the viewer can modify the bodies, face, skin coloring, and the hairstyles of these models. In others, the consumer can project his *own* likeness into the space by scanning a photo into a "makeover" program. Visit LandsEnd.com or another site that offers a personalized mannequin. Surf around. Try on some clothes. How was your experience? How helpful was this mannequin? When you shop for clothes online, would you rather see how they look on a body with dimensions the same as yours or on a different body? What advice can you give Web site designers who personalize these shopping environments when they create lifelike models to guide you through the site?

6   Interview people when they sell items at a flea market or garage sale. Ask them to identify some items to which they had a strong attachment. Then, see if you can prompt them to describe one or more divestment rituals they went through as they prepared to offer these items for sale.

7   Identify three people who own electric coffeemakers. Then, "go to the gemba" by observing them as they actually prepare coffee in the appliance at home. Based on these experiences, what recommendations might you make to the designer of a new coffeemaker model that would improve customers' experiences with the product?

Case Study

GIVING AND RECEIVING ON FREECYCLE.ORG

Like it or not, we live in a disposable society. And it isn't just paper products and fast-food containers we throw away. We use our televisions, computers, cell phones, furniture, clothing, and other products until something better comes along, and then we toss them. Landfills everywhere reel under the onslaught of trash we create.

But what if people could find someone to take their old junk off their hands? Or what if individuals could find a needed item that someone just so happens to be throwing away? Freecycle.org meets this need. This Web site came into being as a recycling concept to reduce the strain on landfills and cut down on consumer wastefulness. Freecycle, which uses a bulletin board structure, works so well because it's so simple. It connects people who have items to give away with others who need them, and vice versa. It's basically like an "eBay for free." Indeed, many users call the site by its nickname of "Freebay."

From its humble beginnings in the Tucson, Arizona, area in 2003, today there are millions of members who comprise thousands of user communities in over 75 countries; they say they are "changing the world one gift at a time." Freecycle.org is one of the most popular nonprofit destinations in cyberspace; *Time* dubbed it "one of the 50 coolest" Web sites. This notoriety comes within a few short years and with no promotion other than word of mouth and plenty of free publicity.

Anyone can join this 24/7 virtual garage sale, and membership is free. In fact, the main rule of Freecycle.org is that you can only offer free items. Givers and receivers contact each other via e-mail and then arrange for delivery. The site's founder estimates that the average freecycled item weighs 1 pound. That means that the Freecycle movement keeps 400 tons of "garbage" out of landfills every day.

This is certainly a sign of success. But other measures of success have become apparent as well, like the satisfaction of all those involved. What one person doesn't want, someone else will take off their hands. In this exchange everyone wins. "It's become a huge gift economy and very life affirming for everyone who has given away something. You can't help but get a good feeling when you've helped another person," the founder said.

As long as people want to get rid of or acquire an old couch, a six-year-old husky, a storm door, a van that needs a transmission, or even horse manure, Freecycle has a bright future. "When it comes to the Internet and connecting with one another, there are no limitations," Beal said. "We'll continue growing and experiencing the goodness that comes from giving."

DISCUSSION QUESTIONS

1 Why do you think Freecycle.org has achieved such high levels of growth in such a short period of time?
2 Freecycle created an alternative disposal option that is rapidly growing. Discuss ways that freecycling might affect the purchase habits of consumers.
3 Should for-profit businesses like eBay get into the freecycling business? Should companies motivate more consumers to give things away that they might otherwise be able to sell or auction? Can they still make a profit while they help to eliminate waste?

Sources: Tamsin Kelly, "Multi-Bargain Swap Shop," *Daily Telegraph* (July 7, 2007): 13; "A Brief History," www.freecycle.org, accessed September 2007; "Free Swap Program Finds Homes for Recycled Goods," *Wall Street Journal* (January 2, 2008); Mac McLean, "Don't Throw Unwanted Items Away," *Bristol Herald Courier* (January 13, 2009).

NOTES

1. Keith Naughton, "Revolution in the Showroom," *BusinessWeek* (February 19, 1996): 70.
2. Quoted in "Denny's Targets College Kids with Late-Night Campaign," *PROMO* (April 9, 2007), www.promo.com, accessed April 9, 2007.
3. David Kesmodel, "More Marketers Place Web Ads by Time of Day," *Wall Street Journal* (June 23, 2006): B1.
4. Pradeep Kakkar and Richard J. Lutz, "Situational Influence on Consumer Behavior: A Review," in Harold H. Kassarjian and Thomas S. Robertson, eds., *Perspectives in Consumer Behavior*, 3rd ed. (Glenview, IL: Scott, Foresman, 1981): 204–14.
5. Ibid.
6. Benedict Carey, "TV Time, Unlike Child Care, Ranks High in Mood Study," *New York Times* ((December 3, 2004), www.nytimes.com, accessed December 3, 2004.
7. Carolyn Turner Schenk and Rebecca H. Holman, "A Sociological Approach to Brand Choice: The Concept of Situational Self-Image," in Jerry C. Olson, ed., *Advances in Consumer Research* 7 (Ann Arbor, MI: Association for Consumer Research, 1980): 610–14.
8. Peter R. Dickson, "Person–Situation: Segmentation's Missing Link," *Journal of Marketing* 46 (Fall 1982): 56–64.
9. Ellen Byron, "How Coach Won a Rich Purse by Inventing New Uses for Bags: What Was a Semiannual Buy Is Now a Regular Ritual; Wristlets, Clutches, Totes, Fresh Competition from Gap," *Wall Street Journal* (November 17, 2004): A1.
10. Alan R. Hirsch, "Effects of Ambient Odors on Slot-Machine Usage in a Las Vegas Casino," *Psychology & Marketing* 12 (October 1995): 585–94.
11. Daniel Stokols, "On the Distinction Between Density and Crowding: Some Implications for Future Research," *Psychological Review* 79 (1972): 275–77.
12. Carol Felker Kaufman, Paul M. Lane, and Jay D. Lindquist, "Exploring More Than 24 Hours a Day: A Preliminary Investigation of Polychronic Time Use," *Journal of Consumer Research* 18 (December 1991): 392–401.
13. Laurence P. Feldman and Jacob Hornik, "The Use of Time: An Integrated Conceptual Model," *Journal of Consumer Research* 7 (March 1981): 407–19; see also Michelle M. Bergadaa, "The Role of

Time in the Action of the Consumer," *Journal of Consumer Research* 17 (December 1990): 289–302.

14. Alan Zarembo, "What If There Weren't Any Clocks to Watch?" *Newsweek* (June 30, 1997): 14; based on research reported in Robert Levine, *A Geography of Time: The Temporal Misadventures of a Social Psychologist, or How Every Culture Keeps Time Just a Little Bit Differently* (New York: Basic Books, 1997).

15. Deborah Kotz, "Wives Do More Housework, Study Shows," *U.S. News & World Report* (April 7, 2008), http://health.usnews.com/blogs/on-women/2008/04/07/wives-do-more-housework-study-shows.html, accessed June 8, 2009; John P. Robinson, "Time Squeeze," *Advertising Age* (February 1990): 30–33.

16. Quoted in Stephanie Rosenbloom, "www.FriesWithThat?.com," *New York Times* (August 5, 2007), www.nytimes.com, accessed August 5, 2007.

17. June S. Cotte, S. Ratneshwar, and David Glen Mick, "The Times of Their Lives: Phenomenological and Metaphorical Characteristics of Consumer Timestyles," *Journal of Consumer Research* 31 (September 2004): 333–45.

18. James Gorman, "Does This Mean People Turned Off, Tuned Out and Dropped In?" *New York Times* (June 27, 2006), www.nytimes.com, accessed June 27, 2006.

19. Robert J. Graham, "The Role of Perception of Time in Consumer Research," *Journal of Consumer Research* 7 (March 1981): 335–42; Esther S. Page-Wood, Paul M. Lane, and Carol J. Kaufman, "The Art of Time," *Proceedings of the 1990 Academy of Marketing Science Conference*, ed. B. J. Dunlap, Vol. XIII, Cullowhee, NC: Academy of Marketing Science (1990): 56–61.

20. Dhruv Grewal, Julie Baker, Michael Levy, and Glenn B. Voss, "The Effects of Wait Expectations and Store Atmosphere Evaluations on Patronage Intentions in Service-Intensive Retail Store," *Journal of Retailing* 79 (2003): 259–68; cf. also Shirley Taylor, "Waiting for Service: The Relationship Between Delays and Evaluations of Service," *Journal of Marketing* 58 (April 1994): 56–69.

21. "We're Hating the Waiting; 43% Prefer Self-Service," *Marketing Daily* (January 23, 2007), www.mediapost.com, accessed January 23, 2007.

22. David H. Maister, "The Psychology of Waiting Lines," in John A. Czepiel, Michael R. Solomon, and Carol F. Surprenant, eds., *The Service Encounter: Managing Employee/Customer Interaction in Service Businesses* (Lexington, MA: Lexington Books, 1985): 113–24.

23. David Leonhardt, "Airlines Using Technology in a Push for Shorter Lines," *New York Times* (May 8, 2000), www.nytimes.com, accessed May 8, 2000.

24. Jennifer Ordonez, "An Efficiency Drive: Fast-Food Lanes, Equipped with Timers, Get Even Faster," *Wall Street Journal* (May 18, 2000), www.wsj.com, accessed May 18, 2000.

25. Quoted in A. Pawlowski, "Queuing Psychology: Can Waiting in Line Be Fun?" *CNN* (November 26, 2008), www.cnn.com/2008/TECH/science/11/20/queuing.psychology/index.html?eref=rss...; accessed November 26, 2008; Dawn C. Chmielewski, "Disney, Verizon to Turn the Cellphone into a Theme-Park Visitor's Tool," *Los Angeles Times*, November 12, 2008, www.latimes.com/business/La-Fi-Disney12-2008nov12,0,4711602.Story?Track=Rss, accessed November 12, 2008.

26. Henry Fountain, quoted in "The Ultimate Body Language: How You Line Up for Mickey," *New York Times* (September 18, 2005), accessed September 18, 2005.

27. Christine Bittar, "Massage in Aisle 7: Whole Foods Opens Spa," *Marketing Daily* (December 13, 2006), www.mediapost.com, accessed December 13, 2006.

28. Laurette Dube and Bernd H. Schmitt, "The Processing of Emotional and Cognitive Aspects of Product Usage in Satisfaction Judgments," in Rebecca H. Holman and Michael R. Solomon, eds., *Advances in Consumer Research* 18 (Provo, UT: Association for Consumer Research, 1991): 52–56; Lalita A. Manrai and Meryl P. Gardner, "The Influence of Affect on Attributions for Product Failure," in Rebecca H. Holman and Michael R. Solomon, eds., *Advances in Consumer Research* 18 (Provo, UT: Association for Consumer Research, 1991): 249–54.

29. Kevin G. Celuch and Linda S. Showers, "It's Time to Stress Stress: The Stress–Purchase/Consumption Relationship," in Rebecca H. Holman and Michael R. Solomon, eds., *Advances in Consumer Research* 18 (Provo, UT: Association for Consumer Research, 1991): 284–89; Lawrence R. Lepisto, J. Kathleen Stuenkel, and Linda K. Anglin, "Stress: An Ignored Situational Influence," in Rebecca H. Holman and Michael R. Solomon, eds., *Advances in Consumer Research* 18 (Provo, UT: Association for Consumer Research, 1991): 296–302.

30. Velitchka D. Kaltcheva and Barton A. Weitz, "When Should a Retailer Create an Exciting Store Environment?" *Journal of Marketing* 70 (January 2006): 107–118.

31. John D. Mayer and Yvonne N. Gaschke, "The Experience and Meta-Experience of Mood," *Journal of Personality and Social Psychology* 55 (July 1988): 102–11.

32. Meryl Paula Gardner, "Mood States and Consumer Behavior: A Critical Review," *Journal of Consumer Research* 12 (December 1985): 281–300; Scott Dawson, Peter H. Bloch, and Nancy M. Ridgway, "Shopping Motives, Emotional States, and Retail Outcomes," *Journal of Retailing* 66 (Winter 1990): 408–27; Patricia A. Knowles, Stephen J. Grove, and W. Jeffrey Burroughs, "An Experimental Examination of Mood States on Retrieval and Evaluation of Advertisement and Brand Information," *Journal of the Academy of Marketing Science* 21 (April 1993): 135–43; Paul W. Miniard, Sunil Bhatla, and Deepak Sirdeskmuhk, "Mood as a Determinant of Postconsumption Product Evaluations: Mood Effects and Their Dependency on the Affective Intensity of the Consumption Experience," *Journal of Consumer Psychology* 1, no. 2 (1992): 173–95; Mary T. Curren and Katrin R. Harich, "Consumers' Mood States: The Mitigating Influence of Personal Relevance on Product Evaluations," *Psychology & Marketing* 11 (March–April 1994): 91–107; Gerald J. Gorn, Marvin E. Goldberg, and Kunal Basu, "Mood, Awareness, and Product Evaluation," *Journal of Consumer Psychology* 2, no. 3 (1993): 237–56.

33. Gordon C. Bruner, "Music, Mood, and Marketing," *Journal of Marketing* 54 (October 1990): 94–104; Basil G. Englis, "Music Television and Its Influences on Consumers, Consumer Culture, and the Transmission of Consumption Messages," in Rebecca H. Holman and Michael R. Solomon, eds., *Advances in Consumer Research* 18 (Provo, UT: Association for Consumer Research, 1991): 111–14.

34. Marvin E. Goldberg and Gerald J. Gorn, "Happy and Sad TV Programs: How They Affect Reactions to Commercials," *Journal of Consumer Research* 14 (December 1987): 387–403; Gorn, Goldberg, and Basu, "Mood, Awareness, and Product Evaluation"; Curren and Harich, "Consumers' Mood States."

35. Rajeev Batra and Douglas M. Stayman, "The Role of Mood in Advertising Effectiveness," *Journal of Consumer Research* 17 (September 1990): 203; John P. Murry, Jr., and Peter A. Dacin, "Cognitive Moderators of Negative-Emotion Effects: Implications for Understanding Media Context," *Journal of Consumer Research* 22 (March 1996): 439–47; see also Curren and Harich, "Consumers' Mood States"; Gorn, Goldberg, and Basu, "Mood, Awareness, and Product Evaluation."

36. Jeffrey Zaslow, "Happiness Inc.," *Wall Street Journal* (March 18, 2006): P1.

37. For a scale to assess these dimensions of the shopping experience, see Barry J. Babin, William R. Darden, and Mitch Griffin, "Work and/or Fun: Measuring Hedonic and Utilitarian Shopping Value," *Journal of Consumer Research* 20 (March 1994): 644–56.

38. Kaltcheva and Weitz "When Should a Retailer Create an Exciting Store Environment?"

39. Babin, Darden, and Griffin, "Work and/or Fun."

40. Edward M. Tauber, "Why Do People Shop?" *Journal of Marketing* 36 (October 1972): 47–48.

41. Ann Zimmerman and Laura Stevens, "Attention, Shoppers: Bored College Kids Competing in Aisle 6," *Wall Street Journal* (February 23, 2005).

42. Robert C. Prus, *Making Sales: Influence as Interpersonal Accomplishment* (Newbury Park, CA: Sage Publications, 1989): 225.

43. Michael-Lee Johnstone and Denise M Conroy, "Dressing for the Thrill: An Exploration of Why Women Dress Up to Go Shopping," *Journal of Consumer Behaviour* 4, no. 4 (2005): 234.

44. Some material in this section was adapted from Michael R. Solomon and Elnora W. Stuart, *Welcome to Marketing.com: The Brave New World of E-Commerce* (Upper Saddle River, NJ: Prentice Hall, 2001).

45. June Cotte and Kathryn A. Latour, "Blackjack in the Kitchen: Understanding Online Versus Casino Gambling," *Journal of Consumer Research* 35 (February 2009): 742–58.

46. Rebecca K. Ratner, Barbara E. Kahn, and Daniel Kahneman, "Choosing Less-Preferred Experiences for the Sake of Variety," *Journal of Consumer Research* 26 (June 1999): 1–15.

47. www.allurent.com/newsDetail.php?newsid=20, accessed January 29, 2007.

48. Stephanie Rosenbloom, "Malls Test Experimental Waters to Fill Vacancies," *New York Times* (April 4, 2009), www.nytimes.com/2009/04/05/business/05mall.html?_r=1, accessed April 4, 2009.

49. Vanessa O'Connell, "Fictional Hershey Factory Will Send Kisses to Broadway," *Wall Street Journal* (August 5, 2002), www.wsj.com, accessed August 5, 2002.

50. Millie Creighton, "The Seed of Creative Lifestyle Shopping: Wrapping Consumerism in Japanese Store Layouts," in John F. Sherry Jr., ed., *Servicescapes: The Concept of Place in Contemporary Markets* (Lincolnwood, IL: NTC Business Books, 1998): 199–228; also cf. Robert V.

Kozinets, John F. Sherry, Diana Storm, Adam Duhachek, Krittinee Nuttavuthisit, and Benet DeBerry-Spence, "Ludic Agency and Retail Spectacle," *Journal of Consumer Research* 31 (December 2004): 658–72.

51. Jennifer Saranow, "Retailers Give It the Old College Try," *Wall Street Journal* (August 28, 2008): B8; *March 2007 Trend Briefing*, www.trend-watching.com/briefing, accessed March 30, 2007.

52. Most measures of store image are quite similar to other attitude measures discussed in Chapter 7. For an excellent bibliography of store image studies, see Mary R. Zimmer and Linda L. Golden, "Impressions of Retail Stores: A Content Analysis of Consumer Images," *Journal of Retailing* 64 (Fall 1988): 265–93.

53. Spiggle and Sewall, "A Choice Sets Model of Retail Selection."

54. Robin Sidel, "WaMu's Branches Lose the Smiles," *Wall Street Journal* (April 7, 2009), http://online.wsj.com/article/SB123906012127494969.html, accessed April 7, 2009.

55. "The Science of Shopping: The Way the Brain Buys," *The Economist* (December 18, 2008), www.economist.com, accessed February 2, 2009.

56. Philip Kotler, "Atmospherics as a Marketing Tool," *Journal of Retailing* (Winter 1973–74): 10; Anna Mattila and Jochen Wirtz, "Congruency of Scent and Music as a Driver of In-Store Evaluations and Behavior," *Journal of Retailing* 77, no. 2 (2001): 273–89; J. Duncan Herrington, "An Integrative Path Model of the Effects of Retail Environments on Shopper Behavior," in Robert L. King, ed., *Marketing: Toward the Twenty-First Century* (Richmond, VA: Southern Marketing Association, 1991): 58–62; see also Ann E. Schlosser, "Applying the Functional Theory of Attitudes to Understanding the Influence of Store Atmosphere on Store Inferences," *Journal of Consumer Psychology* 7, no. 4 (1998): 345–69.

57. Joseph A. Bellizzi and Robert E. Hite, "Environmental Color, Consumer Feelings, and Purchase Likelihood," *Psychology & Marketing* 9 (September–October 1992): 347–63.

58. See Eric R. Spangenberg, Ayn E. Crowley, and Pamela W. Henderson, "Improving the Store Environment: Do Olfactory Cues Affect Evaluations and Behaviors?" *Journal of Marketing* 60 (April 1996): 67–80, for a study that assessed olfaction in a controlled, simulated store environment.

59. Robert J. Donovan, John R. Rossiter, Gilian Marcoolyn, and Andrew Nesdale, "Store Atmosphere and Purchasing Behavior," *Journal of Retailing* 70, no. 3 (1994): 283–94.

60. www.buildabear.com, accessed June 9, 2009.

61. Deborah Blumenthal, "Scenic Design for In-Store Try-ons," *New York Times* (April 9, 1988): N9.

62. John Pierson, "If Sun Shines in, Workers Work Better, Buyers Buy More," *Wall Street Journal* (November 20, 1995): B1.

63. Charles S. Areni and David Kim, "The Influence of In-Store Lighting on Consumers' Examination of Merchandise in a Wine Store," *International Journal of Research in Marketing* 11, no. 2 (March 1994): 117–25.

64. Jean-Charles Chebat, Claire Gelinas Chebat, and Dominique Vaillant, "Environmental Background Music and In-Store Selling," *Journal of Business Research* 54 (2001): 115–23; Judy I. Alpert and Mark I. Alpert, "Music Influences on Mood and Purchase Intentions," *Psychology & Marketing* 7 (Summer 1990): 109–34.

65. "Slow Music Makes Fast Drinkers," *Psychology Today* (March 1989): 18.

66. Brad Edmondson, "Pass the Meat Loaf," *American Demographics* (January 1989): 19.

67. "Through the Looking Glass," *Lifestyle Monitor* 16 (Fall–Winter 2002).

68. Jennifer Lach, "Meet You in Aisle Three," *American Demographics* (April 1999): 41.

69. Ernest Beck, "Diageo Attempts to Reinvent the Bar in an Effort to Increase Spirits Sales," *Wall Street Journal* (February 23, 2001), www.wsj.com, accessed October 1, 2007.

70. Easwar S. Iyer, "Unplanned Purchasing: Knowledge of Shopping Environment and Time Pressure," *Journal of Retailing* 65 (Spring 1989): 40–57; C. Whan Park, Easwar S. Iyer, and Daniel C. Smith, "The Effects of Situational Factors on In-Store Grocery Shopping," *Journal of Consumer Research* 15 (March 1989): 422–33.

71. Yinlong Zhang and L. J. Shrum, "The Influence of Self-Construal on Impulsive Consumption" *Journal of Consumer Research* 35 (February 2009): 838–50; Kathleen D. Vohs and Ronald J. Faber, "Spent Resources: Self-Regulatory Resource Availability Affects Impulse Buying, *Journal of Consumer Research* 33 (March 2007): 537–47; Dennis W. Rook and Robert J. Fisher, "Normative Influences on Impulsive Buying Behavior," *Journal of Consumer Research* 22 (December 1995): 305–13; Francis Piron, "Defining Impulse Purchasing," in Rebecca H. Holman and Michael R. Solomon, eds., *Advances in Consumer Research* 18 (Provo, UT: Association for Consumer Research, 1991): 509–14; Dennis W. Rook, "The Buying Impulse," *Journal of Consumer Research* 14 (September 1987): 189–99.

72. Matt Richtel, "At Starbucks, Songs of Instant Gratification," *New York Times* (October 1, 2007), www.nytimes.com, accessed October 1, 2007.

73. www.shoptext.com, accessed June 9, 2009; Louise Story, "New Form of Impulse: Shopping via Text Message," *New York Times* (April 16, 2007), www.nytimes.com, accessed April 16, 2007.

74. Ellen Byron and Suzanne Vranica, "Scanners Check Out Who's Browsing Marketers, Retailers Test Sensors to Weigh Reach of In-Store Promotions," *Wall Street Journal* (September 27, 2006): B2; cf. also www.popai.com/index.php?option=com_content&view=frontpage&Itemid=1, accessed June 9, 2009.

75. Quoted in Louise Story, "Product Packages Now Shout to Get Your Attention," *New York Times* (August 10, 2007), www.nytimes.com, accessed August 10, 2007.

76. See Robert B. Cialdini, *Influence: Science and Practice*, 2nd ed. (Glenview, IL: Scott, Foresman, 1988).

77. Richard P. Bagozzi, "Marketing as Exchange," *Journal of Marketing* 39 (October 1975): 32–39; Peter M. Blau, *Exchange and Power in Social Life* (New York: Wiley, 1964); Marjorie Caballero and Alan J. Resnik, "The Attraction Paradigm in Dyadic Exchange," *Psychology & Marketing* 3, no. 1 (1986): 17–34; George C. Homans, "Social Behavior as Exchange," *American Journal of Sociology* 63 (1958): 597–606; Paul H. Schurr and Julie L. Ozanne, "Influences on Exchange Processes: Buyers' Preconceptions of a Seller's Trustworthiness and Bargaining Toughness," *Journal of Consumer Research* 11 (March 1985): 939–53; Arch G. Woodside and J. W. Davenport, "The Effect of Salesman Similarity and Expertise on Consumer Purchasing Behavior," *Journal of Marketing Research* 8 (1974): 433–36.

78. www.customerssuck.com, accessed June 9, 2009; Keith Naughton, "Tired of Smile-Free Service," *Newsweek* (March 6, 2000): 44–45. www.protest.net, accessed July 1, 2009.

79. Mary Jo Bitner, Bernard H. Booms, and Mary Stansfield Tetreault, "The Service Encounter: Diagnosing Favorable and Unfavorable Incidents," *Journal of Marketing* 54 (January 1990): 7–84; Robert C. Prus, *Making Sales* (Newbury Park, CA: Sage Publications, 1989); Arch G. Woodside and James L. Taylor, "Identity Negotiations in Buyer–Seller Interactions," in Elizabeth C. Hirschman and Morris B. Holbrook, eds., *Advances in Consumer Research* 12 (Provo, UT: Association for Consumer Research, 1985): 443–49.

80. Barry J. Babin, James S. Boles, and William R. Darden, "Salesperson Stereotypes, Consumer Emotions, and Their Impact on Information Processing," *Journal of the Academy of Marketing Science* 23, no. 2 (1995): 94–105; Gilbert A. Churchill, Jr., Neil M. Ford, Steven W. Hartley, and Orville C. Walker, Jr., "The Determinants of Salesperson Performance: A Meta-Analysis," *Journal of Marketing Research* 22 (May 1985): 103–18.

81. Siew Meng Leong, Paul S. Busch, and Deborah Roedder John, "Knowledge Bases and Salesperson Effectiveness: A Script-Theoretic Analysis," *Journal of Marketing Research* 26 (May 1989): 164; Harish Sujan, Mita Sujan, and James R. Bettman, "Knowledge Structure Differences Between More Effective and Less Effective Salespeople," *Journal of Marketing Research* 25 (February 1988): 81–86; Robert Saxe and Barton Weitz, "The SOCCO Scale: A Measure of the Customer Orientation of Salespeople," *Journal of Marketing Research* 19 (August 1982): 343–51; David M. Szymanski, "Determinants of Selling Effectiveness: The Importance of Declarative Knowledge to the Personal Selling Concept," *Journal of Marketing* 52 (January 1988): 64–77; Barton A. Weitz, "Effectiveness in Sales Interactions: A Contingency Framework," *Journal of Marketing* 45 (Winter 1981): 85–103.

82. Jagdish N. Sheth, "Buyer-Seller Interaction: A Conceptual Framework," in *Advances in Consumer Research* 3 (Cincinnati, OH: Association for Consumer Research, 1976): 382–86; Kaylene C. Williams and Rosann L. Spiro, "Communication Style in the Salesperson-Customer Dyad," *Journal of Marketing Research* 22 (November 1985): 434–42.

83. Marsha L. Richins, "An Analysis of Consumer Interaction Styles in the Marketplace," *Journal of Consumer Research* 10 (June 1983): 73–82.

84. Calmetta Y. Coleman, "A Car Salesman's Bizarre Prank May End Up Backfiring in Court," *Wall Street Journal* (May 2, 1995): B1.

85. "Woman Stabbed over McDonald's Meal Dispute," *Opelika/Auburn News* (April 13, 2002).

86. Rama Jayanti and Anita Jackson, "Service Satisfaction: Investigation of Three Models," in Rebecca H. Holman and Michael R. Solomon, eds., *Advances in Consumer Research* 18 (Provo, UT: Association for Consumer Research, 1991): 603–10; David K. Tse, Franco M. Nicosia, and Peter C. Wilton, "Consumer Satisfaction as a Process," *Psychology & Marketing* 7 (Fall 1990): 177–93. For a recent treatment of satisfaction issues from a more interpretive perspective, see Susan Fournier and David Mick, "Rediscovering Satisfaction," *Journal of Marketing* 63 (October 1999): 5–23.

87. Bruce Cooil, Timothy L. Keiningham, Lerzan Aksoy, and Michael Hsu, "A Longitudinal Analysis of Customer Satisfaction and Share of Wallet: Investigating the Moderating Effect of Customer Characteristics," *Journal of Marketing* 71 (January 2007): 67–83. For a study that looks at consumer variables moderating this relationship, cf. Kathleen Seiders, Glenn B. Voss, Dhruv Grewal, and Andrea L. Godfrey, "Do Satisfied Customers Buy More? Examining Moderating Influences in a Retailing Context," *Journal of Marketing* 69 (October 2005): 26–43.

88. Constance L. Hayes, "Service Takes a Holiday," *New York Times* (December 23, 1998): C1.

89. Leslie Kaufman, "Enough Talk," *Newsweek* (August 18, 1997): 48–49.

90. Robert Jacobson and David A. Aaker, "The Strategic Role of Product Quality," *Journal of Marketing* 51 (October 1987): 31–44. For a review of issues regarding the measurement of service quality, see J. Joseph Cronin, Jr., and Steven A. Taylor, "Measuring Service Quality: A Reexamination and Extension," *Journal of Marketing* 56 (July 1992): 55–68.

91. Amna Kirmani and Peter Wright, "Money Talks: Perceived Advertising Expense and Expected Product Quality," *Journal of Consumer Research* 16 (December 1989): 344–53; Donald R. Lichtenstein and Scot Burton, "The Relationship Between Perceived and Objective Price-Quality," *Journal of Marketing Research* 26 (November 1989): 429–43; Akshay R. Rao and Kent B. Monroe, "The Effect of Price, Brand Name, and Store Name on Buyers' Perceptions of Product Quality: An Integrative Review," *Journal of Marketing Research* 26 (August 1989): 351–57; Shelby Hunt, "Post-Transactional Communication and Dissonance Reduction," *Journal of Marketing* 34 (January 1970): 46–51; Daniel E. Innis and H. Rao Unnava, "The Usefulness of Product Warranties for Reputable and New Brands," in Rebecca H. Holman and Michael R. Solomon, eds., *Advances in Consumer Research* 18 (Provo, UT: Association for Consumer Research, 1991): 317–22; Terence A. Shimp and William O. Bearden, "Warranty and Other Extrinsic Cue Effects on Consumers' Risk Perceptions," *Journal of Consumer Research* 9 (June 1982): 38–46.

92. "Voice of the Consumer Not Leveraged," Center for Media Research (February 3, 2009), www.mediapost.com, accessed February 3, 2009.

93. Holbrook and Corfman, "Quality and Value in the Consumption Experience"; Robert M. Pirsig, *Zen and the Art of Motorcycle Maintenance: An Inquiry into Values* (New York: Bantam Books, 1974).

94. Gilbert A. Churchill, Jr., and Carol F. Surprenant, "An Investigation into the Determinants of Customer Satisfaction," *Journal of Marketing Research* 19 (November 1983): 491–504; John E. Swan and I. Frederick Trawick, "Disconfirmation of Expectations and Satisfaction with a Retail Service," *Journal of Retailing* 57 (Fall 1981): 49–67; Peter C. Wilton and David K. Tse, "Models of Consumer Satisfaction Formation: An Extension," *Journal of Marketing Research* 25 (May 1988): 204–12. For a discussion of what may occur when customers evaluate a new service for which comparison standards do not yet exist, see Ann L. McGill and Dawn Iacobucci, "The Role of Post-Experience Comparison Standards in the Evaluation of Unfamiliar Services," in John F. Sherry, Jr., and Brian Sternthal, eds., *Advances in Consumer Research* 19 (Provo, UT: Association for Consumer Research, 1992): 570–78; William Boulding, Ajay Kalra, Richard Staelin, and Valarie A. Zeithaml, "A Dynamic Process Model of Service Quality: From Expectations to Behavioral Intentions," *Journal of Marketing Research* 30 (February 1993): 7–27.

95. Jagdish N. Sheth and Banwari Mittal, "A Framework for Managing Customer Expectations," *Journal of Market Focused Management* 1 (1996): 137–58.

96. Ariel Sabar, "In Case of Missing Trousers, Aggrieved Party Loses Again," *New York Times* (June 26, 2007), www.nytimes.com, accessed June 26, 2007.

97. Mary C. Gilly and Betsy D. Gelb, "Post-Purchase Consumer Processes and the Complaining Consumer," *Journal of Consumer Research* 9 (December 1982): 323–28; Diane Halstead and Cornelia Droge, "Consumer Attitudes Toward Complaining and the Prediction of Multiple Complaint Responses," in Rebecca H. Holman and Michael R. Solomon, eds., *Advances in Consumer Research* 18 (Provo, UT: Association for Consumer Research, 1991): 210–16; Jagdip Singh, "Consumer Complaint Intentions and Behavior: Definitional and Taxonomical Issues," *Journal of Marketing* 52 (January 1988): 93–107.

98. Gary L. Clark, Peter F. Kaminski, and David R. Rink, "Consumer Complaints: Advice on How Companies Should Respond Based on an Empirical Study," *Journal of Services Marketing* 6 (Winter 1992): 41–50.

99. Alan Andreasen and Arthur Best, "Consumers Complain—Does Business Respond?" *Harvard Business Review* 55 (July–August 1977): 93–101.

100. Tibbett L. Speer, "They Complain Because They Care," *American Demographics* (May 1996): 13–14.

101. Ingrid Martin, "Expert-Novice Differences in Complaint Scripts," in Rebecca H. Holman and Michael R. Solomon, eds., *Advances in Consumer Research* 18 (Provo, UT: Association for Consumer Research, 1991): 225–31; Marsha L. Richins, "A Multivariate Analysis of Responses to Dissatisfaction," *Journal of the Academy of Marketing Science* 15 (Fall 1987): 24–31.

102. John A. Schibrowsky and Richard S. Lapidus, "Gaining a Competitive Advantage by Analyzing Aggregate Complaints," *Journal of Consumer Marketing* 11 (1994): 15–26; Clay M. Voorhees, Michael K. Brady, and David M. Horowitz, "A Voice from the Silent Masses: An Exploratory and Comparative Analysis of Noncomplainers," *Journal of the Academy of Marketing Science* 34 (Fall 2006): 514–27.

103. Emily Steel, "How to Handle 'IHateYourCompany.com' Some Firms Buy Up Negative Domain Names to Avert 'Gripe Sites,'" *Wall Street Journal* (September 5, 2008), http://online.wsj.com/article_email/SB122057760688302147-lMyQjAxMDI4MjAwNTUw..., accessed September 5, 2008.

104. Material adapted from a presentation by Glenn H. Mazur, QFD Institute, 2002.

105. Russell W. Belk, "The Role of Possessions in Constructing and Maintaining a Sense of Past," in Marvin E. Goldberg, Gerald Gorn, and Richard W. Pollay, eds., *Advances in Consumer Research* 17 (Provo, UT: Association for Consumer Research, 1989): 669–76.

106. David E. Sanger, "For a Job Well Done, Japanese Enshrine the Chip," *New York Times* (December 11, 1990): A4.

107. Rob Walker, "The Worm Turns," *New York Times Magazine* (May 20, 2007), accessed May 20, 2007; www.terracycle.net, accessed June 9, 2009.

108. Jacob Jacoby, Carol K. Berning, and Thomas F. Dietvorst, "What About Disposition?" *Journal of Marketing* 41 (April 1977): 22–28.

109. Brian Wansink, S. Adam Brasel, and Steven Amjad, "The Mystery of the Cabinet Castaway: Why We Buy Products We Never Use," *Journal of Family and Consumer Sciences* 92, no. 1 (2000): 104–7.

110. Jennifer Lach, "Welcome to the Hoard Fest," *American Demographics* (April 2000): 8–9.

111. Norimitsu Onishi, "How Do Japanese Dump Trash? Let Us Count the Myriad Ways," *New York Times* (May 12, 2005), accessed May 12, 2005.

112. Debra J. Dahab, James W. Gentry, and Wanru Su, "New Ways to Reach Non-Recyclers: An Extension of the Model of Reasoned Action to Recycling Behaviors," paper presented at the meetings of the Association for Consumer Research, 1994.

113. Bagozzi and Dabholkar, "Consumer Recycling Goals and Their Effect on Decisions to Recycle," *Psychology & Marketing* 11, no. 4 (1994): 313–40; see also L. J. Shrum, Tina M. Lowrey, and John A. McCarty, "Recycling as a Marketing Problem: A Framework for Strategy Development," *Psychology & Marketing* 11 (July–August 1994): 393–416; Dahab, Gentry, and Su, "New Ways to Reach Non-Recyclers."

114. John F. Sherry, Jr., "A Sociocultural Analysis of a Midwestern American Flea Market," *Journal of Consumer Research* 17 (June 1990): 13–30.

115. Allan J. Magrath, "If Used Product Sellers Ever Get Organized, Watch Out," *Marketing News* (June 25, 1990): 9; Kevin McCrohan and James D. Smith, "Consumer Participation in the Informal Economy," *Journal of the Academy of Marketing Science* 15 (Winter 1990): 62.

116. John F. Sherry, Jr., "Dealers and Dealing in a Periodic Market: Informal Retailing in Ethnographic Perspective," *Journal of Retailing* 66 (Summer 1990): 174.

117. www.redo.org, accessed June 9, 2009.

118. Bob Tedeschi, "I'll Trade You My 'Titanic' for Your 'Spider-Man,'" *New York Times*, www.nytimes.com/2006/10/16/technology/16ecom.html?ex=1318651200&en=135f6f837373ce00&ei=5088&partner=rssnyt&emc=rss&pagewanted=print, accessed October 16, 2006.

119. http://freegan.info/?page_id=2, accessed June 9, 2009; Steven Kurutz, "Not Buying It," *New York Times* (June 21, 2007), www.nytimes.com, accessed June 21, 2007.

120. Russell W. Belk, Joon Yong Seo, and Eric Li. "Dirty Little Secret: Home Chaos and Professional Organizers, *Consumption, Markets and Culture* 10 (June 2007): 133–40.

121. John L. Lastovicka and Karen V. Fernandez, "Three Paths to Disposition: The Movement of Meaningful Possessions to Strangers," *Journal of Consumer Research* 31 (March 2005): 813–23.

122. Ray A. Smith, "Belly Up to the Bar and Buy Some Jeans," *Wall Street Journal* (April 2, 2009), http://online.wsj.com/article/SB123862311574879951.html, accessed April 2, 2009.

123. Shelly Branch, "Maybe Sex Doesn't Sell, A&F Is Discovering," *Wall Street Journal* (December 12, 2003), www.wsj.com, accessed December 12, 2003.

10

Groups

Chapter
Objectives

When you finish this chapter you will understand:

1. Why do others, especially those who possess some kind of social power, often influence us?

2. Why do we seek out others who share our interests in products or services?

3. Why are we motivated to buy or use products in order to be consistent with what other people do?

4. Why are certain people particularly likely to influence others' product choices?

5. Why are the things that other consumers tell us about products (good and bad) often more influential than the advertising we see?

6. How do online technologies accelerate the impact of word-of-mouth communication?

7. How is social networking changing the way companies and consumers interact?

Zachary leads a secret life. During the week, he is a straitlaced stock analyst for a major investment firm. He spends a big chunk of the week worrying about whether he'll have a job, so work is pretty stressful these days. The weekend is another story. Come Friday evening, it's off with the Brooks Brothers suit and on with the black leather, as he trades in his Lexus for his treasured Harley-Davidson motorcycle. A dedicated member of HOG (Harley Owners Group), Zachary belongs to the "RUBs" (rich urban bikers) faction of Harley riders. Everyone in his group wears expensive leather vests with Harley insignias and owns customized "Low Riders." Just this week, Zach finally got his new Harley perforated black leather jacket at the company's Motorclothes Merchandise Web page.[1] Surfing around the site makes him realize the lengths to which some of his fellow enthusiasts go to make sure others know they are HOG riders. As one of the Harley Web pages observed, "It's one thing to have people buy your products. It's another thing to have them tattoo your name on their bodies." Zach had to restrain himself from buying more Harley stuff; there were vests, eyewear, belts, buckles, scarves, watches, jewelry, even housewares ("home is the road") for sale. He settled for a set of Harley salt-and-pepper shakers that would be perfect for his buddy Dan's new crib.

Zach spends a lot of money to outfit himself to be like the rest of the group. But it's worth it. He feels a real sense of brotherhood with his fellow RUBs. The group rides together in two-column formation to bike rallies that sometimes attract up to 300,000 cycle enthusiasts. What a sense of power he feels when they all cruise together—it's them against the world!

Of course, an added benefit is the business networking he's accomplished during his jaunts with his fellow professionals who also wait for the weekend to "ride on the wild side—these days it would be professional suicide to let your contacts get cold, and you can't just count on LinkedIn to stay in the loop."[2]

Reference Groups

OBJECTIVE

Why do others, especially those who possess some kind of social power, often influence us?

Humans are social animals. We belong to groups, try to please others, and look to others' behavior for clues about what we should do in public settings. In fact, our desire to "fit in" or to identify with desirable individuals or groups is the primary motivation for many of our consumption behaviors. We may go to great lengths to please the members of a group whose acceptance we covet.[3]

Zachary's biker group is an important part of his identity, and this membership influences many of his buying decisions. He has spent many thousands of dollars on parts and accessories since he became a RUB. His fellow riders bond via their consumption choices, so total strangers feel an immediate connection with one another when they meet. The publisher of *American Iron*, an industry magazine, observed, "You don't buy a Harley because it's a superior bike, you buy a Harley to be a part of a family."[4]

Zachary doesn't model himself after just *any* biker—only the people with whom he really identifies can exert that kind of influence on him. For example, Zachary's group doesn't have much to do with outlaw clubs whose blue-collar riders sport big Harley tattoos. The members of his group also have only polite contact with "Ma and Pa" bikers, whose rides are the epitome of comfort and feature such niceties as radios, heated handgrips, and floorboards. Essentially, only the RUBs comprise Zachary's *reference group*.

A **reference group** is "an actual or imaginary individual or group conceived of having significant relevance upon an individual's evaluations, aspirations, or behavior."[5] Reference groups influence us in three ways: *informational, utilitarian,* and *value-expressive.* Table 10.1 describes these influences. In this chapter we'll focus on how other people, whether fellow bikers, coworkers, friends, family, or simply casual acquaintances, influence our purchase decisions. We'll consider how our group memberships shape our preferences because we want others to accept us or even because we mimic the actions of famous people we've never met. Finally, we'll explore why some people in particular affect our product preferences and how marketers find those people and enlist their support to persuade consumers to jump on the bandwagon.

When Are Reference Groups Important?

OBJECTIVE

Why do we seek out others who share our interests in products or services?

Recent research on smoking cessation programs powerfully illustrates the impact of reference groups. The study found that smokers tend to quit in groups, and when one person quits this creates a ripple effect that motivates others in his social network to give up the death sticks also. The researchers followed thousands of smokers and nonsmokers for over 30 years, and they also tracked their networks of relatives, coworkers, and friends. They discovered that over the years the smokers tended to cluster together (on average in groups of three). As the overall U.S. smoking rate declined dramatically during this period, the number of clusters in the sample decreased but the remaining clusters stayed the same size—this indicated that people quit in groups rather than as individuals. Not surprisingly, some social connections were more powerful than others. A spouse who quit had a bigger impact than did a friend, while friends had more influence than siblings. Coworkers had an influence only in small firms where everyone knew one another.[6]

TABLE 10.1	Three Forms of Reference Group Influence
Informational Influence	• The individual seeks information about various brands from an association of professionals or independent group of experts. • The individual seeks information from those who work with the product as a profession. • The individual seeks brand-related knowledge and experience (such as how Brand A's performance compares to Brand B's) from those friends, neighbors, relatives, or work associates who have reliable information about the brands. • The brand the individual selects is influenced by observing a seal of approval of an independent testing agency (such as *Good Housekeeping*). • The individual's observation of what experts do (such as observing the type of car that police drive or the brand of television that repairmen buy) influences his or her choice of a brand.
Utilitarian Influence	• So that he or she satisfies the expectations of fellow work associates, the individual's decision to purchase a particular brand is influenced by their preferences. • The individual's decision to purchase a particular brand is influenced by the preferences of people with whom he or she has social interaction. • The individual's decision to purchase a particular brand is influenced by the preferences of family members. • The desire to satisfy the expectations that others have of him or her has an impact on the individual's brand choice.
Value-Expressive Influence	• The individual feels that the purchase or use of a particular brand will enhance the image others have of him or her. • The individual feels that those who purchase or use a particular brand possess the characteristics that he or she would like to have. • The individual sometimes feels that it would be nice to be like the type of person that advertisements show using a particular brand. • The individual feels that the people who purchase a particular brand are admired or respected by others. • The individual feels that the purchase of a particular brand would help show others what he or she is or would like to be (such as an athlete, successful business person, good parent, etc.).

Source: Adapted from C. Whan Park and V. Parker Lessig, "Students and Housewives: Differences in Susceptibility to Reference Group Influence," *Journal of Consumer Research* 4 September 1977): 102. Copyright © 1977 JCR, Inc. Reprinted with permission of The University of Chicago Press.

Reference group influences don't work the same way for all types of products and consumption activities. For example, we're not as likely to take others' preferences into account when we choose products that are not very complex, that are low in perceived risk (see Chapter 8), or that we can try before we buy.[7] In addition, knowing what others prefer may influence us at a general level (e.g., owning or not owning a computer, eating junk food versus health food), whereas at other times this knowledge guides the specific brands we desire within a product category (e.g., if we wear Levi's jeans versus Diesel jeans, or smoke Marlboro cigarettes rather than Virginia Slims).

Two dimensions that influence the degree to which reference groups are important are whether we consume the item publicly or privately and whether it is a luxury or a necessity. As a rule, reference group effects are more robust for purchases that are (1) luxuries rather than necessities (e.g., sailboats) because products that we buy with our discretionary income are subject to individual tastes and preferences, whereas necessities do not offer this range of choices, and (2) socially conspicuous or visible to others (e.g., living room furniture or clothing) because we don't tend to be swayed as much by the opinions of others if no one but ourselves will ever see what we buy. (Note: In the old days this was true of underwear, but some of today's styles have changed all that!)[8] Table 10.1 shows the relative effects of reference group influences on some specific product classes.

Why are reference groups so persuasive? The answer lies in the potential power they wield over us. **Social power** is "the capacity to alter the actions of others."[10] To the degree to which you are able to make someone else do something, regardless of whether they do it willingly, you have power over that person. The following classification of power bases helps us to distinguish among the reasons a person exerts power over another, the degree to which the influence is voluntary, and whether this influence will continue to have an effect even when the source of the power isn't around.[11]

- **Referent power**—If a person admires the qualities of a person or a group, he tries to copy the referent's behaviors (e.g., choice of clothing, cars, leisure activities)—just as Zack's fellow bikers affected his preferences. Prominent people in all walks of life affect our consumption behaviors by virtue of product endorsements (e.g., 50 Cent for Reebok), distinctive fashion statements (e.g., Fergie's displays of high-end designer clothing), or championing causes (e.g., Lance Armstrong's work for cancer). Referent power is important to many marketing strategies because consumers voluntarily modify what they do and buy to identify with a referent.

- **Information power**—A person can have power simply because she knows something others would like to know. Editors of trade publications such as *Women's Wear Daily* often possess tremendous power because of their ability to compile and disseminate information that can make or break individual designers or companies. People with information power are able to influence consumer opinion by virtue of their (assumed) access to the "truth."

- **Legitimate power**—Sometimes we grant power by virtue of social agreements, such as the authority we give to police officers, soldiers, and yes, sometimes even professors. The legitimate power a uniform confers wields authority in consumer contexts including teaching hospitals where medical students don white coats to enhance their standing with patients.[12] Marketers "borrow" this form of power to influence consumers. For example, an ad that shows a model who wears a white doctor's coat adds an aura of legitimacy or authority to the presentation of the product ("I'm not a doctor, but I play one on TV").

- **Expert power**—To attract the casual Internet user, U.S. Robotics signed up British physicist Stephen Hawking to endorse its modems. A company executive commented, "We wanted to generate trust. So we found visionaries who use U.S. Robotics technology, and we let them tell the consumer how it makes their lives more productive." Hawking, who has Lou Gehrig's disease and speaks via a synthesizer, said in one TV spot, "My body may be stuck in this chair, but with the Internet my mind can go to the end of the universe."[13] Hawking's expert power derives from the knowledge he possesses about a content area. This helps to explain the weight many of us assign to professional critics' reviews of restaurants, books, movies, and cars—even though with the advent of blogs and open-source references such as Wikipedia it's getting a lot harder to tell just who is really an expert![14]

- **Reward power**—A person or group with the means to provide positive reinforcement (see Chapter 3) has **reward power**. The reward may be the tangible kind such as the contestants on *Survivor* experience when their comrades vote them off the island. Or it can be more intangible, such as the approval the judges on *American Idol* (except Simon) deliver to contestants.

- **Coercive power**—We exert coercive power when we influence someone because of social or physical intimidation. A threat is often effective in the short term, but it doesn't tend to stick because we revert back to our original behavior as soon as the bully leaves the scene. Fortunately, marketers rarely try to use this type of power unless you count those annoying calls from telemarketers! However, we can see elements of this power base in the fear appeals we talked about in Chapter 8 as well as in intimidating salespeople who try to succeed with a "hard sell."

A physician has expert power, and a white coat reinforces this expertise by conferring legitimate power.

Source: Courtesy Jupiter Unlimited.

Types of Reference Groups

Although two or more people normally form a group, we often use the term *reference group* a bit more loosely to describe *any* external influence that provides social cues.[15] The referent may be a cultural figure who has an impact on many people (e.g., Osama bin Laden) or a person or group whose influence only operates in the consumer's immediate environment (e.g., Zachary's biker club). Reference groups that affect consumption can include parents, fellow motorcycle enthusiasts, the Democratic Party, or even the Chicago Bears, the Dave Matthews Band, or Spike Lee.

Some people influence us simply because we feel similar to them. Have you ever experienced a warm feeling when you pull up at a light next to someone who drives the exact car as yours? One reason that we feel a bond with fellow brand users may be that many of us are a bit narcissistic (not you, of course); we feel an attraction to people and products that remind us of ourselves. That may explain why we feel a connection to others who happen to share our name. Research on the **name-letter effect** finds that all things equal we like others who share our names or even initials better than those who don't. When researchers look at large databases like Internet phone directories or Social Security records, they find that Johnsons are more likely to wed Johnsons, women named Virginia are more likely to live in (and move to) Virginia, and people whose surname is Lane tend to have addresses that include the word *lane*, not *street*. During the 2000 presidential campaign, people whose surnames began with B were more likely to contribute to George Bush, while those whose surnames began with G were more likely to contribute to Al Gore.[16]

Obviously, some groups and individuals are more powerful than others and affect a broader range of our consumption decisions. For example, our parents may play a pivotal role as we form our values on many important issues, such as attitudes

Marketing Opportunity

A recent real-life experiment demonstrates the potential social value of harnessing reference group power. For years the Sacramento, California, Municipal Utility District tried various tactics to goad people into using less energy, such as awarding rebates to residents who buy energy-saving appliances. These efforts weren't working too well, so the district tried something new: It told people how their energy consumption compared to their neighbors' energy consumption. Thirty-five thousand randomly selected customers received statements that rated their energy use compared to 100 of their neighbors who lived in homes of a similar size. The relatively energy-efficient customers earned two smiley faces on their statements, and those whose usage was higher than average opened their envelopes to see frowns (they had to delete the frown part after customers got too upset with this criticism). After six months, the utility found that customers who got these report cards reduced energy use by 2 percent compared to the rest of the district. Some colleges employ a similar technique when they create a competition among dormitories to identify which residence hall does the best job of conserving resources. At Central College in Pella, Iowa, students who live in a "green dorm" can access a Web site that tells them how much power their specific suite uses compared to the other suites in the building. Peer pressure is powerful.[18]

An electricity bill compares a homeowner's power usage with the amount neighbors use to encourage energy conservation.
Source: Courtesy of Redux Pictures/Photo by Max Whittaker.

about marriage or where to go to college. We call this **normative influence**—that is, the reference group helps to set and enforce fundamental standards of conduct. In contrast, a Harley-Davidson club exerts **comparative influence** because it affects members' decisions about specific motorcycle purchases.[17]

Brand Communities and Consumer Tribes

Before it released the popular Xbox game *Halo 2*, the company put up a Web site to explain the story line. However, there was a catch: The story was written from the point of view of the Covenant (the aliens who are preparing to attack Earth in the game)—and in *their* language. Within 48 hours, avid gamers around the world shared information in gaming chat rooms to crack the code and translate the text. More than 1.5 million people preordered the game before its release.[19] This cooperative effort illustrates a major trend in consumer behavior.

A **brand community** is a group of consumers who share a set of social relationships based on usage or interest in a product. Unlike other kinds of communities, these members typically don't live near each other—except when they may meet for brief periods at organized events or **brandfests** that community-oriented companies such as Jeep or Harley-Davidson sponsor. These events help owners to "bond" with fellow enthusiasts and strengthen their identification with the product as well as with others they meet who share their passion. In virtually any category you'll find passionate brand communities (in some cases devoted to brands that don't even exist anymore); examples include the 3Com Ergo Audrey (discontinued Internet appliance), Apple Newton (discontinued personal digital assistant), BMW MINI (car), Garmin (GPS device), Jones Soda (carbonated beverage), Lomo and Holga (cameras), Tom Petty and the Heartbreakers (musical group), StriVectin (cosmeceutical), and *Xena: Warrior Princess* (TV program).

Researchers find that people who participate in these events feel more positive about the products as a result, and this enhances brand loyalty. They tend to forgive product failures or lapses in service quality, and they're less likely to switch brands even if they learn that competing products are as good or better. Furthermore, these community members become emotionally involved in the company's welfare, and they often serve as brand missionaries as they carry its marketing message to others.[20]

The notion of a **consumer tribe** is similar to a brand community; it is a group of people who share a lifestyle and who can identify with each other because of a

CB AS I SEE IT

Professor John Schouten, *University of Portland*

There is no such thing as purely personal significance. To the extent that we create individual meaning at all, we do so from a shared language of objects, words, feelings, and experiences whose meanings have already been constructed by social groups. Similarly, there is no such thing as an individual consumer decision. We make our choices from assortments that society has provided, based on values and expectations that we have learned, questioned, embraced, or rejected as members of social groups.

Some groups or communities we choose. Others choose us. Ultimately, the character of our membership in any group is a matter of constant negotiation. Communities of any kind often coincide with or create markets. In response to shared needs and desires, humans come together, harness creativity and labor, and produce new goods and services. In the best cases, the creative power of community can accomplish tremendous good through cultural change. The LOHAS (Lifestyles of Health and Sustainability) community is one such social group, made up of both consumers and businesses. See lohas.com for more about the community's goals and impact.

Our biggest challenge today, in my view, is the collision between escalating human consumption and the rapidly declining capacity of the earth's natural systems to support it. I believe the best real hope for a tolerable human future lies in the ability of communities to redefine acceptable modes of consumer behavior and to participate actively and creatively in making them not only possible but also preferable to those practices that currently undermine the foundation of our existence.

For me, the most exciting aspects of communities are their dynamism and their power to effect change at levels ranging from individual purchases to global movements for social and environmental justice. Recently my studies have turned to such "communities of purpose." For example, for over three years now Diane Martin and I have been engaged with groups of people determined to make Wal-Mart more environmentally sustainable. Self-selecting community members include Wal-Mart executives and associates, key members of its supply chain, environmental activists, academics, and others. Uniting these diverse participants are shared goals of carbon neutrality, zero waste, and products that support the sustainable use of the earth's finite resources. So far these groups have achieved impressive results, helping Wal-Mart to divert millions of tons of waste from landfills, radically reduce its use of fossil fuels, develop more sustainable products and, true to Wal-Mart's mission, continue to profit, even in times of economic recession, with low prices to its customers. Explore walmartstores.com/sustainability and its link to Sustainable Value Networks for more about the results of these ongoing efforts.

shared allegiance to an activity or a product. Although these tribes are often unstable and short-lived, at least for a time members identify with others through shared emotions, moral beliefs, styles of life, and of course the products they jointly consume as part of their tribal affiliation.

Some companies, especially those that are more youth-oriented, use a **tribal marketing strategy** that links their product to, say, a group of shredders. However, there also are plenty of tribes with older members, such as car enthusiasts who gather to celebrate such cult products (see Chapter 4) as the Citroën in Europe and the Ford Mustang in the United States, or "foodies" who share their passion for cooking with other Wolfgang Puck wannabes around the world.[22]

Membership Versus Aspirational Reference Groups

A **membership reference group** consists of people we actually know, whereas we don't know those in an **aspirational reference group**, but we admire them anyway. These people are likely to be successful businesspeople, athletes, performers, or whoever rocks our world. Not surprisingly, many marketing efforts that specifically adopt a reference group appeal concentrate on highly visible, widely admired figures (such as well-known athletes or performers); they link these people to brands so that the products they use or endorse also take on this aspirational quality. For

Marketing Opportunity

Most consumers only admire their aspirational reference groups from afar, but more and more of them shell out big bucks to get up close and personal with their heroes. *Fantasy camps* today are a $1 billion industry as people pay for the chance to hang out—and play with—their idols. Baseball camps that mix retired players with fans have been around for many years, but now other types to let people mingle with their favorite hockey players, poker players, even members of the U.S. women's national soccer team. At one camp, 80 people each paid about $8,000 to jam with rock stars including Nils Lofgren, Dickey Betts, and Roger Daltrey. One enthusiastic novice gushed afterward, "We all grow up with heroes and never get to share a moment with them. But I got to live out my fantasy."[29]

The Tangled Web

The Web encourages the rise of a new kind of avoidance group—**antibrand communities**. These groups also coalesce around a celebrity, store, or brand—but in this case they're united by their disdain for it. The Rachael Ray Sucks Community on the blogging and social-networking site *LiveJournal* claims more than 1,000 members who don't hesitate to post their latest thoughts about the various shortcomings, flaws, and disagreeable traits of the (otherwise popular) television food personality. They criticize Ray's overuse of chicken stock, her kitchen hygiene, her smile (posters like to compare it to The Joker's of Batman fame), her penchant for saying "Yum-o!" and so on. The community has a basic rule for membership: "You must be anti-Rachael!"[32]

One team of researchers that study these communities observes that they tend to attract social idealists who advocate nonmaterialistic lifestyles. After they interviewed members of online communities who oppose Wal-Mart, Starbucks, and McDonald's, they concluded that these antibrand communities provide a meeting place for those who share a moral stance; a support network to achieve

example an amateur basketball player who idolizes Allen Iverson might strongly identify with Reebok because Iverson endorses these shoes.[23] One study of business students who aspired to the "executive" role found a strong relationship between products they associated with their *ideal selves* (see Chapter 5) and those they assumed real executives own.[24]

Because we tend to compare ourselves to similar others, many promotional strategies include "ordinary" people whose consumption activities provide informational social influence. How can we predict which people you know will be part of your membership reference group? Several factors make it more likely:

- **Propinquity**—As physical distance between people decreases and opportunities for interaction increase, they are more likely to form relationships. We call this physical nearness **propinquity**. An early study on friendship patterns in a housing complex showed this factor's strong effects: All things equal, residents were much more likely to be friends with the people next door than with those who lived only two doors away. Furthermore, people who lived next to a staircase had more friends than those at the ends of a hall (presumably, they were more likely to "bump into" people as they used the stairs).[25]

- **Mere exposure**—We come to like persons or things if we see them more often. Social scientists call this tendency the **mere exposure phenomenon**.[26] Greater frequency of contact, even if unintentional, may help to determine one's set of local referents. The same effect holds when we evaluate works of art or even political candidates.[27] One study predicted 83 percent of the winners of political primaries solely by the amount of media exposure each candidate received.[28]

- **Group cohesiveness**—**Cohesiveness** refers to the degree to which members of a group are attracted to each other and how much each values their membership in this group. As the value of the group to the individual increases, so too does the likelihood that the group will influence his or her consumption decisions. Smaller groups tend to be more cohesive because in larger groups the contributions of each member are usually less important or noticeable. By the same token, groups often try to restrict membership to a select few, which increases the value of membership to those who do get in.

Positive Versus Negative Reference Groups

Reference groups impact our buying decisions both positively and negatively. In most cases, we model our behavior to be in line with what we think the group expects us to do. Sometimes however we also deliberately do the *opposite* if we want to distance ourselves from *avoidance groups*. You may carefully study the dress or mannerisms of a group you dislike (e.g., "nerds," "druggies," or "preppies") and scrupulously avoid buying anything that might identify you with that group. For example, rebellious adolescents do the opposite of what their parents desire to make a statement about their independence.

Your motivation to distance yourself from a negative reference group can be as or more powerful than your desire to please a positive group.[30] That's why advertisements occasionally show an undesirable person who uses a competitor's product. This kind of execution subtly makes the point that you can avoid winding up like *that* kind of person if you just stay away from the products he buys. As a once-popular book reminded us, "Real men *don't* eat quiche!"[31]

We Like to Do It in Groups. We get away with more when we do it in a group. One simple reason: The more people who are together, the less likely that any one member gets singled out for attention. That helps to explains why people in larger groups have fewer restraints on their behavior. For example, we sometimes behave more wildly at costume parties or on Halloween than we do when others can easily identify us. We call this phenomenon **deindividuation**—a process where individual identities become submerged within a group.

Social loafing is a similar effect; it happens when we don't devote as much to a task because our contribution is part of a larger group effort.[35] You may have experienced this if you've worked on a group project for a class! Waitpersons are painfully aware of social loafing: People who eat in groups tend to tip less per person than when they eat alone.[36] For this reason, many restaurants automatically tack on a fixed gratuity for groups of six or more.

Furthermore, the decisions we make as part of a group tend to differ from those each of us would choose on our own. The **risky shift effect** refers to the observation that group members tend to consider riskier alternatives after the group discusses an issue than they would if each member made his or her own decision without talking about it with others.[37] Psychologists propose several explanations for this increased riskiness. One possibility is that something similar to social loafing occurs. As more people are involved in a decision, each individual is less accountable for the outcome so this results in *diffusion of responsibility*.[38] The practice of placing blanks in at least one of the rifles a firing squad uses diffuses each soldier's responsibility for the death of a prisoner because it's never certain who actually shot him. Another explanation is the *value hypothesis*, which states that our culture values risky behavior, so when people make decisions in groups they conform to this expectation.[39]

Research evidence for the risky shift is mixed. A more general finding is that group discussion tends to increase **decision polarization**. This means that the direction the group members leaned before discussion began (whether a risky choice

common goals; a way to cope with workplace frustrations (many members actually work for the companies they bash!); and a hub for information, activities, and related resources.[33] Another study chronicles the level of opposition the Hummer inspires. For example, whereas brand enthusiasts celebrate the Hummer's road safety because of its size and weight, antibranders who drive smaller cars slam the vehicle's bulk. One driver posted this message: "The H2 is a death machine. You'd better hope that you don't collide with an H2 in your economy car. You can kiss your ass goodbye thanks to the H2's massive weight and raised bumpers. Too bad you couldn't afford an urban assault vehicle of your own."[34]

An avoidance group appeal.
Source: © Michelin North America, Inc.

Costumes hide our true identities and encourage deindividuation.
Source: Courtesy Shutterstock. Photo by Sergei Bachlakov.

or a conservative choice) becomes even more extreme in that direction after the group talks about it. Group discussions regarding product purchases tend to create a risky shift for low-risk items, but they yield even more conservative group decisions for high-risk products.[40]

Even shopping behavior changes when people do it in groups. For example, people who shop with at least one other person tend to make more unplanned purchases, buy more, and cover more areas of a store than do those who browse solo.[41] Both normative and informational social influence explains this. A group member may buy something to gain the approval of the others, or the group may simply expose her to more products and stores. Either way, retailers are well advised to encourage group-shopping activities.

The famous Tupperware party is a successful example of a **home shopping party** that capitalizes on group pressures to boost sales.[42] In this format a company representative makes a sales presentation to a group of people who gather at the home of a friend or acquaintance. The shopping party works due to informational social influence: Participants model the behavior of others who provide them with information about how to use certain products, especially because a relatively homogeneous group (e.g., neighborhood homemakers) attends the party. Normative social influence also operates because others can easily observe our actions. Pressures to conform may be particularly intense and may escalate as more and more group members "cave in" (we call this process the *bandwagon effect*).

In addition, these parties may activate deindividuation or the risky shift. As consumers get caught up in the group, they may agree to try new products they would not normally consider. These same dynamics underlie the latest wrinkle on the Tupperware home-selling technique: the Botox party. The craze for Botox injections that paralyze facial nerves to reduce wrinkles (for 3 to 6 months anyway) is fueled by gatherings where dermatologists or plastic surgeons redefine the definition of house calls. For patients, mixing cocktail hour with cosmetic injections takes some of the anxiety out of the procedure. Egged on by the others at the party, a doctor can dewrinkle as many as 10 patients in an hour. An advertising executive who worked on the Botox marketing strategy explained that the membership reference group appeal is more effective than the traditional route that uses a celebrity spokesperson to tout the injections in advertising: "We think it's more persuasive to think of your next-door neighbor using it."[43] The only hitch is that after you get the injections your face is so rigid your friends can't tell if you're smiling!

3

OBJECTIVE

Why are we motivated to buy or use products in order to be consistent with what other people do?

Conformity

The early Bohemians who lived in Paris around 1830 made a point of behaving, well, differently from others. One flamboyant figure of the time earned notoriety because he walked a lobster on a leash through the gardens of the Royal Palace. His friends drank wine from human skulls, cut their beards in strange shapes, and slept in tents on the floors of their garrets.[45] Sounds a bit like some frats we've visited.

Although in every age there certainly are those who "march to their own drummers," most people tend to follow society's expectations regarding how they should act and look (with a little improvisation here and there, of course). **Conformity** is a change in beliefs or actions as a reaction to real or imagined group pressure. In order for a society to function, its members develop **norms**, or informal rules that govern behavior. Without these rules, we would have chaos. Imagine the confusion if a simple norm such as stopping for a red traffic light did not exist.

We conform in many small ways every day—even though we don't always realize it. Unspoken rules govern many aspects of consumption. In addition to norms regarding appropriate use of clothing and other personal items, we conform to rules that include gift-giving (we expect birthday presents from loved ones and get upset if they don't materialize), sex roles (men often pick up the check on a first date), and personal hygiene (our friends expect us to shower regularly).

We don't mimic others' behaviors all the time, so what makes it more likely we'll conform? These are some common culprits:[46]

- **Cultural pressures**—Different cultures encourage conformity to a greater or lesser degree. The American slogan "Do your own thing" in the 1960s reflected a movement away from conformity and toward individualism. In contrast, Japanese society emphasizes collective well-being and group loyalty over individuals' needs.
- **Fear of deviance**—The individual may have reason to believe that the group will apply *sanctions* to punish nonconforming behaviors. It's not unusual to observe adolescents who shun a peer who is "different" or a corporation or university that passes over a person for promotion because she is not a "team player."
- **Commitment**—The more people are dedicated to a group and value their membership in it, the greater their motivation to conform to the group's wishes. Rock groupies and followers of TV evangelists may do anything their idols ask of them, and terrorists willingly die for their cause. According to the **principle of least interest**, the person who is *least* committed to staying in a relationship has the most power because that party doesn't care as much if the other person rejects him.[47] Remember that on your next date.
- **Group unanimity, size, and expertise**—As groups gain in power, compliance increases. It is often harder to resist the demands of a large number of people than only a few—especially when a "mob mentality" rules.
- **Susceptibility to interpersonal influence**—This trait refers to an individual's need to have others think highly of him or her. Consumers who don't possess this trait are *role-relaxed*; they tend to be older, affluent, and to have high self-confidence. Subaru created a communications strategy to reach role-relaxed consumers. In one of its commercials, a man proclaims, "I want a car. . . . Don't tell me about wood paneling, about winning the respect of my neighbors. They're my neighbors. They're not my heroes."[48]

Marketing Opportunity

In a new twist on a group experience, an audience in a movie theater uses their bodies as a collective joystick to move a game piece on the screen. The interactive games use a motion sensor to read body movements and move an object such as a ping-pong paddle or a car. These diversions enable advertisers such as MSNBC.com and Volvo to provide a fun group experience as they get their messages across.[44]

OBJECTIVE

Why are certain people particularly likely to influence others' product choices?

Opinion Leadership

As Cold Stone Creamery expands to Japan, the ice cream store projects a somewhat different image than it has in the United States. The chain wants to be ultracool as it generates a buzz among fashion-conscious "office ladies"—as the Japanese call young, single, female professionals. These women are very influential in Japan; their reactions to a new product can make or break it. To woo this group, Cold Stone sponsored a fashion show for young women (assuming the models can fit into the dresses after sampling a few of the chain's caloric creations), and fashion magazines staged photo shoots at the stores.[49]

Although consumers get information from personal sources, they do not usually ask just *anyone* for advice about purchases. If you decide to buy a new stereo, you will most likely seek advice from a friend who knows a lot about sound systems. This friend may own a sophisticated system, or he may subscribe to specialized magazines such as *Stereo Review* and spend his free time browsing through electronics stores. However, you may have another friend who has a reputation for being stylish and who spends his free time reading *Gentleman's Quarterly* and shopping at trendy boutiques. You might not bring up your stereo problem with him, but you may take him with you to shop for a new fall wardrobe.

Everyone knows people who are knowledgeable about products and whose advice others take seriously. Like one of the Japanese office ladies, this individual is an **opinion leader**, a person who is frequently able to influence others' attitudes or behaviors.[50] Clearly, some people's recommendations carry more weight than others. Opinion leaders are extremely valuable information sources because they possess the social power we discussed earlier in the chapter:

- They are technically competent so they possess expert power.[51]
- They prescreen, evaluate, and synthesize product information in an unbiased way, so they possess knowledge power.[52]
- They are socially active and highly interconnected in their communities.[53]
- They are likely to hold offices in community groups and clubs and to be active outside of the home. As a result, opinion leaders often wield legitimate power by virtue of their social standing.
- They tend to be similar to the consumer in terms of their values and beliefs, so they possess referent power. Note that although opinion leaders are set apart by their interest or expertise in a product category, they are more convincing to the extent that they are *homophilous* rather than *heterophilous*. **Homophily** refers to the degree to which a pair of individuals is similar in terms of education, social status, and beliefs.[54] Effective opinion leaders tend to be slightly higher in terms of status and educational attainment than those they influence but not so high as to be in a different social class.
- Opinion leaders are often among the first to buy new products, so they absorb much of the risk. This experience reduces uncertainty for the rest of us who are not as courageous. Furthermore, whereas company-sponsored communications tend to focus exclusively on the positive aspects of a product, the hands-on experience of opinion leaders makes them more likely to impart *both* positive and negative information about product performance. Thus, they are more credible because they have no "axe to grind."

How Influential Is an Opinion Leader?

Ford's prelaunch campaign for its crossover SUV Flex model aimed to get buzz going as it gave opinion leaders an exclusive look at the new car. In five cities, the company invited radio deejays, musicians, and other creative people to take a tour of the

Flex. These influentials went on an urban odyssey as fleets of the vehicles took them to art galleries, nightclubs, and other hot spots. In a separate campaign to plug its Fiesta model, the carmaker selected 100 young people who got free use of a car for six months in return for blogging about it.[55]

When social scientists initially developed the concept of the opinion leader, they assumed that certain influential people in a community would exert an overall impact on group members' attitudes. Later work, however, questioned the assumption that there is such a thing as a *generalized opinion leader* whose recommendations we seek for all types of purchases. Very few people are capable of being expert in a number of fields (even though they believe otherwise). Sociologists distinguish between those who are *monomorphic*, or expert in a limited field, and those who are *polymorphic*, or expert in several fields.[56] Even opinion leaders who are polymorphic, however, tend to concentrate on one broad domain, such as electronics or fashion. For example, Mediamark Research & Intelligence estimates that 10.5 percent of the U.S. adult population, who it labels "Big Circle Influentials" are the key influencers for personal finance decisions.[57]

Research on opinion leadership generally indicates that although opinion leaders do exist for multiple product categories, expertise tends to overlap across similar categories. It is rare to find a generalized opinion leader. An opinion leader for home appliances is likely to serve a similar function for home cleaners but not for cosmetics. In contrast, we may consult a fashion opinion leader whose primary influence is on clothing choices for recommendations on cosmetics purchases but not necessarily for her opinions on microwave ovens.[58]

A recent reexamination of the traditional perspective on opinion leadership reveals that the process isn't as clear-cut as some researchers thought.[59] The original framework is called the **two step flow model of influence**. It proposes that a small group of *influencers* disseminate information since they can modify the opinions of a large number of other people. When the authors ran extensive computer simulations of this process, they found that the influence is driven less by influentials but more by the interaction among those who are easily influenced; they communicate the information vigorously to one another and they also participate in a two-way dialogue with the opinion leader as part of an **influence network**. These conversations create **information cascades**, which occurs when a piece of information triggers a sequence of interactions (much like an avalanche). Figure 10.1 contrasts the old and new perspectives on social networks.

Types of Opinion Leaders

We've seen that early conceptions of the opinion leader role assumed a static, one-way process: The opinion leader absorbs information from the mass media and in turn transmits data to opinion receivers. This view also confuses the functions of several different types of consumers.

Opinion leaders may or may not be purchasers of the products they recommend. Early purchasers also tend to be *innovators*; they like to take risks and try new things. Researchers call opinion leaders who also are early purchasers *innovative communicators*. One study identified characteristics of college men who were innovative communicators for fashion products. These men were among the first to buy new fashions, and other students were likely to follow their lead when they made their own purchases. Other characteristics of the men included the following:[60]

- They were socially active.
- They were appearance conscious and narcissistic (i.e., they were quite fond of themselves and self-centered).
- They were involved in rock culture.

Figure 10.1 OLD AND NEW MODELS OF SOCIAL NETWORKS
Source: Duncan J. Watts and Peter Sheridan Dodds. "Influentials, Networks, and Public Opinion Formation"
Journal of Consumer Research, 34 (December 2007): 441-458, University of Chicago Press.

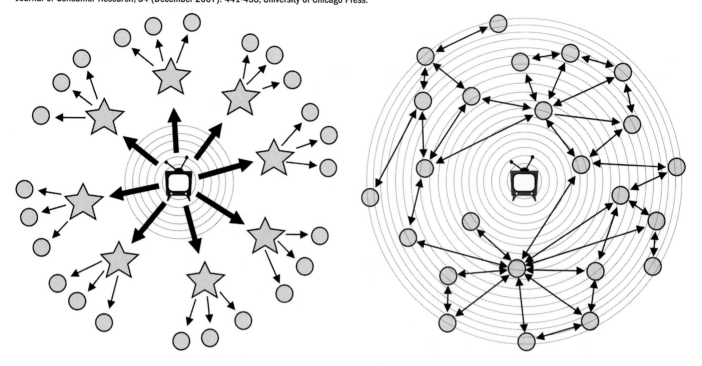

- They were heavy readers of magazine like *Playboy* and *Sports Illustrated.*
- They were likely to own more clothing, and a broader range of styles, than other students.

Opinion leaders also are likely to be *opinion seekers*. They are generally more involved in a product category and actively search for information. As a result, they are more likely to talk about products with others and to solicit others' opinions as well.[61] Contrary to the older, static view of opinion leadership, most product-related conversation does not take place in a "lecture" format where one person does all the talking. A lot of product-related conversation occurs in the context of a casual interaction rather than as formal instruction.[62] One study, which found that opinion seeking is especially high for food products, revealed that two-thirds of opinion seekers also view themselves as opinion leaders.[63]

The Market Maven

To publicize Clinical Therapy, a new lotion from Vaseline, an advertising campaign mapped the social network of a small town in Alaska. In Kodiak, reps took over a storefront and gave away free bottles. In return the recipients had to identify the person in town who recommended the product to them. Through this process they found a woman who many of the townspeople named as their source. The social map with this person at the center appears on a Web site that displays this network, prescribethenation.com.[64]

The Alaskan woman Vaseline found (no, she isn't Sarah Palin) is a **market maven**—she is a person who likes to transmit marketplace information of all types. These shopaholics are not necessarily interested in certain products and they may not necessarily be early purchasers; they're simply into staying on top of what's happening in the marketplace. They come closer to the function of a generalized opinion leader because they tend to have a solid overall knowledge of how and where to procure products. They're also more confident in their own ability to make smart purchase decisions. Researchers use the following scale items, to which respondents indicate how much they agree or disagree, to identify market mavens:[65]

1 I like introducing new brands and products to my friends.
2 I like helping people by providing them with information about many kinds of products.
3 People ask me for information about products, places to shop, or sales.
4 If someone asked me where to get the best buy on several types of products, I could tell him or her where to shop.
5 My friends think of me as a good source of information when it comes to new products or sales.

The Surrogate Consumer

In addition to everyday consumers who influence others' purchase decisions, a class of marketing intermediary we call the **surrogate consumer** often guides what we buy. A surrogate consumer is a person whom we retain to provide input into our purchase decisions. Unlike the opinion leader or market maven, we usually compensate the surrogate for his or her advice. Interior decorators, stockbrokers, professional shoppers, and college consultants are surrogate consumers.

Regardless of whether they actually make the purchase on behalf of the consumer, their recommendations can be enormously influential. The consumer, in essence, relinquishes control over several or all decision-making functions, such as information search, the evaluation of alternatives, or the actual purchase. For example, a client may commission an interior decorator to redo her house, and we may entrust a broker to make crucial buy/sell decisions on our behalf. Marketers tend to overlook surrogates when they try to convince consumers to buy their goods or services. This can be a big mistake because they may mistarget their communications to end consumers when they should focus on the surrogates who actually sift through product information and recommend a purchase to their clients.[66]

How Do We Find Opinion Leaders?

Companies that want to connect with teens are turning up on the cheerleading circuit. They recognize that cheerleaders often are among the most popular kids in high school, and they're able to influence their classmates' opinions about which personal care products or beverages are the coolest. That's why makeup artists who work for P&G's Cover Girl line of cosmetics show up at cheerleading clinics to offer makeup tips to some of the 350,000 people per year who attend these training sessions. PepsiCo promotes its Propel brand via workshops at cheerleader events to teach teens about nutrition and the value of drinking water.[67]

Unfortunately, because most opinion leaders are everyday consumers rather than celebrities, they are hard to find. A celebrity or an influential industry executive is by definition easy to locate. That person has national or at least regional visibility or is listed in published directories. In contrast, opinion leaders tend to operate at the local level and may influence only a small group of consumers rather than an entire market segment. When PepsiCo recently launched its new Sierra Mist Ruby Splash flavor, the company hired a firm to identify local people in different cities who could help it recruit a select group of "influencers" to spread the word as they offer the soft drink at events they host or attend. The requirements were specific: Influencers had to love lemon-lime beverages, be ages 18 to 34, and be musicians, skateboard shop owners, people who love to throw backyard barbeques, or others who had laid-back lifestyles and who were well-known in their communities. One influencer for example is a musician who hosted a backyard jam session for 20 friends—prior to the event a crew dropped off ice-cold cans of the soft drink as well as branded sunglasses, misters, and car fresheners with a Ruby Splash scent.

Another opinion leader owns a skateboard store; he hosted an outdoor movie night to debut a new surf film. In all the company sponsored over 300 of these minievents in a two-month period. Nice job if you can get it.[68]

Because it's difficult to identify specific opinion leaders in a large market, most attempts to do so focus instead on *exploratory studies*. In these cases researchers identify the profile of a representative opinion leader and then generalize these insights to a larger market. For example, one company that sought out financial opinion leaders found that these consumers were more likely to manage their own finances and tended to use a computer to do so. They also were more likely to follow their investments on a daily basis and to read books and watch television shows devoted to financial issues.[69]

Self-Designation

The most commonly used technique to identify opinion leaders is simply to ask individual consumers whether *they* consider themselves to be opinion leaders. Although respondents who report a greater degree of interest in a product category are more likely to be opinion leaders, we must view the results of surveys that discover *self-designated opinion leaders* with some skepticism. Some people have a tendency to inflate their own importance and influence, whereas others who really are influential might not admit to this quality or be conscious of it if they are.[70]

Here's the problem: The fact that we transmit advice about products does not mean other people *take* that advice. For someone to be considered a *bona fide* opinion leader, opinion seekers must actually heed his advice. An alternative is to select certain group members (*key informants*) whom we ask to identify opinion leaders. The success of this approach hinges on locating those who have accurate knowledge of the group.

The self-designating method is not as reliable as a more systematic analysis (where we can verify an individual's self-designation when we ask others if they agree), but the advantage is that we can easily apply it to a large group of potential opinion leaders. Figure 10.2 shows one of the measurement scales researchers use for this kind of self-designation.

Sociometry

The play *Six Degrees of Separation* is based on the premise that everyone on the planet indirectly knows everyone else—or at least knows people who in turn know them. Indeed, social scientists estimate that the average person has 1,500 acquaintances and that five to six intermediaries could connect any two people in the United States.[71] A popular game challenges players to link the actor Kevin Bacon with other actors in much the same way.

Sociometric methods trace communication patterns among members of a group. These techniques allow researchers to systematically map out the interactions among group members. Like the Vaseline campaign in Alaska we described earlier, this means we interview consumers and find out who they ask for product information. In many cases one or a few people emerge as the "nodes" in a map; we've found our opinion leaders. This method is the most precise, but it is very difficult and expensive to implement because it involves very close study of interaction patterns in small groups. For this reason, it's best to apply a sociometric technique in a closed, self-contained social setting, such as in hospitals, in prisons, and on army bases, where members are largely isolated from other social networks.

A recent sociometric study on obesity (similar to the one we read about earlier regarding clusters of smokers) provides a striking example of how our social networks influence what we do. The researchers analyzed a sample of more than 12,000 people who participated in the Framingham Heart Study, which closely documented their health from 1971 to 2003. They discovered that obesity can spread from person to person, much like a virus (we'll talk more about how consumer trends spread in this fashion in Chapter 16). The investigators knew who was friends

Figure 10.2 OPINION LEADER SCALE

Please rate yourself on the following scales relating to your interactions with friends and neighbors regarding _____.

1. In general, do you talk to your friends and neighbors about _____:

very often				never
5	4	3	2	1

2. When you talk to your friends and neighbors about _____ do you:

give a great deal of information				give very little information
5	4	3	2	1

3. During the past six months, how many people have you told about a new _____?

told a number of people				told no one
5	4	3	2	1

4. Compared with your circle of friends, how likely are you to be asked about new _____?

very likely to be asked				not at all likely to be asked
5	4	3	2	1

5. In discussion of new _____, which of the following happens most?

you tell your friends about _____				your friends tell you about _____
5	4	3	2	1

6. Overall in all of your discussions with friends and neighbors are you:

often used as a source of advice				not used as a source of advice
5	4	3	2	1

with whom as well as who was a spouse or sibling or neighbor, and they knew how much each person weighed at various times over 3 decades so they could reconstruct what happened over the years if study participants became obese. Guess what? When one person gains weight, close friends tend to gain weight, too—a person's chances of being obese if a close friend put on the pounds increased by 57 percent! The friend's influence remained even if he lived hundreds of miles away. The researchers speculated that the reason for this *social contagion* effect is that when our best buds get fat, this alters our perception of normal body weight so we aren't as concerned when we put on a few pounds as well. The moral of the story: Hang out with thin people![72]

Many professionals, such as doctors, accountants, and lawyers, as well as services marketers like lawn-care companies and cleaning services, depend primarily on word of mouth to generate business. In many cases, consumers recommend a service provider to a friend or coworker, and in other cases businesspeople make recommendations to their customers. For example, only 0.2 percent of respondents in one study reported that they choose a physician based on advertising. Instead they rely primarily on advice from family and friends.[73]

We use sociometric analyses to better understand *referral behavior* and to locate strengths and weaknesses in terms of how one's reputation flows through a community.[74] *Network analysis* focuses on communication in social systems, considers the relations among people in a *referral network*, and measures the *tie strength* among them. To understand how a network guides what we buy, consider a study researchers conducted among women who lived together in a sorority house. They found evidence that subgroups, or *cliques*, within the sorority were likely to share preferences for various products. In some cases, the sisters even shared their choices of "private" (i.e., socially inconspicuous) products (probably because of shared bathrooms in the sorority house).[75]

Tie strength refers to the nature of the bond between people. It can range from *strong primary* (e.g., one's spouse) to *weak secondary* (e.g., an acquaintance that one rarely sees). Although strong ties are important, weak ties are too because they perform a *bridging function*. This type of connection allows a consumer access between subgroups. For example, you might have a regular group of friends that is a primary reference group (strong ties). If you have an interest in tennis one of these friends might introduce you to a group of people in her dorm who play on the tennis team. As a result, you gain access to their valuable expertise through this bridging function. This referral process demonstrates the *strength of weak ties.*

Word-of-Mouth Communication

OBJECTIVE

Why are the things that other consumers tell us about products (good and bad) often more influential than the advertising we see?

Altoids breath mints have been around for 200 years, but it's only recently they've been a big hit. How did this happen? The revival began when the mint started to attract a devoted following among smokers and coffee drinkers who hung out in the blossoming Seattle club scene during the 1980s. Until 1993, when Kraft bought manufacturer Callard & Bowers, only those "in the know" sucked the mints. The brand's marketing manager persuaded Kraft to hire advertising agency Leo Burnett to develop a modest promotional campaign. The agency decided to publicize the candy with subway posters sporting retro imagery and other "low-tech" media to avoid making the product seem mainstream—that would turn off the original audience.[76] As young people started to tune into this "retro" treat, its popularity skyrocketed.

As the Altoids success story illustrates, "buzz" makes a hit product. **Word of mouth (WOM)** is product information individuals transmit to other individuals. Because we get the word from people we know, WOM tends to be more reliable and trustworthy than messages from more formal marketing channels. And unlike advertising, WOM often comes with social pressure to conform to these recommendations.[77]

Ironically, despite all the money marketers pump into lavish ads, WOM is far more powerful: It influences two-thirds of all consumer-goods sales.[78] In one recent survey, 69 percent of interviewees said they relied on a personal referral at least once over the course of a year to help them choose a restaurant, 36 percent reported they used referrals to decide on computer hardware and software, and 22 percent got help from friends and associates to decide where to travel.[79]

If you think carefully about the content of your own conversations in the course of a normal day, you will probably agree that much of what you discuss with friends, family members, or coworkers is product-related: When you compliment someone on her dress and ask her where she bought it, recommend a new restaurant to a friend, or complain to your neighbor about the shoddy treatment you got at the bank, you engage in WOM. Recall, for example, that comments and suggestions his fellow RUBs made drove many of Zachary's biker purchases. Marketers have been aware of the power of WOM for many years, but recently they've been more aggressive about trying to promote and control it instead of sitting back and hoping people will like their products enough to talk them up. Companies like BzzAgent enlist as many as hundreds of thousands of "agents" who try new products and spread the word about those they like.[80] And, many sophisticated marketers today also precisely track WOM. For example, the ongoing TalkTrack study reports which brands consumers mention the most in different categories. Based on online surveys of 14,000 women, it reports that middle-aged (baby boomer) women talk about Kraft more than any other packaged goods food brand, while they discuss Olay the most among beauty products.[81]

As far back as the Stone Age (well, the 1950s anyway), communications theorists challenged the assumption that advertising primarily determines what we buy. As a

As its name suggests, BzzAgent recruits consumers to create a "buzz" for clients. You can sign up at bzzagent.com.

Source: © 2009 Bzzagent.

rule, advertising is more effective when it reinforces our existing product preferences than when it tries to create new ones.[82] Studies in both industrial and consumer purchase settings underscore the idea that, although information from impersonal sources is important to create brand awareness, consumers rely on WOM in the later stages of evaluation and adoption.[83] Quite simply, the more positive information consumers get about a product from peers, the more likely they will be to adopt the product.[84]

The influence of others' opinions is at times even more powerful than our own perceptions. In one study of furniture choices, consumers' estimates of how much their friends would like the furniture was a better predictor of purchase than what they thought of it.[85] In addition, consumers may find their own reasons to push a brand that take the manufacturer by surprise: That's what happened with Mountain Dew—we trace its popularity among younger consumers to the "buzz" about the soda's high caffeine content. As an advertising executive explained, "The caffeine thing was not in any of Mountain Dew's television ads. This drink is hot by word-of-mouth."[86]

WOM is especially powerful when the consumer is relatively unfamiliar with the product category. We would expect such a situation in the case of new products (e.g., medications to prevent hair loss) or those that are technologically complex (e.g., laptops). One way to reduce uncertainty about the wisdom of a purchase is to talk about it. Talking gives the consumer an opportunity to generate supporting arguments for the purchase and to garner support for this decision from others. For example the strongest predictor of a person's intention to buy a residential solar water-heating system is the number of solar-heat users the person knows.[87]

You talk about products for several reasons:[88]

- You might be highly involved with a type of product or activity and enjoy talking about it. Computer hackers, avid football fans, and "fashion plates" seem to share the ability to steer a conversation toward their particular interests.
- You might be knowledgeable about a product and use conversations as a way to let others know it. Thus, word-of-mouth communication sometimes enhances the ego of the individual who wants to impress others with her expertise.

Wal-Mart recently contended with a widespread text-messaging hoax that warns women to stay away from its stores or risk death. The digital rumor apparently originated in an **urban myth** (an unsubstantiated "fact" that many people accept as true) that circulated via e-mail several years ago. As a reflection of how widespread this myth became, at one point Wal-Mart was number 5 on Twitter's list of trending topics.[90]

A new form of malicious rumor is **Web bullying**, where one or more people post malicious comments about someone else in a coordinated effort to harass them. In South Korea, a famous actress named Choi Jinsil hung herself after online rumors claimed she had driven another actor to take his life. A Korean singer killed herself because rumors claimed she had plastic surgery. In the United States, the most high-profile case involved the suicide of a 13-year-old girl after classmates created a fake boy online who first flirted with the girl and then taunted her with the claim that the world would be better off without her. The hoax allegedly began because the mother of one of the classmates wanted to find out what the victim was saying about her daughter online.

There is a long tradition of inventing fake stories to see who will swallow them—like the one in 1824 when a man convinced 300 New Yorkers to sign up for a construction project. He claimed all the new building in the lower part of Manhattan (what is now the Wall Street area) was making the island bottom-heavy. So, they needed to saw off this section of town and tow it out to sea to prevent New York City from tipping over!

The Web is a perfect medium to spread rumors and hoaxes, and we can only guess how much damage this "project" would cause today if the perpetrator recruited construction crews via e-mail! Modern-day hoaxes abound; many of these are in the form of e-mail chain letters promising instant riches if you pass the message on to 10 friends. Your professor will love one variation of this hoax:

● You might initiate a discussion out of genuine concern for someone else. We like to ensure that people we care about buy what is good for them or that they do not waste their money.

Negative WOM and the Power of Rumors

WOM is a two-edged sword that cuts both ways for marketers. Informal discussions among consumers can make or break a product or store. Furthermore, consumers weigh **negative word of mouth** more heavily than they do positive comments. According to a study by the White House Office of Consumer Affairs, 90 percent of unhappy customers will not do business with a company again. Each of these people is likely to share his grievance with at least nine other people, and 13 percent of these disgruntled customers tell more than 30 people about their negative experience.[89]

Especially when we consider a new product or service, we're likely to pay more attention to negative information than to positive information and to tell others about our nasty experience.[91] Research shows that negative WOM reduces the credibility of a firm's advertising and influences consumers' attitudes toward a product as well as their intention to buy it.[92] Dell found this out the hard way when bloggers denounced the computer maker's quality and service levels; then the popular media picked up this discontent and magnified it.[93]

As Dell discovered, it's incredibly easy to spread negative WOM online. Many dissatisfied customers and disgruntled former employees create Web sites simply to share their tales of woe with others. For example, a Web site for people to complain about the Dunkin' Donuts chain got to be so popular the company bought it in order to control the bad press it got. A man created the site because he couldn't get skim milk for his coffee.[94] An in-depth study of 40 complaint Web sites such as walmartsucks.com identified three basic themes.[95]

1 **Injustice**—Consumer protestors frequently talk about their fruitless attempts to contact the company.
2 **Identity**—Posters characterize the violator (often top management) as evil, rather than simply incompetent.
3 **Agency**—Individual Web site creators try to create a collective identity for those who share their anger with a company. They evoke themes of crusade and heroism to rally others to believe that they have the power to change the *status quo*—where companies can wrong consumers without retribution.

In the 1930s, some companies hired "professional rumormongers" to organize word-of-mouth campaigns that pushed their clients' products and criticized competitors.[96] More recently, Bio Business International, a small Canadian company that markets 100 percent cotton nonchlorine-bleached tampons under the name Terra Femme, encouraged women to spread a message that the tampons its American competitors make contain dioxin. There is very little evidence to support the claim that these products are dangerous, but as a result of this rumor, Procter & Gamble received thousands of complaints about its feminine hygiene products.[97] More recently Domino's Pizza dealt with a public relations crisis after two employees in a North Carolina outlet posted a prank YouTube video. More than a million viewers watched in horror as one of the workers shoved cheese up his nose and spread nasal mucus on sandwiches—ostensibly before they went out for delivery. The two were slapped with a felony charge for delivering prohibited foods. Although the hapless duo insisted they never actually sent out the contaminated food, consumers' perceptions of Domino's plummeted in just a few days. P.S. Surprise: Both employees were fired.[98]

As we transmit information to one another, it tends to change. The resulting message usually does not at all resemble the original. The British psychologist Frederic Bartlett used the method of *serial reproduction* to examine how content

Hoaxkill.com is a Web site dedicated to tracking hoaxes and debunking product rumors.

Source: Courtesy of Joroen Siking Hoaxkill.com.

mutates. Like the game of "Telephone" many of us played as kids, he asked a subject to reproduce a stimulus, such as a drawing or a story. He then gave another subject this reproduction and asked him to copy it, and repeated this process several times. Figure 10.3 illustrates how a message changes as people reproduce it. Bartlett found that distortions almost inevitably follow a pattern: They tend to change from ambiguous forms to more conventional ones as subjects try to make them consistent with their preexisting schemas (see Chapter 2). He called this process *assimilation* and he noted that it often occurs as people engage in *leveling* when they omit details to simplify the structure, or *sharpening* when they exaggerate prominent details.

OBJECTIVE

How do online technologies accelerate the impact of word-of-mouth communication?

Cutting-Edge WOM Strategies

In the "old days" (i.e., a few years ago), here's how a toy company would launch a new product: Unveil a hot holiday toy during a spring trade fair, run a November– December saturation television ad campaign during cartoon prime time to sell the toy to kids, then sit back and watch as desperate parents scramble through the aisles at Toys "R" Us. Then, wait for the resulting media coverage to drive still more sales.

Fast-forward to a current strategy: A Hong Kong company called Silverlit Toys makes the $30 Picoo Z helicopter. At one point a Google search for the term Picoo produced more than 109,000 URLs, and with many of those links pointed to major online global gift retailers like Hammacher-Schlemmer and Toys "R" Us. Do you think this huge exposure was the result of a meticulously planned promotional strategy? Think again. By most accounts, a 28-year-old tech worker in Chicago started the Picoo Z buzz; he bought his helicopter after he read about it on a hobbyist message board. A few months later he uploaded his homemade video of the

In a scam called "Win Tenure Fast," academics were told to add their names to a document and then cite it in their own research papers. The idea is that everyone who gets the letter cites the professor's name and with so many citations you're guaranteed to get tenure! If only it were that easy.

Other hoaxes involve major corporations. A popular one promised that if you try Microsoft products you would win a free trip to Disneyland. Nike received several hundred pairs of old sneakers a day after the rumor spread that you would get a free pair of new shoes in exchange for your old, smelly ones (pity the delivery people who had to cart these packages to the company!). Procter & Gamble received more than 10,000 irate calls after a rumor began to spread on newsgroups that its Febreze fabric deodorant kills dogs. In a preemptive strike, the company registered numerous Web site names such as febrezekillspet.com, febrezesucks.com, and ihateprocterandgamble.com to be sure angry consumers didn't use them. The moral: Don't believe everything you click on.

Figure 10.3 THE TRANSMISSION OF MISINFORMATION

toy on YouTube. Within 2 weeks, 15 of his friends bought the toy and they in turn posted their own videos and pointed viewers to the original video. Internet retailers who troll online conversations for fresh and exciting buzz identified the toy and started to add their own links to the clips. Within a few short months there were hundreds of Picoo Z videos and more than a million people viewed them (find one at: youtube.com/watch?v=y6t1R3yB-cs). As marketers increasingly recognize the power of WOM to make or break a new product, they come up with new ways to get consumers to help them sell. Let's review some successful strategies.

OBJECTIVE

How is social networking changing the way companies and consumers interact?

Social Networking

The Skittles candy brand changed its Web site into a social media hub and in the process significantly boosted consumers' awareness of the product. Instead of seeing corporate-produced content, a visitor to the site finds links to Twitter to read tweets about Skittles (good and bad). Another link guides him to Skittles videos and photos on YouTube and Flickr, and if he clicks "Friends," he'll go directly to the brand's Facebook area.[99]

Skittles successfully tapped into the consumer engine we call **social networking**. Today nearly one in three consumers consider themselves media "broadcasters"—rather than passively taking it all in, they actively contribute to online conversations as they post their own commentary, video, photos, and music.[100]

Here's how some smart marketers play the social networking game:

- As part of Hallmark's promotion of (Product) Red (Bono's campaign to fight AIDS), the card company created <u>Hallmark.com/red</u>. The site includes a blog, a calculator that determines the impact (Product) Red purchases have on AIDS-related efforts, customizable greeting cards, an opportunity for consumers to share their stories, contests, video sharing, graphics downloads, networking on the microsite and at Facebook and Flickr, and an e-mail newsletter.[101]

- In a first for a major group, R.E.M. debuted its album *Accelerate* on the social networking application iLike. This arrangement allowed fans to stream and share the entire album before the band releases to the public.[102]

- DiGiorno launched a new flatbread pizza product on Twitter. The company contacted tweeters with a lot of followers and offered to provide free pizza for *tweetups* (face-to-face meetings of Twitterers).[103]

- Want to find out where the hot spots are tonight? The Citysense tool uses GPS data and real-time feeds that link to search engines like Yelp. This information then displays on a "heat map" that shows you where people in the network hang out. An alarm-clock feature goes off if an exceptionally large number of people are swarming into the city to help clubbers avoid traffic.[104]

- SocialVibe, a company that provides incentives for members of social networks to interact and endorse consumer brands, launched a new service that includes a patented micropayment system. It enables marketers to offer incentives—usually charitable donations to favored causes—directly to the members of social

The Citysense app pinpoints locations where others in your network hang out.

Source: Courtesy of Citysense.

The Whopper Sacrifice was an advertising campaign Burger King launched to promote its new Angry Whopper sandwich. You could earn a free burger, but to get it you had to sacrifice ten of your Facebook friends. After you delete these names, you get a coupon in the mail. Your ex-friends get a note that informs them they were dumped for a freebie sandwich. The burger costs $3.69 so when you do the math, each former friend is worth about 37 cents. Although it sounds cruel to give up a friend for this amount, many Facebookers jumped at the chance to purge their friend lists. As one student with several hundred friends commented, "It's a good excuse to get rid of old girlfriends and their families on my account and get a Whopper out of it."[106]

networks who promote their brands on their personal pages. As marketers like Adobe and Coca-Cola sign on, this new platform has the potential to let companies boost their presence on Facebook and other networks without being too intrusive.[105]

Did you tweet today? Although most of us participate in social networks for fun (and some of us seem addicted), these platforms also offer some really serious marketing implications. Indeed, it's fair to say that aspects of this technology revolution will fundamentally change business models in many industries—especially because they empower end consumers to literally become partners and shape markets. It's hard to overstate the impact this change will have on how we create, distribute, promote, and consume products and services.

Social networking is an integral part of what many call **Web 2.0**, which is the Internet on steroids. The key change is the interactivity among producers and users, but these are some other characteristics of a Web 2.0 platform:[107]

- It improves as the number of users increases. For example, Amazon's ability to recommend books to you based on what other people with similar interests buy gets better as it tracks more and more people who enter search queries.
- Its currency is eyeballs. Google makes money as it charges advertisers according to the number of people who see their ads after they type in a search term.
- It's version-free and in perpetual beta. *Wikipedia*, the online encyclopedia, gets updated constantly by volunteer editors who "correct" others' errors.
- It categorizes entries according to "folksonomy" rather than "taxonomy." In other words, sites rely on users rather than preestablished systems to sort contents. Listeners at <u>Pandora.com</u> create their own "radio stations" that play songs by artists they choose as well as other similar artists.[108]

Crowd Power

This last point highlights a key change in the way some new media companies approach their businesses: Think of it as marketing strategy by committee. The **wisdom of crowds** perspective (from a book by that name) argues that under the right circumstances, groups are smarter than the smartest people in them. If this is true, it implies that large numbers of consumers can predict successful products.[109]

Social networking sites have the power to let their members dictate purchase decisions. At <u>Threadless.com</u>, customers rank T-shirt designs ahead of time, and the company prints the winning ideas. Every week, contestants upload T-shirts designs to the site, where about 700 compete to be among the six that it will print during that time. Threadless visitors score designs on a scale of 0 to 5, and the staff selects winners from the most popular entrants. The six lucky artists each get $2,000 in cash and merchandise. *Threadless sells out of every shirt it offers.* This business model has made a small fortune for a few designers "the crowd" particularly likes. One pair of Chicago-based artists sold $16 million worth of T-shirts. To keep the judges and buyers coming back, the owners offer rewards—upload a photo of yourself wearing a Threadless T-shirt and you get a store credit of $1.50. Refer a friend who buys a T-shirt and you get $3. The site sells more than 1,500 T-shirts in a typical day.[110]

Here are some more crowd-based sites to watch:

- At the French CrowdSpirit site, participants submit ideas for consumer electronics products, and the community votes for the best ones. Those go to the site's R&D partners and investors who then decide which to finance for further development. Community members test and fine-tune a prototype, and then they can buy the products that go to market. The community handles product support and recommends the new products to retailers.[111]
- Sermo is a social network for physicians. It has no advertising, job listings, or membership fees. It makes its money (about $500,000 a year so far) by charging

CB AS I LIVE IT

Ted Powers, *Washington State University*

When I'm not in the classroom, I am usually playing drums in my band Yarn Owl. I constantly promote and try to draw interest to Yarn Owl by utilizing inexpensive social networking sites such as Facebook and MySpace. Although these sites have proven to be effective, they have their pitfalls—too much clutter and a lack of intimate interaction with fans. My band wanted to differentiate itself within the online community by building a strong fan base at our concerts. Knowing some of the techniques marketers use from previous classes, my band decided to develop a strategy to draw a distinctive identity that people would be interested and committed to. By using a simple symbol as a visual representation, we developed yarn bracelets that the public directly links to my band Yarn Owl. This is a unique, yet easy token that represents fans who are committed to the music of Yarn Owl. We give away yarn bracelets for free at concerts to individuals who interact with us and show enjoyment in our music. People then wear these bracelets around the venue and tell their friends about us.

This small-scale group influence of friends leads to a word-of-mouth buzz in the venue. Additionally a small-scale brand community develops as people begin to see others wearing the bracelets and relating the bracelet to Yarn Owl's music.

This has been proven to be an effective way to engage our listeners and build a strong fan base. My experience is closely tied to the development of a brand community and also the impact of WOM. The Harley (HOG) users group mentioned in the chapter is spot on in comparison to my experience (if you missed it, I would strongly suggest rereading). When people come and show interest in us, we give them a bracelet, however, in doing so, they also purchase CD's, T-shirts and other merchandise to show commitment to the band, similar to the Harley community identifying with a family of users.

The book's description of a brand community is accurate as it discusses similar users relating to one another through the consumption of a product. However, the book's definition lacks the interpretation to relate a brand community to a smaller-scale community. The Harley example is informative however—it is associated with a long-time company that has been successful for ages. My experience is tied to a smaller-scale

community, one which you may be more inclined to use. The book also fails to mention the importance of time in developing a brand community. It is crucial as a marketer to understand the element of time and that it may take an abundant amount to establish a user community with a strong attachment to your product. An overnight success is very rare and it is vital to be aware of this aspect. My experience is also associated with WOM. Descriptions in the book are exceedingly self-explanatory, as WOM is defined as users transferring information to others about a product or service. WOM may be a beneficial asset when the opinion of credible individuals holds more value than an advertisement.

What can you take from this? If you want to get the word out about a club or organization at your university, try to find something that is tied to your mission or product and is an easily transmitted message. A simple message will spread through WOM and lead to a larger group. In my case the essence of the yarn bracelet is still small scale but has been effective to spread throughout a crowd using WOM and developing Yarn Owl's unique brand community.

To listen and find out more about Yarn Owl visit myspace.com/yarnowl.

institutional investors for the opportunity to listen in as approximately 15,000 doctors chat among themselves. Say, for example, a young patient breaks out in hives after he takes a new prescription. A doctor might post whether she thinks this is because of a rare symptom or perhaps the drug's side effect. If other doctors feel it's the latter, this negative news could affect the drug manufacturer's stock so their opinions have value to analysts. Doctors who ask or answer a question that paying observers deem especially valuable receive bonuses of $5 to $25 per post.[112]

● How about social networking sites that "create" a concert as they persuade an artist to perform in a certain city or country? At Eventful.com, fans demand events and performances in their town and spread the word to make them happen. Or how about actually buying a piece of the bands you like? Go to

At threadless.com, users vote on which T-shirt designs the company will print and sell.
Source: © Threadless.com, 2009.

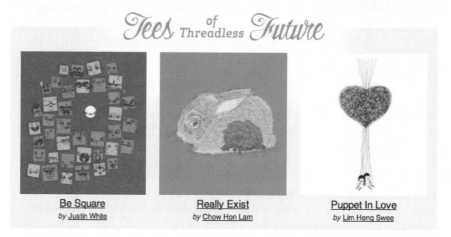

SellaBand where fans ("believers") buy "parts" in a band for $10 per share. Once the band sells 5,000 parts, SellaBand arranges a professional recording, including top studios, A&R (Artists & Repertoire) managers (industry talent scouts), and producers. Believers receive a limited edition CD of the recording. Believers get a piece of the profits, so they're likely to promote the band wherever they can.[113]

● Individual consumers gain crowd clout when they **shopmob** with strangers. So far this is most popular in China where the *tuangou* ("team purchase") phenomenon involves strangers who organize themselves around a specific product or service. Members who meet online at sites such as TeamBuy.com, Taobao.com, and Liba.com arrange to meet at a certain date and time in a real-world store and literally mob the unsuspecting retailer—the bargain-hungry crowd negotiates a group discount on the spot.[114]

● The St. Louis Cardinals invited fans to send the team scouting reports on promising college players. The idea is to collect intelligence on talent at small colleges that scouts don't routinely visit. One of the team's executives explained, "We don't have a monopoly on baseball knowledge. Just looking at the fan sites and posting boards, you see an amazing amount of energy. Why not harness it?"[115]

Guerrilla Marketing

To promote their hip-hop albums, Def Jam and other labels start building a buzz months before a release as they leak advance copies to deejays who put together "mix tapes" they sell on the street. If the kids seem to like a song, *street teams* then push it to club deejays. As the official release date nears, these groups of fans start to slap up posters around the inner city. They plaster telephone poles, sides of buildings, and car windshields with promotions that announce the release of new albums.[117] These streetwise strategies started in the mid-1970s, when pioneering deejays like Kool DJ Herc and Afrika Bambaataa promoted their parties through graffiti-style flyers. As Ice Cube observed, "Even though I'm an established artist, I still like to leak my music to a kid on the street and let him duplicate it for his homies before it hits radio."[118]

This type of grassroots effort epitomizes **guerrilla marketing**: promotional strategies that use unconventional means and venues to push products. The term implies that the marketer "ambushes" the unsuspecting recipient. These campaigns often recruit legions of real consumers who agree to engage in some kind of street theater or other activity to convince others to use the product or service. Scion for example often reaches out to its young buyers with street teams that distribute merchandise and hang wild posters wherever they can to encourage twentysomethings to check out the carmaker's videos and multiplayer games on its Web site.[119]

Net Profit

A **virtual community of consumption** is a collection of people who interact online to share their enthusiasm for and knowledge about a specific consumption activity. Like the brand communities we discussed earlier, these groups form around common love for a product, whether it's Barbie dolls or BlackBerry PDAs. However, members remain anonymous because they only interact with each other in cyberspace.

These online communities often start organically as consumers create forums to identify people who share a similar passion. Of late however marketers who understand the power of these groups more proactively create their own communities to encourage positive WOM, solicit new product and advertising ideas, and locate loyal customers. Dove recently invested several million dollars to build a community for women. At its Web site Dove.msn.com, members can watch original programming such as the miniseries *Fresh Takes* that stars singer Alicia Keys. The site also offers skin care advice from a doctor and forums devoted to how people today think of beauty. On the "In the MotherHood" community for women that Sprint and Suave shampoo cosponsor, mothers submit short scripts about their lives and see them acted out by Hollywood stars such as Jenny McCarthy.[116]

Role-playing games involve thousands of players worldwide who belong to virtual communities.
Source: Courtesy of Zuma Wire West Photos/Newscom.

Today, big companies buy into guerrilla marketing strategies big-time, especially to snag younger consumers who they don't reach with more traditional advertising. Here are some guerrilla campaigns that built buzz:

- Procter & Gamble's Tremor division spreads the word about its products among young people. It recruits almost 300,000 kids between the ages of 13 and 19 to deliver endorsements in school cafeterias, at sleepovers, by cell phone, and by e-mail. It taps these Tremorites to talk up just about everything, from movies and music (such as new releases by artists like Lenny Kravitz and Coldplay) to milk and motor oil—and they do it free. Tremor looks for kids with a wide social circle and a gift of gab. To register, kids fill out a questionnaire, which asks them, among other things, to report how many friends, family members, and acquaintances they communicate with every day. (Tremorites have an average of 170 names on their buddy lists; a typical teen has 30.) P&G rewards the kids for their help with exclusive music mixes and other trinkets such as shampoo and cheap watches.[120]
- Kayem Foods, which makes Al Fresco chicken sausage, hired a company to organize a guerrilla campaign called the Great Sausage Fanout. On a July 4 weekend, legions of people who went to cookouts showed up with packages of Al Fresco chicken sausage for their hosts to throw on the grill. The company sent the "agents" coupons for free sausage and a set of instructions for the best ways to talk up the product.[121]
- The train line CSX launched a safety-awareness campaign when it hired people to throw eggs at the company's outdoor billboards. The billboards carry the stark

black-on-white words "Cars hitting trains." Eggs smashing against the billboard demonstrate the impact of a car hitting a train. The idea is to get people to be careful when they cross railroad tracks.[122]

● *Brand ambassadors* pop up in eye-catching outfits to announce a new brand or service. AT&T sent its ambassadors to high-traffic areas of California and New Jersey, where they did random favors such as handing dog biscuits to people as they walked their dogs and providing binoculars to concertgoers to promote its new AT&T Local Service. Hyatt Hotels unleashed 100 bellhops in Manhattan—they opened doors, carried packages, and handed out pillow mints to thousands of consumers.[123]

Viral Marketing

Many students are big fans of Hotmail, a free e-mail service. But there's no such thing as a free lunch: Hotmail inserts a small ad on every message it sends; each user acts as a salesperson when he or she spreads the message to friends. The company had 5 million subscribers in its first year and it continues to grow exponentially.[125] **Viral marketing** refers to the strategy of getting visitors to a Web site to forward information on the site to their friends in order to make still more consumers aware of the product—usually when an organization creates online content that is entertaining or just plain weird.

Kodak Gallery's viral campaign at <u>makemesuper.com</u> takes a photo a user uploads and pastes it onto a superhero's body. The site then creates a cheesy video that shows the super-user as he engages in such "super tasks" as mowing the lawn or parallel parking.[126] In a successful application of viral marketing on YouTube, many viewers checked out a three-minute short film called *Extreme Sheep LED Art*. It featured a nighttime scene—Welsh shepherds wrangle a huge herd of sheep draped with LED jackets into moving formations that create a series of images such as the Mona Lisa and a fireworks display. The video turned out to be an ad for a new line of HD televisions from Samsung Electronics that are backlit by LEDs.

Virtual Worlds: The Next (Digital) Frontier

The influential cyberpunk novel *Snow Crash* by author Neal Stephenson envisioned the **Metaverse**; a virtual world where everyday people take on glamorous identities in a 3-D immersive digital environment. The book's main character delivers pizza in RL (real life), but in the Metaverse he's a warrior prince and champion sword fighter.[127] The hugely popular *Matrix* movie trilogy paints a similar (though more sinister) picture of a world that blurs the lines between physical and digital reality.[128]

The majority of **virtual worlds** are 3-D and employ sophisticated computer graphics to produce photo-realistic images. Furthermore, unlike most of today's relatively static networking sites, individuals enter the world in the form of a a digital persona that they create themselves. As we saw in Chapter 5, these *avatars* walk, fly, teleport, try on clothes, try out products, attend in-world events (educational classes, concerts, political speeches, etc.), and they interact in real time (via textchat, IM, and VoIP) with other avatars around the world. This unprecedented level of interactivity facilities consumers' engagement and often creates the *flow state* we discussed in Chapter 4.

Analysts claim that the market for **virtual goods**—digital items that people buy and sell online—is worth at least $1.5 billion and is growing rapidly. Many thousands of in-world residents design, create, and purchase clothing, furniture, houses, vehicles, and other products their avatars need—and many do it in style as they acquire the kind of "bling" they can only dream about in real life. Some forward-thinking marketers understand that these platforms are the next stage they can use to introduce their products into people's lives, whether real or virtual. Today for example, people who play *The Sims* can import actual pieces of furniture from IKEA into their

Marketing Pitfall

Is any publicity good publicity? One of the most widely publicized guerrilla marketing stunts in recent years illustrates the potential for a good idea to go bad in a hurry. To promote its *Aqua Teen Hunger Force* show on the Adult Swim segment of its Cartoon Network, Turner Broadcasting hired a company to plant flashing light boards in public areas such as bridges around several cities. Observers in Boston thought they saw terrorist bombs instead, and the city essentially shut down as officials dealt with what they thought was a national security issue. Turner had to pay hefty fines and endure a lot of criticism for this stunt. However, the Adult Swim Web site boosted its traffic by 77 percent on the day after the story broke.[124]

virtual homes; the use of this sort of platform to accelerate purchases for real homes is unplowed ground.

With more than 150 of these immersive 3-D environments now live or in development, we may well see other social networks like Facebook migrate to these platforms in the near future. Whether via your computer or even your cell phone, you and your "friends" will hang out together (or at least your avatars will), and you'll shop and compare your choices wherever you are (hopefully not in class!). According to one estimate, by 2012 53 percent of kids and 80 percent of active Internet users will belong to at least one virtual world.

CHAPTER SUMMARY

Now that you have finished reading this chapter you should understand why:

 Others, especially those who possess some kind of social power, often influence us.

We belong to or admire many different groups, and a desire for them to accept us often drives our purchase decisions. Individuals or groups whose opinions or behavior are particularly important to consumers are reference groups. Both formal and informal groups influence the individual's purchase decisions, although such factors as the conspicuousness of the product and the relevance of the reference group for a particular purchase determine how influential the reference group is.

Individuals have influence in a group to the extent that they possess social power; types of social power include information power, referent power, legitimate power, expert power, reward power, and coercive power.

 We seek out others who share our interests in products or services.

Brand communities unite consumers who share a common passion for a product. Brandfests, when companies organize to encourage this kind of community, can build brand loyalty and reinforce group membership.

 We are motivated to buy or use products in order to be consistent with what other people do.

We conform to the desires of others for two basic reasons: (1) People who model their behavior after others because they take others' behavior as evidence of the correct way to act are conforming because of informational social influence, and (2) those who conform to satisfy the expectations of others or to be accepted by the group are affected by normative social influence. Group members often do things they would not do as individuals because their identities become merged with the group; they become deindividuated.

 Certain people are particularly likely to influence others' product choices.

Opinion leaders who are knowledgeable about a product and whose opinions are highly regarded tend to influence others' choices. Specific opinion leaders are somewhat hard to identify, but marketers who know their general characteristics can try to target them in their media and promotional strategies. Other influencers include market mavens, who have a general interest in marketplace activities, and surrogate consumers, who are compensated for their advice about purchases.

 The things that other consumers tell us about products (good and bad) are often more influential than the advertising we see.

Much of what we know about products we learn through word-of-mouth (WOM) communication rather than formal advertising. We tend to exchange product-related information in casual conversations. Guerrilla marketing strategies try to accelerate the WOM process when they enlist consumers to help spread the word.

Although WOM often is helpful to make consumers aware of products, it can also hurt companies when damaging product rumors or negative WOM occurs.

 Online technologies accelerate the impact of word-of-mouth communication.

The Web greatly amplifies our exposure to numerous reference groups. Virtual consumption communities unites those who share a common bond—enthusiasm about or knowledge of a specific product or service. Emerging marketing strategies try to leverage the potential of the Web to spread information from consumer to consumer extremely quickly. Viral marketing techniques enlist individuals to tout products, services, Web sites, and so on to others on behalf of companies. Blogging allows consumers to easily post their thoughts about products for others to see.

7 Social networking is changing the way companies and consumers interact.

Social networking, where members post information and make contact with others who share similar interests and opinions, changes the way we think about marketing. As Web 2.0 continues to develop, companies and consumers increasingly interact directly. The wisdom of crowds perspective argues that under the right circumstances, groups are smarter than the smartest people in them. If this is true, it implies that large numbers of consumers can predict successful products.[129] In a sense, a lot of social networking sites let their members dictate purchase decisions.

KEY TERMS

Antibrand communities, 388
Aspirational reference group, 387
Brand community, 386
Brandfests, 386
Cohesiveness, 388
Comparative influence, 386
Conformity, 391
Consumer tribe, 386
Decision polarization, 389
Deindividuation, 389
Guerrilla marketing, 407
Home shopping party, 390
Homophily, 392
Influence network, 393
Information cascades, 393
Market maven, 394
Membership reference group, 387

Mere exposure phenomenon, 388
Metaverse, 409
Name-letter effect, 385
Negative word mouth, 400
Normative influence, 386
Norms, 391
Opinion leader, 392
Principle of least interest, 391
Propinquity, 388
Reference group, 382
Reward power, 384
Risky shift effect, 389
Shopmobbing, 406
Social loafing, 389
Social networking, 402
Social power, 383

Sociometric methods, 396
Surrogate consumer, 395
Susceptibility to interpersonal influence, 391
Tie strength, 398
Tribal marketing strategy, 387
Two step flow model of influence, 393
Urban myth, 400
Viral marketing, 409
Virtual community of consumption, 407
Virtual goods, 409
Virtual worlds, 409
Web 2.0, 404
Web bullying, 400
Wisdom of crowds, 404
Word-of-mouth (WOM), 398

REVIEW

1 Name two dimensions that influence whether reference groups impact an individual's purchase decisions.
2 List three types of social power, and give an example of each.
3 Which tend to influence our behavior more: large formal groups or small informal groups? Why?
4 What is a brand community, and why is it of interest to marketers?
5 Describe the difference between a membership and an aspirational reference group and give an example of each kind.
6 Name one factor that makes it more likely a person will become part of a consumer's membership reference group.
7 Define *deindividuation* and give an example of this effect.
8 What is the risky shift, and how does it relate to shopping with friends?
9 What is the difference between normative and informational social influence?

10 Define *conformity* and give an example of it. Name three reasons why people conform.
11 How does the *principle of least interest* relate to your success in a romantic relationship?
12 What is *social comparison*? To what type of person do we usually choose to compare ourselves?
13 What is the difference between independence and anticonformity?
14 What is word of mouth, and how can it be more powerful than advertising?
15 Which is more powerful: positive or negative word of mouth?
16 Describe some ways marketers use the Internet to encourage positive WOM.
17 What is viral marketing? Guerrilla marketing? Give an example of each.
18 What is an opinion leader? Give three reasons why they are powerful influences on consumers' opinions. What are some characteristics of opinion leaders?

19 Is there such a thing as a generalized opinion leader? Why or why not?

20 What is the relationship between an opinion leader and an opinion seeker?

21 What is the difference between a market maven and a surrogate consumer?

22 How can marketers use opinion leaders to help them promote their products or services?

23 What are sociometric techniques? Under what conditions does it make sense to use them?

CONSUMER BEHAVIOR CHALLENGE

■ DISCUSS

1 Although social networking is red-hot, could its days be numbered? Many people have concerns about privacy issues. Others feel platforms like Facebook are too overwhelming. As one media executive comments, "Nobody has 5,000 real friends. At the end of the day it just becomes one big cauldron of noise." What's your stand on this: Can we have too much of a good thing? Will people start to tune out all of these networks?[130]

2 The average Internet user in the United States spends 3 hours a day online, with much of that time devoted to work and more than half of it to communications. Researchers report that the Internet has displaced television watching and a range of other activities. Internet users watch television for 1 hour and 42 minutes a day, compared with the national average of 2 hours. One study reported increasing physical isolation among Internet users; it created a controversy and drew angry complaints from some users who insisted that time they spent online did not detract from their social relationships. However, the researchers said they had now gathered further evidence showing that Internet use has lowered the amount of time people spend socializing with friends and even sleeping. According to the study, an hour of time spent using the Internet reduces face-to-face contact with friends, coworkers, and family by 23.5 minutes; lowers the amount of time spent watching television by 10 minutes; and reduces sleep time by 8.5 minutes.[131] What's your perspective on this issue—does increasing use of the Internet have positive or negative implications for interpersonal relationships in our society?

3 The Word-of-Mouth Marketing Association announced a set of rules and guidelines for word-of-mouth advertising. The trade group maintains that marketers must make sure that people talking up products or services disclose for whom they work. They also must use real consumers, not actors, who discuss what they really believe about a product.[132] The rules were prompted by several controversial incidents, such as a campaign the U.S. arm of Sony Ericsson Mobile Communications created for a camera phone. The company hired 60 actors to hang out at tourist attractions and ask unsuspecting passersby to take their pictures with the Sony Ericsson devices. It told the actors to identify themselves only when asked directly. What do you think about "stealth" campaigns such as this? Should marketers be required to disclose their true intentions when they try to initiate positive word of mouth?

4 Do you agree that deindividuation encourages binge drinking on campus? What can or should a college do to discourage this behavior?

5 The adoption of a certain brand of shoe or apparel by athletes can be a powerful influence on students and other fans. Should high school and college coaches be paid to determine what brand of athletic equipment their players wear?

6 The strategy of *viral marketing* gets customers to sell a product to other customers on behalf of the company. That often means convincing your friends to climb on the bandwagon, and sometimes you get a cut if they buy something.[133] Some might argue that that means you're selling out your friends (or at least selling to your friends) in exchange for a piece of the action. Others might say you're simply sharing the wealth with your buddies. Have you ever passed along names of your friends or sent them to a Web site such as hotmail.com? If so, what happened? How do you feel about this practice?

7 Are home shopping parties that put pressure on friends and neighbors to buy merchandise ethical?

8 The high-profile stunt to publicize *Aqua Teen Hunger Force* created a massive public disruption. When does a guerrilla marketing tactic go too far—or is anything fair game in the heated competition to capture jaded consumers' attention?

9 Mobile social networking is the next frontier in technology as companies race to adapt platforms like Facebook to our cell phones. Marketers are not far behind, especially because there are 3.3 billion cell phone subscribers worldwide—that number is far greater than the number of Internet users. One report says that about 2 percent of all mobile users already use their cell phones for social networking such as chat and multimedia sharing; it forecasts this proportion will zoom to at least

12.5 percent in a few years. Mobile social networks are appealing in part because companies can identify precisely where users are in the physical world. For example the SpaceMe service from GyPSii displays a map that identifies your friends' locations as well as photos, videos, and other information about them. A Dutch network called Bliin lets users update their location every 15 seconds.[134] This enhanced capability creates some fascinating marketing possibilities—but perhaps it also raises some ethical red flags. What do you see as the opportunities and the threats as we inevitably move to a world where our whereabouts are known to others?

■ APPLY

1 The power of unspoken social norms often becomes obvious only when we violate them. To witness this result firsthand, try one of the following: Stand facing the back wall in an elevator, serve dessert before the main course, offer to pay cash for dinner at a friend's home, wear pajamas to class, or tell someone *not* to have a nice day.

2 Identify a set of avoidance groups for your peers. Can you identify any consumption decisions that you and your friends make with these groups in mind?

3 Identify fashion opinion leaders on your campus. Do they fit the profile the chapter describes?

4 Conduct a sociometric analysis within your dormitory or neighborhood. For a product category such as music or cars, ask each individual to identify other individuals with whom they share information. Systematically trace all of these avenues of communication, and identify opinion leaders by locating individuals who others say provide helpful information.

5 See if you can demonstrate the risky shift. Get a group of friends together and ask each to privately rate the likelihood on a scale from 1 to 7 that they would try a controversial new product (e.g., a credit card that works with a chip implanted in a person's wrist). Then ask the group to discuss the product and rate the idea again. If the average rating changes, you've just observed a risky shift.

6 Trace a referral pattern for a service provider such as a hair stylist; track how clients came to choose him or her. See if you can identify opinion leaders who are responsible for referring several clients to the businessperson. How might the service provider take advantage of this process to grow his or her business?

Case Study

PARROT HEADS UNITE!

Are you a Parrot Head? If you don't know what that is, then you definitely are not. Jimmy Buffett fans all over the world proudly refer to themselves by this name. And in many respects, they represent one of the most dedicated fan bases anywhere. Why the name Parrot Head? In a 1985 concert, a member of the Eagles looked at the audience with their bright Hawaiian shirts. He announced that they "looked like Deadheads in tropical suits. They're like Parrot Heads."

Some critics think Jimmy Buffett's career peaked in the late 1970s, though between 1978 and 2006 he released eight gold, six platinum, and three multiplatinum records. During this period he gained a reputation for his concerts, wrote five best sellers, and he opened a chain of restaurants. Wal-Mart sells Margaritaville salsa and Target carries Margaritaville calamari.

Buffett fans gather by the thousands at concerts. A Buffett concert is like a beach party, with fans decked out in Hawaiian shirts and parrot hats. But the concert itself is only part of the event. Fans get to know each other year after year at tailgate parties. So many people party before Buffett concerts, in fact, that many venues charge admission now just to get into the tailgating area.

How die-hard are Buffett fans? Consider that many plan regular vacations around a Buffett concert (some have racked up dozens) or special trips to visit Buffett-themed restaurants in Caribbean destinations. Houses, boats, and RVs decked out in tropical Buffet décor are not uncommon, and there have been a good number of Parrot Head–themed weddings.

Buffett fans come from all walks of life, age groups, and occupations; they typically cite "escapism" as a reason for their devotion. But Parrot Heads do much more than just "wasting away again in Margaritaville." Many spend their free time as volunteers at blood drives, raise thousands of dollars to grant the wishes of sick kids, or build houses for the needy. Parrot Heads in Paradise, a group of fans with more than 220 chapters, has donated more than $10 million to charity.

And Buffett's management recognizes the charitable efforts of the Buffett community. Parrot Head Clubs get a certain amount of tickets allocated to them. Members still have to pay for them, but they get first dibs on the best seats depending on how many Parrot Points (doled out to members when they participate in charitable or volunteer efforts) they earn. As tickets have become harder and harder to obtain, this is indeed a welcome bonus.

DISCUSSION QUESTIONS

1 How can we consider Jimmy Buffett fans as members of a reference group? A brand community? A consumer tribe?

2 Refer to your responses to question 1. What kind of opportunities does the existence of the Buffett community present to marketers? Develop a list of specific marketing and promotional tactics.

Sources: Douglas Hanks, "Jimmy Buffett Represents Florida Culture, Lifestyle," *McClatchy Tribune Business News* (May 17, 2009); Alexis Garrobo, "Tropical Tuesday Brings out the Parrot Heads," *McClatchy Tribune Business News* (July 16, 2008); Geoff Gehman, "A Buffet of Buffett: Tropical Troubadour Sets Sail to Philly," *McClatchy Tribune Business News* (June 5, 2008).

NOTES

1. www.google.com/search?rlz51C1CHMB_enUS307US310&sourceid5 chrome&ie5UTF-8&q5davidson, accessed July 1, 2009.
2. Details adapted from John W. Schouten and James H. McAlexander, "Market Impact of a Consumption Subculture: The Harley-Davidson Mystique," in Fred van Raaij and Gary Bamossy, eds., *Proceedings of the 1992 European Conference of the Association for Consumer Research* (Amsterdam, 1992); John W. Schouten and James H. McAlexander, "Subcultures of Consumption: An Ethnography of the New Bikers," *Journal of Consumer Research* 22 (June 1995): 43–61. See also Kelly Barron, "Not So Easy Riders," *Forbes* (May 15, 2000).
3. Joel B. Cohen and Ellen Golden, "Informational Social Influence and Product Evaluation," *Journal of Applied Psychology* 56 (February 1972): 54–59; Robert E. Burnkrant and Alain Cousineau, "Informational and Normative Social Influence in Buyer Behavior," *Journal of Consumer Research* 2 (December 1975): 206–15; Peter H. Reingen, "Test of a List Procedure for Inducing Compliance with a Request to Donate Money," *Journal of Applied Psychology* 67 (1982): 110–18.
4. Dyan Machan, "Is the Hog Going Soft?" *Forbes* (March 10, 1997): 114–19.
5. C. Whan Park and V. Parker Lessig, "Students and Housewives: Differences in Susceptibility to Reference Group Influence," *Journal of Consumer Research* 4 (September 1977): 102–10.
6. Gina Kolata, "Study Finds Big Social Factor in Quitting Smoking," *New York Times* (May 22, 2008), www.nytimes.com/2008/05/22/science/ 22smoke.html?ex=1369195200&en=0a10910fcde1a1ac&ei=5124& partner=permalink&exprod=permalink, accessed May 22, 2008.
7. Jeffrey D. Ford and Elwood A. Ellis, "A Re-examination of Group Influence on Member Brand Preference," *Journal of Marketing Research* 17 (February 1980): 125–32; Thomas S. Robertson, *Innovative Behavior and Communication* (New York: Holt, Rinehart and Winston, 1980): Chapter 8.
8. William O. Bearden and Michael J. Etzel, "Reference Group Influence on Product and Brand Purchase Decisions," *Journal of Consumer Research* 9 (1982): 183–94; also cf. A. E. Schlosser and S. Shavitt, "Anticipating Discussion About a Product: Rehearsing What to Say Can Affect Your Judgments," *Journal of Consumer Research* 29, no. 1 (2002): 101–15.
9. Sam Schechner, "When Your Political Opinion Isn't Yours Alone Broadcasts of Political Debates That Include Live Audience Feedback Can Influence What You're Thinking—Hecklers Can, Too," *Wall Street Journal* (October 10, 2008), http://online.wsj.com/article/ SB122359949981721549.html, accessed October 11, 2008.
10. Kenneth J. Gergen and Mary Gergen, *Social Psychology* (New York: Harcourt Brace Jovanovich, 1981): 312.
11. J. R. P. French, Jr., and B. Raven, "The Bases of Social Power," in D. Cartwright, ed., *Studies in Social Power* (Ann Arbor, MI: Institute for Social Research, 1959): 150–67.
12. Michael R. Solomon, "Packaging the Service Provider," *The Service Industries Journal* 5 (March 1985): 64–72.
13. Tamar Charry, "Advertising: Hawking, Wozniak Pitch Modems for U.S. Robotics," *New York Times* (February 5, 1997).
14. Patricia M. West and Susan M. Broniarczyk, "Integrating Multiple Opinions: The Role of Aspiration Level on Consumer Response to Critic Consensus," *Journal of Consumer Research* 25 (June 1998): 38–51.
15. Gergen and Gergen, *Social Psychology*.
16. Stephanie Rosenbloom, "Names That Match Forge a Bond on the Internet," *New York Times,* (April 10, 2008), www.nytimes.com/2008/04/ 10/us/10names.html?ref=us, accessed April 10, 2008.

17. Harold H. Kelley, "Two Functions of Reference Groups," in Harold Proshansky and Bernard Siedenberg, eds., *Basic Studies in Social Psychology* (New York: Holt, Rinehart and Winston, 1965): 210–14.
18. Leslie Kaufman, "Utilities Turn Their Customers Green, With Envy," *New York Times* (January 30, 2009), www.nytimes.com/2009/01/ 31/science/earth/31compete.html?_r=1, accessed January 31, 2009.
19. Kris Oser, "Microsoft's Halo 2 Soars on Viral Push," *Advertising Age* (October 25, 2004): 46.
20. Hope Jensen Schau, Albert M. Muñiz, Jr., and Eric J. Arnould, "How Brand Community Practices Create Value." *Journal of Marketing,* forthcoming; John W. Schouten, James H. McAlexander, and Harold F. Koenig. "Transcendent Customer Experience and Brand Community." *Journal of the Academy of Marketing Science,* 35 (2007): 357–368; James H. McAlexander, John W. Schouten, and Harold F. Koenig, "Building Brand Community," *Journal of Marketing* 66 (January 2002): 38–54; Albert Muñiz and Thomas O'Guinn, "Brand Community," *Journal of Consumer Research* (March 2001): 412–32; Scott A. Thompson and Rajiv K. Sinha. "Brand Communities and New Product Adoption: The Influence and Limits of Oppositional Loyalty," *Journal of Marketing,* 72 (November 2008): 65–80.
21. Stephen Baker, "Following the Luxury Chocolate Lover," *BusinessWeek* (March 25, 2009), www.businessweek.com/technology/content/ mar2009/tc20090325_892605.htm, accessed March 25, 2009.
22. Veronique Cova and Bernard Cova, "Tribal Aspects of Postmodern Consumption Research: The Case of French In-Line Roller Skaters," *Journal of Consumer Behavior* 1 (June 2001): 67–76.
23. Jennifer Edson Escalas and James R. Bettman, "You Are What You Eat: The Influence of Reference Groups on Consumers' Connections to Brands," *Journal of Consumer Psychology* 13, no. 3 (2003): 339–48.
24. A. Benton Cocanougher and Grady D. Bruce, "Socially Distant Reference Groups and Consumer Aspirations," *Journal of Marketing Research* 8 (August 1971): 79–81.
25. L. Festinger, S. Schachter, and K. Back, *Social Pressures in Informal Groups: A Study of Human Factors in Housing* (New York: Harper, 1950).
26. R. B. Zajonc, H. M. Markus, and W. Wilson, "Exposure Effects and Associative Learning," *Journal of Experimental Social Psychology* 10 (1974): 248–63.
27. D. J. Stang, "Methodological Factors in Mere Exposure Research," *Psychological Bulletin* 81 (1974): 1014–25; R. B. Zajonc, P. Shaver, C. Tavris, and D. Van Kreveid, "Exposure, Satiation and Stimulus Discriminability," *Journal of Personality and Social Psychology* 21 (1972): 270–80.
28. J. E. Grush, K. L. McKeogh, and R. F. Ahlering, "Extrapolating Laboratory Exposure Research to Actual Political Elections," *Journal of Personality and Social Psychology* 36 (1978): 257–70.
29. Barry Rehfeld, "At These Camps, Everybody Is a Star (If Only for a Day)," *New York Times* (June 12, 2005), www.nytimes.com, accessed June 12, 2005.
30. Basil G. Englis and Michael R. Solomon, "To Be and Not to Be: Reference Group Stereotyping and the Clustering of America," *Journal of Advertising* 24 (Spring 1995): 13–28; Michael R. Solomon and Basil G. Englis, "I Am Not, Therefore I Am: The Role of Anti-Consumption in the Process of Self-Definition" (special session at the Association for Consumer Research meetings, October 1996, Tucson, Arizona); cf. also Brendan Richardson and Darach Turley, "Support Your Local Team: Resistance, Subculture and the Desire for Distinction," *Advances in Consumer Research* 33, no. 1 (2006): 175–180.

31. Bruce Feirstein, *Real Men Don't Eat Quiche* (New York: Pocket Books, 1982); www.auntiefashions.com, accessed December 31, 2002; Katherine White and Darren W. Dahl, "Are All Out-Groups Created Equal? Consumer Identity and Dissociative Influence," *Journal of Consumer Research* 34 (December 2007): 525–36.

32. Rob Walker, "Anti-Fan Club," *New York Times* (November 26, 2006), www.nytimes.com, accessed November 26, 2006.

33. Candice R. Hollenbeck and George M. Zinkhan, "Consumer Activism on the Internet: The Role of Anti-brand Communities," *Advances in Consumer Research* 33, no. 1 (2006):479–485.

34. Marius K. Luedicke, "Brand Community Under Fire: The Role of Social Environments for the Hummer Brand Community," *Advances in Consumer Research* 33, no. 1 (2006): 486–493.

35. B. Latane, K. Williams, and S. Harkins, "Many Hands Make Light the Work: The Causes and Consequences of Social Loafing," *Journal of Personality and Social Psychology* 37 (1979): 822–32.

36. S. Freeman, M. Walker, R. Borden, and B. Latane, "Diffusion of Responsibility and Restaurant Tipping: Cheaper by the Bunch," *Personality and Social Psychology Bulletin* 1 (1978): 584–87.

37. Nathan Kogan and Michael A. Wallach, "Risky Shift Phenomenon in Small Decision-Making Groups: A Test of the Information Exchange Hypothesis," *Journal of Experimental Social Psychology* 3 (January 1967): 75–84; Nathan Kogan and Michael A. Wallach, *Risk Taking* (New York: Holt, Rinehart and Winston, 1964); Arch G. Woodside and M. Wayne DeLozier, "Effects of Word-of-Mouth Advertising on Consumer Risk Taking," *Journal of Advertising* (Fall 1976): 12–19.

38. Kogan and Wallach, *Risk Taking*.

39. Roger Brown, *Social Psychology* (New York: The Free Press, 1965).

40. David L. Johnson and I. R. Andrews, "Risky Shift Phenomenon Tested with Consumer Product Stimuli," *Journal of Personality and Social Psychology* 20 (1971): 382–85; see also Vithala R. Rao and Joel H. Steckel, "A Polarization Model for Describing Group Preferences," *Journal of Consumer Research* 18 (June 1991): 108–18.

41. Donald H. Granbois, "Improving the Study of Customer In-Store Behavior," *Journal of Marketing* 32 (October 1968): 28–32; Tamara F. Mangleburg, Patricia M. Doney, and Terry Bristol, "Shopping with Friends and Teens' Susceptibility to Peer Influence," *Journal of Retailing* 80 (2004): 101–16.

42. Len Strazewski, "Tupperware Locks in New Strategy," *Advertising Age* (February 8, 1988): 30.

43. Melanie Wells, "Smooth Operator," *Forbes* (May 13, 2002): 167–68.

44. Abbey Klaassen, "A Collective Human Joystick Media Morph: Audience Games," *Advertising Age* (March 24, 2008), http://adage.com/Article?Article_Id=125863, accessed March 24, 2008.

45. Luc Sante, "Be Different! (Like Everyone Else!)," *New York Times Magazine* (October 17, 1999), www.nytimes.com, accessed October 3, 2007.

46. For a study attempting to measure individual differences in proclivity to conformity, see William O. Bearden, Richard G. Netemeyer, and Jesse E. Teel, "Measurement of Consumer Susceptibility to Interpersonal Influence," *Journal of Consumer Research* 15 (March 1989): 473–81.

47. John W. Thibaut and Harold H. Kelley, *The Social Psychology of Groups* (New York: Wiley, 1959); W. W. Waller and R. Hill, *The Family, a Dynamic Interpretation* (New York: Dryden, 1951).

48. Bearden, Netemeyer, and Teel, "Measurement of Consumer Susceptibility to Interpersonal Influence"; Lynn R. Kahle, "Observations: Role-Relaxed Consumers: A Trend of the Nineties," *Journal of Advertising Research* (March–April 1995): 66–71; Lynn R. Kahle and Aviv Shoham, "Observations: Role-Relaxed Consumers: Empirical Evidence," *Journal of Advertising Research* (May–June 1995): 59–62.

49. Amy Chozick, "Cold Stone Aims to Be Hip in Japan Ice-Cream Chain, Uses Word-of-Mouth as Part of Bid for an Urban Image," *Wall Street Journal* (December 14, 2006): B10.

50. Everett M. Rogers, *Diffusion of Innovations*, 3rd ed. (New York: Free Press, 1983); cf. also Duncan J. Watts and Peter Sheridan Dodds. "Influentials, Networks, and Public Opinion Formation" *Journal of Consumer Research* 34 (December 2007): 441–58; cf. also Morris B. Holbrook and Michela Addis. "Taste Versus the Market: An Extension of Research on the Consumption of Popular Culture." *Journal of Consumer Research* 34 (October 2007): 415–24.

51. Leonard-Barton, "Experts as Negative Opinion Leaders in the Diffusion of a Technological Innovation"; Rogers, *Diffusion of Innovations*.

52. Herbert Menzel, "Interpersonal and Unplanned Communications: Indispensable or Obsolete?" in Edward B. Roberts, ed., *Biomedical Innovation* (Cambridge, MA: MIT Press, 1981), 155–63.

53. Meera P. Venkatraman, "Opinion Leaders, Adopters, and Communicative Adopters: A Role Analysis," *Psychology & Marketing* 6 (Spring 1989): 51–68.

54. Rogers, *Diffusion of Innovations*.

55. Karl Greenberg, "Ford Puts Trendsetters Behind Wheel in VIP Events," *Marketing Daily* (November 11, 2008), www.mediapost.com/publications/?fa=Articles.san&s=94582&Nid=49281&p=407...; accessed November 11, 2008.

56. Robert Merton, *Social Theory and Social Structure* (Glencoe, IL: Free Press, 1957).

57. "Inconspicuous, But Influential," Center for Media Research (December 26, 2008), www.mediapost.com, accessed December 26, 2008.

58. King and Summers, "Overlap of Opinion Leadership across Consumer Product Categories"; see also Ronald E. Goldsmith, Jeanne R. Heitmeyer, and Jon B. Freiden, "Social Values and Fashion Leadership," *Clothing and Textiles Research Journal* 10 (Fall 1991): 37–45; J. O. Summers, "Identity of Women's Clothing Fashion Opinion Leaders," *Journal of Marketing Research* 7 (1970): 178–85.

59. Duncan J. Watts and Peter Sheridan Dodds. "Influentials, Networks, and Public Opinion Formation" *Journal of Consumer Research* 34 (December 2007): 441–58.

60. Steven A. Baumgarten, "The Innovative Communicator in the Diffusion Process," *Journal of Marketing Research* 12 (February 1975): 12–18.

61. Laura J. Yale and Mary C. Gilly, "Dyadic Perceptions in Personal Source Information Search," *Journal of Business Research* 32 (1995): 225–37.

62. Russell W. Belk, "Occurrence of Word-of-Mouth Buyer Behavior as a Function of Situation and Advertising Stimuli," in Fred C. Allvine, ed., *Combined Proceedings of the American Marketing Association*, series no. 33 (Chicago: American Marketing Association, 1971): 419–22.

63. Lawrence F. Feick, Linda L. Price, and Robin A. Higie, "People Who Use People: The Other Side of Opinion Leadership," in Richard J. Lutz, ed., *Advances in Consumer Research* 13 (Provo, UT: Association for Consumer Research, 1986): 301–5.

64. Stephanie Clifford, "Spreading the Word (and the Lotion) in Small-Town Alaska," *New York Times* (October 8, 2008), www.nytimes.com/2008/10/09/business/media/09adco.html, accessed October 9, 2008.

65. For discussion of the market maven construct, see Lawrence F. Feick and Linda L. Price, "The Market Maven," *Managing* (July 1985): 10; scale items adapted from Lawrence F. Feick and Linda L. Price, "The Market Maven: A Diffuser of Marketplace Information," *Journal of Marketing* 51 (January 1987): 83–87; Ronald A. Clark, Ronald E. Goldsmith, and Elizabeth B. Goldsmith, "Market Mavenism and Consumer Self-Confidence," *Journal of Consumer Behavior* 7 (2008): 239–48.

66. Michael R. Solomon, "The Missing Link: Surrogate Consumers in the Marketing Chain," *Journal of Marketing* 50 (October 1986): 208–18.

67. Brian Steinberg, "Gimme an Ad! Brands Lure Cheerleaders Marketers Try to Rally Influential Teen Girls Behind New Products," *Wall Street Journal* (April 19, 2007): B4.

68. Patricia Odell, "Pepsi Uses "Influencers" to Launch a New Product," *PROMO* (June 18, 2009), www.promomagazine.com, accessed June 18, 2009.

69. Barbara Stern and Stephen J. Gould, "The Consumer as Financial Opinion Leader." *Journal of Retail Banking* 10 (1988) 47–49.

70. William R. Darden and Fred D. Reynolds, "Predicting Opinion Leadership for Men's Apparel Fashions," *Journal of Marketing Research* 1 (August 1972): 324–28. A modified version of the opinion leadership scale with improved reliability and validity appears in Terry L. Childers, "Assessment of the Psychometric Properties of an Opinion Leadership Scale," *Journal of Marketing Research* 23 (May 1986): 184–88.

71. Dan Seligman, "Me and Monica," *Forbes* (March 23, 1998): 76.

72. Gina Kolata, "Find Yourself Packing It On? Blame Friends," *New York Times* (July 26, 2007), www.nytimes.com, accessed July 26, 2007.

73. "Referrals Top Ads as Influence on Patients' Doctor Selections," *Marketing News* (January 30, 1987): 22.

74. Peter H. Reingen and Jerome B. Kernan, "Analysis of Referral Networks in Marketing: Methods and Illustration," *Journal of Marketing Research* 23 (November 1986): 370–78.

75. Peter H. Reingen, Brian L. Foster, Jacqueline Johnson Brown, and Stephen B. Seidman, "Brand Congruence in Interpersonal Relations: A Social Network Analysis," *Journal of Consumer Research* 11 (December 1984): 771–83; see also James C. Ward and Peter H. Reingen, "Sociocognitive Analysis of Group Decision-Making among Consumers," *Journal of Consumer Research* 17 (December 1990): 245–62.

76. Pat Wechsler, "A Curiously Strong Campaign," *BusinessWeek* (April 21, 1997): 134.

77. Johan Arndt, "Role of Product-Related Conversations in the Diffusion of a New Product," *Journal of Marketing Research* 4 (August 1967): 291–95.

78. John Gaffney, "Enterprise: Marketing: The Cool Kids Are Doing It. Should You?" *Asiaweek* (November 23, 2001): 1.

79. Douglas R. Pruden and Terry G. Vavra, "Controlling the Grapevine," *MM* (July–August 2004): 23–30.

80. www.bzzagent.com, accessed June 12, 2009.

81. Les Luchter, "Kraft, Folgers, Olay Top Baby Boomer Gals' WOM," *Marketing Daily,* (November 18, 2008), www.mediapost.com/publications/?fa=Articles.showArticle&art_aid=95000, accessed November 18, 2008.

82. Elihu Katz and Paul F. Lazarsfeld, *Personal Influence* (Glencoe, IL: Free Press, 1955).

83. John A. Martilla, "Word-of-Mouth Communication in the Industrial Adoption Process," *Journal of Marketing Research* 8 (March 1971): 173–78; see also Marsha L. Richins, "Negative Word-of-Mouth by Dissatisfied Consumers: A Pilot Study," *Journal of Marketing* 47 (Winter 1983): 68–78.

84. Arndt, "Role of Product-Related Conversations in the Diffusion of a New Product."

85. James H. Myers and Thomas S. Robertson, "Dimensions of Opinion Leadership," *Journal of Marketing Research* 9 (February 1972): 41–46.

86. Ellen Neuborne, "Generation Y," *BusinessWeek* (February 15, 1999): 86.

87. Dorothy Leonard-Barton, "Experts as Negative Opinion Leaders in the Diffusion of a Technological Innovation," *Journal of Consumer Research* 11 (March 1985): 914–26.

88. James F. Engel, Robert J. Kegerreis, and Roger D. Blackwell, "Word-of-Mouth Communication by the Innovator," *Journal of Marketing* 33 (July 1969): 15–19; cf. also, Rajdeep Growl, Thomas W. Cline, and Anthony Davies, "Early-Entrant Advantage, Word-of-Mouth Communication, Brand Similarity, and the Consumer Decision Making Process," *Journal of Consumer Psychology* 13, no. 3 (2003): 187–97.

89. Chip Walker, "Word-of-Mouth," *American Demographics* (July 1995): 38–44; Albert M Muñiz, Jr., Thomas O'Guinn, and Gary Alan Fine, "Rumor in Brand Community," in Donald A. Hantula, ed., *Advances in Theory and Methodology in Social and Organizational Psychology: A Tribute to Ralph Rosnow* (Mahwah, NJ: Erlbaum, 2005).

90. Jack Neff, "Will Text Rumor Scare Off Wal-Mart Customers? Messaging Hoax in at Least 16 States Warns Women They Could Be Killed," *Advertising Age* (March 19, 2009), www.adage.com; accessed March 19, 2009; Choe Sang-Hun, "Web Rumors Tied to Korean Actress's Suicide," *New York Times* (October 2, 2008), www.nytimes.com/2008/10/03/World/Asia/03actress.Html?_R=1&Scp=1&Sq=Korea, accessed October 3, 2008; The Associated Press, "Fighting the Web Bullying That Led to a Suicide," *New York Times* (June 1, 2008), www.nytimes.com/2008/06/01/Us/01internet.Html?Scp=1&Sq=Cyberbullying&St=Nyt, accessed June 1, 2008.

91. Richard J. Lutz, "Changing Brand Attitudes Through Modification of Cognitive Structure," *Journal of Consumer Research* 1 (March 1975): 49–59. For some suggested remedies to bad publicity, see Mitch Griffin, Barry J. Babin, and Jill S. Attaway, "An Empirical Investigation of the Impact of Negative Public Publicity on Consumer Attitudes and Intentions," in Rebecca H. Holman and Michael R. Solomon, eds., *Advances in Consumer Research* 18 (Provo, UT: Association for Consumer Research, 1991): 334–41; Alice M. Tybout, Bobby J. Calder, and Brian Sternthal, "Using Information Processing Theory to Design Marketing Strategies," *Journal of Marketing Research* 18 (1981): 73–79; see also Russell N. Laczniak, Thomas E. DeCarlo, and Sridhar N. Ramaswami, "Consumers' Responses to Negative Word-of-Mouth Communication: An Attribution Theory Perspective," *Journal of Consumer Psychology*, 11, no. 1 (2001): 57–73.

92. Robert E. Smith and Christine A. Vogt, "The Effects of Integrating Advertising and Negative Word-of-Mouth Communications on Message Processing and Response," *Journal of Consumer Psychology* 4, no. 2 (1995): 133–51; Paula Fitzgerald Bone, "Word-of-Mouth Effects on Short-Term and Long-Term Product Judgments," *Journal of Business Research* 32 (1995): 213–23.

93. Keith Schneider, "Brands for the Chattering Masses," *New York Times* (December 17, 2006), www.nytimes.com, accessed October 3, 2007.

94. "Dunkin' Donuts Buys Out Critical Web Site," *New York Times* (August 27, 1999), www.nytimes.com, accessed August 27, 1999. For a discussion of ways to assess negative WOM online, cf. David M. Boush and Lynn R. Kahle, "Evaluating Negative Information in Online Consumer Discussions: From Qualitative Analysis to Signal Detection," *Journal of EuroMarketing* 11, no. 2 (2001): 89–105.

95. James C. Ward and Amy L. Ostrom, "Complaining to the Masses: The Role of Protest Framing in Customer-Created Complaint Web Sites," *Journal of Consumer Research* 33, no. 2 (2006): 220.

96. Charles W. King and John O. Summers, "Overlap of Opinion Leadership Across Consumer Product Categories," *Journal of Marketing Research* 7 (February 1970): 43–50.

97. Michael Fumento, "Tampon Terrorism," *Forbes* (May 17, 1999): 170.

98. Stephanie Clifford, "Video Prank at Domino's Taints Brand," *New York Times* (April 15, 2009), www.nytimes.com/gst/fullpage.html?res=9A04E4DD173FF935A25757C0A96F9C8B63, accessed April 15, 2009.

99. Karlene Lukovitz, "Marketers Praise Skittles' Gutsy Site Move," *Marketing Daily* (March 3, 2009), www.mediapost.com, accessed March 3, 2009.

100. Gavin O'Malley, "Generation Flex: Xers, Millennials Show Media Muscle, Deem Themselves 'Broadcasters,'" *Marketing Daily* (February 28, 2007), www.mediapost.com, accessed February 28, 2007.

101. Kelly Shermach, "Low-Hanging Fruit Can Feed Brands Well into the Future," *Marketing Daily* (April 16, 2008), http://publications.mediapost.com/index.cfm?fuseaction=Articles.san&s=80742&Nid=415.., accessed April 16, 2008.

102. Jessica Letkemann, "R.E.M. Debuts Album on Social Networking Site," MSNBC (March 11, 2008), www.msnbc.msn.com/id/23575134, accessed March 11, 2008.

103. Emily Bryson York, "DiGiorno Turns to Twitter for Flatbread-Pizza Launch: Kraft Will Deliver Frozen Pies to Tweetups to Generate Word-of-Mouth," *Advertising Age* (April 8, 2009), www.adage.com, accessed April 8, 2009.

104. Rupal Parekh, "How to Follow (or Avoid) the Crowds, Media Morph: Citysense," *Advertising* Age (August 25, 2008), http://adage.com/article?article_id=130487, accessed August 25, 2008

105. Joe Mandese, "Interpublic Unveils New Lab Initiative, Backs Platform That Links Brands with Social Networks," *Online Media Daily* (August 25, 2008), www.mediapost.com/publications/?fa=Articles.san&s=89121&Nid=46432&p=407056, accessed August 25, 2008.

106. Jenna Wortham, "What's the Value of a Facebook Friend? About 37 Cents," *New York Times* (January 9, 2009), www.nytimes.com, accessed January 9, 2009.

107. Some material adapted from a presentation by Matt Leavey, Prentice Hall Business Publishing, July 18, 2007.

108. www.pandora.com, accessed July 1, 2009.

109. Jeff Surowiecki, *The Wisdom of Crowds* (New York: Anchor, 2005); Jeff Howe, "The Rise of Crowdsourcing," *Wired* (June 2006), www.wired.com/wired/archive/14.06/crowds.html, accessed October 3, 2007.

110. Mark Weingarten, "Designed to Grow," *Business 2.0* (June 2007): 35–37.

111. www.crowdspirit.com, accessed July 1, 2009.

112. www.sermo.com, accessed July 1, 2009; Susanna Hamner, "Cashing in on Doctor's, Thinking," *Business 2.0* (June 2006): 40.

113. www.sellaband.com, accessed July 1, 2009.

114. "Shopmobbing," *Fast Company* (April 2007): 31.

115. Quoted in Darren Everson, "Baseball Taps Wisdom of Fans," *Wall Street Journal* (March 7, 2008): W4.

116. Suzanne Vranica, "Can Dove Promote a Cause and Sell Soap? Web Site Is Devoted to 'Real Beauty' . . . and Product Placement," *Wall Street Journal* (April 10, 2008): B6.

117. Sonia Murray, "Street Marketing Does the Trick," *Advertising Age* (March 20, 2000): S12.

118. "Taking to the Streets," *Newsweek* (November 2, 1998): 70–73.

119. Karl Greenberg, "Scion's Web-Based Pre-Launch Scorns Tradition," *Marketing Daily* (March 6, 2007), www.mediapost.com, accessed March 6, 2007.

120. Melanie Wells, "Wabbing," *Forbes* (February 2, 2004): 84–88; Jeff Leeds, "The Next Hit Song? Ask P&G," *New York Times* (November 8, 2004), www.nytimes.com, accessed November 8, 2004.

121. Rob Walker, "The Hidden (in Plain Sight) Persuaders," *New York Times* (December 5, 2004), www.nytimes.com, accessed December 5, 2004.

122. Suzanne Vranica, "Guerrilla Marketing Takes a Soft-Boiled Approach: Public-Service Campaigns Are Now Using the Tactic; Smashing Eggs for Safety," *Wall Street Journal* (July 8, 2004): B4.

123. Kate Fitzgerald, "Branding Face to Face," *Advertising Age* (October 21, 2002): 47.

124. David Goetzl, "Boston Bomb Stunt Drove Online Traffic to Cartoon Network," *Marketing Daily* (February 5, 2007), www.mediapost.com, accessed February 5, 2007.

125. Jared Sandberg, "The Friendly Virus," *Newsweek* (April 12, 1999): 65–66.

126. Aaron Baar, "Kodak Lets People Make Superheroes of Themselves," *Marketing Daily* (October 3, 2008), www.mediapost.com/publications/?fa=Articles.san&s=92022&Nid=48009&p=407056, accessed October 3, 2008; Jenna Wortham, "Do TV Buyers Dream of Electric Sheep?" *New York Times* (March 24, 2009), www.nytimes.com, accessed March 24, 2009.

127. Neal Stephenson, *Snow Crash* (New York: Bantam Books, 1992).

128. This section is adapted from Natalie T. Wood and Michael R. Solomon, "Adonis or Atrocious: Spokesavatars and Source Effects in Immersive Digital Environments," in Matthew S. Eastin, Terry Daugherty, and Neal M. Burns, eds., *Handbook of Research on Digital Media and Advertising: User Generated Content Consumption* (Hershey, PA: IGI Global, 2010).

129. Jeff Surowiecki, *The Wisdom of Crowds* (New York: Anchor, 2005); Jeff Howe, "The Rise of Crowdsourcing," *Wired* (June 2006): 176(8).

130. Quoted in Suzanne Vranica, "Ad Houses Will Need to Be More Nimble, Clients Are Demanding More and Better Use of Consumer Data, Web," *Wall Street Journal* (January 2, 2008): B3.

131. John Markoff, "Internet Use Said to Cut into TV Viewing and Socializing," *New York Times on the Web* (December 30, 2004).

132. Suzanne Vranica, "Getting Buzz Marketers to Fess Up," *Wall Street Journal* (February 9, 2005): B9.

133. Thomas E. Weber, "Viral Marketing: Web's Newest Ploy May Make You an Unpopular Friend," *Wall Street Journal* (September 13, 1999), www.wsj.com, accessed September 13, 1999.

134. Victoria Shannon, "Social Networking Moves to the Cellphone," *New York Times* (March 6, 2008), www.nytimes.com/2008/03/06/technology/06wireless.html?ex=1362459600&en=571b090085db559d&ei=5088&partner=rssnyt&emc=rss, accessed March 6, 2008.

11

Organizational and Household Decision Making

Chapter
Objectives

When you finish this chapter you will understand:

1 Why do marketers often need to understand *consumers'* behavior rather than consumer behavior?

2 Why do companies as well as individuals make purchase decisions?

3 Why are our traditional notions about families outdated?

4 How do many important demographic dimensions of a population relate to family and household structure?

5 How do members of a family unit play different roles and have different amounts of influence when the family makes purchase decisions?

6 How do children learn over time what and how to consume?

*A*manda is about as nervous as she can be. Tonight she and her partner are throwing their first party in their new apartment, and it's really coming down to the wire. Some of her friends and family who were skeptical about Amanda's plan to move out of her parents' house to live with a man will have the chance to say "I told you so" if this debut of her new living arrangement self-destructs.

Life hasn't exactly been a bed of roses since she and Orlando moved in together. It's a bit of a mystery—although his desk is tidy and organized at the publishing company where they both work, his personal habits are another story. Orlando's really been making an effort to clean up his act, but Amanda has taken on more than her share of cleaning duties—partly out of self-defense because they have to share a bathroom! And she's learned the hard way not to trust Orlando to do the grocery shopping—he goes to the store with a big list of staples and returns with beer and junk food. You would think that a man who negotiates major computer purchases for his company would have a bit more sense when it comes to sticking to a budget and picking out the right household supplies. What's even more frustrating is that although Orlando can easily spend a week digging up information about the new big-screen TV they're buying (with her bonus!), she has to virtually drag him by the ear to look at dining room furniture. Then, to add insult to injury, he's quick to criticize her choices—especially if they cost too much.

So, how likely is it that while she's at work Orlando has been home cleaning up the apartment and making some *hors d'oeuvres* as he promised? Amanda did her part by downloading a recipe for crabmeat salad and wasabi caviar from the entertaining section on <u>epicurious.com</u>. She even jotted down some adorable table setting ideas such as napkin holders made out of homegrown bamboo at Martha Stewart's Web site.[1] The rest is up to him—at this point she'd be happy if Orlando remembers to pick up his underwear from the living room couch. This *soiree* could turn out to be a real proving ground for their relationship. Amanda sighs as she walks into an editors' meeting. She sure has learned a lot about relationships since she set up a new household; living together is going to be a lot bumpier than romance novels make it out to be.

Organizational Decision Making

Amanda's trials and tribulations with Orlando illustrate the joint nature of many consumer decisions. The individual decision-making process we described in detail in Chapter 8 is overly simplistic. This is because more than one person often participates in the problem-solving sequence—from initial problem recognition and information search to evaluation of alternatives and product choice. To further complicate matters, these decisions often include two or more people who may not have the same level of investment in the outcome, the same tastes and preferences, or the same consumption priorities. If you've ever debated where to go out to eat with your friends or perhaps bickered about whose turn it is to do the dishes, you get the picture.

In this chapter we examine *collective decision making*—situations where more than one person chooses the products or services that multiple consumers use. In the first part of the chapter we look at organizational decision making, where one person or a group decides on behalf of a larger group. We then move on to focus more specifically on one of the most important organizations to which we belong—the family unit. We'll consider how members of a family negotiate among themselves and how important changes in modern family structure affect this process. We conclude with a look at how "new employees"—children—learn to be consumers.

Why do we lump together big corporations and small families? One important similarity is that in both cases individuals or groups play a number of specific roles when they choose products or services for their organizational unit.[2] Depending on the decision, the choice may include some or all of the group members, and different group members play important roles in what can be a complicated process. These roles include the following:

- **Initiator**—The person who brings up the idea or identifies a need.
- **Gatekeeper**—The person who conducts the information search and controls the flow of information available to the group. In organizational contexts the gatekeeper identifies possible vendors and products for the rest of the group to consider.
- **Influencer**—The person who tries to sway the outcome of the decision. Some people may be more motivated than others to get involved, and participants also possess different amounts of power to get their point across.
- **Buyer**—The person who actually makes the purchase. The buyer may or may not actually use the product.
- **User**—The person who actually consumes the product or service.

Organizational Decision Making

Many employees of corporations or other organizations make purchase decisions on a daily basis. **Organizational buyers** are people like Orlando who purchase goods and services on behalf of companies for their use in manufacturing, distribution, or resale. These individuals buy from **business-to-business (B2B) marketers** who must satisfy the needs of organizations such as corporations, government agencies, hospitals, and retailers. In terms of sheer volume, *B2B marketing* is where the action is: Roughly $2 trillion worth of products and services change hands among organizations, which is actually *more* than end consumers purchase.

Organizational buyers have a lot of responsibility. They decide on the vendors with whom they want to do business and what specific items they require from these suppliers. The items they consider range in price and significance from paper clips

(by the case, not the box) to Orlando's multimillion-dollar computer system. Obviously, there's a lot of good reasons (about two trillion to be exact) for marketers to understand how these organizational consumers make these important decisions.

A number of factors influence the organizational buyer's perception of the purchase situation. These include his *expectations* of the supplier (e.g., product quality, the competence and behavior of the firm's employees, and prior experiences in dealing with that supplier), the *organizational climate* of his own company (i.e., how the company rewards performance and what it values), and the buyer's *assessment* of his own performance (e.g., whether he believes in taking risks).[3]

Like other consumers, organizational buyers engage in a learning process where employees share information with one another and develop an "organizational memory" that consists of shared beliefs and assumptions about the best choices to make.[4] Just as our "market beliefs" influence him when he goes shopping with the family on the weekend (see Chapter 8), the same thing happens at the office. He (perhaps with fellow employees) solves problems as he searches for information, evaluates alternatives, and makes decisions.[5] There are, of course, some important differences between the two situations.

How Does Organizational Decision Making Compare to Consumer Decision Making?

Let's summarize the major differences between organizational and industrial purchase decisions versus individual consumer decisions:[6]

- Purchase decisions companies make frequently involve many people, including those who do the actual buying, those who directly or indirectly influence this decision, and the employees who will actually use the product or service.
- Organizations and companies often use precise technical specifications that require a lot of knowledge about the product category.
- Impulse buying is rare (industrial buyers do not suddenly get an "urge to splurge" on lead pipe or silicon chips). Because buyers are professionals, they base their decisions on past experience and they carefully weigh alternatives.
- Decisions often are risky, especially in the sense that a buyer's career may ride on his judgment.
- The dollar volume of purchases is often substantial—it dwarfs most individual consumers' grocery bills or mortgage payments. One hundred to 250 organizational customers typically account for more than half of a supplier's sales volume, which gives the buyers a lot of influence over the supplier.
- Business-to-business marketing often involves more of an emphasis on personal selling than on advertising or other forms of promotion. Dealing with organizational buyers typically requires more face-to-face contact than when marketers sell to end consumers.

We must consider these important features when we try to understand the purchasing decisions organizations make. Having said that, however, there are actually more similarities between organizational buyers and ordinary consumers than many people realize. True, organizational purchase decisions do tend to have a higher economic or functional component compared to individual consumer choices, but emotional aspects do play a role. Organizational buyers may appear to the outsider to be models of rationality—but at times they base their decisions on brand loyalty, on long-term relationships with particular suppliers or salespeople, or even on aesthetic preferences.

How Do Organizational Buyers Operate?

Like end consumers, both internal and external stimuli influence organizational buyers. Internal stimuli include the buyer's unique psychological characteristics, such as his willingness to make risky decisions, job experience, and training. External stimuli include the nature of the organization for which he works as well as the overall economic and technological environment in which the industry operates. Another set of factors is cultural—we find vastly different norms for doing business in different countries. For example, Americans tend to be less formal in their interactions than are many of their European or Asian counterparts.

As you'd expect, the organizational buyer's decision-making process depends on just what he needs to buy. As with consumer purchases, the more complex, novel, or risky the decision, the more effort he devotes to information search and to evaluating his alternatives. However, if he relies on a fixed set of suppliers for routine purchases, he greatly reduces his information search and effort.[8] Typically, a group of people (members of a **buying center**) play different roles in more complex organizational decisions. As we will see later on, this joint involvement is somewhat similar to family decision making, where family members are likely to participate in more important purchases.

Marketing Pitfall

Everyone likes to get "swag," but critics in the medical community object to the huge pile of premiums like Viagra pens, Zoloft soap dispensers, and Lipitor mugs that the pharmaceutical industry bestows on physicians to encourage them to prescribe their drugs—in addition to the $16 billion worth of free drug samples that wind up in doctors' offices each year. A physician who started No Free Lunch, a nonprofit group that encourages doctors to reject drug company giveaways observes, "Practically anything you can put a name on is branded in a doctor's office, short of branding, like a NASCAR driver, on the doctor's white coat." The Pharmaceutical Research and Manufacturers of America, an industry group in Washington, has imposed a voluntary moratorium on this practice to discourage the conclusion that drug makers try to influence medical decisions. Some feel this ban doesn't go far enough because drug reps are still allowed to provide free lunches for doctors and their staffs or to sponsor dinners for doctors at restaurants, as long as an educational presentation accompanies the meal.[7]

Call the experts© for more
power at high reach.

Reach further with Komatsu's telescopic handlers. With lifting heights from 9 to over 16 metres and lifting capacities from 3500 to 4500 kg, the range includes machines to suit every application. The state-of-the-art hydraulic system and single PPC joystick let you get the most from the huge power available and deliver precise control of the working equipment even during simultaneous operations. To complete the package, each of these highly versatile machines offers exceptional stability, high travel speed, superb manoeuvrability and best-in-class all-round visibility. Not bad for a telescopic.

KOMATSU

Komatsu Europe International nv - Mechelsesteenweg 586 - B-1800 Vilvoorde - Belgium

Industrial marketers can be creative when they want to be, as this European ad for a heavy equipment manufacturer demonstrates.
Source: Used courtesy of Komatsu Europe.

The Buyclass Framework

When we apply the **buyclass theory of purchasing**, we divide organizational buying decisions into three types ranging from the least to the most complex. Three decision-making dimensions describe the purchasing strategies of an organizational buyer:[9]

1 The level of information he must gather before he makes a decision.
2 The seriousness with which he must consider all possible alternatives.
3 The degree to which he is familiar with the purchase.

In practice these three dimensions relate to how much cognitive effort the buyer expends when he decides. Three types of "buyclasses," or strategies these dimensions determine, encompass most organizational decision situations.[10] Each type of purchase corresponds to one of the three types of decisions we discussed in Chapter 8: habitual decision making, limited problem solving, and extensive problem solving. Table 11.1 summarizes these strategies.

● A **straight rebuy** is a habitual decision. It's an automatic choice, as when an inventory level reaches a preestablished reorder point. Most organizations maintain an approved vendor list, and as long as experience with a supplier is satisfactory, there is little or no ongoing information search or evaluation.

TABLE 11.1	Types of Organizational Buying Decisions		
Buying Situation	**Extent of Effort**	**Risk**	**Buyer's Involvement**
Straight rebuy	Habitual decision making	Low	Automatic reorder
Modified rebuy	Limited problem solving	Low to moderate	One or a few
New task	Extensive problem solving	High	Many

Source: Adapted from Patrick J. Robinson, Charles W. Faris, and Yoram Wind, *Industrial Buying and Creative Marketing* (Boston: Allyn & Bacon, 1967).

- A **modified rebuy** situation involves limited decision making. It occurs when an organization wants to repurchase a product or service but it wants to make some minor modifications. This decision might involve a limited search for information among a few vendors. One or a few people will probably make the final decision.
- A **new task** involves extensive problem solving. Because the company hasn't made a similar decision already, there is often a serious risk that the product won't perform as it should or that it will be too costly. The organization designates a buying center with assorted specialists to evaluate the purchase, and they typically gather a lot of information before they come to a decision.

B2B E-Commerce

Business-to-business (B2B) e-commerce refers to Internet interactions between two or more businesses or organizations. This includes exchanges of information, products, services, or payments. The Web revolutionizes the way companies communicate with other firms and even the way they share information with their own people. Roughly half of B2B e-commerce transactions take the form of auctions, bids, and exchanges where numerous suppliers and purchasers interact.[11] For example, more than 50 major corporations such as CVS Corporation, Best Buy, Target, Tesco, JCPenney, and The Gap that belong to *The Worldwide Retail Exchange* (WWRE) participate in an online exchange community to complete their commercial transactions. This collaboration allows the members to work together on product development, production planning, and inventory replenishment.[12]

The Open-Source Revolution

In the simplest form of B2B e-commerce, the Internet provides an online catalog of products and services businesses need. Companies like Dell Computer use their Internet site to deliver online technical support, product information, order status information, and customer service to corporate customers. Early on, Dell discovered that it could serve the needs of its customers more effectively if it tailored its Internet presence to different customer segments. Today Dell's Internet site allows shoppers to get recommendations based on their customer segment (home, home office, government, small business, and education). The company saves millions of dollars a year as it replaces hard-copy manuals with electronic downloads. For its larger customers, Dell provides customer-specific, password-protected pages that allow business customers to obtain technical support or to place an order.

As social networking technologies proliferate (see Chapter 10), businesses adopt these approaches also. The advertising agency Avenue A Razorfish has adopted an open-source **wiki** platform as its intranet; this lets several people change a document on a Web page and then track those changes (of course the most famous wiki is *Wikipedia*). High-tech companies like Intel, SAP, and IBM are experimenting with recording meetings that get downloaded to iPods, blogs where employees can talk back to their bosses, and internal Web pages like Google Docs that allow people to read their colleagues' meeting notes and add their own. A few companies even use Facebook as an intranet site for their employees.[13]

Prediction Markets

Are all of us smarter than each of us? A **prediction market** is one of the hottest new trends in organizational decision-making techniques; it's one outgrowth of the *wisdom of crowds* phenomenon we discussed in Chapter 10. This approach asserts that groups of people with knowledge about an industry collectively are better predictors of the future than are any of them as individuals.

In a prediction market framework, companies from Microsoft to Eli Lilly and Hewlett-Packard empower their employees as "traders." Like a stock market, traders place bets on what they think will happen regarding future sales, the success of new products, or how other firms in a distribution channel will behave—and they often receive a cash reward if their "stock picks" pan out. For example, the pharmaceutical giant Eli Lilly routinely places multimillion-dollar bets on drug candidates that face overwhelming odds of failure—the relatively few new compounds that do succeed need to make enough money to cover the losses the others incur. Obviously, the company will benefit if it can separate the winners from the losers earlier in the process. Lilly ran an experiment where about 50 of its employees involved in drug development, including chemists, biologists, and project managers, traded six mock drug candidates through an internal market. The group correctly predicted the three most successful drugs.[14] At the publicly accessible prediction market Intrade (intrade.com) participants bet on the outcomes of political races, financial activities or even the market value of rare wines and artwork. Or, surf over to the Hollywood Stock Exchange (hsx.com) to check out which celebrities and new movie releases traders think will succeed or bomb—you can bet Hollywood executives do.[15]

Crowdsourcing

In another emerging application, many companies find that it's both cost efficient and productive to call on outsiders from around the world to solve problems their own scientists can't handle. Just as a firm might outsource production to a subcontractor, they are **crowdsourcing**. For example, InnoCentive is a network of more than 90,000 "solvers" whose member companies, such as Boeing, DuPont, Procter & Gamble, and Eli Lilly, are invited to tackle problems they are wrestling with internally. If a "solver" finds a solution, he or she gets a $10,000 to $100,000 reward.[16] Dell's Ideastorm site solicits solutions and new product ideas from geeks worldwide.[17]

The open-source revolution is part of a seismic shift in the way some cutting-edge companies think about their business model. One label for this new approach is **freemium**—you distribute a free version of your product that's supported by a paid premium version. The idea is to encourage the maximum number of people to use your product and eventually convert a small fraction of them to paying customers. In the process you accumulate a sizable customer base that has value to advertisers (Exhibit A: Google). This also creates a **network effect**—each person who uses the product or service benefits as more people participate. For example, if you check out restaurant reviews on *Zagat*, you'd rather know what 1,000 diners thought of a place than to settle for feedback from just 10 cranky people. The freemium model pops up in all sorts of places—people play free online games, they listen to free music on *Pandora* (legally), they trash their cable service and watch free TV shows and movies on *Hulu*, and they cancel their landlines in favor of free international calls on *Skype*. The new and booming market for iPhone apps follows the freemium principle also when you download a program like *Tap Tap Revenge*. Like the popular game *Guitar Hero*, you have to hit notes that stream down your screen. Millions of people downloaded the app, and then some of them forked over cash when the creator offered paid versions built around real bands like Weezer and Nine Inch Nails.[18] In the wacky world of Web 2.0, you give something away to make money. Go figure.

3

OBJECTIVE

Why are our traditional notions about families outdated?

The Family

Sometimes we read in newspapers and magazines about the death of the family unit. Although it is true that the proportion of people who live in a traditional family structure consisting of a married couple with children continues to decline, the reality is that many other types of families continue to grow rapidly. Indeed, some experts argue that as traditional family living arrangements wane, we place even greater emphasis on siblings, close friends, and other relatives who provide companionship and social support.[19] Some people join *intentional families*: groups of unrelated people who meet regularly for meals and who spend holidays together.[20] Indeed, for some the act of meeting together to consume homemade food plays a central role in defining family—it is a symbolic way to separate a family unit from other social groups by allowing the cook(s) to personalize the meal and express affection via the effort that went into preparing the feast.[21]

OBJECTIVE

How do many important demographic dimensions of a population relate to family and household structure?

The Modern Family

The **extended family** used to be the most common family unit. It consists of three generations who live together and it often includes grandparents, aunts, uncles, and cousins. Like the Cleavers of *Leave It to Beaver* and other TV families of the 1950s, the **nuclear family**—a mother, a father, and one or more children (perhaps with a sheepdog thrown in for good measure)—largely replaced the extended family at least in American society. However, we've witnessed many changes since the days of Beaver Cleaver. Although many people continue to base their image of the typical family on old TV shows, demographic data tell us this ideal image of the family is no longer realistic. The U.S. Census Bureau regards any occupied housing unit as a **household**, regardless of the relationships among people who live there. Thus, one person living alone, three roommates, or two lovers (whether straight or gay) constitute a household.

In 2005 we hit a watershed event: the U.S. Census Bureau announced that married couples officially make up a minority (49.7 percent) of American households. The agency's American Community Survey reported that overall nearly 1 in 10 couples who live together are not married. The proportion of married couples ranged from more than 69 percent in Provo, Utah, to only 26 percent in Manhattan.[22]

What's more, for the first time a majority (51 percent) of American women now live without a spouse (up from 35 percent in 1950). This is because younger women choose to marry later or to live with unmarried partners longer, while older women live longer as widows and are more likely than men to delay remarriage if they divorce. Five percent of households consist of unmarried opposite-sex partners the government euphemistically calls **POSSLQ**, which stands for *Persons of Opposite Sex Sharing Living Quarters*. Like Amanda and Orlando, many of us have this kind of arrangement. Nearly half of Americans aged 25 to 40 have at some point lived with a person of the opposite sex.[23]

These changes are part of a broader shift toward nonfamily and childless households. There are also sizable numbers of same-sex couples who live together. Some of these changes came from unexpected places; for example, in the rural Midwest the number of households made up of male partners rose 77 percent since 2000.[24] Same-sex households are increasingly common and as a result more marketers target them as a family unit. E-commerce sites like gayweddings.com and twobrides.com specialize in wedding decorations and gifts for gay couples.[25]

Another 5 percent of U.S. households consist of people who live alone. A large number of these singles appear to have two things in common: financial success and the willingness to spend to satisfy their desires. Single-person households spend 153 percent more per person on rent than those who live in households of two people or more. They also spend more on alcohol ($314 per year compared with $181). And they shell out more per person for reading materials, health care, and tobacco products.[26]

Family Size

Family size depends on such factors as educational level, the availability of birth control, and religion. Demographers define the **fertility rate** as the number of births per year per 1,000 women of childbearing age. Marketers keep a close eye on the population's birthrate to gauge how the pattern of births will affect demand for products in the future. The U.S. fertility rate increased dramatically in the late 1950s and early 1960s, when the parents of so-called *baby boomers* began to reach childbearing age. It declined in the 1970s and began to climb again in the 1980s as *baby boomers* began to have their own children in a new "baby boomlet." More on these groups in Chapter 14.

Worldwide, surveys show that many women want smaller families today. This trend is a problem for European countries whose fertility rates have plummeted during past decades. Ironically, while populations boom in many underdeveloped parts of the world, industrialized countries face future crises because there will be relatively fewer young people to support their elders. In order for population levels to remain constant, the fertility rate needs to be 2.0 so that the two children can replace their parents. That's not happening in places such as Spain, Sweden, Germany, and Greece, where the fertility rate is 1.4 or lower. As a benchmark, the U.S. rate is 2.1. More babies were born in the United States in 2007 than in any other year in American history—but this figure mostly reflects a greater number of women of childbearing age.[28]

Some countries are weighing measures to encourage people to have more children. For example, Spain is looking at cheaper utility bills for large families, assisting young couples trying to afford homes, and creating hundreds of thousands of new preschools and nursery schools. The Italian government provides mothers with nearly full salary compensation for about a half year of maternity leave, but women still stubbornly refuse to have more kids. There are many reasons for this shift from past eras where heavily Catholic countries tended to have large families: Contraception and abortion are more readily available, divorce is more common, and older people who used to look after grandchildren now pursue other activities such as travel. And some experts cite the fact that many Italian men live with their mothers into their 30s so when they do get married they're not prepared to help out at home. One analyst commented, "Even the most open-minded guy—if you scratch with the nail a little bit, there's the mother who did everything for him."[29]

In the United States, the National Center of Health Statistics confirms that the percentage of women of childbearing age who define themselves as *voluntarily childless* is rising. Twenty percent of women ages 40 to 44 have no children, double the level of 30 years ago. Women with advanced degrees are more likely to be childless, the study found. Of women who gave birth in 2006, 36 percent were separated, widowed, divorced, or never married.[30]

Childless couples are an attractive market segment for some companies (but obviously not for others, such as Gerber Baby Food). So-called **DINKS** (double income, no kids) couples are better educated on average than are two-income couples with children. According to the U.S. Census Bureau, 30 percent of childless couples consist of two college graduates, compared with 17 percent of those with kids. The childless are more likely to have professional or managerial occupations (24 percent versus 16 percent of dual-employed couples with children). Dave and Buster's, a Dallas-based restaurant chain, caters to this group as it enforces strict policies to deter families with small children. However, many childless couples feel snubbed by a child-oriented society. In recent years they have formed networking organizations such as Childfree by Choice to support this lifestyle choice.[31]

The Sandwich Generation

Although the number of traditional families is shrinking, ironically in other cases the traditional extended family is very much a reality. Many adults care for their own parents as well as for their children. In fact, Americans on average spend 17 years caring for children, but 18 years assisting aged parents.[32] Some label middle-aged people the **Sandwich Generation** because they must attend to those above and below them in age. In addition to dealing with live-in parents, many adults find to their surprise that their children live with them longer or move back in well after their "lease" has expired.[33] As an Argentinean jeans ad asked, "If you are over 20 and still live with your parents, this is wrong. Isn't it high time you started looking for an apartment for them?"

Animals Are People Too! Nonhuman Family Members

Almost one-third of all U.S. households have at least one pet, and 92 percent of pet owners consider their furry friends members of the family—83 percent call themselves

ECONsumer Behavior

Demographers call these returnees **boomerang kids**. In today's shrinking job market (and in some cases the lucky few who do get job offers find out they have been rescinded!) many young people are forced to redefine the assumption that college graduation automatically means living on their own. Even before the recession we saw this trend quickening—as of 2007, 55 percent of men and 48 percent of women ages 18 to 24 lived with their parents.[34]

Young adults who do leave the nest to live by themselves are relatively unlikely to return, whereas those who move in with roommates are more likely to come back. And young people who move in with a romantic partner are more likely than average to end up back home if the relationship fails![35] If the dismal economic environment continues, it will affect a variety of markets as boomerang kids spend less on housing and staples and more on discretionary purchases such as entertainment.

Many boomerang kids today return home to live with their parents–voluntarily or not.
Source: Copyright Cdp-Travissully Ltd.

"Mommy" or "Daddy" when they talk to their pets.[36] Many of us assume pets share our emotions—perhaps that helps to explain why more than three-quarters of domestic cats and dogs receive presents on holidays and birthdays.[37] We've doubled our spending on our pets in the past decade, and today the pet industry pulls in more revenue (almost $40 billion annually) than either the toy or candy industries. Even in the recession, consumers don't make their pets pay the price—we pay more for pet food, supplies, and services than ever. Here are a few examples of pet-smart marketing:[38]

● Kennels look a lot more like spas for the furry. At some of them, dogs can hike, swim, listen to music, watch TV, and even get a pedicure—complete with nail polish. Heated tile floors and high-tech ventilation systems are common. When a dog stays in the "ambassador suite" at Club Bow-Wow, a staff member sleeps overnight in the room. PetSmart, the largest U.S. pet-store chain, opened a chain of PetsHotels, where furry guests lounge on hypoallergenic lambskin blankets and snack on lactose-free, fat-free ice cream. The suites feature raised dog beds and a television that plays videos, such as *Lady and the Tramp* and *101 Dalmatians.*
● Companies that make human products, such as Gucci, Juicy Couture, Harley-Davidson, IKEA, Lands' End, Paul Mitchell, and Ralph Lauren, also sell products for

The author's pug, Kelbie Rae.

pets—from shampoos to nail polish to gold-plated bowls. Harley-Davidson started its pet collection after it noticed that customers at rallies and other events bring along their dogs—some ride shotgun in the motorcycles' saddle bags or side cars. Customers can buy denim and leather jackets for their pets, as well as riding goggles, bandanas, spiked leather collars, and even squeaky toys shaped like oil cans.

● Designer water for dogs? A California company started things off when it introduced a vitamin-enriched water product for dogs. A Florida company sells "DogWater" in containers that double as throwing toys. Then there's K9 Water Inc., a company whose catalog lists products such as "Gutter Water" and chicken-flavored "Toilet Water." Make that a double.

● Pet Airways is the first pets-only airline. The "pawsengers" fly in pet carriers aboard Beechcraft planes along with a pet attendant. There are separate sections for cats and dogs—but no first-class cabin.

● And what happens when our four-legged companion goes to the great kennel in the sky? One trend is to freeze-dry the departed pet rather than bury it or cremate it. The bereaved say turning furry friends into perma-pets helps them deal with loss and maintains a connection to their former companions. Once dried, the animal's body doesn't decay, so it can continue to occupy that special place on the couch.

The Family Life Cycle

Many factors affect what a family spends, including the number of people (children and adults) in the family, their ages, and whether one, two, or more adults work outside of the home. Two especially important factors that determine how a couple spends time and money are (1) whether they have children and (2) whether the woman works.

Family Life Cycle Models

Because they recognize that family needs and expenditures change over time, marketers apply the **family life cycle (FLC)** concept to segment households. The FLC combines trends in income and family composition with the changes these

This Spanish public service ad promotes pet sterilization via a fake ad for dog condoms.
Source: Tiempo BBDO Barcelona.

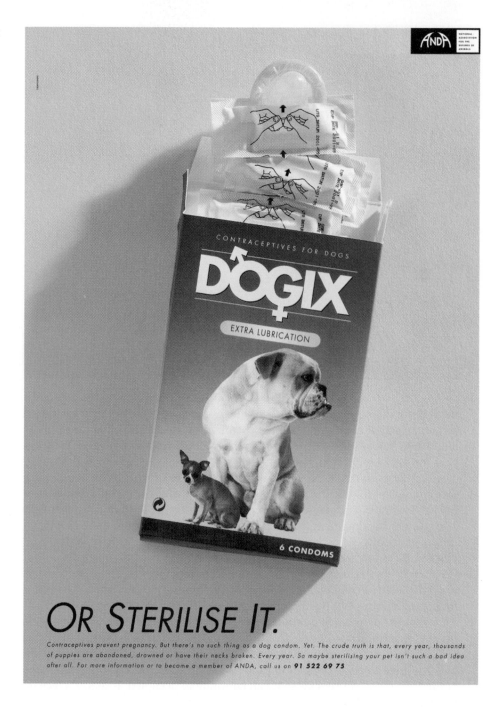

demands place on this income. As we age, our preferences and needs for products and activities tend to change. Twentysomethings spend less than average on most products and services because their households are small and their incomes are low (especially today!). Income levels tend to rise (at least until retirement), so that people can afford more over time. Older consumers spend more *per capita* on luxury items such as gourmet foods and upscale home furnishings.[39] In addition, we don't need to repeat many purchases we make when we start out. For example, we tend to accumulate durable goods such as large appliances and only replace them as necessary.

As Amanda and Orlando discovered when they moved in together, a life-cycle approach to the study of the family assumes that pivotal events alter role relationships and trigger new stages of life that alter our priorities. In addition to the birth of a first child, other pivotal events include the departure of the last child from the

This ad from Chile illustrates that many of us treat our pets like royalty.
Source: Courtesy TBWA Chile.

house, the death of a spouse, retirement of the principal wage earner, and divorce. At Web sites like The Bump women find tools like an Ovulation Calculator and lists of baby names, while The Knot offers a range of wedding-related services when those babies grow up and get hitched. As people move through these life stages, we observe significant changes in expenditures in leisure, food, durables, and services, even after we adjust the figures to reflect changes in income.[40]

Life-Cycle Effects on Buying

It's particularly useful to get a handle on longitudinal changes in priorities when we want to predict demand for specific product categories over time. For example, the money a couple with no children spends on dinners out and vacations will go to quite different purchases after the birth of a child—when a night on the town becomes a distant memory. Ironically, although the entertainment industry focuses on winning the hearts and wallets of young consumers, it's the senior citizens who have become America's true party animals. The average household headed by a 65- to 74-year-old spends more on entertainment than does the average household where the primary wage earner is under age 25 (more on this in Chapter 14).[41]

Researchers over the years proposed several models to describe family life-cycle stages, but with limited effect because most failed to take into account such important social trends as the changing role of women, the acceleration of alternative lifestyles, childless and delayed-child marriages, and single-parent households. We need to focus on four variables to adequately describe these changes: (1) age, (2) marital status, (3) the presence or absence of children in the home, and (4) the ages of children, if present. In addition, we have to relax our definition of marital status to include *any* couple living together in a long-term relationship. Thus, although we might not consider roommates "married," for marketing purposes a man and woman who have established a household would be, as would two homosexual men who have a similar understanding. When we update our outlook, we identify a set of categories that includes many more types of family situations.[42] Consumers we classify into these categories show marked differences in consumption patterns:

- Young bachelors and newlyweds are the most likely to exercise; to go out to bars, concerts, movies, and restaurants; and to drink alcohol. Although people in their 20s account for less than 4 percent of all household spending in the United States, their expenditures are well above average in such categories as apparel, electronics, and gasoline.[43]
- Families with young children are more likely to consume health foods such as fruit, juice, and yogurt; those made up of single parents and older children buy more junk foods. The dollar value of homes, cars, and other durables is lowest for bachelors and single parents but increases as people go through the full nest and childless couple stages.
- Partly because they score wedding gifts, newlyweds are the most likely to own appliances such as toaster ovens and electric coffee grinders. Babysitter and day-care usage is, of course, highest among single-parent and full-nest households, whereas older couples and bachelors are most likely to employ home maintenance services (e.g., lawn mowing).

OBJECTIVE

How do members of a family unit play different roles and have different amounts of influence when the family makes purchase decisions?

The Intimate Corporation: Family Decision Making

The decision process within a household unit resembles a business conference. Certain matters go on the table for discussion, different members have different priorities and agendas, and there may be power struggles to rival any tale of corporate intrigue. In just about every living situation, whether it's a conventional family or students who share a sorority house or apartment, group members assume different roles just as purchasing agents, engineers, account executives, and others do within a company.

When Chevrolet wanted to win drivers over to its Venture minivan, the company sent teams of anthropologists to observe families in their natural habitats. Conventional wisdom says that minivan buyers are practical; they care about affordability, lots of features, and plenty of room. But these researchers discovered a different story: People see the vehicles as part of the family. When they asked consumers to identify the best metaphor for a minivan, many picked a photo of a hang glider because it represents freedom and families on the go. The advertising slogan for the Venture became, "Let's go."[45]

Families make two basic types of decisions:[46]

1 In a **consensual purchase decision**, members agree on the desired purchase; they disagree only in terms of how they will make it happen. In these circumstances, the family will most likely engage in problem solving and consider alternatives until they find a way to satisfy everyone in the group. For example in a family that decides to get a dog, some of the members (you can guess who) voice concerns about who will take care of it. The solution is to draw up a chart that assigns family members to specific duties.

2 In an **accommodative purchase decision** however, group members have different preferences or priorities and they can't agree on a purchase to satisfy everyone's needs. It is here that they use bargaining, coercion, and compromise to achieve agreement on what to buy or who gets to use it. Conflict occurs when

there is incomplete correspondence in family members' needs and preferences. Although household spending and budgeting is the most common source of conflict in these disputes, TV-viewing choices come in a close second![47]

Decisions involve conflict among family members to the extent that the issue is somehow important or novel, or if individuals have strong opinions about good and bad alternatives. The degree to which these factors generate conflict determines the type of decision the family will make.[48] Some specific factors that determine how much family decision conflict there will be include the following:[49]

- **Interpersonal need**—(a person's level of investment in the group): A teenager may care more about what her family buys for the house than will a college student who lives in a dorm.
- **Product involvement and utility**—(the degree to which a person will use the product to satisfy a need): A mother who is an avid coffee drinker will obviously be more interested in the purchase of a new coffeemaker than will her teenage son who swigs Coke by the gallon.
- **Responsibility**—(for procurement, maintenance, payment, and so on): People are more likely to have disagreements about a decision if it entails long-term consequences and commitments. For example, a family decision about getting a dog may involve conflict over who will be responsible for walking and feeding it.
- **Power**—(or the degree to which one family member exerts influence over the others): In traditional families, the husband tends to have more power than the wife, who in turn has more than the oldest child, and so on. Conflict can arise when one person continually uses the power he has within the group to satisfy his priorities. For example, if a child believed that his life would end if he did not receive a Wii for his birthday, he might be more willing to "cash in some chips" and throw a tantrum.

A recent analysis of family decision making takes a closer look at the idea that family members mutually construct a **family identity** that defines the household both to members and to insiders.[50] According to this perspective (which is similar to the role theory approach to consumer behavior we discussed in Chapter 1), family rituals, narratives (stories the members tell about the family), and everyday interactions help families maintain their structure, maintain their family character (day-to-day characteristics of family life), and clarify members' relationships to one another. The value of this approach to marketers is that it reminds us of how often products and services help to define the family identity. For example, a father might take his young children out for ice cream every Saturday afternoon so this becomes a predictable ceremony that defines their relationship. Or, a mom might seek the comfort of her iPod to shield her from the noise when her kids play after school, while a TiVo "saves marriages" because it allows family members to compromise when they decide who gets access to the TV. Figure 11.1 summarizes this framework.

Sex Roles and Decision-Making Responsibilities

When the Indian composer A. R. Rahman accepted two Oscars for his work on the hit movie *Slumdog Millionaire*, he thanked his mother—as an afterthought he also remembered to thank his wife. India's culture strongly encourages a doting relationship between mothers and sons. It's common for many successful men to consult their mothers for advice daily, and some tycoons put their mothers on their boards of directors. Hinduism stresses powerful female gods, and many citizens refer to the country as Mother India. Clearly, older decision makers in the family unit carry a lot of weight, both in the house and out: Young people often take their parents to their first job interview.[51] Americans may not lag far behind if the number of **helicopter**

Figure 11.1 FAMILY IDENTITY
Source: Amber M. Epp and Linda L. Price, "Family Identity: A Framework of Identity Interplay in Consumption Practices." *Journal of Consumer Research,* Vol. 35 (June 2008): 50–70, Fig 1, p. 52.

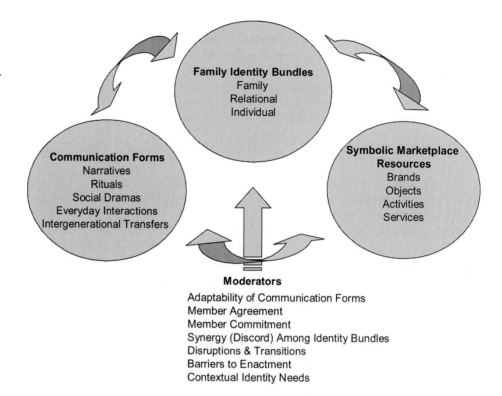

moms continues to swell: These are overprotective mothers who "hover" around their kids and insert themselves into virtually all aspects of their lives—including in some cases job interviews![52]

So, who "wears the pants" in the family? Sometimes it's not obvious which spouse makes the decisions. Indeed, although many men still wear the pants, it's women who buy them. Haggar's research showed that nearly half of married women bought pants for their husbands without them being present, so the firm started to advertise its menswear products in women's magazines. When one family member chooses a product, we call this an **autonomic decision**. In traditional households, for example, men often have sole responsibility to select a car, whereas decorating choices fall to women. **Syncretic decisions**, such as a vacation destination, might involve both partners.

According to a study Roper Starch Worldwide conducted, wives still tend to have the most say when families buy groceries, children's toys, clothes, and medicines. Syncretic decisions are common for vacations, homes, appliances, furniture, home electronics, and long-distance phone services. As the couple's education increases, they are more likely to make decisions together.[54] Roper sees signs of a shift in marital decision making toward more compromise and turn-taking. For example, the survey finds that wives tend to win out in arguments about how the house is kept, whereas husbands get control of the remote![55]

To what degree are traditional sex roles changing? Recent evidence says quite a bit; men and women increasingly express similar attitudes about how they prefer to balance home life and work. Some experts argue that the gender revolution is developing into **gender convergence**. A comprehensive view of current research reported more similarities than differences between American men and women; most people recognize that mothers work more and do less housework, and men work less and do more housework and childcare than their fathers—although they still shoulder significantly less of the burden than do women.[56]

In any case, spouses typically exert significant influence on decision making—even after one of them has died. An Irish study found that many widows claim to sense the continued presence of their dead husbands and to regularly conduct "con-

CB AS I LIVE IT

Allissa Goldberg, *The University of Maryland*

*M*y experience with families and the roles that a parent plays has always been a little bit different than that of my peers because I come from a single parent household. As I heard my friends talk about how their parents went shopping together and came back with a new television for the living room, I marveled at the idea that these children had no say in the purchasing decisions their parents made. While it was technically not an *autonomic* decision in the pure sense of the definition because their mother and father made the decision together, it seemed autonomic to the children because they were not involved. My mother on the other hand, would always consult me before purchasing something we would share. We went grocery shopping together, comparison shopped for digital cameras, and the final decision we made in a *syncretic* matter was where I would go for college. We visited school after school and decided together that I would spend my undergraduate years at the University of Maryland. Now that I am living out of the house at my own apartment at school, I make my own autonomic decisions, as does my mother, but I will always remember how different it was to be involved in each purchase decision when my peers had been left of out of the mix by their traditional two parent households.

versations" with them about household matters![57] Comments from married women who participated in focus groups *Redbook* magazine conducted illustrate some of the dynamics of autonomic versus syncretic decision making:

- "We just got our steps done and that was a big project. The contractor would talk (to my husband) and not talk to me. And I said, 'Excuse me, I'm here, too.'"
- "We are looking for a house now, and we're making decisions on which side of town we want it on, what size house do we want, and it's a together decision. That's never how my mother did it."
- "My husband did not want a van, because we have just one child, but I said, 'I want a van. And it's not because everyone else has a van. I want comfort.' He wanted a convertible. And we got a van."[58]

Marketers need to figure out who makes the buying decisions in a family because this information tells them who to target and whether they need to reach both spouses to influence a choice. For example, marketing research in the 1950s indicated that women were beginning to play a larger role in household purchasing decisions. In response, lawn mower manufacturers emphasized the rotary mower over other power mowers to downplay women's fears of injury. Rotary models, which conceal the cutting blades and engine, began to pop up in ads that depicted young women and smiling grandmothers as they cut the grass.[59]

Researchers pay special attention to which spouse plays the role of the **family financial officer (FFO)**—the individual who keeps track of the family's bills and decides how to spend any surplus funds. Newlyweds tend to share this role, and then over time one spouse or the other takes over these responsibilities.[60] In traditional families (and especially those with low educational levels), women are primarily responsible for family financial management—the man makes it, and the woman spends it. Each spouse "specializes" in certain activities.[61]

The pattern is different among families where more modern sex-role norms operate. These couples believe both people should participate in family maintenance activities. In these cases, husbands assume more responsibility for laundering, housecleaning, grocery shopping, and so on, in addition to such traditionally "male" tasks as home maintenance and garbage removal.[62] Shared decision making is the norm for most American couples today—a Roper poll reported that 94 percent of

Mothers take on many responsibilities as they care for the family unit.

Source: Courtesy KidCare TV.

partnered women say they make the decision or share equally in home furnishings selections (not a huge surprise), but in addition, 81 percent said the same for financial savings/investments and 74 percent participate when the couple decides what car to buy.[63]

Working mothers often struggle with what one researcher calls the **juggling lifestyle**—a frenzied, guilt-ridden compromise between conflicting cultural ideals of motherhood and professionalism.[65] This frantic way of life isn't surprising in light of a recent survey by the U.S. Department of Labor that shows that the average working woman spends about twice as much time as the average working man on household chores and the care of children. And she also gets about an hour less sleep each night than the average stay-at-home mom.[66]

Cultural background plays a big role in determining whether husbands or wives control purchase decisions. For example, husbands tend to dominate decision making among couples with a strong Hispanic ethnic identification. Vietnamese Americans also are more likely to adhere to the traditional model: The man makes the decision for any large purchase, whereas the woman gets a budget to manage the home. In a study that compared marital decision making in the United States and China, American women reported more "wife decides" situations than did the Chinese. Advertising and marketing strategies often reflect assumptions about "who's the boss." These examples illustrate some cross-cultural differences:[67]

● The Coca-Cola Company developed a campaign to appeal to Latin American women based on a big research project the company conducted in Brazil. It found that a motherly female kangaroo was most likely to appeal to women who shop for their families—and who happen to account for 80 percent of Coke's $3.5

billion in Brazilian sales. Coke used the theme "Mom knows everything," after women in focus groups said they felt the media neglected them even though they purchased virtually every product in their households.

● Butterfly, an Indian program, enlists village medicine men to convince local women to take birth control pills. A big obstacle is that women are not accustomed to making these decisions. The response of one village resident is typical: "I have never taken contraceptives. My husband is my master—he will decide."

● Traditional sex-role norms also influenced a commercial Procter & Gamble produced for its Ariel laundry detergent in India. It shows a man named Ravi doing the laundry, which is highly unusual there. A female voice questions, "Where's the wife? Are you actually going to wash them? . . . a man should not wash clothes . . . [he is] sure to fail."

● Ads showing men doing housework are risky in Asia as well, even though today more Asian women work outside the home. A South Korean vacuum cleaner ad flashed to a woman who lies on the floor; she gives herself a facial with slices of cucumber while her husband vacuums around her. Women there didn't appreciate this ad. As a local ad executive put it, they regarded the ad as a challenge to "the leadership of women in the home."

In general, four factors appear to determine the degree to which one or the other spouse or both jointly will decide what to buy:[68]

1   **Sex-role stereotypes**—Couples who believe in traditional sex-role stereotypes tend to make individual decisions for sex-typed products (i.e., those they consider "masculine" or "feminine," as we discussed in Chapter 5).

2   **Spousal resources**—The spouse who contributes more resources to the family has the greater influence.

3   **Experience**—Couples who have gained experience as a decision-making unit make individual decisions more frequently.

4   **Socioeconomic status**—Middle-class families make more joint decisions than do either higher- or lower-class families.

Despite recent changes in decision-making responsibilities, women are still primarily responsible for the continuation of the family's **kin-network system**: They maintain ties among family members, both immediate and extended. Women are more likely to coordinate visits among relatives, stay in touch with family members, send greeting cards, and arrange social engagements.[69] This organizing role means that women often make important decisions about the family's leisure activities, and they are more likely to decide with whom the family will socialize.

Heuristics in Joint Decision Making

The **synoptic ideal** calls for the husband and wife to take a common view and to act as joint decision makers. According to this view, they would very thoughtfully weigh alternatives, assign one another well-defined roles, and calmly make mutually beneficial consumer decisions. The couple would act rationally, analytically, and use as much information as possible to maximize joint utility. Do you know anyone who does that? In reality, spousal decision making may be more about choosing whatever option will result in less conflict. A couple "reaches" rather than "makes" a decision. Researchers simply describe this process as "muddling through."[70]

One common technique to simplify the decision-making process uses *heuristics* (see Chapter 8). The following decision-making patterns realtors frequently observe when a couple decides on a new house illustrate how couples use heuristics.

The couple defines their areas of common preference on obvious, objective dimensions rather than subtler, hard-to-define cues. For example, they may easily

CB AS I SEE IT

Professor Alladi Venkatesh, *University of California, Irvine*

*A*s new technologies diffuse into the home, new terminology has begun to emerge as, for example, in smart homes, home automation, digital home, digital living, networked home, home of the future, smart appliances, and so on. To further complicate the technological scene we are witnessing growth of social media (Facebook, MySpace, YouTube, etc.). We will use the term *smart home technologies* to describe these and other similar technologies. Although smart home technologies have developed in different directions because of the types of industry players involved, some common themes underlie these developments. For example, family shopping behavior from online product information search to payments, vacation planning and communication are some of the many activities that families undertake using these new technologies. They all seem to point to a great sense of anticipation that home life as we have understood in the past fifty or sixty years will undergo some fundamental changes. It is claimed that some of the changes may be the result of advances at the technological frontier.

Embedded in the concept of the smart home are smart appliances, multimedia systems, energy devices, sensors, lighting systems, sensors and control systems, and home robots that manifest basic qualities of programmable machine intelligence. However, their implementation has not been very successful and has been a little slow. Recent developments however seem to suggest that smart home concepts are closer to reality and must be taken seriously.

To put these developments in a historical perspective, one can trace all such advances to the early 1980s with the introduction of the PC into the home. This was also the period when various electronic gadgets entered the domestic space: VCRs, microwave ovens, answering machines, cable TV to name important few. A lot has happened since then. In the 1990s the technological scene changed dramatically with the arrival of the Internet connecting the household to the external environment in some fundamental views. In the beginning of the twenty-first century, the introduction of mobile phones and wireless technologies have further opened up the technological boundaries. The possibilities seem endless. In this ever-increasing technological frenzy, some caution must be exercised as new technologies knock on the door to gain acceptance by families. Our previous studies show that families are reluctant to "overtechnologize" their homes, but at the same time are quite open to technologies that fit with their current patterns of behaviors and possibly add value to the family life. It is this balance between too much and too little technology that one must seek.

Given the developments described previously, technology diffusion into the home remains an unexplored area in the field of consumer research. For consumer researchers, the challenging questions are:

- How are smart home technologies diffusing into the home?
- How is the family changing as a result of new technologies coming into the home?
- Who are the innovators? And what are their characteristics?
- What are the models of technology and appropriate adoption and use?
- How are the family roles transformed in light of these new changes?
- What are the implications for product advertising in light of social media?

agree on the number of bedrooms they need in the new home, but they have a harder time when they need to agree on how the home should look.

The couple negotiates a system of *task specialization* in which each is responsible for certain duties or decision areas and does not intrude on the other's "turf." For many couples, sex roles often dictate just what these territories are. For example, the wife may scout out houses that meet their requirements in advance, and the husband determines whether the couple can obtain a mortgage.

The likelihood of one partner conceding to the wishes of the other depends on how passionately each person desires a specific outcome. One spouse yields to the influence of the other in many cases simply because his or her preference for a certain attribute is not particularly intense. In other situations he is more willing to fight for what he wants (in other words, "choose your battles").[71] In cases where intense preferences for different attributes exist, rather than attempt to influence each other, spouses will "trade off" a less-intense preference for a more strongly felt one. For example, a husband who is somewhat indifferent about kitchen design may give in to his wife in exchange for permission to design his own garage workshop.

OBJECTIVE

How do children learn over time what and how to consume?

Children as Decision Makers: Consumers-in-Training

As they struggle to convince us to buy new cars, carmakers also take time out to woo some people who are still too young to drive. Many advertise in child-oriented areas such as gyms that cater to kids, social networking sites young people visit, and the Saturday morning cartoons. In Whyville. net, a virtual world where nearly 2 million children aged 8 to 15 hang out, kids can buy virtual Scion xBs if they have enough "clams" (Whyville's monetary unit). If not, they can meet with Eric, a virtual Toyota Financial Services advisor, to finance an xB replica they can use to tool around while in-world. Small wonder: A study Nickelodeon conducted reported that almost two-thirds of parents now say their children "actively participate" in car-buying decisions.[72]

Anyone who has had the "delightful" experience of grocery shopping with children in tow knows that kids often have a say (sometimes a loud, whiney one) in what their parents buy. Children make up three distinct markets:[73]

1 **Primary Market**—Kids spend a lot on their own wants and needs that include toys, apparel, movies, and games. When marketers at M&Ms candy figured out who actually buys a lot of their products, they redesigned vending machines with coin slots lower to the ground to accommodate shorter people, and sales rose dramatically.[74] Most children choose their own brands of toothpaste, shampoo, and adhesive bandage.[75]

2 **Influence Market**—**Parental yielding** occurs when a parental decision maker "surrenders" to a child's request.[76] Yielding drives many product selections because about 90 percent of these requests are for a specific brand. Researchers estimate that children directly influence about $453 billion worth of family purchases in a year. They report that on average children weigh in with a purchase request every 2 minutes when they shop with parents.[77] In recognition of this influence, Mrs. Butterworth's Syrup created a $6 million campaign to target kids directly with humorous ads that show the lengths to which adults will go to get the syrup bottle to talk to them. An executive who worked on the campaign explained, "We needed to create the *nag factor* [where kids demand their parents buy the product]."[78]

    The likelihood of yielding depends partly on the dynamics within a particular family. As we all know, parental styles range from permissive to strict, and they also vary in terms of the amount of responsibility parents give their children.[79] Income level also comes into play; kids at the lower end of the spectrum have a greater say in brand purchases than those from high income families. Parents whom children can most easily influence also tend to be highly receptive to advertising; according to a major research firm, these "child influenced shoppers" are twice as likely as the average U.S. adult to agree that if they see a brand name product on a TV show this reassures them it's a good product. They're also twice as likely to say that they'll probably try a new product if they see a character in a movie use it.

    One study documented the strategies kids use to request purchases. Although most children simply ask for things, some other common tactics included saying they had seen it on TV, saying that a sibling or friend has it, or offering to do chores in exchange. Other actions were less innocuous—they included directly placing the object in the cart and continuous pleading—often a "persuasive" behavior![80] In addition, the amount of influence children have over consumption is culturally determined. Children who live in individualistic cultures such as the United States have more direct influence, whereas kids in collective cultures such as Japan get their way more indirectly.[81]

3 **Future Market**—Kids have a way of growing up to be adults—so savvy marketers try to lock in brand loyalty at an early age. That explains why Kodak encourages kids to become photographers. Currently, only 20 percent of children aged 5 to 12 own cameras, and they shoot an average of only one roll of film a year. The company produces ads that portray photography as a cool pursuit and as a form of rebellion. It packages cameras with an envelope to mail the film directly back so parents can't see the photos.

Consumer Socialization

We've seen that kids are responsible for a lot of marketplace activity, but how do they know what they like and want? Children do not spring from the womb with consumer skills in place. **Consumer socialization** is the process "by which young people acquire skills, knowledge, and attitudes relevant to their functioning in the marketplace."[82] From where does this knowledge come? Friends and teachers certainly participate in this process. For instance, children talk to one another about consumer products, and this tendency increases with age.[83] Especially for young children, though, the two primary socialization sources are the family and the media.

Parents' Influence

Parents influence consumer socialization both directly and indirectly. They deliberately try to instill their own values about consumption in their children ("You're going to learn the value of a dollar!"). Parents also determine the degree to which their children come into contact with other information sources such as television, salespeople, and peers.[84] Cultural expectations regarding the involvement of children in purchase decisions influence when and how parents socialize their kids as consumers. For example, parents in traditional cultures such as Greece and India rely on later development timetables for consumer-related skills and understanding advertising practices than do American and Australian parents.[85]

Grown-ups also serve as significant models for observational learning (see Chapter 3). Children learn about consumption as they watch their parents' behaviors and imitate them. Marketers encourage this process when they package adult products in child versions. This "passing down" of product preferences helps to create brand loyalty—researchers find evidence of intergenerational influence when they study the product choices of mothers and their daughters.[86]

The process of consumer socialization begins with infants; within the first 2 years, children request products they want. By about age 5, most kids make purchases with the help of parents and grandparents, and by age 8 most buy things on their own.[87] Figure 11.2 summarizes the sequence of stages as kids turn into consumers.

Parents exhibit different styles when they socialize their children:[88]

- *Authoritarian parents* are hostile, restrictive, and emotionally uninvolved. They do not have warm relationships with their children, they censor the types of media their children see, and they tend to have negative views about advertising.
- *Neglecting parents* also are detached from their children, and the parents don't exercise much control over what their children do.
- *Indulgent parents* communicate more with their children about consumption-related matters and are less restrictive. They believe that children should be allowed to learn about the marketplace without much interference.

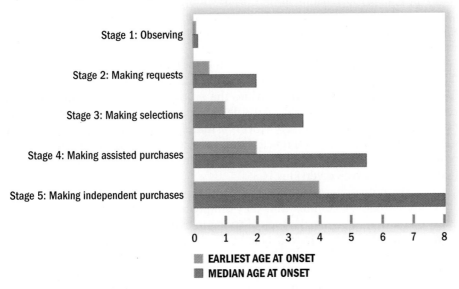

A CONSUMER IS BORN

Children start accompanying parents to the marketplace as early as one month old and begin to make independent purchases as early as four years old.

Figure 11.2 FIVE STAGES OF CONSUMER DEVELOPMENT BY EARLIEST AGE AT ONSET AND MEDIAN AGE AT ONSET

Television and the Web: Electric Babysitters

Advertising starts to influence us at a very early age. As we've seen, many marketers push their products on kids to encourage them to build a lifelong habit. One controversial exception occurred in France. An ad McDonald's placed in the magazine *Femme Actuelle* actually encouraged parents to limit kids' visits to its outlets when it proclaimed, "There is no reason to eat excessive amounts of junk food, nor go more than once a week to McDonald's." A spokesperson for McDonald's in the United States said the company did not agree with the views the ad expressed.[89] That's unfortunate—a recent study the National Institutes of Health funded projected that a ban on fast-food advertising to children would cut the national obesity rate by as much as 18 percent.[90]

In two studies, British researchers compared the effects of television advertising on the eating habits of 152 kids between the ages of 5 and 11. In both studies, the kids watched 10 ads followed by a cartoon. In one session, the kids saw ads for toys before they watched a video. But in another session, they replaced the toy ads with food ads that commonly run during children's programs. After both viewings, held 2 weeks apart, the kids were allowed to snack as much as they wanted from a table of low-fat and high-fat snacks, including grapes, cheese-flavored rice cakes, chocolate buttons, and potato chips. The 5- to 7-year-old kids who saw the food ads ate 14 to 17 percent more calories than those who saw the toy ads. The results were even more dramatic among 9- to 11-year-olds. Those in the food ad condition ate from 84 to 134 percent more calories than did those in the toy ad condition.[91]

And, as we've already seen, a lot of kids divide their time between their TV set and their computer (and their cell phone as well). Many major companies such as Disney are beefing up their presence on the Web to be wherever kids spend their time.[92] At BarbieGirls.com a girl can customize her avatar and shop for furniture and clothes in a virtual mall using "B-bucks" she earns playing games and watching product promotion videos. Mattel hopes these girls, who have outgrown their traditional toys, will want to customize their Barbie Girls' devices as they would their cell phones or iPods. One device is a Barbie-inspired handheld MP3 music device to interact with the Web site and unlock even more content.[93]

The Tangled Web

It comes as no surprise that aggressive advertising drives kids to online locations. A recent study reported that more than 4 out of 10 children ages 6 to 11 visited a Web site they saw or heard about in an ad.[94] Another annual survey highlights the unease many parents feel about cyberspace—one-fourth of adult respondents agreed that their children spend too much time on the Internet. The 2008 study also showed an increase in the number of parents who said their children's grades declined since they went online, and over half of those surveyed said that online predators are a threat.[95]

Marketing Pitfall

Do marketers try to turn girls into women before they should? Adult products and practices increasingly trickle down to the younger set. Analysts estimate that girls 11 to 14 see about 500 advertisements a day. We read about elementary school students who spend the afternoon at the beauty salon and even 5-year-olds who have spa days and pedicure parties. In 2005 the NPD group reported that the average age that women began to use beauty products was 17. In 2009, that average dropped to 13. Another study by Experian found that 43 percent of 6- to 9-year-olds use lipstick or lip gloss, and 38 percent use hairstyling products. In addition to adult shows like *Extreme Makeover*, youngsters learn about makeup from the girls of *Toddlers & Tiaras*, and *Little Miss Perfect*.[98]

Sex-Role Socialization

Children pick up on the concept of gender identity (see Chapter 5) at an earlier age than researchers previously believed—by as young as age 1 in some cases. By the age of 3, most children categorize driving a truck as masculine and cooking and cleaning as feminine.[96] Even characters that cartoons portray as helpless are more likely to wear frilly or ruffled dresses.[97]

One function of child's play is to rehearse for adulthood. Children act out different roles they might assume later in life and learn about the expectations others have of them. The toy industry provides the props children use to perform these roles.[99] Depending on which side of the debate you're on, these toys either reflect or teach children about what society expects of males and females. Preschool boys and girls do not exhibit many differences in toy preferences, but after the age of 5 they part company: Girls tend to stick with dolls, whereas boys gravitate toward "action figures" and high-tech diversions.

Industry critics charge this is because males dominate the toy industry, but toy company executives counter that they simply respond to kids' natural preferences.[100] Indeed, after two decades of trying to avoid boy-versus-girl stereotypes, many companies seem to have decided that differences are inevitable. Toys "R" Us unveiled a new store design after it interviewed 10,000 kids; the chain now has separate sections it calls Girls' World and Boys' World. According to the president of Fox Family Channels, "Boys and girls are different, and it's great to celebrate what's special about each."[101] Boys tend to be more interested in battle and competition; girls are more interested in creativity and relationships. This is what experts refer to as "male and female play patterns."[102]

Some doll manufacturers recognize the powerful role toys play in consumer socialization, so they create characters they hope will teach little girls about the real world—not the fantasy "bimbo" world that many dolls represent. Barbie's rebirth as a career woman illustrates how a firm takes concerns about socialization to heart. Although Mattel introduced a Barbie doll astronaut in 1964 and an airline pilot in 1999, it never provided much detail about the careers themselves. Today girls can choose to play with Working Woman Barbie. She comes with a miniature computer and cell phone as well as a CD-ROM about understanding finances. She dresses in a gray suit, but the skirt reverses to a red dress for her to wear with red platform shoes when she goes on after-work adventures with Ken.[103]

Cognitive Development

A child's ability to make mature, "adult" consumer decisions obviously increases with age (not that grown-ups always make mature decisions). Marketers segment kids in terms of their **stage of cognitive development**, or their ability to comprehend concepts of increasing complexity. Some evidence indicates that very young children learn consumption-related information surprisingly well.[105]

The Swiss psychologist Jean Piaget was the foremost proponent of the idea that children pass through distinct stages of cognitive development. He believed that a certain cognitive structure characterizes each stage as the child learns to process information.[106] In one classic demonstration of cognitive development, Piaget poured the contents of a short, squat glass of lemonade into a taller, thinner glass that actually held the same amount of liquid. Five-year-olds, who still believed that the shape of the glass determined its contents, thought this glass held more liquid than the first glass. They are in what Piaget termed a *preoperational stage of development*. In contrast, 6-year-olds tended to be unsure, but 7-year-olds knew the amount of lemonade had not changed.

Many developmental specialists no longer believe that children necessarily pass through these fixed stages at the same time. An alternative view proposes that they differ in information-processing capability, or ability to store and retrieve information from memory (see Chapter 3). Researchers who advocate this approach identify three developmental stages:[107]

1 **Limited**—Children who are younger than age 6 do not employ storage and retrieval strategies.
2 **Cued**—Children between the ages of 6 and 12 employ these strategies but only when prompted.
3 **Strategic**—Children 12 and older spontaneously employ storage and retrieval strategies.

This sequence of development underscores the notion that children do not think in the same way adults do, and we can't expect them to use information the same way either. It also reminds us that they do not necessarily form the same conclusions as adults when they encounter product information. For example, kids are not as likely to realize that something they see on TV is not "real," and as a result they are more vulnerable to persuasive messages. Younger kids aren't able to distinguish media depictions from reality, so the more a child watches MTV's *Laguna Beach* or *SpongeBob SquarePants*, the more he will accept the images it depicts as real.[108] Kids also see idealized images of what it is like to be an adult. Because children over the age of 6 do about a quarter of their television viewing during prime time, adult programs and commercials have a big affect on them. For example, young girls who see adult lipstick commercials associate lipstick with beauty.[109]

Recent research underscores the idea that children's understanding of brand names evolves as they age. Kids learn to relate to brand names at an early age; they recognize brand names in stores, develop preferences for some brands over others, and request branded items by name. However, brand names function as simple perceptual cues for these children that let them identify a familiar object with particular features. *Conceptual brand meanings*, which specify the nonobservable abstract features of the product, enter into the picture in middle childhood (about age 8); children incorporate them into their thinking and judgments a few years later. By the time a child reaches 12 years of age, she thinks about brands on a conceptual or symbolic level and she's likely to incorporate these meanings into brand-related judgments.[110]

Several new business ventures illustrate that using sound principles of consumer psychology can also make good financial sense. The trend started a long time ago with public television's *Sesame Street*, but today the for-profit networks are in the game as well. The first successful foray into the preschool market was *Blue's Clues* in 1996, which turned into a huge hit as viewers abandoned the smarmy *Barney & Friends*.

Now, when millions of preschoolers tune in to Nickelodeon's hit show *Dora the Explorer*, they don't realize that they view content based on **multiple-intelligence theory**. This influential perspective argues for other types of intelligence, such as athletic prowess or musical ability, beyond the traditional math and verbal skills psychologists use to measure IQ. Thus, when Dora consults her map, she promotes "spatial" skills. And when she asks her young viewers to help her count planks to build a bridge, Dora builds "interpersonal intelligence."[111]

Marketing Research and Children

The Walt Disney Co. recently assembled a team of anthropologists who spent 18 months studying 6- to 14-year-old boys. The company, which has tended toward girl-friendly fare like *Hannah Montana* and *The Little Mermaid* in recent years, wanted to get a better handle on a market segment that spends about $50 billion every year (it recently bought Marvel Comics to expand its reach to boys). After team

Marketing Pitfall

Toys are fun to play with, but often a hidden agenda is that they're also socialization agents that teach kids about life. Sometimes, perhaps they can be a bit *too* realistic. Some critics object to a new doll called Baby Alive Learns to Potty. She comes with a pink plastic toilet. When a child presses the doll's bracelet she chirps, "Sniff sniff. I made a stinky!" The doll also comes with "green beans" and "bananas" that the child feeds to the doll—then they come out the other end. Put Baby Alive on her toilet and a magnet triggers a change in the bowl: The "water" is replaced with "potty waste," which the child can flush (with appropriate sound effects). Critics charge that some things are better left to the land of make-believe. Indeed, most child psychologists agree that the best toys encourage children to use their imaginations.[104]

members observed boys in their natural habitats, they recommended subtle but important changes to programs that better capture this world.

- The central character on the show *Aaron Stone* is a mediocre basketball player. The team learned that boys identify more with characters who try to improve than to those who easily win.
- Actors on the show now carry their skateboards with the bottoms facing outward because boys in real life do that to show off how they personalize their boards.
- The games section of the Disney XD Web site includes trophy cases because the researchers found that players like to share their achievements with others.[112]

Compared to adults, kids are difficult subjects for market researchers. They tend to be unreliable reporters of their own behavior, they have poor recall, and they often do not understand abstract questions.[113] Some European countries restrict marketers' ability to interview children so it's even harder to collect this kind of data there. Still, as Disney discovered market research can pay off.[114]

Product Testing

A particularly helpful type of research with children is product testing. Young subjects provide a valuable perspective on what products will succeed with other kids. Marketers obtain these insights as they watch kids play with toys or talk to them in focus groups. The Fisher-Price Company maintains a nursery it calls the Playlab. Children it chooses from a waiting list of 4,000 play with new toys while staff members watch from behind a one-way mirror.[115]

Message Comprehension

Because children differ in their abilities to process product-related information, when advertisers try to appeal directly to them this raises many serious ethical issues.[116] Children's advocacy groups argue that kids younger than age 7 do not understand the persuasive intent of commercials and (as we've seen) younger children cannot readily distinguish between a commercial and programming. Kids' cognitive defenses are not yet sufficiently developed to filter out commercial appeals, so in a sense, altering their brand preferences may be likened to "shooting fish in a barrel," as one critic put it.[117] Figure 11.3 shows one attempt to assess whether kids can tell that a commercial is trying to persuade them.

Beginning in the 1970s, the Federal Trade Commission (FTC) took action to protect children. The agency limited commercials during "children's" programming

LEGO did research to learn how boys and girls play with its building toys. When executives watched girls play with the toys they noticed they were more likely to build living areas while boys tended to build cars. The company introduced a new version of its product called Paradisa to entice girls to buy more LEGOs. This set emphasizes the ability to build "socially oriented structures" such as homes, swimming pools, and stables. Sales to girls picked up, though the company still sells most of its sets to boys.
Source: PhotoEdit, Inc./Tom Prettyman.

Figure 11.3 EXAMPLES OF SKETCHES RESEARCHERS USE TO MEASURE CHILDREN'S PERCEPTIONS OF COMMERCIAL INTENT

(most often Saturday morning television) and required "separators" to help children discern when a program ended and a commercial began (e.g., "We'll be right back after these commercial messages"). The FTC reversed itself in the early 1980s during the deregulatory, probusiness climate of the Reagan administration. The 1990 Children's Television Act restored some of these restrictions. Still, critics argue that rather than sheltering children from marketplace influences, the dominant way that marketers view them is as what one calls "kid customer."[118]

CHAPTER SUMMARY

Now that you have finished reading this chapter you should understand why:

 Marketers often need to understand *consumers'* behavior rather than consumer behavior because in many cases more than one person decides what to buy.

More than one person actually makes many purchasing decisions. Collective decision making occurs whenever two or more people evaluate, select, or use a product or service. In organizations and in families, members play several different roles during the decision-making process. These roles include the gatekeeper, influencer, buyer, and user.

 Companies as well as individuals make purchase decisions. The decision-making process differs when people choose what to buy on behalf of a company versus a personal purchase.

Organizational buyers are people who make purchasing decisions on behalf of a company or other group. Although many of the same factors that affect how they make decisions in their personal lives influence these buyers, their organizational choices tend to be more rational. They are also likely to involve more financial risk, and as they become more complex, it is probable that a greater number of people will be involved in making the decision. The amount of cognitive effort that goes into organizational decisions relates to internal factors, such as the individuals' psychological characteristics, and external factors, such as the company's willingness to tolerate risk. One of the most important determinants is the type of purchase the company wants to make: The extent of problem solving required depends on whether the product or service it procures is simply a reorder (a straight rebuy), a reorder with minor modifications (modified rebuy), or something it never bought before or something complex and risky (new task). Online purchasing sites revolutionize the way organizational decision makers collect and evaluate product information in business-to-business (B2B) e-commerce.

Our traditional notions about families are outdated.

The number and type of U.S. households is changing in many ways, including delays in getting married and having children, and in the composition of family households, which a single parent increasingly heads. New perspectives on the family life cycle, which focuses on how people's needs change as they move through different stages in their lives, are forcing marketers to more seriously consider consumer segments such as gays and lesbians, divorced persons, and childless couples when they develop targeting strategies.

 Many important demographic dimensions of a population relate to family and household structure.

Demographics are statistics that measure a population's characteristics. Some of the most important of these relate to family structure (e.g., the birthrate, the marriage rate, and the divorce rate). A household is an occupied housing unit.

 Members of a family unit play different roles and have different amounts of influence when the family makes purchase decisions.

Marketers have to understand how families make decisions. Spouses in particular have different priorities and exert varying amounts of influence in terms of effort and power. Children are also increasingly influential during a widening range of purchase decisions.

 Children learn over time what and how to consume.

Children undergo a process of socialization, where they learn how to be consumers. Parents and friends instill some of this knowledge, but a lot of it comes from exposure to mass media and advertising. Because it's so easy to persuade children, consumers, academics, and marketing practitioners hotly debate the ethical aspects of marketing to them.

KEY TERMS

Accommodative purchase
  decision, 432
Autonomic decision, 434
Boomerang kids, 428
Business-to-business (B2B)
  e-commerce, 424
Business-to-business (B2B)
  marketers, 420
Buyclass theory of purchasing, 423
Buyer, 420
Buying center, 422
Consensual purchase decision, 432
Consumer socialization, 440
Crowdsourcing, 425
DINKS, 427

Extended family, 426
Family financial officer (FFO), 435
Family identity, 433
Family life cycle (FLC), 429
Fertility rate, 426
Freemium, 425
Gatekeeper, 420
Gender convergence, 434
Helicopter moms, 433
Household, 426
Influencer, 420
Initiator, 420
Juggling lifestyle, 436
Kin-network system, 437
Modified rebuy, 424

Multiple-intelligence theory, 443
Network effect, 425
New task, 424
Nuclear family, 426
Organizational buyers, 420
Parental yielding, 439
POSSLQ, 426
Prediction market, 425
Sandwich Generation, 427
Stage of cognitive development, 442
Straight rebuy, 423
Syncretic decisions, 434
Synoptic ideal, 437
User, 420
Wiki, 424

REVIEW

1 What are some factors that influence how an organizational buyer evaluates a purchase decision?
2 What is a prediction market?
3 Summarize the buyclass model of purchasing. How do decisions differ within each class?
4 What are some of the ways organizational decisions differ from individual consumer decisions? How are they similar?
5 List at least three roles employees play in the organizational decision-making process.
6 What is a nuclear family, and how is it different from an extended family?
7 How do we calculate a nation's fertility rate? What fertility rate is required to ensure that population size does not decline?
8 What are boomerang kids?
9 What is the FLC, and why is it important to marketers?

10 List some variables we must consider when we try to understand different stages in the FLC.
11 What is the difference between a consensual and an accommodative purchase decision? What are some factors that help to determine how much conflict the family will experience when it makes a decision?
12 What is the difference between an autonomic and a syncretic decision?
13 What are some differences between "traditional" and "modern" couples in terms of how they allocate household responsibilities?
14 What factors help to determine if decisions will be made jointly or by one spouse or the other?
15 What is a kin-network system?
16 Describe a heuristic a couple might use when they make a decision, and provide an example of it.

17 What are three reasons why children are an important segment to marketers?

18 What is consumer socialization? Who are some important players in this process? How do toys contribute?

19 Discuss stages of cognitive development and how these relate to the comprehension of marketing messages.

20 Why is it difficult to conduct marketing research with children?

CONSUMER BEHAVIOR CHALLENGE

■ DISCUSS

1 The promotional products industry thrives on corporate clients that order $19 billion per year of T-shirts, mugs, pens, and other branded items in order to keep their organizations at the forefront of their customers' minds. As a result of the voluntary ban on these products by the pharmaceutical industry, these businesses will lose around $1 billion per year in sales. What do you think about this initiative—is it fair to deprive an industry of its livelihood in this way? Why or why not?[119]

2 Is the family unit dead?

3 Discuss the pros and cons of the voluntarily childless movement. Are followers of this philosophy selfish?

4 Do marketers rob kids of their childhood?

5 The Defense Department shut down a controversial research program following a public outcry. Its intent was to create a prediction market to forecast terrorist activities. Was the decision to terminate the program warranted? Why or why not?

6 The chapter cites parents' worries about the amount of time their kids spend online. Is this just old-fashioned concern that ignores the benefits kids get when they explore cyberspace?

7 Do you think market research should be performed with children? Give the reasons for your answer.

8 Marketers have been criticized when they donate products and services to educational institutions in exchange for free promotion. Is this a fair exchange, in your opinion, or should corporations be prohibited from attempting to influence youngsters in school?

9 For each of the following five product categories—groceries, automobiles, vacations, furniture, and appliances—describe the ways in which you believe having children or not affects a married couple's choices.

10 When they identify and target newly divorced couples, do you think marketers exploit these couples' situations? Are there instances in which you think marketers may actually be helpful to them? Support your answers with examples.

11 Industrial purchase decisions are totally rational. Aesthetic or subjective factors don't—and shouldn't—play a role in this process. Do you agree?

12 We can think of college students who live away from home as having a substitute "family." Whether you live with your parents, with a spouse, or with other students, how are decisions made in your college residence "family"? Do some people take on the role of mother or father or child? Give a specific example of a decision that had to be made and the roles members played.

13 Stanford University Medical Center prohibits its physicians from accepting even small gifts such as pens and mugs from pharmaceutical sales representatives under a new policy it hopes will limit industry influence on patient care and doctor education. The new policy is part of a small but growing movement among centers (Yale and the University of Pennsylvania have similar policies). The policy also prohibits doctors from accepting free drug samples and from publishing articles in medical journals that industry contractors ghostwrite (a fairly common practice). These changes come at a time when many of us are concerned about the safety and rising cost of drugs and medical devices. About 90 percent of the pharmaceutical industry's $21 billion marketing budget targets physicians. Some studies have shown that even small gifts create a sense of obligation; one critical study charged that free drug samples are ". . . a powerful inducement for physicians and patients to rely on medications that are expensive but not more effective." Indeed, some industry documents from a civil lawsuit show that big pharmaceutical companies sometimes calculate to the penny the profits that doctors could make from their drugs. Sales representatives shared those profit estimates with doctors and their staffs, the documents show.[120] Where is the line between legitimately promoting one's products and unethical practice? Should professionals engage in organizational decision making that has such far-reaching medical and financial ramifications?

■ APPLY

1 Arrange to interview two married couples, one younger and one older. Prepare a response form that lists five product categories—groceries, furniture, appliances, vacations, and automobiles—and ask each spouse to indicate, without consulting the other, whether purchases in each category are made by joint or unilateral decisions, and to indicate whether the unilateral decisions are made by the husband or the wife. Compare each couple's responses for agreement between husbands and wives relative to who makes the decisions,

and compare both couples' overall responses for differences relative to the number of joint versus unilateral decisions. Report your findings and conclusions.

2 Collect ads for three different product categories that target families. Find another set of ads for different brands of the same items that don't feature families. Prepare a report comparing the probable effectiveness of the two approaches. Which specific categories would most likely benefit from a family emphasis?

3 Pick three married couples and ask each husband and wife to list the names of all cousins, second cousins, and so on for both sides of the family. Based on the results, what can you conclude about the relative role of men and women in maintaining the kin-network system?

4 Observe the interactions between parents and children in the cereal section of a local grocery store (remember to bring earplugs). Prepare a report on the number of children who expressed preferences, how they expressed their preferences, and how parents responded, including the number who purchased the child's choice.

5 Watch 3 hours of children's programming on commercial television stations. Evaluate the marketing techniques used in the commercials in terms of the ethical issues raised in the final section of this chapter. Report your findings and conclusions.

6 Select a product category, and using the life-cycle stages the chapter describes, list the variables likely to affect a purchase decision for the product by consumers in each stage of the cycle.

7 Consider three important changes in the modern family structure. For each, find an example of a marketer who seems to be conscious of this change in its product communications, retailing innovations, or other aspects of the marketing mix. If possible, also try to find examples of marketers who have failed to keep up with these developments.

Case Study

CHILDREN: THE FINAL FRONTIER . . . FOR CELL PHONES

With the adult and even teen markets for cell phones quickly saturating (over 65 percent of U.S. teens have them now), the industry looks to other segments. The growth market for the cell phone industry in the near future is children, ages 8 to 12—or even younger. Many in the industry see grade school children as the final frontier if phone manufacturers are to continue to grow. Already, parents give children as young as 5 years old their own cell phones.

A host of companies make phones for the younger market. Disney, Hasbro, Mattel, and Firefly Mobile offer models in bright colors that feature graphics of favorite characters such as SpongeBob SquarePants or Barbie. They designed these phones for smaller hands, and many lack traditional keypads. Parents can program what the phones do, control incoming and outgoing calls, and prepay minutes.

But do children really need a cell phone? There are many child advocates, including Ralph Nader, Canadian kids' entertainer Raffi, and various politicians, who say that they do not. Some critics claim that cell phone makers have declared "open season" on children with their aggressive marketing tactics.

The cell phone companies defend their actions. Many released statements saying that they don't market their products (even the kid-friendly ones) to children, but rather to their parents. Disney said it developed the Disney Mobile as a service to address the needs of a family audience, and that its products and services are available to all members of the family including adults. Marketers claim that they simply answer the demands of consumers for services such as the five-key, parent-programmable Firefly.

Of course, children want the phones because they're cool, because their friends have them, and because they want to be more grown-up. In fact, many tweens reject the kiddie versions and demand real adult-style cell phones. According to a spokesman for Verizon Wireless, kids "don't want what we call 'Fisher Price' phones. They want the real deal, with the camera and the QWERTY keyboard for text messaging." Coolness and prestige alone are usually not good enough for parents to give in and buy one of the gadgets for their kids. However, marketers position the phones to Mom and Dad on a different basis: The phones provide an extra layer of security to anxious parents who want to be able to locate their kids at all times. Many of the children's phones offer GPS tracking as well as all the parental control features. When parents are convinced that the increased ability to stay connected with their children enhances safety, the purchase decision is simple. Whether due to safety concerns or simply because parents give in to their kids' demands, the efforts of cell phone marketers appear to be paying off. Already, 55 percent of children ages 9 to 11 and 35 percent of children ages 7 years and younger carry their own mobiles. If companies can get younger children in the habit of using phones, the kids will probably be consumers for life.

DISCUSSION QUESTIONS

1 When it comes to cell phones for kids, who is the customer? Discuss the dynamics of the decision to buy a cell phone for a young child.

2 How do current trends in the family life cycle affect the marketing of cell phones to children?

Sources: Madhusmita Bora, "Must-Have for Tweens: Cell Phone," *St. Petersburg Times* (August 26, 2007): 1A; Allison Ross, "Fast Texting—Tween Market Pumps Cellphone Sales," *McClatchy Tribune Business News* (December 14, 2008); Louise Lee, "Mom, Let's Talk: A Brand New Batch of Cell Phones Takes Aim at Kids as Young as 5," *BusinessWeek*, (August 13, 2007): 82.

NOTES

1. www.epicurious.com, accessed July 1, 2009; www.marthastewart.com, accessed July 1, 2009.
2. Fred E. Webster and Yoram Wind, *Organizational Buying Behavior* (Upper Saddle River, NJ: Prentice Hall, 1972).
3. See J. Joseph Cronin, Jr., and Michael H. Morris, "Satisfying Customer Expectations: The Effect on Conflict and Repurchase Intentions in Industrial Marketing Channels," *Journal of the Academy of Marketing Science* 17 (Winter 1989): 41–49; Thomas W. Leigh and Patrick F. McGraw, "Mapping the Procedural Knowledge of Industrial Sales Personnel: A Script-Theoretic Investigation," *Journal of Marketing* 53 (January 1989): 16–34; William J. Qualls and Christopher P. Puto, "Organizational Climate and Decision Framing: An Integrated Approach to Analyzing Industrial Buying," *Journal of Marketing Research* 26 (May 1989): 179–92.
4. James M. Sinkula, "Market Information Processing and Organizational Learning," *Journal of Marketing* 58 (January 1994): 35–45.
5. Allen M. Weiss and Jan B. Heide, "The Nature of Organizational Search in High Technology Markets," *Journal of Marketing Research* 30 (May 1993): 220–33; Jennifer K. Glazing and Paul N. Bloom, "Buying Group Information Source Reliance," *Proceedings of the American Marketing Association Educators' Conference* (Summer 1994): 454.
6. B. Charles Ames and James D. Hlaracek, *Managerial Marketing for Industrial Firms* (New York: Random House Business Division, 1984); Edward F. Fern and James R. Brown, "The Industrial/Consumer Marketing Dichotomy: A Case of Insufficient Justification," *Journal of Marketing* 48 (Spring 1984): 68–77.
7. Quoted in Natasha Singer, "No Mug? Drug Makers Cut Out Goodies For Doctors," *New York Times* (December 30, 2008), www.nytimes.com, accessed December 30, 2008.
8. Daniel H. McQuiston, "Novelty, Complexity, and Importance as Causal Determinants of Industrial Buyer Behavior," *Journal of Marketing* 53 (April 1989): 66–79.
9. Patrick J. Robinson, Charles W. Faris, and Yoram Wind, *Industrial Buying and Creative Marketing* (Boston: Allyn & Bacon, 1967).
10. Erin Anderson, Wujin Chu, and Barton Weitz, "Industrial Purchasing: An Empirical Examination of the Buyclass Framework," *Journal of Marketing* 51 (July 1987): 71–86.
11. Steven J. Kafka, Bruce D. Temkin, Matthew R. Sanders, Jeremy Sharrard, and Tobias O. Brown, "eMarketplaces Boost B2B Trade," *The Forrester Report* (Cambridge, MA: Forrester Research, Inc., February 2000).
12. http://company.monster.com/wre, accessed June 16, 2009.
13. Sean Silverthorne, "Facebook as Corporate Intranet—It's Starting to Happen," *The View from Harvard Business* (December 18, 2007), http://blogs.bnet.com/harvard/?p=158, accessed June 15, 2009; Vauhini Vara, "Offices Co-Opt Consumer Web Tools Like 'Wikis' and Social Networking," *Wall Street Journal* (September 12, 2006), www.wsj.com, accessed September 12, 2006.
14. Barbara Kiviat, "The End of Management," *Time Inside Business* (July 12, 2004), www.time.com/time/magazine/article/0,9171,994658,00.html, accessed October 5, 2007.
15. www.intrade.com, accessed June 16, 2009; www.hsx.com, accessed June 16, 2009.
16. www.innocentric.com, accessed June 16, 2009; Jeff Howe, "The Rise of Crowdsourcing," *Wired* (June 2006): 176.
17. www.ideastorm.com, accessed June 16, 2009.
18. Chris Anderson, "The Economics of Giving It Away," *Wall Street Journal* (January 31, 2009), http://online.wsj.com/article/SB123335678420235003.html, accessed January 31, 2009.
19. Robert Boutilier, "Targeting Families: Marketing to and Through the New Family," in *American Demographics Marketing Tools* (Ithaca, NY: American Demographics Books, 1993): 4–6; W. Bradford Fay, "Families in the 1990s: Universal Values, Uncommon Experiences," *Marketing Research: A Magazine of Management & Applications* 5 (Winter 1993): 47.
20. Ellen Graham, "Craving Closer Ties, Strangers Come Together as Family," *Wall Street Journal* (March 4, 1996): B1.
21. Risto Moisio, Eric J. Arnould, and Linda L. Price, "Between Mothers and Markets: Constructing Family Identity Through Homemade Food," *Journal of Consumer Culture* 4, no. 3 (2004): 361–84.
22. Sam Roberts, "It's Official: To Be Married Means to Be Outnumbered," *New York Times* (October 15, 2006), www.nytimes.com, accessed October 15, 2006; Sam Roberts, "51% of Women Are Now Living Without Spouse," *New York Times* (January 16, 2007), www.nytimes.com, accessed January 16, 2007.
23. Brad Edmondson, "Inside the New Household Projections," *The Number News* (July 1996).
24. Roberts, "It's Official: To Be Married Means to Be Outnumbered,"; Roberts, "51% of Women Are Now Living without Spouse."
25. http://gayweddings.com, accessed June 16, 2009; http://twobrides.com, accessed June 16, 2009.
26. James Morrow, "A Place for One," *American Demographics* (November 2003): 25–30; Michelle Conlin, "Unmarried America," *BusinessWeek* (October 20, 2003): 106–16.
27. Emily Friedman, "Does Virtual Cheating Still Count? Online Communities Test Boundaries of Infidelity and Relationships," *ABC News* (August 13, 2007), www.abcnews.go.com/Technology/story?id=3473291&page=1, accessed August 13, 2007; Regina Lynn, "Virtual Rape Is Traumatic, but Is It a Crime?" *Wired* (May 4, 2007); www.wired.com/culture/lifestyle/commentary/sexdrive/2007/05/sexdrive_0504, accessed June 16, 2009; "Representative Kirk Wants to Ban Second Life's 'Rape Rooms' from Schools," *Virtual Worlds News* (May 7, 2008), www.virtualworldsnews.com/2008/05/representative.html?cid=113790134, accessed June 16, 2009.
28. Erik Eckholm, "'07 U.S. Births Break Baby Boom Record," *New York Times* (March 18, 2009), www.nytimes.com/2009/03/19/health/19birth.html?_r=1, accessed March 18, 2009.
29. Frank Bruni, "Persistent Drop in Fertility Reshapes Europe's Future," *New York Times* (December 26, 2002), www.nytimes.com, accessed December 26, 2002.
30. Katie Zezima, "More Women Than Ever Are Childless, Census Finds," *New York Times* (August 18, 2008), www.nytimes.com/2008/08/19/Us/19census.Html?_R=1&Scp=1&Sq=Childless&St=Cse, accessed August 19, 2008.
31. P. Paul, "Childless by Choice," *American Demographics* (November 2001): 45–48, 50; www.childfreebychoice.com, accessed June 16, 2009.
32. "Mothers Bearing a Second Burden," *New York Times* (May 14, 1989): 26.
33. Thomas Exter, "Disappearing Act," *American Demographics* (January 1989): 78; see also Kerenami Johnson and Scott D. Roberts, "Incompletely-Launched and Returning Young Adults: Social Change, Consumption, and Family Environment," in Robert P. Leone and V. Kumar, eds., *Enhancing Knowledge Development in Marketing* (Chicago: American Marketing Association), 249–54; John Burnett and Denise Smart, "Returning Young Adults: Implications for Marketers," *Psychology & Marketing* 11 (May–June 1994): 253–69.
34. Bella English, "The Boomerang Kids," *Boston Globe* (January 13, 2009), www.boston.com/lifestyle/family/articles/2009/01/13/the_boomerang_kids/?page=2, accessed June 16, 2009.

35. Marcia Mogelonsky, "The Rocky Road to Adulthood," *American Demographics* (May 1996): 26.

36. Rebecca Gardyn, "Animal Magnetism," *American Demographics* (May 2002): 31–37.

37. For a review cf. Russell W. Belk, "Metaphoric Relationships with Pets," *Society and Animals* 4, no. 2 (1996): 121–46.

38. "Airline Going To The Dogs . . . And Cats, Too," *NPR* (May 12, 2009), www.npr.org, accessed May 12, 2009; "Pets Win Prizes as Recession Bites," *Virgin Money* (April 23, 2009) http://uk.virginmoney .com/virgin/news-centre/press-releases/2009/Pets_win_prizes_as_ recession_bites.jsp, accessed June 16, 2009; Carla Baranauckas, "A Dog's Life, Upgraded," *New York Times* (September 24, 2006), www .nytimes.com, accessed September 24, 2006; Thom Forbes, "PetSmart's Hotels Offer Doggies the Lap of Luxury," *Miami Herald/Bloomberg News Online* (December 28, 2006), accessed December 28, 2006; Stephanie Thompson, "What's Next, Pup Tents in Bryant Park?" *Advertising Age* (January 29, 2007): 4; Maryann Mott, "Catering to the Consumers with Animal Appetites," *New York Times on the Web* (November 14, 2004); Jim Carlton, "For Finicky Drinkers, Water from the Tap Isn't Tasty Enough," *Wall Street Journal* (March 11, 2005), www.wsj.com, accessed March 11, 2005.

39. Brad Edmondson, "Do the Math," *American Demographics* (October 1999): 50–56.

40. Rex Y. Du and Wagner A. Kamakura, "Household Life Cycles and Lifestyles in the United States," *Journal of Marketing Research* 43 (February 2006): 121–132; Mary C. Gilly and Ben M. Enis, "Recycling the Family Life Cycle: A Proposal for Redefinition," in Andrew A. Mitchell, ed., *Advances in Consumer Research* 9 (Ann Arbor, MI: Association for Consumer Research, 1982): 271–76.

41. Cheryl Russell, "The New Consumer Paradigm," *American Demographics* (April 1999): 50.

42. These categories are an adapted version of an FLC model proposed by Gilly and Enis (1982). Based on a recent empirical comparison of several competing models, Schaninger and Danko found that this framework outperformed others, especially in terms of its treatment of nonconventional households, though they recommend several improvements to this model as well. See Gilly and Enis, "Recycling the Family Life Cycle"; Schaninger and Danko, "A Conceptual and Empirical Comparison of Alternate Household Life Cycle Models"; Scott D. Roberts, Patricia K. Voli, and Kerenami Johnson, "Beyond the Family Life Cycle: An Inventory of Variables for Defining the Family as a Consumption Unit," in Victoria L. Crittenden, ed., *Developments in Marketing Science* 15 (Coral Gables, FL: Academy of Marketing Science, 1992): 71–75; George P. Moschis. "Life Course Perspectives on Consumer Behaviour," *Journal of the Academy of Marketing Science* 35 (2007): 295–307.

43. Edmondson, "Do the Math."

44. Amy Harmon, "Grandma's on the Computer Screen," *New York Times* (November 26, 2008), www.nytimes.com/2008/11/27/us/27minicam .html?emc=eta1; accessed November 27, 2008.

45. Jennifer Lach, "Intelligence Agents," *American Demographics* (March 1999): 52–60; for a detailed ethnographic study of how households assimilate products, cf. Jennifer Chang Coupland, "Invisible Brands: An Ethnography of Households and the Brands in Their Kitchen Pantries," *Journal of Consumer Research* 33, no. 2 (2005): 106.

46. Harry L. Davis, "Decision-Making Within the Household," *Journal of Consumer Research* 2 (March 1972): 241–60; Michael B. Menasco and David J. Curry, "Utility and Choice: An Empirical Study of Wife/Husband Decision-Making," *Journal of Consumer Research* 16 (June 1989): 87–97; Conway Lackman and John M. Lanasa, "Family Decision-Making Theory: An Overview and Assessment," *Psychology & Marketing* 10 (March–April 1993): 81–94.

47. Shannon Dortch, "Money and Marital Discord," *American Demographics* (October 1994): 11.

48. For research on factors affecting how much influence adolescents exert in family decision-making, see Ellen Foxman, Patriya Tansuhaj, and Karin M. Ekstrom, "Family Members' Perceptions of Adolescents' Influence in Family Decision-Making," *Journal of Consumer Research* 15 (March 1989): 482–91; Sharon E. Beatty and Salil Talpade, "Adolescent Influence in Family Decision-Making: A Replication with Extension," *Journal of Consumer Research* 21 (September 1994): 332–41; for a recent study that compared the influence of parents versus siblings, cf. June Cotte and S. L. Wood, "Families and Innovative Consumer Behavior: A Triadic Analysis of Sibling and Parental Influence," *Journal of Consumer Research* 31, no. 1 (2004): 78–86.

49. Daniel Seymour and Greg Lessne, "Spousal Conflict Arousal: Scale Development," *Journal of Consumer Research* 11 (December 1984): 810–21.

50. Amber M. Epp and Linda L. Price. "Family Identity: A Framework of Identity Interplay in Consumption Practices." *Journal of Consumer Research* 35 (June 2008): 50–70; Robert Lohrer, "Haggar Targets Women with $8M Media Campaign," *Daily News Record* (January 8, 1997): 1.

51. Heather Timmons, "The Hand That Rocks the Cradle Can Call the Shots," *New York Times* (April 3, 2009), www.nytimes.com/2009/04/ 04/business/global/04indiamom.html, accessed April 3, 2009.

52. www.urbanbaby.com/talk/posts/51108366, accessed June 16, 2009; "Helicopter Moms vs. Free-Range Kids," *Newsweek.com* (April 21, 2008), www.newsweek.com/id/133103, accessed June 16, 2009.

53. Shirley S. Wang, "J&J Pulls Online Motrin Ad After Social-Media Backlash," *Wall Street Journal* (November 18, 2008), http://online.wsj .com/article_email/SB122697440743636123-lMyQjAxMDI4MjE2ODkx ..., accessed November 19, 2008.

54. Diane Crispell, "Dual-Earner Diversity," *American Demographics* (July 1995): 32–37.

55. "Marriage: The Art of Compromise," *American Demographics* (February 1998): 41.

56. Patricia Cohen, "Signs of Détente in the Battle Between Venus and Mars," *New York Times* (May 31, 2007), www.nytimes.com, accessed May 31, 2007; for a detailed look at couples' goal-setting with regard to artificial reproductive technologies, cf. Eileen Fisher, Cele C. Otnes, and Linda Tuncay, "Pursuing Parenthood: Integrating Cultural and Cognitive Perspectives on Persistent Goal Striving," *Journal of Consumer Research* 34, no. 4 (2007): 425–40.

57. Darach Turley, "Dialogue with the Departed," *European Advances in Consumer Research* 2 (1995): 10–13.

58. "Wives and Money," *American Demographics* (December 1997): 34; for a recent study of decision making among lesbian couples, cf. Robert Wilkes and Debra A. Laverie, "Purchasing Decisions in Non-Traditional Households: The Case of Lesbian Couples," *Journal of Consumer Behaviour* 6, no. 1 (2007): 60–73.

59. Thomas Hine, *Populuxe* (New York: Knopf, 1986).

60. Robert Boutilier, "Targeting Families: Marketing to and Through the New Family."

61. Karlene Lukovitz, "Women in Wealthy Homes Make 2 of 3 Buying Decisions," *Marketing Daily* (May 15, 2008), www.mediapost.com, accessed May 15, 2008; Dennis L. Rosen and Donald H. Granbois, "Determinants of Role Structure in Family Financial Management," *Journal of Consumer Research* 10 (September 1983): 253–58; Robert F. Bales, *Interaction Process Analysis: A Method for the Study of Small Groups* (Reading, MA: Addison-Wesley, 1950). For a cross-gender comparison of food shopping strategies, see Rosemary Polegato and Judith L. Zaichkowsky, "Family Food Shopping: Strategies Used by Husbands and Wives," *Journal of Consumer Affairs* 28, no. 2 (1994): 278–99.

62. Alma S. Baron, "Working Parents: Shifting Traditional Roles," *Business* 37 (January–March 1987): 36; William J. Qualls, "Household Decision Behavior: The Impact of Husbands' and Wives' Sex Role Orientation," *Journal of Consumer Research* 14 (September 1987): 264–79; Charles M. Schaninger and W. Christian Buss, "The Relationship of Sex-Role Norms to Household Task Allocation," *Psychology & Marketing* 2 (Summer 1985): 93–104.

63. Jennifer Steinhauer, "Mars and Venus: Who Is 'the Decider'?" *New York Times* (April 26, 2006), www.nytimes.com, accessed April 26, 2006; "Tailor-Made," *Advertising Age* (September 23, 2002): 14.

64. "Moms Shape New Culture by Cutting Back," Center for Media Research (November 13, 2008), www.mediapost.com, accessed November 13, 2008.

65. Craig J. Thompson, "Caring Consumers: Gendered Consumption Meanings and the Juggling Lifestyle," *Journal of Consumer Research* 22 (March 1996): 388–407.

66. Edmund L. Andrews, "Survey Confirms It: Women Outjuggle Men," *New York Times* (September 15, 2004), www.nytimes.com, accessed September 15, 2004.

67. Miriam Jordan, "India's Medicine Men Market an Array of Contraceptives," *Wall Street Journal Interactive Edition* (September 21, 1999); Patricia Winters Lauro, "Sports Geared to Parents Replace Stodgy with Cool," *New York Times* (January 3, 2000), www.nytimes .com, accessed January 3, 2000; Cynthia Webster, "Effects of Hispanic Ethnic Identification on Marital Roles in the Purchase Decision Process," *Journal of Consumer Research* 21 (September 1994): 319–31. For a recent study that examined the effects of family depictions in advertising among Hispanic consumers, see Gary D. Gregory and James M. Munch, "Cultural Values in International Advertising: An Examination of Familial Norms and Roles in Mexico," *Psychology & Marketing* 14 (March 1997): 99–120; John Steere, "How Asian-Americans Make Purchase Decisions," *Marketing News* (March 13, 1995): 9; John B. Ford, Michael S. LaTour, and Tony L. Henthorne, "Perception of Marital Roles in Purchase Decision Processes: A Cross-

Cultural Study," *Journal of the Academy of Marketing Science* 23 (Spring 1995): 120–31; Chankon Kim and Hanjoon Lee, "A Taxonomy of Couples Based on Influence Strategies: The Case of Home Purchase," *Journal of Business Research* 36 (June 1996): 157–68; Claudia Penteado, "Coke Taps Maternal Instinct with New Latin American Ads," *Advertising Age International* (January 1997): 15.

68. Gary L. Sullivan and P. J. O'Connor, "The Family Purchase Decision Process: A Cross-Cultural Review and Framework for Research," *Southwest Journal of Business & Economics* (Fall 1988): 43; Marilyn Lavin, "Husband-Dominant, Wife-Dominant, Joint," *Journal of Consumer Marketing* 10, no. 3 (1993): 33–42.

69. Micaela DiLeonardo, "The Female World of Cards and Holidays: Women, Families, and the Work of Kinship," *Signs* 12 (Spring 1942): 440–53.

70. C. Whan Park, "Joint Decisions in Home Purchasing: A Muddling-Through Process," *Journal of Consumer Research* 9 (September 1982): 151–62; see also William J. Qualls and Francoise Jaffe, "Measuring Conflict in Household Decision Behavior: Read My Lips and Read My Mind," in John F. Sherry Jr. and Brian Sternthal, eds., *Advances in Consumer Research* 19 (Provo, UT: Association for Consumer Research, 1992): 522–31.

71. Kim P. Corfman and Donald R. Lehmann, "Models of Cooperative Group Decision-Making and Relative Influence: An Experimental Investigation of Family Purchase Decisions," *Journal of Consumer Research* 14 (June 1987): 1–13.

72. Jennifer Saranow, "'This Is the Car We Want, Mommy'—Car Makers Direct More Ads at Kids (And Their Parents)," *Wall Street Journal* (November 9, 2006): D1.

73. James U. McNeal, "Tapping the Three Kids' Markets," *American Demographics* (April 1998): 3, 737–41.

74. Harris Curtis, "Making Kids Street Smart," *Newsweek* (September 16, 2002): 10.

75. "Kids Strongly Influence Brand Decisions," Center for Media Research (February 22, 2007), www.marketingpower.com, accessed February 22, 2007.

76. Kay L. Palan and Robert E. Wilkes, "Adolescent-Parent Interaction in Family Decision-Making," *Journal of Consumer Research* 24 (September 1997): 159–69; cf. also Tiffany Meyers, "Kids Gaining Voice in How Home Looks," *Advertising Age* (March 29, 2004): S4.

77. Russell N. Laczniak and Kay M. Palan, "Under the Influence," *Marketing Research* (Spring 2004): 34–39.

78. Stephanie Thompson, "Mrs. Butterworth's Changes Her Target," *Advertising Age* (December 20, 1999): 44.

79. Adrienne W. Fawcett, "Kids Sway One in Three Parents to Buy Stuff (Duh)," available from http://publications.mediapost.com, accessed February 15, 2007; Les Carlson, Ann Walsh, Russell N. Laczniak, and Sanford Grossbart, "Family Communication Patterns and Marketplace Motivations, Attitudes, and Behaviors of Children and Mothers," *Journal of Consumer Affairs* 28, no. 1 (1994): 25–53; see also Roy L. Moore and George P. Moschis, "The Role of Family Communication in Consumer Learning," *Journal of Communication* 31 (Autumn 1981): 42–51.

80. Leslie Isler, Edward T. Popper, and Scott Ward, "Children's Purchase Requests and Parental Responses: Results from a Diary Study," *Journal of Advertising Research* 27 (October–November 1987): 28–39.

81. Gregory M. Rose, "Consumer Socialization, Parental Style, and Development Timetables in the United States and Japan," *Journal of Marketing* 63, no. 3 (1999): 105–19; Gregory M. Rose, Vassilis Dalakis, and Fredric Kropp, "Consumer Socialization and Parental Style Across Cultures: Findings from Australia, Greece, and India." *Journal of Consumer Psychology* 13, no. 4 (2003): 366–76.

82. Scott Ward, "Consumer Socialization," in Harold H. Kassarjian and Thomas S. Robertson, eds., *Perspectives in Consumer Behavior* (Glenview, IL: Scott, Foresman, 1980), 380; cf. also Patricia Robinson, and Steven Maxwell Kates, "Children and Their Brand Relationships," *Advances in Consumer Research* 32, no. 1, (2005); Terry O'Sullivan, "Advertising and Children: What Do the Kids Think?" *Qualitative Market Research* 8, no. 4 (2005): 371.

83. Thomas Lipscomb, "Indicators of Materialism in Children's Free Speech: Age and Gender Comparisons," *Journal of Consumer Marketing* (Fall 1988): 41–46.

84. George P. Moschis, "The Role of Family Communication in Consumer Socialization of Children and Adolescents," *Journal of Consumer Research* 11 (March 1985): 898–913.

85. Gregory M. Rose, Vassilis Dalakas, and Fredric Kropp, "A Five-Nation Study of Developmental Timetables, Reciprocal Communication and Consumer Socialization," *Journal of Business Research* 55 (2002): 943–49.

86. Elizabeth S. Moore, William L. Wilkie, and Richard J. Lutz, "Passing the Torch: Intergenerational Influences as a Source of Brand Equity," *Journal of Marketing* 66 (April 2002): 17–37.

87. James U. McNeal and Chyon-Hwa Yeh, "Born to Shop," *American Demographics* (June 1993): 34–39.

88. Les Carlson, Sanford Grossbart, and J. Kathleen Stuenkel, "The Role of Parental Socialization Types on Differential Family Communication Patterns Regarding Consumption," *Journal of Consumer Psychology* 1, no. 1 (1992): 31–52; cf. also Sonya A. Grier, Janell Mensinger, Shirley H. Huang, Shiriki K. Kumanyika, and Nicolas Stettler. "Fast-Food Marketing and Children's Fast-Food Consumption: Exploring Parents' Influences in an Ethnically Diverse Sample." *Journal of Public Policy & Marketing* 26 (Fall 2007): 221–235.

89. Marian Burros, "McDonald's France Puts Its Mouth Where Its Money Is," *New York Times* (October 30, 2002), www.nytimes.com, accessed October 30, 2002.

90. Emily Bryson York, "NIH: Banning Fast Food Ads Will Make Kids Less Fat," *Advertising Age* (November 19, 2008), http://adage.com/Article?Article_Id=132718; accessed November 24, 2008.

91. Andrew Martin, "Kellogg to Curb Marketing of Foods to Children," *New York Times* (June 14, 2007), www.nytimes.com, accessed June 14, 2007; Tara Parker-Pope, "Watching Food Ads on TV May Program Kids to Overeat," *Wall Street Journal* (July 10, 2007): D1.

92. http://disney.go.com/index, accessed June 16, 2009.

93. http://barbiegirls.com/homemtl.html, accessed June 16, 2009; Associated Press, "Mattel Aims at Preteens with Barbie Web Brand: Toymaker Turns to Tech as Sales Slump for Iconic Fashion Doll," (April 26, 2007), www.msnbc.com, accessed April 26, 2007.

94. "Children Get Product Info Online," *Emarketer.com* (December 24, 2008), www.emarketer.com, accessed December 24, 2008.

95. "The Digital Future Through the Looking Glass," Center for Media Research (December 25, 2008), www.mediapost.com, accessed December 25, 2008.

96. Glenn Collins, "New Studies on 'Girl Toys' and 'Boy Toys'" *New York Times* (February 13, 1984): D1.

97. Susan B. Kaiser, "Clothing and the Social Organization of Gender Perception: A Developmental Approach," *Clothing and Textiles Research Journal* 7 (Winter 1989): 46–56.

98. Jessica Bennett, "Generation Diva: How Our Obsession with Beauty Is Changing Our Kids," *Newsweek* (March 30, 2009), www.newsweek.com/id/191247, accessed April 8, 2009.

99. Lori Schwartz and William Markham, "Sex Stereotyping in Children's Toy Advertisements," *Sex Roles* 12 (January 1985): 157–70.

100. Joseph Pereira, "Oh Boy! In Toyland, You Get More If You're Male," *Wall Street Journal* (September 23, 1994): B1; Joseph Pereira, "Girls' Favorite Playthings: Dolls, Dolls, and Dolls," *Wall Street Journal* (September 23, 1994): B1.

101. Lisa Bannon, "More Kids' Marketers Pitch Number of Single-Sex Products," *Wall Street Journal* (February 14, 2000), accessed February 14, 2000.

102. Ibid.

103. www.amazon.com/Mattel-Working-Woman-Barbie-Doll/dp/B001871UEO, accessed June 16, 2009; Constance L. Hayes, "A Role Model's Clothes: Barbie Goes Professional," *New York Times* (April 1, 2000), www.nytimes.com, accessed April 1, 2000.

104. Brigid Schulte, "Baby Dolls Raise a Stink in More Ways Than One," *Washington Post* (December 21, 2008): A1.

105. Laura A. Peracchio, "How Do Young Children Learn to Be Consumers? A Script-Processing Approach," *Journal of Consumer Research* 18 (March 1992): 425–40; Laura A. Peracchio, "Young Children's Processing of a Televised Narrative: Is a Picture Really Worth a Thousand Words?" *Journal of Consumer Research* 20 (September 1993): 281–93; see also M. Carole Macklin, "The Effects of an Advertising Retrieval Cue on Young Children's Memory and Brand Evaluations," *Psychology & Marketing* 11 (May–June 1994): 291–311.

106. Jean Piaget, "The Child and Modern Physics," *Scientific American* 196, no. 3 (1957): 46–51; see also Kenneth D. Bahn, "How and When Do Brand Perceptions and Preferences First Form? A Cognitive Developmental Investigation," *Journal of Consumer Research* 13 (December 1986): 382–93.

107. Deborah L. Roedder, "Age Differences in Children's Responses to Television Advertising: An Information-Processing Approach," *Journal of Consumer Research* 8 (September 1981): 144–53; see also Deborah Roedder John and Ramnath Lakshmi-Ratan, "Age Differences in Children's Choice Behavior: The Impact of Available Alternatives," *Journal of Marketing Research* 29 (May 1992): 216–26; Jennifer Gregan-Paxton and Deborah Roedder John, "Are Young Children Adaptive Decision Makers? A Study of Age Differences in Information Search Behavior," *Journal of Consumer Research* 21, no. 4 (1995): 567–80.

108. Cf. Patricia M. Greenfield, Emily Yut, Mabel Chung, Deborah Land, Holly Kreider, Maurice Pantoja, and Kris Horsley, "The Program-Length Commercial: A Study of the Effects of Television/Toy Tie-Ins on Imaginative Play," *Psychology & Marketing* 7 (Winter 1990): 237–56 for a study on the effects of commercial programming on creative play.

109. Gerald J. Gorn and Renee Florsheim, "The Effects of Commercials for Adult Products on Children," *Journal of Consumer Research* 11 (March 1985): 962–67. For a recent study that assessed the impact of violent commercials on children, see V. Kanti Prasad and Lois J. Smith, "Television Commercials in Violent Programming: An Experimental Evaluation of Their Effects on Children," *Journal of the Academy of Marketing Science* 22, no. 4 (1994): 340–51.

110. Gwen Bachmannn Achenreiner and Deborah Roedder John, "The Meaning of Brand Names to Children: A Developmental Investigation," *Journal of Consumer Psychology* 13, no. 3 (2003): 205–19.

111. Paula Lyon Andruss, "'Dora' Translates Well," *Marketing News* (October 13, 2003): 8.

112. Brooks Barnes, "Disney Expert Uses Science to Draw Boy Viewers," *New York Times* (April 13, 2009), www.nytimes.com/2009/04/14/arts/television/14boys.html?scp=1&sq=Brooks%20Barnes,%20%93Disney%20Expert%20Uses%20Science%20to%20Draw%20Boy%20Viewers,%94%20&st=cse, accessed April 13, 2009.

113. Janet Simons, "Youth Marketing: Children's Clothes Follow the Latest Fashion," *Advertising Age* (February 14, 1985): 16.

114. See Laura A. Peracchio, "Designing Research to Reveal the Young Child's Emerging Competence," *Psychology & Marketing* 7 (Winter 1990): 257–76 for details regarding the design of research on children.

115. Laura Shapiro, "Where Little Boys Can Play with Nail Polish," *Newsweek* (May 28, 1990): 62.

116. Gary Armstrong and Merrie Brucks, "Dealing with Children's Advertising: Public Policy Issues and Alternatives," *Journal of Public Policy and Marketing* 7 (1988): 98–113.

117. Bonnie Reece, "Children and Shopping: Some Public Policy Questions," *Journal of Public Policy and Marketing* (1986): 185–94.

118. Daniel Cook, University of Illinois, personal communication, December 2002; Daniel Cook, "Contradictions and Conundrums of the Child Consumer: The Emergent Centrality of an Enigma in the 1990s," paper presented at the Association for Consumer Research, October 2002.

119. Natasha Singer, "No Mug? Drug Makers Cut Out Goodies For Doctors," *New York Times* (December 30, 2008), www.nytimes.com, accessed December 30, 2008.

120. Alex Berenson, "Cancer Drug Representatives Spelled Out the Way to Profit," *New York Times* (June 12, 2007), www.nytimes.com, accessed June 12, 2007; Andrew Pollack, "Stanford to Ban Drug Makers' Gifts to Doctors, Even Pens," *New York Times* (September 12, 2006), www.nytimes.com, accessed September 12, 2006.

MINTeL

SECTION 3 MINTEL MEMO AND DATASET EXERCISE

Mintel Memo

TO: Consumer Research Dept.
FROM: The Big Boss
RE: Organic food for the family unit

We're happy with our market share in the organic food and drink category right now, but I have a hunch that we could gain more share if we start to promote to families. I'd like you to create a new promotional campaign with the family unit in mind. Your campaign should focus on triggers that consumers use to recognize their desires for organic food and drink, as well as the criteria that go into their decision to buy a particular organic brand.

Please provide us with actionable recommendations for promotion based on this information. As you analyze the data in the tables provided, remember to focus on general trends with an eye on specific family subgroups (e.g., married, two or more people in the household, children in the household) that show a statistically significant difference in their responses—especially when there is some reason based on what you have learned in this section about consumer behavior to believe that this difference is important.

When you write your memo, please try to incorporate relevant concepts and information you learned when you read the designated chapters!

What can we learn from the following data to help our company promote organic foods/drinks?

Number of Respondents		2000	477	181	1028	314
Respondent Categories				Marital Status		
Respondent Sub-categories		Total	Single	Living with a Partner	Married	Separated, Divorced, Widowed
			(A)	(B)	(C)	(D)
Questions	Answers	%	%	%	%	%
Would you describe your concern about food safety (for food purchased in the grocery store) as:	High	30	24	33	31	37
(Comparison of Column Proportions)						A, C
	Medium	48	55	47	47	42
			D			
	Low	22	22	20	22	21

Comparison of Column Proportions results are based on two-sided tests with significance level $p < 0.05$. Letters appearing in the column category denote a significant difference between the number immediately above the letter and the category associated with that particular letter. For example, the "D" in the Single category above denotes a significant difference between the percentage of Singles who reported a Medium level of concern about food safety (55%) and the percentage of Separated, Divorced, or Widowed respondents who reported the same (42%).

To access the complete Mintel questionnaires and datasets, go to MyMarketingLab at www.mypearsonmarketinglab.com. If you are not using MyMarketingLab, visit this book's Companion Website at www.pearsonhighered.com/solomon.

Section 4 Consumers and Subcultures

In this section we'll focus on the external factors that influence our social identities. In Chapter 12 we'll look at variables that define social class and how our social class exerts a strong pull on what we want to buy with the money we make. Chapter 13 discusses the ways that our ethnic, racial, and religious identifications help to forge who we are. Chapter 14 considers how the bonds we share with others who were born at roughly the same time unite us.

CHAPTERS AHEAD

12

Income and Social Class

When you finish this chapter you will understand:

1 Why do both personal and social conditions influence how we spend our money?

2 How do we group consumers into social classes that say a lot about where they stand in society?

3 Why does a person's desire to make a statement about his social class, or the class to which he hopes to belong, influence the products he likes and dislikes?

*F*inally, the big day has come! Phil is going home with Marilyn to meet her parents. He was doing some contracting work at the securities firm where Marilyn works, and it was love at first sight. Even though Phil attended the "School of Hard Knocks" on the streets of Brooklyn and Marilyn was fresh out of Princeton, somehow they knew they could work things out despite their vastly different backgrounds. Marilyn hinted that her family has money, but Phil doesn't feel intimidated. After all, he knows plenty of guys from his old neighborhood who wheeled-and-dealed their way into six figures. He certainly can handle one more big shot in a silk suit who flashes a roll of bills and shows off his expensive modern furniture with mirrors and gadgets everywhere you look.

When they arrive at the family estate in Connecticut, Phil looks for a Rolls-Royce parked in the circular driveway, but he only sees a beat-up Jeep Cherokee, which must belong to one of the servants. Once inside, Phil is surprised by how simply the house is decorated and by how shabby everything seems. A faded Oriental rug covers the hall entryway and all of the furniture looks really old.

Phil is even more surprised when he meets Marilyn's father, Mr. Caldwell. He had half expected him to be wearing a tuxedo and holding a large brandy snifter like the rich people he's seen in the movies. In fact, Phil had put on his best shiny Italian suit in anticipation, and he wore his large cubic zirconium pinky ring so this guy would know that he had some money too. When Marilyn's father emerges from his study wearing an old rumpled cardigan sweater and tennis sneakers, Phil realizes he's definitely not one of those guys from the old neighborhood.

ECONsumer Behavior

In the current dismal economic climate we have to kick things off by acknowledging that recent changes in consumer spending—prompted by numerous factors including frozen credit markets and massive layoffs—almost overnight altered the landscape of consumer behavior. The "go go" years seem like a distant memory as many people suddenly put the brakes on their BUY NOW mentality. Since the 1980s (when we last experienced economic turbulence) Americans' savings rate dropped steadily—it dipped to less than 1 percent in late 2008. In a few short months this rate rocketed to 5 percent as people cut back wherever they could. The new mantra: Make do with what you have. Save. Question every expense—do you really need that Starbucks latte, that $80 haircut, that fashion magazine? Thriftiness is in, eye-popping bling is out. Even many fashionistas have turned into **frugalistas**—they refuse to sacrifice style but they achieve it on a budget. Now it's cool to visit Web sites and blogs that celebrate frugality—like Dollar Stretcher (stretcher.com), All Things Frugal (allthingsfrugal.com), and Frugal Mom (frugalmom.net)."[1]

Of course, it remains to be seen whether this new frugality will persist when the economy improves (and it will). Young consumers who have grown up with images of (if not actual) affluence and in-your-face bling may not be prepared to pull such an abrupt about-face. In one survey, 91 percent of young adults say they have financial goals, but only 53 percent stick to a monthly budget—and 42 percent give themselves a grade of D or F to describe how well they save.[2]

Contrary to popular wisdom, not everyone suffers in a recession—and consumers don't uniformly cut back on their spending. Many of them just reallocate their priorities (and perhaps buy less on credit). For now, which companies will feel the pain and which will actually gain? A few years ago Citigroup strategists coined the term **plutonomy** to describe an economy that's driven by a fairly small number of rich people. Taking a cue from the Standard & Poor's 500-stock index, they created a "basket" of luxury stocks like Bulgari, Porsche, and Sotheby's. Unfortunately many of those rich people are a lot less rich today—and luxury brands are hurting.

On the other hand another team of analysts created their own Poor Getting Poorer

OBJECTIVE

Why do both personal and social conditions influence how we spend our money?

Consumer Spending and Economic Behavior

As Phil's eye-opening experience at the Caldwells' house suggests, there are many ways to spend money and there's also a wide gulf between those who have it and those who don't. Perhaps an equally wide gap exists between those who have had it for a long time and those who "made it the hard way—by earning it!" This chapter begins as we briefly consider how general economic conditions affect the way we allocate our money. Then, reflecting the adage that says "The rich are different," we'll explore how people who occupy different positions in society consume in very different ways.

Income Patterns

A popular saying goes, "You can never be too thin or too rich." Although conditions are tenuous now, overall the average American's standard of living continues to improve—though many consumers don't get a full ticket to The American Dream. Two factors contribute to an (overall) upward trajectory: a shift in women's roles and increases in educational attainment.[4]

- Mothers with preschool children are the fastest-growing segment of working people. Furthermore, many of them work in high-paying occupations, such as medicine and architecture, which men used to dominate. Although women are still a minority in most professional occupations, their ranks continue to swell. The steady increase in the numbers of working women is a primary cause of the rapid growth of middle- and upper-income families.
- Education also determines who gets a bigger piece of the economic pie. Although picking up the tab for college often entails great sacrifice, it still pays off in the long run. College graduates earn about 50 percent more than those who have only gone through high school during the course of their lives. Women without high school diplomas earn only 40 percent as much as women who have a college degree.[5] So, hang in there!

To Spend or Not to Spend, That Is the Question

Consumer demand for goods and services depends both on our ability and our willingness to buy. Whereas demand for necessities tends to be stable over time, we postpone or eliminate other expenditures if we don't feel that now is a good time to spend money.[6] For example, you may decide to "make do" with your current clunker for another year rather than buy a new car right away. Even businesses like warehouse clubs that sell staples by the case feel the pain when shoppers postpone their purchases; stores like Costco and Sam's Club post big losses when people no longer buy their discounted jewelry and clothing even though sales of paper towels and pickles hold steady.[7]

Discretionary income is the money available to a household over and above what it requires to have a comfortable standard of living. Economists estimate that American consumers wield about $400 billion a year in discretionary spending power. People aged 35 to 55, whose incomes are at a peak, account for about half of this amount. As the population ages and income levels rise, the way a typical U.S. household spends its money changes. The most noticeable shift is to allocate a much larger share of its budget to shelter and transportation, and less to food and apparel. (Note: This doesn't mean that higher income households buy less food and clothing—the *proportion* of dollars that goes toward these categories decreases.)

Individual Attitudes Toward Money

Especially in the wake of the Great Recession of 2009, many consumers experience doubts about their individual and collective futures, and they are anxious to hold on to what they have. Of course, not everyone has the same attitudes about money and its importance. We all know **tightwads** who hate to part with every penny (and who actually experience emotional pain when they hand over their cash) and **spendthrifts** who enjoy nothing more than when they buy everything in sight. Research on this issue finds that (stereotypes aside), American tightwads outnumber spendthrifts. Men are more likely than women to be tightwads, as are older people and those with more education. How do we tell a tightwad from someone who's just being frugal? One of the researchers puts it this way: "The evidence suggests that frugality is driven by a pleasure of saving, as compared with tightwaddism, which is driven by a pain of paying."[8]

Wal-Mart conducted a year of intensive research on its customers to better understand how they think about money and brand names. The company now organizes its products around the shopper groups it identified, which Wal-Mart says represent the majority of its business. A separate team services each group across five so-called "power" product categories: food, entertainment, apparel, home goods and pharmacy.[9] The three groups are:

1 **Brand aspirationals**—People with low incomes who are obsessed with names such as KitchenAid
2 **Price-sensitive affluents**—Wealthier shoppers who love deals
3 **Value-price shoppers**—Those who like low prices and cannot afford much more

Money has many complex psychological meanings; we equate it with success or failure, social acceptability, security, love, freedom and yes, even sex appeal.[10] There are therapists who specialize in treating money-related disorders, and they report that some people even feel guilty about their success and deliberately make bad investments to reduce this feeling! Some other clinical conditions include *atephobia* (fear of being ruined), *harpaxophobia* (fear of becoming a victim of robbers), *peniaphobia* (fear of poverty), and *aurophobia* (fear of gold).[11] A recent study that approached money as a *social resource* explored some interesting links between our need for acceptance and feelings about cash. In one case participants were either led to believe a group had rejected them or that it had accepted them. Then they completed a number of measures that reflected their desire for money. Those who the group rejected expressed a greater desire for money. At another stage subjects counted either real money or pieces of paper and then they experienced physical pain. Those who counted money reported they felt less pain than did those who just counted paper![12]

Consumer Confidence

The field of **behavioral economics**, or *economic psychology*, studies the "human" side of economic decisions (including the decision-making biases we learned about in Chapter 8). Beginning with the pioneering work of psychologist George Katona, this discipline studies how consumers' motives and their expectations about the future affect their current spending, and how these individual decisions add up to affect a society's economic well-being.[13]

Consumers' beliefs about what the future holds are an indicator of **consumer confidence**—this measure reflects how optimistic or pessimistic people are about the future health of the economy and how they predict they'll fare down the road. These beliefs are important because they influence how much money people pump into the economy when they make discretionary purchases.

Many businesses take forecasts about anticipated spending very seriously, and periodic surveys "take the pulse" of the American consumer. The Conference Board conducts a survey of consumer confidence, as does the Survey Research Center at

Index—this basket includes 22 stocks that include retailers, generic brands, repossession agencies, dollar stores, and pawnshops that prosper when others do worse. In a period when the S&P declined by 40 percent, this index actually generated a positive return of about 9 percent. Not everyone is hurting—as consumers downscale their eating habits, for example, fast-food chains like McDonald's pick up the surplus. People may not buy as many expensive concert tickets, but they still treat themselves to a movie—box office receipts are holding up well.

Finally, although people are a lot more conscious of price, it's not clear they've forsaken what was—before the recession hit—a growing emphasis on corporate social responsibility. In one global survey about seven in ten consumers said despite the recession they have given just as much—or more—time and money to causes they deem worthy and more than half still are prepared to pay more for a brand that supports a good cause. Nearly 8 in 10 U.S. consumers who say they are very anxious regarding their personal finances said they would switch to a brand that supports good causes. As an aside, marketers have their work cut out for them if they want to earn brand loyalty and do good at the same time: Only one-third of the respondents worldwide said they were aware of *any* brand that supports a good cause![3]

CB AS I LIVE IT

Dominique Dallas, *University of Tennessee, Knoxville*

As I roll over and rub sleep from my eyes, I realize it is another morning. My roommate is rather quiet and the tenants above me are not heavily walking back and forth. This is a special morning! Birds are chirping, the sun is peeking through my window, and I am waking up, not because of an alarm clock, but because it is Saturday! Saturday mornings are greeted with bright eyes and grinning smiles because it means three things: pancakes and cheesy eggs for breakfast, a day at the mall with the girls, and dinner with the guys! I love pancakes, but more so, I love shopping! It is the perfect time to purchase a nice blouse, or two, or three. My friends always call me "spoiled" and "high maintenance" because I am able to buy what I want with few stipulations when I go to the mall. While I have a decent part-time job and my parents offer funds every now and then, I am truly a "broke college kid." Meanwhile, who cares? Inevitably, there exists the pressing issue to look my best from head to toe and to participate in social activities whether I have a well-paying job or not. Nevertheless, it is not just me

by myself who acts like this. You would think the way my friends carry themselves and spend money that they have full-time jobs and receive weekly bonuses. My friends rely on their credit cards to live the way they want. All in all, by spending money, we prove we have access to a decent amount of discretionary income.

With this discretionary income, my friends and I purchase high-end shoes, clothes, and jewelry. On top of that, we go out to eat often to restaurants like Blue Fin and Wasabi, take road trips at least twice a month to Atlanta and Gatlinburg, and party hardy whenever we get the chance! One could say as college students, we are simply enjoying the best years of our life, but how is it possible to enjoy the best years of one's life without any money or without being a part of a higher social class that can afford such things? It seems despite our financial state as students, especially those with loans, it is important to display financial stability and affluence through the things we acquire. Nowadays, most students have their own cell phones, laptops, MP3 players, and other gadgets. More so, we live in fully furnished apartments and drive our own cars. It seems society has manipulated even the broke college kids to believe buying this or that

represents our rank and social status.

Discretionary income and status symbols are the two concepts that are directly related to my personal example. My friends and I buy certain things that prove us to be financially able. Multiple purchases of these items like DVDs, shoes, and food mean we have money in the bank, which relates us with a social class that has a higher income. The other concepts listed within Chapter 12 seem to hit the head on the nail. There has always been a known correlation between income and social status and how certain materialistic objects and activities indicate your social class.

Nonetheless I still want nice things. I want to look my best and enjoy the finer things in life. It is as though we are trained at birth to want nice, luxury items because they are associated with affluence, glamour, and class. A marketer would be happy to know that making a product seem appealing in terms of luxury, uniqueness, and sheer material comfort will be very advantageous. Society is filled with people who naturally want the best. We seek higher education, to land a better than average job, that will pay an over-the-top salary, so we can ultimately live comfortably to be a part of the upper tier of the social hierarchy.

the University of Michigan. The following are the types of questions they pose to consumers:[14]

- Would you say that you and your family are better off or worse off financially than a year ago?
- Will you be better off or worse off a year from now?
- Is now a good time or a bad time for people to buy major household items, such as furniture or a refrigerator?
- Do you plan to buy a car in the next year?

When, as now, people are pessimistic about their prospects and about the state of the economy, they tend to cut back on what they spend and take on less debt.

However, when they are optimistic about the future, they reduce the amount they save, take on more debt, and buy discretionary items. These factors influence the overall savings rate:

1 Individual consumers' pessimism or optimism about their personal circumstances such as a sudden increase in personal wealth as the result of an inheritance
2 World events such as the recession
3 Cultural differences in attitudes toward saving (e.g., the Japanese have a much higher savings rate than do Americans)[15]

OBJECTIVE

How do we group consumers into social classes that say a lot about where they stand in society?

Social Class Structure

We divide all societies into the "haves" and the "have-nots" (though the amount people "have" is relative). The United States is a place where "all men are created equal," but even so some people seem to be more equal than others. As Phil's encounter with the Caldwells suggests, a complex set of variables, including income, family background, and occupation determines his standing in society.

The place you occupy in the social structure helps to determine not only how much money you spend but also *how* you spend it. Phil was surprised that the Caldwells, who clearly had a lot of money, did not seem to flaunt it. This understated way of living is a hallmark of so-called "old money." People who have had it for a long time don't need to prove they've got it. In contrast, consumers who are relative newcomers to affluence might allocate their booty very differently.

Pick a Pecking Order

In many animal species, a social organization develops whereby the most assertive or aggressive animals exert control over the others and have the first pick of food, living space, and even mating partners. Chickens, for example, exhibit a clearly defined *dominance–submission hierarchy*. Within this hierarchy, each hen has a position in which she is submissive to all the hens above her and she dominates all the ones below her (hence the origin of the term *pecking order*).[17]

People are not much different. We also develop a pecking order that ranks us in terms of our relative standing in society. This rank determines our access to such resources as education, housing, and consumer goods. People try to move up in the social order to improve their ranking. This desire to improve one's lot in life, and often to let others know that one has done so, is at the core of many marketing strategies.

Just as marketers carve society into groups for segmentation purposes, sociologists describe divisions of society in terms of people's relative social and economic resources. Some of these divisions involve political power, whereas others revolve around purely economic distinctions. Karl Marx, the nineteenth-century economic theorist, argued that a person's relationship to the *means of production* determined his position in a society. The "haves" control resources, and they use the labor of others to preserve their privileged positions. The "have-nots" depend on their own labor for survival, so these people have the most to gain if they change the system. The German sociologist Max Weber showed that the rankings people develop are not one dimensional. Some involve prestige or "social honor" (he called these *status groups*), some rankings focus on power (or *party*), and some revolve around wealth and property (*class*).[18]

We use the term **social class** more generally to describe the overall rank of people in a society. People who belong to the same social class have approximately equal social standing in the community. They work in roughly similar occupations,

ECONsumer Behavior

It's naïve to think that everyone reacts the same way to an economic downturn. The U.K.-based firm M&C Saatchi conducted research to identify eight specific consumer segments that each display different attitudes and behaviors regarding spending and saving money:[16]

1 *Crash Dieters* (26 percent): Try to cut out all nonessential spending until things improve.
2 *Scrimpers* (13 percent): Want to maintain their lifestyle and are reluctant to make sacrifices so they will trade down to less expensive brands but not stop buying what they like.
3 *Abstainers* (15 percent): Postpone big purchases but look to buy things on credit and pay later.
4 *Balancers* (9 percent): Sacrifice purchases in some categories in order to buy things in others.
5 *Treaters* (12 percent): They know they have to cut back but they have trouble budgeting; so they reward themselves when they do economize with small treats.
6 *Justifiers* (12 percent): They are willing to spend but they need a good reason to buy something, such as a new model or a deal.
7 *Ostriches* (9 percent): Are in denial; they're mostly younger consumers who continue to buy as long as their credit cards hold out.
8 *Vultures* (4 percent): Circle the market, looking to snap up bargains as businesses offer bargain basement prices.

This ad implies that there are social class differences in leisure activities and preferred beverages.
Source: Courtesy of Libbey Glass Co.

and they tend to have similar lifestyles by virtue of their income levels and common tastes. These people tend to socialize with one another and share many ideas and values regarding the way life should be lived.[19]

Indeed, "birds of a feather do flock together." We tend to marry people in a similar social class to ours, a tendency sociologists call **homogamy**, or "assortative mating." Well over 90 percent of married high school dropouts marry someone who also dropped out or who has only a high school diploma. On the other side of the spectrum, less than 1 percent of the most highly educated Americans have a spouse who did not complete high school.[20]

Social class is as much a state of being as it is of having: As Phil saw, class is also a matter of what you do with your money and how you define your role in society. Although we may not like the idea that some members of society are better off or "different" from others, most consumers do acknowledge the existence of different classes and the effect of class membership on consumption. As one wealthy woman observed when researchers asked her to define social class:

> I would suppose social class means where you went to school and how far. Your intelligence. Where you live. . . . Where you send your children to school. The hobbies you have. Skiing, for example, is higher than the snowmobile. . . . It can't be [just] money, because nobody ever knows that about you for sure.[21]

In school, some kids seem to get all the breaks. They have access to many resources, such as special privileges, fancy cars, large allowances, or dates with other popular classmates. At work, some coworkers get promoted to high-prestige jobs with higher salaries and perks such as a parking space, a large office, or the keys to the executive washroom.

In virtually every context some people rank higher than others. Patterns of social arrangements evolve whereby some members get more resources than others by virtue of their relative standing, power, or control in the group.[22] The process of **social stratification** refers to this creation of artificial divisions: ". . . those processes in a social system by which scarce and valuable resources are distributed unequally to status positions that become more or less permanently ranked in terms of the share of valuable resources each receives."[23] We see these distinctions both in RL and online as the *reputation economy* takes shape—recall that this term refers to the "currency" people earn when they post online and others recommend their comments.[24]

Achieved Versus Ascribed Status

Think back to groups to which you've belonged. You'll probably agree that in many instances some members seem to get more than their fair share of bennies, whereas other individuals aren't so lucky. Some of these resources probably went to people who earned them through hard work or diligent study, or *achieved status*. But someone may have gotten the goodies because she was lucky enough to be born with "a silver spoon in her mouth." Such good fortune reflects *ascribed status*.

Whether rewards go to the "best and the brightest" or to someone who happens to be related to the boss, allocations are rarely equal within a social group. Most groups exhibit a structure, or **status hierarchy**, where some members are better off than others. They may have more authority or power, or other members simply like or respect them.

In our society, wealth is more likely to be earned than inherited.

Source: Courtesy of The Phoenix Companies, Inc.

Social Mobility

We've seen that worldwide there's an upward drift in terms of access to consumer goods. But, to what degree do people actually move from one social class to another? In some societies such as India it's difficult to change one's social class, but in America we like to say, "Any man (or woman?) can grow up to be president" (though being related to a former president doesn't hurt your chances). **Social mobility** refers to the "passage of individuals from one social class to another."[25]

Horizontal mobility occurs when a person moves from one position to another that's roughly equivalent in social status; for instance a nurse becomes an elementary school teacher. *Downward mobility* is of course movement none of us wants but unfortunately we observe this pattern fairly often as farmers and other displaced workers go on welfare rolls or join the ranks of the homeless. By one estimate, between 2.3 million and 3.5 million Americans experience homelessness in a year's time.[26]

Despite that discouraging trend, demographics decree that overall there must be *upward mobility* in our society. The middle and upper classes reproduce less (i.e., have fewer children per family) than the lower classes (an effect demographers call *differential fertility*), and they tend to restrict family size to below replacement level (i.e., they often have only one child). Therefore, so the reasoning goes, over time those of lower status must fill positions of higher status.[27]

Overall, though, the offspring of blue-collar consumers are blue-collar, and the offspring of white-collar consumers are white-collar.[28] People do improve their positions over time, but these increases are not usually dramatic enough to catapult them from one social class to another. The exception is when a person marries someone considerably richer. This "Cinderella fantasy" is a popular theme in our society; we see it in movies (*Pretty Woman* or *Maid in Manhattan*) and popular TV shows such as *The Bachelor*.

Class Structure in the United States

The United States *in theory* does not have a rigid, objectively defined class system. Nevertheless, Americans tend to maintain a stable class structure in terms of income distribution. Unlike some other countries, however, what *does* change are the groups (ethnic, racial, and religious) that occupy different positions within this structure at different times.[29] A sociologist named W. Lloyd Warner proposed the most influential classification of American class structure in 1941. Warner identified six social classes:[30]

1 Upper upper
2 Lower upper
3 Upper middle
4 Lower middle
5 Upper lower
6 Lower lower

These classifications imply that access to resources, such as money, education, and luxury goods increases as you move up the ladder from lower lower to upper upper. For example in 2006 (the most recent year where complete data are available) the richest 20 percent of U.S. households earned half of all the income. In contrast the poorest 20 percent received just over 3 percent. However these figures don't tell the whole story since some poorer families have access to nontaxable income or members may be between jobs so their low income is temporary. When you adjust income for other factors and look at the data on a per person basis (while on average 3.1 people live in a household in the top category, only 1.7 live in one in

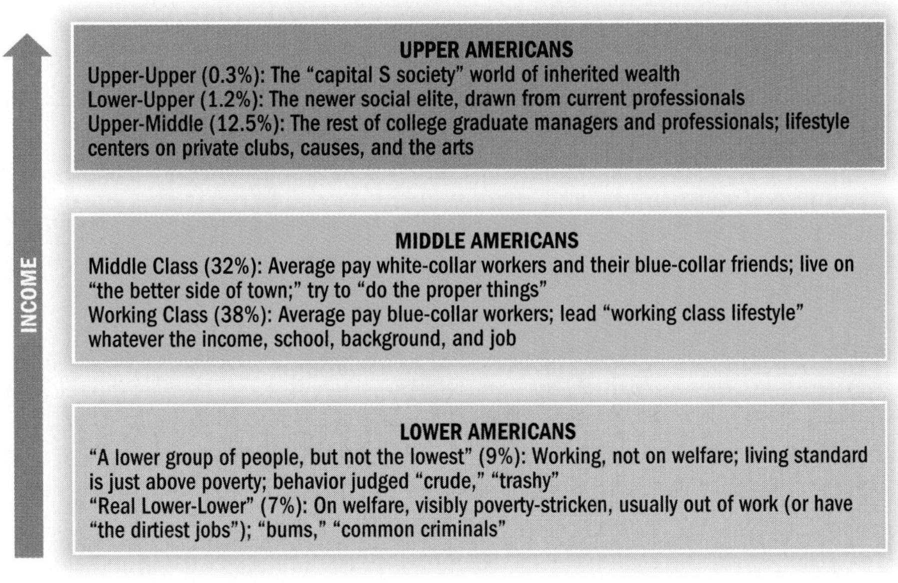

Figure 12.1 A CONTEMPORARY VIEW OF THE AMERICAN CLASS STRUCTURE

INCOME

UPPER AMERICANS
Upper-Upper (0.3%): The "capital S society" world of inherited wealth
Lower-Upper (1.2%): The newer social elite, drawn from current professionals
Upper-Middle (12.5%): The rest of college graduate managers and professionals; lifestyle centers on private clubs, causes, and the arts

MIDDLE AMERICANS
Middle Class (32%): Average pay white-collar workers and their blue-collar friends; live on "the better side of town;" try to "do the proper things"
Working Class (38%): Average pay blue-collar workers; lead "working class lifestyle" whatever the income, school, background, and job

LOWER AMERICANS
"A lower group of people, but not the lowest" (9%): Working, not on welfare; living standard is just above poverty; behavior judged "crude," "trashy"
"Real Lower-Lower" (7%): On welfare, visibly poverty-stricken, usually out of work (or have "the dirtiest jobs"); "bums," "common criminals"

the bottom category), the richest people actually consume four times more than the poorest.[31]

Other social scientists have proposed variations on this system over the years, but these six levels summarize fairly well the way we still think about class—although the proportion of consumers who fall into each category fluctuates over time. Figure 12.1 provides one view of the American status structure.

Class Structure Around the World

Every society has some type of hierarchical class structure that determines people's access to products and services. Let's take a quick look at a few important ones.

China

In China, an economic boom is rapidly creating a middle class of more than 130 million people that analysts project will grow to more than 400 million in 10 years. During the cultural revolution, Mao's Red Guards seized on even the smallest possessions—a pocket watch or silk scarf—as evidence of "bourgeois consciousness." Change came rapidly in the early 1990s, after Mao's successor Deng Xiaoping uttered the phrase that quickly became the credo of the new China: "To get rich is glorious."

Because costs are low, a family with an annual income below the U.S. poverty threshold of about $14,000 can enjoy middle-class comforts, including stylish clothes, Chinese-made color televisions, DVD players, and cell phones. Wealthier Chinese entrepreneurs indulge in Cuban Cohiba cigars that sell for $25 each, a quarter of the average Chinese laborer's monthly wage. In bustling Shanghai, newly minted "yuppies" drop their kids off for golf lessons; visit Maserati and Ferrari showrooms; buy some luxury items from Louis Vuitton, Hugo Boss, or Prada; then pick up some Häagen-Dazs ice cream before they head to an Evian spa to unwind. One cultural difference that may help to account for this love of branded goods is that Asians tend to be highly sensitive to cues that communicate social standing, and well-known brand names help to manage this impression. Indeed, even in the United States researchers report that Asian immigrants and Asian Americans prefer branded goods to generic products compared to other Americans.[32]

Many companies, like this Austrian bank, aggressively pursue the upper class consumer.
Source: Courtesy of Bank Austria Creditanstalt AG. Photo by Gunter Parth.

It's not our job to tell you the best thing to do with your inheritance, but it is our job to advise you the best way of going about it.

Nike, which consumers in a survey named China's coolest brand, profits mightily from the rise of the Chinese middle class. Nike shoes are a symbol of success, and the company opens an average of 1.5 new stores a day there. The company worked for a long time to attain this status—it started when it outfitted top Chinese athletes and sponsored all the teams in China's pro basketball league. Still, becoming a fashion icon (and persuading consumers to spend twice the average monthly salary for a pair of shoes) is no mean feat in a country that's not exactly sports crazy. So Nike affiliated with the NBA (which began to televise games in China) and brought over players such as Michael Jordan for visits. Slowly but surely, in-the-know Chinese came to call sneakers "Nai-ke."[33]

Japan

Japan is a highly brand-conscious society where upscale, designer labels are incredibly popular. The Japanese love affair with top brands started in the 1970s when the local economy was booming and many Japanese could buy Western luxury accessories for the first time. Some analysts say Japan's long slump since that time may have fostered a psychological need to splurge on small luxuries to give people the illusion of wealth and to forget their anxieties about the future. Single, working women are largely responsible for fueling Japan's luxury-goods spending—about three-quarters of Japanese women aged 25 to 29 work outside the home. As we saw in Chapter 10, these "office ladies" save money by living with their parents so this leaves them with cash on hand to spend on clothes, accessories, and vacations.[34]

The Middle East

In contrast to the Japanese, few Arab women work. This makes a search for the latest in Western luxury brands a major leisure activity for those with money. Dressing rooms are large, with antechambers to accommodate friends and family members who often come along on shopping sprees. A major expansion of Western luxury brands is under way across the Middle East, home to some of the fashion industry's best customers. High-end retailers such as Saks Fifth Avenue and Giorgio Armani operate opulent stores that cater to this growing market. However, fashion retailers must take cultural and religious considerations into account. Missoni makes sure that collections include longer pants and skirts, and evening gowns with light shawls to cover heads or bare shoulders. And advertising and display options are more limited: Erotic images don't work. In the strict religious culture of Saudi Arabia, mannequins can't reveal a gender or human shape. At Saks' Riyadh store, models are headless and don't have fingers. Half of the two-level store is off-limits to men.[35]

The United Kingdom

England is an extremely class-conscious country, and at least until recently inherited position and family background largely predetermined consumption patterns. Members of the upper class were educated at schools such as Eaton and Oxford and they spoke like Henry Higgins in *My Fair Lady*. We can still find remnants of this rigid class structure. "Hooray Henrys" (wealthy young men) play polo at Windsor and hereditary peers still dominate the House of Lords.

However, the supremacy of inherited wealth appears to have faded in Britain's traditionally aristocratic society as British entrepreneurs like Richard Branson (of the Virgin empire) redefine the economy. The United Kingdom was particularly hard hit by the recession, like the United States, and a new emphasis on frugality alters people's priorities. In addition populist outrage grew after it came to light in 2009 that legislators had billed the government for excessive expenses—among other abuses, British taxpayers footed a £2,000 bill for one M.P. to clean the moat surrounding his castle.[36]

Some big marketers such as Unilever and Groupe Danone set their sights on a more lower-class group the British call **chavs**. This label refers to young, lower-class men and women who mix flashy brands and accessories from big names such as Burberry with track suits. Their style icons include soccer star David Beckham and his wife, Victoria aka Posh Spice. Despite their (alleged) tackiness, marketers like chavs because they spend a lot of their disposable income on fashion, food, and gadgets. France's Danone, which makes HP Sauce, a condiment the British have poured over bacon sandwiches and fries for a century, launched a series of ads to play up to the chav culture. One features a brawl over the sauce at a wedding buffet; another includes glammy soccer players' wives mingling cattily at a party.[37] Danone found "chavvy" people on the streets of Liverpool to star in the ads.

India

India's economy is booming despite the global recession, and affluent consumers prize higher-end global brands—even though nearly half of India's population live on less than $1.25 a day. Brands like Gucci, Jimmy Choo, and Hermès scramble to open stores in high-end hotels or new superluxury malls, where the management often stations guards at the doors to keep the destitute outside.[38]

One of Bollywood's biggest stars, Shahrukh Khan, is "brand ambassador" for Tag Heuer watches, which cost thousands of dollars. He gives them away on the Indian version of *Who Wants to Be a Millionaire?*—the show that also formed the basis for the hit movie *Slumdog Millionaire*. India's ascendancy is fairly recent; for decades after the country became independent from Britain its economy was socialistic and traditional. Today, young consumers watch MTV, read international fashion magazines, and embrace the power of plastic—credit-card spending in India rose by 30 percent a year for the past 5 years.[39]

Marketing Pitfall

A recent flap illustrates the rapid changes in Indian society. *Vogue India* ran a 16-page spread of poor people surrounded by luxury goods—an old toothless woman holds a child who wears a Fendi bib, a woman and two other people ride on a motorbike as she sports a Hermès bag that sells for more than $10,000, a street beggar grips a Burberry umbrella. A columnist denounced the spread as ". . . not just tacky but downright distasteful." The magazine's editor commented that the shoot's message is simply that ". . . fashion is no longer a rich man's privilege. Anyone can carry it off and make it look beautiful."[40]

Vogue India's emphasis on fashion and luxury illustrates the stark divisions between the haves and the have-nots in that developing country.
Source: Courtesy of Newscom.

Social Class and Consumer Behavior

It's getting more difficult to clearly link certain brands or stores with a specific class. Marketplace changes make it more difficult for the casual observer to accurately place a consumer in a certain class by looking at the products he buys. That's because a lot of "affordable luxuries" now are within reach of many consumers who could not have acquired them in the past. Think of how many college women you know who buy pricey bags from Louis Vuitton or Coach, then eat Ramen noodles for dinner. To make matters even more confusing, a wealthy family may well buy its wine at Costco and its bath towels at Target—and especially in today's economy proudly gloat about the steals they got.[41] Luxury brands slash prices to attract more customers, while mass-market brands move upscale—Disney's new Disney Couture line sells cashmere sweaters "inspired by Tinker Bell," pricey chandeliers patterned after the Art Deco décor in Mr. Disney's former office, and a $1,400 sequined Mickey Mouse T-shirt from Dolce & Gabbana.[42]

Profound changes in global income distribution drive this shift. Traditionally, it was common to find a huge gulf between the rich and the poor—you were either one or the other. Today, rising incomes in many economically developing countries, such as South Korea and China, coupled with decreasing prices for quality consumer goods and services, level the playing field. The current recession aside, more and more con-sumers around the globe participate in the global economy. The biggest emerging markets go by the acronym **BRIC**: Brazil, Russia, India, and China. These four coun-tries today account for 15 percent of the $60 trillion global economy, but analysts pro-ject they will overtake the European and American economies within 20 years.[43]

This change fuels demand for mass-consumed products that still offer some de-gree of *panache*. Companies such as H&M, Zara, EasyJet, and L'Oréal provide crea-ture comforts to a consumer segment analysts label **mass class**. This refers to the hundreds of millions of global consumers who now enjoy a level of purchasing power that's sufficient to let them afford high-quality products—except for big-ticket items such as college educations, housing, or luxury cars. The mass-class mar-ket, for example, spawned several versions of affordable cars: Latin Americans have their Volkswagen Beetle (they affectionately call it *el huevito*, "the little egg"); Indian consumers have their Maruti 800 (it sells for as little as US $4,860); and the Fiat Palio, the company's "world car," targets people in emerging countries such as Brazil, Argentina, India, China, and Turkey.[44]

Components of Social Class

When we think about a person's social class, we consider a number of pieces of information. Two major ones are occupation and income. Let's take a quick look at both.

Occupational Prestige

In a system in which (like it or not) we define people to a great extent by what they do for a living, *occupational prestige* is one way we evaluate their "worth." Hierarchies of occupational prestige tend to be quite stable over time and across cultures. Researchers find similarities in occupational prestige in countries as di-verse as Brazil, Ghana, Guam, Japan, and Turkey.[45]

A typical ranking includes a variety of professional and business occupations at the top (e.g., CEO of a large corporation, physician, and college professor), whereas jobs that hover near the bottom include shoe shiner, ditch digger, and garbage col-lector. Because a person's occupation links strongly to his or her use of leisure time, allocation of family resources, aesthetic preferences, and political orientation, many social scientists consider it the single best indicator of social class.

Income

The distribution of wealth is of great interest to social scientists and to marketers because it determines which groups have the greatest buying power and market potential. Wealth is by no means distributed evenly across the classes. As we have seen, income per se is not often a very good indicator of social class be-cause the way we spend our money is more telling than how much we spend. Still, people need money to obtain goods and services to express their tastes, so obviously income is still very important. American consumers are getting both wealthier and older, and these changes will continue to influence consumption preferences.

How Income Relates to Social Class

Although we equate money with class, the precise relationship between other as-pects of social class and income is not clear, and social scientists debate it.[46] The two are by no means synonymous, which is why many people with a lot of money try to buy their way into a higher social class. One problem is that even if a family adds one or more wage earners and increases its household income, each additional job is likely to be lower in status than the primary wage earner's job. In addition, these members don't necessarily pool their earnings toward the common good of the family.[47]

So which is a better predictor of consumer behavior? The answer partly depends on the type of product we sell—do people buy it largely for its functional value (what it does) or for its symbolic value (the impression it conveys to others)?

● Social class is a better predictor of purchases that have symbolic aspects, but low to moderate prices (e.g., cosmetics, liquor).
● Income is a better predictor of major expenditures that do not have status or symbolic aspects (e.g., major appliances).
● We need both social class and income data to predict purchases of expensive, symbolic products (e.g., cars, homes).

Class Differences in Worldview

A *worldview* is one way to differentiate among social classes. To generalize, the world of the working class (i.e., the lower-middle class) is more intimate and constricted. For example, working-class men are likely to name local sports figures as heroes and are less likely to take long vacation trips to out-of-the-way places.[48] Immediate needs, such as a new refrigerator or TV, tend to dictate buying behavior, whereas the higher classes focus on more long-term goals, such as saving for college tuition or retirement.[49] Working-class consumers depend heavily on relatives for emotional support and tend to orient themselves in terms of the local community rather than the world at large. They are more likely to be conservative and family oriented. Maintaining the appearance of one's home and property is a priority, regardless of the size of the house.

One recent study that looked at social class and how it relates to consumers' feelings of *empowerment* reported that lower-class men aren't as likely to feel they have the power to affect their outcomes. Respondents varied from those who were what the researcher calls *potent actors* (those who believe they have the ability to take actions that affect their world) to *impotent reactors* (those who feel they are at the mercy of their economic situations). This orientation influenced consumption behaviors; for example, the professionals in the study who were likely to be potent actors set themselves up for financial opportunity and growth. They took very broad perspectives on investing and planned their budgets strategically.[50]

Although they would like to have more in the way of material goods, working-class people do not necessarily envy those who rank above them in social standing.[51] They may not view the maintenance of a high-status lifestyle as worth the effort. As one blue-collar consumer commented, "Life is very hectic for those people. There are more breakdowns and alcoholism. It must be very hard to sustain the status, the clothes, and the parties that are expected. I don't think I'd want to take their place."[52]

This person may be right. Although good things appear to go hand-in-hand with higher status and wealth, the picture is not that clear. The social scientist Émile Durkheim observed that suicide rates are much higher among the wealthy; he wrote in 1897, "The possessors of most comfort suffer most."[53] Durkheim's wisdom may still be accurate today. Many well-off consumers seem to be stressed or unhappy despite or even because of their wealth, a condition some call **affluenza**.[54] A *New York Times*/CBS News poll asked kids aged 13 to 17 to compare their lives with what their parents experienced growing up. Forty-three percent said they had a harder time, and upper-income teenagers were the most likely to say that their lives are harder and subject to more stress. Apparently, they feel the pressure to get into elite schools and to maintain the family's status.[55]

Many marketers try to target affluent, upscale markets. This often makes sense because these consumers—those who are still employed in the aftermath of the recession—obviously have the resources to spend on costly products that command higher profit margins. However, it is a mistake to assume that we should place everyone with a high income into the same market segment. As we noted earlier, social class involves more than absolute income. It is also a way of life, and factors including where they got their money, how they got it, and how long they have had it significantly affect affluents' interests and spending priorities.[56]

CB AS I SEE IT

Professor George Loewenstein, *Carnegie Mellon University*

*T*he average American spends more on lottery tickets than on reading materials or movies. In 2003, total spending on lotteries was almost $45 billion, or $155 for every man, woman, and child in the United States. Moreover, people at low income levels play the lottery disproportionately; one study found that those with incomes under $10,000 spent almost three times as much on lottery tickets as those with incomes over $50,000.

Why is playing the lottery so attractive, and why is it especially attractive to low-income individuals? My colleagues Emily Haisley and Romel Mostafa and I explored these questions. We hypothesized that one of the attractions of the lottery is that the typical lottery ticket only costs a dollar—peanuts in the budget of even those with low incomes. We went to the Greyhound bus station in Pittsburgh and asked bus travelers if they would complete a survey about their attitudes toward Pittsburgh in exchange for $5. We then gave them the opportunity to purchase up to five lottery tickets. For some subjects, we handed them the $5 and had them make a single choice of how many tickets to buy (from zero to five). For other subjects, we handed them $1 at a time, five times in a row, and each time asked if they wanted to use the dollar to buy a lottery ticket. Subjects in the latter condition purchased about twice as many lottery tickets. Of course $1 isn't much, but as the statistics document, many people are forking out the money day after day.

This helps to explain the appeal of the lottery, which is the single most popular form of gambling in the United States despite having the lowest payout rate. But, this finding does not explain why low-income individuals are so attracted to playing the lottery. In two follow-up studies we attempted to find out. We reasoned that poor people play the lottery disproportionately because, in contrast to more affluent people, it is their only opportunity, however small, for a dramatic improvement in their economic situation. In the first study we made some Greyhound riders feel rich by asking them in the survey to report their income on a scale that went up in $10,000 increments, peaking at $50,000 or more. We made others feel poor by asking income with a scale that went up in $50,000 increments, peaking at $1,000,000 or more. Those made to feel poor bought, on average, about twice as many tickets. In the second study we reasoned that lottery tickets might be attractive to people with low incomes because they have the same opportunity to win as people with higher incomes (in contrast to other areas of life where rich people have advantages). We reminded them of this fact by asking them to report whether poor people, rich people, or neither had an advantage in different areas of life, with one of the areas being "gambling." Those respondents who received this subtle reminder that lotteries give everyone similar odds of winning once again bought more.

The sad fact is that lotteries return only fifty cents on the dollar, making them one of the worst possible investments, and far less lucrative than playing the stock market—even in a bad year. Yet 21 percent of Americans, and 38 percent of those with incomes less than $25,000— report that the lottery is the only way they would be able to accumulate several thousand dollars for retirement. Along with payday loans, rent-to-own establishments, pawn shops, and instant rebate tax services, lotteries are one of the many ways that commercial and state enterprises may be detrimental to the financial well-being of the poor.

Despite our stereotype of rich people who just party all day long, one study found the typical millionaire is a 57-year-old man who is self-employed, earns a median household income of $131,000, has been married to the same wife for most of his adult life, has children, has never spent more than $399 on a suit or more than $140 for a pair of shoes, and drives a Ford Explorer (the humble billionaire investor Warren Buffett comes to mind). Interestingly, many affluent people don't consider themselves to be rich. One tendency researchers notice is that they indulge in luxury goods while they pinch pennies on everyday items—they buy shoes at Neiman Marcus and deodorant at Wal-Mart, for example.[57]

SRI Consulting Business Intelligence divides consumers into three groups based on their attitudes toward luxury:

1 **Luxury is functional**—These consumers use their money to buy things that will last and have enduring value. They conduct extensive prepurchase

research and make logical decisions rather than emotional or impulsive choices.

2 **Luxury is a reward**—These consumers tend to be younger than the first group but older than the third group. They use luxury goods to say, "I've made it." The desire to be successful and to demonstrate their success to others motivates these consumers to purchase conspicuous luxury items, such as high-end automobiles and homes in exclusive communities.

3 **Luxury is indulgence**—This group is the smallest of the three and tends to include younger consumers and slightly more males than the other two groups. To these consumers, the purpose of owning luxury is to be extremely lavish and self-indulgent. This group is willing to pay a premium for goods that express their individuality and make others take notice. They have a more emotional approach to luxury spending and are more likely than the other two groups to make impulse purchases.[59]

As Phil discovered, people who have had money for a long time use their fortunes a lot differently. *Old money* families (e.g., the Rockefellers, DuPonts, Fords, etc.) live primarily on inherited funds.[60] One commentator called this group "the class in hiding."[61] Following the Great Depression of the 1930s, moneyed families became more discreet about exhibiting their wealth. Many fled from mansions such as those we still find in Manhattan (the renovated Vanderbilt mansion now is Ralph Lauren's flagship store) to hideaways in Virginia, Connecticut, and New Jersey.

Mere wealth is not sufficient to achieve social prominence in these circles. You also need to demonstrate a family history of public service and philanthropy, and tangible markers of these contributions often enable donors to achieve a kind of immortality (e.g., Rockefeller University, Carnegie Hall, or the Whitney Museum).[62] "Old money" consumers distinguish among themselves in terms of ancestry and lineage rather than wealth.[63] And (like the Caldwells) they're secure in their status. In a sense, they have trained their whole lives to be rich.

In contrast to people with old money, today there are many people—including high-profile billionaires such as Bill Gates, Steve Jobs, and Richard Branson—who are "the working wealthy."[64] The Horatio Alger myth, where a person goes from "rags to riches" through hard work and a bit of luck, is still a powerful force in our society. That's why a commercial that showed the actual garage where the two cofounders of Hewlett-Packard first worked struck a chord in so many.

Although many people do in fact become "self-made millionaires," they often encounter a problem (although not the worst problem one could think of!) after they have become wealthy and change their social status. The label *nouveau riche* describes consumers who recently achieved their wealth and who don't have the benefit of years of training to learn how to spend it.

Pity the poor *nouveau riches;* many suffer from *status anxiety.* They monitor the cultural environment to ensure that they do the "right" thing, wear the "right" clothes, get seen at the "right" places, use the "right" caterer, and so on.[65] Their flamboyant consumption is an example of *symbolic self-completion* because they try to display symbols they believe have "class" to make up for an internal lack of assurance about the "correct" way to behave.[66] In major Chinese cities such as Shanghai, some people wear pajamas in public as a way to flaunt their newfound wealth. As one consumer explained, "Only people in cities can afford clothes like this. In farming villages, they still have to wear old work clothes to bed."[67]

"What Do You Use That Fork For?" Taste Cultures, Codes, and Cultural Capital

A **taste culture** describes consumers in terms of their aesthetic and intellectual preferences. This concept helps to illuminate the important, yet sometimes-subtle, distinctions in consumption choices among the social classes.[68] For example, a comprehensive analysis of social class differences using data from 675,000 households supports the mass-class phenomenon we discussed before: Differences in consumption patterns between the upper and upper-middle classes and between the middle and working classes are disappearing. However, strong differences still emerge in terms of how consumers spend their discretionary income and leisure time. Upper- and upper-middle-class people are more likely to visit museums and attend live theater, and middle-class consumers are more likely to camp and fish. The upper classes are more likely to listen to all-news programs, whereas the middle classes are more likely to tune in to country music.[69]

Some social critics don't like the taste culture perspective because they charge it's elitist. Judgments of the relative artistic value of Beethoven versus The Beastie Boys aside, it is very helpful to recognize that we segment ourselves in terms of our shared tastes in literature, art, music, leisure activities, and home decoration. Indeed, all of the thousands of online brand communities we discussed in Chapter 10 are living evidence that we do this all the time!

In one of the classic studies of social differences in taste, researchers cataloged home owners' possessions as they sat in their living rooms and asked them about their income and occupation. They identified clusters of furnishings and decorative items that seemed to appear together with some regularity, and they found different clusters depending on the consumer's social status (see Figure 12.2). For example,

Figure 12.2 LIVING ROOM CLUSTERS AND SOCIAL CLASS

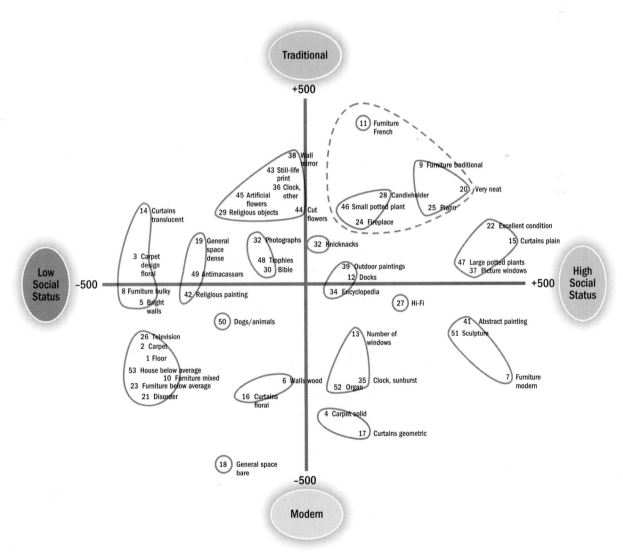

Many consumers still covet luxury products—whether they can afford them or not.
Source: Courtesy of Harry Winston Jewelers.

they tended to find a cluster that consisted of religious objects, artificial flowers, and still-life portraits in relatively lower-status living rooms, whereas they were likely to catalog a cluster of abstract paintings, sculptures, and modern furniture in a higher-status home.[70]

Another approach to social class focuses on the *codes* (the ways consumers express and interpret meanings) people within different social strata use. It's valuable for marketers to map these codes because they can use concepts and terms that target customers will relate to. Marketing appeals we construct with class differences in mind result in quite different messages. For example, a life insurance ad a company targets to a lower-class person might depict in simple, straightforward terms a hard-working family man who feels good immediately after he buys a policy. A more upscale appeal might depict a more affluent older couple surrounded by photos of their children and grandchildren. It might include extensive copy that plugs the satisfaction of planning for the future.

These two ways to communicate product benefits incorporate different types of codes. **Restricted codes** focus on the content of objects, not on relationships among objects. **Elaborated codes**, in contrast, are more complex and depend on a more sophisticated worldview. These code differences extend to the way consumers approach basic concepts such as time, social relationships, and objects. Table 12.1 summarizes some differences between these two code types.

TABLE 12.1	Effects of Restricted Versus Elaborated Codes	
	Restricted Codes	**Elaborated Codes**
General characteristics	Emphasize description and contents of objects	Emphasize analysis and interrelationship between objects; i.e., hierarchical organization and instrumental connections
	Have implicit meanings (context dependent)	Have explicit meanings
Language	Use few qualifiers, i.e., few adjectives or adverbs	Have language rich in personal, individual qualifiers
	Use concrete, descriptive, tangible symbolism	Use large vocabulary, complex conceptual hierarchy
Social relationships	Stress attributes of individuals over formal roles	Stress formal role structure, instrumental relationships
Time	Focus on present; have only general notion of future	Focus an instrumental relationship between present activities and future rewards
Physical space	Locate rooms, spaces in context of other rooms and places: e.g., "front room," "corner store"	Identify rooms, spaces in terms of usage; formal ordering of spaces; e.g., "dining room," "financial district"
Implications for marketers	Stress inherent product quality, contents (or trustworthiness, goodness of "real-type"), spokesperson	Stress differences, advantages vis-à-vis other products in terms of some autonomous evaluation criteria
	Stress implicit of fit of product with total lifestyle	Stress product's instrumental ties to distant benefits
	Use simple adjectives, descriptions	Use complex adjectives, descriptors

Source: Adapted from Jeffrey F. Durgee, "How Consumer Sub-Cultures Code Reality: A Look at Some Code Types," in Richard J. Lutz, ed., *Advances in Consumer Research*, 13 (Provo, UT: Association of Consumer Research, 1986): 332.

Clearly, not all taste cultures are created equal. The upper classes have access to resources that enable them to perpetuate their privileged position in society. Pierre Bourdieu was a French theorist who wrote at length about how people compete for resources, or *capital*. Bourdieu did large-scale surveys to track people's wealth, and he related this "economic capital" to patterns of taste in entertainment and the arts. He concluded that "taste" is a status-marking force, or **habitus**, that causes consumption preferences to cluster together. Later analyses of American consumers largely confirm these relationships; for example, higher-income people are more likely than the average consumer to attend the theater, whereas lower-income people are more likely to attend a wrestling match.[71]

In addition to *economic capital* (financial resources), Bourdieu pointed to the significance of *social capital* (organizational affiliations and networks). The legions of aspiring professionals who take up golf because they conduct so much business on the greens demonstrate how social capital operates. Similarly, as we've seen, respected bloggers acquire social capital when they gain access to business contacts who go online to search for information and advice.[72]

Bourdieu also reminds us of the consequences of **cultural capital**. This refers to a set of distinctive and socially rare tastes and practices—knowledge of "refined" behavior that admits a person into the realm of the upper class.[73] The elites in a society collect a set of skills that enable them to hold positions of power and authority, and they pass these on to their children (think etiquette lessons and debutante balls). These resources gain in value because class members restrict access to them. That's part of the reason why people compete so fiercely for admission to elite colleges. Much as we hate to admit it, the rich *are* different.

Status Symbols

We tend to evaluate ourselves, our professional accomplishments, our appearance, and our material well-being relative to others. The popular phrase "keeping up with the Joneses" (in Japan it's "keeping up with the Satos") refers to a desire to compare your standard of living with your neighbors—and exceed it if you can.

Luxury items like diamond engagement rings are valued as status symbols the world over, as this Brazilian ad for a jeweler reminds us.
Source: Courtesy of Saatchi & Saatchi/Brazil.

Often it's not enough to have wealth or fame—what matters is that you have more of it than others. One study demonstrated how we assign value to *loyalty programs* (e.g., when airlines award you special status based on the number of miles you fly) at least in part based on our level in the hierarchy relative to other members. Subjects were assigned to "gold status" in a program where they were in the only tier or a program where there was also a silver tier. Although both groups were "gold," those in the program that also offered a lower level felt better about it.[74]

A major motivation to buy is not to enjoy these items but rather to let others know that we can afford them. These products are *status symbols.* The popular bumper sticker slogan, "He who dies with the most toys, wins," summarizes the desire to accumulate these "badges of achievement." Status-seeking is a significant source of motivation to procure appropriate products and services that we hope will let others know we've "made it." A recent study demonstrated how people turn to status symbols to prop up their self-concepts, especially when they feel badly or uncertain about other aspects of their lives. When subjects in auctions were made to feel that they had little power, they spent more to purchase items to compensate for this deficit.[75]

We associate status symbols with luxury products, but the reality is that consumers are very good at latching onto all sorts of things that enable them to proclaim their place in a pecking order. In cyberspace, Twitter is the status vehicle *du jour* as actors, politicians, athletes, and millions of the rest of us hop on board the 140-character train. Celebrities including bicyclist Lance Armstrong, actor Ashton Kutcher, basketball player Shaquille O'Neal, and even Oprah are enthusiastic passengers. This social media platform is a way to stay informed, build a following, and perhaps prove that you're cool enough to be a Twitterer. A tweet by design diva Martha Stewart illustrates the "me too" motivation: "Proving that I really am on Twitter!"[76]

As we discussed earlier in the chapter, the rise of a *mass-class* market means that many luxury products have gone down-market. Does this mean Americans no longer yearn for status symbols? Hardly. The market continues to roll out ever-pricier goods and services, from $130,000 Hummers and $12,000 mother–baby diamond tennis bracelet sets to $600 jeans, $800 haircuts, and $400 bottles of wine. Although it seems that almost everyone can flout a designer handbag (or at least a counterfeit version with a convincing logo), our country's wealthiest consumers employ 9,000 personal chefs, visit plastic surgeons, and send their children to $400-an-hour math tutors. A sociologist explained, "Whether or not someone has a flat-screen TV is going to tell you less than if you look at the services they use, where they live and the control they have over other people's labor, those who are serving them."[79]

Of course, the particular products that count as status symbols vary across cultures and locales:

- Although to most Americans the now-defunct Hummer vehicle is a symbol of excess, Iraqis still regard the huge gas-guzzlers as an alluring symbol of power. An Iraqi Hummer dealer observed, "In Iraq, people judge you by your car, and you're not a man without one." People there use an Arabic phrase to explain the need to have the biggest car—*hasad thukuri,* which roughly translates as "penis envy."[80]
- In China, children are status symbols (partly because the government strongly discourages couples from having more than one baby). Parents want to show off their pampered child and are eager to surround their "little emperors" with luxury goods. Chinese families spend one-third to one-half of their disposable income on their children.[81]
- Largely because of an oil boom, there are at least 25 billionaires and 88,000 millionaires in Russia (though the recession has taken a big bite out of the Russian economy also). Muscovites crave luxury goods to show off their newfound wealth. Some buy the GoldVish cell phone that glitters with 120 carats of diamonds encrusting a case of white gold. The desire to spend as much as possible on indulgences fuels a popular joke in Moscow: A wealthy businessman tells a friend he bought a tie for $100. He responds, "You fool. You can get the same tie for $200 just across the street."[82]
- In Indonesia, as in many countries, a cell phone is a status symbol (see Marketing Pitfall box)—but instead of a sleek iPhone, a decade-old Nokia model users call "the Brick" is the one to have. This "smart phone" never took off in the West—its bulky design makes it look dated. But in Jakarta, its heft is what people like about it. At a whopping half-pound, it doesn't fit into a pocket so it's very visible when models, politicians, and other celebrities cart it around with them. Nokia even sells a gold-plated version for $2,500. In the world of status symbols, anything goes as long as others don't have it.[83]

The social analyst Thorstein Veblen first discussed the motivation to consume for the sake of consuming at the turn of the twentieth century. For Veblen, we buy things to create **invidious distinction**—this means we use them to inspire envy in

Marketing Pitfall

Think about those of us who suffer from cell phone envy: Did *you* stake out your place in line when Apple first released its coveted iPhone? British researchers observed how men in clubs used their phones as part of "the mating ritual." Whereas female patrons generally kept their phones in their purses and retrieved them only when needed, most men took their phones out of their jacket pockets or briefcases when they sat down and placed them on the bar counter or table for all to see.

The authors propose that men use their mobile phones just as peacocks use their plumage or male bullfrogs use their croaks—to advertise their status to available mates. They noted that the amount of time the men spent toying with and displaying their phones increased significantly as the number of men relative to women increased—just as male peacocks fan open their feathers more vigorously as the number of competing suitors increases.[77]

Today, the average cell phone user replaces his phone in less than 2 years, and many *aficionados* pant for a new model much sooner than that. It's not about function; it's about fashion and the next best thing. Motorola learned about the status value of phones when its fortunes plunged along with the price of its Razr model (a 30 percent drop in stock price in 6 months). Although the Razr was a big hit when Motorola launched it, the company sat on its laurels and didn't realize that customers soon would crave the latest and greatest. As one industry analyst stated, "Phone manufacturers are only as hot as their last major hit—if they haven't smacked it over the fence in a while, they're in trouble. Motorola failed to follow it up with something similarly as big as the Razr." Motorola hoped that its newer Krzr model would lure back style-conscious consumers because it's got better functionality than the Razr. But the Krzr also looks a lot like a Razr and analysts doubt that phoneaholics are going to buy into a product that looks like it's *so* yesterday.[78]

Marketing Opportunity

About 14 percent of Americans live below the poverty line, and most marketers largely ignore this segment. Still, although poor people obviously have less to spend than do rich ones, they have the same basic needs as everyone else. Low-income families purchase staples, such as milk, orange juice, and tea, at the same rates as average-income families. Minimum wage–level households spend more than average on out-of-pocket health-care costs, rent, and food they eat at home.[89] Unfortunately, they find it harder to obtain these resources because many businesses are reluctant to locate in lower-income areas. On average, residents of poor neighborhoods must travel more than 2 miles to have the same access to supermarkets, large drug stores, and banks as do residents of more affluent areas.[90]

Still, a lot of companies are taking a second look at marketing to the poor because of their large numbers. The economist C.K. Pralahad added fuel to this fire with his book *The Fortune at the Bottom of the Pyramid*, which argued big companies could profit and help the world's 4 billion poor or low-income people by finding innovative ways to sell them soap and refrigerators.[91]

Some companies get into these vast markets as they revamp their distribution systems or make their products simpler and less expensive. When Nestlé Brazil shrank the package size of its Bono cookies (no relation to the U2 singer) from 200 grams to 140 grams and dropped the price, sales jumped 40 percent. Unilever called a new soap brand Ala so that illiterate people in Latin America could easily recognize it. In Mexico, cement company CEMEX improved housing in poor areas after it introduced a pay-as-you-go system to buy building supplies.[92]

Muhammad Yunus, a Bangladeshi economist, won the 2006 Nobel Prize in Economics for pioneering the concept of **microloans**. His Grameen Bank loans small sums—typically less than $100—to entrepreneurs in developing countries. Many of these go to "cell-phone women," who rent time on the phones to others in their remote villages. The bank has issued about 6 million loans to date, and almost 99 percent of recipients repay them (compared to a 50 percent repayment rate for a typical bank in a developing country).[93]

others through our display of wealth or power. Veblen coined the term **conspicuous consumption** to refer to people's desires to provide prominent visible evidence of their ability to afford luxury goods. The material excesses of his time motivated Veblen's outlook. Veblen wrote in the era of the "robber barons," where the likes of J. P. Morgan, Henry Clay Frick, and William Vanderbilt built massive financial empires and flaunted their wealth as they competed to throw the most lavish party. Some of these events were legendary, as this account describes:

> There were tales, repeated in the newspapers, of dinners on horseback; of banquets for pet dogs; of hundred-dollar bills folded into guests' dinner napkins; of a hostess who attracted attention by seating a chimpanzee at her table; of centerpieces in which lightly clad living maidens swam in glass tanks, or emerged from huge pies; of parties at which cigars were ceremoniously lighted with flaming banknotes of large denominations.[84]

Sounds like they really lived it up back in the old days, right? Well, maybe the more things change, the more they stay the same: The recent wave of corporate scandals involving companies such as AIG, Enron, WorldCom, and Tyco infuriated many consumers when they discovered that some top executives lived it up even as other employees were laid off. One account of a $1 million birthday party the chief executive of Tyco threw for his wife is eerily similar to a robber baron shindig: The party reportedly had a gladiator theme and featured an ice sculpture of Michelangelo's David with vodka streaming from his penis into crystal glasses. The company also furnished the executive's New York apartment with such "essentials" as a $6,000 shower curtain, a $2,200 gilt wastebasket, and a $17,100 "traveling toilette box."[85]

This phenomenon of conspicuous consumption was, for Veblen, most evident among what he termed the *leisure class,* people for whom productive work is taboo. In Marxist terms, such an attitude reflects a desire to link oneself to ownership or control of the means of production, rather than to the production itself. Those who control these resources, therefore, avoid any evidence they actually have to work for a living, as the term the *idle rich* suggests.

To Veblen, wives are an economic resource. He criticized the "decorative" role of women as rich men showered them with expensive clothes, pretentious homes, and a life of leisure as a way to advertise their own wealth (note that today he might have argued the same for a smaller number of husbands). Fashions such as high-heeled shoes, tight corsets, billowing trains on dresses, and elaborate hairstyles all conspired to ensure that wealthy women could barely move without assistance, much less perform manual labor. Similarly, the Chinese practice of foot-binding prevented female members of the aristocracy from walking, and servants carried them from place to place.

Veblen's inspiration came from anthropological studies he read of the Kwakiutl Indians, who lived in the Pacific Northwest. At a *potlatch* ceremony, the host showed off his wealth and gave extravagant presents to the guests. The more he gave away, the greater his status. Sometimes, the host employed an even more radical strategy to flaunt his wealth. He would publicly *destroy* some of his property just to demonstrate how much he had.

And the plot thickens: Because guests had to reciprocate by giving a gift of equal value, the host could humiliate a poorer rival with an invitation to a lavish potlatch. The hapless guest would eventually be forced into bankruptcy because he needed to give away as much as the host, even though he could not afford it. If this practice sounds "primitive," think for a moment about many modern weddings. Parents commonly invest huge sums of money to throw a lavish party and compete with others for the distinction of giving their daughter the "best" or most extravagant wedding, even if they have to dip into their retirement savings to do it.

Like the *potlatch* ritual, in modern times our desire to convince others we have a surplus of resources creates the need for us to exhibit the evidence that we do. Accordingly, we may prioritize consumption activities that use up as many resources as possible in nonconstructive pursuits. This *conspicuous waste*, in turn, shows others that we have the assets to spare. Veblen wrote, "We are told of certain

CB AS I LIVE IT

Shannon Fuller, *College of St. Joseph's*

As I live in a world full of *status symbols*, it is extremely hard not to get caught up in the mess of who's who and where everyone ranks in a certain social class. Even in a small town like Rutland, Vermont status still plays a major role in the life of teenagers. Growing up I had three siblings, two of which are also girls. So like every moderate income family that meant lots of hand-me-down clothes, especially because one of my sisters is only thirteen months older than I. This meant a lot of my outfits were already put on display once or twice before, therefore the only way for me to produce a style of my own was to get a job. At the age of fourteen I started my first job at McDonald's.

Jobs are also a status symbol, which meant I was not very high on the list. As the years through high school went on I struggled to maintain a status higher than most kids but I was not popular by any means. I moved on to a better job at a gym and than a furniture store. I was average, I was everyone's friend and I could float among every different group but that didn't place me in any type of status either. The age finally set in where cars, boys, and clothes were on the top of my list. I somehow lucked out and convinced my parents to let me have their car and my mom got a new one. So not only did I have a nicer car than my older sister but I had a nicer car than most of my friends. As the years went on my car and I got older together and three years later I graduated high school. Now I am in college and it is amazing how status symbols change with a complete 360.

Status is now more of who has a higher GPA along with other materialistic items but it is important to be known and top of the class. I still have my same old Honda, but I maintain a positive role in the business department as secretary of Business Club and now just recently voted in as Vice President for the upcoming year. However status means next to nothing now that I realized there is a much bigger picture in life. My GPA is one point away from a perfect 4.0 but the time has arrived where I have realized it is not about the materialist things in life so much anymore. It is about friends, family, and finding happiness in yourself as well as others. To many people status is everything and will remain everything but to me status is what you make it. So I choose to make it nothing and without status, I could not be happier.

Polynesian chiefs, who, under the stress of good form, preferred to starve rather than carry their food to their mouths with their own hands."[87]

As the competition to accumulate status symbols escalates, sometimes the best tactic is to switch gears and go in reverse. One way to do this is to deliberately *avoid* status symbols—that is, to seek status by mocking it. Social scientists call this sophisticated form of conspicuous consumption **parody display**.[88] Hence, the popularity of old, ripped blue jeans (or more likely the ones companies stonewash so they look old and ripped), "utility" vehicles such as Jeeps among the upper classes (like the Caldwells), and brands with a strong blue-collar heritage like Von Dutch truckers' hats and Red Wing boots.

How Do We Measure Social Class?

Because social class is a complex concept that depends on a number of factors, it is not surprising that social scientists disagree on the best way to measure it. Early measures included the Index of Status Characteristics from the 1940s and the Index of Social Position from the 1950s.[94] These indices combined individual characteristics (e.g., income, type of housing) to arrive at a label of class standing. The accuracy of these composites is still a subject of debate among researchers; a study claimed that for segmentation purposes, raw education and income measures work as well as composite status measures.[95] Figure 12.3 shows one commonly used measurement instrument.

American consumers generally have little difficulty placing themselves in either the working class (lower-middle class) or middle class.[96] The proportion of consumers who identify themselves as working class tended to rise until about 1960, but it has declined since then. Blue-collar workers with relatively high-prestige jobs still tend to view themselves as working class, even though their income levels are equivalent to

Marketing Pitfall

Men as trophies? In recent years the tables have turned as older women—who increasingly boast the same incomes and social capital as their male peers—seek out younger men as arm candy. These so-called **cougars** are everywhere; surveys estimate that about one-third of women over age 40 date younger men. One self-professed cougar explained the appeal: "The mentality of having a youthful person on your arm who makes you feel good, who makes you feel ageless, makes you feel desired and desirable." This trend gets carried to the next level at an annual speed-dating event that pairs rich older women with hot younger guys. The "sugar mamas" have to be over age 35 and earn at least $500,000 a year or have a minimum of $4 million in liquid assets. A matchmaker selected 20 "boy toys" out of 5,000 men who applied to meet the cougars.[86]

Ripped jeans (especially the pricey kind that come that way when you buy them) are an example of parody display.
Source: Courtesy of Stock Boston/Photo by Bob Kramer.

many white-collar workers.[97] This fact reinforces the idea that the labels of "working class" or "middle class" are very subjective. Their meanings say at least as much about self-identity as they do about economic well-being.

Problems with Measures of Social Class

Market researchers were among the first to propose that we can distinguish people from different social classes from one another. Some of these class distinctions still exist, but—as we saw earlier—others including brand preferences have changed. Unfortunately, many of these measures are badly dated and are not as valid today.[98]

One reason is that social scientists designed most measures of social class with the traditional nuclear family in mind; this unit included a male wage earner in the middle of his career and a female full-time homemaker. These measures have trouble accounting for two-income families, young singles living alone, or households headed by women, which as we saw in Chapter 11 are so prevalent today.

Another problem with measuring social class is the increasing anonymity of our society. Earlier studies relied on the *reputational method*, where researchers conducted extensive interviews within an area to determine the reputations and backgrounds of individuals (see the discussion of *sociometry* in Chapter 10). When they used information and also traced people's interaction patterns, they could generate a very comprehensive view of social standing within a community. However, this approach is virtually impossible to implement in most communities today. One compromise is to interview individuals to obtain demographic data and to combine these data with the interviewer's subjective impressions of each person's possessions and standard of living.

As an example, refer to the items in Figure 12.3. Note that the accuracy of this questionnaire relies largely on the interviewer's judgment, especially regarding the quality of the respondent's neighborhood. The interviewer's own circumstances can bias these impressions because they can affect her standard of comparison. Furthermore, the instrument uses highly subjective terms: "Slummy" and "excellent" are not objective measures. These potential problems highlight the need to adequately train interviewers, as well as for some attempt to cross-validate such data, possibly by employing multiple judges to rate the same area.

Figure 12.3 EXAMPLE OF A COMPUTERIZED STATUS INDEX

Interviewer circles code numbers (for the computer) that in his/her judgment best fit the respondent and family. Interviewer asks for detail on occupation, then makes rating. Interviewer often asks the respondent to describe neighborhood in own words. Interviewer asks respondent to specify income—a card is presented to the respondent showing the eight brackets—and records R's response. If interviewer feels this is overstatement or understatement, a "better judgment" estimate should be given, along with an explanation.

EDUCATION:

	Respondent	Respondent's Spouse
Grammar school (8 yrs or less)	–1	–1
Some high school (9 to 11 yrs)	–2	–2
Graduated high school (12 yrs)	–3	–3
Some post high school (business, nursing, technical, 1 yr college)	–4	–4
Two, three years of college—possibly Associate of Arts degree	–5	–5
Graduated four-year college (B.A./B.S.)	–7	–7
Master's or five-year professional degree	–8	–8
Ph.D. or six/seven-year professional degree	–9	–9

R's Age ____   Spouse's Age ____

OCCUPATION PRESTIGE LEVEL OF HOUSEHOLD HEAD: Interviewer's judgment of how head of household rates in occupational status.

(Respondent's description—asks for previous occupation if retired, or if R is widow, asks husband's: _____)

Chronically unemployed—"day" laborers, unskilled; on welfare	–0
Steadily employed but in marginal semiskilled jobs; custodians, minimum pay factory help, service workers (gas attendants, etc.)	–1
Average-skill assembly-line workers, bus and truck drivers, police and firefighters, route deliverymen, carpenters, brickmasons	–2
Skilled craftsmen (electricians), small contractors, factory foremen, low-pay salesclerks, office workers, postal employees	–3
Owners of very small firms (2–4 employees), technicians, salespeople, office workers, civil servants with average-level salaries	–4
Middle management, teachers, social workers, lesser professionals	–5
Lesser corporate officials, owners of middle-sized businesses (10–20 employees), moderate-success professionals (dentists, engineers, etc.)	–7
Top corporate executives, "big successes" in the professional world (leading doctors and lawyers), "rich" business owners	–9

AREA OF RESIDENCE: Interviewer's impressions of the immediate neighborhood in terms of its reputation in the eyes of the community.

Slum area: people on relief, common laborers	–1
Strictly working class: not slummy but some very poor housing	–2
Predominantly blue-collar with some office workers	–3
Predominantly white-collar with some well-paid blue-collar	–4
Better white-collar area: not many executives, but hardly any blue-collar either	–5
Excellent area: professionals and well-paid managers	–7
"Wealthy" or "society"-type neighborhood	–9

TOTAL SCORE _____

TOTAL FAMILY INCOME PER YEAR:

Under $5,000	–1	$20,000 to $24,999	–5
$5,000 to $9,999	–2	$25,000 to $34,999	–6
$10,000 to $14,999	–3	$35,000 to $49,999	–7
$15,000 to $19,999	–4	$50,000 and over	–8

Estimated Status _____

(Interviewer's estimate: _____ and explanation _____)

R's MARITAL STATUS: Married ____ Divorced/Separated ____ Widowed ____ Single ____ (CODE: ____)

One problem when we assign any group of people to a social class is that they may not exhibit equal standing on all of the relevant dimensions. A person might come from a low-status ethnic group but have a high-status job, whereas another may live in a fancy part of town but he may not have finished high school. Social scientists use the concept of **status crystallization** to assess the impact of social class inconsistency.[99] The logic is that when these indicators are not consistent stress occurs because the rewards from each part of such an "unbalanced" person's life are variable and unpredictable. People who exhibit such inconsistencies tend to be more receptive to social change than are those whose identities are more firmly rooted.

A related problem occurs when a person's social-class standing creates expectations that he or she can't meet. Some people find themselves in the not-unhappy position of making more money than we expect of those in their social class. This means they are *overprivileged,* a condition we define as an income that is at least 25 to 30 percent greater than the median for one's class.[100] In contrast, *underprivileged* consumers, who earn at least 15 percent less than the median, must often allocate a big chunk of their income toward maintaining the impression that they occupy a certain status. For example, some people talk about being "house-poor;" they pay so much for a lavish home that they can't afford to furnish it. Today many home owners unfortunately find themselves in this position. By the end of 2008 about 2.2 million U.S. homes were in foreclosure.[101]

We traditionally assume that husbands define a family's social class, whereas wives must live it. Women achieve their social status through their husbands.[102] Indeed, the evidence indicates that physically attractive women do tend to "marry up" (*hierogamy*) in social class to a greater extent than attractive men do. Women trade the resource of sexual appeal, which historically has been one of the few assets they were allowed to possess, for the economic resources of men.[103]

We must strongly question the accuracy of this assumption in today's world. Many women now contribute equally to the family's well-being, and they work in positions of comparable or even greater status than their spouses. Employed women tend to average both their own and their husband's positions when they estimate their own subjective status.[104] Nevertheless, a prospective spouse's social class is often an important "product attribute" when someone in the "marriage market" evaluates their options (as Phil and Marilyn found out).

Problems with Social Class Segmentation: A Summary

Social class remains an important way to categorize consumers. Many marketing strategies do target different social classes. However, for the most part marketers fail to use social-class information as effectively as they could because

- They ignore status inconsistency.
- They ignore intergenerational mobility.
- They ignore subjective social class (i.e., the class with which a consumer identifies rather than the one to which he or she actually belongs.
- They ignore consumers' aspirations to change their class standing.
- They ignore the social status of working wives.

CHAPTER SUMMARY

Now that you have finished reading this chapter you should understand why:

 Both personal and social conditions influence how we spend our money.

The field of behavioral economics studies how consumers decide what to do with their money. Consumer confidence—the state of mind consumers have about their own personal situation, as well as their feelings about their overall eco-

nomic prospects—helps to determine whether they will purchase goods and services, take on debt, or save their money.

 We group consumers into social classes that say a lot about where they stand in society.

A consumer's social class refers to his or her standing in society. Factors including education, occupation, and income determine the class to which we belong.

Virtually all groups make distinctions among members in terms of relative superiority, power, and access to valued resources. This social stratification creates a status hierarchy where consumers prefer some goods over others.

Although income is an important indicator of social class, the relationship is far from perfect. Factors such as place of residence, cultural interests, and worldview also determine social class. As income distributions change around the world, it is getting more difficult to distinguish among members of social classes—many products succeed because they appeal to a newly emerging group marketers call the mass class (people with incomes high enough to purchase luxury items, at least on a small scale).

 A person's desire to make a statement about his social class, or the class to which he hopes to belong, influences the products he likes and dislikes.

Conspicuous consumption, where a person flaunts his status by deliberately using up valuable resources, is one way to "buy up" to a higher social class. *Nouveau riches,* whose relatively recent acquisition of income rather than ancestry or breeding accounts for their enhanced social mobility, are the most likely to do this.

We use status symbols (usually scarce goods or services) to communicate our standing to others. Parody display occurs when we seek status by deliberately avoiding fashionable products.

KEY TERMS

Affluenza, 470
Behavioral economics, 459
BRIC, 469
Chavs, 467
Conspicuous consumption, 478
Consumer confidence, 459
Cougars, 479
Cultural capital, 475
Discretionary income, 458
Elaborated codes, 474

Food poverty, 484
Frugalistas, 458
Habitus, 475
Homogamy, 462
Invidious distinction, 477
Mass class, 469
Microloans, 478
Parody display, 479
Plutonomy, 458

Restricted codes, 474
Social class, 461
Social mobility, 464
Social stratification, 463
Spendthrifts, 459
Status crystallization, 482
Status hierarchy, 463
Taste culture, 472
Tightwads, 459

REVIEW

1 How have women contributed to the overall rise in income in our society?
2 Define discretionary income.
3 How does consumer confidence influence consumer behavior?
4 What is a pecking order?
5 What is social class? Is it different from income, and if so how?
6 What is the difference between achieved and ascribed status?
7 What is a chav?
8 Describe what we mean by the term *mass class* and summarize what causes this phenomenon.
9 Define social mobility and describe the different forms it takes.
10 What one variable is the best indicator of social class? What are some other important indicators?

11 Why is it that when a person earns more money his or her social class may not change?
12 What are some of the problems we encounter when we try to measure social class?
13 Define status crystallization and give an example.
14 How does the *worldview* of blue-collar and white-collar consumers differ?
15 What is a taste culture?
16 Describe the difference between a restricted and an elaborated code. Give an example of each.
17 What is cultural capital and why is enrolling in an etiquette class a way to accumulate it?
18 How do you differentiate between "old money" versus "*nouveau riche*" consumers?
19 What is conspicuous consumption? Give a current example.
20 What is a current example of parody display?

CONSUMER BEHAVIOR CHALLENGE

■ DISCUSS

1 Sears, JCPenney, and Wal-Mart tried hard in recent years to upgrade their images and appeal to higher-class consumers. How successful have these efforts been? Do you believe this strategy is wise?

2 What are some of the obstacles to measuring social class in today's society? Discuss some ways to get around these obstacles.

3 What consumption differences might you expect to observe between a family we characterize as under-privileged and one whose income is average for its social class?

4 How do you assign people to social classes, or do you at all? What consumption cues do you use (e.g., clothing, speech, cars, etc.) to determine social standing?

5 In today's economy it's become somewhat vulgar to flaunt your money—if you have any left. Do you think this means that status symbols like luxury products are passé? Why or why not?

6 Thorstein Veblen argued that men used women as "trophy wives" to display their wealth. Is this argument still valid today?

7 This chapter observes that some marketers find "greener pastures" when they target low-income people. How ethical is it to single out consumers who cannot afford to waste their precious resources on discretionary items? Under what circumstances should we encourage or discourage this segmentation strategy?

8 Status symbols are products we value because they show others how much money or prestige we have, such as Rolex watches or expensive sports cars. Do you believe that your peer group values status symbols? Why or why not? If yes, what are the products that you think are status symbols for consumers your age? Do you agree with the assertion in this chapter that a cell phone is a status symbol for many young people?

■ APPLY

1 Use the status index in Figure 12.3 to compute a social-class score for people you know, including their parents, if possible. Ask several friends (preferably from different places) to compile similar information for people they know. How closely do your answers compare? If you find differences, how can you explain them?

2 Compile a list of occupations and ask a sample of students in a variety of majors (both business and non-

business) to rank the prestige of these jobs. Can you detect any differences in these rankings as a function of students' majors?

3 Compile a collection of ads that depict consumers of different social classes. What generalizations can you make about the reality of these ads and about the media in which they appear?

Case Study

AFFORDING JUNK FOOD

The Los Angeles City Council's vote was unanimous. Construction of fast-food restaurants within 32 square miles of the low-income area of South Central Los Angeles would be prohibited for one year.

Why the severe action? It was an attempt by the City Council to improve the public health of its district's citizens. We have all seen the reports on increased adult and childhood obesity. Obesity-related diseases, including cardiovascular disease and type 2 diabetes, are on the rise. But this escalation is not spread evenly among all social classes. Research shows that low-income households exhibit higher levels of obesity than the general population. The factors leading to this outcome are complex and stem from a variety of sociocultural factors.

Low-income neighborhoods suffer from **food poverty**, according to Sustain, a London-based organization that ad-

vocates for food and agricultural policies and practices. This condition describes the inability of consumers to obtain healthy and affordable food. The consumption behavior that drives *food poverty* is impacted by accessibility to healthy versus nonhealthy food, the availability of healthy choices, the affordability of healthy options, and general nutrition awareness.

Accessibility relates to the types of stores and restaurants located within the consumer's reach. If members of households are without cars and have to rely on public transportation, their store choices are limited. The number of supermarkets in low-income urban neighborhoods is far lower than it is in other neighborhoods. Families in low-income neighborhoods often shop at corner convenience stores that offer fewer healthy options, such as fresh fruit and produce, than larger supermarkets. For the rural poor, it can be a very long trip to a supermarket.

Availability addresses the choices and available products within the stores that people can visit. Inner-city convenience stores carry much less fresh fruit and produce than a supermarket. One study showed that fast-food restaurants exist in higher numbers in the poorer, black communities in New Orleans than in other neighborhoods in the city.

Affordability refers to the amount of money families have in their budget to spend on food. A study of a New York neighborhood showed that in the local stores, low-fat milk often cost more than regular milk. As more and more families feel the impact of the recession on their incomes, we can expect further reductions in the consumption of healthier—but more expensive—food. Many food marketers already report dramatic shifts in sales from higher-priced, healthier options to the lower-priced, less healthy options.

Awareness refers to the knowledge people have about nutrition and cooking, and the impact of the media on their food choices. One of the most thorough studies regarding obesity showed that low-income children watch more television than children in other income groups. Increased viewing means greater exposure to junk-food commercials. It is not only the number of ads children watch that makes the difference, it is also how they internalize the advertising messages. Studies have shown that low-income children tend to view the people in the ads as authority figures and are more easily influenced by the advertisement.

DISCUSSION QUESTIONS

1 Can consumption patterns be changed? What can be done to reverse the increase in obesity, especially among low-income children? Should the government follow the example of the Los Angeles City Council and take on a greater role in trying to change consumption patterns, or is education the most effective tool?

2 Discuss the ways that living in a low-income neighborhood contributes to higher obesity rates.

3 In addition to television, why is it that marketers can reach these households so effectively with messages for unhealthy snack foods?

Sources: Jenny Wiggins, "Cheaper Food Buying Raises Obesity Fears," *Financial Times* (November 21, 2008): 4; Shiriki Kumanyika and Sonya Grier, "Targeting Interventions for Ethnic Minority and Low-Income Populations," *The Future of Children* 16, no. 1 (Spring 2006): 187–207; *The Economist,* (February 28, 2009): 4; www.sustainweb.org/page.php?id=187, accessed May 15, 2009.

NOTES

1. Matt Richtel, "Austere Times? Perfect," *New York Times* (April 10, 2009), www.nytimes.com/2009/04/11/business/economy/11cheap.html?_ r=1, accessed April 10, 2009; www.stretcher.com, accessed June 17, 2009; www.allthingsfrugal.com, accessed June 17, 2009; www.frugalmom.net, accessed June 17, 2009.

2. "Financial Security an Elusive Concept," Center for Media Research (November 20, 2008), www.mediapost.com, accessed November 20, 2008.

3. Michael Bush, "Consumers Continue to Stand by Their Causes During Downturn, Survey Says People Will Still Pay More If They Support Brand's Beliefs," *Advertising Age* (November 17, 2008), http://adage.com/Article?Article_Id=132587, accessed November 17, 2008; Rob Cox and Aliza Rosenbaum, "The Beneficiaries of the Downturn," *New York Times* (December 28, 2008), www.nytimes.com, accessed December 28, 2008.

4. Data in this section adapted from Fabian Linden, *Consumer Affluence: The Next Wave* (New York: The Conference Board, 1994). For additional information about U.S. income statistics, access Occupational Employment and Wage Estimates at www.bls.gov/oes/oes_data.htm.

5. Mary Bowler, "Women's Earnings: An Overview," *Monthly Labor Review* 122 (December 1999): 13–22.

6. Christopher D. Carroll, "How Does Future Income Affect Current Consumption?" *Quarterly Journal of Economics* 109 (February 1994): 111–47.

7. "Costco Net Falls on Weak Discretionary Spending," *Reuters* (May 28, 2009), www.reuters.com/article/newsOne/idUSTRE54R1GJ20090528, accessed June 17, 2009.

8. Quoted in Philip Jackman, "What Makes a Tightwad? Study Finds That People Who Are Stingy Report Feeling Emotional Pain When Spending Money," *Toronto Globe and Mail* (March 19, 2008), www.theglobeandmail.com/Servlet/Story/Rtgam.20080319.Wspending19/Emailbn...; accessed March 22, 2008.

9. Michael Barbaro, "It's Not Only About Price at Wal-Mart," *New York Times* (March 2, 2007), http://www.nytimes.com/2007/03/02/business/02walmart.html, accessed March 2, 2007.

10. José F. Medina, Joel Saegert, and Alicia Gresham, "Comparison of Mexican-American and Anglo-American Attitudes Toward Money," *Journal of Consumer Affairs* 30, no. 1 (1996): 124–45.

11. Kirk Johnson, "Sit Down. Breathe Deeply. This Is Really Scary Stuff," *New York Times* (April 16, 1995): F5; cf. also Matthew J. Bernthal, David Crockett, and Randall L. Rose, "Credit Cards as Lifestyle Facilitators," *Journal of Consumer Research* 32 (June 2005): 130–45.

12. Xinyue Zhou, Kathleen D. Vohs, and Roy F. Baumeister, "The Symbolic Power of Money: Reminders of Money Alter Social Distress and Physical Pain," *Psychological Science,* 20, 6 (2009): 700–6.

13. Fred van Raaij, "Economic Psychology," *Journal of Economic Psychology* 1 (1981): 1–24.

14. Richard T. Curtin, "Indicators of Consumer Behavior: The University of Michigan Surveys of Consumers," *Public Opinion Quarterly* (1982): 340–52.

15. George Katona, "Consumer Saving Patterns," *Journal of Consumer Research* 1 (June 1974): 1–12.

16. "Coping with Recession," Center for Media Research (June 3, 2009), www.mediapost.com, accessed June 3, 2009.

17. Floyd L. Ruch and Philip G. Zimbardo, *Psychology and Life,* 8th ed. (Glenview, IL: Scott Foresman, 1971).

18. Jonathan H. Turner, *Sociology: Studying the Human System,* 2nd ed. (Santa Monica, CA: Goodyear, 1981).

19. Richard P. Coleman, "The Continuing Significance of Social Class to Marketing," *Journal of Consumer Research* 10 (December 1983): 265–80; Turner, *Sociology: Studying the Human System.*

20. Rebecca Gardyn, "The Mating Game," *American Demographics* (July–August 2002): 33–34.

21. Richard P. Coleman and Lee Rainwater, *Standing in America: New Dimensions of Class* (New York: Basic Books, 1978), 89.

22. Ibid.

23. Turner, *Sociology: Studying the Human System.*

24. Anya Kamenetz, "The Perils and Promise of the Reputation Economy," *Fast Company* (November 25, 2008), www.fastcompany.com/magazine/131/on-the-internet-everyone-knows-youre-a-dog.html, accessed June 17, 2009.

25. Turner, *Sociology: Studying the Human System,* 260.

26. See Ronald Paul Hill and Mark Stamey, "The Homeless in America: An Examination of Possessions and Consumption Behaviors," *Journal of Consumer Research* 17 (December 1990): 303–21; "Homeless Facts and Figures," NOW (May 2, 2007), www.ask.com/

bar?q=What+Percentage+of+Americans+Are+Homeless&page=1&qsrc=6&ab=0&u=http://www.pbs.org/now/shows/305/homeless-facts.html, accessed June 17, 2009.

27. Joseph Kahl, *The American Class Structure* (New York: Holt, Rinehart and Winston, 1961).

28. Leonard Beeghley, *Social Stratification in America: A Critical Analysis of Theory and Research* (Santa Monica, CA: Goodyear, 1978).

29. James Fallows, "A Talent for Disorder (Class Structure)," *U.S. News & World Report* (February 1, 1988): 83.

30. Coleman, "The Continuing Significance of Social Class to Marketing"; W. Lloyd Warner and Paul S. Lunt, eds., *The Social Life of a Modern Community* (New Haven, CT: Yale University Press, 1941).

31. W. Michael Cox and Richard Alm, "You Are What You Spend," *New York Times* (February 10, 2008), www.nytimesimes.com/2008/02/10/opinion/10cox.html?scp=1&sq=you+are+what+you+...; accessed February 10, 2008.

32. Heejung S. Kim and Aimee Drolet, "Cultural Differences in Preferences for Brand Name Versus Generic Products," *Personality and Social Psychology Bulletin* (forthcoming 2010).

33. Howard W. French, "Chinese Children Learn Class, Minus the Struggle," *New York Times* (September 22, 2006), www.nytimes.com, accessed September 22, 2006; Bay Fang, "The Shanghai High Life," *U.S. News & World Report* (June 20, 2005), www.usnews.com/usnews/biztech/articles/050620/20china.b2.htm, accessed June 20, 2005; http://travel.guardian.co.uk/cities/story/0,7450,489488,00.html, accessed June 20, 2005; Russell Flannery, "Long Live the $25 Cigar," *Forbes* (December 27, 2004): 51; Clay Chandler, "China Deluxe," *Fortune* (July 26, 2004): 149–56; Matthew Forney, "How Nike Figured Out China," *Time* (November 2004): A10–A14; J. David Lynch, "Emerging Middle Class Reshaping China," *USA Today* (November 12, 2002): 13A.

34. Sebastian Moffett, "The Japanese Paradox: Pinched by Economic Slump, Women Buy More Handbags from Vuitton, Prada, Hermes," *Wall Street Journal* (September 23, 2003), www.wsj.com, accessed September 23, 2003.

35. Cecilie Rohwedder, "Design Houses Build Stores, Pamper Demanding Shoppers in Fashion-Industry Hot Spot," *Wall Street Journal* (January 23, 2004), www.wsj.com, accessed January 23, 2004.

36. Frank Skinner, "Take Not the Moat Out of the Tory's Eye," *Times of London* (May 15, 2009), www.timesonline.co.uk/tol/comment/columnists/frank_skinner/article6289313.ece, accessed June 17, 2009.

37. Robert Guy Matthews, "Bawdy British Ads Target Hot Youth," *Wall Street Journal* (April 20, 2005): B9.

38. Heather Timmons, "Vogue's Fashion Photos Spark Debate in India," *New York Times* (August 31, 2008), www.nytimes.com/2008/09/01/business/worldbusiness/01vogue.html?_r=1&ref=busi...; accessed September 1, 2008.

39. Eric Bellman, "Name Game: As Economy Grows, India Goes for Designer Goods," *Wall Street Journal* (March 27, 2007): A1.

40. Quoted in Timmons, "Vogue's Fashion Photos Spark Debate in India."

41. Jennifer Steinhauer, "When the Joneses Wear Jeans," *New York Times* (May 29, 2005), www.nytimes.com, accessed May 29, 2005.

42. Brooks Barnes, "Disney, By Design," *New York Times* (November 5, 2008), www.nytimes.com/2008/11/06/Fashion/06disney.Html?_R=1&Scp=2&Sq=Disney&St=...; accessed November 6, 2008.

43. Gleb Bryanski and Guy Faulconbridge, "BRIC Demands More Clout, Steers Clear of Dollar Talk," *Reuters* (June 16, 2009), www.reuters.com/article/ousiv/idUSTRE55F47D20090616, accessed June 17, 2009; Guy Faulconbridge, "BRIC Seeks Global Voice at First Summit," *Reuters* (June 14, 2009), http://news.yahoo.com/s/nm/20090614/bs_nm/us_russia_bric, accessed June 17, 2009.

44. Paul F. Nunes, Brian A. Johnson, and R. Timothy S. Breene, "Moneyed Masses," *Harvard Business Review* (July–August 2004): 94–104; *Trend Update: Massclusivity*, report from Reinier Evers and Trendwatching.com, Zyman Institute of Brand Science, Emory University, www.zibs.com, accessed February 25, 2005.

45. Coleman and Rainwater, *Standing in America: New Dimensions of Class.*

46. See Coleman, "The Continuing Significance of Social Class to Marketing"; Charles M. Schaninger, "Social Class Versus Income Revisited: An Empirical Investigation," *Journal of Marketing Research* 18 (May 1981): 192–208.

47. Coleman, "The Continuing Significance of Social Class to Marketing."

48. Ibid.

49. Jeffrey F. Durgee, "How Consumer Sub-Cultures Code Reality: A Look at Some Code Types," in Richard J. Lutz, ed., *Advances in Consumer Research* 13 (Provo, UT: Association for Consumer Research, 1986): 332–37.

50. Paul C. Henry, "Social Class, Market Situation, and Consumers' Metaphors of (Dis)Empowerment," *Journal of Consumer Research* 31 (March 2005): 766–78.

51. David Halle, *America's Working Man: Work, Home, and Politics Among Blue-Collar Owners* (Chicago: University of Chicago Press, 1984); David Montgomery, "America's Working Man," *Monthly Review* (1985): 1.

52. Coleman and Rainwater, *Standing in America: New Dimensions of Class*, 139.

53. Roger Brown, *Social Psychology* (New York: Free Press, 1965).

54. Kit R. Roane, "Affluenza Strikes Kids," *U.S. News & World Report* (March 20, 2000): 55.

55. Ibid.

56. "Reading the Buyer's Mind," *U.S. News & World Report* (March 16, 1987): 59.

57. Shelly Reese, "The Many Faces of Affluence," *Marketing Tools* (November–December 1997): 44–48.

58. Ruth LaFerla, "A Facebook for the Few," *New York Times* (September 6, 2007), www.nytimes.com, accessed September 6, 2007; www.smallworld.net, accessed June 17, 2009.

59. Rebecca Gardyn, "Oh, the Good Life," *American Demographics* (November 2002): 34.

60. Paul Fussell, *Class: A Guide Through the American Status System* (New York: Summit Books, 1983): 29.

61. Ibid.

62. Elizabeth C. Hirschman, "Secular Immortality and the American Ideology of Affluence," *Journal of Consumer Research* 17 (June 1990): 31–42.

63. Coleman and Rainwater, *Standing in America: New Dimensions of Class*, 150.

64. Kerry A. Dolan, "The World's Working Rich," *Forbes* (July 3, 2000): 162.

65. Jason DeParle, "Spy Anxiety: The Smart Magazine That Makes Smart People Nervous About Their Standing," *Washingtonian Monthly* (February 1989): 10.

66. For an examination of retailing issues related to the need for status, cf. Jacqueline Kilsheimer Eastman, Leisa Reinecke Flynn, and Ronald E. Goldsmith, "Shopping for Status: The Retail Managerial Implications," *Association of Marketing Theory and Practice* (Spring 1994): 125–30; also cf. Wilfred Amaldoss and Sanjay Jain, "Pricing of Conspicuous Goods: A Competitive Analysis of Social Effects," *Journal of Marketing Research* 42 (February 2005): 30–42.

67. Martin Fackler, "Pajamas: Not Just for Sleep Anymore," *Opelika-Auburn News* (September 13, 2002): 7A.

68. Herbert J. Gans, "Popular Culture in America: Social Problem in a Mass Society or Social Asset in a Pluralist Society?" in Howard S. Becker, ed., *Social Problems: A Modern Approach* (New York: Wiley, 1966).

69. Eugene Sivadas, George Mathew, and David J. Curry, "A Preliminary Examination of the Continuing Significance of Social Class to Marketing: A Geodemographic Replication," *Journal of Consumer Marketing* 41, no. 6 (1997): 463–79.

70. Edward O. Laumann and James S. House, "Living Room Styles and Social Attributes: The Patterning of Material Artifacts in a Modern Urban Community," *Sociology and Social Research* 54 (April 1970): 321–42; see also Stephen S. Bell, Morris B. Holbrook, and Michael R. Solomon, "Combining Esthetic and Social Value to Explain Preferences for Product Styles with the Incorporation of Personality and Ensemble Effects," *Journal of Social Behavior and Personality* 6 (1991): 243–74.

71. Morris B. Holbrook, Michael J. Weiss, and John Habich, "Class-Related Distinctions in American Cultural Tastes," *Empirical Studies of the Arts* 22, no. 1 (2004): 91–115.

72. Charla Mathwick, Caroline Wiertz, and Ko de Ruyter, "Social Capital Production in a Virtual P3 Community," *Journal of Consumer Research* 34 (April 2008): 832–49.

73. Pierre Bourdieu, *Distinction: A Social Critique of the Judgment of Taste* (Cambridge, UK: Cambridge University Press, 1984); see also Douglas B. Holt, "Does Cultural Capital Structure American Consumption?" *Journal of Consumer Research* 1 (June 1998): 1–25.

74. Xavier Drèze and Joseph C. Nunes, "Feeling Superior: The Impact of Loyalty Program Structure on Consumers' Perceptions of Status," *Journal of Consumer Research* (April 2009): 890–905.

75. Derek Rucker and Adam D. Galinsky, "Desire to Acquire: Powerlessness and Compensatory Consumption," *Journal of Consumer Research* 35 (August 2008): 257–67.

76. John Timpane, "All a-Twitter: The Tweet Smell of Success," *Philadelphia Inquirer* (March 5, 2009), www.philly.com/inquirer/front_page/20090305_All_a-Twitter__The_Tweet_smell_of_success.html, accessed March 5, 2009.

77. Natalie Angier, "Cell Phone or Pheromone? New Props for Mating Game," *New York Times* (November 7, 2000), www.nytimes.com, accessed November 7, 2000.

78. Brad Stone, "Cellphone Envy Lays Motorola Low," *New York Times* (February 3, 2007), www.nytimes.com, accessed February 3, 2007.

79. Quoted in Steinhauer, "When the Joneses Wear Jeans."

80. Rod Nordland, "Iraqis Snap Up Hummers as Icons of Power," *New York Times* (March 29, 2009), www.nytimes.com/2009/03/30/world/middleeast/30hummer.html, accessed March 29, 2009.

81. "Western Companies Compete to Win Business of Chinese Babies," *Wall Street Journal Interactive Edition* (May 15, 1998).

82. Andrew E. Kramer, "New Czars of Conspicuous Consumption," *New York Times* (November 1, 2006), www.nytimes.com, accessed November 1, 2006.

83. Tom Wright, "Ringing Up Sales in Indonesia Nokia's Bulky Smart Phones Find Niche Following There as Business Status Symbol," *Wall Street Journal* (May 22, 2007): B1.

84. John Brooks, *Showing Off in America* (Boston: Little, Brown, 1981), 13.

85. Naughton Keith, "The Perk Wars," *Newsweek* (September 30, 2002): 42–46.

86. Jessica Leshnoff, "Cougars and Their Cubs," AARP (February 2008), www.aarp.org/family/love/articles/cougars_and_their.html, accessed June 17, 2009; Robert Campbell, "For the Mature Woman Who Has Everything: A Boy Toy," *Reuters* (January 30, 2008), www.reuters.com/articleprint?Articleid=Usn3061371020080130, accessed January 30, 2008.

87. Thorstein Veblen, *The Theory of the Leisure Class* (1899; reprint, New York: New American Library, 1953): 45.

88. Brooks, *Showing Off in America*.

89. Paula Mergenhagen, "What Can Minimum Wage Buy?" *American Demographics* (January 1996): 32–36.

90. Linda F. Alwitt and Thomas D. Donley, "Retail Stores in Poor Urban Neighborhoods," *Journal of Consumer Affairs* 31, no. 1 (1997): 108–27.

91. C. K. Prahalad, *The Fortune at the Bottom of the Pyramid: Eradicating Poverty Through Profits* (Philadelphia: Wharton School Publishing, 2004).

92. Antonio Regalado, "Marketers Pursue the Shallow-Pocketed," *Wall Street Journal* (January 26, 2007): B3.

93. www.radicalcongruency.com/20061014-microfinance-wins-the-nobel-prize, accessed July 24, 2007.

94. August B. Hollingshead and Fredrick C. Redlich, *Social Class and Mental Illness: A Community Study* (New York: Wiley, 1958).

95. John Mager and Lynn R. Kahle, "Is the Whole More Than the Sum of the Parts? Re-evaluating Social Status in Marketing," *Journal of Business Psychology* 10 (Fall 1995): 3–18.

96. Beeghley, *Social Stratification in America: A Critical Analysis of Theory and Research*.

97. R. Vanneman and F. C. Pampel, "The American Perception of Class and Status," *American Sociological Review* 42 (June 1977): 422–37.

98. Coleman, "The Continuing Significance of Social Class to Marketing." Donald W. Hendon, Emelda L. Williams, and Douglas E. Huffman, "Social Class System Revisited," *Journal of Business Research* 17 (November 1988): 259.

99. Gerhard E. Lenski, "Status Crystallization: A Non-Vertical Dimension of Social Status," *American Sociological Review* 19 (August 1954): 405–12.

100. Richard P. Coleman, "The Significance of Social Stratification in Selling," in Martin L. Bell, ed., *Marketing: A Maturing Discipline: Proceedings of the American Marketing Association 43rd National Conference* (Chicago: American Marketing Association, 1960), 171–84.

101. Edmund L. Andrews, "U.S. Sets Big Incentives to Head Off Foreclosures," *New York Times* (March 4, 2009), www.nytimes.com/2009/03/05/business/05housing.html?_r=1&adxnnl=1&adxnnlx=1245265338-qOCraw3UvILgHzOaTDrTZg, accessed June 17, 2009.

102. E. Barth and W. Watson, "Questionable Assumptions in the Theory of Social Stratification," *Pacific Sociological Review* 7 (Spring 1964): 10–16.

103. Zick Rubin, "Do American Women Marry Up?" *American Sociological Review* 33 (1968): 750–60.

104. K. U. Ritter and L. L. Hargens, "Occupational Positions and Class Identifications of Married Working Women: A Test of the Asymmetry Hypothesis," *American Journal of Sociology* 80 (January 1975): 934–48.

13

Ethnic, Racial, and Religious Subcultures

Chapter Objectives

When you finish this chapter you will understand:

1 Why does our identification with microcultures that reflect a shared interest in some organization or activity also influence what we buy?

2 Why do our memberships in ethnic, racial, and religious subcultures often guide our consumption behaviors?

3 How do many marketing messages appeal to ethnic and racial identity?

4 Why are African Americans, Hispanic Americans, and Asian Americans the three most important ethnic/racial subcultures in the United States?

5 Why do marketers increasingly use religious and spiritual themes when they talk to consumers?

*M*aria wakes up early on Saturday morning and braces herself for a long day of errands and chores. As usual, her mother is at work and expects Maria to do the shopping and help prepare dinner for the big family gathering tonight. Of course, her older brother José would never be asked to do the grocery shopping or help out in the kitchen—these are women's jobs.

Family gatherings make a lot of work, and Maria wishes that her mother would use prepared foods once in a while, especially on a Saturday when Maria has an errand or two of her own to do. But no, her mother insists on preparing most of her food from scratch. She rarely uses any convenience products to ensure that the meals she serves are of the highest quality.

Resigned, Maria watches a *telenovela* (soap opera) on Univision while she dresses, and then she heads down to the *carnicería* (small grocery store) to buy a newspaper—there are almost 40 different Spanish newspapers published in her area, and she likes to pick up new ones occasionally. Then Maria buys the grocery items her mother wants. The list is full of well-known brand names that she gets all the time, such as Casera and Goya, so she's able to finish quickly. With any luck, she'll have a few minutes to go to the *mercado* (shopping center) to pick up that new Reggaeton CD by Daddy Yankee. She'll listen to it in the kitchen while she chops, peels, and stirs.

Maria smiles to herself: Los Angeles is a great place to live and what could be better than spending a lively, fun evening with *la familia.*

1

OBJECTIVE

Why does our identification with microcultures that reflect a shared interest in some organization or activity also influence what we buy?

Subcultures, Microcultures, and Consumer Identity

Si, Maria lives in Los Angeles, not Mexico City. More than one in four Californians are Hispanic, and overall the state has more nonwhite than white residents. In fact, more people watch Spanish-language Univision in LA than any other network.[1]

Maria and other Hispanic Americans have much in common with members of other racial and ethnic groups who live in the United States. They observe the same national holidays, the country's economic health affects what they spend, and they may root for Team USA in the Olympics. Nonetheless, although American citizenship provides the raw material for some consumption decisions, enormous variations in the social fabric of the country profoundly affect many others. The United States truly is a "melting pot" of hundreds of diverse groups, from Italian and Irish Americans to Mormons and Seventh-Day Adventists.

Our group memberships *within* our society-at-large help to define us. A **subculture** is a group whose members share beliefs and common experiences that set them apart from others. Every one of us belongs to many subcultures, depending on our age, race, ethnic background, or place of residence. Maria's Hispanic heritage exerts a huge influence on her everyday experience and consumption preferences.

In contrast to larger, demographically based subcultures (that Nature usually determines), people who are part of a **microculture** freely identify with a lifestyle or aesthetic preference. A good example is the microculture automobile hobbyists call "Tuners." These are single men in their late teens and early 20s, usually in Latino or Asian communities, who share a passion for fast cars, high-tech auto upgrades, and specialized car parts. This microculture started with late-night meets among illegal street racers in New York and LA. Now, Tuners are more mainstream magazines including *Import Tuner* and *Sport Compact Car* and major companies such as Pioneer eagerly court these high-tech hot-rodders. A commercial the Honda Civic targeted to Hispanic American consumers showed a fleet of cars in different colors with customized features such as chrome rims and tinted windows.[2]

Whether Tuners, Dead Heads, or skinheads, each microculture exhibits its own unique set of norms, vocabulary, and product insignias. At the online Redneck Bank ("where bankin's funner"), you can take care of your "personal bankin' bidness" and earn Redneck Rewards.[4] A study of contemporary "mountain men" in the western United States illustrates the binding influence of a microculture on its members. Researchers found that group members shared a strong sense of identity they expressed in weekend retreats, where they reinforced these ties authentic items like as they used *tipis,* buffalo robes, buckskin leggings, and beaded moccasins to create a sense of community among fellow mountain men.[5]

These microcultures often gel around fictional characters and events, and play a key role to define the extended self (see Chapter 5). Many devotees of *Star Trek,* for example, immerse themselves in a make-believe world of starships, phasers, and Vulcan mind melds. Our microcultures typically command fierce loyalty: *Star Trek* fans are notorious for their devotion to the cause, as this excerpt from a fan's e-mail illustrates:

> I have to admit to keeping pretty quiet about my devotion to the show for many years simply because people do tend to view a *Trek* fan as weird or crazy. . . . [after attending her first convention she says] Since then I have proudly worn my Bajoran earring and not cared about the looks I get from others. . . . I have also met . . . other *Trek* fans and some of these people have become very close friends. We have a lot in common and have had some of the same experiences as concerns our love of *Trek*.[6]

Star Trek is a merchandising empire that continues to beam up millions of dollars in revenues. Needless to say, it's not alone in this regard. Numerous other microcultures are out there; they thrive on their collective worship of mythical and not-so-mythical worlds and characters that range from the music group Phish to Hello Kitty.

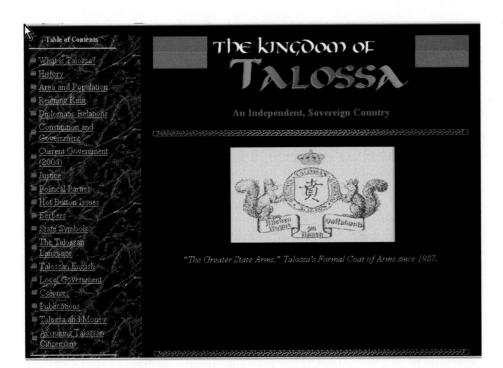

The Kingdom of Talossa home page.
Courtesy of Kingdom of Talossa.

Trend trackers find some of the most interesting—and rapidly changing— microcultures in Japan, where young women start many trends that eventually make their way around the world (more on this in Chapter 16). One is *Onna Otaku* (she-nerds)—girls who get their geek on as they stock up on femme-friendly comics, gadgets, and action figures instead of makeup and clothes. Another is the growing **cosplay** movement, a form of performance art in which participants wear elaborate costumes that represent a virtual world avatar or other fictional character. These outfits often depict figures from *manga, anime,* or other forms of graphic novels but they can also take the form of costumes from movies such as *The Matrix, Star Wars, Harry Potter,* or even *Ace Ventura: Pet Detective* (cosplay cafés in Tokyo feature waitresses who dress as maids). This role-playing subculture appears in various forms in Western culture as well, whether at *anime* or comic conventions, in the popular Goth subculture or as a form of sexual role-playing (e.g., women who dress in nurse's uniforms).[7]

Ethnic and Racial Subcultures

OBJECTIVE

Why do our memberships in ethnic, racial, and religious subcultures often guide our consumption behaviors?

An **ethnic subculture** is a self-perpetuating group of consumers who share common cultural or genetic ties, where both its members and others recognize it as a distinct category.[8] In some countries like Japan, ethnicity is virtually synonymous with the dominant culture because most citizens claim the same homogenous cultural ties (although even Japan has sizable minority populations, most notably people of Korean ancestry). In a heterogeneous society such as the United States, which incorporates many different cultures, consumers expend great effort to keep their subcultural identification from being submerged into the mainstream of the dominant society.

Marketers cannot ignore the stunning diversity of cultures that reshape mainstream society. Ethnic minorities spend more than $600 billion a year on products and services, so firms must tailor products and communications strategies to their unique needs. And this vast market continues to grow: Immigrants now make up 10 percent of the U.S. population and will account for 13 percent by 2050.[9] The U.S. Census calculates that by 2042 Americans who identify themselves as Hispanic, Black, Asian, American Indian, Native Hawaiian, and Pacific Islander will together outnumber

non-Hispanic whites. And the Census Bureau predicts that by 2050 people who identify themselves as multiracial will make up almost 4 percent of the U.S. population.[10]

This important change encourages advertisers to rethink their old strategies,
which assumed that virtually all of their customers were Caucasians who hailed
from Western Europe. For example, as part of Crest toothpaste's fiftieth-anniversary
celebration, Procter & Gamble revived its "Crest Kid," who first appeared as an
apple-cheeked urchin Norman Rockwell illustrated in 1956. Now, a Cuban-born girl
plays the character. An independent panel chose her because of her sparkling smile,
but it's significant that this mainstream American figure now is Hispanic.[11]

It makes good business sense to cater to these segments by (literally) speaking
their language when promoting products and services: Surveys repeatedly show
that members of ethnic groups get much of their product information from specialized ethnic media—one found that 63 percent of ethnic Californians watch native-
language TV daily, and a third of them also read an ethnic newspaper at least once a
week.[12] The advertisements that people who view these media see ideally should
match up with the way they communicate in daily life.

One important subcultural difference is how abstract or literal the group is.
Sociologists make a basic distinction: In a **high-context culture**, group members
tend to be tightly knit, and they infer meanings that go beyond the spoken word.
Symbols and gestures, rather than words, carry much of the weight of the message.
In contrast, people in a **low-context culture** are more literal. Compared to Anglos
(who tend to be low-context), many minority cultures are high-context and have
strong oral traditions, so consumers are more sensitive to nuances in advertisements that go beyond the message copy.[13]

OBJECTIVE

How do many marketing
messages appeal to
ethnic and racial
identity?

Ethnicity and Marketing Strategies

Although some people feel uncomfortable with the notion that
marketers should explicitly take into account people's racial
and ethnic differences when they formulate their strategies, the
reality is that these subcultural memberships do shape many
needs and wants. Research indicates, for example, that members of minority groups find an advertising spokesperson from
their own group more trustworthy, and this enhanced credibility in turn translates into more positive brand attitudes.[14]
However, marketers need to avoid the temptation to paint all members of an ethnic or
racial group with the same brush; these generalizations not only are inaccurate but they
also are likely to turn off the very people a company wants to reach.[15]

Although ethnic marketing is in vogue, it's not always so easy to actually define
and target members of a distinct ethnic group in our "melting pot" society. In the
2000 U.S. Census, some 7 million people identified with two or more races; they refused to describe themselves as only white, black, Asian, Korean, Samoan, or one of
the other racial categories the survey included.[18]

The popularity of golfer Tiger Woods illuminates the complexity of ethnic identity in the United States. Although we laud Tiger as an African American role model,
in reality he is a model of multiracialism. His mother is Thai, and he also has
Caucasian and Indian ancestry. Other popular multiracial celebrities include actor
Keanu Reeves (Hawaiian, Chinese, and Caucasian), singer Mariah Carey (African
American, Venezuelan, and Caucasian), and Dean Cain of *Superman* fame (Japanese and Caucasian).[19]

Products that companies market with an ethnic appeal are sometimes used by
consumers outside of that subculture. **Deethnicization** occurs when a product we
associate with a specific ethnic group detaches itself from its roots and appeals to
other groups as well. Think about the popularity of bagels, a staple of Jewish cuisine
that's mass marketed today. Recent variations include jalapeño bagels, blueberry
bagels, and even a green bagel for St. Patrick's Day.[20] Bagels now account for 3 to 6
percent of all American breakfasts, and bagel franchisers such as Bruegger's

CB AS I SEE IT

Professor Sonya Grier, *American University*

What are the social implications when marketers focus their efforts on specific consumer groups in our increasingly multicultural societies? Target marketing is at the heart of an effective marketing strategy, and it's driven by the recognition that a "one size fits all" approach to marketing no longer works among diverse, sophisticated consumers. Targeted strategies may attempt to affect commercial behavior (e.g., "buy this product") or social behavior (e.g., "increase fruit and vegetable consumption to reduce weight gain") or some combination of the two (e.g., "buy this product and 10 percent of profits go to charity"). Increased competitiveness, product proliferation, and changing economic conditions make it more challenging for marketers to reach those who are potential consumers of their products and services.

Moreover, the emphasis of social marketing as an agent of behavior change has increased the use of target marketing as a tool to address the growing array of social challenges among specific consumer groups. My research investigates the "how" and "to what effect" of target marketing strategies directed at consumers defined by race and ethnicity, especially African Americans. I study diverse domains (e.g., obesity, ethnic product crossover, cancer prevention, and service discrimination) to converge on an understanding of the influence of targeted marketing, both positive and negative, on society.

My initial work in this area asked, "How do consumers respond to targeted advertisements when they are (or *are* not) a member of the targeted group?" Research showed that people used different psychological processes to interpret a racially targeted advertisement, and had different attitudes toward those ads, depending on their own race, the social status of their racial group, and their familiarity with other racial groups.[16] These findings led me to consider how target marketing, with its emphasis on providing different prices, promotions, and access to different consumer segments, might create different marketing environments among targeted consumers and serve as a countervailing force for the socially beneficial behavior changes intended by social marketing efforts.

Currently I am exploring how target marketing may contribute to, as well as help resolve, health disparities between members of ethnic minority and majority groups, with a focus on obesity. The prevalence of obesity in African American and Hispanic children and adults tends to be substantially higher than in white Americans. We know that this disparity is not due solely to differences in income or education, although those factors do play a role. Social marketing programs aimed at obesity prevention often promote the increased intake of healthy foods and decreased intake of less healthy foods. What, then, is the role of target marketing of these less healthy foods in the effectiveness of such strategies (i.e., does it "prevent prevention?"). In a systematic review of the marketing environment of African Americans, a colleague and I found that targeted food marketing strategies, in the aggregate, may challenge the ability of African American consumers to eat healthfully.[17] Marketers' promotional strategies directed toward African Americans emphasize the awareness of low-cost, low-nutrition food products such as candy, soda, and snacks and are less likely to contain health-oriented messages. We also found that distribution and pricing strategies may constrain the ability of African American consumers to purchase healthy food. It is certainly a challenge for any consumer to eat healthfully when their choices are constrained.

My ongoing research further examines how targeted marketing may be used to encourage more health-oriented behaviors at a community level. Such strategies will entail changing not only individual dietary habits, but also support communities when they advocate for increased health-supporting targeted marketing. I am also exploring interactive targeting efforts. As technological advances change the process of targeted marketing, it is important to understand whether consumers' response facilitates or hinders important health behaviors. I believe that through understanding unintended consequences of target marketing, especially aggregate effects among particular target segments, target marketing can be a beneficial strategy for commercial and social marketers alike, and can help address important social challenges. I hope my research contributes to this understanding and to the design of more socially responsible marketing practices, effective social marketing efforts, and conscious, equitable marketplaces worldwide.

CB AS I LIVE IT

Brad Zak, *Boston College*

In an effort to be more marketable to the masses, a lot of companies go through a process of *deethnicization*. When considering a nation as diverse as America, plenty of products get taken from original roots and warped into a more palatable version for the public. Sometimes it may be in an effort to be more politically correct, but in that effort cultural identities become lost and overall quality becomes sacrificed.

When it comes to favorite foods, there might be nothing I enjoy more than a fresh slice of pizza straight out of the oven. However, deethnicization continues to demean the overall quality of this timeless classic. For years, pizza had stayed true to its Italian culture and been a specialty dish of many Italian restaurants. Then with companies such as Domino's and Pizza Hut an era of commercialization dawned on the delicious pizza treat. Pizza was no longer a uniquely Italian food, but a far inferior concoction bastardized by American culture.

Living on a college campus, my food decisions are often based on cost and time because I am never to able to plan ahead for late night hunger needs. The companies around campuses know this and put more resources toward quicker delivery that could be put toward quality. I've complained often about how I can't find a good slice of pizza around my college campus because everything seems as if it was hastily microwaved and thrown into a box before it was delivered to me. Good pizza has become a rarity in my life that I don't feel I deserve. Deethnicization of the pizza industry may have made it more profitable but in that process taste has been kicked to the curb to sit alongside Little Caesar.

The Tangled Web

The release of several popular video games underscores the concern of some critics who argue that these games play on racial stereotypes, including images of African American youths who commit violent street crimes:

- *Grand Theft Auto—San Andreas* is set in a city that resembles gang-ridden stretches of Los Angeles of the 1990s. It features a digital cast of African American and Hispanic men, some who wear braided hair and scarves over their faces and aim Uzis from low-riding cars.
- *Def Jam Fight for NY* features hip-hop-style characters (one with the voice of the rapper Snoop Dogg) who slap, kick, and pummel one another in locations such as the 125th Street train station in Harlem.
- *25 to Life* is an "urban action game" that includes a hip-hop soundtrack. It lets gamers play the role of police officers or criminals, and includes lots of images of young gun-toting African American gangsters.

Corporation and the Einstein/Noah Bagel Corporation operate hundreds of stores in cities that had never heard of a bagel just a few years ago.[21]

The dominant American culture historically exerted pressure on immigrants to divest themselves of their origins and integrate with mainstream society. As President Theodore Roosevelt put it in the early part of the twentieth century, "We welcome the German or the Irishman who becomes an American. We have no use for the German or the Irishman who remains such."[22]

Indeed, there is a tendency for ethnic groups with a relatively longer history in the United States to view themselves as more mainstream as they relax their identification with their country of origin. When the 2000 U.S. Census asked respondents to write up to two ancestries that defined their background, the results showed a clear decline in the number of people who identified themselves as of Irish, German, or other European origin. Compared to other subcultures, more people from these countries simply choose to call themselves "American."[23]

The bulk of American immigrants historically came from Europe, but immigration patterns have shifted dramatically. New immigrants are much more likely to be Asian or Hispanic. As these new waves of immigrants settle in the United States, marketers try to track their consumption patterns and adjust their strategies accordingly. It's best to market to these new arrivals—whether Arabs, Asians, Russians, or people of Caribbean descent—in their native languages. They tend to cluster together geographically, which makes them easy to reach. The local community is the primary source for information and advice, so word of mouth is especially important (see Chapter 10). Figure 13.1 shows how new waves of immigrants are changing the ethnic composition of major American cities.

Ethnic and Racial Stereotypes

A controversial television commercial for Salesgenie.com that ran during Super Bowl XLII in 2008 illustrates how marketers (intentionally or not) use ethnic and racial stereotypes to craft promotional communications. The spot featured two animated pandas who speak in heavy Chinese accents. After complaints from viewers, the company withdrew the commercial.[24]

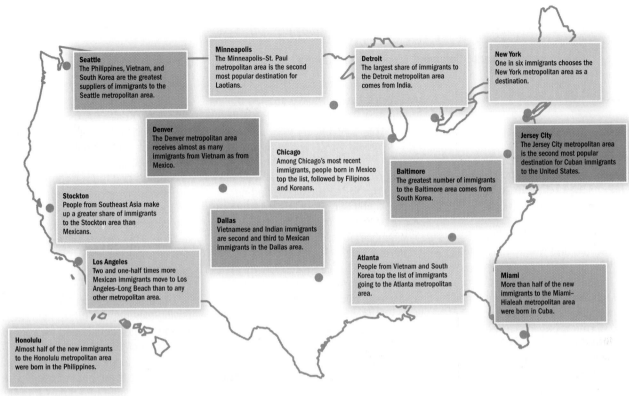

Seattle
The Philippines, Vietnam, and South Korea are the greatest suppliers of immigrants to the Seattle metropolitan area.

Minneapolis
The Minneapolis–St. Paul metropolitan area is the second most popular destination for Laotians.

Detroit
The largest share of immigrants to the Detroit metropolitan area comes from India.

New York
One in six immigrants chooses the New York metropolitan area as a destination.

Denver
The Denver metropolitan area receives almost as many immigrants from Vietnam as from Mexico.

Chicago
Among Chicago's most recent immigrants, people born in Mexico top the list, followed by Filipinos and Koreans.

Jersey City
The Jersey City metropolitan area is the second most popular destination for Cuban immigrants to the United States.

Stockton
People from Southeast Asia make up a greater share of immigrants to the Stockton area than Mexicans.

Baltimore
The greatest number of immigrants to the Baltimore area comes from South Korea.

Dallas
Vietnamese and Indian immigrants are second and third to Mexican immigrants in the Dallas area.

Los Angeles
Two and one-half times more Mexican immigrants move to Los Angeles–Long Beach than to any other metropolitan area.

Atlanta
People from Vietnam and South Korea top the list of immigrants going to the Atlanta metropolitan area.

Miami
More than half of the new immigrants to the Miami–Hialeah metropolitan area were born in Cuba.

Honolulu
Almost half of the new immigrants to the Honolulu metropolitan area were born in the Philippines.

Figure 13.1 AMERICA'S NEWEST MARKETS

Many subcultures have powerful stereotypes the general public associates with them. In these cases outsiders assume that group members possess certain traits. Unfortunately, a communicator can cast the same trait as either positive or negative, depending on his or her biases or intentions. For example, the Scottish stereotype in the United States is largely positive, so we tend to look favorably on their (supposed) frugality. 3M uses Scottish imagery to denote value (e.g., Scotch tape), as does the Scotch Inns, a motel chain that offers inexpensive lodging. However, the Scottish "personality" might carry quite different connotations to the British or Irish. One person's "thrifty" is another's "stingy."

In the past, marketers used ethnic symbolism as shorthand to convey certain product attributes. They often employed crude and unflattering images when they depicted African Americans as subservient or Mexicans as bandits.[26] Aunt Jemima sold pancake mix and Rastus was a grinning black chef who pitched Cream of Wheat hot cereal. The Gold Dust Twins were black urchins who peddled a soap powder for Lever Brothers, and Pillsbury hawked powdered drink mixes via characters such as Injun Orange and Chinese Cherry—who had buck teeth.[27] As the Civil Rights Movement gave more power to minority groups and their rising economic status began to command marketers' respect, these negative stereotypes began to disappear. Frito-Lay responded to protests by the Hispanic community and stopped using the Frito Bandito character in 1971, and Quaker Foods gave Aunt Jemima a makeover in 1989.

For more than 60 years, Mars' Uncle Ben's rice packages featured the black Uncle Ben character. He wore a bow tie evocative of servants and Pullman porters, and his title reflects how white Southerners once used "uncle" and "aunt" as honorary names for older African Americans because they refused to call the African Americans "Mr." and "Mrs." Mars revived the character, but he's been remade as Ben, an accomplished businessman with an opulent office who shares his "grains of wisdom" about rice and life on the brand's Web site.[28]

• *Notorious—Die to Drive* features "gangsta- style car combat" with players who compete to "rule the streets of four West Coast neighborhoods." The game's Web site proclaims, "High-priced honeys, the finest bling, and millionaire cribs are just some of the rewards for the notorious few who can survive this most dangerous game. Once you go Notorious, there's no going back."[25]

CB AS I LIVE IT

Alexandra Solomon, *University of Georgia*

*I*t started as a fantasy. My friend Sara and I schemed for months about making it come true but no one including ourselves actually considered it a realistic possibility. After all, who didn't dream about living in New York City for a whole summer? Then it happened. We both managed to secure internships for the summer and as we made our first payment for the NYU dorms it became a reality. This occurred in February, but living in a college town we got wrapped up in spring break planning and end-of-the year celebrations so the idea that we would soon be moving to the Big Apple quickly escaped our minds. When May rolled around it hit us that we should probably start preparing for our big move. We both started packing our closets, with constant phone calls every five minutes consulting with one another about what to bring. What did girls wear in the north? The question lingered on our minds as we did our best to pack. Although I was born in New Jersey, I grew up in the deep south (Alabama to be exact). New York seemed like a foreign country to me, with the exception of the twice-a-year

visit to relatives who live outside of Manhattan. The extent of these visits was to the local T.G.I.F. restaurant and an occasional movie outing so I was completely oblivious to the fashions of the big city. Although we were clueless about what to bring, still we had no trouble filling two *extra* large duffels to start our voyage.

When we arrived in Manhattan, we soon realized that our nightmare of sticking out like a sore thumb would prove to be correct. It was clear that we dressed and acted differently, and were a little wary of being accepted by our two new roommates who were from the north. The four of us bonded instantly despite our differences and we decided to celebrate our first night in the city together. Sara and I panicked as we got ready and finally we decided to wait and see what our roommates wore before we selected our outfits. After we saw what they wore, we realized that our hopes of fitting in had gone down the drain. While they were dressed to the nines in their finest club gear, we appeared as if we were participating in sorority rush. Shrugging off the differences, we decided to go as we were, adorned in true southern style, proud as can be.

My experience as I tried to learn the ways of the northern culture exemplifies the process of

acculturation. Sara and I come from a completely different culture than the one we would be living in. In order to fit in the best we could, we realized we would have to carefully watch those around us and learn from them. While we obviously weren't going to change who we were, we managed to adapt to the culture around us and do our best to fit in. This chapter's description of acculturation mirrors our own experience and the way it has affected our consumer behavior.

Understanding acculturation and having experienced it firsthand has given me the tools I need in order to survive in cultures unlike my own. With our world changing around us at the pace it is, it is almost impossible to know where one will end up in the future. For this reason I believe it is vital to have an experience such as mine. It's very possible that in the future I could find myself in a culture that varies even more than the southern and northern United States (though when I walk through the streets of Greenwich Village I find this hard to imagine!). It is important for marketers to understand the concept of acculturation so that they can market products to consumers in different cultures while at the same time making those who are not used to that culture comfortable with their products.

The Acculturation Process

Acculturation is the process of movement and adaptation to one country's cultural environment by a person from another country.[29] This is a very important issue for marketers because of our increasingly global society. As people move from place to place, they may quickly assimilate to their new homes or they may resist this blending process and choose to insulate themselves from the mainstream culture. It's typical for a new arrival in the United States for example to feel ambivalence or conflict about relinquishing old ways (and consumer behaviors) for new ones. Home Depot segments its campaigns when the retailer speaks to the Hispanic market; it creates different ads for "acculturated Hispanics" (second- or third-generation Americans) than it shows to consumers who almost always speak Spanish.[30]

A study of Mexican immigrants that used the research technique of *ethnography* probed their acculturation as they adapted to life in the United States.[31] Indeed, after the researchers interviewed these people in their natural settings, they reported a lot of ambivalence. On the one hand, they are happy about the improvements in the quality of their lives because of greater job availability and educational opportunities for their children. On the other hand, they report bittersweet feelings about leaving Mexico. They miss their friends, their holidays, their food, and the comfort that comes from living in familiar surroundings. Another study looked at how Hispanic children responded to a campaign to promote oral hygiene cosponsored by the Boys and Girls Club of America and the American Dental Association. It reported that immigrants who are relatively less acculturated are more motivated to modify their behaviors in line with the campaign's suggestions because they view these changes as important tools for social acceptance.[32]

As Figure 13.2 shows, many factors affect the nature of the transition process. Individual differences, such as whether the person speaks English, influence how rocky the adjustment will be. The person's contact with **acculturation agents**— people and institutions that teach the ways of a culture—are also crucial. Some of these agents come from the *culture of origin* (in this case, Mexico), including family, friends, the church, local businesses, and Spanish-language media that keep the consumer in touch with his or her country of origin. Other agents come from the *culture of immigration* (in this case, America), and help the consumer to learn how to navigate in the new environment. These include public schools, English-language media, and government agencies.

Several processes come into play as immigrants adapt to their new surroundings. *Movement* refers to the factors that motivate people to physically uproot themselves from one location and go to another. In this case, people leave Mexico because of the scarcity of jobs and the desire to provide a good education for their children. On arrival, immigrants encounter a need for *translation*. This means they try to master a set of rules to operate in the new environment, whether they learn how to decipher a different currency or figure out the social meanings of unfamiliar clothing styles. This cultural learning leads to a process of *adaptation*, by which people form new consumption patterns. For example, some of the Mexican women in the study started to wear shorts and pants once they settled in the United States although people in Mexico frown on this practice.

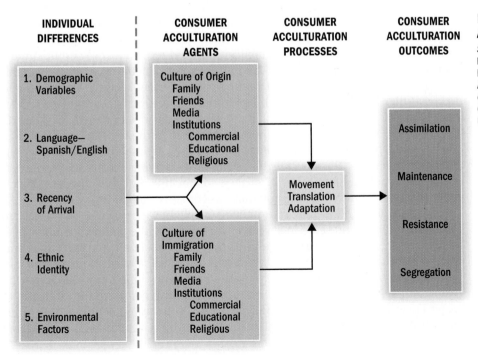

Figure 13.2 A MODEL OF CONSUMER ACCULTURATION

Source: Lisa Peñaloza, : "Atravesando Fronteras/Border Crossings: A Critical Ethnographic Exploration of the Consumer Acculturation of Mexican Immigrants," *Journal of Consumer Research* (June 1994): 32–54. Copyright © 1994 JCR, Inc. Used by permission of University of Chicago Press.

Marketing Pitfall

The mass merchandising of ethnic products is a growing practice. Native American Aztec designs appear on sweaters, gym shoes come in *kente* cloth from an African tribe, and greeting cards bear likenesses of Native American sand paintings. However, some worry about the borrowing—and in some cases, misinterpretation—of distinctive symbolism. Consider, for example, the storm of protest from the international Islamic community over a dress in a House of Chanel fashion show. Supermodel Claudia Schiffer wore a strapless evening gown (with a price tag of almost $23,000) that Karl Lagerfeld designed. The dress included Arabic letters that the designer believed spelled out a love poem. Instead, the message was a verse from the Koran, the Muslim holy book. To add insult to injury, the word *God* happened to appear over the model's right breast. Both the designer and the model received death threats, and the controversy subsided only after the company burned the dress. More recently, Nike caught flak from activists when in late 2007 it introduced an athletic shoe specially designed for Native Americans. Along with its trademark swoosh, the Nike Air Native N7 features feathers and arrowheads. One young Spokane/Coeur d'Alene Indian commented, "The day it was announced, I thought: 'Are they going to have dream catchers on them? Are they going to be beaded? Will they have native bumper stickers on them that say, 'Custer had it coming'?"[33]

During the acculturation process, many immigrants undergo *assimilation,* where they adopt products, habits, and values they identify with the mainstream culture. At the same time, there is an attempt at *maintenance* of practices they associate with the culture of origin. Immigrants stay in touch with people in their country and, like Maria, many continue to eat Spanish foods and read Spanish newspapers. Their continued identification with Mexican culture may cause *resistance,* as they resent the pressure to submerge their Mexican identities and take on new roles. Finally, immigrants (voluntarily or not) tend to exhibit *segregation*; they are likely to live and shop in places physically separated from mainstream Anglo consumers. These processes illustrate that ethnicity is a fluid concept and that members of a subculture constantly recreate its boundaries.

The **progressive learning model** helps us to understand the acculturation process. This perspective assumes that people gradually learn a new culture as they increasingly come in contact with it. Thus, we expect that when people acculturate they will mix the practices of their original culture with those of their new or **host culture.**[34] Research generally supports this pattern when it examines such factors as shopping orientation, the importance people place on various product attributes, media preference, and brand loyalty.[35] When researchers take into account the intensity of ethnic identification, they find that consumers who retain a strong ethnic identification differ from their more assimilated counterparts in these ways:[36]

- They have a more negative attitude toward business in general (probably caused by frustration due to relatively low income levels).
- They access more media that's in their native language.
- They are more brand loyal.
- They are more likely to prefer brands with prestige labels.
- They are more likely to buy brands that specifically advertise to their ethnic group.

The acculturation process occurs even when we relocate from one place to another within the same country. If you have ever moved (and it's likely you have), you no doubt remember how difficult it was to give up old habits and friends and adapt to what people in your new location do.

A study of Turkish people who moved from the countryside to an urban environment illustrates how people cope with change and unfamiliar circumstances. The authors describe a process of **warming,** which they describe as transforming objects and places into those that feel cozy, hospitable, and authentic. The study's informants described what happened as they tried to turn a cold and unfamiliar house into a home that is *güzel* ("beautiful and good," "modern and warm"). In this context that means they integrated symbols of their former village life into their new homes—they blanketed them with the embroidered, crocheted, and lace textiles that people traditionally make by hand for brides' dowries in the villages. The researchers reported that migrants' homes contained far more of these pieces than they would have in their village homes because they used them to adorn their new modern appliances. The dowry textiles symbolize traditional norms and social networks of friends and family in the villages, so they link the "cold" modern objects with the owner's past. Thus, the unfamiliar becomes familiar.[37]

Another group of researchers examined the plight of people who were forced to leave their homes and settle in a foreign country with little planning and few possessions.[38] As "strangers in a strange land," they must essentially start over and completely resocialize. The authors did an in-depth study of refugees from a number of countries who lived in an Austrian refugee shelter. They found that teenagers who were traumatized by their experience turn to adaptive consumption strategies to cope. For example, the adolescents all had stuffed animals (including the boys) they used to comfort themselves. And all of the teenage boys wore earrings to designate their own community.

OBJECTIVE

Why are African Americans, Hispanic Americans, and Asian Americans the three most important ethnic/racial subcultures in the United States?

The "Big Three" American Subcultures

African Americans, Hispanic Americans, and Asian Americans account for much of America's current growth. According to the 2000 U.S. Census, the Hispanic population is now the largest ethnic subculture, with 12.5 percent of Americans.[39] Asian Americans, though much smaller in absolute numbers with only 3.6 percent of the population, are the fastest-growing racial group.[40]

African Americans

On *Harlem Heights*, a reality show that airs on BET, the young, hip stars use a raft of Johnson & Johnson products including Listerine, Zyrtec, and Splenda as part of a partnership between the two companies. Meanwhile the hip-hop impresario Sean "Diddy" Combs appears on TV commercials to plug his new I am King fragrance as a suave, black James Bond—type character. He observes, "When you see Barack Obama, you see a strong, elegant black man and when people see my ad, it's almost like that's the trend."[41]

African Americans comprise a significant racial subculture—they were 12.3 percent of the U.S. population in the 2000 Census.[42] Although African American consumers do differ in important ways from Caucasians, the African American market is hardly as homogenous as many marketers believe. Indeed, some commentators argue that black–white differences are largely illusory. With some exceptions, both groups have the same overall spending patterns; they allocate about two-thirds of their incomes to housing, transportation, and food.[43]

The differences we do observe more likely are the result of differences in income, the relatively high concentration of African Americans in urban areas, and other dimensions of social class we discussed in Chapter 12. And these differences continue to diminish as African American consumers move up the economic ladder. Although it is still lower than the white majority, this group's median household income is at a historic high. We can trace this improvement directly to a steady increase in educational attainment. African Americans had a median household income of $30,439 in 2000, up from $18,676 in 1990, and more than 51 percent of married African Americans make $50,000 or more.[44]

Nonetheless, there clearly are some differences between blacks and whites in consumption priorities and marketplace behaviors that demand marketers' attention.[45] In late 2007, Procter & Gamble launched a new program it calls "My Black Is Beautiful" for African American women after the company's research told it that these women think mainstream media does not represent them very well—three-quarters of the women the company surveyed said programs and ads portray them more negatively than other racial groups and that they worry about the negative impact these messages will have on teens. The campaign includes a discussion guide booklet to encourage women to facilitate dialogue in their local communities and a supporting Web site at <u>myblackisbeautiful.com</u>.[46]

Sometimes these differences are subtle but still important. When Coffee-Mate discovered that African Americans tend to drink their coffee with sugar and cream much more than do Caucasians, the company mounted a promotional blitz in the African American media and in return benefited from double-digit increases in sales volume and market share for this segment.[48] Volvo North America created its first advertising campaign to target African Americans after research showed that car crashes are the leading cause of death among African American children, who are half as likely to use seat belts as other children.[49]

Research by Unilever illustrates how *body cathexis* dynamics (see Chapter 5) vary across subcultures—the personal care products company found that skin takes on a deeper meaning for African Americans. In a poll it ran in *Essence* magazine, the company asked more than 1,400 African American women aged 18 to 64 to describe their

Marketing Pitfall

The good news: In 2009 Congress granted the Food and Drug Administration the authority to regulate tobacco products. The agency will have the power to change existing products and also to ban new products unless it decides they contribute to public health. It will impose a ban on tobacco advertising within 1,000 feet of schools and playgrounds and mandate new graphic warning labels by 2012 that will occupy 50 percent of the space on each pack of cigarettes.

The bad news: As a political compromise the regulations exempt only one form of tobacco flavoring: menthol. This additive is used in about one-quarter of cigarettes sold today. But, three-quarters of black smokers prefer menthol. Antismoking groups that represent African Americans wanted the ban to include menthol because black smokers also have a disproportionate share of lung cancer. The FDA. will, however, study the effects of menthol and it will have the power to ban the additive by 2011 if the evidence supports this change.[51]

skin, and the most common response was "beautiful" (59 percent). Another 30 percent described their skin as "strong." The survey also found that African American women rank skin as "most important to them" (49 percent); more so than their hair, figure, makeup, and clothes. About one-third say their skin is a source of their heritage, one-fourth say it's a source of pride, and "almost half of African American women say their skin tells a story of who they are and identifies them." The survey is part of Unilever's Skinvoice campaign, where the company invites women to talk about their skin at skinvoice.com. This deep attachment is clear in posted comments such as "My skin is my life's historian," and "My skin represents the blending of my parents, an outward expression of their love."[50]

Hispanic Americans

The umbrella term *Hispanic* describes people of many different backgrounds. According to the 2000 U.S. Census, nearly 60 percent of Hispanic Americans are of Mexican descent. The next largest group, Puerto Ricans, make up just fewer than 10 percent of Hispanics. Other groups the Census includes in this category are Central Americans, Dominicans, South Americans, and Cubans.

The Hispanic subculture is a sleeping giant that many U.S. marketers ignored until recently. The growth and increasing affluence of this group now makes it impossible to overlook, and major corporations avidly court Hispanic consumers such as Maria and her family. In Los Angeles where Maria lives, plans are underway for a massive "branded city" called El Portál that expects to attract a 90 percent Latino clientele. Wal-Mart recently opened its first Hispanic-focused supermarkets, Supermercado de Walmart in Phoenix and Houston.[52] No surprise: From 1990 to 2006, Hispanics' disposable income rose by 832 percent, to $798 billion, compared with 154 percent for the rest of the population.[53]

In addition, the Hispanic population is young: Thirty-four percent were younger than age 18 in 2004, compared with 25 percent for the total population. Marketers especially like the fact that Hispanics tend to be brand loyal. In one study, about 45 percent reported that they always buy their usual brand, whereas only one in five said they frequently switch brands.[54] Another study found that Hispanics who strongly identify with their ethnic origin are more likely to seek Hispanic vendors, to be loyal to brands used by family and friends, and to be influenced by Hispanic media.[55] This segment also concentrates geographically by country of origin, which makes them relatively easy to reach. More than 50 percent of all Hispanic Americans live in the Los Angeles, New York, Miami, San Antonio, San Francisco, and Chicago metropolitan areas.[56]

One roadblock for mainstream marketers is the relatively low degree of acculturation among some Hispanic consumers who don't choose to assimilate. About 38 percent of all Hispanics live in *barrios*, or predominantly Hispanic neighborhoods, which tend to be somewhat insulated from mainstream society.[57] For this reason, native language and culture are important components of Hispanic identity and self-esteem (about three-quarters of Hispanics speak Spanish at home), and many Hispanic Americans appreciate marketing efforts that acknowledge their cultural heritage.[58] More than 40 percent say they deliberately attempt to buy products that show an interest in the Hispanic consumer, and this number jumps to more than two-thirds for Cuban Americans.[59] Still, the acculturation process inevitably means that over time these differences will probably narrow. Whereas 73 percent of Hispanic immigrants prefer the Spanish language to English, the number falls to 25 percent of their children and only 1 percent of their grandchildren.

With a larger proportion of Hispanics being born in the United States, experts predict that English will increasingly supplant Spanish as the most effective language for marketing messages. However, third-generation Hispanics, born in the United States, still retain a strong sense of Hispanic identity and heritage that creates demand for publications such as *Urban Latino* that cater to the "new generation Latino." This demand also fuels the emergence of a new, mostly English-language radio genre, "hurban" ("Hispanic Urban").[60]

Hispanic consumers are rapidly entering the mainstream market.
Courtesy of Latina Magazine.

Many initial efforts to market to Hispanic Americans were, to say the least, counterproductive. Companies bumbled in their efforts to translate advertising adequately or to compose copy that captured the nuances advertisers intended. These mistakes do not occur so much anymore because marketers are more sophisticated when they talk to this segment and they tend to involve Hispanics in advertising production to ensure they get it right. These translation mishaps slipped through before Anglos got their acts together:[61]

- The Perdue slogan, "It takes a tough man to make a tender chicken," translated as "It takes a sexually excited man to make a chick affectionate."
- Budweiser was the "queen of beers."
- Braniff (now defunct) promoted the comfortable leather seats on its airplanes with the headline, *Sentado en cuero,* which translates as "Sit naked."
- Coors beer's slogan to "get loose with Coors" appeared in Spanish as "get the runs with Coors."

Even today, confused meanings create problems for some well-intentioned marketers. In 2007, a division of Macy's department stores pulled a T-shirt it intended to sell to Hispanic shoppers in Georgia and Texas that proclaimed "Brown is the New White."[62] In another gaffe, Volkswagen caught flak when it tried to attract Hispanic drivers to its GTI 2006 model with a word they would recognize. Americans use the Spanish word *cojones* to describe a gutsy person, but literally it means testicles. Billboards in huge black letters proclaimed "Turbo-Cojones." VW removed the boards in Cuban-dominated Miami following an outcry. As one local commented, "In English, Turbo-Balls might not sound so offensive. But in the Spanish-speaking community, it will always have a vulgar connotation." It replaced the ads with others that say "Here Today. Gone Tamale" and "Kick a Little Gracias."[63]

In a more sophisticated effort Unilever launched *ViveMejor,* a major digital, print, TV, and retail Hispanic marketing program that combines all of its food and personal care brands together in a single marketing platform for Hispanic consumers. The campaign includes a bilingual Web site (ViveMejor.com), a free bilingual magazine Unilever will distribute in stores, and TV segments to run on Spanish-language television. *ViveMejor* was the result of a major research program where Unilever looked in depth at the shopping habits of more than 800 Hispanic consumers. The company found these consumers shop more often because they prepare more meals at home, but they enjoy their shopping experiences less than general-market shoppers. They also are more receptive to in-store meal suggestions and recipes than the general population.[64]

Some successful advertising campaigns simply don't work in Hispanic subcultures. For example, the California Milk Processor Board discovered that Hispanics did not appreciate its hugely successful "Got Milk?" campaign because biting, sarcastic humor is not part of their culture. In addition, the notion of milk deprivation is not funny to the Hispanic homemaker because if she runs out of milk she has failed her family. To make matters worse, "Got Milk?" translates as "Are you lactating?" so the organization revised Spanish-language ads as, "And you, have you given them enough milk today?" with tender scenes that center on cooking flan in the family kitchen.[65]

However, there are aspects of Hispanic culture that make some products popular for reasons Anglos may not understand. This is the case with Clamato, a clam-flavored tomato juice that has gotten a new lease on life thanks to its popularity among Latino consumers. Many Latinos consider the clam to be an aphrodisiac, and the drink is popular among young people who use it as a base for the seafood cocktail *ceviche* or mix it with beer because they believe it arouses passion.[66]

As we saw earlier, one of the most notable characteristics of the Hispanic market is its youth: The median age of Hispanic Americans is 23.6, compared with the U.S. average of 32. Many of these consumers are "young biculturals" who bounce back and forth between hip-hop and *Rock en Español,* blend Mexican rice with spaghetti sauce, and spread peanut butter and jelly on tortillas.[67] Latino youth are changing mainstream culture. The U.S. Census Bureau estimates that by the year 2020 the number of Hispanic teens will grow by 62 percent compared with 10 percent growth in teens overall. They are looking for spirituality, stronger family ties, and more color in their lives—three hallmarks of Latino culture. Music crossovers are leading the trend, including musicians such as Shakira and Big Pun, the first Latino hip-hop artist to go platinum.

A second notable characteristic of this market is that family size tends to be large. The average Hispanic household contains 3.5 people, compared to only 2.7 for other U.S. households. These differences obviously affect the overall allocation of income to various product categories. For example, Hispanic households spend 15 to 20 percent more of their disposable income than the national average on groceries.[68] That helps to explain why General Mills developed Buñuelitos breakfast cereal specifically for this market. The brand name is an adaptation of *buñuelos,* a traditional Mexican pastry people eat on holidays. Meanwhile, rival Kellogg recently launched Corn Flakes with Honey specifically to attract Hispanics.[69]

We can't overstate the importance of the family to Hispanics such as Maria. Preferences to spend time with family influence the structure of many consumption activities. For this subculture, shopping is a family affair. More than a third (36 percent) of Hispanics say they prefer shopping with their families, and 30 percent report that they like shopping with their children.[70] Hispanic parents gravitate to purchases that underscore their ability to provide well for the family. They regard clothing their children well as a matter of pride.

In contrast, convenience and a product's ability to save time are not terribly important to the Hispanic homemaker. Women like Maria's mother will purchase labor-intensive products if it means that their families will benefit. For this reason, a time-saving appeal short-circuited for Quaker Foods when the company discovered that Hispanic women tend to cook Instant Quaker Oats on the stove as if it were regular oatmeal, refrigerate it, and serve it later as a pudding.[71] Similarly, telephone company promotions that emphasize cheaper rates for calling family members offend many Hispanic consumers to whom deferring a phone call home simply to save money is an insult![72] This orientation also explains why generic products do not tend to do well in the Hispanic market—these consumers value the quality well-known brand names promise.

Asian Americans

Asians are very sensitive to the design and location of a home, especially as these affect the home's *chi*—an invisible energy current they believe brings good or bad luck. Asian home buyers want a house that offers a good *feng shui* environment (translated literally as "the wind and the water"). One home developer in San Francisco sold up to 80 percent of its homes to Asian customers after he made a few minor design changes—he reduced the number of "T" intersections in the houses and added rounded rocks to the garden—harmful *chi* travels in a straight line, whereas gentle *chi* travels on a curved path.[74]

The problems American marketers encountered when they first tried to reach the Hispanic market popped up again when they began to target Asian Americans:[75]

- The Coca-Cola slogan "Coke Adds Life" translated as "Coke brings your ancestors back from the dead" in Japanese.
- Kentucky Fried Chicken described its chicken as "finger-lickin' good" to the Chinese, who don't think it's polite to lick your fingers.
- A footwear ad depicted Japanese women performing foot-binding, which only the Chinese do.

Asians not only make up the fastest-growing population group, they also are the most affluent, best-educated, and most likely to hold technology jobs of any ethnic subculture. Indeed, Asian Americans are much more likely than average Americans to buy high-tech gadgets. They are almost three times as likely to own a digital camcorder and twice as likely to have an MP3 player.[76] About 32 percent of Asian households have incomes of more than $50,000 compared to 29 percent in the entire U.S. population. Estimates put this segment's buying power at $253 billion annually. That explains why the brokerage firm Charles Schwab now employs more than 300 people who speak Chinese, Korean, and Vietnamese at its call centers.[77]

Despite its potential, this group is hard to market to because it's composed of numerous culturally diverse subgroups that use different languages and dialects.[78] The term *Asian* refers to 20 ethnic groups, with Chinese being the largest and Filipino and Japanese second and third, respectively. Filipinos are the only Asians who speak English predominantly among themselves; like Hispanics most Asians prefer media in their own languages. The languages Asian Americans speak most frequently are Mandarin Chinese, Korean, Japanese, and Vietnamese.

Not only are Asian consumers the most frequent shoppers of all racial and ethnic groups but they are also the most brand-conscious. Almost half (43 percent) say they always look for a brand name when they shop. Yet, interestingly, they are also the least brand loyal. Fully a quarter of Asians say they change brands often, compared with 22 percent of Hispanics, 20 percent of African Americans, and 17 percent of whites. Asian consumers are also the most concerned about keeping up appearances. More than a quarter (26 percent) say they buy what they think their neighbors will approve of, compared with 12 percent each of Hispanics and African Americans and only 10 percent of whites. As one Asian American advertising executive noted, "Prosperous Asians tend to be very status-conscious and will spend their money on premium brands, such as BMW and Mercedes-Benz, and the best French cognac and Scotch whiskey."[80] Advertising with Asian celebrities can be particularly effective. When Reebok used tennis star Michael Chang in one advertisement, shoe sales among Asian Americans soared.

Religious Subcultures

In recent years we've seen an explosion of religion and spirituality in popular culture including the box office success of Mel Gibson's movie *The Passion of the Christ* and the book *The Da Vinci Code*.[82] Mainstream marketers that used to avoid religion like the plague (pardon the pun) now actively court church members.

And, mainstream churches market themselves much more aggressively. In the United States there are approximately 400 **megachurches**; each serves 2,000 or more congregants per week (some actually attract more than 20,000 to Sunday services!) and boast a combined annual income of $1.85 billion.[83] As a church marketing consultant observes, "Baby boomers think of churches like they think of supermarkets. They want options, choices, and convenience. Imagine if Safeway was open only one hour a week, had only one product, and didn't explain it in English."[84] Clearly religion is big business.

You don't have to be active in an organized religion to "worship" products. A study of a brand community centered on the Apple Newton illustrates how religious themes spill over into everyday consumption, particularly in the case of "cult products." Apple abandoned the Newton PDA years ago, but many avid users still keep the faith. The researchers examined postings in chat rooms devoted to the product. They found that many of the messages have supernatural, religious, and magical themes, including the miraculous performance and survival of the brand, as well as the return of the brand creator. The most common postings concerned instances where dead Newton batteries magically come back to life. Here is an excerpt from one story, posted on a listserv under the heading "Another Battery Miracle":

> The battery that came with the 2100 that I just received seemed dead. . . . I figured that the battery was fried and I have nothing to lose. While "charging," I unplugged the adapter until the indicator said it was running on batteries again, and then plugged it back in until it said "charging" . . . after a few times, the battery charge indicator started moving from the left to right and was full within 10 minutes! . . . I've been using the Newt for about 4 hours straight without any problems. Strange. It looks like there has been yet another Newton battery miracle! Keep the faith.[85]

How Religion Influences Consumption

Marketers have not studied religion extensively, possibly because many view it as a taboo subject.[87] As one research director noted, "Religion, along with sex and politics, is one of the three taboo topics that we're never supposed to talk about."[88] Taboo or not, at the least dietary or dress requirements do create demand for certain products. For example, less than a third of the 6 million consumers who buy the 86,000 kosher products now on the market are Jewish. Seventh-Day Adventists and Muslims have very similar dietary requirements, and other people simply believe that kosher food is of higher quality. That's why some of the nation's largest manufacturers like Pepperidge Farm offer a wide range of kosher products.[89]

Mindful of the success of kosher certification, some Muslims recognize that *halal* foods also may appeal to mainstream consumers. The Islamic Food and Nutrition Council of America certifies halal products with a "crescent M," much like the circled "O" of the Orthodox Union, the largest kosher certifier. Both kosher and halal followers forbid pork, and both require similar rituals for butchering meat. Religious Jews don't mix milk and meat, nor do they eat shellfish, whereas religious Muslims don't drink alcohol. Neither group eats birds of prey or blood.[90]

In addition to food products, religious subcultures have an impact on consumer variables such as personality, attitudes toward sexuality, birthrates and household formation, income, and political attitudes. Church leaders can encourage consumption, but more importantly, they can *discourage* it—sometimes with powerful effects. The Disney Corporation discovered how effective these movements can be when the Southern Baptist Convention voted to persuade all its members to boycott its operations.[92] The church instituted its anti-Mickey rebellion to protest the "Gay Days" at the theme parks and a view that Disney had a radical homosexual agenda that it promoted through its broadcasts. Soon other organizations joined the cause, including the American Family Association, the General Council of the Assemblies of God, the Congregational Holiness Church, the Catholic League for Religious and Civil Rights, and the Free Will Baptists. The fallout from the boycott was significant; Disney was forced to lay off 4,000 employees.[93]

Born-Again Consumers

In the United States, we trace most religious marketing activity to Born-Again Christians—they follow literal interpretations of the Bible and acknowledge being born again through belief in Jesus. Theirs is among the fastest-growing religious affiliations in the United States. One research company reported that about 72 million of the 235 million Christians in the United States say they are born-again.[95]

The strength of the evangelical movement has caught the attention of many marketers who want to reach these consumers; marketers involved in faith-based marketing strategies include Pfizer, Merck, Tyson, Smucker's, several major automakers, and even the Curves fitness chain. Suzuki sponsored the Christian rock band Kutless on its national tour to promote its motorcycle and SUV lines.[96]

This growing movement also fuels a boom in Christian-related marketing and merchandise. Christian bookstores bring in revenues of well over $2 billion per year, and the proliferation of born-agains (especially younger evangelicals) propels religiously oriented products into more mainstream stores as vendors update their messages for a younger generation (one T-shirt for sale shows a hand with a nail through it along with the caption, "Body Piercing Saved My Life"). C28, a chain of California stores, takes its names from the Bible verse Colossians 2:8, "See to it that no one takes you captive through hollow and deceptive philosophy, which depends

Kingdom, but people in strongly Catholic Italy and Spain didn't appreciate it at all.

- A Brazilian ad for Pirelli tires drew heat from religious leaders. The ad shows a soccer superstar with his arms spread and a tire tread on the sole of his foot as he stands in place of the Christ the Redeemer statue that overlooks Rio de Janeiro.

- The French car manufacturer Renault withdrew an ad in a Danish campaign in response to protests from the local Catholic community. It depicted a dialogue during confession between a Catholic priest and a repenting man. The man atones for his sins as he prays *Ave Marias* until he confesses to having scratched the paint of the priest's new Renault—then the priest shouts "heathen" and orders the man to pay a substantial penalty to the church.

- Burger King had to modify a commercial it aired on U.S. African American radio stations in which a coffeehouse poet reads an ode to a Whopper with bacon. In the original spot the person's name is Rasheed and he uses a common Islamic greeting. The Council on American–Islamic Relations issued a press release noting that Islam prohibits the consumption of pork products. In the new version the poet was renamed Willie.

The Not of This World clothing line targets young, religious consumers.
Courtesy of Not of This World Clothing.

on human tradition and the basic principles of this world rather than on Christ." C28 has its own house brand, Not of This World, that features modern designs coupled with biblical verses. The owner claims that hundreds of people have converted to Born-Again Christianity in his stores: "Our mission is to share the grace, the truth and the love of Jesus. And what better place to do it than a mall?"[97]

CHAPTER SUMMARY

Now that you have finished reading this chapter you should understand why:

 Additional influences come from our identification with microcultures that reflect a shared interest in some organization or activity.

Microcultures are communities of consumers who participate in or otherwise identify with specific art forms, popular culture movements, and hobbies.

 Our memberships in ethnic, racial, and religious subcultures often play a big role in guiding our consumption behaviors.

Consumers identify with many groups that share common characteristics and identities. Subcultures are large groups that exist within a society, and membership in them often gives marketers a valuable clue about individuals' consumption decisions. A person's ethnic origins, racial identity, and religious background often are major components of his or her identity.

 Many marketing messages appeal to ethnic and racial identity.

The three largest ethnic and racial subcultures are African Americans, Hispanic Americans, and Asian Americans, but marketers today focus on consumers with many diverse backgrounds as well. Indeed, the growing numbers of people who claim multiethnic backgrounds will blur the traditional distinctions we draw among these subcultures.

 African Americans, Hispanic Americans, and Asian Americans are the three most important ethnic/racial subcultures in the United States.

African Americans are a very important market segment. In some respects, the market expenditures of these consumers do not differ that much from whites, but African Americans are above-average consumers in such categories as personal care products.

Hispanic Americans and Asian Americans are other ethnic subcultures that marketers actively court. Both groups are growing rapidly, though numerically Hispanics are the nation's single largest ethnic segment. Asian Americans on the whole are extremely well educated, and the socioeconomic status of Hispanics is increasing as well.

Key issues to reach the Hispanic market are consumers' degree of acculturation into mainstream American society and the recognition of important cultural differences among Hispanic subgroups (e.g., Puerto Ricans, Cubans, and Mexicans).

Both Asian Americans and Hispanic Americans tend to be extremely family oriented and are receptive to advertising that understands their heritage and reinforces traditional family values.

 Marketers increasingly use religious and spiritual themes when they talk to consumers.

The quest for spirituality influences demand in product categories including books, music, and cinema. Although the impact of religious identification on consumer behavior is not clear, some differences among religious subcultures do emerge. Marketers need to consider the sensibilities of believers carefully when they use religious symbolism to appeal to members of different denominations.

KEY TERMS

Acculturation, 496
Acculturation agents, 497
Cosplay, 491
Deethnicization, 492
Ethnic subculture, 491

High-context culture, 492
Host culture, 498
Low-context culture, 492
Megachurches, 504

Microculture, 490
Progressive learning model, 498
Subculture, 490
Warming, 498

REVIEW

1 What is a subculture? How does it differ from a microculture?

2 What is the difference between a high-context and a low-context culture? What is an example of this difference?

3 Why is it difficult to identify consumers in terms of their ethnic subculture membership?

4 What is deethnicization? Give an example.

5 Why are Hispanic American consumers attractive to marketers?

6 What is acculturation? How does it differ from enculturation?

7 Who are acculturation agents? Give two examples.

8 Describe the processes involved when a person assimilates into a new host culture.

9 Why are Asian Americans an attractive market segment? Why can they be difficult for marketers to reach?

10 How can we equate consumers' allegiance to some products as a form of religious observance?

11 How do religious subcultures affect consumption decisions?

CONSUMER BEHAVIOR CHALLENGE

■ DISCUSS

1 Some industry experts feel that it's acceptable to appropriate symbols from another culture even if the buyer does not know their original meaning. They argue that even in the host society there is often disagreement about these meanings. What do you think?

2 The prominence of African American characters in video games that contain violent story lines is all the more striking because of the narrow range of video games in which African Americans have been present over the years. One study found that of 1,500 video game characters surveyed, 288 were African American males, and 83 percent of those were athletes.[98] Do you think this is a problem, and if so how would you address it?

3 Should members of a religious group adapt marketing techniques that manufacturers customarily use to increase market share for their secular products? Why or why not?

4 Several years ago R.J. Reynolds announced plans to test market a menthol cigarette called Uptown specifically to African American consumers. According to the company, about 70 percent of African American smokers prefer menthol, more than twice the average rate. After market research showed that blacks tend to open cigarette packs from the bottom, the company decided to pack Uptowns with the filters facing down. Reynolds cancelled its plans after private health groups and government officials protested. Does a company have the right to exploit a subculture's special characteristics, especially to increase sales of a harmful product such as cigarettes? What about the argument that virtually every business that follows the marketing concept designs a product to meet the needs and tastes of a preselected segment?

5 The Uncle Ben campaign described in the chapter gives an attractive "makeover" to a character many found racist. What do you think of this action?

6 RushmoreDrive.com was touted as the first black search engine, but it shut down only a year after its launch. The idea of a site that would look specifically for black-oriented content and data had been the subject of debate in the blogosphere—some critics felt the site was racist and separatist. On the other hand, an African American marketing executive commented, "An African-American search engine not only helps other African Americans find Black-owned business websites, but it can also aid corporations looking for minority companies to hire." What do you think—should companies develop techniques to allow distinct subcultures to access different parts of the Web?[99]

7 Describe the progressive learning model and discuss why this perspective is important when we market to subcultures.

8 General Motors' GMC division launched an advertising campaign it aimed at the African American market to promote its Sierra Crew Cab and Sierra Denali pickup trucks. Pickup ads almost always show the vehicles doing blue-collar work as they charge down rutted back roads or haul bales of hay or boats. In this campaign, however, the trucks cruise in urban settings with a hip-hop soundtrack. As onlookers turn to admire the pickup, it veers off the road and climbs the vertical face of a skyscraper, leaping into the air at the top before it shoots down the other side.[100] How credible is an advertisement that upends such a strongly held stereotype (i.e., "blue-collar" rural men drive pickups)?

9 The humanitarian group Doctors Without Borders set up a camp of tents, medical stations, and latrines in

Central Park to recreate the setting of a refugee camp.[101] What are the pros and cons of subjecting consumers to degrading experiences like these?

10 Born-Again Christian groups have been instrumental in organizing boycotts of products advertised on shows they find objectionable, especially those that they feel undermine family values. Do religious groups have a right or a responsibility to dictate what advertising a network should carry?

11 Religious symbolism appears in advertising, even though some people object to this practice. For example, a French Volkswagen ad for the relaunch of the Golf showed a modern version of *The Last Supper* with the tagline, "Let us rejoice, my friends, for a new Golf has been born."[102] A group of clergy in France sued the company and the ad was removed from 10,000 billboards. One of the bishops involved in the suit said, "Advertising experts have told us that ads aim for the sacred in order to shock, because using sex does not work anymore." Do you agree? Should religion be used to market products? Do you find this strategy effective or offensive? When and where is this appropriate, if at all?

■ APPLY

1 Locate current examples of marketing stimuli that depend on an ethnic or religious stereotype to communicate a message. How effective are these appeals?

2 To understand the power of ethnic stereotypes, conduct your own poll. For a set of ethnic groups, ask people to anonymously provide attributes (including personality traits and products) most likely to characterize each group, using the technique of free association where they simply say what comes to mind when you mention each group. How much agreement do you obtain across respondents? To what extent do the characteristics derive from or reflect negative stereotypes? Compare the associations for an ethnic group between actual members of that group and nonmembers.

3 Locate one or more consumers (perhaps family members) who have emigrated from another country. Interview them about how they adapted to their host culture. In particular, what changes did they make in their consumption practices over time?

Case Study

I'M A PC!

What do age, ethnicity, and lifestyle have to do with personal computer choices? Quite a bit if you watched Apple's advertising for the past several years. You probably know the ads well: "Hi, I'm a Mac . . . and I'm a PC." Two white men in front of a white screen—stereotypes of the computer manufacturer's users and their corporate culture. The Mac guy is young, good-looking, smart, and very cool. Then there's PC, who is chunkier, a little dopey, and dressed in a very uncool business suit. The series of ads, currently over 50 of them, have been wildly successful and have helped to advance Apple to double-digit market share in the home personal computer market.

Microsoft ran some scattered advertising throughout this period, but nothing strong and unified. Then, in 2008, the software giant teamed up with Crispin, Porter + Bogusky with a reported $300 million budget for advertising. The first ads to hit the airwaves featured famous comedian Jerry Seinfeld and Microsoft CEO and founder Bill Gates. In one quirky spot Gates shopped for shoes as Seinfeld accompanied him with clever, Seinfeld-type comments. The ads were poorly received by critics and audiences alike.

The ads stopped running and were replaced by the campaign "Pride," which is commonly referred to as the "I'm a PC" campaign. The first ad begins with an actual Microsoft employee who stands against a white background that mimics the nerdy, white, male stereotype of the PC user the Mac ads depict. He announces, "Hello, I'm a PC. And I've been made into a stereotype." The ad then showcases a variety of people who state they are a PC. The spot features people of different ethnicities, professional interests, and lifestyles throughout the world. The ad ends with mind-body guru Deepak Chopra who states, "I'm a PC and I am a human being. Not a human doing. Not a human thinking. A human being."

One of the main purposes of the ad was to shatter the stereotype of the PC user and to show that PC users cross all ethnic, geographical, age, and lifestyle boundaries. According to Microsoft, the campaign is about ". . . celebrating the individuality within the global Windows community and the pride we have in our own unique passions—and how technology can help us further these interests." To further the message, Microsoft partnered with the social media advertising network Brickfish to create a microsite where consumers can post photos and videos that express their individuality.

Has Microsoft slowed the rapid growth of Apple? According to the research firm NPD, February 2009 U.S. retail sales of Windows PCs grew 22 percent while sales of Macs dropped 16 percent in the same period. There are other factors in play in addition to the advertising. Product choices are changing as new PC-based Netbooks expand within the market. Also updates to the Microsoft operating systems Vista and Windows may have led to increases in PC purchases. But one thing can be said for sure, the face of the PC consumer has certainly changed from the PC guy of the Apple ads.

DISCUSSION QUESTIONS

1 Can we consider avid computer users as a subculture? If so, how can marketers incorporate this bond in their messaging strategies?

2 Was stereotyping effective in the Apple ads? Did they stereotype ethnic or racial groups?

Sources: Daniel Lyons, "I'm a PC. Keep the Change," *Newsweek*, (April 13, 2009); Anonymous, "I'm a PC Campaign Goes Viral with Brickfish," *Business Wire* (December 8, 2008); Peter Burrows, "How Microsft Is Fighting Back (Finally)," *BusinessWeek* (April 20, 2009): 63.

NOTES

1. Jaime Mejia and Gabriel Sama, "Media Players Say 'Si' to Latino Magazines," *Wall Street Journal* (May 15, 2002), www.wsj.com, accessed May 15, 2002.

2. www.bullz-eye.com/cars/tuner_cars.htm, accessed June 18, 2009; Brian Steinberg, "Pioneer's Hot-Rod Ads Too Cool for Mainstream," *Wall Street Journal* (March 14, 2003), www.wsj.com, accessed March 14, 2003; Mireya Navarro, "Advertisers Carve Out a New Segment," *New York Times* (May 22, 2003), www.nytimes.com, accessed May 22, 2003.

3. www.geocities.com/micronations, accessed July 24, 2007; Alex Blumberg, "It's Good to Be King," *Wired* (March 2000): 132–49; http://kingdomoftalossa.net, accessed June 18, 2009; www.freedonia.org, accessed June 18, 2009; www.new-utopia.com, accessed June 18, 2009.

4. www.redneckbank.com, accessed June 18, 2009.

5. Russell W. Belk and Janeen Arnold Costa, "The Mountain Man Myth: A Contemporary Consuming Fantasy," *Journal of Consumer Research* 25 (1998): 218–40.

6. Robert V. Kozinets, "Utopian Enterprise: Articulating the Meanings of *Star Trek*'s Culture of Consumption," *Journal of Consumer Research* 28 (June 2001): 74.

7. "Cosplay," Wikipedia.org, http://en.wikipedia.org/wiki/Cosplay, accessed June 18, 2009; www.cosplay.com, accessed June 18, 2009; www.acparadise.com, accessed June 18, 2009; Lisa Katayama, "Anatomy of a Nerd; Japanese Schoolgirl Watch," *Wired* (March 2006), www.wired.com/wired/archive/14.03/play.html?pg=3, accessed October 6, 2007.

8. See Frederik Barth, *Ethnic Groups and Boundaries: The Social Organization of Culture Difference* (London: Allen and Unwin, 1969); Janeen A. Costa and Gary J. Bamossy, "Perspectives on Ethnicity, Nationalism, and Cultural Identity," in J. A. Costa and G. J. Bamossy, eds., *Marketing in a Multicultural World: Ethnicity, Nationalism, and Cultural Identity* (Thousand Oaks, CA: Sage, 1995): 3–26; Michel Laroche, Annamma Joy, Michael Hui, and Chankon Kim, "An Examination of Ethnicity Measures: Convergent Validity and Cross-Cultural Equivalence," in Rebecca H. Holman and Michael R. Solomon, eds., *Advances in Consumer Research* 18 (Provo, Utah: Association for Consumer Research, 1991): 150–57; Melanie Wallendorf and Michael Reilly, "Ethnic Migration, Assimilation, and Consumption," *Journal of Consumer Research* 10 (December 1983): 292–302; Milton J. Yinger, "Ethnicity," *Annual Review of Sociology* 11 (1985): 151–80.

9. D'Vera Cohn, "2100 Census Forecast: Minorities Expected to Account for 60% of U.S. Population," *Washington Post* (January 13, 2000): A5.

10. Sam Roberts, "In a Generation, Minorities May Be the U.S. Majority," *New York Times* (August 13, 2008), www.nytimes.com/2008/08/14/Washington/14census.Html?_R=1&Hp=&Adxnnl=1&Or . . . , accessed August 14, 2008.

11. Brian Sternberg, "P&G Brushes Up Iconic Image of 'Crest Kid' in New Campaign," *Wall Street Journal* (March 29, 2005), www.wsj.com, accessed March 29, 2005.

12. Pui-Wing Tam, "The Growth in Ethnic Media Usage Poses Important Business Decisions," *Wall Street Journal* (April 23, 2002), www.wsj.com, accessed April 23, 2002.

13. Steve Rabin, "How to Sell Across Cultures," *American Demographics* (March 1994): 56–57.

14. Rohit Deshpandé and Douglas M. Stayman, "A Tale of Two Cities: Distinctiveness Theory and Advertising Effectiveness," *Journal of Marketing Research* 31 (February 1994): 57–64.

15. Warren Brown, "The Potholes of Multicultural Marketing," *Washington Post* (June 10, 2007): G2.

16. Sonya A. Grier and Anne Brumbaugh, "Compared To Whom? The Impact of Status on Third Person Effects in Advertising Persuasion in a South African Context," *Journal of Consumer Behavior* 6, no. 1 (February 2007): 5–18; Sonya A. Grier, Anne Brumbaugh, and C. Thornton "Crossover Dreams: Consumer Responses to Ethnic-Oriented Products," *Journal of Marketing* 70, no. 2 (April 2006): 35–51; Sonya A. Grier and Rohit Deshpandé, "Social Dimensions of Consumer Distinctiveness: The Influence of Social Status on Group Identity and Advertising Persuasion," *Journal of Marketing Research* 38 (May 2001): 216–24; Jennifer A. Aaker, Anne Brumbaugh, and Sony A. Grier, "Non-Target Market Effects and Viewer Distinctiveness: The Impact of Target Marketing on Attitudes," *Journal of Consumer Psychology* 9, no. 3 (2000): 127–40; Sony A. Grier and Anne Brumbaugh, "Noticing Cultural Differences: Advertising Meanings Created by the Target and Non-Target Markets," *Journal of Advertising* 28, no. 1 (Spring 1999): 79–93.

17. Sony A. Grier and S. K. Kumanyika, "The Context for Choice: Health Implications of Targeted Food and Beverage Marketing to African Americans," *American Journal of Public Health* 98, no. 9 (September 2008): 1616–29.

18. J. Raymond, "The Multicultural Report," *American Demographics* (November 2001): S3, S4, S6.

19. Ibid.

20. Eils Lotozo, "The Jalapeño Bagel and Other Artifacts," *New York Times* (June 26, 1990): C1.

21. Dana Canedy, "The Shmeering of America," *New York Times* (December 26, 1996): D1.

22. Peter Schrag, *The Decline of the WASP* (New York: Simon & Schuster, 1971): 20.

23. "Nation's European Identity Falls by the Wayside," *Montgomery Advertiser* (June 8, 2002): A5.

24. Stuart Elliott, "An Ad with Talking Pandas, Maybe, but Not with Chinese Accents," *New York Times* (February 6, 2008), www.nytimes.com/2008/02/06/Business/Media/06adco.Html?Scp=1&Sq=Salesgenie&S . . . , accessed February 6, 2008.

25. Michel Marriott, "The Color of Mayhem, in a Wave of 'Urban' Games," *New York Times* (August 12, 2004), www.nytimes.com, accessed August 12, 2004.

26. Marty Westerman, "Death of the Frito Bandito," *American Demographics* (March 1989): 28.

27. Stuart Elliott, "Uncle Ben, Board Chairman," *New York Times* (March 30, 2007), www.nytimes.com, accessed March 30, 2007.

28. www.unclebens.com, accessed June 18, 2009.

29. See Lisa Peñaloza, "Atravesando Fronteras/Border Crossings: A Critical Ethnographic Exploration of the Consumer Acculturation of

Mexican Immigrants," *Journal of Consumer Research* 21 (June 1994): 32–54; Lisa Peñaloza and Mary C. Gilly, "Marketer Acculturation: The Changer and the Changed," *Journal of Marketing* 63 (July 1999): 84–104; Carol Kaufman-Scarborough, "Eat Bitter Food and Give Birth to a Girl; Eat Sweet Things and Give Birth to a Cavalryman: Multicultural Health Care Issues for Consumer Behavior," *Advances in Consumer Research* 32, no.1 (2005): 226–69; Søren Askegaard, Eric J. Arnould, and Dannie Kjeldgaard, "Postassimilationist Ethnic Consumer Research: Qualifications and Extensions," *Journal of Consumer Research* 32, no. 1 (2005): 160.

30. Stuart Elliott, "1,200 Marketers Can't Be Wrong: The Future Is in Consumer Behavior," *New York Times* (October 15, 2007), www.nytimes.com, accessed October 15, 2007.

31. Peñaloza, "Atravesando Fronteras/Border Crossings."

32. Shuili Du, Sankar Sen and C. B. Bhattacharya. "Exploring the Social and Business Returns of a Corporate Oral Health Initiative Aimed at Disadvantaged Hispanic Families," *Journal of Consumer Research* 35 (October 2008): 483–94.

33. Andrew Adam Newman, "Nike Adds Indian Artifacts to Its Swoosh," *New York Times* (October 3, 2007), www.nytimes.com, accessed October 3, 2007.

34. Wallendorf and Reilly, "Ethnic Migration, Assimilation, and Consumption."

35. Ronald J. Faber, Thomas C. O'Guinn, and John A. McCarty, "Ethnicity, Acculturation and the Importance of Product Attributes," *Psychology & Marketing* 4 (Summer 1987): 121–34; Humberto Valencia, "Developing an Index to Measure Hispanicness," in Elizabeth C. Hirschman and Morris B. Holbrook, eds., *Advances in Consumer Research* 12 (Provo, Utah: Association for Consumer Research, 1985): 118–21.

36. Rohit Deshpandé, Wayne D. Hoyer, and Naveen Donthu, "The Intensity of Ethnic Affiliation: A Study of the Sociology of Hispanic Consumption," *Journal of Consumer Research* 13 (September 1986): 214–20.

37. Güliz Ger, "Warming: Making the New Familiar and Moral," *Journal of European Ethnology* (special issue of the journal *Ethnologia Europea*), Richard Wilk and Orvar Lofgren, eds. (forthcoming).

38. Elisabeth Kriechbaum-Vitellozzi and Robert Kreuzbauer, "Poverty Consumption: Consumer Behavior of Refugees in Industrialized Countries," *Advances in Consumer Research* 33, no. 1 (2006); cf. also L. Wamwara-Mbugua, T. Wakiuru, Bettina Cornwell, and Gregory Boller, "Triple Acculturation: The Role of African Americans in the Consumer Acculturation of Kenyan Immigrants," *Advances in Consumer Research* 33, no. 1 (2006).

39. U.S. Census Bureau, *Census 2000 Brief: Overview of Race and Hispanic Origin* (U.S. Department of Commerce, Economics and Statistics Administration, March 2001).

40. Robert Pear, "New Look at the U.S. in 2050: Bigger, Older and Less White," *New York Times* (December 4, 1992): A1.

41. Brian Stelter, "Product Placements, Deftly Woven into the Story Line," *New York Times* (March 1, 2009), www.nytimes.com, accessed March 1, 2009; Quoted in Teri Agins, "'Diddy' Fragrance Targets Obama Supporters," *Wall Street Journal* (November 13, 2008), http://online.wsj.com/article/sb122652922965222247.html, accessed November 13, 2008.

42. U.S. Census Bureau, *Census 2000 Brief: Overview of Race and Hispanic Origin.*

43. William O'Hare, "Blacks and Whites: One Market or Two?" *American Demographics* (March 1987): 44–48.

44. For an article that examines the impact of political ideologies on the African American community, cf. David Crockett and Melanie Wallendorf, "The Role of Normative Political Ideology in Consumer Behavior," *Journal of Consumer Research* 31 (December 2004): 511–28.

45. For studies on racial differences in consumption, see Robert E. Pitts, D. Joel Whalen, Robert O'Keefe, and Vernon Murray, "Black and White Response to Culturally Targeted Television Commercials: A Values-Based Approach," *Psychology & Marketing* 6 (Winter 1989): 311–28; Melvin T. Stith and Ronald E. Goldsmith, "Race, Sex, and Fashion Innovativeness: A Replication," *Psychology & Marketing* 6 (Winter 1989): 249–62.

46. www.myblackisbeautiful.com, accessed June 18, 2009; Karl Greenberg, "P&G Borrows 'Black Power' Phrase for Campaign," *Marketing Daily,* (August 10, 2007), www.mediapost.com, accessed August 10, 2007.

47. Quoted in Brooks Barnes, "Her Prince Has Come. Critics, Too," *New York Times* (May 31, 2009), www.nytimes.com/2009/05/31/fashion/31disney.html?_r=1&scp=, accessed May 31, 2009.

48. Bob Jones, "Black Gold," *Entrepreneur* (July 1994): 62–65.

49. Jean Halliday, "Volvo to Buckle Up African-Americans," *Advertising Age* (February 14, 2000): 28.

50. www.skinvoice.com, accessed June 18, 2009; Sarah Mahoney, "Unilever Finds Skin Takes on Deep Meaning Among Black Women," *Marketing Daily* (May 23, 2007), www.mediapost.com, accessed May 23, 2007.

51. Duff Wilson, "Congress Passes Measure on Tobacco Regulation," *New York Times* (June 12, 2009), www.nytimes.com/2009/06/13/business/13tobacco.html, accessed June 18, 2009; Stephanie Saul, "Cigarette Bill Treats Menthol with Leniency," *New York Times* (May 13, 2008), www.nytimes.com/2008/05/13/Business/13menthol.Html?_R=1&Oref=Slogin, accessed May 13, 2008.

52. Jonathan Birchall, "Wal-Mart looks to Hispanic Market," *Financial Times* (March 12 2009), www.ft.com/cms/s/0/bd371350-0f2c-11de-ba10-0000779fd2ac,dwp_uuid=02e16f4a-46f9-11da-b8e5-00000e2511c8.html?nclick_check=1, accessed March 12, 2009.

53. "Can't Fight Blade Runner Branded, Cities Are the Future," *NBC News* (February 2, 2009), http://nbclosangeles.com, accessed February 2, 2009.

54. Joe Schwartz, "Hispanic Opportunities," *American Demographics* (May 1987): 56–59.

55. Naveen Donthu and Joseph Cherian, "Impact of Strength of Ethnic Identification on Hispanic Shopping Behavior," *Journal of Retailing* 70, no. 4 (1994): 383–93. For another study that compared shopping behavior and ethnicity influences among six ethnic groups, see Joel Herce and Siva Balasubramanian, "Ethnicity and Shopping Behavior," *Journal of Shopping Center Research* 1 (Fall 1994): 65–80.

56. Amy Cortese, "At the Mall, Mariachi Instead of Muzak," *New York Times* (May 20, 2007), www.nytimes.com, accessed May 20, 2007.

57. Sigfredo A. Hernandez and Carol J. Kaufman, "Marketing Research in Hispanic Barrios: A Guide to Survey Research," *Marketing Research* (March 1990): 11–27.

58. "Dispel Myths Before Trying to Penetrate Hispanic Market," *Marketing News* (April 16, 1982): 1.

59. Schwartz, "Hispanic Opportunities."

60. Erik Sass, "Long-Term Hispanic Trend: Spanish Less Important in Future?" *Marketing Daily* (May 23, 2007), www.mediapost.com, accessed May 23, 2007; Stephanie Kang, "Pitches to Hispanics Get More Nuanced, Ads Incorporate English, Cultural Cues to Reach Children of Immigrants," *Wall Street Journal* (January 8, 2008), http://online.wsj.com/article/sb119976266747873953.html?mod=mm_hs_advertising; accessed January 8, 2008.

61. Schwartz, "Hispanic Opportunities."

62. "Macy's Yanks T-Shirt in Georgia and Texas," *Marketing Daily* (July 25, 2007), www.mediapost.com, accessed July 25, 2007.

63. Miriam Jordan, "VW Rethinks Its High-Testosterone Ads," *Wall Street Journal* (March 17, 2006): B1.

64. Jack Neff, "Unilever Launches Major Hispanic-Aimed Marketing Program *ViveMejor* Brings Together All Food, Personal-Care Brands," *Advertising Age* (May 21, 2007), accessed May 21, 2007.

65. Rick Wartzman, "When You Translate 'Got Milk' for Latinos, What Do You Get?" *Wall Street Journal* (June 3, 1999), www.wsj.com, accessed June 3, 1999.

66. Gabriel Sama, "Appeal of Clamato Isn't Just Its Taste," *Wall Street Journal* (October 23, 2003), www.wsj.com, accessed October 23, 2003.

67. Wartzman, "When You Translate 'Got Milk' for Latinos, What Do You Get?"

68. Cheryl Russell, *Racial Ethnic Diversity: Asians, Blacks, Hispanics, Native Americans, and Whites,* 2nd ed. (Ithaca, NY: American Demographics, 1998).

69. Beth Enslow, "General Mills: Baking New Ground," *Forecast* (November–December 1993): 18; Lindsay Gordon, "Kellogg Adds Honey to Target Hispanics," *Brandweek* (June 18, 2009), www.brandweek.com/bw/content_display/news-and-features/direct/e3i6c3a49109c5609b6e4d10fbf0f59689d, accessed June 18, 2009.

70. Rebecca Gardyn and John Fetto, "Race, Ethnicity and the Way We Shop," *American Demographics* (February 2003): 30–33.

71. Westerman, "Death of the Frito Bandito."

72. Stacy Vollmers and Ronald E. Goldsmith, "Hispanic-American Consumers and Ethnic Marketing," *Proceedings of the Atlantic Marketing Association* (1993): 46–50.

73. Karl Greenberg, "Hispanics' Web Savvy Surpassing Others," *Marketing Daily* (March 25, 2009), www.mediapost.com, accessed March 25, 2009.

74. Dan Fost, "Asian Homebuyers Seek Wind and Water," *American Demographics* (June 1993): 23–25.

75. Marty Westerman, "Fare East: Targeting the Asian-American Market," *Prepared Foods* (January 1989): 48–51; Eleanor Yu, "Asian-American Market Often Misunderstood," *Marketing News* (December 4, 1989): 11.

76. "Made in Japan," *American Demographics* (November 2002): 48.

77. Hassan Fattah, "Asia Rising," *American Demographics* (July–August 2002), www.findarticles.com/p/articles/mi_m4021/is_2002_July_1/ai89374125, accessed October 6, 2007.

78. For a recent discussion of Asian identity, cf. Julien Cayla and Giana M. Eckhardt, "Asian Brands and the Shaping of a Transnational Imagined Community," *Journal of Consumer Research* 35 (August 2008): 216–30.

79. Pui-Wing Tam, "Mandarin Pop Is Looking to Penetrate U.S. Markets," *Wall Street Journal* (March 31, 2000); http://us.yesasia.com, accessed June 18, 2009; www.rockacola.com, accessed June 18, 2009.

80. Donald Dougherty, "The Orient Express," *The Marketer* (July/August 1990): 14.

81. Aaron Baar, "Nationwide Targets South Asians with 'Idol' Contestant Sanjaya," *Marketing Daily* (May 29, 2008), www.mediapost.com, accessed May 29, 2008.

82. Dan Brown, *The Da Vinci Code* (New York: Doubleday, 2003).

83. Patricia Leigh Brown, "Megachurches as Minitowns: Full-Service Havens from Family Stress Compete with Communities," *New York Times* (May 9, 2002): D1; Edward Gilbreath, "The New Capital of Evangelicalism: Move Over, Wheaton and Colorado Springs—Dallas, Texas, Has More Megachurches, Megaseminaries, and Mega-Christian Activity Than Any Other American City," *Christianity Today* (May 21, 2002): 38; Tim W. Ferguson, "Spiritual Reality: Mainstream Media Are Awakening to the Avid and Expanding Interest in Religion in the U.S.," *Forbes* (January 27, 1997): 70.

84. Richard Cimino and Don Lattin, *Shopping for Faith: American Religion in the New Millennium* (New York: Jossey-Bass, 2002).

85. Albert M. Muñiz Jr. and Hope Jensen Schau, "Religiosity in the Abandoned Apple Newton Brand Community," *Journal of Consumer Research* 31 (March 2005): 737–47.

86. Cathy Grossman, "Faithful Build a Second Life for Religion Online," *USA Today* (April 3, 2007), www.usatoday.com, accessed April 3, 2007; Lillian Kwon, "Christians Bring Jesus into Virtual 'Second Life,'" *Christian Post* (April 5, 2007), www.christianpost.com/pages/print.htm?aid=26727, accessed April 5, 2007.

87. For a couple of exceptions, see Michael J. Dotson and Eva M. Hyatt, "Religious Symbols as Peripheral Cues in Advertising: A Replication of the Elaboration Likelihood Model," *Journal of Business Research* 48 (2000): 63–68; Elizabeth C. Hirschman, "Religious Affiliation and Consumption Processes: An Initial Paradigm," *Research in Marketing* (Greenwich, CT: JAI Press, 1983): 131–70.

88. Quoted in Joe Mandese, "MindShare Turns SoulShare, Puts Faith in Evangelicals," *Media Daily News* (May 15, 2008), http://publications.mediapost.com/index.cfm?fuseaction=Articles.showArticle&art_aid=82 . . . , accessed May 15, 2008.

89. Yochi Dreazen, "Kosher-Food Marketers Aim More Messages at Non-Jews," *Wall Street Journal* (July 30, 1999), www.wsj.com, accessed July 30, 1999.

90. Barry Newman, "Halal Meets Kosher in Health-Food Aisle," *Wall Street Journal* (May 5, 2006): B1; Louise Story, "Rewriting the Ad for Muslim-Americans," *New York Times Online* (April 28, 2007), www.nytimes.com, accessed April 28, 2007.

91. Nina M. Lentini, "Dunkin' Donuts Pulls Rachael Ray Spot," *Marketing Daily* (May 29, 2008), www.mediapost.com, accessed May 29, 2008.

92. www.religioustolerance.org/new1_966.htm, accessed October 6, 2007; www.erlc.com/WhoSBC/Resolutions/1997/97Disney.htm, accessed October 6, 2007.

93. Alex Johnson, "Southern Baptists End 8-year Disney Boycott," *MSNBC* (June 22, 2005), www.msnbc.com, accessed October 6, 2007.

94. Jack Neff, "Dip Ad Stirs Church Ire," *Advertising Age* (July 2, 2001): 8; G. Burton, "Oh, My Heck! Beer Billboard Gets the Boot," *Salt Lake Tribune* (November 6, 2001); "Religion Reshapes Realities for U.S. Restaurants in Middle East," *Nation's Restaurant News* 32 (February 16, 1998); Sarah Ellison, "Sexy-Ad Reel Shows what Tickles in Tokyo Can Fade Fast in France," *Wall Street Journal* (March 31, 2000), www.wsj.com, accessed March 31, 2000; Claudia Penteado, "Brazilian Ad Irks Church," *Advertising Age* (March 23, 2000): 11; "Burger King Will Alter Ad That Has Offended Muslims," *Wall Street Journal* (March 15, 2000), www.wsj.com, accessed March 15, 2000.

95. Michael Fielding, "The Halo," *Marketing News* (February 1, 2005): 18–20.

96. Joe Mandese, "MindShare Turns SoulShare, Puts Faith in Evangelicals," *Media Daily News* (May 15, 2008), http://publications.mediapost.com/index.cfm?fuseaction=Articles.showArticle&art_aid=82 . . . , accessed May 15, 2008; Karlene Lukovitz, "Evangelicals More Diverse Than Might Be Assumed," *Marketing Daily* (November 7, 2007), http://publications.mediapost.com/index.cfm?fuseaction=Articles.san&s=70553& . . . , accessed November 7, 2007.

97. Rob Walker, "Cross Selling," *New York Times Magazine* (March 6, 2005), www.nytimes.com, accessed March 6, 20005; John Leland, "At Festivals, Faith, Rock and T-Shirts Take Center Stage," *New York Times* (July 5, 2004), www.nytimes.com, accessed July 5, 2004.

98. Michel Marriott, "The Color of Mayhem, in a Wave of 'Urban' Games," *New York Times* (August 12, 2004), www.nytimes.com, accessed August 12, 2004.

99. Quoted in Pepper Miller and John Parikhal, "Do African-Americans Need a Separate Search Engine?" *Advertising Age* (June 25, 2009), www.adage.com, accessed June 26, 2009.

100. Karl Greenberg, "GM Truck Ads Aim at Urban African-American Market," *Marketing Daily* (May 25, 2007), www.mediapost.com, accessed May 25, 2007.

101. Patrick O'Gilfoil Healy, "Heads Up Hidalgo, Mexico: Run! Hide! The Illegal Border Crossing Experience."

102. Penteado, "Brazilian Ad Irks Church."

14 Age Subcultures

*I*t's the last week of summer vacation and Kurt can't wait to get back to school. It's been a tough summer. Nobody's hiring students for summer jobs (even the worst minimum wage gigs attract several hundred applicants). He seems to be out of touch with his old friends—and with so much time on his hands as he just hangs around the house, he and his mother don't get along too well. Kurt plops on the couch and aimlessly flips channels—from *The Real Housewives of New Jersey* to *Avatar* on Nickelodeon, to a Sony-sponsored beach volleyball tournament on ESPN, back to Bravo. Suddenly, his mother marches in, grabs the remote, and switches the channel to public television. To promote the hype about the 40th anniversary of Woodstock, yet another documentary chronicles the original festival from 1969. When Kurt protests, "Come on Pam, get a life. . . ." his mom snaps back, "Keep your cool. You might learn what it was like to be in college when it really meant something. And what's with the first name stuff? In my day I would never have dreamed of calling my mom or dad by their first name!"

That's when Kurt loses it. He's tired of hearing about the "good old days" of Woodstock, Berkeley, and 20 other places he doesn't care about. Besides, most of his mom's ex-hippie friends who still have jobs work for the very corporations they used to protest about—who are they to preach to him about doing something meaningful with his life? In disgust, Kurt storms into his room, cranks up Korn on his iPod, and pulls the covers up over his head. So much for a constructive use of time. What's the difference, anyway—they'll probably all be dead from global warming by the time he graduates.

OBJECTIVE

Why do people have many things in common with others because they are about the same age?

Age and Consumer Identity

The era in which you grow up bonds you with the millions of others who come of age during the same time period. Obviously, your needs and preferences change as you grow older, often in concert with others of your own age (even though some of us don't really believe we'll ever get older). For this reason, our age is a big part of our identity. All things equal, we are more likely to have things in common with others of our own age than with those younger or older. As Kurt found out, this identity may become even stronger when the actions and goals of one generation conflict with those of others—an age-old battle.

A marketer needs to communicate with members of an age group in their own language. Sony finally figured out that it had to sponsor events like beach volleyball to get young people's attention. When the electronics giant first entered the U.S. car stereo market, it hammered on its usual themes of technical prowess and quality. This got nothing but yawns from the 16- to 24-year-olds who make up half of the consumers who buy these products, and Sony ranked a pitiful seventh in the market after 10 years. Finally, the company got the picture—it totally revamped its approach and eventually doubled its car stereo revenues.[1]

This successful campaign was part of Sony's strategic decision to reorganize its electronics division according to consumers' different life stages. Instead of assigning managers to products, the company groups them in age-related segments such as Gen Y (younger than age 25), young professionals/DINKs (double income no kids, aged 25 to 34), families (35- to 54-year-olds), and zoomers (those older than age 55).[2] In this chapter, we'll explore some of the important characteristics of some key age groups and consider how marketers like Sony modify their strategies to appeal to diverse age subcultures.

An **age cohort** consists of people of similar ages who have similar experiences. They share many common memories about cultural heroes (e.g., John Wayne versus Brad Pitt), important historical events (e.g., the Great Depression versus the Great Recession), and so on. Although there is no universally accepted way to divide up people into age cohorts, each of us seems to have a pretty good idea what we mean when we refer to "my generation."

Marketers often target products and services to a specific age cohort; our possessions help us identify with others of a certain age and express the priorities and needs we encounter at each life stage.[3] An ad campaign for Saturn featured a set of commercials that represent stages in life from childhood and high school to college and marriage. As four friends drive around in the Saturn Ion, they see kids playing on swing sets, students on prom night, partying fraternity members, and young marrieds in tuxedos and wedding gowns. The campaign communicates the idea that the car takes its owner through each life stage.[4]

Although there is general consensus when analysts describe age cohorts, the labels and cutoff dates they use to put consumers into generational categories are subjective. One rough approximation looks like this:[5]

● **The Interbellum Generation**—People born at the beginning of the twentieth century.
● **The Silent Generation**—People born between the two World Wars.
● **The War Baby Generation**—People born during World War II.
● **The Baby Boom Generation**—People born between 1946–1964.
● **Generation X**—People born between 1965–1985.
● **Generation Y**—People born between 1986–2002.
● **Generation Z**—People born 2003 and later.

The same offering probably won't appeal to people of different ages, nor will the language and images marketers use to reach them. In some cases companies develop separate campaigns for age cohorts. For example, Norelco found that younger men are far less likely to use electric shavers than are its core customer base of older men. The firm launched a two-pronged effort, on the one hand, to convince younger men to switch from wet shaving to electric, and on the other hand, to maintain loyalty among its older following. Ads for Norelco's Speedrazor, aimed at males 18 to 35 years old, ran on late-night TV and in *GQ* and *Details*. Messages about the company's triple-head razors, geared to men older than 35, ran instead in publications that attract older readers, such as *Time* and *Newsweek*.

Because consumers within an age group confront crucial life changes at roughly the same time, the values and symbolism marketers use to appeal to them can evoke powerful feelings of *nostalgia* (see Chapter 3). Adults older than 30 are particularly susceptible to this phenomenon.[7] However, references to the past influence young people as well as old. In fact, research indicates that some people are more disposed to be nostalgic than others, regardless of age. Table 14.1 shows a scale researchers use to measure the impact of nostalgia on individual consumers.

Although most products appeal to one age cohort or another, some marketers try to woo people of different ages with a **multigenerational marketing strategy**— this means they use imagery that appeals to consumers from more than one generation. These companies recognize that older baby boomers (more on these guys later) have a youthful attitude and many are quite comfortable with new technology. However, a lot of young people are very sophisticated consumers who don't want companies to talk down to them.

When Honda launched its boxy Element SUV, it was going after young men— but to the company's surprise a lot of middle-aged women also bought the vehicle. Based on that experience, Honda deliberately targeted two age groups at once with its Fit subcompact. It places ads in youth-oriented niche publications such as *Filter* music magazine while it runs others in *Time*. TV commercials include cartoon characters, such as a "speedy demon" monster, that appeal to youth but also resemble creatures you might find in 1970s comic books. Similarly, the Scion tC screams youth—but in reality its buyers' median age is 49. It turns out people in their 50s and 60s like the car's low floor height because it's easy to step into!

In one interesting crossover experiment, *DUB* magazine (which targets Tuner car fanatics like the ones we discussed in the last chapter) pimped out a few Buick Lucernes. Although the average age of the Buick buyer is 65, the cars took on a whole new image when they hit the road with tinted windows and 22-inch chrome wheels. Buick parks the cars outside nightclubs to attract younger drivers. So why did *DUB* initiate this partnership? It turns out that the model is popular among young African Americans in the Oakland area who customize it to make "scrapers." These tricked-out rides feature wheels so big the tires scrape the inside of the car's fender.[8]

TABLE 14.1	The Nostalgia Scale
Scale Items	

They don't make 'em like they used to.
Things used to be better in the good old days.
Products are getting shoddier and shoddier
Technological change will ensure a brighter future (reverse coded).
History involves a steady improvement in human welfare (reverse coded).
We are experiencing a decline in the quality of life.
Steady growth in GNP has brought increased human happiness (reverse coded).
Modern business constantly builds a better tomorrow (reverse coded).

Morris B. Holbrook and Robert M. Schindler, "Age, Sex, and Attitude toward the Past as Predictors of Consumers' Aesthetic Tastes for Cultural Products," *Journal of Marketing Research* 31 (August 1994): 416. Copyright © 1994 American Marketing Association. Reprinted by permission of the *Journal of Marketing Research*. Published by the American Marketing Association.

Note: Items are presented on a nine-point scale ranging from strong disagreement (1) to strong agreement (9), and responses are summed.

The Youth Market

OBJECTIVE

Why are teens an important age segment for marketers?

In 1956, the label *teenage* entered the general American vocabulary when Frankie Lymon and the Teenagers became the first pop group to identify themselves with this new subculture. Believe it or not, the concept of a teenager is a fairly new idea. Throughout most of history a person simply made the transition from child to adult, and many cultures marked this abrupt change in status with some sort of ritual or ceremony, as we'll see in the next chapter.

The magazine *Seventeen* first published in 1944; its founders realized that modern young women didn't want to be little clones of Mom. Following World War II, the teenage conflict between rebellion and conformity began to unfold as teen culture pitted Elvis Presley with his slicked hair and suggestive pelvis swivels against the wholesome Pat Boone with his white bucks (see Figure 14.1). Today, this rebellion continues to play out as pubescent consumers forsake their Barbies for the likes of Paris Hilton, Lindsay Lohan (when they're not in jail or rehab), Nick Jonas, or the teen heartthrob *du jour*.[9]

The global youth market is massive. It represents about $100 billion in spending power! Much of this money goes toward "feel-good" products: cosmetics, posters, and fast food—with the occasional nose ring thrown in. Because teens are interested in so many different products and have the resources to obtain them, many marketers avidly court them.

A major reason for the overwhelming size and future potential of this market is simple: Because of high birthrates (see Chapter 12) in many countries, a large proportion of the population is very young. For example, consider that while 21 percent of U.S. residents are 14 or younger, these are the corresponding percentages in some other countries:[10]

- China: 25 percent
- Argentina: 27 percent
- Brazil: 29 percent
- India: 33 percent
- Iran: 33 percent
- Malaysia: 35 percent
- Philippines: 37 percent

Figure 14.1 THE U.S. TEEN POPULATION

U.S. RESIDENT POPULATION, 13 TO 19 YEARS OLD, 1950–2010

The '50s
1950
14.93
Million

The '60s

The '70s
1976
29.85
Million

The '80s
1991
24.01
Million

The '90s

THE YEARS
2000 TO 2010
2010
30.81
Million

Teen Values, Conflicts, and Desires

As anyone who has been there knows, puberty and adolescence is both the best of times and the worst of times. Many exciting changes happen as we leave the role of child and prepare to assume the role of adult. These transitions create a lot of uncertainty about the self, and the need to belong and to find one's unique identity as a person becomes pressing. At this age, our choices of activities, friends, and clothes are crucial. Teens constantly search for cues for the "right" way to look and behave from their peers and from advertising. Advertising to teens is typically action-oriented and depicts a group of "in" teens that use the product.

Consumers in this age subculture have a number of needs, including experimentation, belonging, independence, responsibility, and approval from others. Product usage is a significant medium that lets them satisfy these needs. For example, many kids view smoking cigarettes as a status activity because of the numerous movies they've seen that glorify this practice. In one study, ninth graders watched original movie footage with either smoking scenes or control footage with the smoking edited out. Sure enough, when the young viewers saw the actors smoking, this enhanced their perceptions of smokers' social stature and increased their own intent to smoke. (The good news: When kids see an antismoking advertisement before the film these effects cancel out.)[11]

Teenagers in every culture grapple with fundamental developmental issues when they transition from childhood to adult. Throughout history young people have coped with insecurity, parental authority, and peer pressure (although each generation has trouble believing it's not the first!). According to Teenage Research Unlimited, the five most important social issues for teens are AIDS, race relations, child abuse, abortion, and the environment. Today's teens often have to cope with additional family responsibilities as well, especially if they live in nontraditional families where they have significant responsibility for shopping, cooking, and housework. It's hard work being a teen in the modern world. The Saatchi & Saatchi advertising agency identified four basic conflicts common to all teens:

- **Autonomy versus belonging**—Teens need to acquire independence, so they try to break away from their families. However, they need to attach themselves to a support structure, such as peers, to avoid being alone. One survey of teens found that only 11 percent view themselves as "popular."[12]
- **Rebellion versus conformity**—Teens need to rebel against social standards of appearance and behavior, yet they still need to fit in and be accepted by others. They prize "in-your-face" products that cultivate a rebellious image, such as those the retail chain Hot Topic sells, for this reason.
- **Idealism versus pragmatism**—Teens tend to view adults as hypocrites, whereas they see themselves as being sincere. They have to struggle to reconcile their view of how the world should be with the realities they perceive around them.
- **Narcissism versus intimacy**—Teens tend to obsess about their appearance and needs. However, they also feel the desire to connect with others on a meaningful level.[13]

These needs often collide, sometimes in unpleasant ways (there's nothing more venomous than a teenager who's having a bad hair day!). One researcher explored the role of *ridicule* as a mechanism through which adolescents exchange information about consumption norms and values. He found that often beginning in middle school, adolescents use ridicule to ostracize, haze, or admonish peers who violate consumption norms. One result of this painful process is that kids internalize their peers' stereotypes about aspirational and avoidance groups (remember Chapter 10) and often significantly alter their consumption patterns to try to align themselves with the former and distance themselves from the latter. For example, one of the kids in the study quickly exchanged a pair of white sneakers for more stylish black ones after his peers ridiculed him.[14]

ECONsumer Behavior

The economy forces a lot of youth retailers into a strategic about-face. In recent years "concept stores" popped up in malls across America to cater to niches of teens like surfers, skaters, and preppies. Now analysts say there are too many of these boutiques that fight over too few customers. Major chains including Pacific Sunwear of California, Abercrombie & Fitch, and American Eagle Outfitters closed new stores as they hoard their dwindling resources to focus on their core brands.[15]

Although teens have the "rep" of always questioning authority, it's also important to keep in mind that one person's rebellion is another's disobedience—there are strong cultural differences when it comes to the desirability of revolting against the establishment.[16] For example many Asian teens don't necessarily value rebellion against a middle class that they are just now starting to join. An MTV executive commented, "Asian youth are schizophrenic. They lead double lives, almost. On one hand, they've got their earrings, belly-button rings and ponytails, but on the other hand, they're completely conformist." In Singapore, Coca-Cola discovered that teen-oriented ads it used successfully elsewhere, such as a shirtless guy who bodysurfs at a rock concert or who recklessly rides a grocery cart down a store aisle, simply didn't make it with local kids who thought the ads were too unruly. One 18-year-old Singaporean's reactions to a scene showing kids head-banging sums up this feeling: "They look like they're on drugs constantly. And if they're on drugs, then how can they be performing at school?"

Gen Y

A recent brand overhaul by Pepsi that includes its new smiley-face logo had the so-called **Gen Y** age segment squarely in its sights. Young people have always been Pepsi's lifeblood, starting with its tagline 'You're in the Pepsi Generation" that over time evolved into "Generation Next" and "The Choice of a New Generation." But, that blood has drained a bit over the last few years as young people gravitate toward energy drinks and fortified waters. The company's research showed it that this age group—that also goes by the labels **Millennials** and **Echo Boomers**—are hopeful about the future; almost all of them agree that it's important to maintain a positive outlook on life. Pepsi also found that 95 percent of Millennials have positive associations with the word *change* and they link the word to others like *new*, *progress*, *hope*, and *excitement*. Presumably this is part of the same sentiment that propelled President Obama's campaign. Indeed, during the 2008 presidential campaign many observers noted striking similarities between the cola brand's logo and the candidate's—and it didn't hurt that the Democratic Convention took place in Denver's Pepsi Center.[17]

Gen Yers were born between 1984 and 2002. They already make up nearly one-third of the U.S. population, and they spend $170 billion a year of their own and their parents' money. They love brands like Sony, Patagonia, Gap, Aveda, and Apple. Echo boomers are a reflection of the sweeping changes in American life during the past 20 years. They are also the most diverse generation ever: Thirty-five percent are non-white, and, as we saw in Chapter 11, they often grow up in nontraditional families: Today one in four 21-year-olds was raised by a single parent, and three out of four have a working mother.

Members of Gen Y are "jugglers" who value being both footloose and connected to their "peeps" 24/7. The advertising agency Saatchi & Saatchi labels this new kind of lifestyle **connexity**. To help Millennials feel connected with one another, companies including Apple and Philips developed miniature devices such as the iPod and MP3 key ring that store music and images for kids on the run—and they plug directly into a USB port for up- and downloading. When Toyota developed its youth-oriented Scion model, researchers learned that Echo boomers practically live in their cars—one-quarter of Gen Yers, for example, keep a full change of clothes in their vehicles. So Toyota's designers made the Scion resemble a home on wheels with fully reclining front seats so drivers can nap between classes and a 15-volt outlet so they can plug in their computers.[18]

Unlike their parents or older siblings, Gen Yers tend to hold relatively traditional values and they prefer to fit in rather than rebel. Their acculturation agents (see Chapter 13) stress teamwork—team teaching, team grading, collaborative sports, community service, service learning, and student juries. Violent crime among teenagers is down 60 to 70 percent. The use of tobacco and alcohol is at an all-time low, as is teen pregnancy. Five out of ten Echo boomers say they trust the government, and virtually all of them trust Mom and Dad.[19]

Digital Natives

Millennials are the first generation to grow up with computers at home, in a 500-channel TV universe. They are *multitaskers* who easily engage their cell phones, music downloads, and IMs at the same time. They are totally at home in a *thumb culture* that communicates online and by cell phone (more likely via text and IM than by voice). These kids truly are **digital natives**. Many young people prefer to use the Internet to communicate because its anonymity makes it easier to talk to people of the opposite sex or of different ethnic and racial groups.[20] A spate of recent studies on how Millennials use technology confirms this profile:[21]

The Tangled Web

Young people today have an unprecedented ability to learn about others—but also to let others learn about them. More than one-quarter of teenagers say they write openly about themselves and friends online, and 17 percent openly share details of their lives. And, almost half of online teens say they have uploaded photos of themselves—most of these say that people comment on the images at least "some of the time."

Parents often are clueless about just how much time their kids devote to cyberspace: A Symantec study found that parents in the United States think their kids are online 2 hours a month, but in reality, kids report spending 20 hours a month online. Four in ten American teens agree that their parent have no idea what they look at online!

- **Texting**—Overall, American cell phone subscribers use their mobiles more to send text messages than to make calls, and teens drive that change. Accenture reports that more than one-half of teens said mobile phones were their preferred means of communication (compared to only 20 percent of psychedelic relics over 45). Young adults spend about 32 minutes a day texting as new acronyms penetrate our language such as *paw* (parents are watching), *lol* (laughing out loud), *g2g* (got to go) and *ooc* (out of control). Harris Interactive found that 42 percent of teens claim they can write text messages while blindfolded.[22]
- **Video**—American Internet users ages 12 and older average more than six hours per day watching video—they devote about four hours of this total to traditional television, including live, digital video recorder (DVR) and video-on-demand (VOD) viewing; video games; and Web and PC videos, DVDs and video on mobile devices accounted for the balance. Analysts project that this total will grow to eight hours per day by 2013, and most of this increase will be due to the boom in online video. And, as a harbinger of the future, Nielsen reports that while kids ages 2 to 11 use the Internet far less than other age groups, they spend almost one-third of their online time watching videos.
- **Online brand WOM**—About one in three Millennials say that within a month they talk about a brand on a discussion forum, about 20 percent put brand-related content on their instant messaging (IM) profile, and the same proportion add branded content to their home page or social networking site. Nearly one-half click on online ads.[23]
- **Consumer-generated content**—About two-thirds of online teens say they participate in one or more content-creating activities on the Internet. One-third creates or works on Web pages or blogs for others, including those for groups they belong to, friends, or school assignments. And about one-quarter remix content they find online into their own creations.

One pair of researchers took an in-depth look at how 13- and 14-year-olds integrate the computer into their lives, and how they use it expresses their *cyberidentities*. These tweens have limited mobility in RL (too young to drive), so they use the computer to transport themselves to other places and modes of being. The researchers explored the metaphors these kids use when they think about their computers. For some, the PC is a "fraternity house" where they can socialize; it also can be a "carnival" where they play games and an "external brain" that helps with homework.[24]

Speak to Teens in Their Language

Because modern teens were raised on TV and tend to be more "savvy" than older generations, marketers must tread lightly when they talk to them. If the message is going to work they have to see it as authentic and not condescending. As one researcher observed, "They have a B.S. alarm that goes off quick and fast. . . . They walk in and usually make up their minds very quickly about whether it's phat or not phat, and whether they want it or don't want it. They know a lot of advertising is based on lies and hype."[25]

So what are the rules of engagement for young consumers?[26]

- **Rule 1: Don't talk down**—Younger consumers want to draw their own conclusions about products. In the words of one teen: "I don't like it when someone tells

Marketing Pitfall

A new study the National Institutes of Health funded reports that young people tend to drink more in areas with more alcohol advertising compared to areas with less advertising. The study looked at alcohol advertising in 24 media markets across the United States, and the researchers collected data on the amount of alcohol people aged 15 to 26 in those markets consume.

On average, young people report they consume about 38.5 drinks per month, and they see an average of 23 ads per month. Respondents who said they saw more ads and who lived in areas with higher-per-capita populations also said they drank more than those who saw fewer ads. The authors estimate that each $1 per-capita increase in alcohol spending boosts drinking by 3 percent in a month. All things being equal, a 20-year-old male who lives in a media market with the highest per capita advertising consumes about 26 drinks per month, compared to his counterpart in an area with less alcohol ads. In addition, this age group's exposure to alcohol advertising climbed sharply between 2001 and 2007. The average 12- to 20-year-old TV viewer saw an average of 301 ads for alcoholic beverages during 2007, up from 217 during 2001 and from 285 during 2006. That increase occurred despite the adoption of standards by alcohol-industry trade groups that instructed members not to advertise where 30 percent or more of the audience was less than 21 years of age.[28]

me what to do. Those drugs and sex commercials preach. What do they know? Also, I don't like it when they show a big party and say come on and fit in with this product. That's not how it works."

- **Rule 2: Don't try to be what you're not. Stay true to your brand image**—Kids value straight talk. Firms that back up what they say impress them. Procter & Gamble appealed to this value with a money-back guarantee on its Old Spice High Endurance deodorant with an invitation to phone 1–800–PROVEIT.
- **Rule 3: Entertain them. Make it interactive and keep the sell short**—Gen Yers like to find brands in unexpected places. The prospect of catching appealing ads is part of the reason they're watching that TV show in the first place. If they want to learn more, they'll check out your Web site.
- **Rule 4: Show that you know what they're going through, but keep it light**—A commercial for Hershey's Ice Breakers mints subtly points out its benefit when it highlights the stress a guy feels as he psyches himself up to approach a strange girl at a club. "I'm wearing my lucky boxers," he reassures himself. "Don't trip. Don't drool. Relax. How's my breath?"

Tweens

Marketers invented the term **tweens** to describe the 27 million children aged 8 to 14 who spend $14 billion a year on clothes, CDs, movies, and other "feel-good" products. Tweens are "between" childhood and adolescence, and they exhibit characteristics of both age groups. As one tween commented, "When we're alone we get weird and crazy and still act like kids. But in public we act cool, like teenagers."[27]

A recent marketing campaign by Victoria's Secret illustrates the fine line marketers must walk when they deal with consumers who are not children but not yet adults, or even full-fledged teens. When the retail chain developed Pink, a lingerie line for younger girls, it wanted to avoid the heat that Abercrombie & Fitch attracted when it sold child-size thong underwear. The company recruited about two dozen (female) students at colleges such as Ohio State, UCLA, and Penn State as brand ambassadors. These older girls became role models for the tween set. Members of Team Pink hand out free gift flyers, give away tickets to special screenings of popular TV shows, and orchestrate stunts such as hiding a thousand pink stuffed animals around campus. "All they are really asking me to do is support another cause," one ambassador explained to her school newspaper, "and the cause happens to be underwear instead of the homeless, child poverty or hunger."[29] Wow.

Youth Tribes

We talked about the emergence of consumer tribes in Chapter 10. Brands with a tribal appeal reinforce belonging when they let people display tribal trappings.[30] In-line roller skaters in France are a great example of the tribal phenomenon at work. There are about 2 million in-line skaters in France today, divided equally by gender. This group has its "in-groups" and "out-groups" within the tribe, but all connect via their shared skating experience. These urban skaters hold national gatherings in Paris that can attract 15,000 people, many of whom belong to associations such as Roller et Coquillages and Paris Roller. Specialized Web sites for members of the skating tribe let them meet to chat and to exchange information. Small tribal divisions exist (e.g., fitness skaters versus stunt skaters), but all identify with the broader skating tribe.

Tribal gatherings provide manufacturers with an opportunity to strengthen the group bond when they offer accessories such as shoes, key chains, belts and hats, backpacks, sunglasses, T-shirts, and other goodies that reinforce membership. For example, although skaters can choose from many brands, K2, Razor, Oxygen, Tecnica, and Nike, the original Rollerblade product still holds cult status within the tribe. Tatoo, the pager arm of France Telecom, builds on tribal bonds with in-line skaters when it sponsors Tatoo Roller Skating in Paris and similar events around the

country. Specialized magazines such as *Crazy Roller, Urban,* and *Roller Saga* carry informational articles as well as celebrity spots.

Closer to home, the American athletic shoe company AND 1 appeals to members of a basketball tribe that admits members if they can blow by a defender on the court. The company carefully cultivates a trash-talking street image (it distributes shirts with slogans such as "I'm sorry. I thought you could play") and it recruits street players to match its renegade brand image.[31]

The tribal phenomenon is very strong in Japan, where teenagers invent, adopt, and discard fads with lightning speed. Teenage girls in Japan exhibit what science fiction writer William Gibson (who invented the term *cyberspace*) calls "techno-cultural suppleness"—a willingness to grab something new and use it for their own ends—matched by no other group on earth. According to one estimate, cell phones sit in the purses and pockets of about 95 percent of all Japanese teenage girls. Unlike American phones, these devices connect constantly to the Internet and plug these girls into a massive network.

Big (Wo)Man on Campus

Advertisers spend approximately $100 million a year on campuses to woo college students, and with good reason: Overall, students spend more than $11 billion a year on snacks and beverages, $4 billion on personal care products, and $3 billion on CDs and tapes. Seventy percent of them own a laptop. Many students have plenty of extra cash and free time (not you, of course . . .): On an average day the average student spends 1.7 hours in class and another 1.6 hours studying. This "average" student (or are all students above average?) has about $287 to spend on discretionary items per month. As one marketing executive observed, "This is the time of life where they're willing to try new products. . . . This is the time to get them in your franchise." The college market is also attractive to many companies because these novice consumers are away from home for the first time, so they have yet to form unshakeable brand loyalty in some product categories such as cleaning supplies (bummer!).[32]

Nevertheless, college students pose a special challenge for marketers because they are hard to reach via conventional media such as newspapers. Of course, online advertising is very effective: Ninety-nine percent of college students go online at least a few times per week, and 90 percent do so daily. Web sites such as mtvU.com and collegehumor.com blossom because they reach students where they live and play.[33] These specialized networks provide college students with irreverent programming that appeals to their sense of humor with shows such as *Bridget the Midget*, which follows the life of a 3-foot-tall former porn star who is now an aspiring rock singer, and an anti–Martha Stewart cooking show called *Half Baked*, which features celebrities such as Shaquille O'Neal and Lisa Loeb who share recipes.[34] To acknowledge the power of this market, Nielsen Media Research now includes college students who live away from home in its television ratings. Nielsen reports that students watch an average of 24.3 hours of television a week.[35]

How Do We Research the Youth Market?

Research firms that specialize in the youth market have to be innovative because many Millennials don't respond well to traditional survey techniques. Pizza Hut invites teens into its boardroom to eat lunch with company executives and share their opinions about the perfect pie. Some research companies give teens video cameras and ask them to record a "typical" day at school—along with play-by-play commentary to help interpret what's going on. Other marketers pay $2,500 a head to spend a day at Trend School, a monthly one-day forum in New York and Los Angeles. The "students" hang out with über-cool kids to learn about the latest tech, music, and fashion trends.[37]

When the Leo Burnett advertising agency revamped Heinz ketchup's image to make it cool, the account research team took teens to dinner to see how they actually use ketchup. These meals opened their eyes; new ads focus on teens' need for control when they show ketchup smothering fries "until they can't breathe" and tout new uses for the condiment on pizza, grilled cheese, and potato chips.[38] Procter & Gamble goes to the Web to learn what kids are thinking. At its Tremor site, P&G recruits teen members and rewards them with merchandise for spreading the word about products.[39]

All of these techniques are about defining what is cool to teens—the Holy Grail of youth marketing. One study asked young people in the United States and the Netherlands to write essays about what is "cool" and "uncool" and to create visual collages that represent what it means to be cool.[40] The researchers found that cool has multiple meanings to kids in these two cultures. Some of the common dimensions include having charisma, being in control, and being a bit aloof. And many of the respondents agreed that being cool is a moving target: The harder you try to be cool, the more uncool you are! Some of their actual responses are as follows:

- "Cool means being relaxed, to nonchalantly be the boss of every situation, and to radiate that" (Dutch female).
- "Cool is the perception from others that you've got 'something' which is macho, trendy, hip, etc." (Dutch male).
- "Cool has something standoffish, and at the same time, attractive" (Dutch male).
- "Being different, but not too different. Doing your own thing, and standing out, without looking desperate while you're doing it" (American male).
- "When you are sitting on a terrace in summer, you see those machos walk by, you know, with their mobile [phones] and their sunglasses. I always think, 'Oh please, come back to earth!' These guys only want to impress. That is just so uncool" (Dutch female).
- "When a person thinks he is cool, he is absolutely uncool" (Dutch female).
- "To be cool we have to make sure we measure up to it. We have to create an identity for ourselves that mirrors what we see in magazines, on TV, and with what we hear on our stereos" (American male).

Marketers view teens as "consumers-in-training" because we often develop strong brand loyalty during adolescence. A teenager who commits to a brand may continue to purchase it for many years to come. Such loyalty creates a barrier to entry for other brands he or she didn't choose during these pivotal years. Thus, advertisers sometimes try to "lock in" consumers so that in the future they will buy their brands more or less automatically. As one teen magazine ad director observed, "We . . . always say it's easier to start a habit than stop it."[41]

Teens also exert a big influence on the purchase decisions of their parents (see Chapter 11).[42] In addition to providing "helpful" advice to parents, teens often buy on behalf of the family. The majority of mothers today work outside the home so they have less time to shop for the family. This fundamental change in family structure changes how marketers need to think about teenage consumers. Although teens are still a good market for discretionary items, now they actually spend more on "basics" such as groceries than for nonessentials. Marketers are responding to these changes—the next time you read through a magazine such as *Seventeen*, notice the large number of ads for food products.

Gen X

Gen X consists of 46 million Americans. This group got the label following publication of the 1991 best-selling novel *Generation X: Tales for an Accelerated Culture* by Douglas Coupland. Some called them "slackers" or "baby busters" because of their supposed alienation and laziness, and these stereotypes live on in movies such as *Clueless* and in music groups such as Marilyn Manson.[43]

Advertisers fell all over themselves to create messages that would not turn off the worldly Generation X cohort. Many of them referenced old TV shows such as *Gilligan's Island* or showed commercials that featured disheveled actors in turned-around baseball caps who tried their best to appear blasé. This approach actually turned off a lot of busters because it implied that they had nothing else to do but sit around and watch old television reruns. Subaru sponsored one of the first commercials of this genre. It showed a sloppily dressed young man who described the Impreza model as "like punk rock" as he denounced the competition as "boring and corporate." The commercial did not play well with its intended audience, and Subaru eventually switched advertising agencies.

Today Gen Xers have grown up and in fact members of this generation are responsible for many culture-changing products and companies such as Google, YouTube, and Amazon. A recent book that laments the bad rap Gen X has gotten sums it up: *X Saves the World: How Generation X Got the Shaft but Can Still Keep Everything from Sucking*.[44]

PepsiCo used a digital campaign to promote its new fruit-flavored and caffeine-free Tava drink—but it targets the beverage primarily to men and women ages 35 to 49.
Source: TAVA is a registered trademark of The Concentrate Manufacturing Company of Ireland. Used with permission.

The Mature Market

Restylane is the top-selling dermal injection to reduce the appearance of wrinkles. The company decided to pitch it directly to consumers for the first time, so in keeping with new media trends it launched a multipronged campaign that recognizes the technical prowess of many middle-aged people. A conventional TV spot features before-and-after results along with women who talk about how frequently men check them out after the treatment. But a second component is a video skit on YouTube that supposedly takes place during a woman's fiftieth birthday party. While her son works on a video birthday card, Mom gets caught smooching with a younger man on a couch. Viewers don't know the skit is an ad until the last 15 seconds. A third prong is a contest to name the "Hottest Mom in America"—contestants submit videos to a Web site and the winner gets cash, free treatments for a year, and an interview with a modeling agency.[45] Today's Mom isn't exactly June Cleaver. Let's take a closer look at the changing face of mature consumers—some of them aren't as mature as they used to be.

now it's Pepsi-for those who **think** young

Thinking young is a wholesome attitude, an enthusiastic outlook. It means getting the most out of life, and everyone can join in. This is the life for Pepsi—light, bracing, clean-tasting Pepsi. Think young. Say "Pepsi, please!"

This 1962 Pepsi ad highlights the emphasis on youth power that began to shape our culture as baby boomers came of age in the 1960s.

Source: Courtesy of Pepsico.

OBJECTIVE

Why do Baby Boomers continue to be the most powerful age segment economically?

Baby Boomers

The **Baby Boomer** age cohort consists of people whose parents established families following the end of World War II and during the 1950s when the peacetime economy was strong and stable. As a general rule, when people feel confident about how things are going in the world, they are more likely to decide to have children so this was a "boom" time for delivery rooms. As teenagers in the 1960s and 1970s, the "Woodstock generation" created a revolution in style, politics, and consumer attitudes. As they aged, they fueled cultural events as diverse as the Free Speech movement and hippies in the 1960s to Reaganomics and yuppies in the 1980s. Now that they are older, they continue to influence popular culture.

ECONsumer Behavior

A study sponsored by AARP divides Boomers into segments based on how they handle the economic downturn.

- **The "yesterday" group**—Their attitude is summed up by the statement, "Life was better in the 1950s." They are concerned about an uncertain future. Members long for a simpler life, feel that they have not accomplished much, and have few goals. About 40 percent say their health has declined. The analysts recommend that marketers reassure these individuals that they are not alone and validate their years of hard work.

- **The "today" group**—This label applies to about 30 percent of boomers. They agree with the statement: "We live in exciting times." They are confident, healthy, and

Many Baby Boomers are interested in maintaining a youthful appearance and will go to great lengths to preserve it.

Source: Botox® Cosmetics ad used with permission of Allergan Inc.

As the Restalyne campaign demonstrates, this generation is much more active and physically fit than its predecessors; baby boomers are 6 percent more likely than the national average to engage in some kind of sports activity.[46] And boomers are now in their peak earning years. As one commercial for VH1, the music video network that caters to those who are a bit too old for MTV, pointed out, "The generation that dropped acid to escape reality . . . is the generation that drops antacid to cope with it."

Consumers aged 35 to 44 spend the most on housing, cars, and entertainment. Baby Boomers are busy "feathering their nests"—they account for roughly 40 percent of all the money consumers spend on household furnishings and equipment. In addition, consumers aged 45 to 54 spend the most of any age category on food (30 percent above average), apparel (38 percent above average), and retirement programs (57 percent above average).[47] To appreciate the impact middle-aged consumers have and will have on our economy, consider this: At current spending levels, a 1 percent increase in the population of householders aged 35 to 54 results in an additional $8.9 billion in consumer spending.

In addition to the direct demand for products and services this age group creates, these consumers have also fostered a new baby boom of their own to keep marketers busy in the future. Because fertility rates have dropped, this new boom is not as big as the one that created the Baby Boom generation; the new upsurge in the number of children is more of a *baby boomlet*. Many boomer couples postponed getting married and having children because of the new opportunities and options for women. They began to have babies in their late 20s and early 30s so there were fewer (but perhaps more pampered) children per family. This new emphasis on children and the family creates opportunities for products such as cars (e.g., the success of the SUV concept among "soccer Moms"), services (e.g., the day-care industry and big chains such as KinderCare), and media (e.g., magazines such as *Working Mother*).

Although youth always lures advertisers, many companies reconsider this fixation in light of boomers' huge spending power. An ad for the Toyota Highlander

shows boomers whose nests are emptying and declares, "For your newfound freedom, it's about how you are going to reinvent yourself for what could be 30 or 40 years of retirement, which is very different from your parents and grandparents."[49] Even mobile marketers who typically blast messages to kids on their cell phones have begun to target the middle-aged. For example, *Redbook* readers can text message to bid on a year's worth of movie tickets.[50]

The Gray Market

4

Why will seniors increase in importance as a market segment?

The old woman sits alone in her dark apartment while the television blares out a soap opera. Once every couple of days, her arthritic hands slowly and painfully open her triple-locked door as she ventures out to the corner store to buy essentials such as tea, milk, and cereal—of course she always picks the least expensive brand. Most of the time she sits in her rocking chair and thinks sadly about her dead husband and the good times they used to have together.

Is this the image you have of a typical elderly consumer? Until recently, many marketers did. They neglected the elderly in their feverish pursuit of the youth market. But as our population ages and we live longer and healthier lives, the game is rapidly changing. A lot of businesses are updating their old stereotype of the poor recluse. The newer, more accurate image is of an active person interested in what life has to offer, and who is an enthusiastic consumer with the means and willingness to buy many goods and services. For example, as we saw earlier in this chapter, Sony targeted zoomers after the company discovered that about a third of its sales come from consumers aged 50 and older. And this market grows even as we speak: An American turns 50 every 7 seconds.[52]

Gray Power: Seniors' Economic Clout

Think about this: The United Nations says that people older than 60 are the fastest-growing age group on earth. There are 700 million of them now, and there will be 2 billion by midcentury. In the United States, by 2030, 20 percent of the population will be over the age of 65.[53] By 2100 there will be 5 million of us who are at least 100 years old.[54] Few of us may be around then, but we can already see the effects of the **gray market** today. Older adults control more than 50 percent of discretionary income, and worldwide consumers over age 50 spend nearly $400 billion a year.[55] The mature market is the second-fastest-growing market segment in the United States, lagging only behind boomers. We're living longer and healthier because of more wholesome lifestyles (at least some of us), improved medical diagnoses and treatment, and changing cultural expectations about appropriate behaviors for the elderly.

Given the economic clout of senior consumers, it's often surprising how many marketers ignore them in favor of younger buyers—even though they are among the most brand loyal of any group. Older consumers repurchase a brand more frequently, consider fewer brands and dealers, and choose long-established brands more often.[56] Still, most contemporary advertising campaigns don't recognize these buyers. Even though people over the age of 50 account for half of all the discretionary spending in the United States, watch more television, go to more movies, and buy more CDs than do the young, Americans over age 50 are the focus of less than 10 percent of the advertising![57]

That focus is indeed changing, as big marketers like Kraft, L'Oréal, Procter & Gamble, and Target set their sights on the over-50 market. Their interest is enhanced by the recession, where people with paid-off mortgages start to look more attractive than younger people who may be laid off tomorrow. In the words of a Nielsen executive, "Especially in this economy, with marketers' budgets under so much stress, they would prefer to spend dollars on today's sales instead of thinking about establishing brand loyalty."[58]

satisfied with their accomplishments. They are more affluent and have planned their financial situation well so they feel they have earned the right to enjoy their retirement. Messages for this group should celebrate their success and encourage members to embrace the moment.

- **The "tomorrow" group**—About 45 percent of boomers live by the philosophy "tomorrow will be better than today." These people are still very optimistic despite recent financial or health setbacks. They are highly connected to their communities, feel young for their age, and many like to try new things. Messages should emphasize optimism and giving back to the community as opposed to "retiring rich."[48]

Marketing Opportunity

As Boomers age, the cosmetics industry is moving away from a singular reliance on young, perfect models. Unilever recently launched a "Pro-Age" line of Dove personal care products that puts a more upbeat spin on the traditional "anti-" advertisers use to describe anti-aging products. Cover Girl hired comedienne Ellen DeGeneres, who at over 50 years old, would seem like an unlikely candidate to represent a major cosmetics brand, to represent its products. You can easily see actress Andie MacDowell's crows' feet in a L'Oréal print campaign for RevitaLift Anti-Wrinkle Concentrate, and Diane Keaton (in her 60s) endorses L'Oréal's hair color and Age-Perfect Pro Calcium moisturizer. The editor of *More*, a magazine for women over 40, explained, "We're getting worn out by the Lindsays and the Britneys, and I think we need a break."[51]

CB AS I LIVE IT

Dan Birnbaum, *Michigan State University*

Woes of a Marketing Student

How can I market a product to all these different groups?

It feels impossible, I am going in loops.

They all have different values, conflicts, and desires,

I'm getting nowhere, like trying to untangle a box of wires.

I would know what to do if a baby boomer was looking for a car,

Or how to target teens that still really don't know who they are.

For college students wall and Internet media may be the best,

But these forms of media won't work as well on all the rest.

I didn't want to sell to the mature market; they have a lot on their plates,

Until I found out they do the most discretionary spending in the whole United States.

I should bribe the "cool hunters" to hype up my stuff as much as they can,

They live in the big city markets; they'll report all the new trends.

I'll target the baby boomers that's definitely my best bet.

It is much harder however to sway an adult whose mind is already set.

Teens want to be independent and buy nonessential stuff,

But making sure I appeal to the youth market could be tough.

They spend 14 billion a year on "feel-good" items like clothes, or DVDs,

This market could definitely be tapped if I am as entertaining and familiar as I can be.

I can't forget about one-third of us that fall under Generation Y,

They're the most diverse group of them all, which is plenty of reason to try.

They are made up of cell phone talkers the music downloaders and Internet users,

All the pressure is on them, they can't afford to be the losers.

I don't know what to do; I'm the one, who's lost,

My benefit here definitely doesn't exceed my cost!

Now let's step back and look at all this in a rational way,

How well a product sells is all about how you act, and what you say.

Teens are interested in forming self-concept and fitting in,

So if we target their new-found independence, there is no way we can't win.

As for college students with a bit of free time and some extra cash,

They have no brand loyalty, and their decisions are often rash.

The baby boomers stress about staying young and being physically fit,

Expressing the youthfulness of the product is an aspect that we must hit.

These age subcultures are something very real,

But remember age is a state of mind and is all about how you feel.

If you learn how to implement this in your marketing strategy,

You will market your product much better than me!

Some of the important areas that stand to benefit from the surging gray market include exercise facilities, cruises and tourism, cosmetic surgery and skin treatments, and "how-to" books and university courses that offer enhanced learning opportunities. In many product categories seniors spend their money at an even greater rate than other age groups: Householders aged 55 to 64 spend 15 percent more than average per capita. They shell out 56 percent more than the average consumer on women's clothing, and as new grandparents they actually spring for more toys and playground equipment than people aged 25 to 44.[59] In fact, the average grandparent spends an average of about $500 per year on gifts for grandchildren—have you called yours today?[60]

Perceived Age: You're Only as Old as You Feel

Research confirms the popular wisdom that age is more a state of mind than of body. A person's mental outlook and activity level have a lot more to do with longevity and quality of life than does *chronological age*, the actual number of years the person has actually been alive. That's why **perceived age**, or how old a person *feels*, is a better yardstick to use. Researchers measure perceived age on several dimensions, including "feel-age" (i.e., how old a person feels) and "look-age" (i.e., how old a person

☐ wrinkled?

☐ wonderful?

Will society ever accept old can be beautiful?

looks).[61] The older consumers get, the younger they feel relative to their actual age. For this reason, many marketers emphasize product benefits rather than age-appropriateness in marketing campaigns because many consumers will not relate to products that target their chronological age.[62]

How Should Marketers Talk to Seniors?

Hallmark's marketing group thought it stumbled on a gold mine. When it realized that about 78 million baby boomers are hitting age 50, the company created "Time of Your Life" cards to subtly flatter the aging ego. They depicted youthful-looking oldsters frolicking on beaches and diving into pools. But Hallmark missed one tiny yet crucial psychological detail: No self-respecting senior wants his friends to catch him shopping in the "old-people's card" section. It had to scrap the line.[63]

This debacle underscores how important it is to understand the psyche of older people. Researchers point to a set of key values relevant to mature consumers. For marketing strategies to succeed, they should link to one or more of these factors:[64]

● **Autonomy**—Mature consumers want to lead active lives and to be self-sufficient. The advertising strategy for Depends, undergarments for incontinent people

Echoing the saying, "You're only as old as you feel," this ad reminds us that a person's perceived age often does not correspond to his or her chronological age.
Source: Courtesy of Atena US Healthcare.

A ROCKING CHAIR IS A PIECE OF FURNITURE.

NOT A STATE OF MIND.

We know people whose lust for life has not and will not diminish because it's the morning after their 65th birthday. They're too busy putting the finishing touches on a book of poems. Tutoring underprivileged kids with their math. Learning the tango. Or taking acting classes. It's an outlook that works rather well with ours. Whether it's annuities, 401(k)s, IRAs, mutual funds or life insurance for your family, we've packaged a unique set of tools to help you realize your life's next great exploit. Which comes naturally when retirement isn't viewed as merely an end. But rather the way you've been living all along: passionately. For a free brochure, call 1-800-AETNA-60 or visit us at http://www.aetna.com.

Build for Retirement. Manage for Life.

Ætna
Retirement Services.

made by Kimberly-Clark, centers on senior celebrities such as actress June Allyson, who plays golf and goes to parties without worrying about her condition.

- **Connectedness**—Mature consumers value the bonds they have with friends and family. Quaker Oats successfully tapped into this value with its ads that feature actor Wilford Brimley, who dispenses grandfatherly advice to the younger generation about eating right.
- **Altruism**—Mature consumers want to give something back to the world. Thrifty Car Rental found in a survey that more than 40 percent of older consumers would select a rental car company if it sponsors a program that gives van discounts to senior citizens' centers. Based on this research, the company launched its highly successful program, "Give a Friend a Lift."

Larger numbers of older people lead more active, multidimensional lives than we assume. Nearly 60 percent engage in volunteer activities, one in four seniors aged 65 to 72 still works, and more than 14 million provide care for their grandchildren.[65] And it is crucial to remember that income alone does not express seniors' spending power. Older consumers are finished with many of the financial obligations that siphon off the income of younger consumers. Eighty percent of consumers older than age 65 own their own homes. In addition, child-rearing costs are over. As the popular bumper sticker proudly proclaims, "We're Spending Our Children's Inheritance!"

Still, outdated images of mature consumers persist. The editors of *AARP Magazine* reject about a third of the ads companies submit to them because they portray older people in a negative light. In one survey, one-third of consumers older than age 55 reported that they deliberately did not buy a product because of the way its ads stereotype older people.[66] To address these negative depictions, some marketers provide more welcoming environments for seniors:

- Wal-Mart hires older people as greeters to be sure their senior customers feel at home.
- The Adeg Aktiv Markt 50+ in Salzburg, Austria, is Europe's first supermarket for shoppers older than age 50. The labels are big; the aisles are wide; the floors are nonskid, even when wet; and there are plenty of places to sit down. The lights are specially calibrated to reduce glare on elderly customers' more sensitive eyes. The shelves are lower so products are within easy reach. And in addition to regular shopping carts, there are carts that hook onto wheelchairs and carts that double as seats for the weary—as soon as a shopper sits down, the wheels lock.[67]
- Japan's population is graying rapidly (21 percent of all Japanese are older than 65 years old), and businesses need to shift gears to keep up with this reality. The Lawson convenience store chain plans to eventually convert 20 percent of its nearly 8,400 stores to senior-friendly centers. These will feature broader aisles to accommodate wheelchairs, lower shelves for easier access, and price tags with enlarged print. The stores stock instant meals that shoppers can consume without chewing.[68]

Products get a more sympathetic reception from seniors when their designers make them sensitive to physical limitations. Packages often are awkward and difficult to manage, especially for those who are frail or arthritic. Also, many serving sizes are too big for people who live alone, and coupons tend to be good for family-sized products rather than for single servings.

Some seniors have difficulty manipulating pull-tab cans and push-open milk cartons. Ziploc packages and clear plastic wrap also can be difficult to handle. Packages need to be easier to read and they need to be lighter and smaller. Finally, designers need to pay attention to contrasting colors. A slight yellowing of the eye's lens as one ages makes it harder to see background colors on packages. Discerning among blues, greens, and violets becomes especially difficult. The closer type colors are to the package or ad background color, the less visibility and attention they will command.

How Can We Segment Seniors?

The senior subculture is an extremely large market: The number of Americans aged 65 and older exceeds the entire population of Canada.[69] Senior consumers are particularly well suited for segmentation because they're easy to identify by age and stage in the family life cycle. Most receive Social Security benefits, so marketers can locate them, and many belong to organizations such as the American Association of Retired Persons (aarp.org), which boasts more than 12 million dues-paying members. *AARP Magazine* (formerly *Modern Maturity*) segments its customers when it prints three outwardly similar but distinct editions: one for readers in their 50s, one for readers in their 60s, and one for those 70 years old or older.[70]

In addition to chronological age, marketers segment the elderly in terms of the particular years a person came of age (his or her age cohort), current marital status (e.g., widowed versus married), and health and outlook on life.[71] One ad agency devised a segmentation scheme for American women over the age of 65 that used two dimensions: self-sufficiency and perceived opinion leadership.[72] It discovered many important differences among the groups. The self-sufficient group was more independent, cosmopolitan, and outgoing. Compared to the other seniors, these women were more likely to read books, attend concerts and sporting events, and dine out.

Several segmentation approaches begin with the premise that a major determinant of elderly marketplace behavior is the way a person deals with being old.[73] **Social aging theories** try to understand how society assigns people to different roles across the life span. For example, when people retire they may reflect society's expectations for someone at this life stage—this is a major transition point when we exit from many relationships.[74]

CB AS I SEE IT

Professor George Moschis, *Georgia State University*

Consumer behavior researchers typically study individuals at a given point in time or stage in life in isolation from events and circumstances they experience or anticipate at various stages in life. While researchers have recognized the importance of prior life experiences in shaping patterns of consumer behavior during later stages in life, they have had inadequate tools to investigate consumer behavior issues over the course of life. Consumer research over the life course has been predominantly cross-sectional; it focuses on the consumer behavior of different age groups, and is confined to describing the observed differences that exist across age categories of individuals. For the most part it does not address how and why changes in consumer behavior occur over the life span.

In recent decades, however, an increasing number of researchers in various disciplines have adopted the **life course paradigm** to study behavior. This perspective views behavior at any stage in life or given point in time as the product of one's actions or responses to earlier life conditions and the way the individual has adapted to social and environmental circumstances. The life course model suggests that changing life conditions in the form of life-event experiences create physical, social, and emotional demands and circumstances to which one must adapt. Development and change in patterns of thought and action may be viewed as an outcome of one's adaptation to various demands and circumstances, with adaptation entailing the change mechanisms or processes of socialization, stress and coping responses, and development/growth or decline.

The life course approach can help researchers understand how experiences at earlier stages in life, including consumer choices, affect current patterns of consumer behavior. We can study consumer behaviors in relation to earlier life stages within historical and cultural contexts and examine the processes that link time and context to change. Specifically, this approach can be used to study issues related to stability, development, and changes in consumer behaviors in later life by considering their timing, duration, sequence, historical contexts, and conditions under which consumers develop or change their consumption patterns. Marketers must appeal to consumers at a given stage in life differently because their needs differ due to life events and circumstances they have experienced. Previous life experiences, such as becoming a widow or a retiree, affect people's mind-sets, consumption needs, and the way they respond to various types of marketing offerings.

A recent study investigated what the authors call **consumer identity renaissance**; this refers to the redefinition process people undergo when they retire. The research identified two different types of identity renaissance: revived (revitalization of previous identities) or emergent (pursuit of entirely new life projects). Even though many retirees cope with losses (of professional identity, spouses, and so on), many of them focus on moving forward. They engage in a host of strategies to do this including *affiliation* where they reconnect with family members and friends (in many cases online) and *self-expression*; this strategy may involve revisiting an activity they never had time to adequately pursue when they were younger, learning new skills, or perhaps moving into an urban area to reengage with cultural activities.[75]

CHAPTER SUMMARY

Now that you have finished reading this chapter you should understand why:

 1   People have many things in common with others because they are about the same age.

Consumers who grew up at the same time share many cultural memories because they belong to a common age co-

hort, so they may respond well to marketers' nostalgia appeals that remind them of these experiences.

 2   Teens are an important age segment for marketers.

Teenagers are in the middle of a transition from childhood to adulthood, and their self-concepts tend to be unstable. They are receptive to products that help them to be accepted and enable them to assert their independence. Because many teens earn money but have few financial obligations, they are a particularly important segment for many nonessential or expressive products, ranging from chewing gum to clothing fashions and music. Because of changes in family structure, many teens also are taking more responsibility for their families' day-to-day shopping. College students are an important but hard-to-reach market. In many cases, they live alone for the first time, so they make important decisions about setting up a household. Tweens are kids aged 8 to 14; they are influential purchasers of clothing, CDs, and other "feel-good" products. Many young people belong to youth tribes that influence their lifestyles and product preferences.

 Baby boomers continue to be the most powerful age segment economically.

Baby boomers are the most powerful age segment because of their size and economic clout. Boomers continue to af-

fect demands for housing, child care, automobiles, clothing, and many other products.

 Seniors will increase in importance as a market segment.

As the population ages, the needs of older consumers will become increasingly important. Many marketers ignore seniors because of the stereotype that they are too inactive and spend too little. This stereotype is no longer accurate. Many older adults are healthy, vigorous, and interested in new products and experiences—and they have the income to purchase them. Marketing appeals to this age subculture should focus on consumers' perceived ages, which tend to be more youthful than their chronological ages. Marketers also should emphasize concrete benefits of products because this group tends to be skeptical of vague, image-related promotions.

KEY TERMS

Age cohort, 514
Baby Boomer, 525
Connexity, 518
Consumer identity renaissance, 532
Digital natives, 519
Echo boomers, 518

Gen X, 523
Gen Y, 518
Gray market, 527
Life course paradigm, 532
Millennials, 518

Multigenerational marketing strategy, 515
Perceived age, 528
Social aging theories, 531
Tweens, 520

REVIEW

1 What is an age cohort, and why is it of interest to marketers?
2 List three basic conflicts that teens face, and give an example of each.
3 How are Gen Yers different from their older brothers and sisters?
4 What are tweens, and why are so many marketers interested in them?

5 How do tribal gatherings represent a marketing opportunity?
6 What are some of the most efficient ways for marketers to connect with college students?
7 What are some industries that stand to benefit most from the increasing affluence and vitality of the senior market?
8 What are some effective ways to segment the senior market?

CONSUMER BEHAVIOR CHALLENGE

■ DISCUSS

1 What are some possible marketing opportunities at reunions? What effects might attending such an event have on consumers' self-esteem, body image, and so on?
2 This chapter describes members of Gen Y as much more traditional and team oriented than their older brothers and sisters. Do you agree?
3 Many parents worry about the time their kids spend online, but this activity may actually be good for them. A study by the MacArthur Foundation claims that

surfers gain valuable skills to prepare them for the future. One of the authors observes, "It may look as though kids are wasting a lot of time hanging out with new media, whether it's on MySpace or sending instant messages. But their participation is giving them the technological skills and literacy they need to succeed in the contemporary world. They're learning how to get along with others, how to manage a public identity, how to create a home page." The study also finds that concerns about online predators are overblown; most kids socialize with friends they know from other situations like school or camp.[76] What's your take on this? Are concerns about excessive Web surfing overblown?

4 What are some of the positives and negatives of targeting college students? Identify some specific marketing strategies you feel have either been successful or unsuccessful. What characteristics distinguish the successes from the failures?

5 An energy drink called Cocaine created quite a buzz before the FDA pulled it from stores. Now, it's back—but this time with changes that allow it to meet the FDA's requirements: It removed the tagline "the legal alternative," added an antidrug warning label on the can, and removed FDA-unapproved health benefits from its Web site.[77] Is this not-too-subtle reference to underground culture a reasonable marketing strategy? Why might it succeed? Should other companies emulate it?

6 Why have baby boomers had such an important impact on consumer culture?

7 How has the baby boomlet changed attitudes toward child-rearing practices and created demand for different products and services?

8 "Kids these days seem content to just hang out, surf the Net, text with their friends, and watch mindless TV shows all day." How accurate is this statement?

9 Is it practical to assume that people age 55 and older constitute one large consumer market? How can marketers segment this age subculture? What are some important variables to keep in mind when we tailor marketing strategies to older adults?

▋ APPLY

1 Find good and bad examples of advertising that targets older consumers. To what degree does advertising stereotype the elderly? What elements of ads or other promotions appear to determine their effectiveness in reaching and persuading this group?

2 If you were a marketing researcher assigned to study what products are "cool," how would you do this? Do you agree with the definitions of "cool" the young people provided in the chapter?

3 Marketers of entrenched brands like Nike, Pepsi, and Levi Strauss tear their hair out over Gen Y consumers.

Image-building campaigns (e.g., 50 Cent endorsing Reebok) are not as effective as they once were. What advice would you give to a marketer who wants to appeal to Gen Y? What are major dos and don'ts? Can you provide some examples of specific marketing attempts that work or don't work?

4 Interview some retired people. How are they reconstructing their identities? What opportunities do their desires present for marketers?

Case Study

SCION'S QUEST TO CRACK GEN Y

How can a big company capture the attention of Gen Y? Toyota created an entirely new division to go after young drivers. Scion (pronounced *sigh-on*) launched in early 2004 with only two models—the small, wedgy four-door xA hatchback, and the odd-looking four-door xB hatchback that looks more like the shipping crate that a real car would come in. Since then, the company added the more stylish tC coupe and the xD hatchback. All are packed with standard features and retail for less than $18,000.

Scion is more than just another car company, however. Jim Farley, vice president of the division, calls Scion a "laboratory for understanding the quirks and demands of Generation Y." Scion's marketers discovered some core characteristics of this group as they developed their marketing strategy:

Gen Yers are impervious to traditional advertising—Like so many other companies, Scion learned that Gen Y consumers resent the mass-media tactics of big brands. Scion instead spends most of its promotional dollars on advertising in obscure lifestyle magazines that target small youth culture niches. In addition, Scion uses grassroots efforts to take the brand to the target market through staged events that seem to just make the vehicle appear in natural situations (e.g., traveling art and music shows).

Gen Yers are individualistic—Young drivers want more than transportation. They want a customized fashion statement. Because of this, Scion's big allure is the huge list of dealer options. This includes everything from spoilers and LED interior lights to custom graphics, leather interiors, engine-performance parts, and custom wheels. Eighty percent of Scion buyers purchase at least one accessory to make their car their own.

Gen Yers are relatively well-off—This age group has more money (though less credit) than did previous generations at the same age. While they are still somewhat limited by their beer-level budgets, they have champagne appetites. That's why Scions come well-equipped with standard features. That's also why Scion has priced its vehicles low. This way, customers can spend their money on custom accessories. And that they do. The average buyer spends $800 to $1,000 on accessories when they buy the car. Many treat their vehicles as works in progress; they add goodies over time as they can afford them.

Gen Yers are Web savvy—Scion has a strong Web presence, including a very well-developed Web site that allows prospective buyers to customize online. Two-thirds of buyers do so prior to visiting the showroom. Scion owners often gather at community Internet sites like Scionlife.com, which gets hundreds of thousands of hits a day.

Have Toyota's efforts to reach America's youth paid off? Sales exceeded expectations from the beginning, with 175,000 Scions flying out of showrooms each year. Scion customers are among the youngest in the industry; the average owner ranges in age from 26 to 38 (the average age for the industry is well over 40). What's more, 85 percent of Gen Y shoppers now recognize the Scion brand. Scion's long-term objective is to reach unit sales of 300,000. If Scion stays on its current course, it's in good shape to command the loyalty of a fickle generation.

DISCUSSION QUESTIONS

1 Is Toyota wasting its time as it pays so much attention to age as a segmentation variable? Explain.

2 When you consider the characteristics of Gen Y, what do you see as some of the challenges that Scion faces in the future as the brand grows?

3 If Gen Yers indeed are "impervious to advertising," how can Scion continue to grow without reaching young people through traditional media outlets?

Sources: Mark Rechtin, "Scion Marketing to Stay Outside Mainstream," *Automotive News* (May 7, 2007): 8; Chris Woodyard, "Outside-the-Box Scion Scores with Young Drivers," *USA Today* (May 2, 2005): 1B; Mark Rechtin, "Which Brand Is Stronger—Scion or Prius?" *Automotive News* (January 21, 2008): 24B.

NOTES

1. Shelly Reese, "The Lost Generation," *Marketing Tools* (April 1997): 50.
2. Toby Elkin, "Sony Marketing Aims at Lifestyle Segments," *Advertising Age* (March 18, 2002): 3.
3. Anil Mathur, George P. Moschis, and Euehun Lee, "Life Events and Brand Preference Changes," *Journal of Consumer Behavior* 3, no. 2 (December 2003): 129–41; James W. Gentry, Stacey Menzel Baker, and Frederic B. Kraft, "The Role of Possessions in Creating, Maintaining, and Preserving Identity: Variations over the Life Course," in Frank Kardes and Mita Sujan, eds., *Advances in Consumer Research* 22 (1995): 413–18.
4. Stuart Elliot, "Saturn Tries Alternate Worlds to Change Its Image," *New York Times* (January 8, 2003), www.nytimes.com, accessed January 8, 2003.
5. Cf. Neil Howe and William Strauss, *Generations: The History of America's Future, 1584 to 2069* (New York: Harper Perennial, 1992). The yearly ranges in this list are the author's synthesis of a variety of generational schemes and as such are approximations.
6. Aaron Baar, "Video Games Becoming a Mainstream Choice," *Marketing Daily* (January 19, 2009), www.mediapost.com, accessed January 19, 2009.
7. Bickley Townsend, "*Ou Sont les Reiges Diantan?* (Where Are the Snows of Yesteryear?)" *American Demographics* (October 1988): 2.
8. Gina Chon and Jennifer Saranow, "Bling-Bling Buick Seeking Younger Buyers, General Motors' Staid Brand Uses Customized Cars, Celebrities to Reach the Hip Hop Crowd," *Wall Street Journal* (January 11, 2007): B1; Gina Chon, "Car Makers Court Two Generations," *Wall Street Journal* (May 9, 2006): B1.
9. Stephen Holden, "After the War the Time of the Teen-Ager," *New York Times* (May 7, 1995): E4.
10. Arundhati Parmar, "Global Youth United," *Marketing News* (October 28, 2002): 1–49.
11. Cornelia Pechmann and Chuan-Fong Shih, "Smoking Scenes in Movies and Antismoking Advertisements Before Movies: Effects on Youth," *Journal of Marketing* 63 (July 1999): 1–13.
12. Maureen Tkacik, "Alternative Teens Are Hip to Hot Topic's Mall Stores," *Wall Street Journal* (February 12, 2002), www.wsj.com, accessed February 12, 2002.
13. Junu Bryan Kim, "For Savvy Teens: Real Life, Real Solutions," *New York Times* (August 23, 1993): S1.
14. Excerpted from David B. Wooten, "From Labeling Possessions to Possessing Labels: Ridicule and Socialization Among Adolescents," *Journal of Consumer Research* 33 (September 2006): 188–98.
15. Nicholas Casey, "Teen Retailers Close 'Concept' Stores to Focus on Main Brand," *Wall Street Journal* (March 13, 2009), http://online.wsj.com/article/SB123690331789113861.html, accessed March 13, 2009.
16. For a look at localized versus global youth culture dynamics in Scandinavia, cf. Dannie Kjeldgaard, and Søren Askegaard, "The Glocalization of Youth Culture: The Global Youth Segment as Structures of Common Difference," *Journal of Consumer Research* 33, no. 2 (2006): 231.
17. Natalie Zmuda, "Pepsi Embraces 'Optimistic' Millennials in New TBWA Work," *Advertising Age* (December 11, 2008), http://adage.com/article?Article_Id=133211, accessed January 12, 2008; James Ledbetter, "Obama, the Pepsi Candidate," *Slate* (August 21, 2008), www.slate.com/id/2198198, accessed June 19, 2009.
18. Michael J. Weiss, "To Be About to Be," *American Demographics* (September 2003): 29–48.
19. Steve Kroft, "The Echo Boomers," *CBS News* (October 3, 2004), www.cbsnews.com, accessed October 3, 2004.
20. Scott McCartney, "Society's Subcultures Meet by Modem," *Wall Street Journal* (December 8, 1994): B1.
21. Quoted in "Millennials' Tech Affects Work, Shopping," (December 1, 2008), www.emarketer.com/Article.Aspx?Id=1006777, accessed December 12, 2008; Suzanne Vranica, "Marketers Try To Be 'Kewl' with Text-Message Lingo," *Wall Street Journal* (April 3, 2008): B1; Video to Consume One-Third of Each Day," (June 25, 2008), www.emarketer.com/Article.Aspx?Id=1006381&Src=Article1_Newsltr, accessed June 25, 2008; Brian Stelter, "Whichever Screen, People Are Watching," *New York Times* (July 8, 2008), accessed July 8, 2008; "Research Brief: Parents in the Dark," Center for Media Research (June 11, 2008), www.mediapost.com, accessed June 11, 2008.
22. Alex Mindlin, "Letting Our Fingers Do the Talking," *New York Times* (September 28, 2008), www.nytimes.com/2008/09/29/Technology/29drill.Html?_R=1&Scp=2&Sq=Text%20m, accessed September 29, 2008.
23. "Are Young Adults Really Brand-Resistant?" (November 20, 2008), www.emarketer.com/Article.Aspx?Id=1006754, accessed November 24, 2008.
24. Laurel Anderson and Julie L. Ozanne, "The Cyborg Teen: Identity Play and Deception on the Internet," *Advances in Consumer Research* 33, no. 1 (2006).
25. Cyndee Miller, "Phat Is Where It's at for Today's Teen Market," *Marketing News* (August 15, 1994): 6; see also Tamara F. Mangleburg and Terry Bristol, "Socialization and Adolescents' Skepticism Toward Advertising," *Journal of Advertising* 27 (Fall 1998): 11; see also Gil McWilliam and John Deighton, "Alloy.com: Marketing to Generation Y," *Journal of Interactive Marketing* 14 (Spring 2000): 74–83.
26. Adapted from Gerry Khermouch, "Didja C That Kewl Ad?" *BusinessWeek* (August 26, 2002): 158–60.
27. Karen Springen, Ana Figueroa, and Nicole Joseph-Goteiner, "The Truth About Tweens," *Newsweek* (October 18, 1999): 62–72.

28. Jeremy Mullman, "Study Says Youth Are Swimming in Alcohol Ads Cable TV Blamed for Increased Exposure; Liquor-Industry Group Says Underage Drinking Is Down," *Advertising Age* (June 24, 2008), http://adage.com/Article?Article_Id=127971, accessed June 25, 2008; Jennifer Corbett Dooren, "Alcohol Ads Impact Consumption Among the Young, Study Shows," *Wall Street Journal* (January 2, 2006), www.wsj.com, accessed January 2, 2006; cf. also Maria G. Piacentini and Emma N. Banister, "Getting Hammered? Students Coping with Alcohol," *Journal of Consumer Behaviour* 5, no. 2 (2006): 145.

29. Rob Walker, "Training Brand," *New York Times Magazine* (February 27, 2005), www.nytimes.com, accessed February 27, 2005.

30. Veronique Cova and Bernard Cova, "Tribal Aspects of Postmodern Consumption Research: The Case of French In-Line Roller Skaters," *Journal of Consumer Behavior* 1 (June 2001): 67–76.

31. Terry Lefton, "Feet on the Street," *Brandweek* (March 2000): 36–40.

32. "Students Rule," Center for Media Research, www.mediapost.com, accessed August 12, 2008. Rebecca Gardyn, "Educated Consumers," *Demographics* (November 2002): 18; Tibbett L. Speer, "College Come-Ons," *American Demographics* (March 1998): 40–46; Fannie Weinstein, "Time to Get Them in Your Franchise," *Advertising Age* (February 1, 1988): S6.

33. www.mtvU.com, accessed June 19, 2009; www.collegehumor.com, accessed June 19, 2009.

34. Laura Randall, "Battle of the Campus TV Networks," *New York Times* (January 12, 2003), www.nytimes.com, accessed January 12, 2003.

35. Maria Aspan, "Nielsen Will Start to Measure TV Habits of College Students," *New York Times* (February 20, 2006), www.nytimes.com, accessed February 20, 2006.

36. "Students Rule," Center for Media Research.

37. Beth Synder Bulik, "Want to Build a Hipper Brand? Take a Trip to Trend School: Intelligence Group Endeavor Gives Marketers a Crash Course in Cool," *Advertising Age* (February 19, 2007), www.adage.com, accessed February 19, 2007.

38. Daniel McGinn, "Pour on the Pitch," *Newsweek* (May 31, 1999): 50–51.

39. www.tremor.com, accessed June 19, 2009; Jack Neff, "P&G Targets Teens via Tremor, Toejam Site," *Advertising Age* (March 5, 2001): 12.

40. Gary J. Bamossy, Michael R. Solomon, Basil G. Englis, and Trinske Antonides, "You're Not Cool If You Have to Ask: Gender in the Social Construction of Coolness," paper presented at the Association for Consumer Research Gender Conference, Chicago, June 2000; see also Clive Nancarrow, Pamela Nancarrow, and Julie Page, "An Analysis of the Concept of Cool and Its Marketing Implications," *Journal of Consumer Behavior* 1 (June 2002): 311–22.

41. Ellen Goodman, "The Selling of Teenage Anxiety," *Washington Post* (November 24, 1979).

42. Ellen R. Foxman, Patriya S. Tansuhaj, and Karin M. Ekstrom, "Family Members' Perceptions of Adolescents' Influence in Family Decision-Making," *Journal of Consumer Research* 15 (March 1989): 482–91.

43. Laura Zinn, "Move Over, Boomers," *BusinessWeek* (December 14, 1992): 7.

44. Jeff Gordinier, *X Saves the World: How Generation X Got the Shaft But Can Still Keep Everything From Sucking* (New York: Viking Adult, 2008); M. J. Stephey, "Gen-X: The Ignored Generation?" *Time* (April 16, 2008), www.time.com/time/arts/article/0,8599,1731528,00.html, accessed June 19, 2009.

45. Angel Jennings, "Contests, YouTube and Commercials Converge for Skin Product," *New York Times Online* (July 26, 2007), accessed July 26, 2007; cf. also Isabelle Szmigin and Marylyn Carrigan, "Consumption and Community: Choices for Women over Forty," *Journal of Consumer Behaviour* 5, no. 4 (2006): 292.

46. John Fetto, "The Wild Ones," *American Demographics* (February 2000): 72.

47. Amy Merrick, "Gap Plans Five Forth & Towne Stores for Fall," *Wall Street Journal* (April 22, 2005): B1.

48. Karlene Lukovitz, "Boomers Can Be Targeted by Economic Outlook," *Marketing Daily* (March 4, 2009), www.mediapost.com, accessed March 4, 2009.

49. Stuart Eliot, "Flower Power in Ad Land," *New York Times* (April 11, 2006), www.nytimes.com, accessed April 11, 2006.

50. Emily Steel, "Grabbing Older Consumers via Cellphone Mobile Marketing Finds Success in Sweepstakes; Teaching How to Text," *Wall Street Journal* (January 31, 2007): B3.

51. Christine Bittar, "Dove 'Pro-Age' Will Woo Menopausal Women," *Marketing Daily* (January 16, 2007), http://publications.mediapost.com/Index.Cfm?Fuseaction=Articles.San&S=53938&Nid=26, accessed January 19, 2009; Quoted in Ruth La Ferla, "Like the Makeup Model, Warts and All?" *New York Times* (September 19, 2008), http://www.nytimes.com/2008/09/21/fashion/21ellen.html?_r=1, accessed September 21, 2008.

52. Elkin Tobi, "Sony Ad Campaign Targets Boomers-Turned-Zoomers," *Advertising Age* (October 21, 2002): 6.

53. Hiawatha Bray, "At MIT's AgeLab Growing Old Is the New Frontier," *Boston Globe* (March 23, 2009), www.boston.com/business/technology/articles/2009/03/23/at_mits_agelab_growing_old_is_the_new_frontier/?s_campaign=8315, accessed March 23, 2009.

54. D'Vera Cohn, "2100 Census Forecast: Minorities Expected to Account for 60% of U.S. Population," *Washington Post* (January 13, 2000): A5.

55. Catherine A. Cole and Nadine N. Castellano, "Consumer Behavior," in James E. Binnen, ed., *Encyclopedia of Gerontology*, vol. 1 (San Diego, CA: Academic Press, 1996), 329–39.

56. Raphaël Lambert-Pandraud, Gilles Laurent, and Eric Lapersonne, "Repeat Purchasing of New Automobiles by Older Consumers: Empirical Evidence and Interpretations," *Journal of Marketing* 69 (April 2005): 97–113.

57. Jonathan Dee, "The Myth of '18 to 34,'" *New York Times Magazine* (October 13, 2002), www.nytimes.com, accessed October 11, 2007; Hillary Chura, "Ripe Old Age," *Advertising Age* (May 13, 2002): 16.

58. Quoted in Stuart Elliott, "The Older Audience Is Looking Better Than Ever," *New York Times* (April 19, 2009), www.nytimes.com/2009/04/20/business/20adcol.html, accessed April 19, 2009.

59. Cheryl Russell, "The Ungraying of America," *American Demographics* (July 1997): 12.

60. Jeff Brazil, "You Talkin' to Me?" *American Demographics* (December 1998): 55–59.

61. Benny Barak and Leon G. Schiffman, "Cognitive Age: A Nonchronological Age Variable," in Kent B. Monroe, ed., *Advances in Consumer Research* 8 (Provo, UT: Association for Consumer Research, 1981): 602–6.

62. David B. Wolfe, "An Ageless Market," *American Demographics* (July 1987): 27–55.

63. Pamela Paul, "Sell It to the Psyche," *Time* (September 15, 2003): Bonus Section inside Business.

64. David B. Wolfe, "Targeting the Mature Mind," *American Demographics* (March 1994): 32–36.

65. Rick Adler, "Stereotypes Won't Work with Seniors Anymore," *Advertising Age* (November 11, 1996): 32.

66. Melinda Beck, "Going for the Gold," *Newsweek* (April 23, 1990): 74.

67. Tania Ralli, "As Europe Ages, a Grocery Chain Extends a Hand," *New York Times* (December 27, 2003), www.nytimes.com, accessed December 27, 2003.

68. Norimitsu Onishi, "In a Graying Japan, Lower Shelves and Wider Aisles," *New York Times* (September 4, 2006), www.nytimes.com, accessed September 4, 2006.

69. Lenore Skenazy, "These Days, It's Hip to Be Old," *Advertising Age* (February 15, 1988): 8.

70. Nat Ives, "AARP Aims to Deliver Message to Marketers," *New York Times* (January 12, 2004), www.nytimes.com, accessed January 12, 2004.

71. L. A. Winokur, "Targeting Consumers," *Wall Street Journal* (March 6, 2000), www.wsj.com, accessed March 6, 2000.

72. Ellen Day, Brian Davis, Rhonda Dove, and Warren A. French, "Reaching the Senior Citizen Market(s)," *Journal of Advertising Research* (December 1987–January 1988): 23–30.

73. Day et al., "Reaching the Senior Citizen Market(s)"; Warren A. French and Richard Fox, "Segmenting the Senior Citizen Market," *Journal of Consumer Marketing* 2 (1985): 61–74; Jeffrey G. Towle and Claude R. Martin, Jr., "The Elderly Consumer: One Segment or Many?" in Beverlee B. Anderson, ed., *Advances in Consumer Research* 3 (Provo, UT: Association for Consumer Research, 1976): 463.

74. Catherine A. Cole and Nadine N. Castellano, "Consumer Behavior," *Encyclopedia of Gerontology* 1 (1996): 329–39.

75. Hope Jensen Schau, Mary C. Gilly, and Mary Wolfinbarger, "Consumer Identity Renaissance: The Resurgence of Identity-Inspired Consumption in Retirement" *Journal of Consumer Research* 36 (August 2009).

76. Quoted in Tamar Lewin, "Teenagers' Internet Socializing Not a Bad Thing," *New York Times* (November 19, 2008), www.nytimes.com/2008/11/20/us/20internet.html?ex=1384923600&en=c3467e945b431625&ei=5124, accessed November 24, 2008.

77. Nina M. Lentini, "Redux Back with Cocaine Energy Drink in Big Way," *Marketing Daily* (February 6, 2008), http://publications.mediapost.com/Index.Cfm?Fuseaction=Articles.San&S=75887&Nid=3907..., accessed February 6, 2008.

MINTEL

SECTION 4   MINTEL MEMO AND DATASET EXERCISE

Mintel Memo

TO: Consumer Research Dept.

FROM: The Big Boss

RE: Premium chocolate

We all love our premium chocolate brand, but we really need to shake up our marketing for it—our sales have been stagnant for quite awhile now. I have no big ideas in mind, so I would consider tweaking any aspect of our marketing strategy to pull our chocolate out of its sales rut. Therefore, please provide us with actionable recommendations for any of our marketing strategy elements based on this information. I have a strong suspicion that we should begin to differentiate our segmentation strategies. As you analyze the data in the tables provided, keep an eye on trends among income/social subcultures, ethnic/racial subcultures, and age subcultures.

When you write your memo, please try to incorporate relevant concepts and information you learned when you read the designated chapters!

Number of Respondents		615	438	80	23	138
Respondent Categories			Ethnicity		Age	
Respondent Sub-categories		Total	Caucasian	African American	25–34	55+
			(A)	(B)	(A)	(B)
Question	**Answers**	%	%	%	%	%
When it comes to premium/gourmet chocolate, which is your favorite type?	Dark chocolate	43	48	28	38	52
(Comparison of Column Proportions)			B			A
	Milk chocolate	42	36	63	48	33
				A	B	
	White chocolate	7	7	5	6	3
	I do not have a favorite type	8	9	5	8	12

Comparison of Column Proportions results are based on two-sided tests with significance level $p < 0.05$. Letters appearing in the column category denote a significant difference between the number immediately above the letter and the category associated with that particular letter. For example, the "B" in the Caucasian category above denotes a significant difference between the percentage of Caucasians who specify dark chocolate as their favorite type (48%) and the percentage of African Americans who specify the same (28%).

What can we learn from these data to help our company's segmentation and market-ing strategies for specific subcultures?

To access the complete Mintel questionnaires and datasets, go to MyMarketingLab at www.mypearsonmarketinglab.com. If you are not using MyMarketingLab, visit this book's Companion Website at www.pearsonhighered.com/solomon.

Section 5 Consumers and Culture

Okay, we're coming up to the finish line. In the final section of the book, we'll consider how we each belong to a bigger cultural system. We'll focus on the "profound" idea that everyday, mundane consumption activities often have deeper meanings. In Chapter 15, we explore some of the basic building blocks of culture and the impact that myths and rituals exert on modern consumers. Chapter 16 focuses on the ways ideas and products spread throughout the members of a culture, and across cultures as well. This final chapter talks about why some consumer products succeed while others don't, and it also examines how successful Western products influence consumer behavior around the world.

CHAPTERS AHEAD

15

Cultural Influences
on Consumer Behavior

When you finish this chapter you will understand:

C h a p t e r
O b j e c t i v e s

Karin is at her wits' end. It's bad enough that she has a deadline looming on that new Christmas promotion for her gift shop. Now, there's trouble on the home front as well: Her son Ken had to go and flunk his driver's license road exam, and he's just about suicidal because he feels he can't be a "real man" if he doesn't have a license. To top things off, now she'll have to postpone her much-anticipated vacation to Disney World with her younger stepchildren because she just can't find the time to get away.

When Karin meets up with her buddy Melissa at their local Starbucks for their daily "retreat," her mood starts to brighten. Somehow the calm of the café rubs off as she savors her *grande cappuccino*. Melissa consoles her with the ultimate remedy to beat the blues: Go home, take a nice long bath, and then consume a quart of Starbucks Espresso Swirl ice cream. Yes, that's the ticket. It's amazing how the little things in life can make such a big difference. As she strolls out the door, Karin makes a mental note to get Melissa a really nice Christmas gift this year. She's earned it.

OBJECTIVE

Why is a culture like a society's personality; how does it shape our identities as individuals?

What Is Culture?

People around the globe mimic Karin's daily coffee "fix" as they take a break from the daily grind and affirm their relationships with others. Of course, the products they consume in the process range from black Turkish coffee to Indian tea, or from lager beer to hashish. Starbucks turns the coffee break into a cultural event that for many is almost like a cult. The average Starbucks customer visits 18 times a month, and 10 percent of the clientele stops by twice a day.[1] Even a simple cup of coffee is more than a simple cup of coffee.

Culture is a society's personality. It includes both abstract ideas, such as values and ethics, and material objects and services, such as the automobiles, clothing, food, art, and sports a society produces. Put another way, it's the accumulation of shared meanings, rituals, norms, and traditions among the members of an organization or society.

We simply can't understand consumption unless we consider its cultural context: Culture is the "lens" through which people view products. Ironically, the effects of culture on consumer behavior are so powerful and far-reaching that it's sometimes difficult to grasp their importance. Like a fish immersed in water, we don't always appreciate this power until we encounter a different culture. Suddenly, many of the assumptions we take for granted about the clothes we wear, the food we eat, or the way we address others no longer seem to apply. The effect when we encounter such differences can be so great that the term *culture shock* is not an exaggeration.

We often discover these cultural expectations only when we violate them. For example, while on tour in New Zealand, the Spice Girls (remember them?) created a stir among New Zealand's indigenous Maoris when they performed a war dance that only men can do. A tribal official indignantly stated, "It is not acceptable in our culture, and especially by girlie pop stars from another culture."[2] Americans had a somewhat similar reaction when Posh Spice came to the United States with her husband David Beckham to teach us Yanks about the joys of soccer! Sensitivity to cultural issues, whether among rock stars or brand managers, can only occur when we understand these underlying dimensions—and that's this chapter's goal.

Our culture determines the overall priorities we attach to different activities and products, and it also helps to decide whether specific products will make it. A product that provides benefits to members of a culture at any point in time has a much better chance to achieve marketplace acceptance. For example, American culture began to emphasize the concept of a fit, trim body as an ideal of appearance in the mid-1970s. The premium consumers put on thinness, which stemmed from underlying values such as mobility, wealth, and a focus on the self, greatly contributed to Miller's success when the brewer launched its Lite beer. However, when Gablinger's introduced a similar low-cal beer in the 1960s the product failed. This beverage was "ahead of its time" because American beer drinkers at that time (who were almost all men) weren't worried about cutting down on calories.

The relationship between consumer behavior and culture is a two-way street. On the one hand, consumers are more likely to embrace products and services that resonate with a culture's priorities at any given time. On the other hand, it's worthwhile for us to understand which products do get accepted because this knowledge provides a window into the dominant cultural ideals of that period. Consider, for example, some American products that successfully reflected dominant values during their time:

- The TV dinner reflected changes in family structure and the onset of a new informality in American home life.
- Cosmetics made from natural materials without animal testing reflected consumers' apprehensions about pollution, waste, and animal rights.
- Condoms marketed in pastel carrying cases for female buyers signaled changes in attitudes toward sexual responsibility and openness.

This ad for a line of veggie foods borrows the look of World War II propaganda art to imply that eating our broccoli is an heroic act.
Source: Courtesy of Fantastic Foods.

   Culture is not static. It is continually evolving, synthesizing old ideas with new ones. A *cultural system* consists of these functional areas:[3]

- **Ecology**—The way a system adapts to its habitat. The technology a culture uses to obtain and distribute resources shapes its ecology. The Japanese, for example, greatly value products that make efficient use of space because of the cramped conditions in their urban centers.[4]
- **Social structure**—The way people maintain an orderly social life. This includes the domestic and political groups that dominate the culture (e.g., the nuclear family versus the extended family; representative government versus dictatorship).

- **Ideology**—The mental characteristics of a people and the way they relate to their environment and social groups. This relates to the idea of a common *worldview* (we discussed this in Chapter 12). Members of a culture tend to share ideas about principles of order and fairness. They also share an *ethos*, or a set of moral and aesthetic principles. A theme park in Bombay called Water Kingdom that caters to India's emerging middle class illustrates how distinctive a culture's worldview can be. Many consumers there are unfamiliar with mixed-sex swimming in public, so the park rents swimsuits to women who have never worn them before. No thongs here, though: The suits cover the women from wrists to ankles.[5]

Although every culture is different, four dimensions account for much of this variability:[7]

1 **Power distance**—The way members perceive differences in power when they form interpersonal relationships. Some cultures emphasize strict, vertical relationships (e.g., Japan), whereas others, such as the United States, stress a greater degree of equality and informality.
2 **Uncertainty avoidance**—The degree to which people feel threatened by ambiguous situations and have beliefs and institutions that help them to avoid this uncertainty (e.g., organized religion).
3 **Masculinity/femininity**—The degree to which a culture clearly defines sex roles (see Chapter 5). Traditional societies are more likely to possess very explicit rules about the acceptable behaviors of men and women, such as who is responsible for certain tasks within the family unit.
4 **Individualism**—The extent to which the culture values the welfare of the individual versus that of the group (see Chapter 10). In **collectivist cultures**, people subordinate their personal goals to those of a stable in-group. In contrast, consumers in **individualist cultures** attach more importance to personal goals, and people are more likely to change memberships when the demands of the group (e.g., workplace, church, etc.) become too costly. Whereas a collectivist society will stress values (see Chapter 4), such as self-discipline and accepting one's position in life, people in individualist cultures emphasize personal enjoyment, excitement, equality, and freedom. Some strongly individualist cultures include the United States, Australia, Great Britain, Canada, and the Netherlands. Venezuela, Pakistan, Taiwan, Thailand, Turkey, Greece, and Portugal are examples of strongly collectivist cultures.[8]

As we saw in Chapter 4, values are very general ideas about good and bad goals. From these flow norms, or rules that dictate what is right or wrong, acceptable or unacceptable. We explicitly decide on *enacted norms*, such as the rule that a green traffic light means "go" and a red one means "stop." Many norms, however, are much more subtle. We discover these **crescive norms** as we interact with others. These are all types of crescive norms:[9]

- A **custom** is a norm that controls basic behaviors, such as division of labor in a household or how we practice particular ceremonies.
- A **more** ("mor-ay") is a custom with a strong moral overtone. It often involves a *taboo*, or forbidden behavior, such as incest or cannibalism. Violation of a more often meets with strong sanctions. In Islamic countries such as Saudi Arabia, people consider it sacrilege to display underwear on store mannequins or to feature a woman's body in advertising, so retailers have to tread lightly—one lingerie store designed special headless and legless mannequins with only the slightest hint of curves to display its products.[10]
- **Conventions** are norms that regulate how we conduct our everyday lives. These rules often deal with the subtleties of consumer behavior, including the "correct" way to furnish one's house, wear one's clothes, or host a dinner party. The Chinese

government tried to change citizens' conventions when the country geared up for the 2008 Olympics in Beijing: Local habits are at odds with what planners knew that foreign visitors expect to encounter. For one, it's common to spit on the sidewalk—the sinus-clearing, phlegmy pre-spit hawking sound is so common that one foreigner dubbed it "the national anthem of China." In addition to the extensive cleanup the government conducted (it even restricted city traffic to reduce smog levels), it imposed a hefty fine for public spitting to get people accustomed to holding in their saliva before hordes of fans descended on the city.[11]

All three types of crescive norms at times operate to completely define a culturally appropriate behavior. For example, a more may tell us what kind of food it's okay to eat. These norms vary across cultures, so a meal of dog is taboo in the United States, Hindus shun steak, and Muslims avoid pork products. A custom dictates the appropriate hour at which we should serve the meal. Conventions tell us how to eat the meal, including such details as the utensils we use, table etiquette, and even the appropriate apparel to wear at dinnertime. We often take these conventions for granted. We just assume they are the "right" things to do (again, until we travel to a foreign country!). Much of what we know about these norms we learn *vicariously* (see Chapter 3) as we observe the behaviors of actors in television commercials, sitcoms, print ads, and other media—that reminds us why the marketing system is such an important element of culture.

Cultural differences show up in all kinds of daily activities. For example, a Big Boy restaurant in Thailand was having trouble attracting customers. After interviewing hundreds of people, the company found out why. Some said the restaurant's "room energy" was bad and that the food was unfamiliar. Others said the Big Boy statue (like the one Dr. Evil rode in the *Austin Powers* movies) made them nervous. One of the restaurant's executives commented, "It suddenly dawned on me that, here I was, trying to get a 3,500-year-old culture to eat 64-year-old food." Once the company put some Thai items on the menu, business picked up.[12] No word yet on the fate of the statue.

Cultural Stories and Ceremonies

Every culture develops stories and ceremonies that help us make sense of the world. When we hear about some strange practice that goes on in another place, it may be hard to figure out just what these people think they're doing. Yet, our own cultural practices seem quite normal—even though a visitor may find them equally bizarre! Just take a European to a NASCAR event and you'll understand that culture is relative.

To appreciate how "primitive" belief systems influence our supposedly "modern" rational society, consider the avid interest many of us have in magic and luck. Marketers of health foods, antiaging cosmetics, exercise programs, and gambling casinos often imply that their offerings have "magical" properties that prevent sickness, old age, poverty, or just plain bad luck. People by the millions play their "lucky numbers" in the lottery, carry rabbits' feet and other amulets to ward off "the evil eye," and own "lucky" clothing.

When the calendar hit July 7, 2007—7/7/07—many people scrambled to take advantage of its link to lucky 777. Our culture associates the number seven with good fortune (like the seven sacraments in Roman Catholicism) and marketers from Wal-Mart to Las Vegas casinos jumped on the bandwagon. The Mandalay Bay Casino hosted a group wedding for more than 100 couples. The New York City Ritz-Carlton even offered a Lucky Number 7 wedding package with a reception for 77, a seven-tier wedding cake, and a seven-night honeymoon at any Ritz in the world for $77,777.[13] Keep in mind that these beliefs are culture centric so they take on different forms around the world. For example, in China eight is the luckiest number. The Chinese word for eight is *ba*, which rhymes with *fa*, the Chinese character for wealth. It's no coincidence that the Summer Olympics in Beijing opened on 8/8/08 at 8 P.M.[14]

FEELING LUCKY?

LuckySurf.com

Interest in the occult tends to spike when members of a society feel overwhelmed or powerless—magical remedies simplify our lives when they give us "easy" answers. Many consumers even regard the computer with awe as a sort of "electronic magician" with the ability to solve our problems (or in other cases to cause data to magically disappear!).[15] Software developers even supply "wizards" that guide the uninitiated through their programs! Or, we may even think a person's soul possesses an object—kids (and maybe some adults as well) believe that when they put on their Air Nikes they magically absorb some of the athletic ability of Michael Jordan. Sound preposterous? The movie *Like Mike* had this exact storyline. In this section, we'll discuss myths and rituals, two aspects of culture common to all societies from the ancients to the modern world.

2
OBJECTIVE

How are myths stories that express a culture's values, and how in modern times do marketing messages convey these values?

Myths

A **myth** is a story with symbolic elements that represents a culture's ideals. The story often focuses on some kind of conflict between two opposing forces, and its outcome serves as a moral guide for listeners. In this way, a myth reduces anxiety because it provides consumers with guidelines about their world. Most members of a culture learn these stories, but usually we don't really think about their origins.

Every culture creates mythical characters to impart moral lessons. The Romans had their gods and goddesses like Artemis, and the Chinese tell of Chang E, whose husband served the mythical Chinese emperor Yao. She drank a stolen elixir of life, then fled to the moon where she became Queen.

Source: a. Photo by Dagli Orti/Courtesy of Picture Desk, Inc./Kobal Collection. b. Photo by Asian Art & Archaeology, Inc./CORBIS-NY.

Consider, for example, a familiar story in our culture: *Little Red Riding Hood*. This myth started as a peasant's tale in sixteenth-century France, where a girl meets a werewolf on her way to granny's house (there is historical evidence for a plague of wolf attacks during this time, including several incidents where men were put on trial because they allegedly turned themselves into the deadly animals). The werewolf has already killed granny, stored her flesh in the pantry, and poured her blood in a bottle. Contrary to the version we know however, when the girl arrives at the house she snacks on granny, strips naked, and climbs into bed with the wolf! To make the story even more scandalous, some versions refer to the wolf as a "gaffer" (a contraction of "grandfather") implying incest as well. This story first appeared in print in 1697; it was a warning to the loose ladies of Louis XIV's court (the author puts her in red in this version because this color symbolizes harlots). Eventually, the Brothers Grimm wrote their own version in 1812, but they substituted violence for sex in order to scare kids into behaving. And to reinforce the sex-role standards of that time, in the Grimm version a man rescues the girl from the wolf.[16] So, this myth sends vivid messages about such cultural no-no's as cannibalism, incest, and promiscuity.

In some cases marketers adapt these stories and (perhaps unconsciously) pattern their messages along a mythic structure. Consider, for example, the way that McDonald's takes on "mythical" qualities.[17] The "golden arches" are a symbol consumers everywhere recognize as virtually synonymous with American culture. They offer sanctuary to Americans around the world; they know exactly what to expect once they enter. Basic struggles involving good versus evil play out in the fantasy world McDonald's advertising creates, for example, when Ronald McDonald confounds the Hamburglar. McDonald's even has a "seminary" (Hamburger University) where inductees go to learn the ways of The Golden Arches.

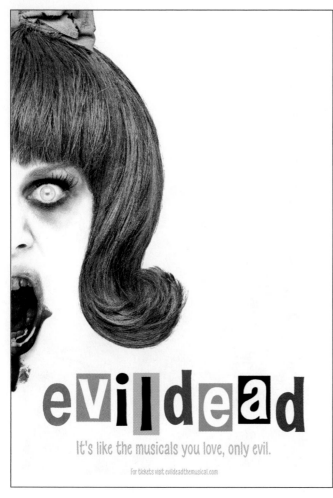

Advertisements like these for Canadian plays build on familiar stories.

Source: Courtesy of Saatchi Toronto.

Corporations often have myths and legends in their history, and some make a deliberate effort to teach them to newcomers. Nike designates senior executives as "corporate storytellers" who explain the company's heritage to the hourly workers at Nike stores. They recount tales about the coach of the Oregon track team who poured rubber into his family waffle iron to make better shoes for his team—the origin of the Nike waffle sole. The stories emphasize the dedication of runners and coaches to reinforce the importance of teamwork. Rookies even visit the track where the coach worked to help them appreciate the importance of the Nike legends. And rumor has it that senior Nike executives (including the CEO) have a "swoosh" tattoo on their backsides.[18]

What Myths Do

Myths serve four interrelated functions in a culture:[19]

1 **Metaphysical**—They help to explain the origins of existence.
2 **Cosmological**—They emphasize that all components of the universe are part of a single picture.
3 **Sociological**—They maintain social order because they authorize a social code for members of a culture to follow.
4 **Psychological**—They provide models for personal conduct.

When we analyze myths, we examine their underlying structures, a technique the French anthropologist Claude Lévi-Strauss (no relation to the blue jeans company) pioneered. Lévi-Strauss noted that many stories involve **binary opposition**, which represents two opposing ends of some dimension (e.g., good versus evil, nature versus technology).[20] Advertisers sometimes define products in terms of what they are *not* rather than what they *are* (e.g., "This is *not* your father's Oldsmobile," "I can't believe it's *not* butter").

Recall from our discussion of Freudian theory in Chapter 6 that the ego functions as a kind of "referee" between the opposing needs of the id and the superego. In a similar fashion, a *mediating figure* typically resolves the conflict between mythical opposing forces; this links the opposites as it shares characteristics of each. For example, many myths are about animals that have human abilities (e.g., a talking snake) to bridge the gap between humanity and nature, just as marketers often give cars (technology) animal names (nature) such as Cougar, Cobra, or Mustang.

Myths in Modern Popular Culture

We associate myths with the ancient Greeks and Romans, but in reality comic books, movies, holidays, and yes, even commercials embody our own cultural myths. And researchers report that some people create their own *consumer fairy tales*—they tell stories that include magical agents, donors, and helpers to overcome villains and obstacles as they seek out goods and services in their quest for happy endings.[21]

Smart marketers are more than happy to help us live out these fairy tales. Consider the popularity of the elaborate weddings Disney stages for couples who want to reenact their own version of a popular myth: At Disney World, the princess bride wears a tiara and rides to the park's lakeside wedding pavilion in a horse-drawn coach, complete with two footmen in gray wigs and gold lamé pants. At the exchange of vows, trumpets blare as Major Domo (he helped the Duke in his quest for Cinderella) walks up the aisle with two wedding bands he gently places in a glass slipper on a velvet pillow. Disney stages about 2,000 of these extravaganzas each year. The company continues to expand the appeal of this myth as it moves into the bridal gown business. It sells a line of billowing princess gowns complete with crystal tiaras. Fairy-tale brides can walk down the aisle costumed as Cinderella, Snow White, Belle, Sleeping Beauty, Jasmine, or Ariel.[22]

Comic book superheroes demonstrate how a culture communicates myths to consumers of all ages. Marvel Comics' Spiderman character tells stories about how he balances the obligations of being a superhero with the need of his alter ego, Peter

This Italian jeans ad evokes imagery from a modern myth that involves an animal character.
Source: Courtesy Meltin' Pot Jeans/Armando Testa, Milan.

Parker, to succeed in school and have a normal love life.[23] Indeed, some of these fictional figures embody such fundamental properties that they become a **monomyth**— a myth that is common to many cultures.[24] Consider Superman—a father (Jor-el) gives his only son to save a world with his supernatural powers. Sound familiar?

Many "blockbuster" movies and hit TV shows draw directly on mythic themes. Although dramatic special effects or attractive stars certainly don't hurt, a number of these movies also owe their huge appeal to their presentation of characters and plot structures that follow mythic patterns. Here are three examples of mythic blockbusters:[25]

- **Gone with the Wind**—Myths often take place in times of upheaval such as wars. In this story, the North (which represents technology and democracy) battles the South (which represents nature and aristocracy). The movie depicts a romantic era (the antebellum South) when love and honor were virtues. Following the war, newer values of materialism and industrialization (i.e., modern consumer culture) replace these priorities. The movie paints a picture of a lost era where man and nature existed in harmony.
- **E.T.: The Extraterrestrial**—E.T. represents a familiar myth involving messianic visitation. The gentle creature from another world visits Earth and performs miracles (e.g., he revives a dying flower). His "disciples" are neighborhood children; they help him combat the forces of modern technology and an unbelieving secular society. The myth teaches that the humans God chooses are pure and unselfish.
- **Star Trek**—The multiple television series and movies, prequels, and sequels that document the adventures of the starship *Enterprise* also link to myths, such as the story of the New England Puritans who explore and conquer a new continent— "the final frontier." Encounters with the Klingons mirror skirmishes with Native Americans. In addition, at least 13 out of the original 79 episodes employed the theme of a quest for paradise.[26] The popular series *Battlestar Galactica* does as well.

Advertisements sometimes represent mythic themes. For example, commercials for Pepperidge Farm ask consumers to "remember" the good old days (lost paradise) when products were wholesome and natural. Avis famously used the theme of the underdog prevailing over the stronger foe (i.e., David and Goliath).[27] A commercial that encouraged Hispanic consumers to buy more milk featured a female phantom who wails as she walks through a home. She is *La Llorona* (the crying one)—a character in a Hispanic myth who murders her children, commits suicide, and roams for all eternity as she seeks her lost family. In this version, however, the moaning phantom makes her way to the refrigerator, only to find an empty milk carton.[28]

Even packages can mythologize a brand, as researchers who analyzed the messages on some "natural" products report. The authors found that many of the packages present a narrative about a romantic past, where values of family, tradition, authenticity, peace, and simplicity reigned. For example, the label on a box of Celestial Seasoning's tea reads: "When you find a quiet moment, ease into a cup of contentment with Honey Vanilla Chamomile Herb Tea." The brand name itself, note the authors, conjures the transcendent possibilities of tea consumption (celestial). The package includes a personally signed guarantee of satisfaction from the company's founder.

(3)

OBJECTIVE

Why are many of our consumption activities— including holiday observances, grooming, and gift-giving—rituals?

These elements subtly invoke the binary opposition to large, impersonal corporations where the founder would never take the time to write a message. Other "natural" product packaging often includes origin myths such as: "It began very simply. In 1960 in the back of a small health food store. . . ."[29]

Rituals

A **ritual** is a set of multiple, symbolic behaviors that occurs in a fixed sequence and is repeated periodically.[30] Bizarre

Koreans are discovering the Western ritual of brunch.
Source: Photo by Chung Sung-Jun/Courtesy of Getty Images, Inc.

tribal ceremonies, perhaps involving animal or human sacrifice, may come to mind when you think of rituals, but in reality many contemporary consumer activities are ritualistic. Just think of Karin's daily "mental health" trip to Starbucks.

Or consider a ritual that many beer drinkers in the United Kingdom and Ireland hold near and dear to their hearts—the spectacle of a pub bartender "pulling" the perfect pint of Guinness. According to tradition, the slow pour takes exactly 119.5 seconds as the bartender holds the glass at a 45-degree angle, fills it three-quarters full, lets it settle, and tops it off with its signature creamy head. Guinness wanted to make the pull faster so the bar could serve more drinks on a busy night so it introduced FastPour, an ultrasound technology that dispenses the dark brew in only 25 seconds. You probably guessed the outcome: The brewer had to scrap the system when drinkers resisted the innovation. Note: Diageo (which owns Guinness) hasn't given up and it continues to experiment with more efficient techniques in markets where this ritual isn't so inbred. A system it calls Guinness Surger shows up in Tokyo bars, many of which are too small to accommodate kegs: The bartender pours a pint from a bottle, places the glass on a special plate, and zaps it with ultrasound waves that generate the characteristic head.[32]

Many colleges boast unique rituals in which students engage in some scripted group activity, but in recent years some institutions abolished these because of safety concerns or because they encourage underage drinking. Casualties include spring couch burning at the University of Vermont and Princeton's Nude Winter Olympics. The death of 12 people from collapsing logs ended the tradition of Texas A&M's bonfire on the eve of the annual football game against the University of Texas (the bonfire ritual has since been revived off campus). Some campus rituals that survive include the following:

- **MIT**—Each spring students haul a steer into a dorm courtyard, put it on a spit, and light a fire under it with a flaming roll of toilet paper they lower from the roof.
- **Wesleyan College (Connecticut)**—Students honor the pot-smoking Doonesbury character Zonker Harris each spring with a day of live music, face painting, and plenty of open marijuana use.
- **Simon Fraser University (British Columbia)**—Costumed engineering students throw one another in the reflection pond during February's Polar Plunge.

Marketing Opportunity

Many Americans treasure the ritual of Sunday brunch. But chowing on a late-morning spread of pancakes, bagels, and other cholesterol-laden goodies was unknown in South Korea until a few years ago. Now it's all the rage; several hundred restaurants offer brunch now after one restaurateur opened a place—decorated with photos of New York City—in 2005 and ignited the trend. One change in Korean society fueled the fire—the government shortened the official workweek from six days to five in 2004 so suddenly people had a weekend to enjoy. Consumers there also like the American show *Sex and the City*, where the characters often drink their way through a long brunch. A consumer ritual is born.[31]

CB AS I SEE IT

Professor Lauren Block, *Baruch College, City University of New York*

Do you have any rituals you perform for good luck? I know a college student who will only walk up the left staircase of her university building on exam days. This student won't take the elevator or use the staircase on the right side of the building for fear that she will jinx her good performance on tests. I know another student who turns off the football game with three minutes left in the fourth quarter if his team is winning. It's not that he doesn't want to watch his team win, it's that he doesn't want to jinx them in the final moments and have a loss be his fault. Make sense? Of course not. But does it feel familiar? Probably.

Research has recently begun to document just how common and ordinary such superstitious or magical thinking is among people. **Superstitions** are beliefs that run counter to rational thought or are inconsistent with known laws of nature. While many superstitions are culturally shared and socially transmitted from generation to generation, others consist of relatively more idiosyncratic beliefs or rituals, like the examples described previously. My colleague Tom Kramer and I study how peoples' superstitious beliefs influence their behavior as consumers. For example, common superstitions among Taiwanese include beliefs about lucky

colors (e.g., red) and lucky numbers (e.g., 8). In research Tom and I conducted in Taiwan, we found that Taiwanese consumers are more likely to purchase a product that is red than the same exact product in another color, and purchasers have higher expectations for the red product than for, say, a green product. In other words, consumers expect the red product to work better than the green one and would be more upset if the product failed or broke. Our research also demonstrated that Taiwanese consumers are willing to pay a higher price for a package with a "lucky" number of items inside (8 tennis balls) than the same package with a greater but neutral number of items (10 tennis balls). Taiwanese consumers were willing to spend over 50 percent more for 25 percent fewer tennis balls because of their positive superstitious beliefs with the number 8 (versus 10). Similarly we found that Taiwanese consumers are willing to pay more to avoid unlucky numbers. They would rather pay TW$555 (5 is a neutral number) than TW$444 (4 is an unlucky number), foregoing a discount for the same product.

Would you be willing to spend more money to avoid unlucky numbers? American consumers don't have the same beliefs as Taiwanese, but they do think 13 is an unlucky number. Many American buildings don't have a 13th floor, and U.S. businesses lose a large amount of money every Friday the 13th

because people avoid important transactions on that day. Tom Kramer and I studied whether superstitious beliefs about Friday the 13th influence the choices American students make. Students were asked to choose between two bets: in the first bet students knew they could win a small sum of money and in the second bet students had to gamble to win either a large amount or nothing. For example, students were asked to choose between receiving $18 for sure versus a 20 percent chance of winning $240 and an 80 percent chance of winning nothing. It turns out that most American students prefer the riskier option in the hopes of winning the large amount of money. But when we asked this question on Friday the 13th, their choice switched to the not-risky smaller amount.

Using this knowledge of how superstitious beliefs influence behavior can help managers make better business decisions. How much more profit could Taco Bell have earned if it had altered its seven-layer Crunchwrap Supreme into an eight-layer one for Chinese consumers? Similarly, the $4/$4/$4 promotion by Domino's Pizza was probably not well received by Chinese consumers. With one of the luckiest days of the century for Western cultures passed (7/7/07) and one of the luckiest days of the century for Eastern cultures still fresh in memory (8/8/08), the study of superstition in the marketplace is both important and timely.

A study the BBDO Worldwide advertising agency conducted illustrates the close relationship between brands and rituals.[33] It labels brands that we use to perform our rituals **fortress brands** because once they become embedded in our ceremonies—whether we use them to brush our teeth, drink a beer, or shave—we're unlikely to replace them. The study ran in 26 countries, and the researchers found that overall people worldwide practice roughly the same consumer rituals. The agency claims that 89 percent of people always use the same brands in their sequenced rituals; three out of four are disappointed or irritated when something disrupts their ritual or their brand of choice isn't available. For example, the report identifies one common ritual category it calls *preparing for battle*. For most of us this means getting ready for work. Relevant rituals include brushing the teeth, taking a shower or bath, having something to eat or drink, talking to a family member or partner, checking e-mail, shaving, putting on makeup, watching TV or listening to the radio, and reading a newspaper.

CB AS I LIVE IT

Julia Koman, *Penn State Behrend*

*B*efore big games or tournaments, the Penn State Behrend softball team organizes team dinners and enjoys a good meal with quality team bonding. As we were preparing to depart for a week-long spring training tournament in Clermont, Florida, we decided to go to Ceci's Pizza, a buffet-style pizzeria with large varieties of pizza and pizza desserts to choose from. Since the team gets together before all big games and tournaments, we have a *ritual* in place. The team dinners have long been a ritual for the softball team because as a senior now, I always remember going to these dinners even as a freshman.

The chapter's definition and explanation of a ritual was much more

broadly defined. After reading about the Starbucks ritual for the demanding businesswoman, I agree that rituals affect my own consumer behavior. I now can see that some of the things that I do can be considered rituals and highly affect my purchase behavior and the money that I spend. This is especially true when it comes to my softball team's dinners. They only happen every so often, but it's money that I never think twice about spending.

Now that I am aware of this concept, I can create a budget to keep a check on how much money I am spending each time I go out to a team dinner. This way, I can save more of my money, especially since I have an extremely limited income due to the fact that I am a typical college student. By keeping track of the reasons I spend money each month, I will have a better grip on my financials, which is very important today.

A marketer can learn from my experience by realizing the number of sports team that have rituals like team dinners. A marketer for a restaurant chain could promote a discount for teams that want to have their team dinners in restaurants. For buffet-style restaurants that are reasonably priced and offer a large selection of food, knowing that teams in the area are willing to come to their establishment for get-togethers, such as team dinners, would be most beneficial. By offering small discounts to sports teams, restaurants like Ceci's and others could benefit by seeing increased sales and traffic. These increases, though they may be small, could help out their advertising efforts by better promoting free word-of-mouth communication by its satisfied customers.

- **Wellesley**—Seniors toss the winner of the annual spring hoop roll into chilly Lake Waban. This ritual has changed to keep up with the times—the winner used to be declared the first to marry—now she's proclaimed the most likely to succeed.
- **University of California at Santa Barbara**—Students run naked across campus on the first rainy day of the year. Princeton and the University of Michigan have banned nude sprints, but at Yale seniors still run naked through two campus libraries at the end of each semester and toss candy at underclass students as they cram for finals.[34]

Table 15.1 notes that rituals can occur at several levels. Some reinforce broad cultural or religious values. Public rituals such as the Super Bowl, presidential inaugurations, and graduation ceremonies are communal activities that affirm our membership in the larger group and reassure us that we are reading from the same script as everyone else.[36] In one recent study, researchers documented the collective ritual of *headbanging* at heavy metal music concerts. They showed how participants, who tend to come from lower economic classes and feel disempowered in other settings, participate collectively in a performance that is a cathartic experience where they are rejuvenated and validated (perhaps this presents an opportunity for companies that sell headache remedies?).[37]

Other rituals occur in small groups or even in isolation. Market researchers discovered that for many people (such as Karin) the act of late-night ice cream eating has ritualistic elements that often involve a favorite spoon and bowl![38] And rituals are not set in stone; they change with the times. For example, when we throw rice at a wedding we express our desire for the couple to be fertile. In recent years, "green"

TABLE 15.1	Types of Ritual Experience	
Primary Behavior Source	**Ritual Type**	**Examples**
Cosmology	Religious	Baptism, meditation, mass
Cultural values	Rites of passage Cultural	Graduation, marriage festivals, holidays (Valentine's Day), Super Bowl
Group learning	Civic	Parades, elections, trials
	Group	Fraternity initiation, business negotiations, office luncheons
	Family	Mealtimes, bedtimes, birthdays, Mother's Day, Christmas
Individual aims and emotions	Personal	Grooming, household rituals

Source: Dennis W. Rook, "The Ritual Dimension of Consumer Behavior," *Journal of Consumer Research* 12 (December 1985): 251–64. Copyright © 1985 JCR, Inc. Reprinted with permission of the University of Chicago Press.

Marketing Opportunity

Tailgating at college and pro football games is one of the most visible group rituals around today. According to legend, this practice started in the nineteenth century when fans had no choice but to cook meals in their carriages after they journeyed to the site of a football game. Now, tailgating is also big business. A survey Coca-Cola sponsored reported that 41 percent of tailgaters spend more than $500 a season on food and supplies, whereas a Ragu survey found that more than half of the fans prefer the party to the actual game! Now, everyone from food conglomerates to camping suppliers tries to get a piece of these boisterous pregame rituals:[35]

- Coleman introduced a special tailgating grill and a complete RoadTrip line.
- The *American Tailgater* catalog sells tailgate flags, tents, and even a gas-powered margarita blender.
- Ragu sponsors training camps, whereas Jack Daniels stages parking-lot contests.
- The NFL sells $100 million a year of tailgating merchandise, including keg-shaped grills. The Buffalo Bills provide showers and changing rooms in the parking lot, and the Denver Broncos pick a "most valuable tailgater" at each home game. The Houston Texans sponsor "Tailgating 101" classes at a local sporting goods store.
- And for the truly hard core: California customizer Galpin Motors sells a tailgaters' pickup truck complete with a huge grill, taps for two beer kegs, a blender, and a flip-down TV screen for "only" $70,000.

newlyweds substitute soap bubbles, jingling bells, or butterflies because birds eat the rice, which expands inside their bodies with nasty results.[39]

Many businesses benefit because they supply **ritual artifacts** to consumers. These are items we need to perform rituals, such as wedding rice, birthday candles, diplomas, specialized foods and beverages (e.g., wedding cakes, ceremonial wine, or even hot dogs at the ball park), trophies and plaques, band uniforms, greeting cards, and retirement watches.[40] In addition, we often follow a *ritual script* to identify the artifacts we need, the sequence in which we should use them, and who uses them. Examples include graduation programs, fraternity manuals, and etiquette books.

Grooming Rituals

Whether you brush your hair 100 strokes a day or give yourself a pep talk in the mirror before a big date, virtually all of us practice private **grooming rituals**. These ceremonies help us to transition from our private self to our public self, or back again. Grooming rituals help to inspire confidence before we face the world, and they "cleanse" us of impurities. When consumers talk about their grooming rituals, some of the dominant themes that emerge from these stories reflect the almost mystical qualities we attribute to grooming products and behaviors. Many people emphasize a before-and-after phenomenon, whereby the person feels magically transformed after she uses certain products (similar to the Cinderella myth).[42]

Some companies that make personal care products understand the power of these rituals and supply the artifacts we need to make them happen. Nair, the depilatory maker, expanded its customer base when it targeted younger girls with its Nair Pretty product—a market the industry calls "first-time hair removers." Researchers conducted focus groups with mothers and their daughters, where they learned that "When a girl removes hair for the first time, it's a life-changing moment." Some of the respondents actually held hair removal slumber parties, where the moms bought products for the teens to remove their hair. So, instead of a focus on boys or romance, ads for Nair Pretty suggest that the depilatory is a stubble-free path to empowerment. "I am a citizen of the world," reads the ad copy. "I am a dreamer. I am fresh. I am so not going to have stubs sticking out of my legs."[43]

Grooming rituals express two kinds of binary opposition: *private/public* and *work/leisure*. Many beauty rituals reflect a transformation from a natural state to the social world (as when a woman "puts on her face") or vice versa. To her, a bath may be a cleansing time—a way to wash away the "sins" of the profane world.[44] In these daily rituals, women reaffirm the value their culture places on personal beauty and the quest for eternal youth.[45] This cleansing ritual is clear in ads for Oil of Olay Beauty Cleanser that proclaim, "And so your day begins. The Ritual of Oil of Olay."

JC Penney partners with a Web site to offer a virtual wedding planner that facilitates nuptial rituals.

Source: Courtesy of JC Penney & ourweddingday .com.

Gift-Giving Rituals

In a **gift-giving ritual**, we procure the perfect object, meticulously remove the price tag, carefully wrap the object (where we symbolically change the item from a commodity to a unique good), and deliver it to the recipient.[46] Gifts can be store-bought objects, homemade items, or services. Some recent research even argues that music file-sharing systems such as Napster, KaZaa, or Morpheus really are all about gifting. This work finds, for example, clear evidence of the gift-giving norm of *reciprocity;* people who download files but who don't leave their own files available to others are "leeches."[47]

Researchers view gift-giving as a form of *economic exchange* where the giver transfers an item of value to a recipient, who in turn must reciprocate. However, gift-giving also involves *symbolic exchange;* for example, when a giver like Karin wants to acknowledge her friend Melissa's intangible support and companionship. In fact, researchers who analyzed the personal memoirs of World War II concentration camp inmates found that even in such a brutal environment where people had to focus on their survival, a need to express humanity through generosity prevailed. The authors find that gift-giving, which symbolized recognition of others' plight as well as one's own, was an act of defiance against the dehumanizing existence the camps forced on their prisoners.[48]

TABLE 15.2	Gift Giving and Relationships	
Relational Effect	**Description**	**Example**
Strengthening	Gift-giving improves the quality of a relationship	An unexpected gift such as one given in a romantic situation
Affirmation	Gift-giving validates the positive quality of a relationship	Usually occurs on ritualized occasions such as birthdays
Negligible Effect	Gift-giving has a minimal effect on perceptions of relationship quality	Informal gift occasions and those in which the gift may be perceived as charity or too good for the current state of the relationship
Negative Confirmation	Gift-giving validates a negative quality of a relationship between the gift giver and receiver	The selection of gift is inappropriate indicating a lack of knowledge of the receiver; alternatively, the gift is viewed as a method of controlling the receiver
Weakening	Gift-giving harms the quality of the relationship between giver and receiver	When there are "strings attached" or the gift is perceived as a bribe, a sign of disrespect, or offensive
Severing	Gift-giving harms the relationship between the giver and receiver to the extent that the relationship is dissolved	When the gift forms part of a larger problem, such as in a threatening relationship; also when a relationship is severed through the receipt of a "parting" gift

Source: Adapted from Julie A. Ruth, Cele C. Otnes, and Frederic F. Brunel, "Gift Receipt and the Reformulation of Interpersonal Relationships," *Journal of Consumer Research* 25 (March 1999): 385–402, Table 1, 389.

Marketing Opportunity

Nestlé's Kit Kat candy bar and its ad agency JWT Japan won the Media Grand Prix at the 2009 Cannes Lions International Advertising Festival—they devised a clever way to capitalize on a Japanese gift-giving ritual. The Japanese translation of Kit Kat is *Kitto Katso,* which means "surely win." Parents in Japan traditionally send students good luck wishes before they take their rigorous higher education entrance exams. So, Nestlé partnered with the Japanese postal service to create "Kit Kat Mail." Sold only in post offices, it resembles a postcard—but it's edible. The promotion was such a huge hit that Nestlé continues to sell the product. As a brand manager observed, "Exams are over but people still send it to wish good luck on any occasion."[52]

Some research indicates that gift-giving evolves as a form of social expression. It is more exchange oriented (instrumental) in the early stages of a relationship (where we keep track of exactly what we give and receive to be sure we're not getting ripped off), but it becomes more altruistic as the relationship develops.[49] Table 15.2 lists the ways giving a gift affects a relationship.

Every culture prescribes certain occasions and ceremonies to give gifts, whether for personal or professional reasons. The birthday gift ritual alone is a significant contributor to our economy. Each American on average buys six birthday gifts a year—about 1 billion gifts in total.[50] Business gifts are an important way to define and maintain professional relationships. Expenditures on business gifts exceed $1.5 billion per year, and givers take great care to ensure that they purchase the appropriate gifts (sometimes with the aid of professional gift consultants). Most executives believe that corporate gift-giving provides both tangible and intangible results, including improved employee morale and higher sales.[51]

The gift-giving ritual proceeds in three distinct stages:[53]

1 During *gestation* the giver procures an item to mark some event. This event may be either *structural* (i.e., prescribed by the culture, as when people buy Christmas presents) or *emergent* (i.e., the decision is more personal and idiosyncratic).
2 The second stage is *presentation*, or the process of gift exchange. The recipient responds to the gift (either appropriately or not), and the donor evaluates this response.
3 In the *reformulation* stage the giver and receiver redefine the bond between them (either looser or tighter) to reflect their new relationship after the exchange. Negativity can arise if the recipient feels the gift is inappropriate or of inferior quality. For example, the hapless husband who gives his wife a vacuum cleaner as an anniversary present is just asking to sleep on the couch, and the new suitor who gives his girlfriend intimate apparel probably won't score many points. The donor may feel the response to the gift was inadequate or insincere or a violation of the **reciprocity norm**, which obliges people to return the gesture of a gift with one of equal value.[54]

Japanese gift-giving rituals show how tremendously important these acts are in that culture, where the wrapping is as important (if not more so) than the gift itself.

The Japanese view gifts as an important aspect of one's duty to others in one's social group. Giving is a moral imperative (*giri*). Highly ritualized acts occur when a person gives both household/personal gifts and company/professional gifts. Each individual has a well-defined set of relatives and friends with which he shares reciprocal gift-giving obligations (*kosai*). People give personal gifts on social occasions, such as at funerals, for a hospitalization, to mark movements from one life stage to another (e.g., weddings, birthdays), and as greetings (e.g., when one meets a visitor). They give company gifts to commemorate the anniversary of a corporation's founding, the opening of a new building, or the announcement of new products. In keeping with the Japanese emphasis on saving face, the recipient doesn't open the present in front of the giver so that he won't have to hide any disappointment with what he gets.[56]

Holiday Rituals

On holidays, we step back from our everyday lives and perform ritualistic behaviors unique to those occasions.[57] Each cultural celebration typically relates to the adventures of one or more special characters, such as St. Patrick in Ireland or Yue Lao in China. These special events require tons of ritual artifacts and scripts. The Thanksgiving holiday script includes serving (in gluttonous portions) foods such as turkey and cranberry sauce that many of us consume only on that day, complaining about how much we've eaten (yet rising to the occasion to find room for dessert), and (for many) a postmeal trip to the couch for the obligatory football game.

Most holidays commemorate a cultural myth, often with a historical (e.g., Miles Standish on Thanksgiving) or imaginary (e.g., Cupid on Valentine's Day) character as the story's hero. These holidays persist because their basic elements appeal to our deep-seated needs.[60]

- **Christmas**—Myths and rituals fill the Christmas holiday, from Santa's adventures at the North Pole to others' adventures under the mistletoe. The meaning of Christmas evolved quite dramatically during the past few hundred years. In colonial times, Christmas celebrations resembled carnivals and public rowdiness was the norm. Most notable was the tradition of "wassailing"—roving packs of rowdy young men laid siege to the rich and demanded food and drink. By the end of the 1800s, the mobs were so unruly that city fathers in Protestant America invented a tradition where families conducted Christmas gatherings around a tree, a practice they "borrowed" from early pagan rites.

  In an 1822 poem Clement Clarke Moore, the wealthy son of a New York Episcopal bishop, invented the modern-day myth of Santa Claus. The Christmas ritual slowly changed to a focus on children and gift-giving.[61] One of the most

Marketing Opportunity

It's no secret that a lot of guys are clueless when they have to choose the right gifts for their significant others. Retailers say that while lingerie is one of the most popular Christmas gifts for women it's also among the most likely to be returned in January. The British retailer Marks & Spencer found that only a third of its female customers were happy with the underwear their partners bought for them, and only a third of the men correctly identified their wife or girlfriend's size or favorite color. Marks & Spencer enlisted its sales force to enlighten male shoppers in the month before Christmas. It deployed salesmen (figuring that men would prefer to talk to a man about such an intimate purchase) who wore purples sashes that say "Stocking Fella—How Can I Help?" to counsel the guys. They educate the shoppers on buying strategies, such as choosing shades like silver or brown since men typically go straight to red items. Who said buying a gift is easy?[55]

At this Web site jilted women vent about their former boyfriends—and perhaps make a little money as they sell gifts they received from them.
Source: Courtesy of www.ExBoyfriendJewelry.com; accessed 3/10/09.

important holiday rituals of course stars Santa, a mythical figure for whose arrival children eagerly await (even if their house doesn't have a fireplace). Indeed, an Australian study that analyzed the letters children write to Santa found they specify their brand preferences quite carefully and often employ sophisticated request strategies to be sure they get what they want from the Big Guy.[62] In opposition to Christ, Santa is a champion of materialism. Perhaps it is no coincidence, then, that he appears in stores and shopping malls—secular temples of consumption. Whatever his origins, the Santa Claus myth socializes children as it reaches them to expect a reward when they are good and that people get what they deserve (which may be a lump of coal).

● **Halloween**—Halloween began as a pagan religious ceremony, but it's clearly a secular event today. However, in contrast to Christmas, the rituals of Halloween (e.g., trick-or-treating and costume parties) primarily involve nonfamily members. Halloween is an unusual holiday because its rituals are the opposite of many other cultural occasions. In contrast to Christmas, it celebrates evil instead of good and death rather than birth. It encourages revelers to extort treats with veiled threats of "tricks" rather than rewards for the good.

Because of these oppositions, Halloween is an **antifestival**—an event that distorts the symbols we associate with other holidays. For example, the Halloween witch is an inverted mother figure. The holiday also parodies the meaning of Easter because it stresses the resurrection of ghosts, and it mocks Thanksgiving as it transforms the wholesome symbolism of the pumpkin pie into the evil jack-o-lantern.[63] Furthermore, Halloween provides a ritualized, and therefore socially sanctioned, context that allows people to *deindividuate* (see Chapter 10) and try on new roles: Children can go outside after dark, stay up late, and eat all the candy they like for a night. The otherwise geeky guy who always sits in the back of class dresses as Jason in *Friday the Thirteenth* and turns out to be the life of the party.

● **Valentine's Day**—On Valentine's Day, we relax our standards about sex and love and we express feelings we may hide during the rest of the year (in Japan, it's the women who send gifts to the men). A study that investigated Valentine's Day rituals explored how marketing communications help to shape the holiday. The authors identify five familiar classes of rituals:

● Exchanging gifts and cards
● Showing affection

Cupid plays a lead role in the Valentine's Day holiday, while in China the mythical figure of Yue Lao performs a similar function.
Source: a. Courtesy of Private Collection/Photo © Christie's Images/The Bridgeman Art Library International. b. Photo by Dawn Sin/Courtesy of Dawn Sin Hui Jie.

- Going out
- Preparing and consuming food and drink
- Special attention to grooming and clothing

Many of their informants (primarily men) understood the holiday as an obligatory occasion for them to buy their partners expensive, "romantic" gifts. One guy posted this warning: "If you want her happy always remember: the gift has to shine or smell [good] or she should be able to wear it! Otherwise, you're doomed." Some informants expressed negative associations with the holiday, including painful emotions because of broken or a lack of relationships and aversion to the "forced" consumption and artificial displays of affection the day requires.[64] But, as much as some of us may grumble about it, this holiday ritual is too powerful to ignore (unless you like sleeping on the couch).

Rites of Passage

What does a dance for recently divorced people have in common with a fraternity Hell Week? Both are modern **rites of passage**—rituals we perform to mark a change in social status. Every society, both primitive and modern, sets aside times for these changes. Some may occur as a natural part of our life cycles (e.g., puberty or death), whereas others are more individual (e.g., getting divorced and reentering the dating market). As Karin's son discovered when he bombed his driving test, the importance of a rite of passage becomes more obvious when you fail to undergo it at the prescribed time.

Much like the metamorphosis of a caterpillar into a butterfly, a rite of passage consists of three phases. Let's see how this works for a young person who changes his social status to become a college student:[65]

1 In the first stage, *separation*, he detaches from his original group or status as a high school kid and leaves home for campus.
2 *Liminality* is the middle stage, where he is in limbo between statuses. Think of those bewildered new first-year students who try to find their way around campus during orientation.
3 In the *aggregation* stage, he returns to society with his new status. Our hero returns home for Thanksgiving break as a cocky college "veteran."

This McDonald's ad from Hong Kong celebrates a holiday. The literal translation is "April Fool's Day: The best day to take the piss out of your friends."
Source: Courtesy of DDB Hong Kong.

Many types of people undergo rites of passage, including fraternity pledges, recruits at boot camp, or novitiates at a convent. We observe a similar transitional state when people prepare for occupational roles. For example, athletes and fashion models typically undergo a "seasoning" process. They leave their normal surroundings (athletes go to training camps, young models move to Paris or New York), they get indoctrinated into a new subculture, and then return to the real world in their new roles (if they successfully pass the trials of their initiation and don't "get cut").

Death also involves rites of passage. Funeral ceremonies help the living organize their relationships with the deceased. Action is tightly scripted, down to the costumes (e.g., the ritual black attire, black ribbons for mourners, the body laid out in its best clothes) and specific behaviors (e.g., sending condolence cards or holding a wake). Passing motorists award special status to the *cortege* (the funeral motorcade) when they obey the strong social norm that prohibits cutting in as the line of cars proceeds to the cemetery.[66]

Forward-thinking funeral directors recognize their role as ritual stagers, so some redefine themselves as party planners. One entrepreneur opened the first nationwide funeral concierge service—for a fee he coordinates tasks that include writing the obituary to negotiating prices with undertakers. Some wealthy people seize the opportunity to go out with a bang: Robert Tisch, who ran the Loews Corporation, had a marching band at his memorial service, and mourners at perfume magnate Estée Lauder's funeral consoled themselves with chocolate-covered marshmallows that waiters passed on silver trays. Other ordinary folks arrange their own special

Cremations will account for a projected 38 percent of all deaths this year, compared with 26 percent in 2000. Consumers can choose to customize their urns, like this one that holds the ashes of a Red Sox fan until the end.
Source: Courtesy of Landov Media/Photo by Boston Globe/John Tlumacki.

send-offs: At a funeral for a former ice cream vendor the deceased's old ice cream truck led the cortege and then it dispensed Popsicles to guests after the ceremony.[67]

Funeral practices vary across cultures, but they're always rich in symbolism. For example, a study of funeral rituals in Ghana found that the community there determines a person's social value *after* he dies; this status depends on the type of funeral his family gives him. One of the main purposes of death rituals is to negotiate the social identities of deceased persons. This occurs as mourners treat the corpse with a level of respect that indicates what they think of him. The Asante people who were the subjects of the study don't view death as something to fear; it's just part of a broader, ongoing process of identity negotiation.[68]

OBJECTIVE

Why do we describe products as either sacred or profane, and why do some products move back and forth between the two categories?

Sacred and Profane Consumption

As we saw when we discussed the structure of myths, many types of consumer activities involve the demarcation, or binary opposition, of categories, such as good versus bad, male versus female—or even regular cola versus diet. One of the most important distinctions we find is between the sacred and the profane. **Sacred consumption** occurs when we "set apart" objects and events from normal activities and treat them with respect or awe. Note that in this context the term *sacred* does not necessarily carry a religious meaning although we do tend to think of religious artifacts and ceremonies as "sacred." **Profane consumption** in contrast describes objects and events that are ordinary or everyday; they don't share the "specialness" of sacred ones. Again, note that in this context we don't equate the word *profane* with obscenity although the two meanings do share some similarities.

Again, often we're unaware of the distinction between these two domains—until they conflict with one another. Then, the sparks fly—sort of like the collision between matter and antimatter on *Star Trek*. A conflict in Thailand illustrates this process. It seems that several Bangkok nightclubs, inspired by the film *Coyote Ugly* about women who dance seductively on a New York bar, began to feature their own "Coyote Girls" dancers. The trend caught on and soon the dancers showed up at auto shows, in shopping malls, and at outdoor festivals. That's when the trouble started: Thailand's queen learned of one performance the girls put on near a Buddhist temple on a holy day that marks the end of a 3-month period where Buddhists refrain from impure thoughts and deeds (sort of like the Christian season of Lent). When the queen saw TV news reports about a motorcycle shop that hired Coyote Girls to promote its wares, she was outraged by the intrusion of profane activity into a sacred domain. Coyote Girls are now banned from dancing in public places.[70]

Sacralization

Sacralization occurs when ordinary objects, events, and even people take on sacred meaning. Many consumers regard events such as the Super Bowl and people such as Michael Jackson as sacred. Indeed, virtually anything can become sacred. Skeptical? Consider the Web site that sells *unlaundered* athletic wear that members of the Dallas Cowboys football team have worn. Former quarterback Troy Aikman's shoes sold for $1,999, and an unwashed practice jersey that retains the sweat of an unknown player goes for $99. Used socks fly out the door at $19.99 a pair. Says the owner, "Fans who have never been able to touch the Cowboys before now have an opportunity."[71]

Objectification occurs when we attribute sacred qualities to mundane items (such as smelly socks). One way that this process occurs is via **contamination**, where objects we associate with sacred events or people become sacred in their own right. This explains the desire by many fans for items that belonged to (or were even touched by) famous people. Even the Smithsonian Institution in Washington, DC, maintains a display that features such "sacred items" as the ruby slippers from *The Wizard of Oz*, a phaser from *Star Trek*, and Archie Bunker's chair from the television show *All in the Family*—all reverently protected behind sturdy display glass.

In addition to museum exhibits that display rare objects, we often set apart mundane, inexpensive things in *collections;* when we do so we transform them from profane items to sacred ones. An item is sacralized as soon as it enters a collection, and it takes on special significance to the collector that outsiders may find hard to comprehend. For example, you may know someone who collects matchbooks that mark their visits to out-of-town restaurants: Just try to use one of these books if you actually need to light a match.

Collecting refers to the systematic acquisition of a particular object or set of objects. We distinguish this from **hoarding**, which is merely unsystematic collecting.[72] Hoarding is a problem in some cities where residents' refusal to discard things properly results in fires, eviction, and even the removal of children from the home. A dozen cities run hoarding task forces to combat this problem.[73]

Collecting typically involves both rational and emotional components. On the one hand, avid collectors carefully organize and exhibit their treasures.[74] On the other hand, they are ferociously attached to their collections. A teddy bear collector summed up this fixation: "If my house ever burns down, I won't cry over my furniture, I'll cry over the bears."[75]

Some consumer researchers feel that collectors acquire their "prizes" to gratify their materialism in a socially acceptable manner. When he systematically amasses a collection, the collector "worships" material objects but he doesn't have to feel guilty or petty. Another perspective argues that collecting is actually an aesthetic experience; for many collectors the pleasure comes from creating the collection. Whatever the motivation, hard-core collectors often devote a great deal of time and energy to maintaining and expanding their collections, so for many this activity becomes a central component of their extended selves (see Chapter 5).[76]

Name an item, and the odds are that a collector lusts after it. You can find collections of just about anything, from movie posters, rare books, and autographs to *Star Wars* dolls, Elvis memorabilia, old computers, and even junk mail.[77] The 1,200 members of the McDonald's collectors' club trade "prizes" such as sandwich wrappers and Happy Meal trinkets—rare ones like the 1987 Potato Head Kids Toys sell for $25.[78] And other consumers collect experiences rather than products: Consider the man who visited more than 10,000 McDonald's restaurants. He keeps a list of unusual menu items and decor, and he defends his hobby this way: "I'm not an oddball or weirdo. I'm a collector of the McDonald's dining experience. So many issues from the last half of the twentieth century can be understood, at least partially, from a seat inside a McDonald's. What could be more quintessentially American?" Supersize that?[79]

Domains of Sacred Consumption

Sacred consumption events permeate many aspects of our lives. We find ways to "set apart" all sorts of places, people, and events. In this section, we'll look at ways that "ordinary" consumption is sometimes *not* so ordinary after all.

Sacred Places

A society "sets apart" sacred places because they have religious or mystical significance (e.g., Bethlehem, Mecca, Stonehenge) or because they commemorate some aspect of a country's heritage (e.g., the Kremlin, the Emperor's Palace in Tokyo, the Statue of Liberty, or, more recently, Ground Zero in Manhattan). *Contamination* makes these places sacred—something sacred happened on that spot, so the place itself takes on sacred qualities. Hard-core Yankees' fans now can buy Yankees Sod—the first officially licensed grass. Although it will cost a few thousand dollars to fill out a good-sized lawn, proud fans can boast a lawn that grows from the same seeds the groundskeepers use at the stadium, and the sod comes with a certificate of

CB AS I LIVE IT

Amanda Deutchman, *The University of Arizona*

*M*aterial objects often are a source of security and expression of values or beliefs. In this way, one might say that the objects you choose to attach yourself to are a result of your culture. In my experience, it seems that *collecting* material objects and the subsequent *sacralization* of such items is a shared value and norm within a culture—a small culture, the family. Many people casually own a series of related items, often rationalized by adding deep meaning to the objects. On occasion, these may be justified as a symbol of an experience, keeping memories alive. This is the basis behind souvenir purchases. However, for some, this act is purely an interest that results in adding value or meanings to objects, meaning that others may not understand.

Family, as an example, can lead to a subculture of values and beliefs, including collecting. Many members of my extended family collect various items, mostly related to pop culture memorabilia. This sense of valuing material objects related to entertainment was passed down as a norm within our family culture for at least three generations. My father collects soundtracks, and my uncle and grandfather collect Disney memorabilia, as well as other items. I collect many things as well, including T-shirts that remind me of places I've been, events I have experienced, or particular stages of my life. These act as a reminder of my past. However, other collections are based on the simple worship of material items that hold no personal

historical value. I collect anything and everything that has to do with the television show *Friends*. This includes books, DVDs, posters, autographs, and games. My interest in the show and interest in working in television led me to begin this collection. This was, in fact, a way of acquiring related objects that illogically held emotional value. I allow myself to value these objects, which results in certain consumption patterns that others without these same cultural collecting values may not follow.

Such collecting and sacralization of a specific set of objects can be used as a way to express oneself by portraying interests to others through material objects. It is an excuse to consume items that may not seem a reasonable or rational expense. This opens a door for marketers who gain the opportunity to build off of these obsessions and add value to items. First, sales of many collections have become an act of consumer-to-consumer sales with electronic resources such as eBay. Individuals market their personal collections, describing products in such a way that adds value to them, despite the value someone may not originally hold. This explanation of the importance of the goods may help the original consumer justify their prior worship of the objects, proving that these items have value. The explanation may also work to convince others who may have a slight interest in a set of objects to increase their interest. It can convince these consumers that such objects have value and *should* be worshipped, bringing them into the collecting culture.

Mass marketers (business-to-consumer marketers) can also exploit this cultural value within certain

families using a *tribal marketing strategy*. They can hold events to increase interest and convince "fans" of things or objects to "worship" these objects. The collector culture has also led to Web sites devoted to memorabilia, allowing businesses to reach the mass consumer who may choose one item and collectors who may purchase multiple items. These new businesses open up the opportunity to market to collectors and justify this sacralization as a common act, enough to justify entire Web sites devoted to this culture. Businesses and marketers can use the collecting habit to capitalize on this culture and create new products to increase profits. They can produce many objects with few moderations and sell, essentially, multiples of the same item. I own two complete sets of the *Friends* DVD sets, one as originally released season by season, and a "collector's box" edition. Sales of the same product, but in different packaging, are a great tool marketers use in targeting collectors in addition to the mass consumers. Many consumers will buy the less expensive item version, while collectors may repurchase an item as each new version of the product is released. As a consumer, it is important to beware of personal interests and desires for objects versus the valuing of objects as a result of observing others actions, purchases, and values. Marketers can easily strengthen a weak or moderate interest and convince a consumer to create value around an object, leading to future expenditures and allow for multiple product sales leading to profits. One must also consider their family cultural influence on this action and how this affects personal purchases.

authenticity from Major League Baseball and a counterfeit-proof hologram that declares it the official grass of the New York Yankees.[80]

Still other places start out as profane but we endow them with sacred qualities. Graumann's Chinese Theater in Hollywood, where movie stars leave their footprints in concrete for posterity, is one such place. Theme parks are a form of mass-produced fantasy that takes on aspects of sacredness. In particular, Disney World and Disneyland (and their outposts in Europe and Japan) are destinations for "pilgrimages" by consumers around the globe. Disney World displays many characteristics of more traditional sacred places. Some even believe it has healing powers, which helps to explain why a trip to the park is the most common "last wish" for terminally ill children.[81]

As the saying goes, "Home is where the heart is."[82] In many cultures, the home is a particularly sacred place. It's a barrier between the harsh, external world and consumers' "inner space." Americans spend more than $50 billion a year on interior decorators and home furnishings, and our home is a central part of our identity. People all over the world go to great lengths to create a feeling of "homeyness." They personalize their dwellings with door wreaths, mantle arrangements, and a "memory wall for family photos."[83] Even public places such as Starbucks cafés strive for a homelike atmosphere to shelter customers from the harshness of the outside world.

Sacred People

At her Web site livingoprah.com, superfan Robyn Okrant blogs about her devotion to Oprah Winfrey—and the year she spent living her life completely guided by Oprah's advice about what to eat, wear, and read. In her mission statement she speculates, "I wonder, will I find bliss if I commit wholeheartedly to her lifestyle suggestions?"[84]

We idolize sacred people as we set them apart from the masses, and sometimes people believe they have "superhuman" abilities. Souvenirs, memorabilia, and even mundane items these celebrities touch acquire special meanings (the celebrities "contaminate" the items). Newspapers pay *paparazzi* hundreds of thousands of dollars for candid shots of stars or royalty. Indeed, many businesses thrive on our desire for products we associate with the famous. There is a flourishing market for celebrity autographs, and objects celebrities owned such as Princess Diana's gowns or John Lennon's guitars sell on eBay for astronomical prices.

Sacred Events

Sometimes public events resemble sacred, religious ceremonies—think about fans who hold their hands over their hearts and solemnly recite the "Pledge of Allegiance" before a ballgame, or how others reverently light matches (or hold up illuminated cell phones) during a rock concert.[85]

The world of sports is sacred to many of us (recent doping and gambling scandals aside). We find the roots of modern sports events in ancient religious rites, such as fertility festivals (e.g., the original Olympics).[86] And it's not uncommon for teams to join in prayer prior to a game. The sports pages are like the scriptures (and we all know ardent fans who read them "religiously"), the stadium is a house of worship, and the fans are members of the congregation. Devotees engage in group activities, such as tailgate parties and the "Wave," where sections of the stadium take turns standing up. The athletes and coaches that fans come to see are godlike; devotees believe they have almost superhuman powers. One study documented more than 600 children whose parents named them after the legendary University of Alabama coach Paul "Bear" Bryant![87]

Athletes are central figures in a common cultural myth—the *hero tale*. In these stories, the player must prove himself under strenuous circumstances, and he achieves victory only through sheer force of will. On a more mundane level, devotees consume certain ritual artifacts during these ceremonies (such as hot dogs at the ballpark). Sales of snack foods and beverages spike around the time of the Super Bowl—people spend $10 million more on tortilla chips than during a normal 2-week period and more than $15 million extra on beer in the weeks surrounding the big game.[88]

Tourism is another example of a sacred experience. People occupy sacred time and space when they travel on vacation (though you may not think so if you get stuck sleeping on an airport floor because of a plane delay). The tourist searches for "authentic" experiences that differ from his normal world (think of Club Med's motto, "The antidote to civilization").[89] This traveling experience involves binary oppositions between work and leisure and being "at home" versus "away." Often, we relax everyday (profane) norms regarding appropriate behavior as tourists—we participate in illicit or adventurous experiences we would never engage in at home ("What happens in Vegas, stays in Vegas").

The desire of travelers to capture these sacred experiences in objects forms the bedrock of the souvenir industry, which really sells sacred memories. Whether it's a personalized matchbook from a wedding or New York City salt-and-pepper shakers, a souvenir represents a tangible piece of the consumer's sacred experience.[90] In addition to personal mementos, such as ticket stubs you save from a favorite concert, these are some other sacred souvenir icons:[91]

- Local products (e.g., wine from California)
- Pictorial images (e.g., postcards)
- "Piece of the rock" (e.g., seashells, pine cones)
- Symbolic shorthand in the form of literal representations of the site (e.g., a miniature Statue of Liberty)
- Markers (e.g., Hard Rock Cafe T-shirts)

From Sacred to Profane, and Back Again

Just to make life interesting, some consumer activities move back and forth between the sacred and profane spheres over time.[92] A recent study of tea preparation in Turkey illustrates this movement. Although we are more likely to think of thick Turkish coffee, in reality Turks consume more tea *per capita* than any other country. In Turkish culture people drink tea continuously, like (or instead of) water. Tea is an integral part of daily life; many households and offices boil water for tea in the traditional *çaydanlik* (double teapot) first thing in the morning, and keep it steaming all day so that the beverage is ready at any time. The tea drinking process links to many symbolic meanings—including the traditional glasses, clear to appreciate the tea's color, and hourglass-shaped like a woman's body—and rituals, such as blending one's own tea, knowing how finely to grind the tea leaves, and how long to steep the tea for optimal flavor. When Lipton introduced the modern tea bag in 1984, Turkey was intent on modernization and soon consumers snapped up electric *çaydanliks* and mugs instead of small, shapely tea glasses. Tea became a symbol of the quick and convenient, and the drinking act became more of a fashion statement. Now, many Turkish consumers opt to return to the sacred, traditional rituals as a way to preserve authenticity in the face of rapid societal changes.[93]

The transition of Turkish tea to a mass market product illustrates the process of **desacralization**—this occurs when we remove a sacred item or symbol from its special place or duplicate it in mass quantities so that it loses its "specialness" and becomes profane. Souvenir reproductions of sacred monuments such as the Washington Monument or the Eiffel Tower, artworks such as the *Mona Lisa* or Michelangelo's *David*, or reproductions of sacred symbols such as the American flag on T-shirts eliminate their special aspects—they become inauthentic commodities with relatively little value.

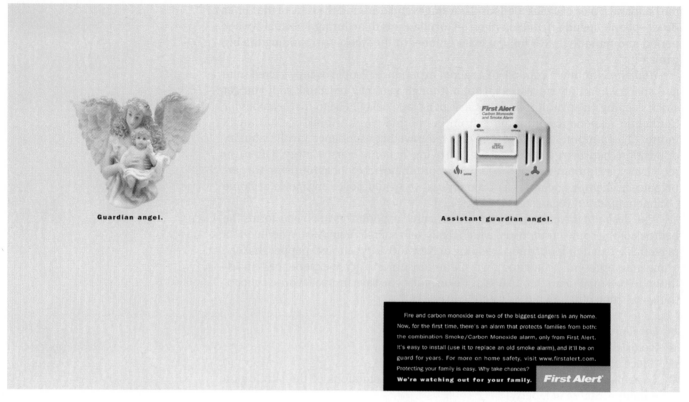

Guardian angel.

Assistant guardian angel.

Fire and carbon monoxide are two of the biggest dangers in any home. Now, for the first time, there's an alarm that protects families from both: the combination Smoke/Carbon Monoxide alarm, only from First Alert. It's easy to install (use it to replace an old smoke alarm), and it'll be on guard for years. For more on home safety, visit www.firstalert.com. Protecting your family is easy. Why take chances?
We're watching out for your family.   *First Alert*

This ad for an alarm system uses sacred imagery to sell a profane product.
Source: Courtesy of First Alert Corp.

Religion itself has to some extent become desacralized. Religious symbols like stylized crosses or New Age crystals often pop up on fashion jewelry.[94] Critics often charge that Christmas has turned into a secular, materialistic occasion devoid of its original sacred significance. A similar process occurs in relatively Westernized parts of the Islamic Middle East, where the holy month of Ramadan (that people traditionally observe by fasting and praying) is starting to look like Christmas: People buy lights in the shape of an Islamic crescent moon, send Ramadan cards to one another, and attend lavish fast-breaking feasts at hotels.[95]

CHAPTER SUMMARY

Now that you have finished reading this chapter you should understand why:

1 A culture is a society's personality; it shapes our identities as individuals.

A society's culture includes its values, ethics, and the material objects its members produce. It is the accumulation of shared meanings and traditions among members of a society. We describe a culture in terms of ecology (the way people adapt to their habitat), its social structure, and its ideology (including moral and aesthetic principles).

2 Myths are stories that express a culture's values, and in modern times marketing messages convey these values.

Myths are stories with symbolic elements that express the shared ideals of a culture. Many myths involve a binary opposition—they define values in terms of what they are and what they are not (e.g., nature versus technology). Advertising, movies, and other media transmit modern myths.

3 Many of our consumption activities including holiday observances, grooming, and gift-giving are rituals.

A ritual is a set of multiple, symbolic behaviors that occur in a fixed sequence and that we repeat periodically. Ritual is related to many consumption activities that occur in popular culture. These include holiday observances, gift-giving, and grooming.

A rite of passage is a special kind of ritual that marks the transition from one role to another. These passages typically entail the need to acquire ritual artifacts to facilitate the transition. Modern rites of passage include graduations, fraternity initiations, weddings, debutante balls, and funerals.

We describe products as either sacred or profane, and it's not unusual for some products to move back and forth between the two categories.

We divide consumer activities into *sacred* and *profane* domains. Sacred phenomena are "set apart" from everyday activities or products. *Sacralization* occurs when we set apart everyday people, events, or objects from the ordinary. *Objectification* occurs when we ascribe sacred qualities to products or items that sacred people once owned. *Desacralization* occurs when formerly sacred objects or activities become part of the everyday, as when companies reproduce "one-of-a-kind" works of art in large quantities.

KEY TERMS

Antifestival, 558
Binary opposition, 548
Collecting, 562
Collectivist cultures, 544
Contamination, 561
Conventions, 544
Crescive norms, 544
Culture, 542
Custom, 544
Desacralization, 565
Fortress brands, 552

Gift-giving ritual, 555
Grooming rituals, 554
Hoarding, 562
Individualism, 544
Individualist cultures, 544
Masculinity/femininity, 544
Monomyth, 550
More, 544
Myth, 546
Objectification, 561
Power distance, 544

Profane consumption, 561
Reciprocity norm, 556
Rites of passage, 559
Ritual, 550
Ritual artifacts, 554
Sacralization, 561
Sacred consumption, 561
Superstitions, 552
Uncertainty avoidance, 544

REVIEW

1 What is culture? List three dimensions social scientists use to describe a culture and give an example of each.
2 A myth is a special kind of story. What makes it special? What is an example of a modern myth?
3 Give an example of a marketer that uses the principle of binary opposition.
4 What is a ritual? Describe three kinds of rituals and provide an example of each.

5 List the three stages of a ritual.
6 What is the difference between sacred and profane consumption? Provide one example of each.
7 How is a collection sacred? What is the difference between collecting and hoarding?

CONSUMER BEHAVIOR CHALLENGE

■ DISCUSS

1 A culture is a society's personality. If your culture were a person, how would you describe its personality traits?
2 This chapter argues that not all gift-giving is positive. In what ways can this ritual be unpleasant or negative?
3 For many, Disney is a sacred place. Do you agree? Why or why not?
4 Describe the three stages of the rite of passage associated with graduating from college.
5 Have you ever given yourself a gift? If so, why did you do it and how did you decide what to get?
6 "Fraternity hazing is simply a natural rite of passage that universities should not try to regulate." Do you agree?
7 Identify the ritualized aspects of football that advertising uses.

8 "Christmas has become simply another opportunity to exchange gifts and stimulate the economy." Do you agree? Why or why not?
9 Bridal registries specify very clearly the gifts that the couple wants. How do you feel about this practice—should people actually specify what you should buy for them, or should a gift be a more personal expression from you?
10 Rituals provide us with a sense of order and security. In a study of the drinking rituals of college students, the researchers found that drinking imposed order in students' daily lives—from the completion of assignments to what and when to eat. In addition, ritualizing an activity such as drinking provides security and fellowship at a time fraught with confusion and turbulent change. Obviously, though, there's a dark side to drinking rituals.

Consider the highly publicized death of an MIT student who died 3 days after he fell into an alcohol-induced coma as the result of a fraternity pledge.[96] Indeed, while binge drinking is a ritual many college students practice, critics have described it as the most significant health hazard on college campuses today.[97] What role does drinking play in the social life on your campus? Based on your experience, how does it fit into rituals of college life? Should these practices be changed? If so, how?

11 The chapter describes a new wave of commercials that give voice to products and practices people didn't use to discuss in polite conversation. Are any products out-of-bounds to advertising? Can these messages boomerang if they turn off consumers?

■ APPLY

1 When you go out on a first date, identify the crescive norms that you follow. Write a report (preferably when the date is over) describing specific behaviors each person performed that made it clear you were on a first date. What products and services do those norms affect?

2 Interview people you know about any "magic" items they own (e.g., How many of your friends have a lucky charm or hang a St. Christopher's medal or some other object from their rearview mirrors?). Get them to describe their feelings about these objects and tell how they acquired their magical properties. How would they feel if they lost these special items?

3 Identify modern-day myths that corporations create. How do they communicate these stories to consumers?

4 Interview people you know who collect some kind of object. How do they organize and describe their collections? Do you see any evidence of sacred versus profane distinctions?

5 Ask friends to describe an incident where they received a gift they thought was inappropriate. Why did they feel this way, and how did this event influence the relationship between them and the gift giver?

Case Study

MOBILE PHONES INVADE THE WORLD

The cell phone is a marvel of modern technology, and consumers all over the world certainly welcome this high-tech accessory. According to Gartner, Inc., worldwide sales of mobile phones reached 1.28 billion units in 2008. As the popularity of these phones grows, their features also multiply. E-mail functions, calendars, Internet, GPS tracking, and cameras are built into many mobiles. But members of various cultures differ in the attributes they most desire in a phone, and how they choose which phone is best for them. A 2008 study by Mintel reported that the size, shape, and style of the phone are most important to American consumers. They rate BlackBerry and Apple as very stylish while many feel that Palm and Nokia are more traditional and behind the times.

Russia boasts a high level of cell phone penetration. Experts say that between 60 to 80 percent of Russians own phones. But, phone preferences there differ from the American market. Attributes like durability and reliability are extremely important. Incomes are lower in Russia and a traditional value of thriftiness prevails so consumers there tend to keep their phones for a longer period of time. On the other hand, in recent years the economy has boomed due to rising oil prices, so people value phones as status symbols—they are quick to jump to a higher-end product.

A different set of circumstances applies in Arab countries. In particular, the integration of the cell phone with a personal camera hits a wall in cultures where picture-taking is frowned upon. Some Arabic countries impose strict penalties for people who use a camera phone in public. In conservative Saudi Arabia, the sexes are segregated in public places and women must be covered head-to-toe in public with veils and robes. So, it's not surprising that Saudi women are sensitive about being photographed, especially without their veils.

DISCUSSION QUESTIONS

1 Why do you think that Saudi Arabia and other Middle Eastern countries have taken a stronger stance on regulating the use of camera phones? Discuss this question in the context of sacred and profane consumption.

2 Consumer choice for cell phones appears to be different in Russia. What do you think that this says about the culture in that country?

3 How might cell phones influence cultural rituals or introduce new ones? Can phone marketers boost phone usage (including video, texting, etc.) if they encourage the development of these rituals? How?

Sources: Abdullah Shihri, "Camera-Equipped Cell Phones Banned by Religious Edict in Saudi Arabia," *Associated Press* (September 29, 2004); Asta Salmi and Elmira Sharafutdinova, "Culture and Design in Emerging Markets: The Case of Mobile Phones in Russia," *Journal of Business & Industrial Marketing* 23, no. 6 (2008): 384–94; "Mobil Phones—US—September 2008," *Mintel Oxygen*, accessed May 23, 2009.

NOTES

1. Bill McDowell, "Starbucks Is Ground Zero in Today's Coffee Culture," *Advertising Age* (December 9, 1996): 1. For a discussion of the act of coffee drinking as ritual, cf. Susan Fournier and Julie L. Yao, "Reviving Brand Loyalty: A Reconceptualization Within the Framework of Consumer–Brand Relationships," working paper 96-039, Harvard Business School, 1996.

2. "Spice Girls Dance into Culture Clash," *Montgomery Advertiser* (April 29, 1997): 2A.

3. Clifford Geertz, *The Interpretation of Cultures* (New York: Basic Books, 1973); Marvin Harris, *Culture, People and Nature* (New York: Crowell, 1971); John F. Sherry, Jr., "The Cultural Perspective in Consumer Research," in Richard J. Lutz, ed., *Advances in Consumer Research* 13 (Provo, UT: Association for Consumer Research, 1985): 573–75.

4. William Lazer, Shoji Murata, and Hiroshi Kosaka, "Japanese Marketing: Towards a Better Understanding," *Journal of Marketing* 49 (Spring 1985): 69–81.

5. Celia W. Dugger, "Modestly, India Goes for a Public Swim," *New York Times* (March 5, 2000), www.nytimes.com, accessed March 5, 2000.

6. Nina M. Lentini, "Products No Longer So Personal," *Marketing Daily* (February 9, 2007), www.mediapost.com, accessed February 9, 2007; Karin Bittar, "'Pee Ship' Enterprise for Clearblue Pregnancy Test," *Marketing Daily* (December 20, 2006), www.mediapost.com, accessed December 20, 2006.

7. Geert Hofstede, *Culture's Consequences* (Beverly Hills, CA: Sage, 1980); see also Laura M. Milner, Dale Fodness, and Mark W. Speece, "Hofstede's Research on Cross-Cultural Work-Related Values: Implications for Consumer Behavior," in W. Fred van Raaij and Gary J. Bamossy, eds., *European Advances in Consumer Research* (Amsterdam: Association for Consumer Research, 1993): 70–76.

8. Daniel Goleman, "The Group and the Self: New Focus on a Cultural Rift," *New York Times* (December 25, 1990): 37; Harry C. Triandis, "The Self and Social Behavior in Differing Cultural Contexts," *Psychological Review* 96 (July 1989): 506; Harry C. Triandis, Robert Bontempo, Marcelo J. Villareal, Masaaki Asai, and Nydia Lucca, "Individualism and Collectivism: Cross-Cultural Perspectives on Self–Ingroup Relationships," *Journal of Personality and Social Psychology* 54 (February 1988): 323.

9. George J. McCall and J. L. Simmons, *Social Psychology: A Sociological Approach* (New York: The Free Press, 1982).

10. Arundhati Parmar, "Out from Under," *Marketing News* (July 21, 2003): 9–10.

11. Jim Yardley, "No Spitting on the Road to Olympic Glory, Beijing Says," *New York Times* (April 17, 2007), www.nytimes.com, accessed April 17, 2007.

12. Robert Frank, "When Small Chains Go Abroad, Culture Clashes Require Ingenuity," *Wall Street Journal* (April 12, 2000), www.wsj.com, accessed April 12, 2000.

13. Laura Petrecca, "Ad Track: Marketers Bet on Lucky 777; That's July 7, 2007," *USA Today* (May 29, 2007), www.usatoday.com, accessed May 29, 2007.

14. Jim Yardley, "First Comes the Car, Then the $10,000 License Plate," *New York Times* (April 16, 2006), www.nytimes.com, accessed April 16, 2006.

15. Molly O'Neill, "As Life Gets More Complex, Magic Casts a Wider Spell," *New York Times* (June 13, 1994): A1.

16. Susannah Meadows, "Who's Afraid of the Big Bad Werewolf?" *Newsweek* (August 26, 2002): 57.

17. Conrad Phillip Kottak, "Anthropological Analysis of Mass Enculturation," in Conrad P. Kottak, ed., *Researching American Culture* (Ann Arbor: University of Michigan Press, 1982), 40–74; cf. also Teresa Davis and Olga Kravets, "Bridges to Displaced Meaning: The Reinforcing Roles of Myth and Marketing in Russian Vodka Labels," *Advances in Consumer Research* 32, no. 1 (2005): 480.

18. Eric Ransdell, "The Nike Story? Just Tell It!" *Fast Company* (January–February 2000): 44.

19. Joseph Campbell, *Myths, Dreams, and Religion* (New York: E. P. Dutton, 1970).

20. Claude Lévi-Strauss, *Structural Anthropology* (Harmondsworth, England: Peregrine, 1977).

21. Tina Lowrey and Cele C. Otnes, "Consumer Fairy Tales and the Perfect Christmas," in Cele C. Otnes and Tina M. Lowrey, eds., *Contemporary Consumption Rituals: A Research Anthology* (Mahwah, NJ: Lawrence Erlbaum, 2003).

22. Merissa Marr, "Fairy-Tale Wedding? Disney Can Supply the Gown," *Wall Street Journal* (February 22, 2007): B1; Laura M. Holson, "For

23. Jeff Jensen, "Comic Heroes Return to Roots as Marvel Is Cast as Hip Brand," *Advertising Age* (June 8, 1998): 3.

24. Jeffrey S. Lang and Patrick Trimble, "Whatever Happened to the Man of Tomorrow? An Examination of the American Monomyth and the Comic Book Superhero," *Journal of Popular Culture* 22 (Winter 1988): 157.

25. Elizabeth C. Hirschman, "Movies as Myths: An Interpretation of Motion Picture Mythology," in Jean Umiker-Sebeok, ed., *Marketing and Semiotics: New Directions in the Study of Signs for Sale* (Berlin: Mouton de Gruyter, 1987), 335–74.

26. See William Blake Tyrrell, "Star Trek as Myth and Television as Mythmaker," in Jack Nachbar, Deborah Weiser, and John L. Wright, eds., *The Popular Culture Reader* (Bowling Green, OH: Bowling Green University Press, 1978): 79–88.

27. Bernie Whalen, "Semiotics: An Art or Powerful Marketing Research Tool?" *Marketing News* (May 13, 1983): 8.

28. Eduardo Porter, "New 'Got Milk?' TV Commercials Try to Entice Hispanic Teenagers," *Wall Street Journal* (December 28, 2001), www.wsj.com, accessed December 28, 2001.

29. Maria Kniazeva and Russell W. Belk, "Packaging as a Vehicle for Mythologizing the Brand," *Consumption, Markets and Culture* 10, no. 1 (2007): 51.

30. See Dennis W. Rook, "The Ritual Dimension of Consumer Behavior," *Journal of Consumer Research* 12 (December 1985): 251–64; Mary A. Stansfield Tetreault and Robert E. Kleine, III, "Ritual, Ritualized Behavior, and Habit: Refinements and Extensions of the Consumption Ritual Construct," in Marvin Goldberg, Gerald Gorn, and Richard W. Pollay, eds., *Advances in Consumer Research* 17 (Provo, UT: Association for Consumer Research, 1990): 31–38.

31. Su Hyun Lee, "A New Lifestyle in South Korea: First Weekends, and Now Brunch," *New York Times* (November 2, 2007), www.nytimes.com/ 2007/11/02/World/Asia/02brunch.Html?_R=1&Oref=Slogin, accessed November 2, 2007.

32. Deborah Ball, "British Drinkers of Guinness Say They'd Rather Take It Slow," *Wall Street Journal* (May 22, 2003), www.wsj.com, accessed May 22, 2003.

33. Karl Greenberg, "BBDO: Successful Brands Become Hard Habit for Consumers to Break," *Marketing Daily* (May 14, 2007), www.mediapost.com, accessed May 14, 2007.

34. Laura Randall, "Things You Do at College," *New York Times* (August 1, 2004): 24.

35. Nancy Keates and Charles Passy, "Tailgating, Inc.," *Wall Street Journal* (August 29, 2003), www.wsj.com, accessed August 29, 2003; www .tailgating.com, accessed June 23, 2009.

36. Virginia Postrel, "From Weddings to Football, the Value of Communal Activities," *New York Times* (April 25, 2002), www.nytimes.com, accessed April 25, 2002.

37. Paul Henry and Marylouise Caldwell, "Headbanging as Resistance or Refuge: A Cathartic Account," *Consumption, Markets, and Culture,* 10 (June 2007): 159–74.

38. Kim Foltz, "New Species for Study: Consumers in Action," *New York Times* (December 18, 1989): A1.

39. For a study that looked at updated wedding rituals in Turkey, see Tuba Ustuner, Güliz Ger, and Douglas B. Holt, "Consuming Ritual: Reframing the Turkish Henna-Night Ceremony," in Stephen J. Hoch and Robert J. Meyers, eds., *Advances in Consumer Research* 27 (Provo, UT: Association for Consumer Research, 2000): 209–14.

40. For a study that looked specifically at rituals pertaining to birthday parties, see Cele Otnes and Mary Ann McGrath, "Ritual Socialization and the Children's Birthday Party: The Early Emergence of Gender Differences," *Journal of Ritual Studies* 8 (Winter 1994): 73–93.

41. Karl Greenberg, "JC Penney Inks Deal with Wedding Site," *Marketing Daily* (March 27, 2009), www.mediapost.com, accessed March 27, 2009.

42. Dennis W. Rook and Sidney J. Levy, "Psychosocial Themes in Consumer Grooming Rituals," in Richard P. Bagozzi and Alice M. Tybout, eds., *Advances in Consumer Research* 10 (Provo, UT: Association for Consumer Research, 1983): 329–33.

43. Quoted in Andrew Adam Newman, "Depilatory Market Moves Far Beyond the Short-Shorts Wearers," *New York Times* (September 14, 2007), www.nytimes.com, accessed September 14, 2007.

44. Diane Barthel, *Putting on Appearances: Gender and Advertising* (Philadelphia: Temple University Press, 1988).

45. Ibid.

46. Russell W. Belk, Melanie Wallendorf, and John F. Sherry, Jr., "The Sacred and the Profane in Consumer Behavior: Theodicy on the

$38,000, Get the Cake, and Mickey, Too," *New York Times Web* (May 24, 2003), www.nytimes.com, accessed May 24, 2003.

Odyssey," *Journal of Consumer Research* 16 (June 1989): 1–38; Jean-Sebastien Marcoux, "Escaping the Gift Economy," *Journal of Consumer Research*, 36 (December 2009), in press.

47. Markus Giesler and Mali Pohlmann, "The Anthropology of File Sharing: Consuming Napster as a Gift," in Punam Anand Keller and Dennis W. Rook, eds., *Advances in Consumer Research* 30 (Provo, UT: Association for Consumer Research 2003); Markus Giesler, "Consumer Gift Systems," *Journal of Consumer Research* 33 no. 2 (2006): 283.

48. Jill G. Klein and Tina M. Lowrey, "Giving and Receiving Humanity: Gifts Among Prisoners in Nazi Concentration Camps," *Advances in Consumer Research* 33, no. 1 (2006): 659.

49. Tina M. Lowrey, Cele C. Otnes, and Julie A. Ruth, "Social Influences on Dyadic Giving over Time: A Taxonomy from the Giver's Perspective," *Journal of Consumer Research* 30 (March 2004): 547–58; Russell W. Belk and Gregory S. Coon, "Gift Giving as Agapic Love: An Alternative to the Exchange Paradigm Based on Dating Experiences," *Journal of Consumer Research* 20 (December 1993): 393–417. See also Cele Otnes, Tina M. Lowrey, and Young Chan Kim, "Gift Selection for Easy and Difficult Recipients: A Social Roles Interpretation," *Journal of Consumer Research* 20 (September 1993): 229–44; Burcak Ertimur and Ozlem Sandikci, "Giving Gold Jewelry and Coins as Gifts: The Interplay of Utilitarianism and Symbolism," *Advances in Consumer Research* 32, no. 1 (2005).

50. Monica Gonzales, "Before Mourning," *American Demographics* (April 1988): 19.

51. Alf Nucifora, "'Tis the Season to Gift One's Best Clients," *Triangle Business Journal* (December 3, 1999): 14.

52. Quoted in Laurel Wentz, "Kit Kat Wins Cannes Media Grand Prix for Edible Postcard," *Advertising Age* (June 23, 2009).

53. John F. Sherry, Jr., "Gift Giving in Anthropological Perspective," *Journal of Consumer Research* 10 (September 1983): 157–68.

54. Daniel Goleman, "What's Under the Tree? Clues to a Relationship," *New York Times* (December 19, 1989): C1; John F. Sherry, Jr., Mary Ann McGrath, and Sidney J. Levy, "The Dark Side of the Gift," *Journal of Business Research* (1993): 225–44.

55. Cecilie Rohwedder, "For a Delicate Sale, a Retailer Deploys 'Stocking Fellas,'" *Wall Street Journal* (December 21, 2006), A1.

56. Colin Camerer, "Gifts as Economics Signals and Social Symbols," *American Journal of Sociology* 94 (Supplement 1988): 5, 180–214; Robert T. Green and Dana L. Alden, "Functional Equivalence in Cross-Cultural Consumer Behavior: Gift Giving in Japan and the United States," *Psychology & Marketing* 5 (Summer 1988): 155–68; Hiroshi Tanaka and Miki Iwamura, "Gift Selection Strategy of Japanese Seasonal Gift Purchasers: An Explorative Study," paper presented at the Association for Consumer Research, Boston, October 1994.

57. See, for example, Russell W. Belk, "Halloween: An Evolving American Consumption Ritual," in Richard Pollay, Jerry Gorn, and Marvin Goldberg, eds., *Advances in Consumer Research* 17 (Provo, UT: Association for Consumer Research, 1990): 508–17; Melanie Wallendorf and Eric J. Arnould, "We Gather Together: The Consumption Rituals of Thanksgiving Day," *Journal of Consumer Research* 18 (June 1991): 13–31.

58. Rick Lyte, "Holidays, Ethnic Themes Provide Built-in F&B Festivals," *Hotel & Motel Management* (December 14, 1987): 56; Megan Rowe, "Holidays and Special Occasions: Restaurants Are Fast Replacing 'Grandma's House' as the Site of Choice for Special Meals," *Restaurant Management* (November 1987): 69; Judith Waldrop, "Funny Valentines," *American Demographics* (February 1989): 7.

59. Quoted in Jeremy Mullman, "Hallmark Reminds Consumers That Little Things Mean a Lot," *Advertising Age* (March 27, 2009), www.adage.com, accessed March 27, 2009.

60. Bruno Bettelheim, *The Uses of Enchantment: The Meaning and Importance of Fairy Tales* (New York: Alfred A. Knopf, 1976).

61. Kenneth L. Woodward, "Christmas Wasn't Born Here, Just Invented," *Newsweek* (December 16, 1996): 71.

62. Aron O'Cass and Peter Clarke, "Dear Santa, Do You Have My Brand? A Study of the Brand Requests, Awareness and Request Styles at Christmas Time," *Journal of Consumer Behavior* 2 (September 2002): 37–53.

63. Theodore Caplow, Howard M. Bahr, Bruce A. Chadwick, Reuben Hill, and Margaret M. Williams, *Middletown Families: Fifty Years of Change and Continuity* (Minneapolis: University of Minnesota Press, 1982).

64. Angeline Close and George M. Zinkhan, "A Holiday Loved and Loathed: A Consumer Perspective of Valentine's Day," *Advances in Consumer Research*, 33, no. 1 (2006). 356–59.

65. Arnold Van Gennep, *The Rites of Passage*, trans. Maika B. Vizedom and Shannon L. Caffee (London: Routledge and Kegan Paul, 1960; orig. published 1908); Michael R. Solomon and Punam Anand, "Ritual Costumes and Status Transition: The Female Business Suit as Totemic

Emblem," in Elizabeth C. Hirschman and Morris Holbrook, eds., *Advances in Consumer Research* 12 (Washington, DC: Association for Consumer Research, 1995): 315–18.

66. Walter W. Whitaker, III, "The Contemporary American Funeral Ritual," in Ray B. Browne, ed., *Rites and Ceremonies in Popular Culture* (Bowling Green, OH: Bowling Green University Popular Press, 1980): 316–25. For a recent examination of funeral rituals, see Larry D. Compeau and Carolyn Nicholson, "Funerals: Emotional Rituals or Ritualistic Emotions," paper presented at the Association of Consumer Research, Boston, October 1994.

67. Gabrielle Glaser, "The Funeral: Your Last Chance to Be a Big Spender," *New York Times* (April 18, 2009), www.nytimes.com/2009/04/19/business/19death.html?_r=1&scp=1&sq=Gabrielle%20Glaser,%20%93The%20Funeral:%20Your%20Last%20Chance%20to%20Be%20a%20Big%20Spender&st=cse, accessed April 19, 2009; John Leland, "It's My Funeral and I'll Serve Ice Cream If I Want To," *New York Times* (July 20, 2006).

68. Samuel K. Bonsu and Russell W. Belk, "Do Not Go Cheaply into That Good Night: Death-Ritual Consumption in Asante, Ghana," *Journal of Consumer Research* 30 (June 2003): 41–55; cf also Stephanie O'Donohoe and Darach Turley, "Till Death Do Us Part? Consumption and the Negotiation of Relationships Following a Bereavement," *Advances in Consumer Research* 32, no. 1 (2005): 625–626.

69. www.sierraclub.typepad.com/greenlife/2007/03/10_steps_to_a_g.html, accessed June 23, 2009; www.greenweddings.net, accessed June 23, 2009; Mireya Navarro, "How Green Was My Wedding," *New York Times* (February 11, 2007), www.nytimes.com, accessed February 11, 2007.

70. "Queen Prompts Thailand to Restrict 'Coyote Ugly' Dance Troupes," *New York Times* (December 28, 2006), www.nytimes.com, accessed December 28, 2006.

71. J. C. Conklin, "Web Site Caters to Cowboy Fans by Selling Sweaty, Used Socks," *Wall Street Journal* (April 21, 2000), www.wsj.com, accessed April 21, 2000.

72. Dan L. Sherrell, Alvin C. Burns, and Melodie R. Phillips, "Fixed Consumption Behavior: The Case of Enduring Acquisition in a Product Category," in Robert L. King, ed., *Developments in Marketing Science* 14 (1991): 36–40.

73. Anne Underwood, "Hoarders Pack It In," *Newsweek* (July 26, 2004): 12.

74. Belk, "Acquiring, Possessing, and Collecting: Fundamental Processes in Consumer Behavior," in Ronald F. Bush and Shelby D. Hunt, eds., *Marketing Theory: Philosophy of Science Perspectives* (Chicago: American Marketing Association, 1982): 85–90; cf. 74.

75. Ruth Ann Smith, *Collecting as Consumption: A Grounded Theory of Collecting Behavior* (unpublished manuscript, Virginia Polytechnic Institute and State University, 1994): 14.

76. For a discussion of these perspectives, see Smith, "Collecting as Consumption."

77. For an extensive bibliography on collecting, see Russell W. Belk, Melanie Wallendorf, John F. Sherry, Jr., and Morris B. Holbrook, "Collecting in a Consumer Culture," in Russell W. Belk, ed., *Highways and Buyways* (Provo, UT: Association for Consumer Research, 1991): 178–215. See also Belk, "Acquiring, Possessing, and Collecting: Fundamental Processes in Consumer Behavior"; Werner Muensterberg, *Collecting: An Unruly Passion* (Princeton, NJ: Princeton University Press, 1994); Melanie Wallendorf and Eric J. Arnould, "'My Favorite Things': A Cross-Cultural Inquiry into Object Attachment, Possessiveness, and Social Linkage," *Journal of Consumer Research* 14 (March 1988): 531–47.

78. Calmetta Y. Coleman, "Just Any Old Thing from McDonald's Can Be a Collectible," *Wall Street Journal* (March 29, 1995): B1; Ken Bensinger, "Recent Boom in Toy Collecting Leads Retailers to Limit Sales," *Wall Street Journal* (September 25, 1998), www.wsj.com, accessed September 25, 1998; "PC Lovers Loyal to Classics," *Montgomery Advertiser* (April 2, 2000): 1.

79. Philip Connors, "Like Fine Wine, a 'Collector' Visits McDonald's for Subtle Differences," *Wall Street Journal* (August 16, 1999), www.wsj.com, accessed August 16, 1999.

80. John Branch, "Yankees Grass Is Now a Brand," *New York Times* (March 21, 2009), www.nytimes.com/2009/03/22/sports/baseball/22grass.html?sq=Yankees%20Grass%20Is%20Now%20a%20Brand&st=cse, accessed March 21, 2009.

81. Kottak, "Anthropological Analysis of Mass Enculturation."

82. Joan Kron, *Home-Psych: The Social Psychology of Home and Decoration* (New York: Clarkson N. Potter, 1983); Gerry Pratt, "The House as an Expression of Social Worlds," in James S. Duncan, ed., *Housing and Identity: Cross-Cultural Perspectives* (London: Croom Helm, 1981): 135–79; Michael R. Solomon, "The Role of the Surrogate Consumer in Service Delivery," *The Service Industries Journal* 7 (July 1987): 292–307.

83. Grant McCracken, "'Homeyness': A Cultural Account of One Constellation of Goods and Meanings," in Elizabeth C. Hirschman, ed., *Interpretive Consumer Research* (Provo, UT: Association for Consumer Research, 1989): 168–84.

84. Quoted in Jessica Grose, "Life in the Time of Oprah," *New York Times* (August 15, 2008), www.nytimes.com/2008/08/17/fashion/17oprah.html?scp=1&sq=Jessica%20Grose,%20%93Life%20in%20the%20Time%20of%20Oprah&st=cse, accessed August 17, 2008.

85. Emile Durkheim, *The Elementary Forms of the Religious Life* (New York: Free Press, 1915).

86. Susan Birrell, "Sports as Ritual: Interpretations from Durkheim to Goffman," *Social Forces* 60, no. 2 (1981): 354–76; Daniel Q. Voigt, "American Sporting Rituals," in Browne, ed., *Rites and Ceremonies in Popular Culture.*

87. Ronald W. Pimentel and Kristy E. Reynolds, "A Model for Consumer Devotion: Affective Commitment with Proactive Sustaining Behaviors," *Academy of Marketing Science Review* 5 (2004): 1.

88. Mark A. Stein, "Block That Snack," *New York Times* (February 4, 2007): 2.

89. Dean MacCannell, *The Tourist: A New Theory of the Leisure Class* (New York: Shocken Books, 1976).

90. Belk et al., "The Sacred and the Profane in Consumer Behavior."

91. Beverly Gordon, "The Souvenir: Messenger of the Extraordinary," *Journal of Popular Culture* 20, no. 3 (1986): 135–46.

92. Belk et al., "The Sacred and the Profane in Consumer Behavior."

93. Güliz Ger and Olga Kravets, "Rediscovering Sacred Times in the Mundane: Tea Drinking in Turkey," Consuming Routines: Rhythms, Ruptures, and the Temporalities of Consumption, International Workshop, European University Institute, Florence, Italy, May 3–5, 2007; cf. also Güliz Ger "Religion and Consumption: The Profane Sacred," *Advances in Consumer Research* 32, no. 1 (2005): 79–81.

94. Deborah Hofmann, "In Jewelry, Choices Sacred and Profane, Ancient and New," *New York Times* (May 7, 1989), www.nytimes.com, accessed October 11, 2007.

95. Lee Gomes, "Ramadan, a Month of Prayer, Takes on a Whole New Look," *Wall Street Journal* (December 4, 2002), www.wsj.com, accessed December 4, 2002.

96. Debbie Treise, Joyce M. Wolburg, and Cele C. Otnes, "Understanding the 'Social Gifts' of Drinking Rituals: An Alternative Framework for PSA Developers," *Journal of Advertising* 28 (Summer 1999): 17–31.

97. Ibid.

16 Global Consumer Culture

When you finish this chapter you will understand:

1. Why are styles like mirrors that reflect underlying cultural conditions?

2. How do we distinguish between high and low culture?

3. Why are many modern marketers reality engineers?

4. How do new products, services, and ideas spread through a population? Why are different types of people more or less likely to adopt them?

5. How do many people and organizations play a role in the fashion system that creates and communicates symbolic meaning to consumers?

6. Why do fashions follow cycles?

7. Why is it that products that succeed in one culture may fail in another if marketers fail to understand the differences among consumers in each place?

8. How does Western (and particularly American) culture have a huge impact around the world, although people in other countries don't necessarily ascribe the same meanings to products as we do?

s Alexandra browses through the racks at her local Abercrombie & Fitch store in Wichita, Kansas, her friend Chloe yells to her, "Alex, check this out! This pencil skirt and animal print blouse outfit is, like, so tight!"[1] From watching MTV, Alex knows *tight* means *cool*, and she agrees. As she takes the pants to the cash register, she looks forward to wearing them to school the next day. All of her girlfriends in junior high compete with each other to dress just like Rihanna, Ciara, Eve, and other hot hip-hop ladies—her friends just won't believe their eyes when they see her tomorrow. Maybe some of the younger kids in her school will even think she's fresh off the mean streets of New York City! Even though she has never been east of the Mississippi, Alex just knows she would fit right in with all of the Bronx "sistahs" she reads about in *Twist, J-14,* and *Yo! Raps.*

Where Does Popular Culture Come From?

OBJECTIVE

Why are styles like mirrors that reflect underlying cultural conditions?

Even though inner-city teens represent only 8 percent of all people in that age group and have incomes significantly lower than their white suburban counterparts, their influence on young people's musical and fashion tastes is much greater than these numbers suggest. Turn on MTV, and it won't be long before a rap video fills the screen. Go to the newsstand, and magazines like *XXL* and *The Source* await you. Numerous Web sites such as allhiphop. com and undergroundhiphop.com pay homage to hip-hop culture.[2]

"Urban" fashion now is a mainstay in the heartland as major retail chains pick up on the craze and try to lure legions of young middle-class shoppers. Macy's and JCPenney carry Sean John and FUBU ("for us by us"); labels like Versace, Tommy Hilfiger, Enyce, Ecko, Nautica, and Affliction are standard issue for junior high kids. Web sites such as hiphopcapital.com sell other emblems of hip-hop such as "pimp cups," gold plated "grillz," and Bellagio spoke rims.[3] Why does this subculture influence the mass market so strongly?

Outsider heroes—whether John Dillinger, James Dean, or Dr. Dre—who achieve money and fame without being hemmed in by societal constraints have always fascinated Americans. That helps to explain the devotion of many white suburban teens to the urban music scene. As one executive of a firm that researches urban youth noted, "People resonate with the strong anti-oppression messages of rap, and the alienation of blacks."[4]

Ironically, the only time Alex experienced "oppression" was when her parents grounded her after her mom found a half-smoked cigarette in her room. She lives in a white middle-class area in the Midwest but "connects" symbolically with millions of other young consumers when she wears styles from "the hood"—even though the original meanings of those styles have little relevance to her. As a privileged member of "white bread" society, her hip-hop clothes mean something much different in her sheltered suburban world than they would to street kids in New York City or LA. In fact, these "cutting-edge" types might even decide that since a kid like Alex now wears their styles that's a sign it's time to move on to something else.

How did hip-hop music and fashions, which began as forms of expression in the African American urban subculture, make it to mainstream America? Here's a brief chronology:

- 1968: Bronx DJ Kool Herc invents hip-hop.
- 1973–1978: Urban block parties feature break dancing and graffiti.
- 1979: Sugar Hill becomes the first rap label.
- 1980: Manhattan art galleries feature graffiti artists.
- 1981: Blondie's song "Rapture" hits number one on the charts.
- 1985: Columbia Records buys the Def Jam label.
- 1988: MTV begins *Yo! MTV Raps*, featuring Fab 5 Freddy.
- 1990: Hollywood produces the hip-hop film *House Party*; Ice-T's rap album is a big hit on college radio stations; amid controversy, white rapper Vanilla Ice hits the big time; NBC launches a new sitcom, *Fresh Prince of Bel Air*.
- 1991: Mattel introduces its Hammer doll (a likeness of the rap star Hammer, formerly known as M. C. Hammer); designer Karl Lagerfeld shows shiny vinyl raincoats and chain belts in his Chanel collection; designer Charlotte Neuville sells gold vinyl suits with matching baseball caps for $800; Isaac Mizrahi features wide-brimmed caps and takeoffs on African medallions; Bloomingdale's launches Anne Klein's rap-inspired clothing line with a rap performance in its Manhattan store.
- 1992: Rappers turn to low-fitting baggy jeans, sometimes worn backward; white rapper Marky Mark appears in a national campaign wearing Calvin Klein underwear, exposed above his hip-hugging pants; composer Quincy Jones launches *Vibe* magazine and it wins over many white readers.[5]

- 1993: Hip-hop fashions and slang continue to cross over into mainstream consumer culture. An outdoor ad for Coca-Cola proclaims, "Get Yours 24–7." The company is confident that many viewers in its target market will know that the phrase is urban slang for "always" (24 hours a day, 7 days a week).[6]

- 1994: The (late) Italian designer Versace pushes oversized overalls. In one ad, he asks, "Overalls with an oversize look, something like what rappers and homeboys wear. Why not a sophisticated version?"[7]

- 1996: Tommy Hilfiger, a designer who was the darling of the preppie set, turns hip-hop. He gives free wardrobes to rap artists such as Grand Puba and Chef Raekwon, and in return they mention his name in rap songs—the ultimate endorsement. The September 1996 issue of *Rolling Stone* features the Fugees; several band members prominently display the Hilfiger logo. In the same year, the designer uses rap stars Method Man and Treach of Naughty by Nature as runway models. Hilfiger's new Tommy Girl perfume plays on his name but also is a reference to the New York hip-hop record label Tommy Boy.[8]

- 1997: Coca-Cola features rapper LL Cool J in a commercial that debuts in the middle of the sitcom *In the House*, a TV show starring the singer.[9]

- 1998: In its battle with Dockers for an increased share of the khaki market, Gap launches its first global ad campaign. One of the commercials, "Khakis Groove," includes a hip-hop dance performance set to music by Bill Mason.[10]

- 1999: Rapper turned entrepreneur Sean (Puffy) Combs introduces an upscale line of menswear he calls "urban high fashion." New companies FUBU, Mecca, and Enyce attain financial success in the multibillion-dollar industry.[11] Lauryn Hill and the Fugees sing at a party upscale Italian clothier Emporio Armani sponsors and she proclaims, "We just wanna thank Armani for giving a few kids from the ghetto some great suits."[12]

- 2000: 360hip-hop.com, a Web-based community dedicated to the hip-hop culture, launches. The site lets consumers purchase clothing and music online while they watch video interviews with artists such as Will Smith and Busta Rymes.[13]

- 2001: Hip-hop dancing becomes the rage among China's youth, who refer to it as *jiew*, or street dancing.[14]

- 2002–2003: Toy manufacturers mimic the hip-hop practice of using the letter *Z* instead of the letter *S* in names. This trend started with the 1991 film *Boyz N the Hood* (a title the movie borrowed from a 1989 song by the rap group N.W.A.). It caught on with other hip-hop terms such as *skillz*, *gangstaz*, and *playaz*. Musical artists including 504 Boyz, Kidz Bop Kidz, Xzibit, the Youngbloodz, and Smilez incorporate the popular *Z* into their names. During the 2002 Christmas season, Target creates its "Kool Toyz," kids' section where parents buy dolls with names such as Bratz (Girlz and Boyz), Diva Starz, and Trophy Tailz—and a Dinky Digz dollhouse to store them. There is a "Scannerz" toy; a Loud Lipz karaoke machine; Marble Moovz, a toddlers' marble set, as well as Rescue Rigz, ControlBotz, 4Wheelerz, and American Patriotz action figures.[15]

- 2005–2006: Successful artists begin to expand their empires into other categories. Jay-Z uses his hip-hop fortune to become part owner of the New Jersey Nets basketball team, Nelly buys into the Charlotte Bobcats, and Usher does the same with the Cleveland Cavaliers.[16] Nelly branches out into the beverage business with Pimp Juice, a hip-hop inspired energy drink, and 50 Cent invests in vitaminwater. Trina and Usher each create their own fragrances, and Gwen Stefani starts her own clothing line. *Esquire* names Andre 3000 of Outkast the world's best-dressed man.

- 2007–2008: Hip-hop disengages from its American roots as artists around the world develop their own localized interpretations. An aboriginal Australian hip-hop dancer tells a crowd the FUBU brand shirt he is wearing means "full blood."[17] Home-grown European artists are popular, such as Jokeren and Den Gale Pose in Denmark, Static and NATiLL in Germany, and Sway in the United Kingdom. Central and eastern European countries develop their own hip-hop subculture with acts such as Parazitii in Romania and Bad Balance/Bad B. in Russia.[18]

● 2009: *Vibe*, the flagship magazine of the hip-hop movement, ceases print publication after 16 years. Slow ad sales due to the recession, a decline in the number of chart-topping artists, and competition contributed to its demise. It was in a sense a victim of its own success; hip-hop is now so mainstream that fans no longer need a single, specialized outlet to access the coverage they crave.[19]

It's common for mainstream culture to modify symbols from "cutting-edge" subcultures for a larger audience to consume. As this occurs, these cultural products undergo a process of **cooptation**, where outsiders transform their original meanings.[20] One writer sees the white part of the "hip-hop nation" as a series of concentric rings. In the center are those who actually know African Americans and understand their culture. The next ring consists of those who have indirect knowledge of this subculture via friends or relatives but who don't actually rap, spray paint, or break dance. Then, there are those a bit farther out who simply play hip-hop between other types of music. Finally we have the more suburban "wiggers," who simply try to catch on to the next popular craze.[21] The spread of hip-hop fashions and music is only one example of what happens when the marketing system takes a set of subcultural meanings, reinterprets them, and reproduces them for mass consumption.

The countercultures that originate these movements of course don't just sit still for this. They develop strategies to reclaim and repoliticize their symbols and practices. For example, large food manufacturers and retailers today recognize shifting consumer tastes as they co-opt vegan or organic food cultures and repackage food products for mainstream grocery shoppers. Wal-Mart sells organic food and the huge conglomerate ConAgra purchased Ben & Jerry's ice cream. In response adherents of a "locavore" lifestyle that emphasizes locally produced meat and vegetables may find alternative channels of distribution like farmers' markets to sell their "authentic" versions to true believers.[22]

In this chapter we'll look at how our culture creates these meanings—which often reside in everyday products—and how these meanings move through a society. As Figure 16.1 shows, the advertising and fashion industries play a key role in this process; they link functional products with symbolic qualities such as sexiness, sophistication, or just plain "cool." These goods, in turn, impart their meanings to us as we use these products to create and express our identities.[23] Recall that in Chapter 1 we learned that "one of the fundamental premises of the modern field of consumer behavior [is that] people often buy products not for what they *do* but for what they *mean*." This closing chapter brings us full circle as we explore how product symbolism evolves and spreads through our culture.

Figure 16.1 THE MOVEMENT OF MEANING

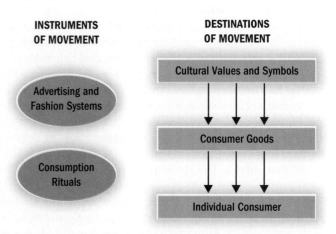

How Do We Know What's "In?"

Aztec tats. Vuitton handbags. Cage-free eggs. Soulja Boy. High-tech furniture. Flash mobs. Postmodern architecture. Twittering. Nettops. Hybrid cars. Costa Rican eco-tours. Gladiator sandals. We inhabit a world that brims with different styles and possibilities. The food we eat, the cars we drive, the clothes we wear, the places we live and work, the music we listen to—the ebb and flow of popular culture and fashion influences all of them.

At times we may feel overwhelmed by the sheer number of choices available to us in the marketplace. A person who wants to choose something as routine as a necktie or a color of lipstick may look at hundreds of alternatives! Despite this seeming abundance, however, the options available to us at any point in time actually represent only a small fraction of the *total* set of possibilities. Figure 16.2 shows that when we select certain alternatives over others—whether automobiles, dresses, computers, recording artists, political candidates, religions, or even scientific methodologies—our choice actually is only the culmination of a complex filtration process that resembles a funnel. Many possibilities initially compete for adoption; most of them drop out of the mix as they make their way down the path from conception to consumption. We call this winnowing out process **cultural selection**.

We don't form our tastes and product preferences in a vacuum. The many images mass media present to us drive our choices, as well as our observations of those around us, and even our desires to live in the fantasy worlds marketers create in the ads we see all around us. These options constantly evolve and change. A clothing style or type of cuisine that is "hot" one year may be "out" the next.

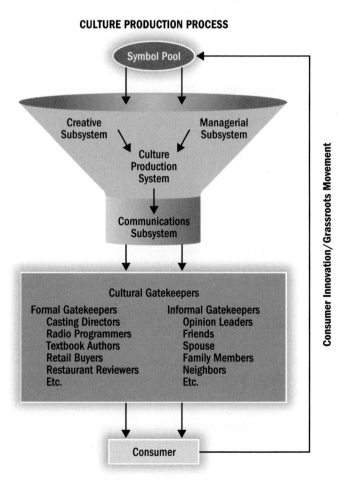

CULTURE PRODUCTION PROCESS

Figure 16.2 THE CULTURE PRODUCTION PROCESS

Alex's emulation of hip-hop style illustrates some of the characteristics of fashion and popular culture:

- Styles reflect more fundamental societal trends (e.g., politics and social conditions).
- A style begins as a risky or unique statement by a relatively small group of people and then spreads as others become aware of it.
- Styles usually originate as an interplay between the deliberate inventions of designers and businesspeople and spontaneous actions by ordinary consumers who modify these creations to suit their own needs. Designers, manufacturers, and merchandisers who anticipate what consumers want will succeed in the marketplace. In the process, they help to fuel the fire when they encourage distribution of the item—especially if they persuade opinion leaders to use it first.
- These cultural products travel widely, often across countries and even continents.
- Influential people in the media play a significant role in deciding which will succeed.
- Most styles eventually wear out as people continually search for new ways to express themselves and marketers scramble to keep up with these desires.
- The cultural selection process never stops, so when styles become obsolete others wait to replace them in popular culture.

No single designer, company, or advertising agency creates popular culture. Instead, many parties contribute to every hit CD, hot car, or new clothing style. A **culture production system (CPS)** is the set of individuals and organizations that create and market a cultural product.[24] The structure of a CPS determines the types of products it creates. Factors such as the number and diversity of competing systems and the amount of innovation versus conformity each influence the selection of products from which choose at any point in time. For example, an analysis of the country/western music industry showed that the hit records it produces are similar to one another when a few large companies dominate the industry, but when a greater number of labels compete we see more diversity in musical styles.[25]

A culture production system has three major subsystems:

1. A *creative subsystem* to generate new symbols and products
2. A *managerial subsystem* to select, make tangible, produce, and manage the distribution of new symbols and products
3. A *communications subsystem* to give meaning to the new product and provide it with a symbolic set of attributes

An example of the three components of a culture production system for a music release would be (1) a singer (e.g., rapper Akon, a creative subsystem); (2) a company (e.g., Umvd Labels that distributes Akon's CDs, a managerial subsystem); and (3) NYLA Entertainment Group, the PR agency that promotes the CDs (a communications subsystem). Table 16.1 illustrates some of the many cultural specialists that create a hit CD.

Many judges or "tastemakers" have a say in the products we consider. These **cultural gatekeepers** filter the overflow of information as it travels down the "funnel." Gatekeepers include movie, restaurant, and car reviewers; interior designers; disc jockeys; retail buyers; and magazine editors. Collectively, social scientists call this set of agents the *throughput sector*.[26] These people play a role in decision making similar to the *surrogate consumers* we discussed in Chapter 8.

We've already encountered numerous examples of the minirevolution we call consumer-generated content; companies today pay attention to everyday people's opinions when they design new products, create advertising messages, or im-

TABLE 16.1	Cultural Specialists in the Music Industry
Specialist	**Functions**
Songwriter(s)	Compose music and lyrics; must reconcile artistic preferences with estimates of what will succeed in the marketplace
Performer(s)	Interpret music and lyrics; may be formed spontaneously, or may be packaged by an agent to appeal to a predetermined market (e.g., The Monkees, Menudo, and New Kids on the Block)
Teachers and coaches	Develop and refine performers' talents
Agents	Represent performers to record companies
A&R (artist & repertoire) executives	Acquire artists for the record label
Publicists, image consultants, designers, stylists	Create an image for the group that is transmitted to the buying public
Recording technicians, producers	Create a recording to be sold
Marketing executives	Make strategic decisions regarding performer's appearances, ticket pricing, promotional strategies, and so on
Video directors	Interpret the song visually to create a music video that will help to promote the record
Music reviewers	Evaluate the merits of a recording for listeners
Disc jockeys, radio program directors	Decide which records will be given airplay and/or placed in the radio stations' regular rotations
Record store owners	Decide which of the many records produced will be stocked and/or promoted heavily in the retail environment

prove on shopping experiences. The rise of social networking changes the basic process of innovation, as the consumer feedback loop in Figure 16.1 grows stronger and stronger. This shift from a top-down to a bottom-up process is a symptom of the transition from *marketerspace* where companies exert total control over the market.

Instead, we now live in consumerspace, where customers act as partners with companies to decide what the marketplace will offer.[27] Innovative companies understand the value of involving their most forward-thinking customers in business decisions before they introduce the final product. More than 650,000 customers tested a beta version of Microsoft Windows 2000. Many were even prepared to pay Microsoft a fee to do this because when they worked with the program they would understand how it could create value for their own businesses. The value of the research and development investment by customers to Microsoft was more than $500 million. Similarly, Cisco gives its customers open access to its resources and systems so that they can solve the problems other customers encounter.

This approach is more prevalent in high-tech industries that routinely invite their most experienced and knowledgeable customers (or **lead users**) to suggest ideas. Indeed, it's common for these people to propose product improvements—because they have to live with the consequences. According to one estimate, users rather than manufacturers developed 70 percent of the innovations in the chemical industry![28] Xerox uses **voice of the consumer** data in its R&D process, which means that it solicits feedback from end customers well before it puts a new product on the market. The company's standard development process is to design and build a prototype and *then* get customer feedback. Xerox is a pioneer in what the company calls "customer-led innovation" that encourages engineers to "dream with the customer." Company engineers meet face-to-face with some of the 1,500 to 2,000 customers who visit showrooms at the company's four global research facilities each year. Others work on-site for a week or two with corporate clients to understand how they behave with the product in real situations to see how they actually use the company's products.[29] Welcome to consumerspace.

As this AT&T ad demonstrates, many styles and products are destined to become obsolete.
Source: Courtesy of AT&T Archives and History Center.

High Culture and Popular Culture

OBJECTIVE

How do we distinguish between high and low culture?

Question: What do Beethoven and Kanye West have in common? Although we associate both the famous composer and the rap singer with music, many would argue that the similarity stops there. Culture production systems create many kinds of products, but we make some basic distinctions.

Arts and Crafts

An **art product** is an object we admire strictly for its beauty or because it inspires an emotional reaction in us (perhaps bliss, or perhaps disgust). In contrast, we admire a **craft product** because of the beauty with which it performs some function (e.g., a ceramic ashtray or hand-carved fishing lures).[30] A piece of art is original, subtle, and valuable, and typically we associate it with society's elite (see Chapter 12). A craft tends to follow a formula that permits rapid production.[31]

To appreciate this distinction, consider the phenomenal success of artist Thomas Kinkade. This painter has sold 10 million digital reproductions of his work. He manufactures the pictures at a factory in California, where workers reproduce a digital photograph of each original thousands of times onto thin plastic film they glue to canvasses. Then "high-lighters" sit along an assembly line where they dab oil paint onto set spots. Each of the 10,000 pieces the factory produces each month is signed in ink that contains drops of the artist's blood, although he never actually touches most of these works. Kinkade also licenses images that appear on coffee mugs, La-Z-Boy recliners, and even a romance novel cover.[32]

High Art Versus Low Art

As Kinkade's "formula for success" demonstrates, the distinction between high and low culture is not as clear as it used to be. In addition to the possible class bias that drives such a distinction (i.e., we assume that the rich have culture but the poor do not), today high and low culture blend together in interesting ways. In addition to the appliances, tires, and cereals it sells by the case, the warehouse club Costco stocks fine art, including limited-edition lithographs by Pablo Picasso, Marc Chagall, and Joan Miró.[33]

Marketers often invoke high-art imagery to promote products. They may feature works of art on shopping bags or sponsor artistic events to build public goodwill.[34] When observers from Toyota watched customers in luxury car showrooms, the company found that these consumers view a car as an art object. The company then used this theme in an ad for the Lexus with the caption, "Until now, the only fine arts we supported were sculpture, painting, and music."[35]

Cultural Formulae

Mass culture, in contrast, churns out products specifically for a mass market. These products aim to please the average taste of an undifferentiated audience. Rather than being unique, they are predictable because they follow a well-defined pattern.

As this British ad illustrates, high art merges with popular art in interesting ways.
Source: Courtesy of Eddis Trailers c/o The Explorer Group.

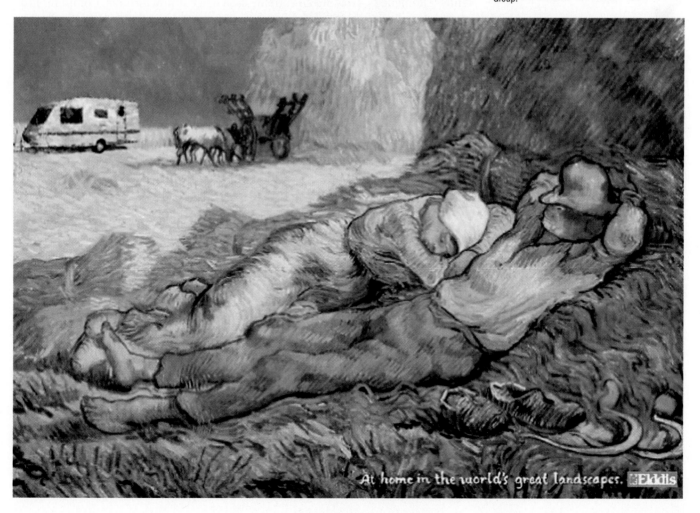

At home in the world's great landscapes. Eddis

TABLE 16.2	Cultural Formulae in Public Art Forms			
Art Form/Genre	**Classic Western**	**Science Fiction**	**Hard-Boiled Detective**	**Family Sitcom**
Time	1800s	Future	Present	Anytime
Location	Edge of civilization	Space	City	Suburbs
Protagonist	Cowboy (lone individual)	Astronaut	Detective	Father (figure)
Heroine	Schoolmarm	Spacegal	Damsel in distress	Mother (figure)
Villain	Outlaws, killers	Aliens	Killer	Boss, neighbor
Secondary characters	Townfolk, Indians	Technicians in spacecraft	Cops, underworld	Kids, dogs
Plot	Restore law and order	Repel aliens	Find killer	Solve problem
Theme	Justice	Triumph of humanity	Pursuit and discovery	Chaos and confusion
Costume	Cowboy hat, boots, etc.	High-tech uniforms	Raincoat	Regular clothes
Locomotion	Horse	Spaceship	Beat-up car	Station wagon
Weaponry	Sixgun, rifle	Rayguns	Pistol, fists	Insults

Source: Arthur A. Berger, *Signs in Contemporary Culture: An Introduction to Semiotics,* 2/e, p.118. Copyright © 1984 by Sheffield Publishing Company, Salem, Wisconsin. Reprinted with permission of the publisher.

Marketing Opportunity

The Bill and Melinda Gates Foundation is a *reality engineer* for good causes—it helps to influence viewers' attitudes toward public health and HIV prevention when it shapes story lines and inserts prosocial messages in popular TV shows like *Law & Order: SVU.* The foundation recently made a deal with Viacom, the parent company of MTV and its sister networks VH1, Nickelodeon, and BET to expand this program. Instead of paying to have colas or cars featured in shows, marketers will sponsor messages that promote education and healthy living.[42]

As Table 16.2 illustrates, many popular art forms, such as detective stories or science fiction, follow a **cultural formula**, where familiar roles and props occur consistently.[36] Romance novels are an extreme case of a cultural formula. Computer programs even allow users to "write" their own romances when they systematically vary certain set elements of the story.

As members of the creative subsystem rely on these formulae, they tend to *recycle* images as they reach back through time for inspiration. Thus, young people watch retro shows like *Gilligan's Island* as well as remakes such as *The Real Gilligan's Island*; designers modify styles from Victorian England or colonial Africa; hip-hop deejays sample sound bits from old songs and combine them in new ways; and Gap runs ads that feature (deceased) celebrities in khaki pants including Humphrey Bogart, Gene Kelly, and Pablo Picasso. With easy access to CD burners, digital cameras, and imaging software, virtually anyone can "remix" the past.[37]

OBJECTIVE

Why are many modern marketers reality engineers?

Reality Engineering

People love the GEICO caveman. He appears in commercials as a throwback who dresses in "yuppie" clothing as he struggles against GEICO's insensitivity when its ads claim, "It's so easy even a caveman can do it." How much do viewers love him? ABC developed a (short-lived) sitcom about a group of caveman roommates who battle prejudice in modern-day America. GEICO receives hundreds of letters and e-mails about the characters, and fans at college sporting events hold up signs that say "Beating [team name] is so easy, even a caveman can do it." The cavemen continue to appear in commercials and in a music video by the band 3 Doors Down.[38] Similarly, the mythical Simpsons family debuted in real life as 7-Eleven transformed many of its stores into Kwik-E-Marts to promote the cartoon series' movie. During the promotion customers snapped up Krusty O's cereal, Buzz Cola, and ice Squishees, all products from the show.[39]

Reality engineering occurs when marketers appropriate elements of popular culture and use them as promotional vehicles.[40] It's hard to know what's real anymore; specialists even create "used jeans" when they apply chemical washes, sandpaper, and other techniques to make a new pair of jeans look like they're ready for retirement. The industry even has a term for this practice that sums up the contradiction: *new vintage*![41]

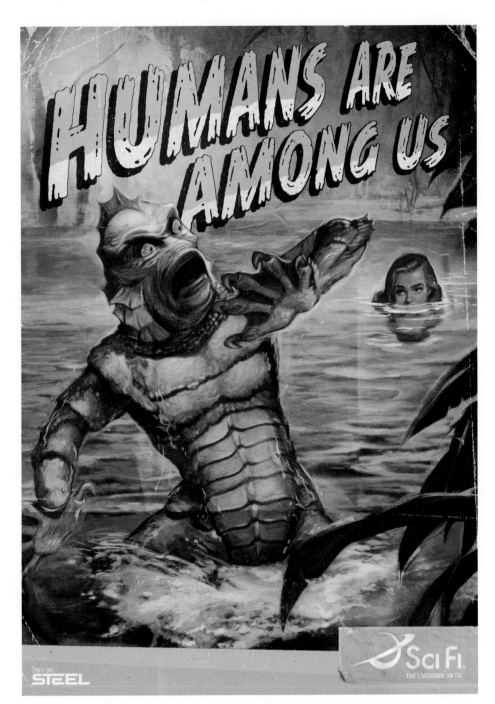

Horror movies tend to follow a cultural formula.

Source: Courtesy of Saatchi & Saatchi, Milan © Steel is an NBC Universal Global Network.

Reality engineers have many tools at their disposal; they plant products in movies, pump scents into offices and stores, attach video monitors in the backs of taxicabs, buy ad space on police patrol cars, or film faked "documentaries" such as *The Blair Witch Project*.[43] This process is accelerating—historical analyses of Broadway plays, best-selling novels, and the lyrics of hit songs, for example, clearly show large increases in the use of real brand names over time.[44] Here are some examples of reality engineering:

● Bravo develops real-world products based on some of its TV programs that it promotes on air and sells on its Web site. These include pricey Kooba bags contestants on *The Fashion Show* created, *Top Chef*–themed flower arrangements from Teleflora, *Top Chef*–branded wines from Terlato Wines International, *Top*

One of the most controversial intersections between marketing and society occurs when companies provide "educational materials" to schools.[61] Many firms including Nike, Hershey, Crayola, Nintendo, and Foot Locker provide free book covers swathed in ads. Standard art supplies, blocks, trucks, and dolls get supplemented with Milton Bradley and Care Bears worksheets, Purell hand-cleaning activities, and Pizza Hut reading programs. Walt Disney advertised its *Little Einsteins* DVDs for preschoolers on the paper liners of examination tables in 2,000 pediatricians' offices, whereas Hasbro introduced the Play-Doh McDonald's Restaurant Playset (with which kids can "extrude Play-Doh shakes and fries") and the Play-Doh George Foreman Grill. Clearasil provides sample packets of its acne medication along with brochures to educate high school students about proper skin care; the handouts also direct students to the Clearasil Web site where they can also register for music downloads and iPods.

Other companies contract with schools to run focus groups with their students during the school day in order to get reactions to new product ideas. Some schools encourage kids to practice their math as they count Tootsie Rolls, and the kids use reading software that bears the logos of Kmart, Coke, Pepsi, and Cap'n Crunch cereal. Entire schools are branded—one in New Jersey awarded naming rights for its gym to the local ShopRite grocery store. Several Texas high schools sold naming rights to their football stadiums for more than a million dollars. At Vernon Hills High outside Chicago, fans watch their players run up and down Rust-Oleum Field.

Corporate involvement with schools is hardly new—in the 1920s Ivory Soap sponsored soap-carving competitions for students. But the level of intrusion is sharply increasing as companies scramble to compensate for the decrease in children's viewership of television on Saturday mornings and weekday afternoons and they try to compete with videos and computer games for kids' attention. Many educators argue that these materials are a godsend for resource-poor schools that otherwise could not provide computers and other goodies to their students. However, a California law bans the use of textbooks with brand names and company logos. This legislation was prompted by complaints from parents about a middle school math book that uses names such as Barbie, Oreos, Nike, and Sony PlayStation in word problems.

Chef knives from Master Cutlery, and online cooking classes conducted by *Top Chef* contestants.[45]

● The Alibi Network provides "excuses" for people who need to cover their tracks. Clients can purchase a fake doctor's note, a virtual travel service that furnishes a fake itinerary and receipts, and a rescue call service that gets you out of boring meetings (classes don't qualify). Reputation Defender will scour the Web to identify your embarrassing entries and delete them (or you can just say no when you post all those photos on Facebook you'll regret later).[46]

● Actress Demi Moore and her fiancé heartthrob Ashton Kutcher appeared on the cover of *Star* magazine, under the headline "$1 Million Wedding of the Year!" She's wearing a sexy white fitted dress, and he's decked out in a white suit. But wait—it turns out Ms. Moore's dress was really chocolate brown and Mr. Kutcher's suit was really pink. The magazine digitally altered the colors before it went to press.[47]

● A father named his baby boy ChamberMaster after a software company won the naming rights in a charitable auction. In one survey, about half of the respondents said they would consider accepting money from corporations in exchange for naming rights to their babies. Others do it for free: In 2000, the latest year for which data are available, 571 babies in the United States were named Armani, 55 were named Chevy, and 21 were named L'Oréal.[48]

● A New York couple funded their $80,000 wedding when they sold corporate plugs; they inserted coupons in their programs and tossed 25 bouquets from 1-800-FLOWERS.

● The TV series *Trust Me* chronicles life in a fictional Chicago advertising agency that competes for accounts against real agencies like Leo Burnett and DDB. The clients are real as well—some like the Dove line of hair care products sold by Unilever also happen to sponsor the show. A real-life brand manager for Dove hair care appears on the show, and to promote the series viewers can play an online game where they pretend to be creative directors for Dove.[49]

Product Placement

Back in the day, TV networks demanded that producers "geek" (alter) brand names before they appeared in a show, as when *Melrose Place* changed a Nokia cell phone to a "Nokio."[50] Today, real products pop up everywhere. Many are well-established brands that lend an aura of realism to the action, while others are upstarts that benefit tremendously from the exposure. For example, in the movie version of *Sex and the City* Carrie's assistant admits that she "borrows" her expensive pricey handbags from a rental Web site called Bag Borrow or Steal. The company's head of marketing commented, "It's like the *Good Housekeeping* Seal of Approval. It gives us instant credibility and recognition."[51]

Bag Borrow or Steal got a free plug (oops, they got another one here!). In many cases, however, these "plugs" are no accident. **Product placement** is the insertion of real products in fictional movies, TV shows, books, and plays. Many types of products play starring (or at least supporting) roles in our culture; the most visible brands range from Coca-Cola and Nike apparel to the Chicago Bears football team and the Pussycat Dolls band.[52] The TV shows that feature the most placements include *The Biggest Loser* (it showed about 4,000 brands in just a three-month period), *American Idol* (how subtle is that Coca-Cola glass each judge holds?), *The Apprentice*, *America's Next Top Model*, and *One Tree Hill*. This practice is so commonplace (and profitable) now that it's evolved into a new form of promotion we call **branded entertainment**, where advertisers showcase their products in longer-form narrative films instead of brief commercials. For example, *SportsCenter* on ESPN showed installments of "The Scout presented by Craftsman at Sears," a 6-minute story about a washed-up baseball scout who discovers a stunningly talented stadium groundskeeper.[53]

Product placement is by no means a casual process: Marketers pay about $25 billion per year to plug their brands in TV and movies. Several firms specialize in ar-

A dining room influenced by the TV show *Dexter* that features a serial killer.
Source: Photo by Adam Chinitz/Courtesy of A C Imaging, LLC.

ranging these appearances; if they're lucky they manage to do it on the cheap when they get a client's product noticed by prop masters who work on the shows. For example, in a cafeteria scene during an episode of *Grey's Anatomy* it was no coincidence that the character Izzie Stevens happened to drink a bottle of Izze Sparkling Pomegranate fruit beverage. The placement company that represents PepsiCo paid nothing to insert the prop in that case, but it probably didn't get off so easily when the new brand also showed up in HBO's *Entourage, Big Bang Theory,* and *The New Adventures of Old Christine* on CBS.[54]

Today most major releases brim with real products, even though a majority of consumers believe the line between advertising and programming is becoming too fuzzy and distracting (though as we might expect, concerns about this blurring of boundaries are more pronounced among older people than younger).[55] A study reported that consumers respond well to placements when the show's plot makes the product's benefit clear. Similarly, audiences had a favorable impression of when a retailer provided furniture, clothes, appliances, and other staples for struggling families who get help on ABC's *Extreme Makeover: Home Edition.*[56]

Although we hear a lot of buzz today about product placement, in reality it's a long-standing cinematic tradition. The difference is that today the placements are more blatant and financially lucrative. In the heyday of the major Hollywood studios, brands such as Bell telephone, Buick, Chesterfield cigarettes, Coca-Cola, De Beers diamonds, and White Owl cigars regularly appeared in films. For example, in a scene in the classic *Double Indemnity* (1944) that takes place in a grocery store, the director Billy Wilder made some products such as Green Giant vegetables face the camera whereas others "mysteriously" were turned around to hide their labels. Indeed, the practice dates at least as far back as 1896, when an early movie shows a cart bearing the brand name Sunlight (a Lever Brothers brand) parked on a street.[58] Perhaps the greatest product placement success story was Reese's Pieces; sales jumped by 65 percent after the candy appeared in the film *E.T.*[59]

Some researchers claim that product placement aids consumer decision making because the familiarity of these props creates a sense of cultural belonging while they generate feelings of emotional security. Another study found that placements consistent with a show's plot do enhance brand attitudes, but incongruent placements that aren't consistent with the plot affect brand attitudes *negatively* because they seem out of place.[60]

Marketing Pitfall

The product placement industry has come under government scrutiny as pressure grows from consumer groups to let viewers know when companies pay to use their products as props. The Federal Communications Commission (FCC) is considering whether it should regulate this practice. Currently shows have to disclose this information but only at the end of the show and in small print. An FCC official says, "You shouldn't need a magnifying glass to know who's pitching you."[57]

Advergaming

If you roar down the streets in the *Need for Speed Underground 2* video racing game, you'll pass a Best Buy store as well as billboards that hawk Old Spice and Burger King.[62] *America's Army*, produced by the U.S. government as a recruitment tool, is one of the most successful advergames. Twenty-eight percent of those who visit the *America's Army* Web page click through to the recruitment page.

About three-quarters of American consumers now play video games, yet to many marketers the idea of integrating their brands with the stories that games tell is still a well-kept secret. Others including Axe, Mini Cooper, and Burger King have figured this out—they create game narratives that immerse players in the action. Orbitz offers playable banner-games that result in the highest click-through rate of any kind of advertising the online travel site does. Even though the game industry brings in more revenue than feature films or music sales, only about 10 percent of marketers execute any promotions in this space.

Even so, it's likely that the future is bright for **advergaming**—where online games merge with interactive advertisements that let companies target specific types of consumers. These placements can be short exposures such as a billboard that appears around a racetrack, or they can take the form of branded entertainment and integrate the brand directly into the action. For example, a game that Dairy Queen helped to create called *DQ Tycoon* lets players run their own fast-food franchise. The game requires players to race against the clock to prepare Peanut-Buster Parfaits, take orders, restock the refrigerator, and dip cones.[63]

The mushrooming popularity of user-generated videos on YouTube and other sites creates a growing market to link ads to these sources as well. This strategy is growing so rapidly that there's even a new (trademarked) term for it. **Plinking™** is the act of embedding a product or service link in a video.

Why is this new medium so hot?[64]

- Compared to a 30-second TV spot, advertisers can get viewers' attention for a much longer time. Players spend an average of 5 to 7 minutes on an advergame site.
- Physiological measures confirm that players are highly focused and stimulated when they play a game.
- Marketers can tailor the nature of the game and the products in it to the profiles of different users. They can direct strategy games to upscale, educated users, while they can gear action games to younger users.

Mead's branded video game attracted over 10 million players.

Source: Courtesy www.mediapost.com accessed 12/15/08.

- The format gives advertisers great flexibility because game makers now ship PC video games with blank spaces in them to insert virtual ads. This allows advertisers to change messages on the fly and pay only for the number of game players that actually see them. Sony Corp. now allows clients to directly insert online ads into PlayStation 3 videogames—the in-game ads change over time through a user's Internet connection.
- There's great potential to track usage and conduct marketing research. For example, an inaudible audio signal coded into Activision's *Tony Hawk's Underground 2* skating game on PCs alerts a Nielsen monitoring system each time the test game players view Jeep product placements within the game.

The Diffusion of Innovations

OBJECTIVE

How do new products, services, and ideas spread through a population? Why are different types of people more or less likely to adopt them?

The originators of skateboarding in 1970s Southern California (who were portrayed in the popular documentary *Dogtown and Z-Boys*) wouldn't recognize the sport today. At that time boarders were outlaws; as one of the main characters in the film says, "We get the beat-down from all over. Everywhere we go, man, people hate us."

Now skateboarding is about as countercultural as *The Simpsons*. More kids ride skateboards than play basketball, and many of them snap up pricey T-shirts, skate shoes, helmets, and other accessories. In fact, boarders spend almost six times as much on "soft goods" such as T-shirts, shorts, and sunglasses (about $4.4 billion in a year) than on hard-core equipment including the boards themselves.[65]

The progression of skateboarding from a cult-like activity with rebellious undertones to a mainstream hobby mirrors the journey many products and services take through popular culture. **Diffusion of innovations** refers to the process whereby a new product, service, or idea spreads through a population. An **innovation** is any product or service that consumers perceive to be new. It may take the form of an activity (skateboarding), a clothing style (Ed Hardy T-shirts), a new manufacturing technique (the ability to design your own running shoe at nike.com), a new variation on an existing product (Parkay Fun Squeeze Colored Margarine in electric blue and shocking pink), a new way to deliver a product (ordering groceries online and having Peapod deliver them to your home), or a new way to package a current product (Campbell's Soup at Hand Microwaveable Soup that comes in a travel mug).[66]

If an innovation is successful (most are not!), it spreads through the population. First only a trickle of people decides to try it. Then, more and more consumers decide to adopt it, until sometimes it seems that almost everyone is buying it—if it's a "hit." The rate at which a product diffuses varies. For example, within 10 years after introduction, 40 percent of U.S. households watched cable TV, 35 percent listened to compact disks, 25 percent used answering machines, and 20 percent bought color TVs. It took radio 30 years to reach 60 million users and TV 15 years to reach this number. In contrast, within 3 years 90 million of us surfed the Web.[67]

How Do We Decide to Adopt an Innovation?

Our adoption of an innovation resembles the decision-making sequence we discussed in Chapter 8. We move through the stages of awareness, information search, evaluation, trial, and adoption. The relative importance of each stage differs, however, depending on how much we already know about an innovation as well as on cultural factors that affect our willingness to try new things.[68]

A study of 11 European countries found that consumers in individualistic cultures are more innovative than consumers in collective cultures (see Chapter 15).[69] However, even within the same culture, not all people adopt an innovation at the

Figure 16.3 TYPES OF ADOPTERS

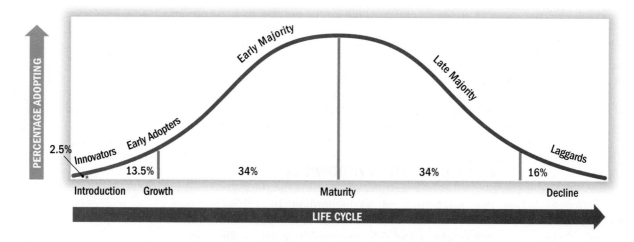

same rate. Some do so quite rapidly, and others never do at all. We place consumers into approximate categories based on the likelihood they will adopt something new.

As Figure 16.3 shows, roughly one-sixth of the population (innovators and early adopters) are very quick to adopt new products, and one-sixth (**laggards**) are very slow. The other two-thirds, so-called **late adopters**, are somewhere in the middle. These consumers are the mainstream public. They are interested in new things, but they do not want them to be *too* new. In some cases, people deliberately wait to adopt an innovation because they assume that the company will improve its technology or that its price will fall after it has been on the market awhile. (have you been holding off on that iPhone purchase to see what Apple will come up with next?)[70] Keep in mind that the proportion of consumers who fall into each category is an estimate—the actual size of each depends on such factors as the complexity of the product, its cost, and how much risk people associate with it.

Even though **innovators** represent only about 2.5 percent of the population, marketers are eager to identify them. These are the brave souls who are always on the lookout for novel products or services and who are first to try something new. Just as generalized opinion leaders do not appear to exist (see Chapter 10), innovators tend to be category-specific as well. A clotheshorse who prides himself as being on the cutting edge of fashion may have no conception of new developments in recording technology—he may still stubbornly cling to his antique phonograph albums even as he searches for the latest avant-garde clothing styles in trendy boutiques. Despite this qualification, we can summarize the profile of someone who's a good candidate to be an innovator.[71] Not surprisingly, for example, he tends to be a risk-taker. He's also likely to have a relatively high educational and income level and to be socially active.

How do we locate innovators? Ad agencies and market research companies are always on the prowl for people who stay on top of developing trends. One ad agency surveys taxi drivers about what they see on the streets every day. Others get more sophisticated and use the Internet and their global networks to monitor what "people in the know" do. The agency DDB runs a service it calls SignBank, which collects thousands of snippets of information from its 13,000 employees around the world about cultural change in order to advise their clients on what it all means for them. For example, sign spotters in several markets noticed that dinner party guests tended to bring their hosts flowers instead of chocolate because of concerns about health and obesity—that's valuable information for a client that makes chocolate.[72]

Early adopters share many of the same characteristics as innovators. But an important difference is their high degree of concern for social acceptance, especially with regard to expressive products such as clothing and cosmetics. Generally speaking, an early adopter is receptive to new styles because she is involved in the product category and she values being in fashion.

CB AS I SEE IT

Professor Gordon Bruner, *Southern Illinois University*

*S*everal years ago, Professor Kumar (University of South Florida) and I were working with Sprint to develop a way for the company to measure a person's technological innovativeness such that it could be easily implemented in the surveys the company routinely conducted. Sprint's primary interest was in *innovators*— the small group of consumers who have a tendency to be among the first to adopt high-tech goods and services. At the same time, Dr. Kumar and I wanted to learn more about a similar group of adopters we called **gadget lovers**. The term *gadget lover* has been tossed around in our country for many decades but no scientific study of them had occurred. We wondered if they were pretty much the same people as tech innovators or if they were different.

After we conducted several studies, the results were rather clear: While there is overlap between the two groups of consumers, there are also key differences. As a group, innovators adopt a little more quickly than gadget lovers. While gadget lovers tend to adopt much more rapidly than the average consumer, they don't all qualify as innovators. On the other hand, more gadget lovers qualify as *opinion leaders* than innovators. The reasons for this are not perfectly clear, but it seems that gadget lovers, as the name implies, genuinely enjoy playing with technology. That experience and expertise is visible to other consumers who then feel comfortable to seek the gadget lovers' advice. In contrast, innovators seem to be more interested in the status that comes from being first to adopt. Although they like high-tech toys, they don't appear to be as expert at using them as are gadget lovers, nor do they tend to exhibit the infectious enthusiasm that gadget lovers do.

When the gadget lover scale was administered to a large nationally representative sample of U.S. consumers, the results indicated that males scored much higher than females, younger adults scored slightly higher than older adults, those with greater education scored higher than those with less education, and the major ethnic groups scored higher than white/non-Hispanics.

The bottom line is that even though gadget lovers are similar to innovators in several ways, we believe they are distinct enough to deserve as much or more attention from marketers of high-tech innovations, particularly because of the group's seemingly greater influence on what others do.[73]

What appears on the surface to be a fairly high-risk adoption (e.g., wearing a skirt three inches above the knee when most people wear them below the knee) is actually not *that* risky. Innovators who truly took the fashion risk have already "field-tested" the style change. We're likely to find early adopters in "fashion-forward" stores that feature the latest "hot" designer brands. In contrast, we're more likely to find true innovators in small boutiques that carry merchandise from as-yet-unknown designers.

Behavioral Demands of Innovations

We categorize innovations by the degree to which they demand adopters to change their behavior. Researchers identify three major types of innovations, though these three categories are not absolutes. They refer, in a relative sense, to the amount of disruption or change they bring to people's lives.

A **continuous innovation** is a modification of an existing product, such as when General Mills introduces a Honey Nut version of Cheerios or Levi's promotes shrink-to-fit jeans. The company makes small changes to position the product, add line extensions, or merely to alleviate consumer boredom. Most product innovations are of this type; they are *evolutionary* rather than *revolutionary*.

When a consumer adopts this kind of new product, she only has to make minor changes in her habits. A typewriter company, for example, many years ago modified its product to make it more "user friendly" to secretaries. Its engineers made the tops of the keys concave because women told them it was hard to type with long fingernails on a flat surface. This change endures today on our computer keyboards.

Some innovations present us with a new way to use an existing product. This may be more effective—but we still have to alter our habits to use it. A Japanese clothing company recently introduced a line of Shower Clean business suits that allow traveling executives to bypass the dry cleaner; they wash their suit in a warm shower and it needs no pressing. Similarly, R.J. Reynolds sells a cigarette in Japan it calls Kool Boost—it's made with a menthol-infused internal "powerball" that allows the smoker to choose his own level of menthol as he squeezes the filter.[74] As these examples suggest, a **dynamically continuous innovation** is a significant change to an existing product. When IBM introduced its Selectric typewriter that used a typing ball rather than individual keys, the new design permitted secretaries to instantly change the typeface of manuscripts as they replaced one Selectric ball with another.

A **discontinuous innovation** creates really *big* changes in the way we live. Major inventions, such as the airplane, the car, the computer, and the television, radically changed modern lifestyles. The personal computer replaced the typewriter, and it also allows some of us to "telecommute" from our homes. Of course, the cycle continues, as new continuous innovations (e.g., new versions of software) constantly update our computers. Dynamically continuous innovations such as the Nintendo Wii and now Microsoft's motion sensitive control for Xbox offer new ways to maneuver in cyberspace.[75]

Prerequisites for Successful Adoption

Regardless of how much we have to change what we do, a successful innovation should possess these attributes:[76]

- **Compatibility**—The innovation should be compatible with consumers' lifestyles. A manufacturer of personal care products tried unsuccessfully several years ago to introduce a cream hair remover for men as a substitute for razors and shaving cream. This formulation was similar to what many women use to remove hair from their legs. Although the product was simple and convenient to use, it failed because men were not interested in a product they perceived to be too feminine and thus a threat to their masculine self-concepts.

- **Trialability**—Because we think an unknown product is risky, we're more likely to adopt an innovation if we can experiment with it prior to making a commitment. To reduce this risk, companies may spend a lot of money to distribute free "trial-size" samples of new products.

- **Complexity**—The product should be low in complexity. All things being equal, we will choose a product that's easier to understand and use rather than a more complex one. This strategy requires less effort from us and it also lowers our perceived risk. Manufacturers of DVD recorders, for example, put a lot of effort into simplifying usage (e.g., on-screen programming) to encourage nontechies to adopt them.

- **Observability**—Innovations that are readily apparent are more likely to spread because we can learn about them more easily. The rapid proliferation of fanny packs (pouches people wear around the waist in lieu of wallets or purses) was a result of their high visibility. It was easy for others to see the convenience this alternative offered (even if they were a bit nerdy).

- **Relative Advantage**—Most importantly, the product should offer relative advantage over other alternatives. The consumer must believe that it will provide a benefit other products cannot offer. For example, the Bugchaser is a wristband that contains insect repellent. Mothers with young children like it because it's nontoxic and nonstaining—these are clear advantages over alternatives. In contrast, the Crazy Blue Air Freshener, which emits a fragrance when you turn on your car wipers, fizzled: People didn't see the need for the product and felt there were simpler ways to freshen their cars.

The Fashion System

OBJECTIVE

How do many people and organizations play a role in the fashion system that creates and communicates symbolic meaning to consumers?

The **fashion system** includes all the people and organizations that create symbolic meanings and transfer those meanings to cultural goods. Although we often equate fashion with clothing, it's important to keep in mind that fashion processes affect *all* types of cultural phenomena, including music, art, architecture, and even science (i.e., certain research topics and individual scientists are "hot" at any point in time). Even business practices are subject to the fashion process—they evolve and change depending on which management techniques are in vogue, such as TQM (total quality management), JIT (just-in-time inventory control), or MBWO (managing by walking around).

It helps to think of fashion as a *code*, or a language, that helps us to decipher these meanings.[77] Unlike a language, however, fashion is *context-dependent*. Different consumers interpret the same style differently.[78] In semiotic terms (see Chapter 2), fashion products are *undercoded*. There is no one precise meaning but rather plenty of room for interpretation among perceivers.

At the outset, let's distinguish among some confusing terms. **Fashion** is the process of social diffusion by which some group(s) of consumers adopts a new style. In contrast, *a fashion* (or style) is a particular combination of attributes (say, stovepipe jeans women wear with a tunic top). And to be *in fashion* means that some reference group positively evaluates this combination (i.e., *Vogue* endorses this look as "in" for this season). Thus, the term *Danish Modern* refers to particular characteristics of furniture design (i.e., a fashion in interior design); it does not necessarily imply that Danish Modern is a fashion that consumers currently desire.[79]

Cultural Categories

The meanings we give to products reflect underlying **cultural categories** that correspond to the basic ways we characterize the world (like the schemas we discussed way back in Chapter 2).[80] Our culture distinguishes between different times of day (brunch, happy hour), between leisure and work, and between genders. The fashion system provides us with products that signify these categories. For example, the

Fashion is a key part of popular culture. This fashion show, hosted by Target at Grand Central Terminal in Manhattan, used digital holograms instead of live human models to display the latest styles by Isaac Mizrahi and other major designers.
Source: Photo by Jacob Silberberg/Reuters/ Courtesy of Landov Media.

apparel industry gives us clothing to denote certain situations (e.g., evening wear, resort wear); it differentiates between leisure clothes and work clothes, and it offers masculine versus feminine styles.

These cultural categories affect many different kinds of products. As we saw in Chapter 15, the way that companies design and market their products reflects the dominant values of a culture at a point in time. This concept is a bit hard to grasp because on the surface a clothing style has little in common with a piece of furniture or a car. However, an overriding concern with a value such as achievement or environmentalism determines the types of products consumers look for across many industry sectors. These underlying themes then surface in a variety of designs. A few examples of this interdependence demonstrate how a dominant fashion *motif* reverberates across industries.

- Costumes that politicians or movie and rock stars wear affect the fortunes of the apparel and accessory industries. A movie appearance by actor Clark Gable without a T-shirt (unusual at that time) dealt a severe setback to the men's apparel industry; whereas Jackie Kennedy's famous pillbox hat prompted a rush for hats by women in the 1960s. Other cross-category effects include the craze for ripped sweatshirts the movie *Flashdance* (1983) instigated, a boost for cowboy boots from the movie *Urban Cowboy* (1980), and the large number of women who wear lingerie on the street due to the singer Madonna. . . . More recently Michelle Obama single-handedly sent J.Crew's sales through the roof as she and her kids wear their clothes in many public settings. When the First Lady wore a J.Crew outfit to breakfast with the British Prime Minister and his wife while in London, it sold out on the company's Web site by 10:00 that morning.[81]
- The architect I. M. Pei's remodeling of the Louvre in Paris included a controversial glass pyramid at the entrance. Shortly thereafter, several clothing designers unveiled pyramid-shaped dresses at Paris fashion shows.[82]
- In the 1950s and 1960s, America was preoccupied with science and technology. The Russians' launching of the *Sputnik* satellite fueled a sense of urgency as people feared that the United States was falling behind in the technology race (and that we were also losing the Cold War). The theme of technical mastery of nature and of futuristic design became a motif that cropped up in many aspects of American popular culture—from car designs with prominent tail fins to high-tech kitchen styles.
- At any point in time a small number of colors dominate in the design world. Many companies actually buy color forecasts from specialists, such as Pantone, that rank the top 10 fashion colors for each season. These charts influence mass-market fashion companies, as well as other industries such as automotive, home furnishings, and home appliances. A dominant color often takes years to emerge. For example, when black was prominent during the 1980s and 1990s, designers snubbed brown as a "dirty" color. Then, Starbucks began to take off and espresso, latte, and other coffee colors seeped into mass culture. In addition, consumers rediscovered gourmet chocolates such as Godiva and (at least in some circles) fur regained its popularity. Color forecasts put brown back on the fast track. Sure enough, now the United Parcel Service asks, "What can Brown do for You?" while BMW's 2009 Mini Cooper Clubman hit the streets in its new "Hot Chocolate" color.[83]

Remember that creative subsystems within a culture production system succeed when they anticipate the tastes of the buying public. Despite their unique talents, however, members of this subsystem also live in the same culture as do their customers—and they often go to the same schools, see the same movies, read the same magazines, and listen to the same music as do their competitors. Cultural gatekeepers draw from a common set of cultural categories, so it's not surprising that their choices often converge—even though they compete against one another to offer the consumer something new or different. **Collective selection** is the process by which CPS members choose some symbolic alternatives over others.[84] Although rivals within each category compete for acceptance, we can usually group them because they follow a dominant theme or motif—be it "The Western Look," "New Wave," "Danish Modern," or "Nouvelle Cuisine."

Behavioral Science Perspectives on Fashion

Fashion is a very complex process that operates on many levels. At one extreme, it's a societal phenomenon that affects many of us simultaneously. At the other, it exerts a very personal effect on individual behavior. Many of us desire to be in fashion, and this motivates us as to what we buy. Fashion products also are aesthetic objects—they reflect a culture's artistic traditions and history. For this reason, there are many perspectives on the origin and diffusion of fashion. Let's summarize some major approaches.[85]

Psychological Models of Fashion

Many psychological factors help explain what motivates us to be fashionable. These include conformity, desires for variety seeking, the need to express personal creativity, and sexual attraction. For example, many consumers seem to have a "need for uniqueness": They want to be different (though not necessarily *too* different!).[86] As a result people may conform to the basic outlines of a fashion, but still improvise to make a personal statement within these general guidelines.

One of the earliest theories of fashion argued that "shifting *erogenous zones*" (sexually arousing areas of the body) accounted for fashion changes and that different zones become the object of interest because they reflect societal trends. J. C. Flugel, a disciple of Freud, proposed in the 1920s that sexually charged areas wax and wane as we grow bored with them; clothing styles change to highlight or hide the parts that currently are the focus of attention. For example, it was common for Renaissance-era women to drape their abdomens in fabrics in order to give a swollen appearance—successful childbearing was a priority in the disease-ridden fourteenth and fifteenth centuries. Now, some suggest that the current prevalence of the exposed midriff in women's fashion reflects the premium our society places on fitness.[87]

Economic Models of Fashion

Economists approach fashion in terms of the model of supply and demand. Items in limited supply have high value, whereas our desire decreases for readily available products. Rare items command respect and prestige. As we discussed in Chapter 12, the writer Thorstein Veblen argued that the wealthy practice *conspicuous consumption* to display their prosperity. As we also noted, this approach is somewhat outdated; upscale consumers today engage in *parody display* where they deliberately buy inexpensive products (especially during a recession). Other factors also influence the demand curve for fashion-related products. These include a *prestige–exclusivity effect*, where high prices still create high demand, and a *snob effect*, whereby lower prices actually reduce demand ("If it's that cheap, it can't be any good").[88]

Sociological Models of Fashion

The *collective selection model* we discussed previously is a sociological approach to fashion. This perspective focuses on a subculture's adoption of a fashion (idea, style, etc.) and its subsequent diffusion into society as a whole. This process often begins with youth subcultures such as the hip-hop segment. The integration of Goth culture into the mainstream is another current example. This fashion started as an expression of rebellion by young outcasts who admired nineteenth-century romantics and who defied conventional styles with their black clothing (often including over-the-top fashion statements such as Count Dracula capes, fishnet stockings, studded collars, and black lipstick) and punk music from bands such as Siouxsie & the Banshees and Bauhaus. Today, music stores sell vampire-girl lunchboxes, and mall outlets sell tons of clunky cross jewelry and black lace. You can find a T-shirt that looks like a corset at Kmart. At the Hot Topic Web site, teen surfers can buy a "multiring choker." Hard-core Goths are not amused, but hey, that's fashion for you.[89]

Trickle-down theory, which the sociologist Georg Simmel first proposed in 1904, is one of the most influential fashion perspectives. It states that there are two conflicting

This ad for Maidenform illustrates that fashions have accentuated different parts of the female anatomy throughout history.
Source: Courtesy of Maidenform Inc.

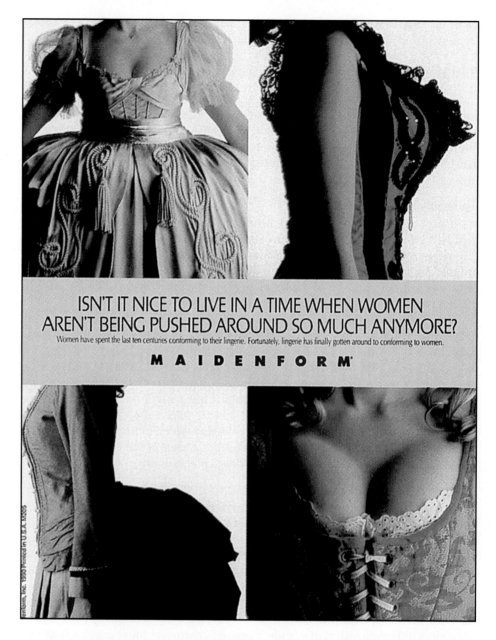

forces that drive fashion change. First, subordinate groups adopt the status symbols of the groups above them as they attempt to climb up the ladder of social mobility. Dominant styles thus originate with the upper classes and *trickle down* to those below.

Now the second force kicks in: Those people in the superordinate groups keep a wary eye on the ladder below them to be sure followers don't imitate them. When lower-class consumers mimic their actions, they adopt new fashions to distance themselves from the mainstream. These two processes create a self-perpetuating cycle of change—the machine that drives fashion.[90]

The integration of hip-hop phrases into our vocabulary illustrates how people who set fashions resist mainstream adoption by the broader society. The street elite shunned some slang terms such as *bad*, *fresh*, and *jiggy* once they became too mainstream. The rap community even held a funeral (with a eulogy by Reverend Al Sharpton) for the word *def* once the *Oxford English Dictionary* included it in its new edition.[91]

Trickle-down theory applies to a society with a stable class structure that allows us to easily identify lower- versus upper-class consumers. This task is no longer so easy. In contemporary Western society, we have to modify this theory to account for new developments in mass culture:[92]

● A perspective we base on class structure can't account for the wide range of styles now available. We have many more choices today because of technological advances that let manufacturers drastically speed up production times and real-time media that keep us informed of style changes in minutes. Stores such as Zara and H&M can replenish their inventories in weeks rather than months. An adolescent like Alex simply watches MTV or chats on Facebook or Stardoll.com to stay on top of the latest trends; *mass fashion* thus replaces elite fashion because our media allows many market segments to learn about a style simultaneously.

● Consumers today are more influenced by opinion leaders who are similar to them—even if these innovators don't live in the same town or even country. As a result each social group has its own fashion innovators who determine fashion trends. It's more accurate to speak of a *trickle-across effect*, where fashions diffuse horizontally among members of the same social group.[93]

● Finally, current fashions often originate with the lower classes and *trickle up*. Grassroots innovators typically are people who lack prestige in the dominant culture (e.g., urban youth). Because they are less concerned with maintaining the status quo, they are free to innovate and take risks.[94]

A "Medical" Model of Fashion

For many years, the lowly Hush Puppy was a shoe for nerds. Suddenly—almost overnight—the shoe became a chic fashion statement even though its manufacturer did nothing to promote this image. Why did this style diffuse through the population so quickly? **Meme theory** explains this process with a medical metaphor. A *meme* is an idea or product that enters the consciousness of people over time—examples include tunes, catch-phrases ("You're fired!"), or styles such as the Hush Puppy.

In this view, memes spread among consumers in a geometric progression just as a virus starts off small and steadily infects increasing numbers of people until it becomes an epidemic. Memes "leap" from brain to brain via a process of imitation. The memes that survive tend to be distinctive and memorable, and the hardiest ones often combine aspects of prior memes. For example, the *Star Wars* movies evoke prior memes that relate to the legend of King Arthur, religion, heroic youth, and 1930s adventure serials. Indeed, George Lucas studied comparative religion and mythology as he prepared his first draft of the *Star Wars* saga, *The Story of Mace Windu*.[95]

The diffusion of many products in addition to Hush Puppies seems to follow the same basic path. A few people initially use the product, but change happens in a hurry when the process reaches the moment of critical mass—what one author calls the **tipping point**. For example, Sharp introduced the first low-priced fax machine in 1984 and sold about 80,000 in that year. There was a slow climb in the number of users for the next 3 years. Then, suddenly in 1987 enough people had fax machines that it made sense for everyone to have one—Sharp sold a million units. Cell phones followed a similar trajectory.[96] Do you remember when you first heard about Twitter?

6
OBJECTIVE
Why do fashions follow cycles?

Cycles of Fashion Adoption

In the early 1980s, Cabbage Patch dolls were all the rage among American children. Faced with a limited supply of the product, some retailers reported near-riots among adults as they tried desperately to buy the dolls for their children. A Milwaukee deejay jokingly announced that people should bring catcher's mitts to a local stadium because an airplane was going to fly overhead and drop 2,000 dolls. He told his listeners to hold up their American Express cards so their numbers could be photographed from the plane. More than two dozen anxious parents apparently didn't get the joke—they showed up in subzero weather, mitts in hand.[97]

The Cabbage Patch craze lasted for a couple of seasons before it eventually died out, and consumers moved on to other things, such as Teenage Mutant Ninja Turtles, which grossed more than $600 million in 1989. The Mighty Morphin Power

Figure 16.4 A NORMAL FASHION LIFE CYCLE

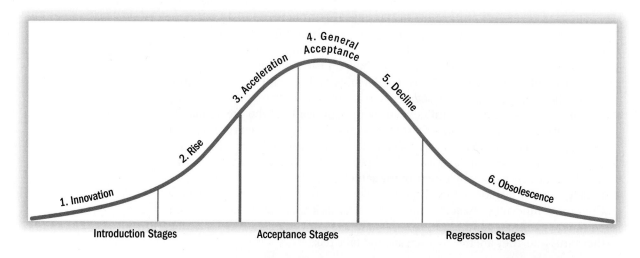

Rangers eventually replaced the Turtles, and Beanie Babies and Giga Pets in turn deposed them before the invasion of Pokémon followed by Yu-Gi-Oh! Cards, Webkinz, and now *Guitar Hero.*[98] What will be next?

Although the longevity of a particular style can range from a month to a century, fashions tend to flow in a predictable sequence. The fashion life cycle is quite similar to the product life cycle you (hopefully!) learned about in your basic marketing course. As Figure 16.4 shows, an item or idea progresses through basic stages from birth to death as it makes its way through the fashion life cycle.

The diffusion process we discussed earlier in this chapter applies to the popularity of fashion items. To illustrate how this process works, consider how the **fashion acceptance cycle** works in the popular music business. In the *introduction stage,* a small number of music innovators hear a song. Clubs or college radio stations may play it—which is how "grunge rock" groups such as Nirvana got their start. Increasingly, the band posts its songs on MySpace and recruits "friends" who will help it get known. During the *acceptance stage,* the song enjoys increased social visibility as large segments of the population start to check it out. Top 40 stations may start to give it wide airplay as it climbs the charts "like a bullet." In the *regression stage,* the song reaches a state of social saturation as Top 40 stations play it once an hour for several weeks. At some point listeners tire of it and focus their attention on newer releases. The former hit record eventually winds up in the discount rack at the local record store.

Figure 16.5 illustrates that fashions begin slowly, but if they "make it," they diffuse rapidly through a market, peak, and then retreat into obscurity. We identify different classes of fashion when we look at the relative length of their **acceptance cycles**. Many fashions have a moderate cycle—they take several months or even years to work their way through the stages of acceptance and decline; others are extremely long lived or short lived.

A **classic** is a fashion with an extremely long acceptance cycle. It is in a sense "antifashion" because it guarantees stability and low risk to the purchaser for a long period of time. Keds sneakers, introduced in 1917, appeal to those who are turned off by the high fashion, trendy appeal of Nike or Reebok. When researchers asked consumers in focus groups to imagine what kind of building Keds would be, a common response was a country house with a white picket fence. In other words, consumers see the shoes as a stable, classic product. In contrast, participants described Nikes as steel-and-glass skyscrapers to reflect their more modern image.[99]

Fads: Here Today, Gone Tomorrow

A theme park in Japan offers "amusement baths" to visitors that include a wine bath, a green-tea bath, a coffee bath, a sake bath, and even a ramen-noodle bath. When

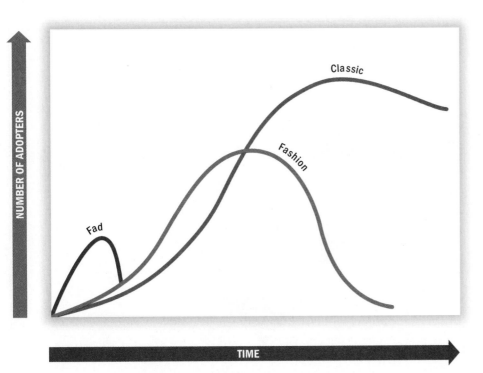

Figure 16.5 COMPARISON OF THE ACCEPTANCE CYCLES OF FADS, FASHIONS, AND CLASSICS

they don their bathing suits and jump into the ramen bath (which looks like a soup bowl), they frolic in pepper-flavored water that contains collagen and garlic extracts the Japanese believe will improve the skin. A man dressed as a chef dispenses noodle-shaped bath additives and soy sauce to everyone in the tub.[100] A **fad** is a very short-lived fashion. Relatively few people adopt a fad product, but it can spread very quickly. Adopters may all belong to a common subculture, and the fad "trickles across" members but rarely breaks out of that specific group. Figure 16.6 illustrates

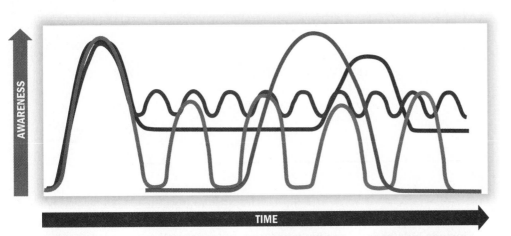

Figure 16.6   THE BEHAVIOR OF FADS

TRUE FAD	**CYCLICAL FAD**	**FAD-TO-FRANCHISE**	**GENERATIONAL FAD**
Life Span: One year or less	**Life Span:** One year or less at each spike	**Life Span:** One to five years	**Life Span:** One year or less at each spike
Top Sources: Toy/novelty, TV, dance/music, fashion	**Top Sources:** Toy/novelty	**Top Sources:** Toy/novelty, publishing, movies	**Top Sources:** Toy/novelty
Demographics: All	**Demographics:** All	**Demographics:** All	**Demographics:** Children and nostalgic adults
Example: Pet Rock	**Example:** Yo-yos	**Example:** Barbies	**Example:** Trolls

This Jim Beam ad illustrates the cyclical nature of fashion.
Source: Courtesy of Jim Beam Brands.

that some types of fads have longer life spans than others. Notable past fad products include hula hoops, snap bracelets, and pet rocks; to learn more about these and other "must have" products, visit <u>badfads.com</u>.[101]

Fads often involve frivolous or "weird" behavior, and many consumers may not conform (see Chapter 10) as they refuse to participate (this may make the fad even more appealing to devotees). A pair of researchers recently studied adults who resist the Harry Potter craze. They find some of these consumers avoid the Hogwarts world because they pride themselves on "not being taken in." These adults react negatively to the "evangelical" enthusiasts who try to convert them to fandom. They recount the resentment of one newlywed on her honeymoon (as her new husband related in

A sommelier pours wine into a "Beaujolais Nouveau bath" at a Tokyo resort.
Source: Photo by Shizuo Kambayash/Courtesy of AP Wide World Photos.

an essay): "My new page turning obsession did not go down too well with my new life partner. When on our first night in the Maldives and expecting some form of conjugal rites [she found] herself in second place to a fictional 11-year-old trainee wizard and something called the Sorting Hat."[102]

The *streaking* fad hit college campuses in the mid-1970s. This term described students who ran nude through classrooms, cafeterias, dorms, and sports venues. Although the practice quickly spread across many campuses, it was primarily restricted to college settings. Streaking highlights several of a fad's "naked truths:"[103]

- The fad is nonutilitarian—it does not perform any meaningful function.
- The fad often spreads impulsively—people do not undergo stages of rational decision making before they join in.
- The fad diffuses rapidly, gains quick acceptance, and dies.

Fad or Trend?

Chrysler's PT Cruiser was the talk of the town when it came out in 2000. With its 1930s-gangster getaway-car looks, cutely compact size, and innovative features— such as a panel in the back that you can use as a picnic table—the PT was hot. Chrysler sold 145,000 of them in 2001. By 2003, PT Cruiser sales slumped to 107,759 cars, and Chrysler offered discounts to keep the miniwagon moving. In fall 2005, Chrysler launched a revamped version—the grille and front end looked more like other new Chrysler models, and it upgraded the interior. The PT Cruiser's sales curve—a 25 percent fall from peak to trough—suggests the market for funky, retro three-quarter-sized wagons generated a lot of excitement at the beginning. But instead of being a hot new model for young trendsetters, the car appealed to graying baby boomers—the median age of owners is 50 years old. Are retro cars a fad or a trend? The jury is still out—especially because General Motors also launched its Chevy HHR—a retro car that according to GM executives was inspired by a 1949 Chevrolet Suburban, *not* the PT Cruiser.[104]

The first company to identify a trend and act on it has an advantage, whether the firm is Starbucks (gourmet coffee), Nabisco (Snackwells low-fat cookies and crackers), Taco Bell (value pricing), or Chrysler (retro cars). Nothing is certain, but

Johnny Earle turned his nickname—
"Cupcake"—into a booming business. His
T-shirts featured cupcakes in unlikely places
(for example, one with a cupcake and
crossbones) and became a popular fad.
Source: Courtesy of JohnnyCupcakes.com.

some guidelines help to predict whether the innovation will endure as a long-term trend or if it's just a fad destined to go the way of hula hoops, pet rocks, and little rubber spiders called Wally Wallwalkers that slowly crawled down walls.[105]

● Does it fit with basic lifestyle changes? If a new hairstyle is hard to care for, this innovation isn't consistent with women's increasing time demands. However, the movement to shorter-term vacations is more likely to last because this innovation makes trip planning easier for harried (and broke) consumers who want to get away for a few days at a time.

● What are the benefits? The switch to poultry and fish from beef came about because these meats are healthier.

● Can we personalize it? Enduring trends tend to accommodate a desire for individuality, whereas styles such as Mohawk haircuts or the grunge look are inflexible and don't allow people to express themselves.

● Is it a trend or a side effect? An increased interest in exercise is part of a basic trend toward health consciousness, although the specific form of exercise that is "in" at any given time will vary (e.g., low-impact aerobics versus Pilates).

● What other changes occurred in the market? Sometimes *carryover effects* influence the popularity of related products. The miniskirt fad in the 1960s boosted hosiery purchases substantially. Now, sales of these items are in decline because of today's more casual styles.

● Who adopted the change? If working mothers, baby boomers, or some other important market segment don't adopt the innovation, it is not likely to become a longer-term trend.

Global Diffusion

Innovations know no geographic boundaries; in modern times they travel across oceans and deserts with blinding speed. Just as Marco Polo brought noodles from China and colonial settlers introduced Europeans to the "joys" of tobacco, today multinational firms conquer new markets when they convince legions of foreign consumers to desire what they make.

As if understanding the dynamics of one's culture weren't hard enough, these issues get even more complicated when we consider what drives consumers in other cultures. The consequences of ignoring cultural sensitivities can be costly. Think about problems a prominent multinational company such as McDonald's encounters as it expands globally:

- During the 1994 soccer World Cup, the fast-food giant reprinted the Saudi Arabian flag, which includes sacred words from the Koran, on disposable packaging it used in promotions. Muslims around the world protested this borrowing of sacred imagery, and the company had to scramble to correct its mistake.
- In 2002, McDonald's agreed to donate $10 million to Hindu and other groups as partial settlement of litigation involving its mislabeling of French fries and hash browns as vegetarian (it cooked them in oil tainted with meat residue).
- Also in 2002, the company abruptly cancelled its plans to introduce its new McAfrika sandwich in its Norwegian restaurants. The CEO of McDonald's in Norway acknowledged on national television that introducing this menu item at a time of growing famine in Africa was "coincidental and unfortunate."
- In India, the company doesn't sell any of its famous beef hamburgers. Instead, it offers customized entrees such as a Pizza McPuff, McAloo Tikki (a spiced-potato burger), Paneer Salsa McWrap, and even a Crispy Chinese burger, to capitalize on the great popularity of Chinese food in India. It makes its mayonnaise without eggs, and all stores maintain separate kitchen sections for vegetarian and non-vegetarian dishes. Workers from the nonvegetarian section must shower before they cross over to the other area.
- In 2005, McDonald's introduced the spicy Prosperity Burger in nine countries from South Korea to Indonesia in recognition of the Lunar New Year.
- The chain's Big Tasty burger is an 840 calorie behemoth that consists of a 5.5 ounce beef patty slathered in smoky barbecue sauce and topped with three slices of cheese. The menu entrée was first introduced in Sweden, and it's now available in other parts of Europe as well as in Latin America and Australia. McDonald's worldwide operations are now far bigger than its U.S. domestic business, and it's no longer the case that menu innovations originate here—regional operations are just as likely to create their own offerings.[106]

In this section, we'll consider some of the issues that confront marketers who want to understand the cultural dynamics of other countries. We'll also consider the consequences of the "Americanization" of global culture. As U.S. (and to some extent, Western European) marketers continue to export Western popular culture to a globe full of increasingly affluent consumers, many customers eagerly replace their traditional products with the likes of McDonald's, Levi's, and MTV. But, as we'll also see, there are plenty of obstacles to success for multinational firms—especially Yankee ones.

Rather than ignore the global characteristics of their brands, firms have to manage them strategically. That's critical because future growth for most companies will come from foreign markets. In 2002, developed countries in North America, Europe, and East Asia accounted for 15 percent of the world's population of 6.3 billion. By 2030, according to the World Bank, the planet's population will rise to 9 billion—and

90 percent of these people will live in developing countries. And, the Web no longer concentrates in the West: According to Jupiter Research, by 2012 there will be 292 million Chinese Internet users compared to 241 million in the United States.

Think Globally, Act Locally

As corporations compete in many markets around the world, the debate intensifies: Should an organization develop separate marketing plans for each culture, or should it craft a single plan to implement everywhere? Let's briefly consider each viewpoint.

Adopt a Standardized Strategy

As Procter & Gamble strategizes about the best way to speak to consumers around the world, the company finds large segments in many countries who share the same outlooks, style preferences, and aspirations. These include teenagers, working women who try to juggle careers and families, and baby boomers. As the head of P&G's Global Health and Feminine Care division explains, "We're seeing global tribes forming around the world that are more and more interconnected through technology. If you focus on the similarities instead of the differences [in these tribes], key business opportunities emerge." Brand managers for example find that teenage girls everywhere have the same concerns and questions about puberty so the company can speak to them on its beinggirl.com Web site and make the same content available in 40 countries.[107]

Proponents of a standardized marketing strategy argue that many cultures, especially those of industrialized countries, are now so homogenized that the same approach will work throughout the world. If it develops one approach for multiple markets, a company can benefit from economies of scale because it does not have to incur the substantial time and expense to develop a separate strategy for each culture.[108] This viewpoint represents an **etic perspective**, which focuses on commonalities across cultures. An etic approach to a culture is objective and analytical—it reflects impressions of a culture as outsiders view it.

Adopt a Localized Strategy

Unlike Disney World in Orlando, visitors to the Walt Disney Studios theme park at Disneyland Paris don't hear the voices of American movie stars narrating their guided tours. Instead, European actors such as Jeremy Irons, Isabella Rossellini, and Nastassja Kinski provide commentary in their native tongues.

Disney learned the hard way about the importance of being sensitive to local cultures after it opened its Euro Disney Park in 1992. The company got slammed because its new location didn't cater to local customs (such as serving wine with meals). Visitors to Euro Disney from many countries took offense, even at what seem to be small slights. For example, initially the park only sold a French sausage, which drew complaints from Germans, Italians, and others who believed their own local version to be superior. Euro Disney's CEO explains, "When we first launched there was the belief that it was enough to be Disney. Now we realize that our guests need to be welcomed on the basis of their own culture and travel habits."[109]

Disney applies the lessons it learned in cultural sensitivity to its newer Hong Kong Disneyland. Executives shifted the angle of the front gate by 12 degrees after they consulted a *feng shui* specialist, who said the change would ensure prosperity for the park (see Chapter 13). Disney also put a bend in the walkway from the train station to the gate to make sure the flow of positive energy, or *chi*, did not slip past the entrance and out to the China Sea. Cash registers are close to corners or along walls to increase prosperity. The company burned incense as it finished each building, and it picked a lucky day (September 12) for the opening. One of the park's main ballrooms measures 888 square meters because eight is a lucky number in Chinese culture.

And because the Chinese consider the number four bad luck, you won't find any fourth-floor buttons in hotel elevators. Disney also recognizes that Chinese family dynamics are different so it revamped its advertising: Print ads showed a grandmother, mother, and daughter who wear tiaras at the park. In China, bonding between parents and children is difficult because of the culture's hierarchical nature so an executive explains, "We want to say it's OK to let your hair down." Camping out with stopwatches, the company's designers discovered that Chinese people take an average of 10 minutes longer to eat than Americans. So they added 700 extra seats to dining areas.

Ironically, some locals feel Disney tries *too* hard to cater to local customs—activists raised a ruckus when the company announced it would serve the traditional Chinese dish of shark's fin soup at wedding banquets held in the park. The species is endangered, and one group distributed T-shirts that depicted Mickey Mouse and Donald Duck holding knives and leering over three bleeding sharks. Nonetheless, Disney forges ahead with localized products. One of its latest ventures is in India, where it's making animated films with the voices of Bollywood stars. It's also making a Hindi version of its TV hit *High School Musical*—set against a backdrop of cricket instead of basketball.

Disney's experience supports the view of marketers who endorse an **emic perspective**, which stresses variations across cultures. They feel that each culture is unique, with its own value system, conventions, and regulations. This perspective argues that each country has a *national character*, a distinctive set of behavior and personality characteristics.[110] A marketer must therefore tailor its strategy to the sensibilities of each specific culture. An emic approach to a culture is subjective and experiential—it attempts to explain a culture as insiders experience it.

Sometimes this strategy means a manufacturer has to modify what it makes or a retailer has to change the way it displays the product so that it's acceptable to local tastes. When Wal-Mart started to open stores abroad in the early 1990s, it offered a little piece of America to foreign consumers—and that was the problem. It promoted golf clubs in soccer-mad Brazil and pushed ice skates in Mexico. It trained its German clerks to smile at customers—who thought they were flirting. Now Wal-Mart tries to adapt to local preferences. Its Chinese stores sell live turtles and snakes and lure shoppers who come on foot or bicycle with free shuttle buses and home delivery for refrigerators and other large items.[111]

In some cases, consumers in one place simply do not like some products that are popular elsewhere, or their different lifestyles require companies to rethink their designs. IKEA finally realized that Americans use a lot of ice in their drinks and so they didn't buy the smaller European glasses the stores stocked. The Swedish furniture chain also figured out that compared to Europeans, Americans sleep in bigger beds, need bigger bookshelves, and like to curl up on sofas rather than sit on them.[112] Snapple failed in Japan because the drink's cloudy appearance and the floating pulp in the bottles were a turnoff. Similarly, Frito-Lay stopped selling Ruffles potato chips (too salty) and Cheetos (the Japanese didn't appreciate orange fingers after they ate a handful).[113] The company still makes Cheetos in China, but the local version doesn't contain any cheese, which is not a staple of the Chinese diet. Instead, local flavors come in varieties such as Savory American Cream and Japanese Steak.[114]

Cultural Differences Relevant to Marketers

So, which perspective is correct—the emic or the etic? As you might guess, the best bet probably is a combination of both. Some researchers argue that the relevant dimension to consider is **consumer style**—a pattern of behaviors, attitudes, and opinions that influences all of a person's consumption activities—including attitudes toward advertising, preferred channels of information and purchase, brand loyalty, and price consciousness. These researchers identified four major clusters of

The Tangled Web

The Web makes it difficult to confine marketing messages to a local area. Absolut vodka and its global advertising agency TBWA discovered this when they ran a print ad they intended only for readers in Mexico City. The ad was a local execution of an international campaign called "In an Absolut World" that includes various depictions of what an ideal world would look like. In this case a map showed much of the United States as part of Mexico. American bloggers soon discovered the ad, and it wasn't long before it enraged U.S. anti-immigration groups and others who called for an Absolut boycott.[115]

consumer styles when they looked at data from the United States, the United Kingdom, France, and Germany:[116]

1 Price-sensitive consumers
2 Variety seekers
3 Brand-loyal consumers
4 Information seekers

Given the sizable variations in tastes within the United States alone, it is hardly surprising that people around the world develop their own unique preferences. Panasonic touted the fact that its rice cooker kept the food from getting too crisp—until the company learned that consumers in the Middle East like to eat their rice this way. Unlike Americans, Europeans favor dark chocolate over milk chocolate, which they think of as a children's food. Sara Lee sells its pound cake with chocolate chips in the United States, raisins in Australia, and coconuts in Hong Kong. Crocodile handbags are popular in Asia and Europe but not in the United States.[117]

The language barrier is one obvious problem that marketers who wish to break into foreign markets must navigate. Travelers abroad commonly encounter signs in tortured English such as a note to guests at a Tokyo hotel that proclaims, "You are invited to take advantage of the chambermaid," a notice at a hotel in Acapulco that reassures people that "The manager has personally passed all the water served here," or a dry cleaner in Majorca who urges passing customers to "drop your pants here for best results." And local product names often raise eyebrows to visiting Americans who might stumble on a Japanese coffee creamer called Creap, a Mexican bread named Bimbo, or even a Scandinavian product to unfreeze car locks named Super Piss.

Chapter 13 noted some gaffes U.S. marketers made when they advertised to ethnic groups in their own country. Imagine how these mistakes multiply outside the United States! One technique marketers use to avoid this problem is *back-translation*, where a different interpreter retranslates a translated ad back into its original language to catch errors. Here are some errors that could have used a bit of back-translation:[118]

- The Scandinavian company that makes Electrolux vacuum cleaners sold them in the United States with this slogan: "Nothing sucks like an Electrolux."
- Colgate introduced Cue toothpaste in France—this also happens to be the name of a well-known porn magazine.
- When Parker marketed a ballpoint pen in Mexico, its ads were supposed to say, "It won't leak in your pocket and embarrass you." The translation actually said "It won't leak in your pocket and make you pregnant."
- Fresca (a soft drink) is Mexican slang for lesbian.
- Ford had several problems in Spanish markets. The company discovered that a truck model it called Fiera means "ugly old woman" in Spanish. Its Caliente model is slang for a streetwalker. In Brazil, Pinto is a slang term for "small male appendage."
- When Rolls-Royce introduced its Silver Mist model in Germany, it found that the word *mist* translates as excrement. Similarly, Sunbeam's hair-curling iron, called the Mist-Stick, translates as manure wand. To add insult to injury, Vicks is German slang for sexual intercourse, so the company had to change its name to Wicks in that country.
- Toyota encountered a similar problem in France, where its MR2 roadster sounds like "M-R-deux," which sounds a lot like *merde*—crap.
- Recently, Buick had to scramble to rename its new LaCrosse sedan the Allure in Canada after discovering that the name comes awfully close to a Québécois word for masturbation.
- IKEA had to explain that the Gutvik children's bunk bed is named "for a tiny town in Sweden" after German shoppers noted that the name sounded a lot like a

phrase that means "good f***." IKEA has yet to issue an explanation for its Fartfull workbench or its Jerker computer table.[119]

Does Global Marketing Work?

So, what's the verdict? Does global marketing work or not? Perhaps the more appropriate question is, "*When* does it work?" Although the argument for a homogenous world culture is appealing in principle, in practice it hasn't worked out too well. One reason is that consumers in different countries have varying conventions and customs, so they simply do not use products the same way. Kellogg, for example, discovered that in Brazil people don't typically eat a big breakfast—they're more likely to eat cereal as a dry snack.

In fact, significant cultural differences even show up within the same country—we certainly feel that we've traveled to a different place as we move around the United States. Advertisers in Canada know that when they target consumers in French-speaking Quebec their messages must be much different from those they address to those in English-speaking regions. Ads in Montreal tend to be a lot racier than those in Toronto, reflecting differences in attitudes toward sexuality between consumers with French versus British roots.[120]

Some large corporations such as Coca-Cola have successfully crafted a single, international image. Still, even the soft drink giant must make minor modifications to the way it presents itself in each culture. Although Coke commercials are largely standardized, the company permits local agencies to edit them so they highlight close-ups of local faces.[121] To maximize the chances of success for these multicultural efforts, marketers must locate consumers in different countries who nonetheless share a common *worldview* (see Chapter 11). This is more likely to be the case among people whose frame of reference is relatively more international or cosmopolitan, or who receive much of their information about the world from sources that incorporate a worldwide perspective.

Who is likely to fall into this category? Two consumer segments are particularly good candidates: (1) affluent people who are "global citizens" and who come into contact with ideas from around the world through their travels, business contacts, and media experiences; and (2) young people whose tastes in music and fashion are strongly influenced by MTV and other media that broadcast many of the same images to multiple countries. For example, viewers of MTV Europe in Rome or Zurich can check out the same "buzz clips" as their counterparts in London or Luxembourg.[122]

A large-scale study with consumers in 41 countries identified the characteristics people associate with global brands, and it also measured the relative importance of those dimensions when consumers buy products.[123] The researchers grouped consumers who evaluate global brands in the same way. They identified four major segments:

1 **Global citizens**—The largest segment (55 percent of consumers) uses the global success of a company as a signal of quality and innovation. At the same time, they are concerned whether companies behave responsibly on issues such as consumer health, the environment, and worker rights.
2 **Global dreamers**—The second-largest segment, at 23 percent, consists of consumers who see global brands as quality products and readily buy into the myths they author. They aren't nearly as concerned with social responsibility as are the global citizens.
3 **Antiglobals**—Thirteen percent of consumers are skeptical that transnational companies deliver higher-quality goods. They dislike brands that preach American values, and they don't trust global companies to behave responsibly. They try to avoid doing business with transnational firms.
4 **Global agnostics**—The remaining 9 percent of consumers don't base purchase decisions on a brand's global attributes. Instead, they evaluate a global product by the same criteria they use to judge local brands and don't regard its global nature as meriting special consideration.

Marketing Opportunity

The huge popularity of a humble local product that Brazilian peasants traditionally wear—*Havaianas*, or flip-flops—illustrates the diffusion of global consumer culture as consumers hunger for fresh ideas and styles from around the globe. Brazilians associate the lowly shoes, which sell for $2 a pair, so strongly with poor people that the expression *pe de chinelo*, or "slipper foot," is a popular slang term for the downtrodden. The main buyers in Brazil continue to be blue-collar workers, but now fashionable men and women in cities from Paris to Sydney wear the peasant shoes to trendy clubs and in some cases even to work.

How did these flip-flops make the leap to fashion statement? In an attempt to boost profit margins, a company named Alpargatas introduced new models in colors such as lime green and fuchsia that cost twice as much as the original black- or blue-strapped sandal with a cream-colored sole. Then, it launched newer styles, including a masculine surf model. Middle-class Brazilians started to adopt the shoes and even the country's president wore them in public. The fashion spread as a few celebrities, including supermodels Naomi Campbell, Kate Moss, and Brazil's own Gisele Bündchen, discovered the flip-flops. Company representatives helped fuel the fire as they gave out free sandals to stars at the Cannes Film Festival. The result: Alpargatas's international sales zoomed from virtually zero to more than 5 million sandals sold around the world.[127]

Marketing Pitfall

Critics in other countries deplore the creeping Americanization of their cultures because of what they view as excessive materialism. City officials in Oaxaca, Mexico, successfully fought to bar McDonald's from installing its arches in the town's central plaza.[132] One French critic summarized this resistance to the diffusion of American culture; he described the Euro Disney theme park as "a horror made of cardboard, plastic, and appalling colors—a construction of hardened chewing gum and idiotic folklore taken straight out of a comic book written for obese Americans."[133] A lot of the criticism focuses on the unhealthy American diet—and its appeal to others.

In the United States, two-thirds of adults and almost one-third of children are overweight. In other countries with traditionally healthy diets, the invasion of fast food and candy has taken its toll. In Greece, considered the birthplace of the Mediterranean diet that emphasizes olive oil, fresh produce, and fish, authorities struggle with an epidemic of obesity (three-quarters of the adult population is overweight or obese) and obesity rates for children skyrocket. Today even small towns overflow with pizza and fast-food outlets. Italy and Spain are not far behind, with more than 50 percent of adults overweight.[134]

The Diffusion of Consumer Culture

Coca-Cola is the drink of choice among young people in Asian countries, and McDonald's is their favorite restaurant.[124] The National Basketball Association sells $500 million of licensed merchandise every year *outside* of the United States.[125] Walk the streets of Lisbon or Buenos Aires, and the sight of Nike hats, Gap T-shirts, and Levi's jeans will accost you at every turn. The allure of American consumer culture spreads throughout the world.

However, it's not simply about exporting American culture. In a global society, people are quick to borrow from *any* culture they admire. For example, the cultural scene in Japan influences many Koreans because they believe the Japanese are sophisticated consumers. Japanese rock bands are more popular in Korea than Korean bands, and shoppers eagerly snap up other exports such as comic books, fashion magazines, and game shows. A Korean researcher explains, "Culture is like water. It flows from stronger nations to weaker ones. People tend to idolize countries that are wealthier, freer, and more advanced, and in Asia that country is Japan."[126]

A survey in Beijing found that nearly half of all children under 12 think McDonald's is a domestic Chinese brand![128] The West (and especially the United States) is a net exporter of popular culture. Many consumers equate Western lifestyles in general and the English language in particular with modernization and sophistication, and numerous American brands slowly but surely insinuate themselves into local cultures. Indeed, some global brands are so widespread that many are only vaguely aware of their countries of origin. In surveys, consumers routinely guess that Heineken is German (it's really Dutch) and that Nokia is Japanese (it's Finnish).[129]

American television inspires knockoffs around the world. But to be fair, many U.S. viewers don't realize that American reality show hits such as *Big Brother* and *American Idol* started out as European concepts that U.S. producers imported. In fact the U.K. version of *Big Brother* briefly went off the air after a fight broke out and housemates threatened to kill each other. The German version attracted accusations of "shameless voyeurism" after a female contestant had her nipple pierced on live TV—without anesthetic.[130]

Still, American TV formats attract many imitators. Some local shows "borrow" from American programs; the German hit *Das Traumschiff* (the "Dream Ship") is a remake of the old American hit *Love Boat*. Versions of *The Apprentice* appear all over the globe— though elsewhere Donald Trump is replaced by local figures such as a German soccer-team manager, a billionaire Arab entrepreneur, and a Brazilian ad agency CEO. Each local version reflects the country's culture—contestants sell flowers in London, hot dogs in Frankfurt, and rolled fish in Finland.[131] Not everyone is treated quite as harshly as the American losers either—in Finland contestants are gently told, "You're free to leave."

8

OBJECTIVE

How does Western (and particularly American) culture have a huge impact around the world, though people in other countries don't necessarily ascribe the same meanings to products as we do?

Emerging Consumer Cultures in Transitional Economies

In the early 1980s the Romanian Communist government broadcast the American TV show *Dallas* to point out the decadence of Western capitalism. This strategy backfired: The devious (but rich!) J. R. Ewing became a revered icon in parts of Eastern Europe and the Middle East. A popular tourist attraction outside of Bucharest includes a big white log gate that announces (in English) the name, "South Fork Ranch."[135] Western "decadence" appears to be infectious.[136]

More than 60 countries have a gross national product of less than $10 billion, and there are at least 135 transnational companies with revenues greater than that. The dominance of these marketing powerhouses creates a **globalized consumption ethic**. Tempting images of luxury cars, glam rock stars on MTV, and modern appliances that make life easier surround us wherever we turn. People the world over begin to share the ideal of a material lifestyle and value well-known brands that symbolize prosperity. Shopping evolves from a wearying, task-oriented struggle to locate even basic necessities to a leisure activity. Possessing these coveted items becomes a mechanism to display one's status (see Chapter 12)—often at great personal sacrifice.

After the downfall of communism, Eastern Europeans emerged from a long winter of deprivation into a springtime of abundance. The picture is not all rosy, however. It's not easy for many people who live in **transitional economies** to attain consumer goods. This term describes countries such as China, Portugal, and Romania that struggle as they adapt from a controlled, centralized economy to a free-market system. In these situations rapid changes occur on social, political, and economic dimensions as the populace suddenly is exposed to global communications and external market pressures.[137]

Some of the consequences of the transition to capitalism include a loss of confidence and pride in the local culture, as well as alienation, frustration, and increased stress as citizens sacrifice their leisure time to work ever harder to buy consumer goods. The yearning for the trappings of Western material culture is perhaps most evident in parts of Eastern Europe, where citizens who threw off the shackles of communism now have direct access to coveted consumer goods from the United States and Western Europe—if they can afford them. One analyst observed, "As former subjects of the Soviet empire dream it, the American dream has very little to do with liberty and justice for all and a great deal to do with soap operas and the Sears Catalogue."[138] A study that looked at how Chinese consumers think about Western brands showed that their interpretations depended on how they think about the

As this Brazilian ad reminds us, globalization is an integral part of the marketing strategy of most major corporations.
Source: Courtesy of Electrolux.

history of relations between China and the West. The researchers in fact identified four different narratives in their sample: West as liberator, as oppressor, as subjugated, and as partner. Depending on the narraitve they endorse, people view Western brands as instruments of democratization, domination, a way to erase past Chinese humiliations, or as instruments of economic progress.[139] A somewhat similar approach identifies various ways that people regard technology in their lives:[140]

- *The Techtopian* sees technology as social progress.
- *The Work Machine* regards it as an economic engine to drive growth and development.
- *The Green Luddite*, blames technology for the destruction of craftsmanship and traditional ways of life.
- *The Techpresssive* regards technology as a way to attain pleasure.

As the global consumption ethic spreads, rituals and product preferences in different cultures become homogenized. For example, some urbanites in Muslim Turkey now celebrate Christmas though gift-giving is not customary in many parts of the country—even on birthdays. In China, Christmas fever grips China's newly rising urban middle class as an excuse to shop, eat, and party. People there snap up Christmas trees, ornaments, and Christian religious objects (even though the street vendors who peddle photos of Jesus and Mary can't always identify who they are). Chinese consumers embrace Christmas because to them the holiday is international and modern, not because it's a traditional Christian celebration. The government encourages this practice because it stimulates consumer spending. To make the holiday even merrier, China exports about $1 billion worth of Christmas products every year, and its factories churn out $7.5 billion of the toys people worldwide put under their trees.[141]

Does this homogenization mean that in time consumers who live in Nairobi, New Guinea, or the Netherlands will all be indistinguishable from those in New York or Nashville? Probably not, because the meanings of consumer goods mutate to blend with local customs and values. For example, in Turkey some urban women use their ovens to dry clothes and their dishwashers to wash muddy spinach. Or a person in Papua New Guinea may combine a traditional clothing style such as a *bilum* with Western items such as Mickey Mouse shirts or baseball caps.[142] These processes make it unlikely that global homogenization will overwhelm local cultures, but it is likely that there will be multiple consumer cultures, each of which blends global icons such as Nike's pervasive "swoosh" with indigenous products and meanings. In Vietnam for example local fast-food chains dominate the market as they duplicate a McDonald's approach—but add a local flavor. The country's hugely successful Kinh Do red and yellow outlets sell specialties like dried squid buns. In the Philippines, the Jollibee Foods Corp. burger chain also copies the McDonald's look—and it outsells McDonald's there.[143]

Creolization occurs when foreign influences integrate with local meanings. Chapter 15 pointed out that modern Christianity adapted the pagan Christmas tree into its own rituals. In India handicapped beggars sell bottles of Coke from tricycles, and Indipop, a popular music hybrid, mixes traditional styles with rock, rap, and reggae.[144] As we saw in Chapter 13, young Hispanic Americans bounce between hip-hop and *Rock en Español*, blend Mexican rice with spaghetti sauce, and spread peanut butter and jelly on tortillas.[145] In Argentina, Coca-Cola launched Nativa, a soft drink flavored with the country's traditional *yerba mate* herbal tea, as part of a strategy to broaden its portfolio with products it makes from indigenous ingredients.[146]

The creolization process sometimes results in bizarre permutations of products and services when locals modify them to be compatible with their customs. Consider these creolized adaptations, for example:[147]

- In Peru, Indian boys carry rocks they paint to look like transistor radios.
- In highland Papua New Guinea, tribespeople put Chivas Regal wrappers on their drums and wear Pentel pens instead of nosebones.

- Bana tribespeople in the remote highlands of Kako, Ethiopia, pay to watch *Pluto the Circus Dog* on a View-Master.
- When an African Swazi princess marries a Zulu king, she wears a traditional costume of red touraco wing feathers around her forehead and a cape of window-bird feathers and oxtails. But guests record the ceremony on a Kodak movie camera while the band plays "The Sound of Music."
- The Japanese use Western words as a shorthand for anything new and exciting, even if they do not understand what they mean. They give cars names such as Fairlady, Gloria, and Bongo Wagon. Consumers buy *deodoranto* (deodorant) and *appuru pai* (apple pie). Ads urge shoppers to *stoppu rukku* (stop and look), and products claim to be *yuniku* (unique).[148] Coca-Cola cans say, "I feel Coke & sound special," and a company called Cream Soda sells products with the slogan, "Too old to die, too young to happy."[149] Other Japanese products with English names include Mouth Pet (breath freshener), Pocari Sweat ("refreshment water"), Armpit (electric razor), Brown Gross Foam (hair-coloring mousse), Virgin Pink Special (skin cream), Cow Brand (beauty soap), and Mymorning Water (canned water).[150]

CHAPTER SUMMARY

Now that you have finished reading this chapter you should understand why:

 Styles are like mirrors that reflect underlying cultural conditions.

The styles prevalent in a culture at any point in time reflect underlying political and social conditions. We term the set of agents responsible for creating stylistic alternatives a culture production system (CPS). Factors such as the types of people involved in this system and the amount of competition by alternative product forms influence the choices that eventually make their way to the marketplace for consideration by end consumers.

 We distinguish between high and low culture.

Social scientists distinguish between high (or elite) forms and low (or popular) forms of culture. Products of popular culture tend to follow a cultural formula and contain predictable components. However, these distinctions blur in modern society as marketers increasingly incorporate imagery from "high art" to sell everyday products.

 Many modern marketers are reality engineers.

Reality engineering occurs when marketers appropriate elements of popular culture to use in their promotional strategies. These elements include sensory and spatial aspects of everyday existence, whether in the form of products that appear in movies, scents pumped into offices and stores, billboards, theme parks, or video monitors they attach to shopping carts.

 New products, services, and ideas spread through a population. Different types of people are more or less likely to adopt them.

Diffusion of innovations refers to the process whereby a new product, service, or idea spreads through a population. Innovators and early adopters are quick to adopt new products, and laggards are very slow. A consumer's decision to adopt a new product depends on his or her personal characteristics as well as on characteristics of the innovation itself. We are more likely to adopt a new product if it demands relatively little behavioral change, is easy to understand, and provides a relative advantage compared to existing products.

 Many people and organizations play a role in the fashion system that creates and communicates symbolic meanings to consumers.

The fashion system includes everyone involved in creating and transferring symbolic meanings. Many different products express common cultural categories (e.g., gender distinctions). Many people tend to adopt a new style simultaneously in a process of collective selection. According to meme theory, ideas spread through a population in a geometric progression much as a virus infects many people until it reaches epidemic proportions. Other perspectives on motivations for adopting new styles include psychological, economic, and sociological models of fashion.

6 Fashions follow cycles.

Fashions follow cycles that resemble the product life cycle. We distinguish the two extremes of fashion adoption, classics and fads, in terms of the length of this cycle.

7 Products that succeed in one culture may fail in another if marketers fail to understand the differences among consumers in each place.

Because a consumer's culture exerts such a big influence on his or her lifestyle choices, marketers must learn as much as possible about differences in cultural norms and preferences when they do business in more than one country. One important issue is the extent to which we need to tailor our marketing strategies to each culture. Followers of an etic perspective believe people in many cultures appreciate the same universal messages. Believers in an emic perspective argue that individual cultures are too unique to permit such standardization; marketers must instead adapt their approaches to local values and practices. Attempts at global marketing have met with mixed success; in many cases this approach is more likely to work if the messages appeal to basic values or if the target markets consist of consumers who are internationally rather than locally oriented.

8 Western (and particularly American) culture has a huge impact around the world, although people in other countries don't necessarily ascribe the same meanings to products as we do.

The United States is a net exporter of popular culture. Consumers around the world eagerly adopt American products, especially entertainment vehicles and items they link to an American lifestyle (e.g., Marlboro cigarettes, Levi's jeans). Despite the continuing "Americanization" of world culture, some people resist globalization because they fear it will dilute their own local cultures. In other cases, they practice creolization as they integrate these products with existing cultural practices.

KEY TERMS

Acceptance cycles, 596
Advergaming, 586
Art product, 580
Branded entertainment, 584
Classic, 596
Collective selection, 592
Consumer style, 603
Continuous innovation, 589
Cooptation, 576
Craft product, 580
Creolization, 608
Cultural categories, 591
Cultural formula, 582
Cultural gatekeepers, 578

Cultural selection, 577
Culture production system (CPS), 578
Diffusion of innovations, 587
Discontinuous innovation, 590
Dynamically continuous innovation, 590
Early adopters, 588
Emic perspective, 603
Etic perspective, 602
Fad, 597
Fashion, 591
Fashion acceptance cycle, 596
Fashion system, 591
Gadget lovers, 589

Globalized consumption ethic, 606
Innovation, 587
Innovators, 588
Laggards, 588
Late adopters, 588
Lead users, 579
Meme theory, 595
Plinking™, 586
Product placement, 584
Reality engineering, 582
Tipping point, 595
Transitional economies, 607
Trickle-down theory, 593
Voice of the consumer, 579

REVIEW

1 What is collective selection? Give an example.
2 Describe a culture production system (CPS) and list its three components. What is an example of a CPS with these three components?
3 Define a cultural gatekeeper, and give three examples.
4 Describe the difference between arts and crafts.
5 What is a cultural formula? Give an example.
6 What is "new vintage?" How is this an example of reality engineering?

7 Define product placement and list three examples of it. How is this practice the same or different from branded entertainment?
8 What is advergaming? Give an example.
9 What is the diffusion of innovations?
10 Who are innovators? Early adopters? Laggards?
11 Describe the differences among continuous innovations, dynamically continuous innovations, and discontinuous

innovations, and provide an example of each. Which type are consumers least likely to adopt as an innovation?

12 What are the differences among *fashion, a fashion,* and *in fashion*?

13 What are cultural categories and how do they influence product designs?

14 Summarize some of the major approaches we can use to understand fashion from the perspectives of psychologists, economists, and sociologists.

15 What is an example of a meme?

16 What is the trickle-down effect? List some reasons why it is no longer as valid as it used to be.

17 What is the difference between a fad, a fashion, and a classic fashion life cycle?

18 What is the difference between an emic and an etic perspective on globalization?

19 Why is the United States a net exporter of popular culture?

20 What country provides an example of a transitional economy?

21 Define creolization and provide an example.

CONSUMER BEHAVIOR CHALLENGE

■ DISCUSS

1 Watchdog groups have long decried product placements because they blur the line between content and advertising without adequately informing viewers. And the networks themselves appear to be divided on how far they want to open the gate. According to one study, the effectiveness of product placements varies by product category and type of placement. Consumers indicate product placements have the most influence on their grocery, electronics, and apparel purchases. The most common platform for a placement is to get a brand shown on a T-shirt or other piece of an actor's wardrobe.[151] What do you think about this practice—under what conditions is product placement likely to influence you and your friends? When (if ever) is it counterproductive?

2 The chapter described a few instances where consumers sold their kids' "naming rights" to corporations—mostly for charitable purposes. Would you do this—why or why not?

3 Is advertising an art or a craft? Which should it be?

4 Movie companies often conduct market research when they produce big-budget films. If necessary they will reshoot part of a movie when viewers say they don't like it. Some people oppose this practice—they claim that movies, or books, songs, plays, or other artistic endeavors should not conform to what the market wants, lest they sacrifice their integrity. What do you think?

5 The chapter describes the traditional acceptance cycle for hit songs. How has the availability of music online altered this cycle? What are the ramifications of these changes for the music acceptance cycle?

6 Because of higher competition and market saturation, marketers in industrialized countries try to develop Third World markets. Asian consumers alone spend $90 billion a year on cigarettes, and U.S. tobacco manufacturers push relentlessly into these markets. We find cigarette advertising, that often depicts glamorous Western models and settings, just about everywhere—on billboards, buses, storefronts, and clothing—and tobacco companies sponsor many major sports and cultural events. Some companies even hand out cigarettes and gifts in amusement areas, often to preteens. Should governments allow these practices, even if the products may be harmful to their citizens or divert money poor people should spend on essentials? If you were a trade or health official in a Third World country, what guidelines, if any, might you suggest to regulate the import of luxury goods from advanced economies?

7 Comment on the growing practice of reality engineering. Do marketers "own" our culture? Should they?

8 Critics of the cultural consequences of standardization often point to Starbucks as an example of a company that succeeds because it obliterates local customs and drives small competitors out of business.[152] Where do you stand on patronizing mom-and-pop stores versus national chains?

9 If you worked in marketing research for a cosmetics firm, how might you apply the lead user concept to help you identify new product opportunities?

10 Boots with 6-inch heels were a fashion rage among young Japanese women a few years ago. Several teens died after they tripped over their shoes and fractured their skulls. However, followers of the style claim they are willing to risk twisted ankles, broken bones, bruised faces, and other dangers the platform shoes cause. One teenager said, "I've fallen and twisted my ankle many times, but they are so cute that I won't give them up until they go out of fashion."[153] Many consumers around the world seem willing to suffer for the sake of fashion. Others argue that we are merely pawns in the hands of designers, who conspire to force unwieldy fashions down our throats. What do you think? What is and what should be the role of fashion in our society? How important is it for people to be in style? What are the pros and cons of keeping up with the latest fashions? Do you believe that we are at the mercy of designers?

■ APPLY

1 The chapter mentions the Hush Puppy shoe fad. Clearly, it's a matter of time before consumers tire of these shoes and move on. What can the company do to prolong the life of this brand?

2 If you were a consultant to a toy company, what would you forecast as the next big trend in this market? Survey toy stores and watch what kids play with to help you with your prediction.

3 How might the rise of peer-to-peer music sharing influence the structure of the music CPS? One guess is that this method erodes the dominance of the big labels because listeners are more likely to access music from lesser-known groups. Survey your friends to determine whether this in fact is happening—do they listen to a wider variety of artists or simply download more from the big-time groups?

4 Read several romance or action novels to see if you can identify a cultural formula at work. Do you see parallels among the roles different characters play (e.g., the hero, the evildoer, the temptress, etc.)?

5 Watch 12 hours of TV and keep a log of all product placements you see. What are the dominant products shows insert?

Case Study

SLUMDOG: FAD OR FASHION?

"And the Oscar goes to . . . *Slumdog Millionaire*." This line was delivered eight times in Hollywood at the 81st Annual Academy Awards. Not bad for a film produced on a mere shoestring by Hollywood standards (budget of $15 million). It is the story of a young man from the slums of Mumbai who overcomes all odds to beat a television quiz show—the Indian equivalent of the show *Who Wants to Be a Millionaire?* and wins an award of 20,000,000 rupees.

The movie was a hit with worldwide critics, but the audience reaction in India was mixed. Many Indians claim that this movie cannot be considered a credit to India because its director is British, and the lead actor, Dev Patel is also from England. However, Indians are proud of A. R. Rahman, a well-known Indian musician, for his Oscar-winning film score.

It's hard to deny that the film turned the world's attention to India. Some were excited by the global interest, but others were not pleased. They felt that the film did not depict the "real" India. Many from Dharavi, the Mumbai slum featured in the film, protested that the name "Slumdog" was derogatory. In an interview, director Danny Boyle responded, ". . . basically it's a hybrid of the word 'underdog'—and everything that means in terms of rooting for the underdog and validating his triumph—and the fact that he obviously comes from the slums."

Whatever one's attitudes toward the filmmakers' rights to portray poverty and injustice in India, it's clear that the film increased awareness of what UNICEF estimates as 11 million children who currently live on the streets of India. *Slumdog* has, in fact, been credited with inspiring a boost in donations to organizations that fight homelessness in India including Railway Children, SOS, Children's Villages of India, and Save the Children. Railway Children reports Web site visits at 10 times what they were before the film, and many groups report an increase in donations.

DISCUSSION QUESTIONS

1 Can you give specific examples of how *Slumdog Millionaire* is part of the culture production system? Specifically, what are the three major subsystems, and who are the cultural gatekeepers in this context?

2 What does it mean that critics of the film are concerned about India's underlying "cultural category"?

3 How do you predict the film's success will influence the popularity of Bollywood productions—will it spark a fad or a fashion?

Sources: Nithin Belle, "New-Found Celebrity Status of the Three Slumdog Children May Get Upset," *McClatchy-Tribune Business News* (February 24, 2009); Gigil Varghese, "Better Times Await Child Stars," *McClatchy-Tribune Business News* (March 3, 2009); Fareed Zakaria, "A Slumdog in Heat," *Newsweek* (February 9, 2009); Niraj Sheth and Eric Bellman, "Slumdog Success Gets Mixed Reviews in India," *Wall Street Journal* (February 24, 2009); "Success of Slumdog Millionaire Is Aiding Charities," *PR Newswire* (March 3, 2009).

NOTES

1. www.abcnews.go.com/GMA/AmericanFamily/Story?id=3397793& page=2, accessed August 15, 2007.
2. www.allhiphop.com, accessed June 25, 2009; www.undergroundhiphop .com, accessed June 25, 2009.
3. www.hiphopcapital.com, accessed June 25, 2009.
4. Marc Spiegler, "Marketing Street Culture: Bringing Hip-Hop Style to the Mainstream," *American Demographics* (November 1996): 29–34.
5. Nina Darnton, "Where the Homegirls Are," *Newsweek* (June 17, 1991): 60; "The Idea Chain," *Newsweek* (October 5, 1992): 32.
6. Cyndee Miller, "X Marks the Lucrative Spot, but Some Advertisers Can't Hit Target," *Marketing News* (August 2, 1993): 1.
7. Ad appeared in *Elle* (September 1994).
8. Spiegler, "Marketing Street Culture: Bringing Hip-Hop Style to the Mainstream"; Joshua Levine, "Badass Sells," *Forbes* (April 21, 1997): 142.

9. Jeff Jensen, "Hip, Wholesome Image Makes a Marketing Star of Rap's LL Cool J," *Advertising Age* (August 25, 1997): 1.

10. Alice Z. Cuneo, "GAP's 1st Global Ads Confront Dockers on a Khaki Battlefield," *Advertising Age* (April 20, 1998): 3–5.

11. Jancee Dunn, "How Hip-Hop Style Bum-Rushed the Mall," *Rolling Stone* (March 18, 1999): 54–59.

12. Teri Agins, "The Rare Art of 'Gilt by Association': How Armani Got Stars to Be Billboards," *Wall Street Journal* (September 14, 1999), www.wsj .com, accessed September 14, 1999.

13. Eryn Brown, "From Rap to Retail: Wiring the Hip-Hop Nation," *Fortune* (April 17, 2000): 530

14. Martin Fackler, "Hip Hop Invading China," *Birmingham News* (February 15, 2002): D1.

15. Maureen Tkacik, "'Z' Zips into the Zeitgeist, Subbing for 'S' in Hot Slang," *Wall Street Journal* (January 4, 2003); Maureen Tkacik, "Slang from the 'Hood Now Sells Toyz in Target," *Wall Street Journal* (December 30, 2002), www.wsj.com, accessed December 30, 2002.

16. www.hiphop-elements.com/article/read/4/6319/1, accessed July 9, 2005; www.bevnet.com/reviews/pimpjuice, accessed July 9, 2005; www.sohh.com/thewire/read.php?contentID=6893, accessed July 9, 2005; www.undercover.com.au/news/2005/mar05/20050324_usher .html, accessed July 9, 2005.

17. Arthur, Damien, "Authenticity and Consumption in the Australian Hip Hop Culture," *Qualitative Market Research* 9 no. 2 (2005): 140.

18. "European Hip Hop," *Wikipedia*, http://en.wikipedia.org/wiki/European_hip_hop, accessed July 30, 2007.

19. David Carr, "Vibe Magazine, Showcase for Hip-Hop and R&B, Dies at 16," *New York Times* (July 2, 2009), www.nytimes.com/2009/07/02/arts/music/02vibe.html?_r=1, accessed July 2, 2009.

20. Elizabeth M. Blair, "Commercialization of the Rap Music Youth Subculture," *Journal of Popular Culture* 27 (Winter 1993): 21–34; Basil G. Englis, Michael R. Solomon, and Anna Olofsson, "Consumption Imagery in Music Television: A Bi-Cultural Perspective," *Journal of Advertising* 22 (December 1993): 21–34.

21. Spiegler, "Marketing Street Culture: Bringing Hip-Hop Style to the Mainstream."

22. Craig Thompson and Gokcen Coskuner-Balli, "Countervailing Market Responses to Corporate Co-optation and the Ideological Recruitment of Consumption Communities," *Journal of Consumer Research*, 34 (August 2007): 135–52.

23. Grant McCracken, "Culture and Consumption: A Theoretical Account of the Structure and Movement of the Cultural Meaning of Consumer Goods," *Journal of Consumer Research* 13 (June 1986): 71–84.

24. Richard A. Peterson, "The Production of Culture: A Prolegomenon," in Richard A. Peterson, ed., *The Production of Culture, Sage Contemporary Social Science Issues* 33 (Beverly Hills, CA: Sage, 1976); Elizabeth C. Hirschman, "Resource Exchange in the Production and Distribution of a Motion Picture," *Empirical Studies of the Arts* 8, no. 1 (1990): 31–51; Michael R. Solomon, "Building Up and Breaking Down: The Impact of Cultural Sorting on Symbolic Consumption," in J. Sheth and E. C. Hirschman, eds., *Research in Consumer Behavior* (Greenwich, CT: JAI Press, 1988), 325–51. For a study that looked at ways consumers interact with marketers to create cultural meanings, cf. Lisa Peñaloza, "Consuming the American West: Animating Cultural Meaning and Memory at a Stock Show and Rodeo," *Journal of Consumer Research* 28 (December 2001): 369–98. Cf. also Markus Giesler, "Conflict and Compromise: Drama in Marketplace Evolution," *Journal of Consumer Research* 34 (April 2007): 739–53. For a study that looked at ways consumers interact with marketers to create cultural meanings, cf. Peñaloza, "Consuming the American West: Animating Cultural Meaning and Memory at a Stock Show and Rodeo."

25. Richard A. Peterson and D. G. Berger, "Entrepreneurship in Organizations: Evidence from the Popular Music Industry," *Administrative Science Quarterly* 16 (1971): 97–107.

26. Paul M. Hirsch, "Processing Fads and Fashions: An Organizational Set Analysis of Cultural Industry Systems," *American Journal of Sociology* 77, no. 4 (1972): 639–59; Russell Lynes, *The Tastemakers* (New York: Harper and Brothers, 1954); Michael R. Solomon, "The Missing Link: Surrogate Consumers in the Marketing Chain," *Journal of Marketing* 50 (October 1986): 208–19.

27. Michael R. Solomon, *Conquering Consumerspace: Marketing Strategies for a Branded World*, (New York: AMACOM, 2003).

28. C. K. Prahalad and Venkatram Ramaswamy, "Co-Opting Customer Competence," *Harvard Business Review* (January–February 2000): 79–87; Eric von Hipple, "Users as Innovators," *Technology Review* 80 (January 1978): 3–11; Jakki Mohr, *Marketing of High-Technology Products and Services* (Upper Saddle River, NJ: Prentice Hall, 2001).

29. Byrnes, Nanette, "Xerox's New Design Team: Customers," *BusinessWeek* (May 7, 2007): 72.

30. Howard S. Becker, "Arts and Crafts," *American Journal of Sociology* 83 (January 1987): 862–89.

31. Herbert J. Gans, "Popular Culture in America: Social Problem in a Mass Society or Social Asset in a Pluralist Society?" in Howard S. Becker, ed., *Social Problems: A Modern Approach* (New York: Wiley, 1966).

32. www.thomaskinkade.com/magi/servlet/com.asucon.ebiz.home .web.tk.HomeServlet, accessed June 25, 2009; Karen Breslau, "Paint by Numbers," *Newsweek* (May 13, 2002): 48.

33. Martin Forstenzer, "In Search of Fine Art Amid the Paper Towels," *New York Times on the Web* (February 22, 2004).

34. Annetta Miller, "Shopping Bags Imitate Art: Seen the Sacks? Now Visit the Museum Exhibit," *Newsweek* (January 23, 1989): 44.

35. Kim Foltz, "New Species for Study: Consumers in Action," *New York Times* (December 18, 1989): A1.

36. Arthur A. Berger, *Signs in Contemporary Culture: An Introduction to Semiotics* (New York: Longman, 1984).

37. Michiko Kakutani, "Art Is Easier the 2d Time Around," *New York Times* (October 30, 1994): E4.

38. www.geico.com/about/commercials/music/cavemen, accessed June 25, 2009.

39. Brooks Barnes and Suzanne Vranica, "Why Advertising's Cavemen Are Going Totally Hollyrock," *Wall Street Journal* (March 5, 2007): B1; Nina M. Lentini, "Doh! Looks Like 7-Eleven Stores May Get Homered," *Marketing Daily* (March 30, 2007), www.mediapost.com, accessed March 30, 2007.

40. Michael R. Solomon and Basil G. Englis, "Reality Engineering: Blurring the Boundaries Between Marketing and Popular Culture," *Journal of Current Issues and Research in Advertising* 16, no. 2 (Fall 1994): 1–17.

41. Austin Bunn, "Not Fade Away," *New York Times* (December 2, 2002), www.nytimes.com, accessed December 2, 2002.

42. Tim Arango and Brian Stelter, "Messages with a Mission, Embedded in TV Shows," *New York Times* (April 1, 2009), www.nytimes.com/2009/04/02/arts/television/02gates.html, accessed April 1, 2009.

43. Marc Santora, "Circle the Block, Cabby, My Show's On," *New York Times* (January 16, 2003), www.nytimes.com, accessed January 16, 2003; Wayne Parry, "Police May Sell Ad Space," *Montgomery Advertiser* (November 20, 2002): A4.

44. This process is described more fully in Michael R. Solomon, *Conquering Consumerspace: Marketing Strategies for a Branded World* (New York: AMACOM, 2003); cf. also T. Bettina Cornwell and Bruce Keillor, "Contemporary Literature and the Embedded Consumer Culture: The Case of Updike's Rabbit," in Roger J. Kruez and Mary Sue MacNealy, eds., *Empirical Approaches to Literature and Aesthetics: Advances in Discourse Processes* 52 (Norwood, NJ: Ablex, 1996), 559–72; Monroe Friedman, "The Changing Language of a Consumer Society: Brand Name Usage in Popular American Novels in the Postwar Era," *Journal of Consumer Research* 11 (March 1985): 927–37; Monroe Friedman, "Commercial Influences in the Lyrics of Popular American Music of the Postwar Era," *Journal of Consumer Affairs* 20 (Winter 1986): 193.

45. Stephanie Clifford, "Bravo Shows Move Further into Licensing Products," *New York Times* (April 12, 2009), www.nytimes.com/2009/04/13/business/media/13bravo.html?scp=1&sq=Stephanie%20Clifford,%20%93Bravo%20Shows%20Move%20Further%20into%20Licensing%20Products&st=cse, accessed April 13, 2009.

46. www.alibinetwork.com/index.jsp, accessed June 25, 2009; www .reputationdefender.com, accessed June 25, 2009.

47. James Bandler, "Only in the *Star!* Demi Moore's Brown Dress Turns White!" *Wall Street Journal* (April 14, 2004): B1.

48. Jeff Zaslow, "Meet John 'Your Ad Here' Smith," *Wall Street Journal* (March 16, 2006): D3.

49. Stuart Elliott, "In 'Trust Me,' a Fake Agency Really Promotes," *New York Times* (January 21, 2009), www.nytimes.com, accessed January 21, 2009.

50. Fara Warner, "Why It's Getting Harder to Tell the Shows from the Ads," *Wall Street Journal* (June 15, 1995): B1.

51. Quoted in Simona Covel, "Bag Borrow or Steal Lands the Role of a Lifetime, Online Retailer Hopes to Profit from Mention in 'Sex and the City,'" *Wall Street Journal* (May 28, 2008), http://online.wsj.com/article/SB121184149016921095.html?mod=rss_media_and_marketing, accessed May 28, 2008; www.bagborroworsteal.com, accessed June 25, 2009.

52. "Top 10 Product Placements in First Half of '07," *Marketing Daily* (September 26, 2007), www.mediapost.com, accessed September 26, 2007.

53. Nat Ives, "'Advertainment' Gains Momentum," *New York Times* (April 21, 2004), www.nytimes.com, accessed April 21, 2004.

54. Brian Steinberg, "Getting Izze to Izzie on 'Grey's Anatomy': How PepsiCo Placed Beverage Brand in ABC Show Without Paying a Thing," *Advertising Age* (April 1, 2009), www.adage.com, accessed April 1, 2009.

55. Claire Atkinson, "Ad Intrusion Up, Say Consumers," *Advertising Age* (January 6, 2003): 1.

56. Motoko Rich, "Product Placement Deals Make Leap from Film to Books," *New York Times* (June 12, 2006), www.nytimes.com, accessed June 12, 2006.

57. Quoted in Amy Schatz And Suzanne Vranica, "Product Placements Get FCC Scrutiny, Concern Focuses on Rise in Use by Advertisers, Disclosure to Viewers," *Wall Street Journal* (June 23, 2008): B3.

58. Stuart Elliott, "Greatest Hits of Product Placement," *New York Times* (February 28, 2005), www.nytimes.com, accessed February 28, 2005.

59. Benjamin M. Cole, "Products That Want to Be in Pictures," *Los Angeles Herald Examiner* (March 5, 1985): 36; see also Stacy M. Vollmers and Richard W. Mizerski, "A Review and Investigation into the Effectiveness of Product Placements in Films," in Karen Whitehill King, ed., *Proceedings of the 1994 Conference of the American Academy of Advertising*, 97–102; Solomon and Englis, "Reality Engineering: Blurring the Boundaries Between Marketing and Popular Culture."

60. Cristel Antonia Russell, "Investigating the Effectiveness of Product Placements in Television Shows: The Role of Modality and Plot Connection Congruence on Brand Memory and Attitude," *Journal of Consumer Research* 29 (December 2002): 306–18; Denise E. DeLorme and Leonard N. Reid, "Moviegoers' Experiences and Interpretations of Brands in Films Revisited," *Journal of Advertising* 28, no. 2 (1999): 71–90; Barbara B. Stern, and Cristel A. Russell "Consumer Responses to Product Placement in Television Sitcoms: Genre, Sex and Consumption," *Consumption, Markets and Culture* 7 (December 2004): 371–94.

61. Jack Neff, "Clearasil Marches into Middle-School Classes, *Advertising Age* (November 2006): 8; Bill Pennington, "Reading, Writing and Corporate Sponsorships," *New York Times on the Web* (October 18, 2004); Caroline E. Mayer, "Nurturing Brand Loyalty: With Preschool Supplies, Firms Woo Future Customers and Current Parents," *Washington Post* (October 12, 2003): F1.

62. Louise Story, "More Marketers Are Grabbing the Attention of Players During Online Games," *New York Times* (January 24, 2007), www.nytimes.com, accessed January 24, 2007; Shankar Gupta, "King of the Advergames," www.mediapost.com, accessed December 22, 2006; "Plinking," *Fast Company* (April 2007): 31; Sarah Sennott, "Gaming the Ad," *Newsweek* (January 31, 2005): E2; "Advertisements Insinuated into Video Games," *New York Times* (October 18, 2004), www.nytimes.com, accessed October 18, 2004; "Advergaming" Center for Media Research (October 24, 2007), www.research@mediapost.com, accessed October 24, 2007; Tim Zuckert, "Become One with the Game, Games Offer Brands a Unique Way to Be the Entertainment—Not Just Sponsor It," *Advertising Age* (June 16, 2008), www.adage.com, accessed June 16, 2008.

63. Stephanie Clifford, "Advertising Dairy Queen, the Video Game," *New York Times* (December 23, 2008), www.nytimes.com, accessed December 23, 2008.

64. Nick Wingfield, "Sony's PS3 to Get In-Game Ads," *Wall Street Journal* (June 4, 2008): B7; Jeffrey Bardzell, Shaowen Bardzell, and Tyler Pace, *Player Engagement and In-Game Advertising*, (November 23, 2008), www.onetooneinteractive.com/otoinsights/research-studies/player-engagement-and-in-game-advertising, accessed June 4, 2008.

65. Damien Cave, "Dogtown, U.S.A.," *New York Times* (June 12, 2005), www.nytimes.com, accessed June 12, 2005.

66. Emily Nelson, "Moistened Toilet Paper Wipes Out After Launch for Kimberly-Clark," *Wall Street Journal* (April 15, 2002), www.wsj.com, accessed April 15, 2002.

67. Robert Hof, "The Click Here Economy," *BusinessWeek* (June 22, 1998): 122–28.

68. Eric J. Arnould, "Toward a Broadened Theory of Preference Formation and the Diffusion of Innovations: Cases from Zinder Province, Niger Republic," *Journal of Consumer Research* 16 (September 1989): 239–67; Susan B. Kaiser, *The Social Psychology of Clothing* (New York: Macmillan, 1985); Thomas S. Robertson, *Innovative Behavior and Communication* (New York: Holt, Rinehart and Winston, 1971).

69. Jan-Benedict E. M. Steenkamp, Frenkel ter Hofstede, and Michel Wedel, "A Cross-National Investigation into the Individual and National Cultural Antecedents of Consumer Innovativeness," *Journal of Marketing* 63, no. 7 (1999): 55–69.

70. Susan L. Holak, Donald R. Lehmann, and Fareena Sultan, "The Role of Expectations in the Adoption of Innovative Consumer Durables: Some Preliminary Evidence," *Journal of Retailing* 63 (Fall 1987): 243–59.

71. Hubert Gatignon and Thomas S. Robertson, "A Propositional Inventory for New Diffusion Research," *Journal of Consumer Research* 11 (March 1985): 849–67.

72. Eric Pfanner, "Agencies Look Beyond Focus Groups to Spot Trends," *New York Times* (January 2, 2006), www.nytimes.com, accessed January 2, 2006.

73. For more details see Gordon C. Bruner II and Anand Kumar, "Gadget Lovers," *Journal of the Academy of Marketing Science* 35, no. 3 (2007): 329–39.

74. Normandy Madden, "Japan's Latest Fads—Marketable in U.S.? While Some Ideas Seem Pretty Out There, Many Are Moving to Mass Market. Here's What to Watch," Advertising Age (June 16, 2008), www.adage.com/results?start=20&endeca=1&...&N54294965798&Ns=P_Ranking|1, accessed June 16, 2008.

75. www.xbitlabs.com/news/multimedia/display/20090601150239_Microsoft_Unveils_Motion_Sensing_Game_Controller_for_Xbox_360.html, accessed June 25, 2009.

76. Everett M. Rogers, *Diffusion of Innovations*, 3rd ed. (New York: The Free Press, 1983).

77. Umberto Eco, *A Theory of Semiotics* (Bloomington: Indiana University Press, 1979).

78. Fred Davis, "Clothing and Fashion as Communication," in Michael R. Solomon, ed., *The Psychology of Fashion* (Lexington, MA: Lexington Books, 1985): 15–28.

79. Melanie Wallendorf, "The Formation of Aesthetic Criteria Through Social Structures and Social Institutions," in Jerry C. Olson, ed., *Advances in Consumer Research* 7 (Ann Arbor, MI: Association for Consumer Research, 1980): 3–6.

80. Grant McCracken, "Culture and Consumption: A Theoretical Account of the Structure and Movement of the Cultural Meaning of Consumer Goods," *Journal of Consumer Research* 13 (June 1986): 71–84.

81. Kimberly Castro, "Michelle Obama Boosts J. Crew," *U.S. News & World Report* (April 3, 2009), www.usnews.com/blogs/luxe-life/2009/04/03/michelle-obama-boosts-j-crew.html, accessed June 25, 2009.

82. "The Eternal Triangle," *Art in America* (February 1989): 23.

83. Elva Ramirez, "How Clothes Make the Car, Fashion Gives Autos Cues on Hues," *Wall Street Journal* (January 11, 2008): B1; Sally Beatty, "Fashion's 'It' Colors: How Runway Dresses, Cars—Even Washer-Dryers—Turned Shades of Blue, Brown," *Wall Street Journal* (February 4, 2005), www.wsj.com, accessed February 4, 2005.

84. Herbert Blumer, *Symbolic Interactionism: Perspective and Method* (Upper Saddle River, NJ: Prentice Hall, 1969); Howard S. Becker, "Art as Collective Action," *American Sociological Review* 39 (December 1974): 767–76; Richard A. Peterson, "Revitalizing the Culture Concept," *Annual Review of Sociology* 5 (1979): 137–66.

85. For more details, see Kaiser, *The Social Psychology of Clothing*; George B. Sproles, "Behavioral Science Theories of Fashion," in Michael R. Solomon, ed., *The Psychology of Fashion* (Lexington, MA: Lexington Books, 1985): 55–70.

86. C. R. Snyder and Howard L. Fromkin, *Uniqueness: The Human Pursuit of Difference* (New York: Plenum Press, 1980).

87. Linda Dyett, "Desperately Seeking Skin," *Psychology Today* (May–June 1996): 14; Alison Lurie, *The Language of Clothes* (New York: Random House, 1981). Note: Until very recently the study of fashion focused almost exclusively on women. Some researchers today also probe the meanings of the fashion system for men, but not nearly to the same extent. Cf. for example Susan Kaiser, Michael Solomon, Janet Hethorn, Basil Englis, Van Dyk Lewis, and Wi-Suk Kwon, "Menswear, Fashion, and Subjectivity," paper presented in Special Session: Susan Kaiser, Michael Solomon, Janet Hethorn, and Basil Englis (Chairs), "What Do Men Want? Media Representations, Subjectivity, and Consumption," at the ACR Gender Conference, Edinburgh, Scotland, June 2006.

88. Harvey Leibenstein, *Beyond Economic Man: A New Foundation for Microeconomics* (Cambridge, MA: Harvard University Press, 1976).

89. Nara Schoenberg, "Goth Culture Moves into Mainstream," *Montgomery Advertiser* (January 19, 2003): 1G.

90. Georg Simmel, "Fashion," *International Quarterly* 10 (1904): 130–55.

91. Maureen Tkacik, "'Z' Zips into the Zeitgeist, Subbing for 'S' in Hot Slang," *Wall Street Journal* (January 4, 2003), www.wsj.com, accessed January 4, 2003; Tkacik, "Slang from the 'Hood Now Sells Toyz in Target."

92. Grant D. McCracken, "The Trickle-Down Theory Rehabilitated," in Michael R. Solomon, ed., *The Psychology of Fashion* (Lexington, MA: Lexington Books, 1985): 39–54.

93. Charles W. King, "Fashion Adoption: A Rebuttal to the 'Trickle-Down' Theory," in Stephen A. Greyser, ed., *Toward Scientific Marketing* (Chicago: American Marketing Association, 1963): 108–25.

94. Alf H. Walle, "Grassroots Innovation," *Marketing Insights* (Summer 1990): 44–51.

95. Robert V. Kozinets, "Fandoms' Menace/Pop Flows: Exploring the Metaphor of Entertainment as Recombinant/Memetic Engineering," *Association for Consumer Research* (October 1999). The new science

of memetics, which tries to explain how beliefs gain acceptance and predict their progress, was spurred by Richard Dawkins who in the 1970s proposed culture as a Darwinian struggle among "memes" or mind viruses. See Geoffrey Cowley, "Viruses of the Mind: How Odd Ideas Survive," *Newsweek* (April 14, 1997): 14.

96. Malcolm Gladwell, *The Tipping Point* (New York: Little, Brown and Co., 2000).
97. "Cabbage-Hatched Plot Sucks in 24 Doll Fans," *New York Daily News* (December 1, 1983).
98. http://hub.guitarhero.com/index_us.html, accessed June 25, 2009; John Lippman, "Creating the Craze for Pokémon: Licensing Agent Bet on U.S. Kids," *Wall Street Journal* (August 16, 1999), www.wsj.com, accessed August 16, 1999; "Turtlemania," *The Economist* (April 21, 1990): 32.
99. Anthony Ramirez, "The Pedestrian Sneaker Makes a Comeback," *New York Times* (October 14, 1990): F17.
100. Madden, "Japan's Latest Fads—Marketable In U.S.?"
101. www.badfads.com, accessed June 25, 2009.
102. Quoted in Stephen Brown and Anthony Patterson, "You're a Wizard, Harry!" Consumer Responses to the Harry Potter Phenomenon," *Advances in Consumer Research* 33, no. 1 (2006): 155–160
103. B. E. Aguirre, E. L. Quarantelli, and Jorge L. Mendoza, "The Collective Behavior of Fads: The Characteristics, Effects, and Career of Streaking," *American Sociological Review* (August 1989): 569.
104. Joseph B. White, "From Fad to Trend," *Wall Street Journal* (June 21, 2005), www.wsj.com, accessed June 21, 2005.
105. Martin G. Letscher, "How to Tell Fads from Trends," *American Demographics* (December 1994): 38–45.
106. Peter Gumbel, "Big Mac's Local Flavor," *CNNmoney.com* (May 2, 2008), http://money.cnn.com/2008/04/29/news/companies/big_macs_local.fortune/index.htm, accessed May 2, 2008; Geoffrey A. Fowler, "For Prosperity Burger, McDonald's Tailors Ads to Asian Tastes," *Wall Street Journal* (January 24, 2005), www.wsj.com, accessed January 24, 2005; Saritha Rai, "Tastes of India in U.S. Wrappers," *New York Times* (April 29, 2003), www.nytimes.com, accessed April 29, 2003; Gerard O'Dwyer, "McD's Cancels McAfrika Rollout," *Advertising Age* (September 9, 2002): 14; McDonald's to Give $10 Million to Settle Vegetarian Lawsuit," *Wall Street Journal* (June 4, 2002), www.wsj.com, accessed June 4, 2002; "Packaging Draws Protest," *Marketing News* (July 4, 1994): 1.
107. www.beinggirl.com/en_US/home.jsp, accessed June 25, 2009; Carol Hymowitz, "Marketers Focus More on Global 'Tribes' Than on Nationalities," *Wall Street Journal* (December 10, 2007): B1.
108. Theodore Levitt, *The Marketing Imagination* (New York: The Free Press, 1983).
109. Geoffrey A. Fowler, "Main Street, H.K.: Disney Localizes Mickey to Boost Its Hong Kong Theme Park," *Wall Street Journal* (January 23, 2008): B1; Merissa Marr, "Small World: Disney Rewrites Script to Win Fans in India; China, Latin America Are also in Turnaround," *Wall Street Journal* (June 11, 2007): A1; Laura M. Holson, "The Feng Shui Kingdom," *New York Times* (April 25, 2005), www.nytimes.com, accessed April 25, 2005; Keith Bradsher, "Disneyland for Chinese Offers a Soup and Lands in a Stew," *New York Times* (June 17, 2005): A1; Paulo Prada and Bruce Orwall, "Disney's New French Theme Park Serves Wine—and Better Sausage," *Wall Street Journal* (March 12, 2002), www.wsj.com, accessed March 12, 2002.
110. Terry Clark, "International Marketing and National Character: A Review and Proposal for an Integrative Theory," *Journal of Marketing* 54 (October 1990): 66–79.
111. Geraldo Samor, Cecilie Rohwedder, and Ann Zimmerman, "Innocents Abroad? Wal-Mart's Global Sales Rise as It Learns from Mistakes; No More Ice Skates in Mexico, *Wall Street Journal* (May 16, 2006): B1.
112. Marc Gobé, *Emotional Branding: The New Paradigm for Connecting Brands to People* (New York: Allworth Press, 2001).
113. Norihiko Shirouzu, "Snapple in Japan: How a Splash Dried Up," *Wall Street Journal* (April 15, 1996): B1.
114. Glenn Collins, "Chinese to Get a Taste of Cheese-Less Cheetos," *New York Times* (September 2, 1994): D4.
115. Laurel Wentz, "Americans Cry 'Racism' over Absolut Poster," *Advertising Age* (April 14, 2008): 6 (2).
116. Martin McCarty, Martin I. Horn, Mary Kate Szenasy, and Jocelyn Feintuch, "An Exploratory Study of Consumer Style: Country Differences and International Segments," *Journal of Consumer Behaviour* 6, no. 1 (2007): 48.
117. Julie Skur Hill and Joseph M. Winski, "Goodbye Global Ads: Global Village Is Fantasy Land for Marketers," *Advertising Age* (November 16, 1987): 22.
118. Shelly Reese, "Culture Shock," *Marketing Tools* (May 1998): 44–49; Steve Rivkin, "The Name Game Heats Up," *Marketing News* (April 22,

1996): 8; David A. Ricks, "Products That Crashed into the Language Barrier," *Business and Society Review* (Spring 1983): 46–50.
119. Mark Lasswell, "Lost in Translation," *Business* (August 2004): 68–70.
120. Clyde H. Farnsworth, "Yoked in Twin Solitudes: Canada's Two Cultures," *New York Times* (September 18, 1994): E4.
121. Hill and Winski, "Goodbye Global Ads."
122. MTV Europe, personal communication, 1994; see also Teresa J. Domzal and Jerome B. Kernan, "Mirror, Mirror: Some Postmodern Reflections on Global Advertising," *Journal of Advertising* 22 (December 1993): 1–20; Douglas P. Holt, "Consumers' Cultural Differences as Local Systems of Tastes: A Critique of the Personality-Values Approach and an Alternative Framework," *Asia Pacific Advances in Consumer Research* 1 (1994): 1–7.
123. Douglas B. Holt, John A. Quelch, and Earl L. Taylor, "How Global Brands Compete," *Harvard Business Review* (September 2004): 68–75.
124. Normandy Madden, "New GenerAsians Survey Gets Personal with Asia-Pacific Kids," *Advertising Age International* (July 13, 1998): 2.
125. Adam Thompson and Shai Oster, "NBA in China Gets Milk to Sell Hoops," *Wall Street Journal* (January 22, 2007): B1; "They All Want to Be Like Mike," *Fortune* (July 21, 1997): 51–53.
126. Calvin Sims, "Japan Beckons, and East Asia's Youth Fall in Love," *New York Times* (December 5, 1999): 3.
127. Miriam Jordan and Teri Agins, "Fashion Flip-Flop: Sandal Leaves the Shower Behind," *Wall Street Journal* (August 8, 2002), www.wsj.com, accessed August 8, 2002.
128. Elisabeth Rosenthal, "Buicks, Starbucks and Fried Chicken, Still China?" *New York Times* (February 25, 2002), www.nytimes.com, accessed February 25, 2002.
129. Special Report, "Brands in an Age of Anti-Americanism," *Business-Week* (August 4, 2003): 69–76.
130. Suzanne Kapner, "U.S. TV Shows Losing Potency Around World," *New York Times* (January 2, 2003), www.nytimes.com, accessed January 2, 2003; "Big Brother Nipple Sparks Outrage," *BBCNews* (September 10, 2004), www.bbcnews.com, accessed September 10, 2004.
131. Laurel Wentz and Claire Atkinson, "Apprentice Translators Hope for Hits All over Globe," *Advertising Age* (February 14, 2005): 3(2).
132. Julie Watson, "City Keeps McDonald's from Opening in Plaza," *Montgomery Advertiser* (December 15, 2002): 5AA.
133. Alan Riding, "Only the French Elite Scorn Mickey's Debut," *New York Times* (1992): A1.
134. Elisabeth Rosenthal, "Fast Food Hits Mediterranean; A Diet Succumbs," *New York Times* (September 23, 2008), www.nytimes.com, accessed September 23, 2008.
135. Professor Russell Belk, University of Utah, personal communication, July 25, 1997.
136. Material in this section adapted from Güliz Ger and Russell W. Belk, "I'd Like to Buy the World a Coke: Consumptionscapes of the 'Less Affluent World,'" *Journal of Consumer Policy* 19, no. 3 (1996): 271–304; Russell W. Belk, "Romanian Consumer Desires and Feelings of Deservingness," in Lavinia Stan, ed., *Romania in Transition* (Hanover, NH: Dartmouth Press, 1997): 191–208; see also Güliz Ger, "Human Development and Humane Consumption: Well Being Beyond the Good Life," *Journal of Public Policy and Marketing* 16 (1997): 110–25.
137. Professor Güliz Ger, Bilkent University, Turkey, personal communication, July 25, 1997.
138. Erazim Kohák, "Ashes, Ashes . . . Central Europe After Forty Years," *Daedalus* 121 (Spring 1992): 197–215; Belk, "Romanian Consumer Desires and Feelings of Deservingness."
139. Lily Dong and Kelly Tian. "The Use of Western Brands in Asserting Chinese National Identity," *Journal of Consumer Research* 36 (October 2009).
140. Robert V. Kozinets. "Technology/Ideology: How Ideological Fields Influence Consumers' Technology Narratives," *Journal of Consumer Research* 34 (April 2008): 865–81.
141. David Murphy, "Christmas's Commercial Side Makes Yuletide a Hit in China," *Wall Street Journal* (December 24, 2002), www.wsj.com, accessed December 24, 2002.
142. This example courtesy of Professor Russell Belk, University of Utah, personal communication, July 25, 1997.
143. James Hookway, "In Vietnam, Fast Food Acts Global, Tastes Local," *Wall Street Journal* (March 12, 2008), http://online.wsj.com/article/Sb120528509133029135.html?mod=mm_hs_marketing_strat, accessed March 12, 2008.
144. Miriam Jordan, "India Decides to Put Its Own Spin on Popular Rock, Rap and Reggae," *Wall Street Journal* (January 5, 2000), www.wsj.com, accessed January 5, 2000; Rasul Bailay, "Coca-Cola Recruits Paraplegics for 'Cola War' in India," *Wall Street Journal* (June 10, 1997).

145. Rick Wartzman, "When You Translate 'Got Milk' for Latinos, What Do You Get?" *Wall Street Journal* (June 3, 1999).

146. Charles Newbery, "Coke Goes Native with New Soft Drink," *Advertising Age* (December 1, 2003): 34

147. Eric J. Arnould and Richard R. Wilk, "Why Do the Natives Wear Adidas: Anthropological Approaches to Consumer Research," *Advances in Consumer Research* 12 (Provo, UT: Association for Consumer Research, 1985): 748–52.

148. John F. Sherry, Jr. and Eduardo G. Camargo, "May Your Life Be Marvelous: English Language Labelling and the Semiotics of Japanese Promotion," *Journal of Consumer Research* 14 (1987): 174–188.

149. Bill Bryson, "A Taste for Scrambled English," *New York Times* (July 22, 1990): 10; Rose A. Horowitz, "California Beach Culture Rides Wave of Popularity in Japan," *Journal of Commerce* (August 3, 1989): 17; Elaine Lafferty, "American Casual Seizes Japan: Teen-agers Go for N.F.L. Hats, Batman and the California Look," *Time* (November 13, 1989): 106.

150. Lucy Howard and Gregory Cerio, "Goofy Goods," *Newsweek* (August 15, 1994): 8.

151. "Product Placement, Sampling, and Word-of-Mouth Collectively Influence Consumer Purchases," Center for Media Research (October 22, 2008), www.mediapost.com, accessed October 22, 2008; Brian Steinberg and Suzanne Vranica, "Prime-Time TV's New Guest Stars: Products," *Wall Street Journal* (January 12, 2004), www.wsj.com, accessed January 12, 2004; Karlene Lukovitz, "'Storyline' Product Placements Gaining on Cable," *Marketing Daily* (October 5, 2007), www.mediapost.com, accessed October 5, 2007.

152. Craig J. Thompson and Zeynep Arsel, "The Starbucks Brandscape and Consumers' (Anticorporate) Experiences of Glocalization," *Journal of Consumer Research* 31 (December 2004): 631–42.

153. Calvin Sims, "For Chic's Sake, Japanese Women Parade to the Orthopedist," *New York Times* (November 26, 1999), www.nytimes.com, accessed November 26, 1999.

SECTION 5 MINTEL MEMO AND DATASET EXERCISE

Mintel Memo

TO: Consumer Research Dept.
FROM: The Big Boss
RE: Sacred food segmentation and positioning

We need to try to expand our presence in the kosher food market. Are we positioning ourselves in this category as effectively as we could? Are we aiming for the right target segments?

Please provide us with actionable recommendations for segmentation and positioning strategies based on this information. As you analyze the data in the tables provided, remember to focus on general trends with an eye on specific subgroups (e.g., age, household income, education, etc.) that show a statistically significant difference in their responses—especially when there is some reason based on what you have learned in this section about consumer behavior to believe that this difference is important.

When you write your memo, please try to incorporate relevant concepts and information you learned when you read the designated chapters!

What can we learn from the following data to help our company position itself in the kosher food market?

Number of Respondents		1,538	441	240	341	335
Respondent Categories			Household Income		Education	
Respondent Sub-categories		Total	$25,000–$49,999	$100,000+	High School or Less	College Graduate
			(A)	(B)	(A)	(B)
Question	Answers	%	%	%	%	%
How much do you know about kosher food?	Know a lot	13	11	18	9	14
(Comparison of Column Proportions)				A		A
	Know some	58	52	65	50	61
				A		A
	Know nothing	30	37	17	40	24
			B		B	

Comparison of Column Proportions results are based on two-sided tests with significance level p < 0.05. Letters appearing in the column category denote a significant difference between the number immediately above the letter and the category associated with that particular letter. For example, the "B" in the High School or Less category above denotes a significant difference between the percentage of participants with an educational level of high school or less who specify knowing nothing about kosher (40%) and the percentage of participants who had graduated from college (24%).

To access the complete Mintel questionnaires and datasets, go to MyMarketingLab at www.mypearsonmarketinglab.com. If you are not using MyMarketingLab, visit this book's Companion Website at www.pearsonhighered.com/solomon.

ABC model of attitudes a multidimensional perspective stating that attitudes are jointly defined by affect, behavior, and cognition

Absolute threshold the minimum amount of stimulation that can be detected on a given sensory channel

Acceptance cycles a way to differentiate among fashions in terms of their longevity

Accommodative purchase decision the process of using bargaining, coercion, compromise, and the wielding of power to achieve agreement among group members who have different preferences or priorities

Acculturation the process of learning the beliefs and behaviors endorsed by another culture

Acculturation agents friends, family, local businesses, and other reference groups that facilitate the learning of cultural norms

Activation models of memory approaches to memory stressing different levels of processing that occur and activate some aspects of memory rather than others, depending on the nature of the processing task

Activity stores a retailing concept that lets consumers participate in the production of the products or services being sold in the store

Actual self a person's realistic appraisal of his or her qualities

Adaptation the process that occurs when a sensation becomes so familiar that it no longer commands attention

Advergaming online games merged with interactive advertisements that let companies target specific types of consumers

Advertising wear-out the condition that occurs when consumers become so used to hearing or seeing a marketing stimulus that they no longer pay attention to it

Affect the way a consumer feels about an attitude object

Affluenza well-off consumers who are stressed or unhappy despite of or even because of their wealth

Age cohort a group of consumers of approximately the same age who have undergone similar experiences

Agentic goals an emphasis on self-assertion and mastery, often associated with traditional male gender roles

AIOs (activities, interests, and opinions) the psychographic variables researchers use to group consumers

Allegory a story told about an abstract trait or concept that has been personified as a person, animal, or vegetable

Allocentric person who has a group orientation

Alternate-reality game an application that blends online and off-line clues and encourages players to collaborate to solve a puzzle

Androgyny the possession of both masculine and feminine traits

Animism cultural practices whereby inanimate objects are given qualities that make them somehow alive

Antibrand communities groups of consumers who share a common disdain for a celebrity, store, or brand

Anticonsumption the actions taken by consumers involving the deliberate defacement or mutilation of products

Antifestival an event that distorts the symbols associated with other holidays

Approach–approach conflict a person must choose between two desirable alternatives

Approach–avoidance conflict a person desires a goal but wishes to avoid it at the same time

Archetypes a universally shared idea or behavior pattern, central to Carl Jung's conception of personality; archetypes involve themes—such as birth, death, or the devil—that appear frequently in myths, stories, and dreams

Art product a creation viewed primarily as an object of aesthetic contemplation without any functional value

Aspirational reference group high-profile athletes and celebrities used in marketing efforts to promote a product

Associative network a memory system that organizes individual units of information according to some set of relationships; may include such concepts as brands, manufacturers, and stores

Atmospherics the use of space and physical features in store design to evoke certain effects in buyers

Attention the assignment of processing activity to selected stimuli

Attentional gate a process whereby information retained for further processing is transferred from sensory memory to short-term memory

Attitude a lasting, general evaluation of people (including oneself), objects, or issues

Attitude object (Ao) anything toward which one has an attitude

Attitude toward the act of buying (A_{act}) the perceived consequences of a purchase

Autonomic decision when one family member chooses a product for the whole family

Autotellics individuals who enjoy touching products to experience them

Avatar manifestation of a Hindu deity in superhuman or animal form. In the computing world it has come to mean a cyberspace presence represented by a character that you can move around inside a visual, graphical world

B2C e-commerce businesses selling to consumers through electronic marketing

Baby boomer a large cohort of people born between the years of 1946 and 1964 who are the source of many important cultural and economic changes

Balance theory a theory that considers relations among elements a person might perceive as belonging together, and people's tendency to change relations among elements in order to make them consistent or "balanced"

Basking in reflected glory the practice of publicizing connections with successful people or organizations to enhance one's own standing

Behavior a consumer's actions with regard to an attitude object

Behavioral economics the study of the behavioral determinants of economic decisions

Behavioral influence perspective the view that consumer decisions are learned responses to environmental cues

Behavioral learning theories the perspectives on learning that assume that learning takes place as the result of responses to external events

Behavioral targeting e-commerce marketers serve up customized ads on Web sites or cable TV stations based on a customer's prior activity

Being space a retail environment that resembles a residential living room where customers are encouraged to congregate

Binary opposition a defining structural characteristic of many myths in which two opposing ends of some dimension are represented (e.g., good versus evil, nature versus technology)

Bioterrorism a strategy to disrupt the nation's food supply with the aim of creating economic havoc

Blissful ignorance effect states that people who have details about a product before they buy it do not expect to be as happy with it as do those who got only ambiguous information

Blogs messages posted online in diary form

Body cathexis a person's feelings about aspects of his or her body

Body image a consumer's subjective evaluation of his or her physical self

Boomerang kids grown children who return to their parents' home to live

Brand advocates consumers who supply product reviews online

Brand community a set of consumers who share a set of social relationships based on usage or interest in a product

Brand equity a brand that has strong positive associations in a consumer's memory and commands a lot of loyalty as a result

Brand loyalty repeat purchasing behavior that reflects a conscious decision to continue buying the same brand

Brand personality a set of traits people attribute to a product as if it were a person

Branded entertainment a format where advertisers showcase their products in longer-form narrative films instead of commercials

Brandfests a corporate-sponsored event intended to promote strong brand loyalty among customers

BRIC the bloc of nations with very rapid economic development: Brazil, Russia, India, and China

Bromance a relationship characterized by strong affection between two straight males

Business ethics rules of conduct that guide actions in the marketplace

Business-to-business (B2B) e-commerce internet interactions between two or more businesses or organizations

Business-to-business (B2B) marketers specialists in meeting the needs of organizations such as corporations, government agencies, hospitals, and retailers

Buyclass theory of purchasing a framework that characterizes organizational buying decisions in terms of how much cognitive effort is involved in making a decision

Buyer the person who actually makes the purchase

Buying center the part of an organization charged with making purchasing decisions

C2C e-commerce consumer-to-consumer activity through the Internet

Carbon footprint the impact human activities have on the environment in terms of the amount of greenhouse gases they produce; measured in units of carbon dioxide

Cascades a piece of information shared in a social network triggers a sequence of interactions (much like an avalanche)

Category exemplars brands that are particularly relevant examples of a broader classification

Chavs British term that refers to young, lower-class men and women who mix flashy brands and accessories from big names such as Burberry with track suits

Chunking a process in which information is stored by combining small pieces of information into larger ones

Classic a fashion with an extremely long acceptance cycle

Classical conditioning the learning that occurs when a stimulus eliciting a response is paired with another stimulus that initially does not elicit a response on its own but will cause a similar response over time because of its association with the first stimulus

Closure principle the *Gestalt* principle that describes a person's tendency to supply missing information in order to perceive a holistic image

Co-branding strategies linking products together to create a more desirable connotation in consumer minds

Co-consumers other patrons in a consumer setting

Cognition the beliefs a consumer has about an attitude object

Cognitive learning theory approaches that stress the importance of internal mental processes. This perspective views people as problem solvers who actively use information from the world around them to master their environment

Cognitive processing style a predisposition to process information. Some of us tend to have a *rational system of cognition* that processes information analytically and sequentially using roles of logic, while others rely on an *experiential system of cognition* that processes information more holistically and in parallel

Cohesiveness the degree to which members of a group are attracted to each other and how much each values their membership in this group

Collecting the systematic acquisition of a particular object or set of objects

Collective selection the process by which certain symbolic alternatives tend to be jointly chosen over others by members of a society

Collectivist culture cultural orientation that encourages people to subordinate their personal goals to those of a stable in-group; values such as self-discipline and group accomplishment are stressed

Communal goals an emphasis on affiliation and the fostering of harmonious relations, often associated with traditional female gender roles

Communications model a framework specifying that a number of elements are necessary for communication to be achieved, including a source, message, medium, receivers, and feedback

Comparative advertising a strategy in which a message compares two or more specifically named or recognizably presented brands and makes a comparison of them in terms of one or more specific attributes

Comparative influence the process whereby a reference group influences decisions about specific brands or activities

Compensatory decision rules a set of rules that allows information about attributes of competing products to be averaged in some way; poor standing on one attribute can potentially be offset by good standing on another

Compliance we form an attitude because it helps us to gain rewards or avoid punishment

Compulsive consumption the process of repetitive, often excessive, shopping used to relieve tension, anxiety, depression, or boredom

Computer-mediated environment immersive virtual worlds

Conditioned response (CR) a response to a conditioned stimulus caused by the learning of an association between a conditioned stimulus (CS) and an unconditioned stimulus (UCS)

Conditioned stimulus (CS) a stimulus that produces a learned reaction through association over time

Conformity a change in beliefs or actions as a reaction to real or imagined group pressure

Connexity a lifestyle term coined by the advertising agency Saatchi & Saatchi to describe young consumers who place high value on being both footloose and connected

Conscientious consumerism a new value that combines a focus on personal health with a concern for global health

Consensual purchase decision a decision in which the group agrees on the desired purchase and differs only in terms of how it will be achieved

Consideration set the products a consumer actually deliberates about choosing

Conspicuous consumption the purchase and prominent display of luxury goods to provide evidence of a consumer's ability to afford them

Consumed consumers those people who are used or exploited, whether willingly or not, for commercial gain in the marketplace

Consumer a person who identifies a need or desire, makes a purchase, and/or disposes of the product

Consumer addiction a physiological and/or psychological dependency on products or services

Consumer behavior the processes involved when individuals or groups select, purchase, use, or dispose of products, services, ideas, or experiences to satisfy needs and desires

Consumer confidence the state of mind of consumers relative to their optimism or pessimism about economic conditions; people tend to make more discretionary purchases when their confidence in the economy is high

Consumer-generated content a hallmark of Web 2.0; everyday people voice their opinions about products, brands, and companies on blogs, podcasts, and social networking sites and film their own commercials they post on Web sites

Consumer hyperchoice a condition where the large number of available options forces us to make repeated choices that drain psychological energy and diminish our ability to make smart decisions

Consumer identity renaissance the redefinition process people undergo when they retire

Consumer satisfaction/dissatisfaction (CS/D) the overall attitude a person has about a product after it has been purchased

Consumer socialization the process by which people acquire skills that enable them to function in the marketplace

Consumerspace marketing environment where customers act as partners with companies to decide what the marketplace will offer

Consumer style a pattern of behaviors, attitudes, and opinions that influences all of a person's consumption activities—including attitudes toward advertising, preferred channels of information and purchase, brand loyalty, and price consciousness

Consumer tribe group of people who share a lifestyle and who can identify with each other because of a shared allegiance to an activity or a product

Consumption communities Web groups where members share views and product recommendations online

Consumption constellation a set of products and activities used by consumers to define, communicate, and perform social roles

Contamination when a place or object takes on sacred qualities because of its association with another sacred person or event

Contemporary Young Mainstream Female Achievers (CYMFA) modern women who assume multiple roles

Continuous innovation a modification of an existing product

Contrast stimuli that differ from others around them

Conventions norms that regulate how we conduct our everyday lives

Co-optation a cultural process by which the original meanings of a product or other symbol associated with a subculture are modified by members of mainstream culture

Core values common general values held by a culture

Cosmopolitanism a cultural value that emphasizes being open to the world and striving for diverse experiences

Cosplay a form of performance art in which participants wear elaborate costumes that represent a virtual world avatar or other fictional character

Cougars older women who date younger men

Country of origin original country from which a product is produced. Can be an important piece of information in the decision-making process

Craft product a creation valued because of the beauty with which it performs some function; this type of product tends to follow a formula that permits rapid production, and it is easier to understand than an art product

Creolization foreign influences are absorbed and integrated with local meanings

Crescive norms unspoken rules that govern social behavior

Crowdsourcing similar to a firm that outsources production to a subcontractor; companies call upon outsiders from around the world to solve problems their own scientists can't handle

Cult products items that command fierce consumer loyalty and devotion

Cultural capital a set of distinctive and socially rare tastes and practices that admits a person into the realm of the upper class

Cultural categories the grouping of ideas and values that reflect the basic ways members of a society characterize the world

Cultural formula a sequence of media events in which certain roles and props tend to occur consistently

Cultural gatekeepers individuals who are responsible for determining the types of messages and symbolism to which members of mass culture are exposed

Cultural selection the process by which some alternatives are selected over others by cultural gatekeepers

Culture the values, ethics, rituals, traditions, material objects, and services produced or valued by the members of a society

Culture jamming the defacement or alteration of advertising materials as a form of political expression

Culture production system (CPS) the set of individuals and organizations responsible for creating and marketing a cultural product

Custom a norm that controls basic behaviors, such as division of labor in a household

Cybermediary intermediary that helps to filter and organize online market information so that consumers can identify and evaluate alternatives more efficiently

Database marketing tracking consumers' buying habits very closely, and then crafting products and messages tailored precisely to people's wants and needs based on this information

Decay structural changes in the brain produced by learning decrease over time

Decision polarization the process whereby individuals' choices tend to become more extreme (polarized), in either a conservative or risky direction, following group discussion of alternatives

Deethnicization process whereby a product formerly associated with a specific ethnic group is detached from its roots and marketed to other subcultures

Deindividuation the process whereby individual identities get submerged within a group, reducing inhibitions against socially inappropriate behavior

Demographics the observable measurements of a population's characteristics, such as birthrate, age distribution, and income

Desacralization the process that occurs when a sacred item or symbol is removed from its special place, or is duplicated in mass quantities, and becomes profane as a result

Determinant attributes the attributes actually used to differentiate among choices

Differential threshold the ability of a sensory system to detect changes or differences among stimuli

Diffusion of innovations the process whereby a new product, service, or idea spreads through a population

Digital native young people who have grown up with computers and mobile technology; multitaskers with cell phones, music downloads, and instant messaging on the Internet. Who are comfortable communicating online and by text and IM rather than by voice

DINKS acronym for Double Income, No Kids; a consumer segment with a lot of disposable income

Discontinuous innovation a new product or service that radically changes the way we live

Discretionary income the money available to a household over and above that required for necessities

Divestment rituals the steps people take to gradually distance themselves from things they treasure so that they can sell them or give them away

Doppelgänger brand image a parody of a brand posted on a Web site that looks like the original but is in fact a critique of it

Drive the desire to satisfy a biological need in order to reduce physiological arousal

Drive theory concept that focuses on biological needs that produce unpleasant states of arousal

Dynamically continuous innovation a significant change to an existing product

Early adopters people who are receptive to new products and adopt them relatively soon, though they are motivated more by social acceptance and being in style than by the desire to try risky new things

Echo Boomers people born between 1986–2002, also known as Gen Y and Millennials

Economics of information perspective in which advertising is an important source of consumer information emphasizing the economic cost of the time spent searching for products

Ego the system that mediates between the id and the superego

Ego-defensive function attitudes we form to protect ourselves either from external threats or internal feelings

80/20 rule a rule-of-thumb in volume segmentation, which says that about 20 percent of consumers in a product category (the heavy users) account for about 80 percent of sales

Elaborated codes the ways of expressing and interpreting meanings that are more complex and depend on a more sophisticated worldview, which tend to be used by the middle and upper classes

Elaboration likelihood model (ELM) the approach that one of two routes to persuasion (central versus peripheral) will be followed, depending on the personal relevance of a message; the route taken determines the relative importance of the message contents versus other characteristics, such as source attractiveness

Elaborative rehearsal a cognitive process that allows information to move from short-term memory into long-term memory by thinking about the meaning of a stimulus and relating it to other information already in memory

Electronic recommendation agent a software tool that tries to understand a human decision maker's multiattribute preferences for a product category by asking the user to communicate his or her preferences. Based on that data, the software then recommends a list of alternatives

sorted by the degree that they fit with the person's preferences

Embeds tiny figures inserted into magazine advertising by using high-speed photography or airbrushing. These hidden figures, usually of a sexual nature, supposedly exert strong but unconscious influences on innocent readers

Emic perspective an approach to studying for (or marketing to) cultures that stresses the unique aspects of each culture

Encoding the process in which information from short-term memory enters into long-term memory in a recognizable form

Enculturation the process of learning the beliefs and behaviors endorsed by one's own culture

Episodic memories memories that relate to personally relevant events; this tends to increase a person's motivation to retain these memories

Esteem need prioritizing the needs of the individual above those of the group

Ethnic subculture a self-perpetuating group of consumers held together by common cultural ties

Ethnocentrism the belief in the superiority of one's own country's practices and products

Etic perspective an approach to studying (or marketing to) cultures that stresses commonalities across cultures

Evaluative criteria the dimensions used by consumers to compare competing product alternatives

Evoked set those products already in memory plus those prominent in the retail environment that are actively considered during a consumer's choice process

Exchange a transaction in which two or more organizations or people give and receive something of value

Expectancy disconfirmation model states that we form beliefs about product performance based on prior experience with the product and/or communications about the product that imply a certain level of quality; when something performs the way we thought it would, we may not think much about it. If it fails to live up to expectations, this may create negative feelings. On the other hand, we are satisfied if performance exceeds our initial expectations

Expectancy theory the perspective that behavior is largely "pulled" by expectations of achieving desirable outcomes, or positive incentives, rather than "pushed" from within

Experience the result of acquiring and processing stimulation over time

Experiential hierarchy of effects an attitude is initially formed on the basis of a raw emotional reaction

Experiential perspective an approach stressing the *Gestalt* or totality of the product or service experience, focusing on consumers' affective responses in the marketplace

Exposure an initial stage of perception during which some sensations come within range of consumers' sensory receptors

Extended family traditional family structure in which several generations live together

Extended problem solving an elaborate decision-making process, often initiated by a motive that is fairly central to the self-concept and accompanied by perceived risk; the consumer tries to collect as much information as possible, and carefully weighs product alternatives

Extended self the external objects we consider a part of our self-identity

Extinction the process whereby a learned connection between a stimulus and response is eroded so that the response is no longer reinforced

Fad a very short-lived fashion

Family branding an application of stimulus generalization when a product capitalizes on the reputation of its manufacturer's name

Family financial officer (FFO) the individual in the family who is in charge of making financial decisions

Family identity the definition of a household by family members that it presents to members and to those outside the family unit

Family life cycle (FLC) a classification scheme that segments consumers in terms of changes in income and family composition and the changes in demands placed on this income

Fantasy a self-induced shift in consciousness, often focusing on some unattainable or improbable goal; sometimes fantasy is a way of compensating for a lack of external stimulation or for dissatisfaction with the actual self

Fashion the process of social diffusion by which a new style is adopted by some group(s) of consumers

Fashion acceptance cycle the diffusion process of a style through three stages: introduction, acceptance, and regression

Fashion system those people and organizations involved in creating symbolic meanings and transferring these meanings to cultural goods

Fear appeals an attempt to change attitudes or behavior through the use of threats or by highlighting negative consequences of noncompliance with the request

Feature creep the tendency of manufacturers to add layers of complexity to products that make them harder to understand and use

Fertility rate a rate determined by the number of births per year per 1,000 women of childbearing age

Figure-ground principle the *Gestalt* principle whereby one part of a stimulus configuration dominates a situation whereas other aspects recede into the background

Fixed-interval reinforcement after a specified time period has passed, the first response an orgamism makes elicits a reward

Fixed-ratio reinforcement reinforcement occurs only after a fixed number of responses

Flow state situation in which consumers are truly involved with a product, an ad, or a Web site

Food culture pattern of food and beverage consumption that reflects the values of a social group

Food poverty the inability of consumers to obtain healthy and affordable food due to limited accessibility to stores, the availability of healthy choices, the affordability of healthy options, and general nutritional awareness

Foot-in-the-door technique based on the observation that a consumer is more likely to comply with a request if he or she has first agreed to comply with a smaller request

Fortress brands brands that consumers closely link to rituals; this makes it unlikely they will be replaced

Freegans a takeoff on *vegans*, who shun all animal products; anticonsumerists who live off discards as a political statement against corporations and materialism

Freemium a free version of a product that's supported by a paid premium version. The idea is to encourage the maximum number of people to use the product and eventually convert a small fraction of them to paying customers

Frequency marketing a marketing technique that reinforces regular purchasers by giving them prizes with values that increase along with the amount purchased

Frugalistas fashion-conscious consumers who pride themselves on achieving style on a limited budget

Functional theory of attitudes states that attitudes exist *because* they serve some function for the person. Consumers who expect that they will need to deal with similar situations at a future time will be more likely to start to form an attitude in anticipation

Gadget lovers enthusiastic early adopters of high-tech products

Gatekeeper the person who conducts the information search and controls the flow of information available to the group

Gemba Japanese term for the one true source of information

Gen X people born between 1965–1985

Gen Y people born between 1986–2002; also known as Echo Boomers and Millennials

Gender convergence blurring of sex roles in modern society; men and women increasingly express similar attitudes about balancing home life and work

Gender-bending products a traditionally sex-typed product adapted to appeal to the opposite gender

Geodemography techniques that combine consumer demographic information with geographic consumption patterns to permit precise targeting of consumers with specific characteristics

Gestalt meaning derived from the totality of a set of stimuli, rather than from any individual stimulus

Gift-giving ritual the events involved in the selection, presentation, acceptance, and interpretation of a gift

Global consumer culture a culture in which people around the world are united through their common devotion to brand name consumer goods, movie stars, celebrities, and leisure activities

Globalized consumption ethic the global sharing of a material lifestyle including the valuing of well-known multinational brands that symbolize prosperity

Goal a consumer's desired end state

Gray market the economic potential created by the increasing numbers of affluent elderly consumers

Green marketing a marketing strategy involving an emphasis on protecting the natural environment

Greenwashing inflated claims about a product's environmental benefits

Gripe sites web sites consumers create specifically to log complaints about a company

Grooming rituals sequences of behaviors that aid in the transition from the private self to the public self or back again

Group dieting online communities devoted to excessive weight loss

Guerrilla marketing promotional strategies that use unconventional locations and intensive word-of-mouth campaigns

Habitual decision making choices made with little or no conscious effort

Habitus ways in which we classify experiences as a result of our socialization processes

Halo effect a phenomenon that occurs when people react to other, similar stimuli in much the same way they responded to the original stimulus

Heavy users a name companies use to identify their customers who consume their products in large volumes

Hedonic consumption the multisensory, fantasy, and emotional aspects of consumers' interactions with products

Helicopter moms overprotective mothers who "hover" around their kids and insert themselves into virtually all aspects of their lives

Heuristics the mental rules of thumb that lead to a speedy decision

Hierarchy of effects a fixed sequence of steps that occurs during attitude formation; this sequence varies depending on such factors as the consumer's level of involvement with the attitude object

High-context culture group members tend to be close-knit and are likely to infer meanings that go beyond the spoken word

Hoarding unsystematic acquisition of objects (in contrast to collecting)

Homeostasis the state of being in which the body is in physiological balance; goal-oriented behavior attempts to reduce or eliminate an unpleasant motivational state and return to a balanced one

Homogamy the tendency for individuals to marry others similar to themselves

Home shopping parties a gathering where a company representative makes a sales presentation to a group of people who have gathered in the home of a friend or acquaintance

Homophily the degree to which a pair of individuals is similar in terms of education, social status, and beliefs

Host culture a new culture to which a person must acculturate

Household according to the U.S. Census Bureau, an occupied housing unit

Hybrid ad a marketing communication that explicitly references the context (e.g., TV show) in which it appears

Hyperopia the medical term for people who have farsighted vision; describes people who are so obsessed with preparing for the future that they can't enjoy the present

Hyperreality the becoming real of what is initially simulation or "hype"

Icon a sign that resembles the product in some way

Id the system oriented toward immediate gratification

Ideal of beauty a model, or exemplar, of appearance valued by a culture

Ideal self a person's conception of how he or she would like to be

Identification the process of forming an attitude to conform to another person's or group's expectations

Identity marketing a practice whereby consumers are paid to alter some aspects of their selves to advertise for a branded product

Idiocentric a person who has an individualist orientation

Illusion of truth effect telling people that a consumer claim is false can make them misremember it as true

Impression management our efforts to "manage" what others think of us by strategically choosing clothing and other cues that will put us in a good light

Impulse buying a process that occurs when the consumer experiences a sudden urge to purchase an item that he or she cannot resist

Incidental brand exposure an experimental technique that involves showing product logos to respondents without their conscious awareness

Incidental learning unintentional acquisition of knowledge

Index a sign that is connected to a product because they share some property

Individualism one of Hofstede's cultural dimensions: The extent to which the culture values the welfare of the individual versus that of the group

Individualist culture cultural orientation that encourages people to attach more importance to personal goals than to group goals; values such as personal enjoyment and freedom are stressed

Inertia the process whereby purchase decisions are made out of habit because the consumer lacks the motivation to consider alternatives

Influence network a two-way dialogue between participants in a social network and opinion leaders

Influencer the person who tries to sway the outcome of the decision

Influencer programs a strategy to start online conversations about brands by encouraging (and perhaps compensating) bloggers to write about them

Information search the process by which the consumer surveys his or her environment for appropriate data to make a reasonable decision

Initiator the person who brings up the idea or identifies a need

Innovation a product or style that is perceived as new by consumers

Innovators people who are always on the lookout for novel developments and will be the first to try a new offering

Insourcing making things yourself that you used to buy from others

Instrumental conditioning also known as operant conditioning, occurs as the individual learns to perform behaviors that produce positive outcomes and to avoid those that yield negative outcomes

Instrumental values goals endorsed because they are needed to achieve desired end states, or terminal values

Intelligent agents software programs that learn from past user behavior in order to recommend new purchases

Interactive mobile marketing real-time promotional campaigns targeted to consumers' cell phones

Interference one way that forgetting occurs; as additional information is learned, it displaces the earlier information

Internalization deep-seated attitudes become part of our value system

Interpretant the meaning derived from a sign or symbol

Interpretation the process whereby meanings are assigned to stimuli

Interpretivism as opposed to the dominant positivist perspective on consumer behavior, instead stresses the importance of symbolic, subjective experience and the idea that meaning is in the mind of the person rather than existing "out there" in the objective world

Invidious distinction the use of status symbols to inspire envy in others through display of wealth or power

Involvement the motivation to process product-related information

j.n.d. (just noticeable difference) the minimum difference between two stimuli that can be detected by a perceiver

Juggling lifestyle working mothers' attempts to compromise between conflicting cultural ideals of motherhood and professionalism

***Kansei* engineering** a Japanese philosophy that translates customers' feelings into design elements

Kin-network system the rituals intended to maintain ties among family members, both immediate and extended

Knowledge function the process of forming an attitude to provide order, structure, or meaning

Knowledge structure organized system of concepts relating to brands, stores, and other concepts

Laddering a technique to uncover consumers' associations between specific attributes and general values

Laggards consumers who are exceptionally slow to adopt innovations

Late adopters the majority of consumers who are moderately receptive to adopting innovations

Lateral cycling a process in which already-purchased objects are sold to others or exchanged for other items

Latitudes of acceptance and rejection in the social judgment theory of attitudes, the notion that people differ in terms of the information they will find acceptable or unacceptable. They form latitudes of acceptance and rejection around an attitude standard. Ideas that fall within a latitude will be favorably received, but those falling outside of this zone will not

Lead users involved, experienced customers (usually corporate customers) who are very knowledgeable about the field

Learning a relatively permanent change in a behavior caused by experience

Licensing popular marketing strategy that pays for the right to link a product or service to the name of a well-known brand or designer

Life course paradigm this perspective views behavior at any stage in life or given point in time as the product of one's actions or responses to earlier life conditions and the way the individual has adapted to social and environmental circumstances

Limited problem solving a problem-solving process in which consumers are not motivated to search for information or to rigorously evaluate each alternative; instead they use simple decision rules to arrive at a purchase decision

List of Values (LOV) scale identifies consumer segments based on the values members endorse and relates each value to differences in consumption behaviors

LOHAS an acronym for "lifestyles of health and sustainability"; a consumer segment that worries about the environment, wants products to be produced in a sustainable way, and who spend money to advance what they see as their personal development and potential

Long tail states that we need no longer rely solely on big hits (such as blockbuster movies or best-selling books) to find profits. Companies can also make money if they sell small amounts of items that only a few people want—if they sell enough different items

Long-term memory (LTM) the system that allows us to retain information for a long period of time

Look-alike packaging putting a generic or private label product in a package that resembles a popular brand to associate the brand with the popular one

Looking-glass self the process of imagining the reaction of others toward oneself

Low-context culture in contrast to high-context cultures that have strong oral traditions and that are more sensitive to nuance, low-context cultures are more literal

Low-involvement hierarchy of effects the process of attitude formation for products or services that carry little risk or self-identity

Low-literate consumer people who read at a very low level; tend to avoid situations where they will have to reveal their inability to master basic consumption decisions such as ordering from a menu

M-commerce the practice of promoting and selling goods and services via wireless devices including cell phones, PDAs, and iPods

Market beliefs a consumer's specific beliefs or decision rules pertaining to marketplace phenomena

Market maven a person who often serves as a source of information about marketplace activities

Market segmentation strategies targeting a brand only to specific groups of consumers who share well-defined and relevant characteristics

Masculinism study devoted to the male image and the cultural meanings of masculinity

Masculinity/femininity one of Hofstede's cultural dimensions: The degree to which a culture clearly defines sex roles

Masked branding strategy that deliberately hides a product's origin

Mass class a term analysts use to describe the millions of global consumers who now enjoy a level of purchasing power that's sufficient to let them afford many high-quality products

Mass customization the personalization of products and services for individual customers at a mass-production price

Materialism the importance consumers attach to worldly possessions

Megachurches very large churches that serve between 2,000 and 20,000 congregants

Membership reference group ordinary people whose consumption activities provide informational social influence

Meme theory a perspective that uses a medical metaphor to explain how an idea or product enters the consciousness of people over time, much like a virus

Memory a process of acquiring information and storing it over time so that it will be available when needed

Mental accounting principle that states that decisions are influenced by the way a problem is posed

Mere exposure phenomenon the tendency to like persons or things if we see them more often

Metaphor the use of an explicit comparison ("A" is "B") between a product and some other person, place, or thing

Metaverse the network of virtual worlds where people interact in 3-D immersive digital environments

Metrosexual a straight, urban male who exhibits strong interests and knowledge regarding product categories such as fashion, home design, gourmet cooking, and personal care that run counter to the traditional male sex role

Microcultures groups that form around a strong shared identification with an activity or art form

Microloans Small sums—typically less than $100—banks lend to entrepreneurs in developing countries

Millennials people born between 1986–2002; also known as Echo Boomers and Gen Y

Minipreneurs one-person businesses

Modeling imitating the behavior of others

Modified rebuy in the context of the buy-class framework, a task that requires a modest amount of information search and evaluation, often focused on identifying the appropriate vendor

Monomyth a myth with basic characteristics that are found in many cultures

More a custom with a strong moral overtone

Motivation an internal state that activates goal-oriented behavior

Motivational research a qualitative research approach, based on psychoanalytic (Freudian) interpretations, with a heavy emphasis on unconscious motives for consumption

Multiattribute attitude models those models that assume that a consumer's attitude (evaluation) of an attitude object depends on the beliefs he or she has about several or many attributes of the object; the use of a multiattribute model implies that an attitude toward a product or brand can be predicted by identifying these specific beliefs and combining them to derive a measure of the consumer's overall attitude

Multigenerational marketing strategy an appeal to people of different ages with imagery from an older generation that also turns on younger consumers

Multiple pathway anchoring and adjustment (MPAA) model a model that emphasizes multiple pathways to attitude formation

Multiple-intelligence theory a perspective that argues for other types of intelligence, such as athletic prowess or musical ability, beyond the traditional math and verbal skills psychologists use to measure IQ

Multitasking processing information from more than one medium at a time

Myth a story containing symbolic elements that expresses the shared emotions and ideals of a culture

Name-letter effect all things equal we like others who share our names or even initials better than those who don't

Narrative product information in the form of a story

Need a basic biological motive

Need for affiliation the need to be in the company of others

Need for power the need to control one's environment

Need for uniqueness the need to assert one's individual identity

Negative reinforcement the process whereby the environment weakens responses to stimuli so that inappropriate behavior is avoided

Negative word of mouth the passing on of negative experiences involved with products or services by consumers to other potential customers to influence others' choices

Network effect each person who uses a product or service benefits as more people participate

Neuromarketing a new technique that uses a brain scanning device called functional magnetic resonance imaging (fMRI), that tracks blood flow as people perform mental tasks. Scientists know that specific regions of the brain light up in these scans to show increased blood flow when a person recognizes a face, hears a song, makes a decision, senses deception, and so on. Now they are trying to harness this technology to measure consumers' reactions to movie trailers, choices about automobiles, the appeal of a pretty face, and loyalty to specific brands

New info shopper consumers who almost automatically search for information online before they buy

New task in the context of the buyclass framework, a task that requires a great degree of effort and information search

Noncompensatory decision rules decision shortcuts a consumer makes when a product with a low standing on one attribute cannot make up for this position by being better on another attribute

Normative influence the process in which a reference group helps to set and enforce fundamental standards of conduct

Norms the informal rules that govern what is right or wrong

Nostalgia a bittersweet emotion; the past is viewed with sadness and longing; many "classic" products appeal to consumers' memories of their younger days

Nuclear family a contemporary living arrangement composed of a married couple and their children

Object in semiotic terms, the product that is the focus of a message

Objectification when we attribute sacred qualities to mundane items

Observational learning the process in which people learn by watching the actions of others and noting the reinforcements they receive for their behaviors

Opinion leader person who is knowledgeable about products and who frequently is able to influence others' attitudes or behaviors with regard to a product category

Organizational buyers people who purchase goods and services on behalf of companies for use in the process of manufacturing, distribution, or resale

Paradigm a widely accepted view or model of phenomena being studied; the perspective that regards people as rational information processors is currently the dominant paradigm, although this approach is now being challenged by a new wave of research that emphasizes the frequently subjective nature of consumer decision making

Parental yielding the process that occurs when a parental decision maker is influenced by a child's product request

Parody display deliberately avoiding status symbols; to seek status by mocking it

Part-list cueing effect a strategy to utilize the interference process in memory; when a marketer presents only a portion of the items in a category to consumers, they don't recall the omitted items as easily

Pastiche mixture of images

Perceived age how old a person feels as compared to his or her true chronological age

Perceived risk belief that a product has potentially negative consequences

Perception the process by which stimuli are selected, organized, and interpreted

Perceptual defense the tendency for consumers to avoid processing stimuli that are threatening to them

Perceptual filters past experiences that influence what stimuli we decide to process

Perceptual map a research tool used to understand how a brand is positioned in consumers' minds relative to competitors

Perceptual selection process by which people attend to only a small portion of the stimuli to which they are exposed

Perceptual vigilance the tendency for consumers to be more aware of stimuli that relate to their current needs

Permission marketing popular strategy based on the idea that a marketer will be much more successful in persuading consumers who have agreed to let them try

Personality a person's unique psychological makeup, which consistently influences the way the person responds to his or her environment

Personality traits identifiable characteristics that define a person

Persuasion an active attempt to change attitudes

Physiological need a basic need required to maintain survival of the organism

Pleasure principle the belief that behavior is guided by the desire to maximize pleasure and avoid pain

Plinking™ act of embedding a product or service link in a video

Plutonomy an economy that a small number of rich people control

Podcasting an audio broadcast that people listen to on portable MP3 players or laptops

Point-of-purchase (POP) stimuli the promotional materials that are deployed in stores or other outlets to influence consumers' decisions at the time products are purchased

Popular culture the music, movies, sports, books, celebrities, and other forms of entertainment consumed by the mass market

Pop-up stores temporary locations that allow a company to test new brands without a huge financial commitment

Positioning strategy an organization's use of elements in the marketing mix to influence the consumer's interpretation of a product's meaning vis-à-vis competitors

Positive reinforcement the process whereby rewards provided by the environment strengthen responses to stimuli and appropriate behavior is learned

Positivism a research perspective that relies on principles of the "scientific method" and assumes that a single reality exists; events in the world can be objectively measured; and the causes of behavior can be identified, manipulated, and predicted

POSSLQ (Persons of Opposite Sex Sharing Living Quarters) U.S. Census designation for unmarried couples who cohabitate

Power distance one of Hofstede's cultural dimensions: The way members perceive differences in power when they form interpersonal relationships

Prediction market an approach based on the idea that groups of people with knowledge about an industry are jointly better predictors of the future than are any individuals

Priming properties of a stimulus that evoke a schema that leads us to compare the stimulus to other similar ones we encountered in the past

Principle of cognitive consistency the belief that consumers value harmony among their thoughts, feelings, and behaviors and that they are motivated to maintain uniformity among these elements

Principle of least interest the person who is least committed to staying in a relationship has the most power

Principle of similarity the *Gestalt* principle that describes how consumers tend to group objects that share similar physical characteristics

PRIZM (Potential Rating Index by Zip Market) clustering technique that classifies every zip code in the United States into one of 66 categories, ranging from the most affluent "Blue-Blood Estates" to the least well off "Public Assistance," developed by Claritas, Inc.

Problem recognition the process that occurs whenever the consumer sees a significant difference between his or her current state of affairs and some desired or ideal state; this recognition initiates the decision-making process

Product complementarity the view that products in different functional categories have symbolic meanings that are related to one another

Product line extension related products to an established brand

Product placement the process of obtaining exposure for a product by arranging for it to be inserted into a movie, television show, or some other medium

Product signal communicates an underlying quality of a product through the use of aspects that are only visible in the ad

Profane consumption the process of consuming objects and events that are ordinary or of the everyday world

Progressive learning model the perspective that people gradually learn a new culture as they increasingly come in contact with it; consumers assimilate into a new culture, mixing practices from their old and new environments to create a hybrid culture

Propinquity as physical distance between people decreases and opportunities for interaction increase, they are more likely to form relationships

Prospect theory a descriptive model of how people make choices

Psychographics the use of psychological, sociological, and anthropological factors to construct market segments

Psychophysics the science that focuses on how the physical environment is integrated into the consumer's subjective experience

Punishment the learning that occurs when a response is followed by unpleasant events

Purchase momentum initial impulses to buy in order to satisfy our needs increase the likelihood that we will buy even more

QR code the next generation of barcodes that activate a browser on a smartphone when photographed

Queuing theory the mathematical study of waiting lines

Rational perspective a view of the consumer as a careful, analytical decision maker who tries to maximize utility in purchase decisions

Reality engineering the process whereby elements of popular culture are appropriated by marketers and become integrated into marketing strategies

Reality principle principle that the ego seeks ways that will be acceptable to society to gratify the id

Recall the process of retrieving information from memory; in advertising research the extent to which consumers can remember a marketing message without being exposed to it during the study

Reciprocity norm a culturally learned obligation to return the gesture of a gift with one of equal value

Recognition in advertising research the extent to which consumers say they are familiar with an ad the researcher shows them

Reference group an actual or imaginary individual or group that has a significant effect on an individual's evaluations, aspirations, or behavior

Refutational arguments calling attention to a product's negative attributes as a persuasive strategy where a negative issue is raised and then dismissed; this approach can increase source credibility

Relationship marketing the strategic perspective that stresses the long-term, human side of buyer-seller interactions

Resonance a literary device, frequently used in advertising that uses a play on words (a double meaning) to communicate a product benefit

Reputation economy a reward system based on recognition of one's expertise by others who read online product reviews

Response bias a form of contamination in survey research in which some factor, such as the desire to make a good impression on the experimenter, leads respondents to modify their true answers

Restricted codes the ways of expressing and interpreting meanings that focus on the content of objects, which tend to be used by the working class

Retail theming strategy where stores create imaginative environments that transport shoppers to fantasy worlds or provide other kinds of stimulation

Retrieval the process whereby desired information is recovered from long-term memory

Retro brand an updated version of a brand from a prior historical period

Reverse product placement fictional products that appear in TV shows or movies become popular in the real world

Reward power a person or group with the means to provide positive reinforcement

RFID (response frequency identification device) a small plastic tag that holds a computer chip capable of storing a small amount of information, along with an antenna that lets the device communicate with a computer network. These devices are being implanted in a wide range of products to enable marketers to track inventory more efficiently

Rich media elements of an online ad that employ movement to gain attention

Risky shift the tendency for individuals to consider riskier alternatives after conferring with a group than if members made their own decisions with no discussion

Rites of passage sacred times marked by a change in social status

Ritual a set of multiple, symbolic behaviors that occur in a fixed sequence and that tend to be repeated periodically

Ritual artifacts items (consumer goods) used in the performance of rituals

Role theory the perspective that much of consumer behavior resembles actions in a play

Sacralization a process that occurs when ordinary objects, events, or people take on sacred meaning to a culture or to specific groups within a culture

Sacred consumption the process of consuming objects and events that are set apart from normal life and treated with some degree of respect or awe

Safety need the need to maintain a secure environment

Salience the prominence of a brand in memory

Sandwich Generation a description of middle-aged people who must care for both children and parents simultaneously

Schema an organized collection of beliefs and feelings represented in a cognitive category

Script a learned schema containing a sequence of events an individual expects to occur

Search engine optimization the process of devising online entries to maximize the likelihood they will appear when consumers search for a term online

Search engines software (such as Google) that helps consumers access information based upon their specific requests

Self-actualization a higher-order need for self-fulfillment and harmony

Self-concept the beliefs a person holds about his or her own attributes and how he or she evaluates these qualities

Self-perception theory an alternative (to cognitive dissonance) explanation of dissonance effects; it assumes that people use observations of their own behavior to infer their attitudes toward some object

Semiotics a field of study that examines the correspondence between signs and symbols and the meaning or meanings they convey

Sensation the immediate response of sensory receptors (eyes, ears, nose, mouth, fingers) to such basic stimuli as light, color, sound, odors, and textures

Sensory marketing marketing strategies that focus on the impact of sensations on our product experiences

Sensory memory the temporary storage of information received from the senses

Sensory overload a condition where consumers are exposed to far more information than they can process

Sensory signature A unique characteristic of a brand conveyed on a perceptual channel (e.g., fragrance)

Sexting the growing trend of young people posting sexually suggestive photos of themselves online

Sex-typed traits characteristics that are stereotypically associated with one gender or the other

Shaping the learning of a desired behavior over time by rewarding intermediate actions until the final result is obtained

Shopmobbing strangers organize online around a specific product or service and arrange to meet at a certain date and time in a real-world store to negotiate a group discount

Shopping orientation a consumer's general attitudes and motivations regarding the act of shopping

Short-term memory (STM) the mental system that allows us to retain information for a short period of time

Shrinkage the loss of money or inventory from shoplifting and/or employee theft

Sign the sensory imagery that represents the intended meanings of the object

Simile comparing two objects that share a similar property

Sleeper effect the process whereby differences in attitude change between positive and negative sources seem to diminish over time

Social aging theories a perspective to understand how society assigns people to different roles across the life span

Social class the overall rank of people in a society; people who are grouped within the same social class are approximately equal in terms of their income, occupations, and lifestyles

Social judgment theory the perspective that people assimilate new information about attitude objects in light of what they already know or feel; the initial attitude acts as a frame of reference, and new information is categorized in terms of this standard

Social loafing the tendency for people not to devote as much to a task when their contribution is part of a larger group effort

Social marketing the promotion of causes and ideas (social products), such as energy conservation, charities, and population control

Social media the set of technologies that enable users to create content and share it with a large number of others

Social mobility the movement of individuals from one social class to another

Social need a need to be accepted by others

Social networking a growing practice whereby Web sites let members post information about themselves and make contact with others who share similar interests and opinions or who want to make business contacts

Social power the capacity of one person to alter the actions or outcome of another

Social pressure the power of others to influence what we do regardless of our internal beliefs

Social stratification the process in a social system by which scarce and valuable resources are distributed unequally to status positions that become more or less permanently ranked in terms of the share of valuable resources each receives

Sociometric methods the techniques for measuring group dynamics that involve tracing communication patterns in and among groups

Sociometry techniques allow researchers to systematically map out communication patterns among group members

Sock puppeting a company executive or other biased source poses as someone else to tout his organization in social media

Source attractiveness the dimensions of a communicator that increase his or her persuasiveness; these include expertise and attractiveness

Source credibility a communications source's perceived expertise, objectivity, or trustworthiness

Spacing effect the tendency to recall printed material to a greater extent when the advertiser repeats the target item periodically rather than presenting it over and over at the same time

Spectacles a marketing message that takes the form of a public performance

Spendthrifts consumers who derive pleasure from large-scale purchasing

Spokescharacters the use of animated characters or fictional mascots as product representatives

Spontaneous recovery ability of a stimulus to evoke a weakened response even years after the person initially perceived it

Spreading activation meanings in memory are activated indirectly; as a node is activated, other nodes linked to it are also activated so that meanings spread across the network

Stage of cognitive development the ability to comprehend concepts of increasing complexity as a person matures

Standard learning hierarchy the traditional process of attitude formation that starts with the formation of beliefs about an attitude object

State-dependent retrieval people are better able to access information if their internal state is the same at the time of recall as when they learned the information

Status crystallization the extent to which different indicators of a person's status (income, ethnicity, occupation) are consistent with one another

Status hierarchy a ranking of social desirability in terms of consumers' access to resources such as money, education, and luxury goods

Stimulus discrimination the process that occurs when behaviors caused by two stimuli are different, as when consumers learn to differentiate a brand from its competitors

Stimulus generalization the process that occurs when the behavior caused by a reaction to one stimulus occurs in the presence of other, similar stimuli

Storage the process that occurs when knowledge in long-term memory is integrated with what is already in memory and "warehoused" until needed

Store image a store's "personality," composed of such attributes as location, merchandise suitability, and the knowledge and congeniality of the sales staff

Straight rebuy in the context of the buyclass framework, the type of buying decision that is virtually automatic and requires little deliberation

Subculture a group whose members share beliefs and common experiences that set them apart from other members of a culture

Subjective norm an additional component to the multiattribute attitude model that accounts for the effects of what we believe other people think we should do

Subliminal perception the processing of stimuli presented below the level of the consumer's awareness

Superego the system that internalizes society's rules and that works to prevent the id from seeking selfish gratification

Superstitions beliefs that run counter to rational thought or are inconsistent with known laws of nature

Surrogate consumer a professional who is retained to evaluate and/or make purchases on behalf of a consumer

Susceptibility to interpersonal influence the extent to which an individual needs to have others think highly of him or her

Symbol a sign that is related to a product through either conventional or agreed-on associations

Symbolic interactionism a sociological approach stressing that relationships with other people play a large part in forming the self; people live in a symbolic environment, and the meaning attached to any situation or object is determined by a person's interpretation of these symbols

Symbolic self-completion theory the perspective that people who have an incomplete self-definition in some context will compensate by acquiring symbols associated with a desired social identity

Syncretic decision purchase decision that is made jointly by both spouses

Synoptic ideal a model of spousal decision making in which the husband and wife take a common view and act as joint decision makers, assigning each other well-defined roles and making mutually beneficial decisions to maximize the couple's joint utility

Taste culture a group of consumers who share aesthetic and intellectual preferences

Terminal values end states desired by members of a culture

Theory of cognitive dissonance theory based on the premise that a state of tension is created when beliefs or behaviors conflict with one another; people are motivated to reduce this inconsistency (or dissonance) and thus eliminate unpleasant tension

Theory of reasoned action an updated version of the Fishbein multiattribute attitude theory that considers factors such as social pressure and A_{act} (the attitude toward the act of buying a product), rather than simply attitudes toward the product itself

Theory of trying states that the criterion of behavior in the reasoned action model of attitude measurement should be replaced with *trying* to reach a goal

Tie strength the nature and potency of the bond between members of a social network

Tightwads consumers who experience emotional pain when they make purchases

Time poverty a feeling of having less time available than is required to meet the demands of everyday living

Tipping point moment of critical mass

Total quality management (TQM) management and engineering procedures aimed at reducing errors and increasing quality; based on Japanese practices

Trade dress color combinations that become strongly associated with a corporation

Transformative Consumer Research (TCR) promotes research projects that include the goal of helping people or bringing about social change

Transitional economies a country that is adapting from a controlled, centralized economy to a free-market system

Tribal marketing strategy linking a product's identity to an activity-based "tribe" such as basketball players

Trickle-down theory the perspective that fashions spread as the result of status symbols associated with the upper classes "trickling down" to other social classes as these consumers try to emulate those with greater status

Tweens a marketing term used to describe children aged 8 to 14

Twitter a popular social media platform that restricts the poster to a 140 word entry

Two-factor theory the perspective that two separate psychological processes are operating when a person is repeatedly exposed to an ad: repetition increases familiarity and thus reduces uncertainty about the product but over time boredom increases with each exposure, and at some point the amount of boredom incurred begins to exceed the amount of uncertainty reduced, resulting in wear-out

Two step flow model of influence proposes that a small group of *influencers* disseminate information since they can modify the opinions of a large number of other people

Übersexual male who is similar to a metrosexual but who also has traditional masculine qualities

U-commerce the use of ubiquitous networks that will slowly but surely become a part of us, such as wearable computers or customized advertisements beamed to us on our cell phones

Uncertainty avoidance one of Hofstede's cultural dimensions: The degree to which people feel threatened by ambiguous situations and have beliefs and institutions that help them to avoid this uncertainty

Unconditioned stimulus (UCS) a stimulus that is naturally capable of causing a response

Underground economy secondary markets (such as flea markets) where transactions are not officially recorded

Unipolar emotions emotional reactions that are either wholly positive or wholly negative

Unplanned buying when a shopper buys merchandise she did not intend to purchase, often because she recognizes a new need while in the store

Urban myth an unsubstantiated "fact" that many people accept as true

User the person who actually consumes a product or service

Utilitarian function states that we develop some attitudes toward products simply because they provide pleasure or pain

VALS2™ the Values and Lifestyles segmentation system developed by SRI International

Value a belief that some condition is preferable to its opposite

Value system a culture's ranking of the relative importance of values

Value-expressive function states we develop attitudes toward products because of what they say about him or her as a person

Variable-interval reinforcement the time that must pass before an organism's response is reinforced varies based on some average

Variable-ratio reinforcement you get reinforced after a certain number of responses, but you don't know how many responses are required

Variety seeking the desire to choose new alternatives over more familiar ones

Video blogging (vlogging) posting video diaries on sites such as YouTube or photos on Flickr

Viral marketing the strategy of getting customers to sell a product on behalf of the company that creates it

Virtual community of consumption a collection of people whose online interactions are based on shared enthusiasm for and knowledge of a specific consumption activity

Virtual goods digital items that people buy and sell online

Virtual identity the appearance and personality a person takes on as an avatar in a computer-mediated environment like Second Life

Virtual worlds immersive 3D virtual environments such as Second Life

Voice of the consumer an approach to new product development that solicits feedback from end customers well before the company puts a new product on the market

Voluntary simplifiers people who believe that once basic material needs are satisfied, additional income does not lead to happiness

Von Restorff effect techniques like distinctive packaging that increase the novelty of a stimulus also improve recall

Want the particular form of consumption chosen to satisfy a need

Warming process of transforming new objects and places into those that feel cozy, hospitable, and authentic

Web 2.0 rebirth of the Internet as a social, interactive medium from its original roots as a form of one-way transmission from producers to consumers

Web bullying one or more people post malicious comments about someone online in a coordinated effort to harass them

Weber's Law the principle that the stronger the initial stimulus, the greater its change must be for it to be noticed

Widgets small programs that users can download onto their desktops, or embed in their blogs or profile pages, that import some form of live content

Wiki online program that lets several people change a document on a Web page and then track those changes

Wisdom of crowds a perspective that argues under the right circumstances, groups are smarter than the smartest people in them; implies that large numbers of consumers can predict successful products

Word of mouth (WOM) product information transmitted by individual consumers on an informal basis

Zipf's Law pattern that describes the tendency for the most robust effect to be far more powerful than others in its class; applies to consumer behavior in terms of buyers' overwhelming preferences for the market leader in a product category

Name

Page numbers with "n" refer to end note number.

Company

Subject